INVESTMENTS

Third Edition

INVESTMENTS

Third Edition

Frank K. Reilly

Bernard J. Hank Professor
University of Notre Dame

The Dryden Press
A Harcourt Brace Jovanovich College Publisher
Fort Worth   Philadelphia   San Diego   New York   Orlando   Austin   San Antonio
Toronto   Montreal   London   Sydney   Tokyo

Acquisitions Editors: Ann Heath, Mike Roche
Developmental Editor: Paula Dempsey
Project Editor: Teresa Chartos
Art and Design Supervisor: Mercedes Santos
Production Manager: Barb Bahnsen
Permissions Editor: Cindy Lombardo
Director of Editing, Design, and Production: Jane Perkins

Cover Illustrator: Greg Couch
Copy Editor and Indexer: David Talley
Compositor: Weimer Typesetting Company, Inc.
Text Type: 10/12 Janson

Library of Congress Cataloging-in-Publication Data

Reilly, Frank K.
        Investments / Frank K. Reilly. — 3rd ed.
           p.   cm.
        Includes bibliographical references and index.
        ISBN 0-03-032663-X
           1. Investments.   2. Investment analysis.   I. title.
HG4521.R397   1992
332.6 — dc20   90-22251
                                    CIP

The paper used in this publication meets the
minimum requirements of American National Standard for
Information Sciences–Permanence of Paper for Printed Library
Materials, ANSI Z39,48-1984.

Printed in the United States of America
234-032-987654321
Copyright © 1992, 1986, 1982 by The Dryden Press.

Address orders:
The Dryden Press
Orlando, FL 32887

Address editorial correspondence:
The Dryden Press
301 Commerce Street, Suite 3700
Fort Worth, TX 76102

The Dryden Press
Harcourt Brace Jovanovich

CFA Examination questions used throughout the text are
reprinted with permission from the Association for Investment
Management and Research, Charlottesville, Virginia.

To My Best Friend and Wife,
Therese
and our greatest gifts,
Frank K. III and Charlotte
Clarence R. II and Whitney
Therese B.
Edgar B. and Michele

The Dryden Press Series in Finance

Preface

The pleasure of writing a textbook comes from writing on a subject that you enjoy and find exciting. As an author, you hope that you can pass on to the reader not only knowledge, but also the excitement that you feel. In addition, writing about investments brings an added stimulant because you are dealing with a subject that can affect the reader during his or her entire business career and beyond. Hopefully, what readers derive from this course will help them enjoy better lives through managing their resources properly. There is nothing sadder than great athletes or entertainers who earn large salaries for a few years, but become destitute later in life. When one hears about such cases, one can only say, "if only they had managed their money properly."

The purpose of this book is to help you, the reader, learn how to manage your money so that you will derive the maximum benefit from what you earn. To accomplish this purpose, you need to learn about the investment alternatives that are available today and, what is more important, to develop a way of analyzing and thinking about investments that will remain with you in the years ahead when new and different investment opportunities become available.

Because of its dual purpose, the book mixes description and theory. The descriptive material discusses available investment instruments and considers the way the capital markets currently work. The theoretical portion details how you should evaluate current investments and future opportunities to develop a portfolio of investments that will satisfy your risk–return objectives.

Preparing this third edition has been challenging for two reasons. First, many changes have occurred in our securities markets during the last four years in terms of theory, new financial instruments, and trading practices. Second, and even more significant, capital markets have become global. Consequently, very early in the book (in Chapter 2) I present the compelling case for global investing. Subsequently, to ensure that you are prepared to function in this new global environment, almost every chapter in this edition discusses how investment practice or theory is influenced by the globalization of investments and capital markets. This completely integrated treatment is a departure from the traditional approach of concentrating the discussion of international investing in a single chapter.

Intended Market

This book is intended for an initial investments course for graduate students or undergraduates who have completed basic course work in financial management and the normal prerequisites of accounting and economics. Technical tools that exceed the scope of these prerequisites are discussed in many appendixes to appropriate chapters.

Throughout the book, you will notice references to empirical studies that have tested various theories. Although the discussion of these studies is limited to their overall conclusions and implications, I believe at least this general coverage is essential so that alternative theories may be exposed to the real world and judged on the basis of their effectiveness in helping us understand and explain actual events in securities markets. The original studies are cited in footnotes for those who want to find and read them.

Major Changes and Additions in the Third Edition

The text has been thoroughly updated. In addition to chapter revisions, we have also greatly enhanced the problem sets. This edition includes approximately 30 new problems and 25 new CFA exam questions. By chapter, some specific changes include the following:

Chapter 1 Consideration of the impact of exchange rate risk on the risk premium; consideration and demonstration of the effects of changes in the market risk premium over time.

Chapter 2 Discussion of why global investing is desirable and a brief description of the world bond and equity markets, along with a description of bonds and equity securities in the United States and the world; discussion of returns on art and antiques.

Chapter 3 Discussion of bond fundamentals is moved up to this chapter and now includes a description of major non-U.S. bond markets and fixed-income instruments in Japan, Germany, and the United Kingdom.

Chapter 4 Combination of Chapters 3 and 4 of the second edition, along with a detailed discussion of equity markets in Japan and the United Kingdom. An appendix describes stock exchanges around the world.

Chapter 5 Consideration of major U.S. bond series and a number of non-U.S. equity and bond series, in addition to the well-known U.S. equity market indexes. More than 25 market indexes are described.

Chapter 6 Extensive discussion of sources of non-U.S. economic data.

Chapter 7 Discussion of the comparative analysis of ratios relative to the industry and the overall market; consideration of factors to consider when analyzing non-U.S. financial statements, including how they differ and the effects of different accounting treatments on various ratios.

Chapter 9 Consideration of the global asset allocation decision and presentation of an example.

Chapter 10 Expansion of the bond valuation chapter to include an extended discussion of bond duration, the price–yield curve for bonds, and its convexity.

Chapter 11 A separate chapter on bond portfolio management strategies; consideration of passive strategies such as indexing, active strategies, and also matched-funding techniques including dedication and immunization.

Chapter 12 Example of the fundamental analysis of a non-U.S. stock market.

Chapter 13 Discussion of industry analysis that considers the industrial life cycle and competitive forces for an industry along with an example of a global industry analysis.

Chapter 14 Discussion of company valuation using the dividend discount model (DDM),

including discussion and demonstration of additional measures of relative value including price/book value and price/cash flow ratios; consideration of an example of global company analysis.

Chapter 15 Discussion of technical analysis includes new technical tools, such as the CBOE put–call ratio, speculators' bullish stock index futures, stocks above 200-day moving averages, and the block uptick–downtick ratio; application of technical analysis to non-equity markets, interest rates, and international markets (non-U.S. equity markets and exchange rates).

Chapter 16 Additional discussion of the use of options to create bullish and bearish spreads, along with graphs of profit profiles for various strategies; expanded discussion of options on indexes and consideration of options on foreign currencies—an important tool for global investors.

Chapter 17 Expanded presentation on breakeven time for convertible bonds, along with consideration of Americus Trusts and foreign currency warrants.

Chapter 18 Expanded presentation on futures contracts concentrating completely on financial futures including stock index futures and currency futures used to reduce exchange rate risk in global portfolios.

Chapter 22 Discussion of evidence on the efficient market hypothesis (EMH), expanded to consider recent evidence on the January effect, the day-of-the-week effect, the Value Line enigma, the small-firm anomaly, and the dividend-yield effect.

Chapter 23 To the discussion of common stock portfolio performance evaluation techniques is added a discussion of techniques to evaluate the performance of bond portfolios.

Ancillaries

The *Instructor's Manual* contains the following aids for each chapter:

1. A fairly detailed outline of the chapter
2. Answers to all of the questions and problems

3. A test bank of multiple-choice questions related to the chapter
4. A set of overhead masters of major exhibits and tables.

The Stock Market Simulation, prepared by Peter Bobko, Guilford College, allows students to select a portfolio of securities, track the performance of the selected portfolio, mutual funds, bonds, and the stock market over a period of time, and then observe the effects of diversification. A master disk is available free to professors who adopt *Investments*, third edition.

Available for Purchase

A student *Study Guide*, prepared by Jeanette Medewitz of the University of Nebraska–Omaha. A four-part presentation for each chapter includes the following:

1. A brief discussion of the main purpose of the chapter
2. The highlights and major points of the chapter
3. Extensive exercises, including true–false, fill-in-the-blank, multiple-choice, and some short-answer questions
4. Answers to all of these exercises.

Security Analysis for Portfolio Construction and Management by Wayne E. Boyet of Nicholls State University is a software and workbook package that allows students to input and manipulate data using sophisticated statistical models and programs used in investment analysis. An accompanying manual gives complete instructions for using the disks, with discussions of each program. The package is an ideal supplement to this text, and is also suitable for use with any investments text.

Managing Investments: A Case Approach, by Michael A. Berry of The Darden School of the University of Virginia and S. David Young of Tulane University, contains 36 Harvard-style cases and 10 technical notes. It is appropriate for use as either a core text or a supplement for investments courses. Based on real-world problems, the book gives students hands-on experience in applying theoretical principles and models to decisions faced by individual investors and portfolio managers. Adoptors of *Managing Investments* have access to a comprehensive *Instructor's Manual*, which includes detailed teaching notes for the cases.

Acknowledgments

So many people have helped me in so many ways that I hesitate to list them, fearing that I may miss someone. I must begin, however, with the University of Notre Dame because of its direct support. Also, I must thank the Bernard J. Hank family, who have endowed the Chair that helped bring me back to Notre Dame and provided support for my work.

I appreciate the understanding of my associates at Notre Dame. In particular, several colleagues have been extremely helpful. Jim Wittenbach did a great job of updating the tax appendix, which makes the "simplified" new tax laws comprehensible, and Shanta Hedge (now at the University of Connecticut) helped a lot on the financial futures chapter. Reviewers for this edition were John Dunkelberg, *Wake Forest University*; John Clinebell, *University of Northern Colorado*; Michael McBain, *Marquette University*; and Jeanette Medewitz, *University of Nebraska–Omaha*.

I was fortunate to have the following excellent reviewers for earlier editions:

Robert Angell, *East Carolina University*
George Aragon, *Boston College*
Brian Belt, *University of Missouri–Kansas City*
Arand Bhattacharya, *University of Cincinnati*
Carol Billingham, *Central Michigan University*
Gerald A. Blum, *Babson College*
Robert J. Brown, *Harrisburg, Pennsylvania*
Dosoung Choi, *University of Tennessee*
Eugene F. Drzycimski, *University of Wisconsin–Oshkosh*
Eric Emory, *Sacred Heart University*
Thomas Eyssell, *University of Missouri–St. Louis*
James Feller, *Middle Tennessee State University*
Eurico Ferreira, *Clemson University*
Michael Ferri, *John Carroll University*
Joseph E. Finnerty, *University of Illinois*
Harry Friedman, *New York University*
R. H. Gilmer, *University of Mississippi*
Stephen Goldstein, *University of South Carolina*
Steven Goldstein, *Robinson-Humphrey/ American Express*
Keshav Gupta, *Oklahoma State University*
Sally A. Hamilton, *Santa Clara University*
Ronald Hoffmeister, *Arizona State University*
Ron Hutchins, *Eastern Michigan University*
A. James Ifflander, *Arizona State University*
Stan Jacobs, *Central Washington University*
Kwang Jun, *Michigan State University*

Jaroslaw Komarynsky, *Northern Illinois University*
Danny Litt, *Century Software Systems/UCLA*
Miles Livingston, *University of Florida*
Christopher Ma, *Texas Tech University*
Steven Mann, *University of South Carolina*
John Matthys, *DePaul University*
Dennis McConnell, *University of Maine*
Jacob Michaelsen, *University of California–Santa Cruz*
Nicholas Michas, *Northern Illinois University*
Lalatendu Misra, *University of Texas–San Antonio*
Michael Murray, *LaCrosse, Wisconsin*
John Peavy, *Southern Methodist University*
George Philippatos, *University of Tennessee*
George Pinches, *University of Kansas*
Rose Prasad, *Central Michigan University*
George A. Racette, *University of Oregon*
Bruce Robin, *Old Dominion University*
James Rosenfeld, *Emory University*
Stanley D. Ryals, *Investment Counsel, Inc.*
Frederic Shipley, *DePaul University*
Douglas Southard, *Virginia Polytechnic Institute*
Harold Stevenson, *Arizona State University*
Donald Thompson, *Georgia State University*
David E. Upton, *Virginia Commonwealth University*
E. Theodore Veit, *Rollins College*
Bruce Wardrep, *East Carolina University*
Rolf Wubbels, *New York University*

Valuable comments and suggestions have come from my former graduate students at the University of Illinois: Paul Fellows, University of Iowa; Wenchi Kao, University of Dayton; and David Wright, University of Notre Dame. Once more, I have been blessed with bright, dedicated research assistants when I needed them most. This includes Rashid Akhtar (R.I.P.), Rich Laberge, Robert Vaio, and Ziaozhong Zhu, all of whom were both careful and creative.

Current and former colleagues have been very helpful: Yu-Chi Chang, Bill McDonald, Rick Mendenhall, Bill Nichols, Juan Rivera, and Norlin Rueschhoff, *University of Notre Dame*; C. F. Lee, *Rutgers University*; Donald Tuttle, *Indiana University*; and John M. Wachowicz, *University of Tennessee*. As always, some of the best insights and most stimulating comments came during my too-infrequent runs with my very good friend, Jim Gentry of the University of Illinois.

I am convinced that a professor who wants to write a book that is both academically respectable and relevant and realistic requires help from the "real world." I have been very fortunate to develop relation-

ships with a number of individuals (including some former students) whom I consider my contacts with reality.

I especially want to thank Robert Conway, who was the managing director of the London office of Goldman Sachs & Company, for suggesting several years ago that it was essential to make the new edition reflect the rapidly evolving global market. This was some of the most important advice I have ever received, and you will note that it has had a profound effect on this book.

The following individuals also graciously provided important insights and material:

Sharon Athey, *Brown Brothers Harriman*
Joseph C. Bencivenga, *Salomon Bros.*
Lowell Benson, *Robert A. Murray Partners*
David G. Booth, *Dimensional Fund Advisors, Inc.*
Leon C. Brand, *Merrill Lynch Pierce Fenner & Smith*
Gary Brinson, *Brinson Partners, Inc.*
Roy D. Burry, *Kidder, Peabody & Co.*
Thomas Coleman, *Adler, Coleman and Co. (NYSE)*
Robert Conway, *Goldman Sachs & Co.*
William Cornish, *Duff & Phelps*
Robert J. Davis, *Crimson Capital Co.*
Robert J. Davis, Jr., *Goldman Sachs & Co.*
Philip Delaney, Jr., *Northern Trust Bank*
William Dwyer, *Moody's Investors Service, Inc.*
Sam Eisenstadt, *Value Line*
Paul Feldman, *Goldman Sachs & Co.*
Kenneth Fisher, *Forbes*
John J. Flanagan, Jr., *Lawrence, O'Donnell, Marcus & Co.*
Martin S. Fridson, *Merrill Lynch Pierce Fenner & Smith*
Patricia A. Genley, *United Mutual Fund Selector*
Eduardo Haim, *Shearson Lehman Brothers*
William J. Hank, *Moore Financial Corporation*
Jim Johnson, *Options Clearing Corporation*
John W. Jordan II, *The Jordan Company*
Andrew Kalotay, *Kalotay Associates*
Debbie Kessler, *Tokyo Stock Exchange*
Luke Knecht, *Harris Trust and Savings Bank*
C. Prewitt Lane, *ICH Companies*
Martin Leibowitz, *Salomon Bros.*
Douglas R. Lempereur, *Templeton Investment Counsel, Inc.*
Robert Levine, *Nomura Securities*
Scott Malpass, *University of Notre Dame*
John Maginn, *Mutual of Omaha*
Richard McCabe, *Merrill Lynch Pierce Fenner & Smith*

Michael McCowin, *Harris Trust & Savings Bank*
Terrence J. McGlinn, *McGlinn Capital Markets*
Robert Milne, *Duff & Phelps*
Robert G. Murray, *First Interstate Bank of Oregon*
John J. Phelan, Jr., *New York Stock Exchange*
Philip J. Purcell III, *Dean Witter Financial Services Group*
Jack Pycik, *Norwest Bank, Indiana*
Robert Quinn, *Salomon Bros.*
Chet Ragavan, *Merrill Lynch Pierce Fenner & Smith*
John C. Rudolf, *Oppenheimer & Co., Inc.*
Stanley Ryals, *Investment Counsel, Inc.*
Ron Ryan, *Ryan Labs, Inc.*
Barry Schnepel, *Merrill Lynch Pierce Fenner & Smith*
Mark H. Sladkus, *Morgan Stanley & Co.*
William Smith, *Dean Witter Financial Services Group*
Shawn St. Clair, *Duff & Phelps*
James Stork, *Duff & Phelps*
Masao Takamori, *Tokyo Stock Exchange*
Richard H. Tierney, *The Bond Buyer*
Anthony Vignola, *Kidder, Peabody & Co.*
William M. Wadden, *Harris Trust & Savings Bank*
Jeffrey M. Weingarten, *Goldman Sachs & Co.*
Thomas V. Williams, *Kemper Financial Services*
Robert Wilmouth, *National Futures Association*
Richard S. Wilson, *Fitch Investors Service, Inc.*

I continue to benefit from the help and consideration of the dedicated people at the Institute of Chartered Financial Analysts, which is now a part of the Association for Investment Management and Research: Darwin Bayston, Tom Bowman, Whit Broome, Hap Butler, Bob Luck, Pete Morley, Sue Martin, Katie Sherrerd, and everybody's favorite, Peggy Slaughter.

Thankfully, Phyllis Sandfort forgets the pain between editions, so she agreed to type this third edition. Her patience, understanding, and willingness to type late at night ensured rapid and accurate turnaround. My secretary, Donna Smith, had the unenviable task of keeping the rest of my life in some sort of order. At The Dryden Press, Ann Heath and Mike Roche were the acquisitions editors; Paula Dempsey was the developmental editor; and Teresa Chartos, the project editor, brought the book from messy manuscript and sloppy exhibits to a bound volume.

As always, my greatest gratitude is to my family—past, present, and future. My parents gave me life and helped me understand love and how to give it. My in-laws created my greatest gift and continuously give through their daughter. Most important is my wife, who provides love, understanding, and support at early morning breakfast and throughout the day and night. We thank God for our children, who make it all worthwhile and ensure that our lives are full of love, fun, and excitement.

Frank K. Reilly
Notre Dame, Indiana
December 1991

About The Author

Frank K. Reilly is the Bernard J. Hank Professor of Business Administration and former dean of the College of Business Administration at the University of Notre Dame. Holding degrees from the University of Notre Dame (B.B.A.), Northwestern University (M.B.A.), and the University of Chicago (Ph.D.), Professor Reilly has taught at the University of Illinois, the University of Kansas, and the University of Wyoming, in addition to the University of Notre Dame. He has several years of experience as a senior securities analyst, as well as experience in stock and bond trading. A Chartered Financial Analyst (CFA), he has been a member of the Council of Examiners, the Council on Education and Research, and the grading committee of the Institute of Chartered Financial Analysts. Professor Reilly has been president of the Financial Management Association, the Midwest Business Administration Association, the Eastern Finance Association, and the Academy of Financial Services. He serves or has served on the boards of directors of the First Interstate Bank of Wisconsin; Norwest Bank, Indiana; and the Investment Analysis Society of Chicago. As the author of more than 100 articles, monographs, and papers, his work has appeared in numerous publications including *Journal of Finance*, *Journal of Financial and Quantitative Analysis*, *Journal of Accounting Research*, *Financial Management*, *Financial Analysts Journal*, *Financial Review*, and *Journal of Portfolio Management*. In addition to *Investments*, Third Edition, Professor Reilly is the author of another textbook, *Investment Analysis and Portfolio Management*, Third Edition (Hinsdale, Ill.: Dryden, 1989).

Professor Reilly was named on the list of *Outstanding Educators in America* and has received both the University of Illinois Alumni Association Graduate Teaching Award and the Outstanding Educator Award from the M.B.A. class at the University of Illinois, and the Outstanding Teacher Award from the M.B.A. class at Notre Dame. He has also received the C. Stewart Sheppard Award from the Association of Investment Management and Research (AIMR) for his contribution to the educational mission of the association. He is editor of *Readings and Issues in Investments, Ethics, and the Investment Industry*, and *High-Yield Bonds: Analysis and Risk Assessment*. He is or has been a member of the editorial boards of *Financial Management*, *The Financial Review*, *The Financial Services Review*, *The Journal of Applied Business Research*, *Journal of Financial Education*, and *Quarterly Review of Economics and Business*. He is included in *Who's Who in Finance and Industry*, *Who's Who in America*, and *Who's Who in the World*.

Opportunities in Investments

Most students take this course because they want to learn to invest excess earnings. In addition, some may consider the investments field as an area for future employment. Over the years, many students have asked me, "What are the job opportunities in the investments area?" Here is a brief discussion of some specific investment-related positions with various financial institutions.

1. **Registered Representative with a Brokerage Firm.** Also referred to as a *broker*, the registered representative is involved in the sale of stocks, bonds, options, commodities, and other investment instruments to individuals or institutions. If you decide to buy or sell stock, you call your broker at the investment firm where you have an account, and he or she arranges the purchase or sale. If you are a regular customer, your broker may call you and suggest that you buy or sell some stock; if you agree, he or she will arrange it. It typically takes several years for a broker to build a clientele, but once this is done, the profession can be very exciting and financially rewarding—for the broker as well as for the clients.

2. **Investment Analysis: Brokerage Firms and/or Investment Bankers.** This field involves analysis of alternative industries, the companies in the industry, and their securities as support for registered representatives. For example, as an employee for Merrill Lynch Pierce Fenner & Smith, you might make an analysis of the computer industry and all the major companies in the industry and then prepare a report. This report would be used by the registered representatives at Merrill Lynch offices all over the country.

   Alternatively, if your firm is an investment banking firm that underwrites new stock or bond issues, you may analyze the industry and companies within the industry regarding a potential securities issue your firm will underwrite in order to determine its needs and to provide suggestions regarding the characteristics of the issue. In addition, investment bankers are heavily involved in finding merger partners for their clients and helping negotiate terms. As an analyst you would help

answer these questions: how much is the potential merger firm worth, and what are reasonable terms?

3. **Investment Analysis: Banks.** Banks require investment analysis in two major areas—loans and trust departments. Obviously a firm that is being considered for commercial loans must be analyzed to find out why the firm needs money, how much money the firm needs, and when and how it will be able to repay the loan.

   Bank trust departments manage trust accounts for individuals and pension funds for companies. The capital is invested in various combinations of stocks and bonds. Again, banks need analysts to examine various industries and individual companies and to recommend securities that should be bought, sold, or held in the trust accounts.

4. **Investment Analysis: Investment Counselors and Mutual Funds.** Both groups manage large portfolios of stocks, bonds, and other assets for clients. Investment counselors manage pension funds and individual accounts (over $1 million) for wealthy individuals. As an investment analyst, you would examine various industries and the companies within them and make recommendations regarding which stocks and bonds should be included in various portfolios.

   In mutual funds (also referred to as *investment companies*), investors pool their money and acquire a portfolio of stocks. The investment company that manages the portfolio will hire analysts to examine industries and companies and to help them select securities for the portfolio.

5. **Investment Analysis: Insurance Companies.** Insurance companies typically have large investment portfolios that they manage in order to derive returns for policyholders. Although the asset mix of the portfolios differs depending upon the type of insurance (life versus property and casualty), the normal emphasis is on fixed-income securities.

6. **Portfolio Managers.** The financial firms mentioned previously (banks, investment counselors, mutual funds, insurance companies) employ port-

folio managers in addition to analysts. The portfolio managers are responsible for gathering information and recommendations from the analysts. On the basis of the information, the recommendations, and the overall needs of the portfolio, they make final decisions about the securities in the portfolio.

7. **Financial Planners.** Because most individuals do not have the time or the desire to learn about stocks, bonds and all the other components of a properly constructed portfolio, recent years have brought significant growth in the number of individuals and firms that provide assistance in personal financial planning. Based upon what a client tells a financial planner about his or her current assets, goals, needs, and constraints, the financial planner provides a blueprint of how that client should invest and in what financial instruments. The point is, financial planning firms need employees to help create appropriate financial plans for clients, and to analyze individual securities and construct portfolios that fulfill the clients' financial plans.

Some Factors to Consider

Many firms hire only investment analysts who have had three or four years of experience. How do you get the experience if nobody will hire you for that first job? It is necessary to contact a large number of firms in the field and show a willingness to apply yourself. Even if you get a job as an analyst, your beginning salary will probably be low compared to those for other jobs. Most investment firms believe that the first few years are almost entirely a training program, which is very costly to the firm. The good news is that once you get the initial position and the necessary experience, the long-run earnings potential for an experienced analyst or portfolio manager is substantial.

For some analyst jobs, firms typically hire individuals with graduate degrees. Often firms also hire undergraduates and encourage them to pursue graduate degrees in evening programs.

Almost anyone considering a career in investment analysis or portfolio management should attempt to become a Chartered Financial Analyst (CFA). This is a professional designation similar to the CPA in accounting. The designation is becoming very well regarded by financial institutions. The program and its requirements are described in an appendix at the back of the book.

Contents

P A R T

6

**Portfolio and Capital Market
Theory and Application** 548

INVESTMENTS

Third Edition

The Investment
Background

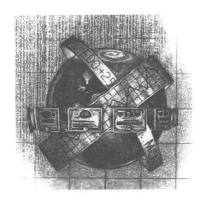

The chapters in this section will provide a background for your study of investments by answering the following questions:

- Why do people invest?
- What investments are available to them?
- How do securities markets function?
- How and why are securities markets in the United States and around the world changing?
- How can you evaluate the market behavior of common stocks and bonds?
- How can you get relevant information to learn about and evaluate potential investments?

In the first chapter we consider why an individual would invest and what factors determine an investor's required rate of return on an investment. The latter point will be very important in subsequent analyses when we work to understand investor behavior, the markets for alternative securities, and the valuation of various investments.

To minimize risk, investment theory supports the need to diversify. To explore the investments available to investors, we discuss several investment instruments found in global markets along with their historical rates of return and measures of risk in Chapter 2.

In Chapters 3 and 4 we examine how markets work in general, and then focus on securities markets specifically. Chapter 4 concentrates on the markets for bonds and common stocks. During the 1980s, significant changes occurred in the operation of the securities market, including a trend toward a global market. After discussing these changes and the globalization of these markets, we will try to predict future changes and envision how global markets will continue to expand available investment alternatives.

This initial section provides the framework for you to understand and analyze various securities, the markets where they are bought and sold, and how you might manage a collection of investments—a portfolio. Specific portfolio management techniques are described in later chapters.

Investors, market analysts, and financial theorists often gauge the behavior of securities markets by evaluating changes in various market indexes. We examine and compare a number of stock-market and bond-market indexes in Chapter 5. Chapter 6, the final chapter in this section, describes sources of information for investors seeking to learn more about various investment opportunities.

1

The Investment Setting

For most of your life, you will be earning and spending money. Rarely, though, will your current income exactly balance with your consumption desires. Sometimes you may have more money than you want to spend; at others you may want to purchase more than you can afford. These imbalances will lead you either to borrow or to save to maximize the benefits from your income.

> **Investment** The current commitment of dollars over time to derive future payments to compensate the investor for the time the funds are committed, the expected rate of inflation, and the uncertainty of future payments.

What Is an Investment?

When current income exceeds current consumption desires, people tend to save the excess. They can do any of several things with these savings. They can put the money under a mattress or bury it in the backyard until some future time when consumption desires exceed current income. When they retrieve their savings from the mattress or backyard, they have the same amount they saved.

Another possibility is that they can give up the immediate possession of these savings for a future, larger amount of money they can use for consumption at that time. This tradeoff of *present* consumption for a higher level of *future* consumption is the reason for saving. What you do with savings to make them increase over time is *investment*.[1]

Those who give up immediate possession of savings (i.e., defer consumption) expect to receive a greater amount in the future than they gave up. Conversely, those who consume more than their current income (i.e., borrow) must be willing to pay back a greater amount in the future.

People's willingness to pay this difference for borrowed funds and their desire to receive a surplus on their savings give rise to the *pure time value of money*. The rate of exchange between certain future consumption (future dollars) and certain current consumption (current dollars) is the *pure rate of interest*. This interest rate is established in the capital market by a comparison of the supply of excess income available to be invested and the demand for excess consumption (borrowing) at a given time. If you can exchange $100 of certain income today for $104 of certain income 1 year from today, then the pure rate of exchange (the pure rate of interest) on a risk-free investment is said to be 4 percent (104/100 − 1).

The investor who gives up $100 today expects to consume $104 of goods and services in the future.

This assumes that the general price level in the economy stays the same. This has rarely been the case during the past several decades when inflation rates have varied from 1.1 percent in 1986 to 13.3 percent in 1979, with an average of 6.2 percent a year from 1970 to 1990. If investors expect a change in prices, they will require a higher rate of return to compensate for it. For example, if the investor expects a rise in prices (i.e., inflation) at the rate of 2 percent during the period of investment, he or she will increase the required interest rate by 2 percent. In our example, the investor would require $106 in the future to defer $100 of consumption during an inflationary period, which implies a 6 percent interest rate instead of the 4 percent in a noninflationary environment.

Further, if the future payment from the investment is not certain, the investor will demand an interest rate that exceeds the pure time value of money plus the inflation rate. The uncertainty of the payments from an investment is the *investment risk*. The excess amount added to the interest rate is called a *risk premium*. In our previous example, the investor would require more than $106 1 year from today, possibly $110 representing a $4, or 4 percent, risk premium.

Investment *Defined*

From our discussion we can create a formal definition of investment. Specifically, an **investment** is the current commitment of dollars for a period of time in order to derive future payments that will compensate the investor for (1) the time the funds are committed, (2) the expected rate of inflation, and (3) the uncertainty of the future payments. Note that the "investor" can be an individual, a government, a pension fund, or a corporation. Similarly, this definition includes all types of investments, including corporate investments in plant and equipment and investments by individuals in stocks, bonds, commodities, or real estate. This text emphasizes the individual investor. In all cases the investor is trading a *known* dollar amount today for some *expected* future stream of payments that will be greater than the current outlay.

At this point, we have answered the questions about why people invest and what they want from their investments. They invest to earn a return from savings due to their deferred consumption. They want a return that compensates them for the time, the expected rate of inflation, and the uncertainty of the return. This return, the investor's **required rate of return**, is discussed throughout this book. A central

---

[1]In contrast, when current income is less than current consumption desires, people borrow to make up the difference. While we will discuss borrowing on several occasions, the major emphasis of this text is how to invest savings.

question of this book is how investors select investments that will give them their required rates of return.

The remainder of this chapter describes how to measure the rate of return on an investment and the uncertainty of its expected returns. You need to understand these techniques for measuring rate of return and uncertainty to evaluate the suitability of a particular investment. Our emphasis will be on financial assets such as bonds and stocks, although we will discuss a range of financial assets and also consider some nonfinancial assets.

Measures of Return and Risk

The purpose of this book is to help you understand how to choose among alternative instruments. As a major part of this selection process, you must evaluate the risk–return tradeoffs for alternative investments. Therefore, it is necessary to understand how to measure the rate of return and the risk involved in an investment accurately. To meet this need, we examine ways to quantify return and risk in this section.

The first measure is the rate of return on an individual investment over the time the investment is held. Next, we consider how to measure the *average* rate of return for an individual investment over a number of time periods, or the average rate of return for a group — or a *portfolio* — of investments. It is important to deal with portfolios of investments for two reasons. First, almost all investors own groups of investments such as several stocks, several bonds, or a collection of stocks and bonds. Second, it is possible to reduce the uncertainty of expected returns by owning a portfolio of investments that have different patterns of return. Combining different types of investments, such as stocks, bonds, and real estate, that have different patterns of returns over time is referred to as *diversification*. This requires that we measure the rate of return on an investment portfolio and relate this rate of return to the overall risk in order to select the best investments.

Measures of Return

When you are evaluating alternative investments for inclusion in your portfolio, you will often be comparing investments with very different prices or lives. As an example, you might want to compare a $10 stock that pays no dividends to a stock selling for $150 that pays dividends of $5 a year. In order to choose be-

Required rate of return The minimum return that will induce the investor to invest.

Holding period return (HPR) The total return from an investment, including all sources of income, for a given period of time. A value of 1.0 indicates no gain or loss.

Holding period yield (HPY) The total return from an investment for a given period of time stated as a percentage.

tween these two investments, you must accurately compare their rates of return. That is the purpose of this section.

The purpose of investing is to defer current consumption and thereby add to our wealth so we can consume more in the future. Therefore, when we talk about a return on an investment, we are concerned with the increase in wealth resulting from this investment.

If you commit $200 to an investment at the beginning of the year and you get back $220 at the end of the year, what is your return for the period? The period during which you own an investment is called its holding period, and the return for that period is the **holding period return (HPR)**. In this example, the HPR is 1.10, calculated as follows:

$$\text{HPR} = \frac{\text{Ending Value of Investment}}{\text{Beginning Value of Investment}}$$
$$= \frac{\$220}{\$200} = 1.10$$

Note that this value will always be zero or greater; it can never be a negative value. A value greater than 1.0 reflects an increase in your wealth, which means that you received a positive rate of return during the period. A value less than 1.0 means that you suffered a decline in wealth, which indicates that you had a negative rate of return during the period. An HPR of zero indicates that you lost all of your money.

Although HPR helps us express the change in value of an investment, investors generally evaluate returns in annual percentage terms. This conversion to annual percentage rates makes it easier to compare alternative investments with very different characteristics directly. The first step in converting a HPR to an annual value is to derive a percentage return, referred to as the **holding period yield (HPY)**. HPY is equal to the HPR minus 1.

$$\text{HPY} = \text{HPR} - 1$$

Mean rate of return The average of an investment's returns over time.
Arithmetic mean A measure of mean return equal to the sum of annual returns divided by the number of years.

In our example:

$$HPY = 1.10 - 1 = 0.10$$
$$= 10 \text{ percent}$$

To derive an annual HPY, you compute an annual HPR and subtract 1. Annual HPR is found by:

$$\text{Annual HPR} = HPR^{1/n}$$

where:

n = number of years the investment is held

Consider an investment that costs $250 and is worth $350 after being held for 2 years:

$$HPR = \frac{\text{Ending Value of Investment}}{\text{Beginning Value of Investment}}$$
$$= \frac{\$350}{\$250} = 1.40$$
$$\text{Annual HPR} = 1.40^{1/n}$$
$$= 1.40^{1/2}$$
$$= 1.1832$$
$$\text{Annual HPY} = 1.1832 - 1 = 0.1832$$
$$= 18.32 \text{ percent}$$

In contrast, consider an investment of $100 that has increased in value to $112 by the end of a 6-month holding period. We would compute the annual HPR and annual HPY as follows:

$$HPR = \frac{\$112}{\$100} = 1.12 \ (n = 0.5)$$
$$\text{Annual HPR} = 1.12^{1/0.5}$$
$$= 1.12^{2}$$
$$= 1.2544$$
$$\text{Annual HPY} = 1.2544 - 1 = 0.2544$$
$$= 25.44 \text{ percent}$$

Note that we made some implicit assumptions when converting HPY to an annual basis. This annualized holding period yield computation assumes a constant annual yield for each year. In the 2-year investment, we assumed an 18.32 percent rate of return

each year, compounded. In the case of a partial year HPR, we assumed that the return is compounded for the whole year. That is, we assumed that the rate of return earned during the first part of the year is likewise earned on the value at the end of the first 6 months. The 12 percent rate of return for 6 months compounds to 25.44 percent for the full year.[2]

Remember one final point. The ending value of the investment can be the result of a change in price for the investment alone, such as a stock going from $20 a share to $22 a share, income from the investment alone, such as a dividend payment, or a combination of price change and income. Ending value includes the value of everything related to the investment.

Computing Mean Returns

Now that we have calculated the HPY for a single investment for a single year, we want to consider **mean rates of return** for a single investment and for a portfolio of investments. Over a number of years, a single investment will likely give high rates of return during some years and low rates of return, or possibly negative rates of return, during others. Your analysis should consider each of these returns, but you also want a summary figure that indicates this investment's typical experience, or the rate of return you should expect to receive if you owned this investment over time. You can derive such a summary figure by computing the mean rate of return for this investment over some period of time.

Alternatively, you might want to evaluate a portfolio of similar investments such as all stocks, or all bonds, or a combination of investments that might include stocks, bonds, and real estate. In this instance, you would calculate the mean rate of return for this portfolio of investments for an individual year or for a number of years.

Single Investment Given a set of annual rates of return for an investment, there are two methods by which we can derive a summary measure of return performance. The first is the arithmetic mean, the second the geometric mean. To find the **arithmetic**

---

[2]To check that you understand the calculations, determine the annual HPY for a 3-year HPR of 1.50. (Answer: 14.47 percent.) Compute the annual HPY for a 3-month HPR of 1.06. (Answer: 26.25 percent.)

mean **(AM)**, the sum (Σ) of annual yields is divided by the number of years (N) as follows:

$$AM = \frac{\Sigma HPY}{N}$$

where:

ΣHPY = the sum of annual holding period yields

An alternative computation, the **geometric mean (GM)**, is the nth root of the product of the HPRs for N years.

$$GM = \pi^{1/n} - 1$$

where:

π = the product of the annual holding period returns $(HPR_1) \times (HPR_2) \ldots (HPR_N)$

To illustrate these alternatives, consider an investment with the following data:

Year	Beginning Value	Ending Value	HPR	HPY
1	100.0	115.0	1.15	0.15
2	115.0	138.0	1.20	0.20
3	138.0	110.4	0.80	−0.20

$$
\begin{aligned}
AM &= \frac{(0.15) + (0.20) + (-0.20)}{3} \\
&= \frac{0.15}{3} \\
&= 0.05 = 5 \text{ percent} \\
GM &= (1.15 \times 1.20 \times 0.80)^{1/3} - 1 \\
&= (1.104)^{1/3} - 1 \\
&= 1.03353 - 1 \\
&= 0.03353 = 3.353 \text{ percent}
\end{aligned}
$$

Investors are typically concerned with long-term performance when comparing alternative investments. GM is considered to be a superior measure of the long-term mean rate of return because it indicates the compound annual rate of return based upon the ending value versus the beginning value.[3] Specifically, using the prior example, if we compounded 3.353 percent for 3 years (1.03353), we would get an ending wealth value of 1.104, which is the actual ending value.

> **Geometric mean** The nth root of the product of the annual holding period returns for N years minus 1.

While the arithmetic average provides a good indication of the expected value for an investment, it is biased upward. This is very obvious for a volatile security. Consider, for example, a security that increases in price from $50 to $100 during year 1 and drops back to $50 during year 2. The annual HPYs would be:

Year	Beginning Value	Ending Value	HPR	HPY
1	50	100	2.00	1.00
2	100	50	0.50	−0.50

This would give an arithmetic mean of:

$$\frac{1.00 + (-0.50)}{2} = \frac{0.50}{2}$$
$$= 0.25 = 25 \text{ percent}$$

This investment brought no change in wealth and therefore no return, yet the arithmetic mean return is 25 percent.

The geometric mean return would be:

$$(2.00 \times 0.50)^{1/2} - 1 = 1.00^{1/2} - 1$$
$$= 1.00 - 1 = 0 \text{ percent}$$

This answer of zero accurately represents the fact that there was no change in wealth from this investment.

When rates of return are the same for all years, the geometric mean will be equal to the arithmetic mean. If the rates of return vary over the years, the geometric mean will be lower than the arithmetic mean. The difference between the two mean values will depend upon the year-to-year changes in rates of return. Larger annual changes, that is, more volatility, give greater differences between the alternative mean values.

---

[3]Note that the GM is the same whether you compute the geometric mean of the individual annual holding period yields, or compute the annual HPY for a 3-year period, comparing the ending value to the beginning value, as discussed earlier under annual HPY for a multiperiod case.

Investment	Number of Shares	Beginning Price	Beginning Market Value	Ending Price	Ending Market Value	HPR	HPY	Market Weight	Weighted HPY
A	100,000	$10	$ 1,000,000	$12	$ 1,200,000	1.20	20%	0.05	0.010
B	200,000	20	4,000,000	21	4,200,000	1.05	5	0.20	0.010
C	500,000	30	15,000,000	33	16,500,000	1.10	10	0.75	0.075
Total			$20,000,000		$21,900,000				0.095

> **Risk** The uncertainty that an investment will earn its expected rate of return.

You should be aware of both methods of computation because published accounts of investment performance or descriptions of financial research will use both AM and GM as measures of average returns. Also, both will be used throughout this book. In the absence of any specific identification, assume the measurement is the arithmetic mean. Some studies dealing with long-run historical return include both arithmetic and geometric mean returns.

A Portfolio of Investments The mean return (HPY) for a portfolio of investments is measured as the weighted average of the returns for the individual investments in the portfolio, or the overall change in value of the original portfolio. The weights of the averages are based upon the relative beginning market values for each investment. This is demonstrated by the following example:

$$HPR = \frac{21,900,000}{20,000,000} = 1.095$$

The purpose of this section has been to help you understand how you can properly measure the *historical* rates of return on alternative investments in order to compare them. While the analysis of historical performance is very useful, selecting investments for your portfolio requires you to *predict* the rates of return you expect to prevail. Numerous economic uncertainties create doubt that past rates of return will be repeated. This uncertainty regarding the future is referred to as the *risk* of the investment. The next section discusses the notion of risk or uncertainty and how you can measure it.

The Impact of Uncertainty

Risk is the uncertainty that an investment will earn its expected rate of return. In the examples in the prior section, we assumed specific historical rates of return.

In contrast, an investor who considers an investment expects or anticipates a particular rate of return. The investor might say the investment will return 10 percent, but this is really the investor's most likely estimate, also referred to as a *point estimate*. Pressed further, the investor would probably acknowledge the uncertainty of this estimated return and the possibility that, under certain conditions, the annual rate of return on this investment might go as low as -10 percent or as high as 25 percent. The point is, a larger range of possible returns from an investment increases the investor's uncertainty regarding the actual return. Therefore, a larger range of returns makes the investment riskier.

An investor determines how certain the expected rate of return on an investment is by analyzing estimates of expected returns. To do this, the investor assigns probability values to all possible returns. These probability values range from zero, which means no chance of the return, to 1, which indicates complete certainty that the investment will provide the rate of return. These probabilities are typically subjective estimates developed from past performance of the investment or similar investments, modified by the investor's expectations for the future. For example, an investor may know that about 30 percent of the time, the rate of return on this particular investment was 10 percent. Using this information along with future expectations regarding the economy, one can derive an estimate of what might happen in the future.

Let us begin our analysis of the effect of risk with an example of perfect certainty. The investor is absolutely certain of a return of 5 percent. A graph to illustrate this situation looks like the graph at the top of p. 11.

Perfect certainty allows only one possible return and the probability of receiving that return is 1.0. Few investments provide certain returns. The *expected* return from an investment is defined as:

Expected Return = Σ (Prob. of Return) (Possible Return)
$$E(R_i) = [(P_1)(R_1) + (P_2)(R_2) + \ldots + (P_nR_n)]$$
$$E(R_i) = \Sigma (P_i)(R_i)$$

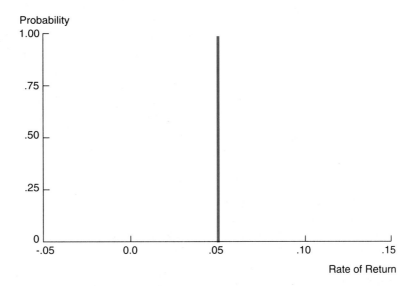

In the case of perfect certainty, there is only one value for P_iR_i:

$$E(R_i) = (1.0)(0.05) = 0.05$$

In an alternative example, suppose an investor believed an investment could provide several different rates of return depending upon different possible economic conditions. As an example, in a strong economic environment with high corporate profits and little or no inflation, the investor might expect the rate of return on common stocks during the next year to reach as high as 20 percent. In contrast, in an economic decline with a higher than average rate of inflation, the investor might expect the rate of return on common stocks during the next year to be a negative 20 percent. Finally, with no major change in the economic environment, the rate of return during next

year would probably approach the long-run average of 10 percent.

The investor might estimate probabilities for each of these economic scenarios based upon past experience and the current outlook as follows:

Economic Conditions	Probability	Rate of Return
Strong economy, no inflation	0.15	0.20
Weak economy, above average inflation	0.15	−0.20
No major change in economy	0.70	0.10

This set of potential outcomes can be visualized as follows:

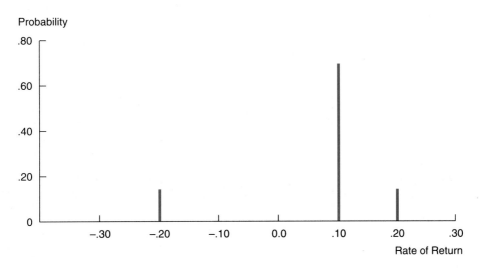

Risk averse The assumption about investors that they will choose the least risky alternative, all else being equal.

The computation of the expected rate of return $[E(R_i)]$ is as follows:

$$E(R_i) = [(0.15)(0.20)] + [(0.15)(-0.20)]$$
$$+ [(0.70)(0.10)]$$
$$= 0.07$$

Obviously, the investor is more uncertain about the expected return from this investment than about the return from the prior investment with its single possible return. An investment with 10 possible outcomes ranging from -40 percent to 50 percent with the same probability for each rate of return would be graphed like the table at the bottom of the page. In this case, there are numerous outcomes from a wide range of possibilities. The expected rate of return $[E(R_i)]$ for this investment would be:

$$E(R_i) = (0.10)(-0.40) + (0.10)(-0.30)$$
$$+ (0.10)(-0.20) + (0.10)(-0.10)$$
$$+ (0.10)(0.0) + (0.10)(0.10) + (0.10)(0.20)$$
$$+ (0.10)(0.30) + (0.10)(0.40) + (0.10)(0.50)$$
$$= (-0.04) + (-0.03) + (-0.02) + (-0.01)$$
$$+ (0.00) + (0.01) + (0.02) + (0.03) + (0.04)$$
$$= 0.05$$

The expected rate of return for this investment is the same as the certain return discussed earlier, but the investor is highly uncertain about the *actual* rate of return. This would be considered a risky investment because of that uncertainty. We would expect an investor faced with the choice between this risky investment and the certain case to select the certain alternative. This expectation is based upon the belief that most investors are **risk averse**, which means that if everything else is the same, they will select the investment with less uncertainty.

Measures of Risk

We have shown that we can evaluate the uncertainty, or risk, of an investment by identifying the range of possible returns from that investment and assigning each a weight based on the probability that it will occur. While the graphs help us visualize the dispersion, most investors want a quantitative measure of this dispersion of returns that uses statistical techniques. These statistical measures allow you to compare the return and risk measures for alternative investments directly. Of several possible measures, two have received support in work on portfolio theory: the variance and the standard deviation of the estimated distribution of expected returns.

In this section, we demonstrate how variance and standard deviation measure the dispersion of possible rates of return around the expected rate of return. We will work with the examples discussed earlier. The formula for variance is as follows:

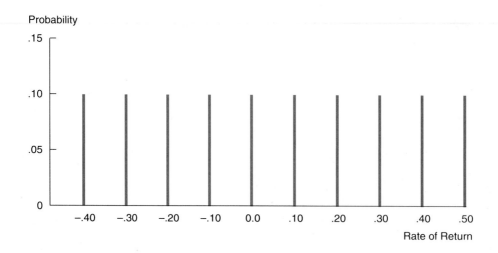

$$\text{Variance } (\sigma^2) = \Sigma(\text{Probability})\left(\begin{array}{c}\text{Possible} \\ \text{Return}\end{array} - \begin{array}{c}\text{Expected} \\ \text{Return}\end{array}\right)^2$$

$$= \Sigma(P_i)[R_i - E(R_i)]^2$$

Variance The larger the **variance** for an expected rate of return, the greater the dispersion of expected returns and the greater the uncertainty, or risk, of the investment. The variance for the perfect-certainty example would be:

$$(\sigma^2) = \Sigma P_i[R_i - E(R_i)]^2$$
$$= 1.0(0.05 - 0.05)^2 = 1.0(0.0) = 0$$

Note that in the case of perfect certainty, there is *no variance of return* because there is no deviation from expectations, and therefore no risk, or uncertainty. The variance for the second example where we were considering expectations for a strong economy, a weak economy, or no change in the economy would be:

$$\sigma^2 = \Sigma P_i[R_i - E(R_i)]^2$$
$$= [(0.15)(0.20 - 0.07)^2 + (0.15)(-0.20 - 0.07)^2$$
$$+ (0.70)(0.10 - 0.07)^2]$$
$$= [0.010935 + 0.002535 + 0.00063]$$
$$= .0141$$

Standard Deviation The **standard deviation** is the square root of the variance:

$$\text{Standard Deviation} = \sqrt{\Sigma P_i[R_i - E(R_i)]^2}$$

For the second example, the standard deviation would be:

$$\sigma = \sqrt{0.0141}$$
$$= 0.11874$$

Interpreting the Results In some cases, an unadjusted variance or standard deviation can be misleading. If conditions are not similar, that is, if returns show major differences, it is necessary to use a measure of *relative variability* to indicate risk per unit of return. This relative measure, the **coefficient of variation,** is found by:

$$\text{Coefficient of Variation (CV)} = \dfrac{\begin{array}{c}\text{Standard Deviation} \\ \text{of Returns}\end{array}}{\begin{array}{c}\text{Expected Rate} \\ \text{of Return}\end{array}}$$

$$= \dfrac{\sigma_i}{E(R)}$$

Variance A measure of variability equal to the sum of the squares of a return's deviation from the mean, divided by N.

Standard deviation A measure of variability equal to the square root of the variance.

Coefficient of variation (CV) A measure of relative variability that indicates risk per unit of return. It is equal to: standard deviation/mean value.

The CV for the example above would be:

$$CV = \dfrac{0.11874}{0.07000}$$
$$= 1.696$$

This measure of relative variability and risk is used by financial analysts to compare alternative investments with very different rates of return and standard deviations of returns. As an illustration, suppose investment A has an expected return of 7 percent and a standard deviation of 5 percent, while investment B has an expected return of 12 percent and a standard deviation of 7 percent. Comparing absolute measures of risk, investment B appears to be riskier because it has a standard deviation of 7 percent versus 5 percent for investment A. In contrast, the CV figures show that investment B has less risk per unit of return as follows:

$$CV_A = \dfrac{0.05}{0.07} = 0.714$$

$$CV_B = \dfrac{0.07}{0.12} = 0.583$$

Determinants of Required Rates of Return

In this section we continue our consideration of techniques for selecting securities for an investment portfolio. You will recall that this selection process involves finding securities that provide a rate of return that compensates you for (1) the time value of money during the period of investment, (2) the expected rate of inflation during the period, and (3) the risk involved.

The summation of these three components is called the required rate of return. This is the minimum rate of return that you should accept from an investment to compensate you for deferring consump-

> **Risk-free rate (RFR)** The basic interest rate with no accommodation for inflation or uncertainty.

tion. Because of the importance of the required rate of return to the total investment selection process, this section contains a detailed discussion of the three components and what influences each of them.

The analysis and estimation of the required rate of return is complicated by the behavior of market rates over time. First, the rates on specific assets change dramatically over time. Second, a wide range of rates is available for alternative investments at any time and the differences between these rates change over time.

An example of these changes can be seen in the promised yield on Moody's Aaa corporate bonds (the highest-grade corporate bonds). Yields were over 5 percent during the 1930s, declined to about 3 percent in the 1940s, rose to over 14 percent in the early 1980s, and then varied between 8 and 9 percent during the late 1980s and early 1990s. When making an investment, it is important to understand why the required rate on a security changes over time and to attempt to estimate such changes.

Table 1.1 gives an example of the range of rates for alternative investments in the form of a list of promised yields on various bonds. All of these bonds have contractual returns and yet their promised yields differ significantly. You could detect even greater differences among promised yields on assets such as common stock and real estate.

Differences in yields result from the riskiness of each investment. Hence, to select an investment that will provide the required rate of return, you must understand the risk factors that affect returns and

include them in your assessment of investment opportunities. Because the required returns on all investments change over time, and because large differences separate individual investments, you should be aware of several components that determine the required rate of return, starting with the risk-free rate.

The Risk-Free Rate

The **risk-free rate (RFR)** is the basic interest rate, assuming no uncertainty about future flows. The investor who knew with certainty the amount and timing of cash flows he or she would receive would demand the risk-free rate on such an investment. Earlier we called this the *pure time value of money*, because the only sacrifice the investor made was deferring the use of the money for a period of time. This risk-free rate of interest is the price charged for the exchange between current goods and future goods.

Two factors, one subjective and one objective, influence this price. The subjective factor is the time preference of individuals for the consumption of income. When individuals give up $100 of consumption this year, how much consumption do they want a year from now to compensate for that sacrifice? The strength of the human desire for current consumption influences the rate of compensation required. Time preferences vary among individuals, and the market creates a composite rate that includes the preferences of all investors. Although this composite rate changes over time, it does so gradually because it is influenced by all the investors in the economy, whose changes in preferences may offset one another.

The objective factor that influences the risk-free rate is the set of investment opportunities available in the economy. The investment opportunities are deter-

Table 1.1 *Promised Yields on Alternative Bonds*

Type of Bond	1982	1983	1984	1985	1986	1987	1988	1989	1990
U.S. government									
3-month Treasury bills	10.61%	8.61%	9.52%	7.48%	5.97%	5.78%	6.67%	8.11%	7.50%
Long-term Treasury bonds	12.23	10.84	11.99	10.75	8.14	8.64	8.98	8.58	8.74
Aaa corporate bonds	12.79	12.04	12.71	11.37	9.02	9.38	9.71	9.26	9.32
Baa corporate bonds	16.11	13.55	14.19	12.72	10.39	10.58	10.83	10.18	10.36

Source: *Federal Reserve Bulletin*, various issues.

Table 1.2		*Average Yields on U.S. Government 3-Month Treasury Bills*					
1967	4.29%	1973	7.03%	1979	10.07%	1985	7.48%
1968	5.34	1974	7.84	1980	11.43	1986	5.98
1969	6.67	1975	5.80	1981	14.03	1987	5.78
1970	6.39	1976	4.98	1982	10.61	1988	6.67
1971	4.33	1977	5.27	1983	8.61	1989	8.11
1972	4.07	1978	7.19	1984	9.52	1990	7.50

Source: *Federal Reserve Bulletin*, various issues.

mined in turn by the long-run real growth rate of the economy. A change in the economy's long-run growth rate causes a change in all investment opportunities, and in the required rates of return on all investments. Three factors influence the real growth rate of the economy: (1) the long-run growth rate of the labor force, (2) the long-run growth rate of the average number of hours worked by the labor force, and (3) the long-run growth rate of the productivity of the labor force (measured by output per hour).[4]

As the investment opportunities in an economy increase or decrease due to changes in the economy's long-run real growth rate, the risk-free rate of return likewise increases or decreases. Thus, there is a *positive* relationship between the real growth rate in the economy and the RFR. Again, while the long-run real growth rate, and, therefore the RFR, can change over time, these changes will be gradual because the three factors that determine this real growth rate (i.e., growth of the labor force, average hours worked, and labor productivity) change very gradually, sometimes offsetting each other.

Factors Influencing the Nominal Risk-Free Rate Earlier we observed that an investor would be willing to forego current consumption in order to increase future consumption at a rate of exchange called the *risk-free rate of interest*. This rate of exchange measured real growth in consumption since the investor wanted to increase the consumption of actual goods and services rather than consuming the same amount

that had come to cost more money. Therefore, when we discuss rates of interest, we need to discuss *real* rates of interest that adjust for changes in the general price level, as opposed to *nominal* rates of interest that are stated in money terms. That is, nominal rates of interest are determined by real rates of interest, plus other factors such as inflation and the monetary environment. It is important to understand these factors.

The variables that determine the risk-free rate change only gradually over the long term. Therefore, you might expect the required rate of return on a risk-free investment to be quite stable over time. As discussed previously, however, rates on long-term, high-grade corporate bonds were not stable over the period from 1930 through 1991. Another example of securities with even lower risk are U.S. government Treasury bills. Table 1.2 shows the average yield on T-bills for the period of 1967 to 1989.

Investors view T-bills as a prime example of a default-free investment because the government has unlimited ability to derive income from taxes or the creation of money from which to pay interest, so we should expect rates on T-bills to change only gradually. In contrast to this expectation, the data show a steady increase in 1968 and 1969 and a sharp decline in 1971, followed by a mammoth increase (close to 75 percent) in 1973. Again, following a decline to below 5 percent in 1976, rates increased to over 14 percent in 1981 before declining to less than 6 percent in 1986 and 1987. In sum, T-bill rates almost tripled in a period of 5 years and then declined by almost 60 percent in 5 more years. This indicates that the nominal rate of interest (the interest rate in money terms) on a default-free investment is definitely not stable in the long run, let alone the short run, even though the underlying determinants of the real RFR are quite stable. Two other factors influence the nominal risk-

[4]For an interesting discussion of the components of real growth and changes in the components over time, see *Economic Report of the President* (Washington, D.C.: U.S. Government Printing Office, 1987).

free rate, also referred to as the *money rate* or *market rate*: (1) the relative ease or tightness in the capital markets, and (2) the expected rate of inflation.

Conditions in the Capital Markets You will recall from prior courses in economics and finance that the purpose of capital markets is to bring together investors who want to invest savings with companies or governments who need capital to expand or to finance budget deficits. The cost of funds at any time (the interest rate) is the price that equates the current supply of capital available and the demand for capital. A change in the relative ease or tightness in the capital market is a short-run phenomenon caused by a temporary disequilibrium in the supply and demand of capital.

As an example, disequilibrium could be caused by an unexpected change in monetary policy (e.g., a change in the growth rate of the money supply) or fiscal policy (e.g., a change in taxes that would affect the federal deficit). Such a change in monetary policy or fiscal policy would produce a change in the risk-free rate of interest, but the change should be short-lived because in the longer run, the higher or lower interest rates would affect capital supply and demand. For example, a decrease in the growth rate of the money supply, which reflects a tightening in monetary policy, will reduce the supply of capital and increase interest rates. In turn, this increase in interest rates will cause an increase in savings and therefore the supply of capital, and a decrease in the demand for this higher-cost capital by corporations or individuals. These changes will bring risk-free interest rates back to the long-run equilibrium, which is based upon the long-run growth rate of the economy.

Expected Inflation Up to this point, we have assumed that the rate of return is unaffected by changes in the price level; that is, we have assumed real rates of interest. In discussing the rate of exchange between current and future consumption, we assumed that a 4 percent required rate of return meant that an investor was willing to give up $1 of consumption today to consume $1.04 worth of goods and services 1 year from now. Because this assumed no change in prices, a 4 percent increase in money wealth would mean a 4 percent increase in potential consumption of goods and services.

If, however, investors expected the prices of these goods and services to increase during the investment period, they would require the rate of return to include compensation for the inflation rate. Assume that you require a 4 percent real rate of return on a risk-free investment, but you expect prices to increase by 3 percent during the investment period. You should increase your required rate of return by this amount to about 7 percent [(1.04 × 1.03) − 1]. If you do not increase your required return, the $104 you receive at the end of the year will represent a real return of only 1 percent, not 4 percent. Since prices have increased by 3 percent during the year, what previously cost $100 now costs $103, so you can consume only about 1 percent more at the end of the year [($104/$103) − 1]. If you had required a 7.12 percent nominal return, your real consumption would have increased by 4 percent [($107.12/$103) − 1]. Therefore, an investor's nominal required rate of return in current dollars on a risk-free investment should be:

$$\text{Nominal RFR} = \left(1 + \text{Real RFR}\right)\left(1 + \text{Expected Rate of Inflation}\right) - 1$$

Rearranging the formula, you can calculate the real risk-free rate of return on an investment as follows:

$$\text{Real RFR} = \left[\frac{(1 + \text{Nominal Risk-Free Rate of Return})}{(1 + \text{Rate of Inflation})}\right] - 1$$

To see how this works, assume that the nominal return on U.S. government T-bills was 9 percent during a given year, when the rate of inflation was 5 percent. In this instance, the real risk-free rate of return on these T-bills was 3.8 percent, as follows:

$$
\begin{aligned}
\text{Real RFR} &= [(1 + 0.09)/(1 + 0.05)] - 1 \\
&= \frac{1.09}{1.05} - 1 \\
&= 1.038 - 1 \\
&= 0.038 = 3.8 \text{ percent}
\end{aligned}
$$

The nominal rate of interest on a risk-free investment is not a good estimate of the real RFR, because the nominal rate can change dramatically in the short run in reaction to temporary ease or tightness in the capital markets or to changes in the expected rate of inflation. The significant changes in the average yields on T-bills shown in Table 1.2 were caused by the large changes in the expected rate of inflation during this period. Table 1.3 shows the volatility of annual rates of inflation.

Table 1.3	*Annual Rates of Inflation: 1969–1989*						
1967	3.0%	1973	8.7%	1979	13.3%	1985	3.8%
1968	4.7	1974	12.3	1980	12.5	1986	1.1
1969	6.2	1975	6.9	1981	8.9	1987	4.4
1970	5.6	1976	4.9	1982	3.8	1988	4.6
1971	3.3	1977	6.7	1983	3.8	1989	4.7
1972	3.4	1978	9.0	1984	3.9	1990	6.1

Based upon December-to-December changes in the Consumer Price Index; 1982–1984 = 100.

Sources: *Federal Reserve Bulletin*, various issues. *Economic Report of the President*, various issues.

The Common Effect All the factors discussed thus far regarding the required rate of return affect all investments equally. Whether an investment is in stocks, bonds, real estate, or machine tools, if the expected rate of inflation increases from 2 percent to 6 percent, the investor's required return on *all* investments should increase by 4 percent. Similarly, if a decline in the expected real growth rate of the economy causes a decline in the real RFR of 1 percent, then the required return on all investments should decline by 1 percent.

Risk Premium

A risk-free investment was defined as one for which the investor is certain of the amount and timing of the expected returns. The returns from most investments do not fit this pattern. An investor typically is not completely certain of the income to be received, or when it will be received. Investments can range in uncertainty from basically risk-free securities like T-bills to highly speculative investments such as the common stock of small companies engaged in high-risk enterprises like oil exploration.

Most investors require higher rates of return on investments to compensate for any uncertainty. This increase in the required rate of return over the nominal risk-free rate is the **risk premium**. While the required risk premium represents a composite of all uncertainty, it is possible to consider several sources of uncertainty. In this section we identify and discuss briefly the major sources, including business risk, financial risk (leverage), liquidity risk, exchange rate risk, and country risk, and describe their effects on the required rate of return.

Risk premium The increase over the nominal risk-free rate that investors demand as compensation for an investment's uncertainty.

Business risk Uncertainty due to the nature of a firm's business.

Financial risk Uncertainty due to the method by which a firm finances its investments.

Business risk is the uncertainty of income flows caused by the nature of a firm's business. The more uncertain the income flows of the firm, the more uncertain the income flows to the investor. Therefore, the investor will demand a risk premium that includes uncertainty caused by the basic business of the firm. As an example, a firm in an industry like retail food that has experienced very stable sales and earnings growth over time, implying low business risk, must pay a lower risk premium than one in the auto industry where sales and earnings fluctuate substantially over the business cycle, implying high business risk.

Financial risk is the uncertainty introduced by the method by which the firm finances its assets. If a firm uses only common stock to finance assets, it incurs only business risk. If, in addition to using common stock, a firm borrows money to finance investments, it must pay fixed financing charges (in the form of interest to creditors) prior to providing income to the owners, who are the holders of common stock. As a result, the uncertainty of returns to the investor in the common stock of the company increases because of the firm's method of financing. This increase in uncertainty due to debt financing,

> **Liquidity risk** Uncertainty due to the ability to buy or sell an investment in the secondary market.
>
> **Exchange rate risk** Uncertainty due to the denomination of an investment in a currency other than that native to the investor.
>
> **Country risk** Uncertainty due to the possibility of major political or economic change in the country where an investment is located.

called *financial risk* or *financial leverage*, causes the investor to demand a larger risk premium.[5]

Liquidity risk is the uncertainty introduced by the secondary market for an investment.[6] An investor who gives up current consumption by investing expects that the investment will mature (as with a bond) or that it will be salable to someone else. In either case, the investor has the ability to convert the security into cash and use the proceeds for current consumption or other investments. An investor must consider two questions about liquidity when assessing the liquidity risk of an investment: (1) How long will it take to convert the investment into cash? (2) How certain is the price? Similar uncertainty faces a new investor: How long will it take to acquire the asset? What will the price be?

The ability to buy or sell an investment quickly without a substantial price concession is known as *liquidity*. Greater uncertainty regarding how fast an investment can be bought or sold, or a larger price concession required to buy or sell it, increases liquidity risk.

A U.S. government Treasury bill has almost no liquidity risk because it can be bought or sold in minutes at a price almost identical to the quoted price. In contrast, examples of illiquid investments include a work of art, an antique, or a parcel of real estate in a remote area. Such an investment may require a long time to find a buyer, and the selling price could vary substantially from expectations. Investors who are uncertain of their ability to buy or sell investments will

increase their required rates of return to compensate for this liquidity risk.

Exchange rate risk is the uncertainty of returns to an investor who acquires securities denominated in a currency different from his own. The likelihood of incurring this risk is becoming greater as investors buy and sell assets around the world, as opposed to only within their own countries. A U.S. investor who buys Japanese stock denominated in yen must consider not only the uncertainty of the return in yen, but also any change in the exchange value of the yen relative to the U.S. dollar. That is, in addition to the foreign firm's business and financial risk as well as the security's liquidity risk, you must consider the uncertainty of the return when converted from yen to U.S. dollars.

To see the effect of exchange rate risk, assume that you buy 100 shares of Mitsubishi Electric at 1,050 yen when the exchange rate is 135 yen to the dollar. The dollar cost of this investment is about $7.78 per share (1,050/135). A year later you sell the 100 shares at 1,200 yen when the exchange rate is 150 yen to the dollar. When you calculate the HPY in yen, you find the stock has increased in value by about 14 percent (1,200/1,050), but this is the HPY for a Japanese investor.

A U.S. investor receives a much lower return because, during this time period, the yen has weakened relative to the dollar by about 11 percent (i.e., it requires more yen to buy a dollar—150 versus 135). At the new exchange rate, the stock is worth $8 per share (1,200/150). Therefore, the return to the U.S. investor would be only about 3 percent ($8.00/$7.78) versus 14 percent for the Japanese investor. The difference in return for the Japanese investor and U.S. investor is because of the decline in the value of the yen relative to the dollar. Clearly, the exchange rate could have gone in the other direction, the dollar weakening against the yen. In this case, a U.S. investor would have experienced a good return, the 14 percent return measured in yen, as well as a gain from the exchange rate change.

Country risk, also called *political risk*, is the uncertainty of returns caused by the possibility of a major change in the political or economic environment of a country. The United States is acknowledged to have the smallest country risk in the world because its political and economic systems are the most stable. Nations with high country risk include South Africa, with its racial tensions, and China, as a result of the

---

[5]For a discussion of financial leverage, see Eugene F. Brigham, *Fundamentals of Financial Management*, 5th ed. (Hinsdale, Ill.: The Dryden Press, 1989): 221–225.

[6]Recall from prior courses that the overall capital market is composed of the primary market and the secondary market. Securities are initially sold in the primary market and then all subsequent transactions take place in the secondary market. These concepts are discussed in more detail in Chapter 3.

1989 unrest. On a single day—June 5, 1989—the Hong Kong stock market declined over 20 percent following student–military confrontations.[7] Investors in these markets, or in other countries that have unstable political–economic systems, must add a country risk premium when determining their required rates of return.

When investing globally (which will be emphasized throughout the book), investors must consider these additional uncertainties. What will happen to exchange rates during the investment period? What is the probability of a political or economic change that will adversely affect the rate of return? Exchange rate risk and country risk differ among countries. Exchange rate risk will depend upon the uncertainty of a given country's exchange rate with the United States (for a U.S. investor). A good measure of exchange rate risk would be the absolute variability of the exchange rate with a composite exchange rate. The analysis of country risk is much more subjective and must be based upon the history of the country.

The risk premium on an investment includes the uncertainty of expected returns to the investor from all sources. This value is determined by (1) the variability of operating earnings (business risk), (2) any added uncertainty of returns caused by how the investment is financed (financial risk), and (3) the uncertainty of buying or selling the investment (liquidity risk). In addition, when investing outside one's own country, one must consider (4) the uncertainty from changing exchange rates (exchange rate risk), and (5) the uncertainty caused by the possibility of a change in the political or economic environment in the other country (country risk).

Risk premium = f (Business risk, Financial risk,
　　　　　　　　　Liquidity risk, Exchange rate risk,
　　　　　　　　　Country risk)

Measures and Sources of Risk In this chapter we have examined both measures and sources of risk arising from an investment.

The *measures* of risk for an investment are:

- Variance of rates of return
- Standard deviation of rates of return

[7]Russell Todd and Robert Sherbin, "Hong Kong Stocks Plunge 22% on China Unrest; Other Asia Markets Fall; London Shares Drop," *The Wall Street Journal*, June 6, 1989: C10.

> **Security market line (SML)** A line that represents the combination of risk and return characteristic of investments in a market.

- Coefficient of variation of rates of return (standard deviation/means)

The *sources* of risk are:

- Business risk
- Financial risk
- Liquidity risk
- Exchange rate risk
- Country risk

Summary for Required Rate of Return

The overall required rate of return on an investment is determined by three factors: (1) the economy's real RFR, which is influenced by the investment opportunities in the economy (i.e., the economy's long-run real growth rate); (2) variables that influence the nominal RFR, which include short-run ease or tightness in the capital market and expected inflation; and (3) variables that influence the risk premium on investments, which include business risk, financial risk, liquidity risk, exchange rate risk, and country risk. The first two sets of variables are the same for all investments. Each source contributes to the risk of an investment, which is measured by the techniques listed above.

Relationship between Risk and Return

Previously, we showed how to measure risk and rates of return for alternative investments and we discussed what determines the rates of return that investors require. This section discusses the risk–return combinations that might be available at a given time and illustrates the factors that can cause changes in these combinations.

Figure 1.1 graphs the expected relationship between risk and return. It shows that investors increase their required rates of return as perceived risk (uncertainty) increases. The line that reflects the combination of risk and return available on alternative investments is typically called the **security market line (SML)** since it is meant to reflect the risk–return

---

Relationship between Risk and Return

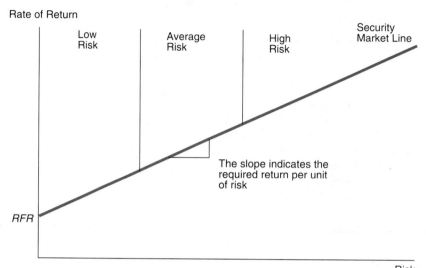

---

combinations available for all securities in the capital market at a given time. Given the security market line prevailing at a point in time, investors would select investments that are consistent with their risk preferences. Some would consider only low-risk investments, while others would welcome high-risk investments.

Beginning with an initial security market line, three changes can occur. First, individual investments can change positions on the line because of changes in their perceived risk. Second, the slope of the SML can change because of changes in the attitudes of investors toward risk, that is, investors can change the returns they require per unit of risk. Third, the SML can experience a parallel shift due to a change in one of the variables that affect all investments such as the real RFR or the expected rate of inflation. Each of these possibilities is discussed in this section.

Movements along the SML

Investors place alternative investments somewhere along the SML based upon their perceptions of the risk of the investments. Obviously, if an investment's risk changes due to a change in one of its risk sources such as its business or financial risk, it will move along the security market line. For example, if a firm in-

creases its financial risk with a large bond issue, investors will perceive its common stock as riskier and the stock will move up the curve to a higher risk position. Investors will then require a higher rate of return. As the common stock becomes more or less risky, it changes its position on the SML.

Changes in the Slope of the SML

The slope of the security market line indicates the return per unit of risk required by all investors. Assuming a straight line, it is possible to select any point on the SML and compute a risk premium (RP) through the equation:

$$RP_i = R_i - RFR$$

where:

RP_i = risk premium for asset i

R_i = the expected return for asset i

RFR = the expected return on a risk-free asset

If a point on the SML is identified as the portfolio that contains all the risky assets in the market (referred to as the market portfolio), it is possible to compute a market risk premium as follows:

$$RP_m = R_m - RFR$$

Figure 1.2   *Time Series Plot of Moody's Corporate Bond Yield Spreads (Baa-Aaa): Monthly 1972–1989*

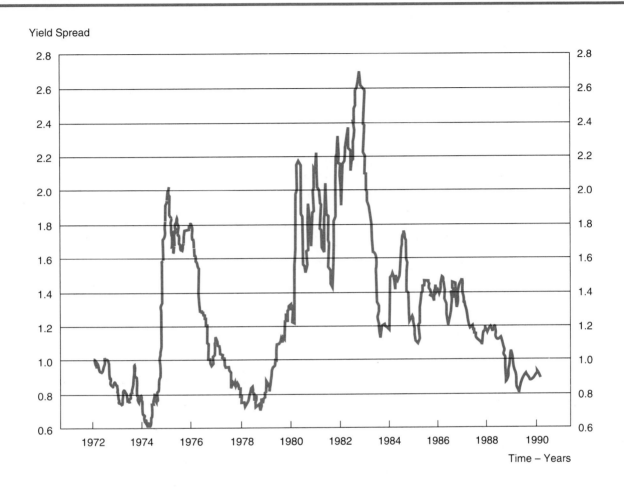

where:

RP$_m$ = the risk premium on the market portfolio

R$_m$ = the expected return on the market portfolio

RFR = the expected return on a risk-free asset

This market risk premium is not constant. The slope of the security market line changes over time. While we do not understand completely what causes such changes, we do know that the differences between the yields of assets with relatively constant risk, called **yield spreads**, change over time. As an example, if the yield on a portfolio of Aaa rated bonds is 7.50 percent and the yield on a portfolio of Baa rated bonds is 9.00 percent, we would say that the yield spread is 1.50 percent.[8] This 1.50 percent is also a risk

Yield spread The difference between yields of investments at a point in time.

premium because the Baa rated bond is considered to have higher risk, that is, greater probability of default. For an example of changes in a yield spread, note the difference in yields on Aaa rated bonds and Baa rated bonds shown in Figure 1.2.

[8]Bonds are rated by rating agencies based upon the credit risk of the securities, that is, the probability of default. Aaa is the top rating Moody's (a prominent rating service) gives to bonds with almost no probability of default. (Only U.S. Treasury bonds are considered to be of higher quality.) Baa is a lower rating Moody's gives to bonds of generally high quality, but with some possibility of default under adverse economic conditions.

Figure 1.3 **Change in Market Risk Premium**

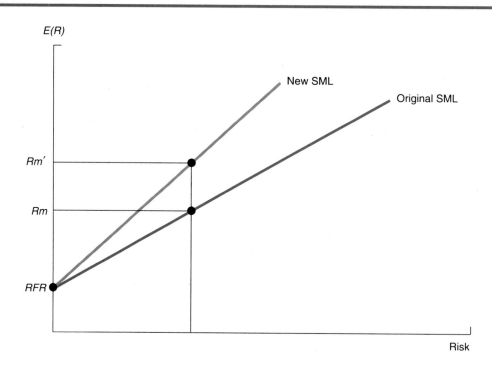

Although the risk levels of portfolios of Aaa bonds and Baa bonds would probably not change dramatically over time, the difference in yields (the yield spread) has changed by over 100 basis points (1 percent) in a short period of time. Such a change in the yield spread would imply a change in the market risk premium because, although the risk levels of the bonds remain relatively constant, investors have changed the spreads they demand to accept this risk.

This change in the risk premium implies a change in the slope of the market line. Such a change is shown in Figure 1.3. The figure assumes that the market risk premium increases, which means an increase in the slope of the market line. Such a change in the slope of the SML will affect the required rate of return for all risky assets. Irrespective of where an investment is on the original SML, its required rate of return will increase, although its risk characteristics remain unchanged.

Changes in Capital Market Conditions or Expected Inflation

The graph in Figure 1.4 shows what happens to the security market line when capital market conditions or the expected rate of inflation change. Either temporary tightness in the capital market or an increase in the expected rate of inflation could cause the SML to shift upward to the dashed line, parallel to the original SML. The parallel shift occurs because changes in market conditions or inflation affect all investments, no matter what their levels of risk.

To summarize this discussion, the relationship between risk and the required rate of return for an investment can change in three ways:

1. Movement *along* the market line demonstrates a change in the risk characteristics of a specific investment, such as a change in business risk or financial risk. This only affects the individual investment.

Figure 1.4   *Capital Market Conditions, Expected Inflation, and the Security Market Line*

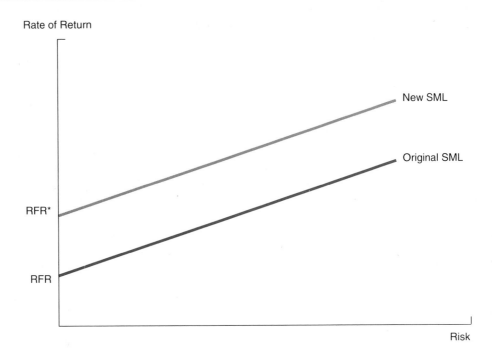

RFR = Nominal risk-free rate.

2. A change in the *slope* of the SML demonstrates a change in the attitudes of investors toward risk. Investors want either higher or lower rates of return for the same risk. This is also described as a change in the market risk premium (R_m − RFR). A change in the risk premium will affect all risky investments.

3. A *shift* in the market line demonstrates a change in market conditions such as ease or tightness of money, or a change in the expected rate of inflation. Again, such a change will affect all investments.

Summary

The purpose of this chapter is to provide a background that can be used in subsequent chapters. To achieve that goal, we covered several topics:

■ We discussed why individuals save part of their income and why they decide to invest their savings.

We defined *investment* as the current commitment of these savings for a period of time in order to derive a rate of return that compensates for the time involved, the expected rate of inflation, and the uncertainty.

■ We examined ways to quantify return and risk to help you analyze alternative investment opportunities. We considered two measures of mean return (arithmetic and geometric) and applied these to an individual investment and to a portfolio of investments during a period of time.

■ We considered the concept of uncertainty and alternative measures of risk (the variance and standard deviation of rates of return). In addition to these absolute measures of risk, we also discussed a relative measure of risk—the coefficient of variation.

■ We discussed in detail the determinants of the required rate of return for an investment. We noted that the estimation of the required rate of return is complicated because the rates on individual investments change over time, because a wide range of rates of return are available on alternative investments, and because the differences between required returns on alternative investments likewise change over time.

■ We examined the specific factors that determine the required rate of return: (a) the real risk-free rate, which is based upon the real rate of growth in the economy, and to some extent on individual preferences for consumption; (b) the nominal risk-free rate, which is influenced by ease or tightness in the capital markets and the expected rate of inflation; and (c) a risk premium, which is a function of risk from several sources, including business risk, financial risk, liquidity risk, exchange rate risk, and country risk.

■ We discussed the risk–return combinations that might be available on alternative investments at a point in time (illustrated by the SML) and the three factors that can cause changes in this relationship. First, a change in the risk related to an investment will cause movement along the security market line. Second, a change in investors' attitudes will cause a change in the required return per unit of risk, that is a change in the market risk premium, which will cause a change in the slope of the SML. Finally, a change in the capital market due to easier or tighter conditions or a change in the expected rate of inflation, will cause a parallel shift of the SML.

Based on this understanding of the investment environment, you are prepared to consider the numerous alternative investments available in the global market. This is the subject of Chapter 2.

Outline of the Book

As discussed earlier, the first section of the book provides an investment background by concentrating on why and how individuals invest, the alternative investments that are available, the functioning of the markets for bonds and stocks, and the indexes that track the performance of the major investments.

The second section gets into investment valuation by discussing how to analyze financial statements. It includes consideration of general valuation principles as applied to bonds and stocks and a presentation on how you might allocate assets in a global market environment.

In the third section, we get into detailed analysis of investments, beginning with fixed-income securities (bonds). We start with bonds because the valuation process for these securities is easier. Assuming that the issuer does not default, an investor in bonds

receives the expected income flows and can concentrate on estimating the required rate of return. We also consider alternative techniques for managing a portfolio of bonds.

The fourth section emphasizes common stocks using the top-down, fundamental approach, which begins with an analysis of the aggregate stock market and then proceeds to various industries and finally to individual companies and stocks within an industry. In contrast to evaluating investments based upon fundamental economic factors, some investors feel that the securities market is its own best predictor and, therefore, you need to examine only trends in alternative market series. This approach to investment selection, called *technical analysis*, is considered at the end of this section.

Besides the trend toward global markets, the other major development in capital markets has been the creation of new investment instruments. The chapters in Section 5 contain descriptions of these alternative investments such as options, warrants, and futures contracts. We consider how to analyze them and how to use them as part of a comprehensive investment program. We also consider investment companies (also known as *mutual funds*) as alternatives to direct investment.

Throughout the book we discuss the construction of a portfolio of investments that provides the best combination of risk and return. The final section of the book discusses this concept in detail, covering developments related to portfolio theory. Closely related to portfolio theory is the notion of efficient capital markets, which has been examined extensively during the past several decades. This theory and the voluminous empirical evidence that both supports and contradicts it are presented in Chapter 22. The final chapter of the book deals with how you can evaluate the risk–return performance of your portfolio.

In summary, the purpose of the book is to help you to understand why you invest, what investments are available to you, how you evaluate investments and make investment decisions, how you combine alternative investments into a portfolio, and how you evaluate the performance of your portfolio of investments to determine if it is meeting your objectives.

Questions

1. Why do people invest? Be specific regarding when they are willing to invest and what they expect to receive in the future.

2. Define *investment*.
3. Why do people borrow? Be specific.
4. As a student, are you saving or borrowing? What do you expect to derive from this activity?
5. Divide a person's life from ages 20 to 70 into 10-year segments and discuss the likely saving or borrowing patterns during each of these periods.
6. Would you expect the saving–borrowing pattern to differ by occupation (e.g., for a doctor versus a plumber)? Why or why not?
7. *The Wall Street Journal* reported that the yield on common stocks is about 4 percent, while a study at the University of Chicago contends that the annual rate of return on common stocks since 1926 has averaged about 9 percent. Reconcile these statements.
8. Some financial theorists consider the variance of the distribution of expected rates of return to be a good measure of uncertainty. Discuss the reasoning behind this measure of risk and its purpose.
9. What are the three components of an investor's required rate of return on an investment? Discuss each briefly.
10. Discuss the two major factors that determine the market nominal risk-free rate (RFR). Which of these factors would be more volatile over the business cycle? Why?
11. List and briefly discuss the five factors that influence the risk premium of an investment.
12. You own stock in the Gentry Company, and you notice that a recent bond offering has raised the firm's debt/equity ratio from 35 percent to 55 percent. Discuss the effect of this change on the variability of the firm's net income stream, other factors being constant. Would this change cause you to adjust your required rate of return on the common stock of the Gentry Company?
13. Draw a properly labeled graph of the security market line (SML) and indicate where you would expect the following investments to fall along that line. Discuss your reasoning.
    a. Common stock of large firms
    b. U.S. government bonds
    c. United Kingdom government bonds
    d. Low-grade corporate bonds
    e. Common stock of a Japanese firm
14. Explain why you would change your nominal required rate of return if you expected the rate of inflation to go from zero (no inflation) to 7 percent. Give an example of what would happen if

you did not change your required rate of return under these conditions.
15. Assume the long-run growth rate of the economy increased by 1 percent and the expected rate of inflation increased by 4 percent. What would happen to the required rates of return on government bonds and common stocks? How would the effects of the above changes differ between these alternative investments? Show these effects graphically.
16. You see in *The Wall Street Journal* that the yield spread between Baa corporate bonds and Aaa corporate bonds has gone from 350 basis points (3.5 percent) to 200 basis points (2 percent). Show graphically the effect of this change in spread on the SML and discuss its effect on the required return for common stocks.
17. Give an example of a liquid investment and an illiquid investment. Why do you consider each to be liquid or illiquid?
18. *CFA Examination III (June 1981)* As part of your portfolio planning process, it is suggested that you estimate the real long-run growth potential of the economy.
    a. Identify and explain three major determinants of the economy's real long-run growth. [5 minutes]
    b. Briefly discuss the outlook for each of these three determinants of long-term growth. Present approximate estimates for each of these components and calculate the composite *real* growth potential for the next 5 years. (While you should provide a calculation, emphasize the process rather than specific numbers.) [10 minutes]

Problems

1. On February 1 you bought some stock in the Wright Corporation for $34 a share and a year later you sold it for $39 a share. During the year you received a cash dividend of $1.50 a share. Compute your HPR and HPY on this stock investment.
2. On August 15, you purchased some stock at $55 a share and a year later you sold it for $51 a share. During the year, you received dividends of $3 a share. Compute your HPR and HPY on this investment.
3. At the beginning of last year you invested $2,000 in 40 shares of the Chang Corporation. During

the year Chang paid dividends of $7 per share. At the end of the year you sold the 40 shares for $59 a share. Compute your total HPY on these shares and indicate how much was due to the price change and how much was due to the dividend income.

4. The rates of return computed in Problems 1, 2, and 3 are nominal rates of return. Assuming that the rate of inflation during the year was 3 percent, compute the real rates of return on these investments. Compute the real rates of return if the rate of inflation were 9 percent.

5. During the past 5 years, you owned two stocks that had the following annual rates of return:

Year	Stock T	Stock B
1	0.17	0.08
2	0.08	0.03
3	−0.12	−0.07
4	−0.03	0.02
5	0.15	0.04

a. Compute the arithmetic mean annual rate of return for each stock. Which is most desirable by this measure?

b. Compute the standard deviation of the annual rate of return for each stock. (Use the Appendix if necessary.) By this measure, which is the preferable stock?

c. Compute the coefficient of variation for each stock. (Use the Appendix if necessary.) By this relative measure of risk, which stock is preferable?

d. Compute the geometric mean rate of return for each stock. Discuss the difference between the arithmetic mean return and geometric mean return for each stock and relate the differences in mean return to the standard deviation of the return for each stock.

6. You are considering acquiring shares of common stock in the Light and Dry Beer Corporation. Your rate of return expectations are as follows:

Possible Rate of Return	Probability
−0.10	0.30
0.00	0.10
0.10	0.30
0.25	0.30

Compute the expected return $[E(R_i)]$ on this investment.

7. A stockbroker calls you and suggests that you invest in the Fast and Powerful Computer Company. After analyzing the firm's annual report and other material, you feel that the distribution of expected rates of return is as follows:

Possible Rate of Return	Probability
−0.60	0.05
−0.30	0.20
−0.10	0.10
0.20	0.30
0.40	0.20
0.80	0.10

Compute the expected return $[E(R_i)]$ on this stock.

8. Without any formal computations, do you consider Light and Dry Beer in Problem 6 or Fast and Powerful Computer in Problem 7 to present greater risk? Discuss your reasoning.

9. During the past year you had a portfolio that contained U.S. government T-bills, long-term government bonds, and common stocks. The rates of return on each of them were as follows:

U.S. government T-bills	7.50%
U.S. government long-term bonds	9.50
Common stocks	12.60

During the year, the consumer price index, which measures the rate of inflation, went from 360 to 387 (1967 = 100). Compute the rate of inflation during this year. Compute the real rates of return on each of the investments in your portfolio based on the inflation rate.

10. You read in Business Week that a panel of economists has estimated that the long-run real growth rate of the U.S. economy over the next 5-year period will average 3 percent. In addition, a bank newsletter estimates that the average annual rate of inflation during this 5-year period will be about 4 percent. What nominal rate of return would you expect on U.S. government T-bills during this period?

11. Assume that the yield on U.S. government T-bills is 8.3 percent. What would your required rate of return be on common stocks if you wanted a 5

percent risk premium to own common stocks? If common stock investors became more risk averse, what would happen to the required rate of return on common stocks? What would the impact on stock prices be?

12. The consensus required rate of return on common stocks is 14 percent. In addition, you read in *Fortune* that the expected rate of inflation is 5 percent and the estimated long-term real growth rate of the economy is 3 percent. What interest

rate would you expect on U.S. government T-bills? What approximate risk premium for common stocks do these data imply?

References

Fama, Eugene F., and Merton H. Miller. *The Theory of Finance.* New York: Holt, Rinehart and Winston, 1972.

Fisher, Irving. *The Theory of Interest.* New York: Macmillan, 1930; reprinted by Augustus M. Kelley, 1961.

1a *Computation of Variance and Standard Deviation*

Variance and standard deviation are measures of how actual values differ from expected values (arithmetic mean) for a given series of values. In this case, we want to measure how rates of return differ from the arithmetic mean value of a series. There are other measures of dispersion, but variance and standard deviation are the best known because they are used in statistics and probability theory. Variance is defined as:

$$\text{Variance } (\sigma^2) = \Sigma(\text{Probability})(\text{Possible Return} - \text{Expected Return})^2$$
$$= \Sigma(P_i)[R_i - E(R_i)]^2$$

Consider the following example, as discussed in the chapter:

Probability of Possible Return (P_i)	Possible Return (R_i)	P_iR_i
0.15	0.20	0.03
0.15	-0.20	-0.03
0.70	0.10	0.07
		$\Sigma = 0.07$

This gives an expected return [E(R_i)] of 7 percent. The dispersion of this distribution as measured by variance is:

Probability (P_i)	Return (R_i)	R_i - E(R_i)	[R_i - E(R_i)]^2	P_i[R_i - E(R_i)]^2
0.15	0.20	0.13	0.0169	0.002535
0.15	-0.20	-0.27	0.0729	0.010935
0.70	0.10	0.03	0.0009	0.000630
				$\Sigma = 0.014100$

The variance (σ^2) is equal to 0.0141. The standard deviation is equal to the square root of the variance:

$$\text{Standard Deviation } (\sigma) = \sqrt{\Sigma P_i[R_i - E(R_i)]^2}$$

Consequently, the standard deviation for the preceding example would be:

$$\sigma_i = \sqrt{0.0141} = 0.11874$$

In this example, the standard deviation is approximately 11.87 percent. Therefore, you could describe this distribution as having an expected value of 7 percent and a standard deviation of 11.87 percent.

In many instances, you might want to compute the variance or standard deviation for a historical series in order to evaluate the past performance of the investment. Assume that you are given the following information on annual rates of return (HPY) for common stocks listed on the New York Stock Exchange (NYSE):

Year	Annual Rate of Return
19__1	0.07
19__2	0.11
19__3	−0.04
19__4	0.12
19__5	−0.06

In this case, we are not examining expected rates of return, but actual returns. Therefore, we can assume equal probabilities, and the expected value (in this case the mean value, R) of the series is the sum of the individual observations in the series divided by the number of observations, or 0.04 (0.20/5). The variances and standard deviations are:

Year	R_i	$R_i - \bar{R}$	$(R_i - \bar{R})^2$	
19__1	0.07	0.03	0.0009	$\sigma^2 = 0.0286/5$
19__2	0.11	0.07	0.0049	$= 0.00572$
19__3	−0.04	−0.08	0.0064	
19__4	0.12	0.08	0.0064	$\sigma = \sqrt{0.00572}$
19__5	−0.06	−0.10	0.0110	$= 0.0756$
			$\Sigma = 0.0286$	

We can interpret the performance of NYSE common stocks during this period of time by saying that the average rate of return was 4 percent and the standard deviation of annual rates of return was 7.56 percent.

Coefficient of Variation

In some instances you might want to compare the dispersion of two different series. Variance and standard deviation are *absolute* measures of dispersion. That is, they can be influenced by the magnitude of the original numbers. To compare series with very different values, you need a *relative* measure of dispersion. A potential measure for this relative dispersion is the coefficient of variation, which is defined as:

$$\text{Coefficient of Variation (CV)} = \frac{\text{Standard Deviation}}{\text{Expected Return}}$$

A larger value indicates greater dispersion relative to the arithmetic mean of the series. For the previous example, the CV would be:

$$CV_1 = \frac{0.0756}{0.0400} = 1.89$$

It is possible to compare this value to a similar figure having a very different distribution. As an example, assume you wanted to compare this investment to another investment that had an average rate of return of 10 percent and a standard deviation of 9 percent. The standard deviations alone tell you that the second series has greater dispersion (9 percent versus 7.56 percent) and might be considered to have higher risk. In fact, the relative dispersion for this second investment is much less.

$$CV_1 = \frac{0.0756}{0.0400} = 1.89$$
$$CV_2 = \frac{0.0900}{0.1000} = 0.90$$

Considering the relative dispersion and the total distribution, most investors would probably prefer the second investment.

Problems

1. Your rate of return expectations for the common stock of Floppy Disc Company during the next year are:

Possible Rate of Return	Probability
−0.10	0.25
0.00	0.15
0.10	0.35
0.25	0.25

Compute the expected return [$E(R_i)$] on this investment, the variance of this return (σ^2), and its standard deviation (σ).
   a. Under what conditions can the standard deviation be used to measure the relative risk of two investments?
   b. Under what conditions must the coefficient of variation be used to measure the relative risk of two investments?
2. Your rate of return expectations for the stock of Turk Computer Company during the next year are:

Possible Rate of Return	Probability
−0.60	0.15
−0.30	0.10
−0.10	0.05
0.20	0.40
0.40	0.20
0.80	0.10

Compute the expected return $[E(R_i)]$ on this stock, the variance (σ^2) of this return, and its standard deviation (σ).

a. On the basis of expected return $[E(R_i)]$ alone, discuss whether Floppy Disc or Turk Computer is preferable.

b. On the basis of standard deviation (σ) alone, discuss whether Floppy Disc or Turk Computer is preferable.

c. Compute the coefficients of variation (CVs) for Floppy Disc and Turk Computer and discuss which stock return series has the greater *relative* dispersion.

3. On the basis of the following annual rates of return, compute the mean rate of return and standard deviation of the returns for U.S. government T-bills and United Kingdom common stocks.

Year	U.S. Government T-Bills	United Kingdom Common Stocks
19__4	0.063	0.150
19__5	0.081	−0.043
19__6	0.076	0.374
19__7	0.090	0.192
19__8	0.085	−0.106

a. Discuss these two alternative investments in terms of their arithmetic average rates of return, their absolute risk, and their relative risk.

b. Compute the geometric mean rate of return for each of these investments. Compare the arithmetic mean return and geometric mean return for each investment and discuss this difference between mean returns as related to the standard deviation of each series.

CHAPTER 2

Selecting Investments in a Global Market

Individuals are willing to defer current consumption for a range of reasons. Some save for their children's college tuition or their own; others wish to accumulate down payments for a home, car, or boat; others want to amass adequate retirement funds for the future. Whatever the reason for an investment program, the techniques we used in Chapter 1 to measure risk and return will help you evaluate investment alternatives.

But what are those alternatives? Thus far we have said very little about the investment opportunities that are available in financial markets. In this chapter, we address this issue by surveying investment alternatives. This background is needed for later chapters where we analyze in detail several individual investments such as bonds, common stock, and other securities and consider how to construct and evaluate portfolios of investments.

As an investor in the 1990s, you have an array of investment choices that were not available only a few decades ago. Together, the dynamism of financial markets, technological advances, and new regulations have resulted in numerous new investment instruments and expanded trading opportunities. Improvements in communications and relaxation of international regulations have made it easier for investors to trade in securities markets around the world, expanding your ability to trade in both domestic and global markets.[1] Telecommunications networks enable U.S. brokers to reach security exchanges in London, Tokyo, and other European and Asian cities, as well as those in New York, Chicago, and other U.S. cities. The competitive environment in the brokerage industry and the deregulation of the banking sector

[1]In this regard, see Scott E. Pardee, "Internationalization of Financial Markets," Federal Reserve Bank of Kansas City, *Economic Review* (February 1987): 3–7.

> **Portfolio** A group of investments. Ideally the investments should have different patterns of returns over time.

have made it possible for more financial institutions to compete for investor dollars. This has spawned investment vehicles with a variety of maturities, risk–return characteristics, and cash flow patterns. In this chapter we will examine some of these choices.

As an investor, you need to understand the differences among investments so you can build a properly diversified **portfolio** that conforms to your objectives. That is, you should seek to acquire a group of investments with different patterns of returns over time. If chosen carefully, such portfolios minimize risk for a given level of return because low or negative rates of return on some investments during a period of time are offset by above average returns on others. The goal is to build a balanced portfolio of investments with a relatively stable overall rate of return. A major goal of this text is to help you understand and evaluate the risk–return characteristics of investment portfolios. An appreciation of alternative security types is the starting point for this analysis.

This chapter is divided into three main sections. In the first section we introduce and briefly describe global capital markets because, as noted earlier, investors can choose securities from financial markets around the world. We look at some reasons why investors should include foreign as well as domestic securities in their portfolios. We continue the investigation of where to invest in Chapter 4 when we examine security markets in more detail.

In the second section we discuss securities found in domestic and global markets, describing their main features and cash flow patterns. From this discussion you will see that the varying risk–return characteristics of alternative investments

suit the preferences of different investors. Some investments are more appropriate for individuals, while others are better suited for financial institutions like insurance companies and pension funds. We conclude the chapter with an assessment of the historical risk and return performance of several investment types. This presentation will examine the relationship among the returns for securities that we describe in this chapter.

Why Global Investments?

A description of investment alternatives written ten years ago would have been much shorter than this one. At that time, the bulk of investments available to individual investors consisted of stocks and bonds sold on U.S. securities markets. Now, however, a call to your broker gives you access to a range of securities sold throughout the world. Currently, you can purchase stock in General Motors or Toyota, U.S. Treasury bonds or Japanese government bonds, a mutual fund invested in U.S. biotechnology companies, a global growth stock fund or a German stock fund, or options on a U.S. stock index or the British pound along with innumerable other investments.

Several changes have caused this explosion of investment opportunities. For one, the growth and development of numerous foreign financial markets such as those in Japan, the United Kingdom, and Germany have made them accessible and viable for U.S. investors. Numerous U.S. investment firms recognized the opportunity in this accessibility and established and expanded facilities in these countries. This expansion was aided by major advances in telecommunications technology that made it possible to maintain constant contact with offices and financial markets around the world.

In addition to the efforts by U.S. firms, foreign firms and global investors undertook counterbalancing initiatives with wealth derived from oil sales and foreign exchange provided by surpluses in balances of payments. As a result, investors and investment firms from around the world found it desirable and possible to trade securities worldwide. Thus the range of investment alternatives extends from the traditional U.S. financial markets to security markets around the world.

For several reasons, U.S. investors should consider adding foreign investments to their portfolios:

1. When investors compare the absolute and relative sizes of U.S. and foreign markets for stocks and bonds, they will see that ignoring foreign markets reduces their choices to less than 50 percent of available investment opportunities. Since more opportunities broaden your range of risk–return choices, it makes sense to evaluate foreign securities in selecting investments to build a portfolio.
2. The rates of return available on non-U.S. securities often have substantially exceeded those on U.S. securities. The higher returns on non-U.S. equities can be justified by the higher growth rates for the countries where they are issued.
3. Diversification with foreign securities reduces portfolio risk.

In this section we will look at each of these reasons in detail to demonstrate the growing role of foreign financial markets for U.S. investors and to assess the benefits and risks of trading in these markets.

Relative Size of U.S. Financial Markets

Prior to 1970, the securities traded in the U.S. stock and bond markets comprised about 65 percent of all the securities available in world capital markets. Therefore, a U.S. investor selecting securities strictly from U.S. markets had a fairly complete range of investment choices. These markets included most of the investments available. Under these conditions, most U.S. investors probably felt it was not worth the time and effort to expand their investment universe to include investments available in foreign markets. That situation has changed dramatically over the last 20 years. Currently, investors who ignore foreign markets limit their investment choices substantially.

Figure 2.1 shows the breakdowns of securities available in world capital markets in 1969 and 1989.

Figure 2.1   *Breakdown of Worldwide Investable Securities: 1969 and 1989*

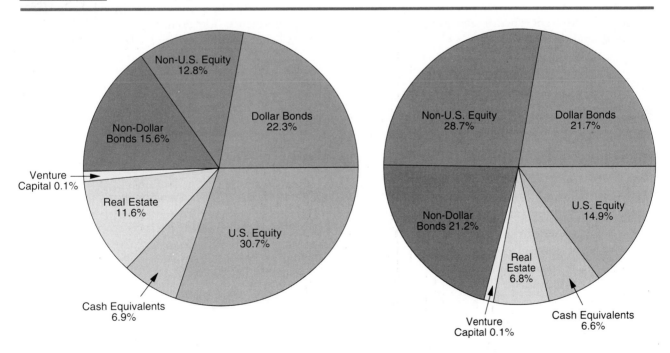

1969 $2.3 Trillion

1989 $24.0 Trillion
(Preliminary)

Source: Brinson Partners, Inc., Chicago, Ill.

Not only has the overall value of all securities increased dramatically (from $2.3 trillion to $24 trillion), but the composition has also changed. Concentrating on proportions of bond and equity investments, the figure shows that in 1969 U.S.-dollar bond and equity securities made up 53 percent of the total versus 28.4 percent for nondollar bonds and equity. By 1989 the U.S. share had become 36.6 percent versus 49.9 percent for nondollar bonds and stocks. These data indicate that the U.S. proportion of only the bond and equity market has declined from 65 percent of the total in 1969 to 42 percent in 1989.

Clearly the U.S. security markets have come to include a smaller proportion of the total world capital market, and it is likely that this trend will continue. The faster economic growth of many other countries compared to the United States will require foreign companies to issue debt and equity securities to finance this growth. Therefore, U.S. investors should consider foreign investments because of their overall importance in world capital markets, and also because of the differing risk–return opportunities they provide. Thus, the investing universe of the 1990s should include many different types of securities available on markets around the world.

Rates of Return on U.S. and Foreign Securities

You need to examine rates of return on U.S. and foreign securities to appreciate that many non-U.S. securities provide superior rates of return, but also to help you recognize the impact of exchange rate risk as discussed in Chapter 1.

Global Bond Market Returns Table 2.1 reports annual compound rates of return for several major international bond markets from 1978 to 1989. You should examine the domestic returns on these bonds and their returns in U.S. dollars. The *domestic return* is the rate of return an investor within the country would earn (e.g., an Australian investor in Australia). In contrast, the return in U.S. dollars is what a U.S. investor would earn after the effects of currency exchange rates during the period.

An analysis of the domestic returns in Table 2.1 indicates that the performance of the U.S. bond market ranked fifth out of the nine countries. When the impact of exchange rates is considered, the U.S. experience was third out of nine. This difference in relative performance for domestic versus U.S.-dollar returns is because the exchange rate effect for a U.S.

Table 2.1 *International Bond Market Compound Annual Rates of Return: 1978–1979*

	Components of Return		
	Total Return in U.S. Dollars	**Total Domestic Return**	**Exchange Rate Effect**
Australia	7.59%	11.07%	−3.13%
Canada	9.92	10.46	−0.49
France	9.46	11.43	−1.77
Germany	8.47	6.58	1.77
Japan	11.65	7.04	4.31
Netherlands	9.39	7.85	1.43
Switzerland	5.73	3.55	2.11
United Kingdom	10.06	11.71	−1.48
United States	9.96	9.96	—

Source: Adam M. Greshin and Margaret Darasz Hadzima, "International Bond Investing and Portfolio Management," in *The Handbook of Fixed-Income Securities*, 3d ed., ed. by Frank J. Fabozzi (Homewood, Ill.: Business One Irwin, 1991).

investor was negative in several cases and offset superior domestic performance.

As an example, the domestic return on Australian bonds of 11.07 percent exceeded the U.S. return of 9.96 percent. The average foreign exchange effect of −3.13 percent, however, reduced this Australian dollar return after conversion to U.S. dollars to only 7.59 percent, dropping it below the return for U.S. bonds. Even with these differences, it appears that investors in non-U.S. bonds from several countries experienced rates of return close to or above those of investors who limited themselves to the U.S. bond market.

Global Equity Market Returns   Table 2.2 (on pp. 36–37) gives annual rates of return in local currencies and in U.S. dollars for 12 major equity markets from 1985 to 1989, identifying the best performing market each year by an asterisk. There are two important observations. First, the U.S. market never experienced the best performance during this 5-year period. Second, the average of the returns for the period indicates that the U.S. performance in local currency was the eighth lowest of the 12 countries. In U.S. dollars, the United States market ranked 11 out of 12. A similar analysis of local currency returns for six countries over a 16-year period indicates that the U.S. market was superior only once in 16 years and had the lowest average return for the period.

Like the results for bond market returns, these results for equity markets around the world indicate that investors who limited themselves to the U.S. market experienced rates of return below those available in most other countries. This is true for both domestic returns and rates of return adjusted for exchange rates.

Individual Country Equity Risk and Return

It has been shown that most countries experienced higher domestic rates of return than the United States. A natural question is whether these superior returns are attributable to higher levels of risk for common stock in these countries.

Table 2.3 (on p. 38) gives figures for total return and risk for a number of individual countries for the 8-year period from 1982 through 1989. (The risk measure, **volatility**, is the standard deviation of returns, as discussed in Chapter 1.) While the risk measure for the U.S. market (16.9) is one of the lowest

| **Volatility** A measure of risk. It is typically equal to the standard deviation of returns.

values, the return is also quite low. A relative measure of performance is derived by dividing the return for each market by its risk measure. These return-to-risk results indicate that the U.S. performance in local currency ranked 10th out of 12. This performance is also shown in Figure 2.2 (on p. 39), which plots the annual compound growth rate of domestic price against the standard deviation of annual return. Figure 2.3 (on p. 40) shows similar results with prices converted to U.S. dollars. Again, the U.S. performance is ranked 10 of 12.

Risk of Combined Country Investments

Thus far, we have discussed the risk and return results for individual countries. In Chapter 1 we considered the idea of combining a number of assets into a portfolio and noted that it would be desirable to diversify the investments in order to reduce the variability of the returns over time. We discussed how proper diversification reduces the variability (our measure of risk) of the portfolio because alternative investments have different patterns of returns over time. When the rates of return on some investments are negative or below average, other investments in the portfolio will be experiencing above average rates of return. This should give a fairly stable rate of return for the total portfolio, which means that it will have a lower standard deviation and, therefore, be considered less risky. While we will discuss and demonstrate portfolio theory in detail in Chapter 20, we need to consider the concept at this point in order to fully understand the benefits of global investing.

The way to measure whether two investments will contribute to diversifying a portfolio is to compute the correlation coefficient between their rates of return over time. Correlation coefficients can range from +1.00 to −1.00. A correlation of +1.00 means that the rates of return for these two investments move exactly together. Combining investments that move together into a portfolio would not help diversify the portfolio because they have identical rate of return patterns over time. In contrast, a correlation coefficient of −1.00 means that the rates of return for two investments move exactly opposite to each other. When one investment is experiencing above-average rates of return, the other is suffering through below average rates of return of the same magnitude.

Table 2.2 *FT-Actuaries World Equity Market Performance: 1985–1989*

Country	1985 Local Currency	1985 U.S. Dollars	1986 Local Currency	1986 U.S. Dollars	1987 Local Currency	1987 U.S. Dollars
Canada	18.3	11.6	6.4	8.0	4.0	10.4
Denmark	31.8	66.0	−15.3	2.6	−4.5	15.5
France	44.9	85.2	45.2	71.0	−27.8	−13.9
Italy	102.8*	133.6*	73.6*	117.1*	−32.4	−22.3
Japan	13.5	42.9	53.9	93.9	8.5*	41.4*
Netherlands	25.7	61.2	4.0	30.7	−18.9	0.3
Norway	25.7	50.7	−8.8	−6.5	−14.0	1.8
Sweden	34.8	59.6	36.1	52.6	−15.1	−0.9
Switzerland	53.8	92.2	9.9	39.9	−34.0	−16.5
United Kingdom	15.6	44.1	20.2	23.2	4.6	32.5
United States	25.6	25.6	14.2	14.2	0.5	0.5
West Germany	72.7	122.8	5.6	34.3	−36.8	−22.7
World Average	24.5	35.8	29.6	39.3	0.9	15.0
Average—12 markets	25.8	40.5	29.6	47.4	1.3	19.7

*Indicates best performing market each year.
Source: "Anatomy of World Markets," (London: Goldman, Sachs International Ltd., June 1990 supplement).

Combining two investments like this in a portfolio would contribute much to diversification because it would stabilize the rates of return over time, reducing the standard deviation of the rate of return for the portfolio and hence its risk. Therefore, to help you diversify your portfolio and reduce your risk, you want an investment that has either low positive correlation, zero correlation, or, ideally, negative correlation with the other investments in your portfolio. With this in mind, the following discussion considers the correlations of returns on U.S. bonds and stocks with returns on foreign bonds and stocks.

Global Bond Portfolio Risk Table 2.4 (on p. 38) lists the correlation coefficients between domestic rates of return for bonds in the U.S. and bonds in major foreign markets from 1978 to 1989. Notice that most of the correlations for returns are below 0.50. These low positive correlations mean that investors have substantial opportunities for risk reduction through global diversification of bond portfolios. A U.S. investor in any market except Canada's would

substantially reduce the standard deviation of the portfolio.

Why do these correlation coefficients for returns between U.S. bonds and those of various foreign countries differ? That is, why is the U.S.–Canada correlation 0.78, while the U.S.–Australia correlation is only 0.8? The answer is that the international trade patterns, economic growth, fiscal policies, and monetary policies of the countries differ. The fact is, we do not have an integrated world economy, but rather a collection of economies that are related to one another in different ways. As an example, the U.S. and Canadian economies are very closely related because of their geographic proximity, similar domestic economic policies, and extensive trade between them. Each is the other's largest trading partner. In contrast, the United States has much less trade with Australia, and the fiscal and monetary policies of the two countries differ dramatically.

A country between these extremes is Japan. The United States has a strong trade relationship with Japan, but each has a fairly independent set of eco-

1988		1989		Average: 1985–1989	
Local Currency	U.S. Dollars	Local Currency	U.S. Dollars	Local Currency	U.S. Dollars
4.4	13.7	17.7	21.2	10.2	13.0
53.1	35.7	36.2	42.0	20.3	32.4
51.5	33.6	29.5	35.6	28.7	42.3
22.8	9.5	12.3	15.6	35.8*	50.7*
39.5	35.4	18.6	3.1	26.8	43.3
26.6	12.1	22.2	28.0	11.9	26.5
43.9	36.5	44.5*	43.9*	18.3	25.3
54.5*	45.9*	34.3	32.8	28.9	38.0
10.2	−6.5	23.7	20.5	12.7	25.9
6.0	2.1	31.6	17.3	15.6	23.8
12.6	12.6	26.4	26.4	15.9	15.9
28.3	13.8	34.1	40.7	20.8	37.8
24.4	21.4	22.8	15.1	20.1	25.3
26.6	23.0	27.6	27.3	22.2	39.7

nomic policies. Therefore, the U.S.–Japan correlation falls between the U.S.–Canada and U.S.–Australia correlations. The point is, macroeconomic differences give the correlation of bond returns between the United States and each other country a unique value. These differing correlations make it worthwhile to diversify with foreign bonds, and they also give guidance regarding which countries will provide the greatest reduction in the standard deviation (risk) of returns.

Table 2.4 also contains correlation coefficients between rates of return that have been adjusted for exchange rates. These results for returns in U.S. dollars are similar to the results for domestic returns except that all correlations are lower, which means that the adjustment for exchange rates reduces the relationship even more.

It is also possible to demonstrate that *the correlation between a single pair of countries changes over time.* The correlation coefficients of returns between countries change because the factors influencing the correlations such as international trade, economic growth, fiscal policy, and monetary policy change over time. A change in any of these variables will produce a change in how the economies are related and in the relationship between returns on bonds, which reflect the future outlook for the economies. As an example, the correlation between the United States and Japan before 1980 was quite low, reflecting limited trade and independent economic policies. During the 1980s, international trade between the two countries increased substantially and so did the correlation between returns on bonds. Specifically, the U.S.–Japan correlation from 1978 to 1981 was 0.34, while from 1986 to 1989 it was 0.58.

We can expect correlations to change among countries that are part of the European Economic Community (EEC). While these countries have always had natural relationships, the extent of their relationships will become more positive after 1992 when they form a united Europe. Part of this transition is the potential for a united monetary system. Clearly, if this economic unification is successful, the correlations between returns for financial investments

| Table 2.3 | *Risk and Return for 12 Major Stock Markets in Local Currency and U.S. Dollars: 1982–1989* |

	Local Currency			U.S. Dollars		
	CGR Return[a]	Risk[b]	Return / Risk	CGR Return	Risk	Return / Risk
Canada	10.7	17.3	0.62	11.7	19.2	0.61
Denmark	20.5	18.9	1.08	24.7	21.3	1.16
France	27.5	21.5	1.28	30.2	24.1	1.25
Italy	26.0	23.9	1.09	27.2	25.7	1.06
Japan	25.4	16.4	1.55	34.5	22.4	1.54
Netherlands	17.2	19.2	0.90	22.6	18.8	1.20
Norway	22.4	26.7	0.91	25.6	27.6	0.93
Sweden	21.6	22.2	0.97	24.5	22.8	1.07
Switzerland	9.5	18.4	0.52	13.6	19.8	0.69
United Kingdom	17.6	18.8	0.94	17.5	21.3	0.82
United States	13.3	16.9	0.79	13.3	16.9	0.79
West Germany	16.8	20.3	0.83	22.6	22.7	1.00

[a]CGR Return = Annual compound growth rate of stock price series

[b]Risk = Standard deviation of annual percentage change in stock price series

Source: "Anatomy of World Markets," (London: Goldman, Sachs International Ltd., June 1990 supplement).

| Table 2.4 | *Correlation Coefficients between Rates of Return on Bonds in the United States and Major Foreign Markets: 1978–1989 (monthly data)* |

	Domestic Returns	Returns in U.S. Dollars
Australia	0.18	0.12
Canada	0.78	0.72
France	0.25	0.28
Germany	0.52	0.32
Japan	0.39	0.28
Netherlands	0.54	0.37
Switzerland	0.35	0.30
United Kingdom	0.34	0.32

Source: Adam M. Greshin and Margaret D. Hadzima, "International Bond Investing and Portfolio Management," in *The Handbook of Fixed-Income Securities*, 3d ed., ed. by Frank J. Fabozzi (Homewood, Ill.: Business One Irwin, 1991).

like bonds and stocks will increase between these countries.

Figure 2.4 (on p. 41) shows what happens to the risk/reward tradeoff when we combine U.S. and foreign bonds. A comparison of a completely non-U.S. portfolio and strictly U.S. portfolio indicates that the non-U.S. portfolio has both a higher rate of return and a higher standard deviation of return than the U.S. portfolio. Combining two portfolios in different proportions gives a very interesting set of points.

The expected rate of return is a weighted average of the two portfolios. In contrast, the risk of the combination is not a weighted average, but also depends upon the correlation between the two portfolios. In this example, the risk levels of the combined portfolios decline below those of either of the individual portfolios. Therefore, a U.S. investor is able not only to increase the rate of return, but also to reduce the risk of a bond portfolio by adding foreign bonds.

Global Equity Portfolio Risk The correlation of world equity markets resembles that for bonds.

Figure 2.2   *Plot of Annual Rates of Return and Risk for Major Stock Markets in Local Currency: 1982–1989*

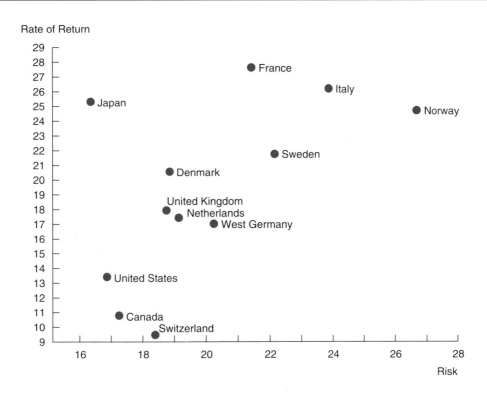

Table 2.5 (on p. 42) lists the correlation coefficients between monthly equity returns of each country and the U.S. market (both domestic and in U.S. dollars) for the 9-year period from 1981 to 1989. About one-half of the correlations between local currency returns top 0.50, with most between 0.30 and 0.60. The correlations among rates of return adjusted for exchange rates were always lower; only 3 of the 11 correlations exceed 0.50 and most were in the range of 0.20 to 0.50.

These relatively small positive correlations between U.S. stocks and foreign stocks have similar implications to those derived for bonds. Investors can reduce the overall risk of their stock portfolios by including foreign stocks.

Figure 2.5 (on p. 43) demonstrates the impact of international equity diversification. These curves demonstrate that as you increase the number of randomly selected securities in a portfolio, the standard deviation will decline due to the benefits of diversifi-

cation within your own country, referred to as *domestic diversification*. After a certain number of securities (30 to 40), the curve will flatten out at a risk level that reflects the basic market risks for the domestic economy. The lower curve illustrates the benefits of international diversification *in addition to* domestic diversification. Adding foreign stocks to a U.S. stock portfolio enables you to reduce the overall risk of your portfolio because foreign stocks are not correlated with our economy.

To see how this works, consider, for example, the effect of U.S. inflation and interest rates on all U.S. securities. As discussed in Chapter 1, all U.S. securities will be affected by these variables. In contrast, a Japanese stock is altered by the Japanese economy and will not be affected by U.S. variables. Thus, adding Japanese, German, and French stocks to a portfolio of U.S. stocks reduces the potential risk to a level that reflects only worldwide systematic factors.

Figure 2.3 *Plot of Annual Rates of Return and Risk for Major Stock Markets in U.S. Dollars: 1982–1989*

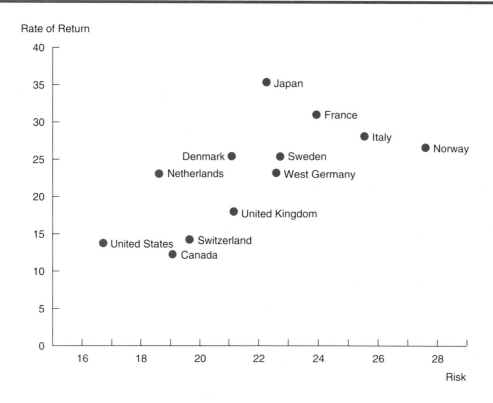

Summary on Global Investing At this point, we have considered the relative size of the market for non-U.S. bonds and stocks and found that it has grown in size and importance, becoming too big to ignore. We have also examined the rates of return for foreign bond and stock investments and determined that, in most instances, their rates of return per unit of risk were superior to those in the U.S. market. Finally, we discussed constructing a portfolio of investments and the importance of diversification in reducing the variability of returns over time, which reduces the risk of the portfolio. It was noted that successful diversification requires the combination of investments with low positive or negative correlations between rates of return.

We then examined the correlation between rates of return on U.S. and foreign bonds and stocks and discovered a consistent pattern of low positive corre-

lations. Therefore, relatively high rates of return combined with low correlation coefficients indicate that adding foreign stocks and bonds to a U.S. portfolio would have increased the average return and reduced the risk of the portfolio.

These are several rather compelling reasons for adding foreign securities to a U.S. portfolio. Therefore, it is important to develop a global investment perspective both because such an approach is justified, and also because this is the trend in the investment world today that will continue in the future. This perspective will not be easy because it requires an understanding of new terms, instruments such as Eurobonds, and institutions like the Japanese stock market. Still, the effort is justified because we are developing a set of skills and a way of thinking that will carry us into the next century and beyond.

| Figure 2.4 | *Risk/Return Tradeoff for International Bond Portfolios* |

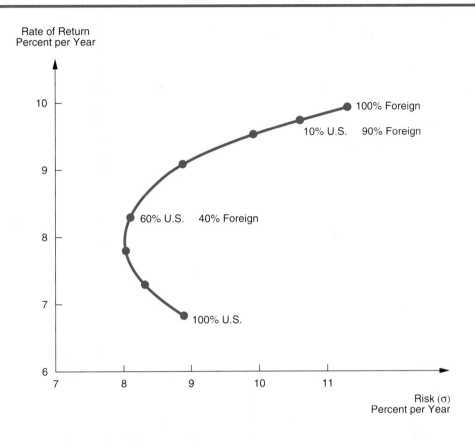

Source: Kenneth Cholerton, Pierre Pieraerts, and Bruno Solnik, "Why Invest in Foreign Currency Bonds?" *Journal of Portfolio Management* 12, no. 4 (Summer 1986): 4–8. Reprinted with permission.

Global Investment Choices

This section presents an overview of investment alternatives from around the world, beginning with fixed-income investments and progressing through numerous alternatives. This is an important overview and foundation for subsequent chapters where we describe techniques to value individual investments and combine alternative investments into properly diversified portfolios that conform to your risk–return objectives.

The investments are divided by asset classes. Specifically, in the first section, we describe fixed-income investments, which offer contractual payment streams that can include a stated interest payment (or no interest payment) and a specified payment at maturity. This section also considers preferred stock, which

involves fixed payments, but does not give the legal protection of bonds. In the second section we discuss equity investments, which do not have specified payments, but involve company ownership. The third section contains a discussion of special equity instruments such as warrants and options, which have characteristics of both fixed-income and equity instruments. Many investors are interested in one or several of these investments, but do not want to analyze individual securities. Such individuals should consider investment companies, which are also described in this section.

All these investments are called *financial assets* because their payoffs are in money. In contrast, a large set of investments, referred to as *real assets*, include such things as grain or real estate. These assets are

Table 2.5 *Correlation Coefficients between Rates of Return on Common Stocks in the United States and Major Foreign Stock Markets: 1981–1989 (monthly data)*

	Local Currency Rates of Return	Rates of Return in U.S. Dollars
Canada	0.79	0.77
Denmark	0.39	0.29
France	0.55	0.46
Germany	0.41	0.30
Italy	0.31	0.25
Japan	0.41	0.27
Netherlands	0.62	0.56
Norway	0.53	0.48
Sweden	0.45	0.35
Switzerland	0.64	0.49
United Kingdom	0.72	0.56

Source: "Anatomy of World Markets," (London: Goldman, Sachs International Ltd., June 1990 supplement).

Fixed-income investments Loans with contractually mandated payment schedules from investors to firms or governments.

Certificates of deposit (CDs) Instruments issued by banks and S&Ls that require minimum deposits for specified terms, and pay higher rates of interest than deposit accounts.

considered in the next section, beginning with contracts for deferred delivery (futures contracts). This is followed by a consideration of alternative opportunities in real estate. We conclude with a group of assets called *low liquidity investments* because of the relative difficulty in buying and selling them. They include art, antiques, coins, stamps, and precious gems.

The purpose of this survey is to briefly introduce each of these investment alternatives to allow you to appreciate the full spectrum of alternatives. The final section of the chapter describes the historical return and risk patterns for many of these investment alternatives. Again, the purpose is to provide additional background to help you evaluate individual investments and build a diversified portfolio of investments from around the world.

Fixed-Income Investments

Fixed-income investments have contractually mandated payment schedules. Their investment contracts promise specific payments at predetermined times, although the legal force behind the promise varies and this affects their risks and required returns. At one extreme, if the issuing firm does not make its payment at the appointed time, creditors can declare the issuing firm bankrupt. In other cases (e.g., income bonds), the issuing firm must make payments only if it earns profits. In yet other instances, such as preferred stock, the issuing firm does not have to make payments unless its board of directors votes to do so.

It is important to recognize that investors who acquire fixed-income securities (except preferred stock) are really lenders to the issuers. Specifically, you lend some amount of money, called the *principal*, to the borrower. In return, the borrower promises to make periodic interest payments, and at the maturity of the loan, to pay back the principal.

Savings Accounts   Savings accounts are so familiar you might not think of them as fixed-income investments, yet an individual who deposits funds in a savings account at a bank or savings and loan association (S&L) is really lending money to the institution and, as a result, earning a fixed payment. These investments are generally considered to be convenient, liquid, and very low-risk because almost all are insured. Consequently, their rates of return are generally low compared to other alternatives. Several versions of these accounts have been developed to appeal to investors with differing objectives.

The passbook savings account has no minimum balance, and funds may be withdrawn at any time with very little loss of interest. Due to its flexibility, the promised interest on passbook accounts is relatively low.

For investors with larger amounts of funds who are willing to give up liquidity, banks and S&Ls developed **certificates of deposit (CDs)**, which require minimum deposits (typically $500) and have fixed durations (usually 3 months, 6 months, 1 year, $2\frac{1}{2}$ years). The promised rates on CDs are higher than those for passbook savings, and the rate increases with the size and the duration of the deposit. An investor who wants to cash in a CD prior to its stated expiration date must pay a heavy penalty in the form of reduced interest.

Figure 2.5   *Risk Reduction through National and International Diversification*

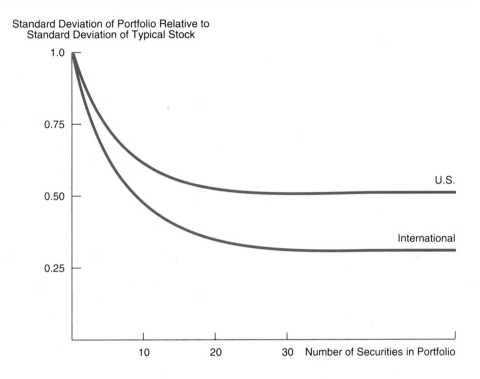

Standard Deviation of Portfolio Relative to
Standard Deviation of Typical Stock

Source: B. H. Solnik, "Why Not Diversify Internationally Rather than Domestically?" *Financial Analyst's Journal*
(July–August 1974): 48–54.

Investors with large sums of money ($10,000 or more) can invest in Treasury bills (T-bills), which are short-term obligations (maturing in from 3 to 12 months) of the U.S. government. To compete against T-bills, banks and S&Ls issue money market certificates, which require minimum investments of $10,000 and have minimum maturities of 6 months. The promised rate on these certificates fluctuates at some premium over the weekly rate on 6-month T-bills. Investors can redeem these certificates only at the bank of issue, and they incur penalties if they withdraw their funds before maturity.

Capital Market Instruments **Capital market instruments** are fixed-income obligations that trade in the secondary market, which means that you can buy them from and sell them to other individuals or institutions. Capital market instruments fall into four categories that we will discuss briefly in turn: U.S. Treasury securities, U.S. government agency securi-

| **Capital market instruments** Fixed-income investments that trade in the secondary market. |

ties, municipal bonds, and corporate bonds. These securities will be discussed in more detail in the next chapter.

U.S. Treasury Securities   Securities issued by the U.S. Treasury may be bills, notes, or bonds depending upon their times to maturity. Specifically, bills mature in less than a year, notes in 1 to 10 years, and bonds in over 10 years from time of issue.

U.S. Government Agency Securities   Agency securities are sold by various agencies of the government to support specific programs, but they are not direct obligations of the Treasury. An example would be the Federal National Mortgage Association (FNMA or Fannie Mae), which sells bonds to the public and uses

> **Debentures** Bonds that promise payments of interest and principal, but pledge no specific assets. Holders have first claim on the issuer's income and unpledged assets.
>
> **Mortgage bonds** Bonds that pledge specific assets, the proceeds of which are used to pay off bondholders in case of bankruptcy.
>
> **Subordinated bonds** Debentures that, in case of default, entitle holders to claims on the issuer's assets only after the claims of holders of senior debentures and mortgage bonds are satisfied.
>
> **Income bonds** Debentures that stipulate interest payments only if the issuer earns the income to make the payments by specified dates.

the proceeds to purchase mortgages from insurance companies or savings and loans. Although the securities issued by federal agencies are not direct obligations of the government, they are virtually default-free, because it is inconceivable that the government would allow them to default, and they are fairly liquid.

Municipal Bonds Municipal bonds are issued by local government entities (states, cities, towns, etc.) as either general obligation or revenue bonds. General obligation bonds are backed by the full taxing power of the municipality, whereas revenue bonds pay the interest from revenue generated by specific projects. For example, the revenue needed to pay the interest on sewer bonds comes from water taxes.

Municipal bonds differ from other fixed-income securities in that they are tax-exempt. The interest earned from them is exempt from taxation by the federal government and by the state that issued the bond, provided the investor is a resident of that state. For this reason, municipal bonds are popular with investors in high tax brackets.

Corporate Bonds Corporate bonds are fixed-income securities issued by industrial corporations, public utility corporations, or railroads to raise funds to invest in plant, equipment, or working capital. Corporate bonds fall into various categories based upon their contractual promises to investors. **Debentures** are promises to pay interest and principal, but they pledge no specific assets (referred to as *collateral*) in case the firm does not fulfill its promise. This means the bondholder depends upon the success of the borrower to make the promised payment. Debenture owners usu-

ally have first call on the firm's earnings and any unpledged assets. If the issuer does not make an interest payment, the debenture owners can declare the firm bankrupt and claim its assets to pay off the bonds.

Mortgage bonds are similar to debentures, but they pledge specific assets such as buildings and equipment. In case of bankruptcy, the proceeds from the sale of these pledged assets are used to pay off the mortgage bondholders.

Subordinated bonds are similar to debentures, but in the case of default, subordinated bondholders have claim to the assets of the firm only after the firm has satisfied the claims of all senior debentures and mortgage bondholders. Within this general category of subordinated issues, you can find senior subordinated, subordinated, and junior subordinated bonds, the last having the weakest claim of all bondholders.

Income bonds stipulate interest payment schedules, but the interest is due and payable only if the issuers earn income to make the payment by stipulated dates. If the company does not earn the required amount, it does not have to make the interest payment and it cannot be declared bankrupt. Instead, the interest payment is considered in arrears and, if subsequently earned, it must be paid off.

Convertible bonds have the interest and principal characteristics of other bonds, with the added feature that they can be turned back to the firm in exchange for its common stock. As an example, a firm could issue a $1,000 face-value bond and stipulate that owners of the bond could, at their discretion, turn the bond in to the issuing corporation and convert it into 40 shares of the firm's common stock. These bonds are very appealing to investors because they combine the features of a fixed-income security with the option of conversion into the common stock of the firm, should it prosper.

International Bond Investing As noted earlier, over half of all fixed-income securities available to U.S. investors are issued by firms in countries outside the United States. Investors identify these securities in different ways: by the country or city of the issuer (e.g., United States, United Kingdom, Japan), by the location of the primary trading market (e.g., United States, London), and by the currency in which the securities are denominated (e.g., dollars, yen, pounds sterling). We will identify foreign bonds by their country of origin and include these other differences in each description.

Eurobonds are international bonds denominated in currencies not native to the countries where they are issued. Specific kinds of Eurobonds include Eurodollar bonds, Euroyen bonds, Eurodeutschemark bonds, and Eurosterling bonds. A Eurodollar bond is denominated in U.S. dollars and sold outside the United States to non-U.S. investors. A specific example would be a U.S. dollar bond issued by General Motors and sold in London. These are typically issued in Europe, with the major concentration in London. Eurobonds can also be denominated in yen or deutschemarks. For example, Nippon Steel can issue Euroyen bonds for sale in London.

Yankee bonds are sold in the United States, denominated in U.S. dollars, but issued by foreign corporations or governments. This allows a U.S. citizen to buy a bond of a foreign firm or government but receive all payments in U.S. dollars, thereby eliminating exchange rate risk. An example would be a U.S. dollar-denominated bond issued by British Airways. Similar bonds are issued in other countries, including the Bulldog Market, which involves British sterling-denominated bonds issued by non-British firms, or the Samurai Market, which involves yen-denominated bonds issued by non-Japanese firms.

International domestic bonds are bonds sold by an issuer within its own country in that country's currency. An example would be a bond sold by a Japanese corporation in Japan denominated in yen. A U.S. investor acquiring such a bond would receive maximum diversification, but would incur exchange rate risk.

Preferred stock is classified a fixed-income security because its yearly payment is stipulated as either a coupon (e.g., 5 percent of the face value) or a stated dollar amount (e.g., $5 preferred). Preferred stock differs from bonds because its payment is legally a dividend and therefore not legally binding. For each period, the firm's board of directors must vote to pay it, similar to a common stock dividend. Although preferred dividends are not legally binding as the interest payments on a bond are, they are considered practically binding because of the credit implications of a missed dividend.

Equity Instruments

This section describes several equity instruments, which differ from fixed-income securities because their returns are not contractual. As a result, you can

Eurobonds Bonds denominated in a currency not native to the country in which they are issued.

Yankee bonds Bonds sold in the United States and denominated in U.S. dollars, but issued by a foreign firm or government.

International domestic bonds Bonds issued by a foreign firm denominated in its native currency and sold within its own country.

Preferred stock An equity investment that stipulates the dividend payment either as a coupon or a stated dollar amount. The firm's directors can withhold payments.

Common stock An equity investment that represents ownership of a firm, with full participation in its success or failure. The firm's directors must approve dividend payments.

receive returns that are much better or much worse than what you would receive on a bond. We begin with common stock, the most popular equity instrument and probably the most popular investment instrument.

Common stock represents ownership of a firm. Owners of the common stock of a firm share in the company's successes and problems. If, like IBM, McDonald's, or Xerox, the company does very well, the investor receives very high rates of return and can become very wealthy. In contrast, the investor can lose money if the firm does not do well or even goes bankrupt, as the once formidable Penn Central, W. T. Grant, and Interstate Department Stores all did. In these instances, the firm is forced to liquidate its assets and pay off all its creditors; the common stock owner receives what is left. The point is, investing in common stock entails all the advantages and disadvantages of ownership and is a relatively risky investment compared to fixed-income securities.

Common Stock Classifications When considering an investment in common stock, there is a tendency to divide the vast universe of stocks into categories based upon general business line and then by industry within these business lines. The division by business line would give classifications for industrial firms, utilities, transportation firms, and financial institutions. Within each of these business lines, there are industries. The most diverse business line — the industrial group — would include industries like automobiles, industrial machinery, chemicals, and beverages.

> **American Depository Receipts (ADRs)** Certificates of ownership of a foreign firm issued by a bank, which holds the firm's common stock in safekeeping.

Utilities would include electrical power companies, gas suppliers, and the water industry. Transportation would include airlines, trucking firms, and railroads. Financial institutions would include several categories of banks, savings and loans, and credit unions.

An alternative classification scheme might separate issues between domestic (U.S.) and foreign common stocks. We will avoid this division because the business line–industry breakdown is more appropriate and useful when constructing a diversified portfolio of common stock investments. With a global capital market, the focus of analysis should be all the companies in an industry, viewed in a global setting. As an example, when one is considering the automobile industry, it is necessary to go beyond General Motors, Ford, and Chrysler and also consider auto firms from throughout the world such as Honda Motors, Porsche, Daimler Benz, Nissan, and Fiat.

Therefore, our subsequent discussion on foreign equities concentrates on how you buy and sell these securities because this procedural information has often been a major impediment. Many investors may recognize the desirability of foreign common stock in terms of its risk and return characteristics, but they may be intimidated by the logistics of the transaction. The purpose of the next section is to alleviate this concern by explaining the alternatives available.

Foreign Equities Many American citizens think nothing of buying TV sets and automobiles produced by companies in Japan, Germany, and France, but as investors, they hesitate to consider the common stock of these firms although foreign stocks offer some attractive alternatives to U.S. stocks. One barrier has been the perceived difficulty of purchasing foreign stocks. Currently, however, there are several ways to acquire foreign common stock:

1. Purchase or sale of American Depository Receipts (ADRs)
2. Purchase or sale of American shares
3. Direct purchase or sale of foreign shares listed on a U.S. or foreign stock exchange
4. Purchase or sale of international mutual funds

Purchase or Sale of American Depository Receipts The easiest way to acquire foreign shares directly is through **American Depository Receipts (ADRs).** These are certificates of ownership issued by a U.S. bank, which holds the shares in safekeeping as a convenience to an investor. ADRs can be issued at the discretion of the bank based upon the demand for the stock. The shareholder absorbs the additional handling costs of an ADR through higher transfer expenses, which are deducted from dividend payments.

ADRs are quite popular in the United States. As of the end of 1990, 110 foreign company stocks were listed on the NYSE, and 64 of these were available through ADRs, including all those listed from Japan, the United Kingdom, Australia, and the Netherlands. In addition, 65 foreign firms are listed on the American Stock Exchange (AMEX) with most of the non-Canadian stocks available through ADRs.

Purchase or Sale of American Shares American *shares* are securities issued in the United States by a transfer agent acting on behalf of a foreign firm. Because of the added effort and expense incurred by the foreign firm, a limited number of American shares are available.

Direct Purchase or Sale of Foreign Shares The most difficult and complicated foreign equity transaction takes place in the country where the firm is located, because it must be carried out in the foreign currency and the shares must then be transferred to the United States. This routine can be cumbersome. A second way to directly buy or sell foreign stock is a transaction on a foreign stock exchange outside the country where the securities originated. As an example, if you acquired shares of a French auto company listed on the London Stock Exchange (LSE), the shares would be denominated in pounds and the transfer would be swift, assuming your broker has a membership on the LSE.

Finally, you could directly buy or sell foreign stocks listed on the NYSE or the AMEX. This is similar to buying a U.S. stock, but only a limited number of foreign firms qualify for, and are willing to accept the cost of, listing. Still, this number is growing. As of the end of 1989, over 30 foreign firms were directly listed on the NYSE, in addition to the firms that were available through ADRs.

Purchase or Sale of International Mutual Funds
Numerous investment companies invest all or a portion of their funds in stocks of firms outside the United States. The alternatives range from global funds, which invest in both U.S. stocks and foreign stocks, to international funds, which invest almost wholly outside the United States. In turn, international mutual funds can: (1) diversify across many countries, (2) concentrate in a segment of the world such as the Pacific basin, or (3) concentrate in a specific country. Examples include the Japan Fund, the Germany Fund, the Italy Fund, or the Korea Fund. A mutual fund is a convenient path to global investing, particularly for a small investor, since the purchase or sale of one of these funds is similar to a transaction for a comparable U.S. mutual fund.

Special Equity Instruments

In addition to common stock investments, it is also possible to invest in equity-derivative securities, which give you a claim on the common stock of a firm. This would include **options**, which are rights to buy or sell common stock at a specified price for a stated period of time. There are two kinds of option instruments: warrants and put and call options.

Warrants A warrant is an option issued by a corporation that gives the holder the right to acquire a firm's common stock from the company at a specified price within a designated time period. The warrant does not constitute ownership of the stock, only the option to buy the stock. Warrants are typically attached to a bond issue and have characteristics of a convertible bond. A bond with warrants provides an opportunity for the investor to acquire a firm's common stock at a specified price.

Call Options A **call option** is similar to a warrant, since it is an option to buy the common stock of a company within a certain period at a specified price called the *striking price*. A call option differs from a warrant because it is not issued by the company but by another investor who is willing to assume the other side of the transaction. Options are also typically valid for a shorter time period than warrants. Call options are generally valid for less than a year whereas warrants extend for over 5 years.

Put Options The holder of a **put option** has the right to sell a given stock at a specified price during a

Options The right to buy or sell a firm's common stock at a specified price for a stated period of time.
Call options Options to buy a firm's common stock within a certain period at a specified price.
Put options Options to sell a firm's common stock within a certain period at a specified price.

designated time period. Puts are used by investors who expect a stock price to decline during the specified period or by investors who own the stock and want protection from a price decline.

Futures Contracts

As discussed, options provide the right to buy or sell common stock at a specified price during some time interval. Another instrument that provides an alternative to the purchase of an investment is a futures contract. This is an agreement that provides for the future exchange of a particular asset at a specified delivery date in exchange for a specified payment at the time of delivery. While the full payment is not made until the delivery date, a good faith deposit called the *margin* is made to protect the seller. This is typically about 10 percent of the value of the contract.

The bulk of trading on the commodity exchanges is in futures contracts, which are contracts for the delivery of a commodity such as wheat or corn at some future date, usually within 9 months. The current price of the futures contract is determined by the participants' beliefs about the future for the commodity. In July of a given year, a trader could speculate on the Chicago Board of Trade on the prices for wheat in the following September, December, March, and May. If the investor expected the price to rise, he or she could buy futures contracts on one of the commodity exchanges for later sale; if the investor expected the price to fall, he or she could sell futures contracts on an exchange and buy similar contracts later when the price had declined to cover the sale.

There are several differences between investing in an asset through a futures contract and investing in the asset itself. One is the use of more borrowed funds to finance the futures purchase, which increases the volatility of returns. Because an investor puts up only a small proportion of the total value of the futures contract (10 to 15 percent), when the price of the commodity changes, the change in the total value of the contract is large compared to the amount invested.

> **Money market funds** Investment companies that hold portfolios of high-quality, short-term securities like T-bills. High liquidity and superior returns make them a good alternative to bank savings accounts.

Another unique aspect is the term of the investment. Although stocks can have infinite maturities, futures contracts typically expire in less than a year.

Financial Futures In addition to futures contracts on commodities, a recent innovation has been the development of futures contracts on financial instruments such as T-bills, Treasury bonds, and Eurobonds. For example, you can buy or sell a futures contract that promises future delivery of $100,000 of Treasury bonds on a given day in the future at a set price and yield. Such a contract is available on the Chicago Board of Trade (CBT). These futures contracts allow individual investors, bond portfolio managers, and corporate financial managers to protect themselves against volatile interest rates. Currency futures can also allow individual investors or portfolio managers to speculate on or to protect against changes in exchange rates. Finally, there are futures contracts on stock market series such as the S&P (Standard & Poor's) 500, the *Value Line* Index, and the Nikkei Average.

Investment Companies

The investment alternatives described so far are individual securities that can be acquired from a government entity, a corporation, or another individual. However, rather than directly buying an individual stock or bond issued by one of these sources, you may choose to acquire these investments indirectly by buying shares in an investment company, also called a *mutual fund*, that owns a number of individual stocks or bonds or a combination of the two. Specifically, an investment company sells shares in itself and uses the proceeds of this sale to acquire bonds, stocks, or other investment instruments. As a result, an investor who acquires shares in an investment company is a partial owner of the investment company's portfolio of stocks or bonds. We distinguish investment companies by the types of investment instruments they acquire. Discussions of some of the major types follow.

Money Market Funds Money market funds are investment companies that acquire high-quality,

short-term investments (referred to as *money market instruments*) like T-bills, high-grade commercial paper (public short-term loans) from various corporations, and large CDs from the major money center banks. The yields on the money market portfolios always surpass those on normal bank CDs, because the investment by the money market fund is larger and the fund can commit to longer maturities than the typical individual. In addition, the returns on commercial paper are above the prime rate. The typical minimum initial investment in a money market fund is $1,000, it charges no sales commission, and minimum additions are $250 to $500. You can always withdraw funds from your money market fund without penalty and you receive interest to the day of withdrawal.

Individuals tend to use money market funds as alternatives to bank savings accounts because they are generally quite safe (since they typically limit their investments to high-quality, short-term investments), they provide yields above what is available on most savings accounts, and the funds are readily available. Therefore, you might use one of these funds to accumulate funds to pay tuition or for a down payment on a car. Because of relatively high yields and extreme flexibility and liquidity, the total value of these funds has grown to assets of over $250 billion in 1990.

Bond Funds Bond funds generally invest in various long-term government, corporate, or municipal bonds. They differ by the quality of the bonds included in the portfolio as assessed by various rating services. Specifically, the bond funds range from those that invest only in risk-free government bonds and high-grade corporate bonds to those that concentrate in lower-rated corporate or municipal bonds, called *high-yield bonds* or *junk bonds*. The expected rate of return on bond funds will vary, with the low-risk government bond funds paying the lowest returns and the high-yield bond funds paying the highest expected returns.

Common Stock Funds Numerous common stock funds invest to achieve the stated investment objectives, which can include aggressive growth, income, precious metals investments, international diversification, and balanced goals. Such funds offer smaller investors the benefits of diversification and professional management. To meet the diverse needs of investors, numerous funds have been created that concentrate in one industry or sector of the economy, such as chemicals, electric utilities, health, housing, and technology. These funds are diversified within a sector or industry, but are not diversified across the total market so they entail more risk.

Also, international funds invest outside the United States and global funds invest in the United States and in other countries. As discussed earlier, these funds offer excellent opportunities for global investing by individual investors.

Balanced Funds   Balanced funds invest in a combination of bonds and stocks of various sorts depending on their stated objectives.

Real Estate

Like commodities, most investors view real estate as an interesting and profitable investment alternative, but believe that it is only available to a small group of experts with a lot of capital to invest. The fact is, some feasible real estate investments do not require detailed expertise or large capital commitments. We will begin by considering low-capital alternatives.

Real Estate Investment Trusts (REITs)   A **real estate investment trust** is basically an investment company designed to invest in various real estate properties. It is similar to a stock or bond mutual fund except that the money provided by the investors is invested in property and buildings rather than in stocks and bonds. There are several types of REITs.

Construction and development trusts lend the money required by builders during the initial construction of a building. Mortgage trusts provide the long-term financing for properties. Specifically, they acquire long-term mortgages on properties once construction is completed. Equity trusts own various income-producing properties such as office buildings, shopping centers, or apartment houses. An investor in an equity real estate trust is buying part of a portfolio of income-producing properties.

REITs have experienced periods of great popularity and significant depression in line with changes in the aggregate economy and the money market. While they are subject to cyclical risks depending on the economic environment, they offer small investors a way to participate in real estate investments.[2]

Real estate investment trusts (REITs)   Investment funds that hold portfolios of real estate investments.

Direct Real Estate Investments   The most common type of direct real estate investment, the purchase of a home, is the largest investment most people ever make. Today, according to the Federal Home Loan Bank, a single-family house usually costs over $95,000. The purchase of a home is considered an investment because, as the buyer, you initially pay a sum of money either all at once or over a number of years. For most people, who are not in a position to pay cash for a house, the financial commitment includes a down payment (typically 10 to 20 percent of the purchase price) and specific mortgage payments over a 20- to 30-year period that include reductions in the loan's principal and also interest on the outstanding balance. Subsequently, they hope to sell the house for what they paid for it, plus a gain.

Raw Land   Another direct real estate investment is the purchase of raw land with the intention of selling it in the future at a profit. During the period of time that you own the land, you have a cash outflow because it is necessary to make mortgage payments, maintain the property, and pay taxes on it. An obvious risk is the possible difficulty of selling it for an uncertain price. Raw land generally has low liquidity compared to most stocks and bonds.

Rental Property   Many investors with an interest in real estate investing acquire apartment buildings or houses with low down payments, with the intention of deriving enough from the rents to pay the expenses of the structure, including the mortgage payments. For the first few years following the purchase, the investor generally has no reported income from the building because of tax deductible expenses including the interest component of the mortgage payment and depreciation on the structure. Subsequently, property provides a cash flow and an opportunity to profit from the sale of the property.[3]

Land Development   Typically, land development involves buying raw land, dividing it into individual lots,

[2]Diane Harris, "Prime REITs for Would-Be Moguls," *Money,* April 1984; 93–96; Jill Bettner, "REITs House Good Value after Recent Price Declines," *The Wall Street Journal,* November 28, 1989: C1, C3.

[3]For a discussion of this alternative, see Diane Harris, "An Investment for Rent," *Money,* April 1984: 87–90.

and building houses on it. (Buying land and building a shopping mall would also be considered land development.) This is a feasible form of investment, but requires a substantial commitment of capital, time, and expertise. While the risks can be high, because of the commitment of time and capital, the rates of return from a successful housing or commercial development can be significant.[4]

Low-Liquidity Investments

Most of the investment alternatives we have described are traded on securities markets. Except for real estate, they have good liquidity. Although many investors view the investments discussed in this section as alternatives to financial investments, financial institutions do not typically acquire them because they are fairly illiquid and have high transaction costs compared to stocks and bonds. Many of these assets are sold at auctions, causing expected prices to vary substantially. The transaction costs are high because there is no national market for these investments, so local dealers must be compensated for the added carrying costs and the cost of searching for buyers or sellers. Given their disadvantages, many financial theorists view low-liquidity investments more as hobbies than investments, even though they can earn substantial rates of return.

Antiques The investors who earn the greatest returns from antiques are dealers who acquire them to refurbish and sell at a profit. If we gauge the value of antiques based upon prices established at large public auctions, it appears that many serious collectors enjoy substantial rates of return. In contrast, the average investor who owns a few pieces to decorate his or her home finds such returns elusive. The high transaction costs and illiquidity of antiques may erode any profit that the individual may earn when selling these pieces. The subsequent discussion of rates of return on various assets will provide some evidence on returns.

Art The entertainment sections of newspapers or the personal finance sections of magazines often carry stories of the results of major art auctions, such as when Van Gogh's *Irises* and *Sunflower* sold for $59 million and $36 million, respectively. Obviously, these examples and others indicate that some paintings have increased significantly in value and thereby generated large rates of return for their owners.[5] However, investing in art typically requires substantial knowledge of art and the art world, a large amount of capital to acquire the work of well-known artists, patience, and an ability to absorb high transaction costs. For investors who enjoy fine art and have the resources, these can be satisfying investments, but for most small investors, this is a difficult area in which to get returns that compensate for the uncertainty and illiquidity.

Coins and Stamps Many individuals enjoy collecting coins or stamps as a hobby, and also as an investment. The market for coins and stamps is fragmented compared to the stock market, but it is more liquid than the market for art and antiques. Indeed, the volume of coins and stamps traded has prompted the publication of weekly and monthly price lists.[6] An investor can get a widely recognized grading specification on a coin or stamp and, once graded, a coin or stamp can usually be sold quickly through a dealer.[7] It is important to recognize that the difference between the bid price the dealer will pay to buy the stamp or coin and the asking or selling price the investor must pay the

---

[4]For a review of studies that have examined returns on real estate, see G. Stacey Sirmans and C. F. Sirmans, "The Historical Perspective of Real Estate Returns," *Journal of Portfolio Management* 13, no. 3 (Spring 1987): 22–31. The implications of these return and risk measures for portfolio management are discussed in James R. Webb and Jack A. Rubens, "How Much in Real Estate? A Surprising Answer," *Journal of Portfolio Management* 13, no. 3 (Spring 1987): 10–14.

[5]For a listing and discussion of art sold at auction, see Jerry E. Patterson, "A Dazzling Year," *Institutional Investor*, International Edition, September 1987: 324–339; and Judith H. Dobrzynski, "Art Collectors May Wish to Stay Close to Home," *Business Week*, December 28, 1988: 184–185. For optimistic views, see Meg Cox, "Art Market Euphoria Is Wearing Off; Realism's Setting in after Stock Drop," *The Wall Street Journal*, October 23, 1987: 22; and John R. Dorfman, "Art of Investing May Mean Avoiding Art," *The Wall Street Journal*, June 6, 1989: C1, C25.

[6]A weekly publication for coins is *Coin World*, published by Amos Press Inc., 911 Vandemark Rd., Sidney, OH 45367. There are several monthly coin magazines, including *Coinage*, published by Behn-Miller Publications, Inc., Encino, CA. Amos Press also publishes several stamp magazines, including *Linn's Stamp News* and *Scott Stamp Monthly*. These magazines provide current prices for coins and stamps.

[7]For an article that describes the alternative grading services, see Diana Henriques, "Don't Take Any Wooden Nickels," *Barron's*, June 19, 1989: 16, 18, 20, 32. For an analysis of experience with commemorative coins, see R. W. Bradford, "How to Lose a Mint," *Barron's*, March 6, 1989: 54, 55.

dealer is going to be fairly large compared to the difference between the bid and ask prices on stocks and bonds.

Diamonds Diamonds can be and have been good investments during many periods. Still, investors who purchase diamonds must realize that: (1) they can be very illiquid, (2) the grading process that determines their quality is quite subjective, (3) most investment-grade gems require substantial investments, and (4) they generate no positive cash flow during the holding period until the stone is sold. In fact, during the holding period the investor must cover costs of insurance and storage. Finally, there are appraisal costs before selling.[8]

In this section, we have described the most common investment alternatives to introduce you to the range of investments available. We will discuss many of these in more detail when we consider how you evaluate them for investment purposes. You should keep in mind that new investment alternatives are constantly being created and developed. You can keep abreast of these by reading business newspapers and magazines.

In our final section, we will present some data on historical rates of return and risk measures for a number of these investments to provide some background on how they have done in the past together with some feel for what kinds of returns you might expect in the future.

Historical Returns on Alternative Investments

How do investors weigh the costs and benefits of owning investments and make decisions to build portfolios that will provide the best risk–return combinations? To help individual or institutional investors answer this question, financial theorists have examined extensive data and attempted to provide information on the return and risk characteristics of various investments.

Many theorists have studied the historical rates of return on common stocks, and a growing interest in bonds has caused investigators to assess their perform-

ance as well. Because inflation has been so pervasive, many studies include both nominal and real rates of return on investments. Still other investigators have examined the performance of such assets as real estate, foreign stocks, art, antiques, and commodities. This section reviews some of the major studies to provide background on the rates of return and risk for these investment alternatives. This should help you to make decisions regarding which of them you might want to examine when building your investment portfolio.

Stocks, Bonds, and T-Bills

A set of studies by Ibbotson and Sinquefield (I&S) examined historical nominal and real rates of return for six major classes of assets in the United States: (1) common stocks, (2) small capitalization common stocks,[9] (3) long-term U.S. government bonds, (4) long-term corporate bonds, (5) U.S. Treasury bills, and (6) consumer goods (a measure of inflation).[10] For each asset, the authors calculated total rates of return before taxes or transaction costs.

These investigators computed geometric and arithmetic mean rates of return and computed nine series derived from the basic series. Four of these series were net returns reflecting different premiums: (1) a risk premium, which I&S defined as the difference in the rate of return that investors receive from investing in common stocks rather than in risk-free U.S. Treasury bills; (2) a small stock premium, which they defined as the return on small capitalization stocks minus the return on total stocks; (3) a horizon premium, which they defined as the difference in the rate of return received from investing in long-term government bonds rather than short-term U.S. Treasury bills; and (4) a default premium, which they defined as the difference between the rates of return on long-term risky corporate bonds and long-term risk-

---

[8]For a discussion of problems and opportunities, see "When to Put Your Money into Gems," *Business Week*, March 16, 1981: 158–161.

[9]Small capitalization stocks were broken out as a separate class of asset because several studies have shown that rates of return on firms with relatively small capitalization (stock with low market value) have been very different from those on stocks in general. Therefore, it is felt that they should be considered a unique asset class.

[10]The original study was Roger G. Ibbotson and Rex A. Sinquefield, "Stocks, Bonds, Bills, and Inflation: Year-by-Year Historical Returns (1926–1974)," *Journal of Business* 49, no. 1 (January 1976): 11–47. While this study was updated in several monographs, the current update is contained in *Stocks, Bonds, Bills, and Inflation: 1990 Yearbook* (Chicago: Ibbotson Associates, 1990).

Table 2.6 *Basic and Derived Series: Historical Highlights (1926–1990)*

Series	Annual Geometric Mean Rate of Return	Arithmetic Mean of Annual Returns	Standard Deviation of Annual Returns
Common stock	10.1%	12.1%	20.8%
Small capitalization stock	11.6	17.1	35.4
Long-term corporate bonds	5.2	5.5	8.4
Long-term government bonds	4.5	4.9	8.5
Intermediate-term government bonds	5.0	5.1	5.5
U.S. Treasury bills	3.7	3.7	3.4
Consumer Price Index	3.1	3.2	4.7
Equity risk premium	6.5	8.6	20.8
Small stock premium	1.8	3.4	18.8
Default premium	0.6	0.6	3.0
Horizon premium	0.9	1.2	7.9
Common stock – inflation adjusted	6.7	8.8	21.0
Small capitalization stock – inflation adjusted	8.2	13.5	34.7
Long-term corporate bonds – inflation adjusted	2.0	2.5	9.9
Long-term government bonds – inflation adjusted	1.4	1.8	10.1
Intermediate-term government bonds – inflation adjusted	1.8	2.0	7.0
U.S. Treasury bills – inflation adjusted	0.5	0.6	4.4

Source: Ibbotson, Roger G., and Rex A. Sinquefield, "Stocks, Bonds, Bills, and Inflation (SBBI)," 1982, updated in *SBBI 1990 Yearbook*, Ibbotson Associates, Inc., Chicago.

free government bonds. I&S also computed the real inflation-adjusted rates of return for common stocks, small capitalization stocks, Treasury bills, long-term government bonds, and long-term corporate bonds.

A summary of the rates of return, risk premiums, and standard deviations for the basic and derived series appears in Table 2.6. As discussed in Chapter 1, the geometric means of the rates of return are always lower than the arithmetic means of the rates of return, and the difference between these two means increases with the standard deviation of returns.

Over the period from 1926 to 1989, all common stocks returned 10.3 percent a year, compounded annually. To compare this to other investments, the results show that common stock experienced a risk premium of 6.5 percent and inflation-adjusted real returns of 7.0 percent per year. In contrast to all common stocks, the small capitalization stocks (which are represented by the smallest 20 percent of stocks listed

on the NYSE measured by market value) experienced a geometric mean return of 12.2 percent, which was a premium compared to all common stocks of 1.8 percent. Although common stocks and small capitalization stocks experienced higher rates of return than the other asset groups, their returns were also more volatile, as measured by the standard deviations of annual returns.

Long-term U.S. government bonds experienced a 4.6 percent annual return, a real return of 1.4 percent, and a horizon premium (compared to Treasury bills) of 0.9 percent. Although the returns on these bonds were lower than those on stocks, they were also far less volatile.

The annual compound rate of return on long-term corporate bonds was 5.2 percent, the default premium compared to U.S. government bonds was 0.6 percent, and the inflation-adjusted return was 2.0 percent. Although corporate bonds provided a higher return, as one would expect, their volatility was slightly lower than government bonds.

The nominal return on U.S. Treasury bills was 3.6 percent a year, while the inflation-adjusted return was 0.5 percent. The standard deviation of nominal returns was the lowest of all series examined, which reflects the low risk of these securities and is consistent with the lowest rate of return.

This study reported the rates of return, return premiums, and risk measures on various asset groups. The rates of return were generally consistent with the uncertainty of annual returns as measured by the standard deviations of annual returns.

World Portfolio Performance

Expanding this analysis from domestic to global securities, Ibbotson, Siegel, and Love examined the performance of numerous assets, not only in the United States, but in the world.[11] Specifically, for the period from 1960 to 1984 they constructed a value-weighted portfolio of stocks, bonds, cash (the equivalent of U.S. T-bills), real estate, and precious metals from the United States, Northern and Western Europe, Japan, Hong Kong, Singapore, Canada, and Australia. They computed annual returns, risk measures, and correlations among the returns for alternative assets. Table 2.7 shows the geometric and arithmetic average annual rates of return and the standard deviations of returns for that period.

Asset Return and Absolute Risk The results in Table 2.7 generally confirm the expected relationship between annual rates of return and the absolute risk of these securities based upon their standard deviations. The riskier assets, those that had higher standard deviations, experienced the highest returns. For example, silver had the highest arithmetic mean rate of return (20.51 percent), but also the largest standard deviation (75.34 percent) while risk-free U.S. cash equivalents (T-bills) had low returns (6.29 percent) and the smallest standard deviation (3.10 percent). The data amassed by Ibbotson et al. could be used to assess the relative risk of assets in a portfolio, as well as risk and return values for each asset.

Relative Asset Risk Calculating the coefficients of variation (CVs), which measure relative variability, Ibbotson et al. found a wide range of values. The lowest CVs were experienced by the cash equivalents (T-bills) and real estate investments. Silver had the highest CV value because of its very large standard deviation, and corporate bonds the next highest because of a relatively small mean return. The CVs for stocks ranged from 1.46 to 2.04, with U.S. stocks about in the middle (1.66). Finally, the world market portfolios had rather low CVs (0.62 and 0.68), which demonstrates the benefits of global diversification.

Correlations between Asset Returns Table 2.8 (on p. 56) is a correlation matrix of selected U.S. and world assets. The first column shows that U.S. equities showed reasonably high correlation with European equities (0.640) and other foreign equities (0.807), but low correlation with Asian equities (0.237). Also, U.S. equities showed a negative correlation with U.S. government bonds (−0.006), farm real estate (−0.171), and gold (−0.088). You will recall from our earlier discussion that you can use this information on correlations to build a diversified portfolio by combining those assets with low positive or negative correlations.

Art and Antiques

Unlike financial securities, where the results of transactions are reported daily, art and antique markets are very fragmented and lack any formal transaction reporting system. This makes it difficult to gather data. The best-known series that attempt to provide information about the changing value of art and antiques were developed by Sotheby Parke Bernet, better known as Sotheby's, a major art auction firm. These value indexes cover 12 areas of art and antiques and a weighted aggregate series that is a combination of the 12.

Reilly examined these series for the period from 1975 to 1989 and computed rates of return, measures of risk, and the correlations among the various art and antique series.[12] Table 2.9 (on p. 57) shows these data and compares them with returns for 1-year Treasury bonds, the Lehman Brothers Government/Corporate

[11]Roger G. Ibbotson, Laurence B. Siegel, and Kathryn S. Love, "World Wealth: Market Values and Returns," *Journal of Portfolio Management* 12, no. 1 (Fall 1985): 4–23.

[12]Frank K. Reilly, "Risks and Returns on Art and Antiques: The Sotheby's Indexes," Eastern Finance Association Meeting, April 1987. The results reported are a summary of the study results and have been updated through September 1989.

Table 2.7   *World Capital Market: Total Annual Returns (1960–1984)*

	Compound Return[a]	Arithmetic Mean	Standard Deviation[b]	Coefficient of Variation[c]
Equities				
United States	8.81%	10.20%	16.89%	1.66
Foreign				
Europe	7.83	8.94	15.58	1.74
Asia	15.14	18.42	30.74	1.67
Other	8.14	10.21	20.88	2.04
Equities total	9.08	10.21	15.28	1.46
Bonds				
United States				
Corporate[d]	5.35	5.75	9.63	1.67
Government	5.91	6.10	6.43	1.05
United States total	5.70	5.93	7.16	1.21
Foreign				
Corporate domestic	8.35	8.58	7.26	0.85
Government domestic	5.79	6.04	7.41	1.23
Crossborder	7.51	7.66	5.76	0.75
Foreign total	6.80	7.01	6.88	0.98
Bonds total	6.36	6.50	5.56	0.86

[a]Equal to geometric mean.

[b]Standard deviation from arithmetic mean.

[c]Coefficient of variation equals standard deviation/arithmetic mean.

[d]Including preferred stock.

[e]United States only.

Source: Robert G. Ibbotson, Laurence B. Siegel, and Kathryn S. Love, "World Wealth: Market Values and Returns," *The Journal of Portfolio Management* 12, no. 1 (Fall 1985): 4–23. Reprinted with permission.

Bond Index, the Standard & Poor's 500 Stock Index, and the annual inflation rate.

These results vary to such a degree that an investor cannot generalize about the performance of art and antiques. As shown, the average annual compound rates of return measured by the geometric means ranged from about 19 percent (American paintings) to about 6 percent (continental silver). Similarly, the standard deviations varied from 21 percent (Chinese ceramics) to about 9.5 percent (American furniture), while the coefficients of variation varied from about 0.65 (American paintings, American furniture, and English furniture) to 2.11 (continental silver). The

annual rankings likewise changed over time. Comparing the art and antique results to the bond and stock indexes indicates that the stocks and bonds experienced results in the middle of the art and antique series.

Analysis of the correlation matrix of these assets reveals several important relationships. First, the correlations among alternative art and antique categories such as paintings and furniture vary substantially (from over 0.90 to some negative correlations). Second, the correlations between rates of return on art and antiques and bonds are generally negative. Third, the correlations of art and antiques with stocks are

	Compound Return[a]	Arithmetic Mean	Standard Deviation[b]	Coefficient of Variation[c]
Cash equivalents				
United States	6.49%	6.54%	3.22%	0.49
Foreign	6.00	6.23	7.10	1.14
Cash total	6.38	6.42	2.92	0.45
Real estate[e]				
Business	8.49	8.57	4.16	0.49
Residential	8.86	8.93	3.77	0.42
Farms	11.86	12.13	7.88	0.65
Real Estate total	9.44	9.49	3.45	0.36
Metals				
Silver	9.14	20.51	75.34	3.67
Gold	9.08	12.62	29.87	2.37
Metals total	9.11	12.63	29.69	2.35
U.S. market wealth portfolio	8.63	8.74	5.06	0.58
Foreign market wealth portfolio	7.76	8.09	8.48	1.05
World market wealth portfolio				
Excluding metals	8.34	8.47	5.24	0.62
Including metals	8.39	8.54	5.80	0.68
U.S. inflation rate	5.24	5.30	3.60	0.68

typically small positive values. These results would suggest that a properly diversified portfolio of art, antiques, stocks, and bonds might provide a fairly low-risk portfolio.

Summary

■ Investors who want the broadest range of choices in investments must consider foreign stocks and bonds in addition to domestic financial assets.

Many foreign securities offer investors higher returns than domestic securities.

The low positive or negative correlations between foreign and U.S. securities make them ideal for building a diversified portfolio.

■ Figure 2.6 (on p. 58) summarizes the risk and return characteristics of the investment alternatives described in this chapter. Some of the differences are due to unique factors that we discussed.

Foreign bonds are considered riskier than domestic bonds because of the unavoidable uncertainty due to exchange rate risk and country risk.

The same is true for foreign and domestic common stocks.

You should divide consideration of real estate investments between your personal home, on which you do not expect as high a return because of nonmonetary factors, and commercial real estate, which requires a higher return due to cash flow uncertainty and illiquidity.

Investments like art, antiques, coins, and stamps require very heavy liquidity risk premiums.

■ Studies on the historical rates of return for common stocks and other investment alternatives

| Table 2.8 | Correlation Matrix of World Capital Market Security Returns |

	U.S. Equities	Total U.S. Bonds	Total Real Estate	U.S. Market Portfolio	World Market Including Metals
U.S. equities	1.000	−0.166	0.054	0.917	0.757
Europe equities	0.640	−0.045	0.156	0.605	0.706
Asia equities	0.237	−0.007	0.033	0.209	0.351
Other equities	0.807	−0.160	0.288	0.754	0.753
Foreign total: equities	0.672	−0.074	0.129	0.626	0.732
World total: equities	0.964	0.075	0.083	0.886	0.805
U.S. corporate bonds and preferred stock	0.323	0.962	−0.123	0.393	0.207
U.S. government bonds	−0.006	0.967	−0.040	0.152	−0.023
U.S. total: bonds	0.166	1.000	−0.082	0.284	0.093
Foreign domestic corporate bonds	0.050	0.180	0.164	0.153	0.380
Foreign domestic government bonds	−0.024	0.192	0.303	0.171	0.426
Foreign total: bonds	0.052	0.242	0.256	0.191	0.429
World total: bonds	0.124	0.646	0.172	0.288	0.389
U.S. cash equivalents (T-bills)	0.079	−0.247	0.405	0.130	−0.004
Foreign cash equivalents	−0.386	−0.192	0.399	−0.233	0.105
World total: cash equivalents	−0.238	−0.141	0.529	0.103	0.046
Business real estate	0.164	0.192	0.518	0.394	0.390
Residential real estate	0.125	0.017	0.916	0.442	0.552
Farm real estate	0.171	−0.274	0.570	−0.019	0.133
U.S. total: real estate	0.054	−0.082	1.000	0.371	0.531
Gold	−0.088	−0.280	0.684	0.104	0.427
Silver	0.116	0.153	0.580	0.291	0.283
World total: metals	−0.086	−0.282	0.696	0.111	0.427
U.S. market wealth portfolio	0.917	0.284	0.371	1.000	0.873
Foreign market wealth portfolio	0.510	0.080	0.177	0.533	0.727
World market wealth portfolio (excluding metals)	0.861	0.231	0.332	0.925	0.924
World market wealth portfolio (including metals)	0.757	0.093	0.531	0.873	1.000

Source: Adapted from Roger G. Ibbotson, Laurence B. Siegel, and Kathryn S. Love, "World Wealth: Market Values and Returns," *The Journal of Portfolio Management* 12, no. 1 (Fall 1985): 19–21. Reprinted with permission.

(including bonds, commodities, real estate, foreign securities, and art and antiques) point toward two generalizations:

A positive relationship typically holds between the rate of return earned on an asset and the variability of its historical rate of return. This is ex-

pected in a world of risk-averse investors, who require higher rates of return to compensate for more uncertainty.

The correlation among rates of return for selected alternative investments is typically quite low, es-

Table 2.9 *Average Annual Rates of Return and Risk Measures for Sotheby's Art and Antique Indexes, Common Stock and Bond Indexes, and Inflation: 1976–1989 (September Year End)*

	Mean Rates of Return		Standard Deviation	Coefficient of Variation
	Arithmetic	Geometric		
Old master paintings	11.92%	10.98%	14.50%	1.22
19th-century European paintings	10.76	9.68	15.84	1.47
Impressionist–post impressionist paintings	17.66	17.04	13.26	0.75
Modern paintings	17.91	17.12	14.93	0.83
American paintings	19.36	18.77	12.62	0.65
Continental ceramics	11.24	10.18	16.09	1.43
Chinese ceramics	16.83	15.26	20.76	1.23
English silver	12.19	10.98	16.49	1.35
Continental silver	6.94	5.99	14.64	2.11
American furniture	13.71	13.40	8.95	0.65
French and continental furniture	10.59	10.15	10.50	0.99
English furniture	16.48	16.01	10.81	0.66
Fixed, weight index	14.31	13.86	10.67	0.75
Unweighted index	13.80	13.45	9.39	0.68
Value weighted index	14.00	13.62	9.75	0.70
1-year Treasury bond	8.53	8.50	3.00	0.35
SLGC bond index	10.66	10.18	10.96	1.03
S&P 500	18.16	17.15	16.30	0.90
Consumer Price Index	6.46	6.40	3.73	0.58

Source: Adapted from Frank K. Reilly, "Risk and Return on Art and Antiques: The Sotheby's Indexes," Eastern Finance Association Meeting, April 1989 (updated October 1989).

pecially for U.S. and foreign stocks and bonds and real assets, as represented by art and antiques. This confirms the advantage of diversification among investments.

■ In addition to describing many direct investments, such as stocks and bonds, we also discussed investment companies that allow investors to buy investments indirectly. These can be very important to investors who want to take advantage of professional management, but also want instant diversification with a limited amount of funds. With $10,000, you may not be able to buy many individual stocks or bonds, but you could acquire shares in a mutual fund which would give you a share of a diversified portfolio that might contain 100 to 150 different stocks or bonds.

■ Now that we know about a range of domestic and foreign investment alternatives, our next task in learning about investments is to turn to the markets in which they are bought and sold. That is the objective of the next two chapters. The discussions in Chapters 3 and 4 will help us to understand how markets match buyers and sellers of investments. Later chapters will describe how investors evaluate the risk and return characteristics of alternative investments to build diversified portfolios to meet their objectives.

Figure 2.6 *Alternative Investments—Risk and Return Characteristics*

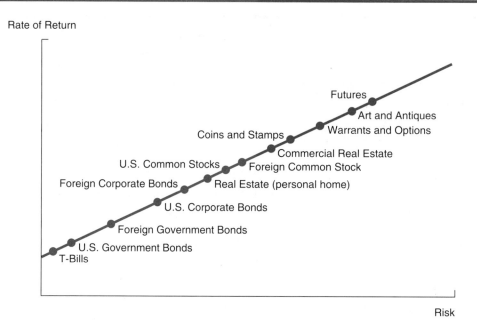

Questions

1. What are the advantages to investing in common stock rather than corporate bonds of the same company? Compare the certainty of returns for a bond with those for a common stock. Draw a line graph to demonstrate the pattern of returns you would envision for each of these assets over time.

2. Discuss three factors that should cause U.S. investors to consider including global securities in their portfolios.

3. Why does international diversification reduce portfolio risk? Specifically, why would you expect low correlation in the rates of return for domestic and foreign securities?

4. Why would you expect a difference in the correlation of returns between securities from the United States and alternative countries such as Japan, Canada, and South Africa? Explain your answer.

5. Would you expect any change in the correlations between U.S. stocks and the stocks for different countries? For example, would you expect the correlation between U.S. and Japanese stock returns to change over time? Explain your answer.

6. If you wanted to invest in U.S. bonds strictly, what proportion of the world bond market would you be ignoring?

7. When you invest in Japanese or German bonds, what is the major risk you must consider besides yield changes within the country? Explain this risk.

8. Some investors believe that international investing introduces additional risk. What is this risk and how can it affect your return? Give an example.

9. What alternatives to direct investment in foreign stocks are available to investors?

10. You are a wealthy individual in a high tax bracket. Why might you consider investing in a municipal bond rather than a straight corporate bond, even though the promised yield on the municipal bond is lower?

11. You can acquire convertible bonds from a rapidly growing company or from a utility. Both firms' debentures have a coupon of 9 percent. Which convertible bond would have the lower yield? What is the reason for this difference?

12. What is an REIT? Describe three alternative types of REITs.

13. Compare the liquidity of an investment in raw land with that of an investment in common stock. Be specific as to why and how they differ. (Hint: Begin by defining *liquidity.*)

14. What are stock warrants and call options? How do they differ?

15. Why do financial analysts consider antiques and art to be illiquid investments? Why do they consider coins and stamps to be more liquid than antiques and art? What must an investor do to sell these assets?

16. You have a fairly large portfolio of U.S. stocks and bonds. You meet a financial planner at a social gathering who suggests that you should diversify your portfolio with an investment in gold. Discuss whether the correlation results in Table 2.8 support this suggestion.

17. You are an avid collector/investor of American paintings. Based upon the results in Table 2.9, how would you describe your results during the period of 1976 to 1989?

Problems

1. Calculate the current horizon premium on U.S. government securities based upon data in *The Wall Street Journal*. The long-term security should have a maturity of at least 20 years.

2. Using a source of international statistics, compare the percentage change in the following economic data for Japan, West Germany, Canada, and the United States for a recent year. What were the differences, and which country or countries differed most from the United States?
   a. Aggregate output (GNP)
   b. Inflation
   c. Money supply growth

3. Using a recent edition of *Barron's*, examine the weekly percentage change in the stock price indexes for Japan, West Germany, Italy, and the United States. For each of three weeks, which foreign series moved most closely with the U.S. series? Which series diverged most from the U.S. series? What would this indicate to you regarding international diversification?

4. Using published sources (e.g., *The Wall Street Journal, Barron's, Federal Reserve Bulletin*), look up the exchange rate for U.S. dollars with Japanese yen for each of the past 10 years (you can use an average for the year or a specific time period each year). Based upon these exchange rates, compute and discuss the yearly exchange rate effect on an investment in Japanese stocks by a U.S. investor. What is the impact of this exchange rate effect on the risk of Japanese stocks?

5. *CFA Examination 1 (June 1980)* The following information is available concerning the historical risk and return relationships in the U.S. capital markets:

U.S. Capital Markets Total Annual Returns, 1947–1978

Investment Category	Arithmetic Mean	Geometric Mean	Standard Deviation of Return[a]
Common stocks	11.80%	10.30%	18.0%
Preferred stocks	3.30	2.90	9.2
Treasury bills	3.53	3.51	2.1
Long government bonds	2.60	2.40	6.2
Long corporate bonds	2.40	2.20	6.7
Real estate	8.19	8.14	3.5

[a]Based upon arithmetic mean.

Source: Adapted from R. G. Ibbotson and C. L. Fall, "The U.S. Market Wealth Portfolio," *The Journal of Portfolio Management*.

a. Explain why the geometric and arithmetic mean returns are not equal and whether one or the other may be more useful for investment decision making. [5 minutes]

b. For the time period indicated, rank these investments on a risk-adjusted basis from most to least desirable. Explain your rationale. [6 minutes]

c. Assume the returns in these series are normally distributed.
   1. Calculate the range of returns that an investor would have expected to achieve 95 percent of the time from holding common stocks. [4 minutes]
   2. Suppose an investor holds real estate for this time period. Determine the probability of at least breaking even on this investment. [5 minutes]

d. Assume you are holding a portfolio composed entirely of real estate. Discuss the justification, if any, for adopting a mixed asset port-

folio by adding long-term government bonds.
[5 minutes]

6. You are given the following long-run annual rates of return for alternative investment instruments:

U.S. government T-bills	8.50%
Common stock	12.25
Long-term corporate bonds	10.25
Long-term government bonds	10.25
Small capitalization common stock	15.60

a. On the basis of these returns, compute the following:
1. The common stock risk premium
2. The small firm stock risk premium
3. The horizon premium
4. The default premium

b. The annual rate of inflation during this period was 7 percent. Compute the real rate of return on these investment alternatives.

References

Brick, John R., H. Kent Baker, and John A. Haslem, eds. *Financial Markets Instruments and Concepts*, 2d ed. Reston, Va.: Reston Publishing, 1986.

Cholerton, Kenneth, Pierre Pieraerts, and Bruno Solnik. "Why Invest in Foreign Currency Bonds?" *Journal of Portfolio Management* 12, no. 4 (Summer 1986).

Fisher, Lawrence, and James H. Lorie, *A Half Century of Returns on Stocks and Bonds*. Chicago: University of Chicago Graduate School of Business, 1977.

Greshin, Adam M., and Margaret D. Hadzima, "International Bond Investing and Portfolio Management," in *The Handbook of Fixed-Income Securities*, 3d ed., ed. by Frank J. Fabozzi. Homewood, Ill.: Business One Irwin, 1991.

Ibbotson, Roger G., Laurence B. Siegel, and Kathryn S. Love. "World Wealth: Market Values and Returns." *Journal of Portfolio Management* 12, no. 1 (Fall 1985).

Lessard, Donald R. "International Diversification," in *The Financial Analyst's Handbook*, 2d ed., ed. by Sumner N. Levine (Homewood, Ill.: Dow Jones-Irwin, 1988).

Reilly, Frank K. "Risks and Returns on Art and Antiques: The Sotheby's Indexes." Eastern Finance Association Meeting, April 1989.

Robinson, Anthony W., and Stephen W. Glover. "International Fixed-Income Markets and Securities," in *The Financial Analyst's Handbook*. 2d ed., ed. by Sumner H. Levine (Homewood, Ill.: Dow Jones-Irwin, 1988).

Rosenberg, Michael R. "International Fixed Income Investing: Theory and Practice," in *The Handbook of Fixed-Income Securities*, 3d ed., ed. by Frank J. Fabozzi. Homewood, Ill.: Business One Irwin, 1991.

Solnik, Bruno, and Bernard Noetzlin. "Optimal International Asset Allocation." *Journal of Portfolio Management* 9, no. 1 (Fall 1982).

Van der Does, Rein W. "Investing in Foreign Securities," in *The Financial Analyst's Handbook*, 2d ed., ed. by Sumner N. Levine (Homewood, Ill.: Dow Jones-Irwin, 1988).

Wilson, Richard S., *Corporate Senior Securities*. Chicago: Probus Publishing, 1987.

Wilson, Richard S., and Frank J. Fabozzi. *The New Corporate Bond Market*. Chicago: Probus Publishing, 1990.

APPENDIX

2a *Covariance and Correlation*

Covariance

Since most students have been exposed to the concepts of covariance and correlation, the following discussion is set forth in intuitive terms with examples to help you recall the concepts.[1]

Covariance is an absolute measure of the extent to which two sets of numbers move together over time, that is, how often they move up or down together. In this regard *move together* means they are generally above their means or below their means at the same time. Covariance between i and j is defined as:

$$COV_{ij} = \frac{\Sigma(i - \bar{i})(j - \bar{j})}{N}$$

[1] A more detailed, rigorous treatment of the subject can be found in any standard statistics text, including S. Christian Albright, *Statistics for Business and Economics* (New York: Macmillan, 1987): 63–67.

If we define $(i - \bar{i})$ as i' and $(j - \bar{j})$ as j', then:

$$COV_{ij} = \frac{\Sigma i'j'}{N}$$

Obviously, if both numbers are consistently above or below their individual means at the same time, their products will be positive, and the average will be a large positive value. In contrast, if the i value is below its mean when the j value is above its mean, or vice versa, their products will be large negative values, giving negative covariance.

Table 2A.1 should make this clear. In this example, the two series generally moved together, so they showed positive covariance. As noted, this is an absolute measure of their relationship and, therefore, can range from $+$infinity (∞), to $-$infinity (∞). Note that the covariance of a variable with itself is its variance.

Correlation

To obtain a relative measure of a given relationship we use the correlation coefficient (r_{ij}) which is a measure of the relationship:

$$r_{ij} = \frac{COV_{ij}}{\sigma_i\sigma_j}$$

You will recall from your introductory statistics course that:

$$\sigma_1 = \sqrt{\frac{\Sigma(i - \bar{i})^2}{N}}$$

If the two series move completely together, then the covariance would equal $\sigma_i\sigma_j$ and:

$$\frac{COV_{ij}}{\sigma_i\sigma_j} = 1.0$$

The correlation coefficient would equal unity in this case, and we would say the two series are perfectly correlated. Because we know that:

$$r_{ij} = COV_{ij}/\sigma_i\sigma_j$$

we also know that $COV_{ij} = r_{ij}\,\sigma_i\sigma_j$. This relationship may be useful when computing the standard deviation of a portfolio, because, in many instances, the relationship between two securities is stated in terms of the correlation coefficient rather than the covariance.

Continuing the example given in Table 2A.1, the standard deviations are computed in Table 2A.2, as is the correlation between i and j. As shown, the two standard deviations are rather large and similar, but not exactly the same. Finally, when the positive covariance is normalized by the product of the two standard deviations, the results indicate a correlation coefficient of 0.898, which is obviously quite large and close to 1.00. Apparently, these two series are highly related.

Table 2A.1   *Calculation of Covariance*

Observation	i	j	$i - \bar{i}$	$j - \bar{j}$	$i'j'$
1	3	8	-4	-4	16
2	6	10	-1	-2	2
3	8	14	$+1$	$+2$	2
4	5	12	-2	0	0
5	9	13	$+2$	$+1$	2
6	11	15	$+4$	$+3$	12
Σ	42	72			34
Mean	7	12			
Cov_{ij}	$= \dfrac{34}{6} = +5.67$				

Table 2A.2   *Calculation of Correlation Coefficient*

Observation	$i - \bar{i}^a$	$(i - \bar{i})^2$	$j - \bar{j}^a$	$(j - \bar{j})^2$
1	-4	16	-4	16
2	-1	1	-2	4
3	$+1$	1	$+2$	4
4	-2	4	0	0
5	$+2$	4	$+1$	1
6	$+4$	16	$+3$	9
		42		34

$\sigma_i^2 = 42/6 = 7.00 \qquad \sigma_j^2 = 34/6 = 5.67$

$\sigma_i = \sqrt{7.00} = 2.65 \qquad \sigma_j = \sqrt{5.67} = 2.38$

$r_{ij} = Cov_{ij}/\sigma_i\sigma_j = \dfrac{5.67}{(2.65)(2.38)} = \dfrac{5.67}{6.31} = 0.898$

^{a}from Table 2A.1

Problems

1. As a new analyst, you have calculated the following annual returns for both Alpha-Omega Corporation and Beta-Tau Industries.

Year	Alpha-Omega's Rate of Return	Beta-Tau's Rate of Return
1988	5	5
1989	12	15
1990	−11	5
1991	10	7
1992	12	−10

Your manager suggests that since these companies produce similar products, you should continue your analysis by computing their covariance. Show all calculations.

2. You decide to go an extra step by calculating the correlation coefficient using the data provided in Problem 1 above. Prepare a table showing your calculations. Add a short analysis to explain how to interpret the results.

2b *Tax Considerations*

This appendix provides an overview of the tax laws about investments in stocks, bonds, options, and futures contracts. It also considers individual retirement accounts and Keogh plans for the self-employed. This information should help you maximize your after-tax rates of return on security transactions and augment your retirement income.

Dividends

Distributed shares of a corporation's current or accumulated earnings and profits to its shareholders are called *dividends*. Any payment in excess of a corporation's current and accumulated earnings and profits is not a dividend but rather a distribution of capital. Capital distributions are usually not taxable to the shareholder, since they reduce the basis of the shareholder's stock. Distributions that exceed the shareholder's basis generate *capital gains*. Dividends are taxable in full as part of a shareholder's gross incomes.

Capital Gains and Losses

Under prior law, individuals preferred to have income classified as capital gains rather than ordinary income because capital gains were taxed more favorably. However, the Tax Reform Act (TRA) of 1986 repealed the 60 percent capital gains exclusion, and now both long-

term and short-term capital gains are taxed like ordinary income. Nevertheless, taxpayers are still required to classify gains and losses as capital gains versus ordinary income. Therefore, it is very important to understand which types of property qualify for capital asset treatment. Section 1221 of the Internal Revenue Code (IRC) requires that you treat investment and personal-use property (stocks, bonds, patents, personal automobiles, personal residences, jewelry, and other personal effects of an individual) in this way.

Items that specifically do not qualify for capital asset treatment include (1) inventory or stock in trade; (2) copyrights, literary compositions, letters or memorandums, and similar property created by the taxpayer; (3) accounts receivable and notes receivable acquired in the ordinary course of business; (4) depreciable or real property used in a trade or business; and (5) certain U.S. government publications. These items, as a general rule, generate ordinary income or loss when sold or exchanged.

Unrealized gain or loss cannot be included in an individual's computation of capital gains or losses. To be included the property must be disposed of in some manner, usually sold or exchanged.

The TRA of 1986 also requires taxpayers to continue the holding-period rules that differentiate long-term gains and losses. If an asset acquired after December 31, 1987, is held for more than 1 year (more than 6 months for property acquired before January 1, 1988), the resulting gain or loss will be classified as long term. An asset held for 1 year or less (6 months or less for property acquired before January 1, 1988) will generate short-term gain or loss. The computation is based on calendar months, with the day the property is acquired not being included and the day of disposal being included in the holding period. Thus, the starting date for determining the holding period is the day after the property's acquisition. Property purchased on January 15, 1991 and disposed of on January 15, 1992 would generate a short-term gain or loss, since the asset was held for exactly 1 year. If the property had been disposed of on January 16, 1992, the resulting gain or loss would have been long term.

Combining Capital Gains and Losses A *net long-term capital gain (NLTCG)* results if gains exceed losses. A *net long-term capital loss (NLTCL)* results if losses exceed gains. Short-term capital gains and short-term capital losses combine to generate either a *net short-term capital gain (NSTCG)* or a *net short-term capital loss (NSTCL)*.

If the above netting process creates either a NSTCG and a NLTCL or a NSTCL and a NLTCG, it is necessary to offset the positive and negative numbers. The Internal Revenue Code defines the excess of NLTCG over NSTCL as a net capital gain (NCG). If a net capital loss (NCL) occurs, the taxpayer will be permitted to offset a portion of ordinary income (explained later). An NCG will be reported as follows.

Tax Treatment of Net Capital Gain (NCG) Prior to 1987 you included any NCG fully in gross income. Then the taxpayer was allowed to deduct 60 percent of the NLTCG in excess of NSTCL as a deduction toward *adjusted gross income (AGI)*. For example, a taxpayer reporting a NLTCG of $36,000 and a NSTCL of $6,000 would increase gross income by $30,000 and be permitted to deduct $18,000 toward AGI because of the 60 percent deduction. As previously noted, the 60 percent exclusion is no longer available; therefore, a NCG is now treated as ordinary income and is taxable in full. Beginning in 1991, the 1990 Revenue Reconciliation Act increases the top tax rate for individuals to 31 percent. However, the act caps the tax rate on net capital gains at 28 percent.

Example: Mr. Jones determines the following information when reviewing transactions for the current year:

Long-term capital gain	$4,600
Long-term capital loss	($4,000)
Short-term capital gain	$ 100
Short-term capital loss	($ 600)

Mr. Jones's net capital gain (NCG) is computed as follows:

LTCG	$4,600	
LTCL	(4,000)	
NLTCG		$ 600
STCG	$ 100	
STCL	(600)	
NSTCL		(500)
NCG		$ 100

The entire NCG of $100 must be included in income and it will be taxed as ordinary income to Mr. Jones.

Net Capital Loss as an Offset against Ordinary Income As mentioned previously, a taxpayer is allowed to deduct all or a portion of any net capital loss (NCL) as a deduction toward AGI. This *net capital loss deduction* cannot exceed $3,000. A taxpayer is permitted to deduct both short-term and long-term losses on a dollar-for-dollar basis. When offsetting ordinary income, the NSTCL is utilized first and then the NLTCL is used.

Example: Assume that Jo Ann Johnson has a STCL of $2,700 and a LTCL of $5,400 generated by 1992 activities. Her NCL for 1992 is computed as follows:

STCG	$ 0	
STCL	(2,700)	
NSTCL		($2,700)
LTCG	$ 0	
LTCL	(5,400)	
NLTCL		($5,400)
NCL		($8,100)

Ms. Johnson's net capital loss deduction for 1992 would be $3,000, consisting of $2,700 of short-term losses and $300 of long-term losses. She would be eligible for a capital loss carryover.

Capital Loss Carryover Because of the ceiling imposed on the net capital loss deduction, it is possible that all of the loss will not be used in the year in which it is generated. In these instances, the individual tax-payer is permitted to carry the loss forward.

Net short-term capital losses that are not fully used up are carried forward indefinitely to subsequent tax years. The NSTCL carryover is treated as a STCL in the carryover periods, and it combines with other short-term items to determine NSTCL or NSTCG for the carryover period.

Net long-term capital losses that are not fully used up are likewise carried forward indefinitely to subsequent tax years. The NLTCL carryover will be treated as a LTCL and will combine with the long-term capital gains and losses of the carryover period to generate NLTCG or NLTCL.

Example: In the preceding example for Jo Ann Johnson, the amount of short-term capital loss carryover that will enter into the computation of 1993 NSTCL or NSTCG will be $0. Since the short-term losses are applied first, the full $2,700 was used. The amount of long-term capital loss carryover that will move into the 1993 computation of NLTCL, or NLTCG, will be $5,100 ($5,400 less $300).

Bonds

Interest income from bonds may be fully included in gross income or totally excluded, depending upon the nature of the obligation. For example, interest on corporate bonds and obligations of the United States represents taxable income. However, interest on obligations of possessions of the United States (e.g., Puerto Rico) is exempt. The increment in the value of U.S. savings bonds (Series E before 1980 and Series EE after 1979) purchased at a discount is taxable as interest income. The period in which this increment is recognized will vary, depending upon whether the taxpayer is on a cash basis or an accrual basis. An *accrual-basis taxpayer* must include annually each year's increment as interest income. On the other hand, a *cash-basis taxpayer* may elect to include annually each year's increment as interest income or defer recognition of the increment until the bonds either mature or are surrendered. Most individuals elect the latter approach. When a taxpayer elects to report interest income annually, the election applies to all bonds owned as well as those acquired in the future.

Example: Karen Brooks, a cash-basis taxpayer, purchased a Series EE bond at a local bank during the current year for $500. When the bond matures in 10 years she will receive $1,000. At the end of the first year the redemption value of the bond is $528. Karen

may elect to recognize the increment in value of $28 as interest income currently. Alternatively, she may defer recognition of any income until the bond matures in 10 years, at which time she would report $500 of interest income ($1,000 proceeds minus $500 cost).

Interest income on obligations of states or any political subdivision (cities, towns, villages, and counties) is exempt. This makes state and local government bonds (*municipal bonds*) very attractive to wealthy tax-payers, because their after-tax rates of return can exceed those of taxable bonds.

In determining whether to invest in a tax-exempt bond, an investor should compute the equivalent yield of a taxable bond. This can be done by subtracting the taxpayer's marginal tax bracket from 1.0 and dividing the result into the yield of a tax-exempt bond. Assume a taxpayer in the 31 percent marginal tax bracket is considering purchasing State of Michigan bonds yielding 7.9 percent. Dividing 0.69 (i.e., 1.00 − 0.31) into 7.9 percent results in a taxable equivalent yield of 11.4 percent.

Amortization of Bond Premium The amount paid in excess of a bond's face value is called a *premium*. Investors in tax-exempt bonds are required to *amortize* (i.e., write off) the bond premium, whereas those who acquire taxable bonds may elect to amortize the bond premium over the remaining life of the bond. In the case of a tax-exempt bond, the amortized premium allowed each year reduces the cost basis of the bond. However, because the interest income on municipal bonds is exempt from taxes, no interest deduction is allowed. With respect to a taxable bond, the amortized premium for the year not only reduces the bond's cost basis, but also results in an interest expense deduction.

Example: On January 1 of the current year, Ed Smith purchased taxable bonds from the XYZ Corporation with face values totaling $80,000 for $86,000. The bonds pay an annual interest rate of 9 percent and mature in 10 years. Mr. Smith elects to amortize the premium of $6,000 over the life of the bonds. Each year until the bonds mature he will report $7,200 of interest income ($80,000 × 0.09) and $600 of amortized premium ($6,000/10) will be treated as an interest deduction. (He will report income of $6,600 each year: $7,200 − $600.) Further, Mr. Smith will reduce his basis in the XYZ Corporation bonds by $600 each year. Consequently, at the end of the first year, his basis for the XYZ Corporation bonds will be $85,400 ($86,000 − $600).

Example: Assume in the previous example that Ed Smith purchased tax-exempt municipal bonds rather than taxable bonds. In this case, he would be required to amortize the bond premium, thereby reducing his cost basis for the bonds by $600 each year. This adjustment of the bond's basis by $600 each year is required so that Mr. Smith will not realize a loss when the face value of the bonds is paid at maturity. However, no interest deduction would be allowed.

Amortization of Original Issue Discount   If an investor pays less than face value for a bond, the difference is called a *discount*. For example, if a cash-basis taxpayer acquired a $10,000 corporate bond paying 8 percent interest and maturing in 20 years for $9,000, the discount, which is referred to as the *original issue discount (OID)*, would amount to $1,000. Assuming the taxpayer was not required to amortize the discount over the life of the bond, he or she would be able to recognize a capital gain of $1,000 when the bond matured in 20 years. The gain of $1,000 represents the difference between the bond's face value at maturity ($10,000) and the taxpayer's basis in the bond ($9,000). In other words, the investor would be able to convert ordinary income into favorable capital gain treatment.

Unfortunately, this strategy will not work, because the Internal Revenue Code requires taxpayers to amortize the original issue discount over the life of the bond. The portion of the discount amortized each year represents ordinary income to the investor and also increases the holder's tax basis in the bonds. The method used to amortize the discount is rather complex and beyond the scope of this appendix. Suffice it to say that the amortization method now required is similar to the results produced by the effective interest method.

The IRC contains an important exception in that a discount that does not qualify as an original issue discount need not be amortized. This exception applies when the discount is less than one-fourth of 1 percent of the redemption price of the bond at maturity, multiplied by the number of years to maturity. Consequently, even with small discounts, it is possible to convert ordinary interest income into a capital gain.

Example: Paula White acquired $60,000 of ABC Corporation bonds for $58,600 during the current year. The bonds pay an annual interest rate of 8 percent and mature in 10 years. The discount of $1,400 does not represent original issue discount because $1,400 is less than $1,500 (i.e., 0.0025 × $60,000 × 10 = $1,500). Therefore, Ms. White will not be required to amortize the discount. As a result, rather than reporting a portion of the discount as interest income each year over the life of the bonds, she will report $1,400 of capital gain when the bond is redeemed at maturity in 10 years. Note that the original issue discount rules are not applicable to state and local bonds or to U.S. savings bonds discussed previously.

Retirement of Bonds   As explained earlier, one of the key elements of a capital gain or loss is the occurrence of a sale or exchange. Although the retirement of a bond does not, under the general rule, represent a sale or exchange, an IRC exception qualifies such retirements for sale or exchange treatment. Consequently, a taxpayer will receive capital gain or loss treatment equal to the difference between the bond's tax basis and its redemption value.

Options

A gain or loss attributable to the sale or exchange of a *purchased option* to buy or sell property, or a loss that results from failure to exercise an option, is considered to have the same character as the property to which the option relates. When a loss results from the failure to exercise an option, the option is deemed to have been sold or exchanged on the date it expired.

Example: Jack Carpenter purchased an option to acquire 100 shares of Appleton Inc. stock. When the value of the Appleton stock appreciated in value, Jack elected to sell the option for more than its cost rather than exercise the option and receive the stock. As a result, he will recognize a capital gain equal to the excess of the sale price of the option minus the cost of the option. This is because the stock (if acquired) would have been a capital asset in Jack's hands. Had Jack sold the option for less than its cost, the resulting loss would be treated as a capital loss.

The tax treatment to an individual who *grants an option* on stocks, securities, commodities, or commodity futures depends upon whether the option is exercised. If the option is not exercised, the amount received for the option is treated as a short-term capital gain upon expiration of the option. On the other hand, if the option is exercised, the amount received for the option is added to the sales proceeds of the option property. In this case, the nature of the gain or loss (i.e., ordinary or capital) depends upon the type of property which is sold. The grantee (option holder) adds the cost of the option to the purchase price of the option property.

Example: Gary Underwood purchased 200 shares of ABC Incorporated stock on January 1, 1989, for $2,500. On March 1, 1992, he wrote a call option on the ABC stock giving Alice Black (the option holder) the right to acquire the 200 shares for $3,500 within the following 150 days. For writing the call option Gary received a call premium of $400.

If Alice Black elects not to exercise the option, Gary will be required to recognize a $400 short-term capital gain on the date the option expires. However, should Alice exercise the option by paying Gary $3,500 for the stock on July 1, 1992, he will have a long-term capital gain of $1,400 ($3,500 + $400 − $2,500). Alice's basis in the ABC stock will amount to $3,900 ($3,500 + $400).

Futures Contracts

A *commodity future* is a contract for the sale or purchase of a specified amount of a commodity at a future date for a fixed price. It is considered to be a capital asset, so a capital gain or loss results from its purchase and sale — unless it is used in *hedging transactions*. When a taxpayer in the ordinary course of a trade or business deals in commodity futures as a form of price insurance, he or she is involved in hedging. An example would be a corn farmer trading in corn futures as will be discussed in Chapter 18. Such hedging transactions generate ordinary gains and losses.

Individual Retirement Accounts

Individual retirement accounts (IRAs) have become very popular in the United States since they were introduced in the middle 1970s. There are two reasons for their popularity: (1) contributions to an IRA are deductible on the taxpayer's federal income tax return and (2) the income earned on the assets placed in an IRA is compounded tax-free. Consequently, an individual who makes annual contributions to an IRA over a period of 20 or more years is able to accumulate a significant nest egg for his or her retirement years.

The TRA of 1986 modified the rules pertaining to IRAs, but left certain provisions unchanged. Basically, a taxpayer is eligible to make a deductible contribution to an IRA if he or she (1) has earned compensation from employment such as wages, salaries, tips, commissions, and bonuses or earnings from self-employment and (2) has not reached age $70\frac{1}{2}$ by the end of the taxable year. Starting in 1985 all taxable

alimony received by a divorced spouse is treated as compensation for IRA purposes.

An eligible individual may deduct up to the lesser of $2,000 or 100 percent of compensation. If both spouses have earned compensation and make contributions to their own individual IRAs, the deduction for each spouse is figured separately. A taxpayer whose spouse has no compensation may establish a *spousal IRA* and contribute up to the lesser of $2,250 or 100 percent of compensation. The contribution may be split in any manner between the working and nonworking spouse, provided no more than $2,000 is placed in either IRA in a given year. Under a special provision included in the TRA of 1986, a nonworking spouse with a small amount of compensation may elect to be treated as having no earned income for the year in order to utilize a spousal IRA. For example, under prior law, if a nonworking spouse received $75 for jury duty, the couple's total IRA contribution for the year was limited to $2,075. The election to ignore the jury-duty fee enables the couple to contribute $2,250 through a spousal IRA.

Example: John Adams is 66 years old and single. During the current year he received $2,800 in wages from part-time work as a maintenance man at his church. He also earned $19,000 in interest on corporate bonds. The maximum amount John can contribute to an IRA and deduct for the current taxable year is $2,000 (i.e., the lesser of $2,000, or 100 percent of his compensation of $2,800).

Example: Assume that John Adams in the previous example is married and that Mrs. Adams, who is also 66 years of age, received $3,000 in wages from part-time employment. Since each spouse has compensation during the current year, both may contribute $2,000 to their own IRAs for a total deduction of $4,000 on a joint return. If Mrs. Adams had no earnings, Mr. Adams could establish a spousal IRA and make a deductible contribution, split between the two spouses, of $2,250.

Beginning in 1987, the rules modified by the TRA of 1986 permit individuals to continue (as under prior law) to make fully deductible contributions to an IRA under either of two conditions:

1. Neither the individual nor the individual's spouse is an active participant in a qualified retirement plan.
2. The individual is an active participant in a qualified retirement plan and has adjusted gross income (AGI) below the "applicable dollar amount."

The "applicable dollar amount" varies depending upon the individual's filing status as follows: (1) $25,000 for an unmarried individual, (2) $40,000 for a married couple filing jointly, and (3) zero for a married couple filing separate returns. On a joint return, if one spouse belongs to a qualified retirement plan, both spouses are deemed to belong. On the other hand, married taxpayers filing separate returns need not take into consideration whether the other spouse is a participant in a qualified plan.

A taxpayer whose adjusted gross income exceeds the levels outlined here must reduce his or her annual IRA deduction by 20 percent of the excess. Consequently, the following individuals who are participants in qualified plans would be unable to make deductible contributions to IRAs: single taxpayers with AGIs of $35,000 or more, married taxpayers filing joint returns with AGIs of $50,000 or more, and married taxpayers filing separate returns with AGIs of $10,000 or more. These individuals can, however, still make nondeductible contributions to an IRA up to the lesser of $2,000 or 100 percent of compensation ($2,250 for a spousal IRA). The earnings on nondeductible contributions will accumulate on a tax-deferred basis. That is, they will not be subject to tax until withdrawn.

Example: John Adams is 45 years old and single. During the current year his compensation amounted to $56,000. Because his employer does not have a pension program, he is allowed to make a deductible contribution of $2,000 to his IRA for 1992.

Example: Ed and Linda Witt received compensation of $25,000 and $13,000, respectively, during 1992. Ed is an active participant in his employer's qualified retirement plan. Because their combined adjusted gross income on a joint return is under $40,000, each is entitled to contribute and deduct $2,000 (i.e., for a total of $4,000) to an IRA for 1992.

Example: Assume in the previous example that Linda's compensation for the year amounts to $21,000 or a combined adjusted gross income on a joint return for 1992 of $46,000. Again, Ed and Linda may each contribute $2,000 to an IRA. However, the deduction for each contribution will be reduced by $1,200 (i.e., $46,000 − $40,000 = $6,000 × 20% = $1,200) to $800. If Ed and Linda elected to file separately, Ed's 1992 contribution of $2,000 to his IRA would be non-deductible. This is because his AGI exceeds $10,000. Linda's $2,000 contribution to her IRA would be fully deductible for 1992 because she is not a participant in a qualified plan.

A taxpayer is deemed to have made a contribution to an IRA on the last day of the preceding taxable year if the contribution is made no later than the due date for filing the individual's return (not including extensions). In other words, a contribution made on April 15, 1992, by a taxpayer accounting by calendar years would be deductible on the taxpayer's 1991 return. Moreover, to receive a deduction for the preceding taxable year, the IRA need not be set up until the due date for filing the income tax return.

An IRA can be established with, for example, a bank, credit union, savings and loan association, brokerage firm, or mutual fund. In addition, insurance companies issue individual retirement annuities.

An individual is entitled to withdraw funds from an IRA once he or she attains the age of $59\frac{1}{2}$. However, to avoid penalties, a taxpayer must begin making withdrawals by April 1 of the year following the year in which he or she reaches age $70\frac{1}{2}$. Payments must be made over the participant's expected lifetime or over the life expectancies of the participant and his or her named beneficiary. Alternatively, payments may be made in a lump sum. Distributions from an IRA, other than nondeductible contributions, which may be recovered tax-free, are taxed in full as ordinary income in the year received.

Keogh (H.R. 10) Plans

A taxpayer who is self-employed is allowed to establish a *Keogh plan* (sometimes referred to as an *H.R. 10 plan*). Self-employed individuals include, among others, sole proprietors, partners in a partnership, independent contractors, consultants, and corporate directors. The maximum contribution to a Keogh plan will vary depending upon whether a defined-benefit plan or a defined-contribution plan has been established.

A *defined-benefit Keogh plan* provides a formula that pre-establishes the annual retirement benefit an individual will receive. A pension actuary computes the amount that must be contributed to the plan each year in order to accumulate the funds needed to pay the retirement benefits. The maximum annual retirement benefit that an individual can receive under a defined-benefit plan for 1990 is limited to the lesser of $102,582 (this amount is indexed annually) or 100 percent of average compensation for the three highest-paid years of employment.

A *defined-contribution Keogh plan* defines the amount to be contributed to the plan each year. An individual's retirement income is not known in advance. Rather, the amount available at retirement depends upon how well contributions to the plan have been invested over the years. The amount contributed each year to a defined-contribution plan is limited to the lesser of 25 percent of net earnings from self-employment or $30,000. However, beginning in 1984, earned income was calculated net of contributions made to the qualified plan.

Example: Dr. C. N. Dubble is a partner in an optometry practice. During 1992 Dr. Dubble had earned income of $150,000. He contributed $30,000 to a defined-contribution Keogh plan during the year. The 25 percent limit would be applied as follows:

Dr. Dubble's earned income before contribution	$150,000
Less: contribution to the H.R. 10 plan	(30,000)
Earned income after contribution	$120,000
25 percent of reduced amount	$ 30,000

Because of the way you must determine the earned income after the contribution, the maximum amount effectively becomes 20 percent of earned income before contribution.

Unlike an IRA, a taxpayer must begin a *new* Keogh plan no later than the last day of the taxable year in order to obtain a deduction for that year. However, subsequent contributions made prior to the due date for filing the return (including extensions) are deductible in the prior year. Thus, for a plan to be eligible for 1992, it must be established by December 31, 1992. Once it is established, subsequent contributions within the limit made up to April 15, 1993, are also deductible for 1992.

Summary

▪ Certain tax laws affect an individual's investment and retirement strategies, and a wide variety of tax-planning opportunities is currently available to taxpayers for reducing their federal income tax liability. Having an appreciation of these opportunities is very important for those who wish to maximize their net worth.

References

Prentice-Hall 1992 Federal Tax Handbook. Englewood Cliffs, N.J.: Prentice-Hall, Inc., 1992.

Your Federal Income Tax for Individuals (Publication 17). Washington D.C.: Department of the Treasury, Internal Revenue Service, 1992.

Hoffman, William H., Eugene Willis, and James E. Smith. *1992 Annual Edition West's Federal Taxation: Individual Income Taxes*. St. Paul, Minn.: West Publishing, Co., 1991.

Planning for Your Retirement: IRA & Keogh Plans. Chicago, Ill.: Commerce Clearing House, 1992.

Pratt, James W., Jane O. Burns, and William N. Kulsrud. *1992 Annual Edition Individual Taxation*. Homewood, Ill.: Richard D. Irwin, 1991.

Individual Retirement Plans after Tax Reform. Chicago, Ill.: Commerce Clearing House, 1992.

Tax-Saving Plans for Self-Employed after Tax Reform. Chicago, Ill.: Commerce Clearing House, 1992.

Problems

1. Assume that Fred Langston's investments for 1992 turn out as follows:

Long-term capital gain	$3,750
Long-term capital loss	($1,250)
Short-term capital gain	$ 200
Short-term capital loss	($ 300)

   a. Determine Mr. Langston's net capital gain (NCG) for 1992.
   b. If Mr. Langston's marginal tax rate is 31 percent, what tax liability do these investments generate?

2. Assume that Jane Renton's investments for 1992 turn out as follows:

Long-term capital gain	$ 750
Long-term capital loss	($1,450)
Short-term capital gain	$ 200
Short-term capital loss	($3,600)

   a. Determine Ms. Renton's net capital loss (NCL) for 1992.
   b. If Ms. Renton's marginal tax rate is 31 percent, what is her 1992 tax savings from these investments?
   c. What is the capital loss carryover?

3. On January 1 of the current year, Sam Cool purchases 75 of Amazon International's $1,000 par bonds for $82,500. These bonds will mature in 15 years and have an annual coupon interest rate of 8 percent. If Sam chooses to amortize the premium,

a. What interest income will he report for the first year?

b. What interest income will he report for the third year?

c. What will his basis be after Year 3?

d. How would these answers differ if the bonds had been municipal bonds?

4. Grace Trent purchased 100 shares of Larchmont Technological Industries for $18 per share. After 1 year she wrote an option giving Rob Rather a 3-month option to purchase these shares at $21.50 per share, for which she received a premium of $350.

   a. What are the tax consequences for Grace Trent if:

      1. Rob does not exercise the option.

      2. Rob exercises the option at the end of 3 months when the shares are selling at $30 per share.

   b. What are the tax consequences for Rob Rather if:

      1. He does not exercise the option.

      2. He exercises the option at the end of 3 months when the shares are selling at $30 per share and then immediately sells the shares.

5. In 1992 Tom Piccard had $127,000 of earned income and contributed $17,000 to a defined-contribution Keogh pension plan. How much additional contribution can he make to the plan before he files his tax return for 1992?

C H A P T E R

3

—

Bond Fundamentals

The global bond market is large and diverse, and represents an important investment opportunity. This chapter is concerned with publicly issued, long-term, nonconvertible debt obligations of public and private issuers in the United States and major global markets. In later chapters, we will consider preferred stock and convertible bonds. An understanding of bonds is helpful in an efficient market because U.S. and foreign bonds increase the universe of investments available for the creation of a diversified portfolio.[1]

In this chapter we review some basic features of bonds and examine the structure of the world bond market. The bulk of the chapter is an in-depth discussion of the major fixed-income investments. The chapter ends with a brief review of the data requirements and information sources for bond investors. Chapter 4 discusses the primary (new issue) and secondary markets for bonds.

---

[1]Meir Statman and Neal L. Ushman, "Bonds versus Stocks: Another Look," *Journal of Portfolio Management* 13, no. 3 (Winter 1987): 33–38.

> **Public bond** A long-term, fixed obligation debt security in a convenient, affordable denomination for sale to individuals and financial institutions.
>
> **Par value** The principal of the debt underlying a bond that is payable at maturity. Rarely less than $1,000.
>
> **Money market** The market for short-term debt securities with maturities of less than 1 year.
>
> **Notes** Intermediate-term debt securities with maturities longer than 1 year, but less than 10 years.
>
> **Coupon** Indicates the interest payment on a debt security. It is the coupon rate times the par value that indicates the interest payments on a debt security.
>
> **Bearer bond** An unregistered bond for which ownership is determined by possession. The holder receives interest payments by clipping coupons attached to the security and sending them to the issuer for payment.

Basic Features of a Bond

Public bonds are long-term, fixed-obligation debt securities packaged in convenient, affordable denominations, for sale to individuals and financial institutions. They differ from other debt, such as individual mortgages and privately placed debt obligations, because they are sold to the public rather than channeled directly to a single lender. Bond issues are considered fixed-income securities because they impose fixed financial obligations on their issuers. Specifically, the issuer agrees to:

1. Pay a fixed amount of *interest* periodically to the holder of record
2. Repay a fixed amount of *principal* at the date of maturity

Normally, interest on bonds is paid every 6 months, although some bond issues pay in intervals as short as a month or as long as a year. The principal is due at maturity; this **par value** of the issue is rarely less than $1,000. A bond has a specified term to maturity, which defines the life of issue. The public debt market is typically divided into three segments based upon an issue's original maturity:

1. Short-term issues with maturities of 1 year or less. The market for these instruments is commonly known as the **money market.**
2. Intermediate-term issues with maturities in excess of 1 year, but less than 10 years. These instruments are known as **notes.**

3. Long-term obligations with maturities in excess of 10 years, called *bonds.*

The lives of debt obligations change constantly as the issues progress toward maturity. Thus, issues that have been outstanding in the secondary market for any period of time eventually move from long-term to intermediate to short-term. This movement is important, because a major determinant of the price volatility of bonds is the remaining maturity of the issue.

Bond Characteristics

A bond can be characterized based upon intrinsic features relating to its own issue, its type, or its indenture provisions.

Intrinsic Features The coupon, maturity, principal value, and the type of ownership are important intrinsic features of a bond. The **coupon** indicates the income that the bond investor will receive over the life (or holding period) of the issue. This is also known as *interest income, coupon income,* or *nominal yield.*

The term to maturity specifies the date on which the bond matures (or expires). Of the two different types of maturity, the most common is a *term bond,* which has a single maturity date. A *serial obligation* bond has a series of maturity dates, perhaps 20 or 25. Each maturity, although a subset of the total issue, is really a small bond issue with, generally, a different coupon. Municipalities issue most serial bonds.

The principal, or par value, of an issue represents the original value of the obligation. This is generally stated in $1,000 increments from $1,000 to $25,000 or more. Principal value is *not* the same as the bond's market value. The market prices of many issues rise above or fall below their principal values because of differences between their coupons and the prevailing market rate of interest. If the market interest rate is above the coupon rate, the bond will sell at a discount to par. If the market rate is below the bond's coupon, it will sell at a premium above par. If the coupon is comparable to the prevailing market interest rate, the market value of the bond will be close to its original principal value.

Finally, bonds differ in terms of ownership form. With a **bearer bond,** the holder, or bearer, is the owner, so the issuer keeps no record of ownership. Interest on a bearer bond is obtained by clipping coupons attached to the bonds and sending them to the issuer for payment. In contrast, the issuers of **regis-**

tered bonds maintain records of owners and pay them their interest by check.

Types of Issues   In contrast to common stock, companies can have many different bond issues outstanding at the same time. Bonds can pledge different types of collateral and be either senior or junior securities. **Secured (senior) bonds** are backed by legal claims on some specified property of the issuer. For example, mortgage bonds are secured by real estate assets, while equipment trust certificates, which are used by railroads and airlines, provide a senior claim on the firm's equipment.

  Unsecured (junior) bonds are backed only by the promise of the issuer to pay interest and principal on a timely basis. Debentures are secured by the general credit of the issuer. *Subordinated debentures* possess a claim on income that is subordinated to other debentures. Income issues are the most junior type of bond because interest on them is only paid if the firm earns enough to pay it. While income bonds are unusual in the corporate sector, the concept is very popular in municipal issues where they are referred to as *revenue bonds.* Finally, refunding issues provide funds to prematurely retire another issue. They remain outstanding after the refunding operation. A refunding bond can be either a junior or senior issue.

  The type of issue has only a marginal effect on comparative yield because it is basically the credibility of the issuer that determines bond quality. A study of corporate bond price behavior found that whether or not the issue pledged collateral did not become important until it approached default.[2] The collateral and security characteristics of a bond influence yield differentials when they affect the bond's quality ratings.

Indenture Provisions   The indenture is the contract between the issuer and the bondholder specifying the issuer's legal obligations. A trustee (usually a bank) acting on behalf of the bondholders ensures that all of the provisions are met, including the timely payment of interest and principal.

  Investors should be aware of the three alternative *call features.* Freely callable provisions allow the issuer to retire the bond at any time, typically after notifying bondholders 30 to 60 days in advance. The issuer can-

> **Registered bond** A bond for which ownership is registered with the issuer. The holder receives interest payments by check directly from the issuer.
> **Secured (senior) bond** A bond backed by a legal claim on specified assets of the issuer.
> **Unsecured (junior) bond** A bond backed only by the issuer's promise of timely interest and principal payments.

not retire a noncallable bond prior to its maturity.[3] Finally, a deferred call provision allows the issuer to call it only after a certain period of time (e.g., 5 to 10 years after issuance). After the deferred call period, the issue becomes freely callable. The call premium is the amount above maturity value that the issuer must pay to the bondholder for prematurely retiring the bond.

  A nonrefunding provision prohibits the retirement of an issue from the proceeds of a lower-coupon refunding bond. That is, it allows a bond to be called and prematurely retired for any reason other than refunding. While this is meant to protect the bondholder, it is not foolproof. A firm that had excess cash, or could acquire funds from the sale of short-term bonds or stock, for example, could retire an issue with a nonrefunding provision prior to maturity. This occurred during 1986 when many issuers retired high-coupon issues early because they had the cash and felt that this was a good financing decision.

  Another important indenture provision mandates a *sinking fund*, to pay off a bond systematically over its life rather than only at maturity. The size of the sinking fund can be a percentage of a given issue or of the total debt outstanding, and it can be a fixed or variable sum stated as a dollar amount or a percentage. The payments may commence at the end of the first year or may be deferred for as long as 5 to 10 years from the date of the issue. The amount of the issue that must be repaid before maturity ranges from a nominal sum to 100 percent.

  Like a call or refunding provision, the sinking-fund feature also carries a nominal call premium (e.g., 1 percent). For example, a bond issue with a 20-year maturity might have a sinking-fund provision that requires that 5 percent of the issue be retired every year beginning in year 10. As a result, by the 20th year,

[2]W. Braddock Hickman, *Corporate Bond Quality and Investor Experience* (Princeton, N.J.: Princeton University Press, 1958).

[3]Currently, most corporate long-term bonds contain some form of call provision.

half of the issue has been retired and the rest is paid off at maturity. While most issues have sinking-fund provisions, many industrial and government issues do not, which means that the total issue is payable at maturity. Sinking-fund provisions affect comparative yields at issue, but have little subsequent impact on prices.

A sinking-fund provision is an obligation and must be carried out regardless of market conditions, which means that a sinking-fund bond issue could be called on a random basis. Most are retired to meet sinking-fund requirements through direct negotiations with institutional holders. Essentially, the trustee negotiates with an institution to buy back the necessary amount of bonds at a price slightly above the current market price.

Rates of Return on Bonds

The rate of return on a bond is computed in the same way as the rate of return on stock or any asset. It is determined by the beginning and ending prices and the cash flows during the holding period. The major difference between stocks and bonds is that the interim cash flows on bonds (i.e., the interest) are specified, while the dividends on stock may vary. Therefore, the holding period return (HPR) for a bond will be:

$$HPR_{i,t} = \frac{P_{i,t+1} + Int_{i,t}}{P_{i,t}}$$

where:

$HPR_{i,t}$ = the holding period return for bond i during period t

$P_{i,t+1}$ = the market price of bond i at the end of period t

$P_{i,t}$ = the market price of bond i at the beginning of period t

$Int_{i,t}$ = the interest payments on bond i during period t

Recall that the holding period yield (HPY) is:

$$HPY = HPR - 1$$

Note that the only contractual factor is the amount of interest payments. The beginning and ending bond prices are determined by market forces, as

discussed in Chapter 10. The ending price is determined by market forces unless the bond is held to maturity, in which case the investor will receive the par value. These price variations in bonds mean that investors in bonds can experience capital gains or losses. Interest rate volatility has increased substantially since the 1960s, and this has caused large price fluctuations in bonds.[4] As a result, capital gains or losses have become major components of the rates of return on bonds.

The Global Bond Market Structure[5]

The market for fixed-income securities is substantially larger than the equity exchanges (NYSE, TSE, LSE), because corporations tend to issue bonds rather than common stock. Federal Reserve figures indicate that in the United States during 1989 only about 20 percent of corporate security issues were equities, including preferred as well as common stock. Corporations issue less common and preferred stock because they derive equity financing from internally generated funds. Also, while the equity market accommodates corporations strictly, the bond market in most countries has some noncorporate sectors, as we will explain shortly.

The size of the global bond market and its distribution among countries can be gleaned from Table 3.1, which lists the dollar value of debt outstanding and the percentage distribution for each of the 18 major bond markets for the years 1985 and 1987.

Participating Issuers

There are five different types of bond issuers: (1) federal governments such as the U.S. Treasury, (2) agencies of the federal government, (3) various state and local political subdivisions (municipalities), (4) corpo-

---

[4]Bond price volatility is discussed in Chapter 12.

[5]For further discussion of global bond markets and specific national bond markets, see *International Bond Handbook* (London: James Capel & Co., 1987); and Adam Greshin and Margaret D. Hadzima, "International Bond Investing and Portfolio Management," in *The Handbook of Fixed-Income Securities*, 3d ed., ed. by Frank J. Fabozzi (Homewood, Ill.: Business One Irwin, 1991).

Table 3.1   *Total Debt Outstanding in the 18 Major Bond Markets, by Year (U.S. dollar terms)*[a]

	1985		1987	
	Total Volume ($ billions)	Percentage of Total	Total Volume ($ billions)	Percentage of Total
U.S. dollar	$2,830	49.8%	$3,717	41.7%
Japanese yen	1,070	18.8	2,033	22.8
Deutschemark	417	7.3	783	8.8
Italian lira	278	4.9	554	6.2
U.K. sterling	207	3.6	310	3.5
French franc	174	3.1	334	3.7
Canadian dollar	171	3.0	228	2.6
Swedish krona	88	1.5	146	1.6
Danish krone	103	1.8	171	1.9
Swiss franc	77	1.4	142	1.6
Dutch guilder	70	1.2	130	1.5
Belgian franc	51	0.9	96	1.1
Australian dollar	60	1.1	91	1.0
Spanish peseta	34	0.6	76	0.8
Norwegian krone	22	0.4	36	0.4
ECU[b]	10	0.2	37	0.4
Irish punt	11	0.2	22	0.2
New Zealand dollar	8	0.1	15	0.2
Total	$5,681	100.0%	$8,920	100.0%

[a]Only includes bonds with maturities over 1 year. (Floating rate notes are excluded.)
[b]ECU = European Community Unit
Source: "Size of the World Bond Markets: 1981–87," Merrill Lynch Capital Markets (February 1988).

rations, and (5) international issuers. The division of bonds among these five types for the three largest markets and the United Kingdom during 1985, 1987, and 1989 appears in Table 3.2.

Government   The market for government securities is the largest sector in the United States, Japan, and the United Kingdom. It involves a variety of debt instruments issued to meet the growing needs of these governments. In Germany, the government sector is smaller, but it is growing in relative size.

Government Agencies   Agency issues have attained and maintained a major position in the U.S. market

(over 20 percent), but a smaller proportion in other countries. They constitute less than 10 percent in Japan, below 4 percent in Germany, and are nonexistent in the United Kingdom. These agencies represent political subdivisions of the government, although the securities are not typically direct obligations of the government.

The U.S. agency market has two types of issuers: government-sponsored enterprises and federal agencies. The proceeds of agency bond issues finance many legislative programs. In the United States many of these obligations carry government guarantees although they are not direct obligations of the government. In other countries, the relationship of an agency

| Table 3.2 | Makeup of Bonds Outstanding in United States, Japan, Germany, United Kingdom: 1985–1989 |

	1985		1987	
	Total Volume ($ billions)	Percentage of Total	Total Volume ($ billions)	Percentage of Total
A. United States				
Government	$1,037.8	35.3%	$1,335.2	35.9%
Federal agency	626.7	20.6	975.1	26.2
Municipal	639.6	22.3	693.0	18.6
Corporate	340.6	11.6	448.7	12.1
International	185.6	10.3	264.7	7.1
Total	$2,830.2	100.0%	$3,716.7	100.0%
B. Japan				
Government	$ 664.0	62.0%	$1,230.5	60.5%
Government associated organization	87.9	8.2	160.0	7.9
Municipal	31.0	2.9	53.6	2.6
Bank debentures	05.7	19.2	411.5	20.2
Corporate	45.9	4.3	74.2	3.6
International	36.0	3.4	103.1	5.1
Total	$1,069.9	100.0%	$2,033.0	100.0%
C. Germany				
Government	$ 74.3	17.8%	$ 171.8	21.9%
Agency	15.0	3.6	34.6	4.4
State and local	11.3	2.7	23.5	3.0
Bank	267.5	64.1	455.8	58.2
Corporate	1.0	0.2	1.6	0.2
International	48.0	11.5	95.5	12.2
Total	$ 417.1	100.0%	$ 782.8	100.0%
D. United Kingdom				
Government	$ 182.6	88.2%	$ 259.3	83.6%
Agency	—	—	—	—
Municipal	0.6	0.3	0.3	0.1
Corporate	11.6	5.3	19.4	6.3
International	12.9	6.2	31.3	10.1
Total	$ 207.1	100.0%	$ 310.2	100.0%

Source: "Size of the World Bond Markets: 1981–87," Merrill Lynch Capital Markets (February 1988).

issue to the government varies. In most countries the market yields of agency obligations generally exceed those attainable from pure government bonds. Thus, they represent a way for investors to increase returns with only marginally higher risk.

Municipalities Municipal debt includes issues of states, cities, school districts, or other political subdivisions. Unlike government and agency issues the interest income on them is not subject to federal income tax, although capital gains are taxable. Moreover, these bonds are exempt from state and local taxes when they are issued by the investor's home state. That is, the interest income on a California issue would not be subject to state tax for a California resident, but it would be taxable to a New York resident. The interest income on Puerto Rican issues enjoys total immunity from federal, state, and local taxes. Also, most U.S. municipal bond issues are serial obligations, which means an investor can select from a number of different maturities from very short (1 or 2 years) to fairly long (20 years).

As shown in Table 3.2, the municipal bond markets in most other countries are much smaller than those in the United States (less than 3 percent). While each country has unique tax laws, typically the income from a non-U.S. municipal bond would not be tax exempt for a U.S. investor.

Corporations The major nongovernmental issuer of debt is the corporate sector. The importance of this sector differs dramatically among countries. It is a significant, but declining factor in the United States; a small, but declining sector in Japan, where it is supplemented by bank debentures; a small, but constant proportion of the U.K. market; and a minuscule part of the German market because most German firms get their financing through bank loans, which explains the very large percentage of bank debt there.

The market for corporate bonds is commonly subdivided into several segments: industrial, public utility, transportation, and financial issues. The specific makeup varies between countries. Most U.S. issues are industrials and utilities. Most foreign corporations do not issue public debt, but borrow from banks.

The corporate sector provides the most diverse issues in terms of type and quality. In effect, the issuer can range from the highest investment-grade firm, such as American Telephone & Telegraph or IBM, to

a relatively new high-risk firm that has defaulted on previous debt securities.[6]

International The international bond sector has two components: (1) foreign bonds such as Yankee bonds and Samurai bonds, and (2) Eurobonds including Eurodollar, Euroyen, Eurodeutschemark, and Eurosterling bonds.[7] While the relative importance of the international bond sector varies by country (12.5 percent in Germany and the United Kingdom, 7 percent in the United States, and 4.3 percent in Japan), it has grown in both absolute and relative terms in all these countries. While Eurodollar bonds have historically made up over 50 percent of the Eurobond market, the proportion has declined as investors have diversified their Eurobond portfolios. Clearly, this desire for diversification increased with the swings in the value of the U.S. dollar.

Participating Investors

Numerous individual and institutional investors with diverse investment objectives participate in the fixed-income security market. Wealthy individual investors are a minor portion, because of the market's complexity and the high minimum denominations of most issues. Institutional investors typically account for 90 to 95 percent of the trading, although different segments of the market are more institutionalized than others. For example, in the agency market, institutions participate heavily, but are much less active in the corporate sector.

A variety of institutions invest in the bond market. Life insurance companies invest in corporate bonds and, to a lesser extent, in Treasury and agency securities. Commercial banks invest in municipal bonds, as well as in government and agency issues. Property and liability insurance companies concentrate on municipal obligations and Treasuries. Private and government pension funds are committed to corporates' Treasuries and agencies. Finally, mutual funds have increased their demand for corporate and mu-

[6]It is possible to distinguish another sector that exists in the United States but not in other countries—institutional bonds. These are corporate bonds issued by private nonprofit institutions such as schools, hospitals, and churches. They are not broken out because they amount to only a minute part of the U.S. market, and do not exist elsewhere.

[7]These bonds will be discussed in more detail later in this chapter.

nicipal bonds. In fact, fixed-income mutual funds experienced higher levels of sales during the period 1986 to 1989 than equity mutual funds.

As suggested, alternative institutions favor certain types of issues based upon (1) the tax code applicable to the investing institution and (2) the nature of the liability stream that the institution has assumed. For example, because commercial banks are subject to normal taxation and have fairly short-term liability structures, they favor short- to intermediate-term municipals. Pension funds are virtually tax-free institutions with long-term commitments, so they prefer high-yielding, long-term government or corporate bonds. Such institutional investment preferences affect the short-run supply of loanable funds and interest rate changes.

Bond Ratings

Agency ratings are an integral part of the bond market since most corporate and municipal bonds are rated by one or more agencies. The exceptions are very small bond issues and bonds from certain industries, like bank issues. These are known as *nonrated bonds*. There are four major rating agencies: (1) Duff and Phelps, (2) Fitch Investors Service, (3) Moody's, and (4) Standard & Poor's.

Bond ratings provide the fundamental analysis data for thousands of issues.[8] The rating agencies analyze an issuing organization and the specific issue to determine the probability of default and inform the market of their analyses through their ratings.

The primary question in bond credit analysis is whether a firm can service its debt in a timely manner over the life of a given issue. Consequently, the rating agencies consider expectations over the life of the issue along with the firm's historical and current financial position. Although the agencies have done an admirable job, mistakes happen.[9] A study suggested that the risk of default has actually been overestimated by the conservative rating agencies and the market, resulting in excessive risk premiums given the true default possibility.[10] We will consider default estimation further when we discuss high-yield (junk) bonds.

Several studies that examined the relationship between bond ratings and issue quality as indicated by financial variables demonstrated that bond ratings have tended to be positively related with profitability, size, cash flow coverage, and earnings coverage. In contrast, ratings were inversely related with financial leverage and earnings instability.[11]

The ratings assigned to bonds when issued have an impact on their marketability and effective interest rates. Generally, the four agencies' ratings agree. When they do not, the issue is said to have *split ratings*. Seasoned issues are regularly reviewed to ensure that the assigned rating is still valid. If not, revisions are made either upward or downward. Revisions are usually done in increments of one rating grade.[12] The ratings are based upon an analysis of both the company and the specific bond issue. After an overall evaluation of the creditworthiness of the total company, a company rating is applied to the most senior unsecured issue outstanding. All junior obligations then receive lower ratings based upon indenture specifications. Also, an issue could receive a higher rating than justified because of credit-enhancement devices such as the attachment of bank letters of credit or surety or indemnification bonds from insurance companies.

The agencies assign letter ratings depicting what they view as the risk of default of an obligation. The letter ratings range from AAA (Aaa) to D. Table 3.3 describes the various ratings assigned by the major services. Except for slight variations in designations, their meanings and interpretation are basically the same. The agencies modify their letter ratings with + and − signs for Duff and Phelps, Fitch, and S&P, or numbers (1, 2, 3) for Moody's. As an example, an A+ bond is at the top of the A rated group.

---

[8]For a detailed listing of rating classes and a listing of factors considered in assigning ratings, see "Bond Ratings," and "Bond Rating Outlines," in *The Financial Analysts Handbook*, 2d ed., ed. by Sumner N. Levine (Homewood, Ill., Dow Jones-Irwin, 1988): 1102–1138.

[9]Hickman, *Corporate Bond Quality*.

[10]Gordon Pye, "Gauging the Default Premium," *Financial Analysts Journal* 30, no. 1 (January–February 1974): 49–52.

[11]See, for example, Robert S. Kaplan and Gabriel Urwitz, "Statistical Models of Bond Ratings: A Methodological Inquiry," *Journal of Business* 52, no. 2 (April 1979): 231–262; Ahmed Belkaoui, "Industrial Bond Ratings: A New Look," *Financial Management* 9, no. 3 (Autumn 1980): 44–52; and James A. Gentry, David T. Whitford, and Paul Newbold, "Predicting Industrial Bond Ratings with Probit Model and Funds Flow Components," *The Financial Review* 23, no. 3 (August 1988): 269–286.

[12]Bond rating changes and bond market efficiency are discussed in Chapter 11. Split ratings are discussed in L. H. Ederington, "Why Split Ratings Occur," *Financial Management* 14, no. 1 (Spring 1985): 37–47; and P. Liu and W. T. Moore, "The Impact of Split Bond Ratings on Risk Premia," *The Financial Review* 22, no. 1 (February 1987).

Table 3.3   *Description of Bond Ratings*

	Duff and Phelps	Fitch	Moody's	Standard & Poor's	Definition
High Grade	AAA	AAA	Aaa	AAA	The highest rating assigned to a debt instrument, indicating an extremely strong capacity to pay principal and interest. Bonds in this category are often referred to as *gilt edge securities.*
	AA	AA	Aa	AA	High-quality bonds by all standards with strong capacity to pay principal and interest. These bonds are rated lower primarily because the margins of protection are less strong than those for Aaa and AAA bonds.
Medium Grade	A	A	A	A	These bonds possess many favorable investment attributes, but elements may suggest a susceptibility to impairment given adverse economic changes.
	BBB	BBB	Baa	BBB	Bonds are regarded as having adequate capacity to pay principal and interest, but certain protective elements may be lacking in the event of adverse economic conditions that could lead to a weakened capacity for payment.
Speculative	BB	BB	Ba	BB	Bonds regarded as having only moderate protection of principal and interest payments during both good and bad times.
	B	B	B	B	Bonds that generally lack characteristics of other desirable investments. Assurance of interest and principal payments over any long period of time may be small.
Default	CCC	CCC	Caa	CCC	Poor-quality issues that may be in default or in danger of default.
	CC	CC	Ca	CC	Highly speculative issues that are often in default or possess other marked shortcomings.
	C	C			The lowest rated class of bonds. These issues can be regarded as extremely poor in investment quality.
		C		C	Rating given to income bonds on which no interest is being paid.
		DDD, DD, D		D	Issues in default with principal or interest payments in arrears. Such bonds are extremely speculative and should be valued only on the basis of their value in liquidation or reorganization.

Sources: *Bond Guide* (New York: Standard & Poor's Corporation, monthly); *Bond Record* (New York: Moody's Investors Services, Inc., monthly); *Rating Register* (New York: Fitch Investors Service, Inc., monthly).

The top four ratings—AAA (or Aaa), AA (or Aa), A, and BBB (or Baa)—are considered investment-grade securities. The next level of securities is known as *speculative bonds* and include the BB (or Ba) and B rated obligations.[13] The C categories include income obligations or revenue bonds, many of which are trading flat. (Flat bonds are in arrears on their interest payments.) D-rated bonds are in outright

[13]Marshall E. Blume and Donald B. Keim, "Lower Grade Bonds: Their Risks and Returns," *Financial Analysts Journal* 43, no. 4 (July/August 1987): 26–33.

Flower bond A Treasury issue that can be redeemed at face value in payment of federal estate taxes.

default, and the ratings indicate the bonds' relative salvage values.

Alternative Bond Issues

At this point, we have described the basic features available for all bonds and the overall structure of the global bond market in terms of the issuers of bonds and investors in bonds. In this section, we provide a detailed discussion of the bonds available from the major issuers. The presentation is longer than you might expect because we discuss each class of issuing units such as government, municipalities, or corporations in several of the major world financial centers — the United States, Japan, Germany, and the United Kingdom.

Domestic Government Bonds

United States   As shown in Table 3.2, the U.S. bond market is dominated by U.S. Treasury obligations. The U.S. government, with the full faith and credit of the U.S. Treasury, issues Treasury bills (T-bills), which mature in less than 1 year, and two forms of long-term obligations: Treasury notes, which have maturities of 10 years or less, and Treasury bonds, with maturities of 10 to about 25 years. Current Treasury obligations come in denominations of $1,000 and $10,000. The interest income from U.S. government securities is subject to federal income tax, but exempt from state and local levies. These bonds are popular because of their high credit quality and substantial liquidity.

Short-term T-bills differ from notes and bonds because they are sold at discounts from par to provide the desired yield. The return is the difference between the purchase price and the par value at maturity. In contrast, government notes and bonds carry semiannual coupons that specify the nominal yields of the obligations.

Government notes and bonds have some unusual features. First, the period specified for the deferred call feature on Treasury issues is very long and is generally measured relative to the maturity date rather than from the date of issue. They cannot generally be

called until 5 years prior to their maturity dates and most recent issues are noncallable.

Certain government issues provide tax breaks to investors because they can be redeemed at par to pay federal estate taxes. Therefore, an investor can acquire a Treasury bond at a substantial discount, with which his or her estate can pay estate taxes equivalent to the bond's par value. Such bonds are called **flower bonds.** Although no new flower bonds can be issued, approximately five such issues are still available in the market. These carry $2\frac{3}{4}$ to $4\frac{1}{2}$ percent coupons with maturities between 1992 and 1998. The lower coupon causes a substantial price discount and more assurance of price appreciation at "time of departure." Recent estate tax law changes have increased the portion of an estate exempt from taxes, reducing the demand for such issues. Also the available supply has declined, because when flower bonds are used to pay estate taxes, they are retired by the government. Therefore, prices have remained steady, and the yields on these bonds are consistently below those on other Treasury issues of comparable maturity. As an example, during 1991 when most Treasury bonds were yielding between 8 and 9 percent, these flower bonds were yielding 4 to 5 percent.

Japan[14]   The second largest government bond market in the world is Japan's. It is controlled by the Japanese government and the Bank of Japan (the Japanese central bank). Japanese government bonds are attractive investments for those favoring the Japanese yen because their quality is equal to that of U.S. Treasury securities since they are guaranteed by the government of Japan. Also, they are very liquid. These bonds fall into three maturity segments: medium term (2, 3, or 4 years), long term (10 years), and super long term (private placements for 15 and 20 years). Bonds are issued in both registered and bearer form, although registered bonds can be converted to bearer bonds through the registrar at the Bank of Japan.

Medium-term bonds are issued monthly through a competitive auction system like U.S. Treasury bonds. Long-term bonds are authorized by the Ministry of Finance (MOF) and issued monthly by the

[14]For additional discussion, see Nicholas Sargan, Kermit L. Schoenhotz, Steven Blitz, and Sahar Elhabashi, *Trading Patterns in the Japanese Government Bond Market* (New York: Salomon Brothers, 1986); and Aron Viner, *Inside Japanese Financial Markets* (Homewood, Ill.: Dow Jones-Irwin, 1988).

Bank of Japan through an underwriting syndicate that includes major financial institutions. Most super-long-term bonds are sold through private placement to a small number of financial institutions. These government bonds, which are the most liquid of all Japanese bonds, account for more than half of the Japanese bonds outstanding and more than 80 percent of Japanese bond trading volume.

At least 50 percent of the trading in Japanese government bonds will be in the so-called **benchmark issue** of the time. (As of late 1990 the benchmark issue was bond number 119, a 4.80 percent coupon bond maturing in 1999.) The selection of the benchmark issue is made from among 10-year coupon bonds in order to assist smaller financial institutions in their trading of government bonds. The specification of such an issue ensured that these institutions would have a liquid market in this particular security. Compared to the benchmark issue, which accounts for approximately 50 percent of total trading in all 10-year Japanese government bonds, the most active bond within a particular class in the United States accounts for only about 10 percent of the volume.

The yield on this benchmark bond is often as much as 50 or 60 basis points below comparable Japanese government bonds, reflecting its superior marketability. In the U.S. market, the most liquid bond sells at a yield differential of only 10 basis points. The benchmark issue changes when a designated issue matures, or because of a decision by the Bank of Japan. Because of the difference in yield and liquidity, institutions that are interested in buying and holding versus trading acquire the nonbenchmark issues for their higher yields. Notably, in taking these nonbenchmark issues out of circulation, they ensure that the issues will not be traded, which confirms assumptions about the lack of liquidity.

Germany[15]   The third largest bond market in the world is the West German market, although the government segment of this market is relatively small. Table 3.2 shows that approximately three-quarters of domestic deutschemark bonds are issued by the major commercial banks, while the federal government (Federal Republic of Germany) issues the remainder through the Deutsche Bundesbank (the German cen-

> **Benchmark issue** A Japanese government bond selected to dominate trading in that market.

tral bank). The capital market in Germany is dominated by commercial banks because no formal distinction separates them into the investment, merchant, or commercial bank divisions found in the United States and the United Kingdom. As a result, firms arrange their financing through bank loans, and the banks in turn raise their capital through public bond issues. Therefore, domestic industrial bonds are substantially less than 1 percent of the total.

Bonds issued by the Federal Republic of Germany, referred to as *bunds*, are issued in amounts up to DM4 billion (4 billion deutschemarks) with a minimum denomination of DM100. Original maturities are normally 10 or 12 years, although 30-year bonds have been issued.

Although bunds are issued as bearer bonds, individual bonds do not exist. A global bond is issued and held in safekeeping within the German securities clearing system (the *Kassenverein*). Contract notes confirming the terms and ownership of each issue are then distributed to individual investors. Sales are based on these contract notes. Bonds are issued through a fixed quota system by the Federal Bond Syndicate, made up of the Bundesbank and 17 commercial banks, including certain resident branches of foreign banks. These government bunds are very liquid because the Bundesbank makes a market at all times. They also offer the highest credit quality since they are guaranteed by the German government.

Bunds are quoted net of accrued interest as percentages of par value on German stock exchanges. An official daily benchmark price is determined by the Bundesbank and market makers use this benchmark level as the base from which to trade. Although listed on the exchanges, government bonds are primarily traded over the counter and interest is paid annually.

United Kingdom[16]   The U.K. government bond market changed dramatically on October 17, 1986 (the day of the Big Bang when the trading rules and organizations in the securities business in the United Kingdom were changed). The roles of jobbers and

---

[15]For additional information on the German bond market, see Graham Bishop, "Deutschemark," in *Salomon Brothers International Bond Manual*, 2d ed. (New York: Salomon Brothers, 1987).

[16]For further discussion, see Ian C. Collier, *An Introduction to the Gilt-Edged Market* (London: James Capel & Co., 1987).

brokers changed so that broker–dealers could act as principals or agents with negotiated commission structures. In addition, the number of primary dealers in the "gilt" market was expanded from 7 gilt jobbers to 27 primary dealers.

The maturities in this market range from short gilts with maturities of less than 5 years to medium gilts (5 to 15 years) to long gilts with maturities of 15 years and longer. These government bonds either have fixed redemption dates or ranges of dates with redemption at the option of the government after appropriate notice. Alternatively, some bonds are redeemable on a given date or at any time afterward at the option of the government. Government bonds are normally registered, although bearer delivery is available.

Gilts are issued through the Bank of England (the British central bank) using the tender method, whereby prospective purchasers tender offers at prices at which they hope to be allotted bonds. The prices cannot be less than the minimum tender prices stated in the prospectuses. If the issue is oversubscribed, allotments are made first to those submitting the highest tenders and continue until a price is reached where only a partial allotment is required to fully subscribe the issue. All successful allottees pay the lowest allotment price.

These issues are extremely liquid, because of the size of the market and the large sizes of the individual issues. They are also highly rated since all payments are guaranteed by the British government. All gilts are quoted and traded net of accrued interest on the London Stock Exchange. Interest is paid semi-annually.

Government Agency Issues

In addition to pure government bonds, the federal government in each country can give its agencies the authority to issue their own bonds. The sizes and importance of these agencies differ among countries. They are a large and growing sector of the U.S. bond market, a smaller component of the bond markets in Japan and Germany, and nonexistent in the United Kingdom.

United States Agency securities are obligations issued by the U.S. government through various political subdivisions, such as a government agency or a government-sponsored corporation. Six government-sponsored enterprises and over two dozen federal

agencies issue these bonds. Table 3.4 lists selected characteristics of the more popular government-sponsored and federal agency obligations, including the recent size of the market, typical minimum denominations, tax features, and the availability of quotes.[17] The issues in the table are representative of the wide variety of different obligations that are available.

Generally, agency issues are similar to those of other issuers; that is, interest is usually paid semi-annually, and the minimum denominations vary between $1,000 and $10,000. These obligations are not direct issues of the Treasury, yet they carry the full faith and credit of the U.S. government. Moreover, unlike government obligations, some of the issues are subject to state and local income tax, while others are exempt.[18]

One agency issue offers particularly attractive investment opportunities: GNMA (Ginnie Mae) pass-through certificates, which are obligations of the Government National Mortgage Association.[19] These bonds represent undivided interest in a pool of federally insured mortgages. The bondholders receive monthly payments from Ginnie Mae that include both principal and interest, because the agency "passes through" mortgage payments made by the original borrowers (the mortgagees) to Ginnie Mae.

These pass-through securities carry coupons that are related to the interest charged on the pool of mortgages. The portion of the cash flow that represents a repayment of principal is a return of capital and is tax-free, while the interest income is subject to federal, state, and local taxes. The issues have minimum denominations of $25,000 with maturities of 25 to 30 years, but an average life of only 12 years, because as pooled mortgages are paid off, payments and prepayments pass through to the investor. Therefore, unlike most bond issues, the monthly payment is not fixed.

---

[17]We will no longer distinguish between federal agency and government-sponsored obligations; instead, the term *agency* shall apply to either type of issue.

[18]Federal National Mortgage Association (Fannie Mae) debentures, for example, are subject to state and local income tax, whereas the interest income from Federal Home Loan Bank bonds is exempt. In fact, a few issues are exempt from federal income tax as well, e.g., public housing bonds.

[19]For a further discussion of mortgage-backed securities, see Linda Lowell, "Mortgage Pass-through Securities," and Gregory Parseghian, "Collateralized Mortgage Obligations," in *The Handbook of Fixed-Income Securities*, 3d ed., ed. by Frank J. Fabozzi (Homewood, Ill.: Business One Irwin, 1991).

Table 3.4 *Agency Issues: Selected Characteristics*

Type of Security	Minimum Denomination	Form	Life of Issue	Tax Status	How Interest Is Earned
Government-Sponsored					
Banks for Cooperatives (Co-ops)	$ 5,000	B, BE	No longer issued. Longest issue due 1/02/86	Federal: Taxable State: Exempt Local: Exempt	Semiannual interest, 360-day year
Federal Farm Credit Banks Consolidated Systemwide Notes	50,000	BE	5 to 365 days	Federal: Taxable State: Exempt Local: Exempt	Discount actual, 360-day year
Consolidated Systemwide Bonds	5,000	BE	6 and 9 months	Federal: Taxable State: Exempt Local: Exempt	Interest payable at maturity, 360-day year
	1,000	BE	13 months to 15 years	Federal: Taxable State: Exempt Local: Exempt	Semiannual interest
Federal Home Loan Bank					
Consolidated Discount Notes	100,000	BE	30 to 360 days	Federal: Taxable State: Exempt Local: Exempt	Discount actual, 360-day year
Consolidated Bonds	10,000[a]	B, BE	1 to 20 years	Federal: Taxable State: Exempt Local: Exempt	Semiannual interest, 360-day year
Federal Home Loan Mortgage					
Corporation Debentures	10,000[a]	BE	18 to 30 years	Federal: Taxable State: Taxable Local: Taxable	Semiannual interest, 360-day year
Participation Certificates	100,000	R	30 years (12-year average life)	Federal: Taxable State: Taxable Local: Taxable	Monthly interest and principal payments
Federal Interstate Credit Banks	5,000	B, BE	No longer issued. Longest issue date 1/05/87	Federal: Taxable State: Exempt Local: Exempt	Semiannual interest, 360-day year
Federal National Mortgage Association Discount Notes	50,000[a]	B	30 to 360 days	Federal: Taxable State: Taxable Local: Taxable	Discount actual, 360-day year
Debentures	10,000[a]	B, BE	1 to 30 years	Federal: Taxable State: Taxable Local: Taxable	Semiannual interest, 360-day year
Government National Mortgage Association					
Mortgage-backed Bonds	25,000	B, R	1 to 25 years	Federal: Taxable State: Taxable Local: Taxable	Semiannual interest, 360-day year
Modified Pass throughs	25,000[a]	R	12 to 40 years (12-year average)	Federal: Taxable State: Taxable Local: Taxable	Monthly interest and principal payments

(continued)

| Table 3.4 | (continued) |

Type of Security	Minimum Denomination	Form	Life of Issue	Tax Status	How Interest Is Earned
Student Loan Marketing Association Discount Notes	100,000	B	Out to 1 year	Federal: Taxable State: Exempt Local: Exempt	Discount actual, 360-day year
Notes	10,000	R	3 to 10 years	Federal: Taxable State: Exempt Local: Exempt	Semiannual interest, 360-day year
Floating Rate Notes	10,000ª	R	6 months to 10 years	Federal: Taxable State: Exempt Local: Exempt	Interest rate adjusted weekly to an increment over the average auction rate on 91-day Treasury bills and payable quarterly
Tennessee Valley Authority (TVA)	1,000	R, B	5 to 25 years	Federal: Taxable State: Exempt Local: Exempt	Semiannual interest, 360-day year
U.S. Postal Service	10,000	R, B	25 years	Federal: Taxable State: Exempt Local: Exempt	Semiannual interest, 360-day year

Notes: Form B = Bearer; R = Registered; BE = Book entry form. Debt issues sold subsequent to December 31, 1982 must be in registered form.

ªMinimun purchase with increments in $5,000.

Source: "United States Government Securities" (New York: Merrill Lynch Government Securities, Inc., 1985); "Handbook of Securities of the United States Government and Federal Agencies," 31st ed. (New York: First Boston Corporation, 1984).

The rates of return on these pass throughs are relatively attractive compared with corporates. Also, most of the return is tax-free in the early years because the tax-free part of the regular payment that is due to the return of principal is large. Also, prepayments are made by homeowners paying off their mortgages when they sell their homes. A major disadvantage of GNMA issues is that they are depleted by prepayments and lack normal maturity values.

Japan   The agencies in Japan, referred to as *government associate organizations*, account for 7 to 8 percent of the total Japanese bond market. This agency market includes a substantial amount of public debt, but almost twice as much is privately placed with major financial institutions. Public agency debt is issued like government bonds.

Germany   The agency market in Germany finances about 4 percent of the public debt. The major agencies

are the Federal Railway, which issues *Bahn* or *Bundesbahn* bonds, and the Federal Post Office, which issues *Post* or *Bundespost* bonds. These Bahns and Posts are issued up to DM 2 billion. The issue procedure is similar to that used for regular government bonds, which involves a fixed-quota system by the Federal Bond Syndicate. Bahns and Posts are quite liquid, on an absolute basis, but less liquid than government bunds, since the market is only about 10 percent as large as the government market. These agency issues are implicitly, though not explicitly, guaranteed by the government.

United Kingdom   As shown in Table 3.2, there are no agency issues in the United Kingdom.

Municipal Bonds

Municipal bonds are issued by states, counties, cities, and other political subdivisions. Again, the size of the municipal bond market (referred to as the *local authority market* in the United Kingdom) varies substantially among countries. It is about 20 percent of the total U.S. market, compared to about 3 percent in Japan and Germany and less than 1 percent in the United Kingdom. Because of the limited size in these other countries, we will discuss only the U.S. municipal bond market.

U.S. municipalities issue two distinct types of bonds: general obligation bonds and revenue issues. **General obligation bonds (GOs)** are essentially backed by the full faith and credit of the issuer and its entire taxing power. **Revenue bonds** are serviced by the income generated from specific revenue-producing projects of the municipality, for example, bridges, toll roads, municipal coliseums, and waterworks. Revenue bonds generally provide higher returns than GOs because of their higher default risk. Specifically, should a municipality fail to generate sufficient income from a project used to service a revenue bond, it has absolutely no legal debt service obligation until the income becomes sufficient.

GO municipal bonds tend to be issued on a serial basis so that the issuer's cash flow requirements will be steady over the life of the obligation. Therefore, the principal portion of the total debt service requirement generally begins at a fairly low level and builds up over the life of the obligation. In contrast, most municipal revenue bonds are term issues, so the principal value is not due until the final maturity date or last few payment dates.

The most important feature of municipal obligations is the exemption of interest payments from federal income tax, as well as from taxes in the locality and state in which the obligation was issued. This means that their attractiveness varies with the investor's tax bracket. You can convert the tax-free yield of a municipal to an equivalent taxable yield using the following equation:

$$TY = \frac{i}{(1 - t)}$$

where:

TY = equivalent taxable yield
 i = coupon rate of municipal obligation
 t = marginal tax rate of investor

An investor in the 35 percent tax bracket would find a 7 percent municipal yield equivalent to a 10.77 per-

General obligation bond (GO) A municipal issue serviced from and guaranteed by the issuer's full taxing authority.
Revenue bond A bond that is serviced by the income generated from specific revenue-producing projects of the municipality.

cent fully taxable yield, according to the following calculation:

$$TY = \frac{0.07}{(1 - 0.35)} = 0.1077$$

Since the tax-free yield is the major benefit of municipal bonds, an investor's marginal tax rate is a primary concern in evaluating them. As a rough rule of thumb, using the tax rates expected in 1991, an investor must be in the 28 to 30 percent tax bracket before municipal bonds offer yields that are competitive with those from fully taxable bonds. However, while the interest payment on municipals is tax-free, any capital gains are not.

Municipal Bond Guarantees   Another unusual and growing feature of the U.S. municipal bond market, municipal bond guarantees, provides the bondholder with assurance of payment by a third party other than the issuer. The guarantees are a form of insurance placed on the bond at date of issue and are irrevocable over the life of the issue. The issuing municipality purchases the insurance for the benefit of the investor, and the municipality benefits from lower issue costs due to lower default risk and increased marketability.

As of 1990, approximately 30 percent of all new municipal bond issues were insured. The four private bond insurance firms include: a consortium of four large insurance companies named the Municipal Bond Insurance Association (MBIA), a subsidiary of a large Milwaukee-based private insurer known as American Municipal Bond Assurance Corporation (AMBAC), Bond Investors Guaranty (BIG), and Financial Guaranty Insurance Company (FGIC). These firms will insure either general obligation or revenue bonds. To qualify for private bond insurance, the issue must carry an S&P rating of BBB or better. Currently, the rating agencies will give AAA ratings to bonds insured by these firms. Issues with private guarantees have gen-

> **Collateral trust bond** A bond secured by financial assets held by a trustee for the benefit of the bondholders.
>
> **Equipment trust certificate** A debt security issued by a transportation firm to finance the purchase of equipment (railroad rolling stock, airplanes), which serves as collateral for the debt.

erally enjoyed a more active secondary market and lower required yields.[20]

Corporate Bonds

Again, the importance of corporate bonds varies across countries. The absolute dollar value of U.S. corporate bonds is substantial, and has grown overall and as a percentage of long-term capital for U.S. firms. At the same time, corporate debt as a percentage of total U.S. debt has declined from 18 percent to 12 percent because of the explosive increase in government debt caused by large government deficits. For comparison, in Japan the pure corporate sector is small and has declined, while bank debentures comprise 20 percent of the market. In Germany the pure corporate sector is almost nonexistent, while bank debentures issued to obtain funds for corporate loans form the largest segment overall. Finally, corporate debt in the United Kingdom is in the 5 to 6 percent range.

U.S. Corporate Bond Market

Utilities dominate the U.S. corporate market. The other important segments include industrials (which rank second to utilities), rail and transportation issues, and financial issues. This market includes debentures, first-mortgage issues, convertible obligations, bonds with warrants, subordinated debentures, income bonds (which are similar to municipal revenue bonds), collateral trust bonds that are typically backed by financial assets, equipment trust certificates, and mortgage-backed bonds.

If we ignore convertible bonds and bonds with warrants, the preceding list of obligations varies by the type of collateral behind the bond. Almost every bond has semiannual interest payments, a sinking fund, and a single maturity date. Maturities range from 25 to 40 years, with public utilities generally on the longer end and industrials preferring the 25- to 30-year range. Nearly all corporate bonds provide for deferred calls after 5 to 10 years. The deferment period varies directly with the level of interest rates such that during periods of higher interest rates an issue will probably carry a 7- to 10-year deferment. On the other hand, corporate notes, with maturities of 5 to 7 years, are generally noncallable. Notes become popular during periods of higher interest rates when issuing firms want to avoid long-term obligations.

Generally, the average yields for industrial bonds will be the lowest of the three corporate sectors, followed by utility returns, with yields on rail and transportation bonds generally being the highest. Yields differ between utilities and industrials because the large supply of utility bonds means that their yields must rise to attract the necessary demand. Some corporate bonds have unique features or security arrangements, which will be discussed in the following subsections.[21]

Mortgage Bonds The issuer of a mortgage bond grants to the bondholder a first-mortgage lien on some piece of property, or possibly all of the firm's property. Such a lien provides greater security to the bondholder and a lower interest rate for the issuing firm. Additional mortgage bonds can be issued, assuming certain protective covenants related to earnings or assets are met by the issuer.

Collateral Trust Bonds As an alternative to pledging fixed assets or property, a borrower can pledge stocks, bonds, or notes as collateral. The bonds secured by these financial assets are termed **collateral trust bonds**. These pledged assets are held by a trustee for the benefit of the bondholder.

Equipment Trust Certificates Equipment trust certificates are issued by railroads (the biggest is-

---

[20]For a discussion of municipal bond insurance, see Sylvan Feldstein and Frank J. Fabozzi, "Municipal Bonds," in *The Handbook of Fixed-Income Securities*, 3d ed., ed. by Frank J. Fabozzi (Homewood, Ill.: Business One Irwin, 1991); and D. S. Kidwell, E. H. Sorenson, and J. M. Wachowicz, "Estimating the Signalling Benefits of Debt Insurance: The Case of Municipal Bonds," *Journal of Financial and Quantitative Analysis* 22, no. 3 (September 1987): 299–313.

[21]For a further discussion of secured bonds, see Frank J. Fabozzi, Richard Wilson, Harry Sauvain, and John Ritchie, "Corporate Bonds," in *The Handbook of Fixed Income Securities*, 3d ed., ed. by Frank J. Fabozzi (Homewood, Ill.: Business One Irwin, 1991).

suers), airlines, and other transportation firms, with the proceeds used to purchase equipment (freight cars, railroad engines, and airplanes), which serve as collateral for the debts. The serial maturities range from 1 to about 15 years. The use of serial maturities reflect the nature of the collateral, which is subject to substantial wear and tear and tends to deteriorate rapidly.

Equipment trust certificates appeal to investors because of their attractive yields and low default records. Although they lack the visibility of other corporate bonds, they are typically fairly liquid.

Collateralized Mortgage Obligations (CMOs)[22]

Earlier we discussed mortgage bonds backed by pools of mortgages which pay bondholders proportionate shares of principal and interest paid on the mortgages in the pool. You will recall that the pass-through monthly payments are necessarily both interest and principal, and the bondholder is subject to early redemption if the mortgagees prepay for any reason such as when they sell the house or refinance the mortgage. As a result, when you acquire the typical mortgage pass-through bonds you receive monthly payments (which may not be ideal), and you would be uncertain about the size and time period of future payments.

Collateralized mortgage obligations (CMOs) were developed to offset some of these problems with mortgage pass-throughs. The first CMO was issued in June 1983, and the present total outstanding exceeds $50 billion. The main innovation of the CMO instrument is the segmentation of the irregular mortgage cash flows into securities that are high-quality, short-, medium-, and long-term mortgage collateralized bonds. Specifically, CMO investors own bonds that are collateralized by a pool of mortgages or by a portfolio of mortgage-backed securities. The bonds are serviced with the cash flows from these mortgages. Rather than the straight pass-through arrangement, however, the CMO substitutes a *sequential distribution process* that creates a series of bonds with varying maturities to appeal to a wider range of investors.

The prioritized distribution process is as follows:

■ Several classes of bonds are issued against a pool of mortgages, which are the collateral. Assuming the

> **Collateralized mortgage obligation (CMO)** A debt security based on a pool of mortgage loans that provides a relatively stable stream of payments for a relatively predictable term.

typical four classes of bonds, the first three (e.g., Classes A, B, and C) would pay interest at their stated rates, beginning at the issue date, while the fourth class would be an accrual bond (referred to as a *Z bond*).

■ The cash flows received from the underlying mortgages are applied first to pay the interest on the first three classes of bonds, and then to retire these bonds.

■ The classes of bonds are retired sequentially. All principal payments are directed first to the shortest-maturity Class A bonds until they are all retired. Then all principal retirement is directed to the next shortest-maturity bonds (i.e., the Class B bonds). The process continues until all the classes have been paid off.

■ During the early periods, the accrual bonds (the Class Z bonds) pay no interest, but the interest accrues as additional principal, while the cash flow from the mortgages that collateralize these bonds is used to pay the interest on and retire the bonds in the other classes. Subsequently, all remaining cash flows are used to pay off the accrued interest and any current interest, and then to retire the Z bonds.

This prioritized sequential pattern means that the A-class bonds have fairly short terms and each subsequent class runs a little longer until the Z-class bond, which is long term. It functions like a zero coupon bond for the initial years.

Besides creating bonds that pay interest in a more normal pattern (quarterly or semiannually) and that have more predictable maturities, these bonds are considered very high-quality securities (AAA) because of the structure and quality of the collateral. In order to obtain an AAA rating, CMOs are structured to ensure that the underlying mortgages will always generate enough cash to support the bonds issued, even under the most conservative prepayment and reinvestment rates. The fact is, most of them are overcollateralized.

Further, the credit risk of the collateral is minimal, since most are backed by mortgages guaranteed by a federal agency (GNMA, FNMA) or the FHLMC. Those mortgages that are not backed by government agencies carry private insurance for principal and in-

[22]For a detailed discussion, see Janet Spratlin and Paul Vianna, *An Investor's Guide to CMOs* (New York: Salomon Brothers, 1986); and Parseghian, "Collateralized Mortgage Obligations." Additional characteristics of the securities are considered in M. D. Youngblood, *The Evolution of CMO Residuals: Economic, Accounting, and Tax Issues* (New York: Salomon Brothers, 1987).

> **Certificates for automobile receivables (CARs)**
> Asset-backed securities backed by pools of loans to individuals to finance car purchases.
>
> **Variable-rate note** A debt security for which the interest rate changes to follow some specified short-term rate (e.g., the T-bill rate).
>
> **Zero coupon bond** A bond that pays its par value at maturity, but no periodic interest payments. Its yield is determined by the difference between its par value and its discounted purchase price.

terest and mortgage insurance. Notably, even with their AAA ratings, the yields on these CMOs have typically been higher than those on AA industrials. This yield premium has, of course, contributed to their popularity and growth.

Certificates for Automobile Receivables (CARs)[23]
A rapidly expanding segment of the securities market is that of asset-backed securities, which involve securitizing debt. This is an important concept since it substantially increases the liquidity of individual debt instruments, whether they are individual mortgages, car loans, or credit card debt. **Certificates for automobile receivables (CARs)** are securities collateralized by loans made to individuals to finance the purchase of cars. They dominate the asset-backed security market except for mortgage-based securities. Auto loans are self-amortizing, with monthly payments and relatively short maturities (i.e., 2 to 5 years).

These auto loans can be either direct loans from lending institutions or indirect loans originated by auto dealers and sold to the ultimate lenders. Given the collateral, CARs typically have monthly or quarterly fixed interest and principal payments, and expected weighted average lives of 1 to 3 years with specified maturities of 3 to 5 years. (Again, the expected actual life of the instrument is shorter than the specified maturity because of early payoffs when cars are sold or traded in.)

The cash flows of CARs make them comparable to short-term corporate debt. They provide a significant yield premium over General Motors Acceptance Corporation (GMAC) commercial paper, which is the most liquid short-term, corporate alternative. The popularity of these collateralized securities makes them important not only by themselves, but also as an indication of the potential for issuing additional collateralized securities backed by other assets and/or debt instruments.[24]

Variable-Rate Notes Available in Europe for decades, **variable-rate notes** were not introduced in this country until the mid-1970s. They became popular during periods of high interest rates. The typical variable-rate note possesses two unique features:

1. After the first 6 to 18 months of the issue's life, during which a minimum rate is often guaranteed, the coupon rate floats, so that every 6 months it changes to follow some standard. Usually it is pegged 1 percent above a stipulated short-term rate. For example, the rate might be the preceding 3 weeks' average 90-day T-bill rate.
2. After the first year or two, the notes are redeemable at par, at the *holder's* option, usually at 6-month intervals.

Such notes represent a long-term commitment on the part of the borrower, yet provide the lender with all the characteristics of a short-term obligation. They are typically available in minimum denominations of $1,000. However, while the 6-month redemption feature provides liquidity, the variable rates can cause the issues to experience wide swings in semiannual coupons.[25]

Zero Coupon and Deep Discount Bonds The typical corporate bond has a coupon and a maturity. In turn, the value of the bond is the present value of the cash flows (the interest payments and the principal payment at maturity) discounted at the required yield to maturity (YTM) for the bond. Alternatively, some bonds have no coupons or have coupons below the

---

[23]For further discussion, see Thomas Delehanty and Michael Waldman, *Certificates for Automobile Receivables (CARs)* (New York: Salomon Brothers, 1986).

[24]For an overview of these securities, see K. Jeanne Person, *A Review of Asset-Backed Securities* (New York: Salomon Brothers, 1987); and Andrew S. Carron, "Asset-Backed Securities," in *The Handbook of Fixed-Income Securities*, 3d ed., ed. by Frank J. Fabozzi (Homewood, Ill.: Business One Irwin, 1991).

[25]For an extended discussion, see Richard S. Wilson, "Domestic Floating-Rate and Adjustable-Rate Debt Securities," in *The Handbook of Fixed-Income Securities*, 3d ed., ed. by Frank J. Fabozzi (Homewood, Ill.: Business One Irwin, 1991). Adjustable rate preferred stocks are also discussed in Richard S. Wilson, *Corporate Senior Securities* (Chicago: Probus Publishing, 1987), Chapter 6.

market rate at the time of issue. Such securities are referred to as **zero coupon bonds,** *minicoupon bonds,* or *original-issue, deep discount (OID) bonds.*

A zero coupon discount bond promises to pay a stipulated principal amount at a future maturity date, but it does not promise to make any interim interest payments. Therefore, the price (value) of such a bond is the present value of the principal payment at the maturity date using the rate of return on this bond as the discount rate. The return on the bond is the difference between what is paid at the time of issue and the principal payment at maturity.

Consider a zero coupon, $10,000 par value bond with a 20-year maturity. If the required rate of return on bonds of equal maturity and quality is 8 percent, and we assume semiannual discounting, the initial selling price would be $2,082.89 (i.e., the present value factor at 8 percent compounded semiannually for 20 years is 0.208289). Note that, from the time of purchase to the point of maturity, the investor would not receive any cash flow from the firm. The investor must pay taxes, however, on the implied interest on the bond, although no cash is received. Because an investor subject to taxes would experience severe negative cash flows during the life of the bond, these bonds primarily benefit investment accounts not subject to taxes, such as pensions, IRAs, or Keogh accounts.[26]

In a modified form of these bonds, the original-issue discount (OID) bond, the coupon is set substantially below the prevailing market rate, for example, a 5 percent coupon when market rates are 12 percent. As a result, the bond is issued at a deep discount from par value. Again, taxes must be paid on the implied 12 percent return rather than the nominal 5 percent, so the cash flow disadvantage of zero coupon bonds, though lessened, remains.

High Yield Bonds A segment of corporate bonds that has grown in size and importance, along with controversy, is **high yield bonds,** also referred to as *speculative grade bonds* and *junk bonds.* These are corporate bonds that have been rated by the rating agencies as noninvestment grade, indicated by ratings

High yield bond A bond rated below investment grade. Also referred to as speculative-grade bonds or junk bonds. These are typically issued by relatively small firms or used to finance leveraged buyouts.

below BBB or Baa. The title *speculative grade bonds* is probably the most objective, based upon the logic that bonds not rated as investment grade are speculative grade. The designation *high yield bonds* was created by Drexel Burnham Lambert as an indication of the returns available for these bonds relative to Treasury bonds and investment grade corporate bonds. The *junk bond* designation is obviously somewhat derogatory, referring to the quality of the issues.

Brief History of the High Yield Bond Market Based upon a definition of bonds rated below BBB as part of the high yield market, this segment has been in existence for as long as there have been rating agencies. A major difference with regard to the bonds in this category occurred in 1980. Prior to 1980, most of the bonds in the high yield group were referred to as *fallen angels.* These are bonds that were originally issued as investment grade securities, but because of changes in the firms over time, the bonds were downgraded into the speculative rating classes (BB and below).

A change in the nature of the market began in the early 1980s when Drexel Burnham Lambert began aggressively underwriting original issue high yield bonds for two groups of clients: (1) small firms that did not have the financial strength to receive investment grade ratings from the rating agencies, and (2) large and small firms that issued high yield bonds in connection with leveraged buyouts (LBOs). The high yield bond market went from a residual market of mainly fallen angels to a new-issue market where bonds were underwritten with below-investment-grade ratings.

The individual who is credited with leading the development of this new-issue, high yield market is Michael Milken, a bond trader/salesman at Drexel Burnham Lambert (DBL). Milken examined the returns and risks related to speculative grade securities before 1975 and became convinced that the promised and realized rates of return on these speculative grade bonds were higher than justified by their default experience. He convinced a number of institutional investors of the superior risk-adjusted returns available on these bonds, which helped create a demand for

---

[26]These bonds will be discussed further in Chapters 10 and 11 in the sections on duration and immunization. The price volatility of these bonds in IRA accounts is discussed in Randall Smith, "Zero Coupon Bonds' Price Swings Jolt Investors Looking for Security," *The Wall Street Journal* (June 1, 1984): 19.

| Table 3.5 | High Yield Bond Issues: Annual Dollar Value, Number, Average Size, and Percentage of All Public Debt Issues ($ millions) |

	Total Par Value: New High Yield Debt Issues			Par Value of New Public Issues	
	Amount	Number	Average Size	Total Value	High Yield as Percentage of Total
1978	$ 1,493	52	$ 28.7	$ 19,944	6.96%
1979	1,307	45	29.0	23,130	5.35
1980	1,374	45	30.5	37,135	3.70
1981	1,284	38	33.8	35,866	3.58
1982	2,518	57	44.2	40,744	6.18
1983	7,534	98	76.9	46,051	16.36
1984	14,111	133	106.1	65,329	21.60
1985	15,043	182	82.7	97,745	15.39
1986	31,965	223	143.3	219,842	14.54
1987	28,925	184	157.2	210,363	13.75
1988	27,804	159	174.9	234,633	11.85
1989	25,232	124	203.5	273,074	9.24
1990	1,297	9	144.1	288,222	0.45

Source: *Investment Dealers Digest* and Martin S. Fridson, "This Year in Highlight," *Extra Credit* (New York: Merrill Lynch & Co., February 1991).

them. At the same time, Milken and DBL became active in underwriting many of these high yield bond issues for small firms and LBOs.[27]

As a result, the high yield bond market exploded in size and activity beginning in 1983. As shown in Table 3.5, while there were a few new, high yield issues in the late 1970s, they were not very large issues (with an average size below $30 million) and they accounted for only about 4 to 7 percent of all public straight debt issues. Beginning in 1983, more larger issues became common (the average size of an issue in 1988 was almost $200 million) and high yield issues came to account for a significant percentage of the total new-issue bond market. High yield bonds rose from about 7 percent of total new bond issues in 1978 to 22 to 25 percent in 1987 to 1988. The cumulative percent column indicates that of all the high yield issues sold since 1978, about 94 percent have been sold since 1983, and about 68 percent were issued during the three years from 1986 to 1988. As of 1989, high yield debt constituted about 21 percent of all public debt in the United States.

An important point bears repeating. While the high yield debt market has been in existence for many years, its real emergence as a significant factor and a major component of the U.S. capital market did not occur until 1983. This is relevant when one considers

[27]Subsequent to the growth and development of the high yield bond market, Michael Milken and DBL were indicted for securities law violations. DBL settled with the SEC and paid a fine without admitting guilt. In early 1990, Milken agreed to a plea bargain with the SEC that involved a fine and a prison term. It is the author's opinion that observers should separate the development of the high yield bond market from the securities law violations. While not condoning the security law violations, almost everyone would acknowledge that the development of the high yield debt market has had a very positive impact on the capital-raising ability of the economy. For an analysis of this impact, see Glenn Yago, *Junk Bonds* (New York: Oxford University Press, 1991).

Table 3.6 *Distribution of Ratings for High Yield Bonds — December 31, 1988*

Average S&P Rating	Percentage	
BB+	13.09%	
BB	3.42	24.88%
BB−	8.37	
B+	12.23%	
B	13.03	49.73%
B−	24.47	
CCC+	15.64%	
CCC	4.09	20.49%
CCC−	0.62	
CC	0.65%	
C	0.19	5.04%
D	4.20	

Source: Martin S. Fridson, Steven B. Jones, and Fritz Wahl, "The Anatomy of the High Yield Debt Market: 1988 Update" (New York: Morgan Stanley & Co., February 1989).

Table 3.7 *Distribution of Ownership of High Yield Bonds: December 31, 1988*

	Percentage Ownership
Mutual funds, money managers	30%
Insurance companies	30
Pension funds	15
Foreign investors	9
Savings and loans	7
Individuals	5
Corporations	3
Securities dealers	1

Source: "1989 High Yield Market Report" (New York: Drexel Burnham Lambert, March 1989).

the liquidity and default experience for these securities.

Distribution of Ratings Table 3.6 shows the distribution of ratings for all outstanding high yield issues as of December 31, 1988. The heavy concentration is in the B class, which contains almost half of all issues. An analysis of new, high yield bond issues by year would indicate a shift toward the lower end of this distribution. Specifically, only about 10 percent of high yield issues in 1987 and 1988 were rated BB, while over 60 percent were rated B.

Ownership of High Yield Bonds As shown in Table 3.7, the major owners of high yield bonds have been mutual funds, insurance companies, and pension funds. As of the end of 1988, almost 100 mutual funds either exclusively invested in high yield bonds, or included such bonds in their portfolios.

This distribution of ownership among a number of groups, including institutions, is an important contributor to the liquidity of this market. Wider distribution gives bondholders more opportunities to find buyers or sellers. Notably, any legislation that would discourage investments by these institutions could

have a significant negative impact on the liquidity of this market.

Major Underwriters Table 3.8 lists the major investment banking firms that acted as lead underwriters for high yield bonds for the 4 years from 1985 to 1988. It demonstrates two important points: (1) the dominant position of Drexel Burnham Lambert (DBL) following its initial efforts to develop this market, and (2) the gradual deterioration of DBL's position as other firms recognized the opportunities to develop research and underwriting capabilities for high yield debt. The point is, while DBL was the major underwriter up to the time that it declared bankruptcy in early 1990, several other firms had clearly established expertise and a clientele for these securities.

Again, it is a positive factor for the liquidity of this market to have more firms involved in underwriting and trading these securities — especially after the bankruptcy of DBL. Therefore, while the market experienced a period from late 1989 to early 1990 of great uncertainty, it did not collapse, and most observers expected it to survive and be a major component of the corporate bond market during the 1990s and beyond.

The purpose of this discussion has been to introduce you to the area of high yield bonds because of the growth in size and importance of these issues for individual and institutional investors. We will revisit

Table 3.8	Lead Underwriters of New High Yield Bond Issues: 1985–1988 ($ millions)

	1988		1987		1986		1985	
	Amount Issued	Percentage of Total[a]	Amount Issued	Percentage of Total[a]	Amount Issued	Percentage of Total[a]	Amount Issued	Percentage of Total[a]
Drexel Burnham Lambert	$12,265	40.8%	$12,089	38.8%	$15,255	45.6%	$7,284	49.7%
Morgan Stanley & Co.	4,265	14.2	5,366	17.2	2,600	7.8	1,050	7.2
First Boston	4,013	13.4	4,301	13.8	1,550	4.6	640	4.4
Merrill Lynch	2,302	7.7	3,657	11.7	3,380	10.1	666	4.5
Salomon Brothers	1,665	5.5	730	2.3	2,434	7.3	1,464	10.0
Prudential-Bache Securities	1,377	4.6	50	0.2	507	1.5	435	3.0
Donaldson, Lufkin & Jenrette	913	3.0	696	2.2	338	1.0	55	0.4
Goldman Sachs & Co.	810	2.7	2,624	8.4	1,278	3.8	615	4.2
Kidder Peabody & Co.	718	2.4	320	1.0	880	2.6	95	0.7
Shearson Lehman Hutton	350	1.2	257	0.8	2,123	6.4	771	5.3

[a]Percentages do not add to 100 because only the top 10 firms are listed.

Source: Martin S. Fridson, Steven B. Jones, and Fritz Wahl, "The Anatomy of the High Yield Debt Market: 1988 Update" (New York: Morgan Stanley & Co., February 1989).

this topic in the chapter on bond portfolio management, where we will review the historical rates of return on these bonds and discuss alternative risk factors that must be considered by potential investors in these securities.[28]

Japanese Corporate Bond Market

The corporate bond market in Japan is made up of two components: (1) bonds issued by industrial firms or utilities and (2) bonds issued by banks to finance loans to corporations. As noted earlier in connection with Table 3.2, the pure, nonbank corporate bond sector was fairly small in 1981 (7.2 percent of all outstanding bonds in Japan) and has declined in relative size over

time to less than 4 percent of all bonds in 1987. In contrast, the dollar amount of bonds issued by banks has increased over time and has maintained its relative position of about 20 percent of the total.

Japanese corporate bonds are monitored by the *Kisaikai*, which is the council for the regulation of bond issues. The council is composed of 22 bond-related banks and 7 major securities companies. It operates under the authority of the Ministry of Finance (MOF) and the Bank of Japan (BOJ) to determine bond-issuing procedures and practices, including issuing conditions for straight corporate debt. Specifically, the Kisaikai fixes the coupons on corporate bonds in relation to coupons on long-term government bonds to prevent any competition with the government bond market.

Because of numerous bankruptcies during the 1930s depression, the government mandated that all corporate debt be secured, and this was enforced by the Kisaikai. There was pressure by the corporations and the securities firms in the late 1970s and early 1980s to relax these requirements. Before this was allowed, domestic Japanese firms began issuing convertible bonds that were not bound by the collateral rule. In addition, foreign firms began issuing Euroyen bonds that were also not restricted, and eventually Japanese firms began to issue straight debt in the

[28]For additional discussion of these bonds, see Kevin J. Perry and Robert A. Taggart, Jr., "The Growing Role of Junk Bonds in Corporate Finance," *Journal of Applied Corporate Finance* 1, no. 1 (Spring 1988): 37–45; Edward I. Altman and Scott A. Nammacher, *Investing in Junk Bonds* (New York: John Wiley & Sons, 1987); Hilary Rosenberg, "The Unsinkable Junk Bond," *Institutional Investor* 23, no. 1 (January 1989): 43–48; Robert Solef, *Historical Perspectives on the Use of High Yield Securities in Corporate Creation: A Hundred Years of Junk* (New York: Drexel Burnham Lambert, 1989); Martin S. Fridson, *High Yield Bonds* (Chicago: Probus Publishing, 1989; and Frank K. Reilly, ed., *High Yield Bonds: Analysis and Risk Assessment* (Charlottesville, Va.: Institute of Chartered Financial Analysis, 1990).

Euroyen market. Finally, early in 1987 numerous firms were permitted to issue unsecured debt in Japan. This allowance was broadened in late 1987 and the restriction was abolished during 1988.

The issuance of unsecured debt has led to a new line of business in Japan — rating agencies. With completely secured debt, there was no need for such firms. The Japan Bond Research Institute was established in 1979 to rate convertible issues. In 1981 Mikuni's Credit Rating Company was established, followed by additional firms in 1985 and 1986, including the Japan Credit Rating Agency, Ltd.; Nippon Investors Service, Inc.; and Moody's Japan K.K. (a subsidiary of Moody's Investors Service, Inc.).

Corporate Bond Segments The corporate debt market in Japan is divided into two major segments: bonds issued by electric power companies, and bonds issued by all other corporations. The nine electric power firms receive preferential treatment because they are regulated public utilities. As a result, about 75 percent of all domestic straight-debt issues are public utility bonds. Corporate bonds for other industrial firms are sold in the domestic market, and also in the Eurobond market.

The Ministry of Finance specifies minimum corporate requirements and issuing requirements, including a stipulation that net corporate assets must exceed 6 billion yen. Also, the ministry controls the month and issuance system that specifies who can issue bonds when. In addition, lead-underwriting managers are predetermined in accordance with a lead manager rotating system that assures balance among the big-four securities firms in Japan (Nomura, Nikko, Daiwa, and Yamaichi Capital Management).

Bank Bonds The substantial issuance of Japanese bank bonds is a function of the banking system in Japan, which is segmented into the following rigidly defined components:

- Commercial banks (13 big-city banks and 64 regional banks)
- Long-term credit banks (3)
- Mutual loan and savings banks (6)
- Specialized financial institutions

During the reconstruction after World War II, several banks were permitted to obtain funding by issuing medium- and long-term debentures at rates above yields on government bonds. The banks were the three long-term credit banks (the Industrial Bank of Japan, the Long-Term Credit Bank of Japan, and the Nippon Credit Bank), the Norinchukin Bank (Central Cooperative Bank for Agriculture and Forestry), the Shako Chukin Bank (Central Bank for Commercial and Industrial Cooperatives), and the Bank of Tokyo. These funds were used to make mortgage loans to firms in the industrial sector to rebuild plant and equipment. Currently these financial institutions sell 5-year coupon debentures and 1-year discount debentures directly to individual and institutional investors. The long-term credit banks are not allowed to take deposits, so they depend upon the debentures to obtain funds. These bonds are traded in the OTC market.[29]

German Corporate Bond Market

Germany likewise has a combination sector in corporates — pure corporates and banks. Here the contrast is even larger, since nonbank corporate bonds are almost nonexistent while the bank bonds make up over 60 percent of the total bond market.

Bank bonds are bearer bonds that may be issued in collateralized or uncollateralized form, with the largest categories being mortgage and commercial bonds, although it is possible to use agricultural loans, industrial loans, and ship mortgages as collateral.

German mortgage bonds are collateralized fixed-income obligations of the issuing bank backed by mortgage loans registered with a government-appointed trustee. The supervision of these bonds and the mortgage loans keep the bonds' quality very high.

They are issued in bearer or registered form. The registered bonds are mainly sold to domestic institutions and cannot be listed on a stock exchange because they are not considered to be securities. Alternatively, the bearer bonds, which are transferred by book-entry, are sold in small denominations, traded on the exchanges, and enjoy an active secondary market.

German commercial bonds are subject to the same regulation as mortgage bonds except that the collateral consists of loans to or guarantees by a German public sector entity rather than first mortgages. Possible borrowers or guarantors include the federal government, its agencies (federal railway agency or post office), federal states, and agencies of the Euro-

---

[29]For further discussion of this market, see Aron Viner, *Inside Japanese Financial Markets* (Homewood, Ill.: Dow Jones-Irwin, 1988): Chapters 5 and 6.

pean Economic Community (EEC). The credit quality of these loans is excellent. Mortgage and commercial bonds have identical credit standing and trade at very narrow spreads.

Schuldscheindarlehen are private loan agreements between borrowers and large investors (usually banks) who make the loans but who can (with the borrowers' permission) sell them or divide them among several investors. These investments resemble negotiable loan participations. All participants receive copies of the loan agreement, and a letter of assignment gives the participant title to a share of principal and interest, although the bank acts as agent for the participants. These loan agreements account for a substantial proportion of all funds raised in Germany. While a large volume of these private loan agreements are outstanding, the market is not very liquid, which means that they are designed for the investment of large sums to maturity.

United Kingdom Corporate Bond Market

Corporate bonds in the United Kingdom are available in three forms, as debentures, unsecured loans, and convertible bonds. The values of securities in each class are about equal (about 3 billion pounds). The corporate bond market was fairly inactive for several years prior to the 1980s because of the high long-term interest rates, but experienced a resurgence in the 1980s with lower inflation. Investment trusts have been very active issuers in this market through the use of preference stock, debentures with floating rate coupons, and zero coupon bonds. Numerous borrowers offered bonds secured by property or prior calls on the revenue of the issuers, but many large corporations and banks raised funds through unsecured borrowing. Also there was significant growth in convertible bonds, although the total proportion related to these securities has remained at about 5 percent.

A indicated, the corporate bond market in the United Kingdom is made up of three sectors: debentures (secured debt), unsecured loans, and convertible bonds. The maturity structure of the corporate bond market is fairly wide and includes a good supply of long maturity bonds. During the 1960s and 1970s most securities were short-term, but this changed during the 1980s when preference shifted toward long maturity bonds. The coupon structure of the corporate bond market features low-coupon bonds issued during the 1960s and 1970s and a number of high-

coupon bonds issued during the 1980s. The higher end of the coupon range, which goes from 10 to 14 percent, is due to the unsecured loan segment of this market with convertible bonds having the low coupons. Almost all U.K. corporate bonds are term bonds with call features.

Corporate bonds have typically been issued by both public offerings underwritten by investment bankers and private placements. Early in the 1980s, the market tended toward the private placement method. Since the "Big Bang" in October 1986, use of public offerings through investment banking firms has increased. Prior to the Big Bang, corporate bonds were traded on the stock exchange by brokers and jobbers. Following the Big Bang, a number of primary dealers have begun trading corporate bonds. Since there are no interdealer brokers, the traders typically deal directly with each other. All corporate bonds are issued in registered form.

International Bonds

Each country's international bond market has two components. The first, foreign bonds, are issues sold primarily in one country and currency by a borrower of a different nationality. An example would be U.S. dollar bonds sold by a Japanese firm in the United States. (As we have explained, these are Yankee bonds.) The second segment, Eurobonds, are underwritten by international syndicates and sold in a number of national markets. For example, Eurodollar bonds are securities denominated in U.S. dollars, underwritten by international syndicates, and sold to non-U.S. investors. As we will discuss, the relative sizes of these two markets vary by country.

United States As of the end of 1989, the Eurodollar bond market was much larger than the Yankee bond market (about $350 billion versus $50 billion). However, the Eurodollar bond market reacts to strength or weakness in the U.S. dollar. For example, the weakness of the dollar during 1986 and 1987 created a desire for diversification into other currencies.

Yankee bonds are issued by foreign firms who register with the SEC and borrow U.S. dollars, through issues underwritten by U.S. syndicates for delivery in the United States. The secondary market for these securities is in the United States and they pay interest semiannually. Over 60 percent of Yankee bonds are issued by Canadian corporations. They typically have shorter maturities than U.S. domestic issues, and they generally offer longer call protection, which increases their appeal.

The Eurodollar bond market is dominated by foreign investors, and the center of trading remains in London. The marketability of these bonds had improved until the slowdown during 1987. Eurodollar bonds pay interest annually, so you must adjust the yield calculation, which typically assumes semiannual compounding. The Eurodollar bond market has historically accounted for almost 50 percent of the total Eurobond market.

Japan Prior to 1984 over 90 percent of the Japanese international bond market was devoted to foreign bonds (Samurai bonds) with the balance in Euroyen bonds. In 1985 the issuance requirements for Euroyen bonds were liberalized. As a result, in 1985 the amounts of Samurai and Euroyen bonds issued were about equal. In 1986, however, the ratio was 4 to 1 in favor of Euroyen bonds, and the ratio was almost 10 to 1 in 1987.

Samurai bonds are yen-denominated bonds issued by non-Japanese issuers and mainly sold in Japan. An example would be a yen-denominated bond sold in Tokyo by IBM. The market is a small portion of the total Japanese bond market and has limited liquidity, but the bonds are exempt from withholding taxes. The Samurai bond market experienced very little growth during 1986 and 1987 in terms of yen, but substantial growth in U.S. dollar terms because of exchange rate changes.

Euroyen bonds are yen-denominated bonds sold outside Japan by international syndicates. As indicated, this market experienced substantial growth during 1985 to 1987 because of the liberalized issue requirements and favorable exchange rate movements. (The rates of return on these bonds from 1985 to 1987 were over 30 percent a year in U.S. dollar terms.)

Germany All deutschemark bonds of foreign issuers can be considered Eurobonds, because the stability of the German currency reduces the importance of the distinction between foreign bonds and Euro-DM bonds. Foreign bonds are deutschemark-denominated bonds sold in Germany by non-German firms such as General Motors and underwritten by domestic institutions. Eurodeutschemark bonds are sold outside Germany and underwritten by international firms. Both sets of bonds share the same primary and secondary market procedures, are free of German taxes, and have similar yields.

A relatively recent innovation was the issuance of a Eurodeutschemark bond secured by a *Schuldscheindarlehen* loan from one of the Federal states (called *lander*). Also, since 1985 the landers have issued Eurodeutschemark floating-rate notes (FRN) fixed to various rates, including the London Inter-Bank Offered Rate (LIBOR), which is considered a world-base loan rate similar to using the 90-day T-bill rate in the United States or the prime rate for bank loans.

United Kingdom U.K. foreign bonds, referred to as *bulldog bonds*, are sterling-denominated bonds issued by non-English firms and sold in London. Eurosterling bonds are sold in markets outside London by international syndicates. As in other countries, the total U.K. international bond market has come to be dominated by this Eurobond segment. In 1981 there were about twice as many Eurosterling bonds outstanding as bulldogs. By 1986 the ratio had grown to almost 5 to 1. In fact, during 1987 about $14 billion in Eurosterling bonds was issued and no bulldogs were issued. Government restrictions on bulldogs implemented in early 1986 made borrowing in this sector very expensive. The procedure for issuing and trading Eurosterling bonds is similar to that for other Eurobonds.

Obtaining Information on Bonds

As might be expected, the data needs of bond investors are considerably different from those of stockholders. For one thing, there is less emphasis on fundamental analysis because, except for speculative-grade bonds and revenue obligations, most fixed-income investors rely on the rating agencies for credit analysis. An exception would be large institutions that employ in-house analysts to confirm agency ratings or to uncover incremental return opportunities. The large investments by these institutions can make the rewards of differences of only a few basis points substantial, and the institutions enjoy economies of scale in research. Finally, several private research firms concentrate on the independent appraisal of bonds.

Required Information

In addition to information on the risk of default, bond investors need information on (1) capital market and economic conditions and (2) intrinsic bond features. Market and economic information allows investors to stay abreast of the general tone of the bond market, overall interest rate developments, and yield-spread behavior in different market sectors. Bond investors also require information on bond indenture provisions such as call features and sinking fund provisions.

Some of this information is readily available in such popular publications as *The Wall Street Journal*, *Barron's*, *Business Week*, *Fortune*, and *Forbes*, which will be discussed in Chapter 6. In addition, two popular sources of bond data are the *Federal Reserve Bulletin* and the *Survey of Current Business*, which are also described in Chapter 6. In addition, a number of other sources of specific information are important to a bond investor. The following publications are specifically concerned with information and analysis of bonds. Some of them are discussed in Chapter 6.

- *Treasury Bulletin* (monthly)
- *Standard & Poor's Bond Guide* (monthly)
- *Moody's Bond Record* (monthly)
- *Moody's Bond Survey* (weekly)
- *Fitch Rating Register* (monthly)
- *Fitch Corporate Credit Analysis* (monthly)
- *Fitch Municipal Credit Analysis* (monthly)
- *Investment Dealers Digest* (weekly)
- *The Bond Buyer* (daily)
- *Credit Markets* (weekly)
- *Duff & Phelps Credit Decisions* (weekly)

Sources of Bond Quotes

The listed information sources fill three needs of investors: evaluating risk of default, staying abreast of the bond market and interest rate conditions, and obtaining information on specific bonds. Another important data need is current market information, that is, bond quotes and prices.

Unfortunately, many of the primary sources are not widely distributed. For example, *Bank and Quotation Record* is a valuable, though not widely circulated, source that provides a monthly summary of price information for government and agency bonds, a large number of listed and OTC corporate issues, municipals, and many money market instruments. Current quotes on municipal bonds are available only through a fairly costly publication (many financial institutions use it, however) called *The Blue List of Current Municipal Offerings*. It contains over 100 pages of price quotes for municipal bonds, municipal notes, and industrial development and pollution-control revenue bonds.

Information on all publicly traded Treasury issues, most important agency obligations, and many corporate issues is published daily in *The Wall Street Journal*. Similar data are available weekly in *Barron's*. Both publications list corporate bond quotes that represent a minor portion of the total market. Finally, major bond dealers maintain firm quotes on a variety of issues for clients.

Interpreting Bond Quotes

Essentially, all bonds are quoted on the basis of either yield or price. Price quotes are always interpreted as a percentage of par. For example, a quote of $98\frac{1}{2}$ is not interpreted as \$98.50, but $98\frac{1}{2}$ percent of par. The dollar price can be derived from the quote, given the par value. If par value is \$5,000 on a particular municipal bond, then the price of an issue quoted at $98\frac{1}{2}$ would be \$4,925. Actually, the market follows three systems of bond pricing: one system for corporates, another for governments (both Treasury and agency obligations), and a third for municipals.

Corporate Bond Quotes   Figure 3.1 is a listing of NYSE corporate bond quotes from *The Wall Street Journal* dated Wednesday, August 8, 1990. The data pertain to trading activity on August 7, 1990. Several quotes have been designated for illustrative purposes. The first, Dayt H (Dayton Hudson), is representative of most corporate price quotes. In particular, "$10\frac{3}{4}$ 13" indicates the coupon and maturity of the obligation; the Dayton Hudson issue carries a $10\frac{3}{4}$ percent coupon and matures in 2013. The next column provides the *current* yield of the obligation, found by comparing the coupon to the current market price. For example, a bond with a $10\frac{3}{4}$ percent coupon selling for $102\frac{1}{2}$ would have a 10.5 percent current yield. This is not the yield to maturity, or even necessarily a good approximation of it. Both of these yields will be discussed in Chapter 9 (especially YTM).

The next column gives the volume of \$1,000 par value bonds traded that day. The next column indicates closing quotes, followed by the column for net change in closing prices from the last day the issue was traded. In this case, there was a $\frac{1}{2}$-point increase in the Dayton Hudson bond from 102 to $102\frac{1}{2}$, which means that the price of the \$1,000 par bond went from \$1,020 to \$1,025.

The second bond in Column 1, identified by "Disney Zr 05," is a Walt Disney zero coupon bond (indicated by "Zr") due in 2005. As discussed, zero

Figure 3.1 *Sample Corporate Bond Quotations*

NEW YORK EXCHANGE BONDS

Quotations as of 4 p.m. Eastern Time
Tuesday, August 7, 1990

Volume $66,090,000

SALES SINCE JANUARY 1
(000 omitted)

1990	1989	1988
$6,968,599	$4,909,895	$4,632,806

	Domestic		All Issues	
	Tue	Mon	Tue	Mon
Issues traded	590	635	596	638
Advances	182	101	184	103
Declines	279	409	281	410
Unchanged	129	125	131	125
New highs	9	11	9	11
New lows	28	38	28	38

Dow Jones Bond Averages

–1989–		–1990–			–––1990–––			––1989––	
High	Low	High	Low		Close	Chg.	%Yld	Close	Chg.
94.15	87.35	93.04	88.48	20 Bonds	91.25	−0.05	9.51	93.62	−0.22
95.26	86.95	94.48	89.23	10 Utilities	92.31	+0.06	9.57	94.68	−0.27
93.26	87.60	91.60	87.55	10 Industrials	90.19	−0.17	9.45	92.56	−0.18

Bonds	Cur Yld	Vol	Close	Net Chg.
CnPw 8⅝03	9.6	6	90⅛	+ ⅛
CnPw 9¾06	9.9	13	98½	...
CnPw 8⅝07	9.9	10	87¼	− ¼
viCtlInf 9s06f	cv	50	1¾	+ ¼
CtlDat 12¾91	12.5	5	101⅝	+ ⅛
CtlDat 8½11	cv	58	80½	− 1½
CrnPd 5¾92	6.2	3	93⅜	+ ⅝
Crane 7s94	7.6	5	91⅝	− ⅜
CritAc 12¼14	11.6	8	105½	+ 1⅝
CritAc 11.85s15	11.6	2	102⅛	− 2⅞
Dana 9s2000	9.5	8	94½	− 1¾
Dana dc5⅞06	cv	27	71½	− 2
Datpnt 8⅞06	cv	232	16	+ 1
DaytH 10¾13	10.5	20	102½	+ ½
DetEd 9s99	9.4	5	96	...
DetEd 9.15s00	9.5	12	96¼	− 1
DetEd 8.15s00	9.1	5	89¼	− 1⅛
DetEd 8⅛01	9.0	14	90	...
Disney zr05	...	163	40¼	+ ½
Divers 10½91	10.8	7	97½	...
Dow 6.70s98	7.7	23	87	...
Dow 8½s05	9.1	4	93	...
Dow 8½s06	9.3	35	91¼	− 2¾
Dow 7⅞07	8.8	8	89	+ 1
Dow 8⅝08	9.3	125	93	− ¼
Dresr 9⅜95	9.2	5	102	+ 2
duPnt 8.45s04	9.1	71	92½	− ½
duPnt 8½06	9.1	53	93¾	− 1⅜
duPnt dc6s01	7.8	197	77	− 1
duPnt 7½93	7.7	10	97	− ⅛
duPnt zr10	cv	751	21¾	− ¼
DukeP 7⅜02	8.7	19	85⅛	− ⅝
DukeP 8⅛03	9.0	5	90⅛	− ¼
DukeP 9¾04	9.5	23	102½	− ⅛
DuqL 8¾00	9.4	1	93¼	− 1¾
DuqL 8⅜07	9.6	2	87½	+ ⅞
EKod 8⅝16	10.0	165	86⅜	− ⅝
Eaton 8¾01	9.3	10	94¼	...
EmbSuit 10½94	10.6	26	99⅛	− ⅜
Exxon 6s97	7.0	30	85⅜	− ⅛
Exxon 6½98	7.5	50	86½	− ½
Exxon 8¼94	8.3	50	99½	...
FMC 7½01	8.5	25	88⅜	+ ⅜
Fairfd 13¼92	31.2	85	42½	+ ½
Farah 5s94	cv	24	58	− 3
Fldcst 6s12	cv	18	51	...
FUnRE 10¼09	cv	10	90	...
FleetFn 8½10	cv	76	92½	+ 1
FrdC 7⅞93	8.1	10	97⅝	+ ½
FrdC 8⅜01	8.9	19	94¼	...
FrdC 8⅜02	9.2	30	91¼	− ¾

EXPLANATORY NOTES
(For New York and American Bonds)

Yield is current yield.

cv-Convertible bond. cf-Certificates. dc-Deep discount. ec-European currency units. f-Dealt in flat. il-Italian lire. kd-Danish kroner. m-Matured bonds, negotiability impaired by maturity. na-No accrual. r-Registered. rp-Reduced principal. st-Stamped. t-Floating rate. wd-When distributed. ww-With warrants. x-Ex interest. xw-Without warrants. zr-Zero coupon.

vj-In bankruptcy or receivership or being reorganized under the Bankruptcy Act, or securities assumed by such companies.

Bonds	Cur Yld	Vol	Close	Net Chg.
GMA dc6s11	9.1	218	66⅛	+ ⅛
GMA zr12	...	170	137½	+ 1¾
GMA zr15	...	83	113	+ 3
GMA 10⅜95	10.0	30	103½	− ⅜
GMA 9¼93	9.2	88	100¼	− ½
GMA 8½91	8.5	12	100	+ 21/32
GMA 8⅞96	8.9	30	99⅜	− ⅛
GMA 8s96	8.5	97	94⅝	− 1
GMA 8¼16	9.5	30	87	− ¼
GMA 8⅛92	8.2	58	99½	− ⅛
GMA 8s93J	8.2	10	97½	− 1½
GMA 7¼90	7.3	10	99 17/32	...
GMA 8s94	8.4	8	95⅝	− 1⅛
GMA 7⅛92i	7.3	10	98¼	...
GM 8⅝s05	9.3	40	92¾	+ ¾
GTE 9⅜99	9.4	11	99¼	− ¾
Gene dc9¾93	10.0	25	97⅜	+ ⅛
GaGlf 15s00	15.2	1099	98⅝	− ⅜
GaPw 7½02D	8.9	15	83⅞	− ¼
GaPw 8⅝04	9.4	10	91⅞	− ⅝
GaPw 11⅝00	11.1	35	104⅝	+ ⅝
GaPw 11¾05	11.2	23	104⅝	...
GaPw 9⅞06	9.8	10	100½	+ ¼
GaPw 9⅝08	9.8	7	97¾	− 1¼
GaPw 10½09	10.3	12	102	− ⅛
GaPw 11s09	10.6	21	103⅜	+ ⅛
GaPw 13⅛12	12.5	68	105	+ ¼
GaPw 10s16J	10.1	26	99⅜	+ ⅛
GaPw 10s16A	10.2	112	98¼	− 1⅜
Getty 14s00	13.1	7	107	+ 3
GldNug 8⅜92	8.7	1	96	+ ½
GdNgF 13¼95	22.0	321	60¼	− 1½
GrnTr dc8¼95	10.7	2	77	− 1
GreyF zr94	...	20	62½	...
Grumn 9¼09	cv	15	77⅝	+ ⅜
GulfMo 5s56f	11.0	10	45¼	+ ¼
GlfRes 10⅞97	13.9	25	78	+ 2⅝
GlfRes 12½04	15.6	214	80	+ 5
HalwdGp 13½09	...	25	74½	+ 3½
Hertz 8⅞s01	9.3	15	95	...
HmeDep 6s97	cv	41	95⅛	− 1⅜
HomFSD 6½11	cv	121	53½	...
HmGrp 14⅞99	16.6	42	89⅜	...
HousF 9s00	9.4	25	95¼	− 1⅜
HudFd 14s08	cv	23	101	...
Humn 10⅛91	10.1	13	100⅝	− 1¼
IBM Cr 8⅜90	8.4	15	99⅞	...
ICI 8⅞03	9.1	25	97	− ½
ITTF 8½02	9.3	3	91½	− ½
ITTR 8s96	8.3	5	96	...
IllBel 7⅝06	8.9	42	86	− ¾
IllBel 8¼16	9.4	9	88⅛	− 2¼
IllPw 7⅝03	9.3	54	82¼	+ ⅛
IllPw 10½04	10.2	10	102½	...
IllPw 8¼07	9.8	12	84	− 3¾
IllPw 10⅛16	10.2	10	99½	− ⅜
IndBel 8⅛11	9.2	22	88	− ¾
Intlgc 11.99s96	28.1	10	42⅝	− 3⅜
IBM 9⅜04	9.3	109	100⅞	− ⅜
IBM 7⅞04	cv	415	96⅜	+ ⅜
IBM 10¼95	9.9	146	104	− ⅛
IBM 9s98	8.9	32	101	− ½
IntRec 9s10	cv	15	73	...
Intnr 11s93	11.2	15	98½	− 1⅝
Jamswy 8s05	cv	21	64	+ 1½
JCP 9¾06	9.8	37	99½	− ½
vjJoneL 9⅞95f	...	10	62	+ 2½
KaufBd zr04	...	7	25½	...
KerrMc 7¼12	cv	25	115	+ 2
KogerP 9¼03	cv	10	82	...

Source: *The Wall Street Journal*, August 8, 1990.

coupon securities do not pay interest, but are redeemed at par at maturity. Because they pay no coupon, they do not report a current yield and they sell at a discount price, which implies a yield to maturity. This bond is selling at $40\frac{1}{2}$, or \$405 for a \$1,000 par bond that will be redeemed in the year 2005.

The third bond in Column 1 is a convertible bond (indicated by "cv") from Fleet Financial. In some instances you will see a "dc" before the coupon, which means "deep discount," indicating that the original coupon was set below the going rate at the time of issue. For example, a coupon might be 5 percent on a bond when market rates are 9 or 10 percent.

In the fourth highlighted quote in Column 2, for the Jone L (Jones & Laughlin) bond, two unique features make a very significant difference. The "vj" in front of the name indicates that the firm is in receivership or bankruptcy. The small letter f that follows the maturity date of the obligation means that the issue is trading *flat*. Simply stated, the issuer is not meeting interest payments on the obligation. Therefore, the coupon of the obligation may be inconsequential, and the dash in the current yield column indicates no payments.

All fixed-income obligations, with the exception of preferred stock, are traded on an *accrued interest basis*. The prices pertain to principal value only and exclude interest that has accrued to the holder since the last interest payment date. The actual price of the bond will, therefore, exceed the quote listed because accrued interest must be added. With the Dayton Hudson $10\frac{3}{4}$ percent issue, if 2 months have elapsed since interest was paid, then the current holder of the bond is entitled to two-sixths or one-third of the normal semiannual interest payment. More specifically, the $10\frac{3}{4}$ percent coupon provides semiannual interest income of \$53.75. The investor who held the obligation for 2 months beyond the last interest payment date is entitled to one-third of that \$53.75 as accrued interest, so to the price of \$1,025.00 ($102\frac{1}{2}$), accrued interest of \$17.92 will be added. In the case of a bond trading flat, you do not add accrued interest because the bond is not paying its interest.

Treasury and Agency Bond Quotes Figure 3.2 illustrates the quote system for Treasury and agency issues. These quotes resemble those for other over-the-counter securities because they contain both bid and ask prices, rather than high, low, and close prices. On U.S. Treasury bond quotes, a small n behind the maturity date indicates that the obligation is actually a Treasury note. A small p indicates a Treasury note on which nonresident aliens are exempt from withholding taxes on the interest.

All other obligations in this section are, of course, Treasury bonds. The first quote is a 7 percent issue. The security identification is different because it is not necessary to list the issuer. Instead, the usual listing indicates the coupon, the month of maturity, the year of maturity, and information on any call feature. For example, the 7 percent issue shows a maturity of "1993–98"; this means that the issue has a deferred call feature until 1993, thereafter being freely callable, and a final maturity date of 1998. The bid–ask figures appear next, also stated as percentages of par. Unlike the current-yield figure for corporate issues, the asking yield is the promised yield to maturity based upon the asking price. This system appears for Treasuries, agencies, and municipals.

This quote also demonstrates the basic difference in the price system of governments (i.e., Treasuries and agencies). The bid quote is 90:04, and the ask is 90:12. Governments are traded in increments of thirty-secondths of a point (rather than eighths), and the figures to the right of the colons indicate the number of thirty-seconds in the fractional bid or ask. The bid price is actually $90\frac{4}{32}$ percent of par.

The lower section of the first column contains quotes for U.S. Treasury securities that have been "stripped." Specifically, the typical bond that promises a series of coupon payments and a principal payment at maturity is divided into two separate units. One contains all the coupon interest payments and no principal, the other contains only the principal payment.

The quotes below the Treasury bond section in Column 2 are for U.S. Treasury bills. Notice that only dates are reported with no coupons. This is because these are pure discount securities, that is, the return is the difference between the price you pay and par at maturity.[30]

Municipal Bond Quotes Figure 3.3 contains municipal bond quotes from *The Blue List of Current Municipal Offerings* for May 4, 1988. These are ordered according to states, and then alphabetically within states. Each issue gives the amount of bonds being

[30]For a discussion on calculating yields, see Bruce D. Fielitz, "Calculating the Bond Equivalent Yield for T-Bills," *Journal of Portfolio Management* 9, no. 3 (Spring 1983): 58–60.

Figure 3.2 *Sample Quotes for Treasury and Agency Issues*

TREASURY BONDS, NOTES & BILLS

Tuesday, August 7, 1990

Representative Over-the-Counter quotations based on transactions of $1 million or more.

Treasury bond, note and bill quotes are as of mid-afternoon. Colons in bid-and-asked quotes represent 32nds; 101:01 means 101 1/32. Net changes in 32nds. n-Treasury note. Treasury bill quotes in hundredths, quoted on terms of a rate of discount. Days to maturity calculated from trading date. All yields are to maturity and based on the asked quote. For bonds callable prior to maturity, yields are computed to the earliest call date for issues quoted above par and to the maturity date for issues below par. *-When issued.

Source: Federal Reserve Bank of New York.

U.S. Treasury strips as of 3 p.m. Eastern time, also based on transactions of $1 million or more. Colons in bid-and-asked quotes represent 32nds; 101:01 means 101 1/32. Net changes in 32nds. Yields calculated on the bid quotation. ci-stripped coupon interest. bp-Treasury bond, stripped principal. np-Treasury note, stripped principal.

Source: Bear, Stearns & Co. via Street Software Technology Inc.

GOVT. BONDS & NOTES

Rate	Maturity	Bid	Asked	Chg.	Ask Yld.
7 7/8	Aug 90n	100:00	100:02	+ 1	3.95
9 7/8	Aug 90n	100:01	100:03	....	4.02
10 3/4	Aug 90n	100:01	100:03	− 1	4.84
8 5/8	Aug 90n	100:01	100:03	....	6.79
6 3/4	Sep 90n	99:25	99:27	− 1	7.68
8 1/2	Sep 90n	100:01	100:03	− 1	7.60
11 1/2	Oct 90n	100:19	100:21	− 1	7.59
8 1/4	Oct 90n	100:02	100:04	....	7.52
8	Nov 90n	100:01	100:03	....	7.50
9 5/8	Nov 90n	100:14	100:16	− 1	7.54
13	Nov 90n	101:10	101:12	− 1	7.51
8 7/8	Nov 90n	100:09	100:11	− 1	7.60
6 5/8	Dec 90n	99:17	99:19	− 1	7.64
9 1/8	Dec 90n	100:16	100:18	− 1	7.57
11 3/4	Jan 91n	101:21	101:23	− 1	7.58
9	Jan 91n	100:18	100:20	− 1	7.62
7 3/8	Feb 91n	99:26	99:28	− 1	7.63
9 1/8	Feb 91n	100:21	100:23	− 1	7.68
9 3/8	Feb 91n	100:27	100:29	− 1	7.69
6 3/4	Mar 91n	99:11	99:13	− 1	7.71
9 3/4	Mar 91n	101:06	101:08	− 1	7.72
12 3/8	Apr 91n	102:30	103:00	− 2	7.79
9 1/4	Apr 91n	100:31	101:01	− 2	7.77
8 1/8	May 91n	100:07	100:09	− 1	7.74
14 1/2	May 91n	105:02	105:06	....	7.43
8 3/4	May 91n	100:22	100:24	− 2	7.78
9 1/4	Jan 96n	103:03	103:07	− 16	8.50
8 7/8	Feb 96n	101:19	101:23	− 12	8.48
9 3/8	Apr 96n	103:22	103:26	− 14	8.52
7 3/8	May 96n	94:22	94:26	− 13	8.53
7 7/8	Jul 96n	96:26	96:30	− 12	8.54
8	Oct 96n	97:07	97:11	− 13	8.56
7 1/4	Nov 96n	93:20	93:24	− 10	8.56
8	Jan 97n	97:00	97:04	− 12	8.59
8 1/2	Apr 97n	99:05	99:07	− 18	8.66
8 1/2	May 97n	99:08	99:12	− 15	8.62
8 1/2	Jul 97n	99:09	99:11	− 15	8.63
8 5/8	Aug 97n	99:25	99:29	− 14	8.64
8 7/8	Nov 97n	100:31	101:03	− 17	8.67
8 1/8	Feb 98n	96:31	97:03	− 17	8.66
7	May 93-98	90:04	90:12	− 8	8.73
9	May 98n	101:12	101:16	− 18	8.73
9 1/4	Aug 98n	102:25	102:29	− 15	8.74
3 1/2	Nov 98	94:10	95:10	....	4.18
8 7/8	Nov 98n	100:18	100:22	− 14	8.76
8 7/8	Feb 99n	100:19	100:23	− 13	8.75
8 1/2	May 94-99	98:00	98:08	− 33	8.79
9 1/8	May 99n	101:31	102:03	− 11	8.78
8	Aug 99n	95:08	95:12	− 10	8.75
7 7/8	Nov 99n	94:05	94:07	− 13	8.80
7 7/8	Feb 95-00	93:17	93:21	− 13	8.88
8 1/2	Feb 00n	98:04	98:08	− 13	8.78
8 7/8	May 00n	100:19	100:21	− 15	8.77

U.S. TREASURY STRIPS

Mat.	Type	Bid	Asked	Chg.	Bid Yld.
Aug 90	ci	99:28	99:28	....	7.65
Nov 90	ci	97:31	98:00	− 1	7.73
Feb 91	ci	96:04	96:04	− 2	7.80
May 91	ci	94:09	94:10	− 2	7.84
Aug 91	ci	92:14	92:15	− 4	7.87
Nov 91	ci	90:18	90:20	− 4	7.97
Feb 92	ci	88:22	88:23	− 4	8.08
May 92	ci	86:30	87:00	− 5	8.08
Aug 92	ci	85:05	85:07	− 6	8.13
Nov 92	ci	83:16	83:18	− 7	8.12
Feb 93	ci	81:21	81:23	− 9	8.21
May 93	ci	80:00	80:02	− 9	8.23
Aug 93	ci	78:08	78:10	− 11	8.30
Nov 93	ci	76:25	76:28	− 13	8.25
Feb 94	ci	74:24	74:26	− 10	8.45
May 94	ci	73:05	73:08	− 11	8.47
Aug 94	ci	71:19	71:21	− 12	8.50
Nov 94	ci	70:04	70:07	− 13	8.49
Nov 94	np	70:03	70:05	− 11	8.51
Feb 95	ci	68:15	68:18	− 16	8.56
Feb 95	np	68:18	68:21	− 13	8.53
May 95	ci	66:31	67:02	− 17	8.59
May 95	np	67:02	67:05	− 14	8.56
Aug 95	ci	65:15	65:19	− 19	8.62
Aug 95	np	65:20	65:23	− 16	8.58
Nov 95	ci	64:04	64:07	− 20	8.62
Nov 95	np	64:09	64:12	− 17	8.57
Feb 96	ci	62:14	62:17	− 2	8.72
Feb 96	np	62:15	62:19	− 6	8.71
May 96	ci	61:04	61:07	− 2	8.72
May 96	np	61:03	61:06	− 5	8.73

TREASURY BILLS

Maturity	Days to Mat.	Bid	Asked	Chg.	Ask Yld.
Aug 09 '90	2	7.45	7.43	+0.12	0.00
Aug 16 '90	9	7.31	7.27	+0.06	7.38
Aug 23 '90	16	7.38	7.34	+0.12	7.46
Aug 30 '90	23	7.22	7.16	+0.02	7.29
Sep 06 '90	30	7.18	7.16	−0.01	7.30
Sep 13 '90	37	7.35	7.31	+0.06	7.46
Sep 20 '90	44	7.66	7.64	+0.11	7.82
Sep 27 '90	51	7.41	7.39	+0.09	7.57
Oct 04 '90	58	7.39	7.37	+0.09	7.56
Oct 11 '90	65	7.43	7.41	+0.12	7.61
Oct 18 '90	72	7.42	7.40	+0.11	7.61
Oct 25 '90	79	7.42	7.40	+0.10	7.62
Nov 01 '90	86	7.41	7.39	+0.11	7.62
Nov 08 '90	93	7.37	7.35	+0.11	7.59
Nov 15 '90	100	7.35	7.33	+0.06	7.58
Nov 23 '90	108	7.39	7.37	+0.09	7.64
Nov 29 '90	114	7.34	7.32	+0.06	7.59
Dec 06 '90	121	7.37	7.35	+0.11	7.64
Dec 13 '90	128	7.40	7.38	+0.12	7.68
Dec 20 '90	135	7.40	7.38	+0.11	7.69
Dec 27 '90	142	7.37	7.35	+0.11	7.67
Jan 03 '91	149	7.35	7.33	+0.11	7.66
Jan 10 '91	156	7.37	7.35	+0.13	7.69
Jan 17 '91	163	7.36	7.34	+0.12	7.69
Jan 24 '91	170	7.38	7.36	+0.14	7.73
Jan 31 '91	177	7.36	7.34	+0.14	7.72
Feb 07 '91	184	7.34	7.32	+0.15	7.71
Feb 14 '91	191	7.34	7.32	+0.12	7.71
Mar 14 '91	219	7.29	7.27	+0.09	7.66
Apr 11 '91	247	7.30	7.28	+0.08	7.69

Source: *The Wall Street Journal*, August 8, 1990.

Figure 3.3 *Quotes for Municipals*

```
                           CONNECTICUT - CONTINUED
   50 COLCHESTER CONN              "B/B" MBIA     8.000  03/15/91      5.25 ROOSEVLT
   15 DARIEN CONN                                 5.750  03/15/91      5.00 ROOSEVLT
+  25 GUILFORD CONN                "B/B"          4.900  05/15/90       100 OPCOFTL
+  15 HARTFORD CNTY CONN MET DIST  "B/B"          3.000  10/01/91      6.00 ROOSEVLT
+   5 HARTFORD CNTY CONN MET DIST  "B/B"          3.250  11/01/96      6.75 ROOSEVLT
+   8 HARTFORD CNTY CONN MET DIST  "B/B"          3.250  11/01/98      7.00 ROOSEVLT
   95 HEBRON CONN                  "B/E" AMBAC    6.400  04/15/90      5.00 CBT
   10 MONTVILLE CONN                               6.700  03/15/02      6.85 ABROWNBO
   70 MONTVILLE CONN                               7.000  03/15/08      7.25 CNB
    5 NEW HAVEN CONN COLISEUM AUTH                 5.600  09/01/94      6.00 DWRBOS
   25 NEW HAVEN CONN PKG REV       "B/B"          5.700  09/01/95      6.25 DWRBOS
   65 SIMSBURY CONN                                6.600  04/15/95      5.90 FLEETNTL
  600 SOUTH CENT CONN REGL WTR AUTH P/R @ 102     8.500  08/01/03 C93  6.00 CBT
  750 SOUTH CENT CONN REGL WTR AUTH P/R @ 102     8.500  08/01/03 C93  6.00 WERTHEIM
   25 STAMFORD CONN                                6.500  07/15/95 N/C  5.90 CONNSEC
   15 STONINGTON CONN              "B/E"          6.300  03/15/90      5.05 CBT
   10 WEST HAVEN CONN                              5.700  03/01/00      7.00 FLEETNTL

                               DELAWARE

  115 DELAWARE ST                  "B/E" W.I.     6.200  04/01/90      5.10 WHEATPH
   25 DELAWARE ST                                 9.600  07/01/90 N/C  5.30 ABROWNBA
   10 DELAWARE ST                                 6.250  04/01/93      5.90 WHEATPH
   40 DELAWARE ST                                 6.300  04/01/94      6.00 WERTHEIM
   25 DELAWARE ST                  P/R @ 103      9.700  07/01/95 C91  5.60 ABROWNBA
   20 DELAWARE ST                  "B/E"          7.250  04/01/03 C00   100 PERSH
      (CA @ 100)
   25 DELAWARE RIV & BAY AUTH DEL                 3.750  01/01/04        82 BEARSTER
  100 DELAWARE RIV & BAY AUTH DEL                 3.750  01/01/04        82 PETERS
   25 DELAWARE ST ECONOMIC DEV AUTH  MULTI-FAM   10.750  11/01/14      9.65 WHEELER
+  50 DELAWARE ST HEALTH FACS AUTH  "REG" MBIA    9.250  10/01/15 C95  7.20 MOORESCH
      (P/C @ 102)
    5 DELAWARE ST HSG AUTH REV                    8.000  01/01/89       103 SMITHB
    5 DELAWARE ST SOLID WASTE AUTH  CA @ 103      9.250  07/01/03 C89  6.50 MEYERND
  175 DELAWARE TRANSN AUTH TRANSN &               6.750  07/01/00      7.00 PRUBAPHL
  175 DELAWARE TRANSN AUTH TRANSN &               6.750  07/01/00      7.00 PRUBAPHL
   25 DOVER DEL                                   5.500  07/01/92       100 JANNEYPH
   50 DOVER DEL                    BK.QD B/E      5.500  07/01/92       100 NEWBOLDW
   25 DOVER DEL                                   5.900  07/01/94       100 JANNEYPH
   15 DOVER DEL                                   6.100  07/01/95       100 JANNEYPH
    5 DOVER DEL                    BK.QD  B/E     6.250  07/01/96       100 NEWBOLDW
   50 DOVER DEL                                   6.250  07/01/96       100 WHEATPH
   25 DOVER DEL                                   6.400  07/01/97       100 JANNEYPH
   10 DOVER DEL                                   6.550  07/01/98       100 WHEATPH
  250 KENT CNTY DEL                CA @ 100       8.000  06/15/06 C96  7.00 MOORESCH
   20 NEW CASTLE CNTY DEL                         1.875  05/01/89 ETM  6.25 RAMIREZ
  100 NEW CASTLE CNTY DEL          "REG"          8.500  10/15/05 C95  7.00 MOORESCH
      (CA @ 102)
+ 300 NORTHERN DEL INDL DEV CORP   (PHOENIX)      5.750  11/01/99   #    73 BEARSTER
   10 NORTHERN DEL INDL DEV CORP   PHOEN.STL      5.750  11/01/99        65 MABONIDB
   25 NORTHERN DEL INDL DEV CORP   PHNX.STL.      5.750  11/01/99    67 1/2 PETERS
   10 NORTHERN DEL INDL DEV CORP                  5.750  11/01/99        68 WMBLBONN
   20 WILMINGTON DEL                 AMBAC        9.000  03/01/92 C91  5.75 SHEARPHL
      (P/R @ 101)
  200 WILMINGTON DEL                              7.300  03/15/95 N/C  6.60 ABROWNBA

                          DISTRICT OF COLUMBIA

   10 DISTRICT COLUMBIA                           7.750  06/01/91      6.00 BARRBROS
+ 850 DISTRICT COLUMBIA              AMBAC        7.900  06/01/98      7.10 PRUBANY
    5 DISTRICT COLUMBIA            SER D          7.100  06/01/00      7.50 IREC
  300 DISTRICT COLUMBIA              MBIA         9.900  12/01/00 C95  6.60 FIRSTCHI
      (P/R @ 102)
  525 DISTRICT COLUMBIA              MBIA         7.650  06/01/03       100 RODMANNY
+ 300 DISTRICT COLUMBIA            CA @ 102       7.375  06/01/05 C96  8.10 FMS
   65 DISTRICT COLUMBIA            P/R @ 102      9.750  06/01/05 C95 # 6.75 DREXELPH
+ 255 DISTRICT COLUMBIA            CA @ 102       7.875  06/01/06 C96  8.00 FMS
..PAGE      8 A          Wednesday, May  4, 1988
```

Source: *The Blue List of Current Municipal Offerings*, May 4, 1988, p. 8A. The Blue List Division of Standard & Poor's Corp., New York. Reprinted with permission.

offered (in thousands of dollars), the name of the security, the coupon rate, the maturity (which includes month, day, and year), the yield or price, and finally, the dealer offering the bonds. Bond quote 1 covers $95,000 of Hebron, Connecticut, bonds. The "AMBAC" indicates that the bonds are guaranteed by this firm, as described earlier. They have a 6.40 percent coupon and were due April 15, 1990. In this instance, the yield to maturity is given (5.00 percent). To determine the price, you would either compute or look up in a yield book the price of a 6.40 percent bond, due in about 2 years to yield 5.00 percent. The dealer offering the bonds is CBT. A list in the back of the publication gives the name of the firm and its phone number.

The second bond quoted is a $5,000 Delaware State Housing Authority revenue bond with an 8.00 percent coupon. This is somewhat unusual since a price is listed rather than the current yield to maturity. The quote indicates that the bond is selling for 103, or 103 percent of par. These are called *dollar bonds*.

The third quote lists a $100,000 New Castle County bond that is registered (indicated by "*REG*") and callable at 102. The "C95" indicates that issue is callable after 1995. It is necessary to contact the dealer, Mooresch, for details.

A "+" in the far-left column indicates a new item since the prior issue of *The Blue List*. A "#" in the column prior to the yield to maturity or price indicates that these data have changed since the last issue. In all instances it is necessary to call the dealer to determine the current yield/price, since these quotes are at least one day old when they are published.

Summary

■ We considered the basic features of bonds: their interest, principal, and maturity. Certain key relationships affect price behavior.

Price is essentially a function of coupon, maturity, and prevailing market interest rates.

Bond price volatility depends on coupon and maturity — that is, bonds with longer maturities and/or lower coupons respond most vigorously to a given change in market rates.

Each bond has unique intrinsic characteristics and can be differentiated by type of issue and indenture provisions (security, call features, and sinking funds).

■ Major benefits to bond investors include high returns for nominal risk, the potential for capital gains, certain tax advantages, and possible additional returns from aggressive trading of bonds. An aggressive bond investor must consider secondary-market activity, investment risks, and interest rate behavior. We introduced high yield (junk) bonds because of the growth in size and status of this segment of the bond market.

■ The global fixed-income market, including some 18 countries, has experienced several significant trends, including the strong relative growth of the Japanese market and the decline in relative terms of the U.S. market. There are four major bond markets — the United States, Japan, Germany, and the United Kingdom.

Each of these markets has a different proportion of government, agency, municipal, corporate, and international issues. In addition, the various market sectors are unique in terms of liquidity, yield spreads, tax implications, and market operating features.

Beyond the four major bond markets discussed, similar securities are available from a number of other countries. As shown in Chapter 2, the benefits from global diversification in bonds are similar to those available from stocks.

■ To gauge default risk, most bond investors rely on agency ratings. For additional information on the bond market, prevailing economic conditions, and intrinsic bond features, individual and institutional investors rely on a host of readily available publications.

Questions

1. How does a bond differ from other types of debt instruments?
2. Explain the difference between calling a bond and a bond refunding.
3. Identify the three most important determinants of the price of a bond. Describe the effect of each.
4. Given a change in the level of interest rates, what two major factors will influence the relative change in price for individual bonds? What is their impact?
5. Define two different types of bond yields.
6. What factors determine whether a bond is senior or junior? Give examples of each type.
7. What is a bond indenture?

8. Explain the differences in taxation of income from municipal bonds and income from U.S. Treasury bonds and corporate bonds.
9. List several types of institutional participants in the bond market. Explain what type of bond each is likely to purchase and why.
10. Why should investors be aware of the trading volume for a particular bond in which they are interested?
11. What is the purpose of bond ratings? What are they supposed to indicate?
12. Based upon the data in Table 3.1, which is the fastest-growing bond market in the world? Which markets seem to be losing market share?
13. Based upon the data in Table 3.2, discuss how the makeup of the German bond market differs from that of the U.S. market. Briefly discuss the reasons for this difference.
14. Discuss how a mortgage pass-through bond differs from a collateralized mortgage obligation.
15. Some contend that the modern high yield bond market was born about 1983. Describe the evidence in favor of this contention.
16. Discuss the distribution of high yield bond holdings among various groups and how this has affected the liquidity of these securities.
17. Discuss the difference between a foreign bond (e.g., a Samurai) and a Eurobond (e.g., a Euro-deutschemark issue).
18. The latter part of this chapter listed many sources of information on bonds, yet the statement was made earlier that, "it is almost impossible for individual investors . . . to keep abreast of the price activity of municipal bond holdings." Discuss this apparent paradox, explaining how such a condition might exist.
19. Using various sources of information described in the chapter, name at least five bonds rated B or better that have split ratings.
20. Select five bonds that are listed on the NYSE. Using various sources of information, prepare a brief description of each bond, including such factors as its rating, call features, collateral (if any), interest payment dates, and refunding provisions.

Problems

1. An investor in the 28 percent tax bracket is trying to decide which of two bonds to purchase. One is a corporate bond carrying an 8 percent coupon and selling at par. The other is a municipal bond with a $5\frac{1}{2}$ percent coupon, and it, too, sells at par. Assuming all other relevant factors are equal, which bond should the investor select?
2. What would be the initial offering prices for the following bonds (assume semiannual compounding):
   a. A 15-year zero coupon bond with a yield to maturity (YTM) of 12 percent
   b. A 20-year zero coupon bond with a YTM of 10 percent
3. An 8.4 percent coupon bond issued by the state of Indiana sells for $1,000. What coupon rate on a corporate bond selling at its $1,000 par value would produce the same after-tax return to the investor as the municipal bond if the investor were in:
   a. The 15 percent tax bracket?
   b. The 25 percent tax bracket?
   c. The 35 percent tax bracket?
4. The Shamrock Corporation has just issued a $1,000 par value zero coupon bond with an 8 percent yield to maturity that is due to mature 15 years from today. Assuming semiannual compounding:
   a. What is the market price of the bond?
   b. If interest rates remain constant, what will the price of the bond be in 3 years?
   c. If interest rates rise to 10 percent, what will the price of the bond be in 3 years?
5. Complete the information requested for each of the following $1,000 par value zero coupon bonds, assuming semiannual compounding.

Bond	Maturity (years)	Yield (percent)	Price ($)
A	20	12%	?
B	?	8	$601
C	9	?	350

References

Altman, Edward I., ed. *The High Yield Debt Market.* Homewood, Ill.: Dow Jones-Irwin, 1990.

Altman, Edward I., and S. Katz. "Statistical Bond Ratings Classification Using Financial and Accounting Data." In *Proceedings of the Conference on Topical Research in Accountancy.* Ed. by Michael Schiff and George Sorter. New York: New York University School of Business, 1976.

Altman, Edward I., and Scott A. Nammacher. *Investing in Junk Bonds.* New York: John Wiley & Sons, 1987.

Ang, James S., and K. A. Patel. "Bond Rating Methods: Comparison and Validation." *Journal of Finance* 30, no. 2 (May 1975).

Beidleman, Carl, ed. *The Handbook of International Investing*. Chicago: Probus Publishing, 1987.

Belkaoui, Ahmed. "Industrial Bond Ratings: A New Look." *Financial Mangement* 9, no. 3 (Autumn 1980).

Darst, David M. *The Handbook of the Bond and Money Markets*. New York: McGraw-Hill, 1981.

Elton, Edwin J., and Martin J. Gruber, eds. *Japanese Capital Markets*. New York: Harper & Row, 1990.

European Bond Commission. *The European Bond Markets*. Chicago: Probus Publishing, 1989.

Fabozzi, Frank J., ed. *Advances and Innovations in the Bond and Mortgage Markets*. Chicago: Probus Publishing, 1989.

Fabozzi, Frank J., ed. *The Handbook of Fixed-Income Securities*, 3d ed. Homewood, Ill.: Business One Irwin, 1991.

Fabozzi, Frank J., ed. *The Japanese Bond Markets*. Chicago: Probus Publishing, 1990.

Fisher, Lawrence. "Determinants of Risk Premiums on Corporate Bonds." *Journal of Political Economy* 67, no. 3 (June 1959).

Fridson, Martin S. *High Yield Bonds*. Chicago: Probus Publishing, 1989.

Gentry, James A., David T. Whitford, and Paul Newbold. "Predicting Industrial Bond Ratings with Probit Model and Funds Flow Components." *The Financial Review* 23, no. 3 (August 1988).

Grabbe, J. Orlin. *International Financial Markets*. New York: Elsevier, 1986.

Howe, Jane Tripp. *Junk Bonds: Analysis and Portfolio Strategies*. Chicago: Probus Publishing, 1988.

Kaplan, Robert S., and Gabriel Urwitz. "Statistical Models of Bond Ratings: A Methodological Inquiry." *Journal of Business* 52, no. 2 (April 1979).

Reilly, Frank K., and Michael D. Joehnk. "Association between Market Determined Risk Measures for Bonds and Bond Ratings." *Journal of Finance* 31, no. 5 (December 1976).

Van Horne, James C. *Financial Market Rates and Flows*, 2d ed. Englewood Cliffs, N.J.: Prentice-Hall, 1984.

Viner, Aron. *Inside Japanese Financial Markets*. Homewood, Ill.: Dow Jones-Irwin, 1988.

Wilson, Richard S. *Corporate Senior Securities*. Chicago: Probus Publishing, 1987.

Wilson, Richard S., and Frank J. Fabozzi. *The New Corporate Bond Market*. Chicago: Probus Publishing, 1990.

Yago, Glenn. *Junk Bonds*. New York: Oxford University Press, 1991.

4

Organization and Functioning of Securities Markets

The stock market, Wall Street, and the Dow Jones Industrials are part of our everyday experience. Each evening we find out how they fared on the television news broadcasts; each morning we read about their prospects for a rally or decline in the pages of our daily newspapers. Yet how the domestic and world markets actually function is imperfectly understood by most. To be a successful investor, you must know which financial markets are available around the world, how these markets function, and how they are changing. Chapter 3 contained an overview of the world bond markets and discussed the available fixed-income investments. The purpose of this chapter is to take a broader view of securities markets than we have taken so far, and then provide a detailed discussion of how the stock markets function and how they are changing.

We begin with a discussion of securities markets and the characteristics of a good market. Two components of the securities market are described: primary and secondary markets. Our main emphasis is on secondary stock markets. We consider the national equity markets around the world and how they are becoming linked to form a 24-hour market. We also consider regional stock markets and the over-the-counter market, and then provide a detailed analysis of how exchange markets operate. The final section considers the many changes that have taken place in financial markets since the mid-1970s, changes that are occurring now, and significant changes that will continue into the next century. These changes in our securities markets will have a profound effect on which investments are available to you from around the world and how you buy and sell them.

In the first section we provide some basic background that is necessary for understanding the subsequent discussion of the different markets around the world. First we consider the general concept of a market and its function, then we describe the characteristics that determine how well a particular market will fulfill its function. The third part of the section describes the two main components of the securities market and how they interact and depend on one another.

> **Price continuity** A feature of a liquid market in which prices change little from one transaction to the next.
>
> **Transaction cost** The cost of executing a trade. Low costs characterize good markets.

What Is a Market?

A market is the means through which buyers and sellers are brought together to aid in the transfer of goods and/or services. Several aspects of this general definition seem worthy of emphasis. First, a market need not have a physical location. It is only necessary that the buyers and sellers can communicate regarding the relevant aspects of their transactions.

Second, the market does not necessarily own the goods or services involved. When we discuss what is required for a good market, you will note that ownership is not involved; the basic criterion is the smooth, cheap transfer of goods and services. In the case of most financial markets, those who establish and administer the markets do not own the assets. They simply provide a physical location or electronic system that allows potential buyers and sellers to interact, and they help the markets to function by providing information and transfer facilities.

Finally, a market can deal in any variety of goods and services. For any commodity or service with a diverse clientele, a market should evolve to aid in the transfer of that commodity. Both buyers and sellers will benefit from its existence. Basically, we take markets for granted since they are vital to a smoothly operating economy.

Characteristics of a Good Market

In this chapter and throughout this book we will be discussing securities markets in the United States and throughout the world that deal in financial assets such as stocks, bonds, and futures. On occasion we will refer to these markets using various terms of quality

such as strong, active, liquid, or illiquid. The point is, there are many markets, but they are not all equal — some are active and liquid, others are relatively inactive, illiquid, and not very efficient. To appreciate these discussions you should be aware of the characteristics that investors look for when they evaluate the quality of a market.

One enters a market in order to buy or sell a commodity quickly at a price justified by prevailing supply and demand. To determine this price, one must have timely and accurate information on the volume and prices of past transactions and on all currently outstanding bids and offers. Therefore, one attribute of a good market is *availability of information*.

Another prime requirement, *liquidity*, is the ability to buy or sell an asset (1) quickly and (2) at a known price, that is, a price not substantially different from the prices for prior transactions, assuming no new information is available. An asset's likelihood of being sold quickly, sometimes referred to as its *marketability*, is a necessary, but not a sufficient, condition for liquidity. The price must be certain, as well, based on the recent history of transaction prices and current bid–ask quotes.[1]

A component of liquidity, is **price continuity,** which means that prices do not change much from one transaction to the next, unless substantial new information becomes available. Suppose no new information is forthcoming, and the last transaction had a price of \$20; if the next trade were at $20\frac{1}{8}$, the market would be considered reasonably continuous.[2] Obviously, a continuous market without large price changes between trades is necessary in order to have a liquid market.

A continuous market requires *depth*, which means that numerous potential buyers and sellers must be willing to trade at prices above and below the current market price. These buyers and sellers enter the market in response to changes in supply and/or demand and thereby prevent drastic price changes.

Another factor contributing to a good market is the **transaction cost.** Lower costs (as a percentage of the value of the trade) make for a more efficient mar-

---

[1] For a more formal discussion of liquidity and the impact of different market systems, see Sanford J. Grossman and Merton H. Miller, "Liquidity and Market Structure," *Journal of Finance* 43, no. 3 (July 1988): 617–633.

[2] The reader should be aware that common stocks are sold in increments of eighths of a dollar, or \$0.125. Therefore, $20\frac{1}{8}$ means the stock sold at \$20.125 per share.

ket. An individual comparing the costs of a transaction between markets would choose one that charged 2 percent of the value of the trade over one that charged 5 percent. Most microeconomic textbooks define an efficient market as one in which the cost of the transaction is minimal. This attribute is referred to as *internal efficiency*.

Finally, a buyer or seller wants the prevailing market price to adequately reflect all the available supply and demand factors in the market. If such conditions change as a result of new information, the price should change accordingly. Therefore, prices should adjust quickly to new information regarding supply or demand. This attribute is referred to as *external efficiency* or *informational efficiency*.

In summary, a good market for goods and services has the following characteristics:

1. Timely and accurate information is available on the price and volume of past transactions and on prevailing supply and demand.
2. It is liquid, meaning an asset can be bought or sold quickly (has marketability) at a price close to the prices for previous transactions, assuming no new information has been received. (The market has price continuity.) Price continuity requires depth, meaning a number of buyers and sellers are willing and able to enter the market at prices above and below the current price.
3. Transaction cost is low (creating internal efficiency), meaning that all aspects of the transaction entail low costs, including the cost of reaching the market, the actual brokerage cost involved in the transaction, as well as the cost of transferring the asset.
4. Prices rapidly adjust to new information (creating external efficiency), meaning that the prevailing price reflects all available information regarding the asset.

Organization of the Securities Market

Before discussing the specific operation of the securities market, you need to understand its overall organization. The principal distinction is between **primary markets,** where new securities are sold, and **secondary markets,** where outstanding securities are bought and sold. Each of these markets is further divided based upon the economic unit that issued the security (the federal government, states or municipalities, or corporations). The following discussion considers each of these major segments of the securities market

Primary market The market in which newly issued securities are sold by their issuers.

Secondary market The market in which outstanding securities are bought and sold by owners other than the issuers.

Treasury bill A negotiable U.S. government security with a maturity less than 1 year that pays no periodic interest, but yields the difference between its par value and its discounted purchase price.

Treasury note A U.S. government security with a maturity between 1 year and 10 years that pays interest periodically.

Treasury bond A U.S. government security with a maturity longer than 10 years that pays interest periodically.

with an emphasis on the individuals involved and the functions they perform.

Primary Financial Market

The primary market is where new issues of bonds, preferred stock, or common stock are sold by government units, municipalities, or companies to acquire new capital.[3]

U.S. Government Bond Issues

U.S. government bond issues are subdivided into three segments based upon their original maturities. **Treasury bills** are negotiable, noninterest-bearing securities with original maturities of 1 year or less. They are currently issued for 3 months, 6 months, or 1 year. **Treasury notes** have original maturities of 2 to 10 years, and they have generally been issued with 2-, 3-, 4-, 5-, 7-, and 10-year terms. Finally, **Treasury bonds** have original maturities of more than 10 years.

To sell bills, notes, and bonds, the Treasury relies upon Federal Reserve System auctions. That is, the Treasury specifies how much it wants and when the bills, notes, or bonds will mature. After receiving the competitive bids, the Treasury determines the stop-out bid (the lowest price or highest yield it will accept)

---

[3]For an excellent set of studies related to the primary market, see Michael C. Jensen and Clifford W. Smith, Jr., eds., "Symposium on Investment Banking and the Capital Acquisition Process," *Journal of Financial Economics* 15, no. 1/2 (January/February 1986).

> **New issue** Securities issued for the first time by the firm or other entity that underlies them.

based upon the bids received and how much it wants to borrow. The Fed also receives many noncompetitive bids on bills, notes, and bonds from bidders who are willing to pay the average price of the accepted competitive tenders.

Municipal Bond Issues

New municipal bond issues are sold by one of three methods: competitive bid, negotiation, or private placement. Competitive bid sales typically involve sealed bids, the bond issue being sold to the bidding syndicate of underwriters that submits the bid with the lowest interest cost in accordance with the stipulations set forth by the issuer. Negotiated sales are contractual arrangements between underwriters and issuers wherein the underwriter helps the issuer prepare the bond issue and has the exclusive right to sell the issue. Private placements involve the sale of a bond issue by the issuer directly to an investor or group of investors (usually institutions).

Note that two of the three methods require an underwriting function. Specifically, in the case of a competitive bid or negotiated sale, the underwriter typically purchases the entire issue, relieving the issuer from the risk and responsibility of selling and distributing the bonds. Subsequently, the underwriter sells the issue to the investing public. In the case of municipal bonds, this underwriting function is performed by both investment banking firms and commercial banks.

The underwriting function can involve three services: origination, risk-bearing, and distribution. Origination involves the design of the bond issue and initial planning. In risk-bearing, the underwriter acquires the total issue and accepts the responsibility and risk of reselling it for more than the purchase price. Distribution means selling the bonds, typically with the help of a selling syndicate that includes other investment banking firms.

In the case of a negotiated sale, the underwriter will carry out all three services. In a competitive bid, the issuer specifies the characteristics of the issue in terms of amount, maturities, and call features prior to bidding on coupons. The issuer may have received advice on desirable characteristics, but this advice would have been on a fee basis, not involving the un-

derwriter. Finally, a private placement involves no risk-bearing, but an investment banker could assist in locating potential buyers and negotiating the characteristics of the issue.

You will recall from Chapter 3 that municipal bonds are either general obligation bonds (GOs) or revenue bonds. Commercial banks dominate the management of GO bond sales and investment banking firms dominate revenue bond sales.

The municipal bond market has experienced two major trends during the decade. First, it has shifted toward negotiated bond issues versus competitive bids. Currently, about 75 percent of issues are negotiated deals. The second trend, the shift toward revenue bonds, has left almost 70 percent of the market in revenue issues. These two trends are related, since revenue issues tend to be negotiated underwritings. Further, many states require that GO bond issues be sold through competitive bidding, but they seldom impose such a requirement on revenue issues.[4]

Corporate Issues

Corporate security issues include both bond and stock issues. Corporate bond issues are almost always sold through negotiated arrangements with investment banking firms that maintain relationships with the issuing firms. In a global capital market with an explosion of new instruments, the origination function is becoming more important because the corporate financial officer will probably not be completely familiar with the availability and issuing requirements of new instruments and alternative markets around the world. One of the ways an investment banking firm can compete is through creating a new instrument that appeals to existing investors or a new set of investors. In either case, the expertise of the investment banker reduces the cost of new capital to the issuer. Once an issue is specified, the bond underwriter puts together a syndicate of other major underwriters and a selling group for the distribution.

In the case of common stock, **new issues** are typically divided into two groups. The first and largest group, seasoned new issues, are offered by companies that have securities trading in public markets. For ex-

---

[4]For a further discussion, see David S. Kidwell and Eric H. Sorenson, "Investment Banking and the Underwriting of New Municipal Issues," in *The Municipal Bond Handbook* ed. by F. J. Fabozzi, S. G. Feldstein, I. M. Pollack, and F. G. Zarb (Homewood, Ill.: Dow Jones-Irwin, 1983).

ample, General Motors might sell a new issue of common stock. There is an existing public market for General Motors common stock, and the company is issuing new shares (increasing the number of outstanding shares) to acquire new equity capital.

In a second major category of new issues, referred to as **initial public offerings (IPOs),** a small company might sell common stock to the public for the first time. There is no existing public market for the stock; that is, the company has been closely held. An example would be a 1982 IPO by Genentech, which had been a successful privately held firm prior to the offering.

New issues (seasoned or IPOs) are typically underwritten by investment bankers, who acquire entire issues from companies and sell the securities to interested investors. The underwriter gives advice to the corporation on the general characteristics of the issue, its pricing, and the timing of the offering. The underwriter also accepts the risk of selling the new issue after acquiring it from the corporation.[5]

Relationships with Investment Bankers Underwriting typically takes one of three forms: negotiated underwritings, competitive bid underwritings, or best-efforts arrangements. Negotiated underwritings, the most common, are the same as those for municipal issues.

A corporation may also specify the type of securities to be offered (common stock, preferred stock, or bonds) and then solicit competitive bids from investment banking firms. This is typical for utilities, in line with state laws. While the use of competitive bidding typically reduces the cost of the issue, it also brings fewer services from the investment banker. The banker gives less advice, but still underwrites the issue.

Alternatively, an investment banker can agree to support an issue and sell it on a best-efforts basis. This is usually done with speculative new issues. The investment banker does not really underwrite the issue since it does not buy any securities. The stock is owned by the company, and the investment banker acts as a broker to sell whatever it can at a stipulated price. The investment banker earns a lower commission on such an issue than on an underwritten issue.

Initial public offering (IPO) A new issue by a firm that has no existing public market.

With either negotiated or best-efforts arrangements, lead investment bankers typically form underwriting syndicates of other investment bankers to spread the risk and help in the sales. In addition, if the issue is very large, the lead underwriter and underwriting syndicate will form a selling group of smaller firms to help in the distribution.

This typical practice of negotiated arrangements involving numerous investment banking firms in syndicates and selling groups has changed with the introduction of Rule 415. Introduced by the SEC during 1982 on an experimental basis and subsequently approved on a permanent basis, it basically allows large firms to register security issues and sell them piecemeal during the following 2 years. These are referred to as *shelf registrations* because the issues lie on the shelf and can be taken down and sold on short notice whenever it suits the issuing firm. As an example, IBM could register an issue of 5 million shares of common stock during 1992 and sell a million shares in early 1992, another million late in 1992, 2 million shares in early 1993, and the rest in late 1993.

Each such offering can be made with little notice or paperwork by one underwriter or several. In fact, the lead underwriter often handles the whole deal without a syndicate or by using only one or two other firms. This arrangement has benefited large corporations because it provides great flexibility, reduces registration fees and expenses, and allows firms issuing securities to request competitive bids from several investment banking firms.

On the other hand, some fear that shelf registrations do not allow investors enough time to examine the firm issuing the securities. Also, they reduce the participation of small underwriters since syndicates are smaller, and selling groups are almost nonexistent. Shelf registrations have typically been used for the sale of straight debentures rather than common stock or convertible issues.[6]

[5]For an extended discussion of the underwriting process, see Richard A. Brealey and Stewart C. Myers, *Principles of Corporate Finance*, 3d ed. (New York: McGraw-Hill, 1988): Chapter 15.

[6]For further discussion of Rule 415, see A. F. Ehbar, "Upheaval in Investment Banking," *Fortune*, August 23, 1982: 90; Beth McGoldrick, "Life with Rule 415," *Institutional Investor* 17, no. 2 (February 1983): 129–133; and Robert J. Rogowski and Eric H. Sorensen, "Deregulation in Investment Banking: Shelf Registrations, Structure and Performance," *Financial Management* 14, no. 1 (Spring 1985): 5–15.

> **Private placement** A new issue sold directly to a small group of investors, usually institutions.

Rather than being sold publicly by one of these arrangements, primary offerings can be sold privately. In such an arrangement, referred to as a **private placement,** the firm, with the assistance of an investment banker, designs an issue and sells it to a small group of institutions. The firm enjoys lower costs, since it is not necessary to prepare the extensive registration statement required for a public offering. The institution typically benefits, because the issuing firm passes some of these savings on as a higher return. In fact, the institution should require a higher return because of the lower liquidity of these securities in the absence of any secondary market for them.

The private placement market could be changed dramatically by the introduction of Rule 144A by the SEC. This rule would allow corporations, including non-U.S. firms, to place securities privately with large, sophisticated institutional investors without extensive registration documents. The SEC intends to provide more financing alternatives for U.S. and non-U.S. firms and possibly increase the number, size, and liquidity of private placements.[7]

Secondary Financial Markets

In this section we consider the purpose and importance of secondary markets and provide an overview of the secondary markets for bonds, financial futures, and stocks. The next section considers national stock markets around the world. The subsequent section discusses regional and over-the-counter stock markets and provides a detailed presentation on the functioning of stock exchanges.

Secondary markets permit trading in outstanding issues, that is, stocks or bonds already sold to the public traded between current and potential owners. The proceeds from a sale in the secondary market do not go to the issuing unit (i.e, the government, municipality, or company), but rather to the current owner of the security.

Why Secondary Markets Are Important

Before discussing the various segments of the secondary market, we must consider its overall importance. Because the secondary market involves the trading of securities initially sold in the primary market, it provides liquidity to the individuals who acquired these securities. After acquiring securities in the primary market, the owner wants to be able to sell them again in order to acquire other securities, buy a house, or go on a vacation. The primary market benefits greatly from the liquidity provided by the secondary market, because investors would hesitate to acquire securities in the primary market if they felt they could not subsequently sell them in the secondary market.

Secondary markets are also important to issuers because the prevailing market prices of their securities are determined by action there. New issues of outstanding stocks or bonds that are to be sold in the primary market are necessarily priced in the secondary market. As a result, capital costs for the government, municipalities, and corporations are determined in the secondary market.

Bond Markets

The secondary market for bonds distinguishes among bonds issued by the federal government, municipalities, or corporations.

U.S. Government and Municipal Bond Markets U.S. government bonds are traded by bond dealers that specialize in either Treasury bonds or agency bonds. Treasury issues are sold through a set of 35 primary dealers, including large banks in major cities like New York and Chicago and some of the large investment banking firms (e.g., Merrill Lynch, First Boston, Morgan Stanley). These institutions and other firms also make markets for government agency issues, but there is no formal set of dealers for agency securities.[8]

---

[7]For a discussion of the rule and private placements, see Michael Siconolfi and Kevin Salwen, "SEC Ready to Ease Private-Placement Rules," *The Wall Street Journal,* April 13, 1990: C1, C5. For a discussion of some reactions to Rule 144A, see Ida Picker, "Watch out for Linda Quinn," *Institutional Investor* 23, no. 8 (July 1989): 77, 78, 83; John W. Milligan, "Two Cheers for 144A," *Institutional Investor* 24, no. 9 (July 1990): 117–119; and Sara Hanks, "SEC Ruling Creates a New Market," *The Wall Street Journal,* May 16, 1990: A12.

[8]For a discussion of non-U.S. markets, see European Bond Commission, *The European Bond Markets* (Chicago: Probus Publishing, 1989).

Banks are active in municipal bond trading because they commit large parts of their investment portfolios to these securities. Also, many large investment banking firms have municipal bond departments because they are active in underwriting these issues.

Corporate Bond Markets The secondary market for corporate bonds has two major segments: security exchanges and the over-the-counter market. The major exchange for bonds is the New York exchange. As of the end of 1990, almost 2,000 corporate bond issues were listed on this exchange with a combined par value of about $290 billion and a combined market value of approximately $226 billion.[9] A typical day sees about 2,000 trades with a total volume of about $43 million. In addition, about 260 issues are listed on the American Stock Exchange (AMEX) with a total market value of $29 billion and a typical daily trading volume over $3 million.

All corporate bonds not listed on one of the exchanges are traded over the counter by dealers who buy and sell for their own accounts. In the United States, most corporate bond trades occur on this OTC market. Virtually all large trades are OTC.

The major bond dealers are the large investment banking firms that underwrite the issues, such as Merrill Lynch, Goldman Sachs, Salomon Brothers, Kidder Peabody, and Morgan Stanley. Because of the limited trading in corporate bonds compared to government bonds, dealers do not carry extensive inventories of specific issues. Instead, they attempt to hold the bonds desired by their clients. As such, they work more like brokers than dealers.

Financial Futures Market In addition to the market for the bonds, recently a market has developed for futures contracts related to these bonds. These contracts allow holders to buy or sell specified amounts of given bond issues at stipulated prices. These futures contracts and the futures market are discussed in detail in Chapter 18.

Equity Markets

The secondary equity market is usually broken down into three major segments: (1) the major national stock exchanges, including the New York, American, Tokyo, and London Stock Exchanges; (2) regional stock exchanges in cities like Chicago, San Francisco, Boston, Osaka and Nagoya in Japan, and Dublin in Ireland; and (3) the over-the-counter stock market, which involves trading in stock not listed on an organized exchange.

The first two groups, referred to as *listed stock exchanges*, differ only in size and geographic emphasis. Both are composed of formal organizations with specific members and specific stocks that have qualified for listing. While stock exchanges are similar because they have listing and membership requirements, the prices of listed stocks are determined via several different systems that will be discussed in the next section.

National Equity Exchanges The secondary stock market is composed of three segments: national stock exchanges, regional stock exchanges, and the over-the-counter market. We need to discuss each of these markets separately because they differ in importance within countries and have different trading systems. As an investor interested in trading global securities, you need to be aware of these differences. This section is devoted to a discussion of the major national stock exchanges in the world because they typically are the dominant markets within their native countries. The next section will consider the regional exchanges and the over-the-counter (OTC) market.

While these exchanges are similar in that only certain stocks can be traded only by individuals who are members of the exchanges, they can differ in their pricing systems. Two major pricing systems exist and an exchange can use one of these or a combination of them. One is a pure auction process, in which interested buyers and sellers submit bid and ask prices for a given stock to a central location where they are matched. The shares of stock are sold to the highest bidder and bought from the seller with the lowest selling price. The other major system is the dealer market, in which individual dealers buy and sell the shares of stock for themselves. When investors want to buy or sell shares of a stock, they go to a dealer. Ideally, a number of dealers will be competing against each other, thus providing the highest bid prices when you are selling and the lowest asking price when you are buying stock. When we discuss the various exchanges, we will indicate the pricing systems they use.

Two U.S. securities exchanges are generally considered national in scope: the New York Stock Ex-

[9]*NYSE Fact Book* (New York: NYSE 1990): 41. If you include U.S. government issues and non-U.S. issues of companies, banks, and governments, there are over 3,300 issues with a par value and market value of over $1,600 billion.

	NYSE	AMEX

Table 4.1	Listing Requirements for Stocks on the NYSE and the AMEX

	NYSE	AMEX
Pretax income last year	$ 2,500,000	$ 750,000
Pretax income last 2 years	2,000,000	400,000[b]
Net tangible assets	16,000,000	4,000,000
Shares publicly held	1,100,000	500,000
Market value of publicly held shares	18,000,000[a]	3,000,000[c]
Minimum number of holders of round lots (100 shares or more)	2,000	800

[a]This minimum required market value varies over time, depending upon the value of the NYSE Common Stock Index. For specifics, see the *1990 NYSE Fact Book* (New York: NYSE, 1991): 28–29.

[b]For AMEX, this is *net* income last year.

[c]The AMEX only has one minimum.

Sources: *NYSE Fact Book* (New York: NYSE, 1990); and *AMEX Fact Book* (New York: AMEX, 1990).

change (NYSE) and the American Stock Exchange (AMEX). Outside the United States, each country typically has one national exchange, such as the Tokyo Stock Exchange (TSE), the London Stock Exchange, the Frankfurt Stock Exchange, and the Paris Bourse. These are considered national because of the large number of listed securities, the reputation of the firms listed, the wide geographic dispersion of the listed firms, and their diverse clienteles of buyers and sellers.

New York Stock Exchange (NYSE) The New York Stock Exchange (NYSE), the largest organized securities market in the United States, was established in 1817 as the New York Stock and Exchange Board. The name was changed to the New York Stock Exchange in 1863.

At the end of 1990, 1,774 companies had stock listed on the NYSE for a total of 2,284 stock issues (common and preferred) with a total market value of over $2.8 trillion. The specific listing requirements for the NYSE as of 1991 appear in Table 4.1.

The average number of shares traded daily on the NYSE has increased steadily and substantially, as shown in Table 4.2. Prior to the 1960s, the daily volume averaged less than 3 million shares, compared to current average volumes of approximately 170 million shares and a record volume of over 600 million shares.

The NYSE has dominated the other exchanges in the United States in terms of trading volume. During the past decade, the NYSE has consistently accounted

for about 80 percent of all shares traded on U.S. listed exchanges, as compared with about 10 percent for the American Stock Exchange and about 10 percent for all regional exchanges combined. Because share prices on the NYSE tend to be higher than those on the AMEX, the trading on the NYSE has averaged about 85 percent of the total value of U.S. trades, compared with less than 5 percent for the AMEX and a little over 10 percent for the regional exchanges.[10]

The volume of trading and relative stature of the NYSE is reflected in the price of membership on it (referred to as a *seat*). As shown in Table 4.3 on p. 114, the price of membership has fluctuated in line with trading volume and other factors that influence the profitability of membership.

American Stock Exchange (AMEX) The American Stock Exchange (AMEX) was begun by a group of persons who traded unlisted shares at the corner of Wall and Hanover Streets in New York. It was originally called the Outdoor Curb Market. In 1910 it established formal trading rules and changed its name to the New York Curb Market Association. The members moved inside a building in 1921 and continued to trade mainly in unlisted stocks (i.e., stocks not listed

---

[10]For a breakdown of shares traded and their value, see Securities and Exchange Commission, *Annual Report* (Washington, D.C.: U.S. Government Printing Office, annual); and *NYSE Fact Book* (New York: NYSE, annual).

Table 4.2	Average Daily Reported Share Volume Traded on Selected National Stock Exchanges ($000)		
Year	**NYSE**	**AMEX**	**TSE**
1940	$ 751	$ 171	$ N.A.
1945	1,422	435	N.A.
1950	1,980	583	N.A.
1955	2,578	912	90,000
1960	3,042	1,113	90,000
1965	6,176	2,120	116,000
1970	11,564	3,319	144,000
1975	18,551	2,138	183,000
1980	44,871	6,427	359,000
1981	46,853	5,310	377,000
1982	65,052	5,287	275,000
1983	85,334	8,225	365,000
1984	91,190	6,107	361,000
1985	109,169	8,337	428,000
1986	141,028	11,773	709,000
1987	188,938	13,858	962,000
1988	161,461	9,941	1,035,000
1989	165,470	12,401	894,000
1990	156,777	13,158	500,000

N.A. = not available

Sources: *NYSE Fact Book* (New York: NYSE, various issues); *AMEX Fact Book* (New York: AMEX, various issues); *Tokyo Stock Exchange Fact Book* (Tokyo: TSE, various issues).

on one of the registered exchanges) until 1946, when its volume in listed stocks finally outnumbered that in unlisted stocks. The current name was adopted in 1953.

The AMEX is a national exchange, distinct from the NYSE because except for a short period in the late 1970s, no stocks have been listed on both the NYSE and AMEX at the same time. The AMEX has emphasized foreign securities, listing about 65 foreign issues in 1989, with trading in these issues constituting about 14 percent of total volume.[11] Warrants were listed on the AMEX for a number of years before the NYSE would list them.

Also, the AMEX has become a major options exchange since January 1975 when it began listing options on six NYSE-listed securities. Since then it has added a number of other options on stocks and interest rates, as discussed in Chapter 16.

At the end of 1989, 1,058 stock issues were listed on the AMEX.[12] As shown in Table 4.2, average daily trading volume has fluctuated substantially over time, growing overall from below 500,000 shares to over 12 million shares a day in 1989. Because of the differences between the NYSE and AMEX, most large brokerage firms are members of both exchanges.

Tokyo Stock Exchange (TSE)   Of the eight stock exchanges in Japan, Tokyo, Osaka, and Nagoya are the largest. The TSE dominates its country's market much as the NYSE does. Specifically, about 83 percent of trades in both volume and value occur on the TSE. The value of stocks listed on the TSE surpassed that of NYSE shares during 1987 but fell below it when Japanese stocks declined in late 1989 and 1990. As of 1991, the two exchanges were very close in terms of total value of stocks listed.

The Tokyo Stock Exchange Co. Ltd., established in 1878, was replaced in 1943 by the Japan Securities Exchange, a quasi-governmental organization that absorbed all existing exchanges in Japan. The Japan Securities Exchange was dissolved in 1947, and the Tokyo Stock Exchange in its present form was established in 1949. It currently lists about 1,600 companies with a total market value of 611,000 billion yen. As shown in Table 4.2, average daily share volume has increased more than 10 times, from 90 million shares per day in 1960 to over a billion shares a day in 1988 prior to a decline to 500 million shares in 1990. The value of shares traded has increased much faster, 50 times from 1960 to 1990, because the prices of the shares have risen, as will be discussed in Chapter 5.

Both domestic and foreign stocks are listed on the Tokyo Exchange. The domestic stocks are further divided between the First and Second Sections. The first section contains about 1,700 stocks. The 150 most active stocks on the First Section are traded on the trading floor. Trading in all other stocks and all foreign stocks is conducted by computer. From on-line terminals in their offices, member firms enter buy and sell orders that are received at the exchange. A clerk employed by a *Saitori* member, the TSE member firm

[11]*AMEX Fact Book* (New York: AMEX, 1990).

[12]The requirements for listing on the AMEX appear in Table 4.1.

Table 4.3	Membership Prices on the NYSE and the AMEX ($000)

	NYSE		AMEX				NYSE		AMEX	
	High	Low	High	Low			High	Low	High	Low
1925	$150	$ 99	$ 38	$ 9		1981	$ 285	$220	$274	$200
1935	140	65	33	12		1982	340	190	285	180
1945	95	49	32	12		1983	425	310	325	261
1955	90	49	22	12		1984	400	290	255	160
1960	162	135	60	51		1985	480	310	160	115
1965	250	250	80	55		1986	600	455	285	145
1970	320	130	185	70		1987	1,150	605	420	265
1975	138	55	72	34		1988	820	580	280	180
1980	275	175	252	95		1989	675	420	215	155
						1990	430	250	170	84

Sources: *NYSE Fact Book* (New York: NYSE, various issues); *AMEX Fact Book* (New York: AMEX, various issues).

Table 4.4	Volume and Value of Foreign Stocks Listed on the Tokyo Stock Exchange

Year	Number of Listed Companies at Year-End	Volume (000)		Value ($ million)	
		Total	Daily Average	Daily Total	Average
1982	12	1,271	5	$ 18,257	$ 64
1983	11	4,974	17	126,858	443
1984	11	4,522	16	93,118	324
1985	21	131,424	461	853,336	2,994
1986	52	309,701	1,110	1,151,863	4,128
1987	88	755,203	2,756	3,469,228	12,661
1988	112	216,332	792	795,252	2,913
1989	119	480,193	1,928	2,797,627	11,235
1990	125	256,252	1,042	2,015,601	8,194

Source: *TSE Fact Book* (Tokyo: TSE, various issues).

responsible for this function, matches buy and sell orders on the electronic book-entry display screen and returns confirmations to the trading parties. The same information is also recorded on the trade-report printer and displayed on all stock-quote screens on the trading floor.

Besides domestic stocks, foreign company stocks are listed and traded on the TSE foreign stock market, which was opened in December 1973. As shown in Table 4.4, only a limited number of foreign companies were listed before 1985. The share volume value of daily average trading in these stocks has increased since then to almost 2 million shares a day in the 125 listed foreign corporations. Trading in foreign stocks declined sharply in 1988 due to poor markets in the original countries and the strength of the yen in the foreign exchange market. There was a rebound in 1989 prior to another decline in 1990.

London Stock Exchange (LSE)   The largest established securities market in the United Kingdom, generally referred to as "The Stock Exchange," is the London Stock Exchange. Since 1973 it has served as the stock exchange of Great Britain and Ireland, with operating units in London, Dublin, and six other cities. Both listed securities (bonds and equities) and unlisted securities are traded on the LSE. The listed equity segment involves over 2,500 companies (2,700 security issues) with a market value in excess of 374 billion pounds (approximately $711 billion). Of the 2,600 companies listed on the exchange, about 600 are foreign firms, the largest number on any exchange.

The stocks listed on the LSE are divided into three groups: Alpha, Beta, and Gamma. The Alpha stocks are the 65 most actively traded stocks, and the Betas are the 500 next most active stocks. In Alpha and Beta stocks, the several competing market-makers are required to offer firm bid–ask quotes to all members of the exchange. For the rest of the stocks, Gamma stocks, market quotations are only indicative and must be confirmed before a trade. All equity trades must be reported to the Stock Exchange Automated Quotation (SEAQ) system within 5 minutes, although only trades in Alpha stocks are reported in full on the screen.

In the pricing system on the LSE, competing dealers communicate via computers in offices away from the stock exchange. This system is similar to the system used in the OTC market in the United States, as described in the next section.

Started by the LSE in 1980, the Unlisted Securities Market (USM) handles smaller companies that do not have sufficiently long trading records for full listing. As of 1989, about 400 companies were traded on the USM with a total market value of over 5,000 million pounds.

Other National Exchanges   Other national exchanges are located in Frankfurt, Toronto, and Paris. In addition, the International Federation of Stock Exchanges was established in 1961. Members include 35 exchanges or national associations of stock exchanges in 29 countries. Located in Paris, the federation's 29 full members and 6 associate members meet every autumn to promote closer collaboration among themselves and to stimulate the development of securities markets.[13]

One of the newest national stock exchanges is in Shanghai, People's Republic of China, established in 1986 in response to the opening up of the Chinese economy. As of 1990 only three stocks were listed, and almost no trading was taking place, although the members of the exchange met daily. In contrast to China, very viable exchanges have been established in Indonesia (Jakarta) and in Thailand (Bangkok).

Global 24-Hour Market   Our discussion of the global securities market will tend to emphasize the three markets in New York, London, and Tokyo because of their relative size and importance, and also because they represent the major segments of a worldwide 24-hour market. You will often hear about a continuous market where investment firms "pass the book" around the world. This means that the major active market in securities moves around the globe as trading hours for these three markets begin and end. Consider the individual trading hours for each of the three exchanges, translated into a 24-hour Eastern Standard clock:

	Local Time (24-hr. notation)	24-Hour EST
New York Stock Exchange	0930–1600	0930–1600
Tokyo Stock Exchange	0900–1100	2300–0100
	1300–1500	0300–0500
London Stock Exchange	0815–1615	0215–1015

Conceive of trading starting in New York and going until 1600 in the afternoon, being picked up by Tokyo late in the evening and going until 0500 in the morning, and continuing in London (with some overlap) until it begins in New York again (with some overlap) at 0930. Alternatively, envision trading as beginning in Tokyo at 2300 hours and continuing until

---

[13]For further discussions of equity markets around the world, see Thomas J. Carroll, ed. *International Guide to Security Exchanges* (New York: Peat, Marwick, Mitchell, 1986); and David Smyth, *Wordly Wise Investor* (New York: Franklin Watts, 1988); *The Spicer and Oppenheim Guide to Securities Markets around the World* (New York: John Wiley & Sons, 1988); Bryan deCaires, ed. *The Kidder Peabody Guide to International Capital Markets* (London: Euromoney Publications, 1988). Appendix 4A summarizes information about the major stock exchanges around the world.

0500, when it moves to London, then it ends the day in New York. This model seems the most relevant since the first question a London trader asks in the morning is, "What happened in Tokyo?" and the U.S. trader asks "What happened in Tokyo and what is happening in London?" The point is, the markets operate almost continuously and they are certainly related in economic events. Therefore, as an investor you are not dealing with three separate and distinct exchanges, but one interrelated world market.[14]

Regional Securities Exchanges Within most countries, regional stock exchanges compete with and supplement the national exchanges by providing secondary markets for the stocks of smaller companies. Beyond these exchanges, trading occurs off the exchange in what is called the over-the-counter (OTC) market, which includes all stocks that are not listed on one of the formal exchanges as well as trading in some listed stocks. The size and significance of the two segments of the overall secondary stock markets vary among countries.

Regional exchanges typically have the same operating procedures as the national exchanges in the same countries, but differ in terms of their listing requirements and the geographic distributions of the listed firms. There are two main reasons for the existence of regional stock exchanges. First, they provide trading facilities for local companies that are not large enough to qualify for listing on one of the national exchanges. Their listing requirements are typically less stringent than those of the national exchanges, as presented in Table 4.1.

Second, regional exchanges in some countries list firms that are also listed on one of the national exchanges to give local brokers who are not members of a national exchange access to these securities. As an example, American Telephone & Telegraph and General Motors are both listed on the NYSE, and also on several regional exchanges. This dual listing allows a local brokerage firm that is not large enough to pur-

chase a membership on the NYSE to buy and sell shares of a dual-listed stock (e.g., General Motors) without going through the NYSE and giving up part of the commission. Currently, about 90 percent of the volume on regional exchanges is attributable to trading in dual-listed issues. The regional exchanges in the United States are:

- Midwest Stock Exchange (Chicago)
- Pacific Stock Exchange (San Francisco–Los Angeles)
- PBW Exchange (Philadelphia–Baltimore–Washington)
- Boston Stock Exchange (Boston)
- Spokane Stock Exchange (Spokane, Washington)
- Honolulu Stock Exchange (Honolulu, Hawaii)
- Intermountain Stock Exchange (Salt Lake City)

The first three exchanges (Midwest, Pacific, and PBW) account for about 90 percent of all regional exchange volume. In turn, total regional exchange volume is 9 to 10 percent of total exchange volume in the United States.

In Japan seven regional stock exchanges supplement the Tokyo Stock Exchange. The exchange in Osaka accounts for about 12 percent and that in Nagoya for about 4.5 percent of the total volume. The remaining exchanges in Kyoto, Hiroshima, Fukuoto, Niigata, and Sapporo together account for less than 1 percent of volume.

The United Kingdom has one stock exchange in London with operating units in seven cities, including Dublin, Belfast, Birmingham, Manchester, Bristol, Liverpool, and Glasgow. West Germany has eight stock exchanges, with its national exchange in Frankfurt where about 50 percent of the trading occurs. There are regional exchanges in Düsseldorf, Munich, Hamburg, Berlin, Stuttgart, Hanover, and Bremen.

Without belaboring the point, each country typically has one national exchange that accounts for the majority of trading and several regional exchanges with less stringent listing requirements to allow trading in smaller firms. Recently, several national exchanges have created second-tier markets that are divisions of the national exchanges to allow smaller firms to be traded as part of the national exchanges.[15]

---

[14]For an example of global trading, see "How Merrill Lynch Moves Its Stock Deals All around the World," *The Wall Street Journal*, November 9, 1987: 1, 19; *Opportunity and Risk in the 24-Hour Global Marketplace* (New York: Coopers & Lybrand, 1987); and "Worldwide Trading," *Chicago Tribune Magazine*, May 1, 1988: 10, 12, 13, 14, 18, 34, 36. In response to this trend toward global trading, the International Organization of Securities Commissions (IOSCO) has been established. For a discussion of it, see David Lascelles, "Calls to Bring Watchdogs into Line," *Financial Times*, August 14, 1989: 10.

[15]An example of this is the second section on the TSE and the Unlisted Stock Market on the LSE. Both exchanges are attempting to provide trading facilities for smaller firms without changing their listing requirements for the national exchanges.

In general, the fortunes of the regional exchanges have fluctuated substantially over time, based upon interest in small, young firms and/or institutional interest in dually listed stocks.

Over-the-Counter (OTC) Market   The over-the-counter (OTC) market includes trading in all stocks not listed on one of the exchanges. It can also include trading in listed stocks. This arrangement, referred to as the third market, is discussed in the following section. The OTC market is not a formal organization with membership requirements or a specific list of stocks deemed eligible for trading.[16] In theory, it is possible to trade any security on the OTC market as long as someone else is willing to take the opposite position (i.e., make a market in the security).

Size   The U.S. OTC market is the largest segment of the secondary stock market in terms of the number of issues traded. It is also the most diverse in terms of quality. As noted earlier, about 2,000 issues are traded on the NYSE and about 1,000 issues on the AMEX. In contrast, almost 3,000 issues are actively traded on the OTC market's NASDAQ National Market System (NMS)[17]. (A firm on the NMS must have a certain size and trading activity and at least four active market-makers). Another 2,000 stocks are traded on the NASDAQ system independent of the NMS. Finally, 1,000 OTC stocks are regularly quoted in *The Wall Street Journal* but not included in the NASDAQ system. The total comes to about 6,000 issues traded on the OTC market—substantially more than on the NYSE and AMEX combined.

Table 4.5 sets forth the growth in the number of companies and issues and the volume of trading on NASDAQ. As of the end of 1990, almost 300 issues on NASDAQ were either foreign stocks or American Depository Receipts (ADRs), both of which trade in the United States just like U.S. stocks. Trading in these securities and ADRs represented about 6 percent of total NASDAQ share volume in 1990. About 200 of these issues trade on both NASDAQ and a foreign exchange like Toronto. In March 1988 NASDAQ developed a link with the Singapore Stock Exchange

> **National Association of Securities Dealers Automated Quotation (NASDAQ) system**   An Electronic system for providing bid–ask quotes on OTC securities.

that allows 24-hour trading going from NASDAQ in New York to Singapore to a NASDAQ/London link and back to New York.

While the OTC market is dominant in terms of the number of issues, the TSE and the NYSE are still dominant in terms of the total value of trading. In 1989 the approximate value of equity trading on the TSE was $2,380 billion, while that on the NYSE was $1,556 billion, and that on the NASDAQ was $431 billion.

There is tremendous diversity in the OTC market because it imposes no minimum requirements. Stocks range from those of small, unprofitable companies to large, very profitable firms. On the upper end, all U.S. government bonds are traded on the OTC market, as are the majority of bank and insurance stocks. Finally, about 100 exchange-listed stocks are also traded on the OTC—this is referred to as the third market.

Operation of the OTC Market   As noted, any stock can be traded on the OTC as long as someone indicates a willingness to take the opposite position. In making a market in this way, the party buys or sells for his or her own account, acting as a dealer.[18] This differs from most transactions on the listed exchanges, where the specialists keep the books and attempt to match buy and sell orders. Therefore, the OTC market is referred to as a *negotiated market*, in which investors directly negotiate with dealers. Most exchanges are auction markets, with specialists acting as intermediaries (auctioneers).

The NASDAQ System   The **National Association of Securities Dealers Automated Quotation (NASDAQ)** system is an automated, electronic quotation system that serves the vast OTC market. Any number of dealers can elect to make markets in an OTC stock. The actual number depends on the activity in the stock. The average for all stocks on the NASDAQ system was 10 in 1989 according to the *NASDAQ Fact Book*.

---

[16]Requirements of trading for different segments of the OTC trading system will be discussed later in this section.

[17]NASDAQ is an acronym for National Association of Securities Dealers Automated Quotations. The system is discussed in detail in a later subsection.

---

[18]*Dealer* and *market-maker* are synonymous.

Table 4.5 *Number of Companies and Issues and Average Daily Volume of Trading on NASDAQ: 1974–1990*

Year	Number of Companies	Number of Issues	Average Daily Volume (millions of shares)
1974	2,463	2,564	4.7
1975	2,467	2,579	5.5
1976	2,495	2,627	6.7
1977	2,456	2,575	7.6
1978	2,475	2,582	11.0
1979	2,543	2,670	14.4
1980	2,894	3,050	26.5
1981	3,353	3,687	30.9
1982	3,264	3,664	33.3
1983	3,901	4,467	62.9
1984	4,097	4,723	59.9
1985	4,136	4,784	82.1
1986	4,417	5,189	113.6
1987	4,706	5,537	149.8
1988	4,451	5,144	122.8
1989	4,293	4,963	133.1
1990	4,132	4,706	131.9

Source: *NASDAQ Fact Book* (Washington, D.C.: National Association of Securities Dealers, 1991): 5.

Historically, a broker trying to buy or sell an OTC stock for a customer had trouble determining current quotations by specific market-makers. NASDAQ makes all dealer quotes available immediately. The broker can check the quotation machine and call the dealer with the best market, verify that the quote has not changed, and make the sale or purchase. The NASDAQ system works on three levels to serve firms with different needs and interests.

Level 1 provides a single median representative quote for firms that want current quotes on OTC stocks but do not consistently buy or sell OTC stocks for their customers and are not market-makers. This composite quote changes constantly to adjust for any changes by individual market-makers.

Level 2 provides instantaneous current quotations by all market-makers in a stock for firms that consistently trade OTC stocks. Given an order to buy or sell, brokers check their quotation machines and call the market-maker with the best market for their purposes

(highest bid if they are selling, lowest offer if buying) and consummate the deal.

Level 3 is for OTC market-makers. Such firms want Level 2 features, but they also need the capability to change their own quotations, which Level 3 provides.

Listing Requirements for NASDAQ Quotes and trading volume for the OTC market are reported in two lists: a National Market System (NMS) list and a regular NASDAQ list. As of 1990, there were four sets of listing requirements. The first, for initial listing on any NASDAQ system, is the least stringent. The second, for automatic (mandatory) inclusion on the NASDAQ/NMS system, provides up-to-the-minute volume and last-sale information for the competing market-makers as well as end-of-the-day information on total volume and high, low, and closing prices.

In addition, two sets of criteria govern voluntary participation on the NMS by companies with differ-

Table 4.6   *Qualification Standards for Inclusion in NASDAQ and NMS*

Standard	Initial NASDAQ Inclusion (Domestic Common Stocks)	Mandatory NASDAQ/NMS Inclusion	Voluntary NASDAQ/NMS Inclusion	
			Alternative 1	Alternative 2
Total assets	$2 million	—	$2 million	$2 million
Net tangible assets	—	$2 million	$4 million	$12 million
Capital and surplus	$1 million	$1 million	$1 million	$8 million
Net income	—	—	$400,000 in latest or last 2 of 3 fiscal years	—
Operating history	—	—	—	4 years
Public float (shares)	100,000	500,000	500,000	$1 million
Market value of float	—	—	$3 million	$15 million
Minimum bid	—	$10 for 5 business days	$5	—
Trading volume	—	Average 600,000 shares/month for 6 months	—	—
Shareholders of record	100	300	400	400
Market-makers	2	Four for 5 business days	2	2

Source: *NASDAQ Fact Book* (Washington, D.C.: National Association of Securities Dealers, 1990): 43.

ent characteristics. Alternative 1 accommodates companies with limited assets or net worth but substantial earnings, while Alternative 2 is for large companies that are not necessarily as profitable. The four sets of criteria are set forth in Table 4.6.

A Sample Trade Assume you are considering the purchase of 100 shares of Apple Computer. Although Apple is large enough and profitable enough to be listed on a national exchange, the company has never applied for listing because it enjoys a very active market on the OTC. (It is one of the volume leaders with daily volume typically above 500,000 shares and often in excess of 1 million shares.)

When you contact your broker, he or she will consult the NASDAQ electronic quotation machine to determine the current markets for AAPL, the trading symbol for Apple Computer.[19] The quote shows about 20 dealers making markets in AAPL. An example of differing market quotes might be as follows:

Dealer	Bid	Ask
1	$44\frac{1}{2}$	$44\frac{3}{4}$
2	$44\frac{3}{8}$	$44\frac{5}{8}$
3	$44\frac{1}{4}$	$44\frac{5}{8}$
4	$44\frac{3}{8}$	$44\frac{3}{4}$

Assuming that these are the best markets available from the total group, your broker would call either Dealer 2 or 3 because they have the lowest offering prices. After verifying the quote, your broker would give one of these dealers an order to buy 100 shares of

[19]Trading symbols are one- to four-letter codes used to designate stocks. Whenever a trade is reported on a stock ticker the trading symbol appears with the figures. Many are obvious, like GM (General Motors), F (Ford Motors), GE (General Electric), and T (American Telephone & Telegraph).

| **Fourth market** Direct trading of securities between owners, usually institutions, without any broker's intermediation.

AAPL at $44\frac{5}{8}$ ($44.625 a share). Because your firm was not a market-maker in the stock, it would act as a broker and charge you $4,462.50 plus a commission for the trade. If your firm had been a market-maker in AAPL with an asking price of $44\frac{5}{8}$, he or she would have sold the stock to you at $44\frac{5}{8}$ net (without commission). If you had been interested in selling 100 shares of Apple Computer instead of buying, the broker would have contacted Dealer 1, who made the highest bid.

Changing Dealer Inventory Let us consider the quotation an OTC dealer would give to change inventory on a given stock. For example, assume Dealer 4, with a current quote of $44\frac{3}{8}$ bid–$44\frac{3}{4}$ ask, decides to increase its holdings of AAPL. The NASDAQ quotes indicate that the highest bid is currently $44\frac{1}{2}$. Increasing the bid to $44\frac{1}{2}$ would bring some of the business currently going to Dealer 1. Taking a more aggressive action, the dealer might raise the bid to $44\frac{5}{8}$ and buy all the stock that is offered, including some from Dealers 2 or 3, who are offering it at $44\frac{5}{8}$. In this example, the dealer raises the bid price but does not change the asking price, which was above those of Dealers 2 or 3. This dealer will buy stock but probably not sell any. A dealer that had excess stock would keep the bid below the market (lower than $44\frac{1}{2}$) and reduce the asking price to $44\frac{5}{8}$ or less. Dealers constantly change their bid and/or ask prices, depending upon their current inventories or the outlook for the stock.[20]

Third Market As mentioned, the term **third market** describes over-the-counter trading of shares listed on an exchange. While most transactions in listed stocks take place on an exchange, an investment firm that is not a member of an exchange can make a market in a listed stock. Most of the trading on this market is in well-known stocks like AT&T, IBM, and Xerox. Success or failure depends on whether the

OTC market in these stocks is as good as the exchange market and on the relative cost of the OTC transaction compared to the cost on the exchange. While current third market volume is below that experienced in 1975 prior to negotiated commissions, this market is very important during rare periods when trading is not available on the NYSE either because trading is suspended or the exchange is closed.[21]

Fourth Market The term **fourth market** describes direct trading of securities between two parties with no broker intermediary. In almost all cases, both parties involved are institutions. When you think about it, a direct transaction is really not that unusual. If you own 100 shares of AT&T and decide to sell it, there is nothing wrong with simply offering it to your friends or associates at a mutually agreeable price and making the transaction directly.

Investors typically buy or sell stock through brokers because it is faster and easier. Also, you would expect to get a better deal because the broker has a good chance of finding the best buyer. You are willing to pay a commission for these liquidity services.

The fourth market evolved because of the substantial brokerage fees charged institutions with large orders. At some point it becomes worthwhile for institutions to attempt to deal directly with each other and save the brokerage fees. Assume an institution decides to sell 100,000 shares of AT&T, which is selling for about $30 a share, for a total value of $3 million. The average commission on such a transaction prior to the advent of negotiated rates in 1975 was about 1 percent of the value of the trade, or about $30,000. This cost made it attractive for a selling institution to spend some time and effort finding another institution interested in increasing its holdings of AT&T and negotiating a direct sale. Currently, such transactions cost about 5 cents a share, which implies a cost of $5,000 for the 100,000 share transaction. This is lower, but still not trivial.

Because of the diverse nature of the fourth market and the lack of reporting requirements, no data are available regarding its specific size or growth. Apparently, it still exists, but is smaller than it was prior to negotiated commissions.

---

[20]A number of studies have examined the determinants of dealers' bid–ask spreads, including H. R. Stoll, "Inferring the Components of the Bid–Ask Spread: Theory and Empirical Tests," *Journal of Finance* 44, no. 1 (March 1989): 115–134.

[21]Rhonda L. Rundle, "Jefferies 'Third Market' Trading Often Steals Show from Exchanges," *The Wall Street Journal*, July 12, 1984: 29.

Detailed Analysis of Exchange Markets

Because of the importance of the listed exchange markets, they must be dealt with at some length. In this section we discuss the major types of orders, the several types of membership on the exchanges including the function of the specialist, or the equivalent central market-maker in non-U.S. markets. These individuals are a critical component of a good exchange market.

Types of Orders

It is important to understand the different types of orders entered by investors and the specialist as a dealer.

Market Orders   The most frequent type of order, a **market order,** is an order to buy or sell a stock at the best price currently prevailing. An investor who enters a market sell order indicates a willingness to sell immediately at the highest bid available at the time the order reaches the specialist on the exchange. A market buy order indicates that the investor is willing to pay the lowest offering price available at the time the order reaches the floor of the exchange. Market orders allow quick execution of a transaction (giving immediate liquidity) for someone willing to accept the prevailing market price.

Assume you are interested in General Electric (GE) and you call your broker to find out the current "market" on the stock. The quotation machine indicates that the prevailing market is 65 bid–$65\frac{1}{4}$ ask. This means that the highest current bid on the books of the specialist is 65; that is, $65 is the most that anyone has offered to pay for GE. The lowest offer is $65\frac{1}{4}$; that is the lowest price anyone is willing to accept to sell the stock. If you placed a market buy order for 100 shares, you would buy 100 shares at $65.25 a share (the lowest ask price) for a total cost of $6,525 plus commission. If you submitted a market sell order for 100 shares, you would sell the shares at $65 each and receive $6,500, less commission.

Limit Orders   The individual placing a **limit order** specifies the buy or sell price. You might submit a bid to purchase 100 shares of Coca-Cola stock at $50 a share when the current market is 55 bid–$55\frac{1}{4}$ ask, with the expectation that the stock will decline to $50 in the near future.

> **Market order** An order to buy or sell a security immediately at the best price available.
>
> **Limit order** An order to buy or sell a security when and if it trades at a specified price.
>
> **Short sale** Sale of borrowed stock with the intention of repurchasing it later at a lower price and earning the difference.

You must also indicate how long the limit order will be outstanding. Alternative time specifications are basically boundless. A limit order can be instantaneous ("fill" or kill," meaning fill the order instantly or cancel it). It can also be good for part of a day, a full day, several days, a week, or a month. It can also be open-ended, or good until canceled (GTC).

Rather than wait for a given price on a stock, your broker will give the limit order to the specialist, who will put it in a limit order book and act as the broker's representative. When and if the market price reaches your limit order price, the specialist will execute the order and inform your broker. The specialist receives a small part of the commission for rendering this service.

Short Sales   Most investors purchase stock (i.e., "go long") expecting to derive their return from an increase in value. If you believe that a stock is overpriced, however, and want to take advantage of an expected decline in the price, you can sell the stock short. A **short sale** is the sale of stock that you do not own with the intent of purchasing it back later at a lower price. Specifically, you would borrow the stock from another investor through your broker, sell it in the market, and subsequently replace it at (you hope) a price lower than the price at which you sold it. The investor who lent the stock has the proceeds of the sale as collateral. In turn, this investor can invest these funds in short-term, risk-free securities. While there is no time limit on a short sale, the lender of the shares can indicate a desire to sell the shares, in which case your broker must find another investor to make the loan.[22]

---

[22]For a discussion of short selling strategies and some profitable results, see Brett Duval Fromson, "Shortseller in the Bull Market," *Fortune,* August 31, 1987: 52, 53, 54, 56; Gary Putka, "Fortune Smiles on Short Side of Market," *The Wall Street Journal,* October 27, 1987: 5; and John R. Dorfman, "Short Sellers Stand Tall, Shrug off Market's Resilience," *The Wall Street Journal,* January 24, 1991: C1, C2.

> **Margin** The amount of cash a buyer pays for a security, borrowing the balance from the broker. This leverage increases the risk of the transaction.

Two technical points affect short sales. First, a short sale can be made only on an *uptick trade*, meaning the price of the short sale must be higher than the last trade price. Exchanges impose this restriction because they do not want traders to be able to force a profit on a short sale by pushing the price down through continually selling short. Therefore, the transaction price for a short sale must be an uptick or, without any change in price, the previous price must have been higher than the security's previous price (a zero uptick). For an example of a zero uptick, consider the following set of transaction prices: 42, $42\frac{1}{4}$, $42\frac{1}{4}$. You could sell short at $42\frac{1}{4}$ even though it is no change from the previous trade at $42\frac{1}{4}$.

The second technical point concerns dividends. The short seller must pay any dividends due to the investor who lent the stock. The purchaser of the short-sale stock receives the dividend from the corporation, so the short seller must pay a similar dividend to the lender.

Special Orders In addition to these general orders, there are several special types of orders. A *stop loss order* is a conditional market order whereby the investor directs the sale of a stock if it drops to a given price. Assume you buy a stock at 50 and expect it to go up. If you are wrong, you want to limit your losses. To protect yourself, you could put in a stop loss order at 45. In this case, if the stock dropped to 45, your stop loss order would become a market sell order, and the stock would be sold at the prevailing market price. The stop loss order does not guarantee that you will get the $45; you can get a little bit more or a little bit less. Because of the possibility of market disruption caused by a large number of stop loss orders, exchanges have, on occasion, canceled all such orders on certain stocks and not allowed brokers to accept further stop loss orders on those issues.

A related type of stop loss tactic for short sales is a stop buy order. An investor who has sold stock short and wants to minimize any loss should the stock begin to increase in value would enter this conditional buy order at a price above that at which the investor sold the stock short. Assume you sold a stock short at 50, expecting it to decline to 40. To protect yourself from an increase, you could put in a stop buy order to pur- chase the stock using a market buy order if it reached a price of 55. This conditional market buy order would hopefully limit any loss on the short sale to approximately $5 a share.

Margin Transactions On any type of order, an investor can pay for the stock with cash or borrow part of the cost, leveraging the transaction. Leverage is accomplished by buying or selling on **margin,** which means that the investor pays some cash and borrows the rest through the broker, putting up the stock for collateral.

As shown in Figure 4.1, the dollar amount of margin credit extended by brokers and dealers increased substantially between early 1985 and late 1987. The interest rate charged on these loans by brokers is typically 1 percent above the rate charged by the bank making the loan. The bank rate, referred to as the *call money rate*, is generally about 1 percent below the prime rate. For example, in January 1991 the prime rate was $9\frac{1}{2}$ percent, and the call money rate was 9 percent.

Federal Reserve Board Regulations T and U determine the maximum proportion of any transaction that can be borrowed. These regulations were enacted during the 1930s because it was contended that the excessive credit extended for stock acquisition contributed to the stock market collapse of 1929. Since the enactment of the regulations, this *margin requirement* (the proportion of total transaction value that must be paid in cash) has varied from 40 percent (allowing loans of 60 percent of the value) to 100 percent (allowing no borrowing). As of June 1991, the initial margin requirement specified by the Federal Reserve was 50 percent, although individual investment firms can require higher rates.

After the initial purchase, changes in the market price of the stock will cause changes in the *investor's equity* that is equal to the market value of the collateral stock minus the amount borrowed. Obviously, if the stock price increases, the investor's equity as a proportion of the total market value of the stock increases (that is, the investor's margin will exceed the initial margin requirement).

Assume you acquired 200 shares of a $50 stock for a total cost of $10,000. A 50 percent initial margin requirement allowed you to borrow $5,000, making your initial equity $5,000. If the stock price were to increase to $70 a share, the total market value of your position would be $14,000, and your equity would be $9,000, or 64 percent ($9,000/$14,000). In contrast, if

Figure 4.1 **_Borrowing against Stocks—Amount of Margin Credit Extended by Brokers and Dealers at End of Month ($ billions)_**

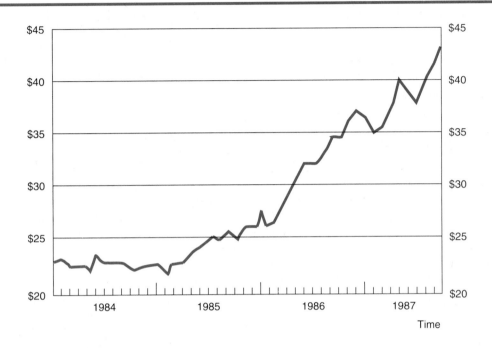

Source: Federal Reserve Board, Washington, D.C., 1988.

the stock price were to decline to $40 a share, the total market value would be $8,000, and your equity would be $3,000 or 37.5 percent ($3,000/$8,000).

At this point, the *maintenance margin*, which is the required proportion of your equity to the total value of the stock becomes important. At present, the minimum maintenance margin specified by the Federal Reserve is 25 percent, but, again, individual brokerage firms can dictate higher margins for their customers. If the stock price declines to the point where your equity drops below 25 percent of the total value of the position, the account is considered undermargined, and you will receive a margin call to provide more equity. If you do not respond with the required funds in the time allotted, the stock will be sold to pay off the loan. The time allowed to meet the call varies between investment firms and is affected by market conditions. Under volatile conditions, the time allowed to respond to a margin call can be shortened drastically.

To continue the previous example, if the stock were to decline to $30 a share, its total market value

would be $6,000 and your equity would be $1,000, which is only about 17 percent of the total value ($1,000/$6,000). You would receive a margin call for approximately $667, which would give you equity of $1,667, or 25 percent of the total value of the account ($1,667/$6,667).[23]

You should recognize that buying on margin provides all the advantages, and the disadvantages, of leverage. Lower margin requirements allow you to borrow more, increasing the percentage of gain or loss on your investment when the stock price increases or decreases. The leverage factor equals 1/percent margin. Thus, if the margin is 50 percent, the leverage factor is 2, that is 1/.50. This means that if the rate of return on the stock is plus or minus 10 percent, the

[23]For a discussion of margin calls following market declines in 1987 and 1990, see Karen Slater, "Margin Calls Create Dilemma for Investors," *The Wall Street Journal*, October 23, 1987: 21; and William Power, "Stocks' Drop Spurs Margin Calls Less Severe than in Earlier Falls," *The Wall Street Journal*, August 15, 1990: C1.

return on the equity for an investor who borrowed 50 percent of the purchase price would be plus or minus 20 percent. If the margin declines to 33 percent, you can borrow more (67 percent), and the leverage factor is 3 (1/.033).

When you acquire stock or other investments on margin, you are increasing the financial risk of the investment beyond the risk inherent in the security itself. You should increase your required rate of return accordingly.[24]

Exchange Membership

Listed U.S. securities exchanges typically offer four major categories of membership: (1) commission broker, (2) floorbroker, (3) registered trader, and (4) specialist.

Commission brokers are employees of a member firm who buy or sell for the customers of the firm. When you place an order to buy or sell stock through a registered representative of a brokerage firm that is a member of the exchange, it contacts its commission broker on the floor of the exchange. That broker goes to the appropriate post on the floor and buys or sells the stock as instructed.

Floor brokers are independent members of an exchange who act as brokers for other members. As an example, when commission brokers for Merrill Lynch become too busy to handle all of their orders, they will ask one of the floor brokers to help them. At one time these people were referred to as *$2 brokers* because that is what they received for each order. Currently they receive about $4 per 100-share order.

Registered traders are allowed to use their memberships to buy and sell for their own accounts. They therefore save commissions on their own trading, and observers believe they have an advantage from their position on the trading floor. The exchanges and others recognize and allow these advantages because these traders provide the market with added liquidity, but regulations limit how they trade and how many registered traders can be in a trading crowd around a specialist's booth at any time. In recent years, registered traders have become registered competitive market-makers (RCMM), who have specific trading

obligations set by the exchange. Their activity is reported as part of the specialist group.[25]

The Central Exchange Market-maker

This person's role differs among exchanges. For example, on U.S. exchanges this person is the *specialist*, while on the TSE it is the *Saitori*. These individuals are critical to the smooth and efficient functioning of these markets.

The stock exchange specialist, or the equivalent on other exchanges, has been justifiably considered the center of the auction market. As noted, a major requirement for a good market is liquidity, which depends heavily upon how the specialist or a counterpart does this job. Our initial discussion centers on the specialist's role in U.S. markets, followed by a consideration of comparable roles on exchanges in other countries.

U.S. Markets The specialist is a member of the exchange who applies to the exchange to be assigned stocks to handle.[26] The typical specialist will handle about 15 stocks. The capital requirement for specialists changed in April 1988 in response to the October 1987 market crash.[27] Specifically, the minimum capital required of each specialist unit was raised to $1 million or they had to be able to support a minimum of 15,000 shares of each stock assigned, whichever is greater.

Functions of the Specialist Specialists have two major functions. First, they serve as brokers to match buy and sell orders. They also handle limit orders or special orders placed with member brokers. An indi-

---

[24]For a further discussion see Jill Bettner, "Brokers Begin Pushing Margin Loans—But Critics Say Borrowers Should Beware," *The Wall Street Journal*, August 26, 1987: 17.

[25]Prior to the late 1970s, there were also odd-lot dealers who bought and sold to individuals with orders for less than round lots (usually 100 shares). Currently, this function is handled by either the specialist or some large brokerage firm.

[26]Most specialists are part of a specialist unit that can be a formal organization of specialists (a specialist firm) or a set of independent specialists who join together to spread the workload and the risk of the stocks assigned to the unit. At the end of 1989 a total of 446 individual specialists made up 53 specialist units (about 8 specialists per unit).

[27]For a detailed presentation on the 1987 crash, see *Report of the Presidential Task Force on Market Mechanisms* (Washington, D.C.: Superintendent of Documents, U.S. Government Printing Office, January 1988). The chairman of the task force was Nicholas Brady, so it is sometimes referred to as "The Brady Report."

vidual broker who receives a limit order to purchase a stock at $5 below the current market does not have the time or inclination to watch the stock constantly for the decline to take place. Therefore, the broker leaves the limit order (or stop loss or stop buy order) with the specialist, who enters it in his book and executes it when and if the specified price occurs. For this service, the specialist receives a portion of the broker's commission on the trade.

The second major function of specialists on U.S. exchanges is to act as *dealers* in the stocks assigned to them in order to maintain fair and orderly markets. They must buy and sell for their own accounts when public supply or demand is insufficient to provide a continuous, liquid market. In this function they act like dealers (market-makers) on the OTC market.

If a stock is currently selling for about $40 per share, the current bid and ask in an auction market (without the intervention of the specialist) might be a 40 bid–41 ask. Under such conditions, random market buy and sell orders might cause the price of the stock to fluctuate between 40 and 41 constantly—a movement of 2.5 percent between trades. Most investors would probably consider such a price pattern too volatile; the market would not be considered continuous. The specialist is expected to provide alternative bids and/or asks to narrow the spread and provide greater price continuity over time. In this example, the specialist would enter a bid of $40\frac{1}{2}$ or $40\frac{3}{4}$ or an ask of $40\frac{1}{2}$ or $40\frac{1}{4}$ to narrow the spread to one-half or one-quarter point.

The specialist can enter either side of the market, depending upon several factors including the trend of the market. Since specialists are committed to being a stabilizing force in the market, they are expected to buy or sell against the market when prices are clearly moving in one direction. They are required to buy stock for their own inventories when there is an excess of sell orders and the market is definitely declining. They must sell stock from their inventories or sell it short to accommodate an excess of buy orders when the market is rising. Note that they are not expected to prevent prices from rising or declining, but only to ensure that the prices change in an orderly fashion, i.e., to maintain price continuity. For an indication of how well this works, consider that during recent years NYSE stocks traded unchanged from, or within one-eighth point of, the price of the previous trade about 95 percent of the time.

Another factor affecting what side of the market specialists enter when they have a choice is their current inventory positions in their stocks. If they have large inventories of a given stock, all other factors being equal, they would probably enter on the ask (sell) side in order to reduce these heavy inventories. In contrast, if previous market action had required heavy selling from their inventories, or even short sales, they would tend toward the bid (buy) side of the market to rebuild their inventories or close out their short positions.

Finally, the position of the limit order book which contains information on all limit orders for a stock will influence these actions. Numerous limit buy orders (bids) close to the current market and very few limit sell orders (asks) might indicate that the most likely future move for the stock, in the absence of any new information, is toward a higher price because demand is apparently heavy and supply limited. Under such conditions, a specialist who is not bound by one of the other factors would probably be on the bid side of the quote to accumulate stock in anticipation of an increase. In this function as a dealer, the specialists on the NYSE have historically participated in 10 to 12 percent of all trades.

Sources of Income The specialist derives income from both being a broker and being a dealer. The actual breakdown between the two depends upon the specific stock. A specialist in a very actively traded stock such as IBM faces little need to act as a dealer because substantial public interest in the issue creates a tight market. In this case the major concern (and main source of income) is maintaining the limit orders for the stock.

In contrast, for a stock with low trading volume and substantial price volatility, the specialist would have to be an active dealer. The specialist's income from that stock would depend upon the ability to trade in it profitably. Specialists have a major advantage in this effort because of their limit order books. Theoretically, only specialists are supposed to see their books, giving them a monopoly on a source of very important information. In practice, they are typically willing to share this information with brokers who come to the trading post and request it. Still, they have this information on a continuous basis. A full set of limit orders, representing the current supply and demand curve for a stock, provides the specialist with a good idea of the probable future direction of that stock. This information should allow a specialist firm to profit on its dealer trades despite being forced to buy or sell against the market for short periods of time.[28]

In addition, the income derived from acting as a broker can be substantial and is basically without risk. Most specialists attempt to balance their portfolios between strong broker stocks that provide steady, riskless income and stocks that require active dealer roles.

An SEC study done in 1972 indicated substantial returns on investment for all specialist units.[29] It is unlikely that specialists are earning returns of such magnitude in the late 1980s and early 1990s because the 1972 returns preceded negotiated commission rates, which have affected the fees paid to specialists. Also, as indicated earlier, following the October 1987 market crash, specialists were required to increase their capital positions substantially, which would reduce their return on investment.[30]

Tokyo Stock Exchange (TSE) As of November 1990, the TSE had a total of 124 "regular members" (99 Japanese members and 25 foreign members) and 4 *Saitori* members. As in the United States, a membership requires the purchase of a seat, which currently costs about 1.15 billion yen (about $8 million). For each membership, the firm is allowed several people on the floor of the exchange, depending upon its trading volume and capital position. The average number of employees on the floor is 20 per firm for a regular member and almost 90 employees per *Saitori* member. The employees of a regular member are called *trading*

clerks, while the employees of a *Saitori* member are called *intermediary clerks*.

Regular members buy and sell securities on the TSE either as agents or principals (i.e., brokers or dealers). *Saitori* members specialize in acting as intermediaries (brokers) for transactions among regular members, and they also maintain the books for limit orders. (Stop loss and stop buy orders as well as short selling are not allowed.) Therefore, *Saitori* members are similar to U.S. exchange specialists because they match buy and sell orders for customers, handle limit orders, and are not allowed to deal with public customers. They differ from U.S. exchange specialists since they do not act as dealers to maintain an orderly market. Only regular members are allowed to buy and sell for their own accounts. Therefore, the TSE is a pure auction market with the *Saitori* acting only as the auctioner. Also, you should remember that although there are about 1,700 listed domestic stocks and 119 foreign stocks on the first section, only the largest 150 largest volume stocks are traded on the floor of the exchange. All other stocks are traded via a computer system called CORES, which stands for Computer-assisted Order Routing and Execution System.

TSE membership is available to corporations licensed by the Minister of Finance. Member applicants may request any of four licenses: (1) to trade securities as a dealer, (2) to trade as a broker, (3) to underwrite new securities on secondary offerings, or (4) to handle retail distribution of new or outstanding securities. While a firm may have more than one license, it cannot act as principal and agent in the same transaction. The minimum capital requirements for these licenses vary from 200 million to 3 billion yen ($1 million to $15 million) depending upon the type of license.

Although Japan's securities laws allow foreign securities firms to obtain membership on the exchanges, the individual exchanges determine whether membership will be granted. Currently 25 foreign firms are members on the TSE. All have joined in since 1986.[31]

London Stock Exchange (LSE) Historically, members on the LSE were either brokers, who could act

---

[28]For evidence that the specialists do not fare too badly, even when they are forced to trade against the market, see Frank K. Reilly and Eugene F. Drzycimski, "The Stock Exchange Specialist and the Market Impact of Major World Events," *Financial Analysts Journal* 31, no. 4 (July–August 1975): 27–32. Also, if a major imbalance in trading arises due to new information, the specialist can request a temporary suspension of trading. For an analysis of what occurs during these trading suspensions, see Michael H. Hopewell and Arthur L. Schwartz, Jr., "Temporary Trading Suspensions in Individual NYSE Securities," *Journal of Finance* 33, no. 5 (December 1978): 1355–1373; and Frank J. Fabozzi and Christopher K. Ma, "The Over-the-Counter Market and New York Stock Exchange Trading Halts," *The Financial Review* 23, no. 4 (November 1988): 427–437.

[29]U. S. House Committee on Interstate and Foreign Commerce, Subcommittee on Commerce and Finance, *Securities Industry Study: Report and Hearings*, 92d Congress, 1st and 2d sessions, 1972: Chapter 12.

[30]For a discussion of the recent problems facing specialists, see Edward A. Wyatt, "Eye of the Hurricane," *Barron's*, February 19, 1990: 28.

[31]Some observers have questioned the pure economics of these memberships, but the firms have defended them as a means of becoming a part of the very lucrative Japanese financial community. In this regard, see Kathryn Graven, "Tokyo Stock Exchange's Broker-Fees Cut Is Seen Trimming Foreign Firms' Profits," *The Wall Street Journal*, October 2, 1987: 17; and Marcus W. Brauchli, "U.S. Brokerage Firms Operating in Japan Have Mixed Results," *The Wall Street Journal*, August 16, 1989: A1, A8.

only as agents trading shares on behalf of customers, or jobbers, who could act as market-makers buying and selling shares as principals. The exchange went through a major deregulation (the "Big Bang") on October 27, 1986. Currently brokers are allowed to make markets in various equities and gilts (British government bonds). Jobbers can deal with nonstock exchange members including the public and institutions. A further discussion of changes after the Big Bang appears in the following section on changes in the capital markets.

Membership in the LSE is granted based upon experience and competence, and there are no citizenship or residency requirements. Currently, over 5,000 individual memberships are held by 214 broker firms and 22 jobbers. While individuals gain membership, the operational unit is a firm. It joins and pays membership fees based upon the number of exchange-approved members it employs during its first year of membership. Subsequently each member firm pays an annual charge equal to 1 percent of its gross revenues.

Changes in the Securities Markets

Prior to 1965 the operations of the securities markets were fairly stable, but since then there have been numerous significant changes. Many of the changes since 1965 were prompted by the growth of trading by large financial institutions like banks, insurance companies, pension funds, and investment companies, whose trading patterns and requirements differ from those of individual investors, for whom the market mechanism was originally developed. In addition, since the mid-1980s additional changes have transpired because of the globalization of capital markets. In this section we discuss why some of these changes occurred in the United States and their impact on the market. We will also consider several changes related to the global market and speculate about future changes.

Evidence and Effects of Institutionalization

The growing impact of large financial institutions is evidenced by data on block trades (transactions involving at least 10,000 shares) and the sizes of trades, in general, as seen in Table 4.7. Financial institutions are the main source of large block trades and the number of block trades on the NYSE has grown steadily from an average of 9 per day in 1965 to almost 3,500 a day

in 1989. On average, such trades constitute half of all the volume on the exchange. Institutional involvement is also reflected in the average size of trades, which has grown consistently from about 200 shares in 1965 to over 2,100 shares in 1989.[32]

Several major effects of this institutionalization of the market have been identified:

1. Negotiated (competitive) commission rates
2. The influence of block trades
3. The creation of a tiered trading market
4. The impact on stock price volatility
5. The development of a National Market System (NMS)

In the following sections we will discuss each of these effects and how they affect the operation of the U.S. securities market.

Negotiated Commission Rates

Background   When the NYSE was formally established in 1792, it was agreed that the members would carry out all trades in designated stocks on the exchange, and that they would charge nonmembers on the basis of a *minimum commission schedule*. This meant that members could engage in price cutting. Because the market was designed for individual investors, the minimum commission schedule was developed to compensate for handling small orders and made no allowance for trading large orders for institutions. When institutions became more active in the mid-1960s, they were paying substantially more in commissions than the costs of their transactions justified.

The initial reaction to the excess commissions was give-ups, wherein brokers agreed to pay part of their commissions (sometimes as much as 80 percent) to other brokerage houses or research firms designated by the institution making the trades. These firms provided services to the institution. These commission transfers were referred to as *soft dollars*.

Another response was the increased use of the third market, where commissions were not fixed as they were on the NYSE. As a result, from 1965 to 1972, third-market volume grew steadily both in ab-

---

[32]While the influence of institutional trading is greatest on the NYSE, it is also a major factor on the AMEX where block trades constituted almost 40 percent of share volume in 1989, and on the NASDAQ–NMS, where block trades accounted for almost 43 percent of share volume in 1989.

| Table 4.7 | Block Transactions[a] and Average Shares per Sale on the NYSE |

Year	Total Number of Block Transactions	Total Number of Shares in Block Trades (000)	Percentage of Reported Volume	Average Number of Block Transactions per Day	Average Shares per Sale
1965	2,171	48,262	3.1%	9	224
1966	3,642	85,298	4.5	14	240
1967	6,685	169,365	6.7	27	257
1968	11,254	292,680	10.0	50	302
1969	15,132	402,063	14.1	61	357
1970	17,217	450,908	15.4	68	388
1971	26,941	692,536	17.8	106	428
1972	31,207	766,406	18.5	124	443
1973	29,233	721,356	17.8	116	449
1974	23,200	549,387	15.6	92	438
1975	34,420	778,540	16.6	136	495
1976	47,632	1,001,254	18.7	188	559
1977	54,275	1,183,924	22.4	215	641
1978	75,036	1,646,905	22.9	298	717
1979	97,509	2,164,726	26.5	305	787
1980	133,597	3,311,132	29.2	528	872
1981	145,564	3,771,442	31.8	575	1,013
1982	254,707	6,742,481	41.0	1,007	1,305
1983	363,415	9,842,080	45.6	1,436	1,434
1984	433,427	11,492,091	49.8	1,713	1,781
1985	539,039	14,222,272	51.7	2,139	1,878
1986	665,587	17,811,335	49.9	2,631	1,881
1987	920,679	24,497,241	51.2	3,639	2,112
1988	768,419	22,270,680	54.5	3,037	2,303
1989	872,811	21,316,132	51.1	3,464	2,123
1990	843,365	19,681,849	49.6	3,333	2,082

[a]Trades of 10,000 shares or more.

Source: NYSE Fact Book (New York: NYSE, various issues).

solute terms and as a percentage of volume on the NYSE. It declined again after 1972 because of the change in commission structure.

The fixed commission structure also fostered the development and use of the fourth market, where two institutions deal directly with one another, saving the full commission. Finally, some institutions attempted to become members of one of the exchanges. The NYSE and AMEX would not allow institutional members, but some of the regional exchanges admitted the institutions to increase trading volume.

Imposition of Negotiated Commissions Beginning in 1970, the SEC considered allowing brokers and customers to negotiate commissions. The SEC began a program of negotiated commissions on large transactions and finally allowed negotiated commissions on all transactions on May 1, 1975 (the event was called *May Day*).

The effect on commissions charged has been dramatic. Initially, negotiated commissions were stated in terms of discounts from pre-May Day fixed rates. The discounts started at 30 percent and increased to over 50 percent on "no-brainers" (relatively small trades on liquid stocks, such as 2,000 shares of AT&T). Currently, commissions for institutions are stated in the range of 5 to 10 cents per share irrespective of the price of the stock, which implies a very large discount on high-priced shares. Although individuals initially enjoyed little discounting, eventually discount brokers appeared who charged only straight transaction fees and provided no research advice or safekeeping services. These discounts vary depending on the size of the trade. Discount brokerage firms advertise extensively in *The Wall Street Journal* and *Barron's*.

Numerous mergers and liquidations by smaller investment firms after May Day led to fewer, larger, and stronger firms in the industry. During the period of fixed minimum commissions, it was cheaper for most institutions to pay for research with soft dollars than to establish extensive in-house research staffs. Competitive rates substantially reduced excess commissions, and the institutions switched to large brokerage firms that had good trading capabilities plus well-staffed research departments. As a result, many independent research firms either disbanded or merged with full-service brokerage firms.

Regional stock exchanges flourished during the early 1970s because they helped institutions distribute soft dollars, allowed institutions to become members, and facilitated trading in large blocks. When negotiated rates reduced excess commission dollars, there was little incentive for the institutions to maintain memberships and some observers expected regional exchanges to suffer. Apparently, the unique trading capabilities developed by these exchanges and their implementation of block trades prevented this because relative trading on these exchanges as a group has been maintained.[33] As mentioned, trading on the third market declined after May Day, amounting to

only about 1 percent of NYSE volume in 1990 compared to about 7 percent before 1972.

Summary of Effects of Negotiated Commissions
Total commissions paid have shown a significant decline and the size and structure of the industry have changed as a result. While independent research firms and the third market have contracted, regional stock exchanges have felt little impact.

Impact of Block Trades

As noted, increased institutional involvement has caused a significant increase in the number and size of block trades. Since these block trades currently account for more than 50 percent of the volume on the NYSE and 40 percent in other sectors of the market, it is important to consider how they influenced the market and why these changes occurred. It is also necessary to understand how block trades work.

The increase in block trading by institutions has strained the market's liquidity. The specialist system had three problems with block trading: *capital, commitment,* and *contacts* (the three *C*s). First, specialists were undercapitalized to deal in large blocks. They had trouble coming up with the capital needed to acquire 10,000 or 20,000 shares. Second, even when specialists had the capital, they may have been unwilling to take the large risks involved. Finally, specialists are not allowed to deal directly with nonbrokers (by Rule 113 of the NYSE). Because they cannot contact institutions to offer a block brought by another institution, they are cut off from the major source of demand for blocks and are reluctant to take large positions themselves in thinly traded stocks.

Block Houses This lack of capital, commitment, and contacts by specialists created a vacuum in block trading that resulted in the development of block houses. Block houses (also referred to as *upstairs traders* because they are away from the floor of the exchange) help institutions locate other institutions interested in buying or selling given stocks. They are brokerage firms (both members and nonmembers of exchanges) that stand ready to help buy or sell blocks for institutions. A good block house has (1) the capital required to position a large block, (2) the willingness to commit this capital to block transactions, and (3) contacts among institutions.

[33]For a discussion of trading on regional exchanges and the third market, see J. L. Hamilton, "Off-Board Trading of NYSE-Listed Stocks: The Effects of Deregulation and the National Market System," *Journal of Finance* 42, no. 5 (December 1987): 1331–1346.

Example of a Block Trade Assume a mutual fund owns 250,000 shares of Ford Motors and decides to sell 50,000 shares through Goldman Sachs & Company (GS&Co.), a large, active block house that is a lead underwriter for Ford and knows institutions interested in the stock. The trader for the mutual fund tells a block trader at Goldman Sachs that the fund wants to sell the 50,000 share block, and asks what GS&Co. can do about it. Traders at Goldman Sachs contact several institutions that own Ford to see if any of them want to add to their positions and to determine their bids. Assume that the previous sale of Ford on the NYSE was at $39\frac{3}{4}$ and GS&Co. receives commitments from four different institutions for a total of 40,000 shares at an average price of $39\frac{5}{8}$.

Goldman Sachs returns to the mutual fund and bids $39\frac{1}{2}$ minus a negotiated commission for the total 50,000 shares. Assuming the fund accepts the bid, Goldman Sachs now owns the block and immediately sells 40,000 shares to the four institutions that made prior commitments. It also positions 10,000 shares, that is, it owns the 10,000 shares and must eventually sell them at the best price possible. Because GS&Co. is a member of the NYSE, the block will be processed ("crossed") on the exchange as one transaction of 50,000 shares at $39\frac{1}{2}$. The specialist on the NYSE might take some of the stock to fill limit orders on the book at prices between $39\frac{1}{2}$ and $39\frac{3}{4}$.

For working on this trade, GS&Co. receives a negotiated commission, but it has committed almost $400,000 to position the 10,000 shares. The major risk to GS&Co. is the possibility of a subsequent price change on the 10,000 shares. If it can sell the 10,000 shares for $39\frac{1}{2}$ or more, it will just about break even on the position and have the commission as income. If the price were to weaken, it might have to sell the stock at $39\frac{1}{4}$ and take a loss on it of about $2,500, offsetting the income from the commission.

This example indicates the importance of contacts to quickly find interested institutions, capital to position a portion of the block, and willingness to commit that capital to the block trade. Without all three, the transaction would not take place.

Tiered Trading Markets

The increase in trading by institutions has led to a distinction among stocks based upon their size. Specifically, when institutions build their portfolios they do not want to have too many different stock issues. Also, they do not want to own too high a percentage

of a firm's outstanding stock because they subsequently may want or need to sell the position quickly (i.e., they want liquidity). Institutions with large portfolios that want to limit both the number of issues and the percentage of a firm's outstanding stock in their portfolios must give strong preference to investments in large-capitalization firms. As a result, some contend that they tend to concentrate on about 700 stocks from the total universe of about 9,000 U.S. stocks.[34] It is suggested that this strong demand for issues of large firms will improve the secondary markets for these issues and reduce the liquidity for smaller firms.[35]

Institutions and Stock Price Volatility

Some observers have expected a strong positive relationship between institutional trading and stock price volatility, because institutions trade in large blocks and it is speculated that they tend to trade together. Empirical studies have tested these contentions, which are based on intuitive arguments or very ad hoc evidence. These studies, which have examined the relationship between trading by large financial institutions and stock price volatility, have never supported the folklore.[36] In a capital market where trading has come to be dominated by institutions, the best environment is one where all institutions are actively involved, since they provide liquidity for one another and for noninstitutional investors.

National Market System (NMS)

The final effect of institutional trading is the development of a National Market System (NMS). This development has been advocated by the financial institutions because they hope it will provide greater efficiency and competition, thereby reducing the cost of transactions for these institutions.

[34]Frank K. Reilly, "A Three-Tier Stock Market and Corporate Financing," *Financial Management* 4, no. 3 (Autumn 1975): 7–15.

[35]Frank K. Reilly and Eugene F. Drzycimski, "An Analysis of the Effects of a Multi-Tiered Stock Market," *Journal of Financial and Quantitative Analysis* 16, no. 4 (November 1981): 559–575.

[36]In this regard, see Frank K. Reilly and John M. Wachowicz, "How Institutional Trading Reduces Market Volatility," *Journal of Portfolio Management* 5, no. 2 (Winter 1979): 11–17; Neil Berkman, "Institutional Investors and the Stock Market," *New England Economic Review* (November–December 1977): 60–77; and Frank K. Reilly and David J. Wright, "Block Trades and Aggregate Stock Price Volatility," *Financial Analysts Journal* 40, no. 2 (March–April 1984): 54–60.

Table 4.8	*Consolidated Tape Volume (thousands of shares)*

1976	6,281,008	1981	13,679,194	1986	42,478,164
1977	6,153,173	1982	19,203,590	1987	55,472,855
1978	8,147,569	1983	25,362,458	1988	47,390,121
1979	9,254,044	1984	27,455,178	1989	49,794,547
1980	12,935,607	1985	32,988,595	1990	48,188,072

Source: *NYSE Fact Book* (New York: NYSE, 1990): 24.

Table 4.9	*Exchanges and Markets Involved in Consolidated Tape with Percentage of Trades during 1990*

	Percentage		Percentage
AMEX	0.00%	NASD	8.53%
Boston	3.77	NYSE	66.17
Cincinnati	0.63	Pacific	8.14
Instinet	0.03	Philadelphia	3.02
Midwest	9.71		

Source: *NYSE Fact Book* (New York: NYSE, 1991): 23.

Although there is no generally accepted definition of a national market, four major characteristics are typically expected:

1. Centralized reporting of all transactions
2. Centralized quotation system
3. Centralized limit-order book (CLOB)
4. Free and open competition among all qualified market-makers

Centralized Reporting Centralized reporting requires a composite tape to report all transactions in a stock regardless of where the transactions took place. As you watched the tape, you might see a trade in GM on the NYSE, another trade on the Midwest, and a third on the OTC. The intent is to report all completed trades on the tape to provide full information on all securities traded.

As of June 1975, the NYSE began operating a central tape that includes all NYSE stocks traded on other exchanges and on the OTC. The volume of shares reported on the consolidated tape has grown significantly, as shown in Table 4.8. The breakdown

among the seven exchanges and two OTC markets appears in Table 4.9. These data indicate that this aspect of a National Market System (NMS) has already been introduced for stocks listed on the NYSE and that the volume of trading is becoming more dispersed among the exchanges and the NASD.[37]

Centralized Quotation System A centralized quotation system would list quotes for a given stock from all market-makers on the national exchanges, the regional exchanges, and the OTC. A broker who requested the market for IBM would see the prevailing quotes on the NYSE and any regional exchanges on which IBM is listed, along with those from several OTC market-makers. The broker could complete the trade on the market with the best quote for the client.

Intermarket Trading System A centralized quotation system is currently available—the Intermarket Trading System (ITS), developed by the American, Boston, Midwest, New York, Pacific, and Philadelphia Stock Exchanges and the NASD. ITS consists of a central computer facility with interconnected terminals in the participating market centers. As shown in Table 4.10, the number of issues included, the volume of trading and the sizes of trades have all grown substantially. Of the 2,082 issues included on the system in 1989, 1,633 were listed on the NYSE and 449 were listed on the AMEX.

Brokers and market-makers in each market center can indicate specific buying and selling commitments through a composite quotation display showing the current quotes for each eligible stock in all participating market centers. These current quotes can guide a

---

[37]For a discussion of these changes, see Craig Turres and William Power, "Big Board Is Losing Some of Its Influence over Stock Trading," *The Wall Street Journal*, April 17, 1990: A1, A6.

| Table 4.10 | Intermarket Trading System Activity |

		Daily Average		
Year	Issues Eligible	Share Volume	Executed Trades	Average Size of Trades
1978 (April)	300	235,000	377	623
1979	687	827,600	1,402	590
1980	884	1,565,900	2,868	546
1981	947	2,144,700	3,659	586
1982	1,039	3,264,100	4,697	695
1983	1,120	4,104,000	5,645	727
1984	1,160	4,692,200	5,404	868
1985	1,288	5,669,400	5,867	966
1986	1,278	7,222,100	7,712	987
1987	1,537	8,608,559	8,573	1,004
1988	1,816	7,625,926	7,069	1,079
1989	2,082	9,168,867	8,065	1,137
1990	2,126	9,397,114	8,744	1,075

Source: *NYSE Fact Book* (New York: NYSE, 1991): 24.

broker or market-maker in any market center to the best market to execute a customer's orders. The broker sends a message to the chosen market center, committing to buy or sell at the price quoted. When this commitment is accepted, a message reports that the transaction has taken place. The following example illustrates how ITS works.

A broker on the NYSE has a market order to sell 100 shares of IBM stock. The quotation display on the floor of the NYSE shows that the best current bid for IBM has been entered on the Pacific Stock Exchange (PSE), and the broker decides to take advantage of that bid by entering a firm commitment on the NYSE terminal to sell 100 shares at the bid on the PSE. Within seconds, the commitment flashes on the CRT screen and is also printed out at the PSE specialist's post, where it is executed against the PSE bid. After the commitment is accepted, a short message reports an execution back to New York, and the trade is reported on the consolidated tape. Brokers on both sides of the transaction receive immediate confirmation, and a journal of all transactions is transmitted to the appropriate market centers at the end of each day. Thereafter, each broker completes his own clearance and settlement procedure.

The ITS system currently provides centralized quotations for stocks listed on the NYSE. On the NYSE screen, it specifies whether a bid or ask away from the NYSE market is superior to that on the New York market. Note, however, that the system lacks several characteristics. It does not have the capability for automatic execution at the best market. Instead you must contact the market-maker and indicate that you want to buy or sell. When a NYSE broker tries to "hit" another market, the bid or ask may be withdrawn. Also, it is not mandatory that a broker go to the best market. Although the best price may be available at another market center, a broker might consider it inconvenient to transact on that exchange if the price difference is not substantial. It is almost impossible to audit such actions. Still, even with these shortcomings, technical and operational progress on a central quotation system has been substantial.

Central Limit-Order Book (CLOB) Substantial controversy has surrounded the idea of a central limit-order book (CLOB) that would contain all limit orders from all exchanges. Ideally, the CLOB would be visible to everyone, and all market-makers and traders could fill orders on it. Currently most limit orders are placed with specialists on the NYSE and filled when a transaction on the NYSE reaches the stipulated price. The NYSE specialist receives some part of the commission for rendering this service. The NYSE has opposed a CLOB because its specialists do not want to share this very lucrative business. While the technology for a CLOB is available, it is difficult to estimate when it will become a reality.

Competition among Market-Makers (Rule 390)
Market-makers have always competed on the OTC market, but competition has been opposed by the NYSE. The argument in favor of competition among market-makers is that it forces dealers to offer better bids and asks, or they will not do any business. The fact is, several studies have indicated that competition among numerous dealers (as in the OTC market) squeezes the spread. In contrast, the NYSE argues that a central auction market forces all orders to the one central location where they are exposed to all interested participants.

To create a concentrated market, the NYSE's Rule 390 requires members to obtain the permission of the exchange before carrying out a transaction in a listed stock off the exchange. This rule is intended to draw all volume to the NYSE, so that the exchange can provide the most complete auction market. The exchange contends that Rule 390 is necessary to protect the auction market, arguing that its elimination would fragment the market, tempting members to trade off the exchange and to internalize many orders (i.e., to match orders from the holdings of their own customers, which would keep these orders from exposure to the full auction market). Hamilton contends that the adverse effects of fragmentation are more than offset by the benefits of competition.[38] Progress in achieving this final phase of the NMS has been slow because of strong opposition by members of the investment community and caution by the SEC.

New Trading Systems
As daily trading volume has gone from 5 or 10 million shares to over 180 million shares, it has become necessary to introduce new technology into the trading process. Currently, the NYSE is capable of handling

daily volume of over 500 million shares as shown in October 1987. Discussions follow of some recent technological innovations that assist in the trading process.

Super Dot Super Dot is an electronic order-routing system through which a member firm transmits market and limit orders in NYSE-listed securities directly to the posts where the securities are traded or to the member firm's booth. After the order has been executed, a report of execution is returned directly to the member firm office over the same electronic circuit, and the execution is submitted directly to the comparison systems. Member firms can enter market orders up to 2,099 shares and limit orders in round or odd lots up to 30,099 shares. At the end of 1990, 182 member firms participated. An estimated 80 percent of all orders enter the NYSE through the Super Dot system.

Opening Automated Report Service (OARS) OARS, the opening feature of the Super Dot system, is designed to accept member firms' preopening market orders up to 30,099 shares and to provide rapid, systematic execution and immediate reporting. OARS automatically and continuously pairs buy and sell orders and presents the imbalance to the specialist prior to the opening of a stock. This helps the specialist determine the opening price. It is now operational for all issues.

Market Order Processing Super Dot's postopening market order system is designed to accept member firms' postopening market orders up to 2,099 shares. The system guarantees delivery of execution reports within 3 minutes. In fact, during 1990, 98.6 percent were reported within 2 minutes.

Individual Investor Express Delivery Service (IIEDS) This service provides priority delivery via the Super Dot system of simple round-lot and odd-lot market orders up to 2,099 shares for individual investor orders. The service is initiated on any day when the DJIA moves 50 points up or down from the previous day's close and it remains in effect for the rest of the trading day.

Limit Order System The limit order system electronically files orders to be executed when and if a specific price is reached. The system accepts limit orders up to 99,999 shares, appends turnaround numbers and delivers printed orders to the trading posts

[38]James L. Hamilton, "Marketplace Fragmentation, Competition, and the Efficiency of the Stock Exchange," *Journal of Finance* 34, no. 1 (March 1979): 171–187.

or the member firms' booths for storage. Good-until-canceled orders that are not executed on the day of submission are automatically stored until they are executed or canceled.

Electronic Book This system replaces the specialist's hand-written limit order book with electronically generated display screens. It facilitates the recording, execution, and researching of limit and market orders and helps eliminate processing errors. At the end of 1990, there were about 2,000 stocks on Electronic Books on the exchange floor.

Global Market Changes

London Stock Exchange As noted earlier, the London Stock Exchange initiated several major changes on October 27, 1986 (the Big Bang). Beyond the changes to the operations of brokers and jobbers discussed earlier, all commissions have become fully negotiable. In addition, the stock exchange was previously self-regulated. A law established a new body, the Securities and Investments Board (SIB), with powers delegated by the Secretary of State for trade and industry. The SIB is similar to the SEC in the United States. It can delegate its power to a self-regulated organization (SRO), which it has done for the exchange.

The gilt market has been restructured to resemble the U.S. government securities market. The Bank of England has approved a system whereby 27 primary dealers make markets in U.K. government securities and a limited number of interdealer brokers transact with the primary dealers. This new arrangement has created a much more competitive environment.

Trades are reported on a system called *Stock Exchange Automated Quotations (SEAQ) International*, which is an electronic market-price information system similar to NASDAQ that supports off-floor trading and provides price quotations to stock exchange members and institutional investors. In addition, real-time prices are being shared with the NYSE while the NASD provides certain U.S. OTC prices to the London market. Also, as discussed earlier, 35 U.S. OTC stocks are available for 24-hour trading between New York, Tokyo, Singapore, and London.

An important change increased access to membership on the exchange. Foreign firms are now being admitted as members, and member firms can be wholly owned by organizations outside the country.

As a result, some U.S. banks have acquired British stockbrokers, and several major U.S. firms are now members of the exchange.

Some Effects of the Big Bang Clearly an overriding effect has been increased competition at all levels, from the brokers on the floor to the LSE member firms and firms trading gilts. Probably one of the most visually striking changes occurred on the trading floor of the LSE. Prior to October 1986 the activity on the floor of the LSE was similar to that on the NYSE and the TSE — large numbers of people gathered around trading posts and moving between the phones and the posts. Currently, the exchange floor is completely deserted except for some traders in stock options. With the advent of competitive market-makers on the floor of the exchange, it became just as easy to conduct business away from the exchange using the SEAQ system; that is, to buy and sell listed stocks using competitive quotes on SEAQ.

The rest of the Big Bang's effects can be summarized by the phrase "more business, less profit." Specifically, there is more activity throughout the system, but profit margins are much smaller or nonexistent due to the intense competition. In the process, many firms have merged or been acquired by new firms from the United States, Japan, or Germany.[39]

Tokyo Stock Exchange (TSE) Thus far, changes on the TSE have been minimal, because the exchange has resisted competitive pressures through regulation. Trading commissions are still based upon fixed-scale rates that vary by the type and value of the transactions, although the idea of competitive commission rates is being discussed.

As of early 1991, only 25 foreign firms were members of the TSE. Probably the biggest change is the impact of Japanese firms on the rest of the global market. Four Japanese investment firms dominate the Japanese financial market: Nomura, Daiwa, Nikko, and Yamaichi. These firms' equity bases and market values exceed those of most U.S. firms and all firms from other countries. They have become major players in both London and the United States, resulting in increased competition and lower commission rates, es-

[39]Craig Forman, "Britain's Deregulation Leaves a Casualty Trail in Securities Industry," *The Wall Street Journal*, October 14, 1987: 1, 18.

pecially for fixed-income securities, but also for equities.[40]

Paris Bourse As an indication of the awareness of changes taking place, in January 1988 the relatively small Paris Bourse initiated changes similar to the Big Bang in London. Specifically, the monopoly on stock trading held by the big brokerage houses was opened up gradually to French and foreign banks. Also some of these investment firms are expected to merge with banks to acquire the capital needed to trade in a world market. The exchange also began moving to a continuous auction market rather than a 2-hour-a-day call market.[41]

Future Developments

Besides the specific factors discussed (the NMS, a global capital market, etc.), some overall changes are expected in capital markets. Once aware of potential changes, you can concentrate on understanding why they are happening and contemplate their effects.

While more individuals have come to own stocks and bonds, they have increasingly acquired this ownership through mutual funds because most individuals feel that it is too difficult and time-consuming to do their own analysis. This increase in fund sales has caused a proliferation of new funds that provide numerous opportunities to diversify. This includes global stock and bond funds, international funds limited to specific countries (e.g., Korea, Spain, Germany), sector funds that are limited to an industry or economic segment, and alternative fixed-income funds (focusing on government, municipal, and corporate securities).

As an example, Fidelity Management has over 25 common stock funds in sectors ranging from aircraft to bioengineering to telephones to utilities. This trend toward specialized funds will continue, and could expand to include other investment alternatives such as stamps, coins, and art. Because of the lower liquidity of some of the assets involved (foreign securities, stamps, coins, and art), many of these new mutual funds have been and will be closed-end. That is, they trade on exchanges. These funds and their surge in popularity in recent years are discussed extensively in Chapter 19.

Further, a major change is likely in the makeup and type of firms in the financial services industry. Prior to 1960, the securities industry was composed of specialty firms that concentrated on one segment of investments such as stocks, bonds, commodities, real estate, or insurance. A major trend is the ascendancy of financial supermarkets that consider all of these investment alternatives around the world. Prime examples would be Sears Financial Corporation and Merrill Lynch, which have acquired insurance and real estate subsidiaries and would like to move into banking, if allowed. At the other end of the spectrum, large banks such as Citicorp want to become involved in investment banking and all phases of the investment business.

In contrast to supermarkets, some firms will decide not to be all things to all people and will go the specialty, or "boutique" route attempting to provide unique, superior financial products. Examples would include discount brokers or special research firms (e.g., firms that concentrate their research efforts on single industries such as banking, or on one type of investment).

Beyond these changes related to the individual firms, the advances in technology continue to accelerate and promise to affect how the secondary market will be organized and operate. Specifically, computerized trading has made tremendous inroads during the last 3 years and promises to force numerous additional changes during the 1990s in markets around the world. The 24-hour market will require extensive computerized trading.[42]

---

[40]For a further discussion of the impact of the Japanese on the world capital market, see "Japan on Wall Street," *Business Week*, September 7, 1987: 82–90; and "The Evolution of the Tokyo Capital Market and Nomura Securities," a sponsored section in *Institutional Investor* 22, no. 4 (April 1988): 157–168. For an analysis of the rise and fall of this market during 1989 to 1990, see "The Tokyo Stock Market," *Business Week*, February 12, 1990: 74–79; and John J. Curran, "Japan Tries to Cool Money Mania," *Fortune*, January 28, 1991: 66–73.

[41]Fiona Gleizes, "Paris Bourse Begins Its Own 'Big Bang' in Effort to Rival London's Exchange," *The Wall Street Journal*, January 4, 1988: 15; "Plugging into a Pan-European Stockmarket," *The Economist*, March 10, 1990: 83–84.

---

[42]See Michael W. Miller and Matthew Winkler, "Computerized Trading Starts to Make Inroads at Financial Exchanges," *The Wall Street Journal*, April 24, 1989: A1, A5; Saul Hansell, "The Wild, Wired World of Electronic Exchanges," *Institutional Investor* 23, no. 10 (September 1989): 91–98, 101, 102, 107, 111, 114, 115; "Automating Financial Markets," *The Economist*, March 10, 1990: 19–21; Chris Welles, "The Future of Wall Street," *Business Week*, November 5, 1990: 119–124; and David Ziggs and Gary Weiss, "A Trading Floor on Every Screen," *Business Week*, November 5, 1990: 128–130.

Summary

■ The securities market is divided into primary and secondary markets.

Secondary markets provide the liquidity that is critical for primary markets.

The major segments of the secondary markets include listed exchanges (the NYSE, AMEX, TSE, LSE, and regional exchanges), the over-the-counter market, the third market, and the fourth market. Because you will want to invest across these secondary markets within a country as well as among countries, you need to understand how they differ and how they are similar.

■ Many of the dramatic changes in our securities markets since 1965 have been due to an increase in institutional trading, and to rapidly evolving global markets. This discussion is important because numerous changes have occurred and many more changes are yet to come. You need to understand how these changes will affect your investment alternatives and opportunities. You should look for the best investment, but also the best market to use for the transaction. This discussion should provide the background to help you make that trading decision.

Questions

1. Define *market*, and briefly discuss the characteristics of a good market.
2. You own 100 shares of General Electric stock, and you want to sell it because you need the money to make a down payment on a stereo. Assume there is absolutely no secondary market system in common stocks. How would you go about selling the stock? Discuss what you would have to do to find a buyer, how long it might take, and the price you might receive.
3. Define *liquidity* and discuss the factors that contribute to it. Give examples of a liquid asset and an illiquid asset, and discuss why they are considered liquid and illiquid.
4. Define the primary and secondary markets for securities and discuss how they differ. How is the primary market dependent on the secondary market?
5. Give an example of an initial public offering (IPO) in the primary market. Give an example of a seasoned equity issue in the primary market. Discuss which would involve greater risk to the buyer.
6. Find an advertisement for a recent primary offering in *The Wall Street Journal*. Based upon the information in the ad, indicate the characteristics of the security sold and the major underwriters. How much new capital did the firm derive from the offering before paying commissions?
7. Briefly explain the difference between a competitive bid underwriting and a negotiated underwriting.
8. a. How do the two U.S. national stock exchanges differ?
   b. Briefly describe how the TSE differs from the NYSE in size and operation.
9. The figures in Table 4.3 reveal a major difference in the price for a seat on the NYSE compared to one on the AMEX. How would you explain this difference?
10. What are the major reasons for the existence of regional stock exchanges? How do they differ from the national exchanges?
11. How does the OTC market differ from the listed exchanges?
12. Which segment of the secondary market (listed or OTC) is larger in terms of the number of issues? In terms of the value of the issues traded? Discuss which has more diversity in terms of the sizes of the companies and the quality of the issues.
13. What is the NASDAQ system? Discuss the three levels of NASDAQ in terms of what each provides and who would subscribe to each.
14. a. Define the third market. Give an example of a third market stock.
    b. Define the fourth market. Discuss why a financial institution would use the fourth market.
15. Briefly define each of the following terms and give an example:
    a. Market order
    b. Limit order
    c. Short sale
    d. Stop loss order
16. Briefly discuss the two major functions of specialists and two sources of their income.
17. What is the high-risk segment of the specialists' dealer function? Why is it high-risk? What aspect of the specialist position reduces the risk involved and also increases potential return? Be specific.
18. Describe the duties of the *Saitori* member on the TSE and discuss how these duties differ from those of the NYSE specialist.

19. Discuss the overall reason why the secondary equity market has experienced major changes since 1965.
20. Discuss the empirical evidence for growth in institutional trading.
21. What were give-ups? Why did they exist under fixed commissions?
22. What is meant by the term *negotiated commissions*? When was May Day? When was the Big Bang?
23. The discussion of block trades and the specialist noted that the specialist is hampered by the three Cs. Discuss each of the three Cs as it relates to block trading.
24. Describe block houses, and explain why they evolved. Describe what is meant by *positioning* part of a block.
25. Define a tiered trading market. Discuss why size is important to an institutional portfolio manager.
26. a. Describe the major attributes of the National Market System (NMS).
    b. Briefly describe the ITS and what it contributes to NMS. Discuss the growth of the ITS.
    c. What is the CLOB and why does the NYSE object to it?

Problems

1. In the section of *The Wall Street Journal* on government bonds with the title "Treasury Bonds, Notes and Bills," what are the current bid and yield figures on the $8\frac{1}{2}$ of 1997?
2. The initial margin requirement is 60 percent. You have $40,000 to invest in a stock selling for $80 a share. Ignoring taxes and commissions, show in detail the impact on your rate of return if the stock rises to $100 a share and also if it declines to $40 a share assuming: (a) you pay cash for the stock, and (b) you buy it using maximum leverage.
3. Shawn has a margin account and deposits $50,000. Assuming that the prevailing margin requirement is 40 percent, commissions are ignored, and The Gentry Shoe Corporation is selling at $33 per share:
   a. How many shares can Shawn purchase using the maximum allowable margin?
   b. What is Shawn's profit (loss) if Gentry's price:
      1. Rises to $45?
      2. Falls to $25?
   c. If the maintenance margin is 30 percent, to what price can Gentry Shoe fall before Shawn will receive a margin call?

4. Suppose you buy a round lot of Maginn Industries stock on 55 percent margin when it is selling at $20 a share. The broker charges a 10 percent annual interest rate, and commissions are 3 percent of the total stock value on both the purchase and sale. If at year-end you receive a $0.50 per share dividend and sell the stock for $27\frac{5}{8}$, what is your rate of return on the investment?
5. You decide to sell 100 shares of Charlotte Horse Farms short when it is selling at its yearly high of $56\frac{1}{4}$. Your broker tells you that your margin requirement is 45 percent and that the commission on the purchase is $155. While you are short, Charlotte pays a $2.50 per share dividend. At the end of 1 year you buy 100 shares of Charlotte at $46\frac{3}{8}$ to close out your position and are charged a commission of $145 and 8 percent interest on the money borrowed. What is your rate of return on the investment?

References

Amex Fact Book. New York: AMEX, published annually.

Beidleman, Carl, ed. *The Handbook of International Investing*. Chicago: Probus Publishing, 1987.

deCaires, Bryan, ed. *The GT Guide to World Equity Markets, 1987*. London: Euromoney Publications, 1987.

Elton, Edwin J., and Martin J. Gruben. *Japanese Capital Markets*. New York: Harper & Row, 1990.

Fabozzi, Frank J., and Frank G. Zarb, eds. *Handbook of Financial Markets*, 2d ed. Homewood, Ill.: Dow Jones-Irwin, 1986.

Garbade, Kenneth D. *Securities Markets*. New York: McGraw-Hill, 1982.

Grabbe, J. Orlin. *International Financial Markets*. New York: Elsevier, 1986.

Jensen, Michael C., and Clifford W. Smith, eds. "Symposium on Investment Banking and the Capital Acquisition Process." *Journal of Financial Economics* 15, no. 1/2 (January/February 1986).

Loll, Leo M., and Julian G. Buckley. *The Over-the-Counter Securities Markets*, 4th ed. Englewood Cliffs, N.J.: Prentice-Hall, 1981.

Lorie, James H., Peter Dodd, and Mary Hamilton Kimpton. *The Stock Market: Theories and Evidence*, 2d ed. Homewood, Ill.: Richard D. Irwin, 1985.

NASDAQ Fact Book. Washington, D.C.: National Association of Securities Dealers, published annually.

Nikko Research Center, Ltd. *The New Tide of the Japanese Securities Market*. Tokyo: Nikko Research Center, 1988.

NYSE Fact Book. New York: NYSE, published annually.

Schwartz, Robert A. *Equity Markets: Structure, Trading, and Performance.* New York: Harper & Row, 1988.

Smyth, David. *Wordly Wise Investor.* New York: Franklin Watts, 1988.

Sobel, Robert. *N.Y.S.E.: A History of the New York Stock Exchange, 1935–1975.* New York: Weybright and Talley, 1975.

Sobel, Robert. *The Curbstone Brokers: The Origins of the American Stock Exchange.* New York: Macmillan, 1970.

Solnik, Bruno. *International Investments,* 2d ed. Reading, Mass.: Addison-Wesley, 1991.

Spicer and Oppenheim Guide to Securities Markets around the World. New York: John Wiley & Sons, 1988.

Tokyo Stock Exchange Fact Book. Tokyo: TSE, published annually.

Viner, Aron. *Inside Japanese Financial Markets.* Homewood, Ill.: Dow Jones-Irwin, 1988.

APPENDIX 4a   *Characteristics of Stock Exchanges around the World*

(During or End of 1988)

Stock Exchange			Tokyo	New York	Toronto	U.K.	Frankfurt	Paris
Number of stock—listed		[Domestic]	1,571	1,604	1,147	1,993	238	459
Companies		[Foreign]	112	77	67	587	219	217
	[Stocks]	[Domestic]	1,576	2,152	1,584	1,989	422	507
		[Foreign]	112	82	72	732	349	247
Number of listed	[Bonds]	[Domestic]	1,197	2,893	—	2,491	5,825	2,406
Issues		[Foreign]	174	213	—	1,933	958	61
Total market value		[Stocks]	3,789,035	2,366,106	241,469	711,527	221,629	222,893
(Dollars in millions)		[Bonds]	1,135,812	1,561,031	1,136	558,390	N.A.	364,980
Trading value		[Stocks]	2,234,233	1,356,050	55,402	361,820	70,682	69,243
(Dollars in millions)		[Bonds]	699,696	7,702	—	526,431	273,882	574,533
Number of member firms			114	555	78	389	122	45

Stock Exchange	Zurich	Amsterdam	Milan	Australia	Hong Kong	Singapore	Taiwan	Korea
Number of stock—listed	161	232	211	1,393	282	132	163	502
Companies	219	228	—	36	22	194	—	—
	309	209	317	2,073	291	136	171	970
	226	266	—	48	24	196	—	—
Number of listed	1,504	1,147	1,277	1,819	8	114	218	5,809
Issues	840	164	20	—	1		—	—
Total market value	140,359	103,644	135,417	182,755	74,407	53,573	120,102	94,348
(Dollars in millions)	144,614	131,410	414,459	45,048	520	93,032	20,045	49,233
Trading value	389,452	30,636	31,705	38,172	23,635	6,325	275,491	79,457
(Dollars in millions)		52,171	16,796	16,540	56	251	35	11,682
Number of member firms	29	106	125	111	740	25	120	25

Source: *Tokyo Stock Exchange Fact Book* (Tokyo: TSE, 1990), p. 84.

C H A P T E R

5

Security Market Indicator Series

It is fair to say that many people talk about security-market indicator series, including those outside the United States, but few people understand them. Even investors familiar with widely publicized stock market series such as the Dow Jones Industrial Average (DJIA) usually know very little about indicator series for the U.S. bond market or for non-U.S. stock markets such as Tokyo or London.

Although portfolios are composed of individual stocks, investors typically ask, "What happened to the market today?" The reason for this question is that if an investor owns more than a few stocks or bonds, it is cumbersome to follow each individually in order to determine the composite performance of the portfolio. Also it seems intuitive that individual stocks or bonds move with the aggregate market. Therefore, if the overall market rose, an individual portfolio probably also increased in value. To supply investors with a composite report on market performance, financial publications and investment firms have developed stock-market and bond-market indexes.[1]

The initial section of this chapter discusses several ways in which investors use market indicator series. These significant functions provide an incentive for becoming familiar with these series and this is why we present a full chapter on the topic. The second section considers what characteristics cause indexes to differ. In this chapter we will discuss over 20 market indicator series and each of them is different. You should understand how they differ and why one may be

---

[1]Throughout this chapter and the book, we will use the terms *indicator series* and *index* interchangeably, although *indicator series* is more correct, since it refers to a broad class of series. One popular type of indicator series is an index, but other types and many different indexes exist.

preferable for a given task because of its characteristics.

The third section presents the most well-known stock market series, grouped by weighting schemes. The fourth section considers the relatively new topic of bond market indicator series, including series for international bond markets. The topic is relatively new, not because the bond market is new, but because the creation and maintenance of bond indexes that provide information about rates of return over time is new.

In the fifth section we consider global stock indexes and indicator series that combine the stock market and the bond market. Our final section examines how these indexes relate to each other over time. This comparison demonstrates the important factors that cause series to have high or low correlations. With this background you should be able to make an intelligent choice of the series that best suits your needs.

> **Indicator series** A statistical measure of the performance of an entire market based on a sample of securities.

Uses of Market Indicator Series

There are at least four specific uses for security-market **indicator series.** An investor can examine total returns for an aggregate market or some component of a market over a specified time period, then use these derived returns as a benchmark to judge the performance of individual portfolios. This assumes that any investor should be able to derive a rate of return comparable to the market return by randomly selecting a large number of stocks or bonds from the total market. Hence, a superior portfolio manager should consistently do better than the market. Therefore, an indicator series for the aggregate stock or bond markets can support judgments about the performance of professional money managers. However, you should compare the risk for the portfolios being judged to that of the market index, as well.

Indicator series also help investors develop index portfolios. A number of academic studies have demonstrated that few money managers consistently outperform a market indicator series on a risk-adjusted basis over time. Given these findings, an obvious alternative is to invest in a portfolio that emulates this market portfolio. This notion led to the creation of index funds, which are portfolios designed to track the performance of specified market indexes over time.[2] While the concept began with common stocks, the development of comprehensive bond-market indexes and submarket performance by most bond portfolio managers has led to a similar phenomenon in fixed-income securities.[3]

Securities analysts, portfolio managers, and others use security-market indexes as proxies for the stock or bond markets when they attempt to examine the factors that influence aggregate price movements. A related use is to analyze the relationships among stock and bond returns of different countries such as those between U.S., Japanese, and German stock price movements.

Another group interested in an aggregate market series, technicians, believe past price changes can predict future price movements. Therefore, their market analysis involves the analysis of past movements of a market indicator series.

Finally, research in portfolio theory has implied that a relevant measure of risk for an individual risky asset is its systematic risk, which is the relationship between the rate of return for the security and the rate of return for a market portfolio of risky assets.[4] Therefore, to compute the systematic risk for an individual security, you must relate its returns to those for an aggregate market index that serves as a proxy for the market portfolio of risky assets.

How Do Market Indexes Differ?

Indicator series are intended to reflect the overall price or return movements of a group of securities.

---

[2]For a discussion of new developments in indexing, see "New Ways to Play the Indexing Game," *Institutional Investor* 22, no. 13 (November 1988): 92–98.

[3]See Fran Hawthorne, "The Battle of the Bond Indexes," *Institutional Investor* 20, no. 4 (April 1986); and Tom Herman, "Matching the Bond Market, Not Beating It," *The Wall Street Journal*, July 26, 1989: C1.

[4]This concept and its justification are discussed in Chapter 21.

Therefore, you should consider differences in how the indexes determine those movements. This section discusses the factors that cause the differences.

Sample

The size, breadth, and source of the sample used to construct a series are all important. A small percentage of the total population can provide valid indications of the behavior of the total population if the sample is properly selected. In fact, at some point the additional costs of taking a larger sample will almost certainly outweigh any benefits of increased size.

The sample should be representative of the total population, of course, or its size will be meaningless; a large, biased sample is no better than a small, biased sample. The sample can be generated by completely random selection or by a nonrandom selection technique designed to incorporate desired characteristics. Finally, the source of the sample becomes important if there are any differences between segments of the population.

Weighting

Our second concern is with the weight given to each member in the sample. Three principal weighting schemes are used: (1) price-weighted series, (2) value-weighted series, and (3) unweighted, or equally weighted, series.

Computational Procedure

Our final consideration is with the computational procedure. One alternative is to take a simple arithmetic average of the various securities in the series. Another is to compute an index and report all changes, whether of price or value, in terms of the basic index. Finally, some prefer a geometric average of the components rather than an arithmetic average.

Stock-Market Indicator Series

As we mentioned in the introduction to this chapter, we hear a lot about what happened to the Dow Jones Industrial Average (DJIA) each day. Depending upon the source, you might also hear about other stock indexes like the NYSE Composite, the S&P 500 index, the AMEX index, or even the Nikkei average. If you listen carefully you will realize that all of these indexes do not change by the same amount. Some of the

> **Price-weighted series** An indicator series calculated as an arithmetic average of the current prices of the sampled securities.

differences are obvious such as the DJIA versus the Nikkei average, but others are not. The purpose of this section is to briefly review each of the major series and point out how they differ in terms of the characteristics discussed in the prior section. As a result, you should come to understand that index movements over time *should* differ and why they differ.

The discussion of the indexes is organized by the weighting of their samples of stocks. We begin with the price-weighted series because some of the most popular indexes are in this category. Next, we cover the value-weighted series, since this technique has been used for most recently developed indexes. Finally, we will examine the unweighted series.

Price-Weighted Series

A **price-weighted** series is an arithmetic average of current prices. Movements of the series reflect changes in the prices of the securities sampled.

Dow Jones Industrial Average The best-known price series is also the oldest, and certainly the most popular, stock market indicator series, the Dow Jones Industrial Average (DJIA). The DJIA is a price-weighted average of 30 large, well-known NYSE industrial stocks that are generally the leaders in their industries. Such issues are called *blue chips*. The DJIA is derived by totaling the current prices of the 30 stocks and dividing the sum by a divisor adjusted to take account of stock splits and changes in the sample over time.[5] The adjustment of the divisor is demonstrated in Table 5.1.

$$DJIA_t = \frac{\sum_{i=1}^{30} P_{it}}{D_{adj}}$$

where:

$DJIA_t$ = the value of the DJIA on day t

P_{it} = the closing price of stock i on day t

D_{adj} = the adjusted divisor on day t

---

[5] A complete list of all events that have caused changes in the divisor since the DJIA went to 30 stocks on October 1, 1928, is contained in Phyllis S. Pierce, ed., *The Dow Jones Investor's Handbook* (Homewood, Ill.: Dow Jones-Irwin, annual).

Table 5.1	Change in DJIA Divisor When a Stock in the Sample Splits

	Prices before the Stock Split	Prices after a Three-for-One Split by Stock A
A	$30	$10
B	20	20
C	10	10
	$60 ÷ 3 = 20	$40 ÷ D_{adj} = 20
		D_{adj} = 2 (New divisor)

Table 5.2	Impact of Differently Priced Shares on a Price-Weighted Indicator Series

	Period T	Period T + 1	
		Case A	Case B
A	$100	$110	$100
B	50	50	50
C	30	30	33
Sum	$180	$190	$183
Divisor	3	3	3
Average	60.0	63.3	61.0
Percentage change	—	5.5	1.7

Table 5.1 employs three stocks to demonstrate the procedure to derive a new divisor for the DJIA when a stock splits. Basically, when stocks split, the divisor becomes smaller. To get an idea of the cumulative effect of splits, consider that the initial divisor was 30.0, and as of January 1991 it was 0.559. Splits make the divisor smaller and the sizes of the point changes in the DJIA larger. If the divisor were 1.00, the DJIA would be the sum of the prices of the 30 stocks; when it is 0.50 it is approximately two times the sum of the prices, which means that a 60 point change is only an average of $1.00 per stock.

The new divisor ensures that the split doesn't affect the value for the series. In the table, the pre-split index value was 20. After the split, with its effect on the new sum of prices, the divisor is adjusted downward to maintain this value of 20. The divisor is also changed if the sample makeup of the series changes, which does not happen very often.

Because the DJIA is price weighted, a high-priced stock carries more weight than a low-priced stock. As shown in Table 5.2, a 10 percent change in a $100 stock ($10) will cause a larger change in the series than a 10 percent change in a $30 stock ($3). In Case A, a 10 percent increase in the $100 stock causes a 5.5 percent increase in the average; in Case B, a 10 percent increase in the $30 stock raises the average by only 1.7 percent.

The DJIA has been criticized on several counts. First, its sample is limited. It is difficult to conceive that 30 nonrandomly selected blue-chip stocks can represent the 1,800 stocks listed on the NYSE. Beyond the limited number, the stocks included are, by definition, offerings of the largest and most prestigious companies in various industries. Therefore, crit-

ics contend that the DJIA probably reflects price movements for large, mature firms rather than for the typical company listed on the NYSE. Several studies have pointed out that price movements of the DJIA have been less volatile than those for other market indexes. Also, the long-run returns on the DJIA are not comparable to the other NYSE stock indexes.

In addition, when a company has a stock split, its price declines. Because the DJIA is price weighted, the company's weight in the DJIA is reduced, though its size and importance remain unchanged. Therefore, the weighting scheme causes a downward bias in the DJIA, because the stocks with higher growth rates have higher prices, and therefore they tend to split. Thus, they consistently lose weight within the index.[6] Despite the several criticisms of the DJIA, a fairly close relationship holds between its daily percentage price changes and comparable price changes for other NYSE indexes as we will discuss further in a subsequent section of this chapter.

Dow Jones also publishes an average of 20 stocks in the transportation industry and 15 utility stocks. Detailed reports of these averages appear in *The Wall Street Journal* and *Barron's*, including hourly figures.

---

[6]For discussions of these problems, see H. L. Butler, Jr. and J. D. Allen, "The Dow Jones Industrial Average Re-examined," *Financial Analysts Journal* 35, no. 6 (November–December 1979): 37–45; and E. E. Carter and K. J. Cohen, "Stock Averages, Stock Splits, and Bias," *Financial Analysts Journal* 23, no. 3 (May–June 1967): 77–81.

Nikkei–Dow Jones Average   Also referred to as the *Nikkei Stock Average Index*, the Nikkei–Dow Jones Average is an arithmetic average of prices for 225 stocks on the First Section of the Tokyo Stock Exchange (TSE). This is the most well-known series in Japan since it has shown stock price trends since the reopening of the TSE. It was formulated by Dow Jones and Company, and, like the DJIA, it is a price-weighted series. It is also criticized because its 225-stock sample includes only about 15 percent of all stocks on the First Section. The results for this index are reported daily in *The Wall Street Journal* and the *Financial Times* and weekly in *Barron's*.

Value-Weighted Series

A **value-weighted series** is based on the initial total market value of all stocks in the sample (Market value = Number of shares outstanding × Current market price.) This initial total market value is typically established as the base value and assigned an index value. The most popular beginning index value is 100, but it can be varied to other values like 10 or 50. Subsequently, a new aggregate market value is computed for all securities in the index and compared to the initial, base value. The percentage change is multiplied by the beginning index value.

$$\text{Index}_t = \frac{\Sigma P_t Q_t}{\Sigma P_b Q_b} \times \text{Beginning index value}$$

where:

Index_t	=	Index value on day t
P_t	=	ending prices for stocks on day t
Q_t	=	number of outstanding shares on day t
P_b	=	ending price for stocks on base day
Q_b	=	number of outstanding shares on base day

A simple example for a three-stock index is shown in Table 5.3. This value-weighted index adjusts automatically for stock splits and other capital changes because the decrease in the stock price is offset by an increase in the number of shares outstanding. As an example of this, note that Stock B split two for one. The price per share declined from $15 to $10, but the number of shares doubled, so the total value increased from $90 million to $120 million.

In a value-weighted index, the importance of individual stocks in the sample depends on their market values. Therefore, a specified percentage change in the value of a company with a large market value has a greater impact than the same change for a small company. For example, if we use the December 31, 1991 data in Table 5.3, we begin with a base value of $200 million. Then, in contrast to the changes set forth for December 31, 1992, we can assume that the only change is a 20 percent increase in the value of Stock A from its beginning value of $10 million. With this assumption the ending index value would be $202 million and would give an index of 101. In contrast, if we assume that the only change is that Stock C increased by 20 percent from $100 million, the ending index value would be $220 million which would cause an ending index of 110.

Value-weighted series   An indicator series calculated as the total market value of the securities in the sample.

Standard & Poor's Indexes   The first company to employ a market value index widely was Standard & Poor's Corporation (S&P). Using 1935 to 1937 as a base period, the firm computed separate indexes for 425 industrial stocks, 50 utilities, and 25 transportation firms, along with a 500-stock composite index. The base period was subsequently changed to 1941 to 1943 and the base value set at 10. The S&P series was again changed significantly on July 1, 1976 to cover 400 industrial issues, 40 utilities, 20 transportation issues, and 40 financial issues. A number of OTC stocks were added because, as we noted in Chapter 4, most major banks and insurance companies have been traded on the OTC market. Therefore, to construct a relevant financial index, S&P found it necessary to break the tradition of including only NYSE-listed stocks.[7] S&P has also constructed over 90 individual industry indexes.

Daily figures for the major S&P indexes are carried in *The Wall Street Journal*, the *Financial Times*, and other newspapers, and weekly data appear in *Barron's*. S&P's weekly publication, *The Outlook*, contains weekly values for all the industry groups. Extensive historical data on all these indexes and other financial series are contained in S&P's annual publication, *Trade and Securities Statistics*.

---

[7]For a detailed discussion of the computation and potential adjustment of all the S&P series, see *Trade and Securities Statistics* (New York: Standard & Poor's, annual).

Table 5.3 Computation of a Value-Weighted Index

Stock	Share Price	Number of Shares	Market Value
December 31, 1991			
A	$10	1,000,000	$ 10,000,000
B	15	6,000,000	90,000,000
C	20	5,000,000	100,000,000
Total base value set equal to index of 100			$200,000,000
December 31, 1992			
A	$12	1,000,000	$ 12,000,000
B	10	12,000,000[a]	120,000,000
C	20	5,500,000[b]	110,000,000
Total			$242,000,000

$$\text{New index value} = \frac{\text{Current market value}}{\text{Base value}} \times \text{Beginning index value}$$

$$= \frac{\$242,000,000}{\$200,000,000} \times 100$$

$$= 1.21 \times 100$$

$$= 121$$

[a]Stock split 2-for-1 during year.

[b]Company paid a 10 percent stock dividend during the year.

New York Stock Exchange Indexes In 1966 the NYSE derived five market value indexes (industrial, utility, transportation, financial, and a composite index of the other four) with figures available back to 1940. December 31, 1965 figures were set equal to an index of 50. In contrast to other indexes, the various NYSE series are not based upon a sample of stocks, but include all stocks listed on the exchange. Therefore, questions about the size or breadth of the sample do not arise as long as it is recognized that these indexes are limited to stocks listed on the NYSE. However, because the index is value-weighted, the stocks of large companies still control major movements in the index. As an example of this impact, as of the end of 1989, 1,720 companies were listed on the NYSE with a total market value of $3.03 trillion. Still, although the largest 50 stocks on the exchange constitute less than 3 percent of the stocks listed, they have

a total market value of $1.18 trillion, which is 39 percent of the total market value.[8]

NASDAQ Series A comprehensive set of price indicator series for the OTC market was developed by the National Association of Securities Dealers (NASD). These NASDAQ–OTC price indexes begin as of February 5, 1971 with an index value of 100. All domestic OTC common stocks listed on NASDAQ are included in the indexes, and new stocks are included when they are added to the system. The 3,967 issues contained in the NASDAQ–OTC Price Indexes

---

[8]For a listing of daily values for each year and a matrix of growth rates in the NYSE Index for the period 1972 to the present, see *NYSE Fact Book* (New York: NYSE, annual).

as of the end of 1990 have been divided into seven categories:[9]

1. Composite (3,967 issues)
2. Industrials (2,731 issues)
3. Banks (205 issues)
4. Insurance (120 issues)
5. Other finance (689 issues)
6. Transportation (65 issues)
7. Utilities (157 issues)

Because the indexes are value-weighted, they are heavily influenced by the largest 100 stocks on the NASDAQ system. Most of the NASDAQ series are reported daily in *The Wall Street Journal* and the *Financial Times* and weekly in *Barron's*. Further descriptive information about the index along with annual high, low, and close figures for all years since 1974 appear in the *NASDAQ Fact Book*, which is published annually by the NASD.

American Stock Exchange The AMEX developed a Price Change Index in 1966, but subsequently commissioned the creation of a value-weighted series referred to as the *Market Value Index*. This new series was released in September 1973 with a base level of 100 as of August 31, 1973 and figures available back to 1969. On July 5, 1983 the Market Value Index was adjusted to half of its previous level so now it has a base level of 50. The index includes common shares, ADRs, and warrants, but does not include rights, preferred stock, or when-issued stock. Daily figures for the index are available in *The Wall Street Journal*, weekly data are in *Barron's*, and monthly closing values from 1969 are published in the annual *AMEX Fact Book*.

Wilshire 5,000 Equity Index The Wilshire 5,000 Equity Index is a value-weighted index published by Wilshire Associates of Santa Monica, California. It derives the dollar value of 5,000 common stocks, including all NYSE and AMEX issues, plus the most active stocks on the OTC market. The specific weighting of about 82 percent NYSE, 4 percent AMEX, and 14 percent OTC gives the NYSE the greatest influence because of its higher market value.

The index was created in 1974 with month-end history computed back to December 1970. Beginning in December 1979, it was calculated daily. The base value for the Wilshire 5,000 is its December 31, 1980 capitalization of $1,404.596 billion. The index currently appears daily in *The Wall Street Journal* and several other major daily papers and has been published weekly in *Barron's* since January 1975.

Dow Jones Equity Market Index This index was introduced by *The Wall Street Journal* in October 1988 with a base of 100 as of June 30, 1982. This index is made up of a set of stock indexes that measure the daily performance of 700 stocks in 82 industry groups. In contrast to the DJIA, this index is value-weighted and includes stocks from the NYSE, the AMEX, and the OTC.

Russell Indexes These are three separate, but overlapping indexes: the Russell 3,000, the Russell 1,000, and the Russell 2,000. The Russell 3,000 consists of the 3,000 largest U.S. stocks by market capitalization and represents 97 percent of the U.S. equity market in terms of market value. The Russell 1,000 consists of the 1,000 largest U.S. stocks by capitalization. The smallest stock in this index has a market value of $350 million. The Russell 2,000 consists of the smallest 2,000 stocks in the Russell 3,000 index. The firms in the 2,000 series range in size from approximately $350 million to $30 million.

Some characterize the Russell indexes as pure because they include only U.S. stocks. The first is fairly comprehensive, with 3,000 stocks. The size difference between the 1,000 and 2,000 index allows for separate analysis of the institutional segment (using the Russell 1,000) and the smaller-firm segment (using the Russell 2,000). The smaller sector has become popular based upon efficient-market studies as discussed in Chapter 22. The Russell 2,000 is reported daily in *The Wall Street Journal*, and the three indexes are reported weekly in *Barron's*.

Financial Times Actuaries Share Indexes The *Financial Times* Actuaries Share Indexes cover stocks listed on the London Stock Exchange (LSE). They relate current market capitalization of each index to its market capitalization at the base date (April 10, 1962), adjusted for intervening capital changes. Recently LSE stocks broke down as follows:

[9]The NASDAQ Composite Index is composed of all NASDAQ/NMS issues (except warrants) and all other NASDAQ domestic common stocks.

> **Unweighted index** An indicator series affected equally by the performance of each security in the sample regardless of price or market value.

Capital goods	207	
Consumer group	186	
Others	93	
	486	Industrial Group Index
Oils	14	
	500	Share Index
	122	Financial Group Index
Others	78	
	700	All-Share Index

The sample is broken down into 34 subsections. This index is very broad, and therefore reflects the movements of the total London market. It is a value-weighted series that can be used to measure long-term market movements and helps evaluate portfolio performance. The All-Share Index and all of its components are reported daily in the *Financial Times*.

Tokyo Stock Exchange Price Index (TOPIX) This price index of the Tokyo Stock Exchange was devised in July 1969 to take account of various perceived defects in the TSE–Dow Jones Stock Price Average (the NIKKEI Average), namely, limited sample and price-weighting. TOPIX is a composite index of all common stocks listed on the First Section of the TSE, so it measures the changes in the aggregate market value of TSE common stocks. Its base of 100 is its market value at the close on January 4, 1968. Like the S&P indexes, its base market value is adjusted to reflect new listings, delistings, and mergers.

The composite index is supplemented by subgroup indexes for each of 28 industry groups and 3 size groups: large (over 200 million shares listed), medium (between 60 and 200 million shares listed), and small (less than 60 million shares listed). The index results are published daily in *The Wall Street Journal* and the *Financial Times*.

Unweighted Price Indicator Series

In an **unweighted index**, all stocks are equally weighted regardless of price or value. A $20 stock is as important as a $40 stock, and the total market value of the company is not important. Such an index is appropriate for an individual who randomly selects stocks for a portfolio. One way to visualize an equally weighted series is to assume that equal dollar amounts are invested in each stock in the portfolio (e.g., a $1,000 investment in each stock would work out to 50 shares of a $20 stock, 100 shares of a $10 stock, and 10 shares of a $100 stock).

University of Chicago Series The best known equally weighted stock-market series are those constructed by Lawrence Fisher while at the University of Chicago.[10] These series were used in studies conducted by Fisher and Lorie that examined the performance of NYSE stocks.[11] They have been used extensively in subsequent empirical studies.

Value Line Average The Value Line Composite Average is an index based upon an equally weighted geometric average of the percentage changes for approximately 1,700 issues with the June 30, 1961 value set at 100. The average consists of all stocks regularly reviewed in *The Value Line Investment Survey* broken down into the following major categories and 146 subgroups.

	Number of Stocks
Industrials	1,499
Utilities	177
Rails	19
Composite	1,695

More than 80 percent of the stocks that make up the Value Line Average are listed on the NYSE.

The average is computed as follows: Each market day, the closing price of each stock is divided by the preceding day's close. The resulting indexes of change are geometrically averaged for the 1,695 stocks. The geometric average of change for each day is then multiplied by the value of the average on the preceding day to get the latest value.

Table 5.4 gives an example of a computation involving three stocks. Note that there is no consideration of a stock's market value and the price level does

---

[10]Lawrence Fisher, "Some New Stock Market Indexes," *Journal of Business* 39, no. 1, Part II (January 1966 supplement): 191–225.

[11]This work is summarized in Lawrence Fisher and James H. Lorie, *A Half Century of Returns on Stocks and Bonds* (Chicago: Chicago Graduate School of Business, 1977).

	Share Price		Index of Change
Stock	T	T + 1	
X	10	12	1.20
Y	22	20	0.91
Z	44	47	1.07

Table 5.4 **Example of Computation of Value Line Index**

$$TT = 1.20 \times 0.91 \times 1.07$$
$$= 1.168$$
$$1.168^{1/3} = 1.0531$$

Index Value (T) × 1.0531 = Index value (T + 1)

not have an impact because you are dealing with percentage changes. Finally, it is a geometric average of the percentage changes rather than an arithmetic average.

When stock splits or dividends occur, the preceding day's value is adjusted accordingly, after which the index of change is computed. As stocks are added to The Value Line Investment Survey, the average is enlarged. Additions and deletions of stocks present no problem to the average because of its large base and method of construction. Daily figures for the Value Line (VL) composite average appear in *The Wall Street Journal*, and weekly data are in *Barron's*.

Indicator Digest Index All stocks on the NYSE are included in the Indicator Digest Index. Compared to value-weighted series that are heavily influenced by large firms, the series is intended to be more representative of all stocks on the exchange. This index has often reached a trough earlier than other indicator series and continued to be depressed after some more popular market indexes resumed rising during bull markets. Such a difference in performance would indicate that market increases were being heavily influenced by the large, popular stocks in the DJIA or the Standard & Poor's series.

Financial Times Ordinary Share Index Sometimes known as the *30-Share Index* because it includes 30 heavily traded, blue-chip stocks listed on the LSE, the

Financial Times Ordinary Share Index resembles the DJIA because it includes a limited number of blue-chip stocks, but it differs because it is an unweighted index. Like the Value Line indexes, it is a geometric average of the rates of return for the 30 stocks. The index has an unbroken history back to 1935 with a limited number of changes in the sample over time, in fact about half the constituents are unchanged from the beginning. The index includes oils and financial firms, so it is not only an industrial index.

The creators of the index recognize that geometric averages of the rates of return bias the series downward compared to other series (see the discussion in Chapter 1). Therefore, the series is sensitive to the short-term movements moods of the market, but it should not be used as a long-term measure of market returns to evaluate portfolio performance. The *Financial Times* All-Share Index described earlier is considered more appropriate for long-term portfolio performance analysis. Daily figures for this 30-share index appear in the *Financial Times* and *The Wall Street Journal*, with weekly data in *Barron's*.

Bond-Market Indicator Series[12]

While investors may not know a lot about the various stock-market indicator series, most know almost nothing about bond-market indexes because these series that track the performance of the bond market are relatively new and not widely published. Knowledge regarding these bond series is becoming more important because of the growth of bond mutual funds and the consequent need for a reliable set of benchmarks for performance evaluation.[13] Because few fixed-income money managers have been able to match the performance of the aggregate bond market, interest in bond index funds has grown, prompting the development of an index for these funds to emulate.[14]

[12]The discussion in this section draws heavily from Frank K. Reilly, G. Wenchi Kao, and David J. Wright, "An Analysis of Alternative Bond Market Indexes," (January 1991).

[13]For a discussion of the evaluation of bond portfolios, see Peter D. Dietz, Russell Fogler, and Anthony U. Rivers, "Duration, Nonlinearity, and Bond Portfolio Performance," *Journal of Portfolio Management* 7, no. 3 (Spring 1981); and Gifford Fong, Charles Pearson, and Oldrick Vasicek, "Bond Performance: Analyzing Sources of Return," *Journal of Portfolio Management* 9 no. 3 (Spring 1983).

[14]For a discussion of this phenomenon, see Hawthorne, "Battle of the Bond Indexes."

The creation and computation of a bond-market index is more difficult than a stock market series for several reasons. First, the universe of bonds is much broader than that of stocks, ranging from U.S. Treasury securities to bonds in default. Also, the universe of bonds changes constantly, because bond maturities change over time. Further, the volatility of bond prices is affected by duration, which likewise changes constantly because of changes in maturity, coupon, and market yield (see Chapter 10). Finally, significant problems complicate correct pricing of the individual bond issues used in an index.

Total Rate of Return Series

This section briefly describes the major bond indexes created during the past 10 years. They are similar in that all of them indicate total rates of return for portfolios of bonds including price changes, accrued interest, and coupon income reinvestments. Also almost all of them are value weighted using current prices and the par value of bonds that are publicly held.

Merrill Lynch Bond Indexes (ML) The Merrill Lynch Bond Indexes track more than 5,000 issues and consist of several corporate and U.S. government master indexes supplemented by more than 150 subindexes segmenting the market by coupon, quality, industry, and maturity. To qualify for inclusion in the Merrill Lynch sample of taxable bonds, securities must be nonconvertible, have maturities of at least 1 year, have minimum par values of $10 million, and be rated by Standard & Poor's or Moody's. Prices for U.S. Treasury and agency securities come directly from the Merrill Lynch Government Securities trading floor. Prices of corporate bonds are based upon a series of pricing matrices provided by the Merrill Lynch Bond Pricing Service.

The indexes provide a value-weighted average of total rates of return. The index values were set to 100 at their inception dates, which vary. The major government and corporate indexes began in 1976 and the High Yield Master began in 1984. The ML corporate indexes are reported daily in *The Wall Street Journal*.

Ryan Index The Ryan Index is a daily total return series derived by computing the equally weighted average of the daily returns of seven current Treasury auction issues with maturities of 2, 3, 4, 5, 7, 10, and 30 years. The index level is calculated each day by compounding the previous day's index by the current

day's total return. The sample is limited to Treasury auction issues because it is contended that all bonds are priced from the government yield curve so this set of bonds should reflect the prevailing risk–reward environment for the bond market.

Salomon Brothers (SB) Broad Investment-Grade Bond Indexes Salomon Brothers (SB) introduced its monthly value-weighted, total rate-of-return indexes in October 1985, with data available back to 1980. These investment-grade bond indexes include about 3,800 individually priced Treasury/agency, corporate, and mortgage securities with maturities of at least 1 year, and a minimum of $25 million outstanding. Every issue is priced on the bid side by the trader responsible for making a market in that security.

Shearson Lehman (SL) Indexes Over 4,000 issues are included in the Shearson Lehman (SL) indexes, with minimum outstanding principal of $25 million ($15 million for the mortgage index) and minimum maturities of 1 year. All total returns are market value-weighted. Most issues are priced by traders, with prices on small corporate issues set using a proprietary algorithm. The SL Treasury bond indexes are reported daily in *The Wall Street Journal*.

Merrill Lynch Convertible Securities Indexes This set of indexes for convertible securities has data beginning in January 1987. The convertible master index contains 550 to 600 issues in three major subgroups: U.S. domestic convertible bonds, Eurodollar convertible bonds issued by U.S. corporations, and U.S. domestic convertible preferred stocks. The issues included must be publicly held issues of U.S. corporations with minimum par values of $25 million and minimum maturities of 1 year.

Merrill Lynch International Bond Indexes Merrill Lynch has developed a set of indexes to measure the total return performances of the major Eurobond and foreign bond markets. Specifically, it publishes indexes for 11 Eurobond markets, a Eurobond Master Index, and indexes for three foreign bond markets, as shown in Table 5.5.

These indexes measure the total returns of these markets in both local currency and U.S. dollars monthly from December 1985. The Eurodollar Index is available since December 1982. These indexes in-

Table 5.5	*Merrill Lynch International Bond Performance Indexes*

	Number of Issues	Amount (local currency)	Amount (U.S. $)	Percentage of Master[a]	Maturity Date	Adjustment for Call	
						Duration	Yield
Eurobond master index	3,039	—	$334.8	100.0%	1993/07/26	4.1	7.3
Nondollar Eurobond master index	2,190	—	190.0	—	1994/02/21	4.3	6.8
Eurobond Indexes							
Eurodollar	849	144.8	144.8	43.8	1992/10/30	3.8	7.78
Euro-Canadian dollar	180	14.1	10.2	3.1	1992/11/04	4.0	9.65
Euroyen	131	4,355.9	27.5	8.1	1993/10/05	4.9	5.87
Eurosterling	118	7.2	10.7	3.1	1993/08/08	4.3	11.03
Eurodeutschemark	562	106.9	55.6	16.4	1993/04/03	4.2	6.01
Euro-Swiss franc	666	78.9	48.9	14.5	1996/10/05	4.5	4.92
Euro-French franc	45	24.4	3.8	1.1	1993/05/31	4.7	9.17
Euroguilder	78	9.9	4.6	1.3	1991/11/22	3.8	6.16
ECU	223	20.3	21.8	6.4	1993/01/07	4.1	8.32
Euro-Australian dollar	138	8.0	5.3	1.6	1990/09/26	2.8	13.89
Euro-New Zealand dollar	49	2.9	1.6	0.5	1989/10/26	2.3	15.56
			$334.8	100.0			
Foreign Bond Markets							
Samurai	41	5,169.5	32.7	—	1994/02/28	3.5	6.16
Bulldog	27	3.1	4.6	—	2009/12/21	8.2	11.93
Foreign guilder	85	16.5	7.6	—	1995/01/11	5.8	7.35
			44.9				

Note: The sum of the Eurobond indexes ($334.8 billion) uses end-of-month exchange rates, while the U.S. dollar amount of the Eurobond Master Index ($330.6 billion) uses beginning-of-month exchange rates.

[a]The shares of the Eurobond Master Index are the actual shares used to calculate the December Master Index values.

clude all straight bonds in each of the major Eurobond and foreign bond markets with the following criteria: minimum 1 year maturity; 10 million or more units of local currency outstanding; nonconvertible or without warrants. Securities that trade actively need not be rated.

From this universe, a sample is selected with the additional criteria that the issues be publicly traded and have ratings of BBB (Baa) or better, if they are rated. Although the returns are calculated based upon a sample, the weights are based upon the relative value of the entire market of bonds. This ensures that the index reflects the entire universe of bonds and not only bonds for which prices are available.

Salomon Brothers International Bond and Money Market Performance Indexes   These indexes measure the total return performance of high-quality securities in major international sectors of the bond and money markets. The indexes contain historical information dating back to January 1, 1978, at which point they were set equal to 100. For each of eight major countries, the series typically includes indexes for domestic government bonds, Eurocurrency bonds, and domestic money market securities in both local currency and U.S. dollars. It also includes value-weighted and unweighted composite world bond indexes and money market indexes. These indexes are reported monthly in *Global Investor*.

J. P. Morgan Government Bond Indexes   These indexes cover central government bonds in the markets most important to the international investor. Calculated daily, indexes in this family are composed of the regularly traded, fixed rate, domestic government bonds of 11 countries with a minimum liquidity requirement. The index provides total returns including immediate reinvestment into the security. The overall index includes 445 traded issues, 185 of which are considered active, and 43 are included in the benchmark index. Daily data are available back to December 31, 1985. Results are published monthly in the *J. P. Morgan Government Bond Index Monitor*.

Global Equity and Composite Indexes

So far, we have discussed series intended to measure the performance of equity for fixed-income markets in individual countries. In this section we describe global equity series that consider all the equity markets in the world individually and combined. In addition, a composite series reflects the performance of both stocks and bonds in the United States.

Global Equity Indexes

Although stock market indexes like those we described for Japan (the Nikkei and TOPIX) and the United Kingdom (the several *Financial Times* indexes) are available for almost all foreign markets, there can be a problem with these series. Specifically, they typically show no consistency in terms of sample selection, weighting, or computational procedures. To solve these problems, one firm or group can compute a set of country indexes using consistent sample selection criteria, weightings, and computational procedures. Besides providing a set of indexes that can be directly compared, this also makes it possible to combine the series in various ways. We will describe four sets of global equity indexes.

FT Actuaries World Indexes   The FT Actuaries World Indexes are jointly compiled by The Financial Times Limited, Goldman Sachs & Co., and County NatWest/Wood Mackenzie & Co., Ltd. in conjunction with the Institute of Actuaries and the Faculty of Actuaries. Approximately 2,400 equity securities in 23 countries are included, covering at least 70 percent of the total value of all listed companies in each country.

Medium and small capitalization stocks with proven investor interest are included along with major international equities. A major condition for inclusion is that the securities allow direct holdings of shares by foreign nationals.

The indexes are value-weighted arithmetic averages of the price relatives (equal to P_t/P_{t-1}) of the constituents. The value on the base date of December 31, 1986 was set equal to 100. The index results are reported in U.S. dollars, U.K. pounds sterling, yen, deutschemark, and the local currency of the country. Index levels and related performance figures are calculated after the New York markets close, and they are published the following day in the *Financial Times*. The 23 countries and the proportion of market capitalization attributable to the country index in U.S. dollars are as follows (as of December 1990):[15]

Australia	1.29	Mexico	0.08
Austria	0.08	Netherlands	1.42
Belgium	0.60	New Zealand	0.26
Canada	2.19	Norway	0.11
Denmark	0.20	Singapore	0.13
France	2.21	South Africa	0.64
West Germany	4.63	Spain	0.72
Hong Kong	0.89	Sweden	0.36
Ireland	0.10	Switzerland	1.42
Italy	2.35	United Kingdom	8.79
Japan	35.17	United States	36.30
Malaysia	0.06		

In addition to the individual countries and the World Index, the indexes report on several geographic subgroups, as shown in the example in Table 5.6.

Morgan Stanley Capital International Indexes   These indexes are designed to measure the performance of the stock markets of the United States, Europe, Canada, Mexico, Australia, and the Far East, as well as the performance of international industry groups. As a result, there are 3 international, 19 national, and 38 international industry indexes. The indexes are based on the share prices of some 1,411 companies listed on stock exchanges in 19 countries.

---

[15]The proportion of market capitalizations indicated here differ from those shown in other chapters either because of different dates or different samples within countries.

Table 5.6 **FT Actuaries World Indexes**

FT-ACTUARIES WORLD INDICES

Jointly compiled by The Financial Times Limited, Goldman, Sachs & Co., and County NatWest/Wood Mackenzie in conjunction with the Institute of Actuaries and the Faculty of Actuaries

NATIONAL AND REGIONAL MARKETS	US Dollar Index	Day's Change %	Pound Sterling Index	Yen Index	DM Index	Local Currency Index	Local % chg on day	Gross Div. Yield
Australia (80)	145.38	−1.5	110.45	134.59	116.93	116.28	−2.7	6.38
Austria (19)	209.65	−2.3	159.28	194.08	168.62	168.39	−2.8	1.72
Belgium (61)	137.19	−0.1	104.23	126.99	110.34	107.59	−0.5	5.38
Canada (119)	136.75	−1.4	103.89	126.59	109.98	112.05	−1.9	3.63
Denmark (33)	252.50	−1.5	191.83	233.75	203.08	203.48	−2.1	1.46
Finland (26)	121.53	−2.8	92.33	112.51	97.75	93.16	−3.2	2.94
France (124)	133.90	−1.0	101.72	123.94	107.68	109.17	−1.5	3.75
West Germany (92)	117.75	−2.2	89.46	109.02	94.70	94.70	−2.6	2.38
Hong Kong (48)	117.49	−2.9	89.26	108.76	94.50	117.35	−2.9	5.46
Ireland (17)	146.81	−6.9	111.53	135.91	118.08	119.37	−7.3	3.64
Italy (96)	88.58	−1.5	67.30	82.00	71.24	76.29	−2.0	3.09
Japan (454)	118.66	−6.0	90.15	109.85	95.45	109.85	−5.5	0.77
Malaysia (35)	195.23	−6.4	148.32	180.72	157.01	202.56	−6.5	2.92
Mexico (13)	498.57	−1.3	378.77	461.54	400.99	1575.90	−1.3	0.33
Netherland (43)	135.43	−2.0	102.89	125.37	108.92	107.80	−2.4	5.26
New Zealand (17)	61.83	−3.5	46.97	57.24	49.73	51.86	−4.5	6.89
Norway (23)	258.70	−1.5	196.54	239.49	208.07	210.59	−2.0	1.51
Singapore (25)	156.96	−2.6	119.25	145.31	126.24	128.25	−3.3	3.26
South Africa (60)	176.65	−5.2	134.20	163.53	142.07	152.92	−5.2	3.78
Spain (42)	144.03	−4.5	109.43	133.34	115.84	105.95	−4.9	5.18
Sweden (34)	189.69	−4.6	144.11	175.61	152.57	160.77	−5.0	2.52
Switzerland (68)	93.12	−3.6	70.75	86.21	74.91	72.71	−4.7	2.86
United Kingdom (301)	162.57	−0.4	123.51	150.48	130.74	123.51	−1.6	5.56
USA (537)	123.62	−3.1	93.92	114.44	99.43	123.62	−3.1	3.97
Europe (979)	137.34	−1.4	104.34	127.15	110.47	107.54	−2.2	4.30
Nordic (116)	194.33	−2.9	147.63	179.90	156.29	154.08	−3.4	1.97
Pacific Basin (659)	119.53	−5.7	90.81	110.66	96.14	110.17	−5.3	1.20
Euro−Pacific (1638)	127.11	−3.8	96.57	117.66	102.23	109.81	−4.0	2.56
North America (656)	124.33	−3.0	94.45	115.11	100.01	122.92	−3.0	3.94
Europe Ex. UK (678)	121.42	−2.2	92.25	112.43	97.68	97.84	−2.7	3.39
Pacific Ex. Japan (205)	129.03	−2.3	98.02	119.46	103.78	110.68	−3.1	5.78
World Ex. US (1830)	128.14	−3.8	97.35	118.63	103.06	110.72	−3.9	2.61
World Ex. UK (2066)	121.96	−3.9	92.66	112.91	98.10	113.86	−3.9	2.75
World Ex. So. Af. (2307)	125.26	−3.5	95.16	115.97	100.75	114.56	−3.6	3.06
World Ex. Japan (1913)	130.40	−2.3	99.07	120.73	104.90	117.48	−2.7	4.16
The World Index (2367)	125.57	−3.5	95.40	116.25	101.00	114.82	−3.6	3.07

Source: Goldman, Sachs & Co.

The combined market capitalization of these companies represents approximately 60 percent of the aggregate market value of the exchange-listed stock of these countries.

All the indexes are arithmetic averages weighted by the market value of the stocks included. The countries included, the weights for each country based on GDP, and the market values of the stocks and groups appear in Table 5.7.

In addition to reporting the indexes in U.S. dollars and the country's local currency, the following valuation information is available from Morgan Stanley: (1) price-to-book value (P/BV) ratio, (2) price-to-cash earnings (net income plus depreciation) (P/CE) ratio, (3) price-to-earnings (P/E) ratio, and (4) dividend yield (YLD). You can use these ratios when analyzing different valuation levels among countries and over time for specific countries.

	U.S.$ billion	EAFE	World	Europe 13	EAFE	Kokusai	World
Austria	$ 18.0	1.6	1.0	1.2	0.5	0.5	0.3
Belgium	40.3	1.9	1.2	2.6	1.1	1.1	0.7
Denmark	26.0	1.3	0.8	1.7	0.7	0.7	0.5
Finland	10.1	1.4	0.8	0.7	0.3	0.3	0.2
Finland (free)	2.0	—	—	0.1	0.1	0.1	0.0
France	200.6	11.7	7.1	13.1	5.7	5.3	3.6
Germany	245.5	14.9	9.1	16.0	7.0	6.5	4.4
Italy	104.0	10.4	6.3	6.8	2.9	2.8	1.9
Netherlands	89.3	2.8	1.7	5.8	2.5	2.4	1.6
Norway	17.6	1.1	0.6	1.1	0.5	0.5	0.3
Norway (free)	13.3	—	—	0.9	0.4	0.4	0.2
Spain	65.1	4.6	2.8	4.2	1.6	1.7	1.2
Sweden	68.1	2.2	1.3	4.4	1.9	1.8	1.2
Sweden (free)	29.3	—	—	1.9	0.8	0.8	0.5
Switzerland	116.4	2.1	1.3	7.6	3.3	3.1	2.1
Switzerland (free)	92.1	—	—	6.0	2.6	2.5	1.7
United Kingdom	535.3	9.2	5.6	34.8	15.2	14.3	9.6
Europe 13 (free)	1,449.8	—	—	95.1	41.4	39.0	26.2
Europe 13	1,536.2	65.0	39.6	100.0	43.5	41.0	27.6
Australia	79.6	3.1	1.9	—	2.3	2.1	1.4
Hong Kong	48.5	0.7	0.4	—	1.4	1.3	0.9
Japan	1,817.3	30.4	16.5	—	51.5	—	32.6
New Zealand	8.4	0.5	0.3	—	0.2	0.2	0.2
Singapore/Malaysia	40.2	0.3	0.2	—	1.1	1.1	0.7
Pacific	1,993.9	35.0	21.3	—	56.5	—	35.8
EAFE (free)	3,454.7	—	—	—	97.9	—	62.1
EAFE	3,530.2	100.0	60.9	—	100.0	—	63.4
Canada	145.1	—	3.8	—	—	3.9	2.6
United States	1,882.1	—	35.3	—	—	50.2	33.8
South African Gold Mines	9.8	—	—	—	—	0.3	0.2
The World Index (free)	5,491.7	—	—	—	—	—	98.6
The World Index	5,567.2	—	100.0	—	—	—	100.0
Nordic countries (free)	70.6	—	—	4.6	2.0	1.9	1.3
Nordic countries	121.8	5.9	3.6	7.9	3.4	3.2	2.2
Europe 13 ex. UK	1,001.0	55.9	34.0	65.2	28.4	26.7	18.0
Far East	1,996.0	31.4	19.1	—	54.0	—	34.2
EASEA (EAFE ex. Japan)	1,712.9	69.6	42.4	—	48.5	45.7	30.8
North America	2,927.2	—	39.1	—	—	54.1	36.4
Kokusai (World ex. Japan)	3,749.9	—	81.5	—	—	100.0	67.4

Source: Morgan Stanley Capital International (New York: Morgan Stanley & Co., 1990).

Computed daily and monthly, the indexes are reported in Morgan Stanley monthly and quarterly publications, specifically the *Morgan Stanley Capital International Perspective*. Monthly issues focus on recent stock-market performance and on comparisons of market valuation factors within countries and international industry groups. Quarterly issues include graphs on 2,000 of the largest companies in the world. Absolute and relative performance compared to the world index is shown for the latest 22 years, together with operating data for the last 5 years.

The Morgan Stanley group index for Europe, Australia, and the Far East (EAFE) serves as the basis for futures and options contracts on the Chicago Mercantile Exchange and the Chicago Board Options Exchange.

Euromoney–First Boston Global Stock Indexes

The Euromoney–First Boston Global Stock Index is a market value-weighted set of indexes for 17 individual countries together with a composite world index. The series were initiated in 1986 with the December 31, 1985 value set at 100. The results are reported in local currency and also in U.S. dollars. Monthly results for the individual countries are reported in *Global Investor*.

Salomon–Russell World Equity Indexes

A series of indexes for 22 individual countries and a world index called the Salomon–Russell World Equity Index were initiated in 1988. This index combines the Russell 1,000 with the Salomon–Russell Primary Market Index (PMI), which is a value-weighted index of 600 non-U.S. stocks covering about 65 percent of the market capitalization in each of 22 markets. Stocks were selected based on their adjusted capitalizations (considering crossownership) and liquidity (trading volume). All indexes are presented in local currency and U.S. dollar terms with monthly results reported in *Global Investor*.

Composite Stock-Bond Index

Beyond separate stock indexes and bond indexes for individual countries, a natural step is the development of a composite series that measures the performance of all securities in a given country. A composite series on stocks and bonds makes it possible to examine the benefits of diversifying among stocks and bonds in addition to diversifying within these asset classes.

Merrill Lynch–Wilshire Capital Markets Index (MLWCMI)

This market value-weighted index was created to measure the total return performance of the combined U.S. taxable fixed-income and equity markets. It is basically a combination of the Merrill Lynch fixed-income indexes and the Wilshire 5,000 common stock index. It tracks more than 10,000 stocks and bonds.

Its makeup gives a total portfolio performance benchmark that can form the basis both for passive portfolio management and also for active management decisions. The following table breaks down the index's market mix as of June 30, 1987:

Security	$ Billions	Percentage of Total
Treasury bonds	$1,085	20.89%
Agency bonds	166	3.20
Mortgage bonds	467	8.99
Corporate bonds	353	8.72
OTC stocks	331	6.37
AMEX stocks	105	2.02
NYSE stocks	2,586	49.92
	$5,193	100.00%

Comparison of Indicator Series Changes over Time

In this section we discuss price movements in the different series for various daily, monthly, or annual intervals. The first part examines the correlations among the major U.S. equity series and also several major foreign equity indexes. The results confirm the discussion in Chapter 2 regarding international diversification. We also discuss the very consistent correlations among bond market indexes. The third part examines the longer-run results for the various stock indexes, while the final part of the section contains a similar analysis for the major bond indexes.

Correlations among Daily Equity Price Changes

Table 5.8 shows a matrix of the correlation coefficients of the daily percentage price changes for a set of U.S. and non-U.S. equity-market indexes during the period from January 4, 1972 through December 31, 1989 (including 4,463 observations). This recent 18-

Table 5.8	Correlation Coefficients among Daily Percentage Price Changes in Alternative Equity Market Indicator Series: January 4, 1972 to December 31, 1989 (4,463 observations)[a]

	DJIA	S&P 400	S&P 500	NYSE Composite	AMEX Value Index	NASDAQ Industrials
DJIA	—					
S&P 400	0.954	—				
S&P 500	0.949	0.975	—			
NYSE Composite	0.930	0.932	0.945	—		
AMEX Value Index	0.712	0.723	0.744	0.763	—	
NASDAQ Industrials	0.722	0.743	0.763	0.807	0.807	—
NASDAQ Composite	0.749	0.745	0.729	0.817	0.809	0.944
Value Line	0.841	0.785	0.787	0.881	0.824	0.870
Wilshire 5,000	0.905	0.876	0.889	0.861	0.729	0.749
FT 30-Share	0.136	0.165	0.132	0.189	0.216	0.242
FT 500	0.167	0.201	0.157	0.224	0.258	0.273
FT All-Share	0.167	0.200	0.155	0.224	0.258	0.273
Nikkei[b]	0.248	0.281	0.278	0.293	0.214	0.212
TSE Index[b]	0.156	0.176	0.172	0.185	0.141	0.136

[a]Maximum number of observations, some figures are based on fewer observations.

[b]Japanese indexes are lagged.

year period was selected because data were available for most of the major equity series during that time.

Most of the differences in the correlations are apparently attributable to differences in the samples, that is, differences in the firms listed on the alternative stock exchanges. Most of the major series except the DJIA, the Nikkei Stock Average, the Value Line (VL) series, and the FT Ordinary Share Index are market value-weighted indexes of a large number of stocks (the DJIA and Nikkei are price-weighted, and the VL and FT Ordinary Share series are unweighted). Therefore, the computational procedures are generally similar, the sample sizes are large (except for the DJIA and the FT 30-Share Index), and the samples represent either large segments of the total applicable populations in terms of value, or all members of the populations. Thus, the major difference is typically the stocks included in the index; the stocks are from different segments of the market or from different countries.

Series that include almost all NYSE stocks (the DJIA, S&P 400, S&P 500, and the NYSE composite)

show very high positive correlation (0.88 to 0.94) with one another. This indicates that, in the short run, even the DJIA, which has been criticized, is a very adequate indicator of price movements on the NYSE. In contrast, these NYSE series show significantly lower correlations with the AMEX series or the NASDAQ indexes. Further, the relationship between the Value Line Index or the Wilshire 5,000 Index of stocks from all exchanges and the other U.S. series is likewise about 0.64 to 0.85. Besides the difference in sample, recall that the VL Index is an unweighted series while the Wilshire is value weighted with a significant impact from the NYSE.

The importance of recognizing the global investment environment can be seen from the correlations among the U.S. indexes and those from the United Kingdom and Japan. The relationships among the three *Financial Times* series for the LSE varied from 0.88 to 0.96 even though their sample sizes and computational methods differ. The correlations between the two Japanese indexes were lower (0.61), but much higher than their correlations with other indexes.

NASDAQ Composite	Value Line	Wilshire 5,000	FT 30-Share	FT 500	FT All-Share	Nikkei	TSE Index
—							
0.887	—						
0.745	0.793	—					
0.256	0.242	0.301	—				
0.290	0.344	0.105	0.888		—		
0.291	0.282	0.343	0.885	—	0.963		
0.223	0.250	0.395	0.125	0.166	0.159	—	
0.141	0.161	0.207	0.076	0.111	0.105	0.611	—

These results attest to the importance of the basic sample.

The relative strength of the U.S.–London relationship, which ranged from 0.132 to 0.344, and the U.S.–Tokyo relationship, which ranged from 0.136 to 0.395, is not unexpected. This confirms the diversification benefits of global investing, which reduces the variance of returns for a total portfolio.

Correlations among Monthly Bond Series

The correlations among the monthly bond return series are not shown because they were so high and also very consistent. Specifically, the correlations ranged from 0.91 to 0.99, confirming that although the *levels* of interest rates differed due to the risk premium, the overriding factors that cause rate *changes* over time (affecting the rates of return) are systematic macroeconomic variables like changes in the risk-free rate and inflation expectations.

Annual Stock Price Changes

The annual percentage price changes for the major stock indexes are shown in Table 5.9. One would expect differences among the price changes and measures of risk for the various series due to the different samples. For example, the NYSE series should have lower rates of return and risk measures than the AMEX and OTC series. The results generally confirm these expectations. The low rate of return for the Value Line series is due to the geometric average calculation of daily changes. (Recall the discussion in Chapter 1.)

The LSE series had higher rates of change and greater variability than the U.S. series. The TSE likewise had higher average price changes, but its risk measures were not correspondingly higher implying superior risk-adjusted performance. Recall that the Japanese market also had very low correlation with alternative U.S. stock market indexes, which indicates that this market was a prime diversification candidate.

Table 5.9 Percentage Price Changes in Stock Price Indicator Series: 1972–1990

	DJIA	S&P 400	S&P 500	NYSE Composite	AMEX Value Index	NASDAQ Industrials
1972	14.58	16.10	15.63	14.27	10.33	13.63
1973	−16.58	−17.38	−17.37	−19.63	−30.00	−36.88
1974	−27.57	−29.93	−29.72	−30.28	−33.22	−32.44
1975	38.44	31.92	31.55	31.86	38.40	43.38
1976	17.86	18.42	19.15	21.50	31.58	23.68
1977	−17.27	−12.35	−11.50	−9.30	16.43	9.30
1978	−3.15	2.39	1.06	2.13	17.73	15.92
1979	4.19	12.88	12.31	15.54	64.10	38.10
1980	14.93	27.62	25.77	25.68	41.25	49.19
1981	−9.23	−11.22	−9.73	−8.67	−8.13	−12.27
1982	19.60	14.95	14.76	13.95	6.23	19.32
1983	20.27	18.16	17.27	17.46	30.95	18.31
1984	−4.33	−0.40	0.81	0.75	−9.07	−20.00
1985	27.66	25.86	26.33	26.15	20.50	23.78
1986	22.58	17.30	16.87	13.98	7.30	6.06
1987	2.26	3.90	0.06	−0.25	−1.42	−3.21
1988	11.85	12.38	12.40	13.04	17.54	12.03
1989	26.96	25.60	27.25	24.82	23.53	10.30
1990	−4.34	−5.07	−6.56	−7.46	−18.49	−2.86
Average of annual changes (arithmetic mean)	7.30	7.95	7.70	7.66	11.87	9.23
Standard deviation of annual changes	17.24	16.54	16.45	16.47	24.20	22.67
Average annual compound rate of change (geometric mean)	5.85	6.57	6.34	6.28	9.10	6.64

Annual Bond Rates of Return

Table 5.10 gives the annual total rates of return for the Shearson Lehman bond-market indexes.[16] You cannot directly compare the bond and stock results because the bond results are total rates of return versus annual percentage price change results for stocks. (Some of the stock series do not report dividend data.)

Within the bond series, it is important to compare the average rate of return figures and the risk measures, because, although the monthly rates of return are correlated, we would expect a difference in the level of return that would reflect the differential risk premiums. The results generally confirm our expectations. Specifically, lower return and risk measures for the government series were followed by higher returns and risks for corporate bonds and the highest rates of return and risk measures for the mortgage series.

---

[16]As you might expect based upon the high correlations among the monthly rates of return, the results for various bond-market segments (government, corporate, mortgages) are very similar irrespective of their sources (Shearson Lehman, Merrill Lynch, Salomon Brothers, Ryan). Therefore, only the Shearson Lehman results are included.

NASDAQ Composite	Value Line Composite	Wilshire 5,000	FT 30-Share	FT 500	FT All-Share	Nikkei	TSE Index
17.18	0.78	14.86	5.38	9.72	12.11	91.91	101.40
−31.06	−35.46	−20.96	−31.94	−30.84	−31.36	−17.30	−23.71
−35.11	−33.47	−31.49	−53.02	−54.39	−54.34	−11.37	−9.01
29.76	44.35	32.83	132.78	141.35	136.33	19.18	15.99
26.10	32.23	21.69	−5.59	−1.01	−3.87	14.51	18.69
7.33	0.48	−6.98	36.85	41.45	41.18	−2.51	−5.16
12.31	4.31	3.96	−2.99	3.92	2.70	23.33	23.48
28.11	24.44	19.28	−12.04	2.54	4.30	9.46	2.24
33.88	18.28	27.61	14.56	24.57	27.07	3.33	7.50
−3.21	−4.43	−8.43	11.78	7.88	7.24	7.95	15.42
18.67	15.32	12.86	12.50	27.44	22.07	4.36	4.10
19.87	22.28	18.74	30.00	19.27	23.10	23.42	23.26
−11.67	−8.97	−1.25	22.84	29.29	26.02	16.66	24.81
31.86	20.72	27.18	18.73	15.20	15.18	13.61	14.89
7.51	5.01	12.48	16.13	22.18	22.34	42.61	48.31
−5.40	−10.69	1.49	4.52	4.59	4.16	21.35	10.89
15.41	21.77	13.29	5.38	5.35	4.52	42.54	36.57
20.44	17.08	26.69	32.38	29.91	30.01	28.67	22.25
−0.98	−15.97	−10.61	−12.67	−14.01	−14.31	−38.72	−39.83
9.53	6.21	8.07	11.87	14.54	14.44	15.42	15.37
19.37	20.55	17.24	35.65	36.66	36.13	26.24	28.27
7.54	4.03	6.55	6.80	9.61	9.20	12.49	12.05

Summary

■ Given the several uses of security-market indicator series, you should know how they are constructed and the differences among them. The point is, if you want to use one of the many series to learn how the "market" is doing, you need to be aware of what market you are dealing with so you can select the appropriate index. Are you interested only in the NYSE, or do you also want to consider the AMEX and the OTC market? Beyond the U.S. market, are you interested in Japanese or United Kingdom stocks, or the total world market?

■ Indexes are also used to evaluate portfolio performance for an individual or a professional money manager. Again, you want to be sure you choose an index that is consistent with your investing universe. If you are investing worldwide, it doesn't seem reasonable to compare your performance to the DJIA, which is limited to 30 U.S. blue-chip stocks. The same is true for a bond portfolio — you want the bond index to match your investment philosophy. Also, if your portfolio includes some combination of stocks and bonds, you want to evaluate your performance against a similar set of indexes.

Table 5.10   *Annual Percentage Rates of Return; Arithmetic and Geometric Mean Annual Rates of Return and Standard Deviations of Annual and Monthly Rates of Return: 1976–1990*

| | Shearson Lehman | | | | | |
	Government/ Corporate	Government	Corporate	Mortgage- Backed	Yankee Bond	Aggregate Bond
1976	0.1559	0.1235	0.1934	0.1631	0.1508	0.1560
1977	0.0298	0.0281	0.0316	0.0190	0.0523	0.0303
1978	0.0119	0.0180	0.0035	0.0241	0.0291	0.0140
1979	0.0230	0.0540	−0.0211	0.0013	−0.0043	0.0193
1980	0.0306	0.0519	−0.0229	0.0065	0.0193	0.0270
1981	0.0726	0.0936	0.0295	0.0007	0.0348	0.0625
1982	0.3109	0.2774	0.3921	0.4304	0.3582	0.3262
1983	0.0800	0.0739	0.0927	0.1013	0.0943	0.0835
1984	0.1502	0.1450	0.1663	0.1579	0.1638	0.1515
1985	0.2130	0.2043	0.2406	0.2521	0.2599	0.2211
1986	0.1562	0.1531	0.1653	0.1343	0.1627	0.1526
1987	0.0229	0.0220	0.0256	0.0428	0.0189	0.0276
1988	0.0758	0.0703	0.0922	0.0872	0.0881	0.0789
1989	0.1424	0.1423	0.1409	0.1535	0.1542	0.1453
1990	0.0828	0.0872	0.0705	0.1072	0.0705	0.0896
Arithmetic Mean	0.1039	0.1030	0.1067	0.1121	0.1102	0.1057
Standard Deviation	0.0813	0.0700	0.1092	0.1112	0.0969	0.0847
Geometic Mean	0.1010	0.1008	0.1016	0.1070	0.1062	0.1026
Standard Deviation (monthly returns)	0.0216	0.0192	0.0272	0.0289	0.0263	0.0222

Source: Frank K. Reilly, G. Wenchi Kao, and David J. Wright, "An Analysis of Alternative Bond Market Indexes," January 1991.

■ Whenever you invest, you will look to one of a multitude of market indexes to tell you what has happened and how successful you have been. Your selection of indexes for information or evaluation will depend on your knowledge of the available indexes. The purpose of this chapter is to help you understand what to look for and how to make the right decision.[17]

Questions

1. Discuss briefly several uses of security market indicator series.

2. What major factors must be considered when constructing a market indicator series? Put another way, what characteristics differentiate indicator series?

3. Explain price weighting of a market indicator series. In such a case, would you expect a $100 stock to be more important than a $25 stock? Demonstrate the effect.

4. What are the major criticisms of the Dow Jones Industrial Average and the Nikkei Stock Average?

5. Explain how you would compute a value-weighted series. Demonstrate the procedure with a small example.

6. How does a price-weighted series adjust for stock splits? How does a value-weighted series make the adjustment?

[17]An article that discusses this decision as related to stock indexes is Anna Merjos, "How's the Market Doing?" *Barron's*, August 20, 1990: 18–20, 27, 28.

7. Describe an unweighted price indicator series, including how you would construct such a series. Assume a 20 percent price change in both GM ($50/share; 50 million shares outstanding) and Coors Brewing ($25/share; 15 million shares outstanding). Which stock's change will have the greater impact on such an index? Why?

8. If you correlated percentage changes in the Wilshire 5,000 equity index with percentage changes in the NYSE composite, the AMEX index, and the NASDAQ composite index, would you expect differences between the correlations? Why or why not?

9. High correlations hold among the daily percentage price changes for the alternative NYSE price indicator series. What causes this similarity: size of sample, source of sample, or method of computation? Explain.

10. Based upon the results in Table 5.9, how do the historical movements for the various NYSE price indicator series differ in terms of average annual price changes and variability of annual price changes? Are the differences generally consistent with economic theory? Discuss.

11. Using the results in Table 5.9, compare stock price indicator series for the three U.S. equity-market segments (NYSE, AMEX, OTC) for the period 1972 to 1990. Discuss whether the average annual price change and risk (variability of price changes) results were consistent with economic theory.

12. What are the major differences between the three *Financial Times* indexes? Which series is similar to the S&P 500 Index?

13. The Nikkei Stock Average is similar to which U.S. stock price series? How is it similar?

14. Discuss the correlations between the two stock price indicator series for the Tokyo Stock Exchange and the three indicator series for the London Stock Exchange. Do the same for the TSE series and two NYSE series. Explain why these relationships differ.

15. You are informed that the Wilshire 5,000 market value-weighted series increased by 16 percent during a specified period, while a Wilshire 5,000 equal-weighted series increased by 23 percent during the same period. Discuss what this difference in results implies.

16. Briefly discuss the uses for bond-market indexes.

17. Why do some contend that bond-market series are more difficult to construct and maintain than stock-market series?

18. Discuss five alternative subindexes you could construct from a composite corporate bond series.

19. The Wilshire 5,000 market value-weighted index increased by 5 percent while the Merrill Lynch–Wilshire Capital Markets Index increased by 15 percent during the same period. What does this difference in results imply?

20. The Russell 1,000 increased by 8 percent during the past year while the Russell 2,000 increased by 15 percent. Discuss what this implies regarding different segments of the market. Also, discuss whether this difference in performance is what you would expect based upon what you know about these two series.

Problems

1. You are given the following information regarding prices for a sample of stocks:

Stock	Number of Shares	Price T	T + 1
A	1,000,000	$60	$80
B	10,000,000	20	35
C	30,000,000	18	25

a. Construct a price-weighted series for these three stocks, and compute the percentage change in the series for the period from T to T + 1.

b. Construct a value-weighted series for these three stocks, and compute the percentage change in the series for the period from T to T + 1.

c. Briefly discuss the difference in the results for the two series.

2. a. Given the data in Problem 1, construct an equal-weighted series by assuming $1,000 is invested in each stock. What is the percentage change in wealth for this portfolio?

b. Compute the percentage of price change for each of the stocks in Problem 1. Compute the arithmetic average of these changes. Discuss how this answer compares to the answer in 2a.

c. Compute the geometric average of the percentage changes in 2b. Discuss how this compares to the answer in 2b.

3. For the last 5 trading days, on the basis of figures in *The Wall Street Journal*, compute the daily percentage price changes for the following price indicator series:
   a. DJIA
   b. S&P 400
   c. AMEX Market Value Series
   d. NASDAQ Industrial Index
   e. FT 30-Share Index
   f. Nikkei Stock Price Average

   Discuss the difference in results for a and b, a and c, a and d, a and e, a and f, and e and f. What do these differences imply regarding diversifying within the United States versus diversifying between countries?

	Price			**Shares**		
	A	**B**	**C**	**A**	**B**	**C**
Day 1	$12	$23	$52	500	350	250
Day 2	10	22	55	500	350	250
Day 3	14	46	52	500	175[a]	250
Day 4	13	47	25	500	175	500[b]
Day 5	12	45	26	500	175	500

[a] Split at close of Day 2
[b] Split at close of Day 3

4. Using the table above:
   a. Calculate a Dow Jones Industrial Index for Days 1 through 5.
   b. What effects did the splits have in determining the next day's index? (Hint: Think of the relative weighting of each stock.)
   c. From a copy of a recent issue of *The Wall Street Journal*, find the current divisor for calculating the DJIA. (Normally this value can be found on the inside back pages.)

5. Utilizing the price and volume data in the preceding problem:
   a. Calculate a Standard & Poor's Index for Days 1 through 5 using a beginning index value of 10.
   b. Identify the effects of the splits in determining the next day's index. (Hint: Think of the relative weighting of each stock.)

6. Using the data in Table 5.9, calculate the average annual rate of change in five of the indexes for the period 1979 to 1990, using (a) the arithmetic mean and (b) the geometric mean.

References

Fisher, Lawrence, and James H. Lorie. *A Half Century of Returns on Stocks and Bonds.* Chicago: Chicago Graduate School of Business, 1977.

Hawthorne, Fran. "The Battle of the Bond Indexes," *Institutional Investor* 20, no. 4 (April 1986).

Lorie, James H., Peter Dodd, and Mary Hamilton Kimpton. *The Stock Market: Theories and Evidence*, 2d ed. Homewood, Ill.: Richard D. Irwin, 1985.

Mossavar-Rahmani, Sharmin. *Bond Index Funds.* Chicago: Probus Publishing, 1991.

Williams, Arthur III, and Noreen N. Conwell. "Fixed Income Indices." In *The Handbook of Fixed-Income Securities*, 2d. ed. Ed. by Frank J. Fabozzi and Irving M. Pollack. Homewood, Ill.: Dow-Jones Irwin, 1987.

Sources of Information on Investments

In the chapters that follow, we will discuss the factors that influence aggregate security prices and security prices within various industries, as well as the unique factors that influence the returns on individual securities. In this chapter we will describe some of the major sources of information needed for these analyses. Relevant information has always been both important and difficult to obtain, but this has become even more apparent in an environment of global investing. When you only considered U.S. investments, a lot of information was readily available. Now it is necessary to seek information from around the world and interpret it in line with U.S. data.

The presentation in this chapter will follow this outline:

- Aggregate economic analysis
    - U.S. government sources
    - Bank publications
    - Sources for non-U.S. economic data
- Financial market analysis
    - Government publications
    - Commercial publications
    - Brokerage firm reports
- Industry analysis
    - Commercial publications
    - Industry publications
    - Trade associations
- Individual stock analysis
    - Company-generated information
    - Commercial publications
    - Brokerage firm reports
    - Investment magazines
- Computerized data sources
    - Data banks
    - On-line data systems
- Academic journals

Aggregate Economic Analysis

This section covers data used in estimating overall economic changes in the United States and other major countries. A later section will deal with data regarding the aggregate securities markets.

U.S. Government Sources

It should come as no surprise that the main source of information on the U.S. economy is the federal government, which issues a variety of publications on the topic.

The *Federal Reserve Bulletin* is a monthly publication issued by the Board of Governors of the Federal Reserve System. It is the primary source for almost all monetary data, including monetary aggregates, factors affecting member bank reserve requirements, Federal Reserve open market transactions, and loans and investments from all commercial banks. In addition, it contains figures on financial markets, including interest rates and some stock market statistics; data for corporate finance including profits, assets, and liabilities of corporations; extensive nonfinancial statistics on output, the labor force, and the GNP; and a major section on international finance.

Survey of Current Business is a monthly publication issued by the U.S. Department of Commerce that gives details on national income and production. It is probably the best source for current, detailed information on all contributions to the gross national product and national income. It also contains a listing of industrial production for numerous segments of the economy. The survey is an excellent secondary source for labor information (statistics on employment and wages), interest rates, and statistics on foreign economic development. Currently, it also includes data regarding the leading, coincident, and lagging economic series published by the Department of Commerce.[1] These series are considered important by those who attempt to project peaks and troughs in the business cycle.

Economic Indicators is a monthly publication prepared for the Joint Economic Committee by the Council of Economic Advisers. It reports monthly and annual data on output, income, spending, employment, production, prices, money and credit, federal finance, and the international economic situation.

The *Quarterly Financial Report* (QFR) is prepared by the Federal Trade Commission to provide aggregate statistics on the combined financial position of U.S. corporations. Based upon an extensive quarterly sample survey, the QFR presents estimated statements of income and retained earnings, balance sheets, and related financial and operating ratios for all manufacturing corporations. The publication also includes data on mining and trade corporations. The statistical data are classified by industry and, within manufacturing groups, by firm size.

Business Statistics, a biennial supplement to the *Survey of Current Business*, contains extensive historical data for about 2,500 series within the survey. The historical section contains monthly data for the previous 4 or 5 years, quarterly data for the previous 10 years, and annual data back to 1947, as available. A notable feature is a section of explanatory notes that describes each series and indicate the original sources for the data.

The *Historical Chart Book*, which is an annual supplement to the *Federal Reserve Bulletin*, provides long-range financial and business series. An excellent section on the various series indicates the sources of the data.

Each January, the president of the United States prepares and provides to Congress the *Economic Report of the President*. This report indicates what has transpired during the previous year, discusses the current environment, and predicts the major economic problems that will face the country during the following year. This publication includes an extensive document, "The Annual Report of the Council of Economic Advisers," which provides over 150 pages of detailed discussion of domestic and international economic developments monitored by the council (the group that advises the president on economic policy). An appendix contains statistical tables relating to income, employment, and production. The tables typically provide annual data from the 1940s, and in some instances from 1929.

The *Statistical Abstract of the United States*, published annually since 1878, is the standard summary of statistics on the social, political, and economic organization of the United States. It is prepared by the Bureau of the Census to serve as a convenient statistical reference and a guide to other statistical publications and sources.

---

[1] These series are discussed more extensively and related to stock market movements in Chapter 9.

Bank Publications

In addition to the government material, banks publish much data and many comments on the economy. These generally appear monthly and free of charge. They can be categorized as publications of either the Federal Reserve Banks or commercial banks.

Publications of Federal Reserve Banks The Federal Reserve System is divided into 12 Federal Reserve Districts with a major Federal Reserve Bank in each, as follows:[2]

1. Boston	7. Chicago
2. New York	8. St. Louis
3. Philadelphia	9. Minneapolis
4. Cleveland	10. Kansas City
5. Richmond	11. Dallas
6. Atlanta	12. San Francisco

Each of the Federal Reserve district banks has a research department that periodically issues reports. While the various bank publications differ, all publish monthly reviews, which are available to interested parties. These reviews typically contain one or several articles of interest and regional statistics. A major exception is the St. Louis Federal Reserve Bank, which publishes statistical releases weekly, monthly, and quarterly containing extensive national and international data, in addition to its monthly review.[3]

Publications of Commercial Banks A number of large banks make monthly newsletters available to interested individuals. These newsletters generally comment on the current and future outlook of the overall economy and specific industries or segments within it.

Sources for Non-U.S. Economic Data In addition to data on the U.S. economy, you need data on other countries where you might consider investing. Some sources of this information follow.[4]

The Economic Intelligence Unit (EIU) publishes 83 separate quarterly reviews and an annual supplement covering economic and business conditions and future outlooks for 160 countries. The reviews consider each country's economy, trade and finance, and trends in investment and consumer spending along with its political environment. Tables contain data on economic activity and foreign trade. Besides these reviews, the EIU also publishes *European Trends*, which discusses the aggregate economic environment for the European community and the world.

The Organization for Economic Cooperation and Development (OECD) publishes semiannual surveys showing recent trends and policies and assessing short-term prospects for each country. An annual volume, *Historical Statistics*, contains annual percentage change data for the most recent 20 years.

Business International Corporation publishes an annual book entitled *Worldwide Economic Indicators* that contains data for 131 countries on population, gross domestic product (GDP) by activity, wages and prices, foreign trade, and a number of more specific topics for the preceding 4 years.

Demographic Yearbook, published by the United Nations, reports statistics on population, births, deaths, life expectancy, marriages, and divorces for about 240 countries. Also, the *United Nations Statistical Yearbook* is a basic reference volume of extensive economic statistics on all UN countries (population, construction, industrial production, etc.).

Another United Nations publication, the *Yearbook of International Trade Statistics*, is an annual report on import statistics over a 4-year period for 166 countries. The commodity figures for each country appear as commodity codes. The UN's *Yearbook of National Account Statistics* is a comprehensive source of national account data, including detailed statistics for 155 countries on domestic product and consumption expenditures, national income, and disposable income for a 12-year period.

International Marketing Data and Statistics, published by Euromonitor Publications Inc. of London, is an annual source of data for 132 non-European countries. It covers population, employment, production, trade, the economy, and other economic data.

Eurostatistics, a monthly publication of the Statistical Office of the European Communities in Luxembourg, contains statistics for short-term economic analysis of 10 European countries and the United States. It generally gives data for 6 years covering industrial production, employment and unemployment, external trade, prices, wages, and finance.

---

[2]Specific addresses for each of the district banks and names of major personnel appear in the *Federal Reserve Bulletin*.

[3]An individual can get on the mailing list for these publications by writing to Federal Reserve Bank of St. Louis, P.O. Box 442, St. Louis, MO 63166. Most are free.

[4]This discussion draws heavily from P. M. Daniells, *Business Information Sources*, 2d ed. (Berkeley, Calif.: University of California Press, 1986).

The U.S. International Trade Administration publishes *International Economic Indicators* quarterly through the U.S. Government Printing Office. This report gives comparative economic indicators and trends in the United States and its seven principal industrial competitors: France, Germany, Italy, the Netherlands, the United Kingdom, Japan, and Canada. The data are organized into five parts: general indicators, trade indicators, price indicators, finance indicators, and labor indicators. The sources for the data appear at the back of the booklet.

International Financial Statistics is a monthly publication supplemented by a yearbook issue. The International Monetary Fund produces this essential source of current financial statistics on topics such as exchange rates, fund positions, international liquidity, money and banking, interest rates (including LIBOR), prices, and production.[5] The International Monetary Fund's *Balance of Payments Yearbook* is a two-part publication. The first part contains detailed balance-of-payments figures for over 110 countries, while the second part contains world totals for balance-of-payments components and aggregates.

Some individual countries, for example, Brazil, Great Britain, Japan, and Switzerland, publish national income studies. These give detailed breakdowns and annual reports of the more important statistics, including bibliographical sources for the tables.

As in the United States, major banks in various countries publish bulletins or letters with statistical reviews. Examples include:

- Bank of Canada (monthly)
- Bank of England (quarterly)
- Bank of Japan (monthly)
- National Bank of Belgium (monthly)
- Deutsche Bundesbank (monthly)

In addition to the specific sources of data described, you should be aware of the following bibliographies:

- G. R. Dicks, ed. *Sources of World Financial and Banking Information.* Westport, Conn.: Greenwood Press, 1981.
A descriptive list of nearly 5,000 financial and banking sources arranged by country.

- David S. Hoopes, ed. *Global Guide to International Business.* New York: File Publications, 1983.
A descriptive list of source information about individual countries.

- *Index of International Statistics.* Washington, D.C.: Congressional Information Service, monthly.
A monthly descriptive guide and index to statistical publications by the world's major government organizations.

Financial Market Analysis

Several government publications provide useful data on the stock market, but the bulk of detailed information comes from private firms. Some of the government publications discussed earlier, such as the *Federal Reserve Bulletin* and the *Survey of Current Business*, contain financial market data including interest rates and stock prices.

Government Publication

The main source of financial market data from the government is the Securities and Exchange Commission (SEC), the federal agency responsible for regulating the operation of and collecting data about the securities markets. The *Annual Report of the SEC* is published for each fiscal year ending in June. It contains a detailed discussion of important developments during the year and comments on the SEC's disclosure system and regulation of the securities markets. Finally, it includes a statistics section with historical data on many security market series.

Commercial Publications

Considering the numerous advisory services in existence, a section dealing with their publications could become voluminous. Therefore, we intend to list and discuss only major services. You can develop your own list of other available sources. An excellent source of advertisements for these services is *Barron's*. The *Fortune Investment Information Directory* is specifically directed toward listing and briefly describing these publications.[6]

---

[5]*LIBOR* is an acronym for "London Interbank Borrowing Rate." It serves as a base rate for many international financial transactions.

[6]This directory contains extensive listings of print (newspapers, magazines), audio-visual, electronic (software, databases), and interpersonal (seminars) information sources. It is published by the Dushkin Publishing Group, Inc., Sluice Dock, Guilford, CT 06437.

The *New York Stock Exchange Fact Book* is an annual publication of the New York Stock Exchange. The book is an outstanding source of current and historical data on activity on the NYSE, as well as comparative data on the AMEX, the OTC market, and institutional trading.

The *Amex Fact Book* is a comparable data source for the American Stock Exchange. The first book (*Amex Databook*) was published in 1969, 1971, 1973, and 1976. The title was changed to *Amex Statistical Review* in 1981, and to *Amex Fact Book* in 1983. It is now published annually with pertinent information on the exchange and its membership, administration, and trading activities.

The *NASDAQ Fact Book* gives data on the OTC market. First published in 1983 and now issued annually, it contains extensive data on trading volume and information related to the stocks on the NASDAQ system. It also discusses past growth and future plans for the NASDAQ market system.

The *Tokyo Stock Exchange Fact Book* is an annual publication by and about the TSE. Like the fact books prepared by U.S. institutions, it gives extensive data related to members of the exchange, along with information, including price action, about stocks traded on the TSE and other Japanese exchanges.

American Banker Yearbook is an annual publication by the publisher of *American Banker*, a daily newspaper serving the financial services industry. (This newspaper is described later in this section.) The *Yearbook* reviews the events of the year and adds an extensive statistical section that includes operating and size data on commercial banks, finance companies, mortgage bankers, thrifts, and also international banking, covering the top 100 banks in the world.

The *Bond Buyer Yearbook* is another annual publication by a daily newspaper *(The Bond Buyer)* related to the fixed-income market. (This newspaper is described later in this section.) In addition to a review of the major events of the year, it provides extensive statistics related to the municipal bond market such as the volume of long-term and short-term issues in total, by purpose, and by state; the interest rates on alternative issues; the top underwriters; and the top counseling firms. This is the major source of data related to the tax-exempt bond market.

The *Wall Street Journal*, published by Dow Jones & Company, is a national business newspaper published 5 days a week. It contains complete listings for the NYSE, the AMEX, the NASDAQ–OTC market, U.S. bond markets, option markets, and commodities

markets. *The Journal* also gives a limited number of quotes for foreign stocks and a few non-U.S. stock market indicator series. It is recognized worldwide as a prime source of U.S. financial and business information.[7]

The *Asian Wall Street Journal* is a Far East version of *The Wall Street Journal* that concentrates on the Asian region. It includes detailed economic news and stock and bond quotes related to this area of the global market.

Investor Daily, which bills itself as "America's Business Newspaper," was initiated in 1984 as competition to *The Wall Street Journal*. It provides much of the same information, but also attempts to provide added information related to stock prices, earnings, and trading volume. An extensive set of U.S. general market indexes, including several unique to it, are included. It contains little, however, on non-U.S. markets.

The *Financial Times* is published five times a week in London, with issues printed in New York and Los Angeles. While it could be considered a British version of *The Wall Street Journal*, it is actually much more. It takes a true *world* perspective on the financial news. While it does an outstanding job of reporting financial news related to England, it also does very well on U.S. stock and bond quotes and security market indicator series and also contains news and data for Japan and other countries. Most important, however, is its global perspective on discussing and interpreting the news. This is critical to those involved in the rapidly evolving global securities market.

The Bond Buyer is a newspaper published 5 days a week that concentrates on news and quotes related to the overall bond market, with special emphasis on the municipal bond market. It claims to be "The Authority on Municipal Bonds Since 1891." Besides news stories on events that affect bonds, it gives extensive listings of new and forthcoming bond sales, bond calls and redemptions, and information on bond ratings. It also reports numerous market indicator series with emphasis on fixed-income series.

American Banker calls itself "The Daily Financial Services Newspaper." It contains articles on topics of interest to bankers and others involved in the financial

---

[7]A booklet that discusses many features of *The Wall Street Journal* is "A Future Manager's Guide to *The Wall Street Journal*." Copies are available from *The Wall Street Journal*, Educational Service Bureau, P.O. Box 300, Princeton, NJ 08540.

services industry such as legislation and general news of the industry and major banks. It also briefly summarizes the financial markets for Treasuries, financial futures, and mortgage securities.

Barron's is a weekly publication of Dow Jones & Company that typically contains about six articles on topics of interest to investors. It includes the most complete weekly listing available of prices and quotes for all U.S. financial markets. It provides weekly data on individual stocks and the latest information on earnings and dividends as well as quotes on commodities, stock options, and financial futures. Finally, toward the back of each issue (typically the last four pages), an extensive statistical section gives detailed information on the U.S. securities market for the previous week.[8] It also gives a fairly extensive set of world security market indicator series and information on interest rates around the world. Its "International Trader" section discusses price movements in the major global stock markets.

Credit Markets, a weekly newspaper issued by the publishers of *The Bond Buyer*, provides a longer-term overview of the major news items that affect Treasury, corporate, and individual fixed-income securities. An extensive statistical section also lists bond calls and redemptions and reports the long-term calendar of upcoming issues along with several security market series.

Banking World is a concise weekly newspaper from the publishers of *American Banker*. It summarizes all the major news stories from Washington, the Federal Reserve, and all sectors of the financial services industry. It gives news on marketing, technology, federal and state regulations, and specific financial services firms.

Financial Services Week is a weekly publication that its publisher, Fairchild Publications, bills as "The Financial Planner's Newspaper." It contains articles on the overall stock and bond market, but also considers insurance and special features such as "Planning for Dentists" and "Baby Boomers and Financial Services." It also reviews tax changes and other legislation of importance to financial planning.

Bond World describes itself as "the authority on global fixed-income investments." It is published weekly by American Banker-Bond Buyer and IFR Publishing Ltd. It includes pages on U.S. Treasury securities, international bonds, corporate debt, securitized debt, tax exempt bonds, and world bond yields. It also contains discussions on investment management activities.

International Financing Review is a weekly magazine with stories and data regarding international investment banking firms and the international securities markets. It emphasizes fixed-income securities and global economics and politics. It is published by IFR Publishing Ltd.

Equities International, a weekly magazine, is another product of IFR Publishing. It deals with global markets, but concentrates on equity instruments such as common stock, warrants, convertibles, options, and futures. It emphasizes major trends and events in countries around the world, including a complete listing of stock market indicator series for major global markets.

Euro Week, billed as "The Euromarket's First Newspaper," contains discussions related to notes, bonds, and stocks throughout Europe, as well as longer articles on major news from individual countries. A capital market guide provides information on major forthcoming securities issues. Finally, it briefly summarizes the market indicator series for various countries and lists the top investment banking firms in various categories (e.g., Eurobonds and Euro-equities) based upon the value of issues underwritten.

The Dow Jones Investor's Handbook is an annual publication of the complete DJIA results for each year along with earnings and dividends for the series since 1939. Individual reports also cover common and preferred stocks and bonds listed on the NYSE and AMEX, including high and low prices, volume, dividends, and the year's most active stocks.[9]

Business and Investment Almanac is an annual publication of Dow Jones-Irwin edited by Sumner N. Levine. This almanac contains a wide range of information on the economy, various industries, U.S. and foreign securities markets, and individual classes of investments (stocks, bonds, options, futures, real es-

---

[8]A booklet that discusses many features of *Barron's* and how technicians use the series is Martin E. Zweig, "Understanding Technical Forecasting." It is available free of charge from *The Wall Street Journal*, Educational Service Bureau, P.O. Box 300, Princeton, NJ 08540.

[9]Prior to 1980, the firm published handbooks on several other topics, including *Barron's Market Laboratory*, *The Dow Jones Commodities Handbook*, and *The Dow Jones Stock Options Handbook*.

tate, diamonds, and other collectibles). It concludes with a very helpful business and information directory.

The Wall Street Waltz is a book put together by Kenneth Fisher with 90 charts dealing with financial cycles and trends of historical interest. Examples include "Price-to-Book-Value Ratios" from 1921; "Stock Prices Abroad" (giving stock prices for seven foreign countries); and a chart of the "South Seas Bubble" from 1719 to 1720. It provides an excellent historical and current perspective.

S&P Trade and Security Statistics is a service of Standard & Poor's that includes historical data on various economic and security price series and a monthly supplement that updates the series for the recent period. It provides two major sets of data: (1) business and financial data, and (2) a security price index record.

Within the business and finance section it gives long-term statistics on trade, banking, industry, prices, agriculture, and the financial sector. The security price index record contains historical data for all of the Standard & Poor's indexes. This includes its sample of 500 stocks broken down into 88 individual groups. Besides the four main groups (industrials, rails, utilities, and financial firms) it also defines four supplementary group series: capital goods companies, consumer goods, high-grade common stocks, and low-priced common stocks.

In addition to the stock price series, Standard & Poor's has derived a quarterly series of earnings and dividends for each of the four main groups. The earnings series includes data from 1946 to the present. The booklet also contains data on daily stock sales on the NYSE since 1918 and historical yields for a number of corporate and government bond indexes.

Brokerage Firm Reports

As a means of competing for investors' business, brokerage firms provide, among other services, information and recommendations on the outlook for securities markets. These reports are typically prepared monthly and distributed to customers (or potential customers) of the firm free of charge. In the competition for institutional business, investment firms have generated extremely extensive and sophisticated reports. Among the brokerage firms issuing these reports are Goldman Sachs & Company; Kidder Peabody & Co.; Merrill Lynch, Pierce, Fenner & Smith; Morgan Stanley; and Salomon Brothers.

Beyond these reports on the U.S. security markets, several investment banking firms publish extensive reviews of the world capital markets. These discuss the economic outlooks for the major countries along with import/export and exchange rate considerations that culminate in evaluations of the outlooks for specified global industries, and also recommendations related to world bond and stock markets. Examples of such publications include the following:

- Goldman Sachs International Corp.'s monthly publication, *World Investment Strategy Highlights*, begins with coverage of world investment factors, such as economic activity, monetary conditions, and interest rates, and moves to individual reports for about 12 countries and groups of countries. It culminates in a recommended world portfolio strategy.
- Morgan Stanley Capital International has a monthly publication that provides up-to-date pricing and valuation data on individual stocks and world industries. It assumes that an analyst or a portfolio manager would evaluate U.S. firms as part of their global industries rather than isolated national industries. This set of world data allows the analyst or portfolio manager to examine stocks across industries and countries.

Morgan Stanley also issues a quarterly publication that provides over 20 years of share price information (adjusted for capital changes) for 1,700 of the largest companies in the world, representing over 75 percent of the world's market capitalization. It provides firms' most recent balance sheets, along with 5 years of operating data.

- The Fixed Income Group of Kidder Peabody & Co. publishes "The International Report," a monthly publication that suggests a global investment strategy for the fixed-income market. Specifically, it considers global fixed-income returns, yields, and exchange rates including specific country analysis for the United States, Japan, West Germany, the United Kingdom and other countries of current interest. The Fixed Income Group also publishes a weekly "Capital Markets Report" that contains numerous charts on domestic output, personal income, inflation, Federal Reserve data, global interest rates, and international statistics.
- The Merrill Lynch Capital Markets Group publishes "World Bond Market Monitor," a biweekly

analysis of international bond yields, spreads, and yield curves. It specifically considers the U.S. dollar bond market, floating rate note market, U.K. sterling bond market, Japanese yen bond market, Deutschemark bond market, Dutch guilder bond market, and bond markets in several other countries, along with world inflation and yields in currency hedged instruments. The same group also publishes the monthly "International Fixed Income Strategy," which considers the global perspective for the dollar, the world climate for bonds, and specific market perspectives for the Japanese yen, the sterling bond market, and DM bonds. It concludes with an international fixed-income strategy for the following 6 months.

- Salomon Brothers Inc. has three interlocking monthly reports: "Global Fixed-Income Investment Strategy," "Global Equity Investment Strategy," and "Global Economic Outlook and Asset Allocation." Based upon the outlook for the United States and world economies and markets, it makes recommendations for a total world portfolio, including consideration of global fixed-income and equity allocation in light of the exchange rate outlook.

- The Nomura Research Institute (NRI) publishes *Nomura Investment Review*, a monthly publication that analyzes and projects the general investment climate in Japan and the rest of the world.[10] While the publication emphasizes the Japanese economy and its securities markets, it also provides an extensive discussion of the world stock markets and events in various sectors (industries). It provides a world portfolio-structure recommendation as well as suggestions for specific stocks.

- Daiwa Securities Co., Ltd. issues a quarterly publication, *Tokyo Stock Market Quarterly Review*, which includes in-depth analyses of the Japanese economy and securities market along with an extensive discussion of financial markets around the world.

Industry Analysis

Only a few publications provide extensive information on a wide range of industries. Most data on various industries come from industry publications and trade association magazines.

Industry Publications

Standard & Poor's Industry Survey is a two-volume reference work divided into 34 sections that deal with 69 major domestic industries. Coverage in each area is divided into a basic analysis and a current analysis. The annual basic analysis examines the long-term prospects for a particular industry based upon an analysis of historical trends and problems. Major segments of the industry are spotlighted, together with a comparative analysis of its principal companies. The current analysis, which is published quarterly, provides information on recent developments and statistics for the industry and specific companies within it, along with appraisals of the investment outlook for the industry.

Standard & Poor's Analysts Handbook contains information on selected income accounts and balance sheet items along with related financial ratios for Standard & Poor's-defined industry groups. This annual book is typically not available until about eight months after year-end. These fundamental income and balance sheet series allow you to compare the major factors bearing on group stock price movements (e.g., sales, profit margins, earnings). We use such data extensively in our coverage of industry analysis in Chapter 13. Figure 6.1 is a sample page from the *Handbook*.

Value Line Industry Survey is an integral part of the *Value Line Investment Survey*. The reports for the 1,700 companies included are divided into 91 industries and updated by industry. In the binder containing these reports, the industry evaluation precedes the individual company reports. The industry report contains summary statistics for the industry on assets, earnings, and important ratios similar to what is included for companies. There is also an industry stock price index as well as a table that provides comparative data for all the individual companies on timeliness rank, safety rank, and financial strength. The discussion considers the major factors affecting the industry and concludes with a section on investment advice related to the industry.

Industry Journals Journals devoted to various industries are excellent sources of specific data and general information about an industry. Depending upon the industry, several publications may be available; for example, the computer industry has spawned at least five such magazines. Examples of industry publications include the following:

---

[10]The Nomura Research Institute is an independently managed research company affiliated with the Nomura Securities Co., Ltd.

Figure 6.1 **Sample Page from Standard & Poor's Analysts Handbook**

CHEMICALS

Per Share Data—Adjusted to stock price index level. Average of stock price indexes, 1941-1943-10

	Sales	Oper. Profit	Profit Margin %	Depr.	Income Taxes	Cash Flow	Earnings Per Share	Earnings % of Sales	Dividends Per Share	Dividends % of Earn.	Price 1941-1943-10 High	Price 1941-1943-10 Low	Price/Earn. Ratio High	Price/Earn. Ratio Low	Div. Yields % High	Div. Yields % Low	Book Value Per Share	% Return	Working Capital	Capital Expenditures
1959	19.34	5.16	26.68	1.40	1.90		2.23	11.53	1.47	65.92	61.60	48.57	27.62	21.78	3.03	2.39	14.75	15.12	5.76	1.62
1960	19.97	4.82	24.14	1.50	1.65		2.08	10.42	1.46	70.19	60.80	44.15	29.23	21.23	3.31	2.40	15.79	13.17	5.67	2.29
1961	20.67	4.96	24.00	1.66	1.64		2.08	10.06	1.55	74.52	56.69	47.55	27.25	22.86	3.26	2.73	16.66	12.48	5.68	2.17
1962	23.55	5.92	25.14	1.88	2.01		2.42	10.28	1.67	69.01	54.31	39.16	22.44	16.18	4.26	3.07	17.34	13.96	6.75	2.33
1963	26.69	6.60	24.73	2.10	2.22		2.75	10.30	1.83	66.55	62.36	52.50	22.68	19.09	3.49	2.93	18.61	14.78	7.77	2.71
1964	31.88	7.99	25.06	2.41	2.58		3.34	10.48	1.99	59.58	72.87	62.96	21.82	18.85	3.16	2.73	20.09	16.63	8.99	3.85
1965	34.52	8.59	24.88	2.64	2.55		3.41	9.88	1.89	55.43	76.78	68.78	22.52	20.17	2.75	2.46	21.94	15.54	9.90	4.88
1966	38.18	8.97	23.49	2.88	2.58		3.50	9.17	1.94	55.43	75.38	49.82	21.54	14.23	3.89	2.57	23.51	14.89	9.93	5.41
1967	38.63	8.12	21.02	3.15	1.99		2.84	7.35	1.87	65.85	60.53	50.87	21.31	17.91	3.68	3.09	24.40	11.64	10.21	5.07
1968	43.96	9.37	21.31	3.51	2.56		3.16	7.19	2.00	63.29	61.43	50.20	19.44	15.89	3.98	3.26	26.25	12.04	11.21	4.59
1969	47.18	9.55	20.24	3.70	2.52		3.17	6.72	1.94	61.20	57.95	40.08	18.28	12.64	4.84	3.35	27.17	11.67	11.79	5.40
1970	47.51	8.89	18.71	3.90	1.95		2.70	5.68	1.90	70.37	47.11	36.93	17.45	13.68	5.14	4.03	27.77	9.72	11.75	5.95
1971	49.55	9.36	18.89	3.99	2.07		2.93	5.91	1.90	64.85	58.71	47.56	20.04	16.23	3.99	2.93	29.48	9.94	12.97	5.25
1972	54.18	10.77	19.88	4.15	2.66		3.61	6.66	1.97	54.57	67.13	56.40	18.60	15.62	3.49	2.93	30.64	11.78	14.51	5.00
1973	64.00	13.54	21.16	4.23	3.91		5.10	7.97	2.08	40.78	72.95	55.46	14.30	10.87	3.75	2.85	33.84	15.07	16.39	6.39
1974	85.47	17.01	19.90	4.76	5.10		6.79	7.94	2.21	32.55	68.80	47.20	10.13	6.95	4.68	3.21	38.34	17.71	18.71	10.26
1975	80.33	15.24	18.97	4.92	4.18		5.51	6.86	2.18	39.56	74.63	48.76	13.54	8.85	4.47	2.92	39.26	14.03	17.59	11.95
1976	91.16	17.47	19.17	5.49	4.52		6.59	7.23	2.48	37.63	89.70	67.27	13.61	10.21	3.69	2.76	43.27	15.23	18.93	12.97
1977	101.01	18.44	18.26	6.37	4.31	12.52	6.16	6.10	2.78	45.13	72.45	52.70	11.76	8.56	5.28	3.84	46.55	13.23	19.77	12.10
1978	112.76	20.82	18.46	7.21	5.07	14.36	7.16	6.35	3.10	43.30	59.62	46.05	8.33	6.43	6.73	5.20	50.65	14.14	22.27	12.13
1979	129.30	22.59	17.47	7.51	5.13	16.67	9.17	7.09	3.38	36.86	61.04	51.75	6.66	5.64	6.53	5.54	54.58	16.80	24.87	12.48
1980	140.37	20.86	14.86	7.73	4.03	15.79	8.07	5.75	3.56	44.11	64.88	49.70	8.04	6.16	7.16	5.49	60.53	13.33	25.83	15.11
1981	143.65	21.09	14.68	7.72	4.79	15.42	7.71	5.37	3.37	43.71	73.84	52.81	9.58	6.85	6.38	4.56	65.84	11.71	29.45	15.26
1982	159.01	21.85	13.74	9.56	5.52	14.76	5.21	3.28	3.57	68.52	63.30	45.44	12.15	8.72	7.86	5.64	65.63	7.94	26.03	15.89
1983	161.68	23.41	14.48	10.18	6.66	14.46	4.98	3.08	3.66	73.49	81.75	57.95	16.41	11.64	6.32	4.48	66.32	7.51	22.60	12.06
1984	168.26	26.85	15.96	9.84	7.97	17.39	7.39	4.39	4.00	54.13	75.82	61.58	10.26	8.33	6.50	5.28	68.72	10.75	21.35	13.35
1985	151.04	24.21	16.03	10.47	3.84	13.35	2.34	1.55	3.91	167.09	91.58	63.14	39.14	26.98	6.19	4.27	60.10	3.89	18.64	13.90
1986	142.01	27.14	19.11	11.64	5.92	19.59	7.95	5.60	6.04	75.97	132.68	87.43	16.69	11.00	6.91	4.55	58.74	13.53	20.02	13.63
1987	171.62	33.40	19.46	12.25	10.21	24.99	12.75	7.43	4.72	37.02	185.85	118.65	14.58	9.31	3.98	2.54	68.96	18.49	25.94	15.02
1988	200.84	44.65	22.23	13.38	11.09	31.10	17.73	8.83	5.19	29.27	151.64	128.15	8.55	7.23	4.05	3.42	84.36	21.02	21.86	21.12
1989	219.60	47.21	21.50	14.44	11.15	32.59	18.15	8.27	6.88	37.91	184.92	146.63	10.19	8.08	4.69	3.72	74.17	24.47	17.12	24.06

Stock Price Indexes for this group extend back to 1926.

*Air Products & Chemicals (4-10-85)
*Dow Chemical (7-30-47)
*du Pont de Nemours (1-16-35)
*Goodrich (B.F.) (transferred from Tire and Rubber) (7-22-87)
*Hercules Inc. (formerly Hercules Powder) (9-17-30)
*Monsanto Co. (1-16-35)
*NL Industries (transferred from Oil Well Equip. & Services) (1-25-89)
*Quantum Chemicals (formerly National Distillers & Chemicals) (transferred from Beverages (Distillers)) (7-22-87)

*Rohm & Haas (transferred from Chemicals Div.) (4-10-85)
*Union Carbide Co. (12-31-25)
Airco Inc. (formerly Air Reduction) (1-2-18 to 2-5-75)
Allied Chemical Corp. (transferred to Chemicals Div.) (1-2-18 to 7-25-79)
American Cyanamid (9-17-30 to 7-25-79)
American Potash & Chem. (2-14-62 to 1-3-68)
Atlas Powder (1-16-35 to 7-23-47)
Celanese Corp. (4-10-85 to 2-25-87)
Chemetron Corp. (formerly Nat'l Cylinder Gas) (4-16-58 to 2-5-75)
Columbian Carbon (12-31-25 to 2-7-62)

Commercial Solvents (12-31-25 to 6-16-65)
Ethyl Corp (transferred to Chemicals (Specialty)) (2-25-87 to 3-14-90)
G.A.F. Corp. (formerly General Aniline & Film) (6-16-65 to 2-5-75)
Hooker Chemical (1-3-68 to 7-30-68)
Olin Corp. (formerly Olin-Mathieson Chemical) (1-2-18 to 2-5-75)
Stauffer Chemical Co. (7-25-79 to 4-10-85)
United Carbon (1-16-35 to 7-23-47)
U.S. Industrial Chemicals (5-11-38 to 8-1-51)

Source: *Standard & Poor's Analysts Handbook* (New York: Standard & Poor's Corporation, 1990). Reprinted with permission.

> **Prospectus** A condensed version of a new issue's SEC registration statement designed to provide authoritative information about the issue for prospective investors.

- *Computers*
- *Real Estate Today*
- *Chemical Week*
- *Modern Plastics*
- *Paper Trade Journal*
- *Automotive News*

Trade Associations

Trade associations are organizations set up by industry members or firms in a general area of business to provide information for such topics as education, advertising, lobbying for legislation, and problem solving. Trade associations typically gather extensive statistics for the industry. Examples of such organizations include:[11]

- Iron and Steel Institute
- American Railroad Association
- National Consumer Finance Association
- Institute of Life Insurance
- American Bankers Association
- Machine Tool Association

Individual Stock and Bond Analysis

The most extensive material is available on individual firms' stocks and bonds. The sources of these publications include individual companies; commercial publishing firms, which produce a vast array of material; reports provided by investment firms; and several investment magazines, which discuss the overall financial markets and provide opinions on individual companies and their stocks or bonds. While we will discuss each of these sources and specific publications, you should keep in mind that many of the prior sources such as *The Wall Street Journal* and *Barron's* also include discussions of individual stocks or bonds.

---

[11]For a more extensive list, see *Encyclopedia of Associations* (Detroit: Gale Research Company, 1987); and *The World Guide to Trade Associations* (New York: R. R. Bowker, 1986).

Company-Generated Information

An obvious source of information about a specific company is the company itself. Indeed, information about some small firms may be available only from those firms because trading activity in the firm's stock is insufficient to justify inclusion in publications of commercial services or brokerage firms.

Annual Reports Every firm with publicly traded stock must prepare and distribute to its stockholders an annual report of financial operations and current financial position. In addition to basic information, most reports discuss what happened during the year and outline expectations for future prospects. Most firms also publish quarterly financial reports that include brief income statements for the interim period and, sometimes, balance sheets. These reports can be obtained directly from the company. To find an address for a company, consult Volume 1 of *Standard & Poor's Register of Corporations, Directors, and Executives*, which contains an alphabetical listing, by business name, of approximately 37,000 corporations.

Security Prospectus When a firm wants to sell securities (bonds, preferred stock, or common stock) in the primary market to raise new capital, the Securities and Exchange Commission (SEC) requires that it file a registration statement describing the securities being offered. It must provide more extensive financial information than that required in an annual report, as well as nonfinancial information on its operations and personnel. A condensed version of the registration statement, called a **prospectus,** is published by the underwriting firm to report most of the information relevant to the issue. Copies of a prospectus for a current offering can be obtained from the underwriter or from the company. Investment banking firms often advertise offerings in publications like *The Wall Street Journal*, *Barron's*, or the *Financial Times*.

Required SEC Reports In addition to registration statements, the SEC requires three *periodic* statements from publicly held firms. The first, the 8–K form, is filed each month, reporting any action that might significantly affect the firm's debt, equity, amount of capital assets, voting rights, or any other change that might have a significant impact on the stock.

Second, the 9–K form is an unaudited report of revenues, expenses, gross sales, and special items filed every six months. It typically contains more extensive information than the quarterly statement.

Finally, the **10–K form** is an annual version of the 9–K with even more information. The SEC requires that firms indicate in their annual reports that copies of their 10–Ks are available upon request without charge.

Commercial Publications

Numerous advisory services supply information on the aggregate market and individual stocks. Examples include Standard & Poor's Corporation, Moody's Investors Service, and Value Line. We will review some of the publications available from these firms in this section.

Standard & Poor's Publications *Standard & Poor's Corporation Records* is a set of seven volumes. The first six contain basic information on all types of corporations (industrial, financial, etc.) arranged alphabetically. The volumes are in binders to allow updating throughout the year. The seventh volume contains recent data on all companies listed in all the volumes.

Standard & Poor's Stock Reports are comprehensive two-page reports on numerous companies with stocks listed on the NYSE or the AMEX or traded OTC. They include the firms' near-term sales and earnings outlooks, recent developments, key income statement and balance sheet items, and charts of their stock price movements. These reports are kept in bound volumes by exchange and are revised every 3 to 4 months. A sample page is shown in Figure 6.2.

Standard & Poor's Stock Guide is a monthly publication that presents compact reports of pertinent financial data on more than 5,000 common and preferred stocks. A separate section covers over 400 mutual funds. For each stock, the guide contains information on its price ranges (historical and recent), dividends, earnings, financial position, institutional holdings, and a ranking for earning and dividend stability. This publication is a very useful quick reference for almost all actively traded stocks, as is shown by the example in Figure 6.3.

Standard & Poor's Bond Guide, a monthly publication, contains the most pertinent comparative financial and statistical information on a broad list of bonds. It covers domestic and foreign bonds (about 3,900 issues), 200 foreign government bonds, and about 650 convertible bonds.

The Outlook, a weekly publication of Standard & Poor's Corporation, advises investors about the general market environment and specific groups of stocks

> **10–K Form** An annual report required by the SEC of a firm's revenues, expenses, and other pertinent data.

or industries (e.g., high-dividend stocks, stocks with low price-to-earnings ratios, high-yield bonds, stocks likely to increase their dividends, etc.). Weekly stock index figures for 88 industry groups and other market statistics are included.

Daily Stock Price Records is published quarterly by Standard & Poor's, with individual volumes for the NYSE, the AMEX, and the OTC market. Each quarterly book is divided into two parts. The first, "Major Technical Indicators of the Stock Market," is devoted to market indicators widely followed as technical guides to the stock market, including price indicator series, volume series, and data on odd lots and short sales. The second, "Daily and Weekly Stock Action," gives daily high, low, close, and volume information, as well as monthly data on short interest for the stock, insider trading information, a 200-day moving average of prices, and a weekly relative strength series. The books for the NYSE and AMEX are available from 1962; the OTC books began in 1968.

Moody's Publications *Moody's Industrial Manual* resembles the Standard & Poor's Corporation Records service, but it organizes information by type of corporation (i.e., industrial, utility, etc.). The two-volume resource is published once a year and covers industrial companies listed on the NYSE, the AMEX, and regional exchanges. One section focuses on international industrial firms. Like all Moody's manuals, this one includes a news report volume that covers events that occurred after publication of the basic manual.

Moody's OTC Industrial Manual is similar to the corresponding manual for listed firms, but it reports on stocks traded on the OTC market.

Moody's covers various industries, as well. *Moody's Public Utility Manual* provides information on public utilities including electricity and gas suppliers, gas transmission firms, telephone companies, and water companies. *Moody's Transportation Manual* covers the transportation industry, including railroads, airlines, steamship companies, electric railways, bus and truck lines, oil pipelines, bridge companies, and automobile and truck leasing companies. *Moody's Bank and Finance Manual* covers the financial services industry as represented by banks, savings and loan associations,

Figure 6.2 *Sample Page from* Standard & Poor's Stock Reports

Int'l Business Machines 1210

NYSE Symbol IBM Options on CBOE (Jan-Apr-Jul-Oct) In S&P 500

Price	Range	P–E Ratio	Dividend	Yield	S&P Ranking	Beta
Aug. 3'90	1990					
108⅛	123⅛–94½	16	4.84	4.5%	A	0.76

Summary

IBM is the world's dominant manufacturer of mainframe computers and is also a major supplier of minicomputers, computer peripheral equipment, personal computers, networking products, and system software. An earnings recovery is foreseen for 1990, reflecting the absence of restructuring costs and translation gains from a weaker dollar. In August, the company announced it would put its domestic typewriter and small printer products businesses into a new unit to be majority owned by Clayton & Dubilier.

Current Outlook

Earnings for 1990 are expected to increase to $10.00 a share from $6.47 in 1989, which included a $2.58 restructuring charge. Earnings for 1991 are projected at $11.20.

The $1.21 quarterly dividend is the minimum expectation.

Gross income should rise almost 8% in 1990 and slightly less in 1991, benefiting from healthy demand overseas and a modest resurgence in domestic demand for IBM's main hardware products, plus translation gains from a weaker dollar. Profit margins should improve, with gains from the domestic cost containment program more than offsetting pricing pressures in the mainframe and minicomputer markets.

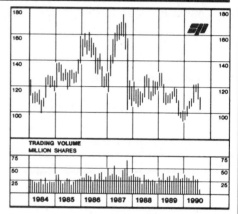

Revenues (Billion $)

Quarter:	1991	1990	1989	1988
Mar.	---	14.19	12.73	12.06
Jun.	---	16.50	15.21	13.91
Sep.	---	---	14.31	13.71
Dec.	---	---	20.46	20.00
	---	---	62.71	59.68

Revenues for the first half of 1990 advanced 10%, year to year, reflecting increased overall hardware sales and significantly higher software and leasing revenues. Profit margins benefited from the higher volume and initial benefits from the cost reduction program. After sharply higher interest expense, net income increased 6.8%, to $4.26 a share (on 1.9% fewer shares) from $3.92.

Capital Share Earnings ($)

Quarter:	1991	1990	1989	1988
Mar.	E1.85	1.81	1.61	1.57
Jun.	E2.55	2.45	2.31	1.63
Sep.	E1.80	E1.70	1.51	2.10
Dec.	E5.00	E4.04	1.04	3.97
	E11.20	E10.00	6.47	9.27

Important Developments

Aug. '90— IBM announced that it will consolidate its domestic typewriter, keyboard, intermediate and personal printers and supplies business into a new subsidiary to be majority owned by Clayton & Dubilier, Inc. IBM may also place the rest of its worldwide information products business in the subsidiary.

Feb. '90— A new line of high performance technical workstations was introduced.

Jan. '90— The company restructured its domestic operations, resulting in a $2.4 billion pretax charge in the fourth quarter of 1989, equal to $2.58 a share after taxes. Savings from expected capacity reductions and technology investment writedowns could add $1.00 to share earnings by 1991.

Nov. '89— Directors approved the repurchase of and additional $4 billion of IBM stock.

Next earnings report expected in mid-October.

Per Share Data ($)

Yr. End Dec. 31	1989	¹1988	1987	1986	1985	1984	1983	1982	1981	1980
Tangible Bk. Val.	66.33	65.78	62.81	55.40	50.60	41.79	38.02	33.13	30.66	28.18
Earnings²	6.47	9.27	8.72	7.81	10.67	10.77	9.04	7.39	5.63	6.10
Dividends	4.73	4.40	4.40	4.40	4.40	4.10	3.71	3.44	3.44	3.44
Payout Ratio	72%	47%	50%	56%	41%	38%	41%	47%	62%	56%
Prices—High	130⅞	129½	175⅞	161⅞	158¾	128½	134¼	98	71½	72¾
Low	93⅜	104¼	102	119¼	117⅜	99	92¼	55⅝	48⅜	50⅜
P/E Ratio—	20–14	14–11	20–12	21–15	15–11	12–9	15–10	13–8	13–9	12–8

Data as orig. reptd. 1. Reflects acctg. change. 2. Bef. spec. item(s) of +0.53 in 1988. E-Estimated.

Source: *Standard & Poor's Stock Reports* (New York: Standard & Poor's Corporation, 1990). Reprinted with permission.

Figure 6.3 *Example from* Standard & Poor's Stock Guide

118 **KAN-KEY** — Standard & Poor's Corporation

Index (¶S&P 500, •Options)	Ticker Symbol	Name of Issue (Call Price of Pfd. Stocks)	Market	Com. Rank. & Pfd. Rating	Par Val.	Inst. Hold Cos	Inst. Hold Shs. (000)	Principal Business	Price Range 1971-88 High	1971-88 Low	1989 High	1989 Low	1990 High	1990 Low	Mar. Sales in 100s	March, 1990 Last Sale Or Bid High	Low	Last	%Div Yield	P-E Ratio
1	KAB	**Kaneb Services**	NY,B,M,P,Ph	C	No	50	8502	Oil&gas expl,dev,drill'g:coal	40⅛	1¼	6½	2⅛	5¾	3⅞	37426	5¾	4½	5¼	...	d
2	KLT	**Kansas City Pwr & Lt**	NY,B,C,M,Ph	A−	No	142	14309	Supplies elec to Kansas City	32¼	10⅝	36⅛	28⅛	35⅛	31⅞	12311	33⅞	32¼	32⅞	7.8	10
3	KSU	**Kansas City So. Ind**	NY,B,M,P,Ph	B	No	73	4733	RR fin'l svcs,mutual funds,RE	79¾	1 9/16	54¾	31½	48	35½	2613	38⅜	35½	38	2.8	8
4	KGE	**Kansas Gas & Elec**	NY,B,M,P	B	No	145	19008	Electric utility-Kansas	26¾	9⅝	24¼	19¼	23¾	20½	23117	21¾	20½	21	8.2	15
5	KAN	**Kansas Pwr & Light**	NY,B,M,P,Ph	A	5	145	9637	Electric & gas utility	32½	7¼	25⅜	21⅝	25⅛	22⅛	6051	23	22¼	23	7.8	11
6	KPA	**Kappa Networks**	AS	NR	No	1	5	Mfr electronic components	10⅝	1⅛	1½	7/16	⅞	½	645	⅞	⅝	¾	...	d
7	KASL	**Kasler Corp**	OTC	B−	No	26	1617	Heavy contstr in west'n U.S.	21½	5¼	11¼	7½	10	8½	4915	10	9⅛	9⅝B	1.0	34
8	KT	**Katy Indus**	NY,B,M,P	B−	1	37	2232	Indus machin'y&components:	45	2	26⅛	18¼	26¾	21	1188	23½	21⅜	22⅜	...	21
9	Pr B	**$1.46 cm Cv B Pfd(25)vtg**	NY	NR	No	4	39	consumer prod:energy res	115	9⅛	66¾	48	62½	55¾	17	59½	56	58	2.5	..
¶10•[1]	KBH	**Kaufman & Broad Home**	NY,Ph	B+	1	128	16185	Single-family home builder	21	7¾	21¾	9⅞	15¼	10¾	23697	13⅜	11⅛	12¾	2.4	5
11•[2]	KJI	**Kay Jewelers**	NY,M,Ph	B	1	28	2093	Operates jewelry stores	15⅞	4¼	24⅜	10⅜	17¾	9¾	23683	12⅝	9¾	12½	...	..
12	KDON	**Kaydon Corp**	OTC	NR	10¢	77	4979	Mfrs bear'gs/filtration prod	34	3¾	38½	26⅞	32½	27¼	4464	32½	29½	30½B	1.3	12
13	KPRQE	**Kaypro Corp**	OTC	↓D	No	6	611	Mfrs personal computer sys	10⅝	¼	½	1/16	¼	1/32	13456	⅛	1/32	1/32B	...	d
14	KEA	**Keane Inc**	AS	B	10¢	12	241	Computer services/systems	5⅜	3/16	14⅝	4½	16⅝	13	6352	15⅛	13½	14	...	15
15	KMCI	**Keegan Management Co**	OTC	NR	0.001	4	110	Oper nutri/weight loss ctrs	....	....	11	9	10¼	4¼	11931	9	4¼	5⅝B	...	10
16	KEI	**Keithley Instruments**	AS	B+	No	24	673	Mfr electronic test instr/sys	19¾	2 7/16	16⅞	11¾	12½	10¾	377	12¼	10¾	12⅛B	1.5	13
17	KLY	**Kelley Oil & Gas Ptnrs**[56]	AS	NR	No	24	1529	Oil & gas explor,dev,prod'n	14½	8	24	13¾	23⅞	20¼	2429	23⅞	20⅝	22	8.0	42
¶18•[3]	K	**Kellogg Co**	NY,B,C,M,P,Ph	A+	25¢	394	85916	Convenience food products	68¾	5⅛	81⅝	57¾	69	58¾	32055	62⅜	58¾	61⅛	3.1	18
19	KWD	**Kellwood Co**	NY,B,M,Ph	A−	1¢	104	7635	Apparel for Sears, Roebuck	41	2 3/16	35⅜	20½	22⅞	15	13875	18¾	15	16⅞	4.7	7
20	KELYA	**Kelly Services'A'**[59]	OTC	A	1	108	8645	Temporary office help	39½	7/16	42	26¾	39⅞	32⅜	5423	36	34¾	35⅜B	1.9	15
21•[1]	KEM	**Kemper Corp**	NY,M,Ph	↑B+	5	171	22512	Insur & fin'l hldg	38¾	1 13/16	51⅞	22¾	51	34	11934	39¾	37¼	38	2.4	6
22	KHI	**Kemper High Income**	NY	NR	1¢	4	2140	Closed-end investment co	12⅜	11¼	12¼	8½	9¼	7⅝	8005	8½	8	8⅛	14.8	..
23	KGT	**Kemper Interm Gvt Tr**	NY,Ph	NR	1¢	9	80	Closed-end diversified inv co	10⅜	9	10	8⅞	9⅞	7⅞	14785	9	7⅞	8⅜	10.5	..
24	KMM	**Kemper Multi-Mkt Income**	NY,M	NR	1¢	4	6	Closed-end diversified inv co	....	....	12⅛	9¼	10¾	8½	6348	9½	8½	9⅛	15.3	..
25	KTF	**Kemper Muni Income**	NY,M	NR	1¢	9	109	Closed-end diversified inv co	12⅛	12	12⅛	10⅞	12	11⅜	5436	11⅝	11⅜	11⅜	7.6	..
26	KSM	**Kemper Strategic Muni Tr**	NY,M,Ph	NR	1¢	..	...	Closed-end investment co	....	....	12⅜	11⅛	12	11	2436	11⅝	11⅛	11⅜	⊙7.9	..
27	KMT	**Kennametal, Inc**	NY,B,M	B	1¼	110	7442	Tungsten-base carbide prod	42¼	5	37⅝	27¼	32	27¾	5129	31⅞	28⅛	30½	3.8	10
28	KEC	**Kent Electronics**	AS	NR	No	25	1440	Dstr variety wiring products	9¾	4	9⅜	5⅝	8¾	7¼	312	8⅝	8	8¼	...	11
29	KENCA	**Kentucky Cent Life Ins**[62]	OTC	B+	1	48	4098	Life,health & accident ins	21¼	1 5/16	21⅝	11⅝	19⅛	13¼	5748	15⅜	13¼	15⅛B	2.6	6
30	KYMDA	**Kentucky Medical Insur'A'**	OTC	B	2.80	3	91	Medl liability insur in Ky	3⅝	2⅝	35	3⅝	24¼	16¼	1146	24	19½	20¼B	...	6
31	KU	**Kentucky Utilities**	NY,B,M,P	↑A	No	114	6201	Electric utility: coal based	24⅛	6⅝	20⅞	17⅞	21	19¼	8716	20⅜	19⅝	19¾	7.4	10
32	KWN	**Kenwin Shops**	AS	C	1	5	45	Ladies & children apparel	24	2¾	10¼	6⅞	7½	6⅝	99	7½	6¾	6⅝B	...	74
33	KPTL	**Keptel Inc**	OTC	NR	No	10	685	Mfr telecommun test equip	8¼	3¾	9⅜	5⅞	8½	5¾	1117	8½	6	6½B	...	12
34	KIX	**Kerkhoff Industries**	AS	NR	No	1	19	Construction,R.E. dvlp,mfg	5⅜	1⅜	2¾	1⅜	2½	1¾	438	2½	1⅞	2¼	...	23
35	KER	**Kerr-Addison Mines**	To	B−	No	37	3808	Canada gold mine: invests	30¾	5⅝	23¾	18¼	21½	18¾	1752	19½	18⅞	19	3.2	26
36	KGM	**Kerr Glass Mfg**	NY,B,M	B−	50¢	25	1545	Glass containers: closures	22	8	14⅞	8⅝	13⅝	9⅞	496	11⅛	10¼	10¾	4.1	d
37	Pr D	**$1.70 cm CvB PfdSerD(20)**	NY	B+	50¢	4	163	packaging products	30⅝	13¼	22⅛	17⅛	21	19½	63	20⅜	19½	19¼B	8.8	..
☆¶38•[4]	**KMG**	**Kerr-McGee**	**NY,B,C,M,P,Ph,To**	**B**	**1**	**352**	**29596**	**Petroleum, chemicals,coal**	**48**	**15⅞**	**52**	**37⅜**	**51¼**	**46¾**	**24805**	**51¼**	**48¾**	**50⅞**	**2.6**	**16**
39	KCH	**Ketchum & Co**	AS	C	1	6	104	Drug distributor & mfr	26¾	1 3/16	7⅝	1⅝	5⅛	2⅛	84	2¾	2⅛	2⅛B	...	d
40	KTM	**Ketema Inc**	AS	NR	1	67	2014	Industrial/engineered prod	14	12	18¾	12¼	15¾	12¾	1085	13¾	12¾	13⅝	...	d
41	KVLM	**Kevlin Microwave**	OTC	B	10¢	7	362	Mfr devices for radar sys	8¼	1/16	3¼	2	2¼	1¼	541	1¾	1⅜	1⅜B	...	12
42	KEQU	**Kewaunee Scientific**	OTC	B	2½	11	373	Furniture & eqp for labs	15¾	1¼	9½	7⅛	7⅝	6	139	6⅞	6	6B	2.7	11
43	KEYC	**Key Centurion Bancshrs**	OTC	B+	3	17	799	Comm'l bkg,West Virginia	19	8½	15¾	12	14¼	12½	4030	14¼	13¼	14¼B	4.2	12
44	KEY	**KeyCorp**	NY,M,Ph	A−	5	133	15919	Comml bkg,Central New York	31	4¼	29¾	19⅝	27⅝	23⅜	5248	25⅞	23⅞	24	5.3	8
45	KYC	**Keystone Camera Prod**	AS,M	C	40¢	15	798	U.S.mfr point/shoot camera	345	¾	2¼	⅞	1⅛	9/16	4828	⅞	9/16	¾	...	d

Uniform Footnote Explanations-See Page 1. Other: [1]Ph:Cycle 1. [2]Ph:Cycle 2. [3]ASE:Cycle 3. [4]CBOE:Cycle 1. [51]Accum on Pfd. [52]△$12.86,'88. [53]®$0.91,'89. [54]Incl Curr Amts. [55]®$2.36,'89. [56]L.P. Dep Units. [57]100% non-taxable,'89. [58]®$2.80,'89. [59]Non-vtg. [60]Excl subsid pfd. [61]©$0.05,'89. [62]Cl A, non vtg. [63]®$0.49,'89. [64]Fiscal Apr'87 & prior. [65]12 Mo Sep'88,fiscal Apr'88 $4.73.
☆ See Directory of Company Investor Contacts in the back of the Guide.

Source: *Standard & Poor's Stock Guide* (New York: Standard & Poor's Corporation, 1990). Reprinted with permission.

credit agencies of the U.S. government, all phases of the insurance industry, investment companies, real estate firms, real estate investment trusts, and miscellaneous financial enterprises.

Moody's Municipal and Government Manual contains data on the U.S. government, the states and their agencies, and over 13,500 municipalities. It also provides some excellent information on foreign governments and international organizations. *Moody's International Manual* provides financial information on about 3,000 major foreign corporations.

Value Line Publications *The Value Line Investment Survey* is published in two parts. Volume 1 contains basic historical information on about 1,700 companies as well as a number of analytical measures of earnings stability, growth rates, a common stock safety factor, and a timing factor rating. A number of studies have examined the usefulness of the timing factor ratings for investment purposes, with results to be discussed in Chapter 22.

The *Investment Survey* also includes extensive 2-year projections for the firms it covers and 3-year estimates of performance. As an example, in early 1992 it will include earnings projections for 1992, 1993, and 1994 to 1996. The second volume includes weekly editions with general investment advice and recommendations of individual stocks for purchase or sale. An example of a Value Line company report is shown in Figure 6.4.

The *Value Line OTC Special Situations Service* is published 24 times a year. It serves the experienced investor who is willing to accept high risk in the hope of realizing exceptional capital gains. Each issue discusses past recommendations and presents 8 to 10 new stocks for consideration.

Brokerage Firm Reports

Besides the products of these information firms, many brokerage firms prepare reports on individual companies and their securities. Some of these reports are rather objective and contain only basic information, but others make specific recommendations.

Investment Magazines

Many periodicals cover the securities industry for the benefit of professionals and individual investors. As noted earlier, while many of these publications emphasize individual companies and their stocks, they also discuss the overall financial markets and indus-

tries. Twice monthly editions of *Forbes* contain 12 to 14 articles on individual companies and industries. Several regular columnists discuss the economy, the aggregate bond and stock markets, and the commodity markets.

Financial World is likewise published twice a month. Each edition generally contains about six articles on companies, industries, and the overall market, along with several regular features on taxes and options. A separate section reports market data.

The Wall Street Transcript is published weekly as a composite of sources of information other than market quotations. It contains text of speeches made at analysts' meetings, copies of brokerage house reports on companies and industries, and interviews with corporate officials. It also includes discussions of forthcoming new stock issues.

The Media General Financial Weekly features a series of articles and columns. Of primary interest is a comprehensive set of financial and statistical information on 3,400 common stocks, including every common stock listed on the NYSE and the AMEX, and over 700 OTC issues. It also presents charts on 60 major industry groups.

Business Week is published weekly by McGraw-Hill. While not strictly an investment magazine, it contains numerous articles on companies and industries, as well as several features of importance to investors including a weekly production index and a leading economic index. The magazine also has initiated several special issues compiling lists such as the top 1,000 U.S. firms, the top 500 global firms, and the wealthiest individuals in the United States and the world.

Fortune, published biweekly by Time Inc., provides extensive articles on the economy, politics, individual companies, securities markets, and personal investing. The magazine is well known for its special annual report on the *Fortune* 500 and the *Fortune* 1,000 largest industrial firms in the country. The magazine also publishes a listing of large nonindustrial firms and major foreign companies. The importance of this information on non-U.S. firms is growing with the increase in global investing.

Pension and Investment Age is a newspaper of corporate and institutional investing published every other Monday. It is intended for those who invest pension fund assets, either as corporate managers or money managers. The paper emphasizes stories and interviews related to pension fund management. There is substantial consideration of personnel changes.

Figure 6.4 **Sample Listing from Value Line**

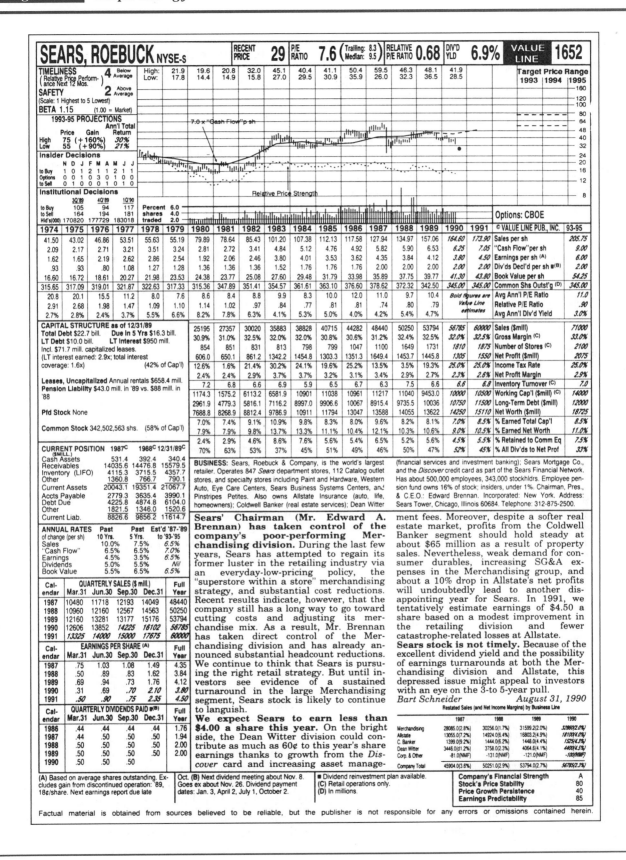

Money, a monthly publication of Time Inc., deals specifically with topics of interest to individual investors, including articles on individual companies and general investment suggestions (e.g., "How to Determine Your Net Worth" or "The Why and How of Investing in Foreign Securities"). Also, each issue presents a financial planning discussion with an individual or couple.

Institutional Investor is a monthly publication of Institutional Investors Systems aimed at professional investors and portfolio managers. It emphasizes events in the investment industry as they relate to corporate finance, pensions, money management, portfolio strategy, and global stock markets. A popular feature is an "All-American Analysts Team" selected by the major institutional investment firms.

OTC Review is a monthly publication devoted to the analysis and discussion of stocks traded on the OTC market. It usually analyzes an industry that is dominated by OTC companies and discusses three or four individual firms. In addition, it publishes numerous earnings reports on OTC firms, name changes, stock exchange listings, and price and volume statistics on OTC stocks.

Financial Planning, a monthly publication billed by its publisher, Financial Services Information Company, as "The Magazine for Financial Service Professionals," is intended for individuals involved in financial planning. It contains a number of feature articles on alternative investment products and procedures, important regulatory information affecting financial planning (e.g., tax legislation), various industries, and specific classes of investments (e.g., mutual funds, real estate, equipment leasing).

Global Finance, a monthly magazine published by Global Information, Inc., contains a number of articles on trends around the world. It is an international version of *Institutional Investor*, since it is written for the practicing money manager or investment professional. It also contains regular columns on topics like venture capital, hedging, and investment strategies.

Global Investor is published monthly, but it produces combined issues for July/August and December/January by Euromoney Publications PLC. Like *Global Finance*, it contains articles on various markets, international instruments, and specific money management firms. It also provides regular columns on the overall bond and stock markets and an extensive section on international bond and stock indicator series.

Academic Journals

Academic journals publish different material than investment magazines in terms of timeliness and general orientation. Investment magazines cover the current investment environment and provide advice for current action. The material is generally nonquantitative. In contrast, academic journals run longer, more theoretical, and more quantitative articles that are typically not intended to be immediately applicable. They typically deal with theoretical or empirical studies related to investments that could have long-run implications.

Journal of Finance is a quarterly published by the American Finance Association. The articles, almost all by academicians, are rather theoretical and empirical. The typical issue includes 15 articles, notes and comments, and book reviews.

Journal of Financial Economics is published quarterly by North Holland Publishing Company in collaboration with the Simon Graduate School of Management of the University of Rochester. It seeks to publish academic research in the areas of consumption and investment decisions under uncertainty, portfolio analysis, efficient markets, and the theory of financial management.

The Review of Financial Studies is published quarterly by Oxford University Press for the Society for Financial Studies. Its purpose is to publish significant new research in financial economics balanced between theoretical and empirical research. While the subject matter appears similar to that of the *Journal of Financial Economics*, it places a stronger emphasis on the theoretical treatment of topics.

Journal of Financial and Quantitative Analysis is a quarterly published by the University of Washington. It is very similar to the *Journal of Finance* in that almost all articles are by academicians. It differs in that it publishes fewer articles on monetary economics.

Financial Analysts Journal is published six times a year by the Financial Analysts Federation. Each issue contains six or seven articles of interest to practicing financial analysts and portfolio managers, a regular feature on securities regulation, and book reviews. The articles are authored by a combination of academicians and practitioners.

Journal of Portfolio Management is published quarterly by Institutional Investors Systems as a forum for academic research of interest to the practicing portfolio manager. Over half the articles are written by academicians, but they are written for the practitioner. Many are less technical and mathematical versions of studies previously published in heavily academic journals.

Financial Management is published quarterly by the Financial Management Association for executives and academicians interested in the financial management of firms. It also runs investment-related articles on topics that are important to the financing decisions of a firm such as stock splits, dividend policy, mergers, initial public offerings, and stock listings.

The Financial Review is a quarterly journal jointly sponsored by the Eastern Finance Association and the Midwest Finance Association. About half of its articles are concerned with capital markets, investments, and portfolio management.

Journal of Financial Research is a joint quarterly publication of the Southern Finance Association and the Southwestern Finance Association. It contains articles on financial management, investments, financial institutions, capital market theory, and portfolio theory.

The C.F.A. Digest is published quarterly by the Institute of Chartered Financial Analysts. Its purpose is to provide about 20 abstracts a quarter of published articles from a wide variety of academic and nonacademic journals of interest to financial analysts and portfolio managers as a service to members of the investment community.

A number of general business and economics journals include articles on finance, and some specifically on investments. One of the foremost, the *Journal of Business* published by the University of Chicago, has run some outstanding articles in the area of investments. Other journals to consider include: *Quarterly Review of Economics and Business* (University of Illinois), *Review of Business and Economic Research* (University of New Orleans), *Journal of Business Research* (North Holland Publishing Co.), *American Economic Review* (American Economic Association), *Journal of Political Economy* (University of Chicago), *Rand Journal of Economics* (American Telephone & Telegraph), and *The Continental Bank Journal of Applied Corporate Finance* (Continental Illinois Bank).

Computerized Data Sources

In addition to the numerous sources of published data, some financial service firms have developed computerized data sources. The discussion considers major

data banks and also some well-known on-line data systems. Space limitations restrict the discussion to major sources.

Data Banks

Compustat is a computerized bank of financial data developed by Standard & Poor's and currently handled by a subsidiary, Investors Management Services. The Compustat tapes contain 20 years of data for approximately 2,220 listed industrial companies, 1,000 OTC companies, 175 utilities, 120 banks, and 500 Canadian firms. Quarterly tapes contain 20 years of quarterly financial data for over 2,000 industrial firms and 12 years of quarterly data for banks and utilities. The financial data on the annual tapes include almost every possible item from each firm's balance sheet and income statement as well as stock market data (stock prices and trading volume).

Value Line Data Base gives historical annual financial and market data for 1,600 industrial and finance companies beginning in 1954. It also provides quarterly data from 1963. In addition to historical data, it gives estimates of dividends and earnings for the coming year and the Value Line opinion regarding stock price stability and investment timing.

Compact Disclosure is a data base on a compact disk with information on over 4,000 public companies filing with the SEC. It is available from Disclosure Information Group of Bethesda, Maryland.

The Center for Research in Security Prices (CRSP) at the University of Chicago Graduate School of Business has developed a set of monthly and daily stock price tapes. The monthly tapes contain month-end prices from January 1926 to the present (updated annually) for every stock listed on the NYSE. Stock prices are adjusted for all stock splits, dividends, and other capital changes. They add monthly AMEX data from July 1962 to the NYSE monthly file to create the current NYSE/AMEX monthly file with information on approximately 6,100 securities.

The daily stock price tape gives daily high, low, and close figures since July 1962 for every stock listed on the NYSE and the AMEX (approximately 5,600 securities). In 1988 the CRSP developed its NASDAQ historical data file with daily price quotes, volume data, and information about capitalization and distributions to shareholders for over 9,600 common stocks traded on the NASDAQ system since December 14, 1972. All of these tapes are updated at the end of each calendar year and supplied to subscribers each spring.

The *Media General Data Bank*, compiled by Media General Financial Services, Inc., includes current price and volume data plus major corporate financial data on 2,000 major companies. In addition, it gives 10 years of daily price and volume information on over 8,000 issues of approximately 4,000 firms on the NYSE, the AMEX, and the OTC market. Finally, it includes price and volume data on several major market indicator series.

ISL Daily Stock Price Tapes are prepared and issued quarterly by Interactive Data Corporation. They include the same information as the *Daily Stock Price Records* published by Standard & Poor's that we discussed earlier.

On-Line Data Systems

A data base called *Bi Data* includes international statistical data such as national accounts, labor statistics, foreign trade, consumption, prices, and production. It is produced by Business International Corporation and sold by General Electric Information Service.

Commodities Market Data Bank provides statistical data on all traded commodities. The producer and vendor is Data Resources Inc. (DRI).

CompuServe provides references, statistical data, and full text retrieval of information on numerous topics, including financial and investment data from the Compustat and Value Line data bases. The producer and vendor is CompuServe, Inc.

The *Quick Quote* service provides current price quotations, trading volume information, and high–low data for securities of U.S. public corporations. The producer and vendor is CompuServe, Inc.

The *Dow Jones News/Retrieval Service* supplies text of articles appearing in major financial publications including *The Wall Street Journal* and *Barron's*. The *Stock Quote Reporters* service provides quotes on stocks, bonds, and mutual funds. The producer and vendor of both is Dow Jones & Co.

The *DRI Capsule/EEI Capsule* service provides over 3,700 U.S. social and economic statistical time series on topics such as population, income, money supply, and interest rates. The producer is DRI and the vendor is Business Information Services.

The *GTE Financial System One Quotation Service* provides current quotations and statistical data on U.S. and Canadian stocks, bonds, options, and com-

modities along with other market data. The producer and vendor is GTE Information Systems, Inc.

The Information Bank provides extensive information on current affairs based upon abstracts from numerous English language publications. The producer and vendor is the New York Times Information Service.

Quotron 800 provides up-to-the-minute quotations and statistics for a broad range of stocks, bonds, options, and commodities. The producer and vendor is Quotron Systems, Inc.[12]

Summary

■ As an investor, you must be aware of sources of information on the U.S. and world economies, the securities markets around the globe, alternative industries, and individual firms. You should use the information in this chapter as a starting point, and spend time in a university library examining these and the many other sources available. Six books that would help in this regard are:

■ Wasserman, Paul, ed. *Encyclopedia of Business Information Sources*, 3d ed. Detroit: Gale Research Co., 1976.

■ Daniells, P. M. *Business Information Sources*, 2d ed. Berkeley, Calif.: University of California Press, 1986.

■ Michanie, Sylvia. *Course Syllabus for Information Sources of Business and Economics*. Brooklyn, N.Y.: Pratt Institute School of Library and Information Science, 1977.

■ Fortune *Investment Information Directory*. Guilford, Conn.: Dushkin Publishing Group, 1988. This booklet contains listings and brief descriptions of numerous newspapers, magazines, investment letters, and books. It also gives an excellent listing of software and data bases of interest to investors in stocks, bonds, futures, and options.

■ *Encyclopedia of Information Systems and Services*. Detroit: Gale Research, 1988.

■ *Guide to American Directories*. Coral Springs, Fla.: B. Klein Publications, 1987.

For other sources, see the References section.

---

[12]An excellent source for additional computer data bases and software, as well as general information on business and economics, is Sumner N. Levine, ed., *The Dow Jones-Irwin Business and Investment Almanac* (Homewood, Ill.: Dow Jones-Irwin, annual).

Questions

1. Name at least three sources of information on the gross national product for the past 10 years.

2. Name two sources of information on rates of exchange with major foreign countries.

3. Assume you want to compare production in the steel and auto industries to industrial production for the economy. Discuss how you would do it, what data you would use, and where you would get the data.

4. You are told that a relationship exists between the growth rate of the money supply and stock price movements. Where would you obtain the data to test this relationship?

5. You are an analyst for Growth Stock Investment Company. The head of research tells you about a tip on an OTC firm, the Shamrock Corporation, for which you need data on sales, earnings, and recent stock price movements. Discuss several sources for this information. (One source is insufficient because the company may not be big enough to be included in some of them.)

6. The head of your research department indicates that the investment committee has decided to become involved in global investing. To get started, they want you to recommend two sources of macroeconomic data for various countries, two sources of industry information, and two sources of company data. Discuss your recommendations.

7. As an individual investor, discuss four publications to which you believe you should subscribe (besides *The Wall Street Journal*). Indicate what each publication can give you and why it is appropriate for you as an individual investor. Be sure that at least two of these sources relate to global investing.

8. As the director of a newly established investment research department at a money management firm, discuss the first four investment services to which you will subscribe, and justify each selection.

9. Select one company each from the NYSE, the AMEX, and the OTC, and look up the name and address of the financial officers you would contact at each firm to obtain recent financial reports.

References

American Banker–Bond Buyer. A division of International Thomson Publishing Corporation, One State Street Plaza, New York, NY 10004.

American Stock Exchange, 86 Trinity Place, New York, NY 10006.

Business Statistics. Superintendent of Documents, U.S. Government Printing Office, Washington, DC 20402. Approximate price, $9.

CompuServe, Inc., 5000 Arlington Centre Boulevard, Columbus, OH 43220.

Data Resources, Inc. (DRI), 29 Hartwell Ave., Lexington, MA 02173.

The Wall Street Journal and *Barron's.* Dow Jones & Co., 200 Burnett Rd., Chicopee, MA 01021.

The Dow Jones Investor's Handbook. Available annually from Dow Jones Books, P. O. Box 455, Chicopee, MA 01021. Approximate price, $10.

Economic Indicators. Superintendent of Documents, U.S. Government Printing Office, Washington, DC 20402. Approximate price, $20/year.

Economic Report of the President. Superintendent of Documents, U.S. Government Printing Office, Washington, DC 20402. Approximate price, $15.

Euromoney Publications PLC, Nestor House, Playhouse Yard, London ECUV 5EX. For North American subscriptions: Reed Business Publishing, 205 East 42d Street, New York, NY 10017.

Federal Reserve Bulletin. Division of Administrative Services, Board of Governors of the Federal Reserve System, Washington, DC 20551. Approximate price, $20/year.

Financial Times. Bracken House, Cannon Street, London EC4P 4BY. U.S. office: 44 East 60th Street, New York, NY 10022.

Global Information, Inc., 55 John Street, New York, NY 10038.

GTE Information Systems, Inc., East Park Drive, Mount Laurel, NJ 08054.

Institutional Investor Systems, Inc., 488 Madison Avenue, New York, NY 10022.

London Stock Exchange, Trogmorton Street, London EG2N 1HP.

Moody's Investors Services, Inc., 99 Church Street, New York, NY 10007.

National Association of Securities Dealers, Inc. (NASD), 1735 K Street N.W., Washington, DC 20006.

New York Stock Exchange, 11 Wall Street, New York, NY 10005.

New York Times Information Services, Inc., 1719-A Route 10, Parsippany, NJ 07054.

Quarterly Financial Report. Superintendent of Documents, U.S. Government Printing Office, Washington, DC 20402. Approximate price, $20/year.

Quotron Systems, Inc., 5454 Beethoven Street, Los Angeles, CA 90066.

Securities and Exchange Commission, 450 5th Street N.W., Washington, DC 20549.

Standard & Poor's Corporation, 345 Hudson Street, New York, NY 10014.

Statistical Abstract of the United States. Superintendent of Documents, U.S. Government Printing Office, Washington, DC 20402. Approximate price, $25 (cloth), $15 (paper).

Statistical Bulletin. Superintendent of Documents, U.S. Government Printing Office, Washington, DC 20402. Approximate price, $20/year.

Survey of Current Business. Superintendent of Documents, U.S. Government Printing Office, Washington, DC 20402. Approximate price, $25/year.

Tokyo Stock Exchange, New York office: TSE, New York Research Office, 100 Wall Street, New York, NY 10005.

Value Line Services. Arnold Bernhard and Company, Inc., 5 East 44th Street, New York, NY 10017.

2

Valuation Principles and Practice

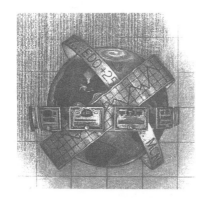

The first part of the book provided the background necessary to learn to make investment decisions. It emphasized defining terms and measures of return and risk, and then describing investment instruments available and the major global capital markets where you would buy and sell these investments.

This second part of the book introduces the valuation process by which you can evaluate alternative investments. Chapter 7 covers the analysis of financial statements. Whatever investment alternative you consider (stocks, bonds, options, or futures), you will use information from financial statements to estimate its risk and return. Therefore, it is important to understand what data are available and how to analyze them to gain insights about a firm such as its operating performance, profitability, growth, business risk, and financial risk.

Chapter 8 explains and presents the case for the top-down approach to the investment process. It covers how and why you evaluate the overall economy, alternative industries, and finally, individual companies when selecting securities for your portfolio. This chapter also discusses the basic valuation model and how one applies this model to bonds, preferred stocks, and common stocks.

In Chapter 9 we initiate the valuation process by considering tools and techniques that support the critical asset allocation decision. We consider how an investor should allocate the funds available among alternative investments (bonds versus stocks versus cash equivalents) and among countries (e.g., the United States versus Japan, the United Kingdom, and Germany). This allocation decision was much easier when an investor had to consider only U.S. assets. Now and in the future, such a decision will have to include a number of countries.

Later parts of the book will discuss the valuation of individual investment alternatives such as bonds, stocks, and options.

CHAPTER

7
___

Analysis of Financial Statements

Financial statements are the main source of information for major investment decisions, including whether to lend money to a firm (invest in its bonds), to acquire an ownership stake in a firm (invest in its preferred or common stock), or to buy warrants or options on a firm's stock.

This chapter has six sections. The first briefly introduces an example corporation's major financial statements, which we will use throughout the chapter. Section two discusses why and how financial ratios are useful. We examine and compute the major financial ratios for our example firm in Section three. Section four includes a comparative analysis of the company ratios relative to the firm's industry and the S&P 400 series. Because you will be dealing with foreign stocks and bonds, Section five contains a discussion of factors that affect analysis of foreign financial statements. In the final section we address four major areas in investments where financial ratios have been effectively employed.

Our example company is Quaker Oats, a worldwide marketer of consumer grocery products including cereals, baking mixes, grain-based snacks, syrup, corn products, edible oils, and pet food. Through its Fisher-Price division, it has been a leading toy maker, but it has recently spun off this division.

> **Balance sheet** A financial statement that shows what assets the firm controls at a point in time and how it has financed these assets.
>
> **Income statement** A financial statement that shows the firm's sales, costs, and earnings over a period of time.
>
> **Statement of cash flows** A financial statement that shows the effect on the firm's cash flows of earnings and changes in its balance sheet.

Major Financial Statements

Financial statements are intended to provide information on the resources available to management, how these resources were financed, and what the firm accomplished with them. The three major accounting statements created to provide this information are the balance sheet, the income statement, and the statement of cash flows.

Balance Sheet

The **balance sheet** shows what resources (assets) the firm controls and how it has financed these assets. Specifically, it indicates the current and fixed assets available to the firm *at a point in time* (the end of the fiscal year or the end of a quarter). In most cases, the firm owns these assets, but some firms lease assets on a long-term basis. How the firm has financed the acquisition of these assets is indicated by its mixture of current liabilities (accounts payable or short-term borrowing), long-term liabilities (fixed debt), and owner's equity (preferred stock, common stock, and retained earnings).

The balance sheet for Quaker Oats in Table 7.1 represents the firm's *stock* of assets and its financing alternatives as of June 30, 1988, 1989, and 1990.

Income Statement

The **income statement** gives information on the efficiency, control, and profitability of the firm during some *period of time* (a quarter or a year). Efficiency is indicated by the sales generated during the period, while expenses indicate control, and the earnings derived from sales indicate profitability. In contrast to the stock concept in the balance sheet, the income statement indicates the *flow* of sales, expenses, and earnings during a period of time. The income statement for Quaker Oats for the years 1988, 1989, and 1990 appears in Table 7.2.

Statement of Cash Flows

The **statement of cash flows** integrates the two prior statements. For a given period, it shows the effects on the firm's cash flow of changes in various items on the balance sheet. This effect is indicated by differences in beginning and ending figures. These changes are combined with relevant data from the income statement to derive a set of cash flow values that help you evaluate risk and return for the firm's bonds and stock. The results show the source of the cash flow (i.e., is it profits from operations or financing?) that will fund expansion (investing activities) and other requirements such as dividends, stock acquisition, or debt retirement.[1] The statement of cash flows for Quaker Oats for 1988, 1989, and 1990 appears in Table 7.3.

Purpose of Financial Statement Analysis

Financial statement analysis seeks to evaluate management performance in several important areas including profitability, efficiency, and risk. While we will necessarily analyze historical data, it serves mainly to let us project future management performance. Expected future performance determines whether you should lend money to a firm or invest in it.

Analysis of Financial Ratios

Why Ratios of Financial Data?

Analysts employ financial ratios because numbers in isolation are typically not very meaningful. Knowing that a firm earned net income of $100,000 is more informative when we also know the sales figure on which it generated this income and the assets or capital committed to the enterprise. Ratios are intended to provide meaningful relationships between individual values in the financial statements.

Because the major financial statements report numerous individual items of data, we can derive numerous potential ratios. You want to limit your examination to the most relevant ratios and categorize them into groups that provide information on important economic characteristics of the firm. It is also important to recognize the need for relative analysis.

---

[1]A complete discussion of this statement and its preparation appears in Erich Helfert, *Techniques of Financial Analysis*, 6th ed. (Homewood, Ill.: Richard D. Irwin, 1987).

| | Table 7.1 | The Quaker Oats Company and Subsidiaries Consolidated Balance Sheet ($ millions) Years Ended June 30, 1988, 1989, and 1990 |

Table 7.1 *The Quaker Oats Company and Subsidiaries Consolidated Balance Sheet ($ millions) Years Ended June 30, 1988, 1989, and 1990*

	1990	1989	1988
Assets			
Current assets			
Cash and short-term investments	$ 18.3	$ 23.7	$ 83.0
Receivables–net of allowances	629.9	594.4	555.0
Inventories:			
Finished goods	324.1	326.0	281.5
Grain and materials	110.7	114.1	95.3
Packaging materials and supplies	39.1	39.0	37.0
Total inventories	473.9	479.1	413.8
Other current assets (including discontinued operations)	359.2	422.7	372.2
Total current assets	1,481.3	1,519.9	1,424.0
Other receivables and investments	63.5	26.4	20.7
Property, plant, and equipment	1,745.6	1,456.9	1,403.1
Less accumulated depreciation	591.5	497.3	480.6
Properties–net	1,154.1	959.6	922.5
Intangible assets–net of amortization	466.7	484.7	414.3
Net noncurrent assets of discontinued operations	160.5	135.3	104.6
Total assets	$3,326.1	$3,125.9	$2,886.1
Liabilities and Common Shareholders' Equity			
Current liabilities			
Short-term debt	$ 343.2	$ 102.2	$ 310.3
Current portion of long-term debt	32.3	30.0	29.2
Trade accounts payable	354.0	333.8	262.2
Accrued payrolls, pensions, and bonuses	106.3	118.1	107.3
Accrued advertising and merchandising	92.6	67.1	70.6
Income taxes payable	36.3	8.0	41.5
Other accrued liabilities	173.8	164.9	185.4
Total current liabilities	1,138.5	824.1	1,006.5
Long-term debt	740.3	766.8	299.1
Other liabilities	100.3	89.5	101.0
Deferred income taxes	327.7	308.4	228.4
Cumulative convertible preferred stock	100.0	100.0	0.0
Deferred compensation	(98.2)	(100.0)	0.0
Common shareholders' equity			
Common stock, $5 par value, 83,989,396 shares issued	420.0	420.0	420.0
Additional paid-in capital	12.9	18.1	19.5
Reinvested earnings	1,164.7	1,106.2	998.4
Cumulative exchange adjustment	(29.3)	(56.6)	(36.5)
Deferred compensation	(164.1)	(165.8)	(17.4)
Treasury common stock, at cost	(386.7)	(184.8)	(132.9)
Total common shareholders' equity	$1,017.5	$1,137.1	$1,251.1
Total liabilities and common shareholders' equity	$3,326.1	$3,125.9	$2,886.1

Table 7.2 *The Quaker Oats Company and Subsidiaries Consolidated Statement of Income*[a] *($ millions) Years Ended June 30, 1988, 1989, and 1990*

	1990	1989	1988
Net sales	$5,030.6	$4,879.4	$4,508.0
Cost of goods sold	2,685.9	2,655.3	2,397.0
Gross profit	2,344.7	2,224.1	2,111.0
Selling, general, and administrative expenses	1,844.1	1,779.0	1,697.8
Operating profit margin	500.6	445.1	413.2
Interest expense–net	101.8	56.4	41.0
Other expense	16.4	149.6	57.6
Income from continuing operations before income taxes	382.4	239.1	314.6
Provision for income taxes	153.5	90.2	118.1
Net income from continuing operations	228.9	148.9	196.5
Net income from discontinued operations	(59.9)	54.1	59.2
Net income from disposal of discontinued operations	0.0	0.0	0.0
Net income	169.0	203.0	255.7
Preferred dividends	4.5	0.0	0.0
Net income available for common shares	$ 164.5	$ 203.0	$ 255.7
Average number of common shares outstanding (000)	76,537	79,307	79,835
Net income per share from continuing operations	$ 2.93	$ 1.88	$ 2.46
Net income per share available for common shares	$ 2.15	$ 2.56	$ 3.20
Dividend per share	$ 1.40	$ 1.20	$ 1.00

[a]Restated to reflect continuing operations only (Fisher-Price is reflected as a discontinued operation).

Importance of Relative Financial Ratios

Just as a single number from a financial statement is not very useful, an individual financial ratio has little value except in perspective relative to other ratios. That is, *only relative financial ratios are relevant!* The important comparisons relate a firm's performance to:

- The aggregate economy
- The firm's industry
- Its major competitors within the industry
- Its past performance

Comparison to the aggregate economy is important because almost all firms are influenced by the economy's expansions and contractions (recessions) in the business cycle. It is not reasonable to expect an increase in a firm's profit margin during a recession; a stable margin might be very encouraging under such

conditions. In contrast, a small increase in a firm's profit margin during a major business expansion may be a sign of weakness. Comparing a firm's financial ratios to a set of ratios for the economy will help you to understand how a firm reacts to the business cycle. This analysis will help you project the future performance of the firm during subsequent business cycles.

Probably the most popular comparison relates a firm's performance to that of its industry.[2] Different

[2]An excellent source of comparative ratios for alternative lines of business is *Industry Norms and Key Business Ratios* (New York: Dun and Bradstreet, annual), 99 Church Street, New York, NY 10007. Another source is "Comparative Financial Ratios," Robert Morris Associates, 1616 Philadelphia National Bank Bldg., Philadelphia, PA 19107.

Table 7.3   The Quaker Oats Company and Subsidiaries Consolidated Statement of Cash Flow ($ millions) Years Ended June 30, 1988, 1989, and 1990

	1990	1989	1988
Cash Flows from Operations			
Net income	$ 169.0	$ 203.0	$ 255.7
Adjustments to reconcile net income to net cash flows (used in) provided from operations			
Depreciation and amortization	162.5	135.5	121.9
Deferred income taxes and other items	15.2	79.9	(20.5)
Provision for restructuring charges	(17.5)	124.3	29.9
Changes in operating assets and liabilities (used in) provided from continuing operations			
(Increase) in receivables	(55.9)	(77.1)	(46.9)
(Increase) in inventories	(2.2)	(90.3)	(32.2)
(Increase) decrease in other current assets	(14.1)	(48.9)	23.3
Increase in trade accounts payable	31.4	102.2	33.9
Increase (decrease) in other current liabilities	83.4	(53.1)	19.6
Other–net	0.4	(8.4)	20.7
(Increase) decrease in net current assets of discontinued operations	74.9	14.5	(103.6)
Net cash flows provided from operations	$ 447.1	$ 381.6	$ 301.8
Cash Flows from Investing Activities			
Additions to property, plant, and equipment	$(275.6)	$(223.2)	$(169.7)
Cost of acquisitions, excluding working capital	–	(112.9)	–
Increase in other receivables and investments	(22.6)	(5.7)	(5.9)
Proceeds of businesses to be sold	–	–	191.6
Disposals of property, plant, and equipment	11.9	26.7	17.5
Other–discontinued operations	(58.4)	(46.7)	(35.4)
Cash used in investing activities	$(344.7)	$(361.8)	$ (1.9)
Cash Flows from Financing Activities			
Cash dividends	$(110.5)	$ (95.2)	$ (79.9)
Net increase (decrease) in short-term debt	(7.2)	42.1	(226.8)
Proceeds from long-term debt	252.1	251.2	25.3
Reduction of long-term debt	(34.8)	(30.1)	(257.4)
Issuance of common treasury stock	12.8	10.1	33.4
Purchase of common stock	(223.2)	(68.5)	(53.6)
Issuance of preferred stock	–	100.0	–
Cash used in financing activities	$(107.3)	$ (38.8)	$(557.5)
Effect of exchange rate changes on cash and cash equivalents	1.6	(7.4)	6.8
Net decrease in cash and cash equivalents	$ (3.3)	$ (26.4)	$(250.8)
Cash and cash equivalents – beginning of year	21.0	47.4	298.2
Cash and cash equivalents – end of year	$ 17.7	$ 21.0	$ 47.4

Time-series analysis Comparison of performance data over alternative time periods.

Internal liquidity (solvency) ratios Relationships between items of financial data that indicate the firm's ability to meet short-term financial obligations.

industries affect the firms within them differently, but this relationship is always significant. The industry effect is strongest for industries with homogenous products such as steel, rubber, glass, and wood products. All firms within these industries experience coincident shifts in demand. In addition, these firms employ fairly similar technology and production processes. The strong industry impact makes isolated analysis of an individual firm in such an industry meaningless. Even the best-managed steel firm experiences a decline in sales and profit margins during a recession. In such a case, the relevant question might be, how did the firm perform relative to the other steel firms? As part of this, you should examine an industry's performance relative to aggregate economic activity to understand how the industry responds to the business cycle. Also, industry comparisons typically look for a ratio that is not too far above or below the industry norm. As we will demonstrate with several ratios, you probably don't want to see ratios too high above the norm even where higher is better, or too far below the norm even where lower is better.

When comparing a firm's financial ratio to an industry ratio, you may not feel comfortable using the average (mean) industry value when ratios for the individual firms within the industry are widely dispersed. Alternatively, you may believe that the firm being analyzed is not typical and has a unique component. Under these conditions, you should probably compare the firm to several firms within the industry that are similar in terms of size or clientele. As an example, within the computer industry you should compare IBM to certain individual firms within the industry such as Burroughs or Unisys rather than to total industry data that include numerous small firms that produce unique products or services. If you were analyzing an electric utility stock, you would probably limit your industry comparison to a set of comparable electric utilities and exclude gas and water utilities. Even within the electric utility segment, you should consider firms from the same geographic area with comparable mixes of residential, commercial, and industrial customers.

Finally, you should examine a firm's relative performance over time to determine if it is progressing or declining. This **time series analysis** helps you estimate future performance. Many investigators calculate average ratios for 5- or 10-year periods without considering trends. This can result in misleading conclusions. For example, an average rate of return of 10 percent can come from rates of return increasing from 5 percent to 15 percent over time, or from a series that begins at 15 percent and declines to 5 percent. Obviously, the difference in the trend for these series would have a major impact on your estimate for the future.

Computation of Financial Ratios

Ratio Categories

We will divide the ratios we will discuss into five major categories that will help us understand the following important economic characteristics of a firm:

1. Internal liquidity (solvency)
2. Operating performance
   a. Operating efficiency
   b. Profitability
3. Risk analysis
   a. Business risk
   b. Financial risk
4. Growth analysis
5. External liquidity (marketability)

Internal Liquidity Ratios

Internal liquidity (solvency) ratios indicate the ability of the firm to meet future short-term financial obligations. They compare near-term financial obligations, such as accounts payable or notes payable, with current assets or cash flows that will be available to meet these obligations.

Current Ratio Clearly the best-known liquidity measure is the current ratio, which examines the relationship between current assets and current liabilities as follows:

$$\text{Current ratio} = \frac{\text{Current assets}}{\text{Current liabilities}}$$

Quaker Oats' current ratios were (in thousands of dollars):

$$1990: \frac{1,481,300}{1,138,500} = 1.30$$

$$1989: \frac{1,519,900}{824,100} = 1.84$$

$$1988: \frac{1,424,000}{1,006,500} = 1.41$$

While these current ratios are adequate, there was a clear decline during 1990 that was due to a large increase in current liabilities caused by an increase in short-term debt. You would need to compare these values to similar figures for the industry and the aggregate market. This comparative analysis is considered in the next section.

Quick Ratio Some observers believe that you should not consider total current assets when gauging ability to meet current obligations, since inventories and some other assets included in current assets might not be very liquid. As an alternative, they prefer the quick ratio, which relates current liabilities to only relatively liquid current assets (cash items and accounts receivable), as follows:

$$\text{Quick ratio} = \frac{\text{Cash} + \text{Receivables}}{\text{Current liabilities}}$$

This ratio is intended to indicate the amount of very liquid assets available to pay near-term liabilities. Quaker Oats' quick ratios were:

$$1990: \frac{648,200}{1,138,500} = 0.57$$

$$1989: \frac{618,100}{824,100} = 0.75$$

$$1988: \frac{638,000}{1,006,500} = 0.63$$

Again, these ratios were adequate, but they also show a definite decline in 1990. As before, the quick assets increased, but the current liabilities rose even faster. Again, you would want to compare them to figures for the industry and the economy.

Cash Ratio The most conservative liquidity ratio, the cash ratio, relates cash and short-term investments (money-market instruments) to current liabilities, as follows:

$$\text{Cash ratio} = \frac{\text{Cash and short-term investments}}{\text{Current liabilities}}$$

Quaker Oats' cash ratios were:

$$1990: \frac{18,300}{1,138,500} = 0.02$$

$$1989: \frac{23,700}{824,100} = 0.03$$

$$1988: \frac{83,000}{1,006,500} = 0.08$$

The cash ratios appear fairly low, and they show continuing declines. These declines would raise concern, except that the firm has strong lines of credit at various banks. Still, as an investor you would want to know the reason for this decline and whether it would affect the firm's ability to respond to unexpected events.

Receivables Turnover In addition to comparing liquid assets to near-term liabilities, it is useful to analyze the liquidity of a firm's accounts receivable. One way to do this is to calculate how often they turn over, which implies their average collection period. The faster they are paid, the sooner the firm gets the funds that can be used to pay off its own current liabilities. Receivables turnover is computed as follows:

$$\text{Receivables turnover} = \frac{\text{Net annual sales}}{\text{Average receivables}}$$

Analysts typically derive the average receivables figure from the beginning figure plus the ending value divided by 2. Quaker Oats' receivables turnover ratios were:

$$1990: \frac{5,030,600}{(629,900 + 594,400)/2} = 8.22$$

$$1989: \frac{4,879,400}{(594,400 + 555,000)/2} = 8.49$$

We cannot compute a turnover value for 1988 because our tables do not include a beginning receivables figure for that year, that is, the ending receivables figure for 1987.

Given these annual receivables turnover figures, you can compute an average collection period, as follows:

$$\text{Average receivables collection period} = \frac{365}{\text{Annual turnover}}$$

$$1990: \frac{365}{8.22} = 44.40 \text{ days}$$

$$1989: \frac{365}{8.49} = 42.90 \text{ days}$$

> **Operating efficiency ratios** Relationships between sales and assets in various categories that indicate how effectively management uses the firm's assets.
>
> **Operating profitability ratios** Relationships of profits to sales and to the capital employed to generate those profits.

These results indicate that Quaker Oats collects its accounts receivable in about 45 days, on average, and this collection record is fairly stable. To determine whether these account collection numbers are good or bad, you need to relate them to the firm's credit policy and to comparable numbers for other firms in the industry. It is important to remember that, although Quaker Oats is mainly in the food business, it was in the toy business, as well, which had different credit policies and characteristics.

The receivables turnover is one of the ratios that you don't want to deviate too much from the norm. In an industry with a norm of 60 days, a collection period of 100 days would indicate slow-paying customers, which increases both the amount of capital tied up in receivables and also the possibility of bad debts. You would want the firm to be somewhat below the norm (e.g., 55 days versus 60 days), but a figure substantially below the norm (e.g., 25 days) might indicate overly stringent credit terms relative to the competition, which could be detrimental to sales.

Investors also compute inventory turnover figures to measure the liquidity of firms' inventories. This inventory ratio can also serve as an operating performance measure and we will consider it in that category.

Working Capital/Sales The working capital/sales ratio goes beyond the balance sheet and relates the firm's net working capital (current assets minus current liabilities) to its sales. This reveals the stock of working capital available to meet any need for excess current assets that might arise from the flow of sales.

$$\frac{\text{Working capital/}}{\text{sales}} = \frac{\text{Current assets} - \text{Current liabilities}}{\text{Net sales}}$$

Like many ratios, we have no guideline number for this value. Your analysis would involve comparing the percentage over time (indicating any trend) to similar ratios for the industry and the aggregate market. The values for Quaker Oats were:

$$1990: \frac{1,481,300 - 1,138,500}{5,030,600} = 6.81 \text{ percent}$$

$$1989: \frac{1,519,900 - 824,100}{4,879,400} = 14.26 \text{ percent}$$

$$1988: \frac{1,424,000 - 1,006,500}{4,508,000} = 9.26 \text{ percent}$$

Generally, a higher percentage for this ratio is better since it reflects more liquidity available. For Quaker Oats, this ratio increased in 1989 but declined significantly in 1990. The real insight will come when we compare these values to similar values for the industry and the market.

Operating Performance Ratios

The ratios that indicate how well management is operating the business can be divided into two subcategories: (1) **operating efficiency ratios** and (2) **operating profitability ratios.** Efficiency ratios show how management uses its assets and capital, measured in terms of the dollars of sales generated by various asset or capital categories. Profitability ratios show profits as a percentage of sales and as a percentage of assets and capital employed.

Operating Efficiency Ratios

Total Asset Turnover The total asset turnover ratio indicates the effectiveness of the firm's use of its total asset base (net assets equal gross assets minus depreciation on fixed assets). It is computed as follows:

$$\text{Total asset turnover} = \frac{\text{Net sales}}{\text{Average total net assets}}$$

Quaker Oats' asset turnover values were:

$$1990: \frac{5,030,600}{(3,326,100 + 3,125,900)/2} = 1.56 \text{ times}$$

$$1989: \frac{4,879,400}{(3,125,900 + 2,886,100)/2} = 1.62 \text{ times}$$

You must compare this ratio to those of other firms in an industry, since it varies substantially between industries. Total asset turnover ranges from about 1 for large, capital-intensive industries (e.g., steel, autos, and other heavy manufacturing) to over 10 for some retailing operations. It can also be affected by leasing facilities.

Again, you should consider a range of turnover values. It is poor management to have an exceedingly high turnover because of too few assets for the potential business (sales) or because the firm is operating with outdated, fully depreciated assets. It is equally poor management to overspend on more assets than the firm needs and have a very low turnover. Beyond the analysis of the total asset base, you can gain insight from examining the utilization of some specific assets, such as inventories and fixed assets.

Inventory Turnover   The inventory turnover ratio indicates the firm's utilization of inventory. It is computed as follows:

$$\text{Inventory turnover} = \frac{\text{Cost of sales}}{\text{Average inventory}}$$

The inventory turnover ratios for Quaker Oats were:

$$1990: \frac{2,685,900}{(473,900 + 479,100)/2} = 5.64 \text{ times}$$

$$1989: \frac{2,655,300}{(479,100 + 413,800)/2} = 5.95 \text{ times}$$

Again, the analysis should emphasize the firm's performance relative to its industry, since inventory turnover ratios vary widely. Also, you should consider the range. Too low an inventory turnover ratio relative to your competitors probably means excess inventory and possibly some obsolete inventory. In contrast, although a high inventory turnover ratio may indicate efficiency, too high a value can indicate inadequate inventory for the sales volume, which can lead to shortages, back orders, and eventually lost sales.

Net Fixed Asset Turnover   The net fixed asset turnover ratio reflects the firm's utilization of fixed assets. It is computed as follows:

$$\text{Fixed asset turnover} = \frac{\text{Net sales}}{\text{Average net fixed assets}}$$

Quaker Oats' fixed asset turnover ratios were:

$$1990: \frac{5,030,600}{(1,154,100 + 959,600)/2} = 4.76 \text{ times}$$

$$1989: \frac{4,879,400}{(959,600 + 922,500)/2} = 5.19 \text{ times}$$

This turnover must be compared to those of firms in the same industry in light of the impact of leased as-

sets. Also, remember that an abnormally high asset turnover ratio can indicate reliance on old, fully depreciated equipment that may be obsolete.

Equity Turnover   In addition to specific asset turnover ratios, it is useful to examine the turnover ratios for alternative capital components. An important one, equity turnover, is computed as follows:

$$\text{Equity turnover} = \frac{\text{Net sales}}{\text{Average equity}}$$

Equity includes preferred and common stock, paid-in capital, and total retained earnings.[3] This ratio differs from total asset turnover in that it excludes capital financed by current liabilities and long-term debt. Therefore, when examining this series, you should consider the capital ratios for the firm, because a firm can increase the equity turnover ratio by increasing its proportion of debt capital (i.e., its debt/equity ratio).

Quaker Oats' equity turnover ratios were:

$$1990: \frac{5,030,600}{(1,019,300 + 1,137,100)/2} = 4.67 \text{ times}$$

$$1989: \frac{4,879,400}{(1,137,100 + 1,251,100)/2} = 4.09 \text{ times}$$

Quaker has experienced a fairly consistent increase in this ratio. In our later analysis of sustainable growth, we will examine the variables that affect the equity turnover ratio to understand what caused the increase.

Given some understanding of the firm's record of operating efficiency, as shown by its ability to generate sales from its assets and capital, the next step is to examine its profitability in relation to sales and capital.

Operating Profitability Ratios

The ratios in this category indicate two facets of profitability: (1) the rate of profit derived from sales (profit margin), and (2) the percentage return on capital employed.

Gross Profit Margin   Gross profit equals net sales minus the cost of goods sold. The gross profit margin is computed as:

---

[3]Some investors prefer to consider only owner's equity, which would not include preferred stock.

$$\text{Gross profit margin} = \frac{\text{Gross profit}}{\text{Net sales}}$$

The gross profit margins for Quaker Oats were:

$$1990: \frac{2,344,700}{5,030,600} = 46.61 \text{ percent}$$

$$1989: \frac{2,224,100}{4,879,400} = 45.58 \text{ percent}$$

$$1988: \frac{2,111,000}{4,508,000} = 46.83 \text{ percent}$$

This ratio indicates the basic cost structure of the firm. An analysis over time relative to a comparable industry figure shows the firm's relative cost-price position. Quaker Oats has maintained a fairly stable margin over the 3 years, but it is important to compare it to industry statistics.

Operating Profit Margin Operating profit is gross profit minus selling, general, and administrative (SG&A) expenses. The operating profit margin equals:

$$\text{Operating profit margin} = \frac{\text{Operating profit}}{\text{Net sales}}$$

Quaker Oats' operating profit margins were:

$$1990: \frac{500,600}{5,030,600} = 9.95 \text{ percent}$$

$$1989: \frac{445,100}{4,879,400} = 9.12 \text{ percent}$$

$$1988: \frac{413,200}{4,508,000} = 9.17 \text{ percent}$$

Variability of the operating profit margin over time is a prime indicator of the business risk for a firm. In the case of Quaker Oats, there was variability, but there was an increase, which is very encouraging. As always, you would want to consider the longer-term trend and also to compare these results to industry results. If the firm has other income or expenses (relatively minor for Quaker Oats except for 1988 and 1989), these amounts are considered in the earnings before interest expense and taxes figure.

Sometimes investors add back depreciation and compute a profit margin based on earnings before depreciation, interest expense, and taxes (EBDIT) as a percentage of sales. This alternative operating profit margin reflects all controllable expenses. It can pro-

vide great insight regarding the profit performance of heavy manufacturing firms with large depreciation charges. It can also indicate earnings available to pay fixed financing costs. This latter use will be discussed in the section on financial risk.

Net Profit Margin This margin relates net income to sales. Net income is earnings after taxes, but before payment of dividends on preferred and common stock. This margin is equal to:

$$\text{Net profit margin} = \frac{\text{Net income}}{\text{Net sales}}$$

Quaker Oats' net profit margins are based upon net income from continuing operations:

$$1990: \frac{228,900}{5,030,600} = 4.55 \text{ percent}$$

$$1989: \frac{148,900}{4,879,400} = 3.05 \text{ percent}$$

$$1988: \frac{196,500}{4,508,000} = 4.36 \text{ percent}$$

This ratio is computed based upon sales and earnings from continuing operations, because our analysis seeks to derive insights about *future* expectations. Therefore, results for continuing operations are relevant, rather than profit or loss that considers discontinued operations or gain or loss from the sale of these operations.

This focus on continuing operations was important in 1987 when Quaker Oats bought and sold several divisions; it was not significant in 1988 and 1989, but it became significant again in 1990 when the firm decided to spin off the Fisher-Price division. The strong recovery of the net profit margin during 1990 was very encouraging after the large decline in 1989.

Common Size Income Statements Beyond these ratios, an additional technique for analyzing operating profitability is a common size income statement, which lists all expense and income items as percentages of sales. Analyzing this statement for several years (5 at least) will provide very useful insights regarding trends in cost figures and profit margins.

Table 7.4 shows a common size income statement for Quaker Oats for the latest 3 years, adjusted for the spin-off. It indicates almost no change overall in the percentage cost of goods and, hence, a stable gross profit margin. Selling, general, and administrative

Table 7.4 *The Quaker Oats Company and Subsidiaries Consolidated Statement of Income ($ millions) Common Size Analysis*

	1990	Percentage	1989	Percentage	1988	Percentage
Net sales	$5,030.6	100.00	$4,879.4	100.00	$4,508.0	100.00
Cost of goods sold	2,685.9	53.39	2,655.3	54.42	2,397.0	53.17
Gross profit	2,344.7	46.61	2,224.1	45.58	2,111.0	46.83
Selling, general, and administrative expenses	1,844.1	36.66	1,779.0	36.46	1,697.8	37.66
Operating profit margin	500.6	9.95	445.1	9.12	413.2	9.17
Interest expense–net	101.8	2.02	56.4	1.16	41.0	0.91
Other expense	16.4	0.33	149.6	3.07	57.6	1.28
Income from continuing operations before income taxes	382.4	7.60	239.1	4.90	314.6	6.98
Provision for income taxes	153.5	3.05	90.2	1.85	118.1	2.62
Net income from continuing operations	228.9	4.55	148.9	3.05	196.5	4.36
Net income from discontinued operations	(59.9)	(1.19)	54.1	1.11	59.2	1.31
Net income from disposal of discontinued operations	0.0	0.00	0.0	0.00	0.0	0.00
Net income	169.0	3.36	203.0	4.16	255.7	5.67
Preferred dividends	4.5	0.09	0.0	0.00	0.0	0.00
Net income available for common shares	$ 164.5	3.27	$ 203.0	4.16	$ 255.7	5.67

(SG&A) expense declined as a percentage of sales from 1988 to 1990. Finally, interest expense has increased consistently during these 3 years, although this was offset somewhat in 1990 by a decline in other expenses that had been quite high in 1988 and 1989. The overall effect is a net profit margin from continuing operations that was at the higher end of its range over the previous 10 years.

Beyond the analysis of earnings on sales, the ultimate measure of the success of management is the profits earned on the assets or capital committed to the enterprise. Several ratios help us evaluate this important relationship.

Return on Total Capital The return on total capital ratio relates the firm's earnings to all of its capital (debt, preferred stock, and common stock). Therefore, the earnings figure used is net income from continuing operations (before any dividends) plus the interest paid on debt:

$$\text{Return on total capital} = \frac{\text{Net income} + \text{interest expense}}{\text{Average total capital}}$$

Quaker Oats incurred interest expenses for long-term and short-term debt. The gross interest expense values used in this ratio ($120,200 for 1990 and $75,900 for 1989) differ from the net interest expense item in the income statement, which is measured as gross interest expense minus interest income. Quaker's rate of return on total capital was:

$$1990: \frac{228,900 + 120,200}{(3,326,100 + 3,125,900)/2} = 10.82 \text{ percent}$$

$$1989: \frac{148,900 + 75,900}{(3,125,900 + 2,886,100)/2} = 7.48 \text{ percent}$$

This ratio indicates the firm's overall return on all the capital it employed. It should be compared to ratios for other firms in the industry and to that for the economy. If this rate of return does not match the perceived risk of the firm, one might question its continued operation, since the capital involved in the enterprise could be used more productively elsewhere in the economy.

Return on Owners' Equity The return on owners' equity (ROE) ratio is extremely important to the owner of the enterprise (the common stockholder), since it indicates the rate of return management has earned on the capital provided by the owners after accounting for payments to all other capital suppliers. If you consider all equity (including preferred stock), this would equal:

$$\text{Return on total equity} = \frac{\text{Net income}}{\text{Average total equity}}$$

If an investor is concerned only with owners' equity (i.e., common shareholders' equity), the ratio would be calculated:

$$\text{Return on owners' equity} = \frac{\text{Net income} - \text{Preferred dividend}}{\text{Average common equity}}$$

Quaker Oats generated return on owners' equity of:

$$1990: \frac{228,900 - 4,500}{(1,017,500 + 1,137,100)/2} = 20.83 \text{ percent}$$

$$1989: \frac{148,900 - 0}{(1,137,100 + 1,257,100)/2} = 12.47 \text{ percent}$$

Although the substantial increase from 1989 to 1990 is very impressive, it reflects a recovery from the low returns in 1989. In the subsequent discussion, we will consider the factors that affect this ratio and examine the longer-term performance of Quaker Oats related to this ratio.

The ratio reflects the rate of return on the equity capital provided by the owners. It should correspond to the firm's overall business risk, but also to any financial risk assumed by the common stockholder because of the prior claims of the firm's bondholders.

The importance of ROE as an indicator of performance makes it desirable to divide the ratio into several components to gain insights into the causes of changes. Specifically, the return on equity (ROE) ratio can be broken down into two previously discussed ratios. To maintain the identity, the calculation uses year-end common equity rather than the average of the beginning and ending values.

$$\begin{aligned} \text{ROE} &= \frac{\text{Net income}}{\text{Common equity}} \\ &= \frac{\text{Net income}}{\text{Net sales}} \times \frac{\text{Net sales}}{\text{Common equity}} \end{aligned}$$

This breakdown is an identity because we have multiplied both the numerator and denominator by net sales. This reveals that ROE equals the net profit margin times the equity turnover. Therefore, a firm can improve its return on equity by either using its equity more efficiently (i.e., increasing its equity turnover) or becoming more profitable (i.e., increasing its net profit margin).

As noted previously, a firm's equity turnover depends on its capital structure. It can increase equity turnover by increasing the proportion of debt capital. We can see this effect in the following relationship.

$$\frac{\text{Sales}}{\text{Equity}} = \frac{\text{Sales}}{\text{Total assets}} \times \frac{\text{Total assets}}{\text{Equity}}$$

Like the prior breakdown, this is an identity because we have multiplied both the top and bottom of the equity turnover ratio by total assets. This equation indicates that the equity turnover ratio equals the firm's total asset turnover (a measure of efficiency) times its ratio of total assets to equity, a measure of financial leverage. The ratio of total assets to equity indicates what proportion of total assets have been financed with debt. Since all assets have to be financed either by equity or some form of debt (either current liabilities or long-term debt), a higher ratio of assets to equity indicates a higher proportion of debt to equity.

A total asset/equity ratio of 2, for example, indicates that the firm financed half of its assets with equity, which implies that it financed the other half with debt. A total asset/equity ratio of 3 means it financed only one-third of total assets with equity, so two-thirds must have been financed with debt. This breakdown of the equity turnover ratio implies that a firm can increase its equity turnover by either increasing its total asset turnover (i.e., becoming more efficient) or increasing its financial leverage ratio (i.e., financing assets with a higher proportion of debt capital).

To further explain this important set of relationships, the figures in Table 7.5 indicate the ROEs and their components for Quaker Oats during the 12 years from 1978 through 1990. As noted, these ratio values employ year-end balance sheet figures (assets and eq-

Table 7.5	Components of Return on Equity for Quaker Oats Company: 1978–1990[a]

	(1) Sales Total Assets	(2) Total Assets Equity	(3)[b] Sales Equity	(4) Net Profit Margin	(5)[c] Return on Equity
1990	1.51	3.27	4.94	4.55	22.48
1989	1.56	2.75	4.29	3.05	13.09
1988	1.56	2.31	3.60	4.36	15.71
1987	1.36	2.99	4.07	4.20	17.08
1986	1.70	2.45	4.17	4.83	20.12
1985	1.82	2.23	4.06	4.48	18.18
1984	1.80	2.38	4.28	4.19	17.95
1983	1.71	2.15	3.68	4.57	16.80
1982	1.68	2.14	3.60	4.55	16.36
1981	1.62	2.21	3.58	4.37	15.65
1980	1.63	2.11	3.44	4.36	15.00
1979	1.56	2.01	3.14	4.65	14.58
1978	1.49	1.97	2.94	4.87	14.29

[a]Ratios use year-end data for total assets and common equity rather than annual averages.

[b]Column 3 equals Column 1 times Column 2.

[c]Column 5 equals Column 3 times Column 4.

uity) rather than averages of beginning and ending data.

These data indicate several important trends. First, prior to 1987, the firm's ROE increased steadily from 14.29 percent in 1978 to over 20 percent in 1986. Analysis of this excellent trend should initially examine the two major ratios—equity turnover and net profit margin. Quaker Oats' profit margin varied over time, finishing in 1986 at about the same level it started at in 1978. Subsequently it experienced an overall decline in 1987, 1988, and 1989, followed by a major recovery in 1990. For the total period, the profit margin was lower at the end of the period than at the beginning. In contrast, the firm's equity turnover series increased steadily from about 3 times in 1978 to almost 5 in 1990 (a 68 percent increase). Therefore, the main cause of the increase in Quaker Oats' ROE was its equity turnover.

What caused this increase in equity turnover? The total asset turnover ratio (sales/total assets) increased consistently from 1978 through 1985, declined in 1986 and 1987, and returned to its beginning

level in 1988 through 1990. In contrast, the financial leverage ratio (total assets/equity) increased steadily throughout the period (from 1.97 to 3.27, over a 50 percent change) and ended at its high value. This increase in the financial leverage ratio implies that the proportion of total assets financed with debt rose from about 50 percent to almost 70 percent. In summary, given the two components of equity turnover, there was almost no change in the total asset turnover ratio over time, which means that virtually all of the change was because of an increase in financial leverage.

A detailed analysis of the firm's performance during 1987 through 1990 is very revealing. In 1987 ROE declined to 17 percent because of a decline in both the total asset turnover and the profit margin. These declines were not offset by the large increase in financial leverage. The firm's ROE declined further in 1988 because the increases in its total asset turnover and profit margin did not offset the large decline in financial leverage. The firm's ROE declined to its lowest level in 1989, because the large decline in its profit margin more than offset the firm's increased financial leverage while its total asset turnover held constant. Finally, the firm's ROE reached its highest level in 1990 due to a combination of a record high level of financial leverage and a strong recovery in its net profit margin.

Therefore, while the overall performance of the firm's ROE looks very good, you as an investor should be concerned about the ability of the firm to increase or maintain its ROE. To judge this, you would need to examine the near-term and longer-term outlook for each component of ROE. Besides providing insights into the firm's ROE, this analysis implies a large change in its financial risk, as analyzed in the next section.

Risk Analysis

Risk analysis examines the uncertainty of income flows both for the total firm and for its individual sources of capital (i.e., debt, preferred stock, and common stock). The typical approach examines the major factors that cause its income flows to vary. More volatile income flows mean greater risk facing the investor.

The total risk of the firm has two components: business risk and financial risk. The next section discusses the concept of business risk, how investors measure this risk, what causes it, and how you can measure its individual causes. The section after that discusses financial risk and describes the ratios by which you measure it.

Business Risk[4]

Recall that business risk is the uncertainty of income common to the firm's industry. In turn, this uncertainty is due to the variability of sales due to products and customers and the way the firm produces its products. Specifically, a firm's earnings vary over time because its sales and production costs vary. As an example, the earnings for a steel firm will probably vary more than those for a grocery chain because, over the business cycle, steel sales are more volatile than grocery sales. Also the steel firm's large fixed production costs make its earnings vary more than its sales.

Business risk is generally measured by the variability of the firm's operating income over time. In turn, earnings variability is measured by the standard deviation of its historical operating earnings series. You will recall from Chapter 1 that standard deviation is influenced by the size of the numbers, so investors standardize this measure of variability by dividing it by the mean value for the series (i.e, the average operating earnings). The resulting ratio of the standard deviation of operating earnings divided by the average operating earnings is the familiar coefficient of variation (CV):

$$
\begin{aligned}
\text{Business risk} &= \text{f(Coefficient of variation of operating earnings)} \\
&= \frac{\text{Standard dev. of operating earnings (OE)}}{\text{Mean operating earnings}} \\
&= \frac{\sqrt{\Sigma_{i=1}^{n}(OE_i - \overline{OE})^2/N}}{\Sigma_{i=1}^{n} OE_i/N}
\end{aligned}
$$

The CV of operating earnings allows very useful comparisons between standardized measures of business risk for firms of different sizes. To compute the CV of operating earnings you need a minimum of 5 years of data, up to about 10 years. Less than 5 years' data is not very meaningful, while data more than 10 years old are typically out of date. We cannot compute the CV of operating earnings for Quaker Oats, since we have data for only 3 years.

Besides measuring overall business risk, we can examine the two factors that contribute to the variability of operating earnings: sales variability and operating leverage.

Sales Variability Sales variability is the primary determinant of earnings variability. Operating earnings must be as volatile as sales. Also, the variability of sales is largely outside the control of management. While the firm's advertising and pricing policy can affect the variability of sales, the major cause is common to the industry. Sales of a firm in a cyclical industry like automobiles or steel will show a very volatile pattern over the business cycle compared to those of a firm in a noncyclical industry, such as retail food or hospital supplies. Like operating earnings, the variability of a firm's sales is typically measured by the CV of sales during the most recent 5 to 10 years. The CV of sales equals the standard deviation of sales divided by the mean sales for the period.

---

[4]For a further discussion on this general topic, see Eugene Brigham, *Financial Management Theory and Practice*, 5th ed. (Hinsdale, Ill.: Dryden Press, 1989): Chapters 6 and 10.

Sales volatility $=$ f (Coefficient of variation of sales)

$$= \frac{\text{Standard deviation of sales (S)}}{\text{Mean sales}}$$

$$= \frac{\sqrt{\Sigma_{i=1}^{n} (S_i - \overline{S})^2/N}}{\Sigma_{i=1}^{n} S_i/N}$$

Operating Leverage The variability of a firm's operating earnings also depends on its mixture of production costs. Total production costs of a firm with no fixed production costs would vary directly with sales, and operating profits would be a constant proportion of sales. The operating profit margin would be constant and operating profits would have the same volatility as sales. Realistically, firms almost always have some fixed production costs (e.g., buildings, machinery, relatively permanent personnel). Fixed production costs cause operating profits to vary more than sales over the business cycle. During slow periods, profits decline by a larger percentage than the percentage sales decline. In contrast, during an economic expansion, profits increase by a larger percentage than sales do.

The amount of fixed production costs is referred to as *operating leverage*. Clearly, greater operating leverage makes the operating earnings series more volatile relative to the sales series.[5] This basic relationship between operating profit and sales leads us to measure operating leverage as the percentage change in operating earnings relative to the percentage change in sales during a specified period, as follows:

$$\text{Operating leverage} = \frac{\sum_{i=1}^{n} \left| \frac{\%\Delta OE}{\%\Delta S} \right|}{N}$$

We take the absolute values of the percent changes because the two series can move in opposite directions. The direction of change is not important, but the relative size of the changes is. More volatile operating earnings as compared to sales indicate greater operating leverage.

Financial Risk

Financial risk, you will recall, is the additional uncertainty of returns to equity holders due to a firm's fixed obligation debt securities. This financial uncertainty is in addition to the firm's business risk. When a firm sells bonds to raise capital, the interest payments on this capital must precede the computation of net earnings available to common stock, and these interest payments are fixed obligations. As with operating leverage, during good times the earnings available for common stock will increase by a larger percentage than operating earnings, while during a business decline the earnings available to stockholders will decline by a larger percentage than operating earnings because of these fixed financial costs.

Two sets of financial ratios help you measure financial risk. The first set indicates the proportions of capital derived from debt securities compared to equity capital (preferred stock and common equity). The second set of ratios considers the flow of earnings, or the cash flow, available to pay fixed financial charges.

Proportion-of-Debt Ratios

Higher proportions of debt capital compared to equity capital make earnings available to common stock more volatile and also increase the probability that the firm will not be able to meet required interest payments and will default on the debt. Therefore, higher debt ratios indicate greater financial risk.

The acceptable level of financial risk for a firm depends upon its business risk. If the firm has low business risk, investors are willing to accept higher financial risk. For example, retail food companies typically have rather stable operating earnings over time and, therefore, relatively low business risk, which means they can support heavy debt in their capital structures, giving them higher financial risk.

Debt/Equity Ratio The debt/equity ratio is equal to:

$$\text{Debt/equity ratio} = \frac{\text{Total long-term debt}}{\text{Total equity}}$$

The numerator includes all long-term fixed obligations including subordinated convertible bonds. The denominator is typically the book value of equity including preferred stock, common stock, and retained

---

[5]For a further treatment of this area, see James C. Van Horne, *Financial Management and Policy*, 7th ed. (Englewood Cliffs, N.J.: Prentice-Hall, 1986): Chapter 27.

earnings. In some cases you may want to exclude preferred stock and consider only common equity. Total equity is preferable if some firms being analyzed have preferred stock outstanding and some do not. Alternatively, if you consider the preferred stock dividend as an interest payment, you might want to compute a ratio of debt plus preferred stock to common equity.

Impact of Deferred Taxes   You need to compute debt ratios both with and without deferred taxes. The balance sheet shows an accumulated deferred tax figure after long-term debt and other liabilities. There is some controversy regarding whether you should treat deferred taxes as a liability or a part of permanent capital. Some argue that if the deferred tax is caused by a difference between depreciation by the accelerated and straight-line methods, this is a liability that may never be paid. That is, as long as the firm continues to grow and add new assets, this total deferred tax figure continues to grow. If, however, the deferred tax arises from differences in methods for recognition of income on long-term contracts such as government contracts, this liability must eventually be paid. To resolve this question, you must determine the reason for the deferred tax account and examine its long-term trend.[6]

Quaker Oats' deferred tax account arose from depreciation calculations and has grown consistently over time. For demonstration purposes, several of the following ratios are computed both with and without deferred taxes as a long-term liability. This dual treatment demonstrates that the impact of this difference can be substantial. The two sets of debt/equity ratios for Quaker Oats were:

Including Deferred Taxes as Long-Term Debt

$$1990: \frac{1,168,300}{1,019,300} = 114.62 \text{ percent}$$

$$1989: \frac{1,164,700}{1,137,100} = 102.43 \text{ percent}$$

$$1988: \frac{628,500}{1,251,100} = 50.24 \text{ percent}$$

Excluding Deferred Taxes from Long-Term Debt

$$1990: \frac{840,600}{1,019,300} = 82.47 \text{ percent}$$

$$1989: \frac{856,300}{1,137,100} = 75.31 \text{ percent}$$

$$1988: \frac{400,100}{1,251,100} = 31.98 \text{ percent}$$

These ratios indicate a steady increase in the firm's debt burden during this recent 3-year period. These results are consistent with the trend for the total asset/equity ratio discussed earlier.

Debt/Total Capital Ratio   The debt/total capital ratio indicates the proportion of long-term capital derived from long-term, fixed-cost debt. It is computed as:

$$\text{Debt/total capital ratio} = \frac{\text{Total long-term debt}}{\text{Total long-term capital}}$$

Long-term capital includes all long-term debt, any preferred stock, and total equity. Again, the ratios are computed both including and excluding deferred taxes. The two sets of debt/total capital ratios for Quaker Oats were:

Including Deferred Taxes as Long-Term Debt

$$1990: \frac{1,168,300}{2,187,600} = 53.41 \text{ percent}$$

$$1989: \frac{1,164,700}{2,301,800} = 50.60 \text{ percent}$$

$$1988: \frac{628,500}{1,879,600} = 33.44 \text{ percent}$$

Excluding Deferred Taxes from Long-Term Debt and Long-Term Capital

$$1990: \frac{840,600}{1,859,900} = 45.20 \text{ percent}$$

$$1989: \frac{856,300}{1,993,400} = 42.96 \text{ percent}$$

$$1988: \frac{400,100}{1,651,200} = 24.23 \text{ percent}$$

These ratios likewise indicate a big increase in the firm's financial risk. They also show the effect of including deferred taxes as both debt and long-term capital.

---

[6]For a further discussion of this, see Leopold A. Bernstein, *Financial Statement Analysis: Theory, Application, Interpretation*, 4th ed. (Homewood, Ill: Richard D. Irwin, 1989): 212–214.

Total Debt Ratios   In some cases it is useful to compare total debt (current liabilities plus long-term liabilities) to total capital. This is especially revealing for a firm that derives substantial funds from short-term borrowing, as Quaker Oats does. The two sets of total debt/total capital ratios for Quaker Oats were:

Including Deferred Taxes as Long-Term Debt

$$1990: \frac{2,306,800}{3,326,100} = 69.35 \text{ percent}$$

$$1989: \frac{1,988,800}{3,125,900} = 63.62 \text{ percent}$$

$$1988: \frac{1,635,000}{2,886,100} = 56.65 \text{ percent}$$

Excluding Deferred Taxes from Long-Term Debt and Long-Term Capital

$$1990: \frac{1,979,100}{2,998,400} = 66.01 \text{ percent}$$

$$1989: \frac{1,680,400}{2,817,500} = 59.64 \text{ percent}$$

$$1988: \frac{1,406,600}{2,657,700} = 52.93 \text{ percent}$$

The ratios indicate that about two-thirds of Quaker Oats' assets are currently financed with debt, which corresponds to the total asset/equity ratio. These ratios should be compared to those of other companies in the industry to judge their consistency with the business risk of this industry. Such a comparison would also indicate how much higher this debt ratio could go. This is important because Quaker Oats has raised its ROE target from 20 percent to 25 percent, and investors need to know how much of the increase in ROE can and should come from additional financial leverage.

Earnings or Cash Flow Ratios

In addition to ratios that indicate the amount of debt on the balance sheet, investors employ ratios that relate the flow of earnings or cash available to meet interest and lease payments. A higher ratio of earnings or cash flow to fixed financial charges signifies lower financial risk.

Interest Coverage   Interest coverage is computed as follows:

$$\text{Interest coverage} = \frac{\text{Income before interest and taxes}}{\text{Debt interest charges}}$$

$$= \frac{\text{Net inc.} + \text{Inc. taxes} + \text{Interest expense}}{\text{Interest expense}}$$

This ratio indicates how many times over earnings available to pay interest cover the fixed interest charges. Alternatively, 1 minus the reciprocal of the coverage ratio indicates how far earnings could decline before the firm could no longer pay interest charges from current earnings. For example, a coverage ratio of 5 means that earnings are 5 times interest payments. This implies that earnings could decline by 80 percent (1 minus $\frac{1}{5}$), and the firm could still pay its fixed financial charges. Quaker Oats had interest coverage ratios (using gross interest expense) of:

$$1990: \frac{228,900 + 153,500 + 120,200}{120,200} = 4.18 \text{ times}$$

$$1989: \frac{148,900 + 90,200 + 75,900}{75,900} = 4.15 \text{ times}$$

$$1988: \frac{196,500 + 118,100 + 62,900}{62,900} = 6.00 \text{ times}$$

The good news is that all the coverage ratios are in excess of 4. The bad news is that they have declined. The trend of Quaker Oats' coverage ratios is consistent with its proportion-of-debt ratios.

Proportion-of-debt ratios and flow ratios do not always give consistent results, because the proportion-of-debt ratios are not sensitive to changes in earnings and cash flow or interest rates on debt. As an example, if interest rates were to increase over time and the firm simply replaced old debt with new debt at higher interest rates, the proportion-of-debt ratios (e.g., the debt/total capital ratio) would not change, but the interest coverage ratio would decline because of the increase in interest expense. Also, the interest coverage ratio is sensitive to positive or negative earnings changes.

Total Fixed Charge Coverage   You might want to determine how well earnings cover total fixed financial charges including any noncancellable lease payments and any preferred dividends paid out of earnings after taxes. To do this, you need to determine the pretax earnings required to meet these dividend payments, as follows:

Fixed charge coverage =

$$\frac{\text{Income before interest, taxes, and lease payments}}{\text{Debt int.} + \text{Lease payments} + (\text{Pref. div.}/1 - \text{Tax rate})}$$

As an alternative to these coverage ratios, cash flow ratios relate the cash flow available from operations to the face value of outstanding debt. These ratios are a combination of a flow ratio (since they include the flow of earnings and noncash expenses) against the stock of outstanding debt. Numerous authors have found that these cash flow/debt ratios have been significant in studies dealing with predicting bankruptcies and bond ratings.[7]

Cash Flow/Long-Term Debt Ratio   The cash flow figure used in several academic studies equals net income plus noncash expenses, which generally include depreciation expense and deferred taxes. Therefore, this ratio would be computed as:

Cash flow/long-term debt =

$$\frac{\text{Net income} + \text{Depreciation} + \text{Deferred taxes}}{\text{Book value of long-term debt}}$$

For Quaker Oats, these ratios were computed based on the net income from continuing operations, plus depreciation expense. Including and excluding deferred taxes, as reported in the financial statement footnotes, the ratios are:

Including Deferred Taxes as Long-Term Debt

$$1990: \frac{228,900 + 162,500 + 18,600}{1,168,300} = 35.09 \text{ percent}$$

$$1989: \frac{148,900 + 135,500 + 40,600}{1,164,700} = 27.90 \text{ percent}$$

$$1988: \frac{196,500 + 121,900 + (20,000)}{628,500} = 47.48 \text{ percent}$$

Excluding Deferred Taxes from Long-Term Debt

$$1990: \frac{410,000}{840,600} = 48.77 \text{ percent}$$

$$1989: \frac{325,000}{856,300} = 37.95 \text{ percent}$$

$$1988: \frac{298,400}{400,100} = 74.58 \text{ percent}$$

Although the values for all three years are good relative to comparable ratios for the economy, the results for 1990 indicate a recovery from 1989, but a decline relative to 1988.

Cash Flow/Total Debt Ratio   Besides relating cash flow to long-term debt, investors also consider its relationship to total debt to check for any increase in or disproportionate amount of short-term borrowing. For Quaker Oats, these ratios were:

Including Deferred Taxes as Long-Term Debt

$$1990: \frac{410,000}{2,306,800} = 17.77 \text{ percent}$$

$$1989: \frac{325,000}{1,988,800} = 16.34 \text{ percent}$$

$$1988: \frac{298,400}{1,635,000} = 18.25 \text{ percent}$$

Excluding Deferred Taxes from Long-Term Debt

$$1990: \frac{410,000}{1,979,100} = 20.72 \text{ percent}$$

$$1989: \frac{325,000}{1,680,400} = 19.34 \text{ percent}$$

$$1988: \frac{298,400}{1,406,600} = 21.21 \text{ percent}$$

The differences in these sets of ratios compared to those with only long-term debt indicate a high proportion of short-term debt for Quaker Oats due to short-term borrowing and trade accounts payable. As before, it is important to compare these flow ratios to similar ratios for other companies in the industry and the overall economy to gauge the firm's relative performance.

Alternative Measures of Cash Flow   The last two ratios used the traditional measure of cash flow. The requirement to report the statement of cash flows to stockholders has raised interest in other measures of cash flow. The first, *cash flow from operations*, is taken directly from the statement of cash flows. The second, *free cash flow*, is a modification of cash flow from operations.

Cash flow from operations includes the traditional measure of cash flow, which is equal to net income, plus adjustments for depreciation and deferred taxes, and restructuring charges (see Table 7.3). Beyond these income statement adjustments, it is necessary to

---

[7]A list of these studies is included in the references.

adjust for operating (current) assets and liabilities that either use or provide cash. For example, if the firm increases accounts receivable, it implies that the firm did not collect all reported sales, which reduces its cash flow from operations. In contrast, an increase in a current liability account like accounts payable means the firm acquired some assets without paying cash for them, which increases cash flow. These changes in operating assets or liabilities can add to or subtract from cash flow estimated strictly from income plus noncash expenses. The table below compares cash flow from operation figures to the traditional cash flow figures for Quaker Oats for 1988 to 1990 as contained in Table 7.3 (this uses net income rather than income from continuing operations):

	Traditional Cash Flow	Cash Flow from Operations
1990	329.2	447.1
1989	542.7	381.6
1988	387.0	301.8

During 1988 and 1989, the true cash flow from operations was much lower than the traditional cash flow value because of increases in current assets and even some reductions in current liabilities. In contrast, cash flow from operations was higher in 1990 due to increases in current liabilities.

Free cash flow further modifies cash flow from operations to recognize investing and financing activities that are critical to the ongoing success of the firm. It is assumed that these needs must be met before a firm can feel free to use its cash flow for other needs. The two additional expenditures considered are: (1) capital expenditures (an investing expenditure) and (2) dividends (a financing activity). These two items are subtracted from cash flow from operations, as follows:

	Cash Flow from Operations	Capital Expenditures	Dividends	Free Cash Flow
1990	447.1	275.6	110.5	61.0
1989	381.6	223.2	95.2	63.2
1988	301.8	169.7	79.9	52.2

For firms acquired in leveraged buyouts, this free cash flow number is critical because the new owners intend to retire outstanding debt with these funds.

Quaker Oats' fairly large, stable free cash flow would be considered a positive attribute.

Analysis of Growth Potential

Importance of Growth Analysis

The analysis of growth potential seeks to examine ratios that indicate how fast a firm can and should grow. Analysis of a firm's growth potential is important for both lenders and owners. Owners know that the value of the firm depends on its future growth in earnings and dividends. In the following chapter, we discuss the dividend discount model, which determines the value of the firm from current dividends, the required rate of return for the stock, and the expected growth rate of dividends.

Creditors are interested in a firm's growth potential because the firm's future success is the major determinant of its ability to pay an obligation, and success depends on growth. Some financial ratios used in credit analysis measure the book value of assets relative to financial obligations, which implies the ability to sell these assets and pay off the loan in case of default. In fact, such a sale of assets in a forced liquidation would typically yield only about 10 to 15 cents on the dollar. The more relevant analysis measures the ability of the firm to pay off its obligations as an ongoing enterprise, and its growth potential indicates its future status as an ongoing enterprise.

Determinants of Growth

The growth of a business firm, like the growth of any economic entity including the aggregate economy, depends on:

1. The amount of resources retained and reinvested in the entity
2. The rate of return earned on the resources retained

The more a firm reinvests, the greater its potential for growth. Further, for a given level of reinvestment, a firm will grow faster if it earns a higher rate of return on the resources reinvested. Therefore, the growth of equity earnings is a function of two variables: (1) the percentage of net earnings retained (i.e., the retention rate), and (2) the rate of return on the firm's equity capital (its ROE).

g = Percentage of earnings retained × Return on equity

= RR × ROE

where:

g = the potential growth rate

RR = the retention rate of earnings

ROE = the firm's return on equity

The retention rate depends on decisions by the board of directors based upon the investment opportunities available to the firm. Theory suggests that the firm should retain earnings and reinvest them as long as the expected rate of return on the investment exceeds the firm's cost of capital.

As discussed, the firm's ROE is a function of three components:

- Net profit margin
- Total asset turnover
- Financial leverage (total assets/equity)

Therefore, a firm can increase its ROE by increasing its profit margin, by becoming more efficient as reflected in an increase in its total asset turnover, or by shifting its capital structure toward increased financial leverage and financial risk. As an investor, you should examine each of the components to project ROE.

The growth potential analysis for Quaker Oats begins with the earnings retention rate (RR):

$$\text{Retention rate} = 1 - \frac{\text{Dividends declared}}{\text{Net income from continuing operations}}$$

Quaker Oats' RR figures were:

$$1990: 1 - \frac{1.40}{2.93} = 1 - 0.48 = 0.52$$

$$1989: 1 - \frac{1.20}{1.88} = 1 - 0.64 = 0.36$$

$$1988: 1 - \frac{1.00}{2.46} = 1 - 0.41 = 0.59$$

These results indicate that Quaker Oats has wanted to maintain a steady, but rising dividend policy during a period of volatile earnings caused by the operating changes. Therefore, although its historical payout before 1988 was consistently about 35 percent, the recent payout has varied, but appears to be moving toward the 50 to 60 percent range.

Table 7.5 on page 197 lists values for the three components of ROE for the period 1978 to 1990. Table 7.6 gives data for the two components of the firm's

| Table 7.6 | *Components of Growth and the Implied Sustainable Growth Rate: 1978–1990* |

	(1) Retention Rate	(2) ROE[a]	(3)[b] Sustainable Growth Rate
1990	0.52%	22.46%	11.62%
1989	0.36	13.09	4.72
1988	0.59	15.71	9.32
1987	0.66	17.09	11.28
1986	0.66	20.14	13.29
1985	0.66	18.19	12.01
1984	0.66	17.93	11.83
1983	0.64	16.82	10.76
1982	0.68	16.38	11.14
1981	0.67	15.64	10.48
1980	0.69	15.00	10.35
1979	0.69	14.60	10.07
1978	0.69	14.42	9.95

[a]Based upon year-end equity

[b]Column 3 equals Column 1 times Column 2.

growth potential and its implied growth rate during the last 13 years. Overall, Quaker Oats increased its growth potential. The potential growth rate declined during the period 1987 to 1989 because of declines in both ROE and retention rate. There was a reversal in both variables during 1990.

This table reinforces our understanding of the importance of the firm's ROE. Quaker Oats' retention rate was quite stable prior to 1988, implying that ROE determines the growth rate. This analysis indicates that the important consideration is the long-run outlook for the components of sustainable growth. As an investor, you need to *project* changes in each of the components and estimate an ROE to use in the growth model.

External Market Liquidity

Market Liquidity *Defined*

In Chapter 1 we discussed liquidity. **Market liquidity** is the ability to buy or sell an asset quickly with little price change from a prior transaction assuming no new information. AT&T and IBM are examples of liquid common stocks because you can sell them very quickly with little price change from prior trades. You might be able to sell shares of an illiquid stock quickly, but the price might differ significantly from prior prices. Alternatively, the broker might be able to get a specified price, but it could take several days.

Determinants of Market Liquidity

Investors should know the liquidity characteristics of securities they own or may buy because it can be important if they want to change the composition of their portfolios. While the major determinants of market liquidity are reflected in market trading data, several internal corporate variables are good proxies for these market variables. The most important determinant of external market liquidity is the number or dollar value of shares traded (dollar value adjusts for different price levels). More trading activity indicates a greater probability that you can find someone to take the other side of a desired transaction. Another measure of market liquidity is the bid–ask spread. Fortunately, certain internal corporate variables correlate highly with these market trading variables:

1. Total market value of outstanding securities (number of common shares outstanding times the market price per share)
2. Number of security owners

Numerous studies have shown that the main determinant of the bid–ask spread after price is the dollar value of trading.[8] In turn, the value of trading is highly correlated with the market value of outstanding securities and the number of security holders. This relationship holds because more shares outstanding implies more stockholders to buy or sell at any time for a variety of purposes. Numerous buyers and sellers provide liquidity.

You can estimate the market value of outstanding Quaker Oats stock as the average number of shares outstanding during the year times the average market price for the year (the high price plus the low price divided by 2) as follows:

1990: 76,537,000 × [(69 + 45)/2] = $4,362,609,000
1989: 79,307,000 × [(66 + 43)/2] = $4,322,231,500
1988: 79,835,000 × [(57 + 31)/2] = $3,512,740,000

---

[8]Studies on this topic were discussed in Chapter 4.

> **Market liquidity** The ability to buy or sell an asset quickly with little price change from a prior transaction assuming no new information.

Quaker Oat's stockholders number 33,859, including numerous institutions that own approximately 50 percent of the outstanding stock.

A final measure, trading turnover (the percentage of outstanding shares traded during a period of time), also indicates relative trading activity. During the calendar year 1990, 60,578,200 shares of Quaker Oats were traded for a turnover of approximately 79 percent (60,578,200/76,537,000). This compares to the average turnover for NYSE stocks of about 60 percent. These large values for market value, number of stockholders, and trading turnover indicate a very liquid market in the common stock of Quaker Oats.

Comparative Analysis of Ratios

We have discussed the importance of comparative analysis, but so far we have concentrated on the selection and computation of specific ratios. Table 7.7 shows most of the ratios discussed for Quaker Oats, the food industry (as derived from the *S&P Analysts Handbook*), and the S&P 400. The 3-year comparison should provide some insights, although you would typically want to examine data for a 5- to 10-year period.

Internal Liquidity

The three basic ratios (current ratio, quick ratio, and cash ratio) all show an overall decline for Quaker Oats. Similarly, relative to its industry and the market, the firm looks weaker in 1990 than it did in 1988. The firm's receivable turnover and collection period have declined, but the collection period is longer than that in the food industry (44 days versus 37 in 1990). Since it is stable, the difference is probably caused by the firm's product mix or its basic credit policy. (It may allow more liberal credit terms to its customers.) The working capital/sales ratio was larger than the industry and market series prior to 1990. Overall, the comparisons are generally inferior, especially relative to the food industry. A positive factor is the firm's ability to sell high-grade commercial paper and the existence of several major credit lines.

Table 7.7 **Summary of Financial Ratios for Quaker Oats, S&P Food Industry, S&P 400 Index: 1988–1990**

	1990			1989			1988		
	Quaker Oats	Food Industry	S&P 400	Quaker Oats	Food Industry	S&P 400	Quaker Oats	Food Industry	S&P 400
Internal Liquidity									
Current ratio	1.30	1.43	1.42	1.84	1.37	1.58	1.41	1.34	1.28
Quick ratio	0.57	0.72	1.01	0.75	0.70	1.12	0.63	0.80	0.72
Cash ratio	0.02	0.19	0.17	0.03	0.20	0.22	0.08	0.35	0.25
Receivables turnover	8.22	9.76	3.84	8.49	11.61	5.26	6.89	12.15	8.24
Average collection period (days)	44.42	37.40	95.05	42.99	31.44	69.39	52.95	30.04	44.30
Working capital/sales	6.81	7.71	13.75	14.26	7.01	17.09	9.26	4.57	7.88
Operating Performance									
Total asset turnover	1.56	1.50	1.00	1.62	1.78	1.09	1.50	1.82	1.13
Inventory turnover (sales)[a]	10.56	8.43	8.99	10.93	9.40	8.49	10.02	9.38	7.57
Working capital turnover	9.69	12.70	6.77	8.77	15.52	8.32	9.74	16.27	13.06
Net fixed asset turnover	4.76	3.90	2.89	5.19	4.63	2.90	4.95	4.57	2.73
Equity turnover	4.67	3.77	3.05	4.09	4.49	3.03	3.86	4.68	2.88
Profitability									
Gross profit margin	46.61	—	—	45.58	—	—	46.83	—	—
Operating profit margin	9.95	12.47	15.08	9.12	11.88	15.49	9.17	11.14	13.70
Net profit margin[b]	4.55	4.24	5.04	3.05	5.10	5.51	4.36	4.76	4.77
Return on total capital[b]	10.82	9.07	8.60	7.48	11.88	10.57	8.61	11.44	8.05
Return on equity[b]	20.83	16.19	15.31	12.47	23.06	16.79	16.80	22.34	13.85
Equity turnover	4.67	3.77	3.05	4.09	4.49	3.03	3.86	4.68	2.88
Financial Risk									
Debt/equity ratio	114.82	77.95	81.69	102.43	56.51	83.39	50.24	66.28	60.08
Long-term debt/long-term capital	53.45	43.80	44.96	50.60	35.24	45.47	33.44	39.86	37.53
Total debt/total capital	69.35	60.96	67.59	63.62	59.43	66.47	56.65	61.20	61.07
Interest coverage[b]	4.18	4.95	3.26	4.15	6.36	3.79	6.00	6.44	4.40
Cash flow/long-term debt[b]	0.35	0.35	0.35	0.38	0.55	0.36	0.75	0.47	0.44
Cash flow/total debt[b]	0.18	0.17	0.14	0.16	0.21	0.15	0.18	0.20	0.17
Growth analysis[c]									
Retention rate[b]	0.52	0.55	0.55	0.36	0.36	0.54	0.59	0.38	0.52
Return on equity[b]	22.46	17.31	15.09	13.09	21.47	16.16	15.71	21.02	13.44
Total asset turnover	1.51	1.53	0.95	1.56	1.69	0.98	1.56	1.71	1.08
Total assets/equity	3.27	2.56	3.09	2.75	2.46	2.98	2.31	2.58	2.57
Net profit margin[b]	4.55	4.24	5.04	3.05	5.10	5.51	4.36	4.76	4.77
Sustainable growth rate[b]	11.62	9.52	8.30	4.72	7.23	8.73	9.32	7.99	6.94

[a]Computed using sales; cost of sales not available.

[b]Calculated using net income from continuing operations.

[c]Using year-end total asset turnover.

Operating Performance

This segment of the analysis employs efficiency (turn-over) ratios and profitability ratios. Given the nature of the ratios, the major comparisons are relative to the industry. Quaker Oats' turnover ratios were generally superior relative to the food industry. This included total asset, inventory, and fixed asset turnovers.

Profitability from sales is best described as adequate. Operating profit margins were consistently below the industry, while the net profit margin fell below the industry in 1988 and 1989, but was higher in 1990. Profit performance related to invested capital was strong. The food industry return on total capital was consistently above the S&P 400, and Quaker Oats was above the food industry in 1990. The food industry turned in ROEs that were consistently above the market's, while Quaker Oats rose above the industry in 1990 after inferior performance in 1988 and 1989.

Financial Risk

Quaker Oats' balance sheet financial risk ratios were above those of the industry and the market in 1989 and 1990, indicating a riskier posture. In contrast, its financial risk flow ratios resembled industry ratios until 1989, when they declined below the industry values. These comparisons confirm that Quaker Oats increased its financial risk position during 1989 and 1990. The financial risk ratios in Table 7.7 include deferred taxes in long-term debt, which is a very conservative assumption for a firm with a strong growth pattern like Quaker Oats.

Growth Analysis

Except for 1989, Quaker Oats has maintained a sustainable growth rate similar to that of its industry, and both have outperformed the aggregate market. The major factor causing a difference in growth for the firm and its industry is ROE. Note that Quaker Oats' ROE components tend to differ from those of its industry. The industry had a higher total asset turnover, while Quaker Oats had higher financial leverage.

In sum, Quaker Oats has shown marginal liquidity, a good operating record, and a strong recovery in its profit margin. Concern arises due to the added debt. As an investor, you would monitor the firm's future ability to service the debt and profit margin. Your success as an investor depends upon how well you use these historical numbers to derive meaningful estimates.

Analysis of Non-U.S. Financial Statements

As we have stressed, your portfolio should encompass economies and markets outside the United States, as well as numerous global industries and many foreign firms in these global industries. You should recognize, however, that non-U.S. financial statements will be very different from those in this chapter or a typical accounting course. Accounting conventions differ substantially between countries. Although it is not possible to discuss alternative accounting conventions in detail, we will consider some of the major differences in format and principle.

Accounting Statement Format Differences

Table 7.8 contains examples of balance sheet formats for several countries and indicates some major differences in accounts and the order of presentation. As an example, in the United Kingdom, fixed assets are presented above current assets, and current liabilities are automatically subtracted from current assets. In Australia, not only are the capital accounts presented first, but the current assets follow long-term assets. The balance sheet items are similar to the U.S. format, but almost exactly opposite in presentation. Clearly, the accounts and presentation in Canada are very similar to the United States, and Germany's are also similar, except for numerous reserve accounts on the liability side. Besides finding similarities to U.S. practices, you need to consider the techniques used to derive individual items.

The comparative income statement formats in Table 7.9 show that U.K. statements have much less detail than U.S. statements. This limits your ability to analyze trends in expense items.

While Japanese statements look like those in the United States, you should be aware of nonoperating income and expense items. These can be substantial because Japanese firms tend to have significant investments in the common stock of suppliers and customers as a sign of goodwill. The income and gains (or losses) from these equity holdings can be a substantial permanent component of a firm's net income.

Australian statements, like the British, combine numerous expense items and add several items concerned with the distribution of the net income. Finally, income statements from Germany are very detailed, and also contain many unusual income and

Table 7.8	Comparative Balance Sheet Formats

United Kingdom

Net assets employed
>   Fixed assets
>   Subsidiaries
>   Associated companies
>   Current assets
>   Less: current liabilities
>   Less: deferred liabilities
Assets represented by
>   Share capital
>   Reserves

Australia

Share capital and reserves and liabilities
>   Share capital and reserves
>   Long-term debt and deferred income taxes
>   Current liabilities
Assets
>   Fixed assets
>   Investments
>   Current assets

Canada

Assets
>   Current assets
>   Investments
>   Fixed assets
>   Other assets
Liabilities and stockholders' equity
>   Current liabilities
>   Long-term debt
>   Deferred income taxes
>   Shareholders' equity

Germany

Assets
>   Outstanding payments on subscribed share capital
>   Fixed assets and investments
>   Revolving assets
>   Deferred charges and prepaid expenses
>   Accumulated net loss (of period)
Liabilities and shareholders' equity
>   Share capital
>   Open reserves
>   Adjustments to assets
>   Reserves for estimated liabilities and accrued expenses
>   Liabilities, contractually payable beyond 4 years
>   Deferred income
>   Accumulated net profit (of period)

Source: *Professional Accounting in 30 Countries*, pp. 51, 125–126, 169, 629, 746–749. Copyright © 1975 by the American Institute of Certified Public Accountants, Inc.

expense items. These details provide numerous opportunities to control the profit or loss for the period.

Differences in Accounting Principles

Beyond the differences in presentation formats, numerous differences characterize accounting principles employed to arrive at the income, expense, and balance sheet items. Choi and Bavishi compared ac-

counting standards for 10 countries and highlighted the differences.[9] Table 7.10 synthesizes the differ-

[9]Frederick D. S. Choi and Vinod B. Bavishi, "Diversity in Multinational Accounting," *Financial Executive* 50, no. 7 (August 1982): 36–39. This table is also presented and discussed in Frederick D. S. Choi and Gerhard G. Mueller, *International Accounting* (Englewood Cliffs, N.J.: Prentice-Hall, 1984): 72–76.

Table 7.9	Comparative Income Statement Formats

United Kingdom

Group turnover

Profit before taxation and extraordinary items

  Less: Taxation based on profit for the year

Profit after taxation and before extraordinary items

  Less: Extraordinary items

Profits attributable to shareholders of parent company

Japan

Sales

  Less: Cost of goods sold

Gross profit on sales

  Less: Selling and administrative expenses

Operating income

  Add: Nonoperating revenue

Gross profit for the period

  Less: Nonoperating expenses

Net income for the period

Australia

Sales and revenue

  Less: Cost of sales

Operating profit

  Add: Income from investments

  Less: Interest to other persons

Pretax profit

  Less: Provision for income tax

Net profit before extraordinary items

  Less: Extraordinary items

Net profit after extraordinary items

Unappropriated profits, previous year

Prior year adjustments

Transfer from general reserve

Available for appropriation

Dividends

Transfer to general reserve

Transfer to capital profits reserve

Unappropriated profits, end of year

Germany

Net sales

Increase or decrease of finished and unfinished products

Other manufacturing costs for fixed assets

Total output

Raw materials and supplies, purchased goods consumed in sale

Gross profit

Income from profit transfer agreements

Income from trade investments

Income from other long-term investments

Other interest and similar income

Income from retirement and appraisal of fixed assets

Income from the cancellation of lump allowances

Income from the cancellation of overstated reserves

Other income, including extraordinary in the sum of DM

Income from loss transfer agreements

Total income

Wages and salaries

Social taxes

Expenses for pension plans and relief

Depreciation and amortization of fixed assets and investments

Depreciation and amortization of finance investments

Losses by deduction or on retirement of current assets

Losses on retirement of fixed assets and investments

Interest and similar expenses

Taxes on income and net assets

Other expenses

Profits transferable to parent company under profit transfer agreement

Profit or loss for the period

Profit or loss brought forward from preceding year

Release of reserves

Amounts appropriated to reserves out of profit of period

Accumulated net profit or loss

Source: *Professional Accounting in 30 Countries*, pp. 52, 350, 351, 630, 750, 753. Copyright © 1975 by the American Institute of Certified Public Accountants, Inc.

ences in 32 specific items. Following a discussion of several major areas, the authors conclude:

> Perhaps the major conclusion drawn from analyzing the annual reports of the world's leading industrial firms is that fundamental differences in accounting practices between each of 10 countries examined are not as extensive as was initially feared. Major differences observed relate to accounting for goodwill, deferred taxes, long-term leases, discretionary reserves, and foreign-currency translation. Having

observed this comforting fact, the user must be cautioned against assuming that consistency and harmonization exists among the annual reports of all foreign companies.[10]

---

[10]Ibid., p. 39. Another comparison of accounting standards for the United States, the United Kingdom, the European Community, and Canada in Thomas G. Evans, Martin E. Taylor, and Oscar Holzmann, *International Accounting and Reporting* (New York: Macmillan, 1985): 106–113.

Table 7.10   *Synthesis of Accounting Differences*

Accounting Principles	United States	Australia	Canada	France	Germany	Japan	Nether-lands	Sweden	Switzer-land	United Kingdom
1. Marketable securities recorded at the lower cost or market?	Yes	Yes	Yes	Yes	Yes	Yes	Yes	Yes	Yes	Yes
2. Provision for uncollectible accounts made?	Yes	Yes	Yes	No	Yes	Yes	Yes	Yes	Yes	Yes
3. Inventory costed using FIFO?	Mixed	Yes	Mixed	Mixed	Yes	Mixed	Mixed	Yes	Yes	Yes
4. Manufacturing overhead allocated to year-end inventory?	Yes	Yes	Yes	Yes	Yes	Yes	Yes	Yes	No	Yes
5. Inventory valued at the lower of cost or market?	Yes	Yes	Yes	Yes	Yes	Yes	Yes	Yes	Yes	Yes
6. Accounting for long-term investments: less than 20 percent ownership: cost method?	Yes	Yes	Yes	Yes*	Yes	Yes	No(K)	Yes	Yes	Yes
7. Accounting for long-term investments: 21–50 percent ownership: equity method?	Yes	No(G)	Yes	Yes*	No(B)	No(B)	Yes	No(B)	No(B)	Yes
8. Accounting for long-term investments more than 50 percent ownership: full consolidation?	Yes	Yes	Yes	Yes*	Yes	Yes	Yes	Yes	Yes	Yes
9. Both domestic and foreign subsidiaries consolidated?	Yes	Yes	Yes	Yes	No**	Yes	Yes	Yes	Yes	Yes
10. Acquisitions accounted for under the pooling of interest method?	Yes	No(C)	No(C)	No(C)	No(C)	No(C)	No(C)	No(C)	No(C)	No(C)

Table 7.10   *(continued)*

Accounting Principles	United States	Australia	Canada	France	Germany	Japan	Nether-lands	Sweden	Switzer-land	United Kingdom
11. Intangible assets: goodwill amortized?	Yes	Yes	Yes	Yes	No	Yes	Mixed	Yes	No**	No**
12. Intangible assets: other than goodwill amortized?	Yes	Yes	Yes	Yes	Yes	Yes	Yes	Yes	No**	No**
13. Long-term debt includes maturities longer than 1 year?	Yes	Yes	Yes	Yes	No(D)	Yes	Yes	Yes	Yes	Yes
14. Discount/premium on long-term debt amortized?	Yes	Yes	Yes	No	No	Yes	Yes	No	No	No
15. Deferred taxes recorded when accounting income is not equal to taxable income?	Yes	Yes	Yes	Yes	Yes	Yes	Yes	No	No	Yes
16. Financial leases (long-term) capitalized?	Yes	No	Yes	No	No	No	No	No	No	No
17. Company pension fund contribution provided regularly?	Yes	Yes	Yes	Yes	Yes	Yes	Yes	Yes	Yes	Yes
18. Total pension fund assets and liabilities excluded from company's financial statement?	Yes	Yes	Yes	Yes	No	Yes	Yes	Yes	Yes	Yes
19. Research and development expensed?	Yes	Yes	Yes	Yes	Yes	Yes	Yes	Yes	Yes	Yes
20. Treasury stock deducted from owner's equity?	Yes	NF	Yes	Yes	No	Yes	Mixed	NF	NF	NF
21. Gains or losses on treasury stock taken to owner's equity?	Yes	NF	Yes	Yes	No	No**	Mixed	NF	NF	NF
22. No general purpose (purely discretionary) reserves allowed?	Yes	Yes	Yes	No	No	No	No	No	No	Yes
23. Dismissal indemnities accounted for on a pay-as-you-go basis?	Yes	Yes	Yes	Yes	Yes	Yes	NF	Yes	NF	Yes
24. Minority interest excluded from consolidated income?	Yes	Yes	Yes	Yes	No	Yes	Yes	Yes	Yes	Yes

(continued)

Table 7.10 (continued)

Accounting Principles	United States	Australia	Canada	France	Germany	Japan	Nether-lands	Sweden	Switzer-land	United Kingdom
25. Minority interest excluded from consolidated owner's equity?	Yes	Yes	Yes	Yes	No	Yes	Yes	Yes	Yes	Yes
26. Are intercompany sales/profits eliminated upon consolidation?	Yes	Yes	Yes	Yes	Yes	Yes	Yes	Yes	Yes	Yes
27. Basic financial statements reflect a historical cost valuation (no price level adjustment)?	Yes	No	Yes	No	Yes	Yes	No**	No	No	No
28. Supplementary inflation adjusted financial statements provided?	Yes	No**	No**	No	No	No	No**	No	No**	Yes
29. Straight-line depreciation adhered to?	Yes	Yes	Yes	Mixed	Mixed	Mixed	Yes	Yes	Yes	Yes
30. No excess depreciation permitted?	Yes	No	Yes	No	Yes	Yes	No	No	No	No
31. Temporal method of foreign currency translation employed?	Yes	Mixed	Yes	No(E)	No(E)	Mixed	No(E)	No(L)	No(E)	No(E)
32. Currency translation gains or losses reflected in current income?	Yes	Mixed	Yes	Mixed	Mixed	Mixed	No(J)	Mixed	No(H)	No

Key

Yes–Predominant practice.
Yes*–Minor modifications, but still predominant practice.
No**–Minority practice.
No–Accounting principle in question not adhered to.
NF–Not found.
Mixed–Alternative practices followed with no majority.
B–Cost method is used.
C–Purchase method is used.
D–Long-term debt includes maturities longer than 4 years.

E–Current rate method of foreign currency translation.
F–Weighted average is used.
G–Cost or equity.
H–Translation gains and losses are deferred.
I–Market is used.
J–Owner's equity.
K–Equity.
L–Monetary/Nonmonetary.

Source: Frederick D. S. Choi and Vinod B. Bavishi, "Diversity in Multinational Accounting." Used by permission from *Financial Executive* 50, no. 7 (August 1982), copyright 1982 by Financial Executives Institute.

International Ratio Analysis

You might tend to analyze non-U.S. accounting statements using financial ratios similar to those discussed in this chapter. While this is certainly legitimate, it is important to recognize that the representative ratio values and trends may differ among countries because of local accounting practices and business norms. Choi et al. compared a common set of ratios for a sample of companies in the United States, Japan, and Korea.[11] Table 7.11 compares mean values for these ratios and the differences among them. These ratios differ substantially for all manufacturing, as well as for specific important industries (chemicals, textiles, and transportation). Following an extensive discussion of the ratios, the authors conclude:

> On the basis of these findings, institutional, cultural, political and tax considerations in Japan and Korea do indeed cause their accounting ratios to differ from U.S. norms without necessarily reflecting better or worse financial risk and return characteristics being measured . . . A major conclusion of our study is that accounting measurements reflected in corporate financial reports represent, in one sense, merely "numbers" that have limited meaning and significance in and of themselves. Meaning and significance come from and depend upon an understanding of the environmental context from which the numbers are drawn as well as the relationship between the numbers and the underlying economic phenomena that are the real items of interest.[12]

Uses of Financial Ratios

We have discussed the role of financial ratios in credit analysis and security valuation. Four major areas in investments invite the use of financial ratios: (1) stock valuation, (2) the identification of internal corporate variables that affect a stock's systematic risk (beta), (3) assigning quality ratings on bonds, and (4) predicting insolvency (bankruptcy) of firms. In this section we discuss how ratios have been used in each of these four areas and the specific ratios found to be most useful.

Stock Valuation Models

Most valuation models attempt to derive an appropriate price/earnings ratio for a stock. As discussed in Chapter 8, this earnings multiple is a function of the expected growth rate of earnings and dividends and the required rate of return on the stock. Clearly, financial ratios can help in making both estimates. The estimate of a growth rate employs the ratios discussed in the growth rate potential section—retention rate and return on equity.

When estimating the required rate of return on an investment (k), remember that it depends on the risk premium for the security, which is a function of business risk and financial risk. Business risk is typically measured in terms of earnings variability, while financial risk is identified by the debt proportion or the flow ratios (i.e., the interest coverage ratios or the cash flow ratios).

The typical empirical valuation model examines a cross section of companies, applying a multiple regression model that relates price–earnings ratios for the sample firms to some of the following corporate variables (most consider data for 5 or 10 years):[13]

1. Operating earnings variability
2. Average debt/equity ratio
3. Average interest coverage ratio
4. Systematic risk (beta) over 5 years
5. Average dividend payout ratio
6. Average rate of earnings growth
7. Average return on equity

Financial Ratios and Systematic Risk

Our discussion of the capital asset pricing model (CAPM) will provide a more detailed discussion, but we can state now that the relevant risk variable is an asset's systematic risk, measured by its beta coefficient relative to the market portfolio of all risky assets. In efficient markets there should be a significant relationship between internal-corporate risk variables and market-determined risk variables such as beta. Numerous studies have examined internal corporate var-

[11]Frederick D. S. Choi, Hisaaki Hino, Sang Kee Min, Sang Oh Nam, Junichi Ujiie, and Arthur J. Stonehill, "Analyzing Foreign Financial Statements: The Use and Misuse of International Ratio Analysis," *Journal of International Business Studies* 14, no. 1(Spring–Summer, 1983): 113–131, reprinted in Frederick D. S. Choi and Gerhard G. Mueller, *Frontiers of International Accounting: An Anthology* (Ann Arbor, Mich.: UMI Research Press, 1985).

[12]Ibid., 131.

[13]A list of studies that have used financial ratios in valuation models appears in the reference section at the end of the chapter.

Table 7.11   *Mean Differences in Aggregate Financial Ratios: United States, Japan, Korea (unadjusted)*

Enterprise Category	Current Ratio	Quick Ratio	Debt Ratio	Times Interest Earned	Inventory Turnover
All Manufacturing					
Japan (976)	1.15	0.80	0.84	1.60	5.00
Korea (354)	1.13	0.46	0.78	1.80	6.60
United States (902)	1.94	1.10	0.47	6.50	6.80
Difference (U.S.–Japan)	40%	26%	(77%)	75%	26%
Difference (U.S.–Korea)	42%	58%	(66%)	73%	2%
Chemicals					
Japan (129)	1.30	0.99	0.79	1.80	7.10
Korea (54)	1.40	0.70	0.59	2.40	7.10
United States (n.a.)	2.20	1.30	0.45	6.50	6.50
Difference (U.S.–Japan)	42%	22%	(74%)	72%	(8%)
Difference (U.S.–Korea)	36%	45%	(31%)	62%	(9%)
Textiles					
Japan (81)	1.00	0.77	0.81	1.10	6.20
Korea (34)	1.00	0.37	0.83	1.30	4.90
United States (n.a.)	2.30	1.20	0.48	4.30	6.50
Difference (U.S.–Japan)	55%	38%	(70%)	74%	5%
Difference (U.S.–Korea)	55%	70%	(74%)	70%	24%
Transportation					
Japan (85)	1.20	0.86	0.83	1.90	3.90
Korea (14)	0.95	0.40	0.91	1.90	18.60
United States (n.a.)	1.60	0.74	0.52	8.70	5.60
Difference (U.S.–Japan)	21%	(16%)	(61%)	78%	28%
Difference (U.S.–Korea)	40%	46%	(75%)	77%	(234%)

Note: Parentheses indicate foreign ratios greater than U.S. ratios.

Source: Frederick D. S. Choi, Hisaaki Hino, Sang Kee Min, Sang Oh Nam, Junichi Ujiie, and Arthur J. Stonehill, "Analyzing Foreign Financial Statements: The Use and Misuse of International Ratio Analysis," *Journal of International Business Studies* (Spring–Summer 1983):113–131.

iables intended to reflect business risk and financial risk.[14] Some significant variables (typically measured by 5-year averages) have emerged, including the following variables:

Financial Ratios

1. Dividend payout
2. Total debt/total assets
3. Cash flow/total debt
4. Interest coverage
5. Working capital/total assets
6. Current ratio

[14]A list of studies in this area appears in the reference section at the end of the chapter.

Average Collection Period	Fixed Asset Turnover	Total Asset Turnover	Profit Margin	Return on Total Assets	Return on Net Worth
86	3.10	0.93	.013	.012	.071
33	2.80	1.20	.023	.028	.131
43	3.90	1.40	.054	.074	.139
(102%)	22%	32%	26%	84%	49%
24%	29%	9%	57%	62%	6%
88	2.80	0.90	.015	.014	.065
33	1.60	0.90	.044	.040	.100
50	2.80	1.10	.073	.081	.148
(75%)	0%	19%	79%	83%	56%
34%	44%	19%	39%	50%	32%
66	3.50	0.92	.003	.003	.017
30	2.20	1.00	.010	.011	.064
48	5.80	1.80	.027	.049	.094
(39%)	40%	50%	87%	93%	82%
36%	63%	44%	62%	78%	32%
116	4.50	0.90	.017	.015	.092
18	1.10	0.80	.026	.021	.221
31	6.50	1.60	.049	.078	.161
278%	30%	44%	65%	80%	43%
40%	84%	50%	47%	73%	(37%)

Variability Measures

1. Variance of earnings multiple
2. Coefficient of variation of operating earnings
3. Coefficient of variation of operating profit margins
4. Operating earnings beta (company earnings compared to aggregate earnings)

Nonratio Variables

1. Asset size
2. Market volume of trading in stock

Financial Ratios and Bond Ratings

As we mentioned in Chapter 3, four financial services assign quality ratings to bonds on the basis of the issuing company's ability to meet all its obligations. An AAA rating or (Aaa) indicates very high quality and almost no chance of default, while a C rating indicates the bond is already in default. A number of studies have used financial ratios to predict the rating to be assigned to a bond.[15] The major financial ratios considered (again, typically in 5-year averages) were as follows:

Financial Ratios

1. Long-term debt/total assets
2. Net income plus depreciation (cash flow)/long-term senior debt
3. Net income plus interest/interest expense (fixed-charge coverage)
4. Market value of stock/par value of bonds
5. Net operating profit/sales
6. Net income/total assets
7. Working capital/sales
8. Sales/net worth (equity turnover)

Variability Measures

1. Coefficient of variation of net earnings
2. Coefficient of variation of return on assets

Nonratio Variables

1. Subordination of the issue
2. Size of the firm (total assets)
3. Issue size
4. Par value of all publicly traded bonds of the firm

Financial Ratios and Insolvency (Bankruptcy)

Analysts have always been interested in using financial ratios to identify which firms might default on a loan or declare bankruptcy.[16] The typical study examines a sample of firms that have declared bankruptcy against a matched sample of firms in the same industry and of comparable size that have continued to operate. The analysis involves examining a number of financial ratios expected to reflect declining liquidity for several

years (usually 5) prior to the declaration of bankruptcy to determine which ratios or set of ratios provide the best predictions. Some of the models can properly classify over 80 percent of the firms the year prior to failure, and some achieve reasonably high classification results 3 to 5 years before failure. The financial ratios typically included in successful models were:[17]

1. Cash flow/total debt
2. Cash flow/long-term debt
3. Net income/total assets
4. Total debt/total assets
5. Working capital/total assets
6. Current ratio
7. Cash/current liabilities
8. Working capital/sales

Limitations of Financial Ratios

We must reinforce the earlier point that you should always consider *relative* financial ratios. In addition, you should keep other limitations of financial ratios in mind:

1. Are alternative firms' accounting treatments comparable? Several generally accepted methods for treating various accounting items can cause a difference in results for the same event. Therefore, you should check on the accounting treatment of significant items to adjust for major differences. This becomes a critical consideration when dealing with non-U.S. firms.
2. How homogeneous is the firm? Many companies have several divisions that operate in different industries. This may complicate deriving comparable industry ratios.
3. Are the implied results consistent? It is important to develop a total profile on the firm rather than depending on only one set of ratios (e.g., internal liquidity ratios). A firm may have short-term liquidity problems, but remain very profitable, and the profitability will eventually alleviate the short-run liquidity problems.
4. Is the ratio within a reasonable range for the industry? As noted on several occasions, you typically want a range of values for a ratio, because a value that

---

[15]A list of studies in this area appears in the reference section at the end of the chapter.

[16]A list of studies on this topic appears in the reference section at the end of the chapter.

[17]In addition to the several studies that have used financial ratios to predict failure, a number of studies have also used cash flow variables or a combination of ratios and cash flow variables. These studies are listed in the reference section at the end of the chapter.

is either too high or too low can be a cause for concern. For example, a low current ratio may indicate a liquidity problem, while a very high current ratio could indicate excessive liquidity and an underutilization of assets.

Summary

■ The overall purpose of financial statement analysis is to help you make decisions about investing in a firm's bonds or stocks. Financial ratios should be examined relative to the economy, the industry, the firm's main competitors, and the firm's past ratios.

■ The ratios can be divided into five categories, depending upon the purpose of the analysis: internal liquidity, operating performance, risk analysis, growth analysis, and external market liquidity. When analyzing the financial statements for non-U.S. firms, you must consider differences in format and accounting principles. These differences give different values for specific ratios in alternative countries. Four major uses of financial ratios are (1) stock valuation, (2) the identification of internal corporate variables affecting a stock's systematic risk (beta), (3) assignment of quality ratings on bonds, and (4) predicting insolvency (bankruptcy).

■ A final caveat; you can envision a huge number of potential financial ratios through which to examine almost every possible relationship. The trick is not to come up with more ratios, but to attempt to limit the number of ratios so you can examine them in a meaningful way. This entails analysis of the ratios over time relative to the economy, the industry, or the past. Any additional effort should be spent on deriving better comparisons for a limited number of ratios.

Questions

1. What is the overall purpose of financial statements?
2. Discuss briefly some decisions that require the analysis of financial statements.
3. Why do analysts employ financial ratios rather than absolute numbers?
4. The Murphy Company, which produces Polish sausage, earned 12 percent on its equity last year. What does this indicate about the firm's management? What other information do you want? Why do you want it?
5. Besides comparing a company's performance to that of its total industry, what other comparisons should be considered *within* the industry? Justify this comparison.
6. What purpose do internal liquidity ratios serve? What information do they provide? Who would be most interested in this information?
7. What are the components of operating performance? Discuss each of them, and the purposes of the ratios involved.
8. How might a jewelry store and a grocery store differ in terms of asset turnover and profit margin? Would you expect their return on equity figures to differ assuming equal risk? Discuss.
9. Describe the components of business risk, and discuss how they affect the variability of operating earnings.
10. Would you expect a steel company or a retail food chain to have greater business risk? Discuss this expectation in terms of the components of business risk.
11. When examining a firm's financial structure, would you be concerned with its business risk? Why or why not?
12. How does the fixed charge coverage ratio differ from the debt/equity ratio? Which would you prefer and why?
13. Why is the analysis of growth potential important to the common stockholder? Why is it important to the debt investor?
14. What general factors determine the rate of growth of any economic unit? Discuss each of the factors.
15. A firm is earning 24 percent on equity and has low risk. Discuss why you would expect it to have a high or low retention rate.
16. The Orange Company earned 18 percent on equity, while the Blue Company earned only 14 percent on equity. Does this mean that Orange is better than Blue?
17. Briefly discuss the two components of external market liquidity. In terms of the components of market liquidity, why do investors consider real estate to be a relatively illiquid asset?
18. Discuss some internal company factors that would indicate the firm's market liquidity.
19. Focusing on one of the four uses of financial ratios, discuss how you would use financial ratios as an investor.

Problems

1. The Whit Vegetable Company has the following results:

Net sales	$6,000,000
Net total assets	4,000,000
Depreciation	160,000
Net income	400,000
Long-term debt	2,000,000
Equity	1,160,000
Dividends	160,000

   a. Compute Whit's ROE directly, and also based upon the three components.
   b. Using the ROE computed in 1a, what is Whit's expected sustainable growth rate?
   c. Assuming the firm's net profit margin went to 0.04, what would happen to its ROE?
   d. Using the ROE in 1c, what is the expected sustainable growth rate? What if dividends were only $40,000?

2. Three companies have the following results during the recent period.

	A	B	C
Net profit margin	0.04	0.06	0.10
Total assets turnover	2.20	2.00	1.40
Total assets/equity	2.40	2.20	1.50

   a. Derive the return on equity for each based upon the three components.
   b. Given the following earnings and dividends, compute the sustainable growth rate for each firm:

Earnings/share	2.75	3.00	4.50
Dividends/share	1.25	1.00	1.00

3. On the following balance sheet, fill in the ratio values for 1992 and discuss how these results compare with both the industry averages and Eddie's past performance.

Eddie's Enterprises Consolidated Balance Sheet ($000) Years Ended December 31, 1991 and 1992

	1992	1991
Assets		
Cash	$ 100	$ 90
Receivables	200	170
Inventories	330	230
Total current assets	650	490
Property, plant, and equipment	1,850	1,650
Depreciation	350	225
Net properties	1,500	1,425
Intangibles	150	150
Total assets	$2,300	$2,065
Liabilities and Shareholders' Equity		
Accounts payable	$ 85	$ 105
Short-term bank note	125	110
Current portion of long-term debt	75	—
Accruals	65	85
Total current liabilities	350	300
Long-term debt	625	540
Deferred taxes	100	80
Preferred stock (10%, $100 par)	150	150
Common stock ($2 par, 100,000 issued in 1988 and 1987)	200	200
Additional paid-in capital	325	325
Retained earnings	550	470
Common shareholders' equity	1,075	995
Total liabilities and shareholders' equity	$2,300	$2,065

*Eddie's Enterprises Consolidated Statement
of Income ($000)
Years Ended December 31, 1991 and 1992*

	1992	1991
Net sales	$3,500.7	$2,990.6
Cost of goods sold	2,135.2	1,823.0
Selling, general and administrative expenses	1,107.3	974.6
Operating profit	258.3	193.0
Net interest expense	62.5	54.0
Income from operations	197.7	139.0
Income taxes	66.5	47.3
Net income	129.2	91.7
Preferred dividends	15.0	15.0
Net income available for common shares	114.2	76.7
Dividends declared	40.0	30.0

	Eddie's Current	Eddie's Average	Industry Average
Current ratio	_____	2.000	2.200
Quick ratio	_____	1.000	1.100
Receivable turnover	_____	18.000	18.000
Average collection period	_____	20.000	21.000
Total asset turnover	_____	1.500	1.400
Inventory turnover	_____	11.000	12.500
Fixed asset turnover	_____	2.500	2.400
Equity turnover	_____	3.200	3.000
Gross profit margin	_____	0.400	0.350
Operating profit margin	_____	8.000	7.500
Return on capital	_____	0.107	0.120
Return on equity	_____	0.118	0.126
Return on common equity	_____	0.128	0.135
Debt/equity ratio	_____	0.600	0.500
Debt/total capital ratio	_____	0.400	0.370
Interest coverage	_____	4.000	4.500
Fixed charge coverage	_____	3.000	4.000
Cash flow/long-term debt	_____	0.400	0.450
Cash flow/total debt	_____	0.250	0.300
Retention rate	_____	0.350	0.400

References

General

Beaver, William H. *Financial Reporting: An Accounting Revolution.* Englewood Cliffs, N.J.: Prentice-Hall, 1981.

Bernstein, Leopold A. *Financial Statement Analysis: Theory Application, and Interpretation*, 4th ed. Homewood, Ill.: Richard D. Irwin, 1989.

Chen, Kung H., and Thomas A. Shimerda. "An Empirical Analysis of Useful Financial Ratios." *Financial Management* 10, no. 1 (Spring 1981).

Foster, George. *Financial Statement Analysis*, 2d ed. Englewood Cliffs, N.J.: Prentice-Hall, 1978.

Gombola, Michael J., and Edward Ketz. "Financial Ratio Patterns in Retail and Manufacturing Organizations." *Financial Management* 12, no. 2 (Summer 1983).

Helfert, Erich A. *Techniques of Financial Analysis*, 6th ed. Homewood, Ill.: Richard D. Irwin, 1987.

Johnson, W. Bruce. "The Cross-Sectional Stability of Financial Ratio Patterns." *Journal of Financial and Quantitative Analysis* 14, no. 5 (December 1979).

Page, John R., and Paul Hooper. "Financial Statements for Security Analysts." *Financial Analysts Journal* 35, no. 5 (September–October 1979).

Analysis of International Financial Statements

Arpan, Jeffrey S., and Lee H. Rodebaugh. *International Accounting and Multinational Enterprises.* New York: John Wiley & Sons, 1981.

Choi, Frederick D. S., ed. *Multinational Accounting: A Research Framework for the Eighties.* Ann Arbor, Mich.: UMI Research Press, 1981.

Choi, Frederick D. S., and Gerhard G. Mueller. *International Accounting.* Englewood Cliffs, N.J.: Prentice-Hall, 1984.

Choi, Frederick D. S., and Gerhard G. Mueller. *Frontiers of International Accounting: An Anthology.* Ann Arbor, Mich.: UMI Research Press, 1985.

Choi, Frederick D. S., and Vinod B. Bavishi. "Diversity in Multinational Accounting." *Financial Executive* 50, no. 7 (August 1982).

Choi, Frederick D. S., H. Hino, S. K. Min, S. O. Nam, J. Ujiie, and A. I. Stonehill. "Analyzing Foreign Financial Statements: The Use and Misuse of International Ratio Analysis." *Journal of International Business Studies* 14, no. 1 (Spring–Summer 1983).

Davidson, Sidney, and John M. Kohlmeier. "A Measure of the Impact of Some Foreign Accounting Principles." *International Journal of Accounting* (Fall 1967).

Drury, D. H. "Effects of Accounting Practice Divergence: Canada and the U.S.A." *Journal of International Business Studies* 10, no. 2 (Fall 1979).

Evans, Thomas G., Martin E. Taylor, and Oscar Holzmann. *International Accounting and Reporting.* New York: Macmillan, 1985.

Fitzgerald, R., A. Stickler, and T. Watts. *International Survey of Accounting Principles and Practices.* Scarborough, Ontario: Price Waterhouse International, 1979.

Gray, S. J., J. C. Shaw, and L. B. McSweeney. "Accounting Standards and Multinational Corporations." *Journal of International Business Studies* 12, no. 1 (Spring–Summer 1981).

Hatfield, H. R. "Some Variations in Accounting Practice in England, France, Germany, and the United States." *Journal of Accounting Research* 4, no. 2 (Autumn 1966).

Nair, R. D., and Werner G. Frank. "The Impact of Disclosure and Measurement Practices in International Accounting Classifications." *Accounting Review* 55, no. 3 (July 1980).

Financial Ratios and Stock Valuation Models

Babcock, Guilford. "The Concept of Sustainable Growth." *Financial Analysts Journal* 26, no. 3 (May–June 1970).

Estep, Tony. "Security Analysis and Stock Selection: Turning Financial Information into Return Forecasts." *Financial Analysts Journal* 43, no. 4 (July–August 1987).

Malkiel, Burton G., and John G. Cragg. "Expectations and the Structure of Share Prices." *American Economic Review* 60, no. 4 (September 1970).

Wilcox, Jarrod W. "The P/B–ROE Valuation Model." *Financial Analysts Journal* 40, no. 1 (January–February 1984).

Financial Ratios and Systematic Risk (Beta)

Beaver, William H., Paul Kettler, and Myron Scholes. "The Association between Market-Determined and Accounting-Determined Risk Measures." *Accounting Review* 45, no. 4 (October 1970).

Edelman, Richard B. "Telecommunications Betas: Are They Stable and Unique?" *Journal of Portfolio Management* 10, no. 1 (Fall 1983).

Harrington, Diana. "Whose Beta is Best?" *Financial Analysts Journal* 39, no. 4 (July–August 1983).

Rosenberg, Barr. "Prediction of Common Stock Investment Risk." *Journal of Portfolio Management* 11, no. 1 (Fall 1984).

Rosenberg, Barr. "Prediction of Common Stock Betas." *Journal of Portfolio Management* 11, no. 2 (Winter 1985).

Thompson, Donald J., II. "Sources of Systematic Risk in Common Stocks." *Journal of Business* 49, no. 2 (April 1976).

Financial Ratios and Bond Ratings

Ang, James S., and A. Kiritkumar. "Bond Rating Methods: Comparison and Validation." *Journal of Finance* 30, no. 2 (May 1975).

Ferri, Michael G., and Charles G. Martin. "The Cyclical Pattern in Corporate Bond Quality." *Journal of Portfolio Management* 6, no. 2 (Winter 1980).

Fisher, Lawrence. "Determinants of Risk Premiums on Corporate Bonds." *Journal of Political Economy* 67, no. 3 (June 1959).

Gentry, James A., David T. Whitford, and Paul Newbold. "Predicting Industrial Bond Ratings with a Probit Model and Funds Flow Components." *The Financial Review* 23, no. 3 (August 1988).

Horrigan, James O. "The Determination of Long-Term Credit Standing with Financial Ratios." *Empirical Research in Accounting: Selected Studies.* Supplement to *Journal of Accounting Research* 4 (1966).

Kaplan, Robert S., and Gabriel Urwitz. "Statistical Models of Bond Ratings: A Methodological Inquiry." *Journal of Business* 52, no. 2 (April 1979).

Pinches, George E., and Kent A. Mingo. "The Role of Subordination and Industrial Bond Ratings." *Journal of Finance* 30, no. 1 (March 1975).

Standard & Poor's Corporation. "Corporation Bond Ratings: An Overview." New York: Standard & Poor's, 1978.

Financial Ratios and Corporate Bankruptcy

Altman, Edward I. "Financial Ratios, Discriminant Analysis, and the Prediction of Corporate Bankruptcy." *Journal of Finance* 23, no. 4 (September 1968).

Altman, Edward I. *Corporate Financial Distress.* New York: John Wiley & Sons, 1983.

Altman, Edward I., Robert G. Haldeman, and P. Narayanan. "Zeta Analysis: A New Model to Identify Bankruptcy Risk of Corporations." *Journal of Banking and Finance* 1, no. 2 (June 1977).

Beaver, William H. "Financial Ratios as Predictors of Failure." *Empirical Research in Accounting: Selected Studies.* Supplement to *Journal of Accounting Research* 4 (1966).

Beaver, William H. "Market Prices, Financial Ratios, and the Prediction of Failure." *Journal of Accounting Research* 6, no. 2 (Autumn 1968).

Beaver, William H. "Alternative Accounting Measures as Predictors of Failure." *The Accounting Review* 43, no. 1 (January 1968).

Casey, Cornelius, and Norman Bartczak. "Using Operating Cash Flow Data to Predict Financial Distress: Some Extensions." *Journal of Accounting Research* 23, no. 1 (Spring 1985).

Gentry, James A., Paul Newbold, and David T. Whitford. "Classifying Bankrupt Firms with Funds Flow Components." *Journal of Accounting Research* 23, no. 1 (Spring 1985).

Gentry, James A., Paul Newbold, and David T. Whitford. "Predicting Bankruptcy: If Cash Flow's Not the Bottom Line, What Is?" *Financial Analysts Journal* 41, no. 5 (September–October 1985).

Mensah, Yaw M. "The Differential Bankruptcy Predictive Ability of Specific Price Level Adjustments: Some Empirical Evidence." *The Accounting Review* 58, no. 2 (April 1983).

Ohlson, J. A. "Financial Ratios and the Probabilistic Prediction of Bankruptcy." *Journal of Accounting Research* 18, no. 2 (Spring 1980).

Scott, J. "The Probability of Bankruptcy: A Comparison of Empirical Predictions and Theoretical Models." *Journal of Banking and Finance* 5 (1981).

Wilcox, Jarrod W. "A Prediction of Business Failure Using Accounting Data." *Empirical Research in Accounting: Selected Studies.* Supplement to *Journal of Accounting Research* 11 (1973).

C H A P T E R

8

Introduction to Security Valuation

Investment decision process Estimation of value for comparison with market price to determine whether or not to invest.

Valuation process Part of the investment decision process in which you estimate the value of a security.

At the start of this book we defined an investment as a commitment of funds for a period of time to derive a rate of return to compensate for the time the funds are invested, the expected rate of inflation during that time, and the uncertainty involved. This definition suggests that the first step in making an investment is determining your required rate of return.

Once you have determined this rate, some investment alternatives, such as savings accounts and T-bills, are fairly easy to evaluate because they provide stated rates of return. Most investments (e.g., common stock) involve expected cash flows and stated market prices and you must evaluate the market prices and determine if they are consistent with your required return. To do this, you estimate the values of the securities based upon the expected cash flows and your required rate of return. This is the process of estimating value. After you have completed this value estimation you compare estimated values to market prices to decide whether you want to buy the securities.

This **investment decision process** resembles your experience on numerous occasions when shopping for a suit or a dress, a stereo, or a car. In each case, you examined the item and subjectively decided how much you thought it was worth (i.e., its value). If the price matched or beat that amount, you bought the item. The same technique applies to a security, except that the determination of value is more formal.

We start our investigation of security valuation by discussing the **valuation process**. While we know that the value of a security is determined by its quality and profit potential, we also know that the economic environment and the performance of the firm's industry influence the security value and rate of return. Because of the importance of these economic and industry factors, our overview of the valuation process describes these influences and explains how they should be incorporated into the analysis of security value. In the following section we describe the theory of value and emphasize the factors that affect the value of securities.

Next we apply these valuation concepts to the valuation of different assets—bonds, preferred stock, and common stock. In this section, we show how the valuation models help investors calculate how much they should pay for these assets. In the final section, we emphasize the estimation of the variables that affect value (required rate of return and the expected growth rate) and discuss what additional factors must be considered when we extend this analysis to the valuation of global securities.

Overview of the Valuation Process

Psychologists suggest that the success or failure of an individual can depend as much on environment as on genetic gifts. If we extend this idea to the valuation of securities, we should consider the economic environment during the valuation process. Regardless of the qualities of a particular issue or the capabilities of the firm, the economic environment will have a major influence on the realized rate of return on the investment.

As an example, assume you own shares of the strongest and most successful firm in the home furnishings industry. If you own the shares during a strong economic expansion, the sales and earnings of the firm will increase and your rate of return on the stock should be quite high. In contrast, if you own the same stock during a major economic recession, the sales and earnings of this firm would probably decline and the stock price would be stable or even decline.

Therefore, when assessing the value of a security, it is necessary to analyze the aggregate economy and the securities markets along with the firm's specific industry.

The valuation process imitates the chicken-and-egg dilemma. Do you start with an analysis of the macroeconomy and various industries and proceed to individual stocks, or do you begin with individual securities and gradually build up to an analysis of the entire economy? We contend that the discussion should begin with aggregate economies and overall securities markets and progress to different industries with a global perspective. Only after a thorough industry analysis can you properly evaluate the securities issued by individual firms within the better industries. Thus, we recommend a three-step valuation process in which you first examine the influence of the general economy on all firms, then analyze the prospects for various industries in this economic environment, and finally turn to the analysis of individual firms in chosen industries.

Why a Three-Step Valuation Process?

General Economic Influences
Monetary and fiscal policy measures enacted by various agencies of national governments influence the aggregate economies of those countries. The resulting economic conditions influence all industries and all companies within the economies.

Fiscal policy initiatives such as tax credits or tax cuts can encourage spending, whereas additional taxes can discourage spending. Increases or decreases in government spending on defense, unemployment insurance, retraining programs, or highways also influence the general economy. All such policies influence the business environment for firms that rely directly on those expenditures for earnings. In addition, government spending has a multiplier effect. For example, increases in road building increase the demand for equipment and materials, and the workers in industries that supply those products have more to spend on consumer goods, which raises the demand for consumer goods, which affects another set of suppliers.

Monetary policy produces similar economic changes. A restrictive monetary policy that reduces the growth rate of the money supply reduces the supply of funds for working capital and expansion for all businesses. This raises market interest rates, and therefore firms' costs, making goods and services more expensive for individuals. Monetary policy therefore affects all segments of an economy, and that economy's relationship with other economies.

Any economic analysis requires consideration of inflation. As we have discussed several times, inflation causes differences between real and nominal interest rates and changes the spending and savings behavior of consumers and corporations. In addition, unexpected changes in the rate of inflation make it difficult for firms to plan, which inhibits growth and innovation. Beyond the impact on the domestic economy, differential inflation and interest rates influence trade balances between countries and exchange rates for currencies.

In addition to government monetary and fiscal policy actions, events such as war, political upheavals, and international monetary devaluations produce changes in the business environment that add to the uncertainty of sales and earnings expectations, and therefore the risk premium required by investors. For example, the reaction of the Chinese government to the student demonstrations in 1989 caused a significant increase in the risk premium for investors in China and a subsequent reduction in investment and spending in China.

In short, it is difficult to conceive of any industry or company that can escape the influence of macroeconomic developments. Because aggregate economic events have a profound effect on all industries and all companies within these industries, these macroeconomic factors must be considered before industries can be analyzed.

Taking a global portfolio perspective, asset allocation within a country will be affected by its economic outlook. An imminent recession in a country should have a negative impact on its security prices. Under these economic expectations, investors would be apprehensive about investing in most industries in the country. Such a country would be **underweighted** in portfolios relative to its weight based on market values. The best investment decision would probably be a smaller allocation to the country, and any funds invested in the country would be directed to low-risk sectors of the economy.

In contrast, optimistic economic and stock-market outlooks for a country should lead an investor to increase overall allocation to this country, (over-weighting the country based upon weights deter-

> **Underweighted** A condition in which a portfolio, for whatever reason, includes less of a class of securities than the relative market value alone would justify.

mined by market values). After allocating funds among countries, the investor next looks for outstanding industries in each country. Economic analysis aids this search for appropriate industries because the future performance of an industry generally depends upon the economic outlook and the particular industry's expected relationship to the economy.

Industry Influences

The next step in the valuation process is to identify industries that will prosper or suffer in the projected aggregate economic environment. Remember that alternative industries react to economic change at different points in the business cycle. For example, construction activity typically lags the business cycle because firms increase capital expenditures when they are operating at full capacity, which happens at the peak of the economic cycle. In addition, alternative industries respond differently to the business cycle. Cyclical industries such as steel or autos typically do much better than the aggregate economy during expansions, but they suffer more during contractions.

Also, firms that sell in international markets can benefit or suffer as foreign economies shift. An industry with a substantial worldwide market might experience low demand in its domestic market, but growing demand in its international market. As an example, much of the growth of the beverage companies, like Coca-Cola and Pepsi, and the fast-food chains, like McDonald's and Burger King, has come from international expansion in Europe and the Far East.

In general, an industry's prospects within the global business environment determine how well or poorly an individual firm will fare, so industry analysis should precede company analysis. Few companies perform well in poor industries, so even the best company in a poor industry is a bad prospect for investment. For example, poor sales and profits in the farm equipment industry during the mid-1980s limited Deere and Co., a very well-managed firm and probably the best firm in its industry, to very poor results. Though Deere performed better than other firms in the industry (some went bankrupt), it fell far short of its past performance and did poorly relative to most firms in other industries.

Company Analysis

After determining that an industry's outlook is good, an investor can analyze and compare individual firms' performance within the entire industry using financial ratios. As stated in Chapter 7, many ratios are valid only for comparing firms' performance to that of their industries.

You undertake company analysis to identify the best company in a promising industry. This involves examining not only a firm's past performance, but also its future prospects. After you understand the firm and its outlook, you are in a position to determine its value. In the final step you compare this estimated value to the firm's market price and decide whether its stock or bonds are good investments.

Your final goal is to select the best stock or bonds within a desirable industry. As we will discuss in more detail in Chapter 11, the best stock or bond may not necessarily be issued by the best company since the stock of the finest company in an industry may be overpriced and a poor investment. You cannot know this until you have analyzed the company, estimated its value, and compared your estimated value to the market price of the stock.

Does the Three-Step Process Work?

Although you might agree with the logic of the three-step valuation process, you might wonder how well it works in selecting investments. Several academic studies have supported this technique. First, studies indicated that most changes in an individual firm's earnings over time could be attributed to changes in earnings for all firms and specific industries with changes to all firms being more important. Although the relative influence of the general economy and specific industries varied among individual firms, the results consistently demonstrated significant effects of the economic environment on firm earnings.

Second, analysts found that stock prices followed cyclical patterns. More specifically, they found relationships between stock prices and various economic variables such as employment, income, or production. These results supported the view that there is a relationship between stock prices and economic expansions and contractions.

Third, analysis of the relationships between rates of return for the aggregate stock market, alternative industries, and individual stocks showed that most changes in rates of return for individual stocks could be explained by changes in rates of return for the aggregate stock market and the stocks' industries. Although the importance of the market effect tended to decline over time, and the significance of the industry effect varied among industries, the combined market–industry effect on individual firms' rates of return was still important.

These results from academic studies support the use of the three-step valuation process. This allocation decision implies that the asset allocation decision is critical. This specifies: (1) what proportion of your portfolio you will invest in various nations' economies; (2) within each country, how you will divide your assets between stocks, bonds, and other investments; and (3) what industries you will analyze based upon which ones are expected to prosper or suffer in the projected economic environment.

Now that we have described and justified the three-step valuation process, in which we evaluate the overall economy, then alternative industries, and finally individual firms and stocks, we need to consider the theory of valuation. The application of this theory allows us to compute values for markets, alternative industries, and individual firms and stocks. Finally, we will compare these estimated values to current market prices and decide whether we want to make particular investments.

Theory of Valuation

You may recall from studies in accounting, economics, or corporate finance that the value of an asset is the present value of its expected returns. Specifically, you expect an investment to provide a stream of returns during the period of time that you own it. To convert this stream of returns to a single value for the security, you must discount the stream at your required rate of return. This process of valuation requires estimates of (1) the stream of expected returns, and (2) your required rate of return on the investment.

Streams of Returns

An estimate of the expected returns from an investment depends not only on the size, but also the form, time pattern, and uncertainty of returns.

Form of Returns The returns from an investment can take many forms, including earnings, dividends, interest payments, or capital gains (i.e., increases in value) during a period. Alternative valuation techniques (called *models*) measure returns of different forms. As an example, one model values common stock by applying a multiplier to a firm's earnings, while another model derives a value by computing the present value of dividend payments. The point is, returns take many forms, and you must consider all of them to evaluate an investment accurately.

Time Pattern of Returns   You cannot calculate an accurate value for a security unless you can estimate when you will receive the returns. Money has a time value which affects the value of the stream of returns relative to alternative investments with different time patterns.

Uncertainty of Returns   You will recall from Chapter 1 that the required rate of return on an investment is determined by (1) the economy's real risk-free rate of return, plus (2) the expected rate of inflation during the holding period, plus (3) a risk premium. All investments are affected by the risk-free rate and inflation (which determine the nominal risk-free rate); the risk premium differentiates alternative investments. In turn, this risk premium depends on the uncertainty of returns on the assets.

We can identify the sources of uncertainty by the internal characteristics of assets or by market-determined factors. Earlier we subdivided the internal characteristics into business risk (BR), financial risk (FR), liquidity risk (LR), exchange rate risk (ERR), and country risk (CR).

Investment Decision Process: Comparison of Estimated Values and Market Prices

To ensure you receive your required return on an investment, you must estimate the value of the investment at your required rate of return, and then compare this estimated value to the investment's prevailing market price. You should not buy an investment with a market price in excess of your estimated value because the difference will prevent you from receiving your required rate of return on the investment. In contrast, if the estimated value of the investment exceeds the market price, you should buy the investment.

Estimated value > Market price = Buy

Estimated value < Market price = Don't buy

Assume, for example, that you read about a publicly traded producer of shoes for running and hiking that has stock listed on the NYSE. Using one of the valuation models we will discuss, and making estimates of earnings and growth based upon the company's annual report and other information, you estimate its value as $20 a share. A look in the paper tells you that the stock is currently trading at $15 a share. You would want to buy the stock because you can buy a share you think is worth $20 for $15. In contrast, if the current market price were $25 a share, you would not consider buying the stock.

The theory of value discussed provides a common framework for the evaluation of all investments. Different applications of this theory produce different techniques to compute estimated values for alternative investments based on the different payment streams and characteristics. The interest and principal payments on a bond differ sharply from the expected dividends and selling prices for a common stock. The initial discussion applies the discounted cash flow method to bonds, preferred stock, and common stock. This demonstrates that the same basic model is useful across a range of investments. Because of the difficulty in estimating the value of common stock, we consider several additional techniques for evaluating this class of security.

Valuation of Alternative Investments

Valuation of Bonds

It is relatively easy to calculate the value of a bond because the size and time pattern of returns over its life are known. A bond typically promises:

1. An interest payment every 6 months equal to one-half its coupon rate times its face value.
2. The payment of the principal on the maturity date.

As an example, in 1992 a $10,000 bond due in 2007 with a 10 percent coupon will pay $500 every 6 months for its 15-year life. In addition, the bond issuer promises to pay the $10,000 principal at maturity in 2007. Assuming the bond issuer does not default, the investor knows what payments will be made and when they will be made.

Applying the valuation theory, which states that the value of any asset is the present value of its returns,

Perpetuity An investment without any maturity date. It provides returns to its owner indefinitely.

the value of the bond is the present value of the interest payments, which we can think of as an annuity of $500 every 6 months for 15 years, plus the present value of the principal payment of $10,000 in 15 years. The only unknown for this asset (assuming the borrower does not default) is the rate of return at which you should discount the expected stream of payments. If the prevailing nominal risk-free rate is 9 percent and you require a 1 percent risk premium as compensation for some probability of default, your required rate of return would be 10 percent.

The present value of the interest payments, that is, of an annuity for 30 periods (15 years every 6 months) at one-half the required return (5 percent), equals:[1]

$$\$500 \times 15.3725 = \$7,686$$

The present value of the principal is likewise discounted at 5 percent for 30 periods:[2]

$$\$10,000 \times 0.2314 = \$2,314$$

This can be summarized as follows:

Present value of interest payments: $500 × 15.3725	$ 7,686
Present value of principal payment: $10,000 × 0.2314	2,314
Present value of bond at 10 percent	$10,000

This is the amount that an investor should be willing to pay for this bond, assuming that the required rate of return on a bond of this risk class is 10 percent. If the market price of the bond is above this value, the investor should not buy it because the promised yield to maturity will be less than the required rate of return.

Assuming an investor wants a 12 percent return on this bond, the value would be:

$500 × 13.7648	$6,882
$10,000 × 0.1741	1,741
Present value of bond at 12 percent	$8,623

This example shows that if you want a higher rate of return, you will not pay as much for an asset; that is, a given stream of returns has a lower value to you. As before, you would compare this computed value to the market price of the bond to determine whether you should invest in it.[3]

Valuation of Preferred Stock

The owner of a preferred stock receives a promise to pay a stated dividend, usually each quarter, for an indefinite period. Preferred stock is a **perpetuity** because it has no maturity. As with a bond, however, it promises stated payments on specified dates, although it does not entail the same legal obligation to pay investors as bonds do. Payments are made only after the firm meets its bond interest payments.

This increases the uncertainty, so investors should require a higher rate of return on a firm's preferred stock than on its bonds. Although this differential should exist in theory, it generally does not exist because of the tax treatment accorded dividends paid to corporations. As described in Chapter 2, 80 percent of intercompany preferred dividends are tax-exempt, making their effective tax rate about 6.8 percent, assuming a corporate tax rate of 34 percent. This stimulates demand for preferred stocks, and their yield has generally been lower than that of the highest-grade corporate bonds.

Because preferred stock is a perpetuity, its value is simply the stated annual dividend divided by the required rate of return on preferred stock (k_p) as follows:

$$V = \frac{\text{Dividend}}{k_p}$$

Assume that a preferred stock has a $100 par value and a dividend of $8 a year. Expected inflation, the uncertainty of the dividend payment, and the tax advantage to you as a corporate investor lead you to set your

---

[1]The annuity factors and present value factors are listed in Appendix A at the end of the book.

[2]With annual compounding this would be 0.239 rather than 0.2314. Semiannual compounding is consistent with the interest payments, and it is used in practice.

[3]To test your mastery of bond valuation, verify that at a required rate of return of 8 percent, the value of this bond would be $11,729.

required rate of return on this stock at 9 percent. Therefore, its value to you is:

$$V = \frac{\$8}{0.09}$$

$$= \$88.89$$

Given this estimated value, you would need to inquire about the current market price in order to decide whether you would want to buy this stock. If the current market price were $95, you would decide against a purchase, while if it were $80 you would want to buy the stock.

Also, given the market price of a preferred stock, you can derive its promised yield. Assuming a current market price of $85, it would be:

$$k_p = \frac{\text{Dividend}}{\text{Price}} = \frac{\$8}{85.00} = 0.0941 \text{ or } 9.41 \text{ percent}$$

Valuation of Common Stock

The valuation of common stocks is much more difficult than valuation of bonds or preferred stock because an investor is uncertain about the size of the returns, their time pattern, and the required rate of return (k_e). In contrast, the only unknown for a bond is the required rate of return, which is the prevailing nominal RFR plus a risk premium. Similarly, for preferred stock the only unknown is the required rate of return on the stock (k_p). Nevertheless, we can find common stock values using the same theory that we applied to bonds and preferred stock.

We can choose either dividends or earnings as the stream of returns to discount. Some investors prefer earnings because they are the source of dividends. Others feel that investors should discount the returns they will receive—dividends. Although we will present models that use both streams, we will introduce the dividend discount model (DDM) first because it is intuitively appealing (dividends *are* the flow received). Also, because the DDM has been used extensively by others, you may be familiar with its reduced form.

[4]This model was initially set forth in J. B. Williams, *The Theory of Investment Value* (Cambridge, Mass.: Harvard University Press, 1938). It was subsequently reintroduced and expanded by Myron J . Gordon, *The Investment, Financing, and Valuation of the Corporation* (Homewood, Ill.: Richard D. Irwin, 1962).

Dividend discount model (DDM) A technique for estimating the value of a stock issue as the present value of all future dividends.

Dividend Discount Model (DDM)

The **dividend discount model** assumes that the value of a share of common stock is the present value of all future dividends as follows:[4]

$$V_j = \frac{D_1}{(1+k)} + \frac{D_2}{(1+k)^2} + \frac{D_3}{(1+k)^3} + \cdots \frac{D_\infty}{(1+k)^\infty}$$

$$= \sum_{t=1}^{\infty} \frac{D_t}{(1+k)^t}$$

where:

V_j = value of common stock j

D_t = dividend during period t

k = required rate of return on stock j

An obvious question is, what happens when the stock is not held indefinitely? A sale of the stock at the end of Year 2 would require the formula:

$$V_j = \frac{D_1}{(1+k)} + \frac{D_2}{(1+k)^2} + \frac{SP_{j2}}{(1+k)^2}$$

where SP_{j2} equals the sale price of stock j at the end of Year 2. The value equals the two dividend payments during Years 1 and 2 plus the sale price (SP) for the stock at the end of Year 2. The expected selling price of the stock at the end of Year 2 is simply the value of all remaining dividend payments:

$$SP_{j2} = \frac{D_3}{(1+k)} + \frac{D_4}{(1+k)^2} + \cdots \frac{D_\infty}{(1+k)^\infty}$$

If SP_{j2} is discounted back to the present by $1/(1+k)^2$, this equation becomes:

$$PV(SP_{j2}) = \frac{\frac{D_3}{(1+k)} + \frac{D_4}{(1+k)^2} + \cdots \frac{D_\infty}{(1+k)^\infty}}{(1+k)^2}$$

$$= \frac{D_3}{(1+k)^3} + \frac{D_4}{(1+k)^4} + \cdots \frac{D_\infty}{(1+k)^\infty}$$

which is simply an extension of the original equation. The point is, whenever the stock is sold, its value (i.e., the sale price at that time) will be the present value of all future dividends. Discounting this ending value back to the present brings you back to the dividend discount model (DDM).

What about stocks that do not pay dividends? The concept is the same, except that some of the early dividend payments equal zero. This assumes expectations that at some point the firm will start paying dividends. Investors who did not have such expectations would be unwilling to buy the security. It would have zero value. A firm with a nondividend-paying stock is reinvesting capital rather than paying current dividend so that its earnings and dividend stream will be larger and grow faster in the future. In this case, we would apply the DDM as:

$$V_j = \frac{D_1}{(1+k)} + \frac{D_2}{(1+k)^2} + \frac{D_3}{(1+k)^3} + \cdots \frac{D_\infty}{(1+k)^\infty}$$

where:

$D_1 = 0$

$D_2 = 0$

The investor expects that when the firm starts paying dividends in period 3, it will pay a large initial amount and dividends will grow faster than those of a comparable stock that had paid out dividends. The stock has value because of these future dividends. If we apply this model with several different holding periods, you can see how it works.

One-Year Holding Period   Assume that an investor wants to buy the stock, hold it for 1 year, and then sell it. To determine the value of the stock, that is, how much the investor should pay for it, using the dividend discount model, we must estimate the dividend to be received during the period, the expected sale price at the end of the period, and its required rate of return.

To estimate the dividend for the coming year, adjust the current dividend for expectations regarding the change in the dividend during the year. Assume that the company we are analyzing earned $2.50 a share last year and paid a dividend of $1 a share. Assume further that the firm has maintained this 40 percent earnings payout level fairly consistently over time. The consensus of financial analysts is that the firm will earn about $2.75 during the coming year and it will raise its dividend to $1.10 per share.

A crucial estimate is the expected selling price for the stock a year from now. You can estimate this expected selling price by either of two alternative procedures. In the first, you can apply the DDM by

estimating the specific dividend payments for a number of years into the future and calculate the value from these estimates. In the second, the earnings multiplier model, you multiply the future expected earnings for the stock by an earnings multiple figure to find an expected sale price.[5] We discuss this model in a later section of the chapter. For now, let's continue with the dividend discount model. Applying this model, you project that the sales price of this stock a year from now will be $22.

Finally, you must determine the required rate of return. As discussed before, the nominal risk-free rate is determined by the real risk-free rate and the expected rate of inflation. A good proxy for this rate is the promised yield on 1-year government bonds because your holding period is also 1 year. You estimate the stock's risk premium by comparing its risk level to those of other potential investments. In later chapters we will discuss how you can make this estimate. For the moment, assume that long-term AAA bonds are yielding 10 percent, and you believe that a 4 percent risk premium over the yield of these bonds is appropriate for this stock. Thus, you specify a required rate of return of 14 percent.

In summary, you have estimated the dividend at $1.10 (payable at year end), an ending sale price of $22, and a required rate of return of 14 percent. Given these inputs, you would estimate the stock's value as follows:

$$\begin{aligned} V_1 &= \frac{\$1.10}{(1+0.14)} + \frac{\$22.00}{(1+0.14)} \\ &= \frac{1.10}{1.14} + \frac{22.00}{1.14} \\ &= 0.96 + 19.30 \\ &= \$20.26 \end{aligned}$$

Note that we have not mentioned the current market price of the stock. The market price is not relevant to the investor except as a comparison to the independently derived value based on estimates of the relevant variables. Once we have calculated V as $20.26, we can compare it to the market price and apply the investment decision rule: If the stock's market price is more than $20.26, do not buy; if it is equal to or less than this amount, buy.

[5]We will discuss the earnings multiplier model in detail in a later section of this chapter.

Multiple-Year Holding Period If you anticipate holding the stock for several years and then selling it, this complicates the valuation estimate because it is necessary to forecast several future dividend payments, and also to estimate the sale price of the stock several years in the future.

The difficulty with estimating future dividend payments is that the future stream can take numerous forms. The exact estimate of the future dividends depends on two projections. The first is your outlook for earnings growth because dividends come from earnings. The second is the firm's dividend policy, which can take several forms. A firm might maintain a constant payout as a percentage of earnings each year, which implies an annual change in dividend. Alternatively the firm could follow a step pattern, increasing the dividend rate by a constant dollar amount each year or every 2 or 3 years. A constant growth rate in earnings and a constant dividend payout level are the easiest dividend policy to analyze. This set of assumptions produces a dividend stream with a constant growth rate equal to the earnings growth rate.

Assume the expected holding period is 3 years, and you estimate the following dividend payments at the end of each year:

Year 1	$1.10/share
Year 2	$1.20/share
Year 3	$1.35/share

You must next estimate the expected sale price (SP) for the stock 3 years in the future. Again, the dividend discount valuation model would require a projection of the dividend growth pattern for this stock beginning 3 years into the future. Assume that you estimate a sale price of $34.

The final estimate is the required rate of return on this stock during this period. Assuming that the 14 percent required rate is still appropriate for this period, the value of this stock is:

$$V = \frac{1.10}{(1 + 0.14)} + \frac{1.20}{(1 + 0.14)^2}$$

$$+ \frac{1.35}{(1 + 0.14)^3} + \frac{34.00}{(1 + 0.14)^3}$$

$$= \frac{1.10}{(1.14)} + \frac{1.20}{(1.2996)} + \frac{1.35}{(1.4815)} + \frac{34.00}{(1.4815)}$$

$$= 0.96 + 0.92 + 0.91 + 22.95$$

$$= \$25.74$$

Again, to make an investment decision you would compare this estimated value for the stock to its market price to determine whether you should buy it or not.

At this point you should recognize that the valuation procedure discussed here is very similar to that for corporate investment decisions, except that our cash flows come from dividends instead of returns to an investment project. Also, rather than estimating the scrap value or salvage value of a corporate asset, we are estimating the ending sale price for the stock. Finally, rather than discounting cash flows using the firm's cost of capital, we employ the individual investor's required rate of return. Both analyses look for excess present value, which means that the present value of expected cash inflows, that is, the estimated value of the asset, exceeds the present value of cash outflows, that is, the market price of the asset.

Infinite Period Model We can extend the multiperiod model by extending our estimates of dividends 5, 10, or 15 years into the future. The benefits derived from these extensions would be minimal, however, and you would quickly become bored with the exercise. Instead, we will move to the infinite period dividend valuation model, which assumes that investors estimate future dividend payments for an infinite number of periods.

Needless to say, this is a formidable task! As mere mortals, we must make some simplifying assumptions about this future stream of dividends to make the task viable. The easiest assumption is that the future dividend stream will grow at a constant rate for an infinite period. This is a rather heroic assumption in many instances, but where it holds, it allows us to derive a model with which we can value individual stocks, as well as the aggregate market and alternative industries. This model is generalized as follows:

$$V_j = \frac{D_0(1 + g)}{(1 + k)} + \frac{D_0(1 + g)^2}{(1 + k)^2} + \cdots \frac{D_0(1 + g)^n}{(1 + k)^n}$$

where:

V_j = the value of stock j

D_0 = the dividend payment in the current period

g = the constant growth rate of dividends

k = the required rate of return on stock j

n = the number of periods, which we assume to be infinite

Growth company A firm that has the opportunity to earn returns on investments that are consistently above its required rate of return.

In the appendix to this chapter, we show that certain assumptions allow us to simplify this model to the following expression:

$$V_j = \frac{D_1}{k - g}$$

You will probably recognize this formula as one that is widely used in corporate finance to estimate the cost of equity capital for the firm.

To use this model, you must estimate: (1) the required rate of return (k), and (2) the expected growth rate of dividends (g). After estimating g it is a simple matter to estimate D_1 as the current dividend (D_0) times $(1 + g)$.

Consider the example of a stock with a current dividend of $1 a share, which you expect to rise to $1.09 next year. You believe that, over the long run, this company's earnings and dividends will continue to grow at 9 percent, so your estimate of g is 0.09. You expect the rate of inflation to decline, so you set your long-run required rate of return on this stock at 13 percent; you estimate k at 0.13. To summarize the relevant estimates:

$$g = 0.09$$

$$k = 0.13$$

$$D_1 = \$1.09(\$1.00 \times 1.09)$$

$$V = \frac{\$1.09}{0.13 - 0.09}$$

$$= \frac{\$1.09}{0.04}$$

$$= \$27.25$$

Any small change in any of the original estimates will have a large impact on V, as shown by the following examples:

1. Assume g = 0.09; k = 0.14 (an increase of 0.01); and D_1 = $1.09.

$$V = \frac{\$1.09}{0.14 - 0.09}$$

$$= \frac{\$1.09}{0.05}$$

$$= \$21.80$$

2. Assume g = 0.10 (an increase of 0.01); k = 0.13 (the original value); and D_1 = $1.10 (an increase of 0.01).

$$V = \frac{\$1.10}{0.13 - 0.10}$$

$$= \frac{\$1.10}{0.03}$$

$$= \$36.67$$

These examples show that as small a change as 1 percent in either g or k produces a large difference in the estimated value of the stock. The crucial relationship that determines the value of the stock is the spread between the required rate of return (k) and the expected growth rate (g). Anything that causes a decline in the spread will increase the computed value, whereas any increase in the spread will decrease the computed value.

Infinite Period DDM and Growth Companies
Recall that the infinite period dividend discount model required assumptions that:

1. Dividends grow at a constant rate.
2. The constant growth rate will continue for an infinite period.
3. The required rate of return (k) is greater than the infinite growth rate (g). If it is not, the model gives meaningless results because the denominator becomes negative.

What do these assumptions mean for valuation of the stock of growth companies such as IBM, Xerox, McDonald's, and Apple Computer? **Growth companies** are firms that have the opportunities and the abilities to earn rates of return that are consistently above their required rates of return.[6] To exploit their outstanding opportunities, these firms generally retain high percentages of earnings for reinvestment, and their earnings grow faster than the typical firm's. These firms' earnings growth patterns are inconsistent with the assumptions of the infinite period dividend discount model.

---

[6]Growth companies are discussed in Ezra Salomon, *The Theory of Financial Management* (New York: Columbia University Press, 1963); and Merton Miller and Franco Modigliani, "Dividend Policy, Growth, and the Valuation of Shares," *Journal of Business* 34, no. 4 (October 1961): 411–433.

First, the infinite period dividend discount model assumes that dividends will grow at a constant rate for an infinite period. This assumption seldom holds for companies that grow at above-average rates. As an example, IBM and McDonald's have both grown at rates in excess of 30 percent a year for several years. It is unlikely that they can maintain such extreme rates of growth indefinitely in an economy where other firms will compete with them for these high rates of return.

Second, when these firms are growing at abnormally high rates, their rates of growth will probably exceed their required rates of return. There is no automatic relationship between growth and risk; a high-growth company is not necessarily a high-risk company. In fact a firm growing at a high but fairly constant rate would have lower risk (less uncertainty) than a low-growth firm with unstable earnings.

In summary, some firms grow at abnormally high rates for some periods of time. The infinite period dividend discount model cannot give values for these firms because their temporary conditions are inconsistent with its assumptions. In a later section of this chapter and in Chapter 14 we introduce models that can give estimates of the stock values of growth companies.

Earnings Multiplier Model

Rather than concentrate on dividends alone, many investors prefer to derive the value of common stock using an **earnings multiplier model.** The reasoning for this approach recalls the basic concept that the value of any investment is the present value of future returns. The returns due to holders of common stock are the net earnings of the firm, so investors can estimate value in terms of the amount they are willing to pay for a dollar of expected earnings (typically represented by the estimated earnings during the following 12-month period). As an example, investors willing to pay 10 times expected earnings would value a stock they expected to earn $2 a share at $20. You can compute the prevailing earnings multiplier, also referred to as the **price–earnings (P/E) ratio,** as follows:

$$\text{Earnings multiplier} = \frac{\text{Price–earnings ratio}}{} = \frac{\text{Current market price}}{\text{Following 12-months' earnings}}$$

This computation of the current earnings multiplier (P/E ratio) indicates the prevailing attitude of investors toward a stock's value. Investors must decide whether they agree with this valuation, that is,

> **Earnings multiplier model** A technique for estimating the value of a stock issue as a multiple of its earnings per share.
> **Price–earnings (P/E) ratio** The number by which earnings per share is multiplied to estimate a stock's value. Also called the *earnings multiplier.*

whether they think the earnings multiplier is too high or too low. In order to answer this question we need to consider what influences the earnings multiplier (P/E ratio) over time. In Chapter 12 the discussion of the valuation of the market shows that the P/E ratio for the aggregate stock market, as represented by the S&P 400 Index, has varied from about 6 times earnings to over 20 times earnings.[7] The infinite period dividend discount model can be used to indicate the variables that should determine the value of the P/E ratio as follows:[8]

$$P_i = \frac{D_1}{k - g}$$

If we divide both sides of the equation by expected earnings during the following 12 months (E_1), the result is:

$$\frac{P_i}{E_1} = \frac{D_1/E_1}{k - g}$$

Thus, the P/E ratio is determined by:

1. The expected dividend payout ratio (dividends divided by earnings)[9]
2. The required rate of return on the stock (k)
3. The expected growth rate of dividends for the stock (g)

As an example, if we assume a dividend payout of 50 percent (which means that the firm pays out 50 percent of its earnings as dividends), a required rate of return of 13 percent, and an expected growth rate for dividends of 9 percent, we get the following:

---

[7]When computing historical P/E ratios, you use earnings for the *previous* 12 months rather than expected earnings. Although this will influence the base level, it should not affect changes over time.

[8]In this formulation of the model, we use P rather than V, i.e., we state value as the estimated price of the stock.

[9]Recall from Chapter 7 that this is the proportion of earnings paid out to stockholders in dividends. Subtracting this proportion from 1 gives the retention rate (RR) used in the growth rate calculation.

234 PART 2 • Valuation Principles and Practice

$$D/E = 0.50; k = 0.13; g = 0.09$$

$$P/E = \frac{0.50}{0.13 - 0.09}$$

$$= \frac{0.50}{0.04}$$

$$= 12.5$$

Again, a small change in either k or g will have a large impact on the multiplier, as shown in the following two examples.

1. $D/E = 0.50;$ $k = 0.14$ (an increase of 0.01); $g = 0.09.$

$$P/E = \frac{0.50}{0.14 - 0.09}$$

$$= \frac{0.50}{0.05}$$

$$= 10.0$$

2. $D/E = 0.50;$ $k = 0.13;$ $g = 0.10$ (an increase of 0.01).

$$P/E = \frac{0.50}{0.13 - 0.10}$$

$$= \frac{0.50}{0.03}$$

$$= 16.7$$

As before, the spread between k and g is the main determinant of the size of the P/E ratio. Although the dividend payout ratio has an impact, it is typically rather stable with little effect on year-to-year changes in the P/E ratio (earnings multiplier).

After estimating the earnings multiplier, you would apply it to your estimate of earnings for the next year (E_1) to arrive at an estimated value. In turn, E_1 is based upon earnings for the current year (E_0) and the expected growth rate of earnings. Using these two estimates you would compute an estimated value of the stock and compare this to its market price.

Consider the following estimates for an example firm: $D/E = 0.50;$ $k = 0.14;$ $g = 0.10;$ $E_0 = \$2.00.$ These estimates would give an earnings multiplier of:

$$P/E = \frac{0.50}{0.14 - 0.10} = \frac{0.50}{0.04} = 12.5$$

Given current earnings (E_0) of \$2.00 and g of 10 percent, you would expect E_1 to be \$2.20. Therefore, you would estimate the value of the stock as:

$$V = 12.5 \times \$2.20$$

$$= \$27.50$$

As before, you would compare this estimated value to the stock's market price to decide if you should buy it.

Valuation with Temporary Supernormal Growth

Thus far, we have considered how to value a firm with different growth rates for short periods of time (1 to 3 years), and with a model that assumes a constant growth rate for an infinite period. Recall that the infinite period dividend discount model assumed an infinite period constant growth rate not greater than the required rate of return (see Appendix 8A). Although a company cannot permanently maintain a growth rate higher than the required rate of return, certain firms may experience temporary supernormal growth. A firm probably cannot grow at a supernormal rate for very long because the lucrative business attracts competition, which reduces profit margins and therefore ROE and the firm's growth rate. Therefore, after a few years of exceptional growth, we would expect a firm's growth rate to decline, eventually stabilizing at a level consistent with the assumptions of the infinite period dividend discount model.

To determine the value of such a company, you should combine the previous models. During stages of exceptional growth, examine each year individually. If there are two or three stages of supernormal growth, then you must examine each year in all of these stages of growth. Subsequently, when the firm's growth rate stabilizes at a rate below the required rate of return, you can compute the value under constant growth and discount this lump-sum value back to the present. The technique should become clear as you work through the following example.

The Bourke Company pays a current dividend (D_0) of \$2.00 a share. The following table shows the expected annual growth rates for dividends.

Year	Dividend Growth Rate
1–3	25%
4–6	20
7–9	15
10 on	9

The required rate of return for the stock is 14 percent. Therefore, the value equation becomes:

$$V_i = \frac{2.00\,(1.25)}{1.14} + \frac{2.00\,(1.25)^2}{1.14^2} + \frac{2.00\,(1.25)^3}{1.14^3}$$

$$+ \frac{2.00\,(1.25)^3(1.20)}{1.14^4} + \frac{2.00\,(1.25)^3(1.20)^2}{1.14^5}$$

$$+ \frac{2.00\,(1.25)^3(1.20)^3}{1.14^6} + \frac{2.00\,(1.25)^3(1.20)^3(1.15)}{1.14^7}$$

$$+ \frac{2.00\,(1.25)^3(1.20)^3(1.15)^2}{1.14^8} + \frac{2.00\,(1.25)^3(1.20)^3(1.15)^3}{1.14^9}$$

$$+ \frac{\dfrac{2.00\,(1.25)^3(1.20)^3(1.15)^3(1.09)}{(0.14 - 0.09)}}{(1.14)^9}$$

As the values in Table 8.1 show, the total value of the stock is $94.36. Needless to say, the difficult part of the evaluation is estimating the supernormal growth rates and determining how long these growth rates will last.

Table 8.1	*Computation of Value for Stock of Company with Temporary Supernormal Growth*

Year	Dividend	Discount Factor (14 percent)	Present Value
1	$ 2.50	0.8772	$ 2.193
2	3.12	0.7695	2.401
3	3.91	0.6750	2.639
4	4.69	0.5921	2.777
5	5.63	0.5194	2.924
6	6.76	0.4556	3.080
7	7.77	0.3996	3.105
8	8.94	0.3506	3.134
9	10.28	0.3075[b]	3.161
10	11.21		
	$224.20[a]	0.3075[b]	68.941
		Total value =	$94.355

[a]Value of dividend stream for Year 10 and all future dividends (i.e., $11.21/(0.14 − 0.09) = $224.20).

[b]The discount factor is the ninth year factor because the valuation of the remaining stream is made at the end of Year 9 to reflect the dividend in Year 10 and all future dividends.

This part of the chapter has demonstrated the application of the valuation model to bonds, preferred stock, and common stock. Valuation of bonds and preferred stock was fairly straightforward because we typically know the amount and timing of the returns and must estimate only the required rate of return. The larger section dealt with the valuation of common stock, which is more difficult because of several unknowns — the amount and timing of flows, in addition to the required rate of return. We considered several common stock valuation models, including the dividend discount model (DDM) and an earnings multiplier model. We noted that the infinite period dividend discount model cannot be used to estimate values for growth companies' stock because of its assumptions, but we were able to adapt it to evaluate companies with temporary supernormal growth.

Estimating the Inputs: The Required Rate of Return and the Expected Growth Rate of Dividends

Now that we have considered the valuation models, this section deals with estimating two inputs that are critical to the process: the required rate of return and the expected growth rate of dividends. In the balance of this chapter we will review these two inputs and also discuss how their estimation differs for domestic versus foreign securities. While the valuation procedure is the same for securities around the world, k and g differ among countries. Therefore, we will review the components of the required rate of return for U.S. securities and for foreign securities, then we will turn to the estimation of the growth rate of earnings and dividends for domestic and foreign stocks.

Required Rate of Return (k)

This discussion reviews the presentation in Chapter 1 dealing with the determinants of the nominal required rate of return on an investment, including a consideration of factors for non-U.S. markets. Recall that three factors influence an investor's required rate of return:

1. The economy's real risk-free rate (RFR)
2. The expected rate of inflation (I)
3. A risk premium (RP)

The economy's real risk-free rate is the absolute minimum rate that an investor should require. It depends on the real growth rate of the economy because capital invested should grow at least as fast as the economy. Recognize though, that the rate can change for short periods of time due to temporary tightness or ease in the capital markets.

The expected rate of inflation is important because investors are interested in real rates of return that will allow them to increase their rates of consumption. Therefore, investors should increase their nominal required risk-free rates of return to reflect any expected inflation, as follows:

$$\text{Nominal RFR} = (1 + \text{Real RFR})[1 + E(I)] - 1$$

where:

$E(I)$ = expected rate of inflation

The two factors that determine the nominal RFR affect all investments, from U.S. government securities to highly speculative land deals. Investors who hope to calculate security values accurately must carefully estimate the expected rate of inflation. Not only does it affect all investments, but its extreme volatility makes its estimation difficult.

Risk Premium The risk premium causes differences in required rates of return between alternative investments ranging from government bonds to corporate bonds to common stocks. This premium also explains the difference in expected returns among securities of the same type. This is the reason corporate bonds with different ratings have different yields and different common stocks have widely varying earnings multipliers despite similar growth expectations.

In Chapter 1 we noted that investors demand a risk premium because of the uncertainty of returns expected from an investment. A measure of this uncertainty was the dispersion of expected returns. We suggested that several internal factors influence the variability of returns, and that you should evaluate the risk of an investment by analyzing factors such as business risk, financial risk, and liquidity risk. Foreign investments bring additional risk factors, including exchange rate risk and country risk. These will be considered in the following section.

Variability of the Risk Premium Because different securities have different patterns of returns and make different guarantees to investors, we expect their risk

premiums to differ. In addition, the risk premium for the same security can change over time. For example, Figure 8.1 graphs the spread between the yields to maturity for Aaa-rated corporate bonds and Baa-rated corporate bonds from 1972 to 1989. This spread, or difference in yield, is a measure of the risk premium for investing in higher-risk bonds (Baa) compared to very low-risk bonds (Aaa). As shown, the difference varied from 0.61 percent to 2.69 percent.

Figure 8.2 plots the ratio of these securities' yields for the same period. These data show the percentage risk premium of Baa bonds compared to Aaa bonds in contrast to the data in Figure 8.1 that show the difference in absolute basis points (100 basis points is 1 percent). You might expect a larger difference in yield between Baa and Aaa bonds if Aaa bonds were yielding 12 percent rather than 6 percent.

The ratio in Figure 8.2 adjusts for this size difference and demonstrates that the risk premium varies over time from about 1.07 to 1.23, or from 7 percent to 23 percent over the base yield on Aaa bonds. This change in risk premium over time occurs because either investors perceive changes in the level of risk of Baa bonds compared to Aaa bonds or the amount of return they want for the same level of risk changes. In either case, this change in the risk premium for a specific asset implies a change in the slope of the security market line (SML). This change in the slope of the SML was demonstrated in Chapter 1.

Estimating Required Return for Foreign Securities Our discussion of the required rate of return for investments has been limited to the domestic market. Although the basic valuation model and its variables are the same around the world, estimates of the variables will differ significantly. This subsection points out where these differences occur and demonstrates how they arise.

Foreign Real RFR Although the real RFR in other countries should be determined by the real growth rates of those countries' economies, the estimated rate can vary substantially among countries due to differences in the three variables that affect the real growth rate: (1) the growth rate of the labor force, (2) the growth rate of the average number of hours worked, and (3) the growth rate of labor productivity. Table 8.2 shows differences in real growth rates of GNP (or GDP—Gross Domestic Product—in some countries). The 1991 data show a range of almost 5.0 percent (i.e., −1.2 percent for the United Kingdom

Figure 8.1   *Plot of Moody's Corporate Bond Yield Spreads (Baa Yield–Aaa Yield): Monthly 1972–1989*

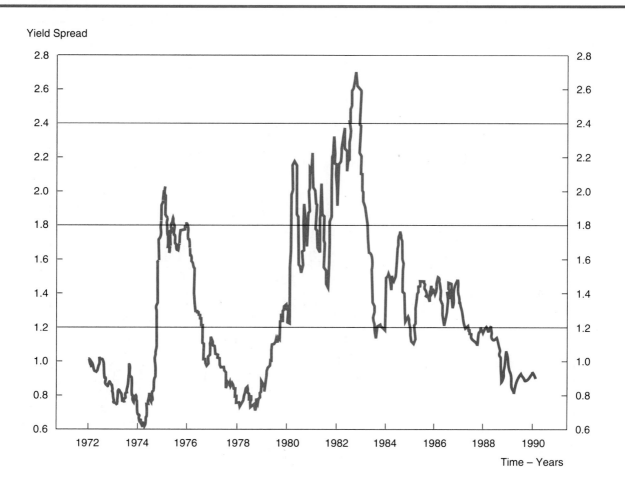

compared to 3.6 percent for Japan). This difference in real GNP growth rates implies a substantial difference in real RFRs for these countries. To estimate real rates of growth, you must examine historical values for the three variables that affect each country's rate.

Inflation Rate   To estimate the nominal RFR for a country, you must also estimate its expected rate of inflation and adjust the real RFR for this expectation. Again, this rate of inflation can vary substantially among countries. The price-change data in Table 8.3 show that the expected rate of inflation during 1991 varied from 3.2 percent in France to 6.9 percent in the United Kingdom. This gives a difference in the nominal required rate of return between these two countries of almost 4 percent. Such a difference in k can

have a substantial impact on estimated values, as demonstrated earlier. Again, you must make a separate estimate of expected inflation for each individual country where you are evaluating securities.

To demonstrate the combined impact of differences in real growth and expected inflation, Table 8.4 shows the results of the following computation for the seven countries based on 1991 estimates:

Nominal RFR =
$$(1 + \text{Real growth})(1 + \text{Expected inflation}) - 1$$

Given the differences between countries in the two components, the range in nominal RFR of about 3.5 percent is not surprising (4.3 percent for the United Kingdom versus 7.8 percent for Italy). As demon-

Figure 8.2 *Plot of the Ratio of Moody's Corporate Bond Yields (Baa Yield–Aaa Yield): Monthly 1972–1989*

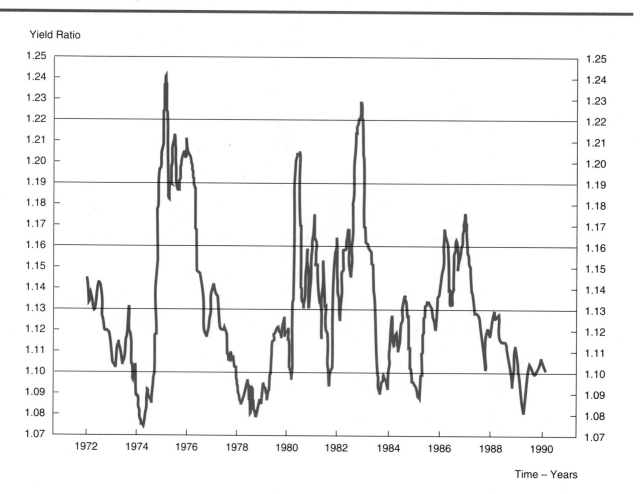

strated earlier, such a difference in k for an investment will have a significant impact on its value.

Risk Premium You must also derive a risk premium for investments in each country. Again, the five risk components differ substantially among countries: business risk, financial risk, liquidity risk, exchange rate risk, and country risk. Business risk can vary because it is a function of the variability of economic activity within a country and of the operating leverage employed by firms within the country. Firms in different countries assume significantly different financial risk, as well. For example, Japanese firms employ substantially more financial leverage than U.S. or U.K. firms. Regarding liquidity risk, the U.S. capital

markets are acknowledged to be the most liquid in the world, with Japan and London being close behind. In contrast, some small, inactive capital markets are quite illiquid.

When investing globally you must also estimate exchange rate risk, which can vary over time and among countries, affecting your required rate of return. Changes over time result from changes in world economies and political conditions. Differences in exchange rates between countries occur because of specific trade relations between them. As an example of exchange rate risk, consider the massive trade imbalances between the United States and Japan during 1985 to 1990. They caused significant fluctuations in the exchange rate of yen to the U.S. dollar, which went

Table 8.2 *Real GNP/GDP (percentage changes from previous year)*

Period	United States	Canada	Japan	Germany	France	United Kingdom	Italy
1987	3.7%	4.5%	4.6%	1.7%	1.9%	4.5%	3.0%
1988	4.4	5.0	5.8	3.6	3.4	4.6	4.2
1989	2.5	2.9	4.8	4.0	3.6	1.9	3.2
1990	0.8	1.0	5.6	4.6	2.5	1.0	1.9
1991[(e)]	0.1	1.6	3.6	3.3	1.2	−1.2	1.5

[(e)] estimate

Source: "World Investment Strategy Highlights" (London: Goldman, Sachs International Ltd., February 1991).

Table 8.3 *Consumer or Retail Price (percentage changes from previous year)*

Period	United States	Canada	Japan	Germany	France	United Kingdom	Italy
1987	3.7%	4.4%	0.1%	0.3%	3.3%	4.1%	4.6%
1988	4.1	4.1	0.7	1.3	2.7	4.9	5.0
1989	4.8	5.0	2.3	2.8	3.4	7.8	6.6
1990	5.4	4.7	3.0	2.7	3.4	9.5	6.1
1991[(e)]	5.4	5.3	3.4	3.5	3.2	6.9	6.2

[(e)] estimate

Source: "World Investment Strategy Highlights" (London: Goldman, Sachs International Ltd., February 1991).

Table 8.4 *Estimates of 1991 Nominal RFR for Major Countries*

Country	Real Growth in GNP/GDP[a]	Expected Inflation[b]	Nominal RFR
United States	0.1%	5.4%	5.5%
Canada	1.6	5.3	7.0
Japan	3.6	3.4	7.1
Germany	3.3	3.5	6.9
France	1.2	3.2	4.4
United Kingdom	−1.2	6.9	4.3
Italy	1.5	6.2	7.8

[a]Taken from Table 8.2.

[b]Taken from Table 8.3.

from 250 down to 110, back up to 155, and down to 125. When the U.S. dollar weakened relative to the yen during 1986 and 1987, Japanese investors in U.S. stocks and bonds suffered significant exchange rate losses that offset or wiped out other returns. Subsequently, the U.S. dollar strengthened in 1988 and 1989 and U.S. owners of Japanese securities suffered.

Recall that country risk arises from events in the political or economic environment in a particular country beyond the normal economic factors that influence exchange rates. As an example, many investors expect country risk to rise in Hong Kong in 1997 when it changes from a territory of the United Kingdom to a province of China. Past examples include the continuing anti-apartheid movement in South Africa and the violent 1989 confrontation between students and the army in Beijing that signaled a major change in the political and economic environment in China.

Such political unrest or economic change creates uncertainties that increase the risk of investments in a country. Before investing in such countries, investors must evaluate the additional returns they should require to accept this increased uncertainty.

Thus, when estimating required rates of return on foreign investments, you must evaluate these differences in fundamental risk factors and assign a unique risk premium for each country.

Expected Growth Rate of Dividends

After arriving at a required rate of return, the investor must estimate the growth rate of dividends, since the valuation models for common stock depend heavily on good estimates of this value. The procedure we describe here is similar to the presentation in Chapter 7 where we used financial ratios to measure a firm's growth potential.

The growth rate of dividends is determined by the growth rate of earnings and the proportion of earnings paid out in dividends, or the payout ratio. Over the short run, dividends can grow faster or slower than earnings if the firm changes its payout ratio. Specifically, if a firm's earnings grow at 6 percent a year and it pays out exactly 50 percent of earnings in dividends, then its dividends will likewise grow at 6 percent a year. Alternatively, if the firm's earnings grow at 6 percent a year and it decides to increase its payout, during the period when the payout ratio is increasing, dividends will grow faster than the earnings. In contrast, if the firm elects to reduce its payout ratio, dividends will grow at a lower rate than earnings. Because there is a limit to how long this difference in growth rates can continue, most investors make the long-run assumption that the dividend payout ratio is fairly stable. Therefore, analysis of the growth rate of dividends is really an analysis of the growth rate of equity earnings.

Assume a firm retains earnings to acquire additional assets. If it earns some positive rate of return on these additional assets, its total earnings will increase because its asset base is larger. How rapidly earnings increase depends upon: (1) the proportion of earnings it retains and reinvests in new assets, and (2) the rate of return it earns on these new assets. Specifically, the growth rate (g) of equity earnings (i.e., earnings per share) without any external financing equals the percentage of net earnings retained (the retention rate, which equals 1 minus the payout ratio), times the rate of return on equity capital:

$$g = \text{Retention rate} \times \text{Return on equity}$$
$$= RR \times ROE$$

A firm can increase its growth rate by increasing its retention rate (reducing its payout ratio) and investing these added funds at its historic ROE. Alternatively, the firm can maintain its retention rate but increase its ROE. As an example, if a firm retains 50 percent of net earnings and consistently earns a 10 percent return on its investments, its net earnings will grow at the rate of 5 percent a year, as follows:

$$g = RR \times ROE$$
$$= 0.50 \times 0.10$$
$$= 0.05$$

If, however, the firm increases its retention rate to 75 percent and invests this money in internal projects that return 10 percent, its growth rate will increase to 7.5 percent, as follows:

$$g = 0.75 \times 0.10$$
$$= 0.075$$

If, instead, the firm continues to reinvest 50 percent of its earnings, but derives a higher rate of return on these investments, say 15 percent, it can likewise increase its growth rate, as follows:

$$g = 0.50 \times 0.15$$
$$= 0.075$$

Breakdown of ROE While the retention rate is a management decision, you will recall from Chapter 7 that changes in the firm's ROE result from changes in its operating performance or its financial leverage. To see what is required, we divide the ROE ratio into the following three components:

$$ROE = \frac{\text{Net income}}{\text{Sales}} \times \frac{\text{Sales}}{\text{Total assets}} \times \frac{\text{Total assets}}{\text{Equity}}$$
$$= (\text{Profit margin}) \times (\text{Total asset turnover}) \times (\text{Financial leverage})$$

As discussed in Chapter 7, this breakdown allows us to consider the three factors that determine a firm's ROE. Since it is a multiplicative relationship, any increase in any of the three ratios will cause an increase in ROE. Two of these three ratios reflect operating performance and one indicates a firm's financing decision.

The first operating ratio, net profit margin, indicates the firm's profitability on sales. This ratio changes over time for some companies, and is very sensitive to the business cycle. For growth companies, this is one of the first ratios to decline as increased competition forces price cutting, reducing profit margins. Also, during recessions profit margins decline because of price cutting or because of higher percentages of fixed costs due to lower sales.

The second component, total asset turnover, is the ultimate indicator of operating efficiency and reflects the asset and capital requirements of the business. While this ratio varies dramatically by industry, within an industry it is an excellent indicator of management's ability.

The final component, total assets/equity, does not measure operating performance, but rather financial leverage, which indicates how management has decided to finance the firm. This management decision regarding the financing of assets has financial risk implications for the stockholder.

Knowing this breakdown of ROE, you must examine past results and expectations for a firm and develop estimates of the three components to derive an estimate of a firm's ROE. This estimate, combined with the firm's retention rate, will indicate its growth potential.

Estimating Dividend Growth for Foreign Stocks

The procedure for finding the growth rates for foreign stocks is similar to that for U.S. stocks, but the value of the equation's components may differ substantially from what is common in the United States. Remember that these differences in the components of ROE result from differences in accounting practices as well as alternative management performance or philosophy.

Retention Rates The retention rates for foreign corporations differ by company within countries, but there are also differences in the averages for all firms due to different countries' investment opportunities. As an example, firms in Japan maintain a much higher average retention rate than U.S. firms, whereas the rate of retention in France is much lower. Therefore, you would need to examine the retention rates for a number of firms in a country as a background for estimating the standard rate within a country.

Net Profit Margins Foreign firms' net profit margins can differ because of differences in accounting conventions between countries. Foreign firms may recognize revenue and allocate expenses differently from U.S. firms. As an example, German firms are allowed to build up large reserves for various reasons so they report very low earnings for tax purposes. Also, different foreign depreciation practices require adjustment of earnings and cash flow values.

Total Asset Turnover Total asset turnover can likewise differ among countries because of accounting conventions on the reporting of asset values at cost or market values. For example, in Japan a large part of the market values for some firms comes from their real estate holdings and their common stock investments in other firms. These assets are reported at cost, which substantially understates their true value. This also makes for substantial overstatement of total asset turnover ratios for these firms.

Total Asset/Equity Ratio This ratio, a measure of financial leverage, differs among countries because of different economic environments, tax laws, management philosophies regarding corporate debt, and accounting conventions. In several countries, firms' attitudes toward debt are much more liberal than those in the United States. A prime example is Japan, where debt as a percentage of total assets is almost 50 percent higher than in the United States. Most corporate debt in Japan entails borrowing from banks at fairly low rates of interest. Balance sheet debt ratios may be higher in Japan than in the United States or other countries, but these lower interest rates may make the fixed-charge flow ratios (e.g., the times interest earned ratio) similar to those in other countries.

Consequently, when analyzing a foreign stock market or an individual foreign stock, you need to estimate the growth rate for earnings and dividends considering the three components of ROE just as you would for a U.S. stock. The point of this brief discussion and the discussion of the analysis of financial statements in Chapter 7 is that you must recognize that financial ratios of foreign firms can differ from those typical for U.S. stocks. Subsequent chapters on stock valuation applied to the aggregate market, various industries, and companies cite examples of these differences.

Summary

■ As an investor, you want to select investments that will provide you with a rate of return that compensates you for your time, the rate of inflation, and the risk involved. To help you find these investments, this chapter considered the theory of valuation by which you derive the value of an investment using your required rate of return. We considered an investment decision process that evaluated the aggregate economy and market, then alternative industries, and finally individual firms and their stocks. This procedure is generally referred to as a *top-down approach*.

■ We applied the valuation theory to a range of investments including bonds, preferred stock, and common stock. In all instances where we used several different valuation models, the trading rule was always the same: if the estimated value of the investment is greater than the market price, you should buy the investment; if the estimated value of an investment is less than its market price, you should not invest in it.

■ We concluded with a review of factors that you consider when estimating your required rate of return on an investment and the growth rate of dividends. Finally, we considered some unique factors that affect the application of these models to foreign stocks.

Questions

1. What is the benefit of analyzing the market and alternative industries before individual securities?
2. Discuss whether you would expect all industries to have a similar relationship to the economy. Give an example involving two industries with different relationships to the economy.
3. Would you expect a U.S. investor's required rate of return on U.S. common stocks to be the same as or different than his or her required rate of return on Japanese common stocks? What factors would determine each rate?
4. Would you expect the U.S. nominal RFR to be the same as that in Germany? Discuss your reasoning.

Problems

1. What is the value to you of a 14 percent coupon bond with a par value of $10,000 that matures in 10 years if you want a 12 percent return? Use semiannual compounding.

2. What would the value of the bond in Problem 1 be if you wanted a 16 percent rate of return?
3. The preferred stock of the Clarence Biotechnology Company has a par value of $100 and a $9 dividend rate. You require an 11 percent rate of return on this stock. What is the maximum price you would pay for it? Discuss whether you would buy it at a market price of $96.
4. The Bozo Basketball Company (BBC) earned $10 a share last year and paid a dividend of $6 a share. Next year you expect the company to earn $11 and continue the previous payout ratio. Assume you anticipate selling the stock at a price of $132 a year from now. If you require 14 percent on this stock, how much would you be willing to pay for it?
5. Given the expected earnings and dividend payments in Problem 4, if you expected a selling price of $110 and required a 10 percent return, what would you pay for the BBC stock?
6. Over the very long run you expect dividends for BBC to grow at 8 percent and you require 12 percent on the stock. Using the infinite period dividend discount model, how much would you pay for this stock?
7. Based upon new information regarding the popularity of basketball, you revise your growth estimate to 10 percent. What is the maximum P/E ratio you will apply to BBC and what is the maximum price you will pay for the stock?
8. The Barking Dogfood Company (BDC) has consistently paid out 40 percent of its earnings in dividends. The company's return on equity is 16 percent. What would you estimate as its dividend growth rate?
9. Given the low risk in dog food, your required rate of return on BDC is 13 percent. What P/E ratio would you apply to the firm's earnings?
10. What P/E ratio would you apply if you learned that BDC had decided to increase its payout to 50 percent?
11. Discuss three ways a firm can increase its ROE. Make up an example to illustrate your discussion.
12. It is widely known that grocery chains have very low profit margins (on average, they earn about 1 percent on sales). How would you explain the fact that their ROE is about 12 percent? Does this seem logical?
13. Compute a recent 5-year average of the following ratios for three companies of your choice (attempt to select diverse firms):

a. Retention rate   d. Total asset turnover
b. Net profit margin   e. Total assets/equity
c. Equity turnover

Based upon these ratios, explain which firm should have the highest growth rate of earnings.

14. You have been reading about the Orange Computer Company, which currently retains 90 percent of its earnings ($5 a share this year). It earns a ROE of almost 40 percent. Assuming a required rate of return of 16 percent, how much would you pay for Orange on the basis of the earnings multiplier model? Discuss the reason for your answer. What would you pay for Orange Computer if its retention rate were 60 percent and its ROE were 19 percent? Show your work.

15. Gentry Can Company paid its latest annual dividend of $1.25 a share yesterday and maintained its historic 7 percent annual rate of growth. You plan to purchase the stock today because you feel that the dividend growth rate will increase to 8 percent for the next 3 years and the selling price of the stock will be $40 per share at the end of that time.
   a. How much should you be willing to pay for the Gentry Can Company stock if you require a 14 percent return?
   b. What is the maximum price you should be willing to pay for the Gentry Can Company stock if you felt that the 8 percent growth rate could be maintained indefinitely and you required a 14 percent return?
   c. If the 8 percent rate of growth is achieved, what will the price be at the end of Year 3 assuming the conditions in problem 15b?

16. In the *Federal Reserve Bulletin*, find the average yield on AAA and BBB bonds for a recent month.

Compute the absolute risk premium (in basis points) and the percentage risk premium on BBB bonds relative to AAA bonds. Discuss how these values compare to those shown in Figures 8.1 and 8.2.

References

Benesh, Gary A., and Pamela P. Peterson. "On the Relation between Earnings Changes, Analysts' Forecasts, and Stock Price Fluctuations." *Financial Analysts Journal* 42, no. 6 (November–December 1986).

Brown, Philip, and Ray Ball. "Some Preliminary Findings on the Association between the Earnings of a Firm, Its Industry, and the Economy." *Empirical Research in Accounting: Selected Studies 1967*, supplement to *Journal of Accounting Research* 5.

Chen, Nui-Fu, Richard Roll, and Stephen A. Ross. "Economic Forces and the Stock Market." *Journal of Business* 59, no. 3 (July 1986).

Fisher, Lawrence. "Determinants of Risk Premiums on Corporate Bonds." *Journal of Political Economy* 67, no. 3 (June 1959).

King, Benjamin F. "Market and Industry Factors in Stock Price Behavior." *Journal of Business* 39, no. 1, Part II (January 1966).

Levine, Sumner N., ed. *The Financial Analysts Handbook*, 2d ed. Homewood, Ill.: Dow Jones-Irwin, 1988.

Reilly, Frank K. "The Misdirected Emphasis in Security Valuation." *Financial Analysts Journal* 29, no. 1 (January–February 1973).

Shaked, Israel. "International Equity Markets and the Investment Horizon." *Journal of Portfolio Management* 11, no. 2 (Winter 1985).

Shiskin, Julius. "Systematic Aspects of Stock Price Fluctuations." In *Modern Developments in Investment Management*, 2d ed. Ed. by James Lorie and Richard Brealey. Hinsdale, Ill.: Dryden Press, 1978.

APPENDIX 8a   *Derivation of Constant Growth Dividend Model*

The basic model is:

$$P_0 = \frac{D_1}{(1+k)^1} + \frac{D_2}{(1+k)^2} + \frac{D_3}{(1+k)^3} + \cdots \frac{D_n}{(1+k)^n}$$

where:

P_0 = Current price

D_i = Expected dividend in period i

k = Required rate of return on asset j

If growth rate (g) is constant:

$$P_0 = \frac{D_0(1 + g)^1}{(1 + k)^1} + \frac{D_0(1 + g)^2}{(1 + k)^2} + \cdots \frac{D_0(1 + g)^n}{(1 + k)^n}$$

This can be written:

(8A.1) $P_0 = D_0 \left[\frac{(1 + g)}{(1 + k)} + \frac{(1 + g)^2}{(1 + k)^2} + \frac{(1 + g)^3}{(1 + k)^3} \right.$

$$\left. + \cdots \frac{(1 + g)^n}{(1 + k)^n} \right]$$

Multiplying both sides of Equation 8A.1 by $(1 + k)/(1 + g)$:

(8A.2) $\left[\frac{(1 + k)}{(1 + g)} \right] P_0 = D_0 \left[1 + \frac{(1 + g)}{(1 + k)} + \frac{(1 + g)^2}{(1 + k)^2} \right.$

$$\left. + \cdots \frac{(1 + g)^{n-1}}{(1 + k)^{n-1}} \right]$$

Subtract Equation 8A.1 from Equation 8A.2:

$$\left[\frac{(1 + k)}{(1 + g)} - 1 \right] P_0 = D_0 \left[1 - \frac{(1 + g)^n}{(1 + k)^n} \right]$$

$$\left[\frac{(1 + k) - (1 + g)}{(1 + g)} \right] P_0 = D_0 \left[1 - \frac{(1 + g)^n}{(1 + k)^n} \right]$$

Assuming $i > g$, as $N \to \infty$, the term in brackets on the right side of the equation goes to 1, leaving:

$$\left[\frac{(1 + k) - (1 + g)}{(1 + g)} \right] P_0 = D_0$$

This simplifies to:

$$\left[\frac{1 + k - 1 - g}{(1 + g)} \right] P_0 = D_0$$

which equals:

$$\left[\frac{k - g}{(1 + g)} \right] P_0 = D_0$$

This equals:

$$(k - g)P_0 = D_0(1 + g)$$

but:

$$D_0(1 + g) = D_1$$

so:

$$(k - g)P_0 = D_1$$

$$P_0 = \frac{D_1}{k - g}$$

Remember, this model assumes:

- A constant growth rate
- An infinite time period
- A required return on investment (k) greater than the expected growth rate (g)

Analysis of Alternative Economies and Security Markets: The Global Asset Allocation Decision

In Chapter 8 we introduced the three-step investment process that begins with economic and market analysis, is followed by industry analysis, and finishes with individual company and stock analysis. Figure 9.1 shows an overview of the process.

We made the point in Chapter 8 that, although we are ultimately interested in securities markets, we analyze economies because of the link between the overall economic environment and the performance of security markets. Security markets reflect what is going on in an economy. This is because the value of an investment is determined by its expected cash flows and required rate of return, and both of these factors are influenced by the economy. Therefore, if you want to estimate cash flows, interest rates, and risk premiums for securities, you need to consider aggregate economic analysis.

Figure 9.1 *Overview of the Investment Process*

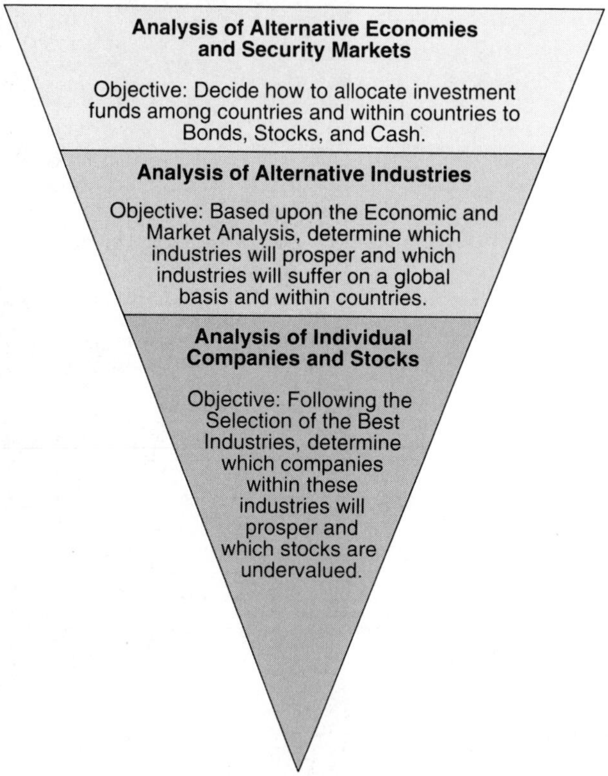

Analysis of Alternative Economies and Security Markets

Objective: Decide how to allocate investment funds among countries and within countries to Bonds, Stocks, and Cash.

Analysis of Alternative Industries

Objective: Based upon the Economic and Market Analysis, determine which industries will prosper and which industries will suffer on a global basis and within countries.

Analysis of Individual Companies and Stocks

Objective: Following the Selection of the Best Industries, determine which companies within these industries will prosper and which stocks are undervalued.

Macroeconomic approach An attempt to project the outlook for securities markets based on their underlying relationship to the aggregate economy.

From this interrelated economic-market perspective, we initiate discussion of the investment process in this chapter by examining various techniques that relate economic variables to security markets. The first section discusses in detail the relationship between economic and security market activity and provides evidence of this relationship. Given this relationship, we consider various techniques used to estimate future market returns concentrating on the macroeconomic approach. Subsequently, we discuss several techniques that are part of this approach including use of leading indicators and the analysis of money supply growth or other measures of monetary conditions. Following from the analysis of monetary variables, we consider the effect of inflation on interest rates, bond prices, and stock returns.

Although most of the discussion focuses on the U.S. economy, we recognize the need to apply these techniques to other countries. To provide insights into this process, we discuss an example of such an analysis by an investment firm. The culmination of this global analysis is a global asset allocation of all investment funds among countries, and further allocation within countries to specific asset classes: bonds, stocks, and cash equivalents.

In Chapter 8 we discussed the importance of analyzing the general economy as part of estimating future aggregate market values, which, in turn, imply future returns from investing in common stocks and/or bonds. Three major techniques are available for analyzing securities markets. A **macroeconomic approach** attempts to project the outlook for securities markets based upon an understanding of their underlying relationship to the aggregate economy. The **microanalysis approach** to market analysis uses the dividend discount model discussed in Chapter 8 to estimate a value for the aggregate stock market. Finally, the **technical analysis approach** assumes that the best way to determine future changes in security market values is to examine past movements in interest rates, security prices, and other market variables. This chapter deals with the macroeconomic approach to security market analysis and subsequently considers the asset allocation decision that flows from this analysis. Chapter 12 presents the microanalysis of the security markets, while technical analysis techniques are discussed and demonstrated in Chapter 15.

Microanalysis approach An attempt to estimate the value of the aggregate stock market based on an application of the dividend discount model.

Technical analysis approach An attempt to predict future behavior of securities markets from their past behavior.

National Bureau of Economic Research (NBER) A nonprofit organization devoted to monitoring business cycles and other economic phenomena.

Cyclical indicator approach An attempt to predict future behavior of securities markets and the economy based on economic series that reflect the business cycle.

Economic Activity and Security Markets

Fluctuations in security markets are related to changes in the aggregate economy. The prices of most bonds depend on the level of interest rates, which, in turn, are influenced by overall economic activity and Federal Reserve policy. The price of a firm's stock reflects investor expectations about the issuing firm's performance in terms of earnings and cash flow, and that performance is likewise affected by the overall performance of the economy.

In its work monitoring business cycles, the **National Bureau of Economic Research (NBER)** has amassed substantial evidence that supports the relationship between security prices and economic behavior. Based on their relationship to the behavior of the entire economy, the NBER has classified numerous economic series into three groups: leading, coincident, and lagging indicator series. Further, extensive analysis of the relationship between the economy and the stock market has shown that the consistency of the relationship makes stock prices one of the better leading indicator series.

The evidence indicates a strong relationship between stock prices and the economy, and also shows that stock prices consistently turn *before* the economy does. The data in Table 9.1 document this relationship over the last 30 years. While this overall relationship appears to hold, the data also show several false signals given by the stock market.

There are two possible reasons why stock prices lead the economy. One is that stock prices reflect expectations of earnings and dividends. As investors attempt to estimate future earnings, their stock price

decisions reveal *expectations* for future economic activity, not current activity. A second possible reason is that the stock market is known to react to other leading indicator series, the most important being corporate earnings, corporate profit margins, and changes in the growth rate of the money supply. Since these series tend to lead the economy, when investors adjust stock prices to follow them, it makes stock prices a leading series as well.

Because stock prices lead the aggregate economy, our macroeconomic approach to market analysis concentrates on economic series that likewise lead the economy, with more advance notice, we hope, than stock prices. First, we will discuss **cyclical indicator approaches** developed by various research groups. These will include the cyclical indicator approach of the National Bureau of Economic Research (NBER) and the *Business Week* leading indicator series, along with several leading series developed by the Center for International Business Cycle Research (CIBCR) at Columbia University. Next we will consider a very popular leading series, the money supply, as well as other measures of monetary liquidity as indicators of economic activity and security market returns. Finally, we will discuss the research related to a number of economic series expected to affect security returns (i.e., production, inflation, risk premiums).

Cyclical Indicator Approach to Forecasting the Economy

The cyclical indicator approach to forecasting the economy is based on the belief that the aggregate economy expands and contracts in discernible periods.

| Table 9.1 | Timing Relationships between Stock Market and Business Cycle Peaks and Troughs |

I.   Stock Market Declines Associated with a Subsequent Recession

Stock Market Cycles[a]				Business Cycles				Lead of Stock Market over Business Cycle[a]	
Peak		**Trough**		**Peak**		**Trough**		**Peak**	**Trough**
Jan.	1953	Sep.	1953	Jul.	1953	May	1954	6.0	8.0
Aug.	1956	Oct.	1957	Aug.	1957	Apr.	1958	11.0	6.0
Aug.	1959	Oct.	1960	Apr.	1960	Feb.	1961	8.0	4.0
Nov.	1968	May	1970	Dec.	1969	Nov.	1970	12.0	6.0
Jan.	1973	Oct.	1974	Nov.	1973	Mar.	1975	10.0	5.0
Feb.	1980	Aug.	1982	Jan.	1980	Nov.	1982	(1.0)	3.0
						Average		7.7	5.3

II.   False Signals

Dec.	1961	Jan.	1962
Apr.	1971	Nov.	1971
Sep.	1976	Mar.	1978

III.   Stock Market Declines Associated with a Subsequent Growth Recession

Feb.	1966	Mar.	1968

[a]Defined as market declines of approximately 15 percent or more.

Source: Jason Benderly and Edward McKelvey, "The Pocket Chartroom" (Economic Research, Goldman, Sachs & Co., December 1987).

This view of the economy has been investigated by the National Bureau of Economic Research (NBER), a nonprofit organization that attempts to interpret important economic facts scientifically and impartially. The NBER explains the business cycle as follows:

> The business cycle concept has been developed from the sequence of events discerned in the historical study of the movements of economic activity. Though there are many cross-currents and variations in the pace of business activity, periods of business expansion appear to cumulate to peaks. As they cumulate, contrary forces tend to gain strength, bringing about a reversal in business activity and the onset of a recession. As a recession continues, forces for an expansion gradually emerge until they become dominant and a recovery begins.[1]

The NBER examined the behavior of hundreds of economic time series in relation to past business cycles. (Recall that a time series reports the values for an economic variable over time, such as the monthly industrial production values for the period 1980 to 1991.) Based upon this analysis, the NBER grouped various economic series into three major categories based on their relationships to the business cycle. The initial list of economic series that could predict turns in the economy was compiled in 1938, and it has undergone numerous revisions over the years. The most recent major revision occurred in 1983 with small modifications in 1987.[2]

[1]Julius Shiskin, "Business Cycle Indicators: The Known and the Unknown," *Review of the International Statistical Institute* 31, no. 3 (1963): 361–383.

[2]For a discussion of these changes, see Marie P. Hertzberg and Barry A. Beckman, "Business Cycle Indicators: Revised Composite Indexes," *Business Conditions Digest* Vol. 17, no. 1 (January 1989): 291–296.

| Table 9.2 | **Economic Series in NBER Leading Indicator Group** |

	Median Lead (−) or Lag (+) (in months)		
	Peaks	Troughs	All Turns
1. Average weekly hours of production workers (manufacturing)	−2	−3	−3
2. Average weekly initial claims for unemployment insurance (inverted)	−5	−1	−3
3. Manufacturers' new orders in 1982 dollars, consumer goods and materials	−2	−2	−2
4. Contracts and orders for plant and equipment in 1982 dollars	−5	+1	−2½
5. Index of raw private housing units authorized by local building permits	−9	−6	−7
6. Index of stock prices, 500 common stocks	−4	−4	−4
7. M2 money supply in 1982 dollars	−5	−4	−5
8. Vendor performance (percentage of firms receiving slower deliveries)	−3	−4	−3
9. Change in sensitive materials, prices smoothed	−4	−8	−5½
10. Changes in business and consumer credit outstanding	−4	−6	−5
11. Changes in manufacturing and trade inventories on hand and on order in 1982 dollars	−2	0	−1½

Source: Geoffrey H. Moore, "The Leading Indicator Approach—Value, Limitations, and Future," presented at Annual Western Economic Association Meeting (June 1984), revised June 1986; and Marie P. Hertzberg and Barry A. Beckman, "Business Cycle Indicators: Revised Composite Indexes," *Business Conditions Digest* 17, no. 1 (January 1989).

Cyclical Indicator Categories

The first category, **leading indicators** of the business cycle, includes economic time series that usually reach peaks or troughs before corresponding peaks or troughs in aggregate economic activity. The group currently includes the 11 series shown in Table 9.2, which indicates the median lead or lag for each series relative to business cycle peaks or troughs. One of the 11 leading economic series, common stock prices, has a median lead of 9 months at peaks and 4 months at troughs.[3] Another leading series, the money supply in constant 1982 dollars, has a median lead of 10 months at peaks and 8 months at troughs.

The second category, **coincident indicators,** includes economic time series peaks and troughs which roughly coincide with the peaks and troughs in the business cycle. The bureau looks to many of these economic time series to help define the different phases of the cycle.

Leading indicators Economic series that reach peaks or troughs in advance of the aggregate economy.

Coincident indicators Economic series that reach peaks or troughs together with the aggregate economy.

Lagging indicators Economic series that reach peaks or troughs after the aggregate economy.

The third category, **lagging indicators,** are series that hit their peaks and troughs after those of the aggregate economy. A listing and the average timing relationships for the coincident and lagging series appear in Table 9.3.

A final category labeled "other selected series" includes economic series that are expected to influence aggregate economic activity, but do not fall neatly into one of the three main groups. This includes such series as U.S. balance of payments, federal surplus or deficit, and military contract awards.

Composite Series and Ratio of Series In addition to the individual economic series in each category, a

[3]A detailed analysis of this relationship is contained in Geoffrey H. Moore and John P. Cullity, "Security Markets and Business Cycles," in *The Financial Analysts Handbook*, 2d ed., ed. by Sumner N. Levine (Homewood, Ill.: Dow Jones-Irwin, 1988).

Table 9.3 **Economic Series in NBER Coincident and Lagging Indicator Series**

	Median Lead (−) or Lag (+) (in months)		
	Peaks	**Troughs**	**All Turns**
A. Coincident Indicator Series			
1. Employees on nonagricultural payrolls	−2	0	0
2. Personal income less transfer payments in 1982 dollars	0	−1	$-\frac{1}{2}$
3. Index of industrial production	−3	0	$-\frac{1}{2}$
4. Manufacturing and trade sales in 1982 dollars	−3	0	$-\frac{1}{2}$
B. Lagging Indicator Series			
1. Average duration of unemployment in weeks (inverted)	+1	+8	$+3\frac{1}{2}$
2. Ratio of manufacturing and trade inventories to sales in 1982 dollars	+2	+3	+3
3. Average prime rate charged by banks	+4	+14	+5
4. Commercial and industrial loans outstanding in 1982 dollars	+2	+5	+4
5. Ratio of consumer installment credit outstanding to personal income	+6	+7	+7
6. Labor cost per unit of output in manufacturing, actual data as percentage of trend	$+8\frac{1}{2}$	+11	+10

Source: Moore, "The Leading Indicator Approach"; and Hertzberg and Beckman, "Business Cycle Indicators."

Composite leading indicator index A combination of leading indicators designed to indicate the likely future state of the economy.

composite time series combines these leading economic series—the **composite leading indicator index.** This composite leading indicator series is reported in the press each month as an indicator of the current and future state of the economy. There are also composite coincident and lagging indicator series.

Some analysts have employed a ratio of these composite series, contending that the ratio of the composite coincident series to the composite lagging series acts like a leading series, in some instances even leading the leading series. The rationale for predicting this relationship is that the coincident series will turn before the lagging series, and the ratio of the two series will be quite sensitive to such changes. As a result, this ratio series is expected to lead both of the individual series.

While this ratio series' movements tend to parallel those of the leading series, its real value comes when it diverges from the pure leading indicator series, signaling a change in the normal relationship between the indicator series. As an example, if the leading indicator series has been rising for a period of time, you would expect both the coincident and lagging series to be rising also, but the coincident series should be rising faster than the lagging series, so the ratio of the coincident to the lagging series should likewise be rising. In contrast, assume the leading indicator series is rising, but the ratio of coincident to lagging series is flattening out or declining. This change in trend in the ratio series could occur because the coincident indicator series is rising more slowly than the lagging indicator series or the coincident series is turning downward. Either scenario would indicate a possible end to an economic expansion, or at least a less robust expansion.

An example of such a divergence appears in Figure 9.2. The pattern indicates that the coincident and lagging series had been moving at about the same rate, causing the ratio series to run flat and even to decline slightly since 1984 although the leading indicator series continued to increase. Apparently this ratio series signaled a change in the economic environment starting in 1984 that was not confirmed by the leading series until late in 1990. Investors should note that,

| Figure 9.2 | *Indicator Series Performance* |

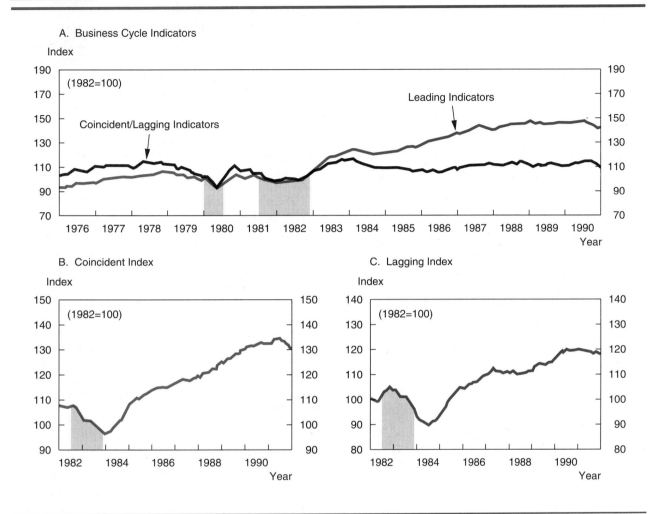

A. Business Cycle Indicators

B. Coincident Index

C. Lagging Index

Source: "Investment Strategy Highlights" (New York: Goldman, Sachs & Co., May 1988).

despite the divergence between the leading indicator series and the ratio series, stock prices declined prior to a downturn in the leading indicator series.

Analytical Measures of Performance

When predicting the future based on an economic series, it is important to consider more than the behavior of the series alone. The NBER has devised certain analytical measures for examining behavior within an alternative economic series.

Diffusion Indexes As the name implies, **diffusion indexes** indicate how pervasive a given series move-

> **Diffusion index** An indicator of the strength of an indicator series movement calculated as the percentage of reporting units with the same result.

ment is. They are measured by computing the percentage of reporting units in a series that indicate a given result. For example, if 100 companies constitute the sample reporting new orders for equipment, the diffusion index for this series would indicate what proportion of the companies were reporting higher orders during an expansion. In addition to knowing that aggregate new orders are increasing, it is helpful to know whether 55 percent or 95 percent of the companies in the sample are reporting higher orders. This information on the pervasiveness of the increase in new orders would help you project the future length and strength of an expansion.

You would also want to know past diffusion index values to determine the prevailing trend for this index. It has been shown that the diffusion index for a series almost always reaches its peak or trough before the peak or trough in the corresponding aggregate series. Therefore, you can use the diffusion index for a series to predict the behavior of the series itself. Assume that you are interested in the leading series labeled Manufacturers New Orders in 1982 dollars—Consumer Goods. If the diffusion index for this series drops from 85 percent to 75 percent and then to 70 percent, it indicates continued widespread receipt of new orders, but it also indicates a diminishing breadth to the increase, and possibly an impending decline in the series itself.

Besides creating diffusion indexes for individual series, the NBER has derived a diffusion index that shows the percentage of the 11 leading indicators rising or falling during a given period.

Rate of Change It is useful to know if a series is increasing, but more helpful to know that a 10 percent increase one month followed a 7 percent increase the previous month. Like the diffusion index, the rate of change values for a series reaches peaks or troughs prior to the peaks or troughs in the aggregate series.

Direction of Change Direction of change tables show which series rose or fell (indicated by plus or minus signs) during the most recent period and how long the movement in the current direction has persisted.

Comparison with Previous Cycles A set of tables and charts shows the movements of individual series during the current business cycle and compares these movements to previous cycles for the same economic series. This comparison reveals whether a given series is moving slower or faster, or more strongly or weakly, than during prior cycles. This information can be useful because, typically, movements in the initial months of an expansion or contraction indicate their ultimate length and strength.[4]

Limitations of the Cyclical Indicator Approach

The NBER has consistently attempted to improve the usefulness of its cyclical indicators while acknowledging some limitations. The most obvious limitation is false signals. Past patterns might suggest that current indicator values signal a contraction, but then they turn up again and nullify previous signals. In a similar problem, the indicators might show hesitancy that is difficult to interpret. Some economic series may exhibit high variability, diminishing confidence in short-run signals as compared to projecting longer-term trends.

Another limitation is the currency of the data and revisions. The problem is that you might not get the original data very soon and then you need to follow subsequent revisions. Many of the series are seasonally adjusted, so you must also watch changes in the seasonal adjustment factors.

Also, no series adequately reflects the service sector, which has grown to become a major factor in our economy. Further, no series represents the very important global economy or world securities markets. Finally, as the NBER points out, numerous political or international developments that significantly influence the economy cannot be incorporated into a statistical system.

Leading Indicators and Stock Prices

We now know that stock prices are part of a composite set of leading indicators, but we wonder whether we can use the composite series without stock prices to predict stock prices. A study that considered this question specified a decision rule in terms of percentage changes in the composite series.[5] Comparing the results of this decision rule to those of a buy-and-hold policy reveals that as long as the analysts had perfect foresight regarding the correct percentage change to use, they beat a buy-and-hold policy. When they used

---

[4]Monthly presentations of all the series and analytical measures previously appeared in the U.S. Department of Commerce publication *Business Conditions Digest*. The government stopped publishing the *Digest* in 1990. The data now appears in the *Survey of Current Business*.

[5]Bryan Heathcotte and Vincent P. Apilado, "The Predictive Content of Some Leading Economic Indicators for Future Stock Prices," *Journal of Financial and Quantitative Analysis* 9, no. 2 (March 1974): 247–258.

the trading rule without foresight as to the best percentage change (merely using the figure that would have worked during the prior market cycle), they were not able to beat a buy-and-hold policy after subtracting commissions. Therefore, although these leading economic series tend to lead the economy, the composite leading indicator series does not consistently lead its own stock price component in a way that is useful for investment decisions.

Other Leading Indicator Series

The NBER leading indicator series employed monthly data. The Center for International Business Cycle Research (CIBCR) at the Columbia Graduate School of Business has developed several additional leading indicator series.

***Business Week* Leading Indicator Series** Developed by the CIBCR and published weekly in *Business Week*, the ***Business Week* Leading Indicator Series** includes seven individual series, as shown in Figure 9.3, along with a bar chart for the leading indicator series and a weekly production series along with other weekly data on foreign exchange, prices, and monetary indicators. This composite weekly leading indicator index can help you gauge upswings and declines in general economic activity. Downturns in the index have preceded every recession since 1948, but some downturns in the leading series have been followed only by slowdowns in the economy rather than recessions.

Long-Leading Index The CIBCR has also developed its **Long-Leading Index** to provide earlier signals of major turning points in the economy than other leading indexes. It includes the following four series: (1) Dow Jones bond prices (20 bonds by percentage of face value); (2) the ratio of price to unit labor cost in manufacturing (1982 = 100); (3) M2 money supply, deflated (1982 $ billions); and (4) new building permits (1967 = 100). This index has anticipated recessions by 14 months, on average, and always by at least 7 months.

Monthly data for these series developed and maintained by the CIBCR are available in "The Leading Indicator Press Release." This release is published about the tenth day of each month with data as of 6 weeks prior to its release.

Leading Employment Index The purpose of the CIBCR's **Leading Employment Index** (1967 = 100)

***Business Week* Leading Indicator Series** An indicator series composed of seven individual series that measure production, foreign exchange, prices, and monetary indicators.
Long-Leading Index An indicator series designed to predict economic movements far in advance of aggregate economic changes based on bond prices, a ratio of prices to labor costs, M2, and building permits.
Leading Employment Index An indicator series designed to forecast changes in U.S. employment.
Leading Inflation Index An indicator series designed to forecast U.S. inflation rates.

is to forecast future changes in U.S. employment. It includes the following six component series:

1. Average workweek in manufacturing
2. Overtime hours in manufacturing
3. Percentage layoff rate (inverted)
4. Voluntary/involuntary part-time employment
5. Percentage short duration unemployment rate (inverted)
6. Initial claims for unemployment insurance (inverted)

Leading Inflation Index The CIBCR **Leading Inflation Index** is intended as a tool for forecasting inflation in the United States. It includes five variables:

1. The percentage employed of the working-age population
2. The growth rate of total debt (including business, consumer, and federal government debt)
3. The growth rate of industrial material prices
4. The growth rate of an index of import prices
5. The percentage of businesspeople anticipating an increase in their selling prices, as determined by a Dun and Bradstreet survey

The leads for this series during the period 1950 to 1990 averaged 7 months at troughs, 4 months at peaks, and 5 months at all turns.

Alternative Leading Indicator of Inflation The Wall Street investment banking firm Kidder, Peabody & Co. has also suggested a model for predicting inflation composed of the following variables:

1. Rate of capacity utilization (lagged 12 months)
2. The Federal Reserve dollar value index (a trade-weighted index of the value of the dollar against 10 other currencies; lagged 14 months)

Figure 9.3 **Business Week *Index***

BusinessWeek Index

PRODUCTION

Change from last week: 0.9%
Change from last year: −1.2%

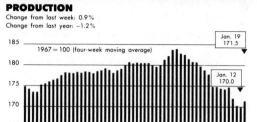

The production index increased for the week ended Jan. 19. Seasonally adjusted auto and truck output were up strongly as many plants reopened. Production of lumber, coal, rail-freight traffic, and crude-oil refining also advanced. Steel output declined. Electric power production was unchanged, and data for paper and paperboard were unavailable. Before calculation of the four-week moving average, the index rose to 176, from 173.1 in the previous week.

BW production index copyright 1991 by McGraw-Hill Inc.

LEADING

Change from last week: 1.0%
Change from last year: −0.8%

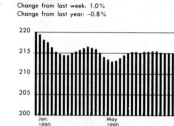

The leading index increased for the week ended Jan. 19. Stock prices rose sharply on news of early military successes in the Persian Gulf war. The growth rates in materials prices and M2 were also up, and the number of business failures was down. The growth rate in real estate loans declined, and bond yields were virtually unchanged from the prior week. Before calculation of the four-week moving average, the index increased to 215.8, from 214.3 in the week before.

Leading index copyright 1991 by Center for International Business Cycle Research

PRODUCTION INDICATORS

	Latest week	Week ago	% Change year ago
STEEL (1/26) thous. of net tons	1,615	1,684 #	−14.8
AUTOS (1/26) units	94,789	111,514r #	−19.4
TRUCKS (1/26) units	50,460	53,813r #	−2.9
ELECTRIC POWER (1/26) millions of kilowatt-hours	59,687	56,636 #	9.3
CRUDE-OIL REFINING (1/26) thous. of bbl./day	12,658	12,585 #	−7.6
COAL (1/19) thous. of net tons	20,360 #	19,008	−2.1
PAPERBOARD (1/19) thous. of tons	NA #	NA	NA
PAPER (1/19) thous. of tons	NA #	NA	NA
LUMBER (1/19) millions of ft.	499.4 #	464.5	−8.5
RAIL FREIGHT (1/19) billions of ton-miles	20.0 #	18.8	−1.5

Sources: American Iron & Steel Inst., *Ward's Automotive Reports*, Edison Electric Inst., American Petroleum Inst., Energy Dept., American Paper Inst., WWPA[1], SFPA[2], Association of American Railroads.

FOREIGN EXCHANGE

	Latest week	Week ago	Year ago
JAPANESE YEN (1/30)	132	132	145
GERMAN MARK (1/30)	1.50	1.49	1.68
BRITISH POUND (1/30)	1.95	1.95	1.68
FRENCH FRANC (1/30)	5.09	5.08	5.71
CANADIAN DOLLAR (1/30)	1.16	1.16	1.19
SWISS FRANC (1/30)	1.27	1.26	1.50
MEXICAN PESO (1/30)[3]	2,948	2,944	2,717

Sources: Major New York banks. Currencies expressed in units per U. S. dollar, except for British pound expressed in dollars.

PRICES

	Latest week	Week ago	% Change year ago
GOLD (1/30) $/troy oz.	367.100	378.300	−11.6
STEEL SCRAP (1/29) # 1 heavy, $/ton	106.00	106.00	−0.5
FOODSTUFFS (1/28) index, 1967 = 100	209.7	208.3	−0.1
COPPER (1/26) ¢/lb.	109.9	113.9	5.3
ALUMINUM (1/26) ¢/lb.	68.5	69.5	2.2
WHEAT (1/26) # 2 hard, $/bu.	2.67	2.67	−37.3
COTTON (1/26) strict low middling 1-1/16 in., ¢/lb.	70.34	70.17	13.7

Sources: London Wed. final setting, Chicago mkt., Commodity Research Bureau, *Metals Week*, Kansas City mkt., Memphis mkt.

LEADING INDICATORS

	Latest week	Week ago	% Change year ago
STOCK PRICES (1/25) S&P 500	336.09	320.52	2.2
CORPORATE BOND YIELD, Aaa (1/25)	9.05%	9.08%	0.0
INDUSTRIAL MATERIALS PRICES (1/25)	98.3	100.5	−4.1
BUSINESS FAILURES (1/18)	364	386	72.5
REAL ESTATE LOANS (1/16) billions	$401.0	$400.4	11.0
MONEY SUPPLY, M2 (1/14) billions	$3,332.9	$3,324.1r	3.0
INITIAL CLAIMS, UNEMPLOYMENT (1/12) thous.	463	396	18.4

Sources: Standard & Poor's, Moody's, *Journal of Commerce* (index: 1980 = 100), Dun & Bradstreet (failures of large companies), Federal Reserve Board, Labor Dept. CIBCR seasonally adjusts data on business failures and real estate loans.

MONTHLY ECONOMIC INDICATORS

	Latest month	Month ago	% Change year ago
12 LEADING INDICATORS COMPOSITE (Dec.) index	140.1	140.0	−3.6
CONSUMER SPENDING (Dec.) billions	$3,746.0	$3,721.5	5.7
ORDERS FOR DURABLE GOODS: MFG. (Dec.) billions	$121.6	$116.4	−7.7
PERSONAL INCOME (Dec.) annual rate, billions	$4,747.3	$4,713.7	5.6

Sources: Commerce Dept.

MONETARY INDICATORS

	Latest week	Week ago	% Change year ago
MONEY SUPPLY, M1 (1/14)	$820.5	$824.7r	3.2
BANKS' BUSINESS LOANS (1/16)	318.7	317.9r	−1.7
FREE RESERVES (1/23)	−205	3,418r	NM
NONFINANCIAL COMMERCIAL PAPER (1/16)	147.1	143.5	10.7

Sources: Federal Reserve Board (in billions, except for free reserves, which are expressed for a two-week period in millions).

MONEY MARKET RATES

	Latest week	Week ago	Year ago
FEDERAL FUNDS (1/29)	7.16%	7.56%	8.24%
PRIME (1/30)	9.50	9.50-10.00	10.00
COMMERCIAL PAPER 3-MONTH (1/29)	6.96	6.96	8.14
CERTIFICATES OF DEPOSIT 3-MONTH (1/30)	6.60	7.05	8.20
EURODOLLAR 3-MONTH (1/25)	7.01	7.41	8.25

Sources: Federal Reserve Board, First Boston

# Raw data in the production indicators are seasonally adjusted in computing the BW index (chart); other components (estimated and not listed) include machinery and defense equipment.
1 = Western Wood Products Assn. 2 = Southern Forest Products Assn. 3 = Free market value NA = Not available r = revised NM = Not meaningful

3. The annual growth rate of the CRB Commodity Spot Index (lagged 8 months)

A graph of the index for the period 1973 to 1987 indicates a strong correlation with inflation.[6]

International Leading Indicator Series In addition to developing leading indicators for the U.S. economy, the CIBCR has also developed a set of composite leading indicators for eight other major industrial countries: Canada, Germany, France, the United Kingdom, Italy, Japan, Australia, and Taiwan (Republic of China). These **International Leading Indicator Series** are part of an ongoing project to develop an international economic indicator (IEI) system. The series are comparable in data and analysis to U.S. leading series.[7]

Monetary Variables, the Economy, and Stock Prices

Many academic and professional observers hypothesize a close relationship between stock prices and various monetary variables that are influenced by monetary policy. The best known of these monetary variables is the **money supply.** You will recall from your economics study that the money supply can be measured in several ways, including currency plus demand deposits (referred to as the *M1 money supply*), and the M1 money supply plus time deposits (referred to as the *M2 money supply*). The government publishes other measures of the money supply, but these are the best known.

The Federal Reserve basically controls the money supply through various tools, the most useful of which is the open market operation. In actuality, the money supply influences stock prices as an offshoot of its influence on the aggregate economy.

Money Supply and the Economy
In their classic work on the monetary history of the United States, Friedman and Schwartz thoroughly

International Leading Indicator Series Indicator series designed to predict economic activity outside the United States.
Money supply A measure of the amount of extremely liquid assets in the economy. Alternative specifications include currency plus demand deposits, sometimes adding time deposits and money market funds.

documented the relationship between changes in the growth rate of the money supply and subsequent changes in the economy.[8] Specifically, they demonstrated that declines in the rate of growth of the money supply have preceded business contractions by an average of 20 months, while increases in the growth rate of the money supply have preceded economic expansions by about 8 months.

Friedman suggests a transmission mechanism through which changes in the growth rate of the money supply affect the aggregate economy. He hypothesizes that, to implement planned changes in monetary policy, the Federal Reserve engages in open market operations, buying or selling Treasury bonds to adjust bank reserves and, eventually, the money supply. Because the Fed deals in government bonds, the initial liquidity impact affects that market, creating excess liquidity when it buys bonds or forcing insufficient liquidity when it sells bonds. Rising or falling government bond prices affect corporate bonds, and subsequently this change in liquidity affects common stocks, and then the real goods market. This liquidity transmission scenario implies that the initial effect of a change in monetary policy appears in financial markets (bonds and stocks) and only later in the aggregate economy.

Money Supply and Stock Prices
Numerous studies have tested the relationship suggested by this transmission mechanism. Do changes in the growth of the money supply precede changes in stock prices? The results of these studies have tended to change over time. The initial studies done in the 1960s and early 1970s generally indicated a strong

[6]Steven R. Ricchiute and Stephen W. Gallagher, "Leading Indicators of Inflation," *Money Market Research*, Kidder, Peabody & Co. (January 1988).

[7]For an extended discussion, see Geoffrey H. Moore, "An Introduction to International Economic Indicators," in *Business Cycles, Inflation, and Forecasting*, 2d ed. (New York: National Bureau of Economic Research, Studies in Business Cycles, No. 24, 1983).

[8]Milton Friedman and Anna J. Schwartz, "Money and Business Cycles," *Review of Economics and Statistics* 45, no. 1, part 2, supplement (February 1963): 32–78, reprinted in Milton Friedman, *The Optimum Quantity of Money and Other Essays* (Chicago: Aldine Publishing, 1969): 189–235.

Excess liquidity The amount of money in excess of that required to support economic growth. It is measured by subtracting the annual percentage change in nominal GNP from the annual percentage change in the M2 money supply measure.

leading relationship between the money supply and stock prices. Such results implied that changes in the growth rate of the money supply could serve as an indicator of stock price changes.

More recent studies have questioned these findings. These recent studies have typically found that there is a relationship between the money supply and stock prices, but the timing of the relationship differs. These studies have found that changes in the growth rate of the money supply consistenty *lagged* stock returns by about 1 to 3 months.

The most recent studies have examined the relationship of stock returns to anticipated and unanticipated money supply growth based on weekly money supply data. The results indicate that money supply changes affect stock prices, but that the securities markets adjust prices very quickly to any expected changes in money supply growth. You can enjoy superior returns only by *forecasting unanticipated changes* in money supply growth.

Excess Liquidity and Stock Prices Some analysts look beyond the growth rate of the money supply. Einhorn contends that **excess liquidity** is the relevant monetary variable that influences stock prices.[9] Excess

---

[9]This work is printed in Goldman, Sachs & Company's monthly publication *Investment Strategy Highlights*.

Figure 9.4 *Relationship of Money, GNP, and Share Prices*

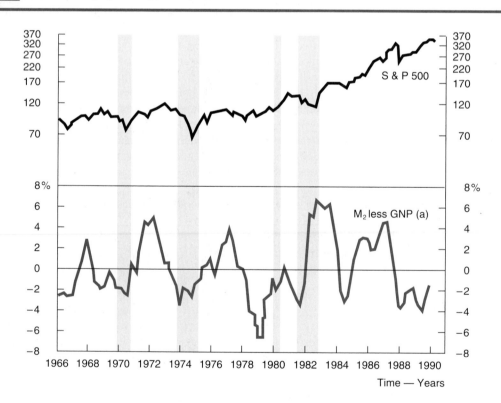

[a]Year-to-year percentage change in M2 growth (as a 6-month moving average) less year-to-year percentage change in nominal GNP.

Note: Shaded areas represent recessions.

Source: "Investment Strategy Highlights" (New York: Goldman, Sachs & Co., February 1990).

liquidity is defined as the year-to-year percentage change in the M2 money supply less the year-to-year percentage change in nominal GNP. It is reason that the growth rate of nominal GNP indicates the need for liquidity in the economy. If the money supply growth rate exceeds the GNP growth rate, this indicates that there is excess money (liquidity) in the economy that is available for securities purchases. This excess liquidity should lead to higher security prices.

Figure 9.4 shows the relationship between this measure of excess liquidity and stock prices. Although it historically tracked the market quite well, this relationship has recently weakened because of non-U.S. excess liquidity that funds U.S. stock and bond purchases. Figure 9.5 shows global excess liquidity. These figures reveal negative liquidity in the United States, but offsetting excess liquidity for non-U.S. countries including Japan, Canada, France, Germany, Italy, and the United Kingdom. This non-U.S. liquidity helped the U.S. stock market continue to rise into 1990 despite negative domestic liquidity.

Other Economic Variables and Stock Prices

Chen, Roll, and Ross examined equity returns relative to a set of macroeconomic variables.[10] They found the following variables to be significant in explaining stock returns:

- Growth in industrial production
- Changes in the risk premium
- Twists in the yield curve
- Measures of unanticipated inflation
- Changes in expected inflation during periods of volatile inflation

The authors did not attempt to predict market returns, but suggested that these variables were important in explaining past returns.

Inflation, Interest Rates, and Security Prices

In this chapter's coverage of macroeconomic analysis of security markets, we should examine the macroeconomic impact of inflation and interest rates. We have noted throughout the book the critical role of expected inflation and nominal interest rates in the required rate of return used to derive the value of all

---

[10]Nai-Fu Chen, Richard Roll, and Stephen A. Ross, "Economic Forces and the Stock Market," *Journal of Business* 59, no. 3 (July 1986).

Figure 9.5 *Plot of Global Excess Liquidity: 1980–1990*

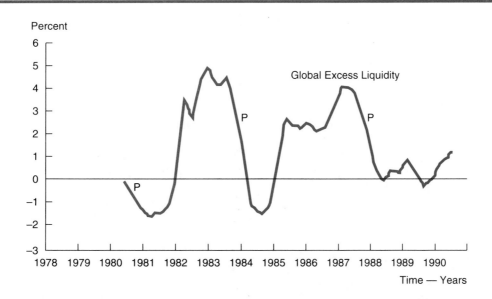

Figure 9.6   *Interest and Inflation: 1975–1989*

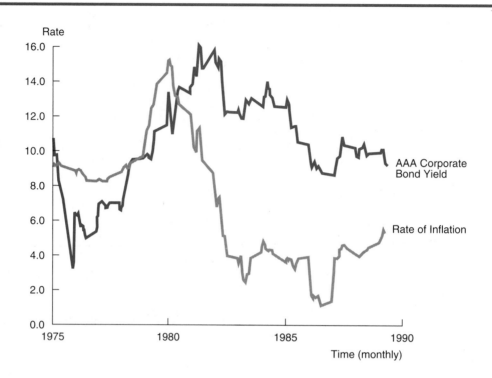

investments. We would expect these variables, with their importance in microeconomic valuation, to also affect changes in the aggregate markets.

Inflation and Interest Rates   Figure 9.6 plots long-term interest rates and the year-to-year percentage change in the consumer price index (CPI, a measure of inflation). This graph demonstrates the strong relationship we have discussed between inflation and interest rates. We contended that investors' anticipation of an increase in the rate of inflation would lead them to increase their required rates of return by similar amounts in order to derive constant real rates of return. The time-series graph of the promised yield of AAA corporate bonds and the annual rate of inflation in Figure 9.6 confirms the expected relationship but also indicates an imperfect relationship between interest rates and inflation. If the relationship were perfect, the difference between the interest rate and the inflation rate (the spread between them) would be fairly constant, reflecting the real return on corporate

bonds. The fact is, the spread between these two curves changes over time.

Figure 9.7 plots this spread to demonstrate the following results. While the two curves move together, in some periods (1975, 1979 to 1980) the inflation rate exceeded the yield on the bonds, which implies that investors received negative real returns on these bonds. In contrast, during 1983 to 1985 the real rate of return on corporate bonds was in the 8 to 10 percent range, which clearly exceeds what most investors would expect on very low risk bonds.

This change in spread does not mean that there is not a relationship between inflation and interest rates; it only shows that investors are not very good at predicting inflation. Recall that the relationship is between *expected* inflation and interest rates in contrast to these data that reflect actual inflation. Apparently, investors underestimated inflation during the periods of negative real returns (1975, 1979–1980), and over-estimated inflation during the periods of abnormally high real rates of return.

Figure 9.7   *Spread between Interest and Inflation Rates: 1975–1989*

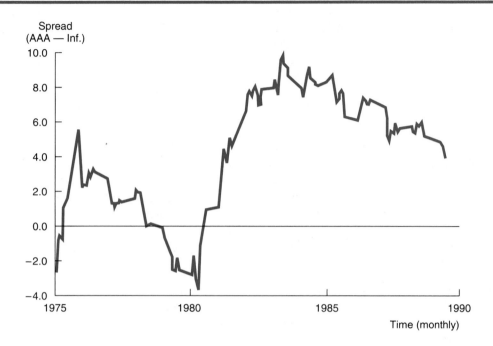

Interest Rates and Bond Prices   The relationship between interest rates and bond prices is clearly negative since the only variable that influences the valuation model is the discount factor. The expected cash flows from a standard bond would not change. Therefore, an increase in interest rates will cause a decline in bond prices and a drop in rates will boost bond prices. For example, if you own a 10-year bond with a coupon of 10 percent, when interest rates go from 10 percent to 12 percent, the price of this bond will go from $1,000 (par) to $885. In contrast, if rates go from 10 percent to 8 percent, the price of the bond will go from $1,000 to $1,136. The size of the price change will depend upon the characteristics of the bond. A longer-term bond shows a larger price change for a change in interest rates.[11] Therefore, we can anticipate a negative relationship between inflation and bond prices and rates of return on bonds because inflation generally has a direct effect on interest rates, and

interest rates have an inverse effect on bond prices and rates of return.

Interest Rates and Stock Prices   The relationship between interest rates and stock prices is not so direct. The cash flows from stocks can change along with interest rates, and we cannot be certain whether this change in cash flow will offset or augment a change in interest rates. To demonstrate this, consider the following illustrative scenarios:

1.   Interest rates rise due to an increase in the rate of inflation and corporate earnings likewise increase as firms boost prices in line with cost increases. In this case, stock prices might be fairly stable because both the required rate of return and the growth rate of corporate earnings and dividends would increase.

2.   Interest rates increase, but expected cash flows change little because firms are not able to increase prices in response to higher costs. This would cause a decline in stock prices by the same mechanism that affects bonds. The required rate of return would increase, but the growth rate of dividends would be constant, that is, the k − g spread would widen.

---

[11]Chapter 10 discusses in detail the specific variables that influence bond price volatility.

3. Interest rates increase while cash flows decline because the factors that cause the rise in interest rates also reduce earnings. For example, during 1981 to 1982 interest rates increased and remained high during a period of economic decline, pushing sales and earnings into a decline. While this set of events does not happen often, its impact can be disastrous. Stock prices decline significantly because k will increase as g declines, causing a large increase in the k − g spread.

In contrast to these three scenarios, you can envision a comparable set of scenarios when interest rates decline. The point is that the relationship between inflation, interest rates, and stock prices is not as direct or consistent as the relationship between interest rates and bonds. The effect of an interest rate change on stock prices depends upon what caused the change and the effect of this cause on the expected returns on common stock.

Further, the actual relationship between inflation, interest rates, and stock prices is an empirical question since it varies over time. Therefore, while an inverse relationship has generally held between inflation, interest rates, and the returns on stocks, this is not always true. In addition, even when it is true for the overall market, certain industries or segments of the economy may still post earnings and dividends that react positively to inflation and interest rate changes, giving their stock prices a positive correlation with inflation and interest rates.

Summary of Macroeconomic Analysis

There is ample evidence of a strong and consistent relationship between economic activity and the stock market, although stock prices consistently seem to turn from 4 to 9 months before the economy does. Therefore, to project the future direction of the stock market using the macroeconomic approach you must either forecast economic activity about 12 months ahead or examine economic indicator series that lead the economy by more than stock prices do.

Work with leading indicator series indicates that only perfect foresight regarding the appropriate data together with a diffusion index of the leading indicator series could allow an investor to improve on a buy-and-hold policy. The results from studies of the relationship between the money supply and stock prices have indicated a significant relationship, but recent research indicates that stock prices generally turn before the money supply does. Therefore, you *cannot* use

Table 9.4   Forecasts for World Economic Activity (percent per annum)

Country	1989	1990E	1991E
United States			
Consumer expenditure	1.9	1.2	0.4
Business fixed investment	3.9	1.7	0.0
GNP	2.5	1.0	0.8
Industrial production	2.9	1.1	0.5
Japan			
Consumer expenditure	3.5	3.7	4.1
Business fixed investment	17.7	14.4	6.2
Domestic demand	5.9	5.8	4.0
GNP	4.9	5.6	3.6
Industrial production	6.1	4.0	3.7
Germany			
Consumer expenditure	1.7	4.7	2.8
Fixed investment	7.1	10.2	7.3
Domestic demand	2.7	4.9	4.1
GNP	3.9	4.5	2.7
Industrial production	4.8	5.0	4.2
United Kingdom			
Consumer expenditure	3.9	2.0	0.7
Fixed investment	4.8	−1.7	−3.4
GDP	2.1	1.1	−0.1
Industrial production	0.5	0.2	−0.8
France			
Consumer expenditure	3.1	2.6	2.0
Fixed investment	5.9	3.5	1.2
GDP	3.6	2.2	1.1
Industrial production	3.9	0.6	0.7
Italy			
Consumer expenditure	3.8	2.8	2.1
Fixed investment	5.1	2.4	0.5
GDP	3.3	2.0	1.2
Industrial production	3.8	0.8	1.1
Canada			
Consumer expenditure	3.8	1.9	1.9
Fixed investment	5.0	1.0	4.6
GDP	3.0	1.1	1.0
Industrial production	1.8	1.1	1.5

Source: "World Investment Strategy Highlights" (London: Goldman, Sachs International Corp., January 1991).

the money supply series to develop a mechanical trading rule that will outperform a buy-and-hold policy.

Alternative measures of the monetary environment were also considered, including U.S. and global excess liquidity. While the historical results with U.S. excess liquidity were interesting, recent results are not as consistent. Some cite positive global liquidity as the cause of this variation. Such a global monetary effect is not surprising in our current environment, and it reemphasizes the need to think in global terms.

Analysis of World Security Markets

While we have focused on the U.S. market to demonstrate the macroeconomic approach to forecasting activity in the securities markets, you must also consider a similar analysis for foreign markets, including those in Japan, Canada, the United Kingdom, and Germany. While it is not feasible to analyze each of these markets in detail, we can provide an example of such an analysis by reviewing the extensive work of Goldman, Sachs & Co. This analysis appears in a monthly Goldman, Sachs publication, "World Investment Strategy Highlights," as part of the firm's international research effort. This publication draws on a number of other Goldman, Sachs publications to outline a world portfolio strategy, as well as strategies for several individual countries.[12]

[12]The other Goldman, Sachs publications used include *The International Economics Analyst, World Markets Monthly, Investment Strategy Highlights, Japan Investment Strategy Highlights,* and *The U.K. Economics Analyst.* The author benefitted from conversations with Jeffrey M. Weingarten, director of international equity research for Goldman, Sachs.

Goldman, Sachs employs a version of the three-step process, initially examining a country's aggregate economy and its components that relate to the valuation of securities—GNP, capital investments, industrial production, inflation, and interest rates. Table 9.4 gives the firm's forecasts of economic activity for several major countries. Note the fairly substantial differences in outlook for GNP/GDP growth during 1991 (e.g., −0.1 percent for the United Kingdom versus 3.6 percent for Japan) and for growth in industrial production (e.g., −0.8 percent for the United Kingdom versus 4.2 percent for Germany). Obviously, several countries face flat economic environments, while Japan and Germany are expected to grow strongly.

Inflation and Exchange Rates
An analysis of historical and expected price changes in Table 9.5 also reveals major differences in the outlook for inflation, ranging from less than 3 percent for Japan to 6.7 percent for the United States. These inflation estimates feed into an interest rate forecast for middle and late 1991 in Table 9.6. This combination of forecasts indicates the expected trend in interest rates. Almost all interest rates were expected to be either stable or expected to decline slightly with ending values ranging from less than 8 percent for Japan to almost 12 percent for Canada and the United Kingdom.

Given these differences in inflation and interest rate levels and trends, you can expect major differences in exchange rates. Table 9.7 presents the firm's exchange rate forecasts for several currencies. The forecasts for 6 and 12 months imply trends during the year. These figures indicate that Goldman, Sachs ex-

Table 9.5 *Consumer or Retail Price Changes (percentage changes on previous year)*

Period	United States	Canada	Japan	Germany	France	United Kingdom	Italy
1988	4.1%	4.1%	0.7%	1.3%	2.7%	4.9%	5.0%
1989	4.8	5.0	2.3	2.8	3.4	7.8	6.6
1990	5.6	4.9	3.0	2.7	3.5	9.5	6.1
1991[e]	6.7	6.0	2.8	3.8	3.5	7.5	6.5

[e]estimate

Source: "World Investment Strategy Highlights" (London: Goldman, Sachs International Ltd., January 1991).

Table 9.6 Interest Rate Forecasts (percent per annum)

Country	Current Rate	Mid-1991	End 1991
United States			
Discount rate	7.0%	6.5%	6.5%
Prime rate	10.0	9.5	9.5
Federal funds	7.6	7.0	7.3
$8\frac{7}{8}$ percent 2000	8.3	8.3	8.5
Germany			
Discount rate	6.0	6.5	6.5
Lombard rate	8.5	9.0	9.0
3-month money market	8.9	9.5	9.0
$8\frac{1}{2}$ percent 2000	8.9	9.2	8.8
Japan			
Discount rate	6.0	6.5	6.5
3-month CD	8.2	8.1	7.9
No. 119 4.8 percent	7.7	7.2	7.6
France			
3-month money market	10.0	9.7	8.8
$8\frac{1}{2}$ percent 2000	10.2	10.6	9.8
United Kingdom			
Banks' base rate	14.0	12.5	11.0
3-month interbank	13.6	12.5	11.0
13 percent 2000	11.6	11.3	12.2
Canada			
Prime rate	13.6	12.7	11.8
3-month T-bill	12.4	11.5	10.8
$10\frac{1}{2}$ percent 2001	10.5	10.3	10.5
Netherlands			
Discount rate	7.3	7.3	7.5
3-month interbank	8.8	9.5	9.0
$7\frac{3}{4}$ percent 2000	9.1	9.3	8.9

Source: "World Investment Strategy Highlights" (London: Goldman, Sachs International Ltd., January 1991).

pects the U.S. dollar to post a strong performance against world currencies during 1991.

Based upon this analysis of underlying economies, Table 9.8 estimates corporate earnings growth rates and ROEs for various countries. It also gives estimates of other stock market variables, including dividend growth, price–earnings ratio, price–cash flow ratio, and dividend yield. Again, all series show major differences among countries. Earnings growth rates vary from negative expected growth for Italy and the United States in 1991 to substantial earnings growth during 1991 for Japan and France. Likewise, the price–earnings ratio is expected to continue its historical variation ranging in 1991 from about 9 times for Italy to 35 times for Japan.

Correlations among Returns

These substantial differences in economic performance and major changes in underlying valuation variables make for fairly low correlations among stock market returns for alternative countries. The correlation matrix of price changes in local currencies in Table 9.9 shows a fairly high correlation of the United States with Canada, and low correlations of the United States with Italy and Japan. Notably, the U.S.–Japan correlation has increased in recent years as our economies have become more interdependent.

Table 9.10, a similar matrix in U.S. dollars, shows that all correlations with the United States decline when one considers the exchange rate effect. Comparisons such as these justify and encourage worldwide diversification of investments.

Individual Country Stock Price Changes

The stock market impact of exchange rates is shown in Table 9.11, which reports percentage changes in stock prices both in the local currency and adjusted for the U.S. dollar. The percentage changes of stock prices in local currency indicate the returns to citizens of the country. The annual averages for 1986 to 1989 range from 7.8 percent (Germany) to 30.1 percent (Japan). The percentage changes of stock prices in U.S. dollars indicate the returns to a U.S. investor in each of these countries. These changes range from 16.5 percent (Germany) to 43.5 percent (Japan).

The significant impact of changes in exchange rates can be seen in a couple of examples. While the rate of change in Japanese stock prices during 1987

| *Table 9.7* | *Forecast Exchange Rates* |

	U.S. Dollar	Canadian Dollar	Japanese Yen	British Pound	German Mark	French Franc	Swiss Franc	Trade-Weighted[a]
Against U.S. Dollar								**U.S. Dollar**
6 month	—	1.17	135	0.56	1.60	5.46	1.33	63
12 month	—	1.18	142	0.62	1.75	5.98	1.38	70
Against Pound								**Pound**
6 month	1.78	2.08	240	—	2.84	9.72	2.37	91
12 month	1.62	1.91	230	—	2.83	9.69	2.24	88
Against Mark								**Mark**
6 month	0.63	0.73	84	0.35	—	3.41	0.83	117
12 month	0.57	0.68	81	0.35	—	3.42	0.79	115
Against Yen								**Yen**
6 month	135	115.4	—	240	84	24.7	103	128
12 month	142	120.3	—	230	81	23.7	102	123

[a]All trade-weighted indices are from the Bank of England (1985 = 100).

Source: "World Investment Strategy Highlights" (London: Goldman, Sachs International Ltd., January 1991).

was 8.5 percent, a U.S. citizen who invested in Japan at the same time would have experienced a change of 41.4 percent because of the significant strength of the yen relative to the dollar. This increase in the rate of return due to exchange rate changes relative to the U.S. dollar was fairly widespread during 1987. In contrast, during 1989, the U.S. dollar was quite strong, and most percentage stock price changes in U.S. dollars were lower. As an example, the change in Japan during 1989 was 18.6 percent in local currency, but only 3.1 percent in U.S. dollars.

Individual Country Analysis

Goldman, Sachs provides a detailed analysis of major countries that include the country's local economy and equity market, and culminates in a portfolio recommendation for investors in that economy. Table 9.12 shows the major economic indicators for Japan reflecting a strong economic recovery following its 1984 recession.

An analysis of the country's equity market follows the economic projections. For example, a summary for the United Kingdom appears in Table 9.13. Goldman,

Normal range The proportion of a portfolio an investor should hold in a particular class of investment assets under normal conditions.

Suggested weighting The proportion of a portfolio an investor should hold in a particular class of investment assets under current and future conditions.

Sachs feels that the overall economic outlook for the United Kingdom is moderate. The firm would recommend cash investments (very short-term bonds) over gilts (long-term U.K. government bonds). For both bonds and stock, it prefers foreign securities to domestic opportunities. This preference is reflected in the recommended portfolio for U.K. investors at the bottom of Table 9.13. It shows a **normal range** for various components of the portfolio (e.g., the range for bonds is 15 to 25 percent) and a **suggested weighting** for the current and future environment. As of early 1991, Goldman, Sachs recommended the midrange proportion of cash (10 percent), a middle weighting in bonds (20 percent), and a middle weighting in equities (70 percent).

| Table 9.8 | Comparative Stock Market Statistics |

	United States	Japan	United Kingdom	Germany[a]	France	Italy[b]
Earnings Growth						
1982–1990 CGR	8.8	9.8	13.2	15.3	15.8	27.8
1989	0.8	16.7	14.0	10.0	18.0	−1.6
1990E	−1.3	9.1	−10.0	0.0	9.7	−9.0
1991E	−1.5	3.6	2.0	3.0	4.1	−4.7
Cash Flow Growth						
1982–1989 CGR	7.9	9.7	10.3	12.3	24.2	24.7
1989	2.5	8.4	10.0	12.0	14.0	6.0
1990E	−2.8	4.0	6.1	12.0	6.5	1.2
Dividend Growth						
1982–1989 CGR	6.6	8.1	14.5	12.1	18.0	24.5
1989	15.0	12.4	12.0	6.2	17.0	14.1
1990E	10.2	1.5	8.0	0.0	9.5	−2.3
Return on Equity						
1982–1989 Avg.	14.1	7.5	15.1	13.8	12.5	8.3
1989	18.1	7.3	19.6	12.8	13.5	11.2
1990E	16.6	7.3	16.9	11.8	14.0	9.3
Price/Earnings						
1982–1990 Avg.	14.3	46.7	11.7	11.5	11.4	10.8
1989	14.3	39.4	10.5	10.7	11.1	7.6
1990E	14.5	36.1	11.7	10.7	10.1	8.3
1991E	14.7	34.8	11.5	10.4	9.7	8.7
Price/Cash Flow						
1982–1989 Avg.	6.4	14.8	5.9	3.5	5.0	2.9
1989	7.1	13.7	6.5	3.0	4.8	2.1
1990E	7.3	13.1	6.2	2.7	4.5	2.1
Dividend Yield						
1982–1989 Avg.	3.4	0.9	4.9	2.8	4.1	4.1
1989	3.0	0.9	5.0	3.0	4.1	5.3
1990E	3.3	0.9	5.4	3.0	4.5	5.2

Aggregates and multiples for earnings, cash flow, book value, and dividends are based on an industrial sample of companies in each country.

[a]Germany calculated with DVFA rules.

[b]Italian averages calculated using period from 1983 to 1988.

All multiples are priced at current prices, 27 November 1990.

Source: "World Investment Strategy Highlights" (London: Goldman, Sachs International Ltd., January 1991).

Table 9.9 *Correlation of Price Returns in Local Currency: 1981–1988*

	United States	Japan	Germany	United Kingdom	Canada	France
United States	—					
Japan	0.39	—				
Germany	0.41	0.27	—			
United Kingdom	0.67	0.40	0.44	—		
Canada	0.77	0.35	0.38	0.64	—	
France	0.49	0.36	0.55	0.43	0.42	—
Italy	0.29	0.34	0.36	0.37	0.37	0.44

Source: "Anatomy of World Markets" (London: Goldman, Sachs International Ltd., October 1989).

Table 9.10 *Correlation of Price Returns in U.S. Dollars: 1981–1988*

	United States	Japan	Germany	United Kingdom	Canada	France
United States	—					
Japan	0.28	—				
Germany	0.33	0.35	—			
United Kingdom	0.54	0.43	0.43	—		
Canada	0.74	0.33	0.30	0.63	—	
France	0.41	0.44	0.61	0.46	0.38	—
Italy	0.24	0.42	0.44	0.38	0.34	0.52

Source: "Anatomy of World Markets" (London: Goldman, Sachs International Ltd., October 1989).

Table 9.11 *World Stock Market Performance: 1986–1989 (in local currency and U.S. dollars)*

Country	1986 Local Currency	1986 U.S. Dollars	1987 Local Currency	1987 U.S. Dollars	1988 Local Currency	1988 U.S. Dollars	1989 Local Currency	1989 U.S. Dollars	Average 1986–1989 Local Currency	Average 1986–1989 U.S. Dollars
United States	14.2	14.2	0.5	0.5	12.6	12.6	26.4	26.4	13.4	13.4
Japan	53.9	93.9	8.5	41.4	39.5	35.4	18.6	3.1	30.1	43.5
Germany	5.6	34.3	−36.8	−22.7	28.3	13.8	34.1	40.7	7.8	16.5
United Kingdom	20.2	23.2	4.6	32.5	6.0	2.1	31.6	17.3	15.6	18.8
France	45.2	71.0	−27.8	−13.9	51.5	33.6	29.5	35.6	24.6	31.6
Italy	73.6	117.1	−32.4	−22.3	22.8	9.4	12.3	15.6	19.1	30.0
World	29.6	39.3	−0.9	15.0	24.4	21.4	22.8	15.1	19.0	22.7

Source: "World Investment Strategy Highlights" (London: Goldman, Sachs International Ltd., July/August 1990).

Table 9.12	Main Japanese Economic Indicators			
	1988	**1989**	**1990**	**1991E**
GDP Components (1980 prices, percentage change from previous year)				
Consumer expenditure	5.1	3.5	3.7	4.1
Fixed investment	15.5	17.7	14.4	6.2
Exports	8.6	15.6	12.1	5.2
Imports	20.7	21.4	12.8	6.5
Output (percentage change from previous year)				
Real GNP	5.7	4.9	5.6	3.6
Industrial production	9.5	6.1	4.0	3.7
Inflation (percentage change from previous year)				
Consumer prices	0.7	2.3	3.0	2.8
Financial Sector (percentage at end of year)				
Discount rate	2.5	4.3	6.0	6.5
3-month CD	4.6	7.0	8.3	7.9
Long bond yield	4.6	5.7	8.0	7.6
Overseas Sector (US $ billions)				
Trade balance	95.0	76.9	61.1	51.3
Current account	79.6	57.2	35.7	28.6
Labor Market (percent)				
Unemployment	2.5	2.3	2.1	2.3

Source: "World Investment Strategy Highlights" (London: Goldman, Sachs International Ltd., January 1991).

World Asset Allocation

The final product of all this analysis is a recommendation for an investor's world asset allocation. Table 9.14 begins with the division among bonds, equities, and cash. As of early 1991, Goldman, Sachs recommended that an investor should be at the middle range for bonds, toward the low end of the equity range, and toward the high end of the cash range.

Within the equity segment of the portfolio, the firm specified a neutral weighting for each country based upon its relative market value. The relative market value of a country's equities is their value as a percentage of the total value of all world equities. A completely neutral portfolio regarding all equity markets would invest a proportion in each country equal to the relative market value of that country's equities.

If the value of stocks in a country constituted 10 percent of the value of all stocks in the world, a neutral outlook would lead you to invest 10 percent of your equity portfolio in that country. If you were bullish toward this country relative to other markets, you would overweight it, investing more than 10 percent of your equity portfolio there.

As of the publication date of this report, Goldman, Sachs was somewhat bearish on the U.S. stock market and recommended underweighting it (32.1 percent invested in the United States versus a 36.5 percent market weighting). Similarly, the firm was bearish regarding Japan and recommended underweighting Japanese stocks (suggesting a 30.2 percent weight versus a market weight of 36.3 percent). In contrast, the firm recommended overweighting the United Kingdom (suggesting 21.6 percent in the United Kingdom versus the neutral weighting of 12.6 percent).

After completing the global market analysis, the next step is to analyze alternative industries worldwide within specific countries. Finally, you should consider alternative firms in the preferred industries. This subsequent analysis is the subject of Chapters 13 and 14.

Summary

▪ In earlier chapters we emphasized the importance of analyzing aggregate markets before beginning any industry or company analysis. You must assess the economic and security market outlooks and their implications regarding the bond, stock, and cash components of your portfolio. Then you proceed to consider the best industry or company.

▪ Three techniques help you make the market decision: (1) the macroeconomic technique, which is based upon the relationship between the aggregate economy and the stock market; (2) the microeconomic technique, which determines future market values by applying the dividend discount model to the aggregate stock market; and (3) technical analysis, which estimates future returns based upon recent past returns. This chapter concentrated on the macroeconomic approach. The microeconomic analysis of equity markets will be considered in Chapter 12 as a prelude to the industry and company analysis in Chapters 13 and 14. Technical analysis is covered in Chapter 15.

▪ The economy and the stock market have a strong, consistent relationship, but the stock market generally

| *Table 9.13* | *United Kingdom* |

| | P/E | | | | P/CF | | | P/B | | | Dividend Yield |
	1989	1990E	1991E	Rel	1989	1990E	Rel	1989	1990E	Rel	1990E
FT–A Industrials	10.5	11.7	11.5	99	6.5	6.2	104	2.1	2.0	113	5.39%

| | Current Price | Performance (% Change) | | | 52-Week Range | | Relative to World | | |
		Last Month	YTD	12 Month	High	Low	Last Month	YTD	12 Month
FT Composite (U.S. dollar)	170.7	5.6	7.6	20.5	176.2	139.9	6.4	32.5	42.4
FT Composite (local currency)	128.1	4.6	−12.2	−4.8	148.6	117.6	5.7	16.9	22.8
FT Industrials (local currency)	129.3	3.8	−11.0	−3.6	148.3	120.2	5.3	13.5	18.8
FT All Share	1,038.6	4.1	−13.8	−6.9	1,226.8	962.1	5.2	14.8	20.1
FT–SE 100	2,159.9	4.7	−10.8	−2.9	2,463.7	1,990.3	5.8	18.7	25.2

Recommended Portfolio for U.K. Investors

	Normal Range (%)	Suggested Weighting (%)
Bonds	**15–25**	**20**
Domestic	10–20	10
Foreign	0–10	10
Equities	**55–85**	**70**
Domestic	40–60	50
Foreign	15–25	20
North America	5–25	10
Japan	5–20	5
Other Europe	0–10	5
Cash	**0–20**	**10**

Source: "World Investment Strategy Highlights" (London: Goldman, Sachs International Ltd., January 1991).

turns before the economy does. Therefore, the best macroeconomic projection techniques use economic series that likewise lead the economy, and possibly the stock market. The NBER leading indicator series (which includes stock prices) is one possibility, but the evidence does not support its use as a predictor of stock prices. Leading series for inflation and for other countries exist, along with a weekly leading indicator series, but none of these series has been examined relative to stock prices.

■ The money supply has been suggested as a predictor of aggregate market behavior based upon its relationship to the economy. Some early studies indicated a strong relationship between the money supply and stock prices, and also suggested that money supply changes turned before stock prices. While more re-

Table 9.14 *Asset Allocation—World Portfolios*

	Normal Range (%)	Weighting (% of index)	Current Suggested Weighting (%)
Bonds	20–40		30
Dollar			30
Nondollar			70
			100
Equities	45–65		50
United States		36.5	32.1
Japan		36.3	30.2
United Kingdom		12.6	21.6
Germany		4.7	4.1
France		3.6	3.2
Italy		1.5	2.2
Netherlands		1.8	2.1
Switzerland		1.5	2.1
Spain		1.1	2.0
Sweden		0.4	0.5
		100.0	100.0
Cash	0–30		20

Source: "World Investment Strategy Highlights" (London: Goldman, Sachs International Ltd., January 1991).

cent studies confirmed the link between money supply and stock prices, they indicated that stock prices turn with or before money supply changes. These recent results imply that, although money supply changes have an important impact on stock price movements, it is not possible to use historical money supply data in a mechanical way to predict stock price changes.

■ The analysis of excess liquidity indicated an impact on stock prices, but also showed that global liquidity weakened the relationship of U.S. markets with U.S. liquidity alone.

■ While we emphasized the U.S. market, we know it is also important to analyze numerous foreign markets. Such an analysis is demonstrated by Goldman, Sachs' application of the three-step, or top-down, approach to major countries. This included economic analysis and market analysis for each country, includ-

ing a recommended portfolio strategy for investors in each country. The analysis culminated with a recommendation for a world portfolio allocation among bonds, stock, and cash. It also recommends an allocation of equity investments among countries. It recommends an equity weighting in comparison to the country's normal weighting based upon its relative market value.

■ This aggregate market analysis should lead you to a decision as to how much of your portfolio should be committed to bonds, stocks, and cash during the forthcoming investment period. The following two chapters deal with the fixed-income portion of your portfolio. Chapter 10 considers the analysis of individual bonds while Chapter 11 presents alternative portfolio strategies for bond investors.

Questions

1. Why would you expect a relationship between economic activity and stock price movements?
2. At a lunch with some business associates you discuss the reason for the relationship between the economy and the stock market. One of your associates believes stock prices typically turn before the economy does. How would you explain this phenomenon?
3. Define *leading*, *lagging*, and *coincident indicators*. Give an example of an economic series in each category and discuss why you think each series belongs in that particular group.
4. Describe a diffusion index of a leading indicator series. Could it help you predict stock market movements? Why or why not?
5. Explain the following statements: There is a strong, consistent relationship between money supply changes and stock prices; money supply changes cannot be used to predict stock price movements.
6. How is excess liquidity measured? Discuss the rationale for the relationship of excess liquidity and security prices.
7. You are informed about the following estimates: nominal money supply is expected to grow at a rate of 8 percent and GNP is estimated to grow at 4.5 percent. Explain what you think will happen to stock prices during this period and why.
8. The current rate of inflation is 3 percent and long-term bonds are yielding 7 percent. You estimate that the rate of inflation will increase to 6

percent. What do you expect to happen to long-term bond yields? Compute the effect of this change in inflation on the price of a 10 year, 10 percent coupon bond.

9. It is fairly easy to determine the effect of a change in interest rates on the price of a bond. In contrast, some contend that it is harder to estimate the effect of a change in interest rates on common stocks. Discuss this contention.

10. Based upon the economic projections in Tables 9.5 through 9.8, would you expect the stock prices for the various countries to be highly correlated? Justify your answer with specific examples.

11. You are informed that a well-respected investment firm projects that the rate of return next year for the U.S. equity market will be 11 percent, while returns for German stocks will be 14 percent. Assume that all risks except exchange rate risk are equal and you expect the DM/U.S. dollar exchange rate to go from 1.60 to 1.35 during the year. Given this information, discuss where you would invest and why. Compute the effect if the exchange rate went from 1.60 to 2.00.

Problems

1. Prepare a table showing the percentage change for each of the last 10 years in (a) the Consumer Price Index (all items), (b) nominal GNP, (c) real GNP (in constant dollars), and (d) the GNP deflator. Discuss how much of nominal growth was due to real growth and how much was due to inflation. Is the outlook for next year any different from last year? Discuss.

2. *CFA Examination I* (June 1983)
   Use of economic analysis in investment management has grown considerably in recent years.

Further significant expansion may lie ahead as financial analysts develop greater skills in economic analysis and these analyses are integrated more completely into the investment decision-making process. The following questions address the use of economic analysis in the investment decision making process:

a. 1. Differentiate among leading, lagging, and coincident indicators of economic activity, and give an example of each.
   2. Indicate whether the leading indicators are one of the best tools for achieving above-average investment results. Briefly justify your conclusion. (8 minutes)

b. Interest rate projections are used in investment management for a variety of purposes. Identify three significant reasons why interest rate forecasts may be important in reaching investment conclusions. (6 minutes)

c. Assume you are a fundamental research analyst following the automobile industry for a large brokerage firm. Identify and briefly explain the relevance of three major economic time series, economic indicators, or economic data items that would be significant to automotive industry and company research. (6 minutes)

3. *CFA Examination III* (June 1985)
   A U.S. pension plan hired two offshore firms to manage the non-U.S. equity portion of its total portfolio. Each firm was free to own stocks in any country market included in Capital International's Europe, Australia, and Far East Index (EAFE) and to use any form of dollar and/or nondollar cash or bonds as an equity substitute or reserve. After 3 years, the records of the managers and the EAFE Index were as shown below:

Summary: Contributions to Return

	Currency	Country Selection	Stock Selection	Cash/ Bond Allocation	Total Return Recorded
Manager A	(9.0)%	19.7%	3.1%	0.6%	14.4%
Manager B	(7.4)	14.2	6.0	2.8	15.6
Composite of A and B	(8.2)	16.9	4.5	1.7	15.0
EAFE Index	(12.9)	19.9	—	—	7.0

You are a member of the plan sponsor's pension committee, which will soon meet with the plan's consultant to review manager performance. In preparation for this meeting, prepare the following analysis:

   a. Briefly describe the strengths and weaknesses of each manager, relative to the EAFE Index data. (5 minutes)

   b. Briefly explain the meaning of the data in the Currency column. (5 minutes)

4. World Stock Market Indexes are published weekly in *Barron's* in the section labeled "Market Laboratory/Stocks." Consult the latest available edition of this publication, and the issue one year earlier to find the following information.

   a. Show the closing value of each index on each date relative to the yearly high for each year.

   b. Name the countries with markets in downtrends. Name those in uptrends.

   c. For the two time periods, calculate the year's change relative to the beginning price. Based on this and the range of annual values, which markets seem the most volatile?

5. Using a source of financial data such as *Barron's* or *The Wall Street Journal:*

   a. Plot the closing S&P index (y-axis) versus the latest M2 money supply figures (x-axis) for the past 10 weeks. Do you see a positive, negative, or zero correlation? (Monetary aggregates will lag the stock market aggregates.)

   b. Examine the trend in money rates (e.g., federal funds, 90-day T-bills, etc.) over the past 10 weeks. Is there a correlation between these money rates? Estimate the correlation between the individual money rates and percentage changes in M1.

   c. For the past 10 weeks, examine the relationship between the weekly percentage changes in the S&P 400 Index and the DJIA. Plot the weekly percentage changes in each index using S&P as the x-axis and DJIA as the y-axis. Discuss your results in terms of diversification. Do a similar comparison for the S&P 400 and the Nikkei Index.

References

Belfer, Nathan. "Economic Indicators and Their Significance." In *The Financial Analysts Handbook*, 2d ed. Ed. by Sumner N. Levine. Homewood, Ill.: Dow Jones-Irwin, 1988.

Chen, Nai-Fu, Richard Roll, and Stephen A. Ross. "Economic Forces and the Stock Market." *Journal of Business* 59, no. 3 (July 1986).

Davidson, Lawrence S., and Richard T. Froyen. "Monetary Policy and Stock Returns: Are Stock Markets Efficient?" *Federal Reserve Bank of St. Louis Review* 64, no. 3 (March 1983).

Friedman, Milton J., and Anna J. Schwartz. "Money and Business Cycles." *Review of Economics and Statistics* 45, no. 1 supplement (February 1963).

Hafer, R. W. "The Response of Stock Prices to Changes in Weekly Money and the Discount Rate." *Federal Reserve Bank of St. Louis Review* 68, no. 3 (March 1986).

Hertzberg, Marie P., and Barry A. Beckman. "Business Cycle Indicators: Revised Composite Indicators." *Business Conditions Digest* 17, no. 1 (January 1989).

Moore, Geoffrey H., and John P. Cullity. "Security Markets and Business Cycles." In *The Financial Analysts Handbook*, 2d ed. Ed. by Sumner N. Levine. Homewood, Ill.: Dow Jones-Irwin, 1988.

Moore, Geoffrey H., ed. *Business Cycles, Inflation, and Forecasting*, 2d ed. New York: National Bureau of Economic Research, Studies in Business Cycles, No. 24, 1983.

P A R T

3

—

Analysis and Management of Bonds

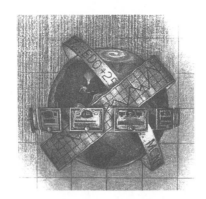

Chapter 2 discussed how the bond market is organized and how it functions, and gave a basic description of the characteristics of bonds. This section completes the consideration of bonds by discussing how to value individual bonds and manage bond portfolios.

In Chapter 10 we apply the valuation principles that we introduced in Chapter 8 to the valuation of bonds. The goal is to help you understand how to value bonds and measure their yields. After this, we discuss why bond values and yields change over time.

Chapter 11 is concerned with bond portfolio management strategies, since there is more to bond investing than selecting attractive individual bonds. To be a successful investor you must understand how to combine good individual securities into a portfolio of securities that will suit your specific return and risk needs and preferences. Given such a goal, this chapter considers a wide range of bond portfolio management strategies through which you can achieve alternative risk–reward objectives using techniques that range from conservative to fairly aggressive.

10

Valuation of Bonds

In this chapter we apply the valuation principles introduced in Chapter 8 to the valuation of bonds. The goal of this chapter is to find the value and yields of bonds, and also to understand why these bond values and yields change over time. To do this, we begin with a review of value estimation for bonds using the present value model introduced in Chapter 8. This background on valuation allows us to understand and compute the expected rates of return on bonds, or their yields. We need to measure yields on bonds because they are very important to a bond investor.

After mastering the measurement of bond yields, we consider what factors influence yield movements over time. We will discuss the effects of various characteristics and indenture provisions that affect the required returns and, therefore, the values of specific bond issues. This includes factors such as time to maturity, coupon, callability, and sinking funds.

With this background we return to the consideration of bond value and examine the characteristics that cause different changes in a bond's price. The point is, when yields change, all bond prices do not change in the same way.

An understanding of the factors that affect the price changes for bonds has become more important during the past several decades because the price volatility of bonds has increased substantially. Before 1950, the yields on bonds were fairly low and both yields and prices were stable. In such an environment, bonds were considered a very safe investment and most investors in bonds intended to hold them to maturity. During the last several decades, the level of interest rates has increased substantially because of inflation, and also have become more volatile because of changes in the rate of inflation and monetary policy. As a result, bond prices have been much more volatile and the rates of return on bond investments have increased. Given these changes, bonds are no longer as safe as they once were.

> **Discount** A bond selling at a price below par value due to capital market conditions.
> **Premium** A bond selling at a price above par value due to capital market conditions.

Fundamentals of Bond Valuation

Similar to valuation procedures in corporate finance, the values of bonds can be described in terms of dollar values or the rates of return they promise under some set of assumptions. In this section we describe both the present value model that computes a specific value for the bond and the yield model that computes the promised rate of return based upon the bond's current price.

Present Value Model

In our introduction to valuation theory in Chapter 8 we saw that the value of a bond (or any asset) equals the present value of its expected cash flows. The cash flows from a bond are the periodic interest payments to the bondholder and the repayment of principal at maturity. Therefore, the value of a bond is the present value of the interest payments plus the present value of the principal payment, where the discount factor is the required rate of return on the bond. We can express this in the following present value formula:

$$(10.1) \qquad V = \sum_{t=1}^{n} C_t \frac{1}{(1 + K_b)^t}$$

where:

n = the number of periods in the holding period

C_t = the cash flow received in period t

K_b = the required rate of return for this bond issue

Essentially, any fixed-income security can be valued on the basis of Equation 10.1. The value computed indicates what an investor would be willing to pay for this bond in order to realize a rate of return that takes into account expectations regarding the RFR, the expected rate of inflation, and the risk of the bond. Many

investors assume a holding period equal to the term to maturity of the obligation. In this case, the number of periods would be the number of years to the maturity of the bond (referred to as the *term to maturity*).

Aggressive bond investors, however, normally do not hold bonds to maturity. They buy bonds with the expectation that they will sell them prior to their maturity. In such a case, the length of time the investor expects to hold the bond determines the number of holding periods. This holding period can range from a few days or weeks to several years, but it would be less than the term to maturity.

Such an investor would estimate cash flows as the periodic interest payments during the holding period and the expected selling price (SP) at the end of the holding period. The expected selling price need not equal the par value of the bond. The bond can sell at a **discount** which means that its market price will be less than its par value, or it can sell at a **premium,** that is, at a market price above its par value. A discount bond with a par value of $1,000 might sell for $900, while a premium bond with the same par value might have a market price of $1,200. When computing the value of a bond you will sell before maturity, it is necessary to estimate both the holding period and the selling price at the end of the holding period. We will discuss how to do this in an example in the next section.

Whether you intend to hold the bond to maturity or for some shorter time period, you will discount the cash flows at your required rate of return on a bond with the given risk. As discussed in Chapter 8, your investment decision will depend on the relationship of your estimated value of the bond and its market price. If the estimated value of the bond equals or exceeds the market price you should buy it; if your estimated value of the bond is less than its market price, you should not buy it.

The present value formula implies that the major determinant of changes in the value of a bond is the discount rate because the cash flows are known. Therefore, we will need to discuss what causes differences in discount rates between bonds and over time. That is, why do interest rates change? These questions will be considered in a subsequent section.

Pricing Bonds from Yields

Instead of determining the value of a bond in dollar terms, investors often price bonds in terms of **yields,** which give the rates of return on bonds under certain assumptions. To this point, we have used known cash flows and our required rate of return to compute an estimated value for the bond, which we then compared to its market price (P). To compute an expected yield, we use the current market price (P) with cash flows. We can express this approach using the present value model as follows:

$$(10.2) \qquad P = \sum_{t=i}^{n} C_t \frac{1}{(1+i)^t}$$

where:

P = the current market price of the bond

C_t = the cash flow received in period t

i = the discount rate at which we will discount the cash flows

This i value gives the yield of the bond. We will discuss several types of bond yields that arise from the assumptions of the valuation model in the next section.

Approaching the investment decision stating the bond's value as a yield figure rather than a dollar amount, you consider the relationship of the computed yield to your required rate of return on this bond. If the computed bond yield is equal to or greater than your required rate of return, you should buy the bond; if the computed yield is less than your required rate of return, you should not buy the bond.

This approach to pricing bonds and making investment decisions is similar to the two alternative approaches by which firms make investment decisions. We referred to one approach, the next present value method, in Chapter 8. With the NPV approach you compute the present value of the net cash flows from the proposed investment at your cost of capital and subtract the present cost of the investment to get the net present value (NPV) of the project. If this NPV is positive, you consider accepting the investment; if it is negative, you reject it. This is basically the way we compared the value of an investment to its market price.

The second approach is to compute the **internal rate of return** (IRR) on a proposed investment project. This is the discount rate that equates the present value of its cash outflows with the present value of its cash inflows. You compare this discount rate, or IRR (which is also the expected rate of return on the project), to your cost of capital, and accept any investment proposal with an IRR equal to or greater than the cost of capital. We do the same thing when we price bonds

Yield The promised rate of return on an investment under certain assumptions.

Internal rate of return The discount rate at which cash outflows of an investment equal cash inflows.

on the basis of yield. If the expected yield on the bond equals or exceeds your required rate of return on the bond, you should invest in it; if the expected yield is less than your required rate of return on the bond, you should not invest in it.

Computing Bond Yields

Bond investors use five types of yields for the following purposes:

Yield Measure	Purpose
Nominal yield	Measures coupon rate
Current yield	Measures current income
Promised yield to maturity	Measures expected rate of return for bond held to maturity
Promised yield to call	Measures expected rate of return for bond held to first call date
Realized yield	Measures expected rate of return for a bond likely to be sold prior to maturity. It considers specific reinvestment assumptions and on estimated sales price. It can also measure the actual rate of return on a bond during some past period of time.

Nominal and current yields are mainly descriptive and contribute little to investment decision making. The last three yields are all derived from the present value model described in Equation 10.2.

When we present the last three yields based on the present value model, we consider two techniques to complete its calculations. First, we consider a fairly simple calculation for the approximate values for each of these yields to provide reasonable estimates. Second, we use the present value model to get accurate values. We provide both techniques because an exact answer with the present value model requires several calculations. In some cases, the easier approximate yield value is adequate.

To measure realized yield, a bond investor must estimate selling price. Following our presentation of bond yields we will present the procedure for finding

> **Nominal yield** A bond's yield as measured by its coupon rate.
>
> **Current yield** A bond's yield as measured by its current income (coupon) as a percentage of its price.
>
> **Promised yield to maturity** The most widely used measure of a bond's yield that states the fully compounded rate of return on a bond bought at market price and held to maturity with reinvestment of all coupon payments at the yield-to-maturity rate.
>
> **Interest-on-interest** Bond income from reinvestment of coupon payments.

these prices. We conclude the section by examining the yields on tax-free bonds.

Nominal Yield

Nominal yield is the coupon rate of a particular issue. A bond with an 8 percent coupon has an 8 percent nominal yield. This provides a convenient way of describing the coupon characteristics of an issue.

Current Yield

Current yield is to bonds what dividend yield is to stocks. You compute it as:

$$(10.3) \qquad CY = C_i/P_m$$

where:

CY = current yield on a bond

C_i = annual coupon payment of bond i

P_m = current market price of the bond

Because this yield measures the current income from the bond as a percentage of its price, it is important to income-oriented investors who want current cash flow from their investment portfolios. An example of such an investor would be a retired person who lives on this investment income. Current yield has little use for most other investors interested in total return because it excludes the important capital gain or loss component.

Promised Yield to Maturity

Promised yield to maturity is the single most widely used bond yield figure, since it indicates the fully compounded rate of return to an investor who buys the bond at prevailing prices, if two assumptions hold true. The first assumption is that the investor holds

the bond to maturity. This assumption gives this value its shortened name, *yield to maturity* (YTM). The second assumption is implicit in the present value method of computation. Referring back to Equation 10.2, recall that it related the current market price of the bond to the present value of all cash flows as follows:

$$P_m = \sum_{t=i}^{n} C_t \frac{1}{(1 + i)^t}$$

To compute YTM for a bond, we solve for the rate i that will equate the current price (P_m) to all cash flows from the bond to maturity. As noted, this resembles the computation of internal rate of return (IRR) on an investment project. Because it is a present value-based computation, it implies a reinvestment rate assumption because it discounts cash flows. That is, the equation assumes that *all interim cash flows (interest payments) are reinvested at the computed YTM*. It is referred to as a *promised* YTM because the bond will provide this YTM if you meet its conditions:

1. You hold it to maturity.
2. You reinvest all the interim cash flows at the computed YTM rate.

If a bond promises an 8 percent YTM, you must reinvest coupon income at 8 percent in order to realize that return. If you spend the coupon payments or you cannot find opportunities to reinvest those coupon payments at rates as high as the promised YTM, then the actual yield you earn will be less than the promised yield to maturity. The income earned on this reinvestment of the interim interest payments is referred to as **interest-on-interest**.[1]

The impact of the reinvestment assumption (i.e., the interest-on-interest earnings) on the actual return from a bond varies directly with coupon and maturity. A higher coupon and/or a longer term to maturity increase the loss in value from failure to reinvest at the YTM. This makes the reinvestment assumption more important.

Figure 10.1 illustrates the impact of interest-on-interest for an 8 percent, 25-year bond bought at par to yield 8 percent. If you invested $1,000 today at 8 percent, and reinvested all the coupon payments at 8 percent, you would have approximately $7,100 at the

[1]This concept is developed in Sidney Homer and Martin L. Leibowitz, *Inside the Yield Book* (Englewood Cliffs, N.J.: Prentice-Hall, 1972): Chapter 1.

Figure 10.1 Effect of Interest-on-Interest on Total Realized Return

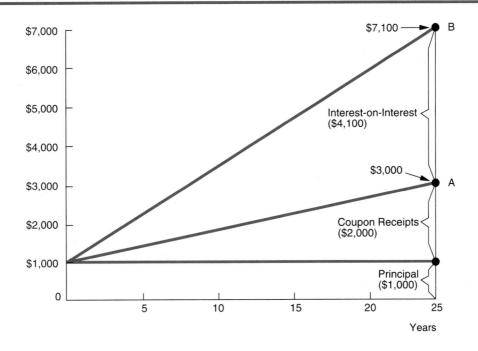

Promised yield at time of purchase: 8.00 percent; realized yield over the 25-year investment horizon with no coupon reinvestment (A): 4.50 percent; realized yield over the 25-year horizon with coupons reinvested at 8 percent (B): 8.00 percent.

end of 25 years. We will refer to this money you have at the end of your investment horizon as your **ending-wealth value.** To prove that you would have an ending-wealth value of $7,100, look up the compound interest factor for 8 percent for 25 periods (6.8493) or 4 percent for 50 periods (assuming semiannual compounding, 7.1073).

Figure 10.1 shows that this $7,100 is made up of the $1,000 principal, $2,000 in coupon payments ($80 a year for 25 years), and $4,100 in interest earned on the coupon payments reinvested at 8 percent. If you had never reinvested any of the coupon payments, you would have an ending-wealth value of only $3,000. This ending-wealth value of $3,000 derived from the beginning investment of $1,000 gives you an actual yield to maturity of only 4.5 percent. That is, the rate that will discount $3,000 back to $1,000 in 25 years is 4.5 percent. Reinvesting the coupon payments at some rate between 0 and 8 percent would place your ending-wealth position above $3,000 and below $7,100; therefore, your actual rate of return would be somewhere between 4.5 and 8 percent. Alternatively, if you man-

Ending-wealth value The total amount of money derived from investment in a bond until maturity, including principal, coupon payments, and income from reinvestment of coupon payments.

Yield illusion The erroneous expectation that a bond will provide its stated yield to maturity without recognizing the implicit reinvestment assumption related to coupon payments.

aged to reinvest the coupon payments at rates consistently above 8 percent, your ending-wealth position would be above $7,100, and your actual rate of return would be above 8 percent.

During periods of very high interest rates, you often hear investors talk about "locking in" high yields. Many of these people are subject to **yield illusion,** because they do not realize that attaining the high promised yields requires that they reinvest all the coupon payments at the same very high yields. As an example, if you buy a 20-year bond with a promised yield to maturity of 15 percent, you can actually realize the 15 percent yield *only* if you reinvest all the coupon payments at 15 percent over the next 20 years.

Computing Promised Yield to Maturity You can compute promised yield to maturity in two ways: finding an approximate annual yield or using the present value model with semiannual compounding.[2] The present value model gives more accurate results and it is the technique used by investment professionals.

The approximate promised yield (APY) measure is easy to calculate, as follows:

$$(10.4) \qquad APY = \frac{C_t + \dfrac{P_p - P_m}{n}}{\dfrac{P_p + P_m}{2}}$$

where:

P_p = par value of the bond
 n = number of years to maturity
C_t = annual coupon of the bond
P_m = current market price of the bond

This approximate value for promised yield to maturity assumes that interest is compounded annually, and it does not require the multiple computations of the present value model. An 8 percent bond with 20 years remaining to maturity and a current price of $900 has an approximate yield of 8.95 percent:

$$APY = \frac{80 + \dfrac{1,000 - 900}{20}}{\dfrac{1,000 + 900}{2}} = \frac{80 + 5}{950}$$

$$= 8.95 \text{ percent}$$

The present value model provides a more accurate promised yield to maturity value. To be consistent with actual practice, we also assume semiannual compounding. Equation 10.5 shows this version of the promised yield valuation model:

$$(10.5) \qquad P_m = \sum_{t=1}^{2n} \frac{C_t/2}{(1 + i/2)^t} + \frac{P_p}{(1 + i/2)^{2n}}$$

All variables are as described previously. This formula reflects the semiannual interest payments. You adjust for these semiannual payments by doubling the number of periods (two times the number of years to maturity) and dividing the annual coupon value in half.

This model is more accurate than the approximate promised yield model, but it is also more complex because the solution requires iteration. The present value equation is a variation of the internal rate of return (IRR) calculation, where we want to find the discount rate (i) that will equate the present value of the stream of coupon receipts (C_t) and the principal value (P_p) with the current market price of the bond (P_m). Using the prior example of an 8 percent, 20-year bond priced at $900, the equation gives us a semiannual promised yield to maturity of 4.545 percent, which implies an annual YTM of 9.09 percent:[3]

$$900 = 40\sum_{t=1}^{40} \frac{1}{(1.04545)^t} + 1,000\frac{1}{(1.04545)^{40}}$$

$$= 40(18.2840) + 1,000(0.1690)$$

The values for $1/(1 + i)$ were taken from the present value interest factor tables in the appendix at the back of the book using interpolation.

Comparing the results of Equation 10.5 with those of the approximate promised yield computation, you find a variation of 14 basis points. As a rule, the approximate promised yield tends to understate the present value promised yield for issues selling below par value (i.e., trading at a discount), and to overstate the promised yield for a bond selling at a premium. The size of the differential varies directly with the length of the holding period. Although the estimated yield values differ, the rankings of yields estimated using the APY formula (Equation 10.4) will generally be identical to those determined by the present value method.

---

[2]You can compute promised YTM assuming annual compounding, but practitioners use semiannual compounding because the interest cash flows arrive semiannually. Even when the cash flows are not semiannual, bond analysts use the assumption for calculating the yield. Therefore, all our calculations employ this assumption.

[3]Recall from your corporate finance studies that you would start with one rate (e.g., 9 percent or 4.5 percent semiannual) and compute the value of the stream. In this example, the value would exceed $900, so you would select successively higher rates until you found a present value for the stream of cash flows below $900. Given the discount rates above and below the true rate, you would do further calculations or interpolate between the two rates to the correct discount rate that would give you a value of $900.

Promised Yield to Call

Although investors use promised YTM to value most bonds, they must estimate the return on certain callable bonds with a different measure—**promised yield to call** (YTC). Whenever a bond with a call feature is selling for a price above par (i.e., at a premium) equal to or greater than its par value plus 1 year's interest, a bond investor should value the bond in terms of YTC rather than YTM. The reason is that the marketplace uses the lowest, most conservative yield measure in pricing a bond. When bonds are trading at or above a specified **crossover point,** which approximates the bond's par value plus 1 year's interest, the yield to call will normally provide the lowest yield measure.[4]

The price at the crossover point is important because when the bond rises this far above par, the computed YTM becomes low enough that it becomes profitable for the issuer to call the bond and finance the call by selling a new bond at the prevailing market interest rate. Therefore, YTC measures the promised rate of return the investor will receive from holding this bond until it is retired at the first available call date, that is, at the end of the deferred call period. Investors need to consider computing YTC after the issuance of numerous high-yield, high-coupon bonds because these have a high probability of being called.

Computing Promised Yield to Call Again, there are two methods for computing promised yield to call: the approximate method and the present value method. Both methods assume that you hold the bond until the first call date. In addition, the present value method also assumes that you reinvest all coupon payments at the YTC rate. The yield to call calculations are variations of Equations 10.4 and 10.5. The approximate yield to call (AYC) is computed as follows:

$$(10.6) \qquad AYC = \frac{C_t + \dfrac{P_c - P_m}{nc}}{\dfrac{P_c + P_m}{2}}$$

where:

AYC = approximate yield to call (YTC)

P_c = call price of the bond (generally equal to par value plus 1 year's interest)

P_m = market price of the bond

C_t = annual coupon payment

nc = number of years to first call date

Promised yield to call A bond's yield if held until the first available call date, with reinvestment of all coupon payments at the yield-to-call rate.

Crossover point The price at which it becomes profitable for an issuer to call a bond. Above this price, yield to call is the appropriate yield measure.

This equation is comparable to the AYM formula, except that P_c has replaced P_p in Equation 10.4, and nc has replaced n.

To find the AYC of a 12 percent, 20-year bond that is trading at 115 ($1,150) with 5 years remaining to first call and a call price of 112 ($1,120), we substitute these values into Equation 10.6:

$$AYC = \frac{120 + \dfrac{1,120 - 1,150}{5}}{\dfrac{1,120 + 1,150}{2}} = 10.04 \text{ percent}$$

This bond's YTC is approximately 10.04 percent, assuming that issue will be called after 5 years at the call price of 112. To confirm that yield to call is the more conservative and more accurate value for a bond you expect to be called in 5 years, you can compute the approximate promised YTM. Equation 10.3 gives a promised YTM of 10.47 percent.

To compute YTC by the present value method, we would adjust the semiannual present value equation (Equation 10.5) to give:

$$(10.7) \qquad P_m = \sum_{t=1}^{2nc} \frac{C_t/2}{(1 + i/2)^t} + \frac{P_c}{(1 + i/2)^{2nc}}$$

where:

P_m = market price of the bond

C_t = annual coupon payment

nc = number of years to first call

P_c = call price of the bond

Following the present value method, we solve for i, which typically requires several computations or extrapolation to get the exact yield.

---

[4]For a discussion of the crossover point, see Homer and Leibowitz, *Inside the Yield Book:* Chapter 4.

Realized yield The expected compounded yield on a bond that is sold before it matures assuming the reinvestment of all cash flows at an explicit rate.

Realized Yield

The final measure of bond yield, **realized yield,** measures the expected rate of return of a bond that is sold prior to its maturity. In terms of the equation, the investor has a holding period (hp) less than n. Using realized yield, we can estimate the rates of return attainable from various trading strategies. This computation requires that the investor estimate the expected selling price of the bond at liquidation. This technique can also help investors measure their actual yields after selling bonds.

Computing Realized Yield   Realized yield requires a variation on the promised yield equations (Equations 10.4 or 10.5). The approximate realized yield (ARY) is calculated as follows:

$$(10.8) \qquad ARY = \frac{C_t + \dfrac{P_f - P_m}{hp}}{\dfrac{P_f + P_m}{2}}$$

where:

ARY = approximate realized yield
C_t = annual coupon payment
P_f = future selling price of the bond
P_m = market price of the bond
hp = holding period of the bond in years

Again, the same two variables change: the holding period (hp) replaces n, and P_f replaces P_p. Keep in mind that P_f is not a contractual value, but is calculated by defining the years remaining to maturity as n − hp, and by estimating a future market interest rate, i. We describe the computation of the future selling price (P_f) in the next section.

Once we determine hp and P_f, we can calculate the approximate realized yield. Assume that you acquired an 8 percent, 20-year bond for $750. Over the next 2 years you expect interest rates to decline. As we know, when interest rates decline, bond prices increase. Suppose you anticipate that the bond price will rise to $900. The approximate realized yield in this case would be:

$$ARY = \frac{80 + \dfrac{900 - 750}{2}}{\dfrac{900 + 750}{2}} = 18.79 \text{ percent}$$

This high estimate of realized yield reflects your expectation of a substantial capital gain in a fairly short period of time.

Similarly, the substitution of P_f and hp into the present value model provides the following realized yield model:

$$(10.9) \qquad P_m = \sum_{t=1}^{2hp} \frac{C_t/2}{(1 + i/2)^t} + \frac{P_f}{(1 + i/2)^{2hp}}$$

Again, this present value model requires that you solve for i to equate the expected cash flows from coupon payments and the estimated selling price to the current market price. Because of the usually small number of periods in hp, the added accuracy of this measure is somewhat marginal. It has been suggested that because realized yield measures are based on an uncertain future selling price, the approximate realized yield method is appropriate under many circumstances. To measure historical performance, you should use the more accurate present value model.

Investors commonly calculate yields to compare bonds and estimate potential returns. In this section, we discussed five yield values, including two (nominal yield and current yield) that are used for description rather than investment decisions. The remaining three yields (promised YTM, promised YTC, and realized yield) are all based upon the present value model and require certain assumptions about the investor's holding period and the reinvestment rate earned on coupon cash flows. We demonstrated that it is possible to compute these last three yields either by a fairly easy approximate method or by the present value model, which is more accurate, but also requires more computations.

Calculating Bond Prices

On several occasions we have discussed the fact that a bond's calculated price varies with the discount rate. This leads to the very important concept that bond prices move inversely to interest rates. You must keep this in mind when valuing individual bonds or making bond portfolio decisions.

In two instances, you will need to calculate dollar prices for bonds. First, when computing realized yield to determine the future selling price P_f, and second, when issues are quoted by practitioners and in financial publications on a promised yield basis, as with municipals. You can convert a yield-based quote to a dollar price through Equation 10.5 simply and without the need for iteration. You only need to solve Equation 10.5 for P_m. The coupon (C_t) is given, as are the par value (P_p), and the promised YTM (i) that functions as the discount rate.

Consider a 10 percent, 25-year bond with a promised YTM of 12 percent. You would compute the price of this issue as:

$$P_m = 100/2 \sum_{t=1}^{50} \frac{1}{\left(1 + \frac{0.120}{2}\right)} + 1,000 \frac{1}{\left(1 + \frac{0.120}{2}\right)^{50}}$$

$$= 50(15.7619) + 1,000(0.0543)$$

$$= \$842.40$$

In this instance, we are determining the prevailing market price of the bond based upon the market YTM. These market figures give us the consensus of all investors regarding the value of this bond. An individual investor whose required rate of return on this bond differed from the market YTM would estimate a different value for the bond.

In contrast to the current market price, you would compute a future price (P_f) when estimating realized yield performance of alternative bonds. Investors or portfolio managers who consistently trade bonds for capital gains need to compute expected realized yield rather than promised yield. They would compute P_f through the following variation of the realized yield equation:

$$(10.10) \qquad P_f = \sum_{t=1}^{2n-2hp} \frac{C_t/2}{(1 + i/2)^t} + \frac{P_p}{(1 + i/2)^{2n-2hp}}$$

where:

P_f = estimated future price of the bond

P_p = par value of the bond

n = number of years to maturity

hp = holding period of the bond in years

C_t = annual coupon payment

i = expected market YTM at the end of the holding period

Equation 10.10 is a version of the present value model that calculates the expected price of the bond at the end of the holding period (hp). The term $2n - 2hp$ equals the bond's remaining term to maturity at the end of the investor's holding period, that is, the number of 6-month periods remaining until the bond's maturity at the time it is sold. Therefore, the determination of P_f is based upon four variables: two that are known and two that must be estimated.

Specifically, the coupon (C_t) and the par value (P_p) are given. The investor must forecast the length of the holding period, and therefore the number of years remaining to maturity at the time the bond is sold (n − hp). The investor must also forecast the expected market YTM at the time of sale (i). With this information you can calculate the future price of the bond. The real difficulty (and the potential source of error) in estimating (P_f) lies in predicting hp and i.

Assume you bought the 10 percent, 25-year bond just discussed at $842, giving it a YTM of 12 percent. Based upon an analysis of the economy and the capital market, you expect this bond's market YTM to decline to 8 percent in 5 years. Therefore, you want to compute its future price (P_f) at the end of year 5 to estimate your expected rate of return, assuming you are correct in your assessment of the decline in overall market interest rates. As noted, you estimate the holding period (5 years, which implies a remaining life of 20 years), and the market YTM of 8 percent. A semiannual model gives a future price of:

$$P_f = 50 \sum_{t=1}^{40} \frac{1}{(1.04)^t} + 1,000 \times \frac{1}{(1.04)^{40}}$$

$$= 50 (19.7928) + 1,000 (0.2083)$$

$$= 989.64 + 208.30$$

$$= \$1,197.94$$

Based upon this estimate of the selling price, you would estimate the approximate realized yield on this investment on an annual basis as:

$$APY = \frac{100 + \frac{1,198 - 842}{5}}{\frac{1,198 + 842}{2}}$$

$$= \frac{100 + 71.20}{1020}$$

$$= 0.1678$$

$$= 16.78 \text{ percent}$$

Fully taxable equivalent yield A yield on a tax-exempt bond that adjusts for its tax benefits to allow comparisons with taxable bonds.

Yield Adjustments for Tax-Exempt Bonds

Municipal bonds, Treasury issues, and many agency obligations possess one common characteristic: their interest income is partially or fully tax-exempt. This tax-exempt status affects evaluation of taxable versus nontaxable bonds. Although you could adjust each present value equation for tax effects, it is not necessary for our purposes. We can envision the approximate impact of such an adjustment, however, by computing the fully taxable equivalent yield, which is one of the most often cited measures of performance for municipal bonds.

The **fully taxable equivalent yield** (FTEY) adjusts the promised yield computation for the bond's tax-exempt status. To compute the FTEY, we determine the promised yield on a tax exempt bond using one of the yield formulas and then adjust the result to reflect the equivalent rate of return

Figure 10.2 ***Samples from a Yield Book***

A — YEARS and MONTHS — 8%

Yield	14-6	15-0	15-6	16-0	16-6	17-0	17-6	18-0
4.00	143.69	144.79	145.88	146.94	147.98	149.00	150.00	150.98
4.20	140.96	141.97	142.97	143.95	144.91	145.84	146.76	147.66
4.40	138.29	139.23	140.14	141.04	141.92	142.78	143.62	144.44
4.60	135.69	136.55	137.39	138.21	139.01	139.80	140.56	141.31
4.80	133.15	133.94	134.71	135.46	136.19	136.90	137.60	138.28
5.00	130.68	131.40	132.09	132.77	133.44	134.09	134.72	135.33
5.20	128.27	128.92	129.55	130.16	130.76	131.35	131.92	132.47
5.40	125.91	126.50	127.07	127.62	128.16	128.69	129.20	129.70
5.60	123.62	124.14	124.65	125.15	125.63	126.10	126.55	127.00
5.80	121.38	121.84	122.30	122.74	123.16	123.58	123.98	124.38
6.00	119.19	119.60	120.00	120.39	120.77	121.13	121.49	121.83
6.10	118.11	118.50	118.87	119.24	119.59	119.93	120.26	120.59
6.20	117.05	117.41	117.76	118.10	118.43	118.75	119.06	119.36
6.30	116.01	116.34	116.67	116.98	117.29	117.58	117.87	118.15
6.40	114.97	115.28	115.58	115.88	116.16	116.43	116.70	116.96
6.50	113.95	114.24	114.51	114.78	115.05	115.30	115.54	115.78
6.60	112.94	113.20	113.46	113.71	113.95	114.18	114.40	114.62
6.70	111.94	112.18	112.42	112.64	112.86	113.07	113.28	113.48
6.80	110.95	111.17	111.39	111.59	111.79	111.99	112.17	112.35
6.90	109.98	110.18	110.37	110.56	110.74	110.91	111.08	111.24
7.00	109.02	109.20	109.37	109.53	109.70	109.85	110.00	110.15
7.10	108.07	108.22	108.38	108.52	108.67	108.80	108.94	109.07
7.20	107.13	107.27	107.40	107.53	107.65	107.77	107.89	108.00
7.30	106.20	106.32	106.43	106.54	106.65	106.75	106.85	106.95
7.40	105.28	105.38	105.48	105.57	105.66	105.75	105.83	105.92
7.50	104.37	104.46	104.54	104.61	104.69	104.76	104.83	104.90
7.60	103.48	103.54	103.61	103.67	103.73	103.78	103.84	103.89
7.70	102.59	102.64	102.69	102.73	102.78	102.82	102.86	102.90
7.80	101.72	101.75	101.78	101.81	101.84	101.87	101.89	101.92
7.90	100.85	100.87	100.88	100.90	100.91	100.93	100.94	100.95
8.00	100.00	100.00	100.00	100.00	100.00	100.00	100.00	100.00
8.10	99.16	99.14	99.13	99.11	99.10	99.09	99.07	99.06
8.20	98.32	98.29	98.26	98.24	98.21	98.18	98.16	98.14
8.30	97.50	97.45	97.41	97.37	97.33	97.29	97.26	97.22
8.40	96.68	96.62	96.57	96.51	96.46	96.41	96.37	96.32
8.50	95.88	95.81	95.74	95.67	95.61	95.55	95.49	95.43
8.60	95.08	95.00	94.91	94.84	94.76	94.69	94.62	94.56
8.70	94.29	94.20	94.10	94.01	93.93	93.85	93.77	93.69
8.80	93.52	93.41	93.30	93.20	93.10	93.01	92.92	92.84
8.90	92.75	92.63	92.51	92.40	92.29	92.19	92.09	92.00
9.00	91.99	91.86	91.73	91.61	91.49	91.38	91.27	91.17
9.10	91.24	91.09	90.96	90.82	90.70	90.57	90.46	90.35
9.20	90.50	90.34	90.19	90.05	89.91	89.78	89.66	89.54
9.30	89.76	89.60	89.44	89.29	89.14	89.00	88.87	88.74
9.40	89.04	88.86	88.69	88.53	88.38	88.23	88.09	87.96
9.50	88.32	88.13	87.96	87.79	87.62	87.47	87.32	87.18
9.60	87.61	87.42	87.23	87.05	86.88	86.72	86.56	86.42
9.70	86.91	86.71	86.51	86.32	86.15	85.98	85.81	85.66
9.80	86.22	86.01	85.80	85.61	85.42	85.24	85.08	84.91
9.90	85.54	85.31	85.10	84.90	84.70	84.52	84.35	84.18
10.00	84.86	84.63	84.41	84.20	84.00	83.81	83.63	83.45
10.20	83.53	83.28	83.05	82.82	82.61	82.41	[illegible]	82.03
10.40	82.23	81.97	81.72	81.48	81.25	81.04	80.84	80.64
10.60	80.96	80.68	80.42	80.17	79.93	79.71	79.50	79.29
10.80	79.72	79.43	79.15	78.89	78.64	78.41	78.19	77.98
11.00	78.50	78.20	77.91	77.64	77.39	77.14	76.91	76.70
11.20	77.31	77.00	76.71	76.43	76.16	75.91	75.67	75.45
11.40	76.15	75.83	75.52	75.24	74.96	74.70	74.46	74.23
11.60	75.02	74.68	74.37	74.07	73.79	73.53	73.28	73.04
11.80	73.90	73.56	73.24	72.94	72.65	72.38	72.13	71.89
12.00	72.82	72.47	72.14	71.83	71.54	71.26	71.00	70.76

8% — YEARS and MONTHS — **B**

Yield	18-6	19-0	19-6	20-0	20-6	21-0	21-6	22-0
4.00	151.94	152.88	153.81	154.71	155.60	156.47	157.32	158.16
4.20	148.54	149.40	150.25	151.08	151.89	152.68	153.46	154.22
4.40	145.24	146.03	146.80	147.56	148.29	149.02	149.72	150.41
4.60	142.05	142.76	143.46	144.15	144.82	145.47	146.11	146.74
4.80	138.95	139.60	140.23	140.85	141.45	142.05	142.62	143.19
5.00	135.94	136.52	137.10	137.65	138.20	138.73	139.25	139.76
5.20	133.02	133.54	134.06	134.56	135.05	135.52	135.99	136.44
5.40	130.18	130.65	131.11	131.56	132.00	132.42	132.84	133.24
5.60	127.43	127.85	128.26	128.66	129.04	129.42	129.79	130.14
5.80	124.78	125.13	125.49	125.84	126.18	126.51	126.84	127.15
6.00	122.17	122.49	122.81	123.11	123.41	123.70	123.98	124.25
6.10	120.90	121.20	121.50	121.78	122.06	122.33	122.59	122.84
6.20	119.65	119.93	120.21	120.47	120.73	120.98	121.22	121.46
6.30	118.42	118.68	118.93	119.18	119.42	119.65	119.87	120.09
6.40	117.21	117.45	117.68	117.91	118.13	118.34	118.55	118.75
6.50	116.01	116.23	116.45	116.66	116.86	117.05	117.24	117.43
6.60	114.83	115.04	115.23	115.42	115.61	115.79	115.96	116.13
6.70	113.67	113.86	114.04	114.21	114.38	114.54	114.70	114.85
6.80	112.53	112.69	112.86	113.01	113.17	113.31	113.46	113.59
6.90	111.40	111.55	111.70	111.84	111.97	112.11	112.23	112.36
[illegible]	110.29	110.42	110.55	[illegible]	110.80	110.92	111.03	111.14
7.10	109.19	109.31	109.42	109.54	109.64	109.75	109.85	109.94
[illegible]	108.11	108.21	108.31	108.41	108.50	108.60	108.68	108.77
7.30	107.04	107.13	107.22	107.30	107.38	107.46	107.54	107.61
7.40	105.99	106.07	106.14	106.21	106.28	106.35	106.41	106.47
7.50	104.96	105.02	105.08	105.14	105.19	105.25	105.30	105.35
7.60	103.94	103.99	104.03	104.08	104.12	104.16	104.20	104.24
7.70	102.93	102.97	103.00	103.04	103.07	103.10	103.13	103.16
7.80	101.94	101.96	101.99	102.01	102.03	102.05	102.07	102.09
7.90	100.96	100.98	100.99	101.00	101.01	101.02	101.03	101.04
8.00	100.00	100.00	100.00	100.00	100.00	100.00	100.00	100.00
8.10	99.05	99.04	99.03	99.02	99.01	99.00	98.99	98.98
8.20	98.11	98.09	98.07	98.05	98.03	98.01	97.99	97.98
8.30	97.19	97.16	97.13	97.10	97.07	97.04	97.01	96.99
8.40	96.28	96.24	96.20	96.16	96.12	96.08	96.05	96.02
8.50	95.38	95.33	95.28	95.23	95.19	95.14	95.10	95.06
8.60	94.49	94.43	94.37	94.32	94.26	94.21	94.16	94.12
8.70	93.62	93.55	93.48	93.42	93.36	93.30	93.24	93.19
8.80	92.76	92.68	92.60	92.53	92.46	92.40	92.34	92.28
8.90	91.91	91.82	91.74	91.66	91.58	91.51	91.44	91.38
9.00	91.07	90.98	90.89	90.80	90.72	90.64	90.56	90.49
9.10	90.24	90.14	90.04	89.95	89.86	89.78	89.70	89.62
9.20	89.43	89.32	89.21	89.11	89.02	88.93	88.84	88.76
9.30	88.62	88.51	88.40	88.29	88.19	88.09	88.00	87.91
9.40	87.83	87.71	87.59	87.48	87.37	87.27	87.17	87.08
9.50	87.05	86.92	86.79	86.68	86.57	86.46	86.36	86.26
9.60	86.27	86.14	86.01	85.89	85.77	85.66	85.55	85.45
9.70	85.51	85.37	85.24	85.11	84.99	84.87	84.76	84.66
9.80	84.76	84.62	84.48	84.34	84.22	84.10	83.98	83.87
9.90	84.02	83.87	83.72	83.59	83.46	83.33	83.21	83.10
10.00	83.29	83.13	82.98	82.84	82.71	82.58	82.45	82.34
10.20	81.86	81.69	81.53	81.38	81.24	81.10	80.97	80.85
10.40	80.46	80.28	80.12	79.96	79.81	79.67	79.53	79.40
10.60	79.10	78.92	78.74	78.58	78.42	78.28	78.13	78.00
10.80	77.78	77.59	77.41	77.24	77.08	76.92	76.78	76.64
11.00	76.49	76.29	76.11	75.93	75.76	75.61	75.46	75.31
11.20	75.23	75.03	74.84	74.66	74.49	74.33	74.17	74.03
11.40	74.01	73.80	73.61	73.42	73.25	73.08	72.93	72.78
11.60	72.82	72.61	72.41	72.22	72.04	71.87	71.71	71.56
11.80	71.66	71.44	71.24	71.05	70.87	70.70	70.53	70.38
12.00	70.53	70.31	70.10	69.91	69.72	69.55	69.39	69.23

Source: Reproduced with permission from Expanded Bond Values Publication #83, pp. 879–880, copyright © 1970 Financial Publishing Co., Boston, Mass.

that must be earned on a fully taxable issue. It is measured as:

$$(10.11) \qquad FTEY = \frac{i}{1 - T}$$

where:

 i = promised yield on the tax exempt bond
 T = amount and type of the tax exemption

The FTEY equation has some limitations. It is applicable only to par bonds or current coupon obligations, such as new issues, because the measure considers only interest income, ignoring capital gains. Therefore, it cannot give values for issues trading at a significant variation from par value.

Bond Yield Books

Collections of bond value tables, commonly known as *bond books* or *yield books*, can eliminate most of the calculations for bond valuation. Figure 10.2 reproduces a page from such a yield book. Like a present value interest factor table, a bond yield table provides a matrix of bond prices for stated coupon rates, various terms to maturity (on the horizontal axis), and promised yields (on the vertical axis). Such a table allows you to determine either the promised yield or the price of a bond.

The example at the left of the figure indicates that a $17\frac{1}{2}$-year, 8 percent coupon bond yielding 10 percent would be priced at 83.63. Likewise, the example at right shows that a 20-year issue priced at 109.54 would have a promised yield to maturity of 7.10 percent. As might be expected, access to sophisticated calculators or computers has substantially reduced the need for and use of yield books.

To truly understand the meanings of yield measures, however, you must master the present value model and its variations that generate values for promised YTM, promised YTC, realized yield, and bond prices.

What Determines Interest Rates?

Now that we have learned to calculate various yields on bonds, the question of the causes of differences and changes in yields over time arises. Market interest rates cause these effects because the interest rates reported in the media are simply the prevailing YTMs for the bonds being discussed. For example, when you

hear on TV that the interest rate on long-term government bonds declined from 8.40 to 8.32 percent, this means that the price of this particular bond increased such that the computed YTM at the former price was 8.40 percent, but the computed YTM at the new, higher price is 8.32 percent. Yields and interest rates are the same. They are different terms for the same concept.

We have discussed the inverse relationship between bond prices and interest rates. When interest rates decline, the prices of bonds increase; when interest rates rise, bond prices decline. It is natural to ask which of these is the driving force, bond prices or bond interest rates? It is a simultaneous change, and you can envision either factor causing it. Most practitioners probably envision the changes in interest rates as causes because they constantly use interest rates to describe changes. They use interest rates because these rates are comparable across bonds, while the price of a bond depends not only on the interest rate, but also upon its specific characteristics including its coupon and maturity. The point is, when you change the interest rate (yield) on a bond, you simultaneously change its price in the opposite direction.

Understanding interest rates and what makes them change is necessary for an investor who hopes to maximize returns from investing in bonds. Therefore, in this section we will review our prior discussion of the following topics: what causes overall market interest rates to rise and fall, why alternative bonds have different rates, and why the differences in rates between alternative bonds change over time. To accomplish this, we begin with a general discussion of the influences on interest rates, and then consider the term structure of interest rates (shown by yield curves), which relates the interest rates on bonds to their terms to maturity. The term structure is important because it reflects what investors expect to happen to interest rates in the future and also dictates their current risk attitudes. Finally, we turn to the concept of yield spreads which measure the differences in yields between alternative bonds. We will describe various yield spreads and also explore changes in them over time.

Forecasting Interest Rates

As discussed, the ability to forecast interest rates and changes in these rates is critical to successful bond investing. While subsequent presentations consider the major determinants of interest rates, you should

Figure 10.3 *International 10-Year Government Bond Yields*

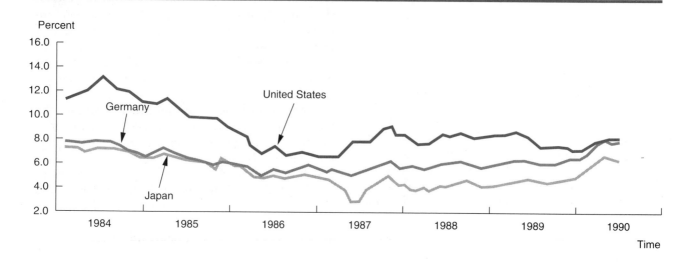

Sources: Federal Reserve Bank, Telerate Service; *Economic Outlook and Chartbook* (New York: Kidder, Peabody & Co., July 1990).

keep in mind that interest rates are the price for loanable funds. Like any price, they depend on the supply and demand for these funds. On one side investors are willing to provide the funds (the supply) at prices based upon their required rates of return for a particular borrower. On the other side borrowers need the funds (the demand) to support budget deficits (governments) or to invest in capital projects (corporations).

Although the lenders and borrowers provide some fundamental determinants of supply and demand curves, the prices for these funds (interest rates) are also affected for short time periods by events that shift the curves such as major government bond issues that affect demand, or significant changes in Federal Reserve monetary policy that affect the supply of money.

Our treatment of interest rate forecasting recognizes that you must be aware of the basic determinants of interest rates and monitor these factors. We also recognize that detailed forecasting of interest rates is a very complex task that is best left to professional economists. Therefore, our goal as bond investors and portfolio managers is to monitor current and expected interest rate behavior. We should continuously assess the major factors that affect interest rate behavior but also rely on others, such as economic consulting firms, banks, or investment banking firms, for detailed insights on topics like the real RFR and the expected

rate of inflation.[5] This is precisely the way most bond portfolio managers operate.

Fundamental Determinants of Interest Rates

As shown in Figure 10.3, average interest rates for long-term U.S. government bonds during 1984 reached almost 14 percent. By early 1987 this bond rate had dropped to under 8 percent. In contrast, the rate on Japanese government bonds peaked at slightly under 8 percent in 1984, dropped to about 3 percent in mid-1987, and rose to almost 8 percent again in 1990. As a bond investor you need to know why interest rates behaved this way.

As you know from your knowledge of bond pricing, bond prices increased dramatically during periods when market interest rates dropped, and some bond investors experienced very attractive returns. In contrast, some investors experienced substantial losses during several periods when interest rates increased. A casual analysis of this chart, which covers only about

[5]Sources of information on the bond market and interest rate forecasts would include Merrill-Lynch's *Fixed Income Weekly* and *World Bond Market Monitor*, Goldman, Sachs' *Financial Market Perspectives*, and Kidder, Peabody & Co.'s *Economic Outlook and Chartbook* and *Capital Market Report*.

6 years, indicates the need for monitoring interest rates. Essentially, the factors causing interest rates (i) to rise or fall are described by the following model:

(10.12) $i = RFR + I + RP$

where:

RFR = real risk-free rate of interest
  I = expected rate of inflation
 RP = risk premium

This relationship should be familiar from our presentations in Chapters 1 and 8. Equation 10.12 is a simple, but complete statement of interest rate behavior. It is more difficult to estimate the future behavior of such variables as real growth, expected inflation, and economic uncertainty. In this regard, interest rates, like stock prices, are extremely difficult to forecast with any degree of accuracy.[6] Alternatively, we can visualize the source of changes in interest rates in terms of economic conditions and issue characteristics that determine the required rate of return on a bond:

$i = f$ (Economic forces + Issue characteristics)
  $= (RFR + I) + RP$

This rearranged version of Equation 10.12 helps us to isolate the determinants of interest rates.[7]

The real risk-free rate of interest (RFR) is the economic cost of money, that is, the opportunity cost necessary to compensate individuals for foregoing consumption. As discussed previously, it is determined by the real growth rate of the economy with short-run effects due to ease or tightness in the capital market.

The expected rate of inflation is the other economic influence on interest rates. We add the expected level of inflation (I) to the real risk-free rate (RFR) to specify the nominal RFR, which is a market rate like the current rate on government T-bills. Given the stability of the real RFR, it is clear that the wide swings in interest rates during the 6 years covered by Figure 10.3 occurred because expected inflation changed.[8] Besides the unique country risk and exchange rate risk we discuss in the section on risk premiums, differences in rates of inflation between countries have a major impact on their levels of interest rates. To sum up, one way to estimate the nominal RFR is to begin with the real growth rate of the economy, adjust for short-run ease or tightness in the capital market, and then adjust this real rate of interest for the expected rate of inflation.

In another approach to estimating the nominal rate or changes in the rate, the macroeconomic view, the supply and demand for loanable funds are the fundamental economic determinants of i. As the supply of loanable funds increases, the level of interest rates declines, other things being equal. Several factors influence the supply of funds. Government monetary policies have a significant impact on the supply of money. The savings pattern of U.S. and non-U.S. investors also affects the supply of funds. Non-U.S. investors have become a stronger influence on the U.S. supply of loanable funds during recent years, as shown by the significant purchases of U.S. securities by non-U.S. investors, most notably the Japanese. It is widely acknowledged that this foreign addition to the supply of funds has been very beneficial to the United States in terms of reducing our interest rates and cost of capital.

Interest rates increase when the demand for loanable funds increases. The demand for loanable funds is affected by the capital and operating needs of the U.S. government, federal agencies, state and local governments, corporations, institutions, and individuals. Federal budget deficits increase the Treasury's demand for loanable funds. Likewise, the level of consumer demand for funds to buy houses, autos, and appliances affects rates, as does corporate demand for funds to pursue investment opportunities. The total for all groups determines the aggregate demand and supply of loanable funds and the level of the nominal RFR.[9]

[6]For an overview of interest rate forecasting, see W. David Woolford, "Forecasting Interest Rates," in *The Handbook of Fixed-Income Securities*, 3d ed., ed. by Frank J. Fabozzi (Homewood, Ill.: Business One Irwin, 1991); and Frank J. Jones and Benjamin Wolkowitz, "The Determinants of Interest Rates on Fixed-Income Securities," in *The Financial Analysts Handbook*, 2d ed., ed. by Sumner N. Levine (Homewood, Ill.: Dow Jones-Irwin, 1988).

[7]For an extensive exploration of interest rates and interest rate behavior, see James C. Van Horne, *Financial Market Rates and Flows*, 3d ed. (Englewood Cliffs, N.J.: Prentice-Hall, 1989).

[8]In this regard, see R. W. Hafer, "Inflation: Assessing Its Recent Behavior and Future Prospects," *Federal Reserve Bank of St. Louis Review* 65, no. 7 (August–September 1983): 36–41.

[9]For an example of the estimate of the supply and demand for funds in the economy, see *Prospects for Financial Markets in 1991* (New York: Salomon Bros., 1990). This annual publication of Salomon Brothers estimates the flow of funds in the economy and discusses its effect on various currencies and interest rates, making recommendations for portfolio strategy on the basis of these expectations.

The interest rate of a specific bond issue is influenced not only by all of these factors that affect the nominal RFR, but also by its characteristics. This influence is measured by the risk premium (RP). The economic forces that determine the nominal RFR affect all securities, while issue characteristics are unique to individual securities, market sectors, or countries. Thus, the differences in the yields of corporate and Treasury bonds are not caused by economic forces, but rather by different issue characteristics that cause differences in risk premiums.

Bond investors separate the risk premium into four components:

1. The quality of the issue as determined by its risk of default relative to other bonds
2. The term to maturity, which can affect yield and price volatility
3. Indenture provisions, including collateral, call features, and sinking-fund provisions
4. Foreign bond risk, including exchange rate risk and country risk

Of these four forces, quality and maturity have the greatest impact on the risk premium, although exchange rate risk and country risk are important components of risk for non-U.S. bonds.

Quality of a bond reflects the ability of the issuer to service outstanding debt obligations. This information is largely captured in the ratings issued by the bond rating firms. As a result, bonds with different ratings have different yields. For example, AAA-rated obligations offer lower risk of default than BBB obligations, so they can provide lower yields. Researchers studying differences in the risk premiums prevailing at a point in time have found them to be largely dependent upon the intrinsic characteristics of the issuers.

At the same time, the risk premium differences between bonds of different quality levels have changed substantially over time depending upon prevailing economic conditions. When the economy experiences a recession or a period of economic uncertainty, the desire for quality increases, and investors bid up prices of higher-rated bonds, which reduces their yields. This variability in the risk premium over time was demonstrated and discussed in Chapter 8.

Term to maturity also influences the risk premium because it affects an investor's level of uncertainty as well as the price volatility of the bond. In the section on the term structure of interest rates, we will discuss the positive relationship that is typical between the term to maturity of an issue and its interest rate.

As discussed in Chapter 3, indenture provisions indicate the collateral pledged for a bond, its callability, and its sinking-fund provisions. Collateral protects the investor if the issuer defaults on the bond since the investor has a specific claim on some asset in case of liquidation.

Call features indicate when an issuer can buy back the bond prior to its maturity. When a bond is called it is typically not to the advantage of the investor. Therefore, more protection against having the bond called reduces the risk premium. The significance of call protection increases during periods of high interest rates. When you buy a bond with a high coupon, you want protection from losing it when rates decline.

A sinking fund reduces the investor's risk and causes a lower yield for several reasons. First, a sinking fund reduces default risk because it requires the issuer to reduce the outstanding issue systematically. Second, repurchases of bonds by the issuer to satisfy sinking-fund provisions provide price support for the bond by boosting demand. These purchases by the issuer also contribute to a more liquid secondary market for the bond because of the increased trading. Finally, sinking-fund provisions require that the issuer retire a bond before its stated maturity which reduces the issue's average maturity. The decline in average maturity tends to reduce the risk premium of the bond much as an issue with a shorter maturity would have a lower yield.

We know that foreign currency exchange rates change over time and that this increases the risk of global investing. Differences in the variability of exchange rates among countries arise because trade balances and rates of inflation differ among countries. More volatile trade balances and inflation rates in a country make its exchange rates more volatile, which will add to the uncertainty of future exchange rates. These factors increase the risk premium due to exchange rates.

In addition to ongoing changes in exchange rates, investors are always concerned with the political and economic stability of a country. If investors are unsure about the political environment or the economic system in a country, they will increase the risk premium they require.

Figure 10.4   **Treasury Yield Curves**

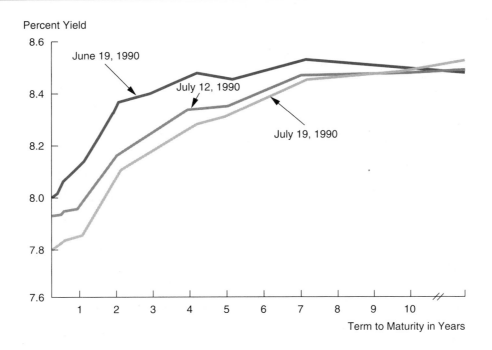

Source: "Capital Market Report," Kidder, Peabody & Co., July 20, 1990.

Term Structure of Interest Rates

The **term structure of interest rates** (which is graphically represented by the *yield curve*) is a static function that relates the term to maturity to the yield to maturity for a sample of bonds at a given time.[10] Thus, it represents a cross section of yields for a category of bonds that are comparable in all respects but their maturities. Specifically, the quality of the issues should be constant, and ideally you should focus on issues with similar coupons and call features within a single industry category. You can construct different yield curves for Treasuries, government agencies, prime-grade municipals, AAA utilities, and so on. The accuracy of the yield curve will depend upon the comparability of the bonds in the sample.

Term structure of interest rates The relationship between term to maturity and yield to maturity for a sample of comparable bonds at a given time.

As an example, Figure 10.4 shows yield curves for a sample of U.S. Treasury obligations. It is based on the yield to maturity information for a set of comparable Treasury issues from a publication like the *Federal Reserve Bulletin* or *The Wall Street Journal*. These promised yields were plotted on the graph, and a yield curve was drawn that represents the general configuration of rates. Kidder Peabody collected these data and constructed yield curves at three different points in time to demonstrate the changes in yield levels and in the shape of the yield curve over time.

All yield curves, of course, do not have the same shape as those in Figure 10.4. The point of the example is that, while individual yield curves are static, their behavior over time is quite fluid. As shown, the curves began at different levels between June 19 and July 19. Also, the shape of the yield curve can undergo

[10]For a discussion of the theory and empirical evidence, see Richard W. McEnally and James V. Jordan, "The Term Structure of Interest Rates," in *The Handbook of Fixed-Income Securities*, 3d ed., ed. by Frank J. Fabozzi (Homewood, Ill.: Business One Irwin, 1991).

Figure 10.5   *Types of Yield Curves*

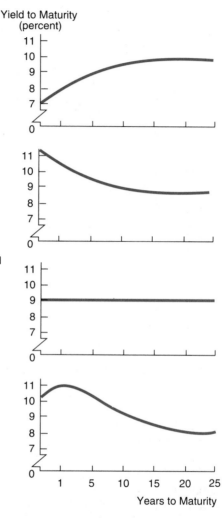

A Rising Yield Curve is formed when the yields on short-term issues are low and rise consistently with longer maturities and flatten out at the extremes.

A Declining Yield Curve is formed when the yields on short-term issues are high and yields on subsequently longer maturities decline consistently.

A Flat Yield Curve has approximately equal yields on short-term and long-term issues.

A Humped Yield Curve is formed when yields on intermediate-term issues are above those on short-term issues; and the rates on long-term issues decline to levels below those for the short-term and then level out.

dramatic alterations, following one of the four patterns shown in Figure 10.5. The ascending curve is the most common and tends to prevail when interest rates are at low or modest levels. The declining yield curve tends to accompany relatively high rates. The humped yield curve prevails when extremely high rates are expected to decline to more normal levels. The flat yield curve rarely exists for any period of time. Note that the slope of the curve tends to level off after 15 years.

Why does the term structure of interest rates as represented by yield curves assume different shapes?

Three major theories attempt to explain this: the expectations hypothesis, the liquidity preference hypothesis, and the segmented market hypothesis.

Expectations Hypothesis   According to the expectations hypothesis, the shape of the yield curve results from the interest rate expectations of market participants. More specifically, it holds that any long-term interest rate simply represents the geometric mean of current and future 1-year interest rates expected to prevail over the maturity of the issue. In essence, the term structure involves a series of intermediate and long-term interest rates, each of which is a reflection of the geometric average of current and expected 1-year interest rates. Under such conditions, the equilibrium long-term rate is the rate the long-term bond investor would expect to earn through successive investments in short-term bonds over the term to maturity of the long-term bond.

The expectations theory can explain any shape of yield curve. Expectations for rising short-term rates in the future cause an ascending yield curve; expectations for falling short-term rates in the future will cause long-term rates to lie below current short-term rates, and the yield curve will descend. Similar explanations account for flat and humped yield curves.

Consider the following explanation by the expectations hypothesis of the shape of the term structure of interest rates:

$1R_1 = 5\frac{1}{2}\%$ The 1-year rate of interest prevailing now (period t)

$t + 1R_1 = 6\%$ The 1-year rate of interest expected to prevail next year (period t + 1)

$t + 2R_1 = 7\frac{1}{2}\%$ The 1-year rate of interest expected to prevail 2 years from now (period t + 2)

$t + 3R_1 = 8\frac{1}{2}\%$ The 1-year rate of interest expected to prevail 3 years from now (period t + 3)

Using these values and the known rate on a 1-year bond, we compute rates on 2-, 3-, and 4-year bonds (designated R_2, R_3, and R_4) as follows:

$R_1 = 5\frac{1}{2}$ percent
$1R_2 = (0.055 + 0.06)/2 = 5.75$ percent
$1R_3 = (0.055 + 0.06 + 0.075)/3 = 6.33$ percent
$1R_4 = (0.055 + 0.06 + 0.075 + 0.085)/4 = 6.88$ percent

In this illustration (which uses the arithmetic average as an approximation of the geometric mean), the yield curve slopes upward because, at present, investors expect future short-term rates to be above current short-term rates. This is not the formal method for constructing the yield curve. Rather, it is constructed as demonstrated in Figure 10.3 on the basis of the prevailing promised yields for bonds with different maturities.

The expectations hypothesis attempts to explain why the yield curve is upward-sloping, downward-

sloping, humped, or flat by explaining the expectations implicit in yield curves with different shapes. The evidence is fairly substantial and convincing that the expectations hypothesis is a workable explanation of the term structure. Because of the supporting evidence, its relative simplicity, and the intuitive appeal of the theory, the expectations hypothesis of the term structure of interest rates is rather widely accepted.

The expectations hypothesis predicts a descending yield curve when interest rates are likely to fall in the future rather than rise. In such a case, long-term bonds may be attractive investments, because the investor would want to lock in prevailing higher yields (and avoid the decline in the future) or capture the increase in bond prices (as capital gains) that should accompany a decline in rates. This means that investor expectations reinforce the predicted descending shape of the yield curve as they bid up prices of long-maturity bonds (forcing yields to decline) and avoid short-term bond issues (making yields rise). These shifts between long- and short-term maturities will continue until equilibrium occurs or expectations change.

Liquidity Preference Hypothesis The theory of liquidity preference holds that long-term securities should provide higher returns than short-term obligations, since investors are willing to sacrifice some yield to avoid the higher price volatility of long-maturity bonds. Another way to interpret the liquidity preference hypothesis states that lenders prefer short-term loans, and to induce them to lend for long terms, it is necessary to offer higher yields.

The liquidity preference theory contends that uncertainty causes investors to favor short-term issues over bonds with longer maturities because short-term bonds can easily be converted into predictable amounts of cash should unforeseen events occur. This theory argues that the yield curve should slope upward and that any other shape should be viewed as a temporary aberration.

This theory is typically set forth as an extension of the expectations hypothesis since the formal liquidity preference position contends that the liquidity premium inherent in the yields for longer-maturity bonds should be added to the expected future rate to calculate long-term yields. Specifically, the liquidity premium (L) compensates the investor in long-term bonds for the added uncertainty because of less stable prices. To see how the liquidity preference theory predicts future yields and how it compares to the pure

> **Yield spread** The difference between the promised yields of alternative bond issues or market segments at a given time.

expectations hypothesis, we might predict future long-term rates from a single set of 1-year rates: 6 percent, 7.5 percent, and 8.5 percent. The liquidity preference theory would suggest that investors add increasing liquidity premiums to successive rates to derive actual market rates. As an example, they might arrive at 6.3 percent, 7.9 percent, and 9.0 percent.

As a matter of historical fact, the yield curve shows a definite upward bias, which implies that some combination of the expectations theory and the liquidity preference theory will more accurately explain the shape of the yield curve than either of them alone. Specifically, actual long-term rates consistently tend to be above what is envisioned from the pure expectations hypothesis, which implies the existence of a liquidity premium.

Segmented Market Hypothesis Despite meager empirical support, a third theory for the shape of the yield curve, the segmented market hypothesis, enjoys wide acceptance among market practitioners. Also known as the *preferred habitat theory*, the *institutional theory*, or the *hedging pressure theory*, it asserts that different institutional investors have different maturity needs that lead them to confine their security selections to specific maturity segments. That is, they focus on either short-term, intermediate-term, or long-term securities. This theory contends that the shape of the yield curve is ultimately a function of these investment policies of major financial institutions.

Financial institutions tend to structure their investment policies to suit conditions such as their tax liabilities, the types and maturity structures of their liabilities, and the level of earnings demanded by their depositors. As an example, because commercial banks are subject to normal corporate tax rates and their liabilities are generally short- to intermediate-term time and demand deposits, they consistently invest in short- to intermediate-term municipal bonds.

The segmented market theory contends that the business environment, along with legal and regulatory limitations, tends to direct each type of financial institution to allocate its resources to particular types of bonds with specific maturity characteristics. In its strongest form, it holds that the maturity preferences of investors and borrowers are so strong that investors would never purchase securities outside their preferred maturity ranges to take advantage of yield differentials. As a result, the short- and long-maturity portions of the bond market are effectively segmented, and yields for a segment depend on the supply and demand within that segment.

Trading Implications of the Term Structure Information on maturities can help you formulate yield expectations by simply observing the shape of the yield curve. If the yield curve is declining sharply, historical evidence suggests that interest rates will probably decline. Expectations theorists would suggest that you need to examine only the prevailing yield curve to predict interest rates in the future.

Based on these theories, bond investors use the prevailing yield curve to predict the shapes of future yield curves. Using these predictions and knowledge of current interest rates, investors can determine expected yield volatility by maturity sector. The maturity segments that experience the greatest yield changes give the investor the largest potential price appreciation.[11]

Yield Spreads

Another technique that can help you make good bond investments is the analysis of **yield spreads**, the differences in promised yields between bond issues or segments of the market at any point in time. Such differences are specific to the particular issues or segments of the bond market so they add to the rates determined by the basic economic forces (RFR + I).

There are four major yield spreads:

1. Different segments of the bond market may have different yields. For example, pure government bonds have lower yields than government agency bonds; government bonds have much lower yields than corporate bonds.
2. Bonds in different sectors of the same market segment may have different yields. For example, prime-grade municipal bonds will have lower yields than good-grade municipal bonds; you will find spreads between AA utilities versus BBB utilities, or AAA industrial bonds versus AAA public utility bonds.

---

[11]Gikas A. Hourdouvelis, "The Predictive Power of the Term Structure during Recent Monetary Regimes," *Journal of Finance* 43, no. 2 (June 1988): 339–356.

Table 10.1 **Selected Mean Yield Spreads (in basis points)**

Comparisons	1984	1985	1986	1987	1988	1989
1. Short governments–Long governments[a]	+10	+111	+108	+96	+72	+3
2. Long governments–Long AAA corporates[b]	+72	+62	+88	+75	+73	+68
3. Long municipals–Long AAA corporates[c]	+272	+226	+170	+174	+203	+203
4. Long AAA municipals–Long BBB municipals[d]	+77	+98	+81	+103	+47	+40
5. AA utilities–BBB utilities[e]	+88	+90	+70	+76	+74	+42
6. AA utilities–AA industrials[e]	−51	−11	+33	+19	−65	−20

[a]Median yield to maturity of a varying number of bonds with 2 to 4 years and more than 10 years to maturity, respectively.

[b]Long AAA corporates based on yields to maturity on selected long-term bonds.

[c]Long-term municipal issues based on a representative list of mixed quality municipal bonds maintaining a 20-year period to maturity.

[d]General obligation municipal bonds only.

[e]Based on a changing list of representative issues.

Source: *Federal Reserve Bulletin*, various issues; Standard & Poor's Statistical Service.

3. Different coupons or seasoning within a given market segment or sector may cause yield spreads. Examples would include current coupon government bonds versus deep-discount governments, or recently issued AA industrials versus seasoned AA industrials.

4. Different maturities within a given market segment or sector also cause differences in yields. You would see yield spreads between short-term agency issues and long-term agency issues, or 3-year prime municipals versus 25-year prime municipals.

The differences among these classes of bonds cause yield spreads, which may be either positive or negative. More important, *the magnitude or direction of a spread can change over time.* These changes in size or direction of yield spreads offer profit opportunities. We say that the spread narrows whenever the differences in yield become smaller, and it widens as the differences increase. Table 10.1 contains data on a variety of past yield spreads.

As a bond investor, you should evaluate yield spread changes because these changes influence bond price behavior and comparative return performance. You should attempt to identify (1) any normal yield spread that is expected to become abnormally wide or narrow in response to an anticipated swing in market interest rates, or (2) any abnormally wide or narrow yield spread that is expected to become normal.

Economic and market analysis would help you develop these expectations of potential yield spread changes. Taking advantage of these changes requires a knowledge of historical spreads and an ability to predict not only future total market changes, but also why and when specific spreads will change.

What Determines the Price Volatility of Bonds?

In this chapter we have learned about alternative bond yields and how to calculate them and about what determines bond yields (interest rates) and what causes them to change. Now that we understand why yields change, we can logically ask, what is the effect of these yield changes on the prices and rates of return for different bonds? We have discussed the inverse relationship between changes in yields and the prices of bonds. We can now discuss the specific factors that affect the amount of changes in price for various bonds due to given changes in interest rates.

The fact is, a given change in interest rates can cause vastly different percentage price changes for alternative bonds. This section will help you understand what causes these differences between price changes. Even if you know that interest rates will decline, in order to maximize your rate of return from this knowledge, you need to know which bonds will benefit the most from the yield change. This section will help you make this bond selection decision.

| **Bond price volatility** The percentage changes in bond prices over time.

Throughout this section, we will talk about bond price changes or bond price volatility interchangeably. A bond price change is measured as the percentage change in the price of the bond, computed as follows:

$$\frac{EPB}{BPB} - 1$$

where:

EPB = ending price of the bond

BPB = beginning price of the bond

Bond price volatility is also measured in terms of percentage changes in bond prices. A bond with high price volatility is one that experiences large percentage price changes for a given change in yields.

Bond price volatility is influenced by more than yield behavior alone. Malkiel used the bond valuation model to demonstrate that the market price of a bond is a function of four factors: (1) its par value, (2) its coupon, (3) the number of years to its maturity, and (4) the prevailing market interest rate.[12] Malkiel's mathematical proofs showed the following relationships between yield (interest rate) changes and bond price behavior:

1. Bond prices move inversely to bond yields (interest rates).
2. For a given change in yields (interest rates), longer-maturity bonds post larger price changes; thus, bond price volatility is directly related to term to maturity.
3. Price volatility (percentage price change) increases at a diminishing rate as term to maturity increases.
4. Price movements resulting from equal absolute increases or decreases in yield are not symmetrical. A decrease in yield raises bond prices by more than an increase in yield of the same amount lowers prices.
5. Higher-coupon issues show smaller percentage price fluctuations for a given change in yield; thus,

bond price volatility is inversely related to coupon.

Homer and Leibowitz showed that the absolute level of market yields also affects bond price volatility.[13] As the level of prevailing yields rises, the price volatility of bonds increases, *assuming a constant percentage change in market yields*. It is important to note that if you assume a constant percentage change in yield, the basis-point change will be larger when rates are high. For example, a 25 percent change in interest rates when rates are at 4 percent will amount to 100 basis points; the same 25 percent change when rates are at 8 percent will be a 200 basis-point change. In the discussion of bond duration, we will see that this difference in basis-point change is important.

Tables 10.2, 10.3, and 10.4 demonstrate these relationships assuming semiannual compounding. Table 10.2 demonstrates the effect of maturity on price volatility. In all four maturity classes, we assume a bond with an 8 percent coupon and a discount rate changing from 7 to 10 percent. The only difference among the four cases is the maturities of the bonds. The demonstration involves computing the value of each bond at a 7 percent yield and at a 10 percent yield and noting the percentage change in price. As shown, this change in yield caused the price of the 1-year bond to decline by only 2.9 percent, while the 30-year bond declined by almost 29 percent. Clearly, the longer-maturity bond experienced the greater price volatility.

Also, price volatility increased at a decreasing rate with maturity. When maturity doubled from 10 years to 20 years, the price increased by less than 50 percent (from 18.5 percent to 25.7 percent). A similar change occurred when going from 20 years to 30 years. Therefore, this table demonstrates the first three of our price–yield relationships: bond price is inversely related to yield, bond price volatility is positively related to term to maturity, and bond price volatility increases at a decreasing rate with maturity.

It is also possible to demonstrate the fourth relationship with this table. Using the 20-year bond, if you computed the percentage change in price related to an increase in rates (e.g., from 7 to 10 percent), you would get the answer reported—a 25.7 percent decrease. In contrast, if you computed the effect on price of a decrease in yield from 10 to 7 percent, you would get a 34.7 percent increase ($1,115 versus $828). This

---

[12]Burton G. Malkiel, "Expectations, Bond Prices, and the Term Structure of Interest Rates," *Quarterly Journal of Economics* 76, no. 2 (May 1962): 197–218.

[13]Homer and Leibowitz, *Inside the Yield Book*.

Table 10.2 *Effect of Maturity on Bond Price Volatility*

	Present Value of 8 Percent Bond ($1,000 par value)							
Term to Maturity	**1 Year**		**10 Years**		**20 Years**		**30 Years**	
Discount rate (YTM)	7%	10%	7%	10%	7%	10%	7%	10%
Present value of interest	$ 75	$ 73	$ 569	$498	$ 858	$686	$1,005	$757
Present value of principal	934	907	505	377	257	142	132	54
Total value of bond	$1,009	$980	$1,074	$875	$1,115	$828	$1,137	$811
Percentage change in total value	−2.9		−18.5		−25.7		−28.7	

Table 10.3 *Effect of Coupon on Bond Price Volatility*

	Present Value of 20-Year Bond ($1,000 par value)							
	0 Percent Coupon		**3 Percent Coupon**		**8 Percent Coupon**		**12 Percent Coupon**	
Discount rate (YTM)	7%	10%	7%	10%	7%	10%	7%	10%
Present value of interest	$ 0	$ 0	$322	$257	$ 858	$686	$1,287	$1,030
Present value of principal	257	142	257	142	257	142	257	142
Total value of bond	$257	$142	$579	$399	$1,115	$828	$1,544	$1,172
Percentage change in total value	−44.7		−31.1		−25.7		−24.1	

Table 10.4 *Effect of Yield Level on Bond Price Volatility*

	Present Value of 20-Year, 4 Percent Bond ($1,000 par value)							
	(1) Low Yields		**(2) Inter-mediate Yields**		**(3) High Yields**		**(4) 100 Basis Point Change at High Yields**	
Discount rate (YTM)	3%	4%	6%	8%	9%	12%	9%	10%
Present value of interest	$ 602	$ 547	$462	$396	$370	$301	$370	$343
Present value of principal	562	453	307	208	175	97	175	142
Total value of bond	$1,164	$1,000	$769	$604	$545	$398	$545	$485
Percentage change in total value	−14.1		−21.5		−27.0		−11.0	

> **Duration** A composite measure of the timing of a bond's cash flow characteristics taking into consideration its coupon and term to maturity.

demonstrates that prices change more in response to a decrease in rates than to a comparable increase in rates.

Table 10.3 demonstrates the coupon effect. In this set of examples, all the bonds have the same maturity (20 years) and react to the same change in YTM (from 7 to 10 percent). The table shows the inverse relationship between coupon rate and price volatility: the smallest-coupon bond (the zero) experienced the largest percentage price change (almost 45 percent), versus a 24 percent change for the 12 percent coupon bond.

Table 10.4 demonstrates the yield level effect. In these examples, all the bonds have the same 20-year maturity and the same 4 percent coupon. In the first three cases the YTM changes by a constant 33.3 percent (i.e., from 3 to 4 percent, from 6 to 8 percent, and from 9 to 12 percent). Note that the first change is 100 basis points, the second is 200 basis points, and the third is 300 basis points. The results in the first three columns confirm that when higher rates change by a constant percentage, the change in the bond price is larger.

The fourth column shows that if you assume a constant basis-point change in yields, you get the opposite results. Specifically, a 100 basis point change in yield from 3 to 4 percent provides a price change of 14.1 percent, while the same 100 basis point change from 9 to 10 percent produces a price change of only 11 percent. Therefore, the yield level effect can differ depending upon whether the yield change is a constant percentage change or a constant basis point change.

Thus, the price volatility of a bond for a given change in yield is affected by the bond's coupon, its term to maturity, the level of yields (depending on the kind of change in yield), and the direction of the yield change. However, while both the level and direction of change in yields affect price volatility, they cannot support trading strategies. When yields change, the two variables with dramatic effects on bond price volatility are coupon and maturity.

Some Trading Strategies

Knowing that coupon and maturity are the major variables that influence bond price volatility, we can de-velop some strategies for maximizing rates of return when interest rates change. Specifically, if you expect a major decline in interest rates, you know that bond prices will increase, so you want a portfolio of bonds with the maximum price volatility so that you will enjoy maximum price changes (capital gains) from the change in interest rates. In this situation, the previous discussion regarding the effect of maturity and coupon indicates that you should attempt to build a portfolio of long maturity bonds with low coupons. A portfolio of such bonds should provide the maximum price appreciation for a given decline in market interest rates.

In contrast, if you expect an increase in market interest rates, you know that bond prices will decline, and you want a portfolio with minimum price volatility to minimize the capital losses caused by the increase in rates. You would want to move your portfolio toward short-maturity bonds with high coupons. This combination should provide minimal price volatility for a change in market interest rates.

Duration Measure

Because the price volatility of a bond varies inversely with its coupon and directly with its term to maturity, it is necessary to determine the best combination of these two variables to achieve your objective. This effort would benefit from a composite measure that considered both coupon and maturity. Fortunately, such a measure, the **duration** of a security, was developed over 50 years ago by Macaulay.[14] Macaulay showed that the duration of a bond was a more appropriate measure of its time characteristics than the term to maturity, because duration takes into account both the repayment of capital at maturity and the size and timing of coupon payments prior to final maturity. Duration is defined as the weighted average time to full recovery of principal and interest payments. Using annual compounding, duration is:

$$(10.13) \qquad D = \frac{\sum_{t=1}^{n} \dfrac{C_t(t)}{(1 + i)^t}}{\sum_{t=1}^{n} \dfrac{C_t}{(1 + i)^t}}$$

[14]Frederick R. Macaulay, *Some Theoretical Problems Suggested by the Movements of Interest Rates, Bond Yields, and Stock Prices in the United States since 1856* (New York: National Bureau of Economic Research, 1938).

where:

t = time period in which the coupon or
   principal payment occurs

C_t = interest or principal payment that occurs
   in period t

i = yield to maturity on the bond

The denominator in Equation 10.13 is the price of a bond as determined by the present value model. The numerator is the present value of all cash flows weighted according to the time of cash receipt. The following example completes the specific computations for two bonds to demonstrate the procedure and highlight some of the properties of duration.

Consider the following two sample bonds:

	Bond A	Bond B
Face value	$1,000	$1,000
Maturity	10 years	10 years
Coupon	4%	8%

Assuming annual interest payments and an 8 percent yield to maturity, duration is computed as shown in Table 10.5. Duration computed by discounting flows using the yield to maturity of the bond is called *Macaulay duration*. We will use Macaulay duration throughout this chapter.

This example illustrates several characteristics of duration. First, the duration of a bond with coupon payments will always be less than its term to maturity, because duration gives weight to these interim payments.

Second, there is an inverse relationship between coupon and duration. A bond with a larger coupon will have a shorter duration because more of the total cash flows come earlier in the form of interest payments. As shown in Table 10.5, the 8 percent coupon bond has a shorter duration than the 4 percent coupon bond.

A bond with no coupon payments (i.e., a zero-coupon bond or another pure discount bond like a Treasury bill) will have a duration equal to its term to maturity. In Table 10.5 if you assume a single payment at maturity, you will see that duration will equal term to maturity.

A positive relationship generally holds between term to maturity and duration, but duration typically increases at a decreasing rate with maturity. There-

Modified duration A measure of Macaulay duration adjusted to help you estimate a bond's price volatility.

fore, all else being the same, a bond with a longer term to maturity will almost always have a higher duration. Note that the relationship is not direct, because as maturity increases, the present value of the principal declines.

As shown in Figure 10.6, the shape of the duration–maturity curve depends upon the coupon and the yield to maturity. The curve for a zero-coupon bond is a straight line, indicating that duration equals term to maturity. In contrast, the curve for a low-coupon bond selling at a deep discount (due to a high YTM) will turn down at long maturities, which gives the longer-maturity bond lower duration.

All else being the same, there is an inverse relationship between YTM and duration. A higher yield to maturity of a bond reduces its duration. As an example, in Table 10.5, if the yield to maturity had been 12 percent rather than 8 percent, the durations would have been about 7.75 and 6.80 rather than 8.12 and 7.25.[15]

Sinking funds and call provisions can dramatically affect a bond's duration. They can accelerate the total cash flows for a bond and, therefore, significantly reduce its duration.[16]

Duration can be very useful to you as a bond investor because it combines the properties of maturity and coupon to measure the time flow of cash from the bond. This is superior to term to maturity, which only considers when the principal will be repaid at maturity. As shown, duration is positively related to term to maturity and inversely related to coupon.

Duration and Bond Price Volatility Duration is more than a superior measure of the time flow of cash from a bond. An adjusted measure of duration called **modified duration** can help you estimate the

[15]These properties are discussed and demonstrated in Frank K. Reilly and Rupinder Sidhu, "The Many Uses of Bond Duration," *Financial Analysts Journal* 36, no. 4 (July–August 1980): 58–72; and Frank J. Fabozzi, Mark Pitts, and Ravi Dattatreya, "Price Volatility Characteristics of Fixed-Income Securities," in *The Handbook of Fixed-Income Securities*, 3d ed., ed. by Frank J. Fabozzi (Homewood, Ill.: Dow Jones-Irwin, 1991).

[16]An example of the computation of duration with a sinking fund and a call feature appears in Reilly and Sidhu, "The Many Uses of Bond Duration."

Table 10.5 *Computation of Duration (assuming 8 percent yield to maturity)*

(1) Year	(2) Cash Flow	(3) PV at 8%	(4) PV of Flow	(5) PV as % of Price	(6) (1) × (5)
Bond A					
1	$ 40	0.9259	$ 37.04	0.0506	0.0506
2	40	0.8573	34.29	0.0469	0.0938
3	40	0.7938	31.75	0.0434	0.1302
4	40	0.7350	29.40	0.0402	0.1608
5	40	0.6806	27.22	0.0372	0.1860
6	40	0.6302	25.21	0.0345	0.2070
7	40	0.5835	23.34	0.0319	0.2233
8	40	0.5403	21.61	0.0295	0.2360
9	40	0.5002	20.01	0.0274	0.2466
10	1,040	0.4632	481.73	0.6585	6.5850
Sum			$ 731.58	1.0000	8.1193

Duration = 8.12 years

(1) Year	(2) Cash Flow	(3) PV at 8%	(4) PV of Flow	(5) PV as % of Price	(6) (1) × (5)
Bond B					
1	$ 80	0.9259	$ 74.07	0.0741	0.0741
2	80	0.8573	68.59	0.0686	0.1372
3	80	0.7938	63.50	0.0635	0.1906
4	80	0.7350	58.80	0.0588	0.1906
5	80	0.6806	54.44	0.0544	0.2720
6	80	0.6302	50.42	0.0504	0.3024
7	80	0.5835	46.68	0.0467	0.3269
8	80	0.5403	43.22	0.0432	0.3456
9	80	0.5002	40.02	0.0400	0.3600
10	1,080	0.4632	500.26	0.5003	5.0030
Sum			$1,000.00	1.0000	7.2470

Duration = 7.25 years

price volatility of a bond. Modified duration equals Macaulay duration (computed in Table 10.5), divided by 1, plus the current yield to maturity, divided by the number of payments in a year. As an example, a bond with a Macaulay duration of 10 years, a yield to maturity (i) of 8 percent, and semiannual payments would have a modified duration of:

$$D_{mod} = \frac{10}{1 + \frac{0.08}{2}}$$

$$= \frac{10}{1.04} = 9.62 \text{ years}$$

It has been shown, both theoretically and empirically, that bond price movements vary proportionally with modified duration.[17] Specifically, as shown in Equation 10.14, an estimate of the percentage change in bond price equals the change in yield times modified duration:

[17]A generalized proof of this is contained in Michael H. Hopewell and George Kaufman, "Bond Price Volatility and Term to Maturity: A Generalized Respecification," *American Economic Review* 63, no. 4 (September 1973): 749–753.

(10.14) $\qquad \dfrac{\Delta P}{P} \times 100 = -D_{mod} \times \Delta i$

where:

ΔP = change in price for the bond

P = beginning price for the bond

$-D_{mod}$ = modified duration of the bond

Δi = yield change in basis points divided by 100. If interest rates go from 8.00 to 8.50 percent, $\Delta i = 50/100 = 0.50$.

Consider a bond with D = 8 years and i = 0.10. Assume that you expect the bond's YTM to decline by 75 basis points (i.e., from 10 to 9.25 percent). The first step is to compute the bond's modified duration as follows:

$$D_{mod} = \dfrac{8}{1 + \dfrac{0.10}{2}}$$

$$= \dfrac{8}{1.05} = 7.62 \text{ years}$$

The estimated percentage change in the price of the bond using Equation 10.14 is as follows:

$$\text{Percentage change in P} = -(7.62) \times \dfrac{-75}{100}$$

$$= (-7.62) \times (-0.75)$$

$$= 5.72 \text{ percent}$$

This indicates that the bond price should increase by about 5.72 percent in response to the 75 basis point drop in YTM. If the price of the bond before the decline in interest rates was $900, the price after the decline should be approximately $900 × 1.0572 = $951.48.

You should put a negative sign in front of modified duration because of the inverse relationship between yield changes and bond price changes. Also, you should remember that this formulation provides an estimate or *approximation* of the percentage change in the price of the bond. The following section on convexity will show that this formula that uses modified duration provides an exact estimate of

Figure 10.6 *Duration versus Maturity*

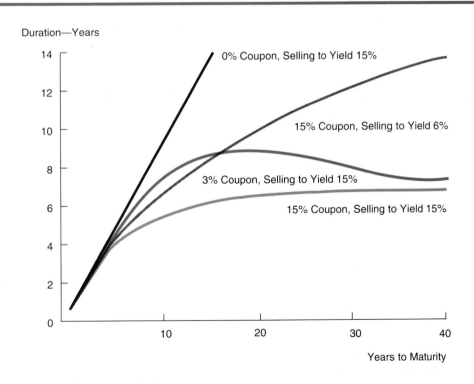

Source: William L. Nemerever, C.F.A., "Managing Bond Portfolios through Immunization Strategies," in *The Revolution in Techniques for Managing Bond Portfolios* (Charlottesville, Va.: Institute of Chartered Financial Analysts, 1983): 42.

| Table 10.6 | *Bond Duration in Years for Bond Yielding 6 Percent under Different Terms* |

Years to Maturity	Coupon Rates			
	0.02	0.04	0.06	0.08
1	0.995	0.990	0.985	0.981
5	4.756	4.558	4.393	4.254
10	8.891	8.169	7.662	7.286
20	14.981	12.980	11.904	11.232
50	19.452	17.129	16.273	15.829
100	17.567	17.232	17.120	17.064
∞	17.167	17.167	17.167	17.167

Source: L. Fisher and R. L. Weil, "Coping with the Risk of Interest Rate Fluctuations: Returns to Bondholders from Naive and Optimal Strategies," *Journal of Business* 44, no. 4 (October 1971): 418.

Convexity A measure of the degree to which a bond's price–yield curve departs from a straight line. This characteristic affects estimates of a bond's price volatility.

the percent price change only for very small changes in yields.

Trading Strategies Using Duration We know from the prior discussion on the relationship between modified duration and bond price volatility that the longest duration security features the maximum price variation. Table 10.6 demonstrates numerous ways to achieve a given level of duration. The duration measure has become increasingly popular because it conveniently specifies the time flow of cash from a security considering both coupon and term to maturity. An active bond investor can use this measure to structure a portfolio to take advantage of changes in market yields.

If you expect a decline in interest rates, you should increase the average duration of your bond portfolio to achieve maximum price volatility. Alternatively, if you expect an increase in interest rates, you should reduce the average duration of your portfolio to minimize your price decline. Note that the duration of a portfolio is the market-value-weighted average of the durations of the individual bonds in the portfolio.

Convexity

Modified duration allows us to derive approximate bond price changes for a change in interest rates. Equation 10.14 is accurate, however, only for *very small changes* in market yields. We will see that the accuracy of the estimate of the price change deteriorates with larger changes in yields because the modified duration calculation is a *linear* approximation of a bond price change that follows a *curvilinear* (convex) function. To understand the effect of this **convexity**, we must consider the price-yield relationships for alternative bonds.[18]

Price–Yield Relationship for Bonds Since the price of a bond is the present value of its cash flows at a particular discount rate, given the coupon, maturity, and yield for a bond, you can calculate a price for it at a point in time. The price–yield curve provides a set of prices for a bond with a specific maturity and coupon at a point in time with a range of yields. As an example, Table 10.7 lists the computed prices for a 12 percent, 20-year bond assuming yields from 1 percent to 12 percent. The table shows that discounting the flows from this 12 percent, 20-year bond at a yield of 1 percent, you get a price of $2,989.47; discounting

[18]For a further discussion of this topic, see Mark L. Dunetz and James M. Mahoney, "Using Duration and Convexity in the Analysis of Callable Bonds," *Financial Analysts Journal* 44, no. 3 (May–June 1988): 53–73.

Table 10.7 *Price–Yield Relationships for Alternative Bonds*

A. 12 Percent, 20-Year		B. 12 Percent, 3-Year		C. Zero Coupon 30-Year	
Yield	Price	Yield	Price	Yield	Price
1.0%	$2,989.47	1.0%	$1,324.30	1.0%	$741.37
2.0	2,641.73	2.0	1,289.77	2.0	550.45
3.0	2,346.21	3.0	1,256.37	3.0	409.30
4.0	2,094.22	4.0	1,224.06	4.0	304.78
5.0	1,878.60	5.0	1,192.78	5.0	227.28
6.0	1,693.44	6.0	1,162.52	6.0	169.73
7.0	1,533.88	7.0	1,133.21	7.0	126.93
8.0	1,395.86	8.0	1,104.84	8.0	95.06
9.0	1,276.02	9.0	1,077.37	9.0	71.29
10.0	1,171.59	10.0	1,050.76	10.0	53.54
11.0	1,080.23	11.0	1,024.98	11.0	40.26
12.0	1,000.00	12.0	1,000.00	12.0	30.31

these same flows at 10 percent gives a price of $1,171.59. The graph of these prices relative to the yields that produced them in Figure 10.7 indicates that the price–yield relationship for this bond is not a straight line, but a curvilinear relationship. That is, it is convex.

Two points are important about the price–yield relationship. First, this relationship can be analyzed for a single bond, a portfolio of bonds, or any stream of future cash flows. Second, the convex price–yield relationship differs depending upon the nature of the cash flow stream, that is, the coupon and maturity of the bond. The price–yield relationship for a high-coupon, short-term security will be almost a straight line because the price does not change much for a change in yield (e.g., the 12 percent, 3-year bond in Table 10.7). In contrast, the price–yield relationship for a low-coupon, long-term bond will curve radically (i.e., be very convex) as shown by the zero-coupon, 30-year bond in Table 10.7. The curved nature of the price–yield relationship is referred to as the bond's *convexity.*

As shown by the graph, because of the convexity of the relationship, as yield increases, the rate at which the price of the bond declines becomes slower. Similarly, when yields decline, the rate at which the price of the bond increases becomes faster. Convexity is, therefore, a desirable trait.

Given this price–yield curve, modified duration is the percentage change in price for a nominal change in yield as follows:[19]

$$(10.15) \qquad D_{mod} = \frac{dP/di}{P}$$

Notice that the dP/di line in Figure 10.7 is tangent to the price–yield curve *at a given yield.* For small changes in yields, this tangent straight line gives a good estimate of the actual price change. For larger changes in yields, the straight line will estimate the new price of the bond at less than the actual price shown by the price–yield curve. The misestimate arises because the modified-duration line is a linear estimate of a curvilinear relationship.

Determinants of Convexity Convexity is a measure of the curvature of the price–yield relationship,[20]

[19]In mathematical terms, modified duration is the first differential of this price–yield relationship with respect to yield.

[20]Mathematically, convexity is the second derivative of price with respect to yield (d^2p/di^2) divided by the price. Put another way, it is the percentage change in dP/di for a given change in yield.

Figure 10.7   *Price–Yield Relationship and Modified Duration at 4 Percent Yield*

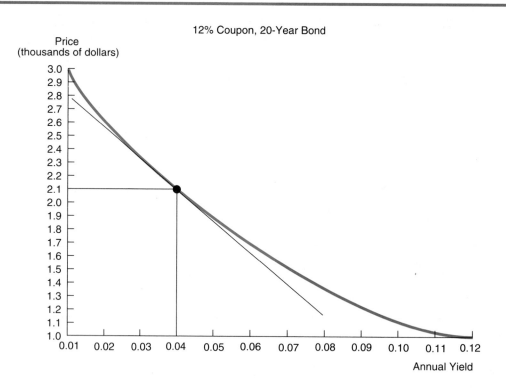

that is, it indicates how much a bond's price–yield curve deviates from the linear approximation of that curve. As indicated by Figure 10.7, for noncallable bonds, convexity is always a positive number, implying that the price–yield curve lies above the modified-duration line. Figure 10.8 illustrates the price–yield relationship for two bonds with very different coupons and maturities. (The yields and prices appear in Table 10.4.)

These graphs demonstrate that the following factors increase convexity:

- Lower coupon (yield and maturity constant)
- Longer maturity (yield and coupon constant)
- Lower yield (coupon and maturity constant). This means that a price–yield curve is more convex in its lower-yield (upper left) segment.

Therefore, a short-term, high-coupon bond such as the 12 percent coupon, 3-year bond in Figure 10.8, has very low convexity—it is almost a straight line. In contrast, the zero-coupon, 30-year bond has high convexity.

In summary, a change in a bond's price resulting from a change in yield can be attributed to two sources: the bond's modified duration and its convexity. The relative effects of these two factors on the price change will depend on the characteristics of the bond (i.e., its convexity) and the size of the yield change. For example, if you were estimating the price change for a 300-basis-point change in yield in a zero-coupon, 30-year bond, the convexity effect would be fairly large, since this bond would have high convexity, and a 300-basis-point change in yield is relatively large.

In conclusion, modified duration can help you derive an approximate percentage bond price change for a given change in interest rates, but you must remember that it is only a good estimate when you are considering small yield changes. You must also consider the convexity effect when you are dealing with large yield changes or when securities or cash flows have high convexity.

Figure 10.8   *Price–Yield Curves for Alternative Bonds*

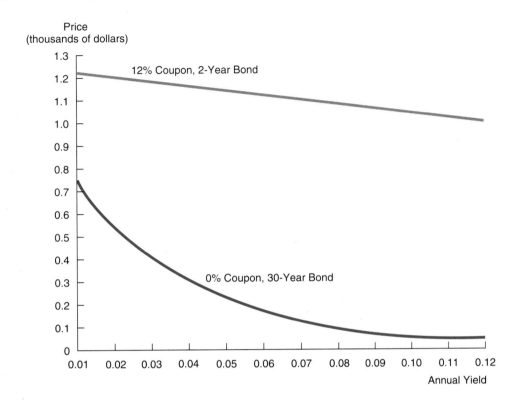

Summary

■ The value of a bond equals the present value of all future cash flows accruing to the investor. Cash flows for the conservative bond investor include periodic interest payments and principal return; cash flows for the aggressive investor include periodic interest payments and the capital gain or loss when the bond is sold prior to its maturity. Bond investors can maximize their yields by accurately estimating the level of interest rates and, more importantly, changes in interest rates and yield spreads. Similarly, they must compare coupon rates, maturities, and call features of alternative bonds.

■ There are five bond yield measures: nominal yield, current yield, promised yield to maturity, promised yield to call, and realized yield. The promised YTM, promised YTC, and realized yield equations include the interest-on-interest, or coupon reinvestment, assumption. The fundamental determinants of

interest rates are the real risk-free rate, the expected rate of inflation, and a risk premium.

■ The yield curve (or the term structure of interest rates) shows the relationships between the yields and the term to maturity on a set of comparable bonds. Yield curves exhibit four basic patterns. Three theories attempt to explain the shapes of yield curves: the expectations hypothesis, the liquidity preference hypothesis, and the segmented market hypothesis.

■ It is important to understand what causes changes in interest rates, and also how these changes in rates affect the prices of bonds. We demonstrated that bond price volatility is mainly a function of differences in yield, coupon, and term to maturity. The duration measure incorporates coupon and maturity in one measure that estimates the responses of bond prices to changes in interest rates. Since modified duration provides a straight-line estimate of the curvilinear price–yield function, you must consider modified duration together with the convexity of a bond for large changes in yields and/or when dealing with securities that have high convexity.

Questions

1. Why does the present value equation appear to be more useful for the bond investor than for the common stock investor?
2. What important assumptions do you make when you calculate promised yield to maturity? What assumptions affect calculation of promised YTC?
3. a. Define the variables in the following model:

$$i = f(RFR, I, RP)$$

   b. You are considering investing in the bonds of a firm that is not expected to break even this year. Discuss which factor will reflect this information.
4. We discussed three alternative hypotheses to explain the term structure of interest rates. Which one do you think best explains the alternative shapes of yield curves? Defend your choice.

5. *CFA Examination I* (1982)
   a. Explain what is meant by the term *structure of interest rates*. Explain the theoretical basis of an upward-sloping yield curve. [8 minutes]
   b. Explain the economic circumstances under which you would expect to see the inverted yield curve prevail. [7 minutes]
   c. Define *real rate of interest*. [2 minutes]
   d. Discuss the characteristics of the market for U.S. Treasury securities. Compare it to the market for AAA corporate bonds. Discuss the opportunities that may exist in bond markets that are less than efficient. [8 minutes]
   e. Over the past several years, fairly wide yield spreads between AAA corporates and Treasuries have occasionally prevailed. Discuss the possible reasons for this. [5 minutes]
6. *CFA Examination III* (1982)
   As the portfolio manager for a large pension fund, you are offered the following bonds:

	Coupon	Maturity	Price	Call Price	Yield to Maturity
Edgar Corp. (new issue)	14.00%	2002	$101.3/4	$114	13.75%
Edgar Corp. (new issue)	6.00	2002	48.1/8	103	13.60
Edgar Corp. (1972 issue)	6.00	2002	48.7/8	103	13.40

Assuming that you expect a decline in interest rates over the next 3 years, identify and justify which of these bonds you would select. [10 minutes]

Problems

1. Your firm issued $1,000 par, 25-year bonds with a 7 percent coupon rate and a 10 percent call premium 4 years ago.
   a. If you call these bonds now, what *approximate* yield to call will the investors who originally purchased them receive?
   b. If you call these bonds now, what yield to call will the investors who originally purchased them at par receive? In this case, compute the yield to call using the present value model.
   c. If the current interest rate were 5 percent and the bonds were not callable, at what price would each bond sell?

2. Assume that you purchase an 8 percent, 20-year, $1,000 par bond with semiannual payments. You pay $1,012.50 for the bond when it has 12 years remaining until maturity. Compute:
   a. Its approximate yield to maturity
   b. Its yield to maturity based upon the present value model
   c. Its yield to call if it were callable in 3 years with an 8 percent premium
3. Calculate the duration of an 8 percent, $1,000 par bond that matures in 3 years if the bond's YTM is 10 percent and it pays interest semiannually.
   a. Calculate this bond's modified duration.
   b. Assuming the bond's YTM goes from 10 to 9.5 percent, calculate an estimate of the price change.
4. Construct a chart demonstrating current ranges of yields for bonds of various ratings. For example, you might want to randomly select three or four bonds in each rating category and show the aver-

age yield on each group, as well as the spread for each group.

5. You are given two 8 percent coupon bonds, one with a term to maturity of 5 years, the second with a term to maturity of 20 years. Assuming that market interest rates go from 8 percent to 12 percent, compute the prices of the two bonds before and after the rate change, and discuss the differential percentage price change.

6. Compute the duration of a 3-year bond with a 7 percent coupon yielding 8 percent. Show all work.

7. You own a bond with a Macaulay duration of 8 years. If market rates are 8 percent, what is the modified duration of this bond? If market rates decline by 2 percent (200 basis points), what will be the estimated percentage change in price for this bond?

8. a. *CFA Examination I* (1984): Assume a $10,000 par value zero-coupon bond with a term to maturity at issue of 10 years and a market yield of 8 percent.
   1. Determine the duration of the bond.
   2. Calculate the initial issue price of the bond at a market yield of 8 percent, assuming semiannual compounding.
   3. This bond is selling to yield 12 percent 12 months after issue. Calculate its then-current market price. Calculate your pre-tax rate of return assuming you owned this bond during the 12-month period.

   b. Assume a 10 percent coupon bond with a Macaulay duration of 8 years, semiannual payments, and a market rate of 8 percent.
   1. Determine the modified duration of the bond.
   2. Calculate the percentage change in price for the bond, assuming market rates decline by 2 percent (200 basis points). Note: In the exam, the candidate received a present value table. You should use the tables at the end of this book. [20 minutes]

9. *CFA Examination I* (1985): Rank the following bonds in descending order of duration. Explain your reasoning (no calculations required). [10 minutes]
   a. 15% coupon, 20-year, yield to maturity at 10%
   b. 15% coupon, 15-year, yield to maturity at 10%
   c. Zero coupon, 20-year, yield to maturity at 10%
   d. 8% coupon, 20-year, yield to maturity at 10%
   e. 15% coupon, 15-year, yield to maturity at 15%

References

Dunetz, Mark L., and James M. Mahoney. "Using Duration and Convexity in the Analysis of Callable Bonds." *Financial Analysts Journal* 44, no. 3 (May–June 1988).

Fabozzi, Frank J., ed. *The Handbook of Fixed-Income Securities*, 3d ed. Homewood, Ill.: Business One Irwin, 1991.

Finnerty, John D. "Evaluating the Economics of Refunding High-Coupon Sinking-Fund Debt." *Financial Management* 12, no. 1 (Spring 1983).

Kalotay, A. J. "On the Structure and Valuation of Debt Refundings." *Financial Management* 11, no. 1 (Spring 1982).

Kalotay, A. J. "Sinking Funds and the Realized Cost of Debt." *Financial Management* 11, no. 1 (Spring 1982).

Macaulay, Frederick R. *Some Theoretical Problems Suggested by the Movements of Interest Rates, Bond Yields, and Stock Prices in the United States since 1856.* New York: National Bureau of Economic Research, 1938.

Reilly, Frank K., and Rupinder Sidhu. "The Many Uses of Bond Duration." *Financial Analysts Journal* 36, no. 4 (July–August 1980).

Van Horne, James C. *Financial Market Rates and Flows*, 3d ed. Englewood Cliffs, N.J.: Prentice-Hall, 1989.

Wilson, Richard S. *Corporate Senior Securities.* Chicago: Probus Publishing, 1987.

Wilson, Richard S., and Frank J. Fabozzi. *The New Corporate Bond Market.* Chicago: Probus Publishing, 1990.

CHAPTER

11

Bond Portfolio Management Strategies

In Chapter 10 we were concerned with the description and measurement of alternative bond yield figures. Knowledge about these yields and the effect of their changes on bonds' prices provided the background needed to evaluate different investments. But there is more to bond investing than just locating and measuring attractive individual bonds. Successful bond investors and portfolio managers understand how to select good individual securities, and how to combine them into portfolios that suit the return and risk preferences of particular investors.

Previously, we discussed the security market line (SML) that related the expected rates of return and risk levels for alternative investments. We made the point that different investors would select different positions on the SML because they would want different returns and would tolerate varying levels of risk. This is as true for bond investors as for any others. Some relatively young bond investors might want to develop bond portfolios for their children's college educations or their own retirements 20 or 30 years away. Such investors could be fairly aggressive because of their long time horizons. In contrast, an older investor planning to retire in a few years would not want to risk the loss of principal needed for retirement. Such a person would be more conservative than the young investor. Finally, a retiree living on the income generated from a bond portfolio would follow a very conservative and extremely risk averse investment policy.

In addition to individual investors, a number of institutional investors trade in the bond market such as banks, insurance companies, and pension plans. Again, they range widely in their goals and tolerance for risk based upon the needs and goals of their clients.

The point is, when discussing bond portfolio management, we must recognize the need to consider a wide range of strategies to achieve the numerous risk–return goals of bond investors.

Bond portfolio management strategies can be divided into three major groups:[1]

1. Passive portfolio management strategies
2. Active portfolio management strategies
3. Matched-funding strategies

In this chapter we will consider a number of specific strategies from the conservative to the fairly aggressive. This includes so-called passive policies in which no investment decisions are made or the decisions are automatic. This includes the simple buy-and-hold strategy where you either buy a portfolio of bonds and hold them to maturity or construct an index portfolio to match the performance of some bond indicator series. In more aggressive strategies, the portfolio manager seeks to buy and sell bonds before maturity to profit from major changes in market interest rates or expected changes in yield spreads.

We will begin the chapter with a discussion of the passive strategies, then we will consider several active management strategies. This will be followed by an examination of matched funding techniques, which can be viewed as a combination of active and passive strategies because they attempt to match a liability stream through fairly active trading.

Like some other topics in investments, bond portfolio management would have required a much shorter chapter 20 years ago because the bond market was very different then. Prior to the 1950s, the bond market was considered very safe and conservative because interest rates were rather low and very steady. Such an environment made a buy-and-hold strategy very reasonable because active trading brought no benefit. In the 1960s the rate of inflation increased substantially, and as a result, the level of interest rates increased. Interest rates also became more volatile, creating opportunities to profit from active bond portfolio strategies that exploited bond price volatility. In the 1970s the duration measure derived by Macaulay was rediscovered. As discussed in Chapter 10, it helped investors to estimate bond price volatility and, therefore, to adjust portfolios to changes in interest rates.

While some portfolio managers viewed the increase in bond price volatility as an opportunity to increase returns through active trading, others were not pleased with the change. Specifically, portfolio managers for insurance companies and pension funds typically faced prespecified future liability streams and the volatility of interest rates made it more difficult to be certain of meeting these obligations. This need led academics and researchers at investment firms to develop various strategies based on duration by which these portfolio managers could match their liabilities with properly constructed bond portfolios.

You can see that the bond market has experienced significant changes during the past 20 years. In response to these changes and the needs of various investors, a number of different bond portfolio management strategies have been developed. This chapter describes these strategies and discusses how to implement them. While these portfolio management strategies can be applied around the globe, we will discuss some additional factors that must be considered when implementing them outside the United States. Specifically, it is necessary to consider the outlook for the local economy and the effect of the economic environment on the country's inflation and interest rates. A

---

[1]For a further discussion of this breakdown see Martin L. Leibowitz, "The Dedicated Bond Portfolio in Pension Funds—Part I: Motivations and Basics," *Financial Analysts Journal* 42, no. 1 (January–February 1986): 61–75.

third factor, one that is unique to this analysis is the impact of these factors on exchange rates.

Given these specific strategies, we will consider some alternative approaches using one or several of them. Finally, we will consider the efficiency of the bond market and its implication for bond portfolio management.

Passive Bond Portfolio Strategies

There are two specific passive portfolio strategies. First is a **buy-and-hold strategy** in which a manager selects a portfolio of bonds based upon the objectives and constraints of the client with the intent of holding these bonds to maturity. In the second passive strategy, **indexing,** the objective is to construct a portfolio of bonds that will equal the performance of a specified bond index such as the Shearson Lehman Government Bond Index.

Buy-and-Hold Strategy

The simplest strategy for managing a bond portfolio is to buy bonds and hold them until maturity. While it is obviously not limited to bond investments, bond investors who employ this strategy look for issues with desired quality ratings, coupon levels, terms to maturity, and such indenture provisions as callability and sinking funds. Based on these features they select appropriate issues for their portfolios. Investors who buy and hold bonds do not trade actively to earn returns, but rather look for vehicles with maturities or durations that approximate their stipulated investment horizons.

Many successful bond investors and institutional portfolio managers follow a modified buy-and-hold strategy in which they buy issues with the intention of holding them until the end of their investment horizons, but they still actively look for opportunities to trade into more desirable positions. Obviously, too much modification would make this an active strategy.

To implement either a strict or modified buy-and-hold strategy, a bond investor seeks vehicles with attractive maturities and yields. Despite the label "passive," these investors are very selective and look for attractive high-yielding issues with desirable features and quality ratings. As an example, most buy-and-hold investors realize that agency issues typically provide higher returns than Treasuries with little sacrifice in quality, that utilities provide higher returns than com-

Buy-and-hold strategy A passive portfolio management strategy in which bonds are bought and held to maturity.

Indexing A passive portfolio management strategy that seeks to copy the composition, and therefore the performance, of a selected market index.

parably rated industrials, and that callability affects the risk and yield of an issue. The successful buy-and-hold investor uses this kind of knowledge of markets and issue characteristics to seek out attractive yields and also to evaluate the timing of cash flows from coupons and principal payments.

Indexing Strategy

As will be discussed in the chapter on efficient capital markets, numerous empirical studies have demonstrated that the majority of money managers have not been able to match the risk–return performance of common stock or bond indexes. As a result, many clients have opted to have some part of their bond portfolios indexed, which means that the portfolio manager builds a portfolio that will match the performance of a selected bond market index such as the Shearson Lehman Index, Merrill Lynch Index, or Salomon Brothers Index. In such a case, the portfolio manager is not judged on the basis of risk and return compared to an index, but by how closely the portfolio tracks the index. Specifically, the analysis examines the tracking error, which equals the difference between the rate of return for the portfolio and the rate of return for the bond market index. For example, if the portfolio experienced an annual rate of return of 8.1 percent during a period when the index had a rate of return of 8.2 percent, the tracking error would be 10 basis points.

Active Management Strategies[2]

In contrast to the passive strategies, several active management strategies require the portfolio manager to make major portfolio changes over time, to analyze

[2]For further discussion on this topic see H. Gifford Fong, "Active Strategies for Managing Bond Portfolios," in *The Revolution in Techniques for Managing Bond Portfolios*, ed. Donald Tuttle (Charlottesville, Va.: Institute of Chartered Financial Analysts, 1983): 21–38.

> **Interest rate anticipation** An active bond portfolio management strategy designed to preserve capital or take advantage of capital gains opportunities by predicting interest rates and their effects on bond prices.
>
> **Valuation analysis** An active bond portfolio management strategy designed to capitalize on expected price increases in temporarily undervalued issues.

and select unique bonds, to trade to take advantage of changing yield spreads, or to buy and sell bonds to benefit from tax laws or other characteristics of bonds.

We will discuss the following portfolio strategies that require constant monitoring and active management:

1. Interest rate anticipation
2. Valuation analysis
3. Credit analysis
4. Yield spread analysis
5. Bond swaps

In all these strategies, the portfolio manager hopes to achieve above-average capital gains by carefully monitoring the economic environment and analyzing bond issues. Following insights from economic and issue analysis, the active portfolio manager is willing and anxious to change the portfolio.

Interest Rate Anticipation

Interest rate anticipation is the riskiest bond portfolio management strategy because the investor must act on uncertain forecasts of future interest rates. This strategy is designed to preserve capital when investors anticipate increasing interest rates and to earn significant capital gains when they expect interest rates to decline.

Investors usually attain these objectives by altering the maturity or duration structures of their portfolios. Specifically, they reduce the duration of the portfolio when interest rates are expected to increase and increase its duration when they expect a decline in yields. The main source of risk in this strategy is the difficulty of interest rate forecasting. When investors concentrate on bonds with short maturities, they can preserve capital, but if rates fail to increase as expected, they can sacrifice substantial income and also lose the opportunity for capital gains if rates decline.

Increasing the maturity or duration of their portfolios in anticipation of a decline in interest rates is likewise very risky. If interest rates are at a peak, the yield curve is likely downward-sloping, so bond coupons will decline with maturity or duration. The investor who extends the maturity of the portfolio sacrifices current income by shifting from high-coupon short bonds to longer-maturity bonds. At the same time, the increase in portfolio maturity or duration exposes the portfolio to greater price volatility, which could diminish its rate of return in case of an unexpected increase in yields.

Interest rate anticipation is a high-risk strategy because it is difficult to project future interest rates. Suppose, however, that you expect interest rates to increase and want to preserve your capital by reducing the duration of your portfolio. You might implement your rate anticipation strategy by selling some long-maturity, high-duration bonds and reinvesting the proceeds in high-yielding, short-term obligations such as Treasury bills. Beyond preserving capital, you want the best return possible within your maturity constraint. You also want liquidity because after the rate increase, yields may stabilize and you want the ability to shift quickly back to a more neutral position (with intermediate-term bonds) or to a long-maturity, high-duration portfolio if you think rates will decline.

When you follow a rate anticipation strategy and you expect lower interest rates, the basic rule is to increase the duration of the portfolio, and with it the price volatility. You would do this by selling your short-duration bonds or notes and reinvesting the proceeds in the longest-maturity, highest-duration bonds you could acquire that would be consistent with your quality constraints. Further, because interest rate sensitivity is critical, high-grade bonds such as Treasuries, agencies, or investment-grade corporates should be used, because higher-quality bonds are more sensitive to interest rate changes. Again, liquidity is important, because you want to be able to close out the position quickly after the rates stop declining and shift your portfolio back to a more neutral position.

Valuation Analysis

With **valuation analysis,** the portfolio manager looks for undervalued bonds, which are bonds with computed values above their current market prices or where the expected YTMs are lower than the prevailing YTM. You will recognize this as similar to the investment decision rule discussed in Chapter 8. The difference here is that this strategy requires continuous evaluations and a lot of trading in response to the results of the analysis. Most practitioners determine bonds' values as computed YTMs. In turn, they derive computed YTMs based upon the average value of bonds with the same characteristics in the marketplace.

As an example, assume that you are evaluating a long-maturity bond with certain features. Long maturity might be worth an added 60 basis points relative to short maturity (this amount gives the maturity spread). Suppose the bond has a long deferred call period; this positive attribute would mean a lower yield. Suppose the bond's sinking fund is very aggressive, reducing its risk and required yield.

Based on all these characteristics and their typical impacts on required yield, you would estimate the required yield for this bond. You would then compare this computed required yield to the prevailing YTM based upon the bond's current market price to determine whether it is undervalued or overvalued. A computed YTM lower than the prevailing YTM indicates an undervalued bond. (If you computed a price for the bond using this computed YTM in the present value model, a value above the current market price would indicate an undervalued bond.) Based upon your confidence in the characteristic costs, you would buy undervalued issues and ignore or sell overvalued issues.

Credit Analysis

Some investors who actively manage bond portfolios become involved in **credit analysis** of bond issuers to identify changes in their default risk levels. Bond investors do this by projecting shifts in the quality ratings assigned to bonds by the four rating agencies discussed in Chapter 3. These rating changes are prompted by internal changes in the issuing companies and also by changes in the external environment.

Changes in financial ratios signal changes in financial risk, profitability, and growth. General economic conditions such as changes in GNP, inflation, and aggregate profits signal changes in the economy that will affect future sales and profits for the firm. During periods of strong economic expansion, even weak firms survive and grow, whereas even normally strong firms may fail to meet financial obligations during severe economic contractions. These theoretical expectations are supported by the historical record, which shows a strong cyclical pattern for rat-

> **Credit analysis** An active bond portfolio management strategy designed to identify bonds that are expected to experience changes in rating. This strategy is critical when investing in high-yield bonds.

ing changes with many more downgradings typical during economic contractions. The period of 1985 to 1990 was an exception, when downgradings increased substantially despite an economic expansion.[3]

To successfully employ credit analysis as a bond management strategy, an investor must project rating changes prior to the actual announcements by the rating agencies. The market adjusts rather quickly to rating changes, especially downgradings, and you gain little from buying or selling bonds after the rating agencies announce changes.

Credit Analysis of High-Yield Junk Bonds One of the most obvious opportunities for credit analysis is the analysis of high-yield junk bonds. Recall that these are bonds rated below BBB by the rating agencies.

Researchers have found that the yield differential between high-yield bonds and Treasury securities ranges from about 250 basis points for BB 10-year bonds to over 700 basis points for CCC, 20-year bonds. Note that these yield spreads vary substantially over time as shown in Figure 11.1. As an example, the spread between B rated, 10-year bonds and Treasury bonds (the dashed line) reached about 600 basis points during 1986, shortly after the 1987 crash, and also during late 1989 and early 1990. In contrast, it got as low as 300 basis points in 1985 and was less than 400 basis points on several occasions. As Altman and Nammacher point out, even considering the default record of high-yield bonds, their net return (i.e., their average gross return less the losses from bonds that defaulted) has been superior to higher-rated debt.[4]

A recent study indicated, however, that the average credit quality of high-yield bonds declined from

---

[3]For a discussion of this pattern, see Frank K. Reilly, "The Critical Importance of Credit Analysis," Working paper, University of Notre Dame (March 1991); and Robin G. Blumenthel, "Quality of Credit Dropped Sharply in '90, S&P Says," *The Wall Street Journal* (January 9, 1991): C12.

[4]Edward I. Altman and Scott A. Nammacher, *Investing in Junk Bonds* (New York: John Wiley & Sons, 1987).

Figure 11.1   *Yield Spread (Basis Points) between 10-Year B, BB, and CCC Corporate Bonds and 10-Year Treasury Bonds*

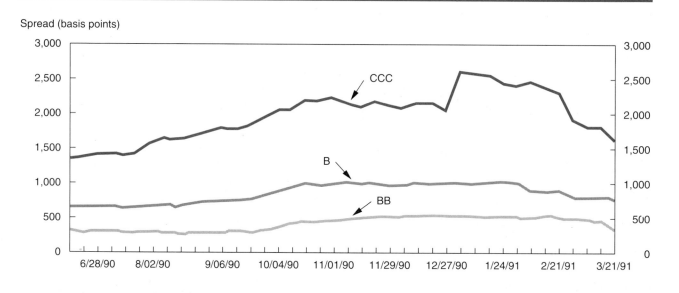

Spread (basis points)

Note: Data include price information through August 9, 1988.

Source: High Yield Securities Research Group, Merrill Lynch & Co., New York.

1980 to 1988.[5] As an example, interest coverage declined from about 2 times in the period from 1980 to 1982 to 0.71 times in the period from 1987 to 1988. This overall decline in the average ratios for all high-yield bonds is due to two factors.[6] First, the distribution of bonds in rating categories has changed. Specifically, the proportion of BB bonds sold compared to the total declined and the proportion of CCC bonds increased during the period 1983 to 1988. Second, the credit quality of bonds *within* rating categories has also declined over time. Specifically, the average values of the financial ratios that determine whether bonds are included in the B or CCC rating classes have declined over time. These two factors explain why overall average credit quality has declined.

These changes in credit quality will make credit analysis of high-yield bonds more important, but also

more difficult. This means that bond analysts–portfolio managers need to engage in detailed credit analysis to select bonds that will survive. Assuming the ability—through rigorous credit analysis—of avoiding bonds with a high probability of default, these bonds will provide substantial rates of return for the investor.

In summary, you can derive substantial rates of return by investing in high-yield bonds assuming that you do the credit analysis required to avoid defaults, which occur with these bonds at substantially higher rates than the overall market. Several recent studies have shown that the average cumulative default rate for high-yield bonds after 10 years is between 30 and 35 percent. Of the high-yield bonds sold in 1980, about 38 percent had defaulted by 1990.[7]

Table 11.1 lists the results for one study that considers the full spectrum of bonds. It shows substantial differences in cumulative default rates for bonds with different ratings for the periods 5, 10, and 15 years after issue. Over 10 years, the holding period that is widely discussed, the default rate for Baa investment grade bonds is only 3.7 percent, but the default rate increases to over 14 percent for Ba and to 25.3 percent for B rated bonds. This analysis does not include Caa issues, which would have even higher default rates.

[5]Roger Lowenstein, "Junk Gets Junkier, and That May Explain Bonds' Current Ills," *The Wall Street Journal* (November 3, 1989): C1, C2. This article discusses Barrie A. Wigmore, "The Decline in Credit Quality of New Issue Junk Bonds," *Financial Analysts Journal* 46, no. 5 (September–October 1990): 53–62.

[6]These changes are demonstrated in Reilly, "The Critical Importance of Credit Analysis."

Table 11.1	*Average Cumulative Default Rates for Corporate Bonds: 1970–1988*		

| | **Years since Issue** | | |
Ratings	**5**	**10**	**15**
Aaa	0.2%	0.8%	2.1%
Aa	0.5	1.4	2.2
A	0.5	1.4	2.7
Baa	1.6	3.7	5.9
Ba	8.3	14.2	18.9
B	22.3	25.3	32.9

Source: K. Scott Douglass and Douglas J. Lucas, "Historical Default Rates of Corporate Bond Issuers, 1970–1988," Moody's Investors Services, 1989.

These default rates do not mean that investors should avoid high-yield bonds, but they do indicate that extensive credit analysis is a critical component for success within this sector. If you can avoid defaults, you can earn substantial rates of return from high-yield bonds.

Because the growth of the high-yield bond market began fairly recently (most occurring since 1982), investors may worry about the availability of information. In fact, the growth of this market has led several investment houses to develop high-yield bond groups that examine such issues and monitor the aggregate junk bond market. Table 11.2 lists the firms and the titles and frequency of their publications.

In summary, the substantial increase in the value of junk bonds outstanding has inspired an increase in

Spread analysis An active bond portfolio management strategy designed to capitalize on corrections in temporarily abnormal yield spreads between alternative issues.

Bond swap An active bond portfolio management strategy that exchanges one position for another to take advantage of some difference between them.

research and credit analysis related to these bonds. In-depth credit analysis of junk bonds is critical because of the large number of high-yield issues, the wide range of quality among them, and the growing complexity of the bonds sold in connection with LBOs. While the task of selecting the better high-yield bonds is not getting any easier, the large yield spreads on these bonds relative to Treasuries indicates that the rewards are also increasing.

Yield Spread Analysis

In Chapter 10 we learned about normal yield spreads for bonds in alternative sectors. For example, yields differ between high-grade versus low-grade industrial bonds, or between industrial versus utility bonds. A portfolio manager using **spread analysis** as an active portfolio strategy would monitor these yield relationships for any abnormalities. The manager would execute various trades that would take advantage of the impending return to a normal spread. This strategy requires enough background to know the normal yield spread relationship and the ability to maintain the liquidity necessary to buy or sell the required issues quickly enough to take advantage of temporary spread abnormalities.

Bond Swaps

Bond swaps are the general name for a group of strategies in which an investor liquidates a current position while simultaneously replacing it with a different issue. The new issue should have similar attributes, but offer a chance for improved return.

Portfolio managers execute swaps to increase current yield, to increase yield to maturity, to take advantage of shifts in interest rates or realignments of yield spreads, to improve the quality of a bond portfolio, or for tax purposes. Some fairly complex swaps require a computer for the necessary calculations. Most, however, are fairly simple transactions, with obvious goals and risks.

[7]While the details of the analysis differ, the overall results for cumulative defaults are quite consistent. See Edward I. Altman, "Measuring Corporate Bond Mortality and Performance," *Journal of Finance* 44, no. 4 (September 1989): 909–922; Paul Asquith, David W. Mullins, Jr., and Eric D. Wolff, "Original Issue High Yield Bonds: Aging Analysis of Defaults, Exchanges and Calls," *Journal of Finance* 44, no. 4 (September 1989): 923–952; K. Scott Douglass and Douglas J. Lucas, "Historical Default Rates of Corporate Bond Issuers, 1970–1988" (New York: Moody's Investors Service, July 1989). The Altman and Douglass–Lucas studies are updated and discussed in Frank K. Reilly, ed., *High Yield Bonds: Analysis and Risk Assessment* (Charlottesville, Va.: Institute of Chartered Financial Analysts, 1990). Another review of these studies is Edward I. Altman, "Setting the Record Straight on Junk Bonds: A Review of the Research on Default Rates and Returns," *Journal of Applied Corporate Finance* 3, no. 2 (Summer 1990): 82–95.

Table 11.12 **Investment Firms with Periodicals on the High-Yield Bond Market**

Firm	Title of Publication	Frequency
Kidder, Peabody & Co.	*High Yield Sector Report*	Biweekly
Merrill Lynch, Pierce, Fenner & Smith, Inc.	*This Week in High Yield*	Weekly
	Extra Credit—The Journal of High Yield Bond Research	Monthly
Salomon Brothers Inc.	*High Yield Market Update*	Monthly
Morgan Stanley & Co.	*High Performance*	Monthly
Standard & Poor's	*Speculative Grade Debt Credit Review*	Monthly
Duff & Phelps	*High Yield Research*	Monthly

They go by such names as profit takeouts, substitution swaps, intermarket spread swaps, or tax swaps. pickup swaps, substitution swaps, and tax swaps.[8] The riskiness of swaps varies from a low-risk pure yield pickup swap to a high-risk rate anticipation swap. Regardless of the risk level, all swaps have one basic purpose: portfolio improvement.

Swapping bonds may entail several different types of risk. The following are examples of potential risk. If the swapping trades are not perfectly simultaneous, the market may move against you between transactions. A rise in interest rates over the holding period would cause you to incur a loss. Alternatively, yield spreads may fail to respond as anticipated, offsetting the benefits of the bond swap. For another possibility, the new bond may not be a perfect substitute for the original bond so, even if your expectations and interest rate formulations are correct, the swap may give unsatisfactory results because you selected the wrong issue. Finally, if it takes longer than expected for the predicted adjustment to occur, the realized yield might be less than expected or a loss may even result. You must be willing to accept such risks if you wish to improve your portfolio using swaps.

Pure Yield Pickup Swap Investors make a pure yield pickup swap when they trade a low-coupon bond for a comparable higher-coupon bond to realize an automatic and instantaneous increase in current yield and yield to maturity. As an example, assume an investor currently holds a 30-year, Aa-rated, 10 percent issue that is trading at a discount to yield 11.40 percent. The investor finds a comparable 30-year, Aa-rated obligation bearing a 12 percent coupon priced to yield 12 percent. The investor would realize and report a book loss assuming the original issue was bought at par, but the swap would improve current yield and yield to maturity assuming that the new obligation were held to maturity.

Notice that the investor did not have to predict rate changes, nor detect any imbalance in yield spread. The object of the swap was simply to seek higher yields. Quality and maturity stay the same, as do all other factors except coupon.

Substitution Swap Investors use substitution swaps to take advantage of short-term abnormalities in yield spreads between substitute issues that they expect to be corrected in the near future. To see how this works, assume an investor holds Bond 1, a 30-year, 12 percent issue that is yielding 12 percent, and locates a comparable 30-year, 12 percent bond that is yielding 12.20 percent (Bond 2). Bond 2 trades at a discount. Thus, for every Bond 1 sold, the investor can buy more than one Bond 2.

Eventually you would expect a correction in the abnormal yield spread to reduce the yield on Bond 2 to the same level as Bond 1. You could realize capital gains by switching out of your current position into the higher-yielding issue before this adjustment.

Only small differences in current income result from corrections in abnormal yields, but investors making substitution swaps can earn capital gains that

[8]For additional information on these and other types of bond swaps, see Robert Kopprasch, John Macfarlane, Janet Showers, and Daniel Ross, "The Interest-Rate Swap Market: Yield Mathematics, Terminology, and Conventions," in *The Handbook of Fixed Income Securities*, 3d ed., ed. by Frank J. Fabozzi (Homewood, Ill.: Business One Irwin, 1991).

cause differentials in the total returns from the swaps. The time necessary for the yields to adjust to correct the abnormal yield spread (called the *work-out time*) is important in order to realize as high a differential return as possible. The correction would give you additional capital for a subsequent swap or other investment.

Substitution swaps are riskier than pure yield pickup swaps. In addition to the concern regarding the work-out time, market interest rates could move against you while you are waiting for the adjustment to occur. Further, the yield spread you find may not be temporary so no correction occurs and you don't receive any capital gain. Also, the spread may be due to lower quality of the issue, which means that you receive a higher yield, but also accept more risk.

Tax Swap The tax swap is popular with individual investors because it is a relatively simple strategy that requires no projections and incurs few risks. Tax treatments of securities differ due to tax laws and realized portfolio capital gains. To see how a tax swap works, assume you acquired $100,000 worth of corporate bonds and after 2 years sold the securities for $150,000, earning a taxable capital gain of $50,000.

One way to eliminate the tax liability of that capital gain is to sell another bond issue in your portfolio that has an equivalent long-term capital loss. If you had another long-term investment of $100,000 with a current market value of $50,000, you could execute a tax swap by selling this second bond in the same tax year to establish the $50,000 capital loss. By offsetting the capital gain on the first transaction with the capital loss on the second transaction, you eliminate the tax you would have had to pay on the gain. Many investors view municipal bonds as attractive tax swap candidates, because they can increase their tax-free income and use the capital loss which is subject to normal federal and state tax treatment, to reduce capital gains tax liability.

An important caveat in executing a swap to reduce taxes is that you cannot swap identical issues. If you do not buy a different issue, the IRS considers the transaction a wash sale and does not allow the loss. It is easier for investors to avoid wash sales in the bond market than in the stock market, because all bond issues, even those with identical coupons and maturities, are considered distinct. Also, it is easier to find comparable bond issues with only modest differences in coupon, maturity, and quality. Many investors commonly execute tax swaps at year-end to establish capital losses, because the capital loss must occur in the same tax year as the capital gain. This strategy differs from other swap transactions in that it takes advantage of tax statutes rather than temporary market anomalies.

Now that we have discussed several active management strategies, we need to consider how to apply them to a global bond market. We must think about what additional factors must be considered when applying these strategies to foreign bonds. That is the topic of the next section.

Applying Active Strategies to Foreign Bond Markets

An active bond portfolio manager who wants to use one or several of these active management techniques will probably want to apply them to a global portfolio. This section discusses the additional analysis that is necessary to implement the strategies in a foreign market.

The implementation of most of the active management techniques is similar across world bond markets. You attempt to anticipate rates in the United Kingdom or Japan in the same way as in the United States; you simply deal with the same set of economic variables for a different country.

The major decision is not whether to attempt a given portfolio strategy in a country, but rather what proportion of your total bond portfolio you should allocate to the country. Therefore, our discussion concentrates on the factors you must consider when making this asset allocation decision. After that, we discuss some examples of such allocations suggested by major investment firms.

An investor who wants to do global fixed-income asset allocation must analyze three interrelated factors: (1) the economy in each country, including the effects of domestic and international demand; (2) the impact of this total economic demand and domestic monetary policy on the rate of inflation and interest rates in the country; and (3) the effect of the economic environment, inflation, and interest rates on the exchange rates among countries. You will notice that the first two factors are considered when you actively manage in the United States, while the third factor is an additional consideration when investing outside your own country. Based on the evaluation of these factors, a bond portfolio manager must decide: (1) the relative weight of each country in the bond portfolio, and (2) the allocation within each country between government, municipal, and corporate bonds.

You should look for securities with yields that are expected to decline relative to Treasury securities so that you will experience larger price gains than Treasuries. You should also search for securities in countries with currencies expected to be strong relative to the U.S. dollar so you would experience currency gains in addition to the normal returns.

Table 11.3 comes from an *International Fixed Income Strategy* report published by Merrill Lynch Capital Markets. The analysis concentrates on economies, foreign trade, inflation, interest rates, and exchange rates. These portfolio recommendations give specific percentages of a portfolio to allocate to each country compared to the proportion each represents in the global bond market. These global market proportions appear below the boldfaced numbers. As an example, the market value of the U.S. bond market is 45 percent

of the world bond market and the Japanese market is 23 percent of the total.

Given these market proportions, the bold numbers indicate Merrill Lynch's investment recommendations. As an example, although the U.S.-dollar market is 45 percent of the global bond market, Merrill Lynch recommended that you underweight it and invest only 40 percent of your portfolio in U.S. bonds. In contrast, Merrill Lynch recommended overweighting the Canadian-dollar bond market by investing 10 percent of your portfolio there although it accounts for only 4 percent of the global bond portfolio.

The next set of columns indicates Merrill Lynch's recommendations regarding the market decision for the country. As shown, it recommends that 23 percent of the 40 percent allocated to the United States be spent on short-term cash equivalent securities with only 17 percent invested in bonds. The next set of columns dealing with the maturity structure indicates

Table 11.3   *Recommended Asset Mix in a Portfolio of Bonds (percentage breakdown)*

Currency Bloc	Market Decision			Bond Selection Decision								
	Gross Currency Position	Cash Equivalents	Bonds	Maturity Structure						Sector Breakdown		Portfolio Duration
				1–3 Years	3–5 Years	5–7 Years	7–10 Years	Long		Government	Euro/ Foreign	
U.S.$	**40**	**23**	**17**	**0**	**0**	**0**	**17**	**0**		**17**	**0**	**2.7**
	45		45	16	9	5	5	10		39	6	4.8
C$	**10**	**4**	**6**	**6**	**0**	**0**	**0**	**0**		**6**	**0**	**1.0**
	4		4	1	1	1	0	1		3	1	4.9
A$/NZ$	**6**	**2**	**4**	**0**	**2**	**0**	**2**	**0**		**4**	**0**	**3.3**
	2		2	1	1	0	0	0		1	1	3.3
Yen	**23**	**13**	**10**	**0**	**0**	**0**	**10**	**0**		**10**	**0**	**3.6**
	23		23	5	5	5	7	1		20	3	4.8
Europe												
STG	**6**	**1**	**5**	**0**	**0**	**0**	**0**	**5**		**5**	**0**	**5.8**
	8		8	1	1	1	2	3		7	1	5.8
DM	**10**	**5**	**5**	**0**	**0**	**0**	**5**	**0**		**5**	**0**	**3.8**
	13		13	2	3	3	4	1		8	5	4.5
FF	**5**	**0**	**5**	**0**	**5**	**0**	**0**	**0**		**5**	**0**	**3.5**
	5		5	1	1	1	2	0		4	1	4.7
Total	**100**	**48**	**52**	**6**	**7**	**0**	**34**	**5**		**52**	**0**	**3.1**
			100	27	21	16	20	16		82	18	4.8

Source: *International Fixed Income Strategy* (New York: Merrill Lynch Capital Markets, 1988).

that Merrill Lynch recommends that all of the 17 percent should be invested in 7- to 10-year bonds and all of these 7- to 10-year bonds should be government securities. Finally, the average duration for the total portfolio should be 2.7 years, compared to an average duration for the market of 4.8 years. Overall, these recommendations imply a very conservative portfolio for the U.S. market composed of high-quality, short-duration bonds. This keeps interest rate risk fairly low.

In summary, you can manage a foreign bond portfolio actively by the same strategies as for U.S. bonds. Before using these strategies on foreign bonds, you must make the overall asset allocation decision to determine what proportion of your total bond portfolio to devote to foreign issues. As with equity securities, global allocation requires more research because you must evaluate each country both individually and relative to other countries. A presentation of some examples of such an allocation shows the impact of the economic environment, inflation, interest rates, and exchange rates.

Matched-Funding Techniques[9]

In the introduction to this chapter we described matched-funding techniques as combining the passive buy-and-hold strategy and active management strategies. In implementing matched-funding techniques, portfolio managers try to match specific liability obligations due at specific times to a portfolio of bonds in a way that minimizes the portfolio's exposure to interest rate risk. **Interest rate risk** is the uncertainty of returns caused by the possibility of changes in interest rates over time.

These matched-funding techniques resemble passive buy-and-hold strategy because they are meant to avoid or offset risk. At the same time, they are like active management techniques because they typically require constant monitoring and numerous transactions to achieve the intended goal. Although the goal is risk aversion, the implementation of the strategy requires very active management.

Interest rate risk The uncertainty of returns on an investment due to possible changes in interest rates over time.
Dedicated portfolio management A bond portfolio management technique designed to service a particular stream of liabilities.

Most matched-funding techniques were developed in the 1980s in response to the needs of portfolio managers who faced streams of known liabilities, such as pension obligations for retired employees, or an individual saving for a child's college education. Before the 1960s, interest rates were stable, so bond portfolio management was fairly easy because bond values did not fluctuate much. In the 1980s volatile interest rates caused bond prices to fluctuate widely. When a liability was due, the value of a portfolio of bonds could be either substantially below or above the needed amount. Therefore, many portfolio managers wanted techniques that would help them match future liability streams with portfolios of bonds that would provide the required funds over time without worrying about interest rate changes.

Our discussion of matched-funding techniques will range from the notion of a dedicated portfolio that exactly matches the liability stream with a stream of cash flows, to immunization, which uses our prior background on modified duration. We finish this section by discussing horizon matching, which is a combination of pure dedication and immunization.

Dedicated Portfolios

Dedicated portfolio management is a set of techniques for servicing a particular stream of liabilities. The returns from the portfolio are dedicated to meet a known stream of liabilities such as a firm's pension obligations for its retired employees. To satisfy these liabilities, the bond portfolio manager wants to construct a bond portfolio having a cash flow that matches this liability stream. Of the several ways to build such a dedicated portfolio, we will discuss two: a pure cash-matched dedicated portfolio and a dedicated portfolio with reinvestment.

A pure cash-matched dedicated portfolio is the most conservative matching strategy. The objective of pure cash matching is to construct a portfolio of bonds with a stream of payments from coupons, sinking funds, and maturing principal payments to match exactly the specified liability schedule. To fund pension

[9]An overview of these strategies appears in Leibowitz, "The Dedicated Bond Portfolio in Pension Funds—Part I: Motivation and Basics," and Martin L. Leibowitz, "The Dedicated Bond Portfolio in Pension Funds—Part II: Immunization, Horizon Matching, and Contingent Procedures," *Financial Analysts Journal* 42, no. 2 (March–April 1986): 47–57.

Figure 11.2   *Estimated Schedule of Liabilities for a Retired Lives Pension Program*

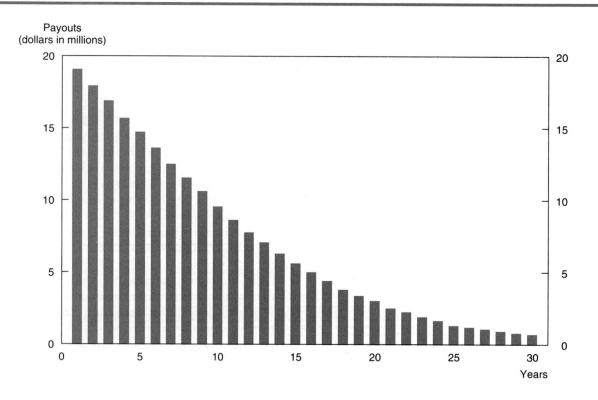

Source: Martin L. Leibowitz, "The Dedicated Bond Portfolio in Pension Funds — Part I: Motivations and Basics," *Financial Analysts Journal* 42, no. 1 (January–February 1986).

payments to a group of retired employees, you consult insurance actuaries who can estimate your future liability stream from knowledge of how much you have promised to each retiree and estimated life expectancies based on the age distribution of the retirees. The typical stream would look like Figure 11.2.

The pension portfolio manager seeks to build a portfolio that generates sufficient funds in advance of each scheduled obligation to ensure that the payment will be met. One way to construct such a portfolio is to find a number of zero-coupon Treasury securities that exactly match the cash needed for each liability. Such an exact cash-match results in a total passive portfolio designed so that receipts are not reinvested. In other words, this portfolio has a zero reinvestment rate.

In contrast, it is possible to construct cash-matched portfolios that plan for reinvestment. The basic portfolio is constructed similarly to the pure cash-matched technique except that the cash flows

need not exactly match the liability stream. Any inflows that precede liability claims can be reinvested at some reasonably conservative rate. A dedicated portfolio with reinvestment allows the portfolio manager to consider a substantially wider set of bonds that may offer higher rates of return than those suitable for a pure cash-matched portfolio. In addition, the assumption of reinvestment also implies a higher total return. This higher return can reduce the original need for funds to set up the portfolio with almost equal safety, assuming the reinvestment assumption is conservative. You might assume a dedicated portfolio with a reinvestment rate of 6 percent when interest rates were ranging from 7 to 10 percent.

Portfolio Immunization

The discussion of dedicated portfolios assumes a liability stream of numerous future payments. Another liability might require a single payment several years into the future. One way to try to meet this obligation is to compute its present value at some conservative rate lower than the prevailing market rate and fund the obligation with this amount of money. Starting with this fund, the portfolio manager could attempt by active management to generate an average rate of return on the portfolio in excess of the original discount rate. As before, the difficulty is the volatility of interest rates, which can work in your favor if you are good at predicting interest rate changes, or cause you to fall short of your goal if you're not.

Given these alternatives, you can imagine that many portfolio managers would welcome the opportunity to lock in an interest rate close to the prevailing market interest rate and not be concerned with subsequent rate changes. To assist portfolio managers who want such a strategy, Fisher and Weil developed the concept of **portfolio immunization**.[10]

The immunization strategy seeks to lock in a specified rate of return that is quite close to the current market rate during a specified investment horizon regardless of what happens to market interest rates; the portfolio manager is attempting to immunize the portfolio from interest rate changes. In this section we will consider how and why immunization works and how investors can immunize their bond portfolios.

Components of Interest Rate Risk   A major problem facing bond portfolio managers is earning a rate of return sufficient to provide the money needed (i.e., the ending-wealth requirement) at a future specific date. This time frame is referred to as your **investment horizon.** If the yield curve remained flat and market rates never changed between the time you acquired your bond and the date you needed funds, you could buy a bond with a term to maturity equal to your investment horizon, and its contribution to ending value would equal the promised wealth value implied by the promised yield to maturity. Specifically, the ending-wealth value would be equal to the beginning value of the bond times the compound value of a dollar at the promised yield to maturity.

As an example, assume that you acquired a 10-year, $1 million bond with an 8 percent coupon at par

Portfolio immunization A bond portfolio management technique of matching modified duration to the investment horizon to eliminate interest rate risk.

Investment horizon The future time at which the investor requires the funds an investment is intended to provide.

Price risk The component of interest rate risk due to the uncertainty of the market price of a bond caused by possible changes in market interest rates.

Coupon reinvestment risk The component of interest rate risk due to the uncertainty of the rate at which coupon payments will be reinvested.

(8 percent YTM). With a flat, stable yield curve and reinvestment of all your coupon income at 8 percent, your ending wealth at the end of your 10-year investment horizon (assuming semiannual compounding) would be:

$$\$1,000,000 \times (1.04)^{20}$$
$$= \$1,000,000 \times 2.1911$$
$$= \$2,191,100$$

You can get the same answer by compounding the $40,000 semiannual interest payment to the end of the period at 8 percent (your reinvestment rate) and adding the $1 million beginning value.

Unfortunately, the real-world term structure (yield curve) is not flat, and interest rates change constantly. Consequently, the bond portfolio manager faces interest rate risk between the time of the investment and the investment horizon date (or target date). This interest rate risk is the uncertainty of achieving the desired ending wealth due to interest rate changes between the time of purchase and the investment horizon date. In turn, interest rate risk has two risk components: price risk and coupon reinvestment risk.

Price risk arises when interest rates change before the target date and the bond is sold before maturity. In this case, the realized market price (i.e., the selling price) for the bond will differ from the expected price, based on the assumption of stable interest rates. If interest rates were to increase after the purchase, the bond would sell in the secondary market at a price below expectations; if interest rates were to decline, the bond would sell at a price above expectations.

Coupon reinvestment risk arises because the yield to maturity computation implicitly assumes that all coupon payments will be reinvested at the prom-

[10]Lawrence Fisher and Roman L. Weil, "Coping with the Risk of Interest Rate Fluctuations: Returns to Bondholders from Naive and Optimal Strategies," *Journal of Business* 44, no. 4 (October 1971): 408–431.

Maturity strategy A portfolio immunization technique in which the investor acquires bonds with maturities that match the investment horizon.

ised yield to maturity. (Recall from Chapter 10 the interest-on-interest assumption built into the calculation.) If, after the purchase of the bond, interest rates were to decline, the coupon cash flows could be reinvested at rates below the promised YTM, and your ending wealth would fall short of expectations. In contrast, if interest rates were to increase after the bond purchase, the interim cash flows could be reinvested at higher than expected rates, and your ending wealth would be above expectations.

Immunization and Interest Rate Risk   Note that price risk and coupon reinvestment risk caused by a change in interest rates have opposite effects on the ending-wealth value of a bond portfolio. An increase in interest rates causes an ending price below expectations, but the reinvestment rate for interim cash flows exceeds expectations. A decline in market interest rates causes the reverse situation.

Clearly, a bond portfolio manager with a specific investment horizon (target date) would like to eliminate these two interest rate risks and earn a specific ending-wealth value. The relationship between the two components of interest rate risk enabled Fisher and Weil to develop a precise immunization process to accomplish this. They defined this technique as follows:

> A portfolio of investments in bonds is *immunized* for a holding period if its value at the end of the holding period, regardless of the course of interest rates during the holding period, must be at least as large as it would have been had the interest-rate function been constant throughout the holding period.[11]

Fisher and Weil showed that an investor can immunize a bond portfolio if the assumption holds that any interest rate changes will affect all rates by the same amount (i.e., there will be a parallel shift of the yield curve). Given this assumption, Fisher and Weil proved that a *portfolio of bonds is immunized from interest rate risk if the modified duration of the portfolio always equals the remaining investment horizon.*

We know that price risk and coupon reinvestment rate risk move in opposite directions in reaction to

changes in interest rates. Fisher and Weil showed that modified duration gives the time period when these two risks are of equal magnitude but opposite in direction. As an example, to immunize a portfolio with an investment horizon of 8 years against interest rate risk, its modified duration should equal 8 years. To attain a given portfolio duration, you set the value-weighted average modified duration of the portfolio at the investment horizon and keep it equal to the remaining horizon value over time.

Example of Immunization   The example in Table 11.4 shows the effect of attempting to immunize a single-bond portfolio by matching its investment horizon and modified duration compared to a **maturity strategy,** where the maturity of the bond is set equal to the investment horizon. This example assumes an investment horizon of 8 years and a current yield to maturity for 8-year bonds of 8 percent. If we assume no change in yields, the expected ending-wealth ratio should be 1.8509, which equals 1.08^8 with annual compounding.[12] As noted, this should also be the expected ending-wealth ratio for a completely immunized portfolio.

The example considers two strategies by which to immunize a portfolio against interest rate risk: (1) the maturity strategy, which sets term to maturity at 8 years, and (2) the duration strategy, which sets the modified duration at 8 years. For the maturity strategy, the portfolio manager acquires an 8-year, 8 percent bond. For the duration strategy the manager acquires a 10-year, 8 percent bond that has approximately an 8-year modified duration (it has a Macaulay duration of 8.12 years, assuming an 8 percent YTM). This is the example in Table 10.2. We assume a single change in the interest rate structure at the end of Year 4, when rates decline from 8 percent to 6 percent and stay there through Year 8.

As shown, the interest rate change reduced the ending-wealth ratio for the maturity strategy bond below the expected wealth ratio because of the shortfall in the reinvestment cash flow after Year 4, when interim coupon payments were reinvested at 6 percent rather than 8 percent. Note that the maturity strategy eliminated the price risk, however, because the bond matured at the end of Year 8.

[11]Ibid.

[12]We use annual compounding to compute the ending-wealth ratio because the example uses annual observations.

Table 11.4 *Effect of Change in Market Rates on a Portfolio That Uses the Maturity Strategy versus a Portfolio Immunized with a Duration Strategy*

	Results with Maturity Strategy			Results with Duration Strategy		
Year	Cash Flow	Reinvestment Rate	End Value	Cash Flow	Reinvestment Rate	End Value
1	$ 80.00	0.08	$ 80.00	$ 80.00	0.08	$ 80.00
2	80.00	0.08	166.40	80.00	0.08	166.40
3	80.00	0.08	259.71	80.00	0.08	259.71
4	80.00	0.08	360.49	80.00	0.08	360.49
5	80.00	0.06	462.12	80.00	0.06	462.12
6	80.00	0.06	596.85	80.00	0.06	596.85
7	80.00	0.06	684.04	80.00	0.06	684.04
8	1,080.00	0.06	1,805.08	1,120.64[a]	0.06	1,845.72

Expected-wealth ratio = 1.8509 or $1,850.90

[a]The bond could be sold at its market value of $1,040.64, which is the value for an 8 percent bond with 2 years to maturity priced to yield 6 percent.

The duration strategy portfolio likewise suffered a shortfall in reinvestment cash flow because of the decline in interest rates. This shortfall due to coupon reinvestment risk was partially offset by an increase in the ending value for the bond because of the decline in market rates. This second bond was sold at the end of Year 8 at 104.06 over par, the price of an 8 percent coupon bond with 2 years to maturity with interest rates at 6 percent. This partial offset due to the price increase gave the duration strategy an ending-wealth value of $1,845.72, which is much closer to the expected-wealth ratio of $1,850.90 than the maturity strategy's ratio of $1,805.08.

If market interest rates had increased during this period, the maturity strategy would have experienced portfolio reinvestment income greater than the expected cash flow, and an ending-wealth ratio above expectations. In contrast, the duration strategy portfolio's excess cash flow from reinvestment would have been partially offset by a decline in the ending price for the bond. The ending-wealth ratio for the duration strategy portfolio, while lower than that for the maturity strategy portfolio, would have been closer to the expected-wealth ratio. The point is, you pursue immunization to eliminate uncertainty due to interest rate changes by producing ending wealth equal to the expected-wealth position. As shown, the duration strategy accomplished this goal.

Another View of Immunization The prior example assumed that both bonds were acquired and held to the end of the investment horizon. An alternative way to envision portfolio immunization is to concentrate on the specific growth path from the beginning-wealth value to the ending-wealth value and examine what happens when interest rates change.

Assume that your initial-wealth value is $1 million, your investment horizon is 10 years, and your coupon and current YTM are both 8 percent. We know that the compound value of a dollar at 4 percent for 20 periods (with semiannual compounding) is 1.04^{20} which equals 2.1911. This implies an expected ending-wealth value of $2,191,100. Figure 11.3A shows the compound growth rate path from $1 million to the expected ending value of $2,191,100.

Figure 11.3B assumes an interest rate increase at the end of Year 2 of 200 basis points to 10 percent. With no prior interest rate changes, the value of the portfolio would have grown at an 8 percent compound interest rate to $1,169,900 [$1.04^4 = 1.1699$]. We know that the change in the interest rate will produce two changes for this portfolio: (1) its price (or value) will decline to reflect the higher rate, and (2) the reinvestment rate, which is the growth rate, will increase to 10 percent. To find the new ending wealth, we must find out how much the portfolio value will decline. The answer depends upon the modified duration of the portfolio at the time of the rate change.

Fisher and Weil showed that if modified duration equals the remaining horizon, the price (value) of the portfolio will grow at the new interest rate (10 percent) to the expected-wealth value. You can approximate the change in portfolio value using modified duration and the change in market rates. (Recall that this will not give an exact estimate because of the convexity of the portfolio.) The new value after the interest rate change would be $1,003,743. If this new portfolio value were to grow at 10 percent a year for 8 years, the ending-wealth value would be:

$1,003,743 × 2.1829 (5% for 16 periods) = $2,191,071

The difference between the expected and projected values is due to rounding.

This example shows that the price (value) decline is exactly offset by the higher reinvestment (growth) rate. It assumes that at the time of the interest rate change, the modified duration of the portfolio was equal to the remaining investment horizon.

What happens if the portfolio is not properly matched? If modified duration exceeds the remaining investment horizon, the price (value) change will be greater than desired. Thus higher interest rates would cause the value after the interest rate change to be below the $1,003,743 in Figure 11.3B. Even if the new value were to grow at 10 percent a year, it would not reach the expected ending-wealth value. As an example, Figure 11.3C assumes that the value of the portfolio declined to $950,000. If this new portfolio value were to grow at 10 percent a year for the remaining 8 years, the ending value would be:

$950,000 × 2.1829 (5% for 16 periods) = $2,073,755

The shortfall of $118,000 between the expected-wealth and realized-wealth values occurs because the portfolio was not properly immunized when interest rates changed. Its modified duration was not equal to its remaining investment horizon.

If interest rates had declined, and modified duration had been longer than 8 years, the new ending value would have exceeded the required value. Figure 11.3D shows what would happen to an improperly matched portfolio when interest rates declined by 200 basis points to 6 percent. A properly matched portfolio's value would increase to $1,365,493. If this new value were to grow at 6 percent for 8 years, the ending value would be:

$1,365,493 × 1.6047 (3% for 16 periods) = $2,191,207

Again, this computed value deviates slightly from the expected ending-wealth value ($2,191,100) due to rounding.

Alternatively, if the modified duration of the portfolio had been above 8 years, the new value would have been greater than the required value of $1,365,493. If we assume the portfolio value increased to $1,450,000, the ending value of the portfolio would be:

$1,450,000 × 1.6047 (3% for 16 periods) = $2,326,815

In this example, the ending-wealth value was greater than the expected-wealth value because the modified duration and the remaining investment horizon were mismatched and interest rates went in the right direction.

The important point is, when the modified duration of your portfolio does not match the remaining investment horizon, you are speculating on interest rate changes. The result can be very good or very bad. The purpose of immunization is to *avoid* these uncertainties and ensure achievement of the expected ending-wealth value ($2,191,100) irrespective of interest rate changes.

Implementing Immunization Implementing immunization to offset components of interest rate risk may seem simple: you merely match modified duration with the investment horizon. You might even consider it a passive strategy; simply match modified duration and the investment horizon, and you can ignore the portfolio until the investment horizon arrives. This is not true, as the following discussion will show. Immunization is neither simple nor passive.

There is one exception to this statement. The zero-coupon bond is unique among bond issues because it is a pure discount bond. As such, it has no reinvestment risk because the price discount assumes that its value will grow at the discount rate. For example, if you discount a future value at 10 percent, the present value factor assumes that the discounted value will grow at a compound rate of 10 percent to maturity. Also, a zero-coupon bond has no price risk if you set its duration (which is its maturity) at your investment horizon. Assuming the issuer does not default, you will certainly receive the face value of the bond at maturity.

An immunized portfolio of other than zero-coupon bonds requires frequent rebalancing to keep its modified duration equal to its remaining investment

Figure 11.3 *Growth Path to the Expected Ending-Wealth Value and the Effect of Matching Modified Duration and the Investment Horizon*

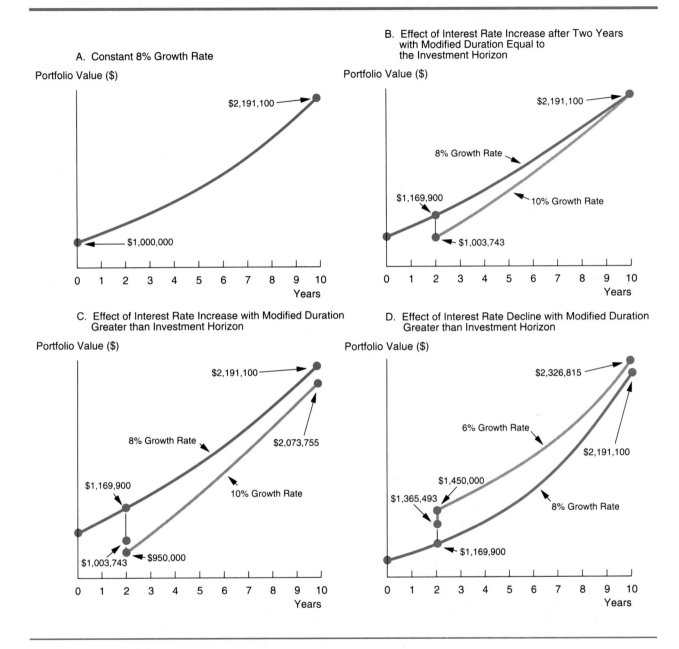

A. Constant 8% Growth Rate

B. Effect of Interest Rate Increase after Two Years with Modified Duration Equal to the Investment Horizon

C. Effect of Interest Rate Increase with Modified Duration Greater than Investment Horizon

D. Effect of Interest Rate Decline with Modified Duration Greater than Investment Horizon

horizon. Several characteristics of the duration of coupon bonds, which constitute the vast majority of bonds outstanding, make it impossible to set the modified duration of the portfolio equal to the remaining investment horizon at the initiation of the portfolio and ignore it thereafter.

First, duration declines more slowly than term to maturity, assuming no change in market interest rates. As an example, suppose you own a bond with a computed duration of 5 years at a 10 percent market yield. A year later, the duration of the security at the same YTM (10 percent) will equal approximately 4.2 years;

although term to maturity has declined by a year, duration declined by only 0.8 years. This means that, assuming no change in interest rates, the portfolio manager will have to rebalance the portfolio to reduce its duration to 4 years. You could do this by selling some long-term bonds and reinvesting in shorter-term bonds, or you could simply reinvest the cash flows from the portfolio in short-term T-bills.

The second characteristic of duration that forces active management is that it changes with a change in interest rates. In Chapter 10 we discussed the inverse relationship between the yields to maturity used to discount cash flows and duration. We demonstrated that higher interest rates will reduce duration and lower interest rates will raise duration. Therefore, a portfolio can start with modified duration matched to the remaining investment horizon, but its duration can change immediately if market rates change, and a portfolio manager would have to rebalance the port-

folio if the difference between modified duration and the investment horizon became too large.

Third, the immunization technique assumes that all market rates change by the same amount and in the same direction, i.e., there is a parallel shift in the yield curve. Based upon observing market interest rates over time, we know that this typically does not happen.

Finally, you always face the problem of acquiring the bonds you want in the market. Can you buy long-duration bonds at the price you consider acceptable? For all these reasons, the implementation of immunization requires active management of the portfolio.

Horizon Matching

Horizon matching combines two of the techniques discussed—cash-matched dedication and immunization. As shown in Figure 11.4, the investor's liability

Figure 11.4 **Horizon Matching**

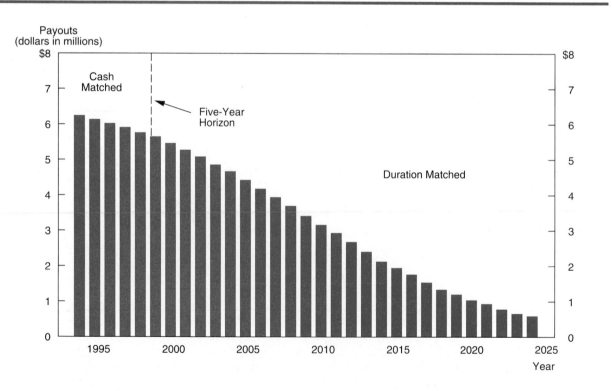

Source: Martin L. Leibowitz, Thomas E. Klaffky, Steven Mandel, and Alfred Weinberger, *Horizon Matching: A New Generalized Approach for Developing Minimum-Cost Dedicated Portfolios* (New York: Salomon Brothers, 1983).

stream is divided into two segments. To fulfill the first segment, the portfolio manager acquires assets that cash-match the liabilities during this portion of the holding period, in this case the first 5 years. In the second segment, the remaining 25-year liability stream, the liabilities are covered by a duration-matched strategy based on the immunization principles discussed earlier. As a result, the investor is certain to cash-match the liabilities during the early years, and still enjoys the cost saving and flexibility of matching the remaining liabilities using a duration strategy.[13]

Investment Objectives and Bond Portfolio Construction

Investors construct bond portfolios to achieve specific investment objectives using some or all of the investment techniques we have discussed. Although portfolio objectives remain fairly fixed over time, investment strategies vary with prevailing conditions in the capital market. To construct and manage a successful bond portfolio, the investor must capture as many beneficial attributes of a market as possible by using alternative investment strategies, while keeping in mind portfolio objectives.

Portfolio objectives vary from maximizing current income to speculation and short-term trading. Strategies vary according to the type of income sought. Although our discussion in this section is limited to three basic portfolio strategies, it is possible to construct a portfolio that falls anywhere along the continuum by emphasizing one strategy over another.

The various bond portfolios can be visualized as points along an upward-sloping security market line. The portfolio that maximizes current income would be at the lowest point because it has low risk and promises the lowest rate of return. Further up we would encounter the portfolio that seeks to maximize total income by maximizing long-term coupon income and capital gains assuming a modest amount of risk. Finally, speculation entails substantial risk, but offers the highest level of expected return. These portfolio

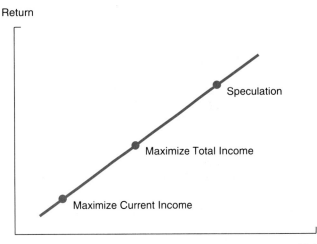

Figure 11.5   *Security Market Line: Bond Portfolios*

Bullet   A portfolio with maturities concentrated in a single sector.

relationships can be seen in Figure 11.5. You can alter your position on the security market line by changing investment tactics and strategy.

Maximizing Current Income

The objective of many bond investors is to build portfolios that generate regular and sizable cash flows. They want to maximize current income. Such an objective might suit a retired person, a college endowment fund that requires an ample cash flow to cover operating expenses, or an insurance company or pension fund that must provide substantial income to beneficiaries. All of these investors require high, certain levels of current cash flow with extreme safety of principal. Given these objectives, a portfolio manager cannot lower bond quality to attain higher returns.

To construct a current-income portfolio, the investor must decide on the maturity structure of the portfolio. This generally takes one of three forms:

- **bullets,** which concentrate maturities in one particular sector

---

[13]This technique is discussed in Martin L. Leibowitz, Thomas E. Klaffky, Steven Mandel, and Alfred Weinberger, *Horizon Matching: A New Generalized Approach for Developing Minimum-Cost Dedicated Portfolios* (New York: Salomon Brothers, 1983).

> **Ladder** A portfolio with approximately equal amounts allotted among various maturity segments.
> **Barbell** A portfolio with capital divided between short and long maturities, avoiding intermediate-term bonds.

- **ladders,** which allot approximately equal amounts of the portfolio to the various maturity segments
- **barbells,** which divide the capital between short maturities and long maturities, avoiding intermediate-term bonds

Once the investor decides on maturities, he or she should consider such factors as call-risk protection to lock in high returns for a maximum period, tax implications, and credit quality.

Income-oriented investors would probably favor a buy-and-hold strategy. Bond selections that required forecasting interest rates would likely be unpopular with such investors.

Speculation and Short-Term Trading

The objective of the speculator is to attain substantial capital appreciation in as little time as possible. Such an investor must possess extensive knowledge of interest-rate behavior, yield spreads, market characteristics, and the effect of issue features. From estimates of short-term interest rates and knowledge of the markets and the alternative investment vehicles available, the speculator seeks to derive maximum capital gains.

Speculating portfolio managers follow a single maturity strategy: maturity concentration. Speculators select bonds based on a forecast of interest rates, and occasionally they swap bonds. This portfolio management approach appeals to highly aggressive investors.

When interest rates are expected to fall, the short-term trader searches for substantial capital gains. Speculators often trade on margin to magnify available returns by increasing the leverage of the portfolio. After the decline in rates, the bond speculator takes any profit and moves to the sidelines to await the next major interest rate swing. Thus as interest rates level off or begin to rise, the trader would assume a more defensive position with short-term securities.

One feature of speculating in bonds is somewhat unique among capital markets. Short-term trading for capital gains usually involves high-grade securities, al-most always A and higher rated bonds, often supplemented by agency and Treasury obligations. Thus risk of default is not a factor in these transactions. High-quality bonds give speculators substantial interest rate sensitivity to help them take advantage of the price behavior when interest rates change. These high-grade bonds also tend to be more liquid.

Maximizing Total Income

Maximizing total income is a middle-of-the-road objective that combines a bit of speculation and a bit of current-income optimization. The investor constructs a portfolio to maximize total income in the form of either current coupon income or capital gains. The portfolio typically has a long-term investment horizon and generally assumes a fairly aggressive investment posture.

Total-income portfolio managers typically select securities on the basis of anticipated interest-rate behavior. They use bond swaps, along with short-term trading strategies to improve returns when conditions are right. No particular maturity strategy dominates the total-income portfolio, just as no specific investment strategy dominates the portfolio. This portfolio approach appeals to both individuals and institutions.

Bonds in a Total Investment Portfolio

The high level of interest rates that has prevailed since the latter part of the 1960s has provided increasingly attractive returns to bond investors. The wide swings in interest rates that have accompanied these high market yields have added opportunities for capital gains. Even with this recent performance, it is necessary to compare the performance of fixed-income securities to that of other investments and examine the place of bonds in a portfolio of all types of securities.

The performance of fixed-income securities has improved even more than returns alone indicate, because bonds offer substantial diversification benefits. Low correlation between the rates of return for stocks and bonds should lead you to focus on neither stocks nor bonds in your portfolio. Rather, some combination of them should provide a superior risk-adjusted return compared to either one alone. Numerous studies have shown that stock returns taken alone have historically outperformed bond returns, but the studies also showed a low correlation between the returns for bonds and equities. The *combination* of these securities in a portfolio will vastly improve the return per unit of risk.

Bonds and Investment Theory

Recall from Chapter 2 that modern investment theory predicts an upward-sloping security market line, meaning that higher rates of return should be accompanied by greater risk. Compared to other market vehicles, fixed-income securities have traditionally been viewed as low risk. Because bonds are considered to be relatively conservative investments, we would expect to find them on the lower end of the security market line.

Soldofsky examined the comparative risk–return characteristics of 28 classes of long-term securities.[14] Figure 11.6 shows the basic findings of the study and confirms the expectations. Specifically, government and high-grade corporate bonds were at the low end of the curve. Following upward, we find regular preferred stocks, high-quality common stocks, convertible securities, and finally lower-quality stocks and deep-discount bonds, which had both high risk levels and substantial rates of return.

An annual analysis of investment returns since 1926 by Ibbotson Associates compared corporate and government bonds with long and intermediate maturities to common stocks (in the form of total NYSE and small-firm results) and Treasury bills. Again, the results confirmed the expected long-run risk–return behavior. As shown in Figure 11.7, Treasury bills have the least risk and return, followed by government bonds, corporate bonds, total common stocks, and finally small capitalization common stocks.

All these results confirm that bonds can serve as the base for a low risk–low return segment of a portfolio. They should be included as part of any well-diversified portfolio.

Active Bond Management and Efficient Markets

Several of our discussions of bond portfolio management techniques indicated that investors could earn above-normal rates of return if they acted on accurate predictions of what the market would do. Specifically, we found that investors would need to forecast interest rate levels and changes, yield spread changes, and bond rating changes. The difficulty of some of these predictions depends upon how fast the market adjusts to various economic events. This is referred to as *market efficiency*. Although we will examine the subject of efficient capital markets in detail in Chapter 22, it is necessary to consider at this point whether expectations of accurate predictions are reasonable.

Studies of market efficiency have focused on bond prices, examining the ability of investors to forecast interest rates. If you can forecast interest rates, you can forecast bond price behavior. Several studies reached the same conclusion: interest rate behavior cannot be consistently and accurately forecast.[15]

The predictive models developed ranged from a naive technique without any forecast to fairly sophisticated techniques. In all cases, the most naive model with no forecast at all tracked future interest rates the best. This implies that interest rates cannot be forecasted using even a fairly sophisticated mechanical forecasting model.

This does not mean that nobody can forecast correctly. It means only that forecasting interest rates is not an easy task or a trivial talent. You need to determine whether you or your portfolio manager can do it consistently. The same statements hold true for predicting changes in yield spreads.

Portfolio managers interested in credit analysis should be aware of the results of bond rating studies. Several studies have examined the informational value of bond rating changes. Analysis of monthly bond returns for the periods surrounding the announcement of bond rating changes indicated no effect from 6 months before to 6 months after the announcement.[16] This implies that the market effect probably occurred over 6 months before the announcement. Alternatively, several studies found a significant im-

[14]Robert M. Soldofsky, "Risk and Return for Long-Term Securities, 1971–1982," *The Journal of Portfolio Management* 11, no. 1 (Fall 1984): 57–64.

[15]See, for example, Stephen K. McNees, "The Recent Record of Thirteen Forecasters," *New England Economic Review*, Federal Reserve Bank of Boston (September–October 1981); and Adrian W. Throop, "Interest Rate Forecasts and Market Efficiency," *Economic Review*, Federal Reserve Bank of San Francisco (Spring 1981): 29–43.

[16]Mark I. Weinstein, "The Effect of a Rating Change Announcement on Bond Price," *Journal of Financial Economics* 5, no. 3 (December 1977): 329–350.

Figure 11.6 *Risk–Return Graph for Long-Term Securities, 1971–1982*

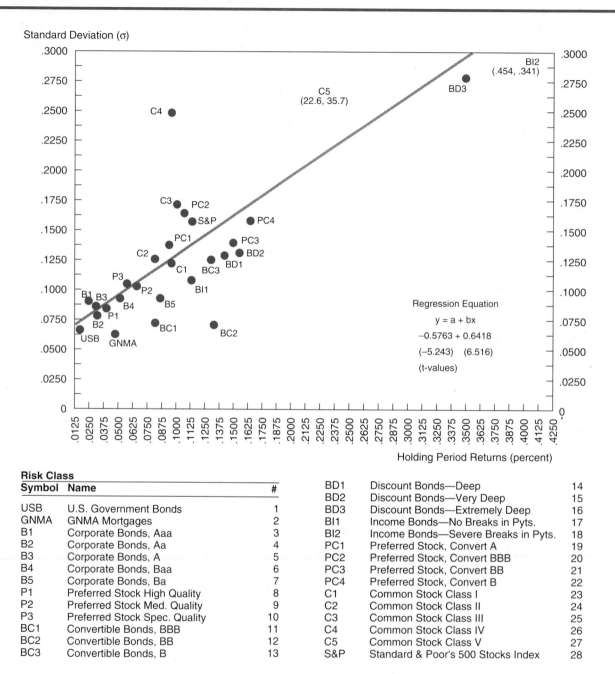

Risk Class Symbol	Name	#
USB	U.S. Government Bonds	1
GNMA	GNMA Mortgages	2
B1	Corporate Bonds, Aaa	3
B2	Corporate Bonds, Aa	4
B3	Corporate Bonds, A	5
B4	Corporate Bonds, Baa	6
B5	Corporate Bonds, Ba	7
P1	Preferred Stock High Quality	8
P2	Preferred Stock Med. Quality	9
P3	Preferred Stock Spec. Quality	10
BC1	Convertible Bonds, BBB	11
BC2	Convertible Bonds, BB	12
BC3	Convertible Bonds, B	13
BD1	Discount Bonds—Deep	14
BD2	Discount Bonds—Very Deep	15
BD3	Discount Bonds—Extremely Deep	16
BI1	Income Bonds—No Breaks in Pyts.	17
BI2	Income Bonds—Severe Breaks in Pyts.	18
PC1	Preferred Stock, Convert A	19
PC2	Preferred Stock, Convert BBB	20
PC3	Preferred Stock, Convert BB	21
PC4	Preferred Stock, Convert B	22
C1	Common Stock Class I	23
C2	Common Stock Class II	24
C3	Common Stock Class III	25
C4	Common Stock Class IV	26
C5	Common Stock Class V	27
S&P	Standard & Poor's 500 Stocks Index	28

Note: Minimum term to maturity on bonds is 15 years.

Source: Robert M. Soldofsky, "Risk and Return for Long-Term Securities, 1971–1982," *The Journal of Portfolio Management* 11, no. 1 (Fall 1984), p. 60. Reprinted by permission.

| Figure 11.7 | Mean Rate of Return and Standard Deviation of Returns for Common Stocks, Government and Corporate Bonds, T-Bills, and Inflation: 1926–1989 |

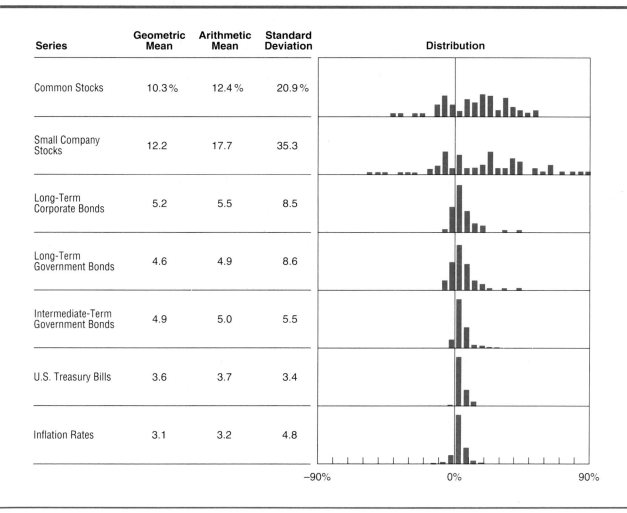

Series	Geometric Mean	Arithmetic Mean	Standard Deviation	Distribution
Common Stocks	10.3%	12.4%	20.9%	
Small Company Stocks	12.2	17.7	35.3	
Long-Term Corporate Bonds	5.2	5.5	8.5	
Long-Term Government Bonds	4.6	4.9	8.6	
Intermediate-Term Government Bonds	4.9	5.0	5.5	
U.S. Treasury Bills	3.6	3.7	3.4	
Inflation Rates	3.1	3.2	4.8	

Note: The 1933 small company stock total return was 142.9 percent.

Source: Roger G. Ibbotson and Rex A. Sinquefield, *Stocks, Bonds, Bills, and Inflation (SBBI)*, 1982, updated in SBBI 1990 Yearbook, Ibbotson Associates, Inc., Chicago.

pact of bond rating downgrades on stock returns, but no impact on stock prices when upgrades were announced.[17]

What does market efficiency imply for bond market strategies, such as bond swaps and yield spreads? Bond swaps suggest some market inefficiency, because they assume temporary abnormalities within or be-tween market segments that provide profitable opportunities. Numerous profitable swap opportunities suggest that price irregularities are neither rare nor random events. Such opportunities may arise from the market's domination by institutional investors and the resulting market segmentation. In effect, artificial constraints, regulations, and statutes may largely create the opportunity for profitable bond swaps.

Alternatively, an increase in yield because of a bond swap for a lower-rated issue does not imply market inefficiency, since the higher default risk accounts for the greater expected return.

[17]See Robert W. Holthausen and Richard W. Leftwich, "The Effect of Bond Rating Changes on Common Stock Prices," *Journal of Financial Economics* 17, no. 1 (September 1986): 57–89.

Yield spreads likewise indicate market efficiency, because they reflect equilibrium yield rates based on differential standards of risk, quality, and other issue characteristics. AAA corporates should yield less than A-rated obligations because of differences in their risk–return profiles. The existence of yield spreads is rational, and their sizes are determined in a highly efficient manner by market participants. Investors must recognize that deriving abnormal returns from this technique requires *predicting* the relevant changes in these spreads. That is not an easy task.

Summary

▪ To help meet the varying objectives of bond investors, the following bond portfolio management strategies have been developed:

1. Passive management strategies
   a. Buy-and-hold
   b. Indexing
2. Active management strategies
   a. Interest rate anticipation
   b. Valuation analysis
   c. Credit analysis including high-yield bonds
   d. Yield spread analysis
   e. Bond swaps
3. Matched-funding strategies
   a. Dedicated portfolios
      1. Cash-matched dedication
      2. Dedication with reinvestment
   b. Immunization
   c. Horizon matching

▪ While you should understand the alternative theoretical strategies available and how to implement them, a specific strategy is based upon the needs and desires of the investor and the background and talents of the portfolio manager. It is possible to conceive of a range of portfolio approaches, including maximizing current income, short-term trading and speculation, or attempting to maximize total income.

▪ The risk–return performance of bonds has been consistent with expectations. They have consistently provided low risk–low return performance relative to stocks and other forms of investments. In addition, including them in portfolios with other assets has enhanced the overall performance of these portfolios because of the low correlation of the bond returns with the returns from other financial assets.

▪ Studies have supported the notion of an efficient market in terms of success predicting interest rates or rating changes. This does not mean that it is not possible to benefit from active management, it just means that the implementation of these active strategies is not easy and requires time and talent.

Questions

1. Explain the difference between a pure buy-and-hold strategy and a modified buy-and-hold strategy.
2. What is an indexing strategy? How do you evaluate the performance of an indexed portfolio?
3. Briefly describe three techniques that are considered active bond portfolio management strategies.
4. What are the incentives for investing in high-yield bonds? Discuss the potential problems from investing in high-yield bonds and how you can avoid them.
5. Describe a cash-matched, dedicated portfolio and discuss the advantages of such a strategy.
6. Describe the two components of interest rate risk.
7. What is meant by "bond portfolio immunization"?
8. If the yield curve were flat and stable, how would you immunize your portfolio?
9. You begin with an investment horizon of 4 years, a portfolio duration of 4 years, and a market interest rate of 10 percent. A year later, what is your investment horizon? Assuming no change in interest rates, what is the duration of your portfolio relative to your investment horizon? What does this difference imply about your ability to immunize your portfolio?
10. Some have contended that a zero-coupon bond is the ideal financial instrument to use for immunizing a portfolio. Discuss the reasoning for this statement in terms of the objective of immunization (i.e., the elimination of interest rate risk).
11. During a conference with a client, the subject of immunization is introduced. The client questions the fee charged for developing and managing an immunized portfolio. Understanding that immunization is basically a passive investment strategy, the client believes the management fee should be substantially lower. How would you explain to the client that immunization is not a passive policy and that it actually requires more time and talent than a buy-and-hold policy?

12. *CFA Examination III* (June 1983)

    The ability to immunize a bond portfolio is very desirable for bond portfolio managers in some instances.

    a. Discuss the components of interest rate risk— i.e., assuming a change in interest rates over time, explain the two risks faced by the holder of a bond.

    b. Define *immunization* and discuss why a bond manager would immunize a portfolio.

    c. Explain why a duration-matching strategy is a superior technique to a maturity-matching strategy for the minimization of interest-rate risk.

    d. Explain in specific terms how you would use a zero-coupon bond to immunize a bond portfolio. Discuss why a zero-coupon bond is an ideal instrument in this regard. [35 minutes]

13. *CFA Examination III* (June 1988)

    The use of bond index funds has grown dramatically in recent years.

    a. Discuss the reasons you would expect it to be easier or more difficult to construct a bond index than a stock index.

    b. It is contended that the operational process of managing a corporate bond index fund is more difficult than managing an equity index fund. Discuss three examples that support this contention.

14. *CFA Examination III* (June 1988)

    Hans Kaufmann is a global fixed-income portfolio manager based in Switzerland. His clients are primarily U.S.-based pension funds. He allocates investments in the following four countries:

    - United States
    - Japan
    - West Germany
    - United Kingdom

    His approach is to make investment allocation decisions between these four countries based on his global economic outlook. In order to develop this, Kaufmann analyzes these five factors for each country:

    - Real economic growth
    - Inflation
    - Monetary policy
    - Interest rates
    - Exchange rates

When Kaufmann believes that the four economies are equally attractive for investment purposes, he equally weights investments in the four countries. When the economies are not equally attractive, he overweights the country or countries where he sees the largest potential returns. Tables 1 through 5 present relevant economic data and forecasts.

a. Indicate, before taking into account currency hedging, whether Kaufmann should overweight or underweight investments in each country. Justify your position. [15 minutes]

b. Briefly describe how your answer to 14a might change with the use of currency hedging techniques. [5 minutes]

Table 1   ***Real GNP/GDP (annual changes)***

	1985	1986	1987	1988E
United States	3.0%	2.9%	2.4%	2.7%
Japan	4.7	2.4	3.2	3.4
West Germany	2.0	2.5	1.5	2.1
United Kingdom	3.4	3.0	3.4	2.3

Sources: World Economic Outlook, October 1987; and Kaufmann's estimates.

Table 2   ***GNP/GDP Deflator (annual changes)***

	1985	1986	1987	1988E
United States	3.2%	2.6%	3.3%	3.8%
Japan	1.5	2.8	3.0	3.0
West Germany	2.2	3.1	2.5	2.2
United Kingdom	6.0	3.5	4.5	4.8

Table 3   ***Narrow Money (M1, annual changes)***

	1985	1986	1987	1988E
United States	9.2%	13.4%	5.5%	7.0%
Japan	5.0	6.9	9.9	10.0
West Germany	4.3	8.5	7.5	8.5
United Kingdom	17.8	25.6	16.5	12.0

Table 4   Long-Term Interest Rates (annual changes)

	1985	1986	1987	1988E
United States	10.6%	7.7%	8.8%	9.0%
Japan	6.5	5.2	6.1	6.1
West Germany	6.9	5.9	6.1	7.0
United Kingdom	10.6	9.9	9.8	9.5

Table 5   Exchange Rates (currency per U.S.$, annual changes)

	1985	1986	1987	1988E
United States (dollars)	1.00	1.00	1.00	1.00
Japan (yen)	228.08	163.87	141.22	140.09
West Germany (marks)	2.80	2.08	1.74	1.67
United Kingdom (pounds)	0.74	0.67	0.58	0.59

15. *CFA Examination III* (1989)
You are a portfolio manager and have a meeting with a client, the very conservative administrator of a pension plan who is interested in segregating the funding liability for a group of current retirees. She has read about alternative versions of dedicated bond portfolios that can be set up to match the required funding.
a. Explain the differences between a pure cash-matched dedication and a cash-matched dedication with reinvestment, including any differences in cost and flexibility.
b. The administrator has heard that a horizon-matched portfolio can involve much lower costs than either a pure cash-match or a cash-match with reinvestment. Explain what is involved in a horizon-matched strategy and compare the risks of this form of dedication to the other dedication techniques.
c. Comment on the potential problems that can arise in the construction and management of a dedicated portfolio. Also comment on how you could actively manage a dedicated port-

folio to improve its return while ensuring its cash flow requirements. [20 minutes]
16. *CFA Examination III* (1990)
The investment committee of the money management firm of Gentry, Inc. has typically been very conservative and has avoided investing in high-yield (junk) bonds, although they have had major positions in investment-grade corporate bonds. Recently, Pete Squire, a member of the committee, suggested that they should review their policy regarding junk bonds because they currently constitute over 25 percent of the total corporate bond market. As a part of this policy review, you are asked to respond to the following questions.
a. Briefly discuss the liquidity *and* pricing characteristics of junk bonds relative to *each* of the following types of fixed income securities:

- Treasuries
- High-grade corporate bonds
- Corporate loans
- Private placements

Briefly discuss the implications of these differences for Gentry's bond portfolio managers.
The committee has learned that the correlation of rates of return between Treasuries and high-grade corporate bonds is approximately 0.98, while the correlation between Treasury/high-grade corporate bonds and junk bonds is approximately 0.45.
b. Briefly explain the reason for this difference in correlations, and briefly discuss its implications for bond portfolios.
The committee has also heard that durations at the times of issue for junk bonds are typically much shorter than for newly issued high-grade corporate bonds.
c. Briefly explain the reason for this difference in duration, and briefly discuss its implication for the volatility of bond portfolios. [15 minutes]

Problems

1. You have a portfolio with a market value of $50 million and a Macaulay duration of 7 years (assuming a market interest rate of 10 percent). If interest rates jump to 12 percent, compute the estimated value of your portfolio using your duration figure. Show all your computations.

2. Assume that at the initiation of an investment account, the market value of your portfolio is $200 million, and you immunize the portfolio at 12 percent for 6 years. During the first year, interest rates are constant at 12 percent.
   a. What is the market value of the portfolio at the end of Year 1?
   b. Immediately after the end of the year, interest rates decline to 10 percent. Estimate the new value of the portfolio assuming you were properly immunized. (Use only modified duration.)
3. Compute the Macaulay durations for the following bonds:
   a. A bond with a 5-year term to maturity, a 12 percent coupon (with annual payments), and a market yield of 10 percent.
   b. A bond with a 4-year term to maturity, a 12 percent coupon (with annual payments), and a market yield of 10 percent.
   c. Compare your answers to 3a and 3b, and discuss their implications for immunization.
4. Compute the Macaulay duration for the following bonds:
   a. A bond with a 4-year term to maturity, a 10 percent coupon (with annual payments), and a market yield of 8 percent.
   b. A bond with a 4-year term to maturity, a 10 percent coupon (with annual payments), and a market yield of 12 percent.
   c. Compare your answers to 4a and 4b. Assuming yields shifted immediately, discuss the implications for immunization.
5. Assume you have a zero-coupon bond with a term to maturity at issue of 10 years (with semiannual compounding):
   a. What is the duration of the bond at issue, assuming a market yield of 10 percent? What is its duration if the market yield is 14 percent? Discuss these two answers.
   b. Compute the initial issue price of this bond at a market yield of 14 percent.
   c. Compute the initial issue price of this bond at a market yield of 10 percent.
   d. A year after issue, the bond in 5c is selling to yield 12 percent. What is its current market price? Assuming you owned this bond during the year, what is your rate of return?

References

Altman, Edward I., and Scott A. Nammacher. *Investing in Junk Bonds.* New York: John Wiley & Sons, 1987.

Babcock, Guilford C. "Duration as a Link between Yield and Value." *Journal of Portfolio Management* 10, no. 4 (Summer 1984).

Barnes, Tom, Keith Johnson, and Don Shannon. "A Test of Fixed Income Strategies." *Journal of Portfolio Management* 10, no. 2 (Winter 1984).

Bierman, Harold. "Investors in Junk Bonds," *Journal of Portfolio Management* 16, no. 2 (Winter 1990).

Bierwag, G. O., George G. Kaufman, and Alden Toevs, eds. *Innovations in Bond Portfolio Management: Duration Analysis and Immunization.* Greenwich, Conn.: JAI Press, 1983.

Bierwag, G. O., George G. Kaufman, and Alden Toevs. "Duration: Its Development and Use in Bond Portfolio Management." *Financial Analysts Journal* 39, no. 4 (July–August 1983).

Choie, Kenneth S. "A Simplified Approach to Bond Portfolio Management: DDS." *Journal of Portfolio Management* 16, no. 3 (Spring 1990).

Fabozzi, Frank J., ed. *The Handbook of Fixed Income Securities*, 3d ed. Homewood, Ill.: Business One Irwin, 1991.

Fridson, Martin. *High Yield Bonds: Assessing Risk and Identifying Value in Speculative Grade Securities.* Chicago: Probus Publishing, 1989.

Goodman, Laurie S. "High-Yield Default Rates: Is there Cause for Concern?" *Journal of Portfolio Management* 16, no. 2 (Winter 1990).

Howe, June Tripp. *Junk Bonds: Analysis and Portfolio Strategies.* Chicago: Probus Publishing, 1988.

Leibowitz, Martin L., William S. Krasker, and Ardavan Nozari. "Spread Duration: A New Tool for Bond Portfolio Management." *Journal of Portfolio Management* 16, no. 3 (Spring 1990).

Reilly, Frank K., ed. *High Yield Bonds: Analysis and Risk Assessment.* Charlottesville, Va.: Institute of Chartered Financial Analysts, 1990.

Reilly, Frank K., and Michael D. Joehnk. "The Association between Market-Determined Risk Measures for Bonds and Bond Ratings." *Journal of Finance* 31, no. 5 (December 1976).

Tuttle, Donald, ed. *The Revolution in Techniques for Managing Bond Portfolios.* Charlottesville, Va.: Institute of Chartered Financial Analysts, 1983.

Van Horne, James. *Financial Market Rates and Flows*, 3d ed. Englewood Cliffs, N.J.: Prentice-Hall, 1989.

Wilson, Richard S., and Frank J. Fabozzi. *The New Corporate Bond Market.* Chicago: Probus Publishing, 1990.

Analysis of Stocks

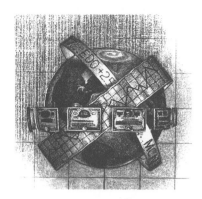

This section is concerned with the analysis of stocks using the tools of both fundamental and technical analysis. The first three chapters present the fundamental approach while the fourth chapter sets forth the technical approach.

As you know from the discussions in Chapters 8 and 9, the fundamental approach moves basically from the top down, emphasizing the need to begin by examining the aggregate economy and market outlook, then proceeding to analyze alternative industries, and, finally, individual companies in the better industries and the stocks of these companies. Therefore, Chapter 12 covers the microanalysis of a country's stock market. You estimate the future value for the stock market using the dividend discount model (DDM) based upon the country's economic outlook. Given this future value, you can estimate the expected rate of return from investing in that stock market during your holding period.

Assuming the initial analysis of the aggregate stock market favors some commitment to this market, the second step is to analyze alternative industries. This is the topic for Chapter 13, in which we discuss why you should undertake industry analysis and how you should analyze an industry in order to arrive at its expected rate of return. This will allow you to decide if the ex-

pected rate of return from investing in the industry is equal to or greater than your required rate of return for it.

Chapter 14 assumes that you have decided to commit funds to a specified stock market and particular industries. This leads to the final two questions in fundamental analysis. First, which are the best companies within the desirable industries? Second, are the common stocks of these companies underpriced, that is, is the value of the stock above its current market price? If so, this implies that the expected rate of return on the stock exceeds your required rate of return on it. In Chapter 14 we discuss how you can use the dividend discount model (DDM) to make this decision.

Chapter 15 concludes the section with a discussion of the technical approach to the analysis of the market, industries, and stocks. As noted, technical analysis makes investment decisions differently than the fundamental approach. To help you understand technical analysis the chapter examines the basic philosophy underlying all technical approaches to valuation, noting its advantages and potential problems. The bulk of the chapter presents and discusses a number of technical trading rules for U.S. and foreign stock markets.

12

Fundamental Analysis of the Stock Market

In earlier chapters we emphasized the importance of analyzing the aggregate economy and security markets before beginning any industry or company analysis. It is very important to determine the economic and market outlooks for investing in stocks, bonds, or cash before you consider in which industry or company to invest.

The techniques for making that security market decision can be described as either macroanalysis, which is based upon the strong relationship between the aggregate economy and the security markets, or microanalysis, which applies basic valuation models to the bond or equity markets. Chapter 9 covered the macroanalysis techniques and discussed world asset allocation. Chapter 10 discussed microanalysis for the valuation of bonds.

This chapter explains the microanalysis of a country's stock market. Your estimate of future value for the stock market in a country implies an estimate of your rate of return if you owned stock during the same period.

This is part of the three-step valuation process introduced in Chapter 8. As noted in the section introduction, this chapter begins the fundamental analysis of stocks with the determination of the value of the market on the basis of sales, earnings, and risk factors. Chapter 13 will then deal with analysis of industries based on the same kinds of data, Chapter 14 will consider how to estimate the value of stock for individual firms.

In order to determine the future value of the aggregate stock market using microanalysis techniques we will apply basic valuation theory to the aggregate stock market. We do this in five sections. The first presents the theoretical background for the multiplier approach. The second section considers the estimation of earnings per share, while the third section deals with the estimation of the earnings multiplier, or the price–earnings ratio. In section four we combine the estimates of earnings per share and the price–earnings ratio to derive a future value for the market on which to base estimates of the expected rate of return on stocks during a holding period. The final section discusses how to apply this approach to foreign markets.

The Valuation Model: Review and Application to the Market

In Chapter 8 we worked with a valuation model that equated the value of an investment to:

1. The stream of expected returns
2. The time pattern of expected returns
3. The required rate of return on the investment

Using this information, we developed the dividend growth model, which estimated the value of a stock (V_j) assuming a constant growth rate of dividends for an infinite period:

$$V_j = \frac{D_0(1 + g)}{(1 + k)} + \frac{D_0(1 + g)^2}{(1 + k)^2} + \cdots \frac{D_0(1 + g)^n}{(1 + k)^n}$$

where:

V_j = value of stock

D_0 = dividend payment in the current period

g = constant growth rate of dividends

k = required rate of return on stock

n = number of periods, assumed to be infinite

We used this model as the basis for the fundamental analysis of common stock. You can also use it to value a stock market series, though we showed in the appendix to Chapter 9 that this model can be simplified to the following expression:

$$V_j = P_j = \frac{D_1}{k - g}$$

where:

P_j = price of stock j

D_1 = dividend in period 1, which equals $D_0 (1 + g)$

k = required rate of return for stock j

g = constant growth rate of dividends

This model suggests parameters to be estimated: (1) the required rate of return (k), and (2) the expected growth rate of dividends (g). After estimating g, it is simple to estimate D_1 as the known current dividend (D_0) times $(1 + g)$.

Recall too that we can transform the dividend growth model into an earnings multiplier model by dividing both sides of the equation by E_1:

$$\frac{P_1}{E_1} = \frac{\dfrac{D_1}{E_1}}{k - g}$$

We call this P_1/E_1 the *earnings multiplier* or the *price–earnings ratio* (P/E ratio). It is determined by:

1. The expected dividend payout ratio (D_1/E_1)
2. The required rate of return on the stock (k)
3. The expected growth rate of dividends for the stock (g)

We will see that the estimation of this earning multiplier is important because it varies between stocks and industries. Also, the multiplier for the aggregate stock market varies widely over time and has a big impact on changes in the value of the market.

We showed previously that the difficult parameters to estimate are k and g, or, more specifically, the spread between k and g. Recall that very small changes in either k or g without any offset in the other variable can affect the spread and change the value of the earnings multiplier substantially.

Two-Part Valuation Procedure

To find a value for the stock market, we use the earnings multiplier version of the dividend valuation model because it is a theoretically correct model of value, assuming constant growth of dividends for an infinite time period. These are reasonable assumptions for the aggregate stock market. Also, this technique of market valuation is consistently used in practice.

Recall that k and g are independent variables because k depends heavily on risk, while g is a function of the retention rate and the ROE. Therefore, the spread between k and g can and does change over time. The following equations show that you can derive an estimate of this spread at a point in time by examining the prevailing dividend yield:

$$P_j = \frac{D_1}{k - g}$$

$$\frac{P_j}{D_1} = \frac{1}{k - g}$$

$$\frac{D_1}{P_j} = k - g$$

While the dividend yield gives an estimate of the size of the prevailing spread, it does not indicate the values for the two individual components (k and g). More important, it says nothing about the future spread, which is the critical value.

Importance of Both Components of Value

The ultimate objective of this microanalysis is to estimate the future market value for some major stock market series, such as the DJIA or the S&P 400. It is important to recognize that this estimation process has two equally important steps:

1. Estimating the future earnings per share for the stock market series
2. Estimating a future earnings multiplier for the stock market series[1]

Some analysts have concentrated on estimating earnings for these series with little consideration of changes in their earnings multipliers. An investor who considers the earnings figure alone and ignores the earnings multiplier implicitly assumes that the earnings multiplier is relatively constant over time. If this were correct, stock prices would generally move in line with earnings. The fallacy of this assumption is obvious when one examines data for the two components during the period since 1970 in Table 12.1.

The earnings per share column gives values during each year for the S&P 400 series. The next column shows the percentage change from the prior year. The third column shows the historical earnings multiplier at the end of the year, which equals the year-end value for the S&P 400 series divided by the earnings for that year. As an example, at the end of 1970, the value of the S&P 400 price series was 100.90 and the earnings

per share for the firms that made up the series came to 5.41. These values imply an earnings multiplier of about 18.65 (100.90/5.41). Although this is not the ideal measure of the multiplier, it is constant in its measurement and shows the changes in the relationship between stock prices and earnings over time.

Many striking examples show annual stock price movements for the S&P 400 series opposite to earnings changes during the same year:

- In 1973 profits increased by 30 percent while stock prices declined by 17 percent.
- In 1974 profits increased by 9 percent while stock prices declined by 30 percent.
- In 1975 profits declined by 10 percent while stock prices increased by 32 percent.
- In 1977 profits increased by 7 percent while stock prices declined by 12 percent.
- In 1980 profits decreased by 1 percent while stock prices increased by over 27 percent.
- In 1982 profits decreased by 21 percent while stock prices increased by 15 percent.
- In 1984 profits increased by almost 23 percent while stock prices were basically unchanged.
- In 1985 profits decreased by 15 percent while stock prices increased by about 26 percent.
- In 1986 profits decreased by almost 5 percent while stock prices increased by over 15 percent.
- In 1989 profits were almost unchanged while stock prices increased by almost 26 percent.

During each of these years, the major influence on stock price movements came from changes in the earnings multiplier. The greater volatility of the multiplier compared to earnings per share can be seen from the summary figures at the bottom of Table 12.1 and from the graph of the earnings multiplier in Figure 12.1 The standard deviation of the annual changes for the earnings multiplier series is much larger than the standard deviation of earnings changes (25.64 versus 16.19). The same is true for the relative measure of variability, the coefficient of variation (9.29 versus 1.83). Also, if you consider the mean annual percentage changes of the two series without signs, the earnings multiplier series has a larger value (18.41 versus 13.30 percent) and it has a larger standard deviation of annual percentage change (15.47 versus 10.91). These figures show that, of the two estimates required for dividend valuation, the earnings multiplier is more volatile and possibly more uncertain.

---

[1]We will emphasize estimating *future* values. While we will show the relevant variables and provide a procedural framework, the final estimate depends upon the ability of the analyst.

Table 12.1	**Annual Changes in Corporate Earnings, the Earnings Multiplier, and Stock Prices: Standard & Poor's 400, 1970–1989**					

	Earnings per Share	Percentage Change	Year-End Earnings Multiple	Percentage Change	Year-End Stock Prices	Percentage Change
1970	5.41	−11.7%	18.65	12.6%	100.90	−0.6%
1971	5.97	10.4	18.88	1.2	112.72	11.7
1972	6.83	14.4	19.31	2.3	131.87	17.0
1973	8.89	30.2	12.28	−36.4	109.14	−17.2
1974	9.61	8.1	7.96	−35.2	76.47	−29.9
1975	8.58	−10.7	11.76	47.8	100.88	31.9
1976	10.69	24.6	11.17	−5.0	119.46	18.4
1977	11.45	7.1	9.14	−18.2	104.71	−12.3
1978	13.04	13.9	8.22	−10.1	107.21	2.4
1979	16.29	24.9	7.43	−9.6	121.02	12.9
1980	16.12	−1.0	9.58	29.0	154.45	27.6
1981	16.74	3.8	8.19	−14.5	137.12	−11.2
1982	13.20	−21.1	11.94	45.8	157.62	15.0
1983	14.78	11.9	12.61	5.6	186.24	18.2
1984	18.11	22.6	10.29	−18.4	186.36	0.1
1985	15.28	−15.6	15.35	49.2	234.56	25.9
1986	14.53	−4.9	18.53	20.7	269.93	15.1
1987	20.28	39.6	14.09	−24.0	285.86	5.9
1988	26.59	31.1	12.08	−14.3	321.26	12.4
1989	26.44	−0.6	15.26	26.3	403.49	25.6
With Signs						
Mean	—	8.83	—	2.76	—	8.45
Standard deviation	—	16.19	—	25.64	—	15.90
Coefficient of variation	—	1.83	—	9.29	—	1.88
Without Signs						
Mean	—	13.30	—	18.41	—	14.55
Standard deviation	—	10.91	—	15.47	—	12.09
Coefficient of variation	—	0.82	—	0.84	—	0.83

Source: *Standard & Poor's Analysts Handbook* (New York: Standard & Poor's Corporation, 1990). Reprinted with permission.

The point is, this calculation of future market value requires two separate estimates. We will begin by considering a procedure for estimating aggregate earnings, but we will also discuss the factors that should be analyzed when estimating the aggregate market earnings multiplier.

Part One: Estimating Expected Earnings per Share

The estimate of expected earnings per share for the market series requires consideration of the outlook for the aggregate economy and for the corporate sector.

Figure 12.1 **Year-End Earnings Multiplier, S&P 400**

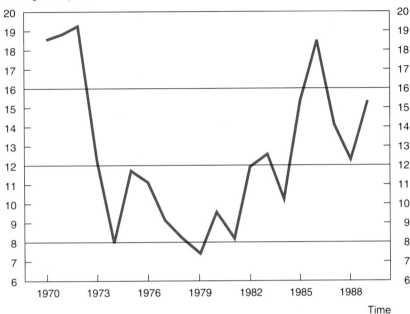

This involves several distinct steps:

1. Estimate sales per share for the stock market series (in our case, the S&P 400). This sales estimate requires an estimate of gross national product (GNP) because of its relationship to the sales of major industrial firms. Therefore, prior to estimating sales per share, we will estimate GNP.
2. Estimate the operating profit margin for the series, which equals operating profit divided by sales. Based on data available from Standard & Poor's, we will define operating profit as earnings before depreciation, interest, and taxes (EBDIT).
3. Estimate depreciation per share for the next year.
4. Estimate interest expense per share for the next year.
5. Estimate the corporate tax rate for the next year.

These steps will lead to an estimate of earnings per share that we will combine with an estimate of the earnings multiplier to arrive at an estimate of the ending price for the stock market series.

Step 1: Estimating Gross National Product

GNP is a measure of aggregate economic output or activity. Therefore, one would expect aggregate corporate sales to be related to GNP. We begin our estimate of sales for a stock market series with a prediction of nominal GNP from one of several banks or financial services that regularly publish such estimates.[2] Based on this estimate of nominal GNP, we can estimate corporate sales through the historical relationship between S&P 400 sales per share and aggregate economic activity (GNP).

---

[2]This would include projections by Standard & Poor's appearing late each year in *The Outlook*, projections by several large investment firms, such as Goldman, Sachs & Co. (*The Pocket Chartbook*) and Merrill Lynch, as well as by banks. An example from a Federal Reserve bank is, J.A. Cacy and Richard Roberts, "The U.S. Economy in 1987 and 1988," Federal Reserve Bank of Kansas City *Economic Review* (December 1987): 3–15.

Figure 12.2   *Scatter Plot of Annual Percentage Changes in S&P 400 Sales and GNP*

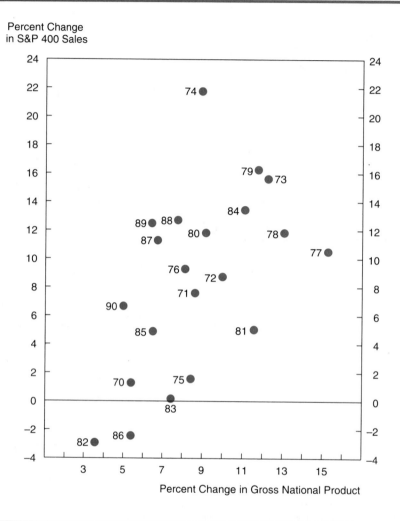

Step 2: Estimating the Market Series Sales per Share

It is best to use sales figures for the stock market series if they are available. Fortunately, we can refer to a sales per share series for the S&P 400 Industrial Index.[3] The plot in Figure 12.2 shows the relationship between annual percentage changes in GNP and S&P sales per share. It indicates a strong relationship between the two series with a few exceptions (most notably 1974). Therefore, it appears that percentage change in nominal GNP explains much of percentage change in S&P 400 sales per share. The scatter plot implies a line with an approximate slope of 1.40, which means that if you expect GNP to increase by 10 percent, you would expect S&P 400 sales per share to increase by about 14 percent.

Step 3: Estimating Operating Profit Margin

Once you have estimated sales per share for the market series, you need to derive an estimate of the net

---

[3]Sales per share figures are available back to 1945 in Standard & Poor's *Analysts Handbook* (New York: Standard & Poor's Corporation, annual). Because the composite series include numerous companies of different sizes, all data are per share. The book is updated annually, and some series are updated quarterly in monthly supplements.

profit margin, or the after-tax profit as a percentage of sales. Multiplying our estimate of sales per share by an estimate of the net profit margin will yield an earnings-per-share estimate for the stock market series.

Although it seems easiest to estimate the net profit margin directly, it is not considered the best procedure. The net profit margin is the most volatile of the profit margin values, so it is the most difficult to estimate. A more detailed procedure produces a more accurate estimate. Therefore, since the operating profit margin is income before depreciation, interest, and taxes as a percentage of sales, we will compute EBDIT per share, then separately estimate depreciation expense, interest expense, and the tax rate. By applying these to EBDIT, we will arrive at the earnings per share.

Four variables have been suggested as influences on operating profit margin:

1. Capacity utilization rate
2. Unit labor cost
3. Rate of inflation
4. Foreign competition[4]

The first two factors (capacity utilization rate and unit labor cost) affect operating profit margin in fairly clear and consistent ways. Agreement is not complete on the effects of the last two factors (inflation and foreign competition).

Capacity Utilization Rate   There is a positive relationship between capacity utilization rate and operating profit margin. An increase in the capacity utilization rate should result in an increase in the operating profit margin. The reasoning is as follows: if production increases as a proportion of total capacity, fixed production costs per unit of output decrease, and so do the fixed financing costs per unit. Therefore, a higher capacity utilization rate reduces unit costs and boosts the operating profit margin. A lower utilization rate raises unit cost and erodes margin. The figures in Table 12.2 indicate that the capacity utilization rate ranged from a peak of 88 percent in 1973 to less than 73 percent during the recession of 1982.

Unit Labor Cost   There is a negative relationship between unit labor cost and operating profit margin.

Table 12.2   *Utilization of Total Manufacturing Capacity: 1970–1990*

	Utilization Rate (Mfg.)
1970	79.7%
1971	78.2
1972	83.7
1973	88.1
1974	83.8
1975	73.2
1976	78.5
1977	82.8
1978	85.1
1979	85.4
1980	80.2
1981	78.8
1982	72.8
1983	74.9
1984	80.4
1985	79.5
1986	79.0
1987	81.4
1988	83.9
1989	83.9
1990	82.2

Source: "Total Manufacturing," Federal Reserve Board series in *Economic Report of the President, 1991* (Washington, D.C.: U.S. Government Printing Office, 1991).

An increase in the unit labor cost produces a decline in the operating profit margin. A change in unit labor cost is a compound effect of: (1) changes in wages per hour and (2) changes in worker productivity. Wage costs per hour typically increase every year by varying amounts depending upon the economic environment. If workers did not become more productive, this increase in per-hour wage costs would increase per-unit labor cost. Fortunately, because of advances in technology and greater mechanization, the units of output produced by the individual worker per hour have increased over time—workers have become more productive. If wages per hour were to increase by 5 percent while labor productivity also increased by 5 percent, unit labor costs would show no increase because the workers would offset the wage increase by producing more.

---

[4]Sidney R. Finkel and Donald L. Tuttle, "Determinants of the Aggregate Profit Margin," *Journal of Finance* 26, no. 5 (December 1971): 1067–1075.

Figure 12.3 *Productivity, Hourly Compensation, and Unit Labor Cost: 1982–1990*

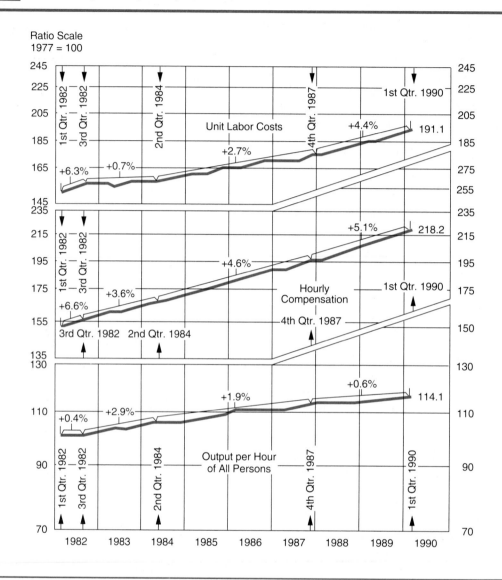

Note: Percentages are annual rates of change for periods indicated. Latest data plotted, first quarter.
Source: Federal Reserve Bank of St. Louis, from U.S. Department of Labor data.

Therefore, the increase in per-unit labor cost is a function of the percentage change in hourly wages minus the increase in productivity during the period. The actual relationship is typically not this exact due to measurement problems, but it is quite close, as indicated by the graphs in Figure 12.3.

Inflation We discuss the effect of inflation, and subsequently the impact of foreign competition, for the sake of completeness, although their relationships to operating profit margin remain unresolved. One can build an argument for a positive relationship between each of these variables and operating profit margin; one can also argue for negative relationships.

Those who expect a positive relationship between inflation and operating profit margin contend that high inflation increases the ability of firms to pass increasing costs on to consumers. Also, assuming the classical demand-pull inflation, higher prices are caused by strong economic activity, which is typically accompanied by higher profit margins.

Those who expect a negative relationship between inflation and profit margins doubt that most businesses can consistently increase prices in line with rising costs. If a firm increases prices at the same rate as costs increase, the result will be a constant profit margin, not an increase. Only by increasing prices by more than the increase in costs can a firm increase its margin. Some contend that many firms will find it difficult to raise prices in line with increased costs because of the elasticity of demand for their products.[5] These firms' profit margins will decline during periods of increased inflation.

Foreign Competition The relationship between foreign competition and operating profit margin would be positive if the profit margin on export sales were lower than on domestic sales. In such a case, a decline in exports signals an increase in foreign competition and would increase overall profit margin. In contrast, the relationship would be negative if foreign competition was reflected in an increase in imports that would increase competition in domestic markets and reduce profit margins.

The empirical evidence on these relationships has generally been consistent with expectations. A positive relationship has held between profit margin and the utilization rate, and a negative relationship has held between profit margin and changes in unit labor cost. The results for inflation and foreign competition have been mixed.

Therefore, when estimating operating profit margin, you should concentrate on the economy's capacity utilization rate and its rate of change in unit labor cost. As an example, consider the two extremes of the business cycle. At the end of an economic recession, the capacity utilization rate is very low. Therefore, the early stages of an economic recovery show a large increase in capacity utilization as firms increase production and sales. At the same time, workers do not ask for very large wage increases, so production increases translate to large increases in labor productivity. As a result, unit labor costs increase very slowly (or even

decline). Therefore, the overall impact of an increase in capacity utilization and a very small increase (or a decline) in unit labor cost should be a large increase in operating profit margin.

At the peak of the business cycle firms operate at full capacity, so capacity utilization shows small increases or even declines. Also, one would expect a higher rate of inflation to prompt demands for large wage increases during a time of small increases in labor productivity because firms are using marginal labor and production facilities. As a result, there are large increases in unit labor cost. The overall effect of very small increases, or decreases, in capacity utilization and large increases in unit labor cost is a major decline in the operating profit margin at the peak of a business cycle.

How do you use this information to estimate an operating profit margin? The most important estimate is the direction of the change from current levels. Assuming that you know the most recent operating profit margin, you need to analyze whether it will increase, decrease, or stay about the same based upon your expectations for capacity utilization and unit labor cost during the next period. The size of the estimated change in operating profit margin will depend upon the economy's point in the business cycle and the size of expected changes in capacity utilization and unit labor cost.

You can derive the dollar value of earnings per share before depreciation, interest, and taxes (EBDIT) by applying your estimated operating profit margin to your previous estimate of sales per share. The next step is to estimate depreciation per share, which you will subtract from operating profits to get earnings before interest and taxes. Data in Table 12.3 give the operating earnings components for the period since 1977 when S&P began to provide this detailed breakdown of earnings.

Step 4: Estimating Depreciation Expense

As shown in Figure 12.4, the depreciation expense per share for the firms in the S&P 400 series has not declined since 1970. (Actually, it has not declined since 1946.) This is not too surprising, because depreciation is an estimate of the annual cost of the total fixed assets held by the 400 industrial firms in this index. Naturally, this fixed asset base increases over time. Therefore, the relevant question when estimating depreciation expense is not whether it

---

[5]For an extreme example of this inability, regulated industries may not be able to raise prices at all without lengthy hearings before regulatory agencies. Even then, increases in rates may not match cost increases.

| Table 12.3 | S&P 400 Sales per Share and Components of Operating Profit Margin: 1977–1989 |

	Sales Per Share	EBDIT		Depreciation		Interest		Income Tax		Net Income	
		Per Share	Percent of Sales	Per Share	Percent of Sales	Per Share	Percent of Sales	Per Share	Percent of Sales	Per Share	Percent of Sales
1977	223.96	34.54	15.42	8.52	3.80	3.22	1.44	11.15	4.98	11.65	5.20
1978	251.88	38.79	15.40	9.64	3.83	3.81	1.51	12.16	4.83	13.18	5.23
1979	292.38	45.86	15.69	10.81	3.70	4.58	1.57	14.02	4.80	16.45	5.63
1980	327.36	48.30	14.75	12.37	3.78	5.95	1.82	13.67	4.18	16.31	4.98
1981	344.31	51.20	14.87	13.82	4.01	7.49	2.18	12.95	3.76	16.94	4.92
1982	333.86	47.89	14.34	15.30	4.58	8.23	2.47	10.95	3.28	13.41	4.02
1983	334.00	50.48	15.11	15.67	4.69	7.62	2.28	12.12	3.63	15.07	4.51
1984	379.70	57.45	15.13	16.31	4.30	8.54	2.25	14.15	3.73	18.95	4.86
1985	398.42	56.71	14.23	18.19	4.57	9.24	2.32	13.68	3.43	15.60	3.92
1986	387.76	54.96	19.17	19.41	5.01	9.75	2.51	11.01	2.89	14.79	3.81
1987	430.45	64.83	15.06	20.21	4.70	10.14	2.36	13.96	3.24	20.52	4.77
1988	486.92	80.41	16.51	23.59	4.84	15.01	3.08	15.00	3.08	26.81	5.51
1989	527.20	84.46	16.02	23.90	4.53	18.57	3.52	15.44	2.93	26.55	5.04

EBDIT = Earnings before depreciation, interest, and taxes. This is used as an estimate of operating earnings.

Source: *Standard & Poor's Analysts Handbook* (New York: Standard & Poor's Corporation, 1990.) Reprinted with permission.

will increase or decrease, but by how much it will increase.

You can use the recent trend as a guide to future increases. Probably the biggest influence on the rate of growth of depreciation expenses is recent capital expenditures. Recently, depreciation expenses have increased by an average of about 8 percent. After estimating the depreciation expense, you subtract it from the operating profit estimate to get an EBIT estimate.

Step 5: Estimating the Interest Expense

As shown in Table 12.3, interest expenses for the companies in the S&P 400 series have consistently increased in absolute value (except for 1983) and also increased as percentages of sales from 1.44 percent in 1977 to 3.52 percent in 1989. This growth in interest expense is consistent with prior discussions of the overall increase in debt financing and financial risk assumed by U.S. firms during the past decade. After estimating interest expense, you subtract it from the EBIT per share to estimate earnings per share before tax (EBT).

Step 6: Estimating the Tax Rate

This is the final step in estimating earnings per share for the S&P 400 series. As shown in Figure 12.5, the average tax rate for the firms in the S&P 400 series during the 1970s was in the 45 to 50 percent range, while during the 1980s it was in the mid-40 percent range. It declined to about 35 percent following the 1986 Tax Reform Act.

Estimating the future tax rate is difficult because it depends on political action. The investor must project any change in the current tax rate in light of recent tax legislation affecting business firms (e.g., tax credits). Once you have estimated the tax rate, you multiply it by EBT per share to derive an estimate of tax per share. Finally, you subtract this from the EBT estimate to arrive at an estimated net income per share for the S&P 400 series.

At this point we have derived an estimate of sales per share for an aggregate stock market series. Following estimates of operating profit margin and several specific expense items, we have estimated earnings per share. We will demonstrate the application of this procedure in the next section, which contains an estimate

Figure 12.4 *Depreciation Expense for S&P 400 Index*

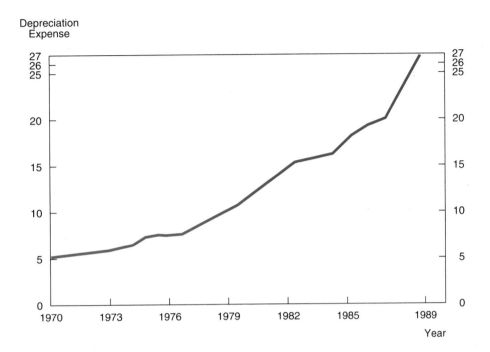

of the S&P 400 earnings per share for 1991 based on 1990 data.

Calculating Earnings per Share: An Example

The following example shows the procedure by which an analyst would estimate earnings per share for the year. We emphasize the procedure rather than the actual numbers. An analyst engaged in this exercise would take much longer and work with minute details.

Step 1 We figure nominal GNP for 1991 based upon an estimate for 1990 of approximately $5,463 billion. In 1991 the economy will be recovering from a recession that began in July 1990. Real GNP during 1991 is expected to increase by about 2 percent with inflation of approximately 5 percent. Therefore, nominal GNP should increase by about 7 percent in 1991 to $5,845 billion.

Step 2 Corporate sales have typically shown a strong relationship with nominal GNP, as was shown in Fig-

ure 12.2. During 1990, nominal GNP increased by about 5 percent and S&P 400 sales were expected to grow by about 7 percent to $564 per share. In 1991, GNP's increase of 7 percent implies an increase in sales of about 9 percent to $615 per share.

Step 3 The operating profit margin declined to about 15.5 percent in 1990, compared to 16.0 percent in 1989. This decline resulted from a lower capacity utilization rate (82.2 percent in 1990 compared to 83.9 percent during 1989), and a similar rate of increase in unit labor cost (4.5 percent in 1990 versus 4.4 percent during 1989). For 1991 we should see a further small decline in the operating profit margin because of a further decline in the utilization rate (to about 81.5 percent) and an increase in unit labor cost. Specifically, compensation per hour will experience a very small increase in 1991 because of the high unemployment rate, but productivity gains will be very small or nonexistent due to the recession that occurred during late 1990 and early 1991. Therefore, we look for a 4 percent increase in unit labor cost. Overall, there would probably be a decline in operating

| Figure 12.5 | *Tax Rate for S&P 400 Index* |

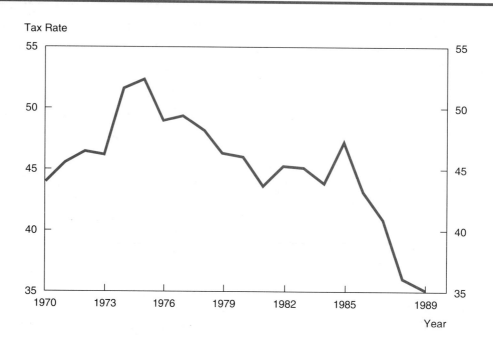

profit margin from 15.5 percent in 1990 to 15.2 percent in 1991. Applying a 15.2 percent operating profit margin to the sales per share figure ($615) results in operating profits (EBDIT) of $93.48 (0.152 × $615).

Step 4   Depreciation during 1990 was approximately $27.00 per share. Because the utilization rate has declined, capital expenditures should increase by about 6 percent during 1991, so depreciation should also increase by 7 percent to about $29.00 per share. Thus the estimated earnings before interest and taxes (EBIT) is $64.48 ($93.48 − $29.00).

Step 5   The interest expense of $18.57 in 1989 was expected to rise to $21.00 in 1990 as firms increased their financial leverage at a slower rate than during 1988 and 1989. During 1991 we envision a very small increase in financial leverage as firms shift to more equity financing and attempt to reduce their proportions of debt financing. Even with the possibility of a lower level of leverage by year end, the dollar value of interest expense for the total year will increase to $22.00. When we subtract interest expense of $22.00

from the EBIT estimate of $64.48 we have an EBT of $42.48.

Step 6   The corporate tax rate during 1990 was slightly lower than that during 1989. The rate is expected to stabilize at about 36 percent in 1991. Applying a 64 percent after-tax retention rate to the EBT figure of $42.48 indicates that net income per share for 1991 will be approximately $27.18. Therefore, future discussions will use an earnings per share estimate of $27.00 a share.

Part Two: Estimating the Earnings Multiplier for a Stock Market Series

Having estimated earnings per share, the next step is to derive an estimate of the earnings multiplier. This value times the estimate of earnings per share will provide an estimate of the future value of the stock market series. From this estimated value for the stock market series and an estimate of dividends during the year, we can compute the expected rate of return for investors in stocks during this holding period.

You will recall from our discussion of Table 12.1 that the earnings multiplier (i.e., P/E ratio) over time has been more volatile than earnings per share. The greater volatility is due to the sensitivity of the multiplier to changes in the spread between k and g, as demonstrated in Chapter 8. Earlier in this chapter we discussed several instances of changes in the earnings multiplier dominating changes in stock prices. Because of its significance, we will examine each of the variables in the P/E ratio equation to identify influences on them and why they change. After we understand how these variables change, we can consider the whole P/E ratio equation and demonstrate how an investor would estimate a value for the earnings multiplier.

Determinants of the Earnings Multiplier

We can identify the variables that influence the earnings multiplier from the equation we generated from the dividend valuation model:

$$P/E = \frac{D_1/E_1}{k - g}$$

where:

D_1 = dividends expected in period 1, which equals $D_0 (1 + g)$

E_1 = earnings expected in period 1

D_1/E_1 = dividend payout ratio expected in period 1

k = required rate of return on the stock

g = expected growth rate of dividends

Therefore, the major variables that affect the earnings multiplier are:

- The dividend payout ratio
- The required rate of return on the stock. Because we are attempting to estimate the earnings multiplier for a stock market series as a proxy for the aggregate stock market, this would be the required rate of return on the common stocks in this market series.
- The expected growth rate of dividends. In this case, it would be the expected growth rate of dividends for the stocks in this market series.

Because this equation is derived from the dividend growth model, you must remember that it assumes constant growth for an infinite period. Also, the required rate of return is applicable to the long-term. Therefore, when estimating k and g, keep in mind that they are long-term estimates. Despite changes in these variables due to near-term events, they should not change much on a year-to-year basis.

It is easier to discuss the dividend payout ratio after we have considered both k and g. Therefore, we will consider these values in the following order:

- Estimating k, the required rate of return
- Estimating g, the growth rate of dividends
- Estimating D_1/E_1, the dividend payout ratio

Step 1: Estimating the Required Rate of Return (k)

The equation shows that the earnings multiplier is inversely related to the required rate of return; an investor with a higher required rate of return will pay less for a future earnings stream. In our discussions of required rate of return (Chapters 1 and 9), we found that k was determined by: (1) the economy's risk-free rate (RFR), (2) the expected rate of inflation during the period of investment (I), and (3) the risk premium (RP) for the specific investment. You will recall that we combined the first two factors (RFR and I) into a nominal risk-free rate for all investments. We saw that changes in inflation determine the bulk of changes in the nominal RFR. A good proxy for the nominal RFR is the current promised yield to maturity of a government bond with a maturity similar to the investor's investment horizon.

The major contribution to differences in required return for alternative investments comes from the risk premium. Ibbotson and Sinquefield calculated an aggregate risk premium for common stocks. They estimated the risk premium on common stocks as the difference in annual rates of return from common stocks and that on Treasury bills.[6] The geometric mean of this risk premium for the period from 1926 to 1990 was 6.6 percent; the arithmetic mean was 8.2 percent. The geometric mean is appropriate for long-run comparisons, while you would use the arithmetic mean to estimate the premium for a given year.

[6]Roger G. Ibbotson and Rex A. Sinquefield, *Stocks, Bonds, Bills, and Inflation: The Past and the Future* (Charlottesville, Va.: Financial Analysts Research Foundation, 1982).

run comparisons, while you would use the arithmetic mean to estimate the premium for a given year.

An investor can determine the "normal" expected return on common stock by combining this long-run, historical risk premium with the nominal RFR. Suppose that the current yield on T-bills is 6 percent. An investor who considered the current equity-market environment to be fairly typical would estimate the current required return on common stock at about 14 percent (6 percent nominal RFR plus an 8 percent equity risk premium).

Once you have derived an estimate of the required rate of return for the current period, you must anticipate changes in the expected rate of inflation or the risk premium on common stock during your investment horizon. From Chapters 1 and 9 we know that several factors influence the risk premium: business risk (BR), financial risk (FR), liquidity risk (LR), exchange rate risk (ERR), and country risk (CR). The last two become important when investing in non-U.S. equities.

To incorporate these forces into the estimate of k, we can express the required return on common stocks as:

$$K_e = f(RFR, I, BR, FR, LR, ERR, CR)$$

where:

k_e = required return on equity

RFR = economy's risk-free rate of return

I = expected rate of inflation

The risk variables are those discussed above.

Step 2: Estimating the Growth Rate of Dividends (g)

The earnings multiple you apply to next year's earnings must take into account the level of and changes in the expected growth rate (g) for the common stock dividend stream because the earnings multiplier has a positive relationship to the rate of growth of earnings and dividends; a higher expected growth rate increases the multiple.[7] Any changes in the relationship be-

tween k and g will also have profound effects on the earnings multiplier.

As discussed in Chapters 7 and 9, a firm's growth rate is equal to the proportion of earnings it retains and reinvests, that is, its retention rate (b) times the rate of return it earns on investments (ROE). An increase in either or both of these variables causes an increase in the expected growth rate (g) and an increase in the earnings multiplier. Therefore, the growth rate can be stated as:

$$g = f(b, ROE)$$

where:

g = expected growth rate

b = expected retention rate, equal to $1 - D/E$

ROE = expected return on equity investments

Your estimate of the market growth rate requires examination of the aggregate retention rate (b) and return on equity (ROE). Figure 12.6 shows that the retention rate was relatively high (56 to 63 percent) during the 1970s, declined to the 50 percent range during the early 1980s, and then increased back to 60 percent at the end of the decade. Because the valuation model is a long-run model, you should attempt to identify relatively permanent changes, although some short-run changes can affect expectations.

To evaluate changes in return on equity (ROE), recall its definition:

$$ROE = \frac{\text{Net income}}{\text{Equity}}$$

The discussion in Chapter 7 broke ROE down as follows:

$$\frac{\text{Net income}}{\text{Equity}} = \frac{\text{Sales}}{\text{Total assets}} \times \frac{\text{Total assets}}{\text{Equity}} \times \frac{\text{Net income}}{\text{Sales}}$$

$$= \begin{pmatrix} \text{Total} \\ \text{asset} \\ \text{turnover} \end{pmatrix} \times \begin{pmatrix} \text{Financial} \\ \text{leverage} \end{pmatrix} \times \begin{pmatrix} \text{Net} \\ \text{profit} \\ \text{margin} \end{pmatrix}$$

This equation shows that ROE increases if either equity turnover or profit margin increases. In turn, you can increase the equity turnover by increasing either total asset turnover or financial leverage or both. Because the S&P 400 series includes historical information on total assets for only a few years, we cannot examine this breakdown of equity turnover. As an alternative, we can examine available data for the For-

---

[7]You know that g in the valuation model is the expected growth rate for dividends. In our discussion, we assume a relatively constant dividend payout ratio (dividends/earnings), so the growth of dividends depends on the growth in earnings, and the growth rates are approximately equal.

| **Figure 12.6** | **Retention Rate for S&P 400 Index** |

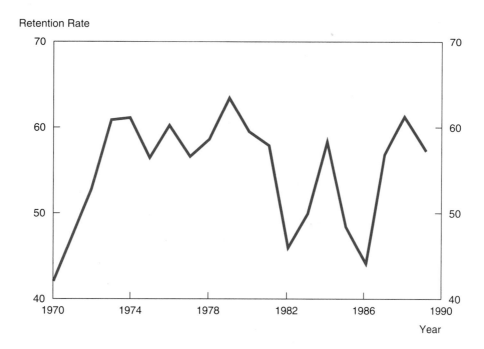

tune 500. It is reasonable to use this alternative series for demonstration purposes because almost all the companies in the S&P 400 are in the Fortune 500 and the specific data are extremely similar.

As shown in Figure 12.7, the ROE for the Fortune 500 companies increased over the 32-year period. Analysis of the three components of ROE indicates what caused this change over time. First, the profit margin (Figure 12.8) showed an overall decline during this period. The second component, total asset turnover (Figure 12.9), increased in the late 1970s, but declined drastically during the last several years to a lower level in 1990 than that in 1956. Therefore, it appears that the major variable driving the increase in ROE has been the third component, the financial leverage ratio (Figure 12.10). It increased from 1.60 to over 3.00 in 1990.

All of this shows the need for an investor to estimate the long-term outlook for ROE. In turn, this requires a long-term estimate for each of its three component ratios. Once you have this long-term estimate of ROE, you multiply it by your estimate of b, the retention rate, to calculate an estimate of g. As an example, if you estimate the firm's long-run retention rate as 60 percent and their ROE at 15 percent, you would expect a long-run growth rate of:

$$g = b \times ROE$$
$$= 0.60 \times 0.15$$
$$= 0.09 = 9 \text{ percent}$$

Step 3: Estimating the Dividend Payout Ratio (D_1/E_1)

The P/E equation reveals a positive relationship between the P/E ratio and the dividend payout ratio. Therefore, if the k − g spread is constant and this dividend payout ratio increases, the earnings multiplier will also increase. At the same time, it is critical to recognize that the dividend payout ratio equals 1 minus the earnings retention rate (b). This means that if the dividend payout increases, the earnings retention rate (b) will decline.

We know that the growth rate (g) equals b times ROE. Therefore, while dividend payout has a positive

Figure 12.7 *ROE for the Fortune 500: 1956–1989*

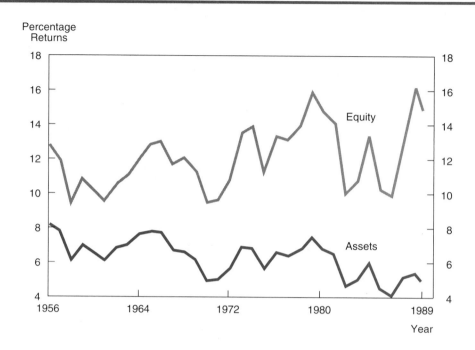

Figure 12.8 *Profit Margin for the Fortune 500: 1956–1989*

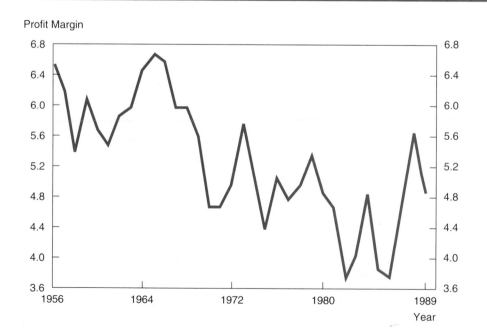

Figure 12.9   *Total Asset Turnover for the Fortune 500: 1956–1989*

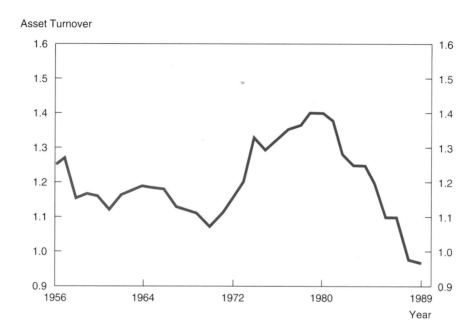

impact on the earnings multiplier, it is partially offset by a decline in expected g due to a lower b.

Our discussion of the growth rate indicated that the retention rate was high in the 1970s, declined in the early 1980s, and increased again during the late 1980s. This implies that the payout ratio has declined recently.

Estimating an Earnings Multiplier: An Example

There are two ways to estimate the earnings multiplier based upon our discussion of the variables that determine it. The first approach is to begin with the current earnings multiplier and attempt to estimate the direction and amount of any change based upon your expectations for changes in the three major components. We will call this the *Direction of Change Approach.*

In the second approach, you estimate a specific value for an earnings multiplier by deriving specific estimates for each of the three components in the P/E ratio equation. When using this approach, most analysts derive several estimates based on alternative

optimistic or pessimistic scenarios. We will call this approach the *Specific Estimate Approach.*

Direction of Change Approach   You begin with the current earnings multiplier and estimate the direction and extent of any change in the dividend payout and the variables that influence aggregate k and g. The direction of the change is more important than its size.

The variables you must estimate include:

1. Changes in the dividend payout ratio

2. Changes in the real RFR
3. Changes in the rate of inflation ⎫
4. Changes in the risk premium   ⎬ Changes in k
   for common stock   ⎭

5. Changes in the earnings   ⎫
   retention rate   ⎬ Changes in g
6. Changes in return on equity ⎭
   (ROE)

The dividend payout ratio is likely to increase in the near future because recent values have been lower

Figure 12.10 *Leverage Ratio for the Fortune 500: 1956–1989*

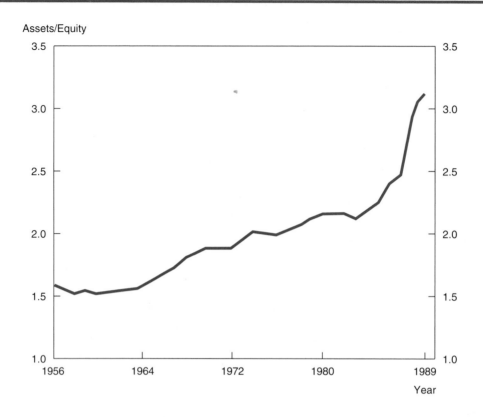

than the historical average. Of the three variables that affect the required rate of return, a decline is probable in the real RFR due to a lower rate of real growth caused by a decline in productivity. The rate of inflation should be fairly stable through 1991 relative to 1990. Finally, the risk premium is expected to increase for two reasons. First, as of early 1991 we were in the late phase of a recession where uncertainty was greater. Second, stock price volatility was higher during the late 1980s. Therefore, k should increase during 1991.

The last two factors in the earnings multiplier estimate relate to the growth rate. A likely small increase in the payout rate implies a decline in the retention rate. The outlook is for a decline in the aggregate ROE during 1991, as well, since it is a function of the profit margin, total asset turnover, and financial leverage. We have already indicated that profit margins in 1991 are expected to decline relative to 1990. One might expect the decline in the total asset turnover to

continue during 1991 because of the recession. Finally, we should see either a small increase or no change in the financial leverage ratio during 1991. The reason is the heavy leverage that already existed in 1990 and the concern with the high leverage during 1989 and early 1990. The lower profit margin, lower asset turnover, and stable financial leverage should cause a decline in ROE during 1991. This scenario of a lower retention rate and a decline in ROE implies a decline in the expected growth rate.[8] In summary, we expect:

- An increase in the payout ratio
- An increase in the required rate of return
- A decline in the growth rate

[8]This is the most reasonable scenario given the economic environment. At the same time, asset write-offs and share repurchases have caused changes in the value of common equity. Both of these events can cause a significant decline in the equity account, but they have little impact on operating earnings. As a result ROE may be higher simply because of a lower equity value.

Overall, this would imply a lower earnings multiplier. An earnings multiplier of about 16 times prevailed late in 1990. Although the multiplier increased to about 18 in early 1991, this discussion would imply that we expect that the multiplier will decline to about 15 times during 1991.

Specific Estimate Approach The purpose of this approach is to derive a set of specific estimates for the earnings multiplier based upon a range of estimates for the three variables: dividend payout (D/E), required rate of return (k), and growth (g).

As indicated earlier, the retention rate has fluctuated between 45 and 60 percent over the past 10 years. Therefore, a reasonable dividend payout ratio (D/E) value would be around 53 percent.

We can estimate required return (k) from knowledge of the interest rate on government bonds plus an estimate of the risk premium for common stocks. An appropriate risk premium could range from 3 to 8 percent, depending upon the government security used as a proxy for the nominal risk-free rate. The 8 percent figure is based upon the long-term arithmetic average risk premium provided by the Ibbotson–Sinquefield studies for the period from 1926 to 1990 using T-bills as the risk-free instrument. Recently (between 1975 and 1990), the risk premium has been in the range of 2.5 to 3.5 percent. As of mid-1991, the rate on T-bills was about 6 percent, the rate on 5-year government bonds was about 7 percent, and the rate on long-term bonds was 8 percent. This gives the following possibilities:

A.	T-bills	6.0%
	Historical risk premium	8.0
	Estimated k	14.0%
B.	5-year government bonds	7.0%
	Low risk premium	2.5
	Estimated k	9.5%
C.	Long-term government bonds	8.0%
	Medium risk premium	4.0
	Estimated k	12.0%

This implies an estimate of the required return (k) in the range of 10 to 14 percent.

Our estimate of growth should be based upon the current and expected return on equity (ROE) and the rate of retention. The graph in Figure 12.7 shows an ROE for the Fortune 500 in the 11 to 16 percent range between 1981 and 1990. Given the decline in the ROE during 1989 and 1990, and assuming the recession will end in 1991, a range of 10 to 13 percent for ROE seems appropriate. As indicated earlier, the retention rate has been between 45 and 60 percent. Therefore, a conservative estimate of the growth rate would combine the 45 percent retention rate and the 10 percent ROE: $0.45 \times 0.10 = 0.045$. An optimistic growth rate estimate would combine the 60 percent retention rate and the 13 percent ROE: $0.60 \times 0.13 = 0.078$. To summarize:

Dividend/Earnings	0.400–0.550
Government securities	0.060–0.080
Equity risk premium	0.025–0.080
Required return (k)	0.100–0.140
ROE	0.100–0.130
Sustainable growth	0.045–0.078

By combining the most optimistic figures we can derive a reasonably generous estimate. Alternatively, we can derive a very conservative estimate from the pessimistic estimates. The D/E figure should be consistent with the retention rate.

High estimate: D/E = 0.40
  k = 0.10
  g = 0.078 (0.60 × 0.13)
$$P/E = \frac{0.40}{0.10 - 0.078} = \frac{0.40}{0.022} = 18.18\times$$

Low estimate: D/E = 0.55
  k = 0.14
  g = 0.045 (0.45 × 0.10)
$$P/E = \frac{0.55}{0.14 - 0.045} = \frac{0.55}{0.095} = 5.79\times$$

These data imply a range of earning multipliers from about 6 times to 18 times with a midrange of about 12. This is reasonably consistent with the expectation of 15 derived from the direction of change approach.

Calculating an Estimate of Value Market Series

Previously, we estimated the earnings per share for Standard & Poor's 400 of $27.00. Clearly, it would have been possible to derive additional earnings estimates.

We developed several estimates for the price–earnings multiple that varied from about 6 to 18. At this point we can combine these estimates of earnings per share and earnings multipliers and calculate the following estimates of value for Standard & Poor's 400 market series:

$$6.0 \times 27.00 = 162$$
$$12.0 \times 27.00 = 324$$
$$15.0 \times 27.00 = 405$$
$$18.0 \times 27.00 = 486$$

This example is intended to help you understand the estimation procedure. The estimation of values for D/E, k, and g was fairly complex, but still not as extensive as the process used by professional analysts. In addition, we used a point estimate for earnings per share rather than a range of estimates (pessimistic, optimistic, and most likely), which would have been preferable.

Our discussion has provided the skeleton of the process, with emphasis on the theoretical background for this first step in the fundamental analysis of stocks. The important point is to understand what variables are relevant and how they relate to either earnings per share or the earnings multiplier.

Calculating the Expected Rate of Return on Common Stocks

From our estimates of the expected value of the stock market series, we can estimate the expected rate of return through the following equation:

$$E(Rt) = \frac{EV - BV + Div.}{BV}$$

where:

E(Rt) = expected rate of return during period t (We will assume a 1-year period.)

EV = ending value for the stock market series (We would use our estimates of the value of the S&P 400 series derived in this subsection.)

BV = beginning value for the stock market series (You would typically use the series' current value under the assumption that you would be committing to a current investment.)

Div. = expected dividend payment on the stock market series during the investment horizon

We will compute four rate of return estimates based upon our four value estimates for the S&P 400. In all cases we will assume the beginning value for the S&P 400 that prevailed at the end of 1990 (387.42) and a single estimate of dividends per share during the next 12 months (13.00). This gives four estimates of expected rate of return:

1. $\frac{162.00 - 387.42 + 13.00}{387.42} = -54.83$ percent

2. $\frac{324.00 - 387.42 + 13.00}{387.42} = -13.01$ percent

3. $\frac{405.00 - 387.42 + 13.00}{387.42} = 7.89$ percent

4. $\frac{486.00 - 387.42 + 13.00}{387.42} = 28.80$ percent

As you would expect, we get a wide range of expected rates of return because of the range of ending values for the S&P 400. At this point, as an investor you must select the most reasonable estimate and use this value and the rate of return it implies to make the investment decision. As discussed previously, you would compare this estimate of the rate of return that you will receive on common stocks to your required rate of return on common stocks. The k from which we calculated the earnings multiplier tells us it is somewhere between 10 and 14 percent. If we assume a rate of 12 percent, our investment decision would depend upon whether the expected return we calculated was equal to or greater than 12 percent, as follows:

Estimate	Estimated Rate of Return	Required Rate of Return	Investment Decision
1	−54.83%	12%	No
2	−13.01	12	No
3	7.89	12	No
4	28.80	12	Yes

Analysis of World Stock Markets

Although we have worked with data from the U.S. market to demonstrate the procedure for analyzing a national stock market, investors should perform a similar analysis for non-U.S. markets, especially the major world markets—Japan, Canada, the United

Table 12.4 Comparative Stock Market Statistics

	United States	Japan	United Kingdom	Germany[a]	France	Italy[b]
Earnings Growth						
1982–1990 CGR	7.9	9.8	13.4	14.2	15.3	25.4
1989	0.8	19.8	14.0	10.0	18.0	−2.0
1990E	−7.2	5.8	−8.5	−7.0	6.2	−19.8
1991E	−1.4	2.3	0.0	2.0	4.1	−12.2
Cash Flow Growth						
1982–1989 CGR	7.9	9.9	10.3	12.3	24.2	24.6
1989	2.5	9.4	10.0	12.0	14.0	5.8
1990E	0.0	2.9	6.1	12.0	4.2	−2.5
Dividend Growth						
1982–1989 CGR	6.6	8.1	14.5	12.1	18.0	24.5
1989	15.0	12.4	12.0	6.2	17.0	14.1
1990E	10.4	2.8	8.0	0.0	9.0	−2.5
Return on Equity						
1982–1989 Avg.	14.1	7.5	15.1	13.8	12.5	8.3
1989	18.1	7.4	19.6	12.8	13.5	11.2
1990E	15.8	7.2	17.2	10.9	13.8	8.3
Price/Earnings						
1982–1990 Avg.	14.4	46.6	11.6	11.6	11.4	11.0
1989	16.3	44.6	11.4	11.3	12.0	8.8
1990E	17.5	42.2	12.5	12.2	11.3	10.9
1991E	17.8	41.2	12.5	11.9	10.9	12.5
Price/Cash Flow						
1982–1989 Avg.	6.4	14.8	5.9	3.5	5.0	2.9
1989	8.0	15.8	7.1	3.2	5.2	2.5
1990E	8.0	15.3	6.7	2.8	4.9	2.5
Dividend Yield						
1982–1989 Avg.	3.4	0.9	4.9	2.8	4.1	4.1
1989	2.6	0.7	4.6	2.9	3.8	4.6
1990E	2.9	0.8	5.0	2.9	4.1	4.5

Aggregates and multiples for earnings, cash flow, book value, and dividend are based on an industrial sample of companies in each country.
[a]Germany calculated with DVFA rules.
[b]Italian averages calculated for the period 1983 to 1988.
All multiples are priced at current prices.
Source: "World Investment Strategy Highlights" (London: Goldman, Sachs International Ltd., July/August 1990).

Kingdom, and Germany. We do not have the space in this text to carry out a detailed analysis of each of these markets, but we can provide an example of such an extensive analysis by a major investment firm. Goldman, Sachs & Company's monthly publication, "World Investment Strategy Highlights," suggests a world portfolio strategy as well as strategies for investors in several individual countries.[9]

Major Stock Markets

Overall, Goldman, Sachs takes a top-down approach, initially examining the components of a country's aggregate economy that relate to the valuation of securities—GNP, capital investments, industrial production, inflation, and interest rates. You will recall that in Chapter 9 we discussed the fairly substantial difference in nations' outlooks for GNP/GDP and industrial production growth during 1991. Likewise, major differences in outlooks for inflation and interest rates indicated major differences in expectations for exchange rates during 1991.

With this background on the macroeconomy, Table 12.4 lists some variables that support a specific market forecast, including corporate earnings growth rates and ROEs for various countries along with stock market expectations for dividend growth and price–earnings ratios. Again, we see major differences among countries. Specifically, earnings growth rates for 1991 vary from negative growth for the United States and Italy, no growth for the United Kingdom, to strong growth for France.

The ROE estimates, which are so critical to estimates of growth, vary from about 7 percent (Japan) to over 17 percent (United Kingdom) with the concentration in the 12 to 19 percent range. These figures should affect dividend growth estimates, which vary from negative growth (Italy) to about 10 percent (the United States and France). These data, along with estimates of required rates of return, could support price–earnings estimates. The prevailing P/E ratios range from about 11 times (France) to 41 times (Japan) with the U.S. P/E ratio above the overall average of about 16 times.

The price–cash flow ratio is also calculated because it is being considered more frequently as cash

flow begins to affect fixed-income credit analysis. Also cash flow appears to be less susceptible to manipulation by management than earnings per share. The range for this ratio is relatively small, from 2.5 times (Italy) to 15 times (Japan).

Individual Country Analysis

Following the summary of equity market statistics for the major equity markets, Goldman, Sachs proceeds to a detailed analysis of each of the major countries. This begins with a discussion of the local economy and continues with analysis of the country's equity market. Table 12.5 shows the major economic indicators for Germany. These projections reflect a strong economy, but government and monetary authorities are concerned about an increase in the rate of inflation.

| Table 12.5 | **Main German Economic Indicators** |

	1988	1989	1990E	1991E
GDP Components (1980 prices, percentage change from previous year)				
Consumer expenditure	2.7	1.7	4.6	4.0
Investment	5.1	7.1	8.8	6.4
Exports	5.7	11.5	8.7	5.6
Imports	6.0	8.8	9.1	9.0
Output (percentage change from previous year)				
Real GNP	3.7	3.9	4.6	3.3
Industrial production	3.6	4.8	5.6	5.3
Inflation (percentage change from previous year)				
Consumer prices	1.3	2.8	2.7	3.5
Financial Sector (percentage at end of year)				
3–month interbank rate	5.1	8.1	9.0	8.0
Long bond yield	6.2	7.6	9.0	7.5
Overseas Sector (DM bn)				
Trade balance	127.5	134.9	103.9	81.6
Current account	88.2	104.7	75.7	33.6
Labor Market (%)				
Unemployment	8.8	7.9	7.3	7.5

Source: "World Investment Strategy Highlights" (London: Goldman, Sachs International Ltd., July/August 1990).

[9]The author benefited from conversations with Jeffrey M. Weingarten, director of international equity research for Goldman, Sachs.

Table 12.6   *Germany*

	P/E				P/CF			P/B			Dividend Yield 1990E
	1989	1990E	1991E	Rel	1989	1990E	Rel	1989	1990E	Rel	
FT–A Industrials	11.3	12.2	11.9	103	3.2	2.8	84	1.4	1.3	86	2.86%

		Performance (% Change)			52-Week Range		Relative to World		
	Current Price	Last Month	YTD	12 Month	High	Low	Last Month	YTD	12 Month
FT Composite (U.S. dollar)	121.7	9.8	8.7	−1.1	144.6	101.4	0.2	−2.7	−2.8
FT Composite (local currency)	96.1	12.2	10.5	−11.1	121.4	82.2	1.5	−0.6	−6.3
FT Industrials (local currency)	93.6	11.6	9.2	−15.5	124.7	81.1	0.6	−1.5	−13.2
FAZ General	663.4	11.6	10.0	−10.5	832.3	569.7	0.9	−1.0	−5.7
DAX	1558.2	12.9	11.4	−12.3	1968.5	1322.7	2.1	0.2	−7.6

New tax package could last longer than 1 year.
Slower domestic demand and higher corporate tax rate will depress earnings.
Tendency could be exaggerated by corporate profit hiding.

Source: "World Investment Strategy Highlights" (London: Goldman, Sachs International Ltd., July/August 1990).

Goldman, Sachs follows the economic projections with an analysis of the country's equity market like the summary for Germany set forth in Table 12.6. Goldman, Sachs feels that the overall economic outlook for Germany is positive, with some pressure on interest rates. In contrast, the suggested investment strategy for Germany is quite negative because they expect relatively weak earnings growth, rising inflation, and little prospect for declining interest rates. Therefore, they feel these shares are overpriced and the firm is recommending that investors underweight German stocks in their world portfolios.

Summary

■   We have consistently emphasized the importance of analyzing overall economies and security markets before analyzing alternative industries or companies. You should determine whether the economic and market outlooks justify investing in stocks, bonds, or cash before you look for the best industry or company. The techniques by which you make the market deci-sion are described as either macroanalysis techniques, which are based upon the strong relationship between the aggregate economy and alternative security markets, or microanalysis techniques, which estimate future market values by applying basic valuation models to equity markets. In Chapter 9 we examined macroanalysis techniques and discussed world asset allocation. Chapter 10 discussed the valuation of bonds. This chapter was devoted to the microanalysis of equity markets in the United States and other countries.

■   We applied the basic dividend discount model discussed in Chapter 8 to a stock market series (the S&P 400) that reflects the U.S. equity market. We estimated earnings per share for a market series and derived a set of estimates for the earnings multiplier. From these two components, we computed an estimate of the future value for the market and used that estimate to derive an expected return for common stocks during the period. It is important to recognize that this procedure generates only an estimate; it is appropriate to make several estimates that reflect various possible conditions.

This microanalysis technique is best summarized by listing its steps:

I. Estimate expected earnings
  A. Estimate nominal GNP for year
  B. Estimate corporate sales based upon the relationship of sales to GNP
  C. Estimate the aggregate operating profit margin (EBDIT/sales)
    1. Utilization rate
    2. Unit labor cost
      a. Wage/hour increases
      b. Productivity changes
    3. Inflation and foreign competition
  D. Estimate net profits
    1. Compute operating profits (operating profit margin times sales)
    2. Subtract estimated depreciation expense
    3. Subtract estimated interest expense
    4. Estimate taxes (tax rate times EBT)
    5. Subtract taxes
II. Estimate the expected earnings multiplier
  A. Estimate changes in the required return (k)
    1. Changes in the risk-free rate (RFR)
    2. Changes in the expected rate of inflation (I)
    3. Changes in the risk premium (RP)
      a. Changes in business risk
      b. Changes in financial risk
      c. Changes in liquidity risk
      d. Changes in exchange rate risk (for non-U.S. equities)
      e. Changes in country risk (for non-U.S. equities)
  B. Estimate changes in the expected growth rate (g)
    1. Changes in the aggregate earnings retention rate
    2. Changes in return on equity
      a. Changes in equity turnover
        1. Changes in total asset turnover
        2. Changes in financial leverage
      b. Changes in profit margin
  C. Estimate changes in the spread between k and g
III. Estimate the future value of a stock market series; multiply earnings per share by the estimated earnings multiplier

■ Finally, although we applied the techniques to the U.S. stock market, it is necessary to do a similar analysis for non-U.S. markets. An example showed such a top-down analysis by Goldman, Sachs.
■ Following this aggregate market analysis, the next step in the procedure, the industry analysis, is considered in the following chapter.

Questions

1. Another investor suggests that the stock market will experience a substantial increase next year because corporate earnings are expected to rise by at least 12 percent. Do you agree or disagree? Why or why not?
2. In the library find at least three sources of historical information on nominal and real GNP. Attempt to find two sources for estimates of nominal GNP for the coming year or the previous year.
3. To arrive at an estimate of the net profit margin, why would you spend time estimating the operating profit margin and working down?
4. You are convinced that capacity utilization next year will decline from 84 percent to about 81 percent. What effect will this change have on the operating profit margin? Explain your reasoning.
5. You see an estimate that hourly wage rates will increase by 6 percent next year. How does this affect your estimate of the aggregate profit margin? What other information do you need in order to use this estimate of a wage rate increase, and why do you need it?
6. You see an estimate that hourly wage rates will increase by 7 percent next year and that productivity will increase by 5 percent. What would you expect to happen to unit labor cost? Discuss how this unit labor cost estimate would influence your estimate of the aggregate profit margin.
7. Assume each of the following changes is independent while all other factors remain unchanged. In each case, indicate what will happen to the earnings multiplier and why.
  a. Return on equity increases.
  b. The aggregate debt–equity ratio declines.
  c. Overall productivity of capital increases.
  d. The dividend payout ratio declines.
8. Based upon the economic projections in Table 12.4, would you expect the stock prices for the various countries to be highly correlated? Explain and justify your answer with specific examples.
9. You are informed that a well-respected investment firm expects that next year's returns for the

U.S. equity market will be 11 percent, while domestic returns for the German market will be 14 percent. Assume that all risks except exchange rate risk are equal and you expect the DM/dollar exchange rate to go from 1.80 to 1.55 during the year. Given this information, discuss where you would invest and why. What if you expected the exchange rate to go from 1.80 to 2.20?

Problems

1. Prepare a table for the last 10 years showing the percentage change each year in (a) the Consumer Price Index (all items), (b) nominal GNP, (c) real GNP (in constant dollars), and (d) the GNP deflator. Discuss what proportion of nominal growth was due to real growth and what part was due to inflation. Is the outlook for the coming year any different from performance during last year? Discuss.

2. You are told that nominal GNP will increase by about 10 percent next year. Using Figure 12.2, what increase in corporate sales would you say is most likely? What would be your most optimistic estimate? Most pessimistic?

3. Currently, the dividend payout ratio (D/E) for the aggregate market is 60 percent, the required return (k) is 15 percent, and the expected growth rate for dividends (g) is 9 percent:

   a. Compute the current earnings multiplier.
   b. You expect the D/E ratio to decline to 50 percent, but you anticipate no other changes. What will be the P/E?
   c. Starting with the initial conditions, you expect the dividend payout ratio to be constant, but the rate of inflation to increase by 4 percent while growth increases by 3 percent. Compute the expected P/E.
   d. Starting with the initial conditions, you expect the dividend payout ratio to be constant, but the rate of inflation to decline by 4 percent while growth declines by 2 percent. Compute the expected P/E.

4. *CFA Examination III* (June 1985)
   A U.S. pension plan hired two offshore firms to manage the non-U.S. equity portion of its total portfolio. Each firm was free to own stocks in any country market included in Capital International's Europe, Australia, and Far East (EAFE) Index. Each was free to use any form of dollar and/or nondollar cash or bonds as an equity substitute or reserve. After 3 years, the records of the managers and the EAFE Index were as shown below:

Summary: Contributions to Return

	Currency	Country Selection	Stock Selection	Cash/ Bond Allocation	Total Return Recorded
Manager A	(9.0)%	19.7%	3.1%	0.6%	14.4%
Manager B	(7.4)	14.2	6.0	2.8	15.6
Composite of A and B	(8.2)	16.9	4.5	1.7	15.0
EAFE Index	(12.9)	19.9	—	—	7.0

You are a member of the plan sponsor's pension committee, which will soon meet with the plan's consultant to review manager performance. In preparation for this meeting, you go through the following analysis:

a. Briefly describe the strengths and weaknesses of each manager, relative to the EAFE Index data. [5 minutes]
b. Briefly explain the meaning of the data in the Currency column. [5 minutes]

5. As an analyst for Middle, Diddle, and O'Leary, you are forecasting the market P/E ratio using the dividend growth model. Since the economy has been expanding for 8 consecutive years, you feel the dividend payout ratio will be at its high of 60 percent and that long-term government bonds will fall to 6 percent. Since investors are becoming more risk averse, the equity risk premium will rise to 7 percent, and investors will require a 13

percent return, while return on equity will be 11 percent.

    a. What growth rate do you expect?

    b. What market P/E ratio do you expect?

    c. What will be the value for the market index if the expectation is for earnings per share of $26.00?

6. World Stock Market Indexes are published weekly in *Barron's* in the section labeled "Market Laboratory/Stocks." Based upon analysis of two issues of this publication (the latest edition available and an issue 1 year earlier) in your college library:

    a. Show the closing position of each index on each date relative to each year's high.

    b. Name the countries whose markets are in a downtrend.

    c. Calculate the percentage range for the last 12 months (High − Low/High + Low/2). Which market seems to be the most volatile?

References

Copeland, Basil L., Jr. "Inflation, Interest Rates, and Equity Risk Premia." *Financial Analysts Journal* 38, no. 3 (May–June 1982).

Fama, Eugene F., and Kenneth French. "Business Conditions and Expected Returns on Stocks and Bonds." *Journal of Financial Economics* 25, no. 1 (November 1989).

Finkel, Sidney R., and Donald L. Tuttle. "Determinants of the Aggregate Profit Margin." *Journal of Finance* 26, no. 5 (December 1971).

Gray, William S., III. "The Anatomy of a Stock Market Forecast." *Journal of Portfolio Management* 16, no. 1 (Fall 1989).

Reilly, Frank K., Frank T. Griggs, and Wenchi Wong. "Determinants of the Aggregate Stock Market Earnings Multiple." *Journal of Portfolio Management* 10, no. 1 (Fall 1983).

Shiller, Robert J., and John Campbell. "Stock Prices, Earnings, and Expected Dividends." *Journal of Finance* 43, no. 3 (July 1988).

Vandell, Robert F., and George W. Keuter. *A History of Risk-Premia Estimates for Equities: 1944–1978.* Charlottesville, Va.: Financial Analysts Research Foundation, 1989.

13

Industry Analysis

Industry analysis Study of the relationships between firms' return and risk levels within an industry and between the industry's levels and those of the aggregate market to identify superior investment opportunities.

When asked about his or her job, a securities analyst will typically reply that he or she is an oil analyst, a retail analyst, or a computer analyst. A widely read trade publication, *The Institutional Investor*, selects an All-American analyst team each year with divisions based upon industry groups. Investment managers talk about being in or out of the metals, the autos, or the utilities. Professional investors refer constantly to industry groups because most are extremely conscious of differences among industries and organize their analyses and portfolio decisions according to industry groups.

We share this appreciation of the importance of **industry analysis** and make it a component of the three-step fundamental analysis initiated in Chapter 12. Industry analysis is the second step as we progress toward selecting specific firms and stocks for our investment portfolios. As the first step, in Chapter 12 we analyzed the stock market in order to decide whether the expected rate of return from investing in common stocks was equal to or greater than our required rate of return. Assuming the answer regarding the stock market was positive, we take the second step in this chapter and analyze different industries in order to decide whether their expected rates of return equal or exceed our required rates of return for them. We will take the final step in Chapter 14 when we analyze individual companies and stocks within acceptable industries.

In the first section we discuss the results of several studies that will help us identify the benefits and uses of industry analysis. Following that, we present a technique for analyzing industries that resembles the process employed in Chapter 12 for analyzing the aggregate stock market. Specifically, we discuss how to estimate earnings per share and an earnings multiplier for an industry, then we combine these two factors to estimate the industry's expected value and rate of return. Another section raises questions unique to industry analysis—the impact of the competitive environment within an industry and the effect of the intensity of competition on potential industry returns. We conclude the chapter with a demonstration of a global industry analysis that recognizes that many industries transcend U.S. borders to compete worldwide.

Why Do Industry Analysis?

Investment practitioners perform industry analysis to isolate profitable investment opportunities. We recommended it as part of our three-step plan for valuing individual stocks. What exactly do we learn from industry analysis? Can we spot trends in industries that make companies within them good investments? Studies of these questions have indicated unique patterns in the rates of return over time in different industries. In this section we survey the results of these studies to answer these questions.

In the research we describe, investigators asked a set of questions designed to pinpoint the benefits and limitations of industry analysis. In particular, they wanted to learn whether returns differed for alternative industries or time periods and whether an industry that performed well in one period continued to perform well in later time periods, that is, whether we can use past relationships between the market and an industry to predict future trends for the industry. They also studied the consistency of the performance of firms within an industry.

In addition, they looked for differences in risk for alternative industries and whether the risk levels for individual industries varied or remained relatively constant over time. We consider the results of these studies and come to some general conclusions about the value of industry analysis. This assessment helps

us interpret the results of our industry valuation in the next section.

Do All Industries Perform Equally Well?

To find out if industry rates of return varied during a given time period, researchers developed performance measures for alternative industries during a specific time period and compared them. Completely consistent performance during specific time periods for different industries would indicate that industry analysis is not necessary. As an example, assume that during 1992 the aggregate stock market returned 10 percent and the returns for all industries were bunched between 9 and 11 percent. If this result persisted for future periods, you might question whether it was worthwhile to conduct an analysis to find an industry that would return 11 percent when random selection would provide about 10 percent (the average return).

Studies of annual performance have found consistently widely dispersed rates of return for different industries. These results imply that industry analysis is necessary to uncover performance differences that give rise to profitable opportunities.[1]

Industry Performance over Time

In another group of investigations, researchers tried to determine whether industries that perform well in one time period continue to perform well, or at least outperform the aggregate market, in later time periods. Investigators found almost no association between industry performance from year to year or over sequential rising or falling markets.

These studies imply that past performance does not help you project future industry performance. They do not, however, negate the usefulness of industry analysis. They simply confirm that investors must project future industry performance on the basis of future estimates of the relevant variables.

Performance of Companies within an Industry

Other studies were designed to identify consistency in the performance of companies within an industry. If

---

[1] Various financial services provide graphs of annual rates of return for alternative industries. These graphical results indicate the substantial variance between industries.

all the firms within an industry performed consistently during a specified time period, investors could skip company analysis. In such a case, industry analysis alone would be enough because selection of a profitable industry would guarantee that all the stocks in that industry would do well.

These studies have typically found widely varied performance among companies in most industries. Another way to measure this same impact is to examine the industry influence on the returns for individual stocks. These studies showed evidence of an industry effect in specific industries such as oil or autos, but most stocks showed small industry effects and these effects generally have declined over time.[2]

Implications of Dispersion within Industries
Citing studies such as these, some theorists feel that industry analysis is useless because all firms in an industry do not move together. Obviously, consistent performance by all firms in an industry would be ideal because you would not need to do company analysis. For industries with strong, consistent influence such as oil, gold, steel, autos, and railroads, you can reduce the extent of your company analysis after your industry analysis.

Most industries do not exert such strong industry influence, however, so thorough company analysis is still necessary. Even for these industries without strong influence, industry analysis is valuable, because it is much easier to select a superior company from a good industry than it is to find a good company in an unhealthy industry. By selecting the best stocks within an industry with good expectations, you avoid the risk that your analysis and selection of a good company will be offset by poor industry performance.

Differences in Industry Risk

Although a number of studies have focused on industry rates of return, few have examined industry risk measures. A study by Reilly and Drzycimski investigated two questions: (1) Did risk differ among industries during a given time period? (2) Were industry risk measures stable over time?[3] The study found a wide range of risk levels among different industries

and the spreads between risk levels typically widened during rising and falling markets. On a positive note, analysis of the risk measures over time indicated reasonable stability.

We can interpret these findings as follows: although risk measures for different industries show substantial dispersion during a period of time, individual industries' risk measures are stable over time. This means that the analysis of past industry risk is necessary, but this historical analysis can aid your attempt to estimate the future risk for an industry.

Summary of Research on Industry Analysis

Earlier we noted that several studies have sought answers to questions dealing with industry analysis. The conclusions of the studies are:

- During any time period, returns vary within a wide range, which means that industry analysis can be useful in targeting investments.
- The rates of return for individual industries vary over time so we cannot simply extrapolate past performance into the future.
- The rates of return of firms within industries also vary, so company analysis is a necessary followup to industry analysis.
- During any time period, different industries' risk levels vary within wide ranges, so we must examine and estimate risk factors for alternative industries, as well as returns.
- Risk measures for different industries remain fairly constant over time so historical risk analysis can be useful when estimating future risk.

These results imply that industry analysis is necessary, both to avoid losses and to find better industries and, subsequently, individual stocks that provide superior risk–return opportunities for investors.

Estimating Industry Rates of Return—A Two-Step Process

Having determined that industry analysis helps an investor select profitable investment opportunities,

[2]For example, see Stephen L. Meyers, "A Re-Examination of Market and Industry Factors in Stock Price Behavior," *Journal of Finance* 28, no. 3 (June 1973): 695–705; and Miles Livingston, "Industry Movements of Common Stocks," *Journal of Finance* 32, no. 2 (June 1977): 861–874.

[3]Frank K. Reilly and Eugene Drzycimski, "Alternative Industry Performance and Risk," *Journal of Financial and Quantitative Analysis* 9, no. 3 (June 1979): 423–446.

| *Table 13.1* | *Composition of Standard & Poor's Composite Retail Store (CRS) Index* |

Department Stores	Drugstores	Food Chains	General Merchandise Chains
Carter Hawley Hale Stores	Longs Drug Stores	Albertson's	K mart
Dayton Hudson	Rite Aid	American Stores (Acme Markets)	J. C. Penney Company
Dillard Department Stores	Walgreen Company	Giant Food Class A	Sears, Roebuck & Company
May Department Stores		Great Atlantic and Pacific	Wal-Mart Stores
Mercantile Stores		Kroger Company	F. W. Woolworth Company
Nordstrom		Winn-Dixie Stores	

Industry life cycle analysis Industry analysis that focuses on the industry's stage of development.

how do we evaluate an industry and compute the rate of return that an investment in it will provide? You estimate the expected value of an industry by a two-step process similar to the microanalysis of the stock market. First, you estimate the expected earnings per share for the industry and then you estimate the expected industry P/E ratio (earnings multiplier). As before, multiplying the expected earnings per share by the expected earnings multiplier gives the expected ending value for the industry index.

We can compute an expected rate of return for the industry by comparing its ending value plus its expected dividend to its beginning value. Comparing this expected rate of return to your required rate of return for this industry allows you to apply the investment decision rule. You would invest in this industry if its expected rate of return equals or exceeds your required rate of return.

To demonstrate industry analysis, we will use Standard & Poor's Composite Retail Store (CRS) index to represent industrywide data. Just as we used the S&P 400 to represent the aggregate stock market, we will take this industry index to indicate the performance of the industry. The composite retail store index covers four subindustries: (1) department stores, (2) retail drugstores, (3) food chains, and (4) general merchandise chains. Most of the companies in this index, which are listed in Table 13.1, should be familiar to you. The variety of stores means that this industry involves a fairly diversified portfolio of companies and stocks.

Step One: Estimating Industry Earnings per Share

To estimate earnings per share, you must start by estimating sales per share. The first part of this section describes three techniques that will provide help and insights for this estimate. Next you must estimate earnings per share, which implies a net profit margin for the industry. As in Chapter 12 where we estimated earnings per share for a stock market series, we begin with the operating profit margin, because it is less volatile and easier to estimate than the net profit margin. Then we subtract estimates of depreciation expense, interest expense, and taxes to find earnings per share.

Forecasting Sales per Share

Three techniques can be used to derive a sales forecast for an industry:

1. Industrial life cycle
2. Input–output analysis
3. Industry–aggregate economy relationship

These techniques are not competing alternatives, but complementary and supplementary. All of them together will help you develop a complete picture of the current position and future outlook of the industry under a variety of scenarios.

Sales Forecasting and the Industrial Life Cycle
We can predict industry sales by viewing the industry over time and dividing its development into stages like those through which humans progress as they move from birth to adolescence to adulthood to middle age to old age. The number of stages in this **industry life**

Figure 13.1   *Life Cycle for an Industry*

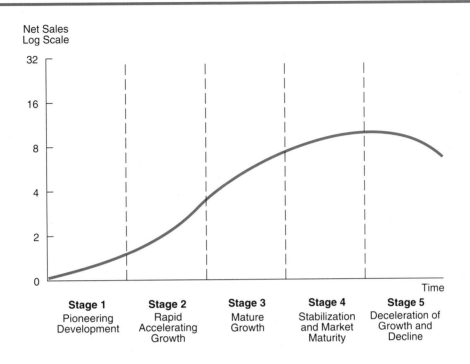

cycle analysis can vary based upon how much detail you want. A five-stage model would include:

1. Early pioneering development
2. Rapidly accelerating growth
3. Mature growth
4. Stabilization and market maturity
5. Deceleration of growth and decline

Figure 13.1 shows the growth path of sales during each stage. The vertical scale in logs reflects rates of growth, whereas the arithmetic horizontal scale's varying widths represent different, unequal time periods. To estimate industry sales, you must predict the length of time for each stage. This requires answers to such questions as: How long will an industry grow at an accelerating rate (Stage 2)? How long will it be in a mature growth phase (Stage 3) before its sales growth stabilizes (Stage 4) and then declines (Stage 5)?

Besides sales estimates, this analysis of life cycle stages can also provide some insights into profit margins and earnings growth, although these measures do

not necessarily parallel the sales growth. The profit margin series typically peaks very early in the total cycle and then levels off and declines as competition is attracted by the early success of the industry.

To illustrate the contribution of life cycle stages to sales estimates, we will briefly describe these stages and their effects on sales growth and profits:

1. Pioneering development. During this startup stage, the industry generates modest sales growth and very small or negative margins and profits. The market for the industry's product or service during this time is small, and firms incur major developmental costs.

2. Rapidly accelerating growth. During this stage, a market develops for the product or service and demand becomes substantial. The limited number of firms in the industry face little competition and individual firms can experience substantial backlogs. Profit margins are very high. The industry builds its productive capacity as sales grow at an increasing rate and the industry attempts to meet excess demand. High sales growth and high profit margins that in-

Input–output analysis Industry analysis that evaluates an industry's prospects based on those of its suppliers and customers.

crease as firms become more efficient cause industry and firm profits to explode. During this phase profits can grow at over 100 percent a year from the low earnings base and because of the rapid growth of sales and net profit margins.

3. Mature growth. The success in Stage 2 has satisfied most of the demand for the industry goods or services. The larger sales base may keep future sales growth above normal, but it no longer accelerates. As an example, if the overall economy is growing at 8 percent, sales for this industry might grow at a stabilizing rate of 15 to 20 percent a year. Also, the rapid growth of sales and high historic profit margins attract competitors to the industry and profit margins stabilize and begin to decline to normal levels.

4. Stabilization and market maturity. During this stage, probably the longest, the industry growth rate matches the growth rate of the aggregate economy or the segment of the economy of which the industry is a part. During this stage, investors can estimate growth easily because sales correlate highly with an economic series. Although sales grow in line with the economy, profit growth varies by industry and by individual firm within the industry because management ability to control costs differs among companies. Competition produces tight profit margins and the rates of return on capital (e.g., return on assets, return on equity) are at or slightly below the competitive level.

5. Deceleration of growth and decline. At this stage of maturity, the industry's sales growth declines because of shifts in demand or growth of substitutes. Profit margins continue to be squeezed, and some firms experience low profits or even losses. Firms that remain profitable may show very low rates of return on capital and investors may begin thinking about alternative uses for the capital tied up in this industry.

While these descriptions of the alternative life cycle stages are general, they should help you identify the stage your industry is in, which should help you to estimate its potential sales growth. Obviously, everyone wants an industry in the early phases of Stage 2 and hopes to avoid industries in Stages 4 or 5. Comparing the sales of an industry to activity in the economy should help you identify the industry's stage within the industrial life cycle.

Sales Forecasting and Input–Output Analysis Input–output analysis is another way to gain insights regarding the outlook for an industry by separating industries that supply its input from those that get its output. In other words, we want to identify an industry's suppliers and customers. This will help us estimate the future demand of customers, and also suppliers' ability to provide needed goods and services.[4] To extend this analysis to global industries, we must include worldwide suppliers and customers.

Sales Forecasting and the Industry–Economy Relationship For a third technique to help you forecast industry sales, you can compare sales for the industry with some aggregate economic series. You try to find a relationship between the industry and the economy. To estimate the value of the retail store industry, we note that it includes the retailers of a range of products from basic necessities such as food and medicine to general merchandise (such as at Sears, Roebuck) to clothing and household products (such as at May Department Stores). Therefore, the economic series we choose to reflect activity in the industry should be equally broad to measure the demand for these products. We would use disposable personal income (DPI) and personal consumption expenditures (PCE).

The scatter plot of CRS sales per share compared to PCE in Figure 13.2 indicates a strong linear relationship between them. Although the graph does not show it, CRS sales also has a good relationship with DPI. Therefore, a good estimate of changes in these economic series should give you a good estimate of expected sales per share for the retail store industry.

We can rely on this relationship between the industry and the aggregate economic series because of the number and diversity of retail stores included in the index. If you want to project sales for a narrower industry group, such as food chains, you should consider a subset of consumer expenditures, such as consumer expenditures for nondurables or personal consumption expenditures for food. As the industry you are analyzing becomes more specialized, you need a more specific economic series to reflect the demand for the industry's product.

[4]For an explanation of input–output analysis, see Howard B. Bonham, Jr., "The Use of Input–Output Economics in Common Stock Analysis," *Financial Analysts Journal* 23, no. 1 (January–February 1967): 27–31.

Figure 13.2   **Scatter Plot of CRS Sales/Share and PCE**

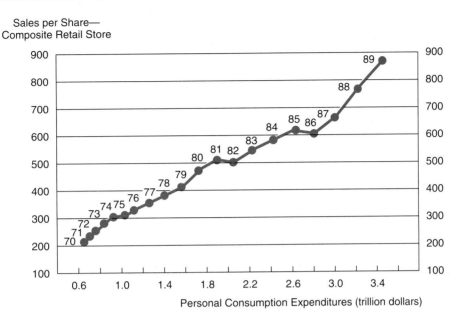

You might also want to evaluate the usefulness of per capita disposable personal income as a predictor of retail demand. Although aggregate DPI increases each year, population increases keep the increase in the DPI per capita (the average DPI for each adult and child) below the increase in the aggregate series. As an example, during 1989, aggregate DPI increased about 8.7 percent, but per capita DPI increased only 7.6 percent. Finally, the relationship between changes in the economic index and in industry sales indicates how well industry sales and the economic index move together and highlights any changes in the relationship.

Summary of Sales Forecasting Techniques
Three techniques used as a group help you arrive at a specific current forecast, and also provide insights on a longer-term perspective on sales. The best specific forecast comes from the industry–economy relationship because this provides specific numbers based upon the near-term outlook for the economy. Once you have this specific estimate of sales per share, you should check to ensure that it is consistent with the overall outlook for the industry based upon its life

cycle stage and with the prospects for its customers based upon input–output analysis.

Assume, for example, that your analysis of an industry relative to an economic series led you to estimate that sales per share should increase by 5 percent this year. Your examination of this industry's industrial life cycle concluded that it was in the middle of Stage 2, where sales growth for the industry should substantially outperform average economic growth. Your analysis of the industry's customers revealed that their outlook was very strong. Putting all of this together, you would probably conclude that your initial forecast of a 5 percent increase in sales was on the low side because of life cycle considerations and input–output analysis. Again, one technique gives you a specific forecast while the other techniques provide confirmation on reasons for an adjustment.

Forecasting an Industry Net Profit Margin

To find earnings per share from a sales projection, we need to know how much of sales revenue goes to profit. As with the aggregate market, the net profit margin for an industry is very volatile and difficult to estimate directly. We can project more accurate net profit margins if we begin with the operating profit margin and then subtract estimates of depreciation expense, interest expense, and taxes. In this subsection we describe the procedure for making these calculations.

Industry Operating Profit Margin Recall that in our analysis of the stock market, we evaluated the factors that should influence the economy's operating profit margin. The most important variables were the capacity utilization rate and changes in unit labor cost. We cannot do such an analysis for an industry because the relevant data are typically not available for individual industries. In many cases, however, we can assume that changes in these industry profit margin variables follow movements in the same variables for the overall economy. As an example, an increase in the capacity utilization rate for the aggregate economy probably implies a comparable increase in the utilization rate for the auto industry or the chemical industry. The same could be true for unit labor cost. If these profit margin variables for the industry and the economy are

related, you would expect a similar relationship between the operating profit margins for the industry and the stock market. Since data are available for these more general variables, you can determine whether a relationship holds between an industry's profit margin and the margin for the stock market series. You should place special emphasis on the stability of the relationship.

A scatter plot of the operating profit margin (OPM) for the S&P 400 industrial index and the S&P composite retail store (CRS) index indicates a poor relationship between these two series. As shown by the time-series plot in Figure 13.3, the S&P 400 OPM has declined over time, while the CRS OPM has been stable (except for 1974) or increased. Therefore, rather than use the S&P series, an alternative is to derive an estimate of the industry OPM from the time-series plot by relying on profit trends in the retail industry.

Beyond this time-series analysis, you should identify any unique factors that affect the specific industry such as price wars, contract negotiations, building plans, or foreign competition. Adjustments for these unique events should complete an estimate of the final

Figure 13.3 *Time-Series Plot of GPM for S&P Composite Retail Store Index and S&P 400*

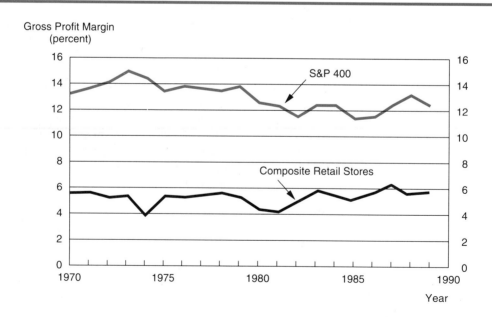

Figure 13.4 *Time-Series Plot of Depreciation for S&P Composite Retail Store Index and S&P 400*

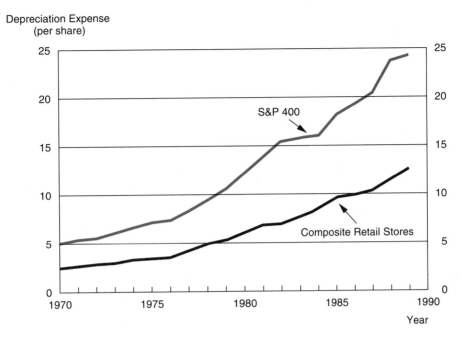

operating profit margin or a range of optimistic, pessimistic, and most likely industry profit margins.

Estimating Industry Depreciation Expense The next step in finding net profit margin is to estimate industry depreciation. This is typically rather easy because you know that it is generally increasing; the only question is by how much. As shown in Figure 13.4, the depreciation series for retail stores has increased every year, maintaining a strong relationship with depreciation for the S&P 400 index. Therefore, our previous estimate of market depreciation should help you to estimate future retail store depreciation. Subtracting depreciation expense from operating profit gives us earnings before interest and tax (EBIT).

Estimating Industry Interest Expense The interest expense graph in Figure 13.5 reflects a fairly stable series from 1984 to 1988 followed by a big increase in 1988 and 1989 that reflected several leveraged buyouts (LBOs) of firms in this industry. It is expected that the financial failures and negative publicity attributed

to high-yield bonds during 1989 will push this series toward stability in 1991. When we subtract our estimate of interest per share, we have earnings before tax (EBT).

Estimating the Industry Tax Rate As the final step in estimating earnings per share, you need to forecast the tax rate for the industry. As you might expect, tax rates differ between industries. In the oil industry heavy depletion allowances causes lower tax rates, for example. In some instances, however, you can assume that tax law changes have similar impacts on all industries. You determine how much the tax rate of the industry you are investigating varies by comparing its rates to the aggregate tax rate over time.

Although the CRS tax rate has historically moved with the economy's tax rate, recently the relationship between the two series has changed. This means that this relationship will not be very useful. Alternatively, the time-series plot of the industry tax rate in Figure 13.6 can be very informative along with a consideration of specific industry factors. Once you have esti-

Figure 13.5   *Interest Expense for S&P Composite Retail Store Index and S&P 400*

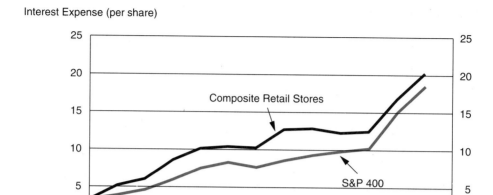

Interest Expense (per share)

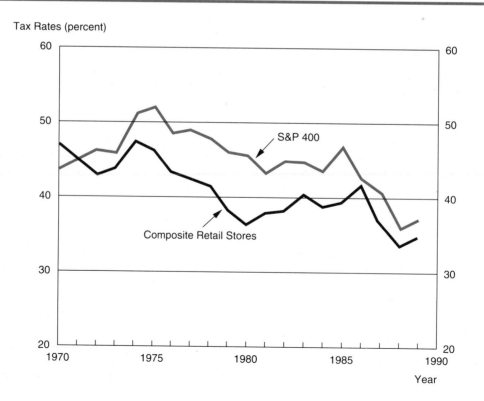

Figure 13.6   *Time-Series Plot of Taxes for S&P Composite Retail Store Index and S&P 400*

Tax Rates (percent)

mated the tax rate, you multiply the EBT per share value by (1 − Tax rate) to get your estimate of earnings per share.

Calculating Industry Earnings per Share: An Example

Now that we have described how to estimate each variable in the equation for earnings per share (EPS), we will use these concepts to estimate EPS for the retail store industry using the economic forecasts from Chapter 12 and the CRS industry series. Our results are not as exact as those of a practicing analyst. We ideally should come close to an analyst's initial estimate, which would be modified based upon the analyst's knowledge of the industry and current events.

The scatter plot in Figure 13.2 indicated that the best sales relationship was between CRS sales and personal consumption expenditures (PCE). During 1991, PCE should post about a 6.0 percent increase.[5] This estimate indicates an increase in retail sales of approximately 4.8 percent (0.80 × 6.0). Therefore, given 1990 retail sales of $970, the 1991 estimate is about $1,017 (1.048 × $970).

The operating profit margin (OPM) for retail stores was 7.0 percent in 1989. During 1990, the OPM for the S&P 400 decreased, so retail store margins probably experienced a decrease to 6.8 percent. The OPM for the market was expected to decline further during 1991. Based upon the graph in Figure 13.3, this would indicate 1991 retail store margins of about 6.7 percent, which implies an operating profit per share for the retail store industry of $68.14. (0.068 × $1,017).

Depreciation per share for the CRS industry during 1990 was estimated to be $11.50. Assuming the industry will maintain the trend exhibited in Figure 13.4, this would imply an estimate for depreciation expense of about $12.25 and earnings before interest and tax of $55.89 ($68.14 − $12.25).

Interest expense increased sharply in 1988 and 1989, but was expected to be stable in 1990 and 1991. Therefore, the estimate for 1991 is for $20.00 per share, so EBT should be $35.89 ($55.89 − $20.00).

The tax rate for the retail store industry has been lower than the market tax rate of about 34 percent during 1990. A rate of about 31 percent seems appropriate for the retail store industry, which implies taxes of $11.13 ($35.89 × 0.31) and earnings per share of $24.76 ($35.89 − $11.13).

Given this estimate of the industry's earnings per share (approximately $25 per share), your next step is to estimate the likely earnings multiplier for this industry. Together the earnings per share and the earnings multiplier provide an estimate of the expected value for the industry index. Given this expected value and an estimate of dividends per share during the holding period, you can compute an expected rate of return from investing in this industry.

Step Two: Estimating an Industry Earnings Multiplier

This section shows how to estimate the earnings multiplier for an industry by two possible techniques: macroanalysis and microanalysis. In macroanalysis, you examine the relationship between the multiplier for the industry and that for the market. In microanalysis, you estimate the industry earnings multiplier by examining the specific variables that influence it—the dividend payout ratio, the required rate of return for the industry(k), and the expected growth rate of earnings and dividends for the industry(g). We analyze each variable and then combine them to estimate a value for the retail store P/E ratio, much as we did in Chapter 12 for the stock market series. In this section we will describe both approaches.

Macroanalysis of an Industry Multiplier

Macroanalysis assumes that the major variables that influence the industry earnings multiplier are related to similar variables for the aggregate stock market. In addition, we expect a relationship between changes in k and g for specific industries and for the aggregate stock market. A similar pattern in the movements of these variables (though not necessarily the same values) would lead us to expect a relationship between changes in the industry P/E ratio and changes in the P/E ratio for the stock market. Macroanalysis requires that we find such a relationship for individual industries and then use it to predict future values of the industry P/E ratio.

Analysis of the relationship between the P/E ratios for 71 industries as defined by Standard & Poor's

---

[5]Steven G. Einhorn, *Portfolio Strategy* (New York: Goldman, Sachs & Co., 1990).

Figure 13.7 *Ratio of Annual Average Multipliers for CRS Industry and S&P 400*

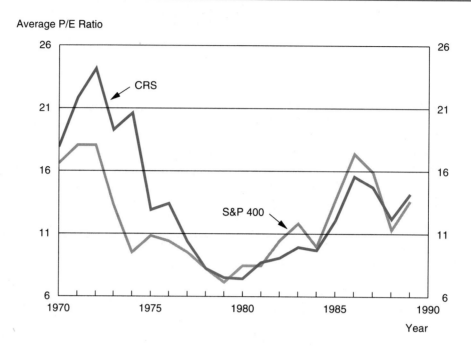

and the S&P 400 index indicated strong correlations for a number of industries, but weak relationships for others, which means that they could not be used for predictive purposes.[6] Therefore, you must evaluate the relationship between P/E ratios for a specific industry and the market before using this technique.

Figure 13.7 shows a graph of the average annual CRS P/E ratio and the average annual S&P 400 multiplier. This plot indicates a fairly stable relationship between these P/E ratios during recent years, so this technique can help us derive an estimate of the industry P/E ratio. Still, you should confirm this macroestimate of the P/E ratio with the results of the microanalysis.

Microanalysis of an Industry Multiplier

In Chapter 12 we estimated the future earnings multiplier for the stock market series in two ways. In the

first, the direction of change approach, we estimated the trends in the changes for the three variables that determine the earnings multiplier—the dividend payout ratio, the required rate of return, and the expected growth rate of earnings and dividends. The consensus of the changes indicated the direction of change for the multiplier from its current value. In the second approach, the specific multiplier estimate technique, we estimated a range of values for the three variables that determine the multiplier and, using several individual estimates, derived a range of P/E ratio estimates from optimistic to pessimistic. These two approaches gave us four multiplier estimates by which we multiplied our EPS estimate to compute a range of expected values for the market index, and subsequently expected rates of return on common stocks.

Our microanalysis of the industry multiplier could use the same two approaches for each industry. Although this would certainly be legitimate and logical, it would not take advantage of our prior work on the stock market multiplier. Since the variables that affect the stock market multiplier also determine the industry multiplier, it should be possible to compare the two sets of variables.

[6]Frank K. Reilly and Thomas Zeller, "An Analysis of Relative Industry Price–Earnings Ratios," *The Financial Review* 4 (1974): 17–33.

Table 13.2 *Earnings Multipliers for S&P 400 Index and S&P Composite Retail Store Index and Influential Variables: 1970 to 1989*

	Mean Earnings Multiplier		Retention Rate		Return on Equity		Equity Turnover		Net Profit Margin	
	S&P 400	Composite Retail Store	S&P 400	Composite Retail Store	S&P 400	Composite Retail Store	S&P 400	Composite Retail Store	S&P 400	Composite Retail Store
1970	16.49	17.72	41.8	52.6	10.28	11.33	2.09	4.84	4.92	2.34
1971	18.02	21.65	47.1	54.8	10.80	11.61	2.14	4.79	5.04	2.43
1972	17.95	24.11	52.9	57.3	11.71	11.39	2.21	4.90	5.30	2.32
1973	13.25	19.24	61.1	61.2	14.15	12.11	2.37	5.03	5.96	2.41
1974	9.43	20.63	61.4	38.3	14.17	7.75	2.69	5.40	5.28	1.43
1975	10.79	12.83	56.6	62.0	12.11	11.72	2.61	5.24	4.63	2.24
1976	10.41	13.39	60.5	66.3	14.02	12.45	2.66	5.25	5.27	2.37
1977	9.55	10.50	56.8	63.8	13.93	13.06	2.73	5.28	5.15	2.48
1978	8.21	8.20	58.8	61.4	14.60	13.19	2.81	5.24	5.19	2.52
1979	7.11	7.48	63.7	60.1	16.50	12.85	2.96	5.23	5.57	2.46
1980	8.44	7.40	59.7	53.8	14.88	11.01	3.02	5.60	4.92	1.97
1981	8.45	8.60	58.1	51.5	14.42	10.31	2.97	5.83	4.86	1.77
1982	10.37	9.05	46.0	59.1	11.13	12.48	2.82	5.65	3.95	2.21
1983	11.84	9.97	50.4	65.8	12.07	14.89	2.73	5.61	4.42	2.65
1984	9.92	9.76	58.5	65.3	14.61	14.63	3.06	5.78	4.77	2.53
1985	13.68	12.04	48.5	63.6	12.14	13.51	3.16	5.71	3.84	2.37
1986	17.47	15.66	44.0	65.5	11.64	13.22	3.11	5.32	3.75	2.48
1987	16.00	14.78	57.0	68.2	15.11	15.72	3.21	5.32	4.71	2.95
1988	11.38	12.31	63.1	68.6	19.06	17.97	3.48	6.37	5.46	2.82
1989	13.79	14.26	57.3	68.1	18.19	17.38	3.63	6.11	4.91	2.84
Mean[a]	12.27	13.10	54.8	61.5	13.76	13.20	2.83	5.43	4.87	2.43
Mean[b]	12.13	11.38	54.3	63.0	14.33	14.11	3.12	5.73	4.56	2.46

[a]Data for 1974 not included.

[b]Results for 10 years from 1980 to 1989.

Source: *Standard & Poor's Analysts Handbook* (New York: Standard & Poor's Corporation, 1990). Reprinted with permission.

Therefore, in our microanalysis, we estimate the three variables that determine the industry earnings multiplier and compare them to the comparable values for the market P/E ratio to determine whether the industry earnings multiplier should be above, below, or equal to the market multiplier. Once we feel confident about this relationship, it is easier to derive a specific estimate for the industry P/E ratio. As a first step, we need to examine the long-run relationship between the industry and market P/E ratios.

Industry Multiplier versus Market Multiplier
The mean high and low multipliers for the aggregate market and the CRS industry appear in Column 1 of Table 13.2. The P/E ratios for the retail store industry exceeded those for the stock market prior to 1978, but the industry multipliers have generally been smaller in recent years. Obvious questions include: Why do the P/E ratios for this industry and the stock market differ over time? Why have investors recently become willing to pay more for a dollar of earnings from the

aggregate market than from retail stores? Why has the relationship between the P/E ratio for this industry and the stock market changed? Analysis of the factors that determine the earnings multiplier should help us answer these questions.

Comparing Dividend Payout Ratios We can discuss the dividend payout ratio directly or in terms of the retention rate because the retention rate equals 1 minus the dividend payout ratio. We see from the second set of columns in Table 13.2 that the retention rates of retail stores and the market index were typically within 2 percentage points prior to the 1970s. Following some large annual changes, the overall averages and recent experience indicate a higher earnings retention rate for the CRS industry (55 versus 62 percent and 54 versus 63 percent). These differences indicate a higher payout ratio for the S&P 400, which would imply a higher multiple for the S&P 400.

Estimating the Required Rate of Return Since the required rate of return (k) on all investments is influenced by the risk-free rate and the expected inflation rate, the differentiating factor between the market and industry rates of return is the risk premium. This is the value we must estimate to arrive at an industry k. To estimate the industry's risk premium, we evaluate business risk (BR), financial risk (FR), liquidity risk (LR), exchange rate risk (ERR), and country risk (CR), then we compare them to those of the aggregate stock market.

Business risk is a function of sales volatility and operating leverage. Historically, retail sales have been about 80 percent as volatile as a measure of aggregate sales. Also, the retail operating profit margin has been less volatile than the operating profit margin for the aggregate stock market. Less volatility in both sales and operating profit margin implies substantially less volatile operating profits, and below-average business risk for the CRS industry.

The financial risk for this industry is difficult to measure because many retail stores lease their premises, so the standard balance sheet ratios underestimate financial leverage. When you consider these long-term lease contracts, the firms in this industry generally have above-average financial risk. As we have discussed earlier, however, below-average business risk means that it is possible to justify above-average financial risk.

To evaluate the liquidity risk for an industry, it is necessary to estimate the liquidity risk for all the individual firms in the industry and derive a composite view because market liquidity can vary substantially among firms. As an example, the stock of Sears, Roebuck is very liquid, whereas the stock for American Stores is quite illiquid. Generally, most of the stocks in this industry have slightly below-average liquidity, so the CRS industry probably has slightly above-average liquidity risk.

Businesses incur exchange rate risk on non-U.S. sales and purchases so it is highest for firms and industries with large proportions of non-U.S. sales or high percentages of non-U.S. sales in countries with volatile exchange rates. The exchange rate risk for the CRS industry is low in comparison to some global industries like chemicals and pharmaceuticals because many of these retail firms operate almost wholly within the United States. Still, some of these firms have been considering the acquisition of foreign firms, so this could change. Still, at the present time, country risk is very low for this industry.

In summary, the CRS industry's business risk is below average, its financial risk is above average, its liquidity risk is slightly above average, and its exchange rate risk and country risk are below average. Assuming that business risk is the most significant variable, we can rate the overall risk for this industry as about equal to that for the market or slightly below it.

Estimating the Expected Growth Rate (g) You will recall that earnings and dividend growth are determined by the retention rate (b) and the return on equity (ROE):

$$g = b \times ROE$$

Therefore, you need to examine each of these variables for the CRS industry contained in Table 13.3 to estimate any difference in its expected growth rate compared to that of the aggregate stock market.

Earnings Retention Rate The earnings retention rate is 1 minus the dividend payout rate. Since the S&P 400 series had a slightly higher payout rate than the CRS industry, the industry has a slightly higher retention rate and a potentially higher growth rate.

Return on Equity Return on equity can be broken down into equity turnover and net profit margin as follows:

$$ROE = \frac{Net\ income}{Equity} = \frac{Sales}{Equity} \times \frac{Net\ income}{Sales}$$

We examine these two variables individually and predict how they will change based upon their relationship to the values for the stock market. The equity turnover series for both the industry and market increased over time, although the CRS series has consistently been higher. The S&P 400 equity turnover series increased from 2.09 in 1970 to 3.63 in 1989. Concurrently, the CRS industry equity turnover went from 4.84 to 6.11. The average for the total period was 2.83 for the S&P 400 versus 5.43 for CRS; during the last 10 years it was 3.12 (S&P) versus 5.73 (CRS). This shows an average equity turnover for the CRS industry almost double that for the aggregate market.

In contrast, the S&P 400 series maintained a consistently higher net profit margin than the CRS industry. The higher profit margin for the aggregate stock market offsets the higher equity turnover for the industry. These differences in equity turnover and net profit margin indicate tactics to generate high ROEs. You can either have a low equity turnover and high net profit margin as in the S&P 400, or a low net profit margin but a higher equity turnover ratio as in the CRS industry.

The return on equity values for the industry and the market from 1979 to 1989 are reasonably close. The average ROE for the period from 1970 to 1989 was 13.76 percent for the S&P 400 versus 13.20 percent for the CRS series; for the last 10 years it was 14.33 (S&P) versus 14.11 (CRS). These average ROEs are quite consistent with the results of multiplying the components, as follows:

Equity turnover (ET)	×	Profit margin (PM)	=	Return on equity (ROE)
	ET	**PM**	**ROE**	
All Years				
S&P 400	2.83	× 4.87	= 13.78	
CRS	5.43	× 2.43	= 13.19	
Last 10 Years				
S&P 400	3.12	× 4.56	= 14.23	
CRS	5.73	× 2.46	= 14.10	

Calculating the Growth Rate   Now that we have estimated the retention rate and the ROE, we can calculate an estimate of the growth rate. As noted, the CRS industry has a higher retention rate while the S&P 400 has a higher return on equity. Using these historical values as estimates, estimated growth rates are as follows:

	RR	ROE	g
All Years			
S&P 400	0.548	× 13.76	= 7.54 percent
CRS	0.615	× 13.20	= 8.12 percent
Last 10 Years			
S&P 400	0.543	× 14.33	= 7.78 percent
CRS	0.630	× 14.11	= 8.89 percent

Clearly, the calculated growth rates based upon historical values are not dramatically different, but they indicate that the CRS industry's implied growth rate is higher due to a higher retention rate.

At this point, we have analyzed the three variables that determine the earnings multiplier (D/E, k, and g) and can interpret our results by discussing the reasons why we would expect a difference in the earnings multiplier for the industry and the stock market.

Interpreting Our Results: Why the Difference in Multipliers?

Because the earnings multiplier is a function of D/E, k, and g, any difference in the multipliers should be explained by the differences in these variables. Our analysis of the historical multiplier series showed a higher earnings multiplier for the CRS industry than for the market during the 1970s, but during most of the 1980s (prior to 1988 and 1989) the industry multiplier was smaller. Why did the CRS industry's multiplier decline relative to the market and then increase during the last 2 years of the decade? A small difference in the payout ratios for the two series favored the S&P 400 series. Analysis of industry risk concluded that the risk premium for the CRS industry should be equal to or below the market risk premium. Finally, analysis of the growth components indicated that the CRS industry's growth rate should be slightly above the stock market's.

In summary, the payout ratio favored the market, while the risk premium and growth rate favored the CRS industry. Overall, this would explain why the

| **Competitive strategy** The search by a firm for a favorable competitive position within an industry, which affects evaluation of the industry's prospects.

earnings multiplier for the CRS industry has risen above the earnings multiplier for the stock market.

Forecasting the Industry P/E Ratio: An Example

The most accurate and consistent estimates of the P/E ratio rely on both macroanalysis and microanalysis. In our example, the macroanalysis showed that the retail store P/E is lower and less volatile than the market P/E. In Chapter 12 we estimated a decline in the market multiplier for 1991 to between 12 and 14 times earnings with a range of 6 to 18 times. A similar decline for the retail store industry multiplier implies an estimate for the CRS industry of about 12.

Microanalysis of individual components indicated that the multiplier for the retail store industry should exceed the market multiplier. This would imply a P/E ratio of about 15 for the CRS industry. For our final estimates of industry value and expected rate of return we will use both of these estimates: 12 and 15.

Forecasting the Industry Value and Return: An Example

To estimate values of the industry index we combine our prior estimate of earnings per share and earnings multipliers for this industry. Our earnings per share estimate for 1991 was $25.00. When we multiply this by our estimated earnings multipliers of 12 and 15, we derive estimates of the value of the industry index as follows:

$$12.0 \times \$25.00 = \$300$$
$$15.0 \times \$25.00 = \$375$$

You can compute your expected return E(R) on an investment in this industry based upon this index value and the expected dividend, as follows:

$$E(R_{CRS}) = \frac{\text{Index (estimated)} - \text{Index (current)} + \text{Dividend}}{\text{Index (current)}}$$

In our demonstration of a technique to estimate the value of an industry index, we relied on probable relationships between an industry and the stock market and focused on the variables that cause industry

values to vary. In estimating future industry values you should never forget that the past alone is an inadequate basis for projecting the future. Past relationships may not hold in the future, especially in the short run. Therefore, when you apply this technique you must determine the *future* values for the relevant variables based upon careful analysis of the industry.

Competition and Expected Industry Returns

In this chapter we have demonstrated the two-step approach to estimating the future value for an industry and the expected rate of return based upon this future value. This analysis provided a specific estimate of the industry's future rate of return based upon its historical relationship with the economy and the aggregate stock market. You should realize that other economic forces can influence the likelihood of realizing these returns. One important factor is the intensity of competition in the industry, as Porter has discussed in a series of books and articles.[7]

Porter's concept of **competitive strategy** is described as the search by a firm for a favorable competitive position in an industry. To create a profitable competitive strategy, a firm must first examine the basic competitive structure of its industry because the potential profitability of a firm is heavily influenced by the inherent profitability of its industry. After determining the competitive structure of the industry, you examine the factors that determine the relative competitive position of a firm within its industry. In this section we consider the competitive forces that determine the competitive structure of the industry. In the next chapter our discussion of company analysis will cover the factors that determine the relative competitive position of a firm within its industry.

Basic Competitive Forces

Porter believes that the **competitive environment** of an industry, or the intensity of competition among the firms in that industry, determines firms' ability to sus-

---

[7]Michael E. Porter, *Competitive Strategy: Techniques for Analyzing Industries and Competitors* (New York: Free Press, 1980); Michael Porter, "Industry Structure and Competitive Strategy: Keys to Profitability," *Financial Analysts Journal* 36, no. 4 (July–August 1980); and Michael Porter, *Competitive Advantage: Creating and Sustaining Superior Performance* (New York: Free Press, 1985): Chapter 1.

tain above-average rates of return on invested capital. He suggests that five competitive forces determine the intensity of competition:

1. Rivalry among existing competitors
2. Threat of new entrants
3. Threat of substitute products
4. Bargaining power of buyers
5. Bargaining power of suppliers

The relative effects of each of these five factors can vary dramatically among industries.

Rivalry among Existing Competitors   For each industry you analyze, you must judge whether the rivalry among firms is intense and growing or polite and stable. Rivalry increases when many firms of relatively equal size compete in an industry. When estimating the number and size of firms, be sure to include foreign competitors. Further, *slow growth* causes competitors to fight for market share and increases competition. *High fixed costs* stimulate the desire to sell at full capacity which can lead to price cutting and greater competition. Finally, look for *exit barriers*, such as specialized facilities or labor agreements. These can keep firms in the industry despite below-average or negative returns.

Threat of New Entrants   Although an industry may have few competitors, you must determine the likelihood of firms entering the industry and increasing competition. High *barriers to entry* such as low current prices relative to costs keep the threat of new entrants low. Other barriers to entry include the need to invest large financial resources to compete and the availability of capital. Also, substantial economies of scale give a current industry member an advantage over a new firm. Further entrants might be discouraged if success in the industry requires extensive distribution channels that are hard to build because of exclusive distribution contracts. Similarly, high costs of switching products or brands like those required to change a computer or telephone system keep competition low. Finally, government policy can restrict entry by imposing licensing requirements or limiting access to materials (lumber, coal). Without some of these barriers it might be very easy for competitors to enter an industry, increasing competition and driving down potential rates of return.

Threat of Substitute Products   Substitute products limit the profit potential of an industry because they

> **Competitive environment** The level of intensity of competition among firms in an industry, determined by an examination of five competitive sources.

limit the prices firms in an industry can charge. While almost everything has a substitute, you must determine how close the substitute is in price and function to the product in your industry. As an example, the threat of substitute glass containers hurt the metal container industry. Glass containers kept declining in price, forcing metal container prices and profits down. In the food industry consumers constantly substitute between beef, pork, chicken, and fish.

Bargaining Power of Buyers   Buyers can influence the profitability of an industry because they can bid down prices or demand higher quality or more services by bargaining among competitors. Buyers become powerful when they purchase a large volume relative to the sales of a supplier. The most vulnerable firm is a one-customer firm that supplies a single large manufacturer, as is common for auto parts manufacturers or software developers. Buyers will be more conscious of costs of items that represent significant percentages of their total costs or if the buying firm is feeling cost pressure from its customers. Also, buyers who know a lot about the costs of supplying an industry will bargain more intensely, as when the buying firms supply some of their own needs and also buy from outside.

Bargaining Power of Suppliers   Suppliers can alter future industry returns if they increase prices or reduce the quality or services they provide. The suppliers are more powerful if they are few and more concentrated than the industry to which they sell, and if they supply critical inputs to several industries for which few if any substitutes exist. In this instance the suppliers are free to change prices and services they supply to the firms in an industry. When analyzing supplier bargaining power, be sure to consider labor's power within each industry.

An investor can analyze these competitive forces to determine the intensity of the competition in an industry and assess its long-run profit potential. You should examine each of these factors for every industry and develop a relative competitive profile. You need to update this analysis of an industry's competitive environment over time because an industry's competitive structure can and will change over time.

| Table 13.3 | Chemical Production Volume (Percentage Change from Previous Year) |

	1983	1984	1985	1986	1987	1988	1989E	1990E
United Kingdom	+7	+7	+5	+2	+7	+5	+4	+2
West Germany	+6	+5	+2	−1	+2	+5	+4	+2
France	+6	+5	−	−	+4	+5	+4	+2
Switzerland	+7	+6	+6	+2	+3	+14	+8	+5
Netherlands	+9	+9	+9	+1	+6	+7	+3	+3
Italy	+1	+6	+3	+1	+3	+7	+4	+3
Europe	+6	+6	+3	−	+4	+6	+4	+3
United States	+10	+6	+4	+4	+6	+8	+5	+2

Source: Chemical industry associations; Goldman, Sachs estimates.

Global Industry Analysis

Because so many firms are active in foreign markets and because the proportion of foreign sales is growing for so many firms, we must expand industry analysis to include the effects of foreign firms on global trade and industry returns. To see why this is so, consider the auto industry. Besides Chrysler, Ford, and General Motors, it includes numerous firms from Japan, Germany, Italy, and Korea among others. Thus, we must extend the analysis described earlier to include additional global factors. This section presents an example of such an analysis for the European chemical industry performed by an industry analyst at Goldman, Sachs & Co.[8] Although the report discusses individual firms in the industry, we will emphasize the overall chemical industry.

An Example: The European Chemical Industry

Production Table 13.3 reports the historical records of chemical production within the major countries from 1983 to 1988 with estimates for 1989 and 1990. It shows very strong sales growth during 1988 and 1989. The outlook for 1990 is for positive growth, but not at the exceptionally high rates that prevailed during 1988 to 1989.

[8]Charles K. Brown and Peter Clark, "European Chemical Majors — Outlook for 1990" (London: Goldman, Sachs International, Ltd., January 1990).

Profit Performance A table in the report shows pretax profit growth for the four major companies, which also reflects conditions for most other firms in this industry. These data in Table 13.4 indicate very good profit results during the 1988 to 1989 expansion. Subsequently the rate of increase declined for most firms and earnings have turned down for some of them.

The final segment of the analysis examines the currency factors involved in forecasting production for each country, and also the export–import possibilities based upon the exchange rate outlook. Table 13.5 lists exchange rates for each of the major countries relative to the U.S. dollar and on a trade-weighted basis to all currencies. The exchange rate changes during 1990 indicated strength in the German mark and French franc. These changes were expected to have an impact, especially on German results.

Overall, prospects for 1990 were considered flat, but not disastrous. The analysts did not expect a collapse in the profitability of major European chemical companies. They envisioned a period of relatively flat performance, with some possibilities of improvement as the year progressed, especially if the U.S. dollar gained in strength.

The rest of the report discussed the major chemical firms and made specific recommendations regarding each of them. This segment of the report on individual companies will be considered in our next chapter on company analysis.

Table 13.4 *Pretax Profit Growth Trends: 1988–1989 (Annual Percentage Changes)*

	1988				1989		
	Q1	Q2	Q3	Q4	Q1	Q2	Q3
BASF	+8	+28	+32	+152	+28	+31	+11
Bayer	+11	+28	+28	+24	+21	+18	—
Hoechst	+20	+41	+40	+25	+23	-2	+1
ICI	+7	+19	+11	+10	+23	+14	-12

Source: Charles K. Brown and Peter Clark, "European Chemical Majors—Outlook for 1990" (London: Goldman, Sachs International, Ltd., January 1990).

Table 13.5 *Exchange Rate Trends: 1988–1990 (Annual Percentage Changes)*

		DM Strength		SFr Strength		FFr Strength		Sterling Strength		
		Versus US$ (%)	Trade-Weighted (%)	Versus US$ (%)	Trade-Weighted (%)	Versus US$ (%)	Trade-Weighted (%)	Versus US$ (%)	Versus DM (%)	Trade-Weighted (%)
1988	Q1	+9	—	+12	+3	+8	-1	+17	+6	+8
	Q2	+6	—	+5	-1	+4	-1	+12	+6	+7
	Q3	-2	-1	-3	-2	-3	-3	+5	+6	+5
	Q4	-4	-2	-7	-4	-5	-3	+2	+6	+4
1989	Q1	-11	-3	-15	-7	-11	-3	-3	+7	+4
	Q2	-13	-2	-19	-7	-13	-2	-11	—	-3
	Q3	-3	—	-6	-3	-3	—	-6	-3	-4
	Q4	-2	+2	-7	-3	-2	+2	-11	-10	-9
1990	Q1E[a]	+9	+6	+3	-1	+8	+5	-8	-15	-11
	Q2E[a]	+12	+6	+9	+2	+12	+4	-1	-13	-8
	Q3E[a]	+12	+6	+7	-1	+11	+4	+1	-11	-6
	Q4E[a]	+7	+3	+4	—	+6	+2	+1	-5	-2

[a]Projections at end-1989 rates of DM1.69/$, SFr1.54/$, FFr5.79/$, $1.61/£, and DM2.73/£ and at trade-weighted indices (Bank of England) of 119.6, 106.6, 103.5, and 86.0 for the DM, SFr, FFr, and £ respectively.

Source: Charles K. Brown and Peter Clark, "European Chemical Majors—Outlook for 1990" (London: Goldman, Sachs International, Ltd., January 1990).

Summary

■ Several studies have examined industry performance and risk. They have found wide dispersion in the performance of alternative industries during specified time periods, implying that industry analysis can help identify superior investments. They also showed inconsistent performance of individual industries over time, implying that only examining the past performance of an industry has little value in projecting future performance. Also, the performance by firms within industries is typically not very consistent, so you must analyze the individual companies in an industry following the industry analysis.

- The analysis of industry risk indicated wide dispersion in the measure of risk for different industries, but a fair amount of consistency in the risk measure over time for individual industries. These results imply that risk analysis and measurement are useful in selecting industries and that past risk measures may be of some use.

- The two-step approach to estimating the value of an industry involves estimating earnings per share, beginning with an estimate of sales. We considered three techniques to estimate sales based on industrial life cycles, input–output analysis, and relationships of industry sales to alternative economic series. We estimated earnings per share based upon estimates of operating profit margin, depreciation expense, interest expense, and the industry tax rate. In the second half of the procedure we estimated the earnings multiplier for the industry through macroanalysis and microanalysis.

- An important part of industry analysis is the examination of five factors that determine the intensity of competition in an industry, which in turn affects its long-run profitability.

- Global industry analysis must consider not only world supply, demand, and cost components for an industry, but also the effects of exchange rates on the total industry and the firms within it.

Questions

1. Briefly describe the results of studies that examined the performance of alternative industries during specific time periods and discuss their implications for industry analysis.
2. Briefly describe the results of the studies that examined industry performance over time and discuss their implications for industry analysis. Do these results complicate or simplify industry analysis?
3. Assume that all the firms in a particular industry have consistently shown rates of return that were very similar to the results for the industry. Discuss what this implies regarding the importance of industry and company analysis for this industry.
4. Some observers have contended that differences in the performance of various firms within an industry limit the usefulness of industry analysis. Discuss this contention.
5. Several studies have examined differences in risk for alternative industries during a specified time

period. Describe the results of these studies and discuss their implications for industry analysis.
6. What were the results of measuring risk for different industries during successive time periods? Discuss the implication of these results for industry analysis.
7. Assume that the industry you are analyzing is in the fourth stage of the industrial life cycle. How would you react if your industry–economic analysis predicted that sales per share for this industry would increase by 20 percent? Discuss your reasoning.
8. Discuss at what stage in the industrial life cycle you would like to discover a firm and justify your decision.
9. Discuss an example of input–output analysis to predict the sales for an industry. Discuss how you would use input–output analysis to predict the costs of production for your industry.
10. Discuss an example of the impact of one of the five competitive forces on an industry's profitability.

Problems

1. Select three industries from the S&P *Analysts Handbook* with different demand factors. For each industry, indicate what economic series you would use in your prediction of growth for the industry. Discuss why the economic series selected is relevant for this industry.
2. Prepare a scatter plot for one of the three industries selected in Problem 1 of industry sales per share and observations from the economic series you suggested for this industry. Do this for the most recent 10 years using information available in the *Analysts Handbook*. Based upon the results of the scatter plot, discuss whether the economic series was closely related to industry sales for this.
3. Using the S&P *Analysts Handbook*, plot the latest 10-year history of the operating profit margin for the S&P 400 versus the S&P-defined industry of your choice. Is there a positive, negative, or zero correlation?
4. Using the *Analysts Handbook*, calculate means for the following variables for the S&P 400 and the industry of your choice during the last 10 years:
   a. Price/earnings multiplier
   b. Retention rate
   c. Return on equity

d. Equity turnover
e. Net profit margin
Note: each of these entries is a ratio, so take care when averaging. Briefly comment on the differences for each of the variables.
5. Industry information can be found in *Barron's* Market Laboratory/Economic Indicators section. Using issues over the past 6 months, plot the trend for:
a. Auto production
b. Auto inventories (domestic and imports)
c. Newsprint production
d. Newsprint inventories
e. Business inventories
What tentative conclusions do these data support regarding the current economic environment?
6. Prepare a table listing variables that influence the earnings multiplier for your chosen industry and the S&P 400 series for the most recent 10 years.
a. Do the average dividend payout ratios for your industry and the S&P 400 differ? How should the dividend payout influence the difference between the multipliers?
b. Would you expect the risk for this industry to differ from that for the market? In what direction, and why? What effect will this difference in risk have on the industry multiplier relative to the market multiplier?
c. Analyze and discuss the components of growth (retention rate, equity turnover, and profit margin) for your chosen industry and the S&P 400 during the most recent 10 years. Based on this analysis, how would you expect the growth rate for your industry to compare to the growth rate for the S&P 400? How

would this difference in expected growth affect the multiplier?
7. Where is your industry in its industrial life cycle? Justify your answer by reference to your prior analysis.
8. Evaluate your industry in terms of the five factors that determine an industry's competitive structure. Discuss your expectations for this industry's long-run profitability.

References

Aber, John. "Industry Effects and Multivariate Stock Price Behavior." *Journal of Financial and Quantitative Analysis* 11, no. 5 (November 1976).

Fruhan, William E., Jr. *Financial Strategy*. Homewood, Ill.: Richard D. Irwin, 1979.

Livingston, Miles. "Industry Movements of Common Stocks." *Journal of Finance* 32, no. 3 (June 1977).

Meyers, Stephen L. "A Re-examination of Market and Industry Factors in Stock Price Behavior." *Journal of Finance* 28, no. 3 (June 1973).

Porter, Michael E. "Industry Structure and Competitive Strategy: Keys to Profitability." *Financial Analysts Journal* 36, no. 4 (July–August 1980).

Porter, Michael E. *Competitive Strategies: Techniques for Analyzing Industries and Competitors*. New York: Free Press, 1980.

Porter, Michael E. *Competitive Advantage: Creating and Sustaining Superior Performance*. New York: Free Press, 1985.

Porter, Michael E. "How to Conduct an Industry Analysis." In *The Financial Analysts Handbook*, 2d ed. Ed. by Sumner N. Levine. Homewood, Ill.: Dow Jones-Irwin, 1988.

Reilly, Frank K., and Eugene Drzycimski. "Alternative Industry Performance and Risk." *Journal of Financial and Quantitative Analysis* 9, no. 3 (June 1974).

APPENDIX

13a *Preparing an Industry Analysis*

What Is an Industry?[1]

Identifying a company's industry can be difficult in today's business world. While airlines, railroads, and utilities may be easy to categorize, what about manufacturing companies with three roughly equal divi-

sions? Perhaps the best way to test whether a company fits into an industry grouping is to compare its oper-

[1]Reprinted and adapted with permission of Stanley D. Ryals, CFA; Investment Counsel, Inc.; Apple Valley, CA 92307.

ating results to those for the industry. For our purposes, an industry is a group of companies with similar operating characteristics.

A set of guidelines for preparing an industry appraisal follows, including the topics to consider and some specific items to include.

Characteristics to Study

1. Price history reveals valuable long-term relationships.
   a. Price–earnings ratios
   b. Common stock yields
   c. Price–book value ratios
   d. Price–cash flow ratios
2. Operating data show comparisons of:
   a. Return on total investment (ROI)
   b. Return on equity (ROE)
   c. Sales growth
   d. Trends in operating profit margin
   e. Trends in net profit margin
   f. Earnings per share growth
   g. Book value growth
3. Comparative results of industries show:
   a. Effects of business cycles on each industry group
   b. Secular trends affecting results
   c. Industry growth compared to other industries
   d. Stage in industrial life cycle
   e. Regulatory changes
   f. Importance of overseas operations
   g. Evaluation of exchange rate risk from foreign sales

Factors in Industry Analysis

Markets for Products

1. Trends in the markets for the industry's major products, historical and projected
2. Industry growth relative to GNP or other relevant economic series; possible changes from past trends
3. Shares of market for major products among domestic and global producers; changes in market shares in recent years; projections
4. Effects of imports on industry markets; share of market taken by imports; price and margin changes caused by imports
5. Effects of exports on industry markets; trends in export prices and units exported; historical trends and expectations for the exchange rates in major countries

Financial Performance

1. Capitalization ratios; ability to raise new capital; earnings retention rates; financial leverage
2. Ratios of fixed assets to capital invested; depreciation policies; capital turnover
3. Return on total capital; return on equity capital; components of ROE
4. Return on foreign investments; need for foreign capital

Operations

1. Degrees of integration; cost advantages of integration; major supply contracts
2. Operating rates as percentages of capacity; backlogs; new order trends
3. Trends in industry consolidation
4. Trends in industry competition
5. New product development; research and development expenditures in dollars and as percentages of sales
6. Diversification; comparability of product lines

Management

1. Management depth and ability to develop from within; board of directors; organizational structures
2. Flexibility to deal with product demand changes; ability to identify and eliminate losing operations
3. Records of and outlooks for labor relations
4. Dividend progression

Sources of Industry Information

1. Independent industry journals
2. Industry and trade associations
3. Government reports and statistics
4. Independent research organizations
5. Brokerage house research

14

Company Analysis and Stock Selection

At this point, you have made two decisions about your investment in equity markets. First, after analyzing the economy and stock markets for several countries you have decided to invest some portion of your portfolio in common stocks. Second, after analyzing a number of industries, you have identified those that offer above-average risk-adjusted performance over your investment horizon. You must now answer the final question in the fundamental analysis procedure: Which are the best companies within these desirable industries, and are their stocks underpriced, which means that their values are above their market prices or their expected rates of return are equal to or exceed your required rate of return on them?

We begin this chapter with a discussion of the difference between company analysis and stock selection. We then present an analysis of a company using the techniques from Chapters 12 and 13 by which we estimated the values of the stock market and an industry. Specifically, we use the dividend discount model to value Walgreen Company shares. Following our valuation example, we consider some other valuation measures that you can use to evaluate stock issues. We then present an example of the analysis of foreign stocks. We conclude the chapter with a discussion of some competitive strategies that can help firms maximize returns in an industry's competitive environment.

> **Growth company** A company that consistently has the opportunities and ability to invest in projects that provide rates of return that exceed the firm's cost of capital. Because of these investment opportunities, it retains a high proportion of earnings and its earnings grow faster than those of average firms.
>
> **Growth stock** A stock issue that generates a higher rate of return than other stocks in the market with similar risk characteristics.

Analysis of Companies versus Selection of Stocks

The title of this chapter, "Company Analysis and Stock Selection," is meant to convey the idea that the common stocks of good companies are not necessarily good investments. In our discussion of firm value, we will analyze a company and its internal characteristics. This analysis should give you opinions about the quality of the firm and its management, and about its outlook for the future.

Remember, however, that the quality of the company need not reflect the desirability of the company's stock as an investment. As a final step, you must compare the intrinsic value of a stock to its market price to determine whether you should invest in it. The stock of a wonderful firm with superior management and performance measures such as sales and earnings can be priced so high that its value falls below its market price. You would not want to buy the stock of this wonderful company. In contrast, the stock of a company with less success as measured by sales and earnings growth may have a computed value above its market price. Although the company is not as good, its stock could be a better addition to your portfolio.

The classic confusion in this regard concerns growth companies versus growth stocks. The stock of a growth company is not necessarily a growth stock. Recognition of this difference is very important for successful investing.

Growth Companies and Growth Stocks

Growth companies have historically been defined as companies that consistently post above-average increases in sales and earnings. This definition has some limitations because many firms could qualify due to certain accounting procedures, mergers, or other external events.

In contrast, financial theorists define a growth company as a firm with the management ability and the opportunities to *make investments that yield rates of return greater than the firm's required rate of return.* Recall from financial management courses that this required rate of return is the firm's average cost of capital. As an example, a growth company might be able to acquire capital at an average cost of 10 percent, and yet have the management ability and the opportunity to invest those funds at rates of return of 15–20 percent. As a result of these investment opportunities, the firm's sales and earnings grow more than those of other firms with equal risk or the overall economy. In addition, a growth company that has above-average investment opportunities should, and typically does, retain a large portion of its earnings to fund these projects.

Growth stocks are not necessarily shares in growth companies. A **growth stock** is a stock with a higher rate of return than other stocks in the market with similar risk characteristics. The stock achieves this superior return because at some point in time the market undervalues it compared to other stocks. While the stock market adjusts stock prices relatively quickly and accurately to reflect new information, available information is very likely not perfect or complete. Imperfect or absent information may cause a given stock to be undervalued or overvalued at a point in time.

If the stock is undervalued, its price should eventually increase to reflect its true fundamental value when the correct information becomes available. During this period of price adjustment, the stock's realized returns will exceed the required returns for a stock with its risk, and it will be considered a growth stock.

Identifying a growth stock as a currently undervalued stock that has a high probability of being properly valued in the near term means that growth stocks are not necessarily limited to growth companies. In fact, if investors recognize a growth company and discount its future earnings stream properly, the current market price of the growth company's stock will reflect its future earnings stream. Thus, those who acquire the stock of a growth company at this *correct* market price will receive a rate of return consistent with the risk of the stock, even after the superior earnings growth. In fact, investors can overprice the stock of a growth company. In turn, investors who acquire the stock at the inflated price will earn a return below the risk-adjusted required rate of return despite the company's bright prospects. A future growth stock can be issued by any type of company; the stock need only be undervalued by the market.

The search for a past growth stock is relatively easy since you only need to examine past rates of return relative to risk. The investor, however, must search for future growth stocks. One who uncovers such stocks consistently is, by definition, a successful investor. A recent study that examined stock price performance for a sample of growth companies found an inverse relationship—i.e., the stocks of growth companies did poorly.[1]

The point is, you must examine a company's characteristics and determine whether it is a cyclical, defensive, or growth company. Following this, estimate the value of its stock and the characteristics of the stock. Then you compare this derived, intrinsic value of the stock to its current market value to determine whether you should acquire it. Based upon a comparison of its estimated intrinsic value and its market price, you must ask this question: Will the stock provide a required rate of return consistent with its risk?

Estimating the Value of a Company

The purpose of this section is to compute a value for a particular company and eventually compare that value to the market price of its stock. To do this, we select a firm and examine its sales and earnings performance, as well as its strategies and policies, relative to its industry and the market. This analysis continues our example from Chapter 13 evaluating a company in the retail drugstore industry.

We selected the Walgreen Company, the largest retail drugstore chain in the United States. It operates 1,484 drugstores in 30 states and Puerto Rico. General merchandise accounts for 29 percent of total sales and the pharmacy generates 27 percent.

While we limit our demonstration to Walgreen, your complete company analysis would cover all of the firms in the retail drugstore industry to determine which stocks should perform best. The objective is to estimate the expected returns and risk levels for all the individual firms over the investment horizon. You

estimate a stock's expected returns by estimating its future values. You derive these future values by predicting the stock's earnings per share and expected earnings multiplier.

Step One: Estimating Company Earnings per Share

Expected earnings per share is a function of the sales forecast and the estimated profit margin.

Company Sales Forecast

The sales forecast includes an analysis of the relationship of company sales to various relevant economic series and to the retail drugstore industry series. These comparisons tell us how the company is performing relative to the economy and its closest competition. Besides providing background on the company, these relationships can help us develop specific sales forecasts for Walgreen.

Table 14.1 contains sales data for Walgreen from its annual report, sales per share for the retail drugstore industry, and several personal consumption expenditure (PCE) series for the period between 1970 and 1989.

To examine the relationship of Walgreen sales to the economy we considered several alternative series. The series that had the strongest relationship was personal consumption expenditures for medical care.[2] The scatter plot of Walgreen sales and the medical care expenditures in Figure 14.1 indicates a strong linear relationship, but it also indicates that Walgreen sales have not grown as fast as medical care expenditures. From 1970 to 1989, Walgreen sales increased by about 624 percent compared to an increase in medical care expenditures of 768 percent. As a result, Walgreen sales have gone from about 1.61 percent of these expenditures to 1.19 percent. The graph in Figure 14.2 compares Walgreen sales and sales per share for the retail drugstore industry, revealing rather weak correlation because of the exceptional growth of industry sales.

The figures in the last column of Table 14.1 indicate that during this period, the proportion of per-

[1]Michael Solt and Meir Statman, "Good Companies, Bad Stocks," *Journal of Portfolio Management* 15, no. 4 (Summer 1989): 39–44. Similar results for "excellent" companies were derived in Michelle Clayman, "In Search of Excellence: The Investor's Viewpoint," *Financial Analysts Journal* (May–June 1987): 54–63.

[2]The relationship between Walgreen sales and total or per capita personal consumption expenditures was significant, but not as strong as medical care expenditures.

Table 14.1 *Data for Comparative Analysis of Sales for Walgreen, the Retail Drugstore Industry, and Various Economic Series: 1970–1989*

	Walgreen Sales ($ million)	Retail Drugstore Industry Sales per Share	Personal Consumption Expenditures ($ billion)	Personal Consumption Expenditures per Capita	Personal Consumption Expenditures—Medical Care ($ billion)	Medical Care Expenditures as Percentage of Total
1970	$ 743.6	$ 12.46	$ 640.0	$ 3,121	$ 46.1	7.2%
1971	817.5	16.79	691.6	3,330	51.8	7.5
1972	863.3	18.58	757.6	3,609	57.8	7.6
1973	930.9	22.43	837.2	3,950	64.4	7.7
1974	996.6	27.61	916.5	4,285	72.4	7.8
1975	1,079.1	25.89	1,012.8	4,689	84.2	8.3
1976	1,169.8	36.40	1,129.3	5,178	95.9	8.5
1977	1,223.2	43.99	1,257.2	5,709	111.5	8.9
1978	1,192.9	49.87	1,403.5	6,403	125.1	9.0
1979	1,344.5	73.39	1,566.8	6,960	141.4	9.0
1980	1,530.7	84.82	1,732.6	7,607	164.2	9.5
1981	1,743.5	95.50	1,915.1	8,320	193.5	10.1
1982	2,039.5	109.22	2,050.7	8,318	217.8	10.6
1983	2,360.6	118.85	2,234.5	9,516	238.3	10.7
1984	2,744.6	135.15	2,430.5	10,253	265.3	10.9
1985	3,161.9	153.30	2,629.0	10,987	291.5	11.1
1986	3,660.6	157.74	2,797.4	11,577	318.4	11.4
1987	4,281.6	191.72	3,009.4	12,336	357.3	11.9
1988	4,883.5	217.80	3,238.2	13,147	398.4	12.3
1989	5,380.1	239.68	3,450.1	13,869	434.3	12.6

Source: Walgreen Company annual reports; *Economic Report of the President,* various issues.

sonal consumption expenditures allocated to medical care rose from about 7 percent in 1970 to almost 13 percent in 1989. This increase reflects the growth of the proportion of the population over 65 and the rising cost of medical care. Although Walgreen sales did not grow as fast as this series, its increases should still benefit Walgreen sales. Notably, these increases continued during economic recessions as data for 1981 to 1982 show.

Table 14.2 shows that internal sales growth for Walgreen resulted from an increase in the number of stores (from 554 in 1970 to 1,484 in 1989) and an increase in annual sales per store due to interior upgrading. The net increase in number of stores reflects numerous large, new stores and the closing of many

smaller stores. As a result, the average size of stores and sales per square foot have increased.

Sample Estimate of Walgreen Sales   The foregoing analysis indicates that you should base projections on medical care expenditures. To estimate this series you should initially project total personal consumption expenditures and then determine how much the medical care component would contribute. Economists were forecasting an increase in PCE of 3.0 percent during 1990. A 1989 preliminary figure of $3,470.3 billion implies a 1990 figure of $3,574.4 billion ($3,470.3 × 1.03). The percentage of personal consumption expenditures spent on medical care has increased steadily to almost 13.0 percent in 1989. An

Figure 14.1 *Scatter Plot of Walgreen Sales and Personal Consumption Expenditures on Medical Care: 1970–1989*

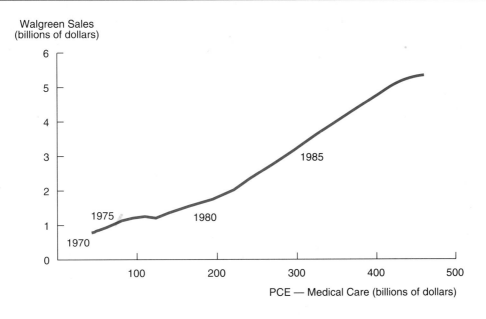

Figure 14.2 *Scatter Plot of Walgreen Sales and Sales for the Retail Drugstore Industry: 1970–1989*

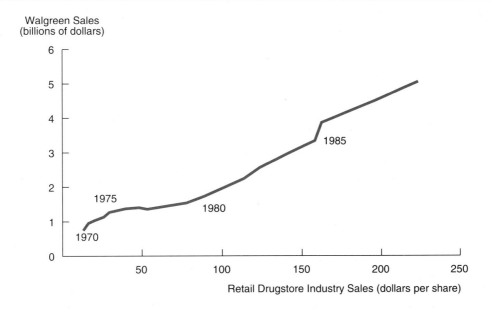

Table 14.2   **Data on Sales, Number of Stores, and Store Area for Walgreen: 1970–1989**

	Sales ($ million)	Number of Stores	Annual Sales per Store ($ million)	Store Area (000 square feet)	Average Area per Store (000 square feet)	Sales per (000 square feet)
1970	$ 743.6	554	$1.34	N.A.	N.A.	N.A.
1971	817.5	561	1.46	N.A.	N.A.	N.A.
1972	863.3	572	1.51	N.A.	N.A.	N.A.
1973	930.9	569	1.64	N.A.	N.A.	N.A.
1974	996.6	616	1.62	N.A.	N.A.	N.A.
1975	1,079.1	633	1.70	6,844	10.81	$157.67
1976	1,169.8	632	1.85	6,961	11.01	168.05
1977	1,223.2	626	1.95	6,917	11.05	176.84
1978	1,192.9	641	1.86	7,187	11.21	165.98
1979	1,344.5	688	1.95	7,801	11.34	172.35
1980	1,530.7	739	2.07	8,407	11.38	182.07
1981	1,743.5	821	2.12	9,610	11.71	181.43
1982	2,039.5	883	2.31	10,420	11.80	195.73
1983	2,360.6	941	2.51	11,203	11.91	210.71
1984	2,744.6	1,002	2.74	12,003	11.98	228.66
1985	3,161.9	1,095	2.89	13,347	12.19	236.90
1986	3,660.6	1,273	2.88	15,860	12.46	230.81
1987	4,281.6	1,356	3.16	17,125	12.63	250.02
1988	4,883.5	1,416	3.45	18,065	12.76	270.33
1989	5,380.1	1,484	3.63	18,896	12.73	284.72

Source: Walgreen Company annual reports.

N.A. = Data not available.

increase in 1990 to 13.5 percent would imply medical care expenditures of $482.5 billion ($3,574.4 × 0.135), a 6.5 percent increase from 1989 ($453.0 billion). The historic relationship in Figure 14.1 between Walgreen sales and medical expenditures implies a 5 percent increase in Walgreen sales to about $5.65 billion ($5.38 billion × 1.05), which is consistent with recent growth.

In this industry firms provide data on square footage and the number of stores. This allows us to compute an alternative estimate using these company data to support the prior estimate based upon economic data. Assuming an increase in store area during 1990 of about 850,000 square feet (following results for 1988 and 1989), the firm's total store area would be about 19.75 million square feet. Since sales per square

foot have likewise experienced a fairly consistent increase, we can assume $300 per square foot. Combining these two estimates implies a sales forecast of about $5,925 million for 1990, a 10 percent increase over 1989 sales of $5,380 million.

Conservatism leads us to prefer the lower of the two estimates, with an upward adjustment to about 7 percent. Therefore our final sales forecast for 1990 is $5,760 million. Next, we want to evaluate the firm's ability to maintain and increase its profit margin.

Estimating Company Profit Margin

The next step in projecting earnings per share, estimating the firm's net profit margin, should consider two goals. (1) The firm's internal performance should

| Table 14.3 | Profit Margins for Walgreen Co. and the Retail Drugstore Industry: 1970–1989 |

	Walgreen			Retail Drugstores		
	Operating Profit Margin	EBT Margin	Net Profit Margin	Operating Profit Margin	EBT Margin	Net Profit Margin
1970	2.57%	2.15%	1.26%	8.83%	7.30%	3.77%
1971	2.62	2.23	1.30	8.46	6.79	3.51
1972	2.63	2.26	1.32	8.93	7.75	4.04
1973	2.97	2.65	1.47	8.87	7.27	3.70
1974	1.58	1.18	0.76	7.57	6.08	3.08
1975	1.78	1.38	0.91	8.65	7.45	3.75
1976	2.97	2.51	1.46	9.18	8.19	4.09
1977	3.11	2.66	1.46	8.96	7.91	4.07
1978	3.86	3.73	2.16	8.78	7.74	4.03
1979	3.86	3.79	2.25	7.24	6.40	3.47
1980	3.56	3.52	2.27	7.07	6.27	3.47
1981	3.40	3.54	2.42	7.17	6.18	3.45
1982	4.32	4.20	2.75	7.30	6.22	3.44
1983	5.16	5.11	2.96	7.98	6.88	3.79
1984	5.57	5.46	3.11	7.19	5.53	3.03
1985	5.63	5.49	2.98	7.00	5.06	2.75
1986	5.37	5.13	2.82	7.37	5.67	3.11
1987	4.92	4.54	2.42	7.08	5.14	2.88
1988	4.59	4.28	2.64	6.70	4.71	2.89
1989	4.71	4.53	2.87	6.71	4.49	2.79
Averages						
1970–1989	3.76	3.52	2.08	7.85	6.45	3.46
1970–1979	2.79	2.45	1.44	8.55	7.29	3.75
1980–1989	4.72	4.58	2.72	7.16	5.61	3.16

Sources: Walgreen Company annual reports; *Analysts Handbook* (New York: Standard & Poor's Corp., 1990).

indicate general company trends and point out any problem areas that might affect future performance. (2) The firm's relationship with its industry should tell us whether its past performance (either good or bad) is attributable to the industry or unique to the firm. These examinations should help us understand the firm's past performance, and also provide the background to make a meaningful estimate for the future. We do not consider the company–economy relationship because significant economywide profit factors are reflected in the industry data.

Profit margin figures for Walgreen and the retail drugstore industry appear in Table 14.3. Walgreen's profit margins increased from 1970 to the mid-1980s, followed by a decline through 1987 and another increase in 1989. In contrast, the margins for the retail drugstore industry followed a relatively flat pattern during the 1970s. We can see that Walgreen's operating profit margin and net margin followed a positive trend over the past 20 years that has brought its net profit margin almost equal to the industry. In order to predict future values, you need to determine the rea-

Figure 14.3   Time-Series Plot of Net Profit Margin for Walgreen and the Retail Drugstore Industry: 1970–1989

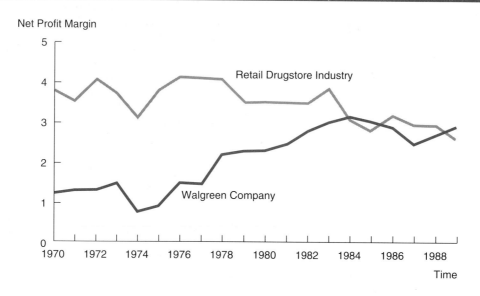

son for the overall decline in the industry profit margin and, more important, what factors have caused Walgreen's strong positive performance.

Industry Factors   Price discounting by aggressive regional drug chains squeezed industry profit margins over the past two decades.[3] The discussion in Chapter 13 suggested this as one of the competitive structure conditions that can affect long-run profitability. Industry analysts have observed, however, that price cutting has subsided and they currently foresee relative price stability. The more profitable product mix in drugstores featuring high-margin items such as cosmetics has positively influenced profit margins.

Company Performance   Walgreen's profit margin has consistently improved due to a change in corporate structure. The outlook for profit margins is good because the firm has developed a strong position in the pharmacy market and has invested in the technology to provide strong margins on this business.

Specific estimates for Walgreen's future margins would typically begin with an analysis of their relationship with drugstore industry margins using time series plots like those in Figure 14.3.[4] They show improved results for Walgreen versus its industry for the period from 1970 to 1989, narrowing the gap between them. You should also consider any unique factors that would influence this long-run relationship, such as any price wars reported in business publications or abnormal numbers of store openings or closings as reported by the firm in quarterly or annual earnings reports.

Following a consideration of the long-run company–industry profit margin relationship, you should analyze the firm's common size income statement for several years. As discussed in Chapter 7, the breakdown of the income statement depends upon the consistent detail provided by the firm.

Table 14.4 shows a common size statement for Walgreen during the period 1986 to 1989. Analysis of the main items of interest, cost of goods sold and operating expenses, is both encouraging and discourag-

---

[3]For a more complete discussion, see "Retailing—Drug Stores," *Standard & Poor's Industry Surveys* (New York: Standard & Poor's Corp., 1990).

[4]Both operating margin and net margin before taxes were analyzed, but the results indicated that the net profit margins yielded the best relationships.

| Table 14.4 | Walgreen Company Common Size Income Statement |

	1989		1988		1987		1986	
	$ million	Percent	$ million	Percent	$ million	Percent	$ million	Percent
Net sales	$5,380.1	100.0%	$4,883.5	100.0%	$4,281.6	100.0%	$3,660.6	100.0%
Cost of sales	3,848.5	71.5	3,469.0	71.0	3,001.0	70.1	2,550.1	69.7
Gross profit	$1,531.6	28.5%	$1,414.5	29.0%	$1,280.6	29.9%	$1,110.5	30.3%
Selling, general, and administrative expense	1,278.1	23.8	1,190.3	24.4	1,069.9	25.0	914.0	25.0
Operating profit	$ 253.5	4.7%	$ 224.2	4.6%	$ 210.7	4.9%	$ 196.5	5.4%
Interest expense	18.8	0.3	19.8	0.4	17.7	0.4	10.8	0.3
Interest income	15.3	0.3	4.5	0.1	1.1	0.0	2.0	0.1
Extraordinary loss	6.1	0.1	0.0	0.0	0.0	0.0	0.0	0.0
Net before taxes	$ 243.9	4.5%	$ 208.9	4.3%	$ 194.1	4.5%	$ 187.7	5.1%
Tax excluding investment credit	89.6	1.7	79.9	1.6	88.4	2.1	90.2	2.5
Investment tax credit	—	0.0	—	0.0	(2.3)	−0.1	5.8	0.2
Net earnings	$ 154.3	2.9%	$ 129.0	2.6%	$ 103.4	2.4%	$ 103.3	2.8%
Tax rate before tax credit		36.7%		38.2%		45.5%		48.1%
Common shares outstanding (000)	61,517		61,514		61,504		61,495	
Net earnings per share	$2.51		$2.10		$1.68		$1.68	

ing. The cost-of-sales percentage's steady increase over time is discouraging. In contrast, the steady decline in selling, general, and administrative expenses is encouraging. Recently flat interest expenses declined in dollar and percentage terms during 1989, while interest income increased substantially in 1989. Finally, the tax rate declined from 48 percent in 1986 to less than 37 percent in 1989.

Estimating Net Profit Margin   Stable prices, increasing mechanization, and the inclusion of high-margin items make for an encouraging overall industry outlook. Therefore, the industry profit margin is expected to stabilize or increase during 1990. Because Walgreen's margin maintains a strong relationship to the industry profit margin and because its margin increased during 1989 as shown in the common size income statement, we estimate that the firm's margin will increase during 1990. Therefore, we estimate Walgreen's net profit margin in 1990 at 3 percent.

Computing EPS   This margin estimate, combined with the prior sales estimate of $5,760 million, indicates net income of $172.8 million. Assuming about 61.25 million common shares outstanding, earnings should be about $2.82 per share for 1990, an increase of about 12 percent over the earnings of $2.51 per share in 1989. To find the value of Walgreen Co., our next step is to estimate its earnings multiplier.

Step Two: Estimating Company Earnings Multipliers

As in our prior analysis of industry multipliers in Chapter 13, to estimate a company multiplier we use two approaches. First, we estimate the P/E ratio from the relationships we observe between Walgreen and its industry and the market through macroanalysis. After that, we compute a multiplier based upon microanalysis of its three components: the dividend payout ratio, the required rate of return, and the rate of

| Table 14.5 | Average Earnings Multipliers for Walgreen, the Retail Drugstore Industry, and the S&P 400: 1970–1989 |

	Walgreen			Retail Drugstore				S&P 400	
	EPS	Mean Price[a]	Mean P/E	EPS	Mean Price[a]	Mean P/E	Company/ Industry Ratio	Mean P/E	Company/ Market Ratio
1970	1.48	21.500	14.53	0.47	10.28	21.87	0.66	16.49	0.88
1971	1.59	27.500	17.30	0.59	18.16	30.78	0.56	18.02	0.96
1972	1.65	27.750	13.79	0.75	28.94	38.59	0.36	17.95	0.77
1973	1.95	17.625	9.04	0.83	26.00	31.33	0.29	13.38	0.68
1974	1.11	13.188	11.88	0.85	11.98	14.09	0.84	9.43	1.26
1975	1.40	11.938	8.53	0.97	13.92	14.35	0.59	10.79	0.79
1976	2.05	15.000	7.32	1.49	19.86	13.33	0.55	10.41	0.70
1977	2.15	16.500	7.67	1.79	18.93	10.58	0.73	9.55	0.80
1978	3.53	23.250	6.59	2.01	22.20	11.05	0.60	8.21	0.80
1979	4.14	29.500	7.13	2.55	22.38	8.78	0.81	7.11	1.00
1980	4.70	33.813	7.19	2.94	24.57	8.36	0.86	8.44	0.85
1981	5.53	46.563	8.42	3.29	34.62	10.52	0.80	8.45	1.00
1982	3.66	40.313	11.01	3.76	41.58	11.06	1.00	10.37	1.06
1983	2.27	33.188	14.62	4.50	56.70	12.60	1.16	11.84	1.23
1984	2.78	36.938	13.29	4.10	58.30	14.22	0.93	9.92	1.34
1985	1.53	25.875	16.91	4.22	68.28	16.18	1.05	13.68	1.23
1986	1.67	31.875	19.09	4.90	83.78	17.10	1.12	17.47	1.09
1987	1.68	34.813	20.72	5.53	98.93	17.89	1.16	16.00	1.30
1988	2.10	32.250	15.36	6.30	93.05	14.77	1.04	11.38	1.35
1989	2.50	40.125	16.05	6.69	107.46	16.06	1.00	13.79	1.16
Means									
1970–1989	N.M.	N.M.	12.32	N.M.	N.M.	16.68	0.81	12.13	1.01
1970–1979	N.M.	N.M.	10.38	N.M.	N.M.	19.48	0.60	12.13	0.86
1980–1989	N.M.	N.M.	14.27	N.M.	N.M.	13.88	1.01	12.13	1.16

[a]The mean price is the average of the high and low prices for the year.

N.M. = Not meaningful.

Source: Walgreen Company annual reports; *Analysts Handbook* (New York: Standard & Poor's Corp., 1990).

growth. We then resolve the estimates derived from each approach to settle on one estimate.

Macroanalysis of the Earnings Multiplier

Table 14.5 shows the mean earnings multipliers for the company, the retail drugstore industry, and the aggregate market for the period from 1970 to 1989.

Walgreen's relationship to its industry has changed dramatically over time. During the 1970s and early 1980s, Walgreen's multiple was consistently below the industry's. After 1983 the Walgreen multiplier has typically exceeded the industry multiplier by 5 to 10 percent although it was almost equal in 1989. Similarly, the Walgreen earnings multiplier fell below the market multiplier until 1982. Since then it has been larger by 10 to 30 percent.

Table 14.6 **Influences on the Earnings Multipliers for Walgreen, Retail Drugstores, and the S&P 400: 1977–1989**

	Walgreen						Retail Drugstores						S&P 400					
	D/E	TAT	TAE	E/T	NPM	ROE	D/E	TAT	TAE	E/T	NPM	ROE	D/E	TAT	TAE	E/T	NPM	ROE
1977	45.80	3.81	2.39	9.08	1.27	11.56	20.11	2.84	1.53	4.35	4.07	17.69	43.23	1.27	2.08	2.64	5.11	13.48
1978	30.31	3.45	2.34	8.16	2.16	17.65	23.88	2.81	1.52	4.27	4.03	17.19	41.18	1.27	2.15	2.72	5.19	14.11
1979	30.33	3.53	2.30	8.18	2.25	18.43	27.45	3.00	1.68	5.02	3.47	17.43	36.34	1.30	2.20	2.85	5.57	15.89
1980	30.47	3.60	2.16	8.00	2.27	18.20	29.25	3.04	1.66	5.06	3.47	17.56	40.26	1.31	2.23	2.93	4.92	14.42
1981	30.42	3.60	2.08	7.62	2.42	18.40	31.00	3.03	1.65	4.99	3.45	17.22	41.88	1.28	2.25	2.87	4.86	13.96
1982	26.93	3.59	2.06	7.42	2.75	20.40	31.12	2.97	1.66	4.93	3.44	16.96	54.02	1.17	2.31	2.70	3.95	10.69
1983	26.33	3.54	2.04	7.25	2.96	21.44	29.33	2.85	1.68	4.81	3.79	18.20	49.56	1.15	2.28	2.63	4.42	11.64
1984	25.84	3.52	2.03	7.16	3.11	22.30	37.56	2.66	1.88	5.00	3.03	15.15	41.47	1.22	2.39	2.91	4.77	13.86
1985	28.68	3.39	2.16	7.08	2.98	21.10	40.76	2.70	2.04	5.50	2.75	15.13	51.51	1.15	2.54	2.92	3.84	11.21
1986	29.81	3.39	2.16	7.08	2.82	19.97	32.86	2.71	2.00	5.44	3.11	16.90	56.94	1.07	2.58	2.76	3.75	10.32
1987	32.08	3.35	2.19	7.28	2.42	17.61	31.65	2.80	2.04	5.72	2.88	16.50	43.00	1.08	2.62	2.83	4.71	13.35
1988	28.59	3.40	2.12	7.32	2.64	19.34	30.63	2.82	2.07	5.83	2.89	16.89	38.54	0.98	3.03	2.96	5.46	16.19
1989	27.12	3.37	2.04	7.01	2.87	20.08	32.29	2.82	2.03	5.72	2.79	15.98	42.70	0.96	3.18	3.04	4.91	14.92
Means	31.26	3.54	2.16	7.70	2.44	18.43	30.61	2.85	1.80	5.13	2.25	16.83	44.75	1.17	2.45	2.83	4.73	13.39

D/E = Dividend payout, equal to dividends/earnings.
TAT = Total asset turnover, equal to sales/total assets.
TAE = Leverage ratio, equal to total assets/equity.
E/T (Equity turnover) = Equity turnover ratio, equal to sales/equity.
NPM = Net profit margin, equal to net income/sales.
ROE = Return on equity, equal to net income/equity.

This pattern raises a question. Is Walgreen's recent P/E premium relative to both the industry and market justified by its expected performance? Microanalysis should provide some insights into these questions.

Microanalysis of the Earnings Multiplier

The historical data for the relevant series are listed in Table 14.6. We need to answer two questions. (1) Why has Walgreen's earnings multiplier tended to be above the market's since the early 1980s? (2) Should this relationship persist? As before, we need estimates of D/E, k, and g to find an earnings multiplier. To do this, we will look at the data in Table 14.6 to identify patterns and develop projections for these relationships.

Comparing Dividend Payout Ratios Walgreen has maintained a lower dividend payout ratio than its industry. The Walgreen–market comparison also shows a generally lower payout. These results by themselves would produce a P/E ratio for Walgreen that is below the industry and the market ratios.

Estimating the Required Rate of Return To find Walgreen's required rate of return (k), we should analyze the firm's internal risk characteristics (BR, FR, LR, ERR, and CR). Walgreen should have relatively low business risk due to expected stable sales growth compared to its industry and the aggregate economy. Unfortunately, analysis of several measures of sales volatility did not support this expectation. The firm's standard deviation of sales was substantially above comparable figures for the industry and the S&P 400. The coefficient of variation of sales adjusts for size, however, and it shows that Walgreen sales were less volatile than those of its industry, but more volatile than those in the market. Since Walgreen's sales were more volatile than expected, we would expect business risk equal to or greater than that in the stock market as a whole.

Several financial risk variables for Walgreen, its industry, and the aggregate market appear in Table 14.7. The firm's financial leverage ratio (total assets/equity) at about 2.00 is comparable to the industry and lower than the aggregate market. Walgreen has an interest coverage ratio of almost 14, a cash flow/long-term debt ratio of over 100 percent, and a cash flow/total debt ratio of about 25 percent. All of these financial risk ratios indicate lower financial risk than its industry or the aggregate stock market.

The firm's external market liquidity risk is quite low compared to its industry and the average firm in the market by several indicators of market liquidity:

(1) the number of stockholders, (2) the number of shares outstanding, (3) the number of shares traded, and (4) institutional interest in the stock. As of January 1, 1990, Walgreen had about 61,500 holders of common stock, a relatively large number. At the end of 1989, about 62 million of its common shares were outstanding with a market value of almost $2.8 billion. Clearly, Walgreen would attract institutions that require firms with large market values. Walgreen stock has a monthly trading volume of almost 1.24 million shares and annual trading turnover of 24 percent. Financial institutions own about 28 million shares of Walgreen stock, or about 45 percent of the outstanding shares. Walgreen's many stockholders, active trading on its stock, and institutional attractiveness indicate very little liquidity risk.

As discussed in Chapter 13, a company's exchange rate risk depends upon what proportion of its sales and earnings it generates outside the United States and the

---

Table 14.7   *Financial Risk Ratios for Walgreen, the Retail Drugstore Industry, and the S&P 400: 1977–1989*

	Walgreen				Retail Drugstores				S&P 400			
	Total Assets/ Equity	Interest Coverage	Cash Flow/ Long-term Debt[a]	Cash Flow/ Total Debt[b]	Total Assets/ Equity	Interest Coverage	Cash Flow/ Long-term Debt[a]	Cash Flow/ Total Debt[b]	Total Assets/ Equity	Interest Coverage	Cash Flow/ Long-term Debt[a]	Cash Flow/ Total Debt[b]
1977	2.39	6.91	0.36	0.13	1.53	28.9	1.76	0.41	2.08	8.0	0.63	0.22
1978	2.34	7.93	—	0.18	1.52	30.9	1.94	0.42	2.15	7.6	0.63	0.22
1979	2.30	8.83	0.50	0.19	1.68	21.2	1.21	0.34	2.20	7.7	0.70	0.22
1980	2.16	9.01	0.60	0.20	1.66	20.1	1.33	0.35	2.23	6.0	0.66	0.21
1981	2.08	10.44	0.91	0.22	1.65	16.2	1.74	0.36	2.25	5.0	0.63	0.21
1982	2.06	13.38	1.40	0.24	1.66	17.4	2.43	0.36	2.31	4.0	0.54	0.18
1983	2.04	19.61	1.76	0.26	1.68	20.2	3.24	0.35	2.28	4.6	0.61	0.19
1984	2.03	25.23	2.14	0.27	1.88	10.6	1.43	0.24	2.33	4.8	0.65	0.19
1985	2.00	28.65	1.79	0.27	2.04	7.8	0.75	0.22	2.48	4.2	0.57	0.16
1986	2.16	17.11	0.90	0.23	2.00	12.7	0.99	0.24	2.53	3.6	0.51	0.15
1987	2.19	11.76	0.94	0.21	2.04	9.4	0.93	0.23	2.57	4.4	0.58	0.17
1988	2.12	11.46	0.99	0.24	2.07	8.2	1.00	0.24	2.98	3.8	0.44	0.15
1989	2.04	13.94	1.21	0.25	2.03	7.5	0.61	0.23	3.09	3.3	0.42	0.14

[a]Long-term debt does not include deferred taxes.

[b]Total debt equals total assets minus total equity including preferred stock.

volatility of the exchange rates in specific countries. Walgreen has very little exchange rate risk or country risk because the firm has virtually no non-U.S. sales.

In summary, Walgreen has above-average business risk, below-average financial risk, low liquidity risk, and very low exchange rate and country risk. This implies overall risk for Walgreen below that of the market, so its risk premium and required rate of return (k) should be lower than the market's. This estimate of k would suggest an earnings multiplier equal to or slightly above the market multiplier.

Expected Growth Rate   Recall that the expected growth rate (g) is determined by the retention rate (b) and the return on equity (ROE). We have already noted Walgreen's low dividend payout compared to the industry or the aggregate market. This implies a higher retention rate.

The firm's ROE is determined by its total asset turnover (TAT), financial leverage (TAE), and net profit margin (NPM). Table 14.6 showed that Walgreen's TAT has consistently exceeded those of its industry and the market. As discussed, Walgreen's financial leverage ratio (TAE) has been slightly above the industry, but definitely lower than the market. As a result, Walgreen's equity turnover (E/T) was above the industry's and substantially above the market's. Walgreen's net profit margin (NPM) has always exceeded its industry's margin, but always fallen short of the S&P 400's margin. Combining the values for total asset turnover (TAT), leverage (TAE), and net profit margin (NPM) gives an ROE for Walgreen of about 19 percent, compared to an industry estimate of about 17 percent and a stock market figure of about 14 percent.

The ROEs and retention rates in Table 14.8 imply the following growth rates:

	Retention Rate	ROE	Expected Growth Rate
Walgreen	0.70	0.1843	0.129
Retail drugstores	0.60	0.1683	0.101
S&P 400	0.56	0.1339	0.075

Table 14.8   *Expected Growth Rate Components for Walgreen, the Retail Drugstore Industry, and the S&P 400: 1977–1989*

	Walgreen			Retail Drugstores			S&P 400		
	Retention Rate	ROE	Expected Growth Rate	Retention Rate	ROE	Expected Growth Rate	Retention Rate	ROE	Expected Growth Rate
1977	0.54	11.56%	6.27%	0.80	17.69%	14.15%	0.57	13.48%	7.68%
1978	0.70	17.65	12.30	0.76	17.19	13.06	0.59	14.11	8.32
1979	0.70	18.43	12.84	0.73	17.43	12.72	0.64	15.89	10.17
1980	0.70	18.20	12.65	0.71	17.56	12.47	0.60	14.42	8.65
1981	0.70	18.40	12.88	0.69	17.22	11.88	0.58	13.96	8.10
1982	0.73	20.40	14.91	0.69	16.96	11.70	0.46	10.69	4.91
1983	0.74	21.44	15.80	0.71	18.20	12.92	0.50	11.64	5.82
1984	0.74	22.30	16.54	0.62	15.15	9.39	0.59	13.86	8.18
1985	0.71	21.10	15.00	0.59	15.13	8.93	0.48	11.21	5.38
1986	0.70	19.97	13.99	0.67	16.90	11.32	0.44	10.32	4.54
1987	0.68	17.61	11.96	0.68	16.50	11.22	0.57	13.35	7.60
1988	0.71	19.34	13.81	0.69	16.89	11.65	0.63	16.19	10.20
1989	0.73	20.08	14.64	0.68	15.98	10.87	0.57	14.92	8.50
Means	0.70	18.43	13.35	0.69	16.83	11.71	0.56	13.39	7.54

These high growth rates would boost Walgreen's multiplier.

Computing the Earnings Multiplier Entering our estimates of D/E, k, and g into the equation for the P/E ratio, we find that microanalysis should give a higher earnings multiplier for Walgreen than those of its industry and the market. The payout ratio points toward a lower multiplier while the risk analysis and the expected growth rate likewise support a multiplier above those of its industry and the market. The growth rate would be the strongest factor.

The macroanalysis suggested that Walgreen's multiplier should be above those of the industry and market. Microanalysis confirms that Walgreen's multiplier should be slightly larger than the market's. Assuming a market multiplier of 12 to 13 and a retail drugstore multiplier of about 13, Walgreen's multiplier should fall between 13 and 14, with a tendency toward the upper end of the range. If we inserted specific values for D/E, k, and g into the P/E ratio formula, however, we would get a multiplier of about 15. Specifically, we would assume a payout ratio of 0.30 based upon the retention rate of 0.70, a k of about 15 percent at current market rates, and an expected growth rate (g) of 13 percent, as shown:

$$P/E = \frac{0.30}{0.15 - 0.13}$$
$$= \frac{0.30}{0.02} = 15\times$$

Estimating Walgreen's Future Value Earlier, we estimated earnings per share for Walgreen of about $2.82 per share. Using the three possible multipliers, we would get the following value estimates:

$$13 \times \$2.82 = \$36.67$$
$$14 \times \$2.82 = \$39.50$$
$$15 \times \$2.82 = \$42.30$$

Making the Investment Decision

In our prior discussions of valuation we set forth the investment decision in two forms:

1. Compute the estimated value for an investment using your required rate of return as the discount rate. If this estimated value is equal to or greater than the current market price of the investment, buy it.
2. Compute the estimated future value for an investment using your required rate of return as one of the components. Given this future value, compute your expected rate of return on the asset at the current market price held for the investment horizon (typically assumed to be a year). If this expected return equals or exceeds your required rate of return, buy the investment; if the expected return falls short of your required rate of return, do not buy it.

We can demonstrate how we would apply these two forms of the investment decision to Walgreen's. We estimated three future values for Walgreen assuming a k of 15 percent: $36.67, $39.50, and $42.30. For the demonstration we will use $40 a share as the future value and an estimated dividend over the next year of $0.85, which assumes a 30 percent payout of the earnings of $2.82.

Comparing Estimated Value to Current Market Price This requires that you remember that the estimated value we have computed is a future value (usually after 1 year). To compare it to a current market price we must discount it by our required rate of return of 15 percent, which gives a current estimated value of:

$$\$40 \times 0.8696 = \$34.78$$

We would compare the current market price of Walgreen stock to this estimated value. As an example, if Walgreen stock were currently priced at $30 a share, you would buy it; if it were currently priced at $40 a share, you would not buy it.

Comparing Expected Rate of Return to Required Rate of Return In past demonstrations of this form of the decision rule, we have computed an expected rate of return using the expected value and dividend. While we will again use this technique, we will also introduce another technique for computing an expected rate of return based upon the dividend growth model.

We can compute the expected rate of return, $E(R_i)$, based upon our expected future value using the formula:

$$E(R_i) = \frac{EV - BV + Div.}{BV}$$

where:

EV = estimated ending value of the stock

BV = beginning value of the stock
(typically current market price)

Div. = expected dividend per share during the
holding period

In our case, EV = \$40.00, BV is unknown, and Div. = \$0.85. For demonstration purposes assume a current market price of \$35 a share.

$$E(R) = \frac{\$40.00 - \$35.00 + \$0.85}{\$35.00}$$

$$= \frac{\$\ 5.85}{\$35.00}$$

$$= 0.167 = 16.7 \text{ percent}$$

Based on the k of 15 percent used in the valuation section, we would buy this stock since its expected rate of return is larger than our required rate of return.

The second technique used to derive an expected rate of return is based upon the dividend growth model. You will recall that the dividend growth model states:

$$P_0 = \frac{D_1}{k - g}$$

Solving to estimate k:

$$K_i = \frac{D_1}{P_0} + g$$

In this equation, k can serve as an estimate of the required rate of return when you assume that you know the firm's future growth rate. Alternatively, k can be used to *estimate* the expected rate of return if you are estimating the future dividend and growth rate. In the case of Walgreen, P_0 would be the current price of the stock, D_1 would be the expected dividend during the investment horizon, and g would be the expected growth rate, as discussed in connection with Table 14.8.

Assume a current price of \$35, an expected dividend of \$0.85 per share, and a growth rate of 13.3 percent. This would imply the following estimate of expected rate of return on Walgreen common stock:

$$k = \frac{0.85}{35.00} + 0.133$$

$$= 0.024 + 0.133$$

$$= 0.157 = 15.7 \text{ percent}$$

This computation shows that you would expect a rate of return from investing in Walgreen stock of 15.7 percent. If your required rate of return were 15 percent, you would buy this stock.

Price/book value ratio The relationship between a firm's stock price and the total book value of its assets, which can indicate its attractiveness as an investment.

Breakup value The estimated value of a firm's divisions if sold to other firms.

Additional Measures of Relative Value

The best-known measure of relative value for common stock is the price–earnings ratio, or the earnings multiplier, because it is derived from the dividend growth model and has stood the test of time as an accurate measure. While not rejecting the P/E ratio, analysts have begun to calculate two additional values they consider reasonable measures of relative value for common stocks—the price/book value ratio and the price/cash flow ratio.

Price/Book Value (P/BV) Ratio

The relationship between the market price of a stock and its book value per share can serve as a relative measure of valuation because, under theoretically ideal conditions, the market value of a firm should reflect its book value. **Price/book value ratio** has been used extensively in valuation of bank stocks since banks' assets often have similar book values and market values. Specifically, bank assets include investments in government bonds, high-grade corporate bonds, or municipal bonds, along with commercial, mortgage, and personal loans that ordinarily are collectible. Under such ideal conditions, the price/book value (P/BV) ratio should be close to 1. Still, even in the banking industry the range of this ratio has increased. You can envision a P/BV ratio of less than 1 for a bank with a lot of problem loans. In the last few years this might include loans to firms in the oil industry, real estate loans in certain areas of the country, and loans to third-world countries. In contrast, you can envision a P/BV ratio above 1 for a bank with significant growth potential due to its location or merger possibilities. As a result, the P/BV ratios for different individual banks have ranged from 0.25 to 2.0.

It is easy to see why the P/BV ratio of an industrial firm might exceed 1.0. The book values of assets will almost always be lower than either their current replacement values or the firm's breakup value. (**Breakup value** is the estimated market value of indi-

Figure 14.4 *Price/Book Value (P/BV) Ratios for the S&P 400, the Retail Drugstore Industry, and Walgreen*

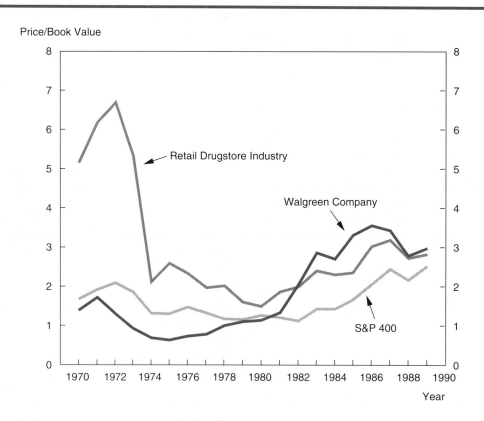

vidual divisions of a firm when sold to others.) Increasing estimates of breakup value have caused the average P/BV ratio for industrial firms to experience a volatile increase over time.

To demonstrate this relationship, Figure 14.4 shows a time-series plot of the historical P/BV ratios for the S&P 400, the retail drugstore industry, and Walgreen. Annual values are represented by mean annual prices/year-end book values. The P/BV ratio for the S&P 400 was about 2.0 in the early 1970s; it declined to about 1.3 during 1974 through 1982, after which it increased to almost 3.0 prior to the October 1987 crash, then declined to about 2.25 during 1988 to 1989 prior to an increase in 1990.

In contrast, the retail drugstore industry had a very high P/BV ratio during 1970 to 1973, followed by a sharp decline in 1974. The industry ratio has

followed the S&P 400 ratio with a premium of about 30 percent in recent years. A higher P/BV ratio for the retail drugstore industry appears reasonable in light of the higher growth rate for the industry's book value. Book value has grown about 5 percent a year for the S&P 400 versus 17.7 percent a year for the retail drugstore industry.

Walgreen's P/BV ratio increased more than both the market and its industry. Walgreen's ratio increased from less than 1.0 in the 1970s to over 3.0 in the late 1980s. As a result, the ratio of Walgreen's P/BV ratio to the market P/BV ratio went from a low of 0.5 to a peak of 2.0 in 1983 and 1985. The ratio of Walgreen's P/BV ratio to its industry's ratio has gone from about 0.2 to a high of 1.4, to about 1.0 in recent years. One can explain the higher P/BV ratio relative to the market based upon Walgreen's higher growth rate of book value. Walgreen's premium relative to its industry is likewise a function of its higher ROE and expected growth rate.

To form this into an investment decision rule, some have suggested that stocks with low P/BV ratios should outperform high P/BV stocks just as stocks with low P/E ratios outperform stocks with high P/E ratios. A study by Rosenberg, Reid, and Lanstein examined this strategy and found that stocks with high book value/price ratios (i.e., low P/BV ratios) experienced significantly higher rates of return than the average stock.[5] Findings like these have made the P/BV ratio an important measure of relative value. Analysts will discuss a stock's P/BV ratio over time and also relative to the market and industry ratios as we have done and consider this as part of the investment decision. This ratio has also been included as a component in other valuation models.

Price/Cash Flow (P/CF) Ratio

Another measure of relative value, the **price/cash flow ratio,** is being used to supplement the P/E ratio because cash flow is typically subject to less accounting manipulation than reported earnings. Also, cash flow has become a more important measure of performance, value, and financial strength because numerous academic studies have shown that cash flow can predict both success and future problems. Also, cash flow data have become more accessible because firms must now publish statements of cash flow along with their income statements and balance sheets.

It is important to develop benchmark values for these relative measures of value. Therefore, you should understand the comparable values over time for the market as represented by the S&P 400 and the relevant industry. For demonstration purposes, availability of data leads us to define cash flow per share as net income per share plus depreciation expense per share. This traditional measure of cash flow is intended to reflect earnings plus noncash expenses; depreciation is the largest such expense that can be identified.

Historical P/CF ratios are plotted in Figure 14.5. These particular ratios are only available beginning in

> **Price/cash flow ratio** The relationship between a firm's stock price and its cash flows. The analysis of this ratio supplements the analysis of price–earnings ratios because cash flows are less easily manipulated by accounting techniques to hide deficiencies than are earnings measures.

1977 because the depreciation expense figures for the S&P 400 and individual S&P industries were not reported prior to this time. Again, both the retail drugstore industry and the Walgreen P/CF ratios are consistently higher than the market ratio. As before, this difference is justified by the higher growth rate of cash flow for the industry versus the market (14.4 versus 6.8 percent) and for the company versus the market (18.3 versus 6.8 percent).

As discussed, both of these ratios (P/BV and P/CF) are considered to be good supplements to the P/E ratio and the fundamental valuation work. Neither gives us the theoretical base that we have with the P/E ratio, but they can provide additional insights into relative valuation changes for a stock. In both instances you would want to examine company ratios over time relative to the same ratio for the market and for the firm's industry. The idea is to look for relationships that are not justified by the fundamentals or for changes in normal relationships that are not supported by changes in the fundamentals. As an example of the first case, assume that a firm's P/BV ratio was 0.8 compared to a market ratio of 2.0 and an industry ratio of 1.9. You would analyze the firm to see if these differences were justified. A difference that was not justified might indicate an underpriced stock. As an example of the second case, if a ratio that had consistently matched the market ratio increased during a period of time by 50 percent relative to the market with no change in fundamentals, you would consider this a possible indicator of overvaluation. Obviously, these are only bits of evidence in a full-scale analysis. Still, they can be additional indicators of relative valuation.

Global Company Analysis

One of our goals in this book is to demonstrate investment techniques for foreign securities, and we have shown on several occasions that these techniques

---

[5]Barr Rosenberg, Kenneth Reid, and Ronald Lanstein, "Persuasive Evidence of Market Inefficiency," *Journal of Portfolio Management* 11, no. 3 (Spring 1985): 9–17.

Time-Series Plot of Price/Cash Flow (P/CF) Ratios for S&P 400, the Retail Drugstore Industry, and Walgreen

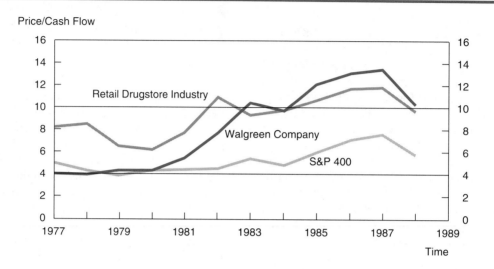

Price/Cash Flow

Earnings per Share Analysis

Table 14.9 gives earnings per share values for the major firms for 1989 and estimates for 1990. These data indicate that the outlook for most of these firms is for little or no growth. The exceptions are Ciba, Solvay, L'Air Liquide, BOC, and Rhone–Poulenc, for which estimates indicate strong gains. The dividend data indicate a tendency toward low payouts (about 35 percent), but a range from 20 percent to over 40 percent.

Profitability and Financial Strength

Table 14.10 contains information on profitability as measured by return on equity (ROE) for the individual

can be applied to foreign markets and industries. The only problem is getting the data required for the analysis.

In this section we will continue the analysis of the European chemical industry we started in Chapter 13 to see how to select individual companies and specific stocks for your investment portfolio. As before, we will work with tables assembled by Goldman, Sachs in its global report. The tables contain data on several companies, though the availability of the data differs among companies.

firms. As stated in the notes to the table, the analysis should concentrate on individual firm performance over time, since the data are not adjusted for accounting differences between firms and countries. The results reflect an increase for almost all the firms, with significant increases by ICI, Hoechst, and AKZO.

You should also examine the financial risk levels of the firms based upon their debt/equity ratios. Again, it is best to limit the analysis to specific firms over time. The discussion by the analyst who prepared the report makes it clear that the changes in these ratios over time reflect operating performance and financial strategy decisions as well as the effects of acquisitions by some firms.

Common Stock Statistics

Table 14.11 lists measures of stock performance and relative value for the firms in the industry. The absolute P/E ratios show the differences in the earnings multipliers among countries. Notably, most are 10 times or lower. There is a very interesting analysis of the P/E ratios for individual stocks relative to the average P/E ratio in the local market. As an example, Bayer's P/E ratio of 8.4 is only 71 percent of the average of all stocks in Germany. In contrast, L'Air

| Table 14.9 | **Earnings and Dividends per Share for Major European Chemical Firms** |

Company	Currency	Earnings per Share		Dividends per Share (1989)	Dividend Payout (1989)
		1989	1990(e)		
ICI	BP	131.0	123.7	56.0	0.427
BASF	DM	39.0	38.5	14.0	0.359
Bayer	DM	36.5	37.0	13.0	0.356
Hoechst	DM	39.0	36.5	13.0	0.333
Ciba	SFr	289.0	324.0	65.0	0.225
AKZO	DFL	20.8[a]	21.9[a]	8.0	0.385
DSM	DFL	29.2[a]	23.8[a]	8.0	0.274
Solvay	BFr	2,278.0[a]	2,330.0[a]	450.0	0.198
L'Air Liquide	FFr	40.0	45.0	14.5	0.363
BOC	BP	53.2	58.4	19.0	0.357
AGA B	SKr	19.9	22.6	7.0	0.352
Rhone–Poulenc–PICs	FFr	70.0	77.0	23.0	0.329

[a]Before extraordinary items.

e = Estimate.

Source: Charles K. Brown and Peter Clark, "European Chemical Majors—Outlook for 1990" (London: Goldman, Sachs International Ltd., January 1990).

| Table 14.10 | **Profitability and Financial Strength for Major European Chemical Firms: 1985–1988** |

	Net Income/Avg. Shareholders' Equity (%)				Net Debt/Shareholders' Equity (%)[a]			
	1985	1986	1987	1988	1985	1986	1987	1988
ICI	15	17	19	24	26[1]	35[2]	39[3]	38
BASF	10	8	9	12	10[4]	− 12	− 16	− 25
Bayer	14	12	12	13	44	2	− 13	− 5
Hoechst	17	15	14	19	23	− 14	32[5]	28
Ciba	8	9	8	9	− 13	− 19	− 20	− 9
AKZO	21	19	15	21	20	21	36[6]	63
L'Air Liquide	16	14	12	14	17	58[7]	49	34
BOC	14	14	18	22	67	56	46	61
Rhone–Poulenc PICs	27	18	15	14	165	129[8]	89[9]	57

Note: These figures are based on reported results and reflect differing accounting practices; they are intended to set out trends over time for the individual companies rather than provide a basis for comparisons between companies.

[a]Note the effect of major acquisitions: 1. Beatrice chemical companies; 2. Glidden; 3. Stauffer agrochemicals; 4. Inmont; 5. Celanese; 6. Stauffer specialty chemicals; 7. Big Three; 8. Union Carbide agrochemicals; 9. Stauffer basic chemicals.

Sources: Company Reports, Goldman, Sachs Analysis; Charles K. Brown and Peter Clark, "European Chemical Industry—Majors Outlook for 1990" (London: Goldman, Sachs International Ltd., January 1990).

| Table 14.11 | Common Stock Statistics for Major European Chemical Firms |

	Cur-rency	Share Priceᵃ	12-Month Range		EPS		DPS (1989E)	P/E (1990E)	P/E–Relative (1990E)	P/CF (1988)	P/BV (1988)	Yield (1989E)
			High	Low	1989	1990E						
ICI	BP	1,140	1,342	1,013	131.0	123.7	56.0	9.2	83%	6.4	2.0	6.5%
BASFᵇ	DM	300	315	256	39.0	38.5	14.0	7.8	66	3.4	1.4	7.3
Bayerᵇ	DM	316	322	275	36.5	37.0	13.0	8.4	71	4.2	1.4	6.4
Hoechstᵇ	DM	291	320	259	39.0	36.5	13.0	8.0	68	3.5	1.7	7.0
Cibaᶜ	SFr	3,740	4,720	2,645	289.0	324.0	65.0	11.5	96	8.9	1.3	1.7
AKZO	DFL	142	154	125	20.8ᵈ	21.9ᵈ	8.0	6.5	74	4.1	1.3	5.7
DSM	DFL	113	142	108	29.2ᵈ	23.8ᵈ	8.0	4.7	54	2.4	1.3	7.1
Solvay	BFr	15,000	15,400	12,725	2,278ᵈ	2,330ᵈ	450.0	6.4	54	4.0	1.7	4.0
L'Air Liquide	FFr	684	685	569	40.0	45.0	14.5	15.2	128	7.8	2.4	3.2
BOCᵉ	BP	559	559	420	53.2ᶠ	58.4ᵍ	19.0ᶠ	10.5	93	7.4	2.6	4.5ᶠ
AGA B	SKr	236	290	208	19.9	22.6	7.0	10.4	85	7.4	2.1	3.0
Rhone–Poulenc PICs	FFr	460	616	451	70.0	77.0	23.0	6.0	49	2.7	0.9	7.5

ᵃPrices at 2 January 1990; all per share figures based on this price.

ᵇEPS is on DVFA-adjusted basis, undiluted; potential dilution for BASF 9%, Bayer 10%, and Hoechst 3%.

ᶜAll figures based on current cost values.

ᵈBefore extraordinary items.

ᵉYears to Sept.

ᶠSept 1990.

ᵍSept 1991.

Source: Charles K. Brown and Peter Clark, "European Chemical Majors—Outlook for 1990" (London: Goldman, Sachs International Ltd., January 1990).

Liquide's P/E ratio of 15.2 is 128 percent of the average for stocks in France. This shows that two stocks with similar P/E ratios could still have different relative valuations in different countries due to variations in accounting conventions or social attitudes. Such a difference in measures of relative valuation among countries might not be possible in the future as accounting practices among countries become more consistent and the global capital markets become more integrated.

The price/book value ratios likewise reflect major differences in relative valuation among countries. Again, these differences could be due to differences in real value or differences in accounting practices. An extreme example of an accounting difference is Ciba, where the book values are based on current costs rather than the historical costs that are used in most accounting presentations.

Share Price Performance

Table 14.12 compares the stock price changes for the major chemical industry firms. Here we can see the impact of exchange rates. Part A shows the stocks' absolute percentage changes as compared to the aggregate market over 1- and 3-year time intervals. Part B converts these stock returns to U.S. dollars to adjust for exchange rate movements and compares them to the U.S. market. These data show us the relative performance for a U.S. investor. For a U.S. investor, this latter comparison is the critical one because it demonstrates the effect of international diversification and

Table 14.12   *Share Price Performance for Major European Chemical Firms*

	Absolute Change (%) over Last		Change Relative to Local Market (%) over Last	
	Year	3 Years	Year	3 Years
A: Domestic Currencies				
ICI	10.9	5.0	−14.4	−27.5
BASF	7.3	9.0	−20.1	1.9
Bayer	2.9	−1.3	−23.0	−7.9
Hoechst	−4.8	8.1	−28.5	0.9
Ciba	41.4	5.1	12.8	−19.3
AKZO	−4.4	−6.3	−21.9	−24.5
Solvay	13.6	90.9	0.2	28.8
L'Air Liquide	15.4	5.7	−14.1	−22.6
BOC	30.0	50.7	0.4	4.1
AGA B	7.3	35.6	−13.6	−22.5
Rhone–Poulenc PICs	−11.5	18.0	−34.1	−13.5
Montedison	−1.8	−28.3	−15.6	−25.3

	Absolute Change (%) over Last		Change Relative to S&P 500 (%) over Last	
	Year	3 Years	Year	3 Years
B: U.S. Dollars				
ICI	−0.1	15.3	−21.1	−20.2
BASF	13.4	25.1	−10.3	−13.4
Bayer	8.8	13.4	−14.0	−21.5
Hoechst	0.7	24.2	−20.4	−14.0
Ciba	38.8	10.5	9.7	−23.5
AKZO	0.9	7.6	−20.2	−25.5
Solvay	20.0	119.3	−5.1	51.8
L'Air Liquide	21.6	17.4	−3.8	−18.7
BOC	17.1	65.5	−7.4	14.6
AGA B	6.6	49.0	−15.7	3.2
Rhone-Poulenc PICs	−6.7	31.0	−26.2	−9.3
Montedison	2.0	−23.5	−19.4	−47.0

Source: Charles K. Brown and Peter Clark, "European Chemical Majors—Outlook for 1990" (London: Goldman, Sachs International Ltd., January 1990).

| Table 14.13 | *Company and Stock Price Data for Bayer* |

Price	DM316
Market value	DM20.1bn
12-Month range	DM322–275
FT-A Germany	108.8

Price relative to market	
1 Month	−3.7%
3 Months	−4.8%
12 Months	−23.0%

Year to December:	Pre-Tax Profit (DMm)	Net Profit (DMm)	EPS[a] (DM)	Net Dividends (DM)	Cash Flow/ Share[b] (DM)	P/E	P/E Rel. (%)	Price/ Cash Flow	Gross Yield (%)
1987	3,066	1,498	30.5	11.0	70	10.3	61%	4.5	5.4
1988	3,776	1,855	34.0	12.0	87	9.3	64	3.6	5.9
1989E	4,300	2,020	36.5	13.0	84	8.6	65	3.8	6.4
1990E	4,450	2,145	37.0	13.0	89	8.4	71	3.5	6.4
1987–1990E composite growth percentage	13.2	12.7	6.7	5.7					

| Options/Convertibles/Warrants: O/C/W | Reuters: BRr/tO |
| Listed ADRs: No | Quotron: BAYR.EU |

[a]DVFA Undiluted—dilution approximately 10%.

[b]Undiluted.

Source: Charles K. Brown and Peter Clark, "European Chemical Majors—Outlook for 1990" (London: Goldman, Sachs International Ltd., January 1990).

Individual Company Analysis

The report concludes with a discussion that summarizes the strengths and potential problems of each individual company. Table 14.13 summarizes results for Bayer, a German firm considered to be one of the world's leading chemical companies. The discussion that accompanies the table indicates what the firm has done and is expected to do given the outlook for this industry. Also, a stock price chart for Bayer (Figure 14.6) shows the absolute and relative movements for the firm's stock.

Identifying and Selecting Competitive Strategies

In describing competition within industries, we identified five conditions that could affect the competitive structure and profits of an industry: current rivalry, threat of new entrants, potential substitute products, bargaining power of suppliers, and bargaining power of buyers. Once you have determined the competitive structure of your industry, you can identify the specific competitive strategy employed by each firm in the industry and evaluate these strategies in terms of the overall competitive structure of the industry. As an investor you must understand the alternatives available, determine each firm's strategy, judge whether the strategy selected by the firm is reasonable for this industry, and finally, evaluate how successfully the firm implements its strategy.

Porter identifies two possible competitive strategies: low-cost leadership or differentiation.[6] These two competitive strategies dictate how a firm has decided to cope with the five competitive conditions that define the industry's environment. Within each industry the strategies available and the ways of implementing them differ.

[6]Michael Porter, *Competitive Advantage: Creating and Sustaining Superior Performance* (New York: Free Press, 1988).

Figure 14.6 *Bayer Share Price Performance*

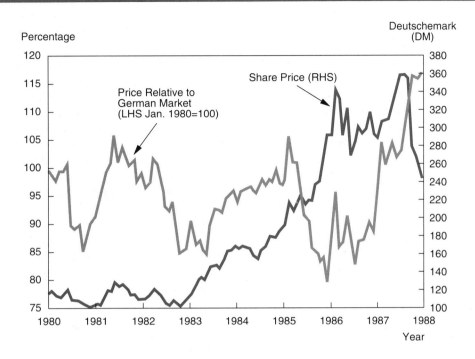

Source: Charles K. Brown, "European Chemical Industry—1988 Prospects" (London: Goldman, Sachs & Co., International Research, February 22, 1988).

Low-Cost Strategy

The firm that pursues the low-cost strategy is determined to become *the* low-cost producer and, hence, the cost leader in its industry. Cost advantages will vary by industry and might include economies of scale, proprietary technology, or preferential access to raw materials. To assert cost leadership, the firm must command prices near the industry average, so it must differentiate itself about as well as other firms. If the firm discounts price too much, it erodes the superior rate of return available because of its low cost. In the retail business both Wal-Mart and K mart are considered low-cost sources. They achieve this by volume purchasing of merchandise and lower-cost operations. As a result, they charge less, but still enjoy higher profit margins and returns on capital.

Differentiation Strategy

With the differentiation strategy, a firm seeks to identify itself as unique in its industry in an area that is important to buyers. Again, the possibilities for dif-

ferentiation vary widely by industry. A company can attempt to differentiate itself based on its product, its distribution system (selling in stores, by mail order, or door-to-door), or some unique marketing approach. A firm employing the differentiation strategy will enjoy above-average rates of return only if its price premium based upon its differentiation exceeds the extra cost of being unique. Therefore, analysis of this strategy must determine whether the differentiating factor is truly unique, whether it is sustainable, what is its cost, and whether the price premium derived from this uniqueness is greater than its cost.

Focusing a Strategy

Whichever strategy it selects, a firm must determine where it will focus this strategy. Specifically, a firm must select a segment or group of segments in the industry and tailor its strategy to serve this specific group. For example, a cost focus would exploit cost advantages for certain segments of the industry, perhaps becoming the low-cost producer for the expensive segment of the market. Similarly, a differentiation focus would attempt to serve the special needs of buyers in specific segments. In the athletic shoe market, companies attempt to develop shoes for unique segments such as tennis, basketball, aerobics, or walkers and hikers, rather than offering only shoes for runners. Firms thought that individuals involved in these other athletic endeavors needed shoes with different characteristics than those used by joggers and they would be willing to pay a premium for these special shoes. Again, you must ascertain whether these special cost or need possibilities exist and that they are not being served by another firm.

Next, you must determine which strategy is being pursued and whether the firm is successful at it. Also, can the strategy be sustained? Further, you should evaluate a firm's competitive strategy over time, because strategies typically change as an industry evolves. The point is, different strategies work during different phases of an industry's life cycle.

Summary

■ The purpose of this chapter was to demonstrate how you complete the fundamental analysis process by analyzing a company and deciding whether you should buy its stock. You must realize that this requires a separate analysis of a company and its stock. A wonderful firm can have an overpriced stock, or a mediocre firm can have an underpriced stock.

■ We demonstrated the dividend growth model using Walgreen Company as an example. We derived an estimate of expected value by computing an earnings per share estimate and the earnings multiplier. The investment decision was based on three comparisons. First we computed the expected value of the stock discounted to the present and compared it to the prevailing market price. If the present value of the expected price exceeded the market price, we would buy the stock. Second, we computed the expected rate of return during our holding period on the basis of the expected value of the stock and the expected dividend. If this expected rate of return exceeded our required rate of return, we would buy it. Finally, we computed an expected rate of return based upon the expected dividend yield plus the expected growth rate and, again, if this expected return exceeded our required rate of return, we would buy the stock.

■ Subsequently, we considered some additional relative valuation variables that affect decisions of inves-

tors in the United States and abroad. Specifically, we computed and analyzed the price/book value ratio and the price/cash flow ratio for the stock market, the retail drugstore industry, and Walgreen. This analysis provided some historical and current perspective for these ratios and Walgreen's relative position.

■ We continued our example of global analysis by reviewing the company analysis related to the European chemical industry. This demonstration showed the importance of differential demand and cost factors among countries, the significance of different accounting conventions, and finally the impact of exchange rate differences.

■ We concluded the chapter with a discussion of the strategic alternatives available to firms in response to different competitive pressures in their industries. The alternative strategies include low-cost leadership or differentiation. Either of these should be focused toward alternative segments of the market and, if properly implemented, should help the company attain above-average rates of return.

Questions

1. Give an example of a growth company, and discuss why you identify it as such.
2. You are told that a biotechnology firm is growing at a compound rate of 22 percent a year. (Its ROE is over 30 percent, and it retains about 70 percent of its earnings.) The stock of this company is currently priced at 74 times next year's earnings. Discuss whether you would consider this a growth company. Discuss whether you would consider it a growth stock.
3. Select a company outside the retail store industry and indicate what economic series you would use for a sales projection. Discuss why this is a relevant series.
4. Select a company outside the retail store industry and indicate what industry series you would use in an industry analysis. (Try to use one of the industry groups designated by Standard & Poor's.) Discuss why this series is most appropriate among the possible alternatives.
5. Select a company outside the retail store industry and, based upon information in its annual report and other public sources (refer to Chapter 6), discuss whether it is pursuing a competitive strategy of low-cost leadership or differentiation.
6. What is the rationale for using the price/book value ratio as a measure of relative value?

7. How would you justify a price/book value ratio of 3.0? What would you expect if a firm had a P/BV ratio of 0.6?
8. Why has the price/cash flow ratio become popular recently? What factors would help explain a difference in this ratio for two firms?
9. Discuss a company known as a low-cost producer in its industry and consider what makes it possible for the firm to be a cost leader. Do the same for a firm known for differentiating.

Problems

1. Select two stocks in an industry of your choice and perform a common size income statement analysis over a 2-year period.
   a. Which firm appears to be more cost effective?
   b. Discuss the relative year-to-year changes for each company.
2. Select a company outside the retail industry and examine its annual operating profit margin relative to the operating margin for its industry for the most recent 10-year period. Discuss these results in terms of levels, percentage changes, and long-run averages.
3. Select any industry except chemicals and provide general background information on two non-U.S. companies from public sources. (See Chapter 6.) This background information should include their products, overall size (sales and assets), growth during the past 5 years (sales and earnings), ROE during the last 2 years, and the current stock price and P/E ratio.
4. Select three companies from an industry and compute their P/E ratios using last year's average price (high plus low/2) and earnings. Also compute the growth rates of their earnings over the last 5 years. Discuss the relationship between the firm's P/E ratio and its growth rate. How do they relate to the company and to the market P/E ratios in Table 14.5?
5. For the three companies in Problem 4, compute the price/book value and price/cash flow ratio and discuss how these have changed over time.
6. *CFA Examination II* (June 1981)
   The value of an asset is the present value of the expected returns from the asset during the holding period. An investment will provide a stream of returns during this period, and it is necessary

to discount this stream of returns at an appropriate rate to determine the asset's present value. A dividend valuation model such as the following is frequently used.

$$P_i = \frac{D_1}{(k_i - g_i)}$$

P_i = current price of common stock i

D_1 = expected dividend in period 1

k_i = required rate of return for stock i

g_i = expected constant growth rate for stock i.

   a. Identify the three factors that must be estimated for any valuation model, and explain why these estimates are more difficult to derive for common stocks than for bonds [9 minutes]
   b. Explain the principal problem involved in using a dividend valuation model to value:
      1. Companies whose operations are closely correlated with economic cycles
      2. Companies that are of giant size and are maturing
      3. Companies that are of small size and are growing rapidly. Assume all companies pay dividends. [6 minutes]
7. *CFA Examination I* (June 1985)
   Your client is considering the purchase of $100,000 in common stock which pays no dividends and will appreciate in market value by 10 percent per year. At the same time, the client is considering an opportunity to invest $100,000 in a lease obligation that will provide the annual year-end cash flows listed in Table 1. Assume that each investment will be sold at the end of 3 years and that you are given no additional information.

Table 1 Annual Cash Flow from Lease

End of Year		
1		$ 0
2	Lease receipts	15,000
3	Lease receipts	25,000
3	Sale proceeds	100,000

(continued)

Table 1 continued

Period	6 Percent	8 Percent	10 Percent	12 Percent
1	0.943	0.926	0.909	0.893
2	0.890	0.857	0.826	0.797
3	0.840	0.794	0.751	0.712
4	0.792	0.735	0.683	0.636
5	0.747	0.681	0.621	0.567

Calculate the present value of each of the two investments assuming a 10 percent discount rate, and state which will provide the higher return over the 3-year period. Use the data in Table 1, and show your calculations. [10 minutes]

References

Cottle, Sidney, Roger F. Murray, and Frank E. Block. *Graham and Dodd's Security Analysis*, 5th ed. New York: McGraw-Hill, 1988.

Fama, Eugene F., and Kenneth R. French. "Dividend Yields and Expected Stock Returns." *Journal of Financial Economics* 22, no. 1 (October 1988).

Hassel, John M., and Robert H. Jennings. "Relative Forecast Accuracy and the Timing of Earnings Forecast Announcements." *The Accounting Review* 61, no. 1 (January 1986).

Hassel, John M., Robert H. Jennings, and Dennis J. Lasser. "Management Earnings Forecasts: Their Usefulness as a Source of Firm-Specific Information to Security Analysts." *Journal of Financial Research* 11, no. 4 (Winter 1988).

Imhoff, Eugene, and G. Lobo. "Information Content of Analysts Composite Forecast Revisions." *Journal of Accounting Research* 22, no. 3 (Autumn 1984).

Jennings, Robert. *Reaction of Financial Analysts to Corporate Management Earnings per Share Forecasts*. Financial Analysts Research Foundation Monograph No. 20, New York, 1984.

Levine, Sumner N., ed. *The Financial Analysts Handbook*, 2d ed. Homewood, Ill.: Dow Jones-Irwin, 1988.

Waymire, G. "Additional Evidence on the Information Content of Management Earnings Forecasts." *Journal of Accounting Research* 22, no. 3 (Autumn 1984).

Technical analysis Estimation of future security
price movements based on past movements.

*The market reacted yesterday to the report of a large
increase in short interest on the NYSE.*

*Although the market declined today, it was not considered
bearish because volume was very light.*

*The market declined today after 3 days of increases due
to profit taking by investors.*

What Is Technical Analysis?

Statements like these appear daily in the financial
news. All of them derive from numerous technical
trading rules. Technical analysts develop technical
trading rules from observations of past price
movements of the stock market and individual
stocks. This investment philosophy contrasts
sharply with the fundamental analysis that we
have been studying. It also contradicts the efficient market hypothesis (we will study this in
Chapter 22), which contends that past performance has no influence on future performance or
market values.

We know from Chapters 11 to 14 that fundamental analysis bases investment decisions upon
fundamental economic and company variables
that lead to an estimate of the intrinsic value for
an investment. In contrast to this approach, and
the efficient market hypothesis, **technical analysis** involves the examination of past market data
such as prices and trading volume to estimate future price as a basis for an investment decision.
While the economic data that fundamental analysts consider are usually independent of the mar-

CHAPTER
15

Technical Analysis[1]

---

[1]The author received very helpful comments and material for this
chapter from Richard T. McCabe, Manager of Market Analysis at
Merrill Lynch Capital Markets.

ket, the technical analyst uses data from the market itself believing that the market is its own best predictor. Therefore, technical analysis is an alternative method of making the investment decision and answering these questions: What securities should an investor buy or sell? When should these investments be made?

Technical analysts see no need to study multitudes of economic and company variables in order to estimate future value because past price movements signal future price movements. Technicians also believe that changes in price trends may predict forthcoming changes in fundamental variables such as earnings and risk earlier than the techniques of most fundamental analysts.

Are technicians correct? Many investors using decision rules based upon technical analysis claim to enjoy superior rates of return on many investments. In addition, many newsletter writers base their recommendations upon technical analysis, and even the major investment firms, which employ many fundamental analysts, also employ technical analysts to provide investment advice. The point is, numerous investment professionals and individual investors alike believe in technical trading rules and base their investment decisions on them. Therefore, you should understand the basic philosophy and reasoning behind these technical approaches.

To help you understand technical analysis, we begin this chapter with an examination of the philosophy and assumptions underlying all technical approaches to market and company analysis. Subsequently we consider the advantages and potential problems of technical analysis. Finally, we present and discuss a number of the alternative technical trading rules that apply to both the U.S. and foreign securities markets.

Underlying Assumptions of Technical Analysis

Technical analysts base trading decisions on examinations of prior price and volume data to determine past market trends, from which they predict future behavior for the market as a whole and for individual securities. They cite several assumptions that support this view of price movements:

1. The market value of any good or service is determined solely by the interaction of supply and demand for it.
2. Supply and demand are governed by numerous factors, both rational and irrational, including the economic variables relied upon by the fundamental analyst, as well as opinions, moods, and guesses. The market weighs all of these factors continually and automatically.
3. Disregarding minor fluctuations, *the prices for individual securities and the overall value of the market tend to move in trends, which persist for appreciable lengths of time.* [Emphasis added]
4. Prevailing trends change in reaction to shifts in supply and demand relationships. These shifts, no matter why they occur, *can be detected sooner or later in the action of the market itself.*[2] [Emphasis added]

Certain aspects of these assumptions make technical analysis controversial, leading fundamental analysts and advocates of efficient markets to question their validity. Those aspects are emphasized above.

The first two assumptions are almost universally accepted by technicians and nontechnicians alike. Almost anyone who has had a basic course in economics would agree that, at any point in time, the price of a security (or any good or service) is determined by the interaction of supply and demand for it. In addition, most observers would acknowledge that supply and demand are governed by many variables. The only difference in opinion might concern the extent of the influence of irrational factors. A technical analyst might expect this influence to persist for some time, whereas other market analysts would expect only a short-run effect with rational beliefs prevailing over

---

[2]These assumptions are summarized in Robert A. Levy, "Conceptual Foundations of Technical Analysis," *Financial Analysts Journal* 22, no. 4 (July–August 1966): 83.

Figure 15.1	**Technicians' View of Price Adjustment to New Information**

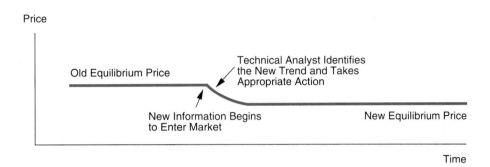

the long run. Certainly, everyone would agree that the market continually weighs all these factors.

A stronger difference of opinion arises over technical analysts' third assumption about the speed of adjustment of stock prices to changes in supply and demand. Technical analysts expect stock price trends to persist for long periods because new information that affects supply and demand does not come to the market at one point in time, but rather enters the market over a period of time. This pattern of information access occurs because of differences in sources of information or because certain investors receive the information and deduce fundamental changes earlier than others. As various groups ranging from insiders to well-informed professionals to the average investor receive information and buy or sell a security accordingly, its price moves toward the new equilibrium. Therefore, technicians do not expect the price adjustment to be as abrupt as fundamental analysts and efficient market supporters do, but expect a gradual adjustment to reflect the gradual flow of information.

Figure 15.1 shows this process. The figure shows that new information causes a decrease in the equilibrium price for a security, but the price adjustment is not rapid. It occurs as a trend that persists until the price reaches its new equilibrium. Technical analysts look for the beginning of a movement from one equilibrium value to a new equilibrium value, they do not attempt to predict the new equilibrium value. They try to get on the bandwagon early and benefit from the change by buying if the trend is up or selling if the trend is down. Rapid adjustment of prices would

keep the ride on the bandwagon very short and thus it would not be worth the effort.

Challenges to Technical Analysis

Those who question the value of technical analysis for investment decisions challenge this technique in two areas. First, they challenge some of its basic assumptions. Second, they challenge some of its specific trading rules. In this section, we consider both of these challenges.

Challenges to Technical Analysis Assumptions

The major challenge to technical analysis is based on the efficient market hypothesis. As we will discuss in Chapter 22, technical trading rules can generate superior returns with similar risk after transactions costs only when the market is slow to adjust prices to the arrival of new information, that is, when it is inefficient. (This is referred to as the weak-form efficient market hypothesis.) The vast majority of studies that have tested the weak-form efficient market hypothesis have found that prices adjust rapidly to stock market information, supporting the efficient market hypothesis.

Critics acknowledge that numerous technical trading rules have not been or cannot be tested. They raise challenges in addition to those based on efficient market arguments.

Challenges to Technical Trading Rules

In an obvious challenge to technical analysis, some contend that past price patterns or relationships between market variables and stock prices may not be repeated. As a result, a technique that previously worked might miss subsequent market turns. This possibility leads most technicians to follow several trading rules and seek a consensus of all of them to predict the future market pattern.

Other critics challenge that many price patterns become self-fulfilling prophecies. Assume that many analysts expect a stock selling at $40 a share to go to $50 or more if it should rise above its current trading pattern of peaking at $45. As soon as it reaches $45, a number of technicians will buy, causing the price to rise to $50, exactly as predicted. In fact, some technicians may place limit orders to buy the stock at such a breakout point. Under such conditions, the increase will probably be only temporary and the price will return to its true equilibrium.

Success with a trading rule will encourage many investors to adopt it. Such popularity and the resultant competition will eventually neutralize the value of the technique. If numerous investors focus on a specific technical trading rule, some of them will attempt to anticipate the expected price pattern and either ruin the expected historical price pattern or eliminate profits for most users of the trading rule by causing the price to change faster than expected.

As an example, suppose that it becomes known that technicians who invest in reaction to the amount of short selling have been enjoying very high rates of return. Based on this knowledge, other technicians will likely start using these data and thus affect the relationship between stock prices and the amount of short selling. The trading rule that provided high rates of return previously may no longer work after the first few investors react.

Further, as we will see when we examine specific trading rules, they all require a great deal of subjective judgment. Two technical analysts looking at the same price pattern may arrive at widely different interpretations of what has happened and, therefore, will come to different investment decisions. This implies that the use of various techniques is neither completely mechanical nor obvious.

Finally, as we will discuss in connection with several trading rules, the standard values that signal investment decisions can change over time. Therefore, technical analysts must adjust the trading rule or the specified values that trigger investment decisions over time to conform to new environments.

Advantages of Technical Analysis

Despite these criticisms, some technical analysts see benefits in their strategy. Most technical analysts admit that a fundamental analyst with good information, good analytical ability, and a keen sense of information's impact on the market should achieve above-average returns. However, this statement requires qualification. According to technical analysts, the fundamental analysts can experience superior returns *only* if they obtain new information before other investors and process it correctly and quickly. Technical analysts do not believe that anyone can consistently get new information and process it correctly and quickly.

Technical analysts claim as a major advantage of their method that it is not heavily dependent on financial accounting statements, the major source of information about the past performance of a firm or industry. As you know from Chapters 13 and 14, the fundamental analyst evaluates such statements to help project future return and risk characteristics for industries and individual securities. The technician points out several major problems with those statements:

1. They do not contain sufficient information to support full security analysis, such as details on sales and general expenses or sales and earnings by product line and customer.
2. Corporations may choose among several procedures for reporting expenses, assets, or liabilities, and these alternative procedures can produce vastly different values for expenses, income, return on assets, and return on equity. As a result, an investor can have trouble comparing the statements of two firms in the same industry, much less firms in different industries.
3. Many psychological factors and other nonquantitative variables do not appear in financial statements. Examples include employee training and loyalty, customer goodwill, and general investor attitude toward an industry. Investor attitudes could become important when, for example, risk concerns arise about further restrictions or taxes on industries such as tobacco or alcohol, or when firms do business in countries that practice repressive policies such as South Africa and China.

Technicians' suspicions of financial statements lead them to consider it an advantage that they generally do not depend upon those statements. As we will show, technicians derive most of their data such as security prices, volume of trading, and other trading information from the stock market itself.

Also, a fundamental analyst must process any new information correctly and very quickly to derive a new intrinsic value for the stock or bond before other investors can. Technicians, on the other hand, need only quickly recognize a movement to a new equilibrium value for whatever reason.

Finally, assume a fundamental analyst determines that a given security is under- or overvalued long before other investors. He or she still must determine when to make the purchase or sale. Ideally, the highest return would come from a transaction just before the change in market value occurs. As an example, assume that based upon your analysis in February, you expect a firm to report substantially higher earnings in June. Although you could buy the stock in February, you would be better off waiting until about May so your funds would not be tied up for an extra 3 months. Since most technicians do not invest until the move to the new equilibrium is under way, they achieve ideal timing more easily than the fundamental analyst.

Some technicians buy stocks that have declined to a stable price level (referred to as a "bottom" or "base"

Trough The culmination of a bear market at which prices cease declining and begin rising.
Declining trend channel The range defined by security prices as they move progressively lower.

pattern) despite continued bad news. They wait for the stock price to respond to anticipated positive information. These people resemble fundamental analysts.

Technical Trading Rules and Indicators

To help you understand the specific technical trading rules, the typical stock price cycle in Figure 15.2 could be an example for the overall stock market or for an individual stock. The graph shows a peak and a trough along with a rising trend channel, a flat trend channel, a declining trend channel, and indications of when a technical analyst would ideally want to trade.

The graph begins as a declining (bear) market that finishes in a **trough** followed by an upward trend that breaks through the **declining trend channel.** Confirmation that the trend had reversed would be a buying signal. The technical analyst would buy stocks

Table 15.2 *Typical Stock Market Cycle*

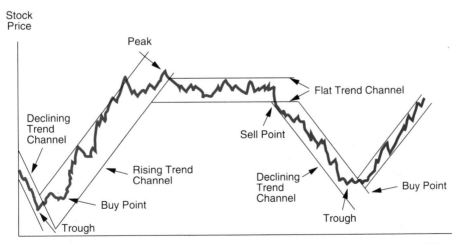

> **Rising trend channel** The range defined by security prices as they move progressively higher.
>
> **Peak** The culmination of a bull market when prices stop rising and begin declining.
>
> **Flat trend channel** The range defined by security prices as they maintain a relatively steady level.

in general or an individual stock that showed this pattern.

The analyst would then look for the development of a **rising trend channel.** As long as the stock's price stays in this rising channel, the technician would hold it for the upward ride. Ideally, you want to sell at the **peak** of the cycle, but you generally cannot identify a peak until after the trend changes.

If the stock begins trading in a flat pattern, it will necessarily break out of its rising trend channel. At this point, some technical analysts would sell, but most would hold to see if the stock would experience a period of consolidation and then break out of the **flat trend channel** on the upside and begin rising again. If the stock were to break out of the channel on the downside, the technician would take this as a sell signal. The next buy signal comes after the trough when the price breaks out of the declining channel and establishes a rising trend. Subsequently, we will consider the importance of volume in this analysis.

There are numerous technical trading rules and a large number of interpretations for each of them. Almost all technical analysts watch many alternative rules. This section discusses most of the well-known techniques, but certainly not all of them, divided into four subsections based upon the attitudes of technical analysts. The first group of trading rules serve analysts who like to trade against the crowd using contrary opinion signals. The second group of rules is intended to emulate very astute investors—i.e., the smart money. The next group of technical indicators are very popular, but not easily classified. The fourth group covers pure price and volume techniques, including the famous Dow Theory. The final subsections describe how these technical trading rules have been applied to foreign securities markets.

Contrary-Opinion Rules

Many technical analysts rely on technical trading rules developed from the premise that the majority of investors are wrong most of the time, or at least at peaks and troughs. These technicians try to determine when most investors are either very bullish or very bearish and then trade in the opposite direction.[3]

Odd-Lot, Short-Sales Theory As we know from Chapter 4, investors make short sales when they expect stock prices to decline. Such behavior is pessimistic or bearish. Compared to ordinary purchases of shares for cash, selling short is a fairly high-risk form of investing because it contradicts the long-run upward trend and you can lose over 100 percent if the stock increases by over 100 percent.

Most small investors are optimists and would consider short selling too risky. Therefore, they do not engage in short selling except when they feel especially bearish. Technical analysts interpret heavy short selling by individuals as a signal that the market is close to a trough because small investors only get pessimistic after a long decline in prices, just when the market is about to turn around.

Technical analysts who translate this into a trading rule contend that a relatively high rate (3 percent or more) of odd-lot short sales as a percentage of total odd-lot sales indicates a very bearish attitude by small investors, which they consider a signal of a near-term trough in stock prices. These technicians become bullish and begin buying stocks. Alternatively, when the ratio declines below 1 percent, technical analysts interpret small investors' behavior as very bullish and become bearish.

Recent very erratic figures for this ratio suggest that it may be necessary to change the investment decision percentages. Specifically, the recent values have very seldom deviated from the 1 percent range so it is difficult to imagine that this series would give a buy signal using the prevailing decision values.

Mutual Fund Cash Positions Mutual funds hold some part of their portfolios in cash for one of several reasons. The most obvious reason is that they need cash to liquidate shares that fundholders sell back to the fund. For another reason, funds from new purchases of the fund may not have been invested. A third reason might be the portfolio manager's bearish out-

---

[3]Prior editions of this book included the percentage of odd-lot purchases and sales as a contrary-opinion rule. It is not included in this edition because it is seldom used since odd-lot volume has come to account for a very small proportion of total trading volume. This trading is no longer considered a valid indication of small investor sentiment.

Figure 15.3 *Time-Series Plot of Dow Jones Industrial Average and Mutual Fund Cash Ratio (Cash/Total assets)*

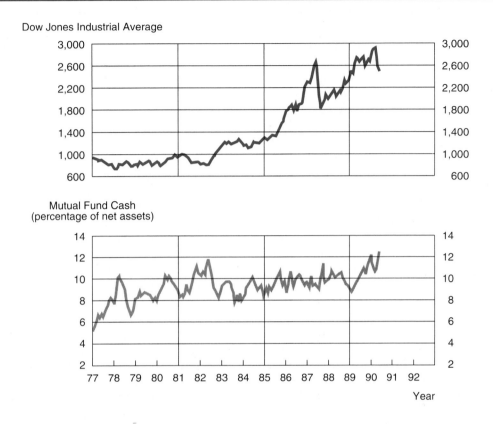

Source: *Where the Indicators Stand* (New York: Merrill Lynch, November 1990).

look for the market, inspiring a buildup in the defensive cash position.

Mutual funds' ratios of cash as percentages of the total assets in their portfolios (the *cash ratio* or *liquid asset ratio*) are reported in the press, including monthly figures in Barron's.[4] This percentage of cash has varied during the last decade from a low of about 8 percent to a high near 12 percent, although the range has increased during the last several years.

Contrary-opinion technicians consider the mutual funds to be a good proxy for the institutional investor group. They also feel that mutual funds are usually

wrong at peaks and troughs. Thus, they expect mutual funds to have high percentages of cash near the trough of a market cycle, being very bearish exactly when they should be fully invested to take advantage of the impending market rise. At the market peak, technicians expect mutual funds to be almost fully invested, with low percentages of cash. This would indicate a bullish outlook when the funds should be selling stocks and realizing gains for some part of their portfolios. Therefore, technicians would watch for the mutual fund cash position to approach one of the extremes and act contrary to the mutual funds. Their trading rule would lead them to buy when the cash ratio approached 12 percent and sell when the cash ratio approached 8 percent.

Figure 15.3 contains a time-series plot of the DJIA and the mutual fund cash ratio. It shows apparent bullish signals in 1970, late 1974, and in 1982 near

---

[4]*Barron's* is a prime source for numerous technical indicators. For a readable discussion of these data and their use, see Martin E. Zweig, *Understanding Technical Forecasting* (New York: Dow Jones & Co., 1987).

market troughs. The ratio was approaching 12 percent in late 1990 after the market had declined from its peak of almost 3,000 on the DJIA. Bearish signals appeared in 1971, 1972 to 1973, and 1976 prior to market peaks.

A high mutual fund cash position can also be considered as a bullish indicator of potential buying power. Whether the cash balances have built up because of stock sales completed as part of selling programs or because investors have been buying the fund, technicians believe that these funds will eventually be invested, boosting stock prices. Alternatively, a low cash ratio would mean that the institutions have bought heavily and are left with little potential buying power.

A couple of studies have examined this mutual fund cash ratio and its components as a predictor of market cycles. They concluded that the mutual fund liquid asset ratio was not as strong a predictor of market cycles as suggested by technical analysts.[5]

Credit Balances in Brokerage Accounts Credit balances result when investors sell stocks and leave the proceeds with their brokers, expecting to reinvest them shortly. The amounts are reported by the SEC and the NYSE in *Barron's*. Technical analysts view these credit balances as pools of potential purchasing power, so they interpret a decline in these balances as bearish because it indicates lower purchasing power as the market approaches a peak. Alternatively, technicians view a buildup of credit balances as an increase in buying power and a bullish signal.

Note that the data by which technicians gauge the market environment are stated in terms of an increase or decline in the credit balance series rather than comparing these balances to some other series. This assumption of an absolute trend could make interpretation difficult as market levels change.

Investment Advisory Opinions Many technicians feel that bearish attitudes of a large proportion of investment advisory services signal the approach of a market trough and the onset of a bull market. They develop this trading rule from the ratio of the number of advisory services that are bearish as a percentage of the number of services expressing an opinion.[6] A "bearish sentiment index" of 50 to 60 percent indicates a pervasive bearish attitude by advisory services, and contrarians would consider this a bullish indicator. In contrast, when this bearish sentiment index declines below 20 percent, it indicates a pervasive bullish attitude by advisory services, which technicians would interpret as a bearish sign. Figure 15.4 shows a time-series plot of the DJIA and both the bearish sentiment index and the bullish sentiment index.

OTC versus NYSE Volume Prior to the 1970s, the accepted measure of speculative trading activity was the ratio of AMEX volume to NYSE volume. This ratio is no longer considered useful because the relationship between the exchanges has changed dramatically over time. The ratio of AMEX to NYSE volume has gone from about 50 percent in the 1950s and 1960s to about 10 percent or less currently. Instead, technicians currently use the ratio of OTC volume on the NASDAQ system to NYSE volume as a measure of speculative trading. They consider speculative activity high when this ratio gets to 80 percent or more. Speculative trading typically peaks at market peaks. Technicians consider the market to be oversold, which means that investors are too bearish, when this ratio drops below 60 percent. Figure 15.5 shows a time-series plot of the NASDAQ Composite Index and the OTC/NYSE volume ratio.

Technicians acknowledge that current decision ratios of 80 percent for a peak and 60 percent for an oversold position may change in the future if individual investors start accounting for a higher proportion of trading because individual investors are more likely to trade the small firms on the OTC market that lack the size and liquidity required by institutions. Also, there is a strong tendency for a faster increase in NASDAQ volume since more firms are being added to this market than to the NYSE. The number of firms listed on the NYSE has been fairly constant over the past 10 years while the number on NASDAQ has increased by over 60 percent (from 2,647 in 1979 to 4,293 in 1989).

Chicago Board Option Exchange (CBOE) Put/Call Ratio The CBOE put/call ratio is a relatively

[5]Paul H. Massey, "The Mutual Fund Liquidity Ratio: A Trap for the Unwary," *Journal of Portfolio Management* 5, no. 2 (Winter 1979): 18–21; and R. David Ranson and William G. Shipman, "Institutional Buying Power and the Stock Market," *Financial Analysts Journal* 37, no. 5 (September–October 1981): 62–68.

[6]This ratio is compiled by Investors Intelligence, Larchmont, N.Y. 10538.

Table 15.4 *Time-Series Plot of Dow Jones Industrial Average and Bullish and Bearish Sentiment Indexes*

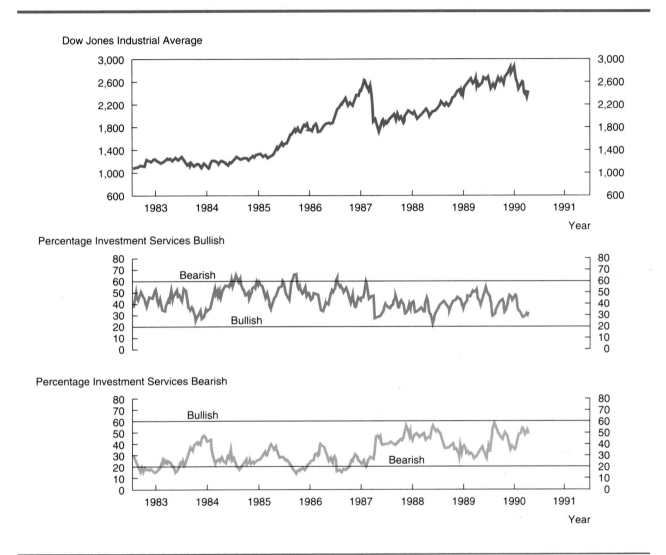

Sources: *Investors' Intelligence*, Larchmont, N.Y. 10538; and *Where the Indicators Stand* (New York: Merrill Lynch, November 1990).

new tool of contrary-opinion technicians. They see put options, which give the holder the right to sell stock at a specified price for a given time period, as signals of a bearish attitude. The technicians reason that a higher put/call ratio indicates a more pervasive bearish attitude, which they consider a bullish indicator.

As shown in Figure 15.6, this ratio typically falls in the range of 0.35 to 0.80. It should typically be substantially less than 1 because investors tend to be bullish and avoid selling short. The widely used deci-

sion rule states that a put/call ratio of 0.60, which means that 60 puts are traded for every 100 calls, is considered bullish. In contrast, a relatively low put/call ratio of 0.40 or less is considered a bearish sign.

Bullish Speculation on Stock Index Futures   Another relatively new measure used by contrary opinion technicians is the percentage of speculators in stock index futures who are bullish. Specifically, an advisory service (Market Vane) surveys other firms that provide advisory services for the futures market along with

Figure 15.5   *Time-Series Plot of NASDAQ Composite Average and the Ratio of OTC Volume to NYSE Volume*

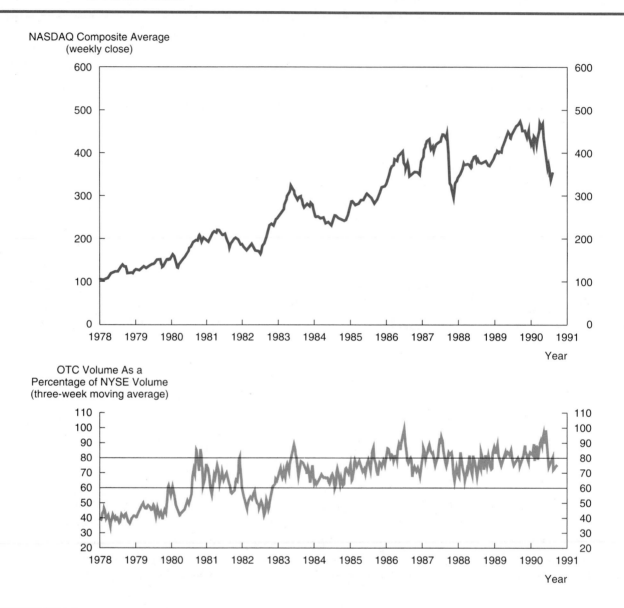

Source: *Where the Indicators Stand* (New York: Merrill Lynch, November 1990).

individual traders involved in the futures market to determine whether these speculators are bearish or bullish regarding stocks. A plot of the series in Figure 15.7 indicates that these technicians would consider it a bearish sign when over 70 percent of the speculators are bullish. In contrast, if the proportion of bullish speculators declines to 30 percent or lower, it is a bullish sign.

As you can see, technicians who seek to be contrary to the market have several series that provide measures of how the majority of investors are investing. They then take the opposite action. They would

Figure 15.6   *Time-Series Plot of Dow Jones Industrial Average and CBOE Put/Call Ratio*

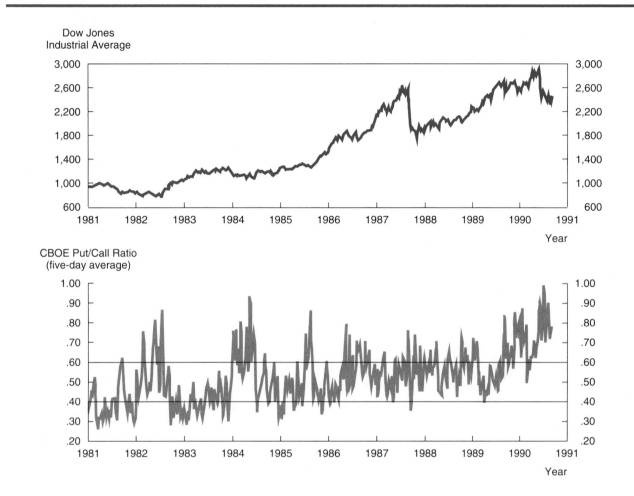

Source: *Where the Indicators Stand* (New York: Merrill Lynch, November 1990).

generally follow several of these series to provide a consensus regarding investors' attitudes.

Follow the Smart Money

Some technical analysts employ an alternative set of indicators that they expect to indicate the behavior of smart, sophisticated investors. After studying the market, these technicians have created indicators that tell what smart investors are doing and rules to follow them. In this section, we discuss some of the more popular indicators.

Confidence Index   Published by *Barron's*, the Confidence Index is the ratio of *Barron's* average yield on 10 top-grade corporate bonds to the yield on the Dow Jones average of 40 bonds to measure the difference in yield spread between high-grade bonds and ordinary bonds.[7] Because the yields on high-grade bonds should always be lower than those on ordinary bonds,

---

[7]Historical data for this series are contained in *The Dow Jones Investor's Handbook* (Princeton, N.J.: Dow Jones Books, annual). Current figures appear weekly in *Barron's*.

Figure 15.7   *Time-Series Plot of Dow Jones Industrial Average and Percentage of Speculators Bullish on Stock Index Futures*

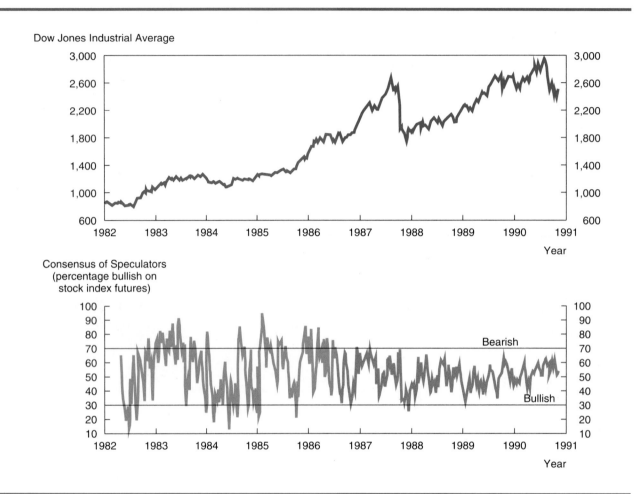

Source: *Where the Indicators Stand* (New York: Merrill Lynch, November 1990).

this ratio should never exceed 100. It approaches 100 as the spread between the two sets of bonds gets smaller.

Technicians feel the ratio is an indicator because, during periods of high confidence, investors are willing to invest more in lower-quality bonds for the added yield. This increased demand for lower-quality bonds should reduce the average yield spread between ordinary bonds and high-grade bonds, so this ratio of yields, and the Confidence Index, will increase. In contrast, when investors are pessimistic about the economic and market outlook, they seek quality and avoid investing in low-quality bonds and increase their investments in high-grade bonds. This shift in

investment preference increases the yield differential between the high-grade bonds and the average bonds, which causes the Confidence Index to decline.

A major problem complicates this interpretation of bond investor behavior: it is almost solely demand-oriented. Specifically, it assumes that changes in the yield spread are caused almost exclusively by changes in investor demand for different quality bonds. In fact, the yield differences have frequently changed because the supply of bonds in one of the groups increased. A large issue of high-grade AT&T bonds could cause a temporary increase in yields on all high-grade bonds, which would reduce the yield spread and increase the Confidence Index without any change in investors' attitudes. Such a change in the supply of bonds can cause the series to generate a false signal of a change in confidence.

Advocates of the index believe that it can indicate future stock-price movements because it reflects investor attitudes toward financial assets. One may ask, however, why investors in bonds would change their attitudes before equity investors. Several studies have found this index not very useful for predicting stock-price movements.

As an alternative measure of investor attitude or confidence, some have suggested the spread between T-bill yields and Eurodollar rates. At times of crisis, this spread widens as money flows to T-bills. The stock market has tended to reach a trough shortly thereafter.

Short Sales by Specialists The NYSE and the SEC report data for total short sales on the NYSE and the AMEX along with short sales attributed to the specialists on the exchanges. This information appears weekly in *Barron's*. It should be no surprise after our discussion in Chapter 4 that technicians who want to follow smart money watch the specialists. Specialists regularly engage in short selling as a part of their market-making function, but they can exercise discretion in this area when they feel strongly about market changes.

The normal ratio of specialists' short sales to total short sales on the NYSE was about 45 percent prior to 1981.[8] Subsequently, the norm has become approximately 40 percent. Technicians view a decline in this ratio below 30 percent as a bullish sign because it means that specialists are attempting to minimize their participation in short sales. In contrast, an increase in the proportion above 50 percent is a bearish sign.

Note two points about this ratio. First, do not expect it to be a long-run indicator; the nature of the specialists' portfolios will probably limit it to short-run movements. Second, there is a 2-week lag in reporting these data. The data for a week ending Friday, April 7, would appear in *Barron's* on Monday, April 24.

A study of a graph of the specialist short sales ratio indicated some support for its use as a buying signal.[9] In contrast, its use as part of a trading rule provided

insignificant excess returns. Also, this ratio has become extremely erratic in recent years, possibly because specialists are using stock index futures and/or options to hedge positions.

Debit Balances in Brokerage Accounts (Margin Debt) Debit balances in brokerage accounts represent borrowing by knowledgeable investors from their brokers. Such borrowing is called *margin debt*. It is contended these balances indicate the attitude of a sophisticated group of investors who engage in margin transactions. Therefore, an increase in debit balances would indicate to technicians an increase in purchasing by this astute group and would be a bullish sign. In contrast, a decline in debit balances would indicate an increase in the supply of stocks as these sophisticated investors liquidate positions. Alternatively, a decline could indicate less capital available for investing. In either case, this would be a bearish indicator.

Monthly data on margin debt is reported in *Barron's*. A potential problem with this series is that it does not include borrowing by investors from other sources such as banks.

Other Market Environment Indicators

In this subsection, we discuss several indicators to support investment decisions related to the aggregate market. These measures are not considered either contrary opinion indicators or useful tools to follow the smart money.

Breadth of Market Breadth of market measures the number of issues that have increased and those that have declined each day. It helps explain the cause of a change of direction in a composite market indicator series like the DJIA or the S&P 400. As discussed in Chapter 5, the major stock market indicator series are either confined to large, well-known stocks or are heavily influenced by the stocks of large firms because most are value-weighted. As a result, a stock market series might go up while most individual issues do not increase. This divergence between a series and its components causes concern because it means that most stocks are not participating in the rising market. Such a situation can be detected by examining the

---

[8]Notably, during the 1960s and early 1970s the norm for this ratio was about 55 percent. This is an example of a technique for which the decision ratio has changed over time.

[9]Frank K. Reilly and David Whitford, "A Test of the Specialists' Short Sale Ratio," *Journal of Portfolio Management* 8, no. 2 (Winter 1982): 12–18.

Table 15.1 *Daily Advances and Declines on the New York Stock Exchange*

	Day				
	1	**2**	**3**	**4**	**5**
Issues traded	1,608	1,641	1,659	1,651	1,612
Advances	1,010	950	608	961	1,025
Declines	309	350	649	333	294
Unchanged	289	341	402	357	293
Net advances (advances minus declines)	+701	+600	−41	+628	+731
Cumulative net advances	+701	+1,301	+1,260	+1,888	+2,619
Changes in DJIA	+20.47	+13.99	−8.18	+9.16	+15.56

Sources: New York Stock Exchange and *Barron's*.

Diffusion index An indicator of the number of stocks rising during a specified period of time relative to the number declining and not changing price.

advance–decline figures for all stocks on the exchange along with the overall market series.

A useful way to specify the advance–decline series for analysis is to create a cumulative series of net advances or net declines. Each day major newspapers publish figures on the number of issues on the NYSE that advanced, declined, or were unchanged. The figures for a 5-day sample, as would be reported in *Barron's*, are shown in Table 15.1. These figures, along with changes in the DJIA listed at the bottom of the table, indicate a strong market advance to a technician because the DJIA's increase was accompanied by a strong net advance figure, indicating that the increase reflected in the stock market series extended to most individual stocks. Even the results on Day 3, when the market declined 8 points, were somewhat encouraging. While the market was down, it was a very small net decline and the individual stocks were split just about 50–50, which points toward a fairly even environment.

An alternative specification of the series, a **diffusion index,** shows the number of stocks advancing plus one-half the number unchanged, divided by the total number of issues traded. To smooth the series, Merrill Lynch computes a 5-week moving average of daily figures, as shown in Figure 15.8.

Unusual or extreme readings indicate changes in the major trend of the market. For example, assume the major trend in the market has been up. The market has experienced intermediate corrections, however, typically accompanied by declines in the advance–decline diffusion index to values of 42 to 45. A subsequent market correction accompanied by a diffusion index value below 42 would suggest that the market's major trend may be turning down. In contrast, assume the major trend in the market had been down with intermediate recoveries typically accompanied by diffusion index values of 50 to 54. A market recovery with a diffusion index of about 59 would indicate to a technician the possibility of a change in the major declining trend.

Crossing from below 50 to above 50 indicates the market's intermediate-term trend if the moving average series turns from down to up. This advance–decline series is also used to measure intermediate trends and to signal overbought or oversold levels if it reaches very low or very high levels.

The usefulness of the advance–decline series is supposedly greatest at market peaks and troughs. At such times the composite value-weighted market series might be moving either up or down, but the move would not be broadly based, and most individual stocks might be moving in the opposite direction. Near a peak, the DJIA would be increasing, but the net advance–decline ratio for individual days would become negative, and the cumulative advance–decline series would begin to level off and decline. The *divergence* between the trend for the stock market series

Figure 15.8 *Time-Series Plot of Dow Jones Industrial Average and Advance–Decline Diffusion Index*

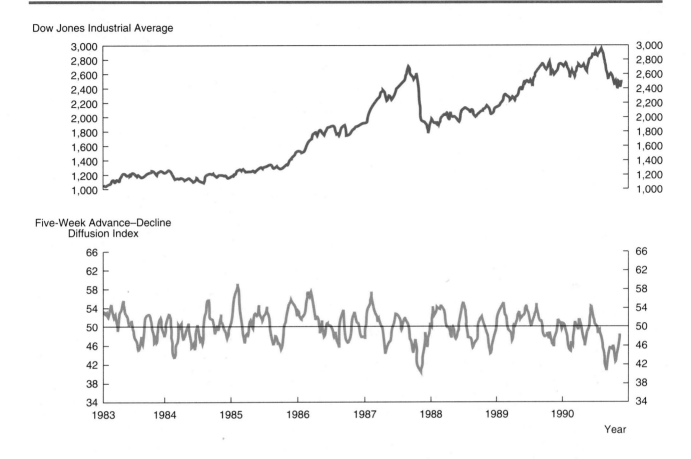

Dow Jones Industrial Average

Five-Week Advance–Decline
Diffusion Index

Year

Source: *Where the Indicators Stand* (New York: Merrill Lynch, November 1990).

and the cumulative advance–decline series signals a market peak.

As the market approached a trough, the composite market series would be declining, but the daily advance–decline ratio would become positive, and the cumulative advance–decline series would level off and begin to turn up before the aggregate market series.[10] In summary, a technician would look for the advance–decline series to indicate a change in trend before the composite stock market series. It is considered to be more useful at peaks than at troughs.[11]

Short Interest   The short interest is the cumulative number of shares that have been sold short by investors and not covered. This means that the investor has not purchased the shares sold short and returned them to the investor from whom they were borrowed. Technicians compute a short-interest ratio as the outstanding short interest divided by the average daily volume

---

[10]Ideally the performance of the series should work at both peaks and troughs. In fact, it appears to work best at peaks. At troughs the secondary stocks, which make up most of the issues, may remain weak until the low point and keep the advance–decline figures negative.

[11]This series has also been used to evaluate non-U.S. indexes. See Linda Sandler, "Advance–Decline Line, a Popular Indicator, Warns of Correction in Tokyo Stock Market," *The Wall Street Journal*, August 26, 1988: C1.

> **Moving average** The continually recalculated average of security prices for a period, often 200 days, to serve as an indication of the general trend of prices and also as a benchmark price.
>
> **Uptick** An incremental movement upward in a transaction price over the previous transaction price.
>
> **Downtick** An incremental movement downward in a transaction price compared to the previous transaction price.

of trading on the exchange. As an example, outstanding short interest on the NYSE of 500 million shares and average daily trading volume on the exchange of 170 million shares would give a short interest ratio of 2.94 (500/170). This means the outstanding short interest equals about 3 days' trading volume.

Technicians probably interpret this ratio contrary to your initial intuition. Because short sales reflect investors' expectations that stock prices will decline, one would typically expect an increase in the short-interest ratio to be bearish. On the contrary, technicians consider a high short-interest ratio bullish because it indicates *potential demand* when those who previously sold short must cover their sales.

The ratio fluctuated prior to 1984 between 1.00 and 1.75. Since about 1985 the ratio has increased, seldom falling as low as 1.50. In fact, its typical range in recent years has been between 2.0 and 3.0. The short-interest position is calculated by the stock exchanges and the NASD as of the 20th of each month and is reported about 2 days later in *The Wall Street Journal.*

This is another example of a change in the decision value over time. Recent experience regarding the range of values for this ratio would make a technician bullish when the short-interest ratio approached 3.0 and bearish if it declined toward 2.0.

A number of studies have examined the short-interest series as a predictor of stock-price movements with mixed results. For every study that supports the technique, another indicates that it should be rejected.[12] Technical analysts have pointed out that this ratio, and any ratio that involves short selling, has been affected by the introduction of other techniques for short-selling such as options and futures.

Stocks' 200-Day Moving Averages Technicians often compute moving averages of a series to determine its general trend. To examine individual stocks, the 200-day **moving average** of prices has been fairly popular. From these moving average series for numerous stocks, Media General Financial Services calculates the number of stocks currently trading above their moving average series as an indicator of general investor sentiment. Specifically, the market is considered to be overbought, with somewhat high prices, when 80 percent or more of the stocks being analyzed are trading above their 200-day moving averages. Technical analysts feel that an overbought market usually signals consolidation or a negative correction. In contrast, if less than 20 percent of the stocks are selling above their 200-day moving averages, the market is described as oversold, with rather low prices, so investors should be buying stocks in anticipation of positive corrections.

Block Uptick–Downtick Ratio As we discussed in Chapter 4, trading in the equity market (especially the NYSE) has come to be dominated by institutional investors who tend to trade in large blocks. As noted, about 50 percent of NYSE volume comes from block trades by institutions. The exchange can determine the price change that accompanied a particular block trade, stating whether the price of the stock involved in the block trade was higher than its price prior to the transaction. If the block trade price is above the prior transaction price, it takes place on an **uptick;** if the block trade price is below the prior transaction price, it takes place on a **downtick.**

Technicians assume, together with most investors, that the price change indicates whether the block trade was initiated by a buyer, in which case you would expect an uptick, or a seller, in which case you would expect a downtick. This line of reasoning led to the development of the uptick–downtick ratio, a measure of the number of buyers (uptick transactions) versus sellers (downtick transactions), to indicate institutional investor sentiment. As shown in Figure 15.9, this ratio has generally fluctuated in the range of 70, which reflects a bearish sentiment, to about 120, which indicates a bullish sentiment.

Stock Price and Volume Techniques

In the introduction to this chapter, we examined a hypothetical stock price chart that demonstrated the market cycle and its peaks and troughs. Also, we con-

---

[12]See, Joseph Vu and Paul Caster, "Why All the Interest in Short Interest?" *Financial Analysts Journal* 43, no. 4 (July–August 1987): 77–79.

Figure 15.9 *Time-Series Plot of Dow Jones Industrial Average and NYSE Block Uptick–Downtick Ratio*

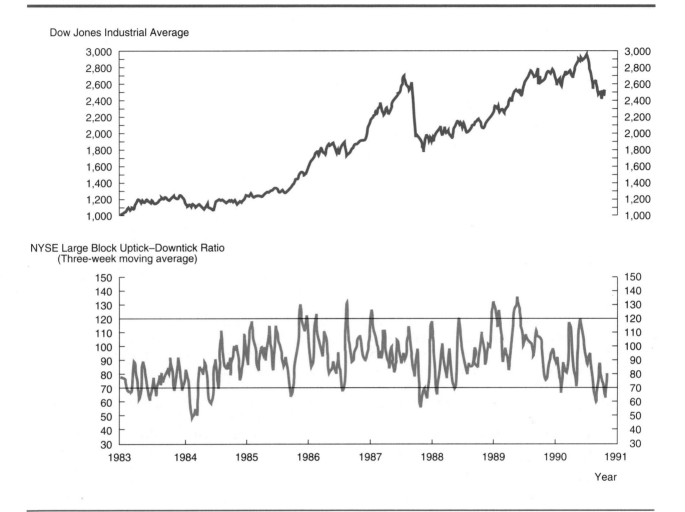

Source: *Where the Indicators Stand* (New York: Merrill Lynch, November 1990).

sidered rising and declining trend channels and breakouts from channels that signal new price trends or reversals of price trends. Although these price patterns are important, most technicians' trading rules for the overall market and individual stocks consider both stock price movements and corresponding volume movements. Because technicians believe that prices move in trends that persist, they seek to predict future price trends from analysis of past price trends along with changes in volume.

Dow Theory Any discussion of technical analysis using price and volume data should begin with a consideration of the Dow Theory because it was some of

the earliest work on this topic and it remains the basis for many indicators. In this section we show how Charles Dow combined price and volume information to analyze both individual stocks and the overall stock market.

Charles Dow published *The Wall Street Journal* during the late 1800s.[13] Dow described stock prices as moving in trends analogous to the movement of water.

---

[13]A study that discusses the theory and provides support for it is David A Glickstein and Rolf E. Wubbels, "Dow Theory Is Alive and Well," *Journal of Portfolio Management* 9, no. 3 (Spring 1983): 28–32.

Figure 15.10 *Sample Bullish Price Pattern*

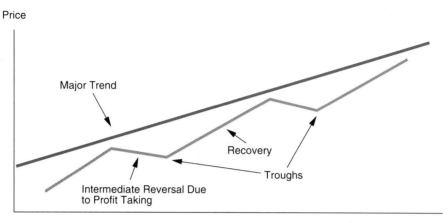

He postulated three types of price movements over time: (1) major trends that resemble tides in the ocean, (2) intermediate trends that resemble waves, and (3) short-run movements that resemble ripples. Followers of the Dow Theory hope to detect the direction of the major price trend (tide), recognizing that intermediate movements (waves) will move in the opposite direction. They recognize that a major market advance does not move in a straight line, but rather shows deviations including small price declines as some investors decide to take profits.

Figure 15.10 shows the typical bullish pattern. The technician would look for every recovery to reach a new peak above the prior peak, and this price rise should be accompanied by heavy trading volume. Alternatively, each reversal that follows an increase to a new peak should reach a trough above the prior trough, with relatively light volume of trading indicating that only a limited number of investors are interested in profit-taking at these levels. When this pattern of price and volume movements changes, the major trend may be entering a period of consolidation or major reversal. When using the Dow Theory to analyze the overall stock market, technicians also look for confirmation of peaks and troughs in the industrial stock price series by subsequent peaks and troughs in the transportation series. Such an "echo" indicates that the change in direction is occurring across the total market.

Importance of Volume As noted in the description of the Dow Theory, technicians watch volume changes along with price movements to detect changes in supply and demand for individual stock or for stocks, in general. A price movement in one direction means that the net effect on price is in that direction, but that does not tell us how widespread the excess demand or supply is at that time. A price increase of one-half point on volume of 1,000 shares demonstrates excess demand, but little overall interest. In contrast, a 1-point increase on volume of 30,000 shares shows a lot of interest and strong demand.

Therefore, a technician looks for a price increase on heavy volume relative to the stock's normal trading volume as an indication of bullish activity. Following the same line of reasoning, a price decline with heavy volume is very bearish, because it reflects a strong and widespread desire to sell the stock. A long-term bullish pattern would show price increases accompanied by heavy volume while small price reversals occur with light trading volume, indicating only limited interest in selling and taking profits.

Technicians also use a ratio of upside–downside volume as an indicator of short-term momentum for the aggregate stock market. Each day the stock exchanges announce the volume of trading in stocks that gained value divided by the volume of trading in stocks that declined. These data are reported daily in *The*

> **Support level** A price at which a technician would expect a substantial increase in demand for a stock to reverse a declining trend that was due to profit taking.
>
> **Resistance level** A price at which a technician would expect a substantial increase in the supply of a stock to reverse a rising trend.
>
> **Relative-strength ratio** The ratio of a stock price or an industry index value to a market indicator series, indicating performance relative to the overall market.

Wall Street Journal and weekly in *Barron's*. Technicians consider this ratio to be an indicator of investor sentiment and use it to pinpoint excesses. The upside–downside ratio typically ranges between 1.50, which technicians feel indicates an overbought position leading them to be bearish, and a value of 0.70, which reflects an oversold position inspiring bullish attitudes.

Support and Resistance Levels A **support level** is named for the price range at which the technician would expect a substantial increase in demand for a stock. Generally, a support level will develop after the price has increased and the stock has begun to reverse because of profit taking. Technicians reason that at some price, other investors will buy who did not buy during the first price increase and have been waiting for a small reversal to get into the stock. When the price reaches the point at which they want to buy, demand surges and price and volume begin to increase again.

A **resistance level** is the name for the price range at which the technician would expect an increase in the supply of stock to cause any price increase to reverse abruptly. A resistance level tends to develop after a stock has declined steadily from a higher price level. In this case, technicians reason that the decline in price leads some investors who acquired the stock at a higher price to look for an opportunity to sell it near their breakeven points. The supply of stock owned by these investors is waiting to be sold. Professionals refer to this stock as *overhanging* the market. When the price rebounds to these investors' target price, there is a resistance to a further increase because this overhanging supply of stock comes to the market and dramatically reverses the price increase.

Moving-Average Line Earlier we discussed how technicians use a moving average of past stock prices as an indicator of long-run trends and how they watch the relationship of current prices to this trend for signals of a change. We also noted that a 200-day moving average is a relatively popular measure for individual stocks and the aggregate market. In this discussion, we want to revisit this moving average price line and add volume to the analysis.

If the overall price trend of the market has been down, the moving-average price line would generally lie above current prices. If prices reverse and break through the moving-average line from below accompanied by heavy trading volume, most technicians would consider this a very positive change and a reversal of the declining trend. In contrast, if the price of a stock had been rising, the moving-average line would also be rising, but it would still lie below current prices. If current prices broke through the moving-average line from above accompanied by heavy trading volume, this would be considered a bearish pattern that would signal a reversal of the long-run rising trend.[14]

Relative Strength Technicians believe that once a trend begins, it will continue until some major event causes a change in direction. This is also true, they believe, of relative performance. If an individual stock or an industry group is outperforming the market, technicians believe it will continue to do so.

Therefore, technicians compute weekly or monthly **relative-strength ratios** for individual stocks and industry groups as the ratio of the price of a stock or an industry index to the value for some stock market series like the DJIA or the S&P 400. If this ratio increases over time, it shows that the stock or industry is outperforming the market, and a technician would expect this superior performance to continue. Relative-strength ratios work during declining as well as rising markets. In a declining market, if the price of the stock does not decline as much as the market does, the stock's relative-strength ratio will continue to rise. Technicians believe that if this ratio is stable or increases during a bear market, the stock

---

[14]This technique is tested in J. C. Van Horne and G. C. Parker, "The Random Walk Theory: An Empirical Test," *Financial Analysts Journal* 23, no. 6 (November–December 1967): 57–64.

Figure 15.11 *How to Read Industry Group Charts*

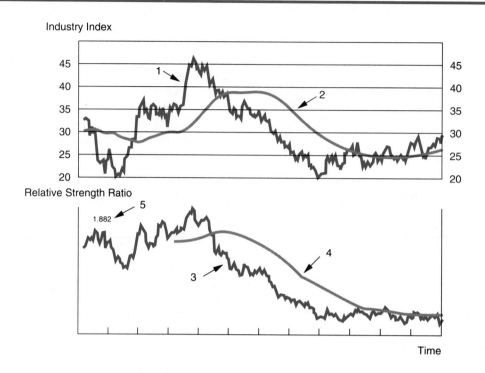

The industry group charts in this report display the following elements:
1. A line chart of the weekly close of the Standard & Poor's Industry Group Index for the last 9½ years, with the index range indicated to the left.
2. A line of the 75-week moving average of the Standard & Poor's Industry Group Index.
3. A relative-strength line of the Standard & Poor's Industry Group Index compared with the New York Stock Exchange Composite Index.
4. A 75-week moving average of relative strength.
5. A volatility reading that measures the maximum amount by which the index has outperformed (or underperformed) the NYSE Composite Index during the time period displayed.

Source: *Technical Analysis of Industry Groups* (New York: Merrill Lynch, monthly).

should do very well during the subsequent bull market.[15]

Merrill Lynch publishes relative-strength charts for stocks and industry groups. Figure 15.11 describes how to read the charts, and Figure 15.12 includes graphs for an industry with strong positive relative strength and one with poor relative strength.

Bar Charting Technicians use charts that show daily, weekly, or monthly time series of stock prices. For a given interval, the technical analyst plots the high and low prices and connects the two points vertically to form a bar. Typically, he or she will also draw a small horizontal line across this vertical bar to indicate the closing price. Finally, almost all bar charts list the volume of trading at the bottom of the chart so that the technical analyst can relate the price and volume movements. A typical bar chart in Figure 15.13 shows data for the DJIA from *The Wall Street Journal* along with the volume figures for the NYSE.

[15]A study that supports the technique is James Bohan, "Relative Strength: Further Positive Evidence," *Journal of Portfolio Management* 7, no. 1 (Fall 1981): 39–46. A study that rejects the technique is Robert D. Arnott, "Relative Strength Revisited," *Journal of Portfolio Management* 6, no. 3 (Spring 1979): 19–23. Finally, a study that combines it with modern portfolio theory is John S. Brush and Keith Boles, "The Predictive Power in Relative Strength and CAPM," *Journal of Portfolio Management* 9, no. 4 (Summer 1983): 20–23.

Figure 15.12   *Example of Relative-Strength Charts for Two Industries*

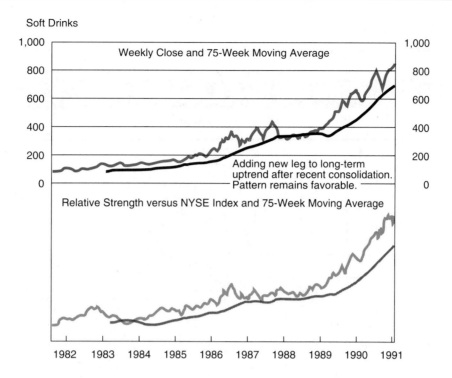

Soft Drinks

Weekly Close and 75-Week Moving Average

Adding new leg to long-term uptrend after recent consolidation. Pattern remains favorable.

Relative Strength versus NYSE Index and 75-Week Moving Average

1982 1983 1984 1985 1986 1987 1988 1989 1990 1991

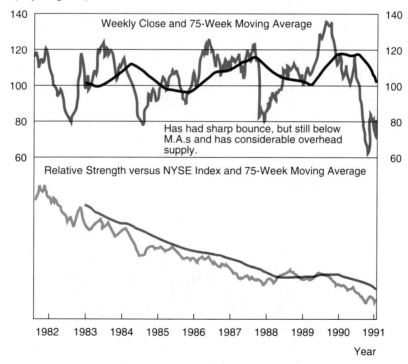

Banks (major regional)

Weekly Close and 75-Week Moving Average

Has had sharp bounce, but still below M.A.s and has considerable overhead supply.

Relative Strength versus NYSE Index and 75-Week Moving Average

1982 1983 1984 1985 1986 1987 1988 1989 1990 1991

Year

Miscellaneous—Pollution Control: Browning-Ferris Industries; Rollins Environmental; Waste Management; Zurn Industries
Financial and Building—Interest Sensitive—Banks (major regional): Bank of Boston; Barnett Banks of Florida; First Interstate Bancorp; First Republic; Mellon Bank; NCNB Corp; NBD Bancorp; Norwest Corp; Wells Fargo

Source: *Technical Analysis of Industry Groups* (New York: Merrill Lynch, February 1991).

Figure 15.13　**A Typical Bar Chart**

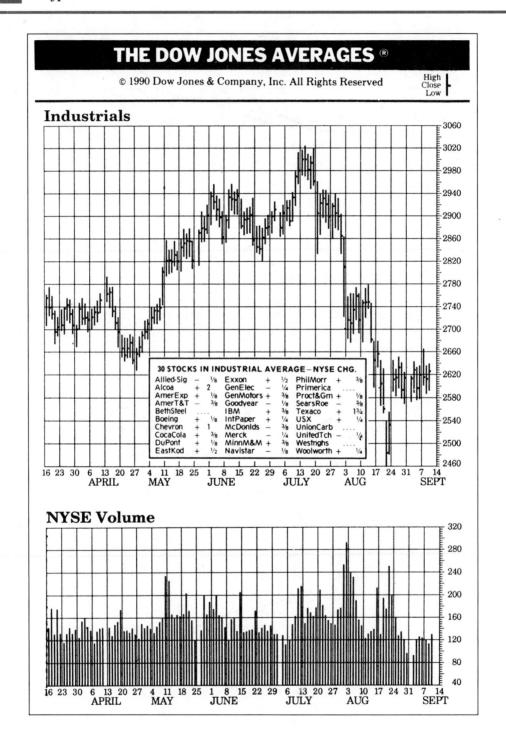

Source: "The Dow Jones Averages," *The Wall Street Journal*, September 13, 1990. Reprinted by permission of *The Wall Street Journal*, © Dow Jones & Company, Inc. 1990. All Rights Reserved.

Figure 15.14   *Sample Point-and-Figure Chart*

```
50  |  |  |  |  |  |  |  |  |
48  |  |  |  |  |  |  |  |  |
46  |  |  X |  |  |  |  |  |
44  |  |  X |  |  |  |  |  |
42  X | X | X |  |  |  |  |  |
40  X | X | X |  |  |  |  |  |
38  |  X | X |  |  |  |  |  |
36  |  X | X |  |  |  |  |  |
34  |  X | X |  |  |  |  |  |
32  |  |  |  |  |  |  |  |  |
30  |  |  |  |  |  |  |  |  |
```

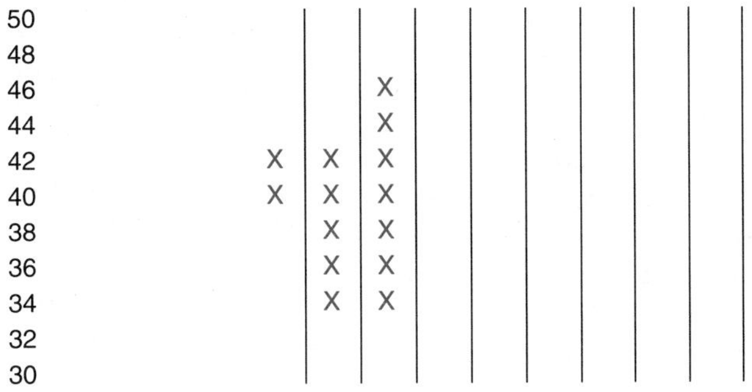

The technical analyst might also include a line to show a 200-day moving average for the series, possibly identifying expected resistance and support levels based upon past price and volume patterns. Finally, a bar chart for an individual stock might add a relative-strength line. Technicians include as many price and volume series as is reasonable on one chart and, based on the performance of several technical indicators, try to arrive at a consensus about the future movement for the stock.

Point-and-Figure Charts   Another graph popular with technicians is the point-and-figure chart.[16] Unlike the bar chart, which typically includes all ending prices and volumes to show a trend, the point-and-figure chart includes only significant price changes, regardless of their timing. The technician determines what price interval to record as significant (1 point, 2 points, etc.) and when to note price reversals.

To demonstrate how a technical analyst would use such a chart, assume that you want to chart a volatile stock that is currently selling for $40 a share. Because of its volatility, you believe that anything less than a 2-point price change is not significant. Also, you consider anything less than a 4-point movement in the opposite direction quite minor. You would set up a chart similar to the one in Figure 15.14, which starts at 40 and progresses in 2-point increments. If the stock moves to 42, you would place an X in the box above 40 and do nothing else until the stock rose to

44 or dropped to 38 (a 4-point reversal from its high of 42). If it dropped to 38, you would move a column to the right, which indicates a reversal in direction, and begin at 38 (fill in boxes at 42 and 40). If the stock price dropped to 34, you would enter an X at 36 and another at 34. If the stock then rose to 38 (another 4-point reversal), you would move to the next column and begin at 38 going up (filling in 34 and 36). If the stock then went to 46, you would fill in more Xs as shown and wait for further increases or a reversal.

Depending upon how fast the prices rise and fall, this process might take anywhere from 2 to 6 months. Given these figures, the technical analyst would attempt to determine trends just as with the bar chart.

As always, you look for breakouts to either higher or lower price levels.[17] A long horizontal movement with many reversals but no major trends up or down would be considered a period of consolidation. The technician would speculate that the stock is moving from buyers to sellers and back again with no strong support from either group that would indicate a consensus about its direction. Once the stock breaks out and moves up or down after a period of consolidation, analysts anticipate a major move because previous trading set the stage for it. Point-and-figure charts differ from bar charts by providing compact records of movements, because they record price changes that are significant for the stock being analyzed. Therefore, some technicians prefer point-and-figure charts

[16]Daniel Seligman, "The Mystique of Point-and-Figure," *Fortune,* March 1962: 113–115.

[17]A study that questions the usefulness of various price patterns is Robert A. Levy, "The Predictive Significance of Five Point Chart Patterns," *Journal of Business* 44, no. 3 (July 1971): 316–323.

> **Group rotation** The tendency for demand to shift among industry groups or other market segments.

because they are easier to work with and give more vivid pictures of price movements.

This section discussed technical indicators that are widely used and alluded to in the financial press. As noted on several occasions, technical analysts do not generally concentrate on only a few indicators or even general categories, but seek to derive a feel for the market or a stock based on a consensus of numerous technical indicators.

Technical Analysis of Foreign Markets

Our discussion thus far has concentrated on U.S. markets, but these techniques apply to foreign markets, as well, as numerous analysts and firms have discovered.

Merrill Lynch, for instance, prepares separate technical analysis publications for individual countries such as Japan, Germany, and the United Kingdom as well as a summary of all world markets. The examples that follow show that many techniques are limited to price and volume data rather than using the more detailed information described for the U.S. market. This emphasis on price and volume data is necessary because the more detailed information that is available on the U.S. market through the SEC, the stock exchanges, the NASDAQ system, and various investment services is not always available in other countries.

Also, individuals who concentrate on the analysis of foreign markets point out that these markets show a greater tendency toward **group rotation,** or major shifts in interest among segments of the market. For example, we observe shifts among industry groups such as autos, construction, and electronics, or among major sectors of the market such as secondary stocks

Figure 15.15 **FTSE 100 Price Index from March 16, 1990 to March 18, 1991, Daily**

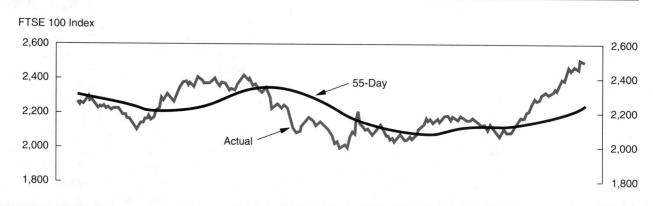
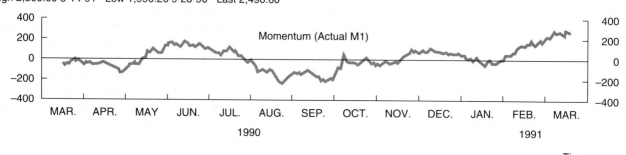

Sources: Datastream; Merrill Lynch Market Analysis/International Research.

versus large, blue-chip stocks. This means that industries or sectors become hot and cool down extremely quickly.

Foreign Stock Market Series   Figure 15.15 displays the time-series plot and moving average series for the Financial Times Stock Exchange 100 Index (FTSE 100). In a separate written analysis, the market analysts at Merrill Lynch estimate support and resistance levels for the London Stock Exchange series and comment on the longer-term outlook for the United Kingdom stock market, the British pound, and various U.K. industries.

Figure 15.16 is a similar chart for the Japanese Nikkei Stock Average. This series has experienced substantial volatility since the 1987 crash. Besides two subsequent periods of substantial price declines, the yen has been weak relative to the U.S. dollar.

Merrill Lynch publishes similar charts and discussions for 10 other countries and a summary release that compares the countries and ranks them by stock and currency performance. The next section discusses the technical analysis of currency markets.

Technical Analysis of Foreign Exchange Rates
On numerous occasions we have discussed the importance of changes in foreign exchange rates and their impact on the rates of return on foreign securities. Because of the importance of these relationships, technicians who trade bonds and stocks in world markets examine the time-series data of various individual currencies such as the British pound. They also analyze the spreads between currencies such as the difference between the Japanese yen (¥) and the German deutschemark (DM).

Figure 15.16   *Japan Nikkei Stock Average (225) Price Index from March 16, 1990 to March 18, 1991, Daily*

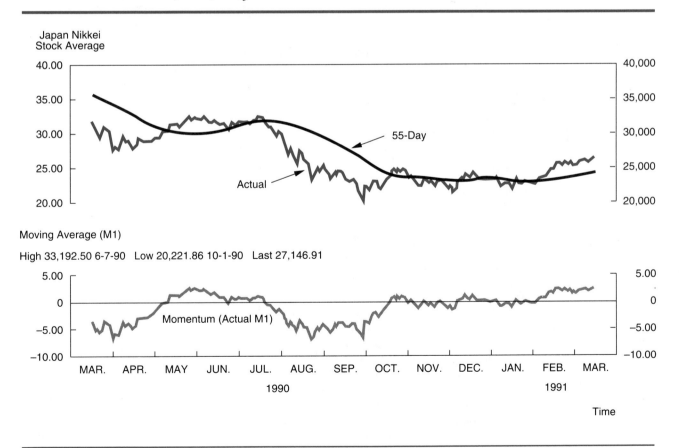

Sources: Datastream; Merrill Lynch Market Analysis/International Research.

Figure 15.17 *Examples of Technical Analysis Charts for the Fixed-Income Market*

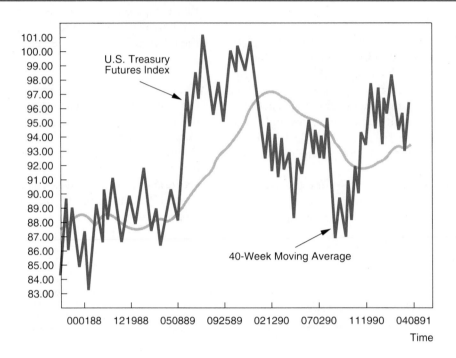

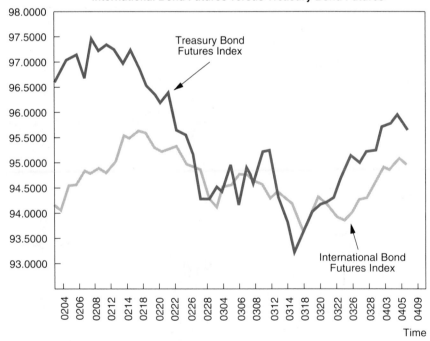

Source: *Interest Rates* (New York: Merrill Lynch, April 10, 1991).

Bonds versus Treasury-Corporate Spread

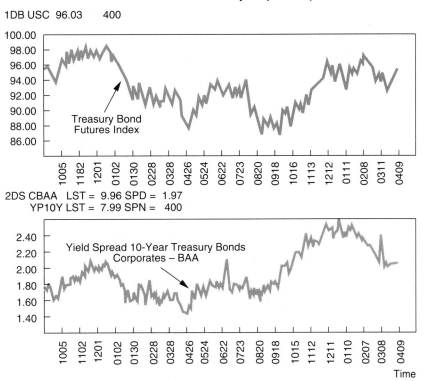

1DB USC 96.03   400

Treasury Bond
Futures Index

2DS CBAA LST = 9.96 SPD = 1.97
      YP10Y LST = 7.99 SPN =   400

Yield Spread 10-Year Treasury Bonds
Corporates – BAA

Time

Bonds versus Stocks

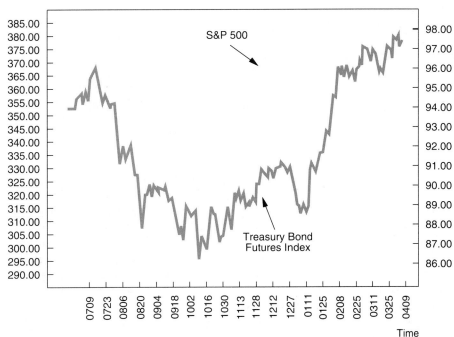

S&P 500

Treasury Bond
Futures Index

Time

Technical Analysis of Bond Markets

Through our description of the technical tools for the analysis of the U.S. and world stock market, we have emphasized the extensive use of technical analysis. You should be aware that technicians also apply these techniques to the bond market. The theory and rationale for technical analysis of bonds is the same as for stocks and many of the same techniques are used. As with stocks, the techniques apply to an individual bond, several bonds, or a bond index. A major difference is that almost no consideration of volume of trading for bonds is possible because these data are not generally available since most bonds are traded OTC, where volume is not reported.

Figure 15.17 gives four sample technical charts for various segments of the bond market. The first chart is the plot of the U.S. Treasury Bond Futures Index, including a 40-week moving average line to indicate the long-term trend for this index. The second chart shows the relationship between the Treasury Bond Futures Index and the yield spread between 10-year Treasury bonds and BAA corporate bonds. This yield spread reflects the required risk premium on corporate bonds.

The third chart shows the prevailing relationship between the U.S. and international bond markets. Finally, Chart 4 indicates the relationship between the stock and bond markets in the United States. As shown, during some periods they are highly correlated, while during the middle time interval there are clear differences.

These examples show how technical analysis can be and is applied to the bond market as well as the stock market.

Summary

■ Whether you want to base your investment decisions on fundamental analysis, technical analysis, or a belief in efficient markets, you should be aware of the principles and practice of technical analysis. Numerous investors do believe in and use technical analysis, the large investment houses provide extensive support for technical analysis, and a large proportion of the discussion related to securities markets in the media, whether written or on TV, is based upon a technical view of the market. Now that you are aware of technical analysis principles, techniques, and indicators, you will recognize this tendency of reporters.

■ Two main differences separate technical analysts and those who believe in efficient markets. The first, related to the information dissemination process, is concerned with whether one assumes that everybody gets information at about the same time. The second difference is concerned with how quickly investors adjust security prices to reflect new information. Technical analysts believe that the information dissemination process differs for different people. They believe that news takes time to travel from the insider and expert to the individual investor. They also believe that price adjustments are not instantaneous. As a result, they contend that security prices move in trends that persist and, therefore, past price trends and volume information along with other indicators can help you determine future price trends.

■ We discussed technical trading rules under four general categories: contrary-opinion rules, follow-the-smart-money tactics, other market indicators, and stock price and volume techniques. These techniques can also be applied to foreign markets and to the analysis of currency exchange rates. In addition, technical analysis has been used to project interest rates and to determine the prevailing sentiment in the bond market.

■ Most technicians follow several indicators and decision rules at any point in time and attempt to derive a consensus decision to buy, sell, or do nothing.[18] Many technicians conclude on many occasions to do nothing.

■ At this point, we have finished our discussion of fundamental analysis and technical analysis. The third approach to making investment decisions is implied by the efficient market hypothesis (EMH). We will discuss this final approach in Chapter 22.

Questions

1. Technical analysts believe that one can use past price changes to predict future price changes. How do they justify this belief?
2. Technicians contend that stock prices move in trends that persist for periods of time. What do technicians believe happens in the real world to cause these trends?

---

[18]An analysis using numerous indicators is Jerome Baesel, George Shows, and Edward Thorp, "Can Joe Granville Time the Market?" *Journal of Portfolio Management* 8, no. 3 (Spring 1982): 5–9.

3. Briefly discuss the problems with fundamental analysis that are considered to be advantages for technical analysis.

4. Discuss some disadvantages of technical analysis.

5. If the mutual fund cash position were to increase close to 12 percent, would a technician consider this bullish or bearish? Give two reasons why the technical analyst would feel this way.

6. Assume a significant decline in credit balances at brokerage firms. Discuss why a technician would consider this to be bearish.

7. If the bearish sentiment index of advisory service opinions were to increase to 61 percent, would a technician consider this to be bullish or bearish? Discuss the reasoning behind your answer.

8. Define the Confidence Index and describe the reasoning behind it. What problem arises because the Confidence Index is demand-oriented?

9. Suppose the ratio of specialists' short sales to total short sales increases to 70 percent. Discuss why a technician would consider this bullish or bearish.

10. Why is an increase in debit balances considered bullish?

11. Describe the Dow Theory and its three components. Which component is most important? What is the reason for an intermediate reversal?

12. Why is trading volume important to a technician? Describe a bearish price and volume pattern, and discuss why it is considered bearish.

13. Describe the computation of the breadth of market index. Discuss the logic behind using it to identify a peak in stock prices.

14. During a 10-day trading period, the cumulative net advance series goes from 1,752 to 1,253. During this same period of time, the DJIA goes from 2,757 to 2,807. As a technician, discuss what this set of events would mean to you.

15. Describe a support level and a resistance level, and explain the reasoning behind each of them.

16. What is the purpose of computing a moving-average line for a stock? Describe a bullish pattern using a moving-average line and the volume of trading. Discuss why this pattern is considered bullish.

17. Explain how you would construct a relative-strength series for an individual stock or an industry group. What would it mean to say a stock experienced good relative strength during a bear market?

18. Discuss why most technicians follow several technical rules and attempt to derive a consensus.

Problems

1. Select a stock on the NYSE and construct a daily high, low, and close bar chart for it that lists volume for 10 trading days.

2. Compute the relative-strength ratio for the stock in Problem 1 relative to the S&P 500 Index, and prepare a table that includes all the data and indicates the computations as follows:

	Closing Price		Relative-Strength Ratio	
Day	Stock	S&P 500	Stock Price	S&P 500

3. Plot the relative-strength ratio computed in Problem 2 on your bar chart. Discuss whether the stock's relative strength is bullish or bearish.

4. Currently, Charlotte Art Importers is selling at $32 per share. While you are somewhat dubious about technical analysis, you feel that you should know how technicians who use point-and-figure charts would view this stock. You decide to note 1-point movements and 3-point reversals. You gather the following price information:

Date	Price	Date	Price	Date	Price
4/1	$23\frac{1}{2}$	4/18	33	5/3	27
4/4	$28\frac{1}{2}$	4/19	$35\frac{3}{8}$	5/4	$26\frac{1}{2}$
4/5	28	4/20	37	5/5	28
4/6	28	4/21	$38\frac{1}{2}$	5/6	$28\frac{1}{4}$
4/7	$29\frac{3}{4}$	4/22	36	5/9	$28\frac{1}{8}$
4/8	$30\frac{1}{2}$	4/25	35	5/10	$28\frac{1}{4}$
4/11	$30\frac{1}{2}$	4/26	$34\frac{1}{4}$	5/11	$29\frac{1}{8}$
4/12	$32\frac{1}{8}$	4/27	$33\frac{1}{8}$	5/12	$30\frac{1}{4}$
4/13	32	4/28	$32\frac{7}{8}$	5/13	$29\frac{7}{8}$

Plot the point-and-figure chart using Xs for uptrends and Os for downtrends. How would a technician evaluate these movements? Discuss why you would expect the technician to buy, sell, or hold.

References

Colby, Robert W., and Thomas A. Mayers. *The Encyclopedia of Technical Market Indicators.* Homewood, Ill.: Dow Jones-Irwin, 1988.

Dines, James. *How the Average Investor Can Use Technical Analysis for Stock Profits.* New York: Dines Chart Corp., 1974.

Edwards, R. D., and John Magee, Jr. *Technical Analysis of Stock Trends*, 5th ed. Springfield, Mass.: John Magee, 1988.

Fosback, Norman G. *Stock Market Logic*. Fort Lauderdale, Fla.: Institute for Economic Research, 1976.

Grant, Dwight. "Market Timing: Strategies to Consider." *Journal of Portfolio Managements*, no. 4 (Summer 1979).

Hardy, C. Colburn. *Investor's Guide to Technical Analysis*. New York: McGraw-Hill, 1978.

Levy, Robert A. *The Relative Strength Concept of Common Stock Price Forecasting*. Larchmont, N.Y.: Investors Intelligence, 1968.

Murphy, John J. *Technical Analysis of the Futures Markets*, 2d ed. New York: McGraw-Hill, 1985.

Pring, Martin J. *Technical Analysis Explained*, 2d ed. New York: McGraw Hill, 1985.

Shaw, Alan R. "Market Timing and Technical Analysis." *Financial Analysts Handbook*, 2d ed. Ed. by Sumner N. Levine. Homewood, Ill.: Dow Jones-Irwin, 1988.

Zweig, Martin E. *Winning on Wall Street*. New York: Warner Books, 1986.

Additional Investment Opportunities

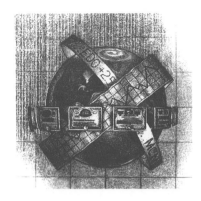

In this section we complete our discussion of investment alternatives by analyzing several investment instruments that will widen your range of risk–return possibilities. In Chapter 16 we discuss stock options, which have become very popular due to their versatility and limited risk. In Chapter 17 we discuss warrants and convertible securities, which reduce the cost of capital for issuing companies by adding features that investors find attractive. Leverage gives appeal to warrants, while convertible securities typically provide downside protection and good upside potential.

In Chapter 18 we consider the general area of futures contracts and the specific topic of financial futures, which have generated substantially increased trading volume since 1979. We discuss how they are traded, who can use them, and how to use them for portfolio insurance, index arbitrage, and foreign currency hedging. We present examples of several typical transactions for U.S. and global investors.

The final chapter in this section (Chapter 19) considers an alternative to analyzing securities and managing your own portfolio—investment companies. After a basic explanation of the concept of investment companies and a description of the major forms, we examine the numerous types available, including money market funds, REITs, high-growth companies, international stocks and bonds, high-yield (junk) bonds, and option funds. It will become clear that almost any investment objective can be met by investing in one or several investment companies. A review of several studies that have examined the performance of funds indicates that on average they are not able to outperform the market, but they are capable of carrying out a number of functions important to investors.

16

Stock Options

An option gives the holder the right to buy or sell a security at a specified price during a designated period of time (usually from 3 to 9 months). Call options give the owner the right to purchase and put options the right to sell a given number of shares. Although these options have been available on the OTC market for many years, they have only become popular since the Chicago Board Options Exchange (CBOE) was established. Actions by the CBOE and other stock exchanges that have listed options have encouraged options trading by individual and institutional investors. Options offer a range of investment alternatives from very speculative to very conservative strategies.

In the first section of this chapter we discuss the creation and operation of option exchanges, including a brief history of the options exchanges, which are relatively new when compared to stock exchanges. We also discuss how those markets operate and the development of competing markets for options. The terminology used to describe options differs from that for stocks and bonds, as we discuss in the second section.

As we point out in the introduction to this part, options have become popular investments because they expand the risk–return alternatives available to investors. In the third section we demonstrate a number of trading strategies ranging from fairly aggressive speculation to conservative hedges. Because many of these strategies depend on the correct valuation of options, in the fourth section we consider the individual variables that determine this value and their expected impact. We present the full valuation model in an appendix.

In the following two sections we discuss two relatively new option contracts. The first are options on stock indexes rather than on individual

Option Clearing Corporation (OCC) A central organization affiliated with the CBOE that guarantees the writer's performance. The OCC is the intermediary in each transaction between the buyer and the writer of an option contract.

stocks. The second, options on foreign currency, are important for global investors. We conclude the chapter with a brief discussion of the risk–return experience for investors in the options markets.

Creation and Operation of Options Exchanges

While the stock exchanges were established in the 18th and 19th centuries, the options exchanges were not created until the 1970s. In this section we discuss the advantages of such exchanges, along with how they are organized and some of their differences from the stock exchanges. We also analyze the growth in total volume of trading and the distribution of trading volume among the exchanges. Finally, we discuss the development of competing markets on alternative exchanges.

Recent History of Options Trading

For a number of years it has been possible to buy and sell put and call options on the OTC market. Investment firms that were members of the Put and Call Association helped investors negotiate specific put and call options on selected stocks. These arrangements were very flexible, but somewhat disorganized. An investor who wanted to buy an option on a stock would contact a member of the association and indicate the stock involved and the desired time period. The investment firm would find an interested seller, and the parties would negotiate the price of the option. Limited secondary trading in these individually negotiated options usually made it difficult to sell them prior to maturity.

The market for stock options changed dramatically when the CBOE was established on April 26, 1973, and began trading options on 16 stocks. The CBOE brought numerous innovations to the OTC system:

1. It created a central marketplace with regulatory, surveillance, disclosure, and price dissemination capabilities.
2. It introduced the **Option Clearing Corporation** as the guarantor of every CBOE option. Standing as the opposite party to every trade, the Clearing Corporation enables buyers and sellers of options to terminate their positions in the market at any time by making offsetting transactions.
3. It standardized expiration dates. Most CBOE options expire in January, April, July, and October, while another set expire in February, May, August, and November. It also standardized exercise prices, which are the prices per share at which holders can buy or sell stock upon exercise of options, as we will explain.
4. It created a secondary market for options. While an option is a contract guaranteeing the owner the right to buy or sell stock at an agreed-upon price, few option buyers actually exercise their options and buy or sell stock. Most sell their options on the exchanges. Before option exchanges were established, the buyers and sellers of OTC options were essentially committed to their positions until the expiration dates if they didn't exercise the options.

Operation of the CBOE

Readers understand well the trading mechanisms on the NYSE and other stock exchanges. You will recall that the specialists at the center of the stock exchanges have two functions: (1) as brokers who maintain the limit-order books, and (2) as market-makers (dealers) who buy and sell for their own accounts to ensure the operation of fair and orderly markets for investors. Some observers have expressed concern because the specialist has monopoly information from the limit-order book and also enjoys a monopoly as the sole market-maker on the exchange.

The structure of the CBOE differs from that of the stock exchange since it separates the broker and dealer functions. The person who handles the limit-order book on the CBOE (called the *board broker*) is not a market-maker. The board broker handles the limit-order book and accepts only public orders, much like the role of the *Saitori* on the Tokyo Stock Exchange. In addition, the limit-order book is public! Above the trading post for a particular option, a video screen shows information regarding the last trade, the current bid and ask price for the option, and the limit orders on the book.

Besides separating the broker role from the market-maker (dealer) role, the CBOE provides competing market-makers for all options. These members can trade only for themselves and are not allowed to handle public orders. As an example, four members are designated as primary market-makers for IBM options.

Each market-maker is assigned three or four primary options and another three or four secondary options. These market-makers must concentrate 70 percent of their trading activity on their primary issues and provide liquidity for individual and institutional investors. The multiple market-makers are expected to provide more funds for trading and to improve markets through added competition.

A third category of CBOE members, floor brokers, only execute orders for their customers in the same manner as floor brokers on stock exchanges.

Volume of Trading

The CBOE started with options on 16 stocks. This number increased gradually and other exchanges were established during 1975 and 1976 as shown in Table 16.1. As of 1990, the various exchanges combined traded in put and call options for 683 stocks. As you might expect, the options are based on stocks of large companies that enjoy active secondary markets. In fact, the criterion for listing an option is the trading activity of the underlying stock.

Trading volume has grown phenomenally. During the first full month of trading on the CBOE (May 1973), about 31,000 contracts were traded. By early 1990, the monthly trading volume on five exchanges was almost 12 million contracts. The annual totals appear in Table 16.2, along with a breakdown for the individual exchanges. This shows that the trading volume in call options is substantially larger than the volume of put options because investors prefer to buy long rather than sell short. As you might expect, the purchase of a call typically reflects a bullish outlook, while you might buy a put if you were bearish on a stock.

Competing Markets for Options

The breakdown of volume among exchanges reflects the initial dominance of the CBOE. While the proportion of options traded on the CBOE has declined, it is still the largest exchange, followed by the AMEX. The CBOE dominates the trading of index options even more. As Table 16.3 shows, the CBOE proportion of index option trading has grown from 76 percent to reach over 87 percent in 1989. Overall volume peaked in 1986, then declined sharply in 1988, followed by a small recovery in 1989.

When the AMEX established its option market in January 1975, it selected 15 stocks that were not traded on the CBOE. The exchanges refrained from establishing competing markets, a practice that continued when the Philadelphia Exchange began trading in options. This changed in late 1976, when the AMEX listed several CBOE issues, and the CBOE responded by listing some AMEX issues. These dual listings were subsequently rescinded, though.

Table 16.1 *Option Stocks Listed on Exchanges: February 1990*

Exchange	Starting Date	Number of Stocks[a]
Chicago Board Option Exchange (CBOE)	April 26, 1973	196
American Stock Exchange	January 13, 1975	169
Philadelphia Exchange	June 29, 1975	138
Pacific Exchange	April 9, 1976	131
Midwest Exchange	December 10, 1976	—[b]
New York Stock Exchange	February 13, 1985	49
Total		683

[a]These are options that are only traded on one exchange.
[b]Merged with CBOE on June 2, 1980

Table 16.2 *Put and Call Equity Option Contracts Traded on Different Exchanges*

	CBOE		AMEX		Philadelphia		Pacific		Midwest[a]		NYSE		
	No.	%	No.	%	No.	%	No.	%	No.	%	No.	%	Total
A. Call Options (thousands)													
1977	23,581	63.0%	9,657	25.8%	2,002	5.3%	1,704	4.6%	497	1.3%	—	—	37,441
1978	30,298	59.2	13,540	26.5	2,974	5.8	2,325	4.5	2,041	4.0	—	—	51,178
1979	30,123	53.7	16,505	29.4	4,527	8.1	3,118	5.6	1,847	3.3	—	—	56,120
1980	42,942	53.6	24,955	31.1	6,705	8.4	4,410	5.5	1,111	1.4	—	—	80,123
1981	40,801	50.4	26,430	32.7	8,104	10.0	5,610	6.9	—	—	—	—	80,945
1982	50,225	53.2	27,665	29.3	9,880	10.5	6,668	7.1	—	—	—	—	94,438
1983	52,595	52.8	26,599	26.7	12,085	12.1	8,255	8.3	—	—	—	—	99,535
1984	42,938	49.0	24,721	28.2	11,348	12.9	8,627	9.8	—	—	—	—	87,634
1985	44,009	48.1	27,979	30.6	9,668	10.6	9,748	10.7	—	—	126	0.1%	91,530
1986	50,023	44.3	38,232	33.9	12,521	11.1	11,215	9.9	—	—	951	0.8	112,942
1987	56,424	43.6	42,381	32.8	14,909	11.5	14,630	11.3	—	—	1,041	0.8	129,385
1988	37,904	41.8	30,190	33.3	10,917	12.0	10,068	11.1	—	—	1,595	1.8	90,674
1989	47,641	42.8	33,131	29.7	13,388	12.0	14,059	12.6	—	—	3,206	2.9	111,425
1990	34,417	44.1	23,454	30.0	8,769	11.2	9,509	12.2	—	—	1,960	2.5	78,109
B. Put Options (thousands)													
1977	1,257	57.2%	423	19.3%	192	8.7%	222	10.1%	103	4.7%	—	—	2,197
1978	3,979	63.5	841	13.4	316	5.0	640	10.2	489	7.8	—	—	6,265
1979	5,250	64.6	961	11.8	423	5.2	736	9.0	763	9.4	—	—	8,133
1980	9,975	60.0	4,093	24.6	1,053	6.3	1,076	6.5	408	2.5	—	—	16,605
1981	16,783	59.0	8,430	29.6	1,906	6.7	1,343	4.7	—	—	—	—	28,462
1982	25,511	60.0	11,102	25.9	3,587	8.4	2,642	6.2	—	—	—	—	42,842
1983	19,101	52.9	9,601	26.6	4,522	12.5	2,900	8.0	—	—	—	—	36,124
1984	15,737	50.3	8,356	26.7	4,634	14.8	2,564	8.2	—	—	—	—	31,291
1985	13,515	50.0	8,124	30.1	2,397	8.9	2,953	10.9	—	—	37	0.1%	27,026
1986	14,722	50.8	8,909	30.7	2,534	8.7	2,726	9.4	—	—	99	0.3	28,990
1987	16,891	48.2	10,389	29.6	3,180	9.1	4,322	12.3	—	—	265	0.8	35,047
1988	11,489	47.4	7,280	30.0	2,176	9.0	3,001	12.4	—	—	307	1.3	24,253
1989	14,262	46.9	8,449	27.8	3,381	11.1	3,807	12.5	—	—	517	1.7	30,416
1990	14,069	42.2	10,744	32.3	3,674	11.0	4,242	12.7	—	—	587	1.8	33,316

[a]The Midwest Options Exchange merged with CBOE on June 2, 1980.

Source: Option Clearing Corporation.

In May 1989 the SEC voted to allow multiple listings.[1] Specifically, beginning in January 1990 all new stock options could be multiple listed. Also, in January 1990 each exchange was allowed to list 10 individual options already listed on another exchange. Finally, as of January 1991, all options could be traded on any options exchange.

[1]Paul Duke, Jr., "SEC Approves Multiple Listing of Stock Options," *The Wall Street Journal*, May 21, 1989: C16.

| Table 16.3 | Index Option Contracts Traded on Different Exchanges (in thousands) |

	CBOE		AMEX		Philadelphia		Pacific[a]		NYSE		
	Number	%	Number	%	Number	%	Number	%	Number	%	Total
1983	10,661	76.1%	2,693	19.2%	6	0.0%	—	—	656	4.7%	14,016
1984	64,357	84.9	7,006	9.2	127	0.2	175	0.2%	4,094	5.4	75,759
1985	90,822	82.5	12,438	11.3	2,321	2.1	93	0.1	4,213	3.8	110,044[b]
1986	114,835	82.9	18,275	13.2	1,399	1.0	134	0.1	3,774	2.7	138,461[b]
1987	108,352	83.6	18,153	14.0	499	0.4	459	0.4	2,193	1.7	129,656
1988	62,250	87.7	7,527	10.6	157	0.2	280	0.4	725	1.0	70,961[b]
1989	64,645	87.5	8,265	11.2	151	0.2	226	0.3	593	0.8	73,897[b]
1990	80,945	91.7	6,690	7.6	219	0.2	130	0.1	271	0.3	88,282[b]

[a]Trading initiated during 1984.

[b]Totals do not equal components due to minor trading on NASD in 1985 and 1986, and the European Options Exchange (EOE) in 1988, 1989, and 1990.

Source: Option Clearing Corporation.

Options Terminology and Quotations

Given the unique nature of the options market, it is hardly surprising that it has developed its own terminology. In this section, we discuss the principal terms and then describe and explain option quotations.

Option Premium

The price paid for the option itself is the option **premium.** This is the amount a buyer must pay for the right to acquire or sell the stock at a given price during some time period. We will study the components of this premium in detail later in the chapter.

The standard **option contract** gives rights for a transaction with 100 shares of a common stock referred to as the **underlying security.** As an example, a call option contract on IBM would give the holder an option to buy 100 shares of IBM common stock. The financial press quotes per-share prices, so the total cost of a contract would be 100 times this amount, plus commission.

Exercise Price

The price at which the stock will be exchanged is the **exercise** (or strike) **price.** If the underlying stock is currently selling for $38 a share, the option may

Premium The price a buyer pays for a stock option.

Option contract An investment vehicle that gives the holder the right to either buy or sell 100 shares of a stock issue at a stated price within a set period of time.

Underlying security The stock to which an option contract gives the holder rights.

Exercise price The transaction price specified in an option contract. Also called the *strike price.*

specify an exercise (strike) price of $40, allowing the holder of a call option to buy the stock for $40 a share, or the holder of a put option to sell the stock for $40 a share for the duration of the option.

Exercise prices are determined by the prices of the underlying stocks. For stocks selling under $100, the exercise prices are set at $5 intervals such as $35, $40, $45. For stocks selling for over $100, they are set at $10 intervals such as $110, $120, $130.

An initial exercise price is set at the interval closest to the current market price of the stock. If a stock were selling for $43 at the time the option was established, the exercise price would be set at $45. If the stock price were to decline to $41 a share, another option would be established at $40 a share; if it increased to $48 a share, an additional option would be established with a strike price of $50. A newspaper

> **Expiration date** The last date before a holder of an option contract loses the right to control the stock.
>
> **In-the-money option** An option with a favorable exercise price in relation to the stock's market price.
>
> **Out-of-the money option** An option with an unfavorable exercise price in relation to the stock's market price.
>
> **At-the-money option** An option with an exercise price approximately equal to the stock's market price.

quote for a stock with options at numerous prices indicates that the stock's price has moved over a wide range during the recent past.

Expiration Date

The date on which the option expires, or the last date on which it can be exercised, is its **expiration date.** For example, assume that in July the exchange establishes a September option on a stock. The holder of a September call option can purchase the stock at the exercise (striking) price at any time between July and September, after which the option expires. Although the expiration dates are designated by month, the actual date of expiration is the Saturday following the third Friday of the specified month. A September option would expire at the close of business on the Saturday following the third Friday in September. Actual trading in the option would cease at the close of the options exchange on the third Friday.

In-, Out-of-, or At-the-Money Options

An **in-the-money option** is an option with a favorable exercise price in relation to the stock's market price. A call option is in the money when the stock's market price is above the exercise price. A put option is in the money when the market price is below the strike price. As an example, if the exercise price of a call option were $30 while the stock was selling for $34 a share, it would be an in-the-money call option. The market price of the stock ($34) exceeds the exercise price of the call option ($30), so the call option has an intrinsic value of $4 a share. An in-the-money put option might have an exercise price of $30 a share while the stock is selling for only $26 a share. This put option has an intrinsic value of $4 a share.

An **out-of-the-money option** has an unfavorable strike price. An out-of-the-money call option would have an exercise price above the market price for the

stock. An out-of-the-money put option would have an exercise price below the stock's market price. For example, a call option with an exercise price of $30 for a stock that is currently selling at $25 a share is out of the money; it has no intrinsic value because it allows you to buy a stock for $30 a share when you can buy it in the open market at only $25.

An investor may be willing to pay something for this option based on the possibility of the stock price increasing. The price you are willing to pay for an out-of-the-money option is based on its time value, or speculative value, because you are paying for the ability to buy the stock at this exercise price for the remaining time to maturity. An out-of-the-money put option might have a strike price of $35 when the stock is selling for $45. Again, it has no intrinsic value; why would you want to sell the stock at $35 a share when its market price is $45?

Finally, an **at-the-money option** is one with a strike price approximately equal to the market price for the stock. An option with a strike price of $50 and a market price of $51 would be considered an at-the-money option.

A Sample Quotation

Refer to Figure 16.1. Assume that in September 1990 you were considering acquiring a call option on Boeing stock. As shown in the left column, the stock is currently priced at $47\frac{5}{8}$. Arrow 1 indicates that you could buy a Boeing October 45 option for $3\frac{1}{2}$. You would pay $3.50 a share for the right to buy a share of Boeing at $45 between the time of the purchase and the expiration of the option during the third week in October. This is an in-the-money option; it has an intrinsic value of $2.625 ($47.625 − $45.00). If you wanted an option with a strike price of 45 that expired in November 1990, it would cost $4.625 a share; the extra $1.125 is the time value of the additional month.

You could also acquire a Caesar's World October 15 option on the American Exchange (Arrow 2) for $1.00 a share. This is an out-of-the-money option because its exercise price of $15 exceeds the current market price of $14. Investors apparently are willing to pay a speculative or time value of $1.00 based upon the possibility that the price of Caesar's World will exceed $15 by the third week in October.

You could also buy or sell put options in these stocks. As an example, consider the Fruit of the Loom (FruitL) options listed on the New York Exchange. In this case, all put options with strike prices below

Figure 16.1 *Listed Options Quotations*

LISTED OPTIONS QUOTATIONS

Wednesday, September 12, 1990

Options closing prices. Sales unit usually is 100 shares.
Stock close is New York or American exchange final price.

CHICAGO BOARD

Option & NY Close	Strike Price	Calls–Last Sep	Calls–Last Oct	Calls–Last Nov	Puts–Last Sep	Puts–Last Oct	Puts–Last Nov
AlexAl	20	r	1 7/16	r	r	r	r
20 7/8	22 1/2	r	r	r	2 9/16	r	r
Amdahl	12 1/2	3/8	13/16	1 3/16	7/16	r	r
12 1/2	15	r	r	7/16	r	r	r
12 1/2	17 1/2	r	s	1/8	r	s	r
AlnGrp	65	1 1/2	2 3/4	r	7/8	1 7/8	r
65 5/8	80	r	s	1/4	r	s	r
Amoco	50	7 1/2	r	r	r	r	r
58	55	3 1/4	3 1/2	3 3/4	1/4	r	1 5/8
58	60	1/4	1 1/8	1 7/8	3	2 7/8	r
A M P	40	r	r	r	r	r	1 3/4
Anadrk	40	r	r	1 1/2	r	r	3 1/4
Baxter	20	r	3 7/8	r	r	r	r
23 3/4	22 1/2	r	r	1 7/8	r	r	1/2
23 3/4	25	r	3/8	5/8	r	r	r
Blk Dk	10	r	r	3 1/8	r	r	r
12 3/4	12 1/2	r	r	1 1/8	r	r	r
12 3/4	15	r	r	1/4	r	r	r
Bng o	53 3/8	s	s	1 7/16	s	s	6 3/4
47 5/8	60	s′	s	7/16	s	s	r
Boeing	40	6 7/8	r	r	1/16	7/16	13/16
①→ 47 5/8	45	3	3 1/2	4 5/8	3/8	1 1/4	1 7/8
47 5/8	50	3/8	1 3/8	2	3 1/8	4	4 1/2
47 5/8	55	1/16	3/8	3/4	8 1/4	r	r
47 5/8	60	r	s	3/8	r	s	13 1/4
47 5/8	65	1/16	s	3/16	r	s	r
Bois C	25	r	4 3/8	r	r	r	r
28 3/4	30	3/8	r	r	1 3/8	r	r
28 3/4	35	1/8	1/2	11/16	6 1/4	r	r
28 3/4	40	r	s	r	r	s	11 1/2
C B S	160	r	r	r	r	r	2 7/8
172 7/8	170	r	r	r	r	r	6 1/8
172 7/8	175	2 3/16	r	r	r	r	r
172 7/8	180	3/4	r	r	r	r	r
Cadenc	17 1/2	r	r	r	r	r	1 3/16

AMERICAN

		Sep	Oct	Nov	Sep	Oct	Nov
A M R	40	r	r	5 3/8	3/16	3/4	1 1/8
44 3/8	45	3/4	1 13/16	2 3/8	1 3/8	2 3/8	2 3/4
44 3/8	50	1/16	r	3/4	6 3/8	r	r
44 3/8	55	r	r	5/16	r	r	r
44 3/8	60	r	s	1/8	r	s	r
44 3/8	70	r	s	1/16	r	s	s
A S A	45	4	5 1/8	5 7/8	5/16	1 3/16	2 3/16
48 5/8	50	1	2 3/8	3 1/4	2 3/8	3 3/8	r
48 5/8	55	1/8	13/16	1 5/8	r	7 1/8	8
48 5/8	60	1/16	r	3/4	11 5/8	r	r
AST Rs	15	4	4	r	r	7/16	9/16
19	17 1/2	1 9/16	2 1/16	r	5/16	15/16	r
19	20	7/16	1	1 5/8	r	r	r
19	22 1/2	r	r	13/16	r	r	r
19	25	r	s	7/16	r	s	r
Allwst	10	r	r	3/8	r	r	r
8 7/8	12 1/2	r	r	1/8	r	r	r
AFamly	12 1/2	r	3 1/4	r	r	r	r
15 5/8	15	7/8	1 3/8	1 3/4	5/16	3/4	r
15 5/8	17 1/2	1/8	1/8	7/16	r	r	r
Avnet	22 1/2	r	r	r	3/16	r	r
24 1/4	25	r	5/8	r	r	r	r
24 1/4	30	r	r	1/4	r	r	r
Bally	5	r	2 1/2	r	r	r	3/16
7 1/2	7 1/2	1/4	1/2	3/4	3/8	1/2	1
7 1/2	10	r	1/8	1/4	2 1/2	r	2 3/4
C&SSov	20	1/4	r	r	r	1 7/8	r
CNA Fn	60	r	5 1/4	r	r	r	r
64	65	r	r	r	2 1/8	r	3 7/8
Cadenc	17 1/2	r	r	r	r	13/16	1 3/16
20 3/8	20	11/16	r	r	r	1 1/2	2 1/4
20 3/8	22 1/2	r	r	r	r	r	3 3/4
CaesrW	10	r	4 5/8	r	r	r	r
14	12 1/2	1 3/4	2 5/8	2 1/2	r	1/2	13/16
②→ 14	15	1/4	1	1 5/8	r	r	2
14	17 1/2	1/8	3/8	5/8	r	r	r
14	20	r	s	7/16	r	s	r
14	22 1/2	s	s	5/16	s	s	r

PHILADELPHIA

		Sep	Oct	Nov	Sep	Oct	Nov
Abbt L	35	r	r	r	r	1/4	r
40 3/4	37 1/2	s	s	4 3/8	s	s	r
40 3/4	40	1 3/8	1 3/4	2 7/8	5/8	1 3/8	1 3/4
40 3/4	45	r	1/4	3/4	r	r	r
A Hess	45	r	s	10 1/2	r	s	r
54 3/4	50	4 3/4	r	6 1/4	3/16	r	1 1/4
54 3/4	55	3/8	2	3	1 1/4	3 1/8	r
Armco	7 1/2	r	r	r	r	r	1 3/8
AutDt	45	r	r	r	r	3/8	r
49 3/8	50	5/8	r	2 1/8	1 1/4	r	2
49 3/8	60	r	s	1/4	r	s	r
BkBost	5	r	3	r	r	r	r
7 7/8	7 1/2	r	7/8	1	5/16	3/4	1 1/8
7 7/8	10	r	r	3/8	2 1/8	2 3/4	2 3/4
7 7/8	12 1/2	r	r	1/8	r	r	4 3/4
7 7/8	15	r	s	1/8	r	s	r
BurlRs	40	7 7/8	r	r	r	r	r
48 1/2	45	2 5/8	4 1/4	4 1/8	r	r	r
48 1/2	50	7/16	1	1 7/8	r	r	r
48 1/2	55	r	s	1/2	r	s	r
CinMil	12 1/2	r	r	15/16	r	r	r
12 5/8	15	r	r	1/8	2 3/8	r	r
12 5/8	17 1/2	r	r	r	r	r	4 3/4
12 5/8	20	r	r	r	7 1/8	r	r
CntlCp	22 1/2	r	1	r	5/8	r	r
22 1/4	25	r	r	r	3 1/8	r	r
Dell	12 1/2	r	5/8	r	r	r	r
11 3/4	15	r	3/16	r	r	r	r
GaGulf	7 1/2	r	r	5/8	r	r	1 3/8
6 5/8	10	r	r	5/16	r	r	r
GoldWF	30	r	5/16	r	r	r	r
Harley	25	r	r	1 1/8	r	r	r
Harnis	20	r	s	1/8	r	s	r
Home o	33 3/8	s	s	2 1/8	s	s	r
HomeD	25	r	r	r	r	7/16	5/8
32 7/8	30	3	3 3/4	4 5/8	5/16	1 1/4	1 1/2
32 7/8	35	3/8	1 7/16	1 7/8	2 5/8	3	4 1/8
32 7/8	40	1/16	1/4	11/16	7 3/4	7 7/8	7 3/4

NEW YORK

		Sep	Oct	Nov	Sep	Oct	Nov
BordCh	10	r	5/16	3/8	r	r	r
CSoup	45	6 1/8	r	7	r	r	r
50 7/8	50	1 1/2	2 9/16	3 3/8	3/4	1 5/8	r
50 7/8	55	1/4	1	1 9/16	r	r	r
50 7/8	60	1/16	r	r	r	r	r
ClairS	17 1/2	r	r	r	r	1 3/8	r
17 1/2	20	r	r	3/4	r	r	r
DigCom	15	r	r	r	r	1	r
15 7/8	17 1/2	r	r	r	r	2 1/2	r
15 7/8	20	r	1/4	5/16	r	r	r
EdisBr	30	r	r	1 3/8	r	r	r
FMC Cp	35	r	r	1	r	r	r
FruitL	10	3/4	1 1/4	1 1/2	1/8	r	r
③→ 10 1/2	12 1/2	r	r	9/16	2	2 1/8	r
QntmCp	12 1/2	4 3/4	r	r	r	r	r
17 5/8	15	2 1/2	r	r	r	r	r
17 5/8	17 1/2	5/8	1 1/2	r	7/8	r	r
17 5/8	20	1/8	r	r	r	3 1/4	r
Sysco	30	r	r	r	r	5/8	r
Trnsco	40	r	r	r	r	3/8	3/16
44 3/4	45	5/8	r	r	1 1/2	2 5/8	r
44 3/4	50	s	r	9/16	s	r	r
VF Cp	20	r	1	r	r	r	r

PACIFIC

		Sep	Oct	Nov	Sep	Oct	Nov
BncOne	22 1/2	r	r	r	r	3/8	r
23 7/8	25	r	r	r	1 1/8	r	2 1/8
23 7/8	30	r	r	1/4	r	r	6
C&SSov	20	r	r	r	r	r	1 15/16
C S X	25	r	r	r	r	r	3/8
28 5/8	30	1/8	r	7/8	r	1 1/4	r
Checkp	12 1/2	r	r	1/4	r	r	r
Dillrd	80	1 5/8	r	r	r	r	r
80 1/2	85	r	2 1/8	r	r	r	r
80 1/2	90	1/16	15/16	r	10	10 1/4	r
E Sys	30	r	5/8	15/16	r	r	r
Mc D D	40	10 3/4	r	11 1/4	r	r	3/8
51	45	6	6 1/2	7 1/2	r	5/8	1
51	50	2	3	4	1	2	2 1/2
51	55	s	s	1 3/4	s	s	r
51	60	s	s	1/2	s	s	r
McKess	35	r	r	r	r	r	2 1/2
Melvil	40	r	1 3/4	r	r	2 1/4	r
39 7/8	50	r	r	r	r	r	10 1/2
39 7/8	55	r	s	r	r	s	16
MurphO	45	r	r	r	1/4	r	r
RynMtl	50	s	s	18 1/4	s	s	r
68 3/8	55	11 1/2	r	14 1/4	r	r	r

Source: "Listed Options Quotations," *The Wall Street Journal*, September 13, 1990.

Figure 16.2 **Profit Line for Buyer of Call Options**

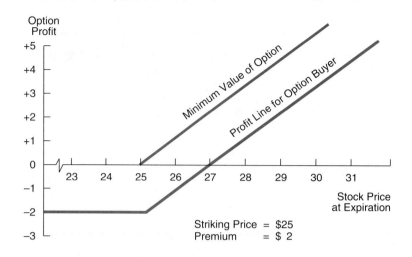

$10.50 are out-of-the-money. Arrow 3 indicates an in-the-money put at $12.50 that allows its owner to sell a stock with a market value of $10.50 for $12.50. Its intrinsic value is therefore $2.00, and the October put is selling for $2.125. Again, a longer-term put option would have greater time value. A November $12.50 put would be priced above $2.125.

Trading Strategies

The introduction of put options has multiplied the number of trading strategies available to an investor enormously, and the range of complexity is substantial. In this section we cannot cover all the strategies, but we will discuss the major alternatives and refer you to articles and books that describe the more sophisticated techniques. Most advanced trading strategies involve the basic techniques discussed in this chapter, and to understand the more sophisticated strategies, you must understand the basic techniques upon which they build.

Buying Call Options

An investor buys a call option expecting the price of the underlying stock to increase prior to the expiration date. If this expectation is fulfilled, the purchase of an option will yield a large return on a small dollar investment. Several strategy alternatives arise from

the relationship of the exercise price to the market price. You can purchase an out-of-the-money option, an at-the-money option, or an in-the-money option.

The out-of-the-money option is the riskiest investment because you can clearly lose the premium if the stock price does not rise sufficiently. At the same time, the rate of return on such an investment can be very large, and it requires the smallest commitment of initial capital of the three alternatives.

To understand the effect of an at-the-money option (without taking commissions or taxes into account) consider the following example.[2] In April, when Avon is selling for $25 a share, assume that an Avon July 25 call option is selling for $2 a share. If you expected an increase in the price of Avon during the next 3 months, you would pay $200 for this option contract. Figure 16.2 indicates your situation at the expiration of the option. If the stock stays at $25 or declines, the option will have no intrinsic value. It will expire worthless and you will lose all of the money you invested in it.

Alternatively, suppose the stock's value rises in a linear fashion beyond this point. For you to recoup your premium, the price would have to rise to at least

---

[2]In all these examples, we ignore commissions and taxes to simplify the computations. This allows us to concentrate on the major impact, but is not intended to deemphasize the importance of these factors in the ultimate investment decision.

$27. If you are correct, and the price of Avon stock goes to $30 within this period (a 20 percent increase), the option contract will be in the money with an intrinsic value of $5. At this point, you could sell the option contract for $500 and enjoy a 150 percent increase on the option from a 20 percent increase in the stock price.

This comparison of returns reflects the leverage available in options. If the stock price never rose above 25, the option would expire worthless and you would lose the full $200. You would break even at $27 a share and begin earning significant returns on your investment at prices of $28 and above.

Note that your maximum loss would be $200 irrespective of what happened to the stock. This loss limit is another major advantage to call options. The point is, an option is a right, not an obligation, so you cannot be forced to exercise the option, which means you cannot lose more than the premium plus transaction costs.

You could also acquire an in-the-money option on the stock. This requires a larger investment than at-the-money or out-of-the-money options because the option has an intrinsic value and a time value. While such an option does not have as much potential leverage, the price of the underlying stock does not have to increase much for you to enjoy a return. Assume that in April, when Avon stock is selling for $25, you buy an Avon July 20 at $5\frac{1}{4}$. This option has an intrinsic value of $5 and a time value of $0.25. Assuming the stock goes to $29, the option will have an intrinsic value of $9. Even if the time value of the option declines to $\frac{1}{8}$ (0.125), the option would sell for $9.125. Therefore, on a 16 percent increase in the stock price ($29 versus $25), the option price increased by 73.8 percent ($9.125 versus $5.25). If the stock price declined below $20, you would lose the full $5.25 per share investment. If the stock price declined from the current price of $25, but remained above $20, the option would have some intrinsic value at expiration, and your loss would be figured accordingly.

Selling (Writing) Covered Call Options[3]

In addition to buying call options, you can also sell call options. Selling an option is referred to as **writ-**

> **Writing an option** Selling an option contract, that is, giving another party control over stock you own, or will acquire if need be.
>
> **Covered call option** Selling an option contract against stock that you own.
>
> **Uncovered (naked) call option** Selling an option contract on a stock that you do not own; you would have to acquire it if the option owner called for the stock.

ing an option. A call option writer enters into a contract to deliver 100 shares of a stock at a predetermined exercise price during some specified time interval. You can write a **call option** either for stock you own, in which case you write a covered call option, or for stock you do not own, in which case you write an **uncovered, or naked, call option.** The option writer is typically looking for extra income from the stock in the form of the premium the buyer pays. The premium also provides some downward protection to offset any price decline in the underlying stock. At the same time, the call option writer gives up some upside profit potential on the stock. If its price rises above the exercise price, the stock might be "called away," which means that the owner of the option decides to exercise the option and buy the stock at the strike price.

Assume that in March you acquired 100 shares of Ford Motor Company stock at $32 a share and could sell a Ford June 35 call option contract for $2 a share. This covered call option would give you an extra income ($200), or you could consider this premium as downside protection because it reduces your net price of the stock to $30 ($32 − $2). If the stock does not change price between March and June (approximately 3 months), you have an additional $200 that you would not have had otherwise, which is a 6.25 percent return during the 3 months.

If the stock price increases to $40, the option holder will exercise the option and call the stock away at $35 a share. In this case, you will have sold the stock at a profit of $3 per share based upon your purchase price of $32 and you still have the premium. You earned a return (before dividends) during the period of $5 a share (the $2 premium plus the $3 capital gain), which would be 15.6 percent for the 3 months. You have given up the gain above $35, however, because you sold the call option. You are protected on the downside by the lower net price, but also restricted on the upside by the exercise price.

---

[3]For further discussions of option writing strategies, see *The Merrill Lynch Guide to Writing Options* (New York: Merrill Lynch, Pierce, Fenner, and Smith, 1987); and *Call Option Writing Strategies* (Chicago: Chicago Board Options Exchange, 1985).

Figure 16.3 *Profit Line for Seller of Call Options*

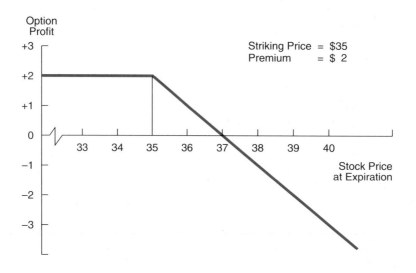

Closing purchase transaction Acquiring an option that exactly offsets another option to which you previously agreed. The purpose is to liquidate the position.

If an option writer (seller) wants to get out of the contract, he or she can simply buy a comparable call option on the exchange, and the two contracts cancel each other. This is referred to as a **closing purchase transaction,** and it liquidates the previous option sale.

Figure 16.3 illustrates the profit potential if you sell a call option. Note that the sale generates a loss at prices above $37 because this offsets the $200 premium received. In the case of a covered call, it is an opportunity loss, because you receive only $35 a share whereas you could have received more if you had not sold the call option contract. If you sell a naked call, the loss is very real and is unlimited. To liquidate an uncovered call, you must go into the market and buy the underlying stock at the prevailing market price.

Writing Call Options in Different Markets Your option-writing strategy should differ depending upon your outlook for the market environment (stable, rising, declining) and also your expectations for the individual stock. In a very stable market, you could continue to sell options over time to supplement dividend income. This strategy requires only that you

watch whether the option you sold becomes an out-of-the-money or at-the-money option, in which case you should consider closing out your position by buying an option to offset the option you wrote prior to its expiration. You can then sell another call option sooner. This action assumes that the price of the option, which is out-of-the-money or at-the-money, gets pretty low near its maturity because it has no intrinsic value and its time value declines.

If the stock price increases you must decide whether you want to continue to own the stock or let it be called away. Assume you sold a $50 option on a stock you bought at $45 a share and the stock subsequently went to $52. If you were satisfied with the $5 capital gain plus the premium, you would allow the stock to be called away and put the money into another stock. Alternatively, if you see further potential in the stock, you might consider buying back your option with its strike price of $50 and selling another call option at $55. You would lose on the repurchase of the first option because what you would have to pay (at least its intrinsic value of $2 plus any time value) would exceed what you received when you sold it as an out-of-the-money option. You would make up some part of this loss on the sale of the second option, and you would still own the stock. The decision would depend upon your valuation of the two options relative to their market prices and your expectation for the stock.

Option Spreads

Rather than simply buying or selling a call option, you can do both by entering into a spread. A spread reduces the risk of either a long or short position alone in the option for a stock.

The first of two basic types of spreads, a **price spread** (also called a *vertical spread*), involves buying the call option for a given stock, expiration date, and strike price, and selling a call option for the same stock and expiration date, but at a different strike price. For example, you might buy a Ford October 35 and sell a Ford October 40. The second type, a **time spread** (also called a *horizontal spread*), involves both buying and selling options for the same stock and strike price, but with different expiration dates. An example would be buying a Ford October 40 and selling a Ford January 40. Option spreads can serve a variety of investment goals.

Bullish Spreads   You might consider a bullish spread strategy if you were generally bullish on the underlying stock, but you wanted to keep the execution of your policy conservative. Assume you are optimistic on the outlook for Ford stock, which is currently selling for $35, and want to enter into a price spread. A Ford October 30 option is currently priced at 7, while a Ford October 40 option is priced at 2.

Your bullish outlook leads you to buy the higher priced Ford October 30 option and sell the lower priced Ford October 40 option. The net cost of 5 ($500) is your maximum loss. If your expectations were correct, and the stock rose from $35 to $45, the October 30 option would be worth about 15, its intrinsic value, and the October 40 would sell for about 6, a slight premium over its intrinsic value. Closing out both positions would give you a $400 gain as follows:

> October 30: bought at 7, sold at 15 = gain 8
>
> October 40: sold at 2, bought at 6   = loss 4
>
> Overall   = gain 4

If the stock were to decline dramatically, your maximum loss would be $500 (your initial cost), even though both options would expire worthless. Your maximum gain would also be $500. At some high stock price, the value of the options will differ by 10, which would give you a gross profit of $1,000 less the $500 initial cost.

> **Price spread** Simultaneously buying and selling options that are identical except for their exercise prices.
>
> **Time spread** Simultaneously buying and selling options that are identical except for their expiration dates.

Bearish Spreads   Assume, on the other hand, that you are generally bearish on a stock or the market and want to act upon your expectation using a conservative strategy. You might set up a bearish spread, selling the higher-priced option and buying the lower-priced option. You would sell the Ford October 30 at 7, then buy the Ford October 40 at 2 generating an immediate gain of $500.

If you are correct, and Ford stock declines below 30, both options will expire worthless and you will have the $500 profit. In contrast, if the stock rises to 45, the results would be as follows:

> October 30: sold at 7, bought at 15 = loss 8
>
> October 40: bought at 2, sold at 6   = gain 4
>
> Overall   = loss 4

The loss of $400 compares favorably with the potential loss of $800 or more if the spread did not offset somewhat the adverse movement. At a very high stock price, the two options will differ in price by 10, so your maximum loss is $500, or a gross loss of $1,000 less a $500 gain on the original transaction.

Option spreads allow numerous other potential transactions to meet almost any possible set of risk–return conditions.[4]

Buying Put Options

You might consider buying a put option on a stock for several reasons. For the most obvious, you might want to profit from an expected stock price decline. The purchase of a put option allows you to do this with the benefits of leverage and yet it limits your potential loss if the stock price does not decline as expected.

Put options can also protect you from a decline in the price of stock you own without selling it. In such a case, you can buy a put option on your stock as a

---

[4]A more extensive discussion appears in M. J. Gombola, R. Roenfeldt, and P. L. Cooley, "Spreading Strategies in CBOE Options: Evidence on Market Performance," *Journal of Financial Research* 1, no. 1 (Winter 1978): 35–44.

Table 16.4 *Profit Line for Buyer of Put Option*

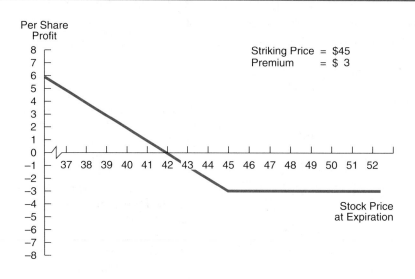

Per Share Profit

Striking Price = $45
Premium = $ 3

Stock Price at Expiration

hedge against the decline. In effect, you offset the decline in the price of the stock with an increase in the value of the put option.

You might also buy a put option when you want to acquire a very volatile stock with a good long-term outlook, but uncertain near-term prospects. You could acquire the stock together with a put option on it as a hedge for the short term. A near-term decline in the price of the stock would be offset by a profit on the put option.

Consider an example of a put acquisition. As of April, General Motors stock is selling for $47, but you feel the stock price could decline. Assume you purchase a July 45 put option on GM for $3 and by May the price for GM stock has declined to $40. At this time, your put option will have a minimum value of $5 (45 − 40), and probably more because 2 months remain before it expires. Assuming a price of 6, you could sell it and realize a gain of $3 (before commission) for a 100 percent return on the option [(6 − 3)/3] during a period when the stock declined by almost 15 percent (7/47). Alternatively, assume that the stock did not decline below 47, or, in fact, increased in price. The put option would expire worthless, and your loss would be limited to the $300 you paid for the option.

Figure 16.4 shows the profit picture at expiration if you bought a put option. Note that at prices above $45, the option would expire worthless, and you would

lose $300; at prices below $42, you would have gains in excess of the cost of the option. Besides the substantial leverage involved, you could benefit from a lower capital commitment and also a lower commission when you react to a bearish outlook with a put option compared to short selling. Also a put option limits your potential loss.

Selling (Writing) Put Options

When you sell (write) a put option you obligate yourself to buy a stock at a specified price during some time period. For accepting this obligation you receive a premium. You might write such an option to increase the return on your portfolio during a period when you expect stock prices to rise. As an example, assume that you own Eastman Kodak (EK) stock, which is selling for $43, and you expect the stock price to rise over the next 6 months. An EK 6-month put with a strike price of $45 is priced at 3, so selling this put option would bring a $300 premium.

If the stock were to rise to $50 as you expect, the put option would expire worthless and you would have the extra $300 in addition to the capital appreciation. In contrast, if EK were to decline to $40, the value of the put option might increase to about 6 if any time remained before it expired because it would have an intrinsic value of 5. You would lose $300 if you bought it back at this time, based upon the $600 cost of the

| Figure 16.5 | *Profit Line for Seller of Put Option* |

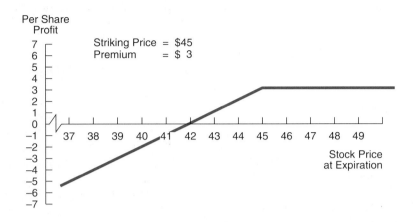

option less the $300 premium received for selling it. Alternatively, you may be called upon to actually buy 100 shares of EK at $45, paying $4,500 for stock worth $4,000 before commissions. Figure 16.5 shows the profit related to the sale of this put option at its expiration.

In another interesting strategy, you could sell a put option as a means of buying stock you want at a price below the current market price. Rather than placing a limit buy order for the stock at a price below the current market price, you can sell a put option with a strike price below the current market price. As an example, assume you want to buy IBM, but you think its current price of $110 is too high. As an alternative to buying the stock directly, you can sell an IBM 100 put option due in about 6 months for 2. If the stock declines below 100 as you expect, you will be called upon to buy 100 shares of IBM at $100 a share. The premium you received reduces your effective cost to 98. You get the IBM stock you want at an effective price that is $12 below the original market price. If the stock were to increase in price, you would miss the chance to buy it, but you would have the $200 premium.

Hedging with Put Options

Beyond using put options as speculative investments or means to acquire stock, you can use them to hedge current stock positions. A **hedge** combines two or more securities into a single position that reduces the overall risk of the portfolio. As we will see, you can

Hedge Combining two or more securities into a single position such that price increases offset decreases to limit the effects of adverse price movements.

hedge a stock position when you first buy stock or after you have owned it for a period of time to protect a profit in it.

Hedging a Long Stock Position Assume that you have been following a stock and decide to buy it. While you feel that the stock has good upside potential, it also can be very volatile and could decline sharply. Therefore, you want to buy the stock, but also want to hedge against a decline. To do this you would:

Buy the common stock	− $30/share
Buy a 6-month put option on the stock with a strike price of $30	− $3/share

If you were correct about the bullish outlook for the stock and it increased to $50 a share, the value of the put option would be zero giving you the following results:

Value of stock	$5,000
Cost of stock	(3,000)
Cost of put option	(300)
Net gain	$1,700

You have a net gain, but you spent an extra $300 for the hedge. Alternatively, if the stock declined to $20 a share, the value of the put would be at least $10 a share, giving you the following results:

Value of stock	$2,000
Value of option	1,000
Cost of stock	(3,000)
Cost of put option	(300)
Net loss	($300)

Your net $300 loss is substantially less than the $1,000 loss you would have experienced without the hedge.

Hedging a Long Profit Position   Assume that you acquired the stock discussed at $30 a share, but did not hedge your position initially. The stock increases consistently to sell for $65/share, which gives you a $3,500 unrealized capital gain. Although you feel the stock has some further upside potential, you don't want to lose your gain as a result of some bad news. To protect your gain, you buy a 6-month put option with a strike price of $65 for $5 a share.

If the price of the stock continues to rise to $80 per share, the 65 put option would have no value and your results would be:

Value of stock	$8,000
Cost of stock	(3,000)
Cost of put option	(500)
Net gain	$4,500

Holding the stock brought you an additional increase in value of $1,500, but the hedge cost you $500, so your net additional gain is $1,000. In contrast, if a negative news release dropped the stock price to $50 a share, your results would be:

Value of stock	$5,000
Value of option	1,500
Cost of stock	(3,000)
Cost of put option	(500)
Net gain	$3,000

You gave up $500 of your prior gain by acquiring the put option, but avoided giving up an additional $1,000 because of the gain on the option.

Again, you can see that put options increase your investment opportunities. Speculative investors who expect price declines use put options to take advantage of their leverage. Conservative investors use them to hedge current stock positions. Finally, you can use them to acquire desired stock at lower effective prices.

Valuation of Call and Put Options

Five factors are needed to calculate the value of an American call or put option, assuming the stock does not pay a dividend: (1) the stock price, (2) the exercise price, (3) the time to maturity, (4) the interest rate, and (5) the volatility of the underlying stock.[5] You can allow for dividends through an additional calculation. The following discussion will relate each of the factors to the value of a call option. After this, we will note how they relate to the value of a put option.

Stock Price

The value of a call option is positively related to the price of the underlying stock. With a given exercise price, the price of the stock determines whether the option is in the money, and therefore has an intrinsic value, or out of the money with only speculative (time) value. In addition, some of the other variables are influenced by the relationship between market price and exercise price.

Exercise Price

The value of a call option is inversely related to its exercise price. For a given stock price, a lower exercise price raises the value of a call on the stock. As an example, consider a stock selling at $70 a share. A call option with an exercise price of $50 would certainly be worth more than a call option with an exercise price of $60. The first option is in the money by $20, the second by only $10.

Time to Maturity

The value of an option depends to a great extent on its time to maturity. All other factors being equal, a longer time to maturity increases the value of the option because the span of time during which gains are possible is longer. The longer option allows investors

---

[5]An American call option can be exercised at any time prior to the expiration date; a European option can be exercised only on the expiration date.

to reap all the benefits of a shorter option for a longer time.

Interest Rate

An investor who acquires an option buys control of the underlying stock for a period of time, with downside risk limited to the cost of the option. The option gives upside potential that grows at an accelerating rate because of its leverage. Therefore, the option resembles buying on margin, except that the interest charge is implicit. A higher market interest rate increases the saving from using options, and therefore the value of the option. This creates a positive relationship between the market interest rate and the value of the call option.

Volatility of Underlying Stock Price

When determining the value of most investments, a high level of price volatility indicates greater risk, which reduces value, all other factors being equal. For call options on a stock, however, the opposite is true; its value has a positive relationship with the volatility of the underlying stock. This is because greater volatility implies greater potential for gain on the upside, and the downside protection of the option is also worth more.[6]

Valuation Factors and Put Options

As noted, the same five factors determine the value of put options although several of the relationships differ. First, the value of put options is *inversely* related to the price of the underlying stock, all else remaining the same.

This is because the intrinsic value of a put option is the difference between the exercise price and the stock price; the exercise price of an in-the-money option exceeds the stock price. Following from this, the value of the put option is *positively* related to the exercise price.

The relationship of put option value to the third factor, time to maturity, is positive, as for a call option. Again, the reasoning is that the longer maturity provides more time for the put option to increase in value.

The effect of the interest rate factor on the value of a put option also differs. The interest rate effect on the value of a put option is *negative* because buying a put option is like deferring the *sale* of stock so you receive the proceeds of the sale in the future. Therefore, we are dealing with the present value of the future proceeds, and a higher interest rate reduces the present value of those proceeds. Finally, the effect of the volatility of the stock price on the value of the put option is the same as for the call option. Higher price volatility increases the value of the put option because it increases the probability of the put option being in the money.

Derivation of the Valuation Formula

Black and Scholes developed a formula for determining the value of American call options in a classic article published in 1973.[7] Merton later refined this formula under less restrictive assumptions.[8] The resulting formula is set forth and demonstrated in Appendix 16A.

As discussed in the appendix, although the formula appears rather forbidding, one can observe almost all the required inputs directly in the market. Further, although the calculations are rather difficult, numerous computer programs can expedite the process, as can programs available for hand-held calculators.

Options on Stock Indexes

In previous sections, we considered various trading strategies for options on individual stocks and also the variables used to derive values for these options. In this section, we move from options on individual stocks to options on stock market indexes that allow you to speculate on the total market or hedge a portfolio of stocks.

Options on stock market indexes work just like options on individual stock issues, except that the ag-

---

[6]For an article that discusses how to estimate volatility, see Galen Burghardt and Morton Lane, "How to Tell If Options are Cheap," *Journal of Portfolio Management* 16, no. 2 (Winter 1990): 72–78.

[7]Fischer Black and Myron Scholes, "The Pricing of Options and Corporate Liabilities," *Journal of Political Economy* 81, no. 2 (May–June 1973): 637–654. For a background discussion, see Fischer Black, "How We Came up with the Option Formula," *Journal of Portfolio Management* 15, no. 2 (Winter 1989): 4–8.

[8]Robert C. Merton, "The Theory of Rational Option Pricing," *Bell Journal of Economics and Management Science* 4, no. 3 (August 1973): 141–183.

Table 16.4 *Description of Major Index Options*

Standard & Poor's 100 Index   These options are underlain by a portfolio of 100 stocks included in the S&P 500 Index. Like the other S&P indexes, the S&P 100 Index is a value-weighted series. A 1-point move in this index equals about a 7.5-point move in the Dow Jones Industrial Average (DJIA). These options are traded on the CBOE.

Standard & Poor's 500 Index   These options are underlain by the 500 stocks in the value-weighted S&P 500 Composite Index. The options are traded on the CBOE.

New York Stock Exchange Composite Index   These options are underlain by a value-weighted index of the 1,500-plus stocks traded on the NYSE. A 1-point move in this index equals about a 6.5-point move in the DJIA. The options trade on the NYSE.

American Stock Exchange Major Market Index (MMI)   These options are underlain by a price-weighted index of 20 blue-chip stocks. Although the options are traded on the AMEX, all stocks in the index are listed on the NYSE. A 1-point movement in this index equals approximately a 5-point move in the DJIA. This index is very highly correlated with the DJIA, because 15 of the 20 stocks are included in that series.

Value Line Composite Index   These options are underlain by the VL Index, which includes the 1,679 stocks followed by Value Line (VL). This VL series is an unweighted sample of stocks from the NYSE, the AMEX, and the OTC. It takes a geometric average of individual percentage price changes rather than an arithmetic average as other series do. These options are traded on the Philadelphia Stock Exchange.

National OTC Index   These options are underlain by the National OTC Index, which includes the 100 stocks with the largest market value traded on the national OTC market. The index is value-weighted and the options are traded on the Philadelphia Stock Exchange.

Subindex Options

Computer Technology Index   These options are underlain by a value-weighted index of 29 computer technology stocks, both listed and unlisted. The index was started with a value of 100 on July 29, 1983. The options are traded on the AMEX.

Financial News Composite Index   These options are underlain by an index of 30 stocks of major companies (e.g., Alcon, Walt Disney). The index is value-weighted with a base value of 100 as of June 30, 1986. The options are traded on the Pacific Stock Exchange.

Oil Index   These options are underlain by a price-weighted index of 15 oil company stocks. Originally the Oil & Gas Index, it was subsequently revised and renamed with a benchmark value of 125 as of August 27, 1984. The options are traded on the AMEX.

Institutional Index   These options are underlain by a value-weighted index of the 75 stocks that represent the largest dollar holdings in major institutional portfolios. These options are traded on the AMEX.

Utilities Index   These options are underlain by a value-weighted index of 120 utility stocks with a benchmark value of 200 as of May 1, 1987. These options are traded on the Philadelphia Stock Exchange.

Gold/Silver Index   These options are underlain by a value-weighted index of seven mining stocks with a benchmark value of 100 as of January 2, 1984. These options are traded on the Philadelphia Stock Exchange.

---

gregate market, as represented by a stock market series, takes the place of the underlying security. The most well-known indexes with options are described in Table 16.4.[9] In addition, a number of subindexes has been created to accommodate strong interest in certain segments of the market with volatile securities.[10]

Quotations for Index Options

Sample quotes for the various index options appear in Figure 16.6. Each point of premium represents $100. The minimum premium quotation is $\frac{1}{16}$ of a point for premiums of less than $3, and $\frac{1}{8}$ of a point for premiums of $3 and above. As shown, based upon volume and open interest, the option on the S&P 100 Index traded on the Chicago Board Options Exchange (CBOE) is the most active.[11] In September, when the

[9]Pamela Sebastian, "Index Options Proliferate: A Guide to Calls, Puts and Striking Prices," *The Wall Street Journal*, March 13, 1985: 35.

[10]Pamela Sebastian, "Exchanges Plan More Sub-Index Options Fearing Aggressive Rivals May Push Issues," *The Wall Street Journal*, December 15, 1983: 33.

[11]Jeffrey Zaslow, "Chicago Exchange Moving to Speed up Index-Options Trades for Small Investors," *The Wall Street Journal*, January 31, 1985: 29. The Value Line series underlies another popular option; see Steve Swartz, "Value Line Stock Index Option Gets Off to a Fast Start in Philadelphia," *The Wall Street Journal*, January 28, 1985: 38.

Figure 16.6 ***Index Option Quotations***

INDEX TRADING

Thursday, September 13, 1990

OPTIONS

Chicago Board

S&P 100 INDEX

Strike Price	Calls—Last Sep	Oct	Nov	Puts—Last Sep	Oct	Nov
270	....	38¼	....	⅜	2⅜	4¼
275	....	....	....	7/16	2 15/16	4¾
280	....	....	....	⅝	3⅝	5⅞
285	21⅞	....	....	⅞	4⅜	7⅛
290	14⅞	19¼	....	1⅜	5½	8¼
295	9¾	16	....	2 1/16	6¾	9⅛
300	6⅛	12	17	3¼	8⅜	11½
305	3¼	9	12	5⅜	10⅛	13½
①→ 310	1⅜	6⅜	9½	8⅝	12⅝	15½
315	½	4⅜	7½	12¾	15¾	17¾
320	3/16	2¾	5⅜	17½	19¼	21¾
325	⅛	1 9/16	3⅝	22½	23	23½
330	1/16	15/16	2⅝	27¼	24⅜	....
335	1/16	½	....	32	....	....
340	....	¼	1	38	36½	....
345	....	⅛	⅝	43	40¼	....
350	....	⅛	....	47	47	47½
355	....	1/16	....	....	....	....
360	....	....	¼	....	....	....
365	....	1/16	....	....	....	....

Total call volume 113,702 Total call open int. 561,201
Total put volume 136,708 Total put open int. 496,645
The index: High 307.12; Low 302.15; Close 302.60, −4.52

S&P 500 INDEX

Strike Price	Calls—Last Sep	Oct	Dec	Puts—Last Sep	Oct	Dec
250	....	....	....	1/16	¾	1⅞
275	44	....	....	⅛	....	4⅜
290	....	....	....	¼	2⅞	6⅞
295	....	....	....	....	3½	....
300	19¼	....	31¼	¾	4½	9⅝
305	....	19¾	....	1¼	5¾	10¾
310	....	....	....	1 13/16	6¼	11
315	6⅜	....	21⅝	3	8¼	14⅜
320	3⅝	9¾	19	4⅞	10	16
325	1½	8¼	14⅝	8	....	18¼
330	7/16	4⅞	12⅜	12	14¾	18⅜
335	3/16	3⅝	10	16½	18⅛	23
340	1/16	1⅞	7⅞	20¾	....	25½
345	1/16	1	5⅞	26	....	27¼
350	....	....	4⅛	31¼	....	32⅛
355	1/16	....	3	36¼	....	32⅜
360	1/16	....	2¼	41	....	38½
365	1/16	¼	....	....	....	....
370	1/16	....	....	....	....	....
375	....	....	11/16	....	....	....
400	....	....	....	....	....	75

Total call volume 34,578 Total call open int. 408,814
Total put volume 59,242 Total put open int. 595,234
The index: High 322.54; Low 318.02; Close 318.65, −3.89

American Exchange

MAJOR MARKET INDEX

Strike Price	Calls—Last Sep	Oct	Nov	Puts—Last Sep	Oct	Nov
440	....	....	....	⅛	1½	....
450	....	....	....	....	2¼	4⅜

Strike Price	Calls—Last Sep	Oct	Nov	Puts—Last Sep	Oct	Nov
460	....	....	....	5/16	2½	....
470	....	....	....	½	3¼	....
480	....	....	....	13/16	5¼	6⅞
490	....	....	....	1 5/16	6	10½
500	29½	37⅞	....	1⅞	8	12¾
505	27¼	....	....	2 7/16	9¼	....
510	....	....	....	2 15/16	8½	13¼
515	21	....	....	3¾	11¾	....
520	12⅝	27	....	4¾	11⅜	15¾
525	9⅛	22⅞	②→	6⅜	11⅞	19⅜
530	6⅜	18⅜	....	8⅛	16⅝	....
535	3⅞	16¾	....	11¼	15½	....
540	2½	11½	18¾	14½	....	....
545	1 7/16	9½	....	18⅞	....	....
550	13/16	7½	....	23¼	27	....
555	7/16	....	....	27	29	....
560	¼	4⅝	....	31¾	....	....
565	⅛	....	....	36½	....	....
570	1/16	2	....	....	....	....
575	1/16	....	....	45½	....	....
580	1/16	15/16	....	45¾	47	....
585	1/16	¾	....	....	....	....
590	....	½	2 1/16	....	....	....
595	1/16	....	1 7/16	....	....	....
600	....	¼	⅞	....	....	....

Total call volume 7,799 Total call open int. 80,997
Total put volume 7,268 Total put open int. 73,610
The index: High 534.95; Low 525.92; Close 526.48, −8.47

INTERNATIONAL MARKET INDEX

Strike Price	Calls—Last Sep	Oct	Nov	Puts—Last Sep	Oct	Nov
280	....	....	....	5/16	....	....
285	....	....	....	½	....	....
290	....	....	....	15/16	....	....
295	6⅞	....	....	....	....	....
300	....	....	....	3⅜	....	....
310	9/16	....	....	....	....	....

Total call volume 15 Total call open int. 391
Total put volume 55 Total put open int. 429
The index: High 302.65; Low 301.15; Close 301.95, −0.68

COMPUTER TECHNOLOGY INDEX

Strike Price	Calls—Last Sep	Oct	Nov	Puts—Last Sep	Oct	Nov
90	3¾	....	....	....	....	....

Total call volume 1 Total call open int. 100
Total put volume 0 Total put open int. 101
The index: High 94.63; Low 92.31; Close 92.56, −1.80

OIL INDEX

Strike Price	Calls—Last Sep	Oct	Nov	Puts—Last Sep	Oct	Nov
245	....	....	....	¼	....	....
250	....	....	....	¼	....	....
255	....	....	....	....	3¼	....
260	....	....	....	1¼	....	....
265	4	....	....	1⅞	....	....
270	2⅛	7¼	....	4½	....	....
275	1	....	....	....	....	....

Total call volume 137 Total call open int. 720
Total put volume 42 Total put open int. 769
The index: High 268.34; Low 266.33; Close 266.62, −1.22

INSTITUTIONAL INDEX

Strike Price	Calls—Last Sep	Oct	Nov	Puts—Last Sep	Oct	Nov
310	....	....	....	11/16	....	....
315	....	....	....	⅞	....	....
320	....	....	....	1 3/16	....	....
325	....	....	....	1¾	....	....
330	9¾	....	....	2⅝	....	....
335	6	....	....	4	....	11½
340	3½	....	....	6	....	....
345	1½	....	11⅝	9⅝	....	....
350	⅝	4¾	8⅞	11⅜	....	....
355	⅜	....	....	....	....	....

Total call volume 716 Total call open int. 38,747
Total put volume 1,629 Total put open int. 46,889
The index: High 341.16; Low 336.29; Close 336.80, −4.36

N.Y. Stock Exchange

NYSE INDEX OPTIONS

Strike Price	Calls—Last Sep	Oct	Nov	Puts—Last Sep	Oct	Nov
160	....	....	....	¼	1 9/16	....
165	....	13½	....	....	2½	4⅛
170	7¾	....	....	1	3⅝	....
175	2⅝	5 5/16	8¼	2 5/16	4¾	6⅞
180	....	3¾	....	4⅜	6⅝	9⅞
182½	3/16	2½	....	....	....	....
185	....	1 5/16	2⅝	....	....	....
187½	1/16	⅝	....	....	....	....
190	....	½	....	....	15	....
200	....	1/16	....	....	....	....

Total call volume 1,137. Total call open int. 9,130.
Total put volume 195. Total put open int. 2,922.
The index: High 177.09; Low 174.88; Close 175.16, −1.93

Philadelphia Exchange

GOLD/SILVER INDEX

Strike Price	Calls—Last Sep	Oct	Nov	Puts—Last Sep	Oct	Nov
105	1⅝	....	....	....	5½	....
110	....	....	4⅜	7⅜	....	....
115	....	1⅝	2⅞	....	....	....
120	....	1	....	....	....	....
125	....	9/16	....	....	....	....

Total call volume 251 Total call open int. 1,383
Total put volume 2 Total put open int. 394
The index: High 103.43; Low 102.12; Close 103.20, +0.05

VALUE LINE INDEX OPTIONS

Strike Price	Calls—Last Sep	Oct	Nov	Puts—Last Sep	Oct	Nov
230	....	....	....	⅜	2¾	....
235	....	....	....	....	3½	....
240	....	....	....	½	....	....

Total call volume 100 Total call open int. 6,368
Total put volume 44 Total put open int. 6,019
The index: High 246.90; Low 244.53; Close 244.76, −2.10

NATIONAL O-T-C INDEX

Strike Price	Calls—Last Sep	Oct	Nov	Puts—Last Sep	Oct	Nov
285	2⅛	....	....	....	....	....

Total call volume 6 Total call open int. 560
Total put volume 0 Total put open int. 4
The index: High 281.76; Low 275.34; Close 276.12, −4.30

UTILITIES INDEX

Strike Price	Calls—Last Sep	Oct	Nov	Puts—Last Sep	Oct	Nov
195	2¾	....	....	....	....	....
205	....	....	1¼	....	....	....

Total call volume 16 Total call open int. 2,443
Total put volume 0 Total put open int. 732
The index: High 199.17; Low 196.78; Close 197.53, −1.70

Pacific Exchange

FINANCIAL NEWS COMPOSITE INDEX

Strike Price	Calls—Last Sep	Oct	Dec	Puts—Last Sep	Oct	Dec
205	....	....	....	¾	....	....
210	8⅛	....	....	....	5¼	....
215	4	7¾	....	3¼	7	....
220	1	5½	....	6⅛	....	....
225	5/16	....	....	10⅛	....	....
230	....	....	....	15⅛	....	....
275	....	....	1/16	....	....	....

Total call volume 151 Total call open int. 4,058
Total put volume 390 Total put open int. 2,692
The index: High 218.16; Low 214.38; Close 214.65, −3.51

Source: "Index Trading," *The Wall Street Journal*, September 14, 1990.

value of the S&P 100 Index was 302.60, you could have acquired a November 310 call option on this index (Arrow 1). This option would have given you the right to acquire this portfolio of stocks at 310 until it expired during the third week in November. The cost of the option, $9\frac{1}{2}$, means that 100 units would cost $950. This out-of-the-money option had no intrinsic value, but investors were willing to pay for its time value.

If you were bearish on the market, you could buy a put like the Major Market Index (MMI) which, though traded on the AMEX, is highly correlated with the DJIA. With the index at 526.48, you could buy a November at-the-money 525 put for $19\frac{3}{8}$ (Arrow 2) and hope for a market decline. You could also use these puts to hedge a portfolio of blue-chip stocks if you were concerned about the possibility of a decline in the aggregate market.

If you have strong feelings about broader market movements rather than individual stock movements, these options give you convenient, low-cost means of investing to act upon those expectations. Also, several subindexes allow you to hedge or speculate on certain volatile industries such as computers, oil, and gold.

Options on Foreign Currencies

Throughout this book we have discussed global investing and the added risks and opportunities caused by changes in exchange rates between currencies. When you invest in Japanese stocks or bonds, in addition to the typical business, financial, and liquidity risks, you must also evaluate the added uncertainty due to changes in currency exchange rates. These changes can work in your favor or against you, as when the Japanese yen–U.S. dollar exchange rate fluctuated dramatically during 1988 through 1990 from over 200 yen per U.S. dollar in 1988, down to about 120 yen, then back up to over 150 yen per dollar in 1990.

Foreign currency options allow you to hedge part of this foreign exchange risk. This section considers options on foreign currencies. We will discuss foreign currency futures contracts in Chapter 18.

In response to the desire for hedging or speculation in foreign currencies, the Philadelphia Stock Exchange began trading options on some foreign currencies in 1982. While options on foreign currencies are traded on the Toronto and Montreal exchanges and the Amsterdam Exchange, the Philadelphia Exchange houses the largest exchange-based market for foreign currency options. As shown in Figure 16.7, options are traded on Australian dollars, British pounds, Canadian dollars, West German marks, Japanese yen, and Swiss francs.

The strike price of each option is the U.S.-dollar price of a unit of a foreign currency. The number of foreign currency units per contract is specified for each currency, for example, 31,250 British pounds or 62,500 West German marks. The strike prices for British pound contracts are quoted in U.S. cents per British pound. For example, the exchange rate closed at 187.64 cents per pound the day before the publication of the chart in Figure 16.7. Arrow 1 indicates an October 185 call option selling for $3.30. This option is slightly in the money with an intrinsic value of $2.64 (187.64 − 185.00), and a speculative value of $0.66 ($3.30 − $2.64).

Foreign Currency Hedging

Consider the following example of a currency option market hedge for the exchange rate risk in a stock or bond investment. Assume that you are interested in buying Japanese stocks traded on the Tokyo Stock Exchange and denominated in yen. You could make money on the stock investment, but lose some or all your return in U.S. dollars if the yen were to weaken relative to the U.S. dollar while you owned the Japanese stock. You want to buy or sell options on the Japanese yen that will offset the currency loss on the stock transaction.

You can do this in one of two ways: sell a call option or buy a put option on the yen. In either case, if the exchange rate for U.S. dollars per Japanese yen declines from the current 0.0078320 (see Figure 16.7) you will benefit. If you sell an in-the-money call option and the yen declines in value, the option could expire worthless, and you would have the premium. For example, if you sell a December 73 call at $1.74 (Arrow 2), you will receive $174 a contract. If you sell a 71 call you will receive $256 a contract. If the exchange rate goes from 0.007320 to 0.0070, the option will expire worthless and the premium will help offset the exchange rate loss. Alternatively, if you buy a December 73 put, and the exchange rate declines to 0.0070, your put option contract will give you a significant gain that will help offset the exchange rate loss on the stock transaction.

The discussion in Chapter 18 on financial futures will consider how to accomplish such a hedge using foreign currency futures.

Investor Experience with Options

Several studies have examined the risks and returns for a fully covered call option program compared to those from a pure stock portfolio. The authors have fairly consistently found reduced rates of return and variability of returns from writing covered call options. This is consistent with expectations because, as we discussed, such a policy provides downside protection through the premium the option writer receives, but also limits upside potential because the stock will be called away if it increases in price.[12]

---

[12]Studies that considered this question include, Frederic S. Dawson, "Risks and Returns in Continuous Option Writing," *Journal*

Figure 16.7 ***Prices on Foreign Currency Options***

CURRENCY MARKETS

OPTIONS

Philadelphia Exchange

Option & Underlying	Strike Price	Calls—Last Sep	Calls—Last Oct	Calls—Last Dec	Puts—Last Sep	Puts—Last Oct	Puts—Last Dec
50,000 Australian Dollars-cents per unit.							
ADollr	...77	r	r	r	r	r	0.42
82.38	79	r	r	3.13	r	r	r
82.38	...80	r	r	r	r	r	1.27
82.38	...81	r	r	r	r	0.89	r
82.38	...82	0.39	0.97	1.48	0.10	1.06	1.91
82.38	...83	0.04	0.60	1.10	r	1.68	2.53
82.38	...84	r	0.23	r	r	r	r
82.38	...86	r	0.07	r	r	r	r
50,000 Australian Dollars-European Style.							
82.38	...79	3.49	r	r	r	r	r
82.38	...80	r	r	r	r	0.48	r
31,250 British Pounds-cents per unit.							
BPound	180	r	r	r	r	0.80	r
187.64	182½	r	r	5.00	r	1.45	3.75
① 187.64	185	r	3.30	r	0.35	2.12	r
187.64	187½	0.95	2.75	r	0.75	3.40	7.20
187.64	.190	0.10	1.65	r	r	r	8.90
187.64	192½	r	r	r	r	r	10.90
187.64	.195	r	r	r	r	r	12.35
50,000 Canadian Dollars-cents per unit.							
CDollr	...82	r	r	r	r	r	0.28
85.95	.82½	r	r	r	r	r	0.42
85.95	...84	r	r	r	r	0.27	0.85
85.95	.84½	r	r	r	r	0.37	1.08
85.95	...85	r	r	r	0.03	0.56	1.20
85.95	.85½	0.24	r	r	0.14	r	r
85.95	...86	0.12	0.53	r	0.37	r	r
85.95	.86½	r	r	r	0.64	r	r
85.95	.87½	r	r	r	1.62	r	r
85.95	...88	r	r	r	2.45	r	r
50,000 Canadian Dollars-European Style.							
CDollar	..84	r	r	r	r	0.28	r
85.95	.85½	0.31	r	r	r	r	r
85.95	.86½	r	0.30	r	r	r	r
62,500 West German Marks-cents per unit.							
DMark	.. 56	6.77	r	r	r	r	r
63.59	...57	r	r	r	r	r	0.09
63.59	...59	3.92	r	r	r	r	r
63.59	...60	3.49	r	r	r	r	0.49
63.59	...61	r	2.68	r	r	0.17	0.63
63.59	.61½	r	s	s	0.02	s	s
63.59	...62	1.51	r	r	0.03	0.36	0.92
63.59	.62½	r	s	s	0.05	s	s
63.59	...63	0.64	1.05	r	0.11	0.66	r
63.59	.63½	0.32	s	s	0.22	s	s
63.59	...64	0.14	0.71	1.30	0.56	1.11	r
63.59	...65	r	0.38	0.87	r	r	r
63.59	.65½	r	0.23	s	r	r	s
63.59	...66	r	0.13	r	r	r	3.55
63.59	...68	r	r	0.29	r	r	r
62,500 West German Marks-European Style.							
63.59	...54	9.41	s	r	r	s	r
6,250,000 Japanese Yen-100ths of a cent per unit.							
JYen	... 68	r	r	r	r	r	0.24
73.20	...69	r	r	4.49	r	r	0.40
73.20	...70	2.91	r	3.50	r	0.18	0.58
73.20	...71	r	r	2.56	0.03	0.32	r
73.20	.71½	r	s	s	0.07	s	s
73.20	...72	r	1.70	1.95	0.06	0.59	r
73.20	.72½	0.36	0.95	s	r	0.90	s
73.20	...73	0.43	r	1.74	0.33	1.15	r
73.20	...74	0.08	0.75	1.35	r	r	r
73.20	...75	0.03	r	0.95	r	r	r
73.20	...76	r	r	0.67	r	r	r
73.20	...77	r	r	0.30	r	r	r
62,500 Swiss Francs-cents per unit.							
SFranc	..69	6.65	r	r	r	r	r
76.39	.74½	r	s	s	0.12	s	s
76.39	...72	r	r	r	r	r	0.55
76.39	...74	r	r	2.52	r	0.54	r
76.39	...75	0.39	1.25	1.96	0.08	1.01	1.82
76.39	...76	r	r	2.14	0.24	r	2.20
76.39	.76½	0.26	r	s	r	r	s
76.39	...77	0.12	0.97	r	r	r	3.01
76.39	.77½	0.06	r	s	r	r	s
76.39	...79	r	0.36	r	r	r	r
76.39	...80	r	r	0.70	r	r	r

Total call vol. 26,298 Call open int. 389,296
Total put vol. 32,085 Put open int. 464,296
r—Not traded. s—No option offered.
Last is premium (purchase price).

Source: "Currency Markets," *The Wall Street Journal*, September 14, 1990.

Summary

■ Options have become popular since the establishment of the CBOE in 1973. They offer a wide range of investment alternatives.

■ Options may be in the money, out of the money, or at the money. We reviewed basic trading strategies including buying call options, writing covered call options, setting up option spreads, and buying and selling put options. You should develop an understanding of each of these strategies in preparation for learning more sophisticated techniques. Also, you should recognize the numerous alternatives these options make available, ranging from high-risk speculation to low-risk hedging.

■ Black and Scholes developed a model that deals with the major variables that influence the value of call and put options and indicates the directions of their effects. In addition to options on individual stocks,

---

of Portfolio Management 5, no. 2 (Winter 1979): 58–63; R. Corwin Grube, Don B. Panton, and J. Michael Terrell, "Risks and Rewards in Covered Call Positions," *Journal of Portfolio Management* 5, no. 2 (Winter 1979): 64–68; Robert Merton, Myron Scholes, and Mathew Gladstein, "A Simulation of the Returns and Risks of Alternative Option Portfolio Investment Strategies," *Journal of Business* 51, no. 2 (April 1978): 183–242; and Ronald T. Slivka, "Risk and Return for Option Investment Strategies," *Financial Analysts Journal* 36, no. 5 (September–October 1980): 67–73.

recent innovations include options on the total stock market as well as options on foreign currencies. Options on aggregate stock market indexes allow you to hedge a total stock portfolio or to speculate on the future returns for the total market. Options on foreign currencies allow you to hedge exchange rate risk, which can benefit an investor who feels confident about the investment outlook for a foreign market, but is less sure of prospects for the currency of the country.

■ Studies that examined the risks and returns from selling covered options have found that the rates of return and the risks are lower from such programs than from pure stock investing.

Questions

1. Define the terms *call option* and *put option*.
2. How is the CBOE different from the original over-the-counter option market?
3. Define the following terms related to options:
   a. premium
   b. exercise price
   c. expiration date
   d. in-the-money option
   e. at-the-money option
   f. out-of-the-money option
4. Differentiate between selling a fully covered call option and a naked (uncovered) call option. Give an example to show why the sale of an uncovered call option is much riskier.
5. Five variables are involved in estimating the value of call or put options. List and discuss each of them and indicate how each influences the value of a call and a put option.
6. Some have contended that selling a fully covered option is a conservative investment strategy. Discuss the reasoning behind this contention based upon the possible distribution of returns from such a strategy. Use an example if it will help.
7. Describe a time spread and a price spread. Discuss why investors engage in spreads. Explain to a friend why a spread has less risk than writing a call option.
8. Assume that you want to buy American Express (AXP) stock, but feel that its current price of 30 is somewhat high. Currently a 6-month AXP 25 put is selling for $1.50. Describe how you would use this put option to accomplish your goal of

buying AXP if the stock declined to 25. What would happen if you sold this put and AXP stock rose to $35?
9. You want to buy the common stock of a German chemical firm, but you are concerned about weakness in the German mark. Discuss how you could use a currency option on the German mark to protect yourself from the exchange rate risk. What would be the effect of a 10 percent increase in the value of the mark relative to the U.S. dollar?

Problems

1. Assume you are bullish on the outlook for the stock market. Look up a 4- to 6-month at-the-money option in *The Wall Street Journal*. If the value of the stock index were to increase by 15 percent, indicate the approximate outcome, including the percentage return, from your option investment.
2. You are bullish on the stock of Peoria Tractor (PT) and want to write a bullish price spread. PT's stock is currently priced at 32 and it has the following 3-month options outstanding:

Peoria Trac

30	4.00
35	2.00
40	1.00

   a. Describe how you would write a bullish spread on PT.
   b. Describe what would happen if the stock price increased to 45 in 3 months.
   c. Describe what would happen if the stock price declined to 25 in 3 months.
3. Look up IBM options in the CBOE listings and discuss how you would write a bullish price spread for 2 months.
   a. Describe what would happen if the price of IBM increased by 30 percent.
   b. Describe what would happen if the price of IBM declined by 15 percent.
4. Look up Phillip Morris (Ph Mor) options in the American Stock Exchange listings and discuss how you would enter into a price spread, assuming you were bearish on the stock.

a. Describe what would happen if the price of Ph Mor increased by 20 percent.

b. Describe what would happen if the price of Ph Mor declined by 35 percent.

5. Assume that you are generally bearish on common stocks, so you buy a General Electric 6-month put at 60 when the stock is at 65. The put contract costs you $200. General Electric subsequently goes to 75. What is your rate of return? What would your rate of return be if GE went to 55?

6. Jack Raider was considering the purchase of 100 shares of Medical Corporation common stock selling at $43 per share on the last day in July. As an alternative Jim Gantry, Jack's neighbor, suggests that Jack consider a Medical Corp. option. They examine the following option table from the local newspaper:

	Calls		Puts	
Price	September	December	September	December
40	$4\frac{1}{2}$	6	$1\frac{1}{4}$	2
45	$2\frac{1}{2}$	$3\frac{1}{2}$	$4\frac{1}{2}$	$4\frac{3}{4}$
40	$1\frac{1}{8}$	$2\frac{1}{8}$	$7\frac{7}{8}$	
45		$\frac{1}{2}$		

Jack decides to buy December options. What are his dollar and percentage gains or losses if he makes the following purchases and subsequently closes his position when the stock is selling for $52?

a. A call with an exercise price of 43?

b. A call with an exercise price of 45?

c. A put with an exercise price of 40?

d. A put with an exercise price of 45?

7. David Right is considering the following alternatives for investing in Jamison Industries, which is now selling for $28 per share:

a. Buy 100 shares for cash

b. Buy 100 shares on 60 percent margin

c. Buy a 6-month call option at $25 for $600

Assuming no commissions or taxes, compute the dollar and annualized percentage returns for each alternative assuming the following:

a. The stock reaches $40 in 4 months and all transactions are completed.

b. The stock falls to $24 in 2 months and all transactions are completed.

References

Articles and Pamphlets

(The address to order pamphlets from the Chicago Board Options Exchange is CBOE, LaSalle at Van Buren, Chicago, IL 60605.)

Biger, N., and J. Hull. "The Valuation of Currency Options." *Financial Management* 2, no. 1 (Spring 1983).

Black, Fischer, and Myron Scholes. "The Pricing of Options and Corporate Liabilities." *Journal of Political Economy* 81, no. 2 (May–June 1973).

Black, Fischer, and Myron Scholes. "The Valuation of Option Contracts and a Test of Market Efficiency." *Journal of Finance* 27, no. 2 (May 1972).

Bodwurtha, J., and G. Courtadon. "Efficiency Tests of the Foreign Currency Options Market." *Journal of Finance* 41, no. 1 (March 1986).

Bookstaber, Richard. "The Use of Options in Performance Structuring." *Journal of Portfolio Management* 11, no. 4 (Summer 1985).

Buying Puts, Straddles and Combinations. Chicago: Chicago Board Options Exchange, 1980.

Evnine, J., and A. Rudd. "Index Options: The Early Evidence." *Journal of Finance* 40, no. 3 (July 1985).

Index Options for Portfolio Management. Chicago: Chicago Board Options Exchange, 1986.

Klemkosky, Robert C., and T. Maness. "The Impact of Options on Underlying Securities." *Journal of Portfolio Management* 6, no. 2 (Winter 1980).

Merton, Robert, Myron Scholes, and Mathew Gladstein. "A Simulation of the Returns and Risks of Alternative Option Portfolio Investment Strategies." *Journal of Business* 51, no. 2 (April 1978).

Merton, Robert, Myron Scholes, and Mathew Gladstein. "The Returns and Risks of Alternative Put Option Portfolio Investment Strategies." *Journal of Business* 55, no. 1 (January 1982).

Option Spreading. Chicago: Chicago Board Options Exchange, 1982.

Option Writing Strategies. Chicago: Chicago Board Options Exchange, 1982.

Rendleman, Richard J., Jr. "Optimal Long-Run Option Investment Strategies." *Financial Management* 10, no. 1 (Spring 1981).

Slivka, Ronald T. "Call Option Spreading." *Journal of Portfolio Management* 7, no. 3 (Spring 1981).

Slivka, Ronald T. "Risk and Return for Option Investment Strategies." *Financial Analysts Journal* 36, no. 5 (September–October 1980).

Tax Considerations in Using CBOE Options. Chicago: Chicago Board Options Exchange, 1987.

Understanding Interest Rate Options. Chicago: Chicago Board Options Exchange, 1987.

Books

Bookstaber, Richard. *Option Pricing and Strategies in Investing.* New York: Addison-Wesley, 1986.

Chance, Don M. *An Introduction to Options and Futures.* Hinsdale, Ill.: Dryden Press, 1989.

Cox, J., and M. Rubinstein. *Option Markets.* Englewood Cliffs, N.J.: Prentice-Hall, 1985.

Fabozzi, F., and G. Kipnis, eds. *Stock Index Futures.* Homewood, Ill.: Dow Jones-Irwin, 1984.

Gibson, Rajna. *Option Valuation.* New York: McGraw-Hill, 1991.

Jarrow, Robert A., and Andrew Rudd. *Option Pricing.* Homewood, Ill.: Richard D. Irwin, 1983.

Kolb, Robert W. *Understanding Futures Markets,* 2d ed. Glenview, Ill.: Scott, Foresman, 1988.

Ritchken, Peter. *Options: Theory, Strategy, and Applications.* Glenview, Ill.: Scott, Foresman, 1987.

APPENDIX

16a *Black–Scholes Option Pricing Formula*

In this appendix we present the Black–Scholes (B–S) valuation formula and identify the variables involved. Subsequently, we discuss how to implement the formula and conclude with an example of its application.

The basic B–S and Merton valuation formula is:[1]

$$P_0 = P_s[N(d_1)] - E[\text{antiln}(-rt)][N(d_2)]$$

where:

P_0 = market value of call option

P_s = current market price of underlying common stock

$N(d_1)$ = cumulative density function of d_1 as defined below

E = exercise price of call option

r = current annualized market interest rate for prime commercial paper

t = time remaining before expiration in years (90 days = 0.25)

$N(d_2)$ = cumulative density function of d_2 as defined below

The cumulative density functions are defined as:

$$d_1 = \left[\frac{\ln(P_s/E) + (r + 0.5\sigma^2)t}{\sigma(t)^{1/2}}\right]$$

$$d_2 = d_1 - [\sigma(t)^{1/2}]$$

where:

$\ln(P_s/E)$ = natural logarithm of (P_s/E)

σ = standard deviation of annual rate of return on underlying stock

Implementing the Option Pricing Formula

Although the formula appears quite forbidding, almost all the required data are observable. The major inputs are current stock price (P_s), exercise price (E), market interest rate (r), time to maturity (t), and standard deviation of annual returns (σ). The only variable that is not observable, the volatility of price changes as measured by the standard deviation of returns (σ), becomes the major variable that you must estimate. It is also the variable that will cause differences in the estimates of market value for the option.

In a subsequent article, Black made several observations regarding how an investor goes about making this estimate.[2] First, he noted that knowledge of past

---

[1] Fischer Black and Myron Scholes, "The Pricing of Options and Corporate Liabilities," *Journal of Political Economy* 81, no. 2 (May–June 1973): 637–654; Robert C. Merton, "The Theory of Rational Option Pricing," *Bell Journal of Economics and Management Science* 4, no. 3 (August 1973): 141–183.

[2] Fischer Black, "Fact and Fantasy in the Use of Options," *Financial Analysts Journal* 31, no. 4 (July–August 1975): 36–41. Also see Galen Burghardt and Morton Lane, "How to Tell If Options Are Cheap," *Journal of Portfolio Management* 16, no. 2 (Winter 1990): 72–78.

price volatility should be helpful, but more is needed because the volatility of an individual stock changes over time. Therefore, in addition to a historical measure of the stock's volatility, you need to consider factors that would make its volatility increase or decrease during the period before expiration. This could include industry factors or internal corporate variables; do you expect any changes in business risk, financial risk, or liquidity risk?

One other variable requires some attention: the interest rate. You should use a rate that corresponds to the term of the option. The most obvious, the interest rate on prime commercial paper, is quoted daily in *The Wall Street Journal* for maturities of 30, 60, 90, and 240 days.

To demonstrate the application of the formula, consider an example with the following variables:

$$P_s = \$36$$
$$E = \$40$$
$$r = 0.10 \text{ (the rate on 90-day prime commercial paper)}$$
$$t = 90 \text{ days (0.25 year)}$$
$$\text{Historical } \sigma = 0.40$$
$$\text{Expected } \sigma = 0.50 \text{ (analysts expect an increase in the stock's beta because of a new debt issue)}$$

All the values except stock price volatility are observable. A historical measure of volatility is given, but the analyst expects the stock's volatility to increase.

Table 16A.1 details the calculations for the option, assuming the historical volatility ($\sigma = 0.40$). Table 16A.2 shows the same calculations, assuming the higher volatility ($\sigma = 0.50$).

These results indicate the importance of estimating stock-price volatility. A 25 percent increase in volatility (0.50 versus 0.40) causes a 36 percent increase in the value of the option. Because everything else is observable, this variable will differentiate estimates.

Table 16A.1   Calculation of Option Value ($\sigma = 0.40$)

$$d_1 = \left[\frac{\ln(36/40) + [0.10 + 0.5(0.4)^2]0.25}{0.4(0.25)^{1/2}} \right]$$
$$= \left[\frac{-0.1054 + 0.045}{0.2} \right]$$
$$= -0.302$$
$$d_2 = -0.302 - [0.4(0.25)^{1/2}]$$
$$= -0.302 - 0.2$$
$$= -0.502$$
$$N(d_1) = 0.3814$$
$$N(d_2) = 0.3079$$
$$P_0 = P_s [N(d_1)] - E[\text{antiln}(-rt)][N(d_2)]$$
$$= [36][0.3814] - [40][\text{antiln}(-0.025)][0.3079]$$
$$= 13.7304 - [40][0.9753][0.3079]$$
$$= 13.7304 - 12.0118$$
$$= 1.7186$$

Table 16A.2   Calculation of Option Value ($\sigma = 0.50$)

$$d_1 = \left[\frac{\ln(36/40) + [0.10 + 0.5(0.5)^2]0.25}{0.5(0.25)^{1/2}} \right]$$
$$= \frac{-0.1054 + 0.05625}{0.25}$$
$$= -0.1966$$
$$d_2 = -0.1966 - [0.5(0.25)^{1/2}]$$
$$= -0.1966 - 0.25$$
$$= -0.4466$$
$$N(d_1) = 0.4199$$
$$N(d_2) = 0.3275$$
$$P_0 = [36][0.4199] - [40][\text{antiln}(-0.025)][0.3275]$$
$$= 15.1164 - [40][0.9753][0.3275]$$
$$= 15.1164 - 12.7764$$
$$= 2.34$$

CHAPTER

17
———

Warrants and Convertible Securities

In prior chapters we considered how you can invest in various bonds, common stocks, and options on both individual common stocks and the aggregate stock market. In this chapter we explore additional investment alternatives that resemble these familiar investments or combinations of them.

We begin with warrants, which are quite similar to options, except that they are issued by the firm that issues the stock and they cover longer periods. Some features make them very appealing to the issuing firm and to potential investors. In connection with our analysis of pure warrants, we discuss Americus Trusts, which combine fairly conservative, dividend-yielding "primes" and price-appreciation "scores" that closely resemble warrants. After discussing warrant valuation and trading strategies, we conclude with a consideration of currency exchange warrants as components of global investment programs.

The second major section of the chapter deals with convertible securities, which typically combine the features of bonds and common stock, since most are bonds that can be converted into common stock. We discuss why these instruments appeal to the firms that issue them and to investors who acquire them. We finish the section by considering how you should view these securities and evaluate them as combination securities. We conclude the chapter with a review of an alternative convertible security, convertible preferred stock.

Throughout the chapter you should keep in mind that these investment instruments assume that you have already decided to invest in a particular company and its stock. This chapter discusses alternative instruments that will help you acquire the stocks or that you can convert to common

Warrant An option to buy a stated number of shares of common stock from the issuing firm at a specified price for a certain period of time.

stock. Some unique characteristics of these vehicles can improve your investment portfolio more than pure common stock.

Warrants

A **warrant** is an option to buy a stated number of shares of common stock from the issuing firm at a specified price for a certain period of time. Although this definition reminds one of the description of a call option, there are several important differences. First, the life of a warrant is much longer than the term of a call option. The typical call option expires from 3 to 9 months after initiation. In contrast, a warrant generally has an original term to maturity of at least 2 years, and most last for between 5 and 10 years. There are even a few perpetual warrants.

A second major difference between warrants and options is that warrants are issued by the company that issues the stock. When you exercise a warrant and buy stock, you acquire the stock from the company, and the proceeds from the sale are new capital for the issuing firm.

In general, companies use warrants to "sweeten" bond or other security issues, since they could have value if the stock price were to increase as expected. The warrant will raise the price of the stock or bond, although most warrants are detachable after the initial sale and they trade separately on stock exchanges or the OTC market. Subsequently, the warrant can be a major source of new equity capital for the company.

Investors are generally interested in warrants because of their leverage possibilities, as we will discuss. Warrants pay no dividends and give the holder no voting rights. Also, you need to determine how a warrant protects you against dilution in the case of stock dividends or stock splits. Such protection either reduces the exercise price or increases the number of shares to be received to compensate for dilution.

An Example Warrant

The following example warrant issue will show how warrants are issued and their advantages for the issu-

ing firm and the investor. Suppose the Bourke Corporation is going to issue $10 million in bonds, but the firm knows that within 5 years it will need an additional $5 million in new external equity beyond expected retained earnings. To make the bond issue more attractive, while at the same time anticipating the need to sell stock in the future, the firm can attach stock warrants to the bonds.

If Bourke common stock were selling at $45 a share, the firm might issue 5-year warrants that allow the holder to acquire the company's common stock at $50 a share. Because the firm wants to raise $5 million from the future stock sale, it must issue warrants for 100,000 shares ($5 million/$50). To raise the initial $10 million, the company will need to sell 10,000 bonds with par values of $1,000, so, in order to sell the desired 100,000 shares of stock, each bond will have 10 warrants attached, assuming each warrant is for one share.

Suppose that the Bourke Corporation is successful and the market price on its common stock reaches $55 a share over the next 5 years. At this point each warrant will have an intrinsic value of $5 ($55 − $50), and all the warrants should be exercised prior to their expiration. As a result, the company will sell 100,000 shares of common stock at $50 a share. The company pays no explicit commission cost, but it does have administrative costs.

Examples of outstanding warrant quotations appear in Figure 17.1, which is a page from the *R. H. M. Survey of Warrants, Options & Low-Price Stocks.* For each warrant, the quote indicates where the stock and warrant are traded, the number of shares involved, price, expiration date if the warrant is not perpetual, and the current prices of the common stock and the warrant.

As an example, consider the Hasbro, Inc. warrants. The table indicates that the stock and the warrants are traded on the AMEX. Four of the 4 million warrants outstanding allow the holder to buy one share of Hasbro common stock from the company for $28.38 a share until July 12, 1994. As of late 1990, the common stock was selling on the AMEX for $14.50 per share and the warrant was selling for $0.43. We will discuss the valuation of the warrant in the following subsection.

Numerous firms have warrants outstanding with wide-ranging expiration dates and varying relationships between stock prices and warrant exercise prices. As of mid-1990, 20 warrant issues were listed on the NYSE, about 35 were listed on the AMEX, and sub-

Figure 17.1 *R·H·M Survey of Warrants·Options & Low-Price Stocks*

THE R·H·M SURVEY
of WARRANTS · OPTIONS & LOW-PRICE STOCKS

September 14, 1990

WARRANT
Explanatory Notes

All the information needed to evaluate each Warrant follows each Name, which is given precisely as each Warrant is traded, and this is followed by two letters indicating where common and Warrant are traded, in that order. S is New York SE, A is American SE, O is over-the-counter, P is Pacific SE, T is Toronto SE., M is Montreal SE and V is Vancouver SE. The symbol for the common follows, and the number of Warrants outstanding. If a senior security is useable at full face value, there will be an "SS" at this point, with a letter indicating where the senior security is traded, and the name of the senior security — coupon and year of maturity in the case of a Bond. There follows a recent price for the senior security, and "EEP," which means Effective Exercise Price in relation to that price. Example: if a Bond sells at 80 and the exercise price for the Warrant is 12, the EEP would be 80 x 12 or 9.6 *at* that price for the Bond. Always check the *current* price of the senior security if considering a commitment. Any "Call" terms or other provisions now follow. The full exercise terms for the Warrant will be at the end of the paragraph in italics, and common and Warrant price, in that order, will be on the last line to the right. Any recommendation to Buy, Hold, or Sell, will be to the left of the common/Warrant prices. **Warrants on Listed Stocks** appear in full in every issue. For all other Warrants, consult the box above, top-right. That box also informs you as to where the latest Index will be found, and coverage of **Currency Exchange Warrants**.

Warrants On Listed Stocks

AM Int'l, S-A, (AM), Callable if com exceeds 200% of exercise price for 20 tdg. days. *5.834 to 2-28-97.*

1.62-0.37

Allou Health & Beauty Care "A" '94, A-A, (ALU), 1,200,000 Warrants. Redeemable at 0.05 per Wt. if com exceeds 7.00/sh. for "A" Wt. & 10.50/sh. for "B" Wt. *5.00 to buy 1 Class 'A' com plus 1 "B" Wt. to 7-10-94.* ("B" Wt. - 7.50 to buy 1 Class 'A' com to 7-10-94)

2.37-0.37

American Capital Corp. '92, A-O, (ACC), 1,064,240 Warrants. *1.5 shs. at 4.00/sh. to 6-15-92.*

0.12-0.01

American Exploration Co., A-A, (AX), 2,000,000 Warrants. Redeemable at 1.00 per Wt. if com exceeds 150% of exercise price for 20 tdg. days. *2.75 to 1-3-93.*

Buy   *3.87-1.62*

American Science & Engineering, A-A, (ASE), 936,000 Warrants. *7.50 to 3-15-91.*

6.87-1.25

Angeles Corp., A-A, (ANG), 1,648,000 Warrants. Callable at 16.80 per Wt. Co. may accelerate expiration date by up to 24 months if com is 31.50/sh. or higher for stated period. *21.00 to 1-15-91.*

4.50-0.06

Asarco Inc. '91, S-O, (AR), 203,809 Warrants. *16.09 to 8-15-91.*

26.87-11.00

Astrotech Int'l Corp., A-A, (AIX), 868,000 Warrants. *6.00 to 3-31-93.*

1.37-0.25

Atlas Corp. S-A, (AZ), 2,800,000 Warrants. *15.625 Perpetual*

13.25-5.37

BSN Corp., A-A, (BSN), 1,000,000 Warrants. Redeemable at 1.00 per Wt. *10.75 to 11-15-96.*

6.00-0.43

Baker Hughes '95, S-O, (BHI), 5,400,000 Warrants. Redeemable at company's option. *36.75 to 3-31-95.*

31.75-7.93

Bank of New York Co. '98, S-O, (BK), 15,121,312 Warrants. *62.00 to 11-14-98*

23.00-3.50

Bond Int'l Gold Inc., S-S, (BIG), 4,862,000 Warrants. *15.25 to 7-31-91.*

6.37-0.37

British Petroleum, S-S, (BP), 21,477,228 Warrants. *80.00 to 1-31-93.*

Buy   *83.12-13.25*

Community National Bancorp, A-A, (CNB), 1,190,000 Warrants. (SS) A, 11's-99, N.A. Redeemable at 0.05 per Wt. if com exceeds 150% of exercise price. Exercise price of Wts. will be adjusted 3-31-92. *8.40 to 10-31-96.*

5.25-0.75

ESI Ind, A-A, (ESI), 669,000 Warrants. Redeemable at 0.25 per Wt. *6.00 to 10-31-91.*

0.75-0.03

Equitable Resources '92, S-O, (EQT), 1,500,000 Warrants. *57.50 to 7-1-92.*

Buy   *39.50-0.87*

Federal National Mtge. "A" 91, S-S, (FNM), 34,500,000 Warrants. *14.75 to 2-25-91.*

28.87-14.75

First Financial Management '95, S-O, (FFM), 8,400,000 Warrants. *6 Wts. to buy 1 com at 40.00/sh. to 4-15-95.*

18.75-0.18

Genesco-Feb. '93, S-O, (GCO), 737,840 Warrants, (SS), S, 14 1/4's-'94 N.A. Redeemable at 2.00 per Wt. if com exceeds 12.00 for stated period. *8.00 to 2-15-93.*

4.00-0.87

Genesco-Oct. '93, S-O, (GCO), 900,000 Warrants. (SS) S, 9 3/4's-'93, 97.37 EEP 10.37. Callable at 5.00 per Wt. if com exceeds 17.50/sh. for stated period. *10.65 to 10-15-93.*

4.00-0.62

Global Marine, S-S, (GLM) 12,700,000 Warrants. Co. may accelerate expiration date after 3-16-91 if com exceeds 150% of exercise price for 20 tdg. days. *3.00 to 3-16-96.*

6.37-4.50

Goldfield Corp '91, A-O (GV), 3,000,0000 Warrants. *0.53 to 5-6-91.*

0.37-0.06

Goldfield Corp. '93, A-O, (GV). *1.25 to 5-6-93.*

0.37-0.12

Granges Inc., A-A, (GXL), 1,000,000 Warrants. 7.50 to 1-21-91.

1.06-0.18

Halsey Drug Co. '91, A-A, (HDG), 976,435 Warrants. *1.05 shares at 1.90/sh. to 3-6-91.*

3.00-1.43

Hanson PLC '94, S-S, (HAN), 24,314,000 Warrants. *18.00 to buy 1 ADS sh. to 9-30-94.*

18.75-4.62

Hasbro Inc., A-A, (HAS), 4,000,000 Warrants. *4 Warrants to buy 1 com at 28.38/sh. to 7-12-94.*

14.50-0.43

Heritage Entertainment, A-A, (HHH), 746,000 Warrants. *5.00 to 12-31-90.*

1.25-0.06

Hotel Investors "B", S-A, (HOT), 1,659,974 Warrants. *16.95 to 9-16-96.*

2.75-0.03

Keystone Camera Products "B", A-A, (KYC), 1,150,000 Warrants. Callable at 0.75 per Wt. if com exceeds 140% of exercise price. 6 Wts. may be exchanged for 1 com. *7.50 to 5-7-91.*

0.56.0.18

Keystone Camera Products '93, A-O, (KYC), 1,250,000 Warrants. Redeemable at 0.05 per Wt. if com exceeds 3.25/sh. for 30 tdg. days. *1.75 to 8-23-93.*

0.56-0.31

Lifetime Corp. '96, S-O, (LFT), 4,530,000 Warrants. *6 Wts. to buy 1 com at 27.00/sh. to 10-28-96.*

24.50-1.62

Lilly (Eli), S-S, (LLY), 13,167,510 Warrants. *2 shs. at 37.99/sh. to 3-31-91.*

73.62-72.87

> **Americus Trust** A trust that holds common stock tendered by investors and in return issues units made up of primes and scores, which may be traded separately.
>
> **Prime** Part of a unit issued by an Americus Trust that entitles the holder to all dividend payments for the term of the trust, plus shares of the common stock at termination worth the number of shares originally tendered times the termination claim price.
>
> **Score** Part of a unit issued by an Americus Trust that entitles the holder at termination to shares of stock worth the number of shares originally tendered times any surplus of the market price of the stock over the termination claim price.

stantially more than 100 were traded on the OTC market.

Americus Trusts

Some individual security instruments have been divided into components, including stripped government bonds, from which security dealers have stripped the interest payments to create separate interest streams and zero coupon bonds. In a similar investment vehicle, an **Americus Trust,** investors tender regular common shares of a selected group of stocks to a trust fund and receive in exchange a "unit," which is a composite of a "prime" and a "score." (These terms will be explained shortly.) These separate components need not be held together, but can be separated and traded in the secondary market, currently the AMEX. While you can divide a unit into a prime and score, you can also combine a prime and a score back into a unit and exchange the unit for a share of the stock.

The SEC has approved 26 blue-chip stocks for inclusion in Americus Trusts. The stocks, their termination prices, and the termination dates of the trusts are listed in Figure 17.2.

The tendered shares are held in an Americus Trust until its termination date (or exercise date), which is always 5 years from the date of its establishment. At the termination date, the shares are divided between the holders of the primes and scores in accordance with the specifications of the trust, which depend upon the market value of the stock at the termination date.

A **prime** entitles the holder to all dividends paid on the stock during the life of the trust plus the mar-

ket value of the underlying stock on the termination date up to the value of the termination claim, which resembles the strike price for an option. This termination claim is set when the trust is established, at a level typically about 25 percent above the market value of the stock at that time. As an example, the trust for American Telephone & Telegraph was established in February 1987, so its termination date is February 20, 1992. Its termination claim is $30.

The holder of the AT&T prime receives all the dividends paid on AT&T common stock during the 5-year period and a maximum of $30 a share at termination. (As of September 1990, AT&T stock was selling for $32.) If the market value is less than $30 at the termination date, the holders of the primes will receive all the shares. If the price of the stock is greater than $30, the holders of the primes will receive enough shares to provide the same value as the original number of shares at $30 a share.

The **score** entitles the holder to all the value of the stock above the termination claim as of the date of termination. Continuing the previous example, if the market price of AT&T were to rise to $50 a share by the termination date (giving 100 shares a total market value of $5,000), the holder of the prime would receive shares worth $3,000 ($30 a share × 100 shares) and the holder of the score would receive shares worth $2,000. As of September 1990, when AT&T was selling for $32 a share, the price of the score was 6, so the score was in the money. In effect, if you acquired an AT&T score in late 1990, you would be buying an 18-month option with a strike price of $30. The price of $6 for the score reflects an intrinsic value of $2 and a time value of $4.

The score option is officially a European option, since it cannot be redeemed for its value over $30 until February 1992. Still, it acts like an American option since you can sell it at any time because it can be recombined with a prime into a unit at any time and exchanged for the original common shares. Therefore, if the combined value of a prime and a score were to fall below the current market price of the stock, a trader could profit by buying a prime and a score and selling the stock short. Suppose, for example, that the AT&T prime was selling for $19 and the score was $5 when the common stock was selling for $27. An investor could sell the stock short at $27 and cover it by purchasing a prime and a score for a total cost of $24. This keeps the sum of the values for the two units at least as high as the stock value. The combined value of the two components can sell at a premium above

Figure 17.2 **Listing of Americus Trust Stocks**

THE R·H·M SURVEY
of WARRANTS · OPTIONS & LOW-PRICE STOCKS

SCORES — Updated Prices

Name (symbol)	Term. Date	Term Price	Com Price	Score Price Ranges High	Low	Last
Amer Express (axp)	8-92	50.00	24.00	10.62	1.37	1.37
Amer Home Prod (ahp)	12-91	45.00	48.00	16.25	5.25	8.25
A T & T (t)	2-92	30.00	31.12	21.00	5.87	6.50
Amoco (an)	3-92	52.50	57.87	12.87	6.50	11.00
Atl Richfield (arc)	7-92	116.00	138.50	36.00	13.62	33.00
Bristol-Myers (bmy)	2-92	55.00	60.75	17.37	8.75	12.75
Chevron (chv)	7-92	75.00	78.00	17.37	6.25	13.37
Coca-Cola (ko)	7-92	28.00	42.12	23.12	9.50	17.75
Dow Chemical (dow)	5-92	73.33	41.37	19.87	2.25	2.62
Du Pont (dd)	3-92	36.66	35.62	11.00	5.12	5.75
Eastman Kodak (ek)	3-92	61.33	40.50	12.50	3.37	4.25
Exxon (xon)*	9-90	60.00	50.87	48.62	28.25	40.50
Ford (f)	6-92	52.00	35.12	12.12	1.87	2.37
GTE (gte)	7-92	22.00	25.87	14.75	4.75	7.25
General Electric (ge)	5-92	70.00	60.62	14.25	6.50	8.37
General Motors (gm)	6-92	53.50	37.62	8.75	2.12	2.87
Hewlett-Packard (hwp)	7-92	90.00	35.25	9.75	1.12	1.75
IBM (ibm)	6-92	210.00	105.50	15.75	1.87	3.00
Johnson & Johnson (jnj)	6-92	59.00	65.62	23.62	9.25	17.50
Merck (mrk)	4-92	66.66	81.12	30.87	13.50	22.87
Mobil (mob)	6-92	60.00	66.50	16.37	8.37	14.00
Philip Morris (mo)	7-92	27.50	45.25	26.62	12.62	20.62
Procter & Gamble (pg)	6-92	52.50	78.00	42.12	15.50	30.25
Sears (s)	7-92	64.00	28.75	6.87	1.12	1.25
Union Pacific (unp)	4-92	87.00	72.50	18.00	4.75	5.12
Xerox (xrx)	7-92	97.00	40.25	9.75	0.93	1.37

* 1 Prime plus 1 Score of Exxon will receive 2 shares of common stock.

Prime/Score Explanatory Notes

Just as, in recent years, *bonds* have been "stripped," so that one can have a claim on either the interest or the principal, *blue chip stocks* have now been similarly "stripped," by the device of the "Americus Trust." The owner of a blue chip stock (A.T. & T., GE, Mobil etc.), turns the stock into the appropriate Americus Trust and receives a "Unit." The Unit consists of a "Prime," entitled to both dividend payments normally paid to the common stock, and a certain payment — the *Termination Claim* — after 5 years, when the Trust is dissolved which is the *Termination Date*, and a "Score," which is entitled to no dividends, but, after the five-year period, is entitled to everything *above* the Termination Claim. In effect, each Score is a *long-term Warrant* on its common stock, with the Termination Claim being the exercise price, but exercise comes only at the *Termination Date*. At any time, a Prime and a Score can be recombined into a Unit and exchanged for a share of common stock, by the Trust. Since the October 1987 crash, Scores have been devastated in price, and many of them have sold below the 10 level, where they can become an outstanding, high-leverage purchase, and we will be following

September 14, 1990

Latest Index   Page 604
Scores   Page 573
Index Warrants Page 574-575
Currency Exchange Warrants
Page 574
Listed Warrants Page 575-577
Over-The-Counter Warrants
Pages 577-580(A-I) 589-592(J-Z)
Canadian Warrants
Page   601-602
Expiring Warrants
Pages 602-603

these developing opportunities in the weekly issues of the Survey. The headings in the box shown are self-explanatory. All Scores trade on the American Stock Exchange under individual "Americus Trusts." Thus, the IBM Score will be found on the ASE under "A-ibm sc."

WARRANT Explanatory Notes

All the information needed to evaluate each Warrant follows each Name, which is given precisely as each Warrant is traded, and this is followed by two letters indicating where common and Warrant are traded, in that order. S is New York SE, A is American SE, O is over-the-counter, P is Pacific SE, T is Toronto SE., M is Montreal SE and V is Vancouver SE. The symbol for the common follows, and the number of Warrants outstanding. If a senior security is useable at full face value, there will be an "SS" at this point, with a letter indicating where the senior security is traded, and the name of the senior security — coupon and year of maturity in the case of a Bond. There follows a recent price for the senior security, and "EEP," which means Effective Exercise Price in relation to that price. Example: if a Bond sells at 80 and the exercise price for the Warrant is 12, the EEP would be 80 x 12 or 9.6 *at* that price for the Bond. Always check the *current* price of the senior security if considering a commitment. Any "Call" terms or other provisions now follow. The full exercise terms for the Warrant will be at the end of the paragraph in italics, and common and Warrant price, in that order, will be on the last line to the right. Any recommendation to Buy, Hold, or Sell, will be to the left of the common/Warrant prices. **Warrants on Listed Stocks** appear in full in every issue. For all other Warrants, consult the box above, top-right. That box also informs you as to where the latest Index will be found, and coverage of **Currency Exchange Warrants.**

the value of the stock because you cannot get new primes and scores by exchanging outstanding stock since the value of each trust is limited to about 5 percent of the outstanding shares. Once this limit is reached, the trust is closed and you can only acquire units or components in the open market.

All of the trusts were closed by the end of 1988. The dealer–manager for these trusts was Alex, Brown & Sons, Inc., a New York investment banking firm. Sample quotes for primes and scores on the AMEX appear in Figure 17.3. Some also give quotes for the units (un), so you can see the relationship. As an example, the Eastman Kodak (Kodak) closing quotes indicate that the unit (Arrow 1) closed at $41, the prime (pm, Arrow 2) at $37.125, and the score (sc, Arrow 3) at $4.25, which means the combination of the components was selling for a small premium over the unit ($41.375 versus $41.00). The common stock, which is listed on the NYSE, was equal to the value of the unit at $41.

This example also indicates the difference in yield on the prime. The dividend payment on the unit (the common stock) and the prime are the same ($1.97), but because the price for the prime is $37.125 versus $41 for the unit, its yield is 5.3 percent versus 4.8 percent on the common stock unit.

Strategies with Americus Trusts If you own shares of one of the stocks eligible for such a trust, you could shift your emphasis by tendering your shares and receiving trust units. For our first example (ignoring commissions), you could conservatively increase your income return by selling the scores in the market and using the proceeds of the sale to buy more primes. Assume you tender stock with a market value of $100,000, which equals the stock price of $100 times the number of shares you owned, 1,000. Assume the stock pays a $4,000 dividend, the primes cost $80, and the scores cost $20. Selling your 1,000 scores would bring you $20,000, which you could use to buy 250 more primes ($20,000/$80), increasing your total dividends to $5,000 (1,250 × $4). As a result of these transactions, you have increased your yield while making your portfolio more conservative because primes would act more like bonds when the market price of the common stock approached the termination price. This is especially true as you get close to the termination date of the trust. The price of the primes must remain close to the termination price because that known figure determines their return.

Figure 17.3 ***Quotations for Americus Trusts***

AMERICAN STOCK EXCHANGE COMPOSITE TRANSACTIONS

Quotations as of 4:30 p.m. Eastern Time
Monday, September 17, 1990

	52 Weeks Hi	52 Weeks Lo	Stock	Sym	Div	Yld %	PE	Vol 100s	Hi	Lo	Close	Net Chg
			-A-A-A-									
	32	21¼	A-TrAmExp pm	XPP	.87	4.0	...	20	22	22	22	+ ¼
	10⅝	**1⅜**	**A-TrAmExp sc**	**XPS**		**...**	**...**	**51**	**1⅝**	**1½**	**1⅝**	**+ ⅛**
s	42½	37¾	A-TrAmHom pm	HPP	2.10	5.2	...	41	40¼	40	40¼	+ ¼
s	**16¼**	**5¼**	**A-TrAmHom sc**	**HPS**		**...**	**...**	**146**	**8¼**	**7⅞**	**8¼**	**+ ½**
	28	24¾	A-TrATT pm	ATP	1.27	5.0	...	453	25¾	25½	25⅝	...
	21	5⅞	A-TrATT sc	ATS		...	...	1497	6½	6⅛	6¼	– ¼
s	47½	39½	A-TrAmoco pm	AOP	2.01	4.3	...	27	46⅝	46⅜	46⅝	+ ⅛
	12⅞	**6½**	**A-TrAmoco sc**	**AOS**		**...**	**...**	**88**	**11¼**	**10⅝**	**11¼**	**+ ⅝**
	108	83½	A-TrArco pm	RFP	4.95	4.7	...	15	106	105⅞	106	+ ½
	36	13⅝	A-TrArco sc	RFS		...	...	199	35	34	34⅞	+ ⅞
s	49⅝	40¾	A-TrBriMyr pm	BYP	2.09	4.3	...	32	48⅝	48¼	48¼	...
	17⅜	8¾	A-TrBriMyr sc	BYS		...	...	294	12⅜	11⅜	12⅛	+ ⅛
	66	48¼	A-TrChevrn pm	CVP	3.05	4.8	...	9	64	63¾	64	+ ⅝
	17⅜	**6¼**	**A-TrChevrn sc**	**CVS**		**...**	**...**	**43**	**13¼**	**12⅝**	**13¼**	**+ ⅝**
s	25⅞	21⅜	A-TrCoke pm	KKP	.77	3.2	...	97	24½	24¼	24¼	...
s	23⅛	9½	A-TrCoke sc	KKS		...	...	156	17	16½	16⅝	...
▼	62¼	38¼	A-TrDowChm pm	DOP	2.57	6.7	...	12	38⅝	38⅛	38⅝	+ ⅜
	19⅞	**2⅛**	**A-TrDowChm sc**	**DOS**		**...**	**...**	**269**	**2⅜**	**2⅛**	**2¼**	**– ⅛**
s	32⅞	29½	A-TrDupont pm	DPP	1.58	5.2	...	50	30½	30¼	30¼	– ¼
s	11	5⅛	A-TrDupont sc	DPS		...	...	89	5⅜	5¼	5¼	– ⅛
s	21¼	19	A-TrGTE pm	LDP	1.56	7.9	...	68	19⅞	19¾	19¾	...
s	14¾	4¾	A-TrGTE sc	LDS		...	...	418	6⅞	6⅝	6⅝	– ¼
	75	54¾	A-TrGE un	GNU	1.86	3.1	...	15	60¼	60¼	60¼	...
s	61⅜	46¼	A-TrGE pm	GNP	1.86	3.5	...	156	53	52½	52¾	– ½
	14¼	6½	A-TrGE sc	GNS		...	...	517	7⅞	7½	7½	– ⅛
s	44⅝	34	A-TrGM pm	GCP	2.97	8.5	...	14	35⅜	34⅞	35⅛	– ⅛
	8⅜	2⅛	A-TrGM sc	GCS		...	...	79	2⅝	2½	2½	– ⅛
①→	52	39¼	A-TrKodak un	KDU	1.97	4.8	...	5	41	41	41	– ¼
②→ s	41⅞	33½	A-TrKodak pm	KDP	1.97	5.3	...	57	37⅝	37⅛	37⅛	– ⅜
③→	11¾	3⅜	A-TrKodak sc	KDS		...	...	162	4¼	4⅛	4¼	...
s	44	31¾	A-TrFord pm	FCP	2.98	9.0	...	9	33	32⅞	33	– ¼
	11¼	1⅞	A-TrFord sc	FCS		...	...	314	2⅛	1⅞	2	...
	46½	30	A-TrHewltP pm	HLP	.37	1.2	...	5	31⅝	31⅝	31⅝	+ ⅛
	9½	1⅛	A-TrHewltP sc	HLS		...	...	9	1½	1⅜	1½	...
	118½	88⅞	A-TrIBM pm	BZP	4.79	4.7	...	173	102¾	100½	102⅜	+1¼
	15½	1⅞	A-TrIBM sc	BZS		...	...	456	2¾	2⅝	2¾	...
s	51½	41	A-TrJ&J pm	JNP	1.33	2.7	...	36	48⅜	48	48⅜	+ ¼
	23⅝	9¼	A-TrJ&J sc	JNS		...	...	247	16⅞	16¼	16⅜	– ⅜
s	60½	52	A-TrMerck pm	MKP	2.23	3.8	...	26	58¼	58	58¼	+ ⅜
	30⅞	13½	A-TrMerck sc	MKS		...	...	97	22⅜	21½	22⅜	+ ½
s	25½	23⅜	A-TrPhMor pm	HMP	1.70	6.7	...	26	25¼	25⅛	25¼	+ ⅛
	26⅝	12⅝	A-TrPhMor sc	HMS		...	...	283	21¼	20⅝	21	+ ⅜
	53¾	43⅞	A-TrMobil pm	MBP	2.85	5.4	...	18	52½	52¼	52½	+ ⅛
	16⅜	8⅜	A-TrMobil sc	MBS		...	...	100	13¾	13¼	13¾	+ ½
s	50	41¼	A-TrPrctrG pm	OGP	1.78	3.8	...	18	47⅛	46⅞	47⅛	+ ¼
s	42⅛	15½	A-TrPrctrG sc	OGS		...	...	332	28⅞	27⅞	28⅞	– ⅛
	6⅝	**1⅛**	**A-TrSears sc**	**RSS**		**...**	**...**	**1**	**1⅛**	**1⅛**	**1⅛**	**– ⅛**
	69¾	59	A-TrUnPac pm	UPP	2.27	3.4	...	14	67¾	67	67¾	+1½
	17⅞	**4¼**	**A-TrUnPac sc**	**UPS**		**...**	**...**	**26**	**4⅞**	**4⅜**	**4⅞**	**+ ⅜**
	59¼	37½	A-TrXerox pm	XXP	2.95	7.8	...	18	38	37¾	37¾	– ½
	9⅝	15/16	A-TrXerox sc	XXS		...	...	60	1¼	1¼	1¼	...

Source: "American Stock Exchange Composite Transactions," *The Wall Street Journal*, September 18, 1990.

If, on the other hand, you want a more aggressive investment, you can use the score like an option or warrant. You could sell your primes and invest the proceeds ($80,000) in 4,000 scores, for a portfolio of 5,000 scores at $20. Your results depend entirely on what happens to the firm's stock price because the scores entitle you to everything over the prime termination price. If the prime termination were $80 and the stock price rose to $120 at the termination date, the prime holder would receive $80, but the holder of the score would receive $40.

Valuation of Warrants

The value of a warrant is determined much like that of a call option. The major difference is the longer term of the warrant. As an investor you do not care whether the option allows you to buy the stock from another investor or directly from the firm. You should consider the two components of the value of a warrant, which are similar to those of a call option: its intrinsic value and its speculative value, which is sometimes referred to as its *premium*. We will discuss each of these components.

Intrinsic Value   The intrinsic value of a warrant is the difference between the market price of the common stock and the warrant exercise price, as follows:

Intrinsic value = (Market price of common stock − Warrant exercise price) × Number of Shares Specified by the Warrant

If the market price of the stock exceeds the warrant exercise price, the warrant has a positive intrinsic value. If the stock price is less than the exercise price, the equation would give a negative value and we would say that the warrant has zero intrinsic value. As an example, Figure 17.1 shows that the Eli Lilly Company warrant allows the holder to buy two shares of Eli Lilly common stock at an exercise price of $37.99 until March 31, 1991; the common stock was selling for $73.62. This gives the warrant an intrinsic value of $71.26 [($73.62 − $37.99) × 2], because each warrant allows the holder to purchase two shares of common stock at a price lower than the current market price. Note that the market price of the warrant ($72.87) is above its intrinsic value ($71.26). This excess market value relative to the intrinsic value is its speculative value, as we discuss next.

Speculative Value   Similar to a call option, a warrant's leverage, which causes the value of the warrant to increase and decline by larger percentages than the value of the underlying stock, is important. As an example, assume a stock is selling for $48, and a warrant for the stock with an exercise price of $50 is selling for $3 on the basis of its speculative value. This warrant would have no intrinsic value because its exercise price is above the market price. If the stock were to increase 15 percent to $55 the warrant would rise to at least $5, its new intrinsic value. Thus, a stock price increase of about 15 percent would cause the price of the warrant to increase by at least 67 percent, from $3 to $5. Any speculative value would boost the price of the warrant even higher.

You can evaluate leverage involved in a warrant by examining the *ratio of the stock price to the warrant price*. A larger ratio of stock price to warrant price means greater leverage. We can demonstrate this relationship with the example in Table 17.1, which assumes that the warrant has an exercise price of $20 and sells at its theoretical value over time. The example demonstrates the effect on the stock price to warrant price (SP/WP) ratio of different percentage changes in the price of the stock and the price of the warrant. A higher SP/WP ratio increases the leverage of the warrant, that is, there is a larger percentage change in the warrant price for a given percentage change in the stock price. At a beginning SP/WP ratio of 11, a 36 percent stock price increase brings a warrant price increase of 400 percent. After this change, when the SP/WP ratio was 3, a 33 percent stock price increase boosted the warrant price by 100 percent.

Note that this leverage works both ways; a decline in the stock price would cause a larger decline in the warrant price.[1] Because investors in warrants typically consider this leverage a positive attribute, a greater SP/WP ratio increases the speculative value of the warrant.

A major factor in the price of a warrant, as in the price of a call option, is the time to maturity. A longer term to maturity increases the value of the warrant. Because warrants typically possess long terms to expiration, they typically have speculative value even when they are deeply out of the money. A 3-year warrant with an exercise price of $50 would have time

---

[1]"Stock Warrants—A Way to Get Leverage," *Forbes*, June 9, 1980: 102–104.

| Table 17.1 | *Warrant Leverage and Ratio of Stock Price to Warrant Price* | | | | |

	Time				
	T	T + 1	T + 2	T + 3	T + 4
Stock price	$22	$30	$40	$50	$60
Warrant price*	$2	$10	$20	$30	$40
Ratio of stock price to warrant price (SP/WP)	11.00	3.00	2.00	1.67	1.50
Percentage change in stock price	—	36.40	33.30	25.00	20.00
Percentage change in warrant price	—	400.00	100.00	50.00	33.30

*Strike price, $20/share.

value even when the stock was selling for $40. As noted, this difference in the original time to maturity is a major factor distinguishing warrants from call options, which typically cover less than 9 months. As Figure 17.1 indicates, newly issued warrants generally do not expire for 2 to 5 years, and some are perpetual.

Another important factor in warrant valuation is the volatility of the stock's price. Higher volatility in the stock price makes a positive move above the exercise price more probable and boosts the value of the warrant. Again, this effect is similar for call options. This volatility factor would not be very important in the valuation of a warrant on a relatively stable stock like AT&T, but it could affect the speculative value for stocks with high price volatility.

The value of the warrant would suffer if the firm paid a dividend on the underlying stock. The dividend payment would reduce the total value of the firm and therefore the stock price, but the warrant holder would not receive any dividend.

To summarize, the value of the warrant is determined by the following factors:

1. Intrinsic value of the warrant, which is based on the difference between the market price of the stock and the exercise price of the warrant times the number of shares per warrant.
2. Speculative value of the warrant, sometimes referred to as its *premium value* or *time value*, which is a function of the following factors:
    a. Potential leverage, which is a function of the ratio of the stock price to the warrant price (SP/WP). More potential leverage means a larger speculative value.
    b. Time to maturity. A longer time to maturity increases speculative (time) value.
    c. Price volatility of the underlying stock. More price volatility increases the premium value.
    d. Dividend paid by the stock. A larger dividend reduces premium value.

Based on these valuation factors, the graph in Figure 17.4 indicates the maximum value the warrant could have, which equals the total value of the stock. It also shows the warrant's minimum value, which is its intrinsic value. Finally, the graph shows how the likely market value for a warrant is affected by the time remaining before expiration. You could envision multiple curves for each maturity to represent different levels of price volatility for the underlying security.

Warrant Strategies

A basic investment philosophy should guide your use of warrants. Once you have analyzed a stock and decided that it would be a good investment over the next several years, you should find out whether the firm has any warrants outstanding. These warrants would allow you to control a large amount of the stock for a fairly long period (possibly several years) for a modest investment.[2] Several considerations influence investment in warrants as part of an overall program:

1. The ultimate performance of the warrant depends on the performance of the stock. Remember that the

[2]For a further discussion on warrant pricing, see Michael G. Ferri, Joseph W. Kremer, and H. Dennis Oberhelman, "An Analysis of

Figure 17.4   ***Graph of Maximum, Minimum, and Actual Warrant Prices***

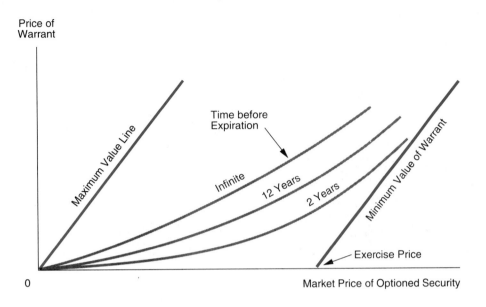

leverage factor works both ways. You should consider buying a warrant only if you are bullish on the stock. The warrant gives you a means to maximize the return from a good stock.

2.   Diversification is as important with warrants as with other investments. If you decide to invest in warrants you should probably consider acquiring a number of them on several desirable stocks.

3.   Once you own a diversified portfolio of warrants with high leverage characteristics, be sure to cut your losses short and let the profits run. This strategy governs any leveraged investment, including options or commodities. Successful warrant investing combines inevitable small losses with a few very big winners. Returns in excess of 100 percent from three warrants can easily compensate for losses on five or six warrant positions of 25 to 30 percent.

4.   The most desirable warrants generally have very little intrinsic value, and therefore large SP/WP ratios, and high leverage. In addition, you probably want a minimum of 2 years remaining to maturity, and preferably 3 or 4 years. Also, look for highly volatile stock prices. These recommendations presuppose the standard protective features against dilution and calls.

Based upon these characteristics, you determine whether the speculative or premium value of a warrant is reasonable. This requires comparing alternative warrants to their underlying stocks. As stated initially, when you buy a warrant, you ultimately invest in the underlying stock.

5.   You can search for desirable warrants in one of two ways. The first is to use the three-step analysis process to put together a list of good stocks in good companies in desirable industries. You then check a warrant reference service such as the *R. H. M. Survey* to see whether any of these desirable stocks have outstanding warrants with the characteristics mentioned previously.

For an alternative approach, you can begin by examining a number of warrants listed in a service such as the *R. H. M. Survey* and select those that have most of the desirable characteristics. Next, you analyze the

the Pricing of Corporate Warrants," *Advances in Futures and Options Research* 1 (1986): 201–225; Michael G. Ferri, Scott B. Moore, and David C. Schirm, "Investor Expectations about Callable Warrants," *Journal of Portfolio Management* 14, no. 3 (Spring 1988): 84–86. For an analysis of hedging with warrants, see Moon K. Kim and Allan Young, "Rewards and Risks from Warrant Hedging," *Journal of Portfolio Management* 6, no. 4 (Summer 1980): 65–68.

> **Currency exchange warrant (CEW)** A warrant that entitles the holder to buy a specific number of U.S. dollars for a non-U.S. currency at a stated exchange rate.

issuing companies and their industries to assess the stocks. We prefer the first approach, which treats warrant selection as part of the total investment process, rather than as an end in itself.

Currency Exchange Warrants

A set of relatively recently developed warrants, **currency exchange warrants (CEWs),** are important to global investors. They allow holders to buy a specific number of U.S. dollars for a non-U.S. currency at a stipulated exchange rate. Figure 17.5 lists the CEWs

available as of September 1990. As an example, the Sallie Mae yen CEW that expires March 1, 1993 has a strike price of 135.92 yen. Each warrant allows the holder to acquire 50 U.S. dollars at an exchange rate of 135.92 yen per dollar. The minimum transaction is for 2,000 warrants or $100,000.

These warrants become profitable when the U.S. dollar strengthens against the yen to a rate in excess of 136. As shown in Figure 17.5, this CEW was selling for $3.75 on September 14, 1990. To find a value for these warrants, you compute their cash settlement values (CSVs), as the greater of:

$$CSV = 0 \text{ or}$$
$$= 50 - \left(50 \times \frac{\text{Strike price}}{\text{Spot rate}}\right)$$

When the spot rate exceeds the strike price, such a warrant has some positive intrinsic value. If the spot

Figure 17.5 *Description of Currency Exchange Warrants*

Currency Exchange Warrants

Name	Exp Date	Exerc Rate	High	Low	Close
A T & T Credit	7-92	158.25 yen	3.50	0.87	1.75
Citicorp Wt M	7-92	1.932 marks	4.00	0.87	2.50
Citicorp Wt Y	7-92	152.50 yen	4.00	1.37	2.37
Citicorp Wt Y	4-93	132.90 yen	3.37	2.87	3.87
Emerson Elec Wt M	7-92	1.918 marks	4.62	1.12	2.50
Ford Motor Cred 92	7-92	152.2 yen	4.50	1.75	2.62
Ford Motor Cred 93	2-93	134.00 yen	4.12	3.12	4.50
General Elec Cr	6-92	149.70 yen	5.00	2.00	2.62
General Elec Cr	7-92	1.9120 marks	4.75	1.37	2.75
Morgan (J.P.)	7-91	1.904 marks	2.75	2.25	2.37
Sallie Mae Wt M	7-92	1.92 marks	4.62	1.25	2.25
Sallie Mae Wt Y	7-92	152.20 yen	4.37	1.25	2.37
Sallie Mae Wt Y	2-93	131.75 yen†	9.37	7.87	7.87
Sallie Mae Wt Y	3-93	135.92 yen	4.00	2.50	3.50
Xerox Credit Wt Y	7-92	154.15 yen	4.12	1.00	1.87

†Minimum expiration value of $9.25; Strike Price varies over life of Warrant

Source: *R·H·M Survey of Warrants·Options & Low-Price Stocks*, September 14, 1990. Reprinted with permission.

yen/U.S. dollar exchange rate went to 150, the CSV on the example warrant would be:

$$\text{CSV} = 50 - \left(50 \times \frac{\text{Strike price: } 135.92}{\text{Spot rate: } 150.00}\right)$$

$$= 50 - (50 \times 0.9061) = \$4.69$$

Table 17.2 indicates the cash settlement values for other exchange rates.

Currency exchange warrants provide long-term options that can be used for speculation or hedging exchange rate risk. The increasing number of warrants and strike prices available increase the opportunities substantially.

Convertible Securities

A convertible security gives the holder the right to convert one type of security into a stipulated amount of another type. Typically, but not invariably, the security is convertible into common stock, but it could be exchanged for preferred stock or a special class of common stock. The most popular convertible securities are convertible bonds and convertible preferred stock. Appendix 17A gives a glossary of terms related to convertibles.

Table 17.2	Cash Settlement Values for Sallie Mae Yen Warrant

Hypothetical Spot Rate (Yen/U.S.$1)	Cash Settlement Value of Warrant*
110.00	$ 0.00
120.00	0.00
130.00	0.00
135.92	0.00
140.00	1.46
150.00	4.69
160.00	7.53
180.00	12.24
200.00	16.02
220.00	19.11
240.00	21.68
260.00	23.86

*Expiration date, 3/1/93; Strike price, 135.92 yen

Convertible bond A bond, usually subordinated, that the holder can exchange for a stated number of shares of the issuer's common stock.

Convertible Bonds

A **convertible bond** is usually a subordinated bond that allows the holder to exchange it for a stated number of shares of common stock in the issuing company. The conversion price is generally set above the price of the common stock at the issue of the bonds. A company with common stock selling for $36 a share might decide to sell a subordinated convertible bond that matures in 20 years and is convertible into common stock at $40 a share. At a par value of $1,000, the bond could be converted into 25 shares of common stock ($1,000/$40). Because the conversion feature is generally considered attractive for reasons to be discussed, these bonds typically pay interest at rates below the required return on the firm's straight debentures. In this case, assume an 8 percent coupon.

Advantages of Convertible Bonds to Issuing Firms

Companies issue convertible bonds for several reasons. First, the interest rate on a firm's convertible bonds is lower than that on its straight debt. The difference in interest rates is usually at least 0.5 percent (50 basis points), but can be much larger depending on the growth prospects of the firm. Interest on convertible bonds is lower despite their higher risk due to being subordinated to straight debt. Bond rating agencies generally rate subordinated issues one class lower than a firm's straight debentures because of this higher risk, raising the interest rates they must pay above those for straight debt. This means that convertibles give even more savings compared to a bond with the same rating than the 50 basis points quoted above. This means that convertible bonds reduce the cost of debt capital to the issuing firm.

Another advantage to the issuing firm is that convertible bonds represent potential common stock sales at a price above the current market price. The bondholder can choose to convert the bond or the firm may force conversion in the future by including a call feature in the indenture. This ability to arrange for a future issue of common stock may be desirable for a firm that would like to finance an investment through common stock rather than bonds, but does not want

> **Conversion value** The value of a convertible bond if converted into common stock at the stock's current market price. It is equal to the market price of the stock times the number of shares into which the bonds convert.
>
> **Investment value** The price at which a convertible bond would be expected to sell as a straight debt instrument.

to dilute per-share earnings during the initial years before the investment begins generating income. After the investment begins generating earnings, the stock price should rise above the conversion value, inducing investors to convert the bonds, or the firm can force conversion by calling the bonds.

Consider an example of forced conversion. Suppose a $1,000 par value bond is convertible into stock at $40 a share, giving the holder 25 shares of common stock. Assume that the bond is callable at 108 percent of par ($1,080), and in the 2 years after the issue is sold, the common stock rises from $36 to $45 a share because of higher earnings. At a stock price of $45, the bond has a minimum market value, or conversion value, of $1,125 (25 × $45). If the firm wants to get the convertible bond issue off the balance sheet by converting it to common stock, it can simply call the bonds at 108 ($1,080). To avoid the call at $1,080, the bondholders should convert their bonds for the 25 shares of stock worth $1,125.

Convertible bonds give a firm low-cost debt when it wants it together with the chance to convert it to future common stock at an implicit price of $40 a share compared with the $36 a share when the bond was issued.

Advantages of Convertible Bonds to Investors

As noted, special features of convertible bonds keep their coupon rates substantially below what you would expect based upon the quality of the issues. Investors are willing to accept these lower interest rates to gain the upside potential of common stock and the downside protection of a bond.

Upside Potential The preceding example showed the upside potential of such bonds. As soon as the price of the common stock exceeded $40 a share, the price of the bond increased by at least the increase in **con-**

version value, which is equal to the number of shares to which the bond converts times the current price of the common stock. In most cases, the market price of the bond will be above its conversion value because it also offers downside protection, and its interest payments typically exceed the dividend payments for the potential common stock.

Downside Protection The convertible bond offers downside protection because, whatever happens to the price of the stock, the price of the bond will not decline below its value as a straight bond. Assume that the 8 percent subordinated convertible bond from the previous example is rated A by the rating services. (The company's nonsubordinated debentures are rated AA.) If the firm's earnings were to decline significantly pushing the price of common stock down to $25 a share, the bond would have a conversion value of $625 (25 shares × $25).[3] The price of the convertible bond would probably not decline to $625 because it would still have value as an A-rated security with an 8 percent coupon. This value as a nonconvertible bond is generally referred to as a bond's **investment value.**

If we assume that the bond has 18 years to maturity and that comparable A-rated, 18-year bonds are yielding 9 percent, the price of this bond will decline below par, but not to $625. The price of this bond should decline to about $938.80 (0.9388 of par), the price of an 18-year, 8 percent coupon bond with a YTM of 9 percent. While the stock price has declined about 30 percent (from $36 to $25), the bond price should decline by only about 6 percent (from $1,000 to $938.80).

Higher Current Returns In addition to their upside potential and downside protection, convertible bonds also typically have higher current returns than the underlying common stock. An annual dividend of $1.50 a share would give a 3.75 percent yield on a $40 stock or a 4.17 percent yield on a $36 stock. Although such dividend yields are reasonable, the bond would pay more total current income.

Total dividends on the 25 shares of stock would be $37.50 a year (25 × $1.50), compared to interest income of $80 from the bond (0.08 × $1,000). Ob-

---

[3]As noted, the bond's conversion value is equal to its conversion ratio (25 in this example) times the current market price of the stock.

viously, the bond would pay more current income until the dividend on the stock were raised to $3.20 a share ($80/25). Even at this higher dividend, the bond would probably be preferred for its downside protection and because the $80 interest payment is a contractual obligation, whereas the $80 dividend payment could be reduced if earnings were to decline. You would probably wait until the common stock dividend reached $3.50 or $4.00 a share before converting the bond to take advantage of the higher yield from the stock.

One advantage that convertible bonds have lost is their former potential for leverage. Prior to the 1970s, investors could borrow on convertible bonds at about the same proportion of value as on straight debentures, which was about 80 percent. This ability to borrow a high proportion of market value allowed people to invest in convertible bonds with little cash, and then to offset part of the interest on the loan with the interest from the convertible bond. Currently, however, margin requirements are the same for convertible bonds and common stock (50 percent), which means that the cash commitment is much greater.

Price-Response of Convertible Bonds

The upside potential–downside protection for convertible bonds can be shown in two ways. First, we can examine the effects on the price of the convertible bond of price changes in the common stock. Second, we can consider what happens to the returns on convertible bonds when we assume a set of returns for straight bonds and for pure common stocks. In this subsection, we consider the price-response curve; in the next subsection, we discuss the differential return patterns for stocks, bonds, and convertible bonds.

Figure 17.6 shows a price-response curve for a convertible bond over a variety of stock prices. The straight, dotted line below the curve shows the pure equity value, or the conversion value, of the convertible bond, as discussed previously. The curve shows the market value of the convertible bond including both the conversion value and the investment value (or bond value) of the security. As discussed, a decline in the stock price leaves the convertible bond with a value as a subordinated bond, so it would not decline together with the pure equity value. The decline in the market value of the bond at the far left of the graph

Figure 17.6 *Convertible Bond Price-Response Curve*

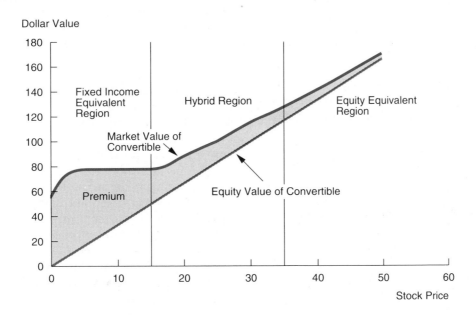

Source: Luke D. Knecht and Michael L. McCowin, "Valuing Convertible Securities," Harris Trust and Savings Bank (1986). Reprinted with permission.

Figure 17.7 **Return Distributions on Stocks, Bonds, and Convertible Securities**

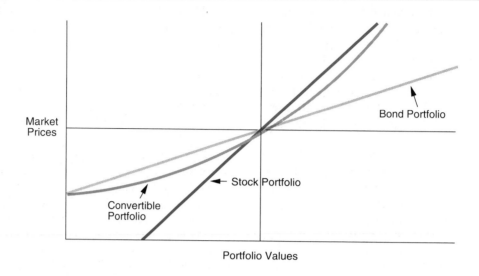

Source: Luke D. Knecht and Michael L. McCowin, "Valuing Convertible Securities," Harris Trust and Savings Bank (1986). Reprinted with permission.

reflects the possibility that at very low stock prices investors might doubt the viability of the firm and its ability to pay off a subordinated bond issue.

The returns on a convertible bond generally fall into three regions. At the far right, when the stock price is substantially above the conversion price, the convertible bond is equivalent to common stock, and its value reflects changes in the stock price. At very high stock prices the premium over the bond's pure equity value, that is, its conversion value, basically disappears. In this zone, the bond moves in close synchronization with the common stock.

At the far left, when the stock price is substantially below the conversion price, the security is equivalent to a straight subordinated bond, and its price moves with interest rates. In this bond-equivalent region, the security's price includes a substantial premium over the conversion value, or pure equity value, of the bond.

Between these two extremes, the convertible bond falls within a hybrid region where it performs like a combination of a bond and common stock. Within this region, valuation of the bond is difficult. In the bond region, the security is valued as a straight bond, while in the equity region its value depends upon its stock conversion value. We discuss some of the factors that must be considered when valuing a bond in this hybrid region in a subsequent section.

Differential Return Pattern of Convertible Bond Components

Figure 17.7 indicates the second way to evaluate the returns on this security. This graph indicates the values and implied rates of return for a straight stock issue, a straight bond, and a convertible bond. As you would expect, the returns for common stock over time are larger and more volatile than the returns for bonds. The graph shows that the convertible bond's returns fall between those of the stock and the bond. Specifically, it acts like common stock when stock prices are increasing, but like the less volatile straight bond when stock prices decline.

This performance makes convertible bonds a desirable investment alternative because they offer upside price appreciation, downside protection, and, typically, higher current income than common stocks.[4] This yield advantage of convertible bonds versus common stock is especially valuable for issues of growth companies that pay low dividends on the stock and have substantial potential for stock price increases. In such cases, institutional investors are will-

---

[4]This is the price of an 18-year, 8 percent coupon bond priced to yield 9 percent.

ing to accept substantially lower coupon rates on a convertible bond than they would accept on straight bonds for the same firm.

Analysis and Valuation of Convertible Bonds

As noted, a convertible bond is actually a combination of a bond and a warrant or option for the common stock of the firm. Therefore, the value of the security is composed of both components. You must first ask, as a straight bond, what should its yield and implied price be? This analysis will indicate your downside risk if the stock were to decline to the point where the convertible bond had value only as a straight bond.

As an example, consider a 7.875 percent convertible bond issue of IBM due in the year 2004. Both Standard & Poor's and Moody's give these bonds AAA ratings and each bond is convertible into 6.508 shares of common stock until maturity. This 6.508 is the bond's **conversion ratio.** To find the straight bond component of value in 1992, you would need to determine the going rate on a AAA-rated bond with about 12 years to maturity. A current yield to maturity on such a bond of about 10 percent would imply a straight bond price (i.e., investment value) of approximately $853, the present value of a 7.875 percent, 12-year bond at a 10 percent yield, assuming semiannual interest payments. Comparing this straight bond price (investment value) to the current market price of the bond tells you the **price risk** of the bond. This difference in price is referred to as the **investment premium.** Assuming a current market price for the bond of 104 of par would imply about a 22 percent price risk (investment premium) (1,040 − 853/1,040). You must decide whether you are willing to accept this downside risk.

In the second part of the analysis, you evaluate the bond's stock value, or its upside potential as a result of the conversion factor. To evaluate this component of the bond, you need to compute the **conversion premium** for the bond, which you find by comparing its conversion parity price to the current stock price. The **conversion parity price** equals the market price of the bond divided by the number of shares you would receive if you converted it into common stock (i.e., its conversion ratio).

As noted, the IBM bond's conversion ratio is 6.508 shares of stock. Therefore, a price of 104 for these bonds would imply a conversion parity price of $159.80 ($1,040/6.508). Comparing this conversion

Conversion ratio The number of shares into which a bond can be converted.

Price risk The uncertainty of a convertible bond's returns because of its market price being different from its investment value. This is also referred to as *investment premium.*

Investment premium The difference between the market price of a convertible bond and its investment value as a straight bond as a percentage of investment value.

Conversion premium The excess of the market value of a convertible bond compared to the market value of the common stock into which it can be converted (i.e., its conversion value). Typically expressed as a percentage of the conversion value.

Conversion parity price The market value of a convertible bond divided by the number of shares into which it can be converted (i.e., its conversion ratio).

Breakeven time The time required for the added income from a convertible bond to offset the conversion premium. Also referred to as *payback period.*

parity price to the current market price of the common stock indicates the conversion premium. A price for the common stock of $120 on the NYSE would indicate a conversion premium over the market price (sometimes referred to as the *parity price premium*) of about 33 percent (the $159.80 conversion parity price is 33 percent higher than the $120 stock price). Obviously, a smaller conversion premium makes a bond more desirable.

Another way to compute this conversion premium is to compare the conversion value of the bond, which equals the market price of the stock times the conversion ratio, to the market price of the bond. The IBM bond's conversion value would be $781 (6.508 × $120) versus the market price of the convertible, $1,040. This gives the same 33 percent premium.

Another factor that affects evaluation of convertible bonds, **breakeven time,** also called the *payback period*, measures how long the difference between the interest income from the convertible bond and the dividend income from the common stock must persist to make up for the difference between the price on the bond and its conversion value. The equation for the breakeven time (BT) is:

$$\frac{\text{Bond price} - \text{Conversion value}}{\text{Bond income} - \text{Income from equal investment in common stock}}$$

You need the following data to make this calculation:

a. Bond price: $1,040.00
b. Conversion value: 780.96 (6.508 × $120)
c. Conversion premium: 259.04 (a − b)
d. Bond income: 78.75
e. Stock income: 41.91 (0.0403 × $1,040)
f. Differential income: 36.84 (d − e)

Note that the stock income (item e) equals the current dividend yield on IBM stock times the dollar amount invested in the convertible bond. The dividend yield on IBM common stock is 0.0403, since the company is paying a dividend of $4.89 per share, and the stock price is $120. This gives the income if the investor bought $1,040 worth of IBM common stock.

With the data above, the breakeven time (BT) would be:

$$BT = \frac{\$259.04}{36.84} = 7.03 \text{ years}$$

This indicates that the higher interest income from the bond relative to the dividend on the stock would make up the conversion premium paid for the bond in about 7 years. Obviously, a shorter breakeven time is better. Also, you should compare this breakeven time to the call date of the bond. As you might expect, you would prefer, but not require, a breakeven time less than the time to first call. This is not true for the IBM bond, which became callable in November 1988.

The conversion premium and the breakeven time are relative indicators of value for comparing several convertible bond issues. Alternatively, you could attempt to value this combination security in terms of its two components: its pure bond (investment) value plus its value as an option. We have discussed the value of the bond component, but the option component is difficult to evaluate because the call feature obscures the true expiration date. As you know, the bonds were callable as of 1988 so they can be called any time between the present and the year 2004 when they mature.

Still, it is interesting to consider the other data for the option-pricing model:

- Strike price: $153.66 ($1,000/6.508)
- Market price of stock: 124.00
- Risk-free interest rate: 9.00 percent
- Expiration date: Unknown (bond maturity = 12 years)
- Standard deviation of stock: 0.40 (based on historical results)

You could simulate several expiration times and stock volatilities and derive some estimates for the value of this option. You know that the bond provides 6.508 options, so its total value would be its value as a straight bond ($853.00) plus the value of the options on the stock (per-option estimate × 6.508).

After analyzing the stock's current price, you should also estimate its future potential. What price do you expect it to reach over your investment horizon? If you expect the stock to go to $175 a share, your upside potential is approximately 9.5 percent, because the bond will sell for at least $1,139 ($175 × 6.508), a 9.5 percent increase from $1,040.

Finally, you should consider the differential income from holding the bond rather than the stock. The bond's 7.875 percent coupon indicates $78.75 a year in interest and a current yield of 7.57 percent at the price of 104 ($78.75/1,040). In contrast, the stock is paying a dividend of $4.84 per share, a 4.03 percent dividend yield, indicating a total dividend payment on the 6.508 shares of $31.50. Therefore, at this time, the current income from the convertible bond substantially exceeds the current income from the shares to which it would convert. You will note that this total dividend income from the 6.508 shares differs from the income calculated in the breakeven analysis where we assumed that the total $1,040 would be invested in IBM stock. If we invested the $1,040 in IBM stock at $120 a share, we would have acquired 8.67 shares ($1,040/$120) compared to the 6.508 from the conversion of the bond.

In summary, the analysis indicates the following characteristics for this bond:

- 22 percent downside risk
- 33 percent conversion premium
- 7 years breakeven time

You expect about a 10 percent increase in the value of the bond during your investment period and, finally, its current yield is substantially higher than the dividend yield on the stock. At this point, you must decide whether this IBM convertible bond is an appropriate way to invest in IBM stock, given your investment objectives and horizon.

Convertible Preferred Stocks

Convertible preferred stock is a preferred stock issue that can be converted into the common stock of the same firm. Much like convertible bonds, it combines preferred stock and common stock issues. Beyond the conversion privileges, these issues typically have the following characteristics:

1. They are cumulative but not participating, which means that any unpaid dividend accumulates, but the preferred stockholders do not participate in earnings beyond the dividend.
2. They have no sinking funds or purchase funds.
3. Conversion rates are fixed.
4. They generally impose no waiting period before conversion.
5. The conversion privilege does not expire.[5]

As pointed out by Pinches, most convertible preferred stock is issued in connection with mergers as a way of providing income without diluting the common equity of the acquiring firm. Although preferred and convertible preferred stock have not been a major source of new financing, a number of convertible preferred issues remain outstanding. Sources of information on these stocks are discussed in the final section of this chapter.

Analysis and Valuation of Convertible Preferred Stocks

Because convertible preferred stock is a hybrid of preferred stock and common stock, the valuation analysis, like that of convertible bonds, involves two steps. Consider a Cummins Engine Corporation convertible preferred stock issue that pays an annual dividend of $3.50 a share. The stock is rated Baa3 by Moody's and BBB by Standard & Poor's and listed on the NYSE. Each share is convertible into 0.649 shares of common stock. As of mid-1990, the common stock was selling for $52 a share and the $3.50 convertible preferred stock was at $46 a share.

As a pure preferred stock issue, it had some downside risk. In mid-1990, when most straight preferred stock issues were yielding between 8 and 9 percent, the yield on the Cummins Engine stock was 7.6 percent. If we use the conservative 9 percent as the required yield, we would find a straight preferred stock price of $38.89 ($3.50/0.09). This represents the pos-

> **Convertible preferred stock** A preferred stock issue that the holder can exchange for a stated number of shares of common stock.

sibility of about an 18 percent decline from the prevailing market price of $46. An 8 percent yield would give a value for the stock of $43.75, which implies a 5 percent downside risk.

Comparing the conversion value of the stock ($33.75 = 0.649 × $52) to its market price of $46 implies a conversion premium of 36 percent ($46 versus $33.75). You can also derive a conversion parity value for the convertible preferred stock by dividing its current market price by the conversion ratio. The conversion parity price of $70.88 ($46/0.649) implies the same 36 percent conversion premium compared to the current stock price of $52. Clearly, the stock is selling on the basis of its investment value, because it currently involves a fairly substantial conversion premium. Put another way, the convertible preferred stock is currently priced in line with its investment value as pure preferred stock, so its price will likely move in line with yields on preferred stock.

You should examine the income relationship between the common and preferred stock. The common stock's recent annual dividend of $2.20 a share indicates a dividend yield of 4.23 percent (2.20/52). In contrast, the preferred stock's annual dividend of $3.50 indicates a 7.6 percent yield ($3.50/$46).

This analysis would indicate limited downside risk for the convertible preferred stock because it is selling close to its investment value. Unfortunately, it has limited upside potential, as well, since it is selling at a fairly large conversion premium. Finally, the convertible preferred stock's current income gives it an advantage over the common stock.

Sources of Information

A comprehensive list of convertible bonds with information about them appears in the convertible bond section of the *Standard & Poor's Bond Guide*. A sample page is shown in Figure 17.8. *Moody's Bond Record* also has a section on convertible bonds. Merrill Lynch publishes a monthly statistical report, *Convertible Securities*, that provides data on almost 500 convertible bonds and 100 convertible preferred stock issues. This report also lists unique convertible securities, such as

[5]George E. Pinches, "Financing with Convertible Preferred Stock, 1960–1967," *Journal of Finance* 25, no. 1 (March 1970): 61; Ronald W. Melicher, "A Comment on Financing with Convertible Preferred Stock, 1960–1967," *Journal of Finance* 26, no. 1 (March 1971): 148–149; George E. Pinches, "Financing with Convertible Preferred Stock, 1960–1967: Reply," *Journal of Finance* 26, no. 1 (March 1971): 150–151.

Figure 17.8 *Sample Page from* **Standard & Poor's Bond Guide**

XVI **STANDARD & POOR'S CORPORATION**

CONVERTIBLE BONDS Issue, Rate, Interest Dates and Maturity	S & P Quality Rating	Bond Form	Outstdg. Mil.-$	Conv. Expires	Shares per $1,000 Bond	Price per Share	Div. Income per Bond	1987 RANGE Hi	Lo	Curr Bid Sale(s) Ask(A)	Curr. Return	Yield to Mat	Stock Value of Bond	Conv. Parity	STOCK DATA Curr. Price	P/E Ratio	Earnings Per Share Yr. End	1986	1987	Last 12 Mos	1986 Dil-u't'n
Waxman Indus.....6¼ s Ms15 2007	B-	R	25.0	2007	69.57	14.375	6.96	100	72	72	8.68	9.43	65¼	10⅜	9⅜	14	Je	0.21	□0.60	[9]0.69	n/r
• Wean Inc[1].................5½ s Ms 1993	NR	R	16.5	1993	41.67	24.00	....	47½	37	43	12.7	26.3	5¼	10⅜	•1¼	d	Dc	△d3.27	....	[9]d1.25	n/r
Welbilt Corp.........6¼ s Ao15 2012	B	R	25.0	2012	38.96	25.67	....	101	58	64	9.77	10.3	....	16⅜	....	..	Dc	1.35	....	[9]1.51	n/r
• Wells Fargo Mtg/Eq12s mN 2005	BBB	R	27.6	2005	39.96	25.025	79.92	118	99	102	11.7	11.7	72⅞	25½	•18¼	15	Je	2.42	1.52	[9]1.19	n/r
• Wendy's Int'l.............7¼ s jD 2010	BBB-	R	55.0	2010	57.34	17.44	13.76	105¾	68½	s71	10.2	10.6	32¼	12⅜	•5⅝	62	Dc	d0.05	E0.09	[9]0.02	n/r
Wessex Corp........8½ s mN15 2006	CC	R	22.1	2006	204.08	4.90	....	98	65	A68	12.5	13.1	20⅜	3⅜	1	d	Mr	*△0.07	....	[9]d0.32	n/r
• Western Union[2]........5¼ s fA 1997	CCC-	R	62.5	1997	....	[3]66.00	....	47½	24	s36¼	14.4	20.9	....	....	....	..	Dc	□d22.7	....	[9]d20.5	n/r
• Westinghouse Elec...9s fA15 2009	AA-	R	123	2009	32.26	31.00	55.49	243	136	160.60	5.60	4.56	160½	49¾	•49¾	10	Dc	4.42	E5.15	[9]4.96	4.31
Weston(Roy F.),Inc.7s Ao15 2002	B+	R	30.0	2002	[4]47.33	21.13	....	118	85	90	7.78	8.20	67½	19	14¼	37	Dc	0.51	....	[9]0.39	n/r
Westwood One.....6¾ s aO15 2011	B+	R	100	2011	40.68	24.58	....	130⅛	75	95	7.11	7.19	75¼	23⅜	18½	24	Nv	0.63	....	[8]0.76	n/r
◆Wherehouse Entmt[5]...6¼ s jJ 2006	B	R	50.0	2006	36.23	27.60	1.81	85	45	s50	12.5	13.7	48⅞	13¾	◆13½	41	Ja	0.58	....	[10]0.33	n/r
• Whittaker Corp...........4½ s jJ 1988	NR	R	3.62	7-1-88	21.28	47.00	21.28	98¾	94	95⅝	4.71	14.0	51⅛	44⅞	•24	5	Oc	d0.44	P4.60	4.60	n/r
Williams(A.L.) ....7¼ s Jd 2006	NR	R	40.3	2006	35.09	28.50	....	104	77	79	9.18	9.72	57⅞	22½	16½	11	Dc	△1.09	....	[9]1.48	n/r
Winners Corp ....8¼ s Jd 2003	NR	R	25.0	2003	56.34	17.75	....	47½	32	33	....	....	12⅝	5⅞	•2¼	d	Dc	d0.54	....	[9]d1.40	n/r
• Witco Corp[6] ....4½ s jD15 1993	A-	R	1.68	1993	67.52	14.81	86.43	287	268	225⅜	2.00	....	225⅜	33⅜	•33⅜	12	Dc	2.93	E2.70	[9]2.89	2.88
• Witco Corp...........5½ s Ms15 2012	A-	R	140	2012	18.33	54.55	23.46	104	70	s78	7.05	7.48	61⅛	42½	•33⅜	12	Dc	2.93	E2.70	[9]2.89	2.88
• WMS Industries[7]..12¾ s mN 1996	NR	R	22.0	1996	49.58	20.17	....	100	81	84	15.1	16.2	20½	17	•4⅛	d	Sp	d0.45	Pd0.29	d0.29	n/r
Worlds of[8]Wonder[9] ......9s Jd 2012	D	R	80.0	2012	58.48	17.10	....	100	7½	7½	....	Flat	3⅝	1¼	⅝	d	Mr	0.85	Edef	[9]d1.60	n/r
Xerox Corp[10] ....5s AnDec 1988	A	C	73.6	12-1-88	6.76	148.00	20.28	98½	95⅜	96⅞	5.16	8.64	38¼	143¼	•56⅝	10	Dc	△3.85	E5.40	[9]4.69	n/r
• Xerox Corp ....6s mN 1995	A	R	100	1995	10.87	92.00	32.61	108¼	83½	s90½	6.63	7.63	61½	83¼	•56⅝	10	Dc	△3.85	E5.40	[9]4.69	n/r
• Zayre Corp.............7¼ s jJ15 2010	BBB+	R	75.0	2010	28.41	35.20	11.36	116	71¼	s72	10.0	10.5	39¾	25⅜	•14	5	Ja	□1.55	E2.80	[10]2.76	1.49
Zehntel, Inc..........9¼ s Ms15 2012	NR	R	15.5	2012	212.77	4.70	....	131⅝	82	92	10.0	10.1	61⅛	4⅜	2⅞	d	Je	d1.52	*0.06	[9]d0.20	n/r
• Zenith Electronics....6¼ s Ao 2011	BB-	R	115	2011	32.00	31.25	....	119	68	s71	8.80	9.32	47¼	22¼	•14¾	d	Dc	d0.43	Ed1.00	[9]0.97	n/r
• Zurn Indus..............5¾ s mN 1994	NR	R	4.70	1994	70.18	14.25	47.72	175	127	134¼	4.28	....	134¼	19⅛	•19⅛	12	Mr	1.43	E1.60	[9]1.53	1.40

Uniform Footnote Explanations—See Page XVI. Other: [1]Was Wean United. [2]Exch offer:1.76 Cl A & 56Cl B Pfd,to Dec 30. [3]Old shares. [4]Into Cl A com. [5]WEI Hldg offers $14 for com, to Jan 22. [6]Was Witco Chemical. [7]Was Williams Electronics. [8]Int of 12-1-87 not pd when due. [9]File bankruptcy Chapt 11. [10]Offered outside U.S.:P&I pay in U.S.$.

EXPLANATION OF COLUMN HEADINGS AND FOOTNOTES

MARKET: Unlisted except where symbols • or ◆ are used:
• –New York Stock Exchange ◆ –American Stock Exchange

ISSUE TITLE: Name of Bond at time of offering; otherwise issue footnoted with name change of obligor. Minor changes with old title indicated in brackets, i.e. Gen Tel (Corp) & Elec.
#Prin & int payable in U.S. funds. §Int. and/or prin. in default.

FORM OF BOND: Letters are used to indicate form of bond: C–Coupon only; CR–Coupon or Registered, interchangeable; R–Registered only.

CONVERSION EXPIRES: Footnote keyed to bottom of page when conversion price changes during life of the privilege; also noted on conversion price.
◉ Indicates a change in next 12 months. a–No fractional shs. issued upon conversion; settlements in cash.

DIVIDEND INCOME PER BOND: If $1,000 Bond were converted, the annual amount of dividends expected to be paid by the company on the stock based on most recent indication of annual rate of payment.
t–Less tax at origin. g–in Canadian funds less 15% or 10% non–residence tax.

STOCK VALUE OF BOND: Price at which bond must sell to equal price of stock i.e., number of shares received on conversion times price of the stock.

CONVERSION PARITY: Price at which stock must sell to equal bond price, i.e., price of bond divided by number of shares received on conversion.

P–E RATIO: (Price–Earnings Ratio) Represents market valuation of any $1 of per share earnings i.e., the price of the stock divided by estimated or latest 12 months per share earnings.

EARNINGS, in general, are per share as reported by company. **FOR YEAR INDICATED:** Fiscal years ending prior to March 31 are shown under preceding year. Net operating earnings are shown for **banks**; net earnings before appropriation to general reserve for **savings & loan associations**; net investment income for **insurance companies**; **railroads'** earnings are as reported to ICC. **Foreign** issues traded **ADR** are dollars per share, converted at prevailing exchange rate. Specific footnotes used:

△Excl extra–ord income
▲Incl extra–ord income
□Excl extra–ord charges
■Incl extra–ord charges
* Excl tax credits
§–Partial Year
‡–New Year Earns
b–Before depletion
d–Deficit
E–S&P Estimate
j–Currency at origin
P–Preliminary
p–Pro forma
R–Fully diluted
n/r–Not reported

LAST 12 Mos. indicates earnings through period indicated by superior number preceding figure: [1]for Jan. for Feb., etc. Figure without superior number indicates fiscal year end.

DILUTION: Earnings on a fully diluted basis, as reported in accordance with Accounting Principles Board opinions.

Source: *Standard & Poor's Bond Guide*, January 1988 (New York: Standard & Poor's Corp.). Reprinted with permission.

issues that are convertible into more than one security and convertible bonds with put features.

The *Value Line Options and Convertibles* service provides analysis beyond the statistical information. This service indicates whether a bond is under- or over-valued along with its upside potential and downside protection. R. H. M. Associates, which provides the warrants and options service to which we referred earlier, also has a convertible bond service.

Various investment firms provide data and charts on heavily traded convertible bonds. For example, Figure 17.9 shows a Merrill Lynch chart for the IBM convertible bond issue that we discussed. The top chart plots the market price of the convertible, its conversion value, and its investment value based upon its AAA rating. It is important to compare the volatility of the bond's conversion value to its investment value. The bottom chart gives a plot of the conversion premium and the premium recovery period, which we have called the *breakeven time.* The parallel movement of the two series reflects the fact it takes longer to recover this conversion premium as it increases based on the differential income.

Summary

■ Based upon analysis in prior chapters, we assume that you have made a decision to invest in the bonds or common stock of individual firms, or possibly the

Figure 17.9 **Merrill Lynch Convertible Research**

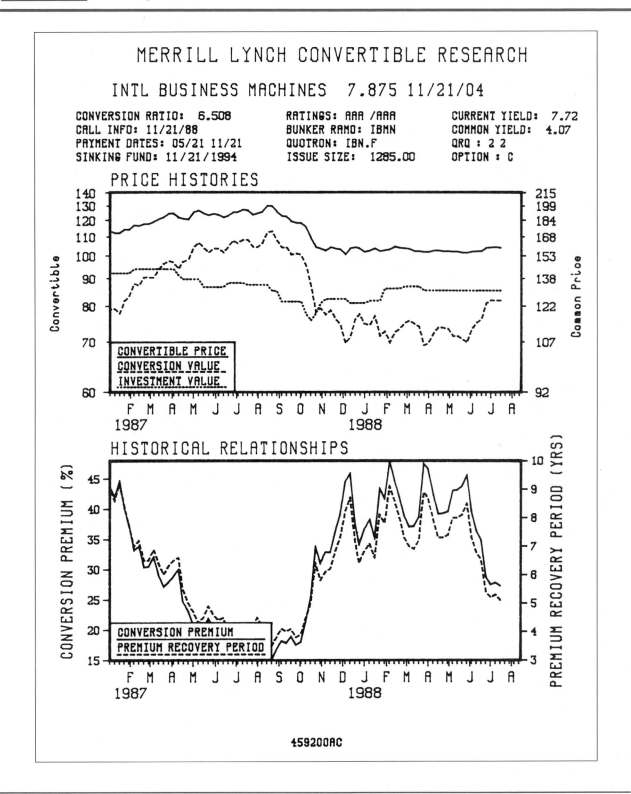

Source: "Convertible Research," (New York: Merrill Lynch Pierce Fenner and Smith, August 1988).

aggregate market. This chapter has explained some additional vehicles through which you can invest. These investment instruments attract interest because they can be beneficial to both the issuing company and the investor.

■ Warrants are long-term call options that allow holders to buy stock directly from the firm, which supplies additional capital to the firm. This basic concept is quite popular and it has generated several similar instruments. One of these, the Americus Trust, combines a dividend yielding prime with a score, which is very similar to a warrant.

■ Warrants are becoming a bigger factor in the global market with the growth of currency exchange warrants (CEWs) through which you can speculate or hedge in the foreign currency market. In addition, several investment firms have issued warrants related to foreign security markets. Our discussion on the valuation of these instruments emphasized the need to consider their intrinsic values and their speculative values, which react to the same variables as call options because a warrant works like an option except that it typically has a longer term.

■ Although our prior analysis generally considered investing in either bonds or stocks, you should also consider convertible bonds, which combine bonds and common stocks, or convertible preferred stock, which combines preferred stock and common stock. Both of these combination securities have significant advantages to the issuing corporation in terms of its cost of funds and flexibility, and to the investor because they combine the upside potential of common stock and the downside protection of bonds or preferred stock. The valuation procedure for a convertible security involves evaluating both of its components: its value as a straight bond or preferred stock and the value of its common stock option.

■ Since these investment instruments provide additional investment opportunities and strategies beyond those available with bonds or common stock alone, after you have evaluated a firm and decided to invest in it, you need to ask how should I invest in this firm? Clearly, if warrants, Americus Trusts, or convertible securities are available, you should consider them as viable alternatives.

Questions

1. What are two major differences between a warrant and a call option?

2. What advantage does a warrant give a corporation in comparison to a listed call option?
3. What advantage does a warrant give an investor in comparison to a listed call option?
4. Define the intrinsic value of a warrant. Give an example of a warrant with positive intrinsic value.
5. Discuss briefly three factors that influence the speculative value of a warrant (that is, the premium over its intrinsic value).
6. As an investor, would you want a high or a low ratio of stock price to warrant price? Why?
7. Describe a score. How does it resemble a warrant?
8. Assuming that you are a conservative investor, discuss why you would want to invest in primes or scores.
9. Describe how a firm forces conversion of a convertible bond. What conditions must exist?
10. The Medical Corporation's debentures, rated Aa by Moody's, are selling to yield 10.00 percent. Its subordinated convertible bonds, rated A by Moody's, are selling to yield 9.10 percent. Explain this phenomenon.
11. Describe what is meant by the *upside potential of convertible bonds*. Give an example. Describe how convertible bonds provide downside protection and give an example.
12. Assume a convertible bond's conversion value is substantially above par. Why might you as an investor continue holding the convertible bond rather than converting it?
13. Explain the term *breakeven time*. Why would you want a high or low value?

Problems

1. The Tree Corporation has a warrant outstanding that allows the holder to acquire two shares of common stock at $20 a share for the next 4 years. The stock is currently selling for $17 and the warrant is selling for $3.
   a. Compute the intrinsic value of the warrant. What difference does it make that the warrant gives rights to two shares?
   b. Compute the speculative value (premium) of this warrant.
   c. Would you expect the premium to be greater if the stock were selling for $19? Why?
2. The Silver Spoon Corporation has a warrant outstanding that allows the holder to buy a share of stock for $35 until 1999. The stock is cur-

rently selling for $38 and the warrant is selling for $5.

   a. Compute the intrinsic value and speculative value of this warrant.

   b. What is the leverage factor for this warrant?

   c. If the stock increases to $45 a share, what will be the percentage change in the stock price and the warrant price, assuming the same premium on the warrant?

   d. Discuss the relationship between your answers to Parts c and b.

3. The Outstanding Education Corporation's 8 percent subordinated convertible debenture is due in 10 years. The current yield to maturity on this A-rated bond is 5 percent. The current yield to maturity on 10-year, nonconvertible, A-rated bonds is 10 percent. The holder can convert this bond into 21 shares of common stock and the company can call it at 106 of par, which is $1,000. The company's common stock is currently selling for $54.

   a. What is the value of the convertible bond as straight debt, assuming semiannual interest payments?

   b. What is its conversion value?

   c. What would you expect for the current price of this bond?

   d. Could the Outstanding Education Corporation remove this convertible debenture from its balance sheet at this time? Discuss specifically how it would do so.

4. Irish Industries has debentures outstanding (par value $1,000) that are convertible into the company's common stock at a price of $25. The convertible issue has a coupon interest rate of 11 percent and matures in 10 years. It pays interest semiannually, and it is callable at 111.

   a. Calculate the issue's conversion value if the stock price is $20 per share.

   b. Calculate the conversion value if the stock price is $28 per share.

   c. Calculate its value as a straight bond, assuming that bonds of equivalent risk and maturity are yielding 12 percent per year compounded semiannually.

   d. Based on your answers to Parts b and c, estimate the market price of the convertible. No calculations are required, but explain your answer.

5. Sitting next to Rashid at a business luncheon,

Therese exclaimed, "I bought American Desk at $20 a share and it has risen to $40." Rashid said, "You would have done better to buy American's warrants, as I did."

   a. Why did Rashid say this?

   b. Calculate Therese's percentage gain on the purchase of the stock.

   c. The exercise price of American Desk warrants is $18. Rashid purchased the warrants for $4 each when American Desk's stock price was $20 a share. Each warrant entitles Rashid to purchase one share of stock. Assuming the $2 warrant premium drops to $1, what is the current price of the warrant?

   d. Calculate Rashid's percentage gain when the stock price is $40 and the warrant premium is $1.

6. The common stock of Interstate Corporation is currently selling at $12 per share, while Interstate's warrants, which have 5 years until expiration, are selling at $3. They permit the purchase of common at $11 per share. By the end of the year you expect the premium on the warrants to decrease by 20 percent with the following probability distribution for prices on the stock:

Probability	Stock Price
0.10	$10
0.30	13
0.40	16
0.15	19
0.05	25

   a. Given the probability distribution for the stock, what is the expected stock price?

   b. Given the probability distribution, what is the expected warrant price?

   c. If average expectations are met, what would be your annual return from an investment in the stock?

   d. If average expectations are met, what would be your annual return from an investment in the warrants?

References

Warrants

Ferri, Michael G., Joseph W. Kremer, and H. Dennis Oberhelman. "An Analysis of the Pricing of Warrants." *Advances in Futures and Options Research* 1 (1986).

Kim, Moon K., and Allan Young. "Rewards and Risks from Warrant Hedging." *Journal of Portfolio Management* 6, no. 4 (Summer 1980).

Convertible Securities

Alexander, Gordon J., and Roger D. Stover. "The Effect of Forced Conversion on Common Stock Prices." *Financial Management* 9, no. 1 (Spring 1980).

Baumol, William J., Burton J. Malkiel, and R. E. Quandt. "The Valuation of Convertible Securities." *Quarterly Journal of Economics* 80, no. 1 (February 1966).

Ritchie, J. C., Jr. "Convertible Securities and Warrants." In *The Handbook of Fixed-Income Securities*, 3d ed. Ed. by Frank J. Fabozzi. Homewood, Ill.: Dow Jones-Irwin, 1991.

Soldofsky, Robert M. "The Risk–Return Performance of Convertibles." *Journal of Portfolio Management* 7, no. 2 (Winter 1981).

Young, Robert A. "Convertible Securities: Definitions, Analytical Tools, and Practical Investment Strategies." In *The Financial Analysts Handbook*. Ed. by Sumner N. Levine. Homewood, Ill.: Dow Jones-Irwin, 1988.

APPENDIX 17a *Convertible Glossary*

Bond equivalent *See* Fixed income equivalent

Bond value *See* Investment value

Breakeven time The time required for the added income from the convertible to offset the conversion premium. Also referred to as *payback period*.

"Busted" convertibles *See* Fixed income equivalent

Call provisions Indenture provisions describing the date, price, and other circumstances under which the issuer may redeem a convertible.

Conditional call *See* Provisional call

Conversion premium The excess of the market value of the convertible over its equity value if immediately converted into common stock. Typically expressed as a percentage of the equity value.

Conversion price (or exercise price) The price at which common stock can be obtained by surrendering the convertible instrument at par value.

Conversion ratio The number of shares of common stock for which a convertible security may be exchanged.

Conversion value *See* Equity value

Equity equivalent A convertible with price behavior dominated by changes in the common stock price, with relatively little sensitivity to changes in interest rates.

Equity value The value of the convertible security if converted into common stock at the stock's current market price. Also referred to as *parity* or *conversion parity*.

Fixed income equivalent A convertible with price behavior dominated by changes in interest rates, with relatively little sensitivity to changes in common stock price.

Floor value *See* Investment value

Forced conversion If an issuer attempts to redeem a convertible for cash by issuing a call, and if the equity value exceeds the redemption price, the investor is "forced" to convert into common stock in order to obtain the higher equity value.

Hard call A convertible that does not have any provisional call feature is said to have *hard call* protection.

Initial premium The conversion premium at the time a new convertible security is offered.

Investment value The price at which a debenture would have to sell as a straight debt instrument. Also referred to as *bond value* or *floor value*.

Investment value premium The difference between a convertible's market price and its investment value, expressed as a percentage of investment value.

Parity (or conversion parity) *See* Equity value

Payback   *See* Breakeven time

Point premium   The conversion premium expressed as *points*, or the dollar price difference between the market price of the convertible and its equity value.

Provisional call   Indenture provision that permits the company to call a convertible security prior to the stated call date if the common stock price rises above a preset level. Typically expressed as a percentage (such as 140 percent or 150 percent) of the specified conversion price.

Unit offering   A combination of notes and warrants that is issued as a unit but may subsequently be traded either separately or as a unit. Also referred to as *synthetic convertibles*.

Yield advantage   The difference between the current yield of the convertible bond and the current yield of the common stock.

Yield to first call   Rate of return at the current price, assuming the issue is called at the first call date and at its call price.

Yield to first put   Rate of return at the current price, assuming the issue is called at the first put date and at its put price.

Source: Luke D. Knecht and Michael L. McCowin. "Valuing Convertible Securities," Harris Trust and Savings Bank (1986). Reprinted with permission.

Futures

When most individuals consider the subject of investments, they think in terms of stocks and bonds bought and sold for cash in the *spot* market. Although stocks and bonds typically constitute the bulk of the investment portfolios of most investors, trading in futures contracts has increased substantially. Futures contracts allow investors to buy and sell stocks, bonds, commodities, or currencies in future periods at future prices. Futures trading provides investment opportunities ranging from relatively conservative hedging transactions by portfolio managers using financial futures to high-risk speculation that can provide very large positive or negative rates of return.

This chapter gives general background on the concept and use of futures contracts with an emphasis on financial futures. While we discuss the application of futures contracts to financial assets, the same principles apply to futures contracts for commodities such as wheat, corn, meat products, and metals.

The discussion on the conceptual background of futures contracts begins with the four contracts available in securities markets: cash contracts for immediate delivery, along with three alternative *deferred delivery* contracts: forward contracts, futures contracts, and options. Given an understanding of the meaning of futures contracts, the next section deals with the mechanics of trading them. To dispel the widespread belief that futures trading is quite unique and specialized, the first part of this section deals with similarities between stock markets and futures markets. The second part of the section then describes the specifics of trading futures contracts.

Armed with this general background about the futures market and its operation, the rest of the chapter considers three specific types of finan-

> **Cash (spot) contract** An agreement for the immediate delivery of some asset.
>
> **Deferred-delivery contract** An agreement for delivery of an asset in the future. Forward and futures contracts are types of deferred-delivery contracts.
>
> **Forward contract** An agreement between two traders for delivery of an asset at a fixed time in the future for a specified price.

cial futures contracts and how you can use them to protect yourself or to speculate. The first, the interest rate futures contract, allows you to hedge against or speculate on movements in interest rates and bond prices. As we know from prior discussions, interest rates have become more volatile during the 1980s, and this has increased the need for instruments with which to hedge and speculate. Second, we will discuss currency futures, which have become important with the globalization of financial markets and increasing exchange rate risk.

A final type of futures contracts, stock index futures, provides an opportunity to hedge against or speculate on movements in various segments of the aggregate stock market. Besides the standard hedges and speculation with stock index futures, these contracts also have been used in program trading to profit from arbitrage between the futures market and the cash stock market. Program trading has become very popular, although it is controversial since some observers contend that it promotes stock price volatility.

We will recall the discussion in Chapter 16 when we consider options on futures contracts. The final section of the chapter compares the major characteristics of options and futures contracts. Since options and futures are available to you as an investor, you should be aware of how they differ to make an informed decision on using either or both of them.

Spot, Forward, and Futures Contracts

In general, there are four types of contracts for the purchase and sale of assets: cash or spot contracts, forward contracts, futures contracts, and option contracts. A **cash** or **spot contract** is an agreement for the immediate delivery of an asset. Transactions in the primary and secondary markets for stocks and bonds represent cash or spot contracts. Similarly, if a food processing firm purchases wheat to fill a flour contract, it completes a cash or spot market transaction, which requires immediate delivery of the wheat to be ground into flour.

In contrast, **deferred-delivery contracts** cover purchase or delivery of a commodity in the future. For example, a mortgage banker might commit to lend money to a builder in the future at a specified rate of interest. For another example of a deferred-delivery contract, an exporter might agree to deliver grain in the future for a specified price. Such deferred-delivery contracts can take one of three forms: forward, futures, or option contracts.

A **forward contract** is an agreement between two traders for delivery of a specific asset at a fixed time in the future for a specified price (called the *exercise price*). The transactions by the mortgage banker and the exporter were forward contracts. Forward contracts state the characteristics of the asset (such as grade), the term to maturity and coupon on any loan, the quantity, the method and place of delivery, the price, and the method of settlement. This makes the forward market *a dealer market where all the details of the transaction are negotiated.* In the forward market, a buyer contracts for a commodity that will meet his or her particular needs, but it is necessary to find another trader willing to agree to the same terms. Because the terms of the contract are unique and specific, there is generally *no secondary market for forward contracts.* As a result, both parties are locked into the contract for its full term. They bear the risk of failure to perform on the contract by either party as well as the uncertainty due to subsequent price fluctuations.

A **futures contract** overcomes many of the shortcomings of forward contracts. It is a deferred-delivery contract between a trader and the *clearinghouse of a futures exchange* in which all terms of trade except the price and the number of contracts are standardized. This means that futures contracts can be traded in auction markets organized by futures exchanges and the clearinghouses can guarantee performance on all contracts. The arrangement with the clearinghouses and the availability of fairly active secondary markets for most futures contracts allow traders to close their positions prior to their contracts' delivery dates by executing reverse transactions.

To see how this works, consider the following example. Assume that in March a mortgage banker makes a commitment to a builder to lend money in June at 12 percent. The mortgage banker assumes the risk that mortgage rates will increase during the following 3 months, which would diminish the value of the mortgage. When arranging this transaction, the banker could use the Treasury bond futures contract for June delivery traded on the Chicago Board of Trade (CBT). The current published quote on the June Treasury bond contract would give the banker the market consensus forecast of long-term interest rates expected in June. From this information, coupled with an estimate of the expected yield spread between the rates on GNMA securities and government bonds, the banker could set the interest rate on the forward mortgage loan.

The banker could use the interest rate futures contract in a second way. The banker could *hedge* the interest rate risk exposure involved in this commitment by selling an appropriate number of June futures contracts upon making the loan commitment and subsequently buying them back before delivery. If mortgage rates were to increase by June, the forward commitment to the builder would generate a loss, but the short futures position would bring a gain. On the other hand, if mortgage rates were to decline from their expected levels, the forward loan would produce a gain, but the short interest rate futures position would show a loss. Thus, whatever happened to mortgage rates between March and June, the gain or loss on the interest rate futures position would reduce the variability of the rate of return on the forward loan.

Notice that the example involves no delivery on the futures contract. This is not unusual; fewer than 5 percent of hedging transactions involve delivery of the underlying asset. Therefore, futures contracts are considered close, but imperfect, substitutes for forward contracts. In addition, as we will discuss in the next section, a futures contract is "marked to market" at the end of every trading day. This means that the gains or losses on futures positions are settled daily while a forward contract is not settled until the delivery date.

Futures contract An agreement between a trader and an exchange clearinghouse for delivery of an asset at a fixed, standardized time in the future for a specified price.

The spot, forward, and futures contracts that we have discussed impose obligations on buyers and sellers to perform on the contracts. The buyer must make payment and the seller must deliver as specified. Sometimes an investor or trader would like to acquire the right to buy or sell an asset without incurring the obligation to do so. As we know from Chapter 16, standardized option contracts, which involve the exchange of such rights, are actively traded in auction markets (exchange markets). You will recall that a call option contract confers a right to purchase (call away) a specified asset from the clearinghouse at a predetermined price (exercise price) during a specified period of time. A put option gives the buyer the right to sell the underlying asset to the clearinghouse at a fixed price during a specified period of time. The buyer of an option contract is entitled to buy or to sell, but does not have to exercise that right. In contrast, the seller of an option has an obligation to perform when the buyer exercises the option.

Mechanics of Futures Trading

Trading in futures contracts differs substantially from trading in the cash market for stocks and bonds. At the same time, the two systems clearly share some attributes. Because it is necessary to understand both the similarities and the differences, this section has two parts. The first part discusses the resemblances between the two markets. The second part describes the specific steps involved in futures trading and shows several differences between the two markets.

Similarities in Stock and Futures Trading Practices

Both types of investments are traded on highly organized exchanges such as the NYSE and the Chicago Board of Trade (CBT). Trading markets for other investment alternatives, such as real estate, coins, or stamps, are highly fragmented.

Trading on a given exchange is limited to specified stocks or financial instruments. Just as the New

| **Futures clearinghouse** A subsidiary of a futures exchange that takes the other side of all trades to ensure a liquid, orderly market.

York, Tokyo, and London stock exchanges allow trading only in listed stocks, the futures exchanges like the CBT, the Chicago Mercantile Exchange (CME), and the New York Futures Exchange (NYFE) limit trading to specified assets. These include commodity futures (wheat, oats, corn), interest rate futures (T-bills, long-term government bonds), currency futures (British pounds, Japanese Yen), and stock index futures (the S&P 500, the Value Line Index). Further, only individuals or firms that have memberships can trade on either stock or futures exchanges for themselves or for others.

The mechanics of buying and selling stocks or futures contracts are quite similar. In both cases, you give an order to your local broker, who then sends it to the floor of the exchange. There a member of the exchange executes the order at a designated spot on the floor of the exchange. Stock orders are executed through the designated specialist for the ordered stock; futures contract orders are executed at the pit where the particular futures contract is traded. The types of orders on the exchanges are substantially similar. Both types of exchange allow market orders, stop orders, and limit orders.

The highly organized exchanges and their communication networks give both classes of investments substantial liquidity. This ability to turn investments into cash almost instantly at a fairly certain price contrasts sharply with many other investments, such as real estate, art, and antiques.

Both the stock and futures markets feature some investors who are fundamentalists, basing their investment decisions on underlying economic variables, and some investors who are technicians, using charts and past price movements to indicate future price movements.

Specifics of Futures Trading

Probably the easiest way to present the specifics of futures trading is to walk through a typical transaction in detail. Assume that in September you expect long-term interest rates to decline during the next 3 months and want to buy a futures contract for long-term U.S. Treasury bonds to profit from this change. In *The Wall Street Journal*, in the section titled "Interest Rate Instruments," you see under the heading "Futures" a quote for the December contract that looks like this:

Treasury Bonds (CBT) — $100,000

Open	High	Low	Settle	Chg.	Yield Settle	Chg.	Open Interest

December
87–23 88–16 87–22 88–15 +28 9.278 −0.108 263,262

This tells you that futures contracts on Treasury bonds are traded on the CBT, and $100,000 of bonds underlie each contract. Prices are quoted in thirty-seconds of a point. You know from reading a description of this contract that it is based on 20-year bonds with an 8 percent coupon.

The open price states what this contract cost when it was established several months earlier. The high and low prices are for the period since the contract was established. These contracts were almost at their low point at the open and have generally increased over this period. The settle price, a consensus of the trades during the final minutes of the most recent trading session, shows that bond prices ended the day on the up side because bond yields were declining. In this case, investors were expecting yields on long-term Treasury bonds of about 9.278 percent, which was a decline from the prior day's yield of 9.386 percent (-0.108). You compute this yield by calculating that an 8 percent coupon, 20-year Treasury bond with a yield to maturity of 9.278 percent would be priced at 88–15, which represents $88\frac{15}{32}$.

With this knowledge, you call your broker with an instruction to buy a Treasury bond futures contract on the CBT at the market. Assuming your investment firm has a membership on the CBT, your broker will phone the firm's representative on the floor of the CBT who will proceed to the Treasury bond pit and give the order to the firm's trader in that pit. Assume that prices have declined slightly since the price close and the order is filled at 88, which means that the value of the contract is $88,000.

At this point, two factors that are unique to this market come into play. First, although your trader bought the contract from another trader, you do not complete the transaction with that person. As in the option market, all transactions go through the **futures clearinghouse**; it takes the other side of both trades. This means that you buy the contract from the clearinghouse and the other trader sells the contract to the clearinghouse. This arrangement guarantees that you will receive the contract, irrespective of what happens to the seller between the time when you buy it and when it matures in the future.

Besides this guarantee, the clearinghouse also makes subsequent transactions much easier. If you decide to liquidate your position, you need only to sell the same contract and this sale will automatically offset your prior purchase through the clearinghouse. This offsetting transaction, called a **reversing trade,** means that you have a net position of zero and do not have to either accept delivery on your original purchase or provide the securities in line with your sale.

The number of contracts outstanding at a point in time is referred to as the **open interest** for that contract. Our example quotation indicated an open interest of 263,262 December contracts. This number will increase after the contract is established and decline as its maturity approaches. By mid-November, many of the traders in the December contract will execute reversing trades in order to realize their profits or cut their losses. This will begin to reduce the open interest in this contract below 100,000. When it matures, very few contracts will remain outstanding — approximately 2 or 3 percent of those written.

The second unique feature of the futures market is the method of payment for the contract. Since this is a futures contract, if you don't reverse the trade, you won't receive the underlying Treasury bonds until after the maturity date in December. You receive shares of stock when you buy them, but in this instance all you have is a future promise of delivery.

Therefore, this transaction requires you to put money into a **margin account,** which is really a good-faith deposit to protect the clearinghouse. The typical margin requirement is between 5 and 10 percent of the value of the contract, depending on the price volatility of the asset. The requirement for Treasury bonds would be toward the lower end of the range, so let us assume it is 5 percent of $88,000 or $4,400. This margin deposit can be in cash or in near-cash securities like T-bills that continue to earn interest for you while in the account.

At this point, you are long on a Treasury bond futures contract and have paid for it with a good-faith deposit of $4,400 in your margin account. The commission on this transaction is computed only after the trade is reversed or closed out so it covers both the

> **Reversing trade** A transaction that offsets a previous transaction leaving a trader with a zero balance between the two trades.
>
> **Open interest** The number of contracts in a particular future outstanding at a point in time.
>
> **Margin account** An account that holds a trader's deposits toward the total cost of his or her position.
>
> **Marked to market** The daily adjustment of the value of a trader's account to reflect that day's price changes.
>
> **Maintenance margin** A minimum amount for a margin account, typically about 75 percent of the initial margin.
>
> **Variable margin** The amount a trader must deposit in cash to return his or her margin account to its initial level.

purchase and sale. It is typically a flat fee that is a very small percentage of the total value of the contract (which is $88,000 in this case).

Marking to Market   As our next step, we must consider what happens over time as interest rates and the price of the futures contract change. When the prices of stocks or bonds that you own move up or down, you know that you have gained or lost on the investment. You never realize the gain or loss, however, until you close out the investment. This is not so with futures contracts because the clearinghouses assure that every contract is **marked to market** every day.

As observed earlier, the clearing corporation guarantees delivery and payment on every futures contract. By marking contracts to market at the end of every trading day, the clearing corporation limits its obligations to the maximum daily price change in the unusual event of default by a member broker and a customer.

If the futures price moves in your favor during the day, the clearinghouse credits your account with the amount of price change, increasing its value from the original $4,400. In contrast, any unfavorable price change is debited to the account, reducing the prior credit balance of $4,400. Your initial margin of $4,400 increases or decreases daily due to the price changes in the contract.

You must maintain a minimum margin, called a **maintenance margin,** which is typically about 75 percent of the initial margin. Whereas you can satisfy the initial margin by posting interest-bearing securities, the subsequent margin, called the **variable**

> **Margin call** Notice that a trader's margin account balance has fallen below the maintenance margin, requiring additional deposits.
>
> **Financial futures contract** An agreement for future delivery of a specified amount of a particular financial instrument at a stated price.

margin, should be paid in cash. You will receive a **margin call** whenever the balance in your account falls to the level of the maintenance margin as a result of daily resettlement. As an example, assume an initial margin of $4,400 and a maintenance margin of $3,300. Losses of $1,200 charged against your margin account would reduce it below the $3,300 maintenance margin and initiate a margin call for $1,200 in cash to rebuild your margin account to $4,400. On top of the exchange-imposed margin requirements, brokerage houses can ask for additional margins depending upon the clients' creditworthiness, the volatility of futures prices, and competition from other firms.

This daily mark-to-market practice generates heavy cash flows for futures traders before contract delivery dates. When futures prices rise, the contract buyer's account accumulates cash, but final settlement of the long position will require a higher price than originally agreed. In contrast, the contract seller will have to meet many margin calls and suffer cash outflows if futures prices rise, but the settlement price will be higher. Notice that at final settlement, the aggregate cash receipt of the seller and net cash payment by the buyer match the originally specified price. Daily marking to market alters only the timing of these cash flows. The clearinghouse maintains a zero net position at all times because changes in the account of every contract buyer are offset by opposite changes in a seller's account.

Regulation The SEC regulates trading in stocks whereas the Commodity Futures Trading Commission (CFTC) regulates futures trading. The futures exchanges must obtain approval from the CFTC before introducing new futures contracts. For some commodities, the CFTC has placed maximum limits on positions of individual traders in order to prevent attempts to corner the market in a commodity or to squeeze traders who are short and want to buy contracts to close out their short positions. Further, the CFTC requires traders with larger positions to file periodic reports on their trading activities in regulated commodities.

The prior discussion should have given you a good background in the basic makeup of the futures markets, as well as an understanding of spot and futures prices. The rest of this chapter applies and extends these concepts to financial futures instruments including interest rate futures, currency futures, and stock index futures. These instruments are changing the way investors and financial managers function, so you need to understand how to use them.

Interest Rate Futures

Futures contracts on various commodities such as corn and wheat have served as a means of hedging against price changes for many decades. Although futures contracts on financial instruments such as government bonds and commercial paper are relatively new, their basic purpose is similar to that of commodity futures contracts.

Specifically, a **financial futures contract** promises the delivery of a specified amount of a particular financial instrument at some future time. In our prior example, you bought a December Treasury bond contract on the Chicago Board of Trade. This futures contract specified that, if you held it to maturity in December, you would receive 8 percent, 20-year U.S. Treasury bonds with face values totaling $100,000. The specific characteristics of the bonds that can be delivered to satisfy the contract are set forth by the exchange.

Such futures contracts were created for the same reason as commodities contracts. They allow participants in the market to hedge against price risk in the underlying instrument. We will discuss some specific hedging techniques in a later section.

Types of Interest Rate Futures Contracts

Each interest rate futures contract specifies a different amount of underlying securities and the characteristics of each financial instrument are unique. As shown in Figure 18.1, 13 different contracts are currently available for a variety of interest rates, including 30-day interest rates, Treasury bills, municipal bonds, and long-term Treasury bonds. The following list details some specific examples of contracts and what they represent:

1. Contracts on 90-day U.S. Treasury bills: $1 million in T-bills

Figure 18.1   *Quotations on Interest Rate Futures Contracts*

INTEREST RATE INSTRUMENTS

Thursday, September 27, 1990
For Notes and Bonds, decimals in closing prices represent 32nds; 1.01 means 1 1/32. For Bills, decimals in closing prices represent basis points; $25 per .01.

FUTURES

TREASURY BONDS (CBT)–$100,000; pts. 32nds of 100%

	Open	High	Low	Settle	Chg	Yield Settle	Chg	Open Interest
Dec	87-23	88-16	87-22	88-15	+ 28	9.278	− .108	263,262
Mr91	87-10	88-03	87-10	88-02	+ 28	9.328	− .108	17,010
June	87-12	87-21	87-02	87-21	+ 27	9.378	− .105	5,789
Sept	87-00	87-09	86-23	87-09	+ 26	9.424	− .102	3,371
Dec	86-24	86-31	86-12	86-31	+ 26	9.463	− .103	1,712
Mr92	86-06	86-21	86-06	86-21	+ 25	9.503	− .099	424
June	....	....	....	86-12	+ 25	9.538	− .100	144

Est vol 235,000; vol Wed 251,299; op int 301,211, +1,276.

TREASURY BONDS (MCE)–$50,000; pts. 32nds of 100%

	Open	High	Low	Settle	Chg	Yield Settle	Chg	Open Interest
Dec	88-05	88-22	87-25	88-18	+ 28	9.267	− .055	12,206

Est vol 7,600; vol Wed 4,237; open int 13,483, −405.

T–BONDS (LIFFE) U.S. $100,000; pts of 100%

	Open	High	Low	Settle	Chg	High	Low	Open Interest
Dec	87-31	88-07	87-29	88-00	+ 0-10	93-21	87-07	6,782

Est vol 3,274; vol Wed 3,887; open int 6,782, +334.

TREASURY NOTES (CBT)–$100,000; pts. 32nds of 100%

	Open	High	Low	Settle	Chg	Yield Settle	Chg	Open Interest
Dec	93-16	94-02	93-16	94-01	+ 18	8.914	− .090	63,413
Mr91	93-11	93-23	93-10	93-23	+ 17	8.964	− .086	3,036

Est vol 15,000; vol Wed 17,047; open int 71,404, +574.

5 YR TREAS NOTES (CBT)–$100,000; pts. 32nds of 100%

	Open	High	Low	Settle	Chg	Yield Settle	Chg	Open Interest
Dec	97-145	97-22	97-125	97-215	+12.5	8.58	− .10	73,704
Mr91	....	....	....	97-165	+12.5	8.62	− .10	1,177

Est vol 5,151; vol Wed 8,292; open int 76,358, +912.

2 YR TREAS NOTES (CBT)–$200,000; pts. 32nds of 100%

	Open	High	Low	Settle	Chg	Yield Settle	Chg	Open Interest
Dec	99-22	99-26	99-21	99-257	+ 7¼	8.108	− .125	8,121

Est vol 768; vol Wed 282; open int 9,622, −73.

30-DAY INTEREST RATE (CBT)–$5 million; pts. of 100%

	Open	High	Low	Settle	Chg	Yield Settle	Chg	Open Interest
Sept	91.75	91.77	91.75	91.77	+ .04	8.23	− .04	1,514
Oct	91.99	92.00	91.99	92.00	+ .04	8.00	− .04	1,622
Nov	92.08	92.09	92.08	92.09	+ .04	7.91	− .04	1,235
Dec	92.07	92.08	92.06	92.08	+ .04	7.92	− .04	818
Ja91	92.17	92.18	92.17	92.18	+ .05	7.82	− .05	357

Est vol 188; vol Wed 522; open int 5,571, +208.

TREASURY BILLS (IMM)–$1 mil.; pts. of 100%

	Open	High	Low	Settle	Chg	Discount Settle	Chg	Open Interest
Dec	93.02	93.20	93.01	93.19	+ .22	6.81	− .22	30,664
Mr91	93.13	93.35	93.12	93.34	+ .27	6.66	− .27	5,395
June	93.08	93.23	93.07	93.22	+ .25	6.78	− .25	355

Est vol 18,523; vol Wed 10,523; open int 36,475, +1,824.

MUNI BOND INDEX (CBT)–$1,000; times Bond Buyer MBI

	Open	High	Low	Settle	Chg	Open High	Low	Interest
Dec	86-28	87-04	86-18	86-26	+ 9	92-21	85-14	7,511

Est vol 1,800; vol Wed 2,292; open int 7,520, +259.
The index: Close 88-01; Yield 8.05.

EURODOLLAR (IMM)–$1 million; pts of 100%

	Open	High	Low	Settle	Chg	Yield Settle	Chg	Open Interest
Dec	91.84	91.91	91.79	91.90	+ .13	8.10	− .13	256,476
Mr91	91.88	91.97	91.83	91.95	+ .16	8.05	− .16	116,101
June	91.75	91.84	91.71	91.83	+ .17	8.17	− .17	66,147
Sept	91.51	91.59	91.48	91.59	+ .15	8.41	− .15	47,988
Dec	91.23	91.31	91.21	91.31	+ .13	8.69	− .13	40,107
Mr92	91.18	91.25	91.17	91.25	+ .12	8.75	− .12	30,862
June	91.09	91.15	91.07	91.15	+ .11	8.85	− .11	22,868
Sept	91.02	91.08	91.00	91.08	+ .11	8.92	− .11	14,534
Dec	90.88	90.94	90.86	90.94	+ .11	9.06	− .11	11,615
Mr93	90.84	90.91	90.84	90.91	+ .11	9.09	− .11	9,789
June	90.75	90.82	90.75	90.82	+ .11	9.18	− .11	7,624
Sept	90.69	90.75	90.68	90.75	+ .11	9.25	− .11	4,657
Dec	90.60	90.64	90.57	90.65	+ .11	9.35	− .11	3,124
Mr94	90.58	90.62	90.57	90.63	+ .11	9.37	− .11	2,920
June	90.49	90.56	90.49	90.57	+ .11	9.43	− .11	1,965
Sept	90.48	90.52	90.47	90.53	+ .11	9.47	− .11	644

Est vol 180,360; vol Wed 118,125; open int 637,421, −822.

EURODOLLAR (LIFFE)–$1 million; pts of 100%

	Open	High	Low	Settle	Change	Lifetime High	Low	Open Interest
Dect	91.81	91.87	91.81	91.82	+ .04	92.40	90.02	20,021
Mr91	91.86	91.90	91.86	91.87	+ .07	92.33	90.11	7,663
June	91.75	91.76	91.74	91.73	+ .06	92.14	90.43	3,526
Sept	91.50	91.54	91.50	91.50	+ .04	91.96	90.54	1,092
Dec	....	....	91.23	91.23	+ .03	91.75	90.58	482
Mr92	....	....	91.18	91.18	+ .03	91.54	90.60	267

Est vol 6,379; vol Wed 6,905; open int 33,123, +287.

STERLING (LIFFE)–£500,000; pts of 100%

	Open	High	Low	Settle	Chg	High	Low	Open Interest
Dec	85.53	85.55	85.46	85.49	− .01	89.37	84.83	59,538
Mr91	86.39	86.45	86.34	86.40	+ .04	89.06	85.27	27,162
June	87.16	87.23	87.13	87.20	+ .05	89.10	85.75	16,162
Sept	87.61	87.69	87.61	87.66	+ .05	89.66	86.23	16,229
Dec	87.81	87.91	87.81	87.88	+ .06	88 57	86.52	13,596
Mr92	87.88	87.94	87.88	87.93	+ .06	88.30	86.68	9,955
June	87.82	87.88	87.82	87.86	+ .04	88.06	87.45	2,342
Sept	87.85	87.88	87.85	87.86	+ .04	88.08	87.46	1,240
Dec	....	....	87.86	87.86	+ .04	88.12	87.55	541
Mr93	....	....	87.86	87.86	+ .04	88.12	87.50	305
June	....	....	87.86	87.86	+ .04	88.11	87.58	552

Est vol 32,410; vol Wed 51,377; open int 147,622, +1,855.

LONG GILT (LIFFE)–£50,000; 32nds of 100%

	Open	High	Low	Settle	Chg	High	Low	Open Interest
Dec	82-01	82-05	81-25	81-30	+ 0-02	87-02	80-17	28,086
Mr91	82-22	82-22	82-22	82-18	+ 0-02	84-03	82-20	107

Est vol 14,344; vol Wed 23,942; open int 28,193, −350.

CBT–Chicago Board of Trade. FINEX–Financial Instrument Exchange, a division of the New York Cotton Exchange. IMM–International Monetary Market at Chicago Mercantile Exchange. LIFFE–London International Financial Futures Exchange. MCE–MidAmerica Commodity Exchange.

Source: "Interest Rate Instruments," *The Wall Street Journal*, September 28, 1990.

2. Contracts on 5-year U.S. Treasury notes: $100,000 in 7 percent coupon securities
3. Contracts on long-term U.S. Treasury bonds: $100,000 in 8 percent, 20-year bonds
4. Contracts on Municipal Bond Index: $100,000 in bonds with a principal value to yield 8 percent. The index equals $1,000 times the current value of the Bond Buyer Municipal Bond Index.

Figure 18.2 *Treasury Bond Contract Volume on the Chicago Board of Trade*

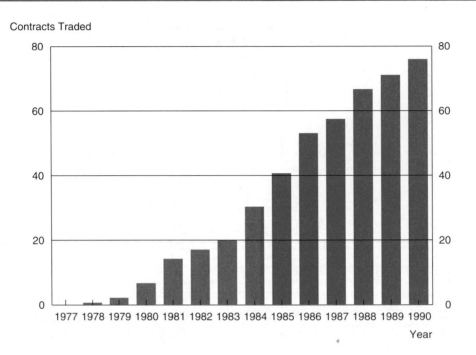

Contracts Traded

Brief History of the Financial Futures Market

Although financial futures contracts have existed since the early 1970s, their widespread use began in January 1976 when the International Monetary Market (IMM), a subsidiary of the Chicago Mercantile Exchange, initiated the 90-day Treasury bill contract, followed by contracts in 1-year T-bills in September 1978 and 4-year Treasury notes in July 1979. The Chicago Board of Trade (CBT) initiated a financial futures market with a long-term Treasury bond contract in August 1977, followed by contracts on 5-year Treasury notes, 2-year Treasury notes, and a Municipal Bond Index.[1]

The exceptional growth in trading on these two exchanges inspired other exchanges to initiate contracts. Specifically, the Financial Instrument Ex-

change (FINEX) was established as a division of the New York Cotton Exchange. The New York Futures Exchange (NYFE, pronounced "knife") was set up as part of the New York Stock Exchange in 1980.

Growth in Trading Volume   Although space prohibits documenting the growth in trading of all contracts, the graph in Figure 18.2 indicates what has happened to the trading volume for Treasury bond contracts on the Chicago Board of Trade since the contract was initiated in August 1977. As of 1991, this long-term Treasury bond contract was the most actively traded financial futures instrument.

Why the Growth in Trading Volume?   The dramatic growth in trading of financial futures raises an obvious question: Why have financial futures become so popular? The explanation is based on the reason for establishing futures exchanges, in general, and financial futures contracts, in particular. The primary function of futures markets, whether for commodities or financial instruments, is to *allow investors to transfer risk*. Financial futures contracts meet the need to

---

[1]See Roger Lowenstein, "Commodities Trader Pushes a New Market for Financial Futures," *The Wall Street Journal*, December 19, 1980: 1.

Figure 18.3 **Average Rate on 90-Day Treasury Bills**

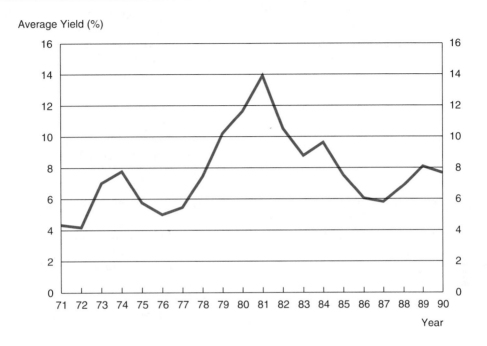

Source: *Federal Reserve Bulletin*, various issues.

hedge the price risk of the underlying financial instruments.

Everyone is aware of the substantial price volatility of commodities such as wheat, corn, and soybeans. Futures contracts allow farmers, processing firms, and others to hedge against this risk. The need for hedging positions in financial instruments has arisen from the *increasing volatility of interest rates*, which has caused an increase in bond price volatility. Investors and money managers involved in the bond market want to protect themselves by hedging their current or future bond positions against this volatility. (We will discuss an example of such a hedge in a subsequent section.)

The volatility of interest rates is demonstrated in the graph in Figure 18.3 of average annual T-bill rates for each year since 1971. One can imagine what happened to bond prices during 1972 and 1973, when rates increased by almost 75 percent from 4.07 to 7.03 percent, and during the period from 1977 to 1981 when rates almost tripled from 5.27 to 14.03 percent. Similarly strong, but opposite, effects were felt from

1981 to 1983 when rates declined from 14.03 to 8.61 percent, while from 1984 to 1986 rates declined by about 30 percent, from 9.52 to 5.97 percent. Even stronger volatility shook the market *within* some of these years.

The point is, the bond market has become more volatile, and this has prompted investors and money managers to consider using financial futures to protect themselves against substantial variation in bond prices. At the same time, this increase in interest rate volatility attracts speculators who are anxious to take the other side of futures transactions to earn substantial profits.[2]

Interest Rate Futures Transactions

Given this background on the operation and historical development of the financial futures market, the following subsections give examples of three types of

---

[2]"An Explosion of Options and Futures," *Business Week*, March 23, 1980: 88.

interest rate futures trades: short hedges, long hedges, and speculation. Understanding these examples requires definition of the term *basis*. **Basis** is the difference in the prices in the cash market and the futures market. As an example, if the current price of a long-term Treasury bond is 85–00 and the price on a 3-month Treasury bond futures contract is 83–00, the basis is 2–0. The important factor is not whether there is a difference in price (basis), but the change in basis over time, as we will demonstrate.

Short Hedge Using Interest Rate Futures

A **short hedge** involves the sale of a financial futures contract to hedge a current position in the underlying financial instrument. The following examples show how various investors might enter into short hedges using interest rate futures.

1.   A dealer with an inventory of bonds could enter into a short hedge to avoid price risk due to volatile interest rates by selling interest-rate futures contracts against that inventory.
2.   An investment banker could sell interest-rate futures contracts against a recent bond issue that was not completely sold out. Selling futures contracts would protect the investment banker against a sudden change in Federal Reserve policy or an international incident that would affect interest rates since any loss

on the unsold issue would be partially offset by a gain on the futures contracts.
3.   A bond portfolio manager could sell interest rate futures contracts against a unique bond issue in the portfolio that is expected to decline. Rather than sell the issue and buy it back later, the portfolio manager would sell futures contracts against it so that any loss on the portfolio issue would be offset by a gain on the futures position.
4.   A bond portfolio manager could enter into a short hedge as protection against a price decline while attempting to liquidate an illiquid issue. As an example, assume a portfolio manager decides to sell a large holding of a bond issue for which the market is thin. It will take about 2 weeks to complete the sale. To protect against a price decline in the bond issue during this period, the manager could sell futures contracts against the position.
5.   A financial manager for a corporation anticipating financing an asset purchase with bonds could use financial futures to hedge against higher interest rates before completion of the financing deal. If interest rates were to increase between the time you decide to sell bonds to get the needed funds and the actual bond issue, the gain on the short hedge would help offset the higher interest costs and the larger amount of bonds needed to get the funds required.

The following table summarizes a fairly typical short hedge transaction:

Example of a Short Hedge
Intent: Sell futures contracts short against a cash position

	Cash	Futures	Basis (Cash–Future)
Nov. 1	You own $1 million of 15-year, 8⅜ percent U.S. Treasury bonds @ 82–17 (Yield 10.45 percent) Value: $825,312.50	You sell 10 March bond futures contracts at 80–09	+ 2–8
Mar. 3	You sell the 8⅜ percent bonds @ 70–26 (Yield 12.31 percent) Value: $708,125	You buy 10 March bond futures contracts at 66–29	+ 3–29
	Loss: 11–23 per bond or $117,187.50	Gain: 13–12 per contract or $133,750	

Conclusion: You had an overall gain on the hedge (before transaction costs) of $16,562.50 because the basis moved in your direction. Specifically, the basis widened, which means that the price on your futures contract declined by more than the price of the bonds in your portfolio.

Long Hedge Using Interest Rate Futures

In a **long hedge,** you purchase financial futures contracts to offset potential adverse price movements related to the future purchase of the actual bonds or a future cash position. Long hedges are not as widespread as short hedges. A long hedge would be useful, for example, when a portfolio manager was expecting to invest some future cash flow in bonds. If the portfolio manager felt that yields might decline before the cash flowed in, it would be possible to lock in the higher yield through a long hedge, i.e., by buying

Basis The difference between an asset's prices in the cash market and the futures market.

Short hedge The sale of a financial futures contract to hedge a current position in the underlying security.

Long hedge The purchase of a financial futures contract to hedge against adverse price movements in a security a trader plans to purchase.

futures contracts on the bonds. The following example of a long hedge shows how this would work:

Example of a Long Hedge
Intent: Buy futures contracts against a future cash position

	Cash	Futures	Basis (Cash–Future)
June 1:	A 20-year Treasury bond is currently yielding 12.45 percent. The price for a 20-year, $8\frac{1}{4}$ percent bond is 67–28 Current cost: $678,750	You buy 10 Dec. bond futures contracts at 66–13	+ 1–15
Dec. 3:	You buy $1 million of 20-year $8\frac{1}{4}$ percent Treasury bonds at 83–23 (Yield: 10.03 percent) Future cost: $837,187.50	You sell 10 Dec. bond futures contracts at 81–22	+ 2–1
	Loss: $837,187.50 678,750.00 $158,437.50	Gain: $81,687.50 66,406.25 $15,281.25/contract or $152,812.50	

Conclusion: You had an overall loss on the hedge (before margin and transaction costs) of $5,625 because the basis moved against you. Specifically, the basis increased, which means that the price of the futures contracts that you were selling did not increase as much as the price of the bonds in the cash market. This loss on the hedge transaction is small compared to the $158,437 opportunity loss you would have experienced without the long hedge, i.e., without the hedge the purchase of these bonds would have cost $158,437.50 more than in June.

Speculative Transactions Using Interest Rate Futures

Investors can speculate with financial futures when they expect a rise or fall in interest rates and want to buy or sell bonds to profit from this change. Interest rate futures contracts allow you to speculate on this expectation with a small capital outlay and to derive all the benefits or risks of substantial leverage.[3]

The following examples demonstrate the large profit or loss potential available through leverage, which allows you to control a large amount of bonds

with a relatively small margin. Because of this leverage, a small change in the price of the bond issue results in a large percentage gain or loss on your capital investment. Never forget that capital markets are very consistent: any potential for a large gain is accompanied by the potential for a large loss.

---

[3]The impact is discussed in Sue Shellenbarger, "Boom in Financial Futures Trading Transforms Commodities Markets," *The Wall Street Journal*, March 23, 1981: 23.

The first example assumes that you want to take advantage of an expected decline in interest rates by buying an interest rate futures contract:

Example of a Speculative Trade
Outlook: *You expect a decline in interest rates over the next 3 months.*

April 1:	You buy a 90-day T-bill futures contract at 87 (for a 13 percent discount). Your initial margin on the $1 million contract is $1,500. A 1-basis-point (b.p.) change on the contract is worth $25.
July 10:	You were correct and rates declined from 13 to 11 percent. You can sell your contract at 89 (for an 11 percent discount). The 200-basis-point change earns you $5,000 (200 b.p. × $25). You have made $5,000 on an investment of $1,500.

Note: If you were wrong, and interest rates had increased to 15 percent, you would have sold the contract for 85 and lost $5,000 on a $1,500 investment.

For a second example of a trade by a speculator, suppose you expect an increase in interest rates. This situation is somewhat unusual because typically you do not have an opportunity to make money when you expect interest rates to increase and bond prices to decline. About all you can do is either avoid buying bonds, or sell those you currently own and invest in very short-term bonds that will experience minimal price declines. This example shows that interest rate

Example of a Speculative Trade
Outlook: *You expect an increase in interest rates over the next 3 months.*

Sept. 1:	You sell a long-term Treasury bond future at 89–00. Your initial margin on this $100,000 contract is $2,000. A 1-basis-point change in this contract is worth $31.25 (0.01/32 × $100,000).
Oct. 15:	You were correct and rates increased dropping the futures price to 86–00. You buy back the contract at that price to offset the original sale. The 3-point change is equal to 96 thirty-seconds (3 × 32), so the total gain is 96 × 31.25 = $3,000. You earned $3,000 on an investment of $2,000.

Note: If you were wrong and interest rates declined, you would have experienced a high percentage loss in your investment.

futures contracts can help you make money on the price decline.

Does Interest Rate Futures Hedging Work?

Two studies that examined this question provided evidence that interest rate futures do provide a good hedge. One study that examined the hedging performance of interest rate futures contracts related to GNMAs and T-bills found that hedging about 80 percent of the spot position reduced the price variability of the unhedged spot portfolio by 66 percent.[4] A second study that considered several alternative hedging techniques found that the most successful technique reduced the variability of the unhedged position by 73 percent.[5] Finally, it is possible to use financial futures to reduce or eliminate interest rate risk by immunizing the portfolio.[6]

Currency Futures

The rapid growth of international trade and travel has led to development of an active market for foreign currencies. Centered primarily in New York, this foreign exchange market facilitates trading in international currencies for both spot and deferred delivery by exporters, importers, banks, and travelers. The spot and forward foreign exchange quotes appear in *The Wall Street Journal*, as illustrated in Figure 18.4. These exchange rates were those that prevailed in transactions among a few large banks that are the major dealers in the forward market. As an example, the figure shows a spot exchange rate for dollars per British pound of $1.6905 (Arrow 1) and a 180-day forward rate (Arrow 2) of $1.6392.

As we have explained, the holder of foreign currencies faces additional risk due to fluctuations in exchange rates. One way to minimize exposure to exchange rate risk is to balance foreign-currency-

[4]Louis H. Ederington, "The Hedging Performance of the New Futures Market," *Journal of Finance* 34, no. 1 (March 1979): 157–170.

[5]Gerald D. Gay, Robert W. Kolb, and Raymond Chiang, "Interest Rate Hedging: An Empirical Test of Alternative Strategies," *Journal of Financial Research* 6, no. 3 (Fall 1983): 187–197.

[6]For a discussion of using futures to immunize bond portfolios, see Gerald D. Gay and Robert W. Kolb, "Interest Rate Futures as a Tool for Immunizing," *Journal of Portfolio Management* 10, no. 1 (Fall 1983): 65–70.

Figure 18.4 Spot and Forward Foreign Exchange Rates

EXCHANGE RATES

Friday, May 18, 1990

The New York foreign exchange selling rates below apply to trading among banks in amounts of $1 million and more, as quoted at 3 p.m. Eastern time by Bankers Trust Co. Retail transactions provide fewer units of foreign currency per dollar.

Country	U.S. $ equiv. Fri.	U.S. $ equiv. Thurs.	Currency per U.S. $ Fri.	Currency per U.S. $ Thurs.
Argentina (Austral) ...	.0002000	.0002000	5000.00	5000.00
Australia (Dollar)	.7615	.7620	1.3132	1.3123
Austria (Schilling)	.08624	.08607	11.60	11.62
Bahrain (Dinar)	2.6522	2.6522	.3771	.3771
Belgium (Franc)				
Commercial rate ...	.02937	.02928	34.04	34.16
Brazil (Cruzeiro)	.01966	.01969	50.87	50.80
① Britain (Pound)	1.6905	1.6915	.5915	.5912
30-Day Forward ...	1.6812	1.6822	.5948	.5945
90-Day Forward ...	1.6636	1.6648	.6011	.6007
180-Day Forward ...	1.6392	1.6412	.6101	.6093
② Canada (Dollar)	.8477	.8511	1.1797	1.1750
30-Day Forward ...	.8440	.8506	1.1849	1.1756
90-Day Forward ...	.8370	.8501	1.1948	1.1763
180-Day Forward ...	.8282	.8498	1.2074	1.1767
Chile (Official rate) ...	.003441	.003441	290.62	290.62
China (Renminbi) ...	.211752	.211752	4.7225	4.7225
Colombia (Peso)	.002107	.002107	474.59	474.59
Denmark (Krone)	.1591	.1594	6.2870	6.2750
Ecuador (Sucre)				
Floating rate	.001195	.001195	837.00	837.00
Finland (Markka)	.25628	.25681	3.9020	3.8940
France (Franc)	.18003	.17974	5.5545	5.5635
30-Day Forward ...	.17982	.17953	5.5612	5.5702
90-Day Forward ...	.17937	.17908	5.5750	5.5840
180-Day Forward ...	.17872	.17843	5.5955	5.6045
Greece (Drachma)	.006146	.006131	162.70	163.10
Hong Kong (Dollar) ..	.12843	.12843	7.7865	7.7865
India (Rupee)	.05800	.05800	17.24	17.24
Indonesia (Rupiah)	.0005507	.0005507	1816.00	1816.00
Ireland (Punt)	1.6243	1.6285	.6156	.6141
Israel (Shekel)	.4980	.4980	2.0081	2.0081
Italy (Lira)	.0008254	.0008237	1211.50	1214.00
Japan (Yen)	.006534	.006572	153.05	152.15
30-Day Forward ...	.006539	.006578	152.93	152.02
90-Day Forward ...	.006550	.006591	152.67	151.73
180-Day Forward ...	.006568	.006610	152.25	151.29
Jordan (Dinar)	1.5076	1.5076	.6633	.6633
Kuwait (Dinar)	3.4536	3.4536	.2896	.2896
Lebanon (Pound)	.001538	.001538	650.00	650.00
Malaysia (Ringgit)	.3701	.3708	2.7020	2.6970
Malta (Lira)	3.0912	3.0912	.3235	.3235
Mexico (Peso)				
Floating rate	.0003549	.0003549	2818.00	2818.00
Netherland (Guilder) ..	.5400	.5385	1.8520	1.8570
New Zealand (Dollar) .	.5725	.5735	1.7467	1.7437
Norway (Krone)	.1563	.1563	6.3980	6.3960
Pakistan (Rupee)	.0459	.0459	21.80	21.80
Peru (Inti)	.00003275	.00003275	30535.28	30535.28
Philippines (Peso)	.04474	.04474	22.35	22.35
Portugal (Escudo)	.006892	.006892	145.09	145.09
Saudi Arabia (Riyal) ..	.26681	.26681	3.7480	3.7480
Singapore (Dollar)	.5394	.5398	1.8540	1.8525
South Africa (Rand)				
Commercial rate	.3785	.3798	2.6420	2.6330
Financial rate	.2505	.2506	3.9920	3.9904
South Korea (Won) ...	.0014332	.0014332	697.73	697.73
Spain (Peseta)	.009747	.009685	102.60	103.25
Sweden (Krona)	.1661	.1659	6.0210	6.0260
Switzerland (Franc) ..	.7121	.7112	1.4043	1.4060
30-Day Forward ...	.7119	.7109	1.4047	1.4068
90-Day Forward ...	.7115	.7105	1.4054	1.4075
180-Day Forward ...	.7114	.7100	1.4056	1.4084
Taiwan (Dollar)	.036778	.036697	27.19	27.25
Thailand (Baht)	.03888	.03888	25.72	25.72
Turkey (Lira)	.0003994	.0003994	2504.00	2504.00
United Arab (Dirham) ..	.2723	.2723	3.6730	3.6730
Uruguay (New Peso)				
Financial	.000917	.000917	1090.00	1090.00
Venezuela (Bolivar)				
Floating rate	.02212	.02212	45.21	45.21
W. Germany (Mark) ..	.6070	.6055	1.6475	1.6515
30-Day Forward	.6071	.6056	1.6472	1.6512
90-Day Forward	.6072	.6058	1.6468	1.6508
180-Day Forward	.6070	.6054	1.6475	1.6518
SDR	1.32444	1.32920	.75504	.75233
ECU	1.24103	1.24681	....	....

Special Drawing Rights (SDR) are based on exchange rates for the U.S., West German, British, French and Japanese currencies. Source: International Monetary Fund.

European Currency Unit (ECU) is based on a basket of community currencies. Source: European Community Commission

Source: *The Wall Street Journal*, May 21, 1990.

Figure 18.5 Prices on Foreign Currency Futures

FUTURES

	Open	High	Low	Settle	Change	Lifetime High	Lifetime Low	Open Interest
JAPANESE YEN (IMM) 12.5 million yen; $ per yen (.00)								
June	.6549	.6557	.6536	.6538	− .0042	.7530	.6254	73,162
Sept	.6567	.6574	.6555	.6555	− .0043	.7410	.6268	8,597
Dec	.6590	.6590	.6583	.6574	− .0044	.7165	.6290	987
Est vol 19,128; vol Thur 24,393; open int 82,757, +187.								
W. GERMAN MARK (IMM)−125,000 marks; $ per mark								
June	.6060	.6078	.6051	.6073	+ .0021	.6153	.5057	66,016
Sept	.6061	.6080	.6054	.6074	+ .0022	.6156	.5410	5,686
Dec	.6065	.6070	.6054	.6073	+ .0024	.6150	.5764	302
Mr91	....	....	....	.6073	+ .0026	.6140	.5820	294
Est vol 29,175; vol Thur 45,436; open int 73,010, −2,876.								
CANADIAN DOLLAR (IMM)−100,000 dlrs.; $ per Can $								
June	.8450	.8465	.8427	.8438	− .0031	.8570	.8088	25,243
Sept	.8350	.8368	.8328	.8339	− .0030	.8471	.8093	5,102
Dec	.8285	.8285	.8250	.8253	− .0029	.8420	.8050	1,648
Mr91	.8190	.8210	.8180	.8175	− .0028	.8365	.7990	1,801
Est vol 5,375; vol Thur 7,208; open int 53,854, +458.								
→ **BRITISH POUND (IMM)−62,500 pds.; $ per pound**								
June	1.6836	1.6854	1.6796	1.6816	− .0012	1.6950	1.4400	34,716
Sept	1.6590	1.6602	1.6540	1.6562	− .0014	1.6616	1.5290	2,427
Dec	1.6340	1.6360	1.6330	1.6324	− .0014	1.6360	1.5640	336
Est vol 5,900; vol Thur 24,757; open int 37,479, +7,111.								
SWISS FRANC (IMM)−125,000 francs-$ per franc								
June	.7121	.7128	.7097	.7121	+ .0010	.7205	.5850	44,126
Sept	.7119	.7123	.7118	.7119	+ .0013	.7202	.6020	2,046
Dec	.7110	.7117	.7100	.7119	+ .0015	.7200	.6300	280
Mr91	....	.7133	+ .0016	.7165	.6500	778		
Est vol 17,900; vol Thur 32,561; open int 47,230, −724.								
AUSTRALIAN DOLLAR (IMM)−100,000 dlrs.; $ per A.$								
June	.7570	.7578	.7568	.7570	+ .0010	.7700	.7260	2,249
Est vol 44; vol Thur 76; open int 2,285, −8.								
U.S. DOLLAR INDEX (FINEX) 500 times USDX								
June	91.53	91.64	91.40	91.45	− .14	100.43	90.70	5,459
Sept	92.20	92.23	92.10	92.05	− .18	100.43	91.25	2,421
Est vol 750; vol Thur 2,245; open int 7,899, −260.								
The index: High 91.45; Low 91.23; Close 91.31 −.03								

Source: *The Wall Street Journal*, May 21, 1990.

denominated assets and liabilities. An investor can cover any net exposure, that is, the excess of foreign assets over foreign liabilities or vice versa, with a long or short hedge in the forward currency market. As noted earlier though, the forward market suffers from low liquidity relative to the currency *futures* market.

The primary currency futures market is the International Monetary Market (IMM), a subsidiary of the Chicago Mercantile Exchange. The sample currency futures quotations from *The Wall Street Journal* in Figure 18.5 show prices for the futures contract on 62,500 British pounds for four delivery months each year: March, June, September, and December. The settle quote on the June contract, $1.6816, gives this contract a value of $105,100 (62,500 × 1.6816). Table 18.1 contains a brief description of major currency futures contracts traded on the International Monetary Market.

Like other futures instruments, currency forward and futures markets serve two major economic purposes: price discovery and hedging. Academic studies have concluded that the current forward rate provides

Table 18.1 *Specifications for Foreign Currency Futures Contracts Traded on the International Monetary Market*[a]

Contract	Contract Size	Minimum Price Change	Margin	
			Initial	Maintenance
Australian dollar	A$100,000	$0.0001/A$ = $10.00	$2,000	$1,500
British pound	£62,500	$0.0002/£ = $12.50	$2,000	$1,500
Canadian dollar	C$100,000	$0.0001/C$ = $10.00	$ 900	$ 700
Deutschemark	DM125,000	$0.0001/DM = $12.50	$2,000	$1,500
Japanese yen	¥12,500,000	$0.000001/¥ = $12.50	$1,500	$1,000
Swiss franc	SF125,000	$0.0001/SF = $12.50	$2,000	$1,500

[a]These specifications are believed to be current as of May 1991, but contract specifications can change, so investors should check for the latest information.

Source: International Monetary Market.

Illustration of a Currency Futures Hedge

Spot Market		Futures Market	
May 18			
Anticipated cost of equipment (£250,000 × $1.6905)	$422,625	Purchase four December contracts @ $1.6905	$422,625
November 15			
Purchase spot currency to pay for imports at £1.5200	380,000	Sell four December contracts @ 1.5210	380,250
Gross savings	$ 42,625	Gross loss on futures	($ 42,375)

Total gains, subject to margin and transaction costs = $250

an unbiased forecast of the future spot rate, but with no better accuracy than projections from the current spot rate. More importantly, the hedging performance of currency futures compares quite favorably with those of commodity futures and interest rate futures.[7]

Sample Hedge Using Currency Futures

Consider the case of a U.S. manufacturer importing industrial equipment from a British firm. On May 18,

[7]Charles Dale, "The Hedging Effectiveness of Currency Futures Markets," *Journal of Futures Markets* 1, no. 1 (Spring 1981): 77–88.

the U.S. importer agrees to pay £250,000 for the equipment to be shipped in November. The quotation in Figure 18.4 gives a current cost of the equipment in U.S. dollars of $422,625 (250,000 × 1.6905). The anticipated cost based upon the expected exchange rate in November is $409,800 (250,000 × 1.6392). Being somewhat apprehensive about carrying an uncovered commitment in British pounds, the importer decides to hedge by buying four December contracts (for £62,500 each) at the rate of $1.6392 per British pound, as detailed in the above illustration.

Assume that the spot exchange rate falls to $1.5200 by November 15. The importer buys £250,000 in the spot market at $1.5200, takes delivery of the equipment, and closes out the futures position at a price of 1.5210 because there is a negative basis of 0.001. The manufacturer gained on the transaction in the spot market because the British pound declined in value, but lost a comparable amount in the futures market. The manufacturer avoided speculating on the chance that the British pound would get stronger, increasing the cost of the equipment in dollars. If the pound had increased in value, the manufacturer's loss on the equipment transaction would be offset by a gain on the futures transaction.

Stock Index Futures

It is well known that stock prices vary less than prices of many commodities, but much more than prices of bonds. An investor with a well-diversified portfolio of stocks bears little unsystematic or firm-specific risk, but is fully exposed to **systematic risk,** that is, the sensitivity of the expected portfolio return to fluctuations in the rate of return of the market portfolio. The owner of a diversified stock portfolio can protect against any expected market decline by selling short shares in a diversified stock mutual fund. Since the returns on the investor's portfolio would correlate highly with the returns on the mutual fund, the loss (gain) on the long stock position would be reduced by the gain (loss) on the short mutual fund position. This strategy is limited by transaction costs and restrictions imposed on short sales, particularly the requirement that a short sale can take place only on an uptick.

An alternate strategy if you have a bearish market outlook is to sell part of your stock portfolio and invest the proceeds in liquid assets. The costs of this strategy would involve commissions, bid–ask spreads, taxes, and potential liquidity costs in thin markets. For yet another alternative, you could buy put options on individual stocks in your portfolio or on a stock market index.[8]

The first two strategies have three major problems: high transaction costs, taxes, and difficulties in their execution. A solution is to trade **stock index futures contracts.** The liquidity and leverage of a stock index futures market provide a convenient, low-cost mechanism for hedging or speculating on market risk. Going short on index futures contracts is as easy as going long.

---

[8]These are discussed later in the chapter.

Systematic risk The uncertainty of the returns on an investor's portfolio due to changes in the rate of return of the market as a whole.

Stock index futures contract An agreement for delivery of cash based on movements in a stock market index.

The next subsection describes the major stock index futures contracts that are available to provide substantial diversity. The alternatives range from a futures contract on all stocks listed on the NYSE or the S&P 500 Index to a contract backed by a very select group of 20 stocks that are intended to track the DJIA or a select sample of large stocks traded on the OTC market.

Alternative Stock Index Futures Contracts

The Kansas City Board of Trade introduced the first stock index futures contract on the Value Line Composite Average (VLA) in February 1982. Currently, three other index futures contracts are also popular: Standard & Poor's 500 (S&P 500) index futures traded on the Chicago Mercantile Exchange (CME), the NYSE Composite Index futures traded on the New York Futures Exchange (NYFE), and the Major Market Index (MMI) of 20 blue-chip NYSE stocks traded on the Chicago Board of Trade (CBT). Table 18.2 lists the major characteristics of these index futures.

As indicated in Table 18.2, the market prices of the futures contracts vary from 100 to 500 times the values of the underlying stock indexes. No specific asset, such as a commodity or a bond that is traded in the spot market, underlies an index futures contract. Because stock index futures are underlain by stock market indexes, they do not require delivery of any financial instrument; instead, they call for cash settlements when the contracts expire. At the end of the last day of trading, the quote on the index futures contract is set equal to the value of the underlying stock index and investors settle gains/losses on their futures positions in cash.

How to Use Stock Index Futures

In this subsection, we discuss three ways you can use stock index futures in your investment program: (1) an ongoing strategy to change the aggressiveness of your overall portfolio, (2) hedging your portfolio, and (3) speculation on overall market trends.

| Table 18.2 | Comparison of Currently Traded Stock Index Futures Contracts |

Feature	Value Line Composite Average (VLA) Contract	Standard & Poor's 500 Index (S&P 500) Contract	NYSE Composite Index Contract
1. Location	Kansas City Board of Trade (KCBT)	Chicago Mercantile Exchange (CME)	New York Futures Exchange (NYFE)
2. Underlying market index	Value Line Composite Average (VLA). This is an equally weighted index of approximately 1700 stocks. Geometric average is used.	Standard & Poor's 500 (S&P 500) Index. This is a value-weighted index of 500 stocks. Arithmetic average is used.	NYSE Composite Index. This is a value-weighted average of *all* common stocks listed on the NYSE. Arithmetic average is used.
3. Contract size (value of contract)	500 times the Value Line Average (about $88,500)	500 times the S&P Index (about $75,000)	500 times the NYSE Composite Index (about $45,000)
4. Minimum price change	Tick size is 0.01 points. This represents a change of $5.	Tick size is 0.05 points. This represents a change of $25 per tick.	Tick size is 0.05 points. This represents a change of $25 per tick.
5. Daily price change limits	Five-point daily price limit is in effect.[a] Each point represents $500.	Five-point daily price limit is in effect.[a] Each point represents $500.	No limits currently in effect.
6. Delivery concept	Cash settlement. Actual value of VLA determines the payment. Final settlement is the last trading day of the expiring month. Delivery months are March, June, September, and December.	Cash settlement. Actual value of S&P 500 Index determines the payment. Final settlement occurs on the third Thursday of the delivery month. Delivery months are March, June, September, and December.	Cash settlement. Actual value of NYSE Composite determines the payment. Settlement is based on the difference between the settlement price on the next to last day of trading in the month and the value of NYSE Composite Index at the close of trading. Delivery months are March, June, September, and December.

[a]If the limit is reached on two consecutive days, the limit on the third day is 7.5 points; if reached for three consecutive days, the limit on the fourth day is 10 points; if reached on four consecutive days, there is no limit on the fifth day.

As we know from our discussion of fundamental analysis, active investment management requires market, industry, and individual company and stock analysis. An active investor or portfolio manager looks for underpriced and overpriced securities.

In addition, market timing is necessary. This calls for predicting the overall movement of the stock market and altering your overall portfolio position accordingly. If you had a bullish market outlook, you would develop an aggressive portfolio of stocks that would respond to market changes to maximize your gain from the expected market rally. In contrast, if you were bearish on the market, you would reduce the proportion of volatile stocks in your portfolio in order to minimize your price loss. Through these two strategies (stock picking and/or market timing), an active investor or portfolio manager with superior skills in forecasting firm-specific factors and/or overall stock market trends would experience above-average risk-adjusted returns.[9]

[9]Stephen Figlewski and Stanley Kon, "Portfolio Management with Stock Index Futures," *Financial Analysts Journal* 38, no. 1 (January–February 1982): 52–60. For an overview of index futures, see Victor Niederhoffer and Richard Zeckhauser, "Market Index Futures Contracts," *Financial Analysts Journal* 36, no. 1 (January–February 1980): 49–55. For a set of readings on this topic, see Frank J. Fabozzi and Gregory M. Kipnis, eds., *Stock Index Futures* (Homewood, Ill.: Dow Jones-Irwin, 1984).

Table 18.2 *continued*

Feature	MMI Futures Contract	MMI Maxi Futures Contract	NASDAQ-100 Index Futures Contract	S&P OTC 250 Futures
1. Location	Chicago Board of Trade (CBT)	Chicago Board of Trade (CBT)	Chicago Board of Trade (CBT)	Chicago Mercantile Exchange (CME)
2. Underlying market index	The Major Market Index (MMI) The following stocks make up the MMI Index: American Express; American Telephone & Telegraph; Chevron; Coca Cola; Dow Chemical; DuPont; Eastman Kodak; Exxon; General Electric; General Motors; IBM; International Paper; Johnson & Johnson; Merck; Minnesota M&M; Mobil; Philip Morris; Procter & Gamble; Sears Roebuck; U.S. Steel.	The Major Market Index (MMI)	The NASDAQ 100 Index. This capitalization-weighted index is composed of 100 of the largest nonfinancial stocks in the NASDAQ National Market System.	The S&P 250 Index of major stocks traded on the NASDAQ system.
3. Contract size (value of contract)	$100 times the MMI (about $25,000)	$250 times the MMI (about $62,500)	$250 times the NASDAQ 100 Index (about $62,500)	$500 times the S&P 250 OTC Index
4. Minimum price change	One-eighth (1/8) of a point. This represents a change of $12.50.	Five one-hundredths of a point (0.05). This represents a change of $12.50.	Five one-hundredths of a point (0.05). This represents a change of $12.50.	Five one-hundredths of a point (0.05). This represents a change of $25.
5. Price change limits	Five points daily. One point equals $100.	Five points. One point equals $250.	Five points. One point equals $250.	Five points. One point equals $500.
6. Delivery concept	Cash settlement based on the closing value of the MMI on the third Friday of the contract month. Contract months are the first three consecutive months plus the next month in the March, June, September, and December quarterly cycle.	Cash settlement based on the closing value of the MMI on the third Friday of the contract month. Contract months are the first three consecutive months, plus the next three months in the March, June, September, and December quarterly cycle.	Cash settlement based on the closing value of the spot NASDAQ 100 Index on the third Friday of the contract month. Contract months are the first three consecutive months, plus the next three months in the March, June, September, and December quarterly cycle.	Cash settlement is based on the actual closing value of the S&P 250 OTC Index on the third Thursday of the delivery month. Contract months are March, June, September, and December.

Altering the Volatility of Your Portfolio In the absence of futures trading, altering the aggressiveness of your portfolio requires shifting funds between low- and high-volatility stocks. This necessitates a large turnover of the portfolio with high accompanying transaction costs, including commissions, liquidity costs, and taxes. As noted previously, stock index futures provide an inexpensive, yet effective way of altering the relative volatility of your portfolio without affecting its essential composition.

An active investor typically does not want to completely hedge a portfolio, but rather wants to hold a portfolio with specific levels of risk and return. Through security analysis, you should attempt to select stocks with desirable firm-specific characteristics. Through market-timing strategies, you should try to control the exposure of your portfolio to general market movements. Before stock index futures trading, it was not feasible to separate overall market risk from risks unique to a stock. For example, a portfolio of

Table 18.3	Stock Hedge Using Index Futures		

Spot Market		Futures Market	
January 16			
Value of spot portfolio	$3,000,000	Sell 26 S&P 500 futures contracts with a total market price of 26 × 150,000	
		Initial margins: 26 × 2,500 = $65,000	$3,900,000
March 10			
Value of spot portfolio	2,960,000	S&P 500 Index futures contract is at 296, so the contract value is $148,000. Buy back 26 futures contracts with a value of 26 × 148,000	3,848,000
Gross loss on value of spot portfolio	($ 40,000)	Gross gain on futures portfolio	$ 52,000

Total gain subject to margin and transaction costs is $12,000.

stocks with desirable firm-specific factors might be very volatile relative to the overall stock market. If you were bearish on the market, you would not want to hold this portfolio because of its high relative volatility risk. By trading index futures, however, you could alter the overall volatility of your portfolio to a desired level and still not have to change the composition of stocks in the portfolio.

Hedging with Stock Index Futures The primary use of stock index futures contracts is to protect a stock portfolio from price fluctuations due to general market movements. In addition, some portfolio managers have used index futures contracts to earn near-arbitrage profits by exploiting transient discrepancies between prices in the cash stock market and those for stock index futures. This is referred to as *program trading*, and we will discuss it later in the chapter.

At this point, let us consider a fairly simple hedging example to illustrate the defensive use of stock index futures. Assume that the price behavior of the stock index futures contract is identical to that of the underlying stock index. Assume, also, a 100 percent margin requirement on futures and measuring percentage instead of dollar price changes.

Now, consider a manager of a diversified $3 million portfolio of stocks that is 30 percent more volatile than the market. The portfolio manager expects the market to decline in the near future. Currently, the S&P 500 stock index futures contract is quoted at

300, for a price of $150,000 (300 × $500). To minimize the variance of this spot–futures portfolio, the portfolio manager needs to sell 26 futures contracts.[10] The hedging transactions are illustrated in Table 18.3.

In this example hedge, the decline in the value of the portfolio because of an overall market decline was offset by a gain on the sale of 26 futures contracts. This example hedge brought an overall gain because the profit on the sale of 26 futures contracts was more than the loss in value of the portfolio (before transaction costs).

If the portfolio manager was incorrect and the market rose during this period, the hedge would have generated an offset in the opposite direction. An increase in value of the stock portfolio would have been partially or completely offset by a loss on the futures transaction. The loss on the futures transaction could have been even greater than the gain on the stock portfolio, in addition to the transaction costs. The portfolio manager is willing to give up the potential gain on the stock portfolio during this period of time to protect against a potential loss from a projected market decline.

[10]The computation of the exact hedge ratio is discussed and illustrated in Frank K. Reilly, *Investment Analysis and Portfolio Management*, 3d ed. (Hinsdale, Ill.: Dryden Press, 1989): Chapter 25. Also see Ira G. Kawaller and Timothy W. Koch, "Managing Cash Flow Risk in Stock Index Futures: The Tail Hedge," *The Journal of Portfolio Management* 15, no. 1 (Fall 1988): 41–44.

Speculation with Stock Index Futures It is also possible to envision this example as a speculative transaction. As an individual bearish investor, you could simply sell some number of futures contracts, as shown on the right-hand side of Table 18.3, and put up the appropriate margin. Subsequently, when the market declined, you would buy the same number of contracts to close out your transaction. In this example with 26 contracts, you would have earned $26,000 (before transaction costs) on a margin of $65,000, for a 40 percent rate of return.

Program Trading or Index Arbitrage

From our prior discussion in this chapter, we know that a futures contract is a very close substitute for a forward contract on the same underlying asset. Therefore, a sufficiently large discrepancy between the futures and forward prices will provide arbitrage opportunities. Similarly, under a set of simplifying assumptions, we can derive an equilibrium relationship between the index futures contract and the stock index taking account of carrying costs and dividends. This derivation of the relationship reveals that index futures should typically trade at a premium over the spot stock index because carrying costs usually exceed the dividend yield.

Knowing these relationships and specific costs, you can construct boundaries between the values of the futures contract and the stock index. If the value of the futures contract should rise so that the premium of futures relative to the stock index exceeded the boundary, you could enter into an arbitrage transaction, selling the overpriced index future contract and buying the portfolio of stocks covered by the index future in the cash market. Subsequently, when the boundary relationship was corrected (i.e., the futures premium declined), you could reverse the transactions and experience a profit equal to the change in the premium spread.

If the price of the index future should decline to a value below the stock index, you could do the opposite, buying the underpriced index future and selling the stock index. Again, when the relationship corrected itself and the index futures returned to a premium position, you could reverse the transaction. This practice of buying and selling index futures and the portfolio of underlying stocks to take advantage of violations of normal boundaries is called **index arbitrage.**

Index arbitrage Simultaneous purchase (sale) and sale (purchase) of stock index futures and the stocks in the index portfolio to profit from price differences between them.

Program trading Index arbitrage using automatic transaction commands according to instructions from sophisticated computer programs.

Using sophisticated computer programs, institutional investors and market professionals continuously monitor the differences between index futures contracts and the underlying stock indexes. Whenever they detect violations of the boundary conditions, the computer programs instantaneously issue market orders to the stock and futures exchanges to lock in nearly riskless returns. Because of the use of these computer programs, the term **program trading** has been coined for this type of arbitrage with coordinated purchases and sales of portfolios of stocks and futures contracts. Program trading has benefited the markets by accelerating the process by which new information is incorporated into stock prices and strengthening the linkages between the stock market and the index futures market. This close linkage in turn enhances the hedging effectiveness of index futures contracts.

Program Trading and the 1987 Crash In sharp contrast to tolerant attitudes toward their traditional beneficial role, stock index futures have been attacked as a culprit that aggravated price volatility during the October 1987 stock-market crash. Briefly, the enormous trading activity during October 19 and 20 swamped the electronic order-processing system used by program traders (the DOT system) and also overpowered the information display capabilities of stock markets. This led to several episodes of disconnections between the spot stock market and futures markets. On top of this mechanical disruption, the uptick rule for short sales drastically reduced the ability of traders to carry out arbitrage-motivated trades. Together, these factors caused stock index futures to trade persistently at substantial discounts from the underlying stock indexes. Under such conditions, program traders sold the overpriced stocks and bought the stock index futures. Instead of protecting investors against market movements, critics charged, program trading caused a dramatic increase in stock-market volatility.

While the debate continues over the role of index futures in stock-market volatility, studies by the Brady Commission, the Commodity Futures Trading Commission, and the Securities and Exchange Commission have generally identified four primary problems: (1) a lack of harmony in operating procedures of the stock and futures markets, (2) a lack of coordination in the regulation of these markets, (3) a failure of the stock exchange order-processing systems, and (4) undercapitalization of specialists on the stock exchanges.

These studies underscore tension between the financial futures and options markets and the trading structures of the stock exchanges. In response to these events, the NYSE and the SEC have introduced rules, called *circuit breakers*, limiting program traders' access to the NYSE's automated super DOT execution system after 50-point swings in the Dow Jones Industrial Average. Such a limitation makes it more difficult for program traders to carry out their coordinated trades on the NYSE. Some speculate that the program traders are doing it by other means using smaller "proxy" portfolios of stocks. Questions have also been raised about whether these circuit breakers, which disrupt the liquidity of the stock market, are the appropriate way to handle market volatility.

Some advocate transferring control over stock index futures trading to the SEC from the CFTC. They contend that centralized control over both instruments (stocks and futures) would enhance coordination between these markets and instruments.

Options on Futures Contracts

In Chapter 16, we discussed options on individual stocks and on stock indexes such as the S&P 500 Index, the S&P 100 Index, and the Major Market Index. In this chapter, we considered futures contracts on various instruments such as bonds, currencies, or stock indexes. In this section, we discuss combinations of these two instruments, or options on futures. The owner of a put (call) option on a financial instrument has the right (but not the obligation) to sell (buy) a futures contract on that instrument at a predetermined strike price during a specified time period. These options expire at the same time as the underlying futures contracts. As American options, they can be exercised prior to their expiration. On exercising a call option, the owner assumes a long position in the futures contract; the owner of a put option takes a short position in the futures contract. Figure 18.6 gives market quotes on some popular options on futures (referred to as *futures options*).

The first set of quotes in Figure 18.6 pertains to puts and calls on the CBT T-bond futures contract. The strike prices range from 88 to 98 per 100 of the futures contract's par value. The quotes are stated in 64ths, so the quote for the June 88 call of 3–57 indicates 249 64ths. Therefore, the premium on the call that expires in June is $3,890.625 (= $100,000 × 249/64 × 1/100) per contract. Suppose that the owner of the June 88 call option exercises the right to buy a June T-bond futures contract at $88,000 in early June when the futures contract is trading at 94. After assuming a long futures position at the strike price of 88, this investor can take a profit by selling a futures contract at the current price of 94, providing a price gain of $6,000 − $3,890.625 = $2,109.375, before adjustment for transaction costs and taxes.

The June 94 put quote of 1–44 represents a premium of $2,109.375 per futures contract. The owner of a put option on T-bonds has the right to sell a T-bonds futures contract at 94. In exercising the put option, the owner assumes a short position in T-bond futures. He or she can close out this short futures position by executing a reverse trade (selling a June 94 put) or by delivering a futures contract for T-bonds at the time of final settlement.

As another example, consider options on the S&P 500 stock index futures. As of May 18, 1990, the S&P 500 Index was at 354.64. The September 350 call and put were quoted at 19.35 and 9.10, which amount to $9,675 (500 × $19.35) and $4,550 (500 × $9.10) per futures contract, respectively. If the S&P 500 index were at 350 when these options expired in September, both would have remained unexercised. If the index were at 340, the 350 call option would have been worthless because it allowed the holder to buy the index at 350 when it was trading for 340. In contrast, the 350 put option would have been worth $5,000 per contract (10 points × $500). If the index were at 370, the put option would have been worthless because it allowed the holder to sell the index at 350 when it was priced at 370. The call option would have been worth $10,000 per contract (20 points × $500).

These examples demonstrate two important characteristics of these options—leverage and limited risk. These example investments required fairly limited capital investments. A movement in the index of 20 points, which is less than 6 percent, gave returns over 100 percent, which indicates substantial leverage. Risk is limited because no matter how badly the market

Figure 18.6 **Quotes for Options on Futures Contracts**

FUTURES OPTIONS

T-BONDS (CBT) $100,000; points and 64ths of 100%

Strike	Calls—Last			Puts—Last		
Price	Jun-c	Sep-c	Dec-c	Jun-p	Sep-p	Dec-p
88	3-57	4-01	4-24	0-01	0-36	1-12
90	1-57	2-33	3-05	0-01	1-05	1-56
92	0-05	1-26	2-02	0-12	1-58	2-47
94	0-01	0-45	1-17	2-07	3-11	3-56
96	0-01	0-20	0-50	4-09	4-48	5-20
98	0-01	0-09	0-30	6-07	6-36	....

Est. vol. 92,000, Thur vol. 69,107 calls, 56,580 puts
Open interest Thur;433,192 calls, 342,893 puts

T-NOTES (CBT) $100,000; points and 64ths of 100%

Strike	Calls—Last			Puts—Last		
Price	Jun-c	Sep-c	Dec-c	Jun-p	Sep-p	Dec-p
92	....	....	....	0-01	0-22	....
93	2-08	2-27	....	0-01	0-35	....
94	1-08	1-47	....	0-01	0-54	....
95	0-12	1-10	....	0-04	1-16	....
96	0-01	0-47	....	0-57	1-51	....
97	0-01	0-30	....	1-59	2-33	....

Est. vol. 5,200, Thur vol. 3,858 calls, 1,672 puts
Open interest Thur;41,710 calls, 35,156 puts

MUNICIPAL BOND INDEX (CBT) $100,000; pts. & 64ths of 100%

Strike	Calls—Settle			Puts—Settle		
Price	Jun-c	Sep-c	Dec-c	Jun-p	Sep-p	Dec-p
88	2-26	....	2-26	0-06	....	1-19
89	1-35	1-48	....	0-15	1-07	....
90	0-54	1-16	1-29	0-33	1-38	2-17
91	0-22	0-55	1-05	1-02	2-11	2-54
92	0-09	0-37	....	1-50	2-55	....
93	0-04	0-25	....	2-41	3-43	....

Est. vol. 100, Thur vol. 11 calls, 0 puts
Open interest Thur;11,655 calls, 10,753 puts

EURODOLLAR (IMM) $ million; pts. of 100%

Strike	Calls—Settle			Puts—Settle		
Price	Jun-c	Sep-c	Dec-c	Jun-p	Sep-p	Dec-p
9100	0.55	0.50	0.51	0.01	0.08	0.24
9125	0.31	0.33	0.36	0.02	0.15	0.34
9150	0.09	0.19	0.25	0.05	0.26	0.47
9175	0.02	0.10	0.17	0.23	0.42	0.63
9200	0.01	0.05	0.10	0.47	0.61	0.81
9225	.0004	0.03	0.07	0.71	0.83	1.00

Est. vol. 24,970, Thur vol. 18,781 calls, 16,395 puts
Open interest Thur; 198,200 calls, 204,081 puts

EURODOLLAR (LIFFE) $1 million; pts. of 100%

Strike	Calls—Settle			Puts—Settle		
Price	Jun-c	Sep-c	Dec-c	Jun-p	Sep-p	Dec-p
9100	0.55	0.51	0.53	0.00	0.08	0.26
9125	0.31	0.34	0.39	0.01	0.16	0.37
9150	0.12	0.20	0.27	0.07	0.27	0.50
9175	0.02	0.10	0.17	0.22	0.42	0.65
9200	0.00	0.05	0.11	0.45	0.62	0.84
9225	0.00	0.02	0.06	0.70	0.84	1.04

Est. Vol. Fri, 2,200 Calls, 100 Puts.
Open interest Thur 3,861, Calls, 2,593 Puts.

LONG GILT (LIFFE) £50,000; 64ths of 100%

Strike	Calls—Settle			Puts—Settle		
Price	Jun-c	Sep-c	....	Jun-p	Sep-p	....
81	2-22	3-52	....	0-04	0-58	....
82	1-30	3-08	....	0-12	1-14	....
83	0-47	2-33	..:.	0-29	1-39	....
84	0-20	2-00	....	1-02	2-06	....
85	0-07	1-36	....	1-53	2-42	....
86	0-04	1-13	....	2-50	3-19	....

Est. Vol. Fri, 3,009 Calls, 4,090 Puts.
Open interest Thur 39,707, Calls, 30,446 Puts.

JAPANESE YEN (IMM) 12,500,000 yen; cents per 100 yen

Strike	Calls—Settle			Puts—Settle		
Price	Jun-c	Jly-c	Sep-c	Jun-p	Jly-p	Sep-p
63	2.42	2.67	2.92	0.05	0.15	0.41
64	1.51	1.83	2.19	0.14	0.41	0.67
65	0.76	1.15	1.58	0.38	0.60	1.03
66	0.30	0.65	1.07	0.92	1.10	1.51
67	0.12	0.35	0.71	1.73	1.78	2.12
68	0.05	0.17	0.46	2.66	2.60	2.85

Est. vol. 7,700, Thur vol. 8,641 calls, 3,852 puts
Open interest Thur; 68,392 calls, 40,052 puts

FUTURES OPTIONS

W. GERMAN MARK (IMM) 125,000 marks; cents per mark

Strike	Calls—Settle			Puts—Settle		
Price	Jun-c	Jly-c	Sep-c	Jun-p	Jly-p	Sep-p
59	1.81	2.01	2.41	0.09	0.27	0.69
60	0.98	1.28	1.78	0.25	0.54	1.05
61	0.40	0.73	1.24	0.67	0.99	1.50
62	0.14	0.39	0.85	1.40	1.53	2.10
63	0.05	0.18	0.58	2.31	2.42	2.80
64	0.03	0.09	0.39	....	....	....

Est. vol. 4,981, Thur vol. 8,929 calls, 12,472 puts
Open interest Thur; 68,127 calls, 62,771 puts

CANADIAN DOLLAR (IMM) 100,000 Can.$, cents per Can.$

Strike	Calls—Settle			Puts—Settle		
Price	Jun-c	Jly-c	Sep-c	Jun-p	Jly-p	Sep-p
835	1.04	0.64	0.94	0.18	0.74	1.02
840	0.67	0.45	0.72	0.32	1.03	1.30
845	0.39	0.29	0.54	0.54	1.38	1.61
850	0.21	0.19	0.39	0.82	1.78	1.96
855	0.10	....	0.30	1.22	....	2.33
860	0.50	....	0.21	1.67	....	2.73

Est. vol. 691, Thur vol. 197 calls, 1,046 puts
Open interest Thur; 8,025 calls, 11,872 puts

BRITISH POUND (IMM) 62,500 pounds; cents per pound

Strike	Calls—Settle			Puts—Settle		
Price	Jun-c	Jly-c	Sep-c	Jun-p	Jly-p	Sep-p
1625	5.80	4.16	5.36	0.18	1.06	2.34
1650	3.54	2.62	3.98	0.40	1.98	3.36
1675	1.74	1.50	2.82	1.12	....	4.68
1700	0.74	0.78	1.98	2.54	5.08	....
1725	0.26	0.40	1.32	....	....	....
1750	0.08	....	0.90	6.86	....	....

Est. vol. 708, Thur vol. 1,101 calls, 1,700 puts
Open interest Thur; 11,569 calls, 13,655 puts

SWISS FRANC (IMM) 125,000 francs; cents per franc

Strike	Calls—Settle			Puts—Settle		
Price	Jun-c	Jly-c	Sep-c	Jun-p	Jly-p	Sep-p
69	2.30	2.46	2.89	0.09	0.30	0.75
70	1.45	1.73	2.24	0.24	0.55	1.08
71	0.77	1.14	1.69	0.56	0.95	1.51
72	0.36	0.70	1.25	1.15	1.50	2.06
73	0.15	0.40	0.90	1.94	2.20	....
74	0.07	0.22	0.63	2.85	....	....

Est. vol. 2,036, Thur vol. 929 calls, 3,334 puts
Open interest Thur; 17,111 calls, 28,638 puts

S&P 500 STOCK INDEX (CME) $500 times premium

Strike	Calls—Settle			Puts—Settle		
Price	May-c	Jun-c	Se-c	May-p	Jun-p	Sep-p
345	10.60	12.80	23.20	0.00	2.25	7.90
350	5.60	8.90	19.35	0.00	3.35	9.10
355	0.60	5.65	15.95	0.00	5.05	10.60
360	0.00	3.15	12.90	4.40	7.55	12.40
365	0.00	1.55	10.20	....	10.85	14.55
370	0.00	0.70	7.80	....	15.00	16.90

Est. vol. 6,008; Thur vol. 3,456 calls; 4,674 puts
Open interest Thur; 36,459 calls; 52,512 puts

—OTHER INDEX FUTURES OPTIONS—

NYSE COMPOSITE INDEX (NYFE) $500 times premium

Strike	Calls—Settle			Puts—Settle		
Price	May-c	Jun-c	Jly-c	May-p	Jun-p	Jly-p
194	0.05	2.65	5.70	0.00	2.65	3.40

Est. vol. 67, Thur vol. 15 calls, 25 puts
Open interest Thur; 575 calls, 677 puts
CBT—Chicago Board of Trade. CME—Chicago Mercantile Exchange. NYFE—New York Futures Exchange, a unit of the New York Stock Exchange.

Source: *The Wall Street Journal*, May 21, 1990.

moves against you, the most you can lose is your premium. Therefore, you have leverage on the upside and limited loss on the downside.

Options and Futures Compared

At this juncture, it is important to note some of the essential similarities and differences between options and futures. Both are deferred-delivery instruments. Positions in both options and futures can be terminated prior to expiration by executing reverse trades.

You deliver on a futures contract only during the delivery period prescribed by the futures exchange. In contrast, American options may be exercised at any time prior to expiration.

The distribution of returns on options is different from that on a futures contract. Ignoring transaction costs and taxes, an option buyer can lose no more than the option premium. Further, the call (put) buyer insures against the downside (upside) variability of the futures price. The downside (upside) risk for a futures contract is the variability of the futures price below (above) the exercise price of the call option.

The maximum possible gain at expiration on a purchased put is the option exercise price; the potential gain on a purchased call option is the excess of the futures price over the option strike price. The option seller's position at expiration is opposite to that of the option buyer: the option seller's maximum possible gain at expiration is the premium received. In contrast, the buyer (seller) of a futures contract gains (loses) dollar-for-dollar with any increase in futures price. All of this means that the distribution of returns on options is different from the distribution of returns from futures contracts.

In general, buying options is less risky than writing them because the maximum possible loss on a purchased option is the premium paid, while the potential loss for a seller of an option is unlimited. Except for some delivery privileges enjoyed by the futures contract seller, a long futures position is about as risky as a short futures position.

The option premium is paid up-front, but the payment on a futures contract is postponed until final settlement. Purchased options do not require any margins and are not marked to market on a daily basis. Margins on options that are sold are generally higher than those on futures, which are marked to market daily. Also, writing (selling) an option generates premium income, but selling a futures contract does not.

Options provide flexible hedging mechanisms. An investor with a long spot position can insure against a price decline by buying a put option with a desired strike price without sacrificing the potential for capital appreciation on the spot position. Alternatively, writing calls against one's own portfolio can give limited protection against price declines since any subsequent price decline will be offset by the premium received. You can also vary the number of calls you write per unit of spot position. Finally, you can purge your spot position of most risk by buying a put and writing a call with identical exercise prices and expiration dates.

Selling an appropriate number of futures contracts against a long spot position is similar to buying a put and selling a call, that is, a single futures trade can minimize the variability of returns on the hedged portfolio.[11] However, the hedger in the futures market gives up any potential for capital appreciation on the spot position. Unlike options, a futures contract cannot separate downside risk from upside potential.

Summary

■   This chapter was concerned with financial futures, one of the fast-growing segments of the securities market. This market has grown rapidly because an increase in interest rate volatility caused an increase in bond price variability.

■   Sections of the chapter considered the three major segments of this market—interest rate futures, currency futures, and stock index futures. For each of these segments, we discussed alternative types of transactions (short hedges, long hedges, and speculation) used in financial futures trading and provided examples of each. We also discussed options on futures contracts for bonds, currency, or stock. The chapter concluded with a consideration of some similarities and several differences between options and futures contracts.

■   As mentioned on numerous occasions, these new instruments serve a very useful function, providing

---

[11]Eugene Moriarty, Susan Phillips, and Paula Tosini, "A Comparison of Options and Futures in the Management of Portfolio Risk," *Financial Analysts Journal* 37, no. 1 (January–February 1981): 61–67.

new risk–return alternatives and liquidity for investors in stocks, bonds, and/or foreign securities.

Questions

1. How do financial futures differ from commodity futures? Give an example of each.
2. What events in the economy have caused an increase in the number of financial futures instruments and the volume of trading in these instruments?
3. Describe a situation in which an investment banker might use interest rate futures. Assume that during the period following the futures transaction, interest rates decline. Describe what would happen to the investment banker.
4. Assume that you are informed that interest rates are going to become very stable during the next several years. What would you expect to happen to the volume of trading in interest rate futures? Discuss your reasoning.
5. You expect interest rates to increase during the next 2 months. Describe how you could use interest rate futures to benefit from this expectation.
6. Currency exchange rates have become more volatile during the past decade. Should this have an impact upon the volume of trading in currency futures? Discuss why or why not.
7. You expect the exchange rate between the U.S. dollar and the British pound to go from $1.65 per pound to $2.00 per pound.
   a. If you planned to travel in England during the next 3 months, what action should you take in the futures market?
   b. What action would you take in the futures market to speculate on this expectation?
8. Differentiate between stock options and stock futures contracts.
9. Assume you are a portfolio manager for a common stock fund composed of high-quality, NYSE stocks. What futures contract would you use to hedge this portfolio against a market decline? Why is this contract appropriate?
10. Describe an option on a futures contract. Discuss two advantages of purchasing this option rather than the futures contract directly.
11. *CFA Examination III (1986)* Your client, for whom you are underwriting a $400 million bond issue, is concerned that market conditions will change before the issue is brought to market. Having heard that it may be possible to reduce risk exposure by hedging in the Government National Mortgage Association (GNMA) futures market, the client asks you to:
   a. Briefly explain how the hedge works.
   b. Describe *four* practical problems that would limit the effectiveness of the hedge.
12. *CFA Examination III (1986)* Futures contracts and options on futures contracts can be used to modify risk. Identify the fundamental distinction between a futures contract and an option on a futures contract, and briefly explain the difference in the way futures and options modify portfolio risk.

Problems

1. *CFA Examination III (1982)* In each of the following cases, discuss how you as a portfolio manager would use financial futures to protect the portfolio. (15 minutes)
   a. You own a large position in a relatively illiquid bond that you want to sell.
   b. You have a large gain on one of your long Treasuries and want to sell it, but would like to defer the gain until the next accounting period, which begins in 4 weeks.
   c. You will receive a large contribution next month that you hope to invest in long-term corporate bonds on a yield basis as favorable as is now available.
2. *CFA Examination III (1983)* In February 1983 the United American Co. is considering the sale of $100 million in 10-year debentures that will probably be rated AAA, as are the firm's other bond issues. The firm is anxious to proceed at today's rate of 10.5 percent. As treasurer, you know that it will take about 12 weeks (until May 1983) to get the issue registered and sold. Therefore, you suggest that the firm hedge the pending bond issue using Treasury bond futures contracts. (Each Treasury bond contract is for $100,000.)

   Explain how you would go about hedging the bond issue, and describe the results, assuming that the following two sets of future conditions actually occur. (Ignore commissions and margin costs, and assume a 1-to-1 hedge ratio.) Show all calculations. (15 minutes)

	Case 1	Case 2
Current Values—February 1983		
Bond rate	10.5%	10.5%
June 1983 Treasury bond futures	78.875	78.875
Estimated Values—May 1983		
Bond rate	11.0%	10.0%
June 1983 Treasury bond futures	75.93	81.84
Present Value of a $1 Annuity		
10 years at 10.5 percent	6.021	6.021

References

Chance, Don M. *An Introduction to Options and Futures.* Hinsdale, Ill.: Dryden Press, 1989.

Dale, Charles. "The Hedging Effectiveness of Currency Futures Markets." *The Journal of Futures Markets* 1, no. 1 (Spring 1981).

Fabozzi, Frank J., and Gregory M. Kipnis, eds. *Stock Index Futures.* Homewood, Ill.: Dow Jones-Irwin, 1984.

Figlewski, Stephen, and Stanley Kon. "Portfolio Management with Stock Index Futures." *Financial Analysts Journal* 38, no. 1 (January–February 1982).

Gay, Gerald D., and Robert W. Kolb, eds. *Interest Rate Futures: Concepts and Issues.* Richmond, Va.: Robert F. Dame, 1982.

Gay, Gerald D., Robert W. Kolb, and Raymond Chiang. "Interest Rate Hedging: An Empirical Test of Alternative Strategies." *Journal of Financial Research* 6, no. 3 (Fall 1983).

Kolb, Robert W. *Understanding Futures Markets,* 2d ed. Glenview, Ill.: Scott, Foresman and Company, 1988.

Kolb, Robert W., and Gerald D. Gay. *Interest Rate and Stock Index Futures and Options: Characteristics, Valuation and Portfolio Strategies.* Charlottesville, Va.: Financial Analysts Research Foundation, 1985.

Modest, David M. "On the Pricing of Stock Index Futures." *Journal of Portfolio Management* 10, no. 4 (Summer 1984).

Moriarty, Eugene, Susan Phillips, and Paula Tosini. "A Comparison of Options and Futures in the Management of Portfolio Risk." *Financial Analysts Journal* 37, no. 1 (January–February 1981).

Powers, Mark J. *Inside the Financial Futures Market,* 2d ed. New York: John Wiley & Sons, 1984.

Rothstein, Nancy H. *The Handbook of Financial Futures.* New York: McGraw-Hill, 1984.

APPENDIX

18a *Commodity and Financial Futures Glossary*

Arbitrage   The simultaneous purchase and sale of similar financial or commodity instruments to benefit from an anticipated change in their price relationship.

Basis   The difference between a spot or cash price and a price of a futures contract.

Buy in   To cover or liquidate a sale.

Carrying charges   Those charges incurred in carrying an actual commodity, generally including interest, insurance, and storage.

CFTC   The Commodity Futures Trading Commission is the independent federal agency created by Congress to regulate futures trading. The CFTC Act of 1974 became effective April 21, 1975.

Clearinghouse   An adjunct to a futures exchange through which transactions executed on the floor of the exchange are settled by matching purchases and sales. A clearing organization is also charged with the proper conduct of delivery procedures and the adequate financing of the entire operation.

Clearing member   A member of the clearinghouse or organization. Each clearing member must also be a member of the exchange. Not all members of the exchange, however, are members of the clearing organization. All trades of a nonclearing member must be registered with, and eventually settled through, a clearing member.

Close   The period at the end of the trading session during which all trades are officially declared as having been executed at or on the close. The closing range is the range of actual sales during the closing period.

Contract   A term describing a unit of trading for a financial or commodity future. Also, the actual bilateral agreement between the buyer and seller of a futures transaction, as defined by an exchange.

Cover   Buying a commodity or a financial instrument to offset a sale previously made.

Current delivery   Delivery during the current month.

Day orders   Limit orders to be executed on a specific day or automatically cancelled at the close of that day.

Delivery   The tender and receipt of an actual commodity or financial instrument or cash in settlement of a futures contract.

Delivery month   The calendar month during which a futures contract matures.

Delivery points   Locations designated by futures exchanges at which the commodity covered by a futures contract may be delivered to fulfill the contract.

Discount   Commodity or bond prices that are below the future's contract price, deliveries at a lower price than others either due to maturity (e.g., May price is below the July price) or because of quality differences.

Evening up   Buying or selling to offset an existing market position.

Floor trader   A member who generally trades only for his or her own account or for an account he or she controls or who has such a trade made. Also referred to as a *local*.

Hedging   The sale of a futures contract against the physical commodity, an existing bond position, or its equivalent as protection against a price decline; alternatively, the purchase of a futures contract against anticipated prices of the physical commodity or bond as protection against a price advance.

Inverted market   A futures market in which the nearer months are selling at premiums to the more distant months.

Last trading day   The final day during which trading may take place in a particular delivery futures month under an exchange's rules. Futures contracts outstanding at the end of the last trading day must be settled by delivery of underlying physical commodities or financial instruments, or by agreement for monetary settlement, if the former is impossible.

Life of delivery (or **contract**)   The period between the beginning of trading in a particular futures contract and the expiration of that contract.

Liquidation   Sale of a previously bought contract, otherwise known as *long liquidation*. It may also be the repurchase of a previously sold contract, generally referred to as *short covering*.

Long hedge   The purchase of futures contracts in anticipation of actual purchases in the cash market. It is used by exporters as protection against advances in cash prices.

Maintenance margin   A sum, usually smaller than, but part of, the original margin. If a customer's equity in any futures position drops to the maintenance margin level, the broker must issue a margin call for the amount of money required to restore the customer's equity in the account to the original margin level.

Margin   The amount deposited by a client with a broker to protect the broker against losses on contracts being carried, or to be carried, by the broker. A margin call is a request to deposit either the original margin at the time of the transaction or funds to restore the margin to the maintenance levels required for the duration of the time the contract is held.

Opening range/closing range   In open auction with many buyers and sellers, commodities are often traded at several prices at the opening or close of the market. Buying or selling orders might be filled at any point within such a price range.

Open interest   The total of unfilled or unsatisfied contracts on either side of the market. In any delivery month, the short interest equals the long interest; in other words, the total number of contracts sold equals the total number bought.

Pit   The location on the trading floor where trading in a specific futures contract (commodity or financial) takes place.

Round-turn   The procedure by which the long or short position of an individual is offset by an opposite transaction, or by accepting or making delivery of the actual financial instrument or physical commodity.

Scalper   A speculator operating on the trading floor who provides market liquidity by buying and selling rapidly, with small profits or losses, holding positions for short periods of time.

Settlement price   The price at which the clearinghouse clears all the day's trades in a given commodity; also the price established by the exchange to settle contracts unliquidated because of acts of God, such as floods or other causes.

Short hedge The sale of futures contracts to eliminate or reduce the possible decline in value of an approximately equal amount of an actual financial instrument or physical commodity.

Speculator A trader who attempts to anticipate price changes and, through market activities, profit from these changes.

Spot commodity Goods available for immediate delivery.

Investment Companies

Up to this point in the book, we have discussed how to analyze the aggregate market, industries, and individual companies as well as their stocks and bonds in order to build a portfolio that serves your investment objectives. The current section has centered on alternative instruments such as options, warrants, convertibles, and futures that provide additional risk–return possibilities beyond those available from a straight stock–bond portfolio. This chapter introduces another investment opportunity: investment companies that sell shares in portfolios of stocks, bonds, or some combination of securities. Investment companies can make up part of a larger portfolio along with investments in individual stocks and bonds, or the investment companies can account for your total portfolio.

Studies of efficient capital markets have indicated that few individual investors can outperform the aggregate market averages. This makes managed investment companies an appealing alternative to direct investment because they provide several helpful services. Many different types of investment companies offer a wide variety of investment instruments with varying risk and return characteristics.

The initial sections in this chapter explain investment companies with examples and discuss the management organizations for investment company groups. The following section breaks investment companies into major types based upon how they are traded in the secondary market and how they charge for their services. The next section divides investment companies into types based upon their investment objectives and the types of securities in their portfolios. This section outlines some very interesting alternatives rang-

> **Investment company** A corporation, trust, or partnership in which investors pool their money to obtain professional management and portfolio diversification.
>
> **Net asset value (NAV)** The market value of an investment company's assets after deducting liabilities divided by the number of shares outstanding.
>
> **Investment management company** A company separate from the investment company that manages the portfolio and performs administrative functions.
>
> **Management fee** The compensation an investment company pays to the investment management company for its services.

ing from unusual types of instruments to securities from around the world.

To choose among more than 2,000 investment companies available, you need to understand how to evaluate their performance. After discussing some major studies of what factors are important and how to examine them, we consider the implications of these results for the investor. We conclude the chapter with a presentation on some sources of information on investment companies, emphasizing how these sources of information can help you to make an investment decision.

What Is an Investment Company?

An **investment company** invests a pool of funds from many individuals in a portfolio of individual securities such as stocks and bonds. An investment company might sell 10 million shares to the public at $10 a share for a total of $100 million. The manager of a common stock fund that emphasizes blue chips would invest the funds in the stock of companies like American Telephone & Telegraph, General Motors, IBM, Xerox, and General Electric. Each individual who bought shares of the investment company would own a percentage of its total portfolio.

The value of these shares depends upon what happens to the portfolio of assets. With no further transactions, if the total market value of the stocks in the portfolio increases to $105 million, then each original share of the investment company would be worth $10.50 ($105 million/10 million shares). This per-

share value is the **net asset value (NAV)** of the investment company. It equals the total market value of all its assets divided by the number of shares outstanding.

Management of Investment Companies

The investment company is typically a corporation that has as its major assets the portfolio, or *fund*, of marketable securities. The management of the portfolio of securities and most other administrative duties are handled by a separate **investment management company** hired by the board of directors of the investment company. This legal description oversimplifies, though. The actual management usually begins with an investment advisory firm that starts an investment company and selects a board of directors. This board of directors hires the investment advisory firm as the fund's portfolio manager.

The contract between the investment company (which owns the portfolio of securities) and the investment management company indicates the duties and compensation of the management company. The major duties include investment research, management of the portfolio, and administrative duties such as issuing shares and handling redemptions and dividends. The **management fee** is generally stated as a percentage of the total value of the fund, typically from one-quarter to one-half of 1 percent, with a sliding scale as the size of the fund increases.

To achieve economies of scale, many management companies start a number of funds with different characteristics. The variety of funds allows the management group to appeal to many investors with different risk–return preferences. The investors can also switch among funds as conditions change. This promotes flexibility and also increases the total capital the firm manages.

Closed-End versus Open-End Investment Companies

Investment companies begin like any other company—someone sells an issue of common stock to a group of investors. An investment company, however, uses the proceeds to purchase the securities of other publicly held companies rather than buildings and equipment. An open-end investment company (often referred to as a *mutual fund*) differs from a closed-end investment company (typically referred to as a *closed-end fund*) in the way each operates *after* the initial public offering.

Closed-End Investment Companies

A **closed-end investment company** operates like any other public firm. Its stock trades on the regular secondary market and the market price of its shares is determined by supply and demand. Such an investment company typically offers no further shares and it does not repurchase the shares on demand. To buy or sell shares in a closed-end fund, you make transactions in the public secondary market. The shares of many of these funds are listed on the NYSE. No new investment dollars are available for the investment company unless it makes another public sale of securities. Similarly, no funds are withdrawn unless the investment company decides to repurchase its stock, which is quite unusual.

The closed-end investment company's net asset value (NAV) is computed twice daily based upon prevailing market prices for the securities in the portfolio. The market price of its shares is determined by the relative supply and demand for the investment company stock in the public, secondary market. When you buy or sell shares of a closed-end fund, you pay or receive this market price plus or minus a regular trading commission. The NAV almost never matches the market price. Over the long run, the market prices of these shares have historically been from 5 to 20 percent below the NAV. Figure 19.1 lists closed-end stock funds, including diversified funds, flexible portfolio funds, and equity and convertible funds, quoted in *Barron's*.

Table 19.1 indicates the dramatic growth in number and dollar value of closed-end funds from 1986 to 1990. As of 1986 there were 8 diversified common stock funds and 18 specialized and convertible funds. By 1990 the number had grown to 24 diversified and flexible funds and 78 equity and convertible funds.

Figure 19.2 shows a listing of closed-end bond funds published in *Barron's*. Again, after many years of relative stability, the number of these funds has shown a major increase from about 20 in 1986 to 96 in 1990 (including 36 municipal bond funds). We discuss several international bond funds later in the chapter.

Some observers expect this growth to slow down because of the substantial discounts on these issues.[1] Besides the long-run discount of price relative to NAV,

Table 19.1 *Closed-End Fund Initial Public Offerings and New Funds Raised*

	Number of Funds	Amount Raised
1981	1	$ 62 million
1982	0	–
1983	4	58 million
1984	4	106 million
1985	3	614 million
1986	28	5 billion
1987	34	9 billion
1988	66	20 billion
1989	39	9 billion
1990	38	6 billion
1991[a]	11	3 billion

[a]Estimate through June 1991.

Source: Thomas J. Herzfeld Advisors, Inc., P.O. Box 161465, Miami, Florida 33116.

Closed-end investment company An investment company that issues only a limited number of shares which it does not redeem (buy back). Shares are traded in secondary securities markets at prices determined by supply and demand.

these funds seem to suffer further discounts following their initial public offerings (IPOs). Several studies have shown that prices of most individual stocks experience positive abnormal returns within a day after they are first offered. In contrast, studies of closed-end fund IPOs show fairly stable prices initially, which then drift to a discount over a 4-month period. This unusual pattern prompted an SEC study of the question.[2] Notably, several of the affected funds are the individual non-U.S. country funds (e.g., Japan, Korea, Germany, Italy, Spain, Thailand, Mexico) that we discuss later in the chapter.

At the time of the quotes in Figures 19.1 and 19.2, most of the funds were selling at discounts to their NAVs. This typical relationship has prompted inves-

[1]Michael Siconolfi, "Launching of Closed-End Funds May Ease," *The Wall Street Journal*, November 30, 1987: 33.
[2]Michael Siconolfi, "SEC Studies Closed-End Fund 'Mystery,'" *The Wall Street Journal*, May 23, 1988: 31.

Figure 19.1 *Closed-End Stock Funds and Convertible Security Funds*

MUTUAL FUNDS/CLOSED-END FUNDS

Fund Name	Exch.	NAV	Price	% Diff.	Fund Name	Exch.	NAV	Price	% Diff.
Put Premier	NYSE	7.80	6⅜	− 18.27	Duff & Phelps Sel Utils	NYSE	7.73	8	+ 03.49
Seligman Select Mun Fd	NYSE	z	z	z	Ellsworth Conv Gr&Inc	AMEX	7.67	6½	− 15.25
Taurus Muni CA Hld	NYSE	10.88	11⅛	+ 02.25	Emerging Germany Fd	NYSE	9.20	7¾	− 15.76
Taurus Muni NY Hld	NYSE	10.71	11⅛	+ 03.87	Engex Inc	AMEX	10.05	7 11/16	− 23.51
Templeton Global Inc-b	NYSE	8.46	7⅜	− 12.83	Europe Fd	NYSE	13.11	10¾	− 18.00
Temp Global Govt-b	NYSE	8.95	8¼	− 07.82	First Financial Fund	NYSE	5.35	4⅝	− 13.55
World Inc Fd	AMEX	9.25	9	− 02.70	First Philippine Fd	NYSE	9.80	7	− 28.57
ZenixIF-a	NYSE	5.84	5	− 14.38	France Growth Fd	NYSE	10.44	8½	− 18.58
Diversified Funds					Future Germany Fd	NYSE	13.90	11¼	− 19.06
Adams Express	NYSE	16.93	15	− 11.40	G.T. Greater Eur. Fd	NYSE	11.55	10¼	− 11.26
Baker Fentress	NYSE	20.42	16¼	− 20.42	Gabelli Equity Trust	NYSE	10.23	9½	− 07.14
Blue Chip Value	NYSE	6.47	6	− 07.26	Germany Fund	NYSE	10.91	11⅜	+ 04.26
Clemente-Global-b	NYSE	10.40	8⅞	− 14.66	Global Utilities Fd Inc	NYSE	10.52	9⅝	− 08.51
GSO Trust	NYSE	10.26	9¾	− 04.97	Growth Fund of Spain	NYSE	10.15	7⅝	− 24.88
Gemini II Capital	NYSE	11.82	10	− 15.40	H&Q Healthcare Inv	NYSE	11.67	9¾	− 16.45
Gemini II Income	NYSE	9.77	12⅜	+ 26.66	Hampton Utils Tr Cap-b	AMEX	10.47	9	− 14.04
General Amer Investors	NYSE	20.58	17½	− 14.97	Hampton Utils Tr Pref-b	AMEX	49.74	48⅜	− 02.74
Liberty All-Star Equity	NYSE	8.33	7¼	− 12.97	India Fund-f	NYSE	18.78	13⅞	− 26.12
Niagara Share Corp	NYSE	16.00	12⅞	− 19.53	Indonesia Fd (The)	NYSE	12.68	10⅞	− 14.24
Nicholas-Applegate Gro	NYSE	9.98	9¾	− 02.30	Inefficient-Mkt Fd	AMEX	9.51	7⅞	− 17.19
Quest For Value Income	NYSE	11.66	12⅜	+ 06.13	Irish Invest. Fd	NYSE	9.30	6⅞	− 26.08
Quest For Value Capital	NYSE	16.01	11¼	− 29.73	Italy Fund-b	NYSE	13.43	11¼	− 16.23
Royce Value Trust	NYSE	9.13	7⅞	− 13.75	Jakarta Growth Fd	NYSE	9.74	7⅜	− 24.28
Salomon Fund	NYSE	13.24	10¾	− 18.81	Japan OTC Equity Fd	NYSE	10.84	8	− 26.20
Source Capital	NYSE	35.77	38	+ 06.23	Korea Fund	NYSE	10.65	14⅜	+ 34.98
Tri-Continental Corp	NYSE	25.13	21½	− 14.44	Latin American Invest.	NYSE	13.13	9¾	− 25.74
Worldwide Value-a	NYSE	15.47	13¾	− 11.12	MG Small Cap	NYSE	9.10	8¾	− 03.85
Zweig Fund	NYSE	10.50	10¾	+ 02.38	Malaysia Fund	NYSE	13.06	11	− 15.77
Flexible Portfolio Funds					Meeschaert G&C	MWST	z	z	z
Amer All Sea Fd	OTC	5.85	4 15/16	− 15/60	Mexico Equity & Inc	NYSE	11.38	10⅜	− 08.83
European Warrant Fd	NYSE	9.59	8⅛	− 15.28	Mexico Fund-b	NYSE	14.01	12⅞	− 08.10
Flexible Bond Tr	AMEX	8.21	7⅞	− 04.08	New Germany Fd	NYSE	12.47	9⅞	− 20.81
Franklin Multi-Inc. Tr-b	NYSE	7.96	6⅞	− 13.63	Put Div Inc Fd	NYSE	9.41	9⅞	+ 04.94
MFS Special Value Tr-b	NYSE	12.30	10¾	− 12.60	Pacific Euro Growth Fd	AMEX	9.43	9	− 04.56
Zweig Total Ret	NYSE	8.94	8⅝	− 03.52	Patriot Select Div Tr	NYSE	13.82	14¾	+ 06.73
					Patriot Premium Div Fd II	NYSE	9.09	10	+ 10.01
Loan Participation Funds					Patriot Premium Div Fd	NYSE	7.85	9⅜	+ 19.43
Eaton Vance PRR		10.00	x	00.00	Petrol & Resources	NYSE	32.48	30	− 07.64
Merrill Lynch Prime Fd		10.00	x	00.00	Pilgrim Reg Bk Shrs	NYSE	7.30	6¾	− 07.53
Pilgrim PRT		10.04	x	00.00	Portugal Fund	NYSE	12.11	8⅞	− 26.71
VKM Prime Rate Inc Tr		10.01	x	00.00	Real Estate Sec Inc Fd	AMEX	5.95	5⅛	− 13.87
					ROCTwn	NYSE	7.31	7	− 04.24
Equity & Convertible Funds					SE Savings Inst. Fd-b	OTC	6.68	5	− 25.15
1st Australian	AMEX	10.07	7⅞	− 21.80	Scudder New Asia	NYSE	16.38	13¼	− 19.11
1st Iberian	AMEX	9.25	8	− 13.51	Scudder New Europe	NYSE	10.66	8¾	− 17.92
ASA Ltd-bc	NYSE	56.40	48½	− 14.01	Singapore Fd-b	NYSE	10.95	8½	− 22.37
Alliance New Europe	NYSE	9.65	8⅝	− 10.62	Spain Fund	NYSE	12.06	11¼	− 06.72
Alliance Global Env	NYSE	12.53	10⅛	− 19.19	Swiss Helvetia Fund	NYSE	13.00	12½	− 03.85
American Capital Conv	NYSE	20.23	17¾	− 12.26	TCW Convertible Secs-b	NYSE	7.32	7⅝	+ 04.17
Asia Pacific	NYSE	12.46	11⅞	− 04.70	Taiwan Fund-b	NYSE	15.90	19⅜	+ 21.86
Austria	NYSE	12.19	11	− 09.76	Thai Capital Fund	NYSE	8.37	6¾	− 19.35
BGR Prec Metals-be	TOR	10.48	9⅜	− 10.54	Thai Fund	NYSE	15.30	15	− 01.96
Bancroft Convertible	AMEX	19.10	16⅜	− 14.27	Temp Emerg Mkts-b	AMEX	14.62	12⅞	− 11.94
Bergstrom Capital	AMEX	59.50	62	+ 04.20	Temp Glob Util	AMEX	10.33	10⅛	− 01.98
Brazil	NYSE	10.16	8¼	− 18.80	Templeton Value Fd-b	NYSE	8.42	8⅛	− 03.50
CNV Holdings Capital	NYSE	8.49	4⅜	− 48.47	Turkish Invest. Fd	NYSE	15.65	10	− 36.10
CNV Holdings Income	NYSE	9.61	10½	+ 09.26	United Kingdom Fund	NYSE	10.38	9½	− 08.48
Castle Convertible	AMEX	19.93	16⅝	− 16.58	Z-Seven	OTC	11.27	13¾	+ 22.01
Central Fund Canada-b	AMEX	4.96	4 11/16	− 05.49					
Central Securities	AMEX	10.06	8	− 20.48					
Chile Fund	NYSE	16.26	12⅝	− 22.36					
Counsellrs Tandem Secs	NYSE	12.11	9½	− 21.55					
Cypress Fund	AMEX	8.33	7⅞	− 05.46					

(a) Ex-dividend (b) As of Thursdays close (c) Translated at Commercial Rand exch. rate (e) In Canadian dollars (f) As of Wednesday close (x) Not applicable (y) On Sept. 21 NAV 11.49 MKT 11½% +0.09 (z) Not available.

Source: *Barron's*, September 24, 1990.

Figure 19.2   *Closed-End Bond Funds*

CLOSED-END FUNDS

LIPPER ANALYTICAL SERVICES LIST

August 31, 1990

Bond Funds

Fund Name	Exch.	NAV	Price		% Diff.
AIM Strategic Inc	AMEX	8.90	7⅞	−	11.52
Allstate Prime		10.00	x		x
Amev Securities	NYSE	9.40	9⅛	−	2.93
Amer Adjust Rate	NYSE	9.63	9¾	+	1.25
Amer Capital Bond	NYSE	ab18.31	16	−	12.62
Amer Capital Inc	NYSE	7.33	6½	−	11.32
Amer Gov Income	NYSE	6.69	7⅛	+	6.50
Amer Gov Portf	NYSE	8.64	8¾	+	1.27
Amer Gov Term	NYSE	8.82	9¾	+	10.54
Amer·Opport Inc	NYSE	9.24	9⅛	−	1.24
Blackstone Advantage	NYSE	9.41	9¾	+	3.61
Blackstone Income	NYSE	8.30	8⅛	−	2.11
Blackstone Target	NYSE	9.07	9⅝	+	6.12
Bunker Hill Inc	NYSE	15.21	13¾	−	9.60
CIGNA High Inc	NYSE	6.08	6¼	+	2.80
CNA Inc Shares	NYSE	9.89	9	−	9.00
Circle Inc Shares	OTC	11.59	10¼	−	11.56
Colonial Intermarket	NYSE	10.87	9¾	−	10.30
Colonial Intrm High	NYSE	a6.03	5½	−	8.79
Current Inc Shrs	NYSE	11.60	11⅜	−	1.94
Dean Witter Gov Inc	NYSE	9.24	8¾	−	5.30
Dreyfus Strat.'Gov't	NYSE	10.88	10⅛	−	6.94
1838 Bond-Debenture	NYSE	19.40	19⅜	−	0.13
Excelsior Inc Shrs	NYSE	17.25	15¼	−	11.59
Fst Boston Income	NYSE	a7.69	6⅞	−	10.60
Fst Boston Strat Inc	NYSE	a9.43	8½	−	9.86
Flexible Bond	AMEX	a8.30	7⅞	−	5.12
Fort Dearborn Inc	NYSE	14.35	14	−	2.44

The data in the Lipper Analytical Services list of closed-end funds is as of August 31, while the information in the Investment Company Institute list is as of September 7.

Closed-end stock funds invest in diversified portfolios. Closed-end bond funds usually have diversified portfolios of debt issues. Closed-end convertible funds invest in preferred stock that is convertible into common shares.

John Hancock Inc	NYSE	15.21	14¼	−	6.31
John Hancock Inv	NYSE	20.18	18¼	−	9.56
Hatteras Inc Secs	NYSE	15.12	15⅛	+	0.03
High Inc Adv Tr	NYSE	a5.35	4⅛	−	22.90
High Inc Adv Tr II	NYSE	a5.83	4⅞	−	16.38
High Inc Adv Tr III	NYSE	a6.45	5¾	−	10.85
Hyperion Total Ret Inc	NYSE	a10.80	9⅝	−	10.88
INA Investment	NYSE	16.90	14⅝	−	13.46
Independence Square	OTC	15.89	14⅛	−	11.11
Intercapital Inc	NYSE	a17.33	20⅛	+	16.13
Lincoln National	NYSE	26.95	24⅛	−	10.48
MFS Spec Value	NYSE	12.38	11⅛	−	10.14
Montgomery Street	NYSE	17.55	15¾	−	10.26
Mutual Omaha Int	NYSE	a13.01	11⅝	−	10.65

New Amer High Inc	NYSE	c4.53	3⅛	−	31.02
Pacific Amer Inc	NYSE	b14.56	14¼	−	2.13
Prospect Street High	NYSE	4.36	3½	−	19.72
Prudential Interm	NYSE	8.54	7¾	−	9.25
Prudential Strat	NYSE	7.54	7⅜	−	2.19
RAC Income Fund	NYSE	11.12	10⅜	−	6.70
State Mutual Secur	NYSE	a10.14	9⅜	−	7.54
Transamerica Inc	NYSE	a22.05	22	−	0.23
USF&G Pacholder	AMEX	16.52	13⅝	−	17.52
USLife Income	NYSE	8.63	7⅝	−	11.65
VanKampen Merritt Int	NYSE	6.07	6	−	1.15
VanKampen Ltd Term	NYSE	7.68	7¼	−	5.60
Vestaur Secur	NYSE	13.63	13	−	4.62

Convertible Bond Funds

Lincoln Nat'l Conv	NYSE	13.85	12	−	13.36

International Bond Funds

F Australia Prime	AMEX	a10.27	9⅛	−	11.15
Global Government	NYSE	7.95	7	−	11.95
Global Yield Fund	NYSE	9.09	8¼	−	9.24
Klein Benson Aust	NYSE	10.53	8⅞	−	15.72

Municipal Bond Funds

Allstate Muni Inc Opp	NYSE	a9.38	10⅜	+	10.61
Allstate Muni Inc Opp II	NYSE	a9.29	9⅛	−	1.78
Allstate Muni Inc Opp III	NYSE	a9.29	9½	+	2.26
Allstate Muni Inc Tr	NYSE	a10.01	10⅛	+	1.15
Allstate Muni Inc II	NYSE	a9.69	9½	−	1.96
Allstate Muni Inc III	NYSE	a9.32	8⅝	−	7.46
Allstate Muni Prem Inc	NYSE	a9.22	8¾	−	5.10
Colonial High Income	NYSE	a9.07	9⅝	+	6.12
Colonial Inv Grade Muni	NYSE	10.82	11⅜	+	5.13
Colonial Muni Income	NYSE	a8.33	8½	+	2.04
Dreyfus Calif. Muni Inc	AMEX	9.30	9¾	+	4.84
Dreyfus Muni Income	AMEX	9.37	9½	+	1.39
Dreyfus NY Muni	AMEX	9.27	9⅛	−	1.56
Dreyfus Strat Muni Bd	NYSE	9.28	9¼	−	0.32
Dreyfus Strat Muni	NYSE	9.82	10¼	+	4.38
Kemper Muni Inc Tr	NYSE	10.99	11⅜	+	3.50
NY Tax-Exempt	AMEX	9.78	9½	−	2.86
Nuveen CA Income	NYSE	11.66	11⅝	−	0.30
Nuveen CA Mkt Opp	NYSE	13.64	14⅝	+	7.22
Nuveen CA Value	NYSE	9.96	10	+	0.40
Nuveen CA Perf Plus	NYSE	13.69	14¼	+	4.09
Nuveen Inv Qual Muni	NYSE	14.03	14⅛	+	0.68
Nuveen Muni Advant	NYSE	13.76	14¼	+	3.56
Nuveen Muni Inc	NYSE	11.49	11¾	+	2.26
Nuveen Muni Mkt Oppor	NYSE	13.93	14¼	+	2.30
Nuveen Muni Value	NYSE	9.94	10	+	0.60
Nuveen NY Income	AMEX	11.45	12	+	4.80
Nuveen NY Muni Mkt	NYSE	13.18	14¾	+	11.91
Nuveen NY Value	NYSE	9.95	10⅛	+	1.76
Nuveen NY Perf Plus	NYSE	13.51	14¾	+	9.18
Nuveen Perf Plus	NYSE	13.42	13⅞	+	3.39
Nuveen Premium Inc	NYSE	14.42	14¾	+	2.29
Seligman Select	NYSE	10.87	10½	−	3.40
VanKampen Merritt CA	AMEX	a8.89	9⅛	+	2.64
VanKampen Merritt Inv	NYSE	a10.85	10⅞	+	0.23
VanKampen Merritt Muni	NYSE	9.40	9¼	−	1.60

a-Ex-Dividend. b-Fully diluted c-As of Thursday. x-Not applicable. z-Not available.

Source: *Barron's*, September 24, 1990.

> **Open-end investment company** A more formal name for a mutual fund, which derives from the fact that it continuously offers new shares to investors and redeems them on demand.
>
> **Load fund** A mutual fund that imposes sales charges on share purchases to compensate salespeople.

tors to inquire about the returns available to investors from funds that sell at large discounts. This question arises because an investor who acquires a portfolio at a price below market value (i.e., below NAV) expects a dividend yield above the average. Still, the total rate of return on the fund depends upon what happens to the discount during the holding period. If the discount relative to the NAV declines, the investment should generate positive excess returns. If the discount increases, expect negative excess returns. The analysis of these discounts remains a major question of modern finance.[3]

Closed-End Fund Index The interest in closed-end funds has led a firm that specializes in these funds (Thomas J. Herzfeld Advisors) to create an index that tracks the market price performance of the following 18 closed-end funds, which invest principally in U.S. equities:

- The Adams Express Company
- Baker, Fentress and Company
- Blue Chip Value Fund, Inc.
- Central Securities Corp.
- Claremont Capital Corp.
- Cypress Fund Inc.
- Gabelli Equity Trust, Inc.
- General American Investors Co.
- Growth Stock Outlook Trust
- Lehman Corp.
- Liberty All-Star Equity Fund
- Morgan Grenfell Cap Fund
- Niagara Share Corp.
- Nicholas–Applegate Growth

- Royce Value Trust
- Source Capital Inc.
- Tri-Continental Corp.
- Zweig Fund Inc.

Of these 18 funds, 17 are listed on either the NYSE or the AMEX, while one trades on NASDAQ. The price-weighted index is based on fund market values rather than NAVs. In addition to its market price index, Herzfeld also computes the average discount from NAV. The graph in Figure 19.3, which is updated weekly in *Barron's*, indicates that the average discount from NAV changes over time, with major effects on the market performance of the index. As an example, during the third quarter of 1990 the average discount was relatively stable with a slight decline. As a result, the performance of the index closely tracked the DJIA during this period.

Open-End Investment Companies

Open-end investment companies are funds that continue to sell and repurchase shares after their initial public offerings. They stand ready to sell additional shares of the fund at the NAV, with or without sales charges, or to buy back (redeem) shares at the NAV, with or without redemption fees.

Open-end investment companies, or mutual funds, have enjoyed substantial growth since World War II, as shown by the figures in Table 19.2. Clearly, open-end funds account for a substantial portion of assets invested, and they provide a very important service for almost 37 million accounts.

Load versus No-Load Open-End Funds One distinction between open-end funds is whether they charge sales fees for share sales. The offering price for a share in a **load fund** equals the NAV of the share plus a sales charge, which is typically 7.5 to 8.0 percent of the NAV. A fund with an 8 percent sales charge (load) would give an individual investing $1,000 shares worth $920. Such funds generally charge no redemption fees, which means the shares can be redeemed at their NAV. These funds are typically quoted with a NAV and an offering price. The NAV price is the redemption price, while the offering price equals the NAV divided by 1.0 minus the load. As an example, if the NAV of a fund with an 8 percent load is $8.50 a share, the offering price would be $9.24 ($8.50/0.92). The 74-cent differential is really 8.7 percent of the NAV. The load percentage typically declines with the size of the order.

[3]Edward F. Cone, "Stocks on Sale," *Forbes*, July 11, 1988: 144–145. For a discussion of bond funds, see Malcolm Richards, Donald Fraser, and John Groth, "The Attractions of Closed-End Bond Funds," *Journal of Portfolio Management* 8, no. 2 (Winter 1982): 56–61. For a discussion of performance and opportunities in closed-end funds, see Thomas J. Herzfeld, "Battered Beauties?" *Barron's*, August 13, 1990; and Thomas J. Herzfeld, "Finding Value in Closed-End Funds," *Investment Adviser*, July 1990.

Figure 19.3   *Herzfeld Closed-End Fund Average*

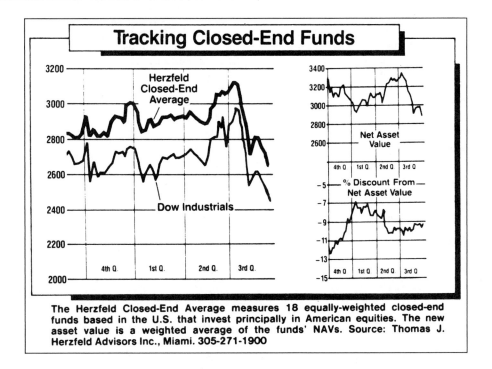

The Herzfeld Closed-End Average measures 18 equally-weighted closed-end funds based in the U.S. that invest principally in American equities. The new asset value is a weighted average of the funds' NAVs. Source: Thomas J. Herzfeld Advisors Inc., Miami. 305-271-1900

Source: *Barron's*, October 1, 1990.

A **no-load fund** imposes no initial sales charge so it sells shares at their NAV. Some of these funds charge small redemption fees, about one-half of 1 percent. In *The Wall Street Journal*, quotes for these no-load funds list bid prices as NAVs with the designation for "no-load" (NL) in the offering price column.

A number of no-load funds have been established in recent years. *The Wall Street Journal* lists more than 350 no-load funds, while *Barron's* lists more than 800. A directory of no-load funds is available from an industry association.[4]

Between the full-load fund and the pure no-load fund, you can find several important variations. The first, the low-load fund, charges a front-end load, the term for the sales charge on fund purchases, but it is typically in the 3 percent range rather than 7 to 8 percent. Generally, low-load funds are offered on bond funds or equity funds by management companies

> **No-load fund**   A mutual fund that sells its shares at net asset value without adding sales charges.

that also offer no-load funds. For example, almost all of the Fidelity Management funds were no-load prior to 1985, but several of their newer funds have carried low loads of 3 percent. Some funds that previously charged full loads have reduced their loads.

The second major innovation is the 12b–1 plan, named after the 1980 SEC rule that permits it. This plan permits funds to deduct as much as 1.25 percent of average net assets *per year* to cover distribution costs, such as advertising, commissions paid to brokers, and general marketing expenses. A large and growing number of no-load funds are adopting these terms, as are a few low-load funds. You can determine if a fund has a 12b–1 plan only by reading the prospectus or using an investment service that reports charges in substantial detail.

Finally, some funds have instituted contingent, deferred sales loads. They charge you sales fees when

[4]No-Load Mutual Fund Association, Inc., 11 Penn Plaza, New York, NY 10001. The cost of the directory is $5.

Table 19.2

	Number of Reporting Funds	Assets ($Billions)		Number of Reporting Funds	Assets ($Billions)
1945	73	$ 1.3	1968	240	$ 52.7
1946	74	1.3	1969	269	48.3
1947	80	1.4	1970	361	47.6
1948	87	1.5	1971	392	55.0
1949	91	2.0	1972	410	59.8
1950	98	2.5	1973	421	46.5
1951	103	3.1	1974	416	34.1
1952	110	3.9	1975	390	42.2
1953	110	4.1	1976	404	47.6
1954	115	6.1	1977	427	45.0
1955	125	7.8	1978	444	45.0
1956	135	9.0	1979	446	49.0
1957	143	8.7	1980	458	58.4
1958	151	13.2	1981	486	55.2
1959	155	15.8	1982	539	76.8
1960	161	17.0	1983	653	113.6
1961	170	22.8	1984	820	137.8
1962	169	21.3	1985	1,071	251.7
1963	165	25.2	1986	1,356	424.2
1964	160	29.1	1987	1,781	453.8
1965	170	35.2	1988	2,109	472.3
1966	182	34.8	1989	2,253	553.9
1967	204	44.7	1990	2,362	570.8

Note: Does not include money market and short-term bond funds.

Sources: *1975 Mutual Fund Fact Book*, *1981 Mutual Fund Fact Book*, and *1991 Mutual Fund Fact Book*, Investment Company Institute, Washington, D.C.

you sell shares in them if you have held them for less than some time period, perhaps 3 or 4 years.

Fund Management Fees

In addition to selling charges (loads or 12b–1 charges), all investment firms charge annual management fees to compensate their professional managers. Such a fee is typically a percentage of the average net assets of the fund, varying from about 0.25 to about 1.00 percent. Most of these management fees are on sliding scales that decline with the sizes of the funds. For example, a fund with assets under $1 billion might charge 1 percent, while one with assets over $1 billion might charge 0.50 percent.

These management fees are a major factor driving the creation of new funds. More assets under management generate more fees, but management costs do not increase at the same rate as the assets managed because there are substantial economies of scale in managing financial assets. Once you have established the research staff and management structure, the incremental costs do not rise in line with assets. The cost of managing $1 billion of assets is definitely not twice the cost of managing $500 million.

Types of Investment Companies Based on Portfolio Makeup

Common Stock Funds

Some funds invest almost solely in common stocks, while others invest in preferred stocks, bonds, etc. Within this category of common stock funds, you find wide differences in emphasis, including funds that focus on growth companies, companies in specific industries (e.g., Chemical Fund, Oceanography Fund), certain classes of industries (e.g., Technology Fund), or even geographic areas (such as the Northeast Fund). Different common stock funds suit almost any taste or investment objective. Therefore, you must decide whether you want a fund that invests only in common stock; then you must consider the type of common stock you desire.

Balanced Funds

Balanced funds diversify outside the stock market by combining common stock with fixed-income securities, including government bonds, corporate bonds, convertible bonds, or preferred stock. The ratio of stocks to fixed-income securities will vary by fund, as stated in each fund's prospectus.

Bond Funds

Bond funds concentrate on various types of bonds in order to generate high current income with minimal risk. As with common stock funds, their investment policies differ. Some funds concentrate on U.S. government or high-grade corporate bonds, others hold a mixture of investment-grade bonds, and some concentrate on high-yield (junk) bonds. Management strategies can also differ ranging from buy-and-hold to extensive trading.

In addition to government, mortgage, and corporate bond funds, a change in the tax law in 1976 caused the creation of numerous municipal bond funds. These funds provide investors with monthly interest payments that are exempt from federal income taxes, although some of the interest may be subject to state and local taxes. To avoid the state tax, some municipal

bond funds concentrate on bonds from specific states. The New York Municipal Bond Fund allows New York residents to avoid most state taxes on the interest income.

Money Market Funds

The first money market funds were initiated during 1973 when short-term interest rates were at record levels. These funds attempt to provide current income, safety of principal, and liquidity by investing in a diversified portfolio of short-term securities such as Treasury bills, bank certificates of deposit, bankers' acceptances, and commercial paper. They are typically no-load funds and impose no penalty for withdrawal at any time. They generally allow holders to write checks against their accounts.[5] Table 19.3 documents the significant growth of these funds. Changes in their growth rate are usually associated with investor attitudes toward the stock market. Investors who are bullish toward stocks withdraw funds from their money market accounts to invest; uncertainty leads them to shift from stocks to the money funds. Because of the interest in money market funds, Monday editions of *The Wall Street Journal* provide a special subsection within the mutual fund section titled "Money Market Funds."

Breakdown by Fund Characteristics

Table 19.4 groups funds in terms of marketing tactics and investment objectives. The two major means of distribution are (1) by sales force and (2) by direct purchase from the fund, or direct marketing. Sales forces would include brokers such as Merrill Lynch, commission-based financial planners, or dedicated sales forces such as those of IDS Financial. Almost all mutual funds acquired from these individuals charge sales fees (loads), from which the salespeople are compensated.

Investors purchase shares of directly marketed funds through the mail, telephone, bankwire, or of-

---

[5]For a list of names and addresses of money market funds, write to Investment Company Institute, 1775 K Street N.W., Washington, DC 20006. A publication that concentrates on money market funds is *Donoghue's Money Letter*, 770 Washington Street, Holliston, MA 01746. For an analysis of performance, see Michael G. Ferri and H. Dennis Oberhelman, "How Well Do Money Market Funds Perform?" *Journal of Portfolio Management* 7, no. 3 (Spring 1981): 18–26.

| Table 19.3 | Statistics on Money Market Funds | | | |

	Total Number of Funds	Total Accounts Outstanding	Average Maturity (Days)	Total Net Assets ($Millions)
1974	15	n.a.	n.a.	1,715.1
1975	36	208,777	93	3,695.7
1976	48	180,676	110	3,685.8
1977	50	177,522	76	3,887.7
1978	61	467,803	42	10,858.0
1979	76	2,307,852	34	45,214.2
1980	96	4,745,572	24	74,447.7
1981	159	10,282,095	34	181,910.4
1982	281	13,101,347	37	206,607.5
1983	307	12,276,639	37	162,549.5
1984	329	13,556,180	43	209,731.9
1985	348	14,425,386	42	207,535.3
1986	360	15,653,595	40	228,345.8
1987	389	16,832,666	31	254,676.4
1988	432	17,630,528	28	272,293.3
1989	463	20,173,265	38	358,719.2
1990	508	21,577,559	41	414,700.0

Source: *1991 Mutual Fund Fact Book*, Investment Company Institute, Washington, D.C.

fices of the funds. These direct sales funds typically impose low sales charges or none at all. Without any sales fees, they have to be sold directly because a broker has no incentive to sell a no-load fund. As seen in Table 19.4, the division between these two major distribution channels is currently about 68 to 28 percent in favor of the sales force method, although a shift has been occurring toward direct marketing.

The breakdown by investment objective indicates investment company response to a shift in investor emphasis. The growth of an investment objective category reflects the overall growth of an industry, but also creation of new funds to meet the evolving demands of investors. Therefore, while aggressive growth, growth, and growth and income funds have continued to proliferate, categories like international global equity, high-yield bonds (pre-1989), municipal bonds, and global bonds have also shown significant growth.[6] Also, while the sale of stock funds has increased, the number and total outstanding value of bond and income funds has exceeded those of equity funds.

Performance of Investment Companies

A number of studies have examined the historical performance of mutual funds because these funds reflect the performance of professional money managers, and data on them are available for a long period. Two of the three major portfolio evaluation techniques (which we will discuss in Chapter 23) were derived in connection with studies of mutual fund performance.

Analysis of Overall Performance

A study by Sharpe evaluated the performance of 34 open-end mutual funds.[7] For the total period, only 11 of the 34 funds outperformed the DJIA. Further, com-

[6]International funds invest only in non-U.S. stocks or bonds, while global funds invest in securities from anywhere in the world, including the United States.

[7]William F. Sharpe, "Mutual Fund Performance," *Journal of Business* 39, no. 1, part 2 (January 1966): 119–138.

Table 19.4   *Total Net Assets by Fund Characteristics ($Millions)*

	1986 Dollars	1986 Percentage	1987 Dollars	1987 Percentage	1988 Dollars	1988 Percentage	1989 Dollars	1989 Percentage
Total net assets	$414,156.4	100.0%	$453,842.4	100.0%	$472,296.6	100.0%	$553,870.9	100.0%
Method of Sale								
Sales force	304,637.3	71.8	331,752.8	73.1	336,184.0	71.2	376,016.9	67.9
Direct marketing	107,911.3	25.4	107,496.1	23.7	120,728.6	25.5	154,769.8	27.9
Variable annuity	9,274.3	2.2	12,730.1	2.8	13,592.8	2.9	20,975.8	3.8
Not offering shares	2,333.5	0.6	1,863.4	0.4	1,791.2	0.4	2,108.5	0.4
Investment Objective								
Aggressive growth	25,006.9	5.9	27,298.1	6.0	29,452.3	6.2	37,209.0	6.7
Growth	43,579.5	10.3	48,037.6	10.6	50,547.2	10.7	66,078.8	11.9
Growth and income	55,944.1	13.2	64,032.5	14.1	70,865.3	15.0	91,362.2	16.5
Precious metals	2,027.1	0.5	4,050.9	0.9	3,171.9	0.7	4,089.3	0.7
International	7,186.1	1.7	6,982.3	1.5	6,831.8	1.4	9,888.3	1.8
Global equity	8,282.0	2.0	10,449.2	2.3	11,151.1	2.4	13,697.0	2.5
Flexible portfolio	1,461.8	0.3	4,287.2	0.9	3,485.7	0.7	4,142.6	0.8
Balanced	7,483.0	1.8	9,024.7	2.0	9,492.9	2.0	13,519.0	2.4
Income equity	12,560.1	3.0	14,745.1	3.2	17,509.5	3.7	22,925.2	4.2
Income–mixed	10,323.7	2.4	11,418.4	2.5	8,768.7	1.9	15,190.8	2.8
Income–bond	11,417.9	2.7	12,580.0	2.8	10,693.3	2.3	13,465.1	2.4
Option/income	6,952.9	1.6	5,095.2	1.2	5,286.3	1.1	3,804.3	0.7
U.S. government income	82,444.2	19.4	88,906.2	19.6	82,688.1	17.5	81,400.7	14.7
Ginnie Mae	39,619.9	9.3	34,204.0	7.5	28,712.0	6.1	28,209.3	5.1
Global bond	523.2	0.1	2,137.1	0.5	3,024.3	0.6	3,063.2	0.6
Corporate bond	9,080.5	2.1	9,470.5	2.1	10,463.9	2.2	11,676.6	2.1
High-yield bond	24,591.6	5.8	24,147.2	5.3	33,425.2	7.1	28,492.4	5.1
Long-term municipal bond	49,857.2	11.8	49,174.6	10.8	54,316.3	11.5	64,450.6	11.6
Long-term state municipal bond	25,814.8	6.1	27,791.6	6.1	22,410.8	6.9	41,206.4	7.4

Sources: *1988 Mutual Fund Fact Book*, and *1990 Mutual Fund Fact Book*, Investment Company Institute, Washington, D.C.

paring the ranks of the funds between the first and second halves of the sample period led Sharpe to conclude that past performance was not the best predictor of future performance.

Good performance was associated, however, with low expense ratios. Finally, analysis of gross performance, with expenses added back to the returns, indicated that 19 of the 34 funds did better than the DJIA.

This led to the conclusion that the average mutual fund manager selected a portfolio at least as good as the DJIA, but after deducting operating costs of the fund, most achieved net returns below those of the DJIA.

Jensen evaluated 115 open-end mutual funds with results that indicated that, on average, the funds earned 1.1 percent less per year than they should have earned for their collective level of risk.[8] Analysis of gross returns with expenses added back indicated that 42 percent did better than the overall market on a risk-adjusted basis, while the analysis of net returns indicated that only 34 percent of the funds outperformed the market. The gross returns indicate the forecasting ability of the funds, since these results do not penalize them for operating expenses (only brokerage commissions). Jensen concluded that, on average, these funds could not beat a buy-and-hold policy.

A comment by Mains questioned several of Jensen's estimates, which apparently biased the results against mutual funds.[9] After adjusting for these biases, he contended that net returns indicated neutral performance, while gross returns indicated that most fund managers outperformed the market.

Carlson examined the overall performance of mutual funds with emphasis on the effects of the market series used for comparison and the time period.[10] The results depended heavily upon which market series was used: the S&P 500, the NYSE composite, or the DJIA. For the total period, most fund groups outperformed the DJIA, but only a few had gross returns better than the S&P 500 or the NYSE composite. Using net returns, *none* of the groups outperformed the S&P 500 or the NYSE composite. Analysis of the factors that determined performance indicated consistency over time for return or risk alone, but no consistency in risk-adjusted performance. Less than one-third of the funds that performed above average during the first half did so in the second half. A more recent study by Lehmann and Modest found substantial differences between benchmarks, but also concluded that average performance was consistently inferior to the overall market.[11]

Impact of Fund Objectives

An investor considering buying a fund needs to know whether its performance is consistent with its stated objective. For example, does the performance of a balanced fund reflect less risk and lower return than an aggressive growth fund? To answer this question, several studies have examined the relationship between funds' stated objectives and their measures of risk and return.

McDonald examined the overall performance of a sample of mutual funds relative to their stated objectives: (1) maximum capital gain, (2) growth, (3) income and growth, (4) balanced, and (5) income.[12] The results revealed a positive relationship between stated objectives and measures of risk, with risk measures increasing as objectives became more aggressive. The study also found a positive relationship between return and risk. Analysis of risk-adjusted performance indicated that the funds with the more aggressive objectives outperformed the more conservative funds during this period.

Martin, Keown, and Farrell examined mutual funds representing five investment objectives (aggressive growth, growth, growth and income, income, and other). They found definite differences in abnormal variability for the funds in alternative classifications.[13]

Market Timing Ability

As noted on several occasions, one way to achieve superior performance is to do a good job of market timing, investing aggressively prior to strong markets and restructuring for very conservative portfolios prior to weak or declining markets. Can mutual fund managers do this on your behalf? Several studies have examined the ability of mutual funds to time market cycles and react accordingly; that is, to increase the relative volatility of the portfolio in anticipation of a bull market and reduce its volatility prior to a bear market.

[8]Michael C. Jensen, "The Performance of Mutual Funds in the Period 1945–1964," *Journal of Finance* 23, no. 2 (May 1968): 389–416.

[9]Norman E. Mains, "Risk, the Pricing of Capital Assets, and the Evaluation of Investment Portfolios: Comment," *Journal of Business* 50, no. 3 (July 1977): 371–384.

[10]Robert S. Carlson, "Aggregate Performance of Mutual Funds, 1948–1967," *Journal of Financial and Quantitative Analysis* 5, no. 1 (March 1970): 1–32.

[11]Bruce N. Lehmann and David M. Modest, "Mutual Fund Performance Evaluations: A Comparison of Benchmarks and Benchmark Comparisons," *Journal of Finance* 42, no. 2 (June 1987): 233–265.

[12]John G. McDonald, "Objectives and Performance of Mutual Funds, 1960–1969," *Journal of Financial and Quantitative Analysis* 9, no. 3 (June 1974): 311–333.

[13]John D. Martin, Arthur J. Keown, Jr., and James L. Farrell, "Do Fund Objectives Affect Diversification Policies?" *Journal of Portfolio Management* 8, no. 2 (Winter 1982): 19–28.

Several studies indicated inability to time market changes and change risk levels accordingly.[14] Veit and Cheney, using four different schemes to define bull and bear markets, concluded that mutual funds do not successfully alter their risk characteristics consistently with timing strategies.[15]

Kon and Jen examined the ability of mutual funds to change portfolio composition to take advantage of market cycles and the ability to select undervalued securities.[16] Although many of the funds' risk levels changed significantly during the test period, implying superior timing ability, no individual fund was able to *consistently* generate superior results. Shawky found that risk was consistent with fund objectives, but overall results indicated that most funds performed poorly, although the funds appeared to have improved the diversification of their portfolios.[17]

Two recent studies examined the overall market forecasting and specific stock selection ability of fund managers. Chang and Lewellen tested for market timing ability and found little market forecasting going on, or, if any was being done, it was overwhelmed by other portfolio decisions.[18] They found evidence of neither skillful market timing nor clever security selection. The authors concurred with the conclusions of prior studies that mutual funds cannot outperform a passive investment strategy.

Henriksson considered a total period and two subperiods to test ability to enjoy consistent success.[19] The results showed little evidence of market-timing ability and the results for each fund for the two periods were independent. Also, it appears that managers could not forecast large changes, and those who were good at stock selection apparently had negative market-timing ability.

Consistency of Performance

Although several studies have considered consistency along with overall performance, some studies have concentrated on it. Klemkosky examined rankings of risk-adjusted performance for adjacent 2-year periods and for two 4-year periods.[20] The results indicated some consistency between the 4-year periods, but relatively low consistency between the adjacent 2-year periods. The author concluded that investors should not use past performance to predict future performance, especially for short periods of time.

Dunn and Theisen examined institutional portfolios over a 10-year period to determine what proportion of managers were consistently successful.[21] The first test, which examined whether managers tend to remain in the same quartile over time, concluded that historical results give little help in explaining future results. The authors felt that "markets make managers"—that is, if the market performed consistently over time, managers showed more consistent performance. The authors concluded that historical performance should carry very little weight when selecting a manager. Ang and Chua examined the consistency of performance of funds with different objectives and found that, while various funds met their stated objectives, they did not do it consistently.[22]

What Performance Studies Mean to You

What functions would you want your own personal portfolio manager to perform for you? The list would probably include:

[14]Jack L. Treynor and Kay K. Mazuy, "Can Mutual Funds Outguess the Market?" *Harvard Business Review* 44, no. 4 (July–August 1966): 131–136; and Frank J. Fabozzi and Jack C. Francis, "Mutual Fund Systematic Risk for Bull and Bear Markets," *Journal of Finance* 34, no. 5 (December 1979): 1243–1250.

[15]E. Theodore Veit and John M. Cheney, "Are Mutual Funds Market Timers?" *Journal of Portfolio Management* 8, no. 2 (Winter 1982): 35–42.

[16]Stanley J. Kon and Frank C. Jen, "The Investment Performance of Mutual Funds: An Empirical Investigation of Timing, Selectivity, and Market Efficiency," *Journal of Business* 52, no. 2 (April 1979): 263–289.

[17]Hany A. Shawky, "An Update on Mutual Funds: Better Grades," *Journal of Portfolio Management* 8, no. 2 (Winter 1982): 29–34.

[18]Eric C. Chang and Wilbur G. Lewellen, "Market Timing and Mutual Fund Investment Performance," *Journal of Business* 57, no. 1, part 1 (January 1984): 57–72.

[19]Roy D. Henriksson, "Market Timing and Mutual Fund Performance: An Empirical Investigation," *Journal of Business* 57, no. 1, part 1 (January 1984): 73–96.

[20]Robert C. Klemkosky, "How Consistently Do Managers Manage?" *Journal of Portfolio Management* 3, no. 2 (Winter 1977): 11–15.

[21]Patricia C. Dunn and Rolf D. Theisen, "How Consistently Do Active Managers Win?" *Journal of Portfolio Management* 9, no. 4 (Summer 1983): 47–50.

[22]James S. Ang and Jess H. Chua, "Mutual Funds: Different Strokes for Different Folks?" *Journal of Portfolio Management* 8, no. 2 (Winter 1982): 43–47.

> **Market index fund** An investment company that attempts to match the composition, and performance, of a chosen market indicator series.

1. Determine your risk–return preferences and develop a portfolio that is consistent with them
2. Diversify your portfolio to eliminate unsystematic risk
3. Maintain your portfolio diversification and risk class while allowing flexibility so you could shift between investment instruments as desired
4. Turn in risk-adjusted performance that is superior to aggregate market performance. As noted, this can be done either by consistently selecting undervalued stocks or by properly timing market swings. Some investors may be willing to sacrifice diversification for superior returns in limited segments of their portfolios.
5. Administer the account, keep records of costs, provide timely information for tax purposes, and reinvest dividends if desired

While most of the performance studies reviewed only risk-adjusted performance, all of these functions should be considered in order to put performance into perspective. Therefore, let us consider each of these functions and discuss how mutual funds fulfill them.

Mutual funds do not determine your risk preference. Once you determine your risk–return preferences, you can choose a mutual fund from a large and growing variety of alternative funds designed to meet almost any investment goal. Recall that the empirical studies indicated that the funds generally consistently met their stated goals for investment strategies, risks, and returns.

Diversifying your portfolio to eliminate unsystematic risk is one of the major benefits of mutual funds. They provide instant diversification. This is especially beneficial to small investors who do not have the resources to acquire 100 shares of 10 or 12 different issues to reduce unsystematic risk. By initiating an investment in a fund with about $1,000, you can participate in a portfolio of securities that is correlated about 0.90 with the market portfolio, which means that it is about 90 percent diversified. Although diversification varies among funds, typically about three-quarters of the funds correlate with the market at rates above 0.90. Therefore, most funds provide excellent

diversification, especially if they state this as an objective.

The third function of your portfolio manager is to maintain diversification and desired risk class. It is not too surprising that mutual funds have generally maintained the stability of their correlations with the market since few change the makeup of reasonably well-diversified portfolios substantially. Strong evidence regarding the consistency of the risk class for individual funds indicated consistency in risk alone, even for studies that indicated inconsistency in risk-adjusted performance.

Mutual funds meet the desire for flexibility to change investment instruments because there are usually numerous funds within a single management company. Typically, investment groups such as T. Rowe Price or Fidelity Investments allow you to shift among their funds without a charge simply by calling the fund. Therefore, you can shift among an aggressive stock fund, a money market fund, and a bond fund for much less than it would cost you in time and money to buy and sell numerous individual issues.

The fourth function is to provide risk-adjusted performance that is superior to the aggregate market, which implies that it is superior to a naive buy-and-hold policy. You will probably not be surprised that the funds do not fulfill this function very well. The evidence indicates that, on average, fund managers' results in selecting undervalued securities or timing the market are about as good as, or only slightly better than, the results of a naive buy-and-hold policy. This conclusion is based upon gross returns. Unfortunately, the evidence from net returns, which are what you as an investor would receive, indicates that most funds do not do as well as a naive buy-and-hold policy. The shortfall in performance of about 1 percent a year roughly matches the average cost of research and trading commissions.

In response to these findings, several investment management firms have started index funds, apparently following the homily "if you can't beat them, join them." These **market index funds** do not attempt to beat the market, but merely to match the composition, and therefore the performance, of some specified market indicator series such as the S&P 500 Index. Since they have no research costs and minimal trading expenses, their returns have typically correlated with the chosen indexes at rates in excess of 0.99 with very low expenses. Also, their management fees are substantially below those charged by active managers.[23]

While institutions have used index funds for many years, such funds have not generally been available for individual investors. This changed during 1989 when several major investment company sponsors, such as Fidelity Management, initiated such funds. Currently six or seven are available.

If you want to find a superior fund, the news is not very good. The only funds to perform consistently over time are the inferior funds. Apparently, if a fund performs poorly because of excessive expenses, it will probably continue to do so. Such funds should be avoided. The overall point is that you should not expect to enjoy consistently superior risk-adjusted performance from an investment in a mutual fund.

The final function of a portfolio manager is account administration. This is another significant benefit of most mutual funds, since they allow automatic reinvestment of dividends with no charge and consistently provide records of total costs. Further, each year they supply statements of dividend income and capital gain distribution that can be used to prepare tax returns.

In summary, as an investor, you probably want your portfolio manager to perform a set of functions. Typically, mutual funds can help you accomplish four of the five functions at a lower cost in terms of time and money than doing the work on your own. Unfortunately, this convenience and service costs about 1 percent a year in terms of performance.

Sources of Information

Because so many funds of such widely varying types are available, you should examine the performance of various funds over time to derive some understanding of their goals and management philosophies. Daily quotations for numerous open-end funds appear in *The Wall Street Journal*. A more comprehensive weekly list of quotations with figures for dividend income and capital gain for the previous 12 months are carried in *Barron's*. In addition, *Barron's* publishes quarterly updates on the performance of a number of funds over the previous 10 years. As shown earlier in Figures 19.1 and 19.2, *Barron's* lists closed-end funds with their current net asset values, current market quotes, and the percentage difference between the two figures. As mentioned, market prices typically run about 5 to 15 percent below NAVs, but this discount varies between funds and over time.

The major source of comprehensive historical information is an annual publication issued by Arthur Wiesenberger Services entitled *Investment Companies*. This book gives statistics for over 600 mutual funds arranged alphabetically. It describes each major fund including a brief history, investment objectives and portfolio analysis, statistical history, special services available, personnel, advisors and distributors, sales charges, and a chart of the value of a hypothetical $10,000 investment over 10 years. Figure 19.4 shows a sample page for the Nicholas II fund. The Wiesenberger book also contains a summary list with annual rates of return and price volatility measures for a number of additional funds.

Wiesenberger has two other services. Every 3 months the firm publishes *Management Results*, which updates the long-term performance of more than 400 mutual funds, arranged alphabetically and grouped by investment objective. The firm's monthly publication *Current Performance and Dividend Record* reports the dividend and short-run performance of more than 400 funds, listed alphabetically with objectives indicated.[24]

Another source of historical, analytical information on funds is *Forbes*. This biweekly financial publication typically discusses individual companies and their investment potential. In addition, the magazine's August issue includes an annual survey of mutual funds. A sample page in Figure 19.5 demonstrates how the survey reports on recent and 10-year returns. The survey also provides information regarding each fund's sales charge and annual expense ratio.

Business Week publishes "Mutual Fund Scoreboards." Figure 19.6 shows a sample of such a scoreboard for open-end, fixed-income funds. The

---

[23]For a discussion of the reasoning behind these index funds (both economic and legal) and their early development, see A. F. Ehrbar, "Index Funds—An Idea Whose Time Is Coming," *Fortune*, June 1976: 146–148.

[24]These reports are currently published by Wiesenberger Investment Companies Services, Warren, Gorham and Lamont, 210 South St., Boston, MA 02111.

Figure 19.4 **Sample Page from** Investment Companies

NICHOLAS II, INC.

Nicholas II is a diversified open-end management investment company pursuing long-term growth of capital through a portfolio of common stocks with growth potentia!. Securities are not purchased with a view to rapid turnover or to obtain short-term trading profits. The fund is one of five managed by Nicholas Company, Inc.

At the close of 1989, the fund was 85.7% invested in common stocks, of which the major portion was in five industry groups: industrial products & services (11.9% of net assets); consumer products (10.1%); insurance (9.3%), and banks and health care (each 9.0%). The five largest individual common stock holdings were Chambers Development (4.3% of net assets), International Dairy Queen (3.0%), Block Drug and Marshall & Ilsley (each 2.5%), and Hamilton Oil (2.2%). The rate of portfolio turnover during the latest fiscal year was 8.2% of average assets. Unrealized appreciation in the portfolio at calendar year-end amounted to 25.3% of net assets.

Special Services: An open account provides for accumulation and dividend reinvestment. The fund offers a prototype Individual Retirement Account (IRA) plan and has available a master Keogh or self-employed IRA plan.

Statistical History

						% of Assets in							
Year	Total Net Assets ($)	Number of Share-holders	Net Asset Value Per Share ($)	Yield (%)	Cash & Gov't	Bonds & Pre-ferreds	Com-mon Stocks	Income Div-idends ($)	Capital Gains Distribu-tion ($)	Expense Ratio (%)	Offering Price ($) High	Low
1989	404,423,252	35,116	20.16	1.5	14	—	86	0.312	0.669*	0.74	21.99	17.95
1988	361,084,568	35,467	17.98	1.9	7	—	93	0.335	0.08	0.77	18.72	15.63
1987	339,942,160	38,211	15.69	2.0	17	1	82	0.245	1.303*	0.74	21.52	14.19
1986	293,041,669	31,334	16.22	2.5	3	2	95	0.42	0.513	0.79	18.62	15.59
1985	232,693,089	25,898	15.54	1.0	39	—	61	0.163	0.061	1.11	15.73	11.69
1984	16,373,024	1,600	11.79	0.8	26	—	74	0.093	0.186	1.85	11.79	9.71
1983	2,612,530	200	10.33	NM	41	—	59	—	—	—	10.33	9.95

Note: Initially offered 10/17/83 at $10.00 per share.
* Includes short-term gains of $0.186 in 1984; $0.028 in 1985; $0.005 in 1987; $0.005 in 1989.
NM. Not meaningful; not a full year.

Directors: Albert O. Nicholas, Pres.; Melvin L. Schultz; Richard Seaman; Robert H. Bock.

Investment Adviser: Nicholas Company, Inc. Compensation to the Adviser is at an annual rate of .75 of 1% of the first $50 million of average net asset value, .6 of 1% of the next $50 million and .5 of 1% on assets in excess of $100 million.

Custodian & Transfer Agent: First Wisconsin Trust Company, Milwaukee. WI.

Distributor: Nicholas Company, Inc., 700 N. Water St., Milwaukee, WI 53202.

Sales Charge: None; shares are offered at net asset value. Minimum initial purchase is $1,000 with $100 the subsequent minimum.
Distribution Plan (12b-1): None.
Dividends: Investment income and net realized capital gains, if any, are distributed in December.
Shareholder Reports: Issued quarterly. Fiscal year ends September 30. The current prospectus was effective in January.
Qualified for Sale: In all states.
Address: 700 N. Water St., Milwaukee, WI 53202.
Telephone: (414) 272-6133.

An assumed investment of $10,000 in this fund, with capital gains accepted in shares and income dividends reinvested, is illustrated below. The explanation in the introduction to this section must be read in conjunction with this illustration.

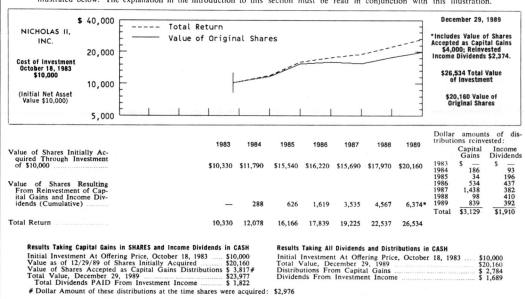

	1983	1984	1985	1986	1987	1988	1989
Value of Shares Initially Acquired Through Investment of $10,000	$10,330	$11,790	$15,540	$16,220	$15,690	$17,970	$20,160
Value of Shares Resulting From Reinvestment of Capital Gains and Income Dividends (Cumulative)	—	288	626	1,619	3,535	4,567	6,374*
Total Return	10,330	12,078	16,166	17,839	19,225	22,537	26,534

Dollar amounts of distributions reinvested:

	Capital Gains	Income Dividends
1983	$	$
1984	186	93
1985	34	196
1986	534	437
1987	1,438	382
1988	98	410
1989	839	392
Total	$3,129	$1,910

Results Taking Capital Gains in SHARES and Income Dividends in CASH
Initial Investment At Offering Price, October 18, 1983 ...... $10,000
Value as of 12/29/89 of Shares Initially Acquired $20,160
Value of Shares Accepted as Capital Gains Distributions $ 3,817#
Total Value, December 29, 1989 .... $23,977
    Total Dividends PAID From Investment Income .... $ 1,822
    # Dollar Amount of these distributions at the time shares were acquired: $2,976

Results Taking All Dividends and Distributions in CASH
Initial Investment At Offering Price, October 18, 1983 ...... $10,000
Total Value, December 29, 1989 .... $20,160
Distributions From Capital Gains .... $ 2,784
Dividends From Investment Income .... $ 1,689

Figure 19.5 **Sample Fund Quote Page from Forbes**

Annual Fund Ratings

Stock funds

FORBES rates stock funds over the three market cycles shown in the chart below. To be rated, a fund must have been in existence for at least two of the market cycles, that is, since June 30, 1983. Foreign stock funds, a category that includes most gold funds, are rated separately against a different benchmark (see page 212). Performance and other data are as of June 30, 1990. For more information about a fund, call or write the distributor listed after the fund name, using the table of distributors that begins on page 248. Closed-end funds have no distributor; they can be bought and sold in the secondary market through a broker, like shares of industrial companies. The average annual total return is compounded; it and other performance numbers are calculated after deducting expenses but before sales load.

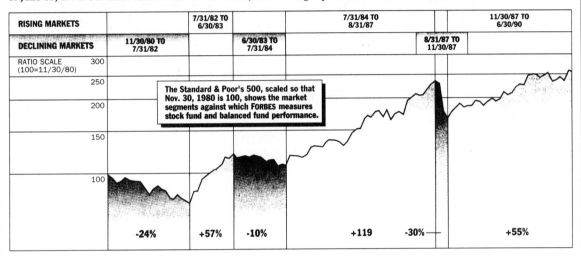

Performance			Fund/distributor	Total return			Assets		Maximum sales charge	Annual expenses per $100
in UP	in DOWN			Annual average 11/80 to 6/90	Last 12 months	Yield	6/30/90 ($mil)	% change '90 vs '89		
---markets---										
			Standard & Poor's 500 stock average	14.9%	16.4%	3.2%				
			Forbes stock fund composite	12.1%	12.3%	2.7%				$1.44
			AAL Capital Growth Fund/AAL Mutual	—*	16.8%	2.1%	$143	155%	4.75%	*$1.40p*
			AARP Growth–Capital Growth/Scudder	—*	1.3	0.6	219	50	none	1.11
			AARP Growth–Growth & Income/Scudder	—*	7.0	4.3	269	23	none	1.08
C	D		**ABT Growth & Income Trust/ABT**	10.0%	5.3	4.4	96	–7	4.75	*1.23*
●A	●D		**ABT Invest–Emerging Growth/ABT**	—*	16.5	none	20	–4	4.75	*1.78*
●D	●A		**ABT Invest–Security Income/ABT**	—*	–4.2	5.9	5	–32	4.75	*2.32*
D	A		**ABT Utility Income Fund/ABT**	11.5	11.6	6.2	144	24	4.75	*1.21*
B	C		**Acorn Fund/Acorn**	14.5	12.3	1.3	953	29	none§	0.73
			Adam Investors/Siebel	—*	17.5	5.1	4	43	none	1.71
D	B		**Adams Express/closed-end**	12.5	16.5	3.9	567	11	NA	0.51
			Advance Amer–Equity Inc/Oppenheimer	—*	2.5	2.5	11	15	4.75	*2.29p*
			Advantage Growth Fund/Advest	—*	13.4	1.2	30	8	4.00b	*2.33*

●Fund rated for two periods only; maximum allowable grade A.   *Fund not in operation for full period.   §Distributor may impose redemption fee whose proceeds revert to the fund.   *Expense ratio is in italics if the fund has a shareholder-paid 12b-1 plan exceeding 0.1% (hidden load) pending or in force.*   b: Includes back-end load that reverts to distributor.   p: Net of partial absorption of expenses by fund sponsor.   NA: Not applicable or not available.

(continued)

Figure 19.5   *(continued)*

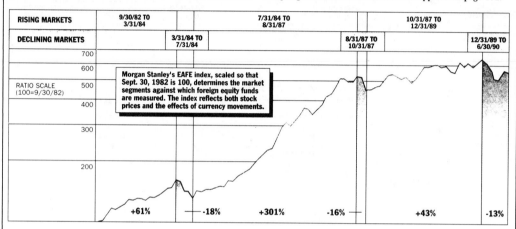

Annual Fund Ratings

Foreign stock funds

U.S.-based stock funds with predominantly foreign portfolios are in this table. The benchmark for measuring foreign fund performance is the Morgan Stanley stock index for Europe, Australia, the Far East and New Zealand. The index aims to show the dollar return that a U.S. investor would have enjoyed in the average foreign stock. Thus, it reflects not only price movements on foreign bourses but also fluctuations in the value of the dollar. The standout performer on this table: the Mexico Fund, the only one in our survey to rate a double-A+. Mexican stocks were severely depressed in 1982, at the beginning of our foreign fund measurement period. Funds based overseas, whether they invest in local makets or in the U.S., are not covered in the main fund tables, although a sampling of British investment trusts appears on page 152.

RISING MARKETS	9/30/82 TO 3/31/84		7/31/84 TO 8/31/87		10/31/87 TO 12/31/89	
DECLINING MARKETS		3/31/84 TO 7/31/84		8/31/87 TO 10/31/87		12/31/89 TO 6/30/90

Morgan Stanley's EAFE index, scaled so that Sept. 30, 1982 is 100, determines the market segments against which foreign equity funds are measured. The index reflects both stock prices and the effects of currency movements.

RATIO SCALE (100=9/30/82)

+61%   -18%   +301%   -16%   +43%   -13%

Performance in UP —markets—	in DOWN	Fund/distributor	Total return Annual average 9/82 to 6/90	Last 12 months	Yield	Assets 6/30/90 ($mil)	% change '90 vs '89	Maximum sales charge	Annual expenses per $100
		Morgan Stanley Capital Intl EAFE index	27.0%	3.3%	1.4%				
		Forbes foreign stock fund composite	17.6%	18.0%	1.4%				$1.94
C	C	Alliance Global–Canadian Fund/Alliance	13.4%	–6.1%	none	$26	–17%	5.50%	*$2.33*
A	C	Alliance International Fund/Alliance	24.5	15.3	0.2%	266	60	5.50	*1.45*
		AMA Family of Funds–Global Growth/AMA	—*	14.2	4.1	109	5	none	*1.69*
D	D	ASA Limited/closed-end	8.0	10.2	6.1	552	4	NA	0.51
		Asia Pacific Fund/closed-end	—*	45.4	0.2	143	40	NA	1.72
		Babson-Stewart Ivory Intl/Jones & Babson	—*	23.4	0.3	11	184	none	2.68
		Boston Co Inv–International/Boston Co	—*	14.6	1.4	35	70	none	*1.77*
		Brazil Fund/closed-end	—*	–29.5	19.2	120	–40	NA	2.01
D	D	Bull & Bear Gold Investors/Bull & Bear	4.3	1.5	1.0	39	3	none	*2.49p*
		Capstone Intl–European Plus/Capstone	—*	22.6	0.3	15	NM	4.75	4.75p
		Clemente Global Growth Fund/closed-end	—*	28.8	none	73	27	NA	3.05
		Colonial Intl Equity Index/Colonial	—*	15.6	none	15	32	4.75	*2.86*
		Counsellors International Equity/Counsellors	—*	28.4	0.8	34	329	none	1.48p

*Fund not in operation for full period.   *Expense ratio is in italics if the fund has a shareholder-paid 12b-1 plan exceeding 0.1% (hidden load) pending or in force.   p: Net of partial absorption of expenses by fund sponsor.   NA: Not applicable or not available.   NM: Not meaningful.

Source: "Annual Fund Ratings—Stock funds/Foreign stock funds," *Forbes*, September 3, 1990, pp. 177, 212. Reprinted by permission of Forbes magazine. © Forbes Inc., 1990.

Figure 19.6   *Mutual Fund Scoreboard*

MUTUAL FUND

FUND	RATING	SIZE ASSETS $ MIL.	% CHG. 1989-90	FEES SALES CHARGE (%)	EXPENSE RATIO (%)	OBJECTIVE	CURRENT RESULTS 1990 TOTAL RET. (%)	YIELD	RANK WITHIN OBJECTIVE
AAL CAPITAL GROWTH		169.6	90	4.75	1.44†	Growth	0.8	2.4	28/198
AARP CAPITAL GROWTH	⇩	173.9	−8	No load	1.11	Growth	−15.8	2.3	186/198
AARP GROWTH & INCOME	AVG	265.2	11	No load	1.03	Growth/income	−2.0	5.2	34/100
ABT GROWTH & INCOME	⇩	81.4	−19	4.75	1.27†	Growth/income	−8.8	4.6	83/100
ABT UTILITY INCOME	AVG	138.8	−3	4.75	1.25†	Utilities	−6.2	5.7	11/16
ACORN (a) 👤	AVG	769.5	−10	2.00‡*	0.77	Small company	−17.5	1.9	38/45
ADVANTAGE INCOME		44.8	−23	4.00**	2.04†	Income	0.8	6.4	5/9
AEGON USA GROWTH (b)	AVG	34.0	−7	4.75	0.99†	Growth	−5.5	4.7	111/198
AFA NATIONAL AVIATION & TECH. (c) 👤	⇩⇩	62.9	−25	4.75	1.28	Technology	−19.3	1.1	11/11
AFFILIATED 👤	AVG	3210.5	−13	6.75	0.50†	Growth/income	−5.3	4.5	67/100
AIM CHARTER 👤	⬆⬆	122.9	59	5.50	1.35†	Growth/income	8.2	2.2	1/100
AIM CONSTELLATION 👤	⇩	108.6	30	5.50	1.40†	Maximum growth	−4.1	0.0	12/33
AIM SUMMIT	⇩	316.1	20	8.50	0.82	Growth	0.9	2.0	25/198
AIM WEINGARTEN 👤	⬆⬆	803.1	84	5.50	1.30†	Growth	5.6	0.7	4/198
ALLIANCE	⇩	620.4	−26	5.50	0.88†	Growth	−4.4	2.7	95/198
ALLIANCE BALANCED SHARES 👤	AVG	146.9	−7	5.50	1.39†	Balanced	−2.2	3.6	27/40
ALLIANCE COUNTERPOINT	⬆	53.3	−11	5.50	2.00†	Growth	−4.6	1.4	101/198
ALLIANCE GLOBAL SMALL CAP. A (d)	⇩⇩⇩	69.6	−31	5.50	2.16†	International	−24.9	0.0	65/67
ALLIANCE GROWTH & INCOME 👤	AVG	330.5	−9	5.50	1.09†	Growth/income	−1.7	3.9	29/100
ALLIANCE INTERNATIONAL A	AVG	213.8	−4	5.50	1.53†	International	−21.0	0.2	62/67
ALLIANCE QUASAR A 👤	⇩⇩⇩	262.6	−9	5.50	1.66†	Maximum growth	−23.4	0.4	29/33
ALLIANCE TECHNOLOGY 👤	⇩⇩⇩	131.8	−7	5.50	1.77†	Technology	−3.1	0.0	5/11
ALTURA GROWTH		54.4	46	No load	0.40	Growth	−3.1	3.8	75/198
AMA GLOBAL GROWTH		91.1	−14	No load	1.74†	International	−10.1	3.0	29/67
AMCAP 👤	AVG	1897.3	−7	5.75	0.76†	Growth	−4.0	2.3	89/198
AMERICAN BALANCED 👤	⬆	370.4	35	5.75	0.84†	Balanced	−1.6	5.9	24/40
AMERICAN CAPITAL COMSTOCK	AVG	812.9	−15	8.50	0.79	Growth	−3.4	3.3	80/198
AMERICAN CAPITAL EMER. GROWTH (e)	⇩⇩	212.6	8	5.75	1.15†	Small company	2.0	0.5	3/45
AMERICAN CAPITAL ENTERPRISE	⇩	542.6	−10	5.75	0.94†	Growth	−2.9	2.1	70/198
AMERICAN CAPITAL EQUITY-INCOME (f) 👤	AVG	85.3	−17	5.75	0.89†	Equity-income	−4.7	5.8	13/30

* Includes redemption fee. ** Includes deferred sales charge. † 12(b)-1 plan in effect. ‡ Not currently accepting new accounts or deposits. NA = Not available. NM = Not meaningful. (a) Redemption fee applies within 60 days of purchase. (b) Formerly MidAmerica Mutual Fund. (c) Formerly National Aviation & Technology. (d) Formerly Surveyor Fund. (e) Formerly American Capital Venture Fund. (f) Formerly Provident Fund For Income.

HOW TO USE THE TABLES

BUSINESS WEEK RATING

Ratings are based on five-year risk-adjusted performance, relative to the S&P 500. Performance is calculated by subtracting a fund's risk-of-loss factor (see RISK) from historic total return. To get a positive rating, a fund must beat the S&P 500 on a risk-adjusted basis.

⬆⬆⬆   Superior performance

⬆⬆   Very good performance

⬆   Above-average performance

AVG   Average performance

⇩   Below-average performance

⇩⇩   Poor performance

⇩⇩⇩   Very poor performance

MANAGEMENT CHANGES

Symbols after some fund names are a useful aid in assessing performance.
👤 indicates that the fund's current manager has held that job for 10 years.
👤 indicates that fund management has changed since Dec. 31, 1989.

S&P 500 COMPARISON

Here are total return figures for the S&P 500 for the four time periods that appear in the tables:

1990	3.1%
Three-year average (1988-90)	14.1%
Five-year average (1986-90)	13.2%
Ten-year average (1981-90)	13.8%

SALES CHARGE

The cost of buying a fund, commonly called the "load." Most funds take loads out of initial investments, and for rating purposes, performance is reduced by the amount of these charges. When loads are levied on withdrawals, they can take two forms. Deferred charges decrease over time, usually ending after shares have been owned five years. Redemption fees arise when investors sell shares.

EXPENSE RATIO

Expenses for 1990 as a percentage of average net assets. This ratio measures how much shareholders pay for fund management. Footnotes indicate that a fund has a 12(b)-1 plan. These allocate shareholder money for distribution costs.

OBJECTIVE

Many funds specialize in one sector, which is indicated in this column. Otherwise, funds are grouped into the following categories. *Asset allocation:* Seeks returns by moving money among stocks, bonds and cash; some also use gold, real

(continued)

Figure 19.6 (continued)

SCOREBOARD

EQUITY FUNDS

HISTORIC RESULTS AVG. ANN'L TOTAL RET. (%) 3 YEARS	5 YEARS	10 YEARS	TREND BW 10-YEAR ANALYSIS	PORTFOLIO DATA TURNOVER	% CASH	P/E RATIO	LARGEST HOLDING COMPANY	% ASSETS	RISK	TELEPHONE TOLL FREE (800)	IN-STATE
13.7				Very low	5	15.7	American Home Prod.	4		553-6319	WI 414 734-7633
12.7	10.7			Average	10	19.1	Tele-Communications	3	High	253-2277	MA 617 330-5400
11.2	10.7			Average	15	14.5	United Illumination	3	Low	253-2277	MA 617 330-5400
7.9	9.0	9.0		Average	15	10.5	IBM	2	Average	289-2281	FL 407 655-7255
13.3	10.6	10.9		Low	1	13.5	Houston Industries	6	Low	289-2281	FL 407 655-7255
8.7	9.4	11.4		Low	15	15.0	Harley-Davidson	2	Average	922-6769	IL 312 621-0630
10.4				Average	3	14.2	Texaco	3		243-8115	MA 617 742-9858
6.6	7.7	10.9		Average	25	17.7	Abbott Laboratories	4	Low	288-2346	IA 319 363-5400
12.1	7.3	7.9		Very low	20	13.3	UAL	18	High	654-0001	NY 212 482-8100
9.7	10.8	13.3		Low	6	12.6	IBM	1	Average	874-3733	NY 212 848-1800
15.9	15.0	12.8		Very high	23	21.3	Philip Morris	4	Low	347-1919	TX 713 626-1919
15.5	15.3	10.1		Very high	1	22.8	St. Jude Medical	3	Very high	347-1919	TX 713 626-1919
15.8	11.1			High	0	17.9	Johnson & Johnson	3	Average	347-1919	TX 713 626-1919
16.9	17.0	15.2		Average	4	19.6	Philip Morris	4	High	347-1919	TX 713 626-1919
11.4	10.2	9.9		Average	12	17.4	Philip Morris	4	High	227-4618	NJ 201 319-4000
9.1	9.2	13.7		Very low	26	16.8	Philip Morris	5	Average	227-4618	NJ 201 319-4000
15.3	12.8			Very low	1	17.9	Philip Morris	4	Low	227-4618	NJ 201 319-4000
6.4	5.6	6.4		Average	5	16.3	Nac Re	2	Very high	227-4618	NJ 201 319-4000
13.0	12.1	14.3		Average	8	16.9	Philip Morris	5	Average	227-4618	NJ 201 319-4000
10.8	12.8			Average	2	NA	Holland Amer. Line Tr.	3	Average	227-4618	NJ 201 319-4000
8.4	6.0	10.9		High	8	17.0	Nac Re	2	Very high	227-4618	NJ 201 319-4000
1.1	6.7			High	19	15.1	Intel	5	Very high	227-4618	NJ 201 319-4000
12.3				Very low	9	15.7	Johnson & Johnson	2		255-9961	OH 800 255-9961
8.7				Low	2	14.4	Pfizer	3		262-3863	PA 215 825-0400
10.0	11.3	13.0		Low	7	16.7	Merck	4	Average	421-0180	CA 213 486-9200
10.5	10.4	13.8		Low	14	13.1	IBM	2	Very low	421-0180	CA 415 421-9360
13.1	10.3	13.8		Low	8	15.5	Philip Morris	3	Average	421-5666	TX 713 993-0500
10.9	8.2	11.8		Average	8	23.1	St. Jude Medical	4	High	421-5666	TX 713 993-0500
12.6	9.7	9.2		High	11	17.4	Wal-Mart Stores	2	High	421-5666	TX 713 993-0500
9.3	8.3	13.2		High	13	15.1	IBM	3	Low	421-5666	TX 713 993-0500

DATA: MORNINGSTAR INC.

estate and foreign stocks. *Balanced:* Attempts to maximize return by buying both stocks and bonds. *Equity-income:* Aims to achieve maximum income by buying high-yield stocks. *Growth:* Seeks long-term growth, with income secondary. *Growth/income:* Tries to combine capital appreciation and current income. *Income:* Tries to maximize current income and may sometimes buy fixed-income securities. *Maximum growth:* Takes larger risks; may borrow money, sell short, and buy options. *Option:* Uses options to augment income.

TOTAL RETURN
A fund's net gain to investors, including reinvestment of dividends and capital gains at month-end prices.

TREND
A fund's relative performance during the four 30-month periods from Jan. 1, 1981, to Dec. 31, 1990. Boxes read from left to right, and the level of red indicates performance relative to all other funds during the period: ■ for the top quartile; ▤ for the second quartile; ▦ for the third quartile; and ☐ for the bottom quartile. An empty box indicates no rating for that time period.

TURNOVER
Trading activity, the lesser of purchases or sales divided by average monthly assets. High turnover can raise expenses.

% CASH
The portion of a fund's assets not currently invested in stocks or bonds. A negative figure can occur as a result of a pending capital gains distribution.

PRICE/EARNINGS RATIO
The average, weighted price/earnings ratio of stocks in a fund's portfolio, based on trailing 12-month earnings.

RISK
The potential for losing money in a fund, or risk-of-loss factor. To derive each fund's level of risk, the monthly Treasury bill return is subtracted from the monthly total return for each fund for each of the 60 months in the rating period. When a fund has not performed as well as Treasury bills, this monthly result is negative. The sum of these negative numbers is then divided by the number of months. The result is a negative number, and the greater its magnitude, the higher a shareholder's risk of loss. This number is the basis for BW ratings and the RISK column. The designations in this column are assigned according to a normal statistical distribution.

Source: Mutual Fund Scoreboard, pp. 80–81. Reprinted from February 18, 1991 issue of *Business Week* by special permission, copyright © 1991 by McGraw-Hill, Inc.

Figure 19.7 *United Mutual Fund Selector: Investment Company Performance Comparisons*

UNITED Mutual Fund Selector Performance Comparisons

No-Load Funds   **May 15, 1990**

	Fund Type§	% Change in Net Asset Value ■ 4 Months 1990	Latest 12 Mos.	Minimum Purchase Init.	Minimum Purchase Sub.	Max. % Sales Load	% Yield○
AARP Investment Program:							
Capital Growth	G	− 12.1	− 4.1	$ 500	$None	None	0.7
GNMA	FI	− 0.4	8.2	500	None	None	8.9
General Bond	FI	− 2.2	6.8	500	None	None	8.2
Growth & Income	GI	− 8.4	2.8	500	None	None	4.7
★Acorn Fund (f)	SG	− 5.3	5.1	4000	1000	None	1.4
Afuture Fund	G	− 5.9	− 5.8	500	30	None	1.0
AMA Advisers:							
Classic Growth (b)	G	− 7.1	2.7	1000	None	None	3.4
US Government Income Plus (b)	I	− 0.6	6.0	1000	None	None	8.8
Armstrong Associates	G	− 2.9	3.2	250	None	None	3.5
Axe-Houghton:							
Fund B (b)	B	− 3.0	9.8	1000	None	None	7.0
Income (b)	FI	− 2.2	5.8	1000	None	None	9.1
Stc.ʸ (b)	G.	− 2.6	9.8	1000	None	None	0.8
Babson:							
Bond Trust (Long)	FI	− 1.6	7.7	500	50	None	9.2
★Enterprise	SG	− 3.5	5.0	1000	100	None	1.5
Growth	G	− 6.5	2.3	500	50	None	3.2
UMB Bond	FI	0.8	9.2	1000	100	None	7.8
UMB Stock	GI	− 3.3	5.2	1000	100	None	4.6
Value	GI	− 5.8	0.3	1000	100	None	2.9
Beacon Hill Mutual	G	− 4.3	7.7	None	None	None	0.0
Benham GNMA Income	FI	− 1.2	9.3	1000	100	None	9.3
Blanchard:							
Precious Metals (b) (m)	AU	− 19.5	− 10.4	3000	200	None	0.5
Strategic Growth Fd (b) (m)	AG	− 6.4	3.9	3000	200	None	8.1
Boston Company:							
Capital Appreciation (b)	G	− 8.0	3.6	1000	None	None	2.2
Special Growth (b)	G	− 10.6	− 6.2	1000	None	None	1.8
Brandywine Fund	G	4.2	16.3	25000	1000	None	0.2
Bruce Fund	G	2.0	21.4	1000	500	None	2.8
Bull & Bear Group:							
Capital Growth (b)	G	− 6.8	5.3	1000	100	None	0.0
Equity Income (b)	EI	− 5.3	− 0.3	1000	100	None	3.7
Gold Investors Ltd (b)	AU	− 14.2	0.4	1000	100	None	1.0
High Yield (b)	FH	− 2.9	− 2.4	1000	100	None	13.5
Calamos Convertible Income	CV	− 4.6	2.6	5000	500	None	6.6
Calvert Washington Area Gro (b) (r)	G	− 9.6	− 8.8	2000	250	None	0.6
Century Shares Trust	S	− 10.1	10.0	500	25	None	2.9
CGM:							
Capital Development (c)	G	0.6	10.1	1000	50	None	1.8
Mutual Fund	B	− 5.7	7.2	1000	50	None	4.5
Clipper Fund (r)	GI	− 9.0	− 0.3	25000	1000	None	2.5
Columbia:							
Fixed Income Secs	FI	− 2.0	8.5	1000	100	None	8.5
Growth Fund	G	− 4.3	9.7	1000	100	None	2.4
Special Fund	SG	− 2.1	9.2	2000	100	None	0.1
Copley Fund	GI	− 5.6	3.9	1000	None	None	0.0
Dean Witter:							
American Value (b) (r)	G	− 6.1	6.3	1000	100	None	2.3
Convertible Securities (b) (r)	CV	− 4.5	− 0.3	1000	100	None	5.5
Developing Growth (b) (r)	SG	2.6	9.7	1000	100	None	0.5
Dividend Growth Secs. (b) (r)	GI	− 7.0	7.6	1000	100	None	3.5
Government Plus (b) (r)	FI	− 3.6	7.4	1000	100	None	8.2
Natural Res. Devel. (b) (r)	NR	− 5.6	10.6	1000	100	None	3.4
Option Income Trust (b) (r)	OI	− 5.7	3.7	1000	100	None	6.3
US Govt. Securities (b) (r)	FI	0.2	8.4	1000	100	None	9.8
Utilities (b) (r)	S	− 7.9	10.0	1000	100	None	6.1
Worldwide Investment Tr (b) (r)	IF	− 8.7	1.3	1000	100	None	1.6

	Fund Type§	% Change in Net Asset Value ■ 4 Months 1990	Latest 12 Mos.	Minimum Purchase Init.	Minimum Purchase Sub.	Max. % Sales Load	% Yield○
Dodge & Cox:							
Balanced	B	− 3.1	9.8	$ 1000	$ 100	None	5.0
Stock	GI	− 4.6	9.1	1000	100	None	2.3
D.R. European Equity	IF	5.6	26.4	100000	5000	None	16.6
Dreyfus:							
A Bonds Plus	FI	− 4.3	5.8	2500	100	None	8.3
Convertible Securities	CV	− 0.4	2.9	2500	100	None	4.5
Fund	GI	− 4.7	9.2	2500	100	None	5.1
GNMA Fund (b)	FI	− 0.7	7.6	2500	100	None	8.4
Growth Opportunity	G	− 4.3	− 1.7	2500	100	None	4.8
New Leaders (b)	SG	− 5.4	11.0	2500	100	None	1.4
Third Century	G	1.4	10.6	2500	100	None	2.8
Equitec Siebel:							
Aggressive Growth (b) (r)	AG	− 1.1	1.2	2500	None	None	0.4
High Yield Bond (b) (r)	FH	− 1.6	0.5	2500	None	None	12.1
Total Return (b) (r)	GI	− 2.3	7.7	2500	None	None	3.1
U. S. Govt. Secs. (b) (r)	FI	2.3	8.2	2500	None	None	9.9
Evergreen:							
★Fund	G	− 7.9	− 4.7	2000	None	None	3.2
★Total Return	GI	− 7.1	− 0.6	2000	None	None	6.3
Value Timing	AG	− 4.7	7.7	2000	None	None	4.6
Fairmont Fund	AG	− 11.2	− 12.0	5000	1000	None	1.5
Farm Bureau Growth (b) (r)	GI	0.4	8.0	250	None	None	5.7
Fidelity Investments:							
Asset Manager	B	− 3.1	5.8	2500	250	None	3.6
Balanced	B	− 3.5	7.5	2500	250	None	9.2
Contrafund (b)	G	− 2.3	17.9	1000	250	None	1.5
Convertible Securities	CV	− 1.5	10.5	2500	250	None	6.8
Flexible Bond	FI	− 2.6	6.8	2500	250	None	8.4
Freedom (b)	AG	− 5.7	8.5	500	250	None	2.7
Fund (b)	GI	− 4.0	10.9	2500	250	None	4.0
GNMA Fund (b)	FI	− 2.1	8.1	1000	250	None	7.8
Global	GL	− 0.4	7.8	2500	250	None	4.4
Government Securities (b)	FI	− 1.8	7.2	2500	250	None	8.0
★High Income	FH	− 5.1	− 8.5	2500	250	None	13.9
Intermediate Bond	FI	− 2.0	6.4	1000	250	None	8.3
Mortgage Securities	FI	− 1.8	8.0	2500	250	None	7.9
Real Estate	S	− 3.6	4.8	2500	250	None	5.7
Trend (b)	G	− 9.6	2.1	2500	250	None	1.4
Utilities Income	GI	− 8.7	11.1	2500	250	None	7.2
Value (b)	AG	− 7.3	2.9	2500	250	None	1.1
Financial Group:							
Dynamics	AG	− 3.1	8.5	250	50	None	1.8
High Yield Bond	FH	− 3.1	− 0.8	250	50	None	14.0
Industrial	GI	− 1.5	16.9	250	50	None	2.2
b— Industrial Income	EI	− 3.8	13.8	250	50	None	4.8
Portfolios:Energy	NR	− 11.3	9.0	250	50	None	2.1
Portfolios:European	IF	0.3	15.0	250	50	None	1.2
Portfolios:Financial Serv	S	− 6.6	10.6	250	50	None	1.1
Portfolios:Gold	AU	− 14.9	7.4	250	50	None	0.4
Portfolios:Health Sci	SH	0.7	30.8	250	50	None	0.5
Portfolios:Leisure	S	− 5.2	6.9	250	50	None	1.6
Portfolios:Pacific Basin	IF	− 15.8	− 8.2	250	50	None	0.2
Portfolios:Technology	ST	11.4	22.6	250	50	None	0.0
Portfolios:Utilities	SU	− 14.1	3.1	250	50	None	2.4
Select Income Bond	FI	− 1.5	4.0	250	50	None	10.3

(continued)

Figure 19.7 (continued)

Load Funds (Continued)

Fund Type§	4 Months 1990	Latest 12 Mos.	Init.	Sub.	Max. % Sales Load	% Yield°
Value Shares	AG	– 4.3	0.0	$ None	$None	6.00	0.0
Venture Shares (b)	SG	– 5.6	5.5	None	None	6.00	0.1
World Fund (b)	IF	– 11.8	– 4.4	None	None	6.00	0.2
Putnam:							
Convertible Inc. Growth (b)	CV	– 4.5	2.2	500	50	5.75	6.2
Energy Resources (b)	NR	– 4.7	10.6	500	50	5.75	3.0
George of Boston (b)	B	– 4.5	9.0	500	50	5.75	6.1
Global Gov't Income Trust (b)	GL	– 1.4	7.0	500	50	4.75	9.9
Growth & Income (b)	GI	– 2.6	8.0	500	50	5.75	5.0
Health Sciences Trust (b)	SH	– 4.0	17.5	500	50	5.75	1.4
High Income Gov't Trust (b)	FI	– 3.8	6.6	500	50	6.75	8.1
High Yield Trust I	FH	– 4.1	– 7.9	500	50	6.75	15.6
High Yield Trust II (b)	FH	– 5.7	– 10.6	500	50	6.75	15.7
Income (b)	FI	– 2.7	5.8	500	50	4.75	10.0
Information Sciences (b)	ST	– 7.9	– 5.3	500	50	5.75	0.5
★International Equities (b)	GL	– 5.1	10.0	500	50	5.75	1.7
Investors (b)	G	– 3.6	14.5	500	50	5.75	3.3
Option Income I	OI	– 5.1	– 0.6	500	50	8.50	3.6
Option Income II (b)	OI	– 4.6	4.7	500	50	8.50	5.4
OTC Emerging Growth (b)	SG	– 4.2	6.0	500	50	5.75	0.0
U.S. Gov't. Guaranteed	FI	– 0.3 *	8.9	500	50	4.75	9.7
Vista Basic Value (b)	AG	– 5.6	5.3	500	50	5.75	3.6
Voyager (b)	AG	– 8.0	5.8	500	50	5.75	1.3
Quest for Value	AG	– 6.9	2.2	2000	25	4.75	2.8
Rea-Graham Balanced Fund	B	– 3.8	1.6	1000	200	8.50	6.9
Rightime Government Secs (b)	FI	– 7.0	4.8	2000	100	4.75	6.8
Security:							
Equity	G	– 5.3	8.5	100	20	8.50	2.9
Income-Bond	FI	– 1.3	5.1	100	20	4.75	9.6
Investment	GI	– 7.1	2.2	100	20	8.50	6.2
Ultra	AG	– 2.5	1.5	100	20	8.50	1.0
Seligman Group:							
Capital	AG	– 2.8	12.4	1000	50	4.75	0.0
Common Stock	GI	– 4.3	10.8	1000	50	4.75	3.5
Communications & Info	ST	– 0.9	10.2	1000	50	4.75	0.0
Growth	G	– 6.9	12.7	1000	50	4.75	1.4
High Yield Bond Series (b)	FH	– 3.4	– 1.4	1000	50	4.75	13.8
Income	I	– 3.8	4.9	None	None	4.75	8.5
Secured Mortgage Inc. Series	FI	– 3.2	4.2	None	None	4.75	9.1
US Gov't Guaranteed Secs (b)	FI	– 3.5	4.0	None	None	4.75	9.2
Sentinel Group:							
Balanced	B	– 3.2	8.0	250	25	8.50	6.1
Bond	FI	– 1.7	7.1	250	25	8.50	8.5
Common	GI	– 6.4	7.7	250	25	8.50	3.7
Growth	G	– 3.0	12.0	250	25	8.50	1.1
Sentry Fund	G	– 1.3	11.9	250	25	8.00	2.7
Shearson Lehman Hutton:							
Aggressive Growth	AG	– 4.8	13.5	500	200	5.00	0.1
Appreciation	G	– 3.5	11.4	500	200	5.00	2.7
Fundamental Value	G	– 1.9	6.6	500	200	5.00	2.9
Global Opportunities	GL	– 6.6	4.9	500	200	5.00	0.8
High Yield	FH	– 3.3	– 7.7	500	200	5.00	16.4
Lehman Capital	AG	– 7.5	6.9	1000	100	5.00	0.0
Lehman Investors	GI	– 5.1	6.2	500	50	5.00	4.1
Managed Government	FI	– 0.6	8.0	500	200	5.00	8.9
Smith, Barney:							
Equity	G	– 4.3	10.1	3000	50	5.75	2.8
Income & Growth	GI	– 7.8	5.4	3000	50	5.75	5.8
Sovereign Investors (b)	GI	– 2.2	12.9	30	30	4.75	4.7
State Bond Common (b)	G	– 5.4	18.7	250	50	4.75	1.9
State Street Investment (r) (c)	GI	– 5.1	11.4	250	25	4.50	3.1
Strategic:							
Gold & Minerals	AU	8.2	– 4.0	500	100	8.50	0.9
Investments	AU	– 36.7	– 1.0	500	100	8.50	4.6
Silver	S	2.0	16.3	500	100	8.50	0.0

Fund Type§	4 Months 1990	Latest 12 Mos.	Init.	Sub.	Max. % Sales Load	% Yield°
Summit Investors Fund	G	– 4.5	9.3	$ 600	$ 600	8.50	2.0
SunAmerica:							
Aggressive Growth (b)	AG	– 2.9	0.2	1000	100	4.75	0.0
Convertible Securities (b)	CV	– 3.7	– 5.4	1000	100	4.75	5.3
Growth (b)	G	– 6.2	13.9	1000	100	4.75	0.7
High Yield (b)	FH	– 4.2	– 9.6	1000	100	4.75	12.3
Templeton Group:							
Foreign	IF	– 0.4	19.0	500	25	8.50	3.0
Global Fund Inc	GL	– 3.4	4.1	500	25	8.50	2.5
Growth	GL	– 5.4	6.2	500	25	8.50	3.8
★World	GL	– 9.8	1.4	500	25	8.50	3.6
Transamerica:							
Gov't Secs Trust (b)	FI	– 3.2	4.8	1000	100	4.75	11.1
Growth & Income (b)	GI	– 3.3	12.0	100	10	4.75	3.5
Investment Quality Bond (b)	FI	– 4.2	3.1	100	10	4.75	9.2
Lowry Market Timing (b)	AG	2.1	12.5	1000	100	4.75	2.6
Sunbelt Growth (b)	G	– 7.8	3.6	100	10	4.75	5.0
Technology (o)	ST	0.8	12.6	100	10	4.75	0.6
Tyndall-Newport Global Growth	GL	– 8.3	– 6.1	1000	100	5.00	0.4
United:							
Accumulative	G	– 4.9	7.0	500	25	8.50	2.2
Bond	FI	– 3.3	4.0	500	25	8.50	8.7
Continental Income	B	– 4.3	10.0	500	25	8.50	5.4
Government Secs	FI	– 2.6	6.7	500	25	4.25	8.4
High Income (c)	FH	– 6.8	– 13.5	500	25	8.50	15.9
Income	EI	– 2.1	11.1	500	25	8.50	3.4
International Growth	IF	– 8.9	– 0.3	500	25	8.50	2.1
New Concepts Fund	SG	1.4	4.4	500	25	8.50	3.1
Science & Energy	ST	– 3.9	11.9	500	25	8.50	1.5
Vanguard	G	– 1.7	5.0	500	25	8.50	3.7
Van Eck:							
Gold/Resources (b)	AU	– 20.3	– 4.1	1000	100	6.75	0.2
International Investors	AU	– 20.5	14.7	1000	100	8.50	2.1
World Trends (b)	GL	– 5.3	8.6	1000	100	5.75	1.3
Van Kampen U.S. Govt (b)	FI	– 1.2	9.8	1500	100	4.90	9.1
Wall Street Fund	G	– 5.8	2.0	2000	500	5.50	0.3
Zweig Series Trust:							
Blue Chip (b)	G	– 16.1	6.0	1000	100	5.00	2.9
Bond Debenture (b)	FI	– 2.0	4.1	1000	100	5.00	7.6
Emerging Growth (b)	SG	0.6	4.7	1000	100	5.00	1.4
Government Securities (b)	FI	– 3.9	5.8	1000	100	5.00	7.0
Option Income (b)	OI	– 4.8	5.3	1000	250	5.00	1.7

Market Yardsticks

	4 Months 1990	Latest 12 Mos.	Divs.	% Yield°
S&P 500 Index	– 5.3	10.4	$ 11.14	3.4
Dow Jones Industrials	– 2.3	14.2	104.22	3.9
Nasdaq OTC Composite	– 7.6	– 1.8	0.00	0.0
Selector Equity-Fund Average	– 4.9	6.7	NA	2.0
Selector Income-Fund Average	– 2.8	3.0	NA	9.6
S.H. Aggregate Bond Index	– 1.8	9.2	9.28	9.6
S.H. Government/Corporate Index	– 2.2	8.6	9.25	9.6
Consumer Price Index ▲	2.1			
T-Bill Rates	(4/30/90) 13 weeks, 7.91%		26 weeks, 8.03%	

▲ For 3 months 1990 ■ Dividends and capital gains included but not reinvested. NA not applicable, not available, or not meaningful. ° Based on latest 12 months dividends. (b) 12b-1 plan. % of fund's assets may be used for marketing purposes. (c) Not available for new purchase. (f) Redemption fee for one year or less. (m) Miscellaneous annual costs. (p) Dividends reinvested at offering price (r) Redemption fee or contingent deferred sales charge may be imposed. ★ Supervised list/purchase recommendation. b—, s— Recent Selector buy/sell recommendation. ‡ Low Loads. † No-Loads. § Fund type: AG Aggressive Growth, AU Gold, B Balanced, CV Convertible Securities, EI Equity-Income, FH High Yield Bond, FI Fixed-Income, G Growth, GI Growth & Income, IF International, NR Natural Resources, OG Option-Growth, OI Option-Income, SG Small Company Growth, S Specialty, SH Health, ST Technology, SU Utility. # $Millions.

Source: United Mutual Fund Selector, a division of Babson-United Investment Advisors, Inc., 101 Prescott Street, Wellesley Hills, MA 02181. Reprinted with permission.

magazine publishes comparable information for closed-end, fixed-income funds and equity funds. Besides information on performance, sales charges (including those for 12b–1 plans), and expenses, an accompanying table lists telephone numbers for all the funds.

To meet the interest in mutual funds, United Business Service Company publishes a semimonthly report called *United Mutual Fund Selector.* Each issue contains several articles on specific mutual funds or classes of mutual funds, such as municipal bond funds. In the first issue of each month, a four-page supplement entitled "Investment Company Performance Comparisons" gives recent and historical changes in NAV for load and no-load funds. A sample page is illustrated in Figure 19.7.[25]

Global Investment Companies

As discussed throughout this text, you should give very serious thought to global diversification of your investment portfolio. Funds that invest in non-U.S. securities are generally called **foreign funds.** More specific designations include *international funds* and *global funds.* **International funds** include only non-U.S. securities such as those from countries like Japan, Singapore, and Korea. **Global funds** hold both U.S. and non-U.S. securities. Ideally, a global fund should invest in a large number of countries. Both international and global funds fall into familiar categories: money funds, long-term government and corporate bond funds, and equity funds. In turn, an international equity fund might limit its focus to a segment of the non-U.S. market, such as the European Fund, or to a single country like Germany, Italy, Japan, or Korea. While most global and international funds are open-end funds (either load or no-load), there are a significant number that are closed-end funds, including most of the single-country funds. These funds have opted to be closed end because they are not subject to major investor liquidations that require the sale of stocks in the portfolio on an illiquid foreign stock exchange. Because of the growth and popularity of foreign funds, most sources of information include separate sections on them.

---

[25]This service is available from United Business Service Company, 210 Newbury St., Boston, MA 02116.

Foreign fund An investment company that holds non-U.S. securities.

International fund An investment company that holds only non-U.S. securities, sometimes focusing on a specific segment of the non-U.S. market.

Global fund An investment company that holds both U.S. and non-U.S. securities.

Summary

- An investment company can be defined as a pool of funds from many individuals that is invested in a collection of individual investments such as stocks, bonds, and other publicly traded securities. Investment companies can be classified as closed-end, or open-end, and the latter as either load or no-load funds. A wide variety of funds are available, so you can find one to match almost any investment objective or combination of objectives.
- Numerous studies have examined the historical performance of mutual funds. Most found that less than half the funds matched the risk-adjusted net returns of the aggregate market. The results with gross returns generally indicated average risk-adjusted returns about equal to the market's, with about half of the funds (or more in some studies) outperforming the market.
- While the returns to average individual investors on funds managed by investment companies will probably not be superior to the average results for a specific U.S. or international market, you should recognize that several other important services are provided by investment companies. Therefore, you should give serious consideration to these funds as a very important alternative to investing in individual stocks and bonds in the United States or worldwide.

Questions

1. How do you compute the net asset value of an investment company?
2. Discuss the difference between an open-end investment company and a closed-end investment company.
3. What two prices are provided in a quote for a closed-end investment company? What is the typical relationship between these prices?
4. What is the difference between a load fund and a no-load fund?

5. What are the differences between a common stock fund and a balanced fund? How would you expect their risk and return characteristics to compare?
6. Why might you buy a money market fund? What would you want from such an investment?
7. Should you care how well a mutual fund is diversified? Why or why not?
8. Discuss why the stability of a risk measure for a mutual fund is important to an investor. Are mutual funds' risk measures generally stable?
9. Should the performance of mutual funds be judged on the basis of return alone or on a risk-adjusted basis? Discuss why, using examples.
10. Define the net return and gross return for a mutual fund. Discuss how you would compute each.
11. As an investor in a mutual fund, is net return or gross return more relevant to you? As an investigator attempting to determine how well mutual fund managers select undervalued stock or project market returns, discuss whether net or gross returns are more relevant.
12. Based upon the numerous tests of mutual fund performance, you are convinced that only about half of the funds do better than a naive buy-and-hold policy. Does this mean you would forget about investing in investment companies? Why or why not?
13. You are told that Fund X experienced above-average performance over the past 2 years. Do you think it will continue over the next 2 years? Why or why not?
14. You are told that Fund Y experienced consistently poor performance over the past 2 years. Do you expect this to continue over the next 2 years? Why or why not?
15. You see advertisements for two mutual funds indicating that they have investment objectives that are consistent with yours.
    a. How would you get a quick view of these two funds' performance over the past 2 or 3 years?
    b. Where would you find more in-depth information on the funds, including addresses so you can write for prospectuses?

Problems

1. Suppose ABC Mutual fund owned only four stocks as follows:

Stock	Shares	Price	Market Value
W	1,000	12	$12,000
X	1,200	15	18,000
Y	1,500	22	33,000
Z	800	16	12,800
			$75,800

The fund began by selling $50,000 of stock at $8 per share. What is its NAV?

2. Suppose you are considering investing $1,000 in a load fund with a fee of 8 percent and you expect your investment to earn 15 percent over the next year. You could invest in a no-load fund with similar risk that charges a 1 percent redemption fee. You estimate that this no-load fund will earn 12 percent. Given your expectations, which is the better investment and by how much?

3. In *Barron's*, look up the NAVs and market prices for five closed-end funds. Compute the difference between the two values for each fund. How many are selling at a premium to NAV? How many are selling at a discount to NAV? What is the overall average premium or discount? How does this compare to the Herzfeld chart published in *Barron's* that tracks the average discount on these funds over time?

References

Anderson, Seth Copeland. "Closed-End Funds vs. Market Efficiency." *Journal of Portfolio Management* 13, no. 1 (Fall 1986).

Ang, James S., and Jess H. Chua. "Mutual Funds: Different Strokes for Different Folks?" *Journal of Portfolio Management* 8, no. 2 (Winter 1982).

Brealey, Richard A. "How to Combine Active Management with Index Funds." *Journal of Portfolio Management* 12, no. 2 (Winter 1986).

Chang, Eric C., and Wilbur G. Lewellen. "Market Timing and Mutual Fund Investment Performance." *Journal of Business* 57, no. 1, part 1 (January 1984).

Henricksson, Roy D. "Mutual Timing and Mutual Fund Performance: An Empirical Investigation." *Journal of Business* 57, no. 1, part 1 (January 1984).

Martin, John D., Arthur J. Keown, Jr., and James L. Farrell. "Do Fund Objectives Affect Diversification Policies?" *Journal of Portfolio Management* 8, no. 2 (Winter 1982).

Richards, Malcolm, Donald Fraser, and John Groth. "The Attractions of Closed-End Bond Funds." *Journal of Portfolio Management* 8, no. 2 (Winter 1982).

Simonds, Richard R. "Mutual Fund Strategies for IRA Investors." *Journal of Portfolio Management* 12, no. 2 (Winter 1986).

Veit, E. Theodore, and John M. Cheney. "Are Mutual Funds Market Timers?" *Journal of Portfolio Management* 8, no. 2 (Winter 1982).

APPENDIX

19a *Mutual Funds Glossary*

This glossary is divided into three parts: (A) general terms used in the mutual funds industry, (B) specific terms for types of mutual funds, and (C) a description of alternative retirement plans, each of which can include mutual funds.

A. General Terms

Accumulation (periodic payment) plan An arrangement through which an investor can purchase mutual fund shares periodically in large or small amounts, usually with provisions for the reinvestment of income dividends and capital gains distributions in additional shares.

Adviser The organization employed by a mutual fund to give professional advice on the management of its assets.

Asked (offering) price The price at which you can purchase a mutual fund's shares equal to the net asset value per share plus, at times, a sales charge.

Automatic reinvestment *See* Reinvestment privilege.

Bid (redemption) price The price at which a mutual fund redeems (buys back) its shares, usually equal to the net asset value per share.

Bookshares A modern share recording system that eliminates the need for share certificates, but gives fund shareowners records of their holdings.

Broker-dealer (dealer) A firm that retails mutual fund shares and other securities to the public.

Capital gains distributions Payments, usually annual, to mutual fund shareholders for gains realized on the sale of the fund's portfolio securities.

Capital growth An increase in the market value of a mutual fund's securities that is reflected in the NAV of its shares. Maximizing this factor is a long-term objective of many mutual funds.

Closed-end investment company An investment company that issues only a limited number of shares, which it does not redeem (buy back). Instead, closed-end shares are traded in securities markets at prices determined by supply and demand.

Contractual plan A program for the accumulation of mutual fund shares in which the investor agrees to invest a fixed amount on a regular basis for a specified number of years. A substantial portion of the sales charge applicable to the total investment is usually deducted from early payments.

Conversion (exchange) privilege A provision that enables a mutual fund shareholder to transfer an investment from one fund to another within the same fund group, sometimes with a small transaction charge, if needs or objectives change.

Custodian The organization (usually a bank) that holds the securities and other assets of a mutual fund in custody and safekeeping.

Dollar-cost averaging Investing equal amounts of money at regular intervals regardless of whether the stock market is moving upward or downward. This reduces the average share costs in periods of lower securities prices, and the number of shares purchased in periods of higher prices.

Exchange privilege *See* Conversion privilege.

Income dividends Payments to mutual fund shareholders of dividends, interest, and short-term capital gains earned on the fund's portfolio after deduction of operating expenses.

Investment adviser *See* Adviser.

Investment company A corporation, trust, or partnership in which investors pool their money to obtain professional management and portfolio diversification. Mutual funds are the most popular type of investment company.

Investment objective   The goal, such as long-term capital growth or current income, that an investor or a mutual fund pursues.

Load   *See* Sales charge.

Management fee   The compensation an investment company pays to the investment management company for its services. The average annual fee is about 0.5 percent of fund assets.

Mutual fund   An investment company that pools money from shareholders and invests in a variety of securities, including stocks, bonds, and money market securities. A mutual fund ordinarily stands ready to buy back (redeem) its shares at their current net asset value, which depends on the market value of the fund's portfolio of securities at the time. Mutual funds generally continuously offer new shares to investors.

Net asset value (NAV) per share   The market value of an investment company's assets (securities, cash, and any accrued earnings) after deducting liabilities, divided by the number of shares outstanding.

No-load fund   A mutual fund that sells its shares at net asset value without adding sales charges.

Open-end investment company   The more formal name for a mutual fund, which derives from the fact that it continuously offers new shares to investors and redeems them (buys them back) on demand.

Payroll deduction plan   An arrangement offered by some employers through which an employee may accumulate shares in a mutual fund. Employees authorize the employer to deduct specified amounts from their salaries at stated times and transfer the proceeds to the designated fund or funds.

Periodic payment plan   *See* Contractual plan.

Prospectus   A booklet that describes a mutual fund and offers its shares for sale. It contains information required by the Securities and Exchange Commission on such subjects as the fund's investment objective and policies, services, investment restrictions, officers and directors, procedures for buying or redeeming shares, charges, and financial statements.

Redemption price   *See* Bid price.

Reinvestment privilege   A provision of most mutual funds by which the investor can automatically reinvest income dividends and capital gains distributions in additional shares.

Sales charge   An amount charged to purchase shares in most mutual funds that are sold by brokers or other members of a sales force. Typical charges range from 4 to 8.5 percent of the initial investment. The charge is added to the net asset value per share to determine the offering price. *See also* No-load fund.

Short-term fund   An industry designation for money market and short-term municipal bond funds.

Transfer agent   The organization employed by a mutual fund to prepare and maintain records relating to the accounts of fund shareholders.

12b–1 fee   A fee charged by some funds, named after the SEC rule that permits it. Such fees pay for distribution costs, such as advertising, or for brokers' commissions. The fund's prospectus details any 12b–1 charges that apply.

Underwriter (principal underwriter)   The organization that acts as the distributor of a mutual fund's shares to broker–dealers and the public.

Unit investment trust   An investment company that purchases a fixed portfolio of income-producing securities to create a trust and sells units in the trust to investors through brokers.

Variable annuity   A contract under which an annuity is purchased with a fixed amount of money that is converted into a varying number of accumulation units. At retirement, the annuitant is paid a fixed number of monthly units, which are converted into varying amounts of money. The value of both accumulation and annuity units varies with the performance of a portfolio of equity securities.

Variable life insurance   An equity-based life insurance policy the reserves of which may be invested in common stocks. The death benefit is guaranteed never to fall below the face value, but it would increase if the value of the securities were to increase. This kind of policy may have no guaranteed cash-surrender value.

Voluntary plan   A flexible accumulation plan that states no definite time period or total amount to be invested.

Withdrawal plan   A mutual fund provision that allows shareholders to receive payments from their investments at regular intervals. These payments typically are drawn from the fund's dividends and capital gains distributions, if any, and from principal, as needed. Many mutual funds offer these plans.

B.   *Types of Mutual Funds*

Aggressive growth fund   A fund that seeks maximum capital gains as its investment objective. Current income is not a significant factor. Some may invest in stocks on the fringes of the mainstream, such as those of fledgling companies, new industries, companies fallen on hard times, or industries temporarily out of favor. They may also use specialized investment techniques such as option writing. The risks are obvious, but the potential for handsome rewards should accompany them.

Balanced fund A fund with, generally, a three-part investment objective: (1) to conserve the investors' principal, (2) to pay current income, and (3) to increase both principal and income. The fund aims to achieve this by owning a mixture of bonds, preferred stocks, and common stocks.

Corporate bond fund Like an income fund, this type of fund seeks a high level of income. It does this by buying bonds of corporations for the majority of the portfolio. Some part of the portfolio may be in U.S. Treasury and other government bonds.

Flexible portfolio fund A fund that invests in common stocks, bonds, money market securities, and other types of debt securities. The portfolio may hold up to 100 percent of any one of these types of securities or any combination of them, depending upon market conditions.

Global bond fund A fund that invests in bonds issued by companies from countries worldwide, including the United States.

Global equity fund A fund that invests in the stock of both U.S. and foreign companies.

GNMA (Ginnie Mae) fund A fund that invests in the government-backed mortgage securities of the Government National Mortgage Association. To qualify for this category, the majority of a fund's portfolio must always be invested in mortgage-backed securities.

Growth and income fund A fund that invests mainly in the common stock of companies with longer track records—companies that combine the expectation of higher share values and solid records of paying dividends.

Growth fund A fund that invests in the common stock of more settled companies, but again, with the primary aim of building the value of its investments through capital gains rather than a steady flow of dividends.

High-yield bond fund A corporate bond fund that invests predominantly in bonds rated below investment grade. In return for a generally higher yield, investors bear greater risk than more highly rated bonds require.

Income equity fund A fund that invests primarily in stocks of companies with good dividend-paying records.

Income-bond fund A fund that invests in a combination of government and corporate bonds to generate income.

Income-mixed fund A fund that seeks a high level of current income, often by investing in the common stock of companies that have good dividend-paying records. Often corporate and government bonds are also part of the portfolio.

International fund A fund that invests in the stocks of companies located outside the United States.

Long-term municipal bond fund A fund that invests in bonds issued by local governments, such as cities and states, which use the money to build schools, highways, libraries, and the like. Because the federal government does not tax the income earned on most of these securities, the fund can pass the tax-free income through to shareholders.

Long-term state municipal bond fund A fund that invests predominantly in long-term municipal bonds issued within a single state. These issues are exempt from both federal income tax and state taxes for residents of the same state.

Money market mutual fund A fund that invests in short-term securities sold in the money market. (Large companies, banks, and other institutions also invest their surplus cash in the money market for short periods of time.) In the entire investment spectrum, these are generally the safest, most stable securities available. They include Treasury bills, certificates of deposit of large banks, and commercial paper (short-term IOUs of large corporations).

Option/income fund A fund that seeks a high current return by investing primarily in dividend-paying common stocks on which call options are traded on national securities exchanges. Current returns generally consist of dividends, premiums from writing call options, but other sources include short-term gains from asset sales, often to satisfy exercised options, and profits from closing purchase transactions.

Short-term national municipal bond fund A fund that invests in municipal securities with relatively short maturities, also known as a *tax-exempt money market fund*.

Short-term state municipal bond fund A fund that invests in municipal securities with relatively short maturities issued in a single state. Such issues are exempt from state taxes for residents of the same state.

U.S. Government Income Fund A fund that invests in a variety of government securities, including U.S. Treasury bonds, federally guaranteed mortgage-backed securities, and other government issues.

C. Retirement Plans

Federal income tax laws permit the establishment of a number of types of tax-deferred retirement plans, each of which may be funded with mutual fund shares.

Corporate and self-employed retirement plan A tax-qualified pension and profit-sharing plan that can be established by corporations or self-employed individuals. Changes in the tax laws have made retirement plans for corporate employees essentially comparable to those for self-employed individuals. Contributions to a plan are tax-deductible and earnings accumulate on a tax-deferred basis. The maximum annual amount that may be contributed to such a plan on behalf of an individual is limited to the lesser of 25 percent of the individual's compensation or $30,000.

Individual retirement account Any wage earner under the age of $70\frac{1}{2}$ may set up an individual retirement account (IRA) and may contribute as much as 100 percent of his or her compensation each year up to $2,000. Income on these contributions is tax-deferred until withdrawal. The amount contributed each year may be wholly or partially tax deductible. Under the Tax Reform Act of 1986, all taxpayers not covered by employer-sponsored retirement plans can continue to take the full deduction for IRA contributions. Those who are covered or who are married to someone who is covered must have adjusted gross incomes of no more than $25,000 if they are single or $40,000 if they are married and filing jointly to take the full deduction. The deduction is phased out for incomes for single people between $25,000 and $35,000 and for married people who file jointly between $40,000 and $60,000. An individual who quali-

fies for an IRA and has a spouse who either has no earnings or elects to be treated as having no earnings may contribute up to 100 percent of his or her income or $2,250, whichever is less.

Qualified retirement plan A private retirement plan that meets the rules and regulations of the Internal Revenue Service. In almost all cases, contributions to a qualified retirement plan are tax deductible and earnings on such contributions are always exempt from taxes until the investor retires.

Simplified employee pension (SEP) An employer-sponsored plan that may be viewed as an aggregation of separate IRAs. In a SEP, the employer contributes up to $30,000 or 15 percent of compensation, whichever is less, to an individual retirement account maintained for the employee.

Section 403(b) plan Section 403(b) of the Internal Revenue Code permits employees of certain charitable organizations and public school systems to establish tax-sheltered retirement programs. These plans may be invested in either annuity contracts or mutual fund shares.

Section 401(k) plan A particularly popular type of plan that may be offered by either corporate or noncorporate entities. A 401(k) plan is a tax-qualified profit-sharing plan that includes a "cash or deferred" arrangement, which permits employees to have a portion of their compensation contributed to a tax-sheltered plan on their behalf or paid to them directly as additional taxable compensation. An employee may elect to reduce his or her other taxable compensation with contributions to a 401(k) plan, where those amounts will accumulate tax-free. The Tax Reform Act of 1986 established new, tighter anti-discrimination requirements for 401(k) plans and curtailed the amount of elective deferrals that may be made by all employees. Nevertheless, 401(k) plans remain excellent and popular retirement savings vehicles.

Portfolio and Capital Market Theory and Application

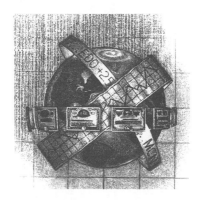

Up to this point in the book we have discussed the analysis and valuation of a number of different individual assets such as stocks, bonds, options, and futures. Throughout this effort, however, we have recognized that our ultimate objective has been to combine those assets into a portfolio that would provide the highest returns available and that is consistent with a given risk level and the basic objective of the investment program. At several points in the book, we have pointed out that the optimum portfolio is more than a collection of desirable individual assets. The discussion in this final section of the book will explain this concept in greater detail and expand upon it.

Chapter 20 provides a detailed discussion of portfolio theory, as derived by Harry Markowitz, and how this theory is applied including how to properly diversify a portfolio. Building upon the Markowitz portfolio theory, Chapter 21 discusses the development of the capital asset pricing model, which implies a specific measure of risk that is used in the valuation of capital assets.

These two theories (portfolio theory and capital asset pricing theory) assume that capital markets are efficient so that all assets are properly priced to maintain consistent relationships between expected rates of return and the expected risk levels of assets. Chapter 22 considers this important topic including descriptions of alternative efficient market hypotheses and how these hypotheses are tested, along with reviews of the results of these tests which both support and attack the hypotheses.

We conclude the section and the book with a chapter that describes how you can evaluate the performance of a portfolio of securities. The notable advance in this area is the development of composite performance models that consider both the rate of return earned over a period of time and the risk of the portfolio.

In summary, the material in this section will help you to understand how to construct a portfolio, why your risk–return results should be consistent, and how to evaluate the performance of your portfolio in terms of its risk-adjusted rate of return.

C H A P T E R

20

Portfolio Theory and Application

At this point, having analyzed the aggregate market, alternative industries, and leading companies and their stocks within the better industries, you need to combine a number of individual securities into an investment portfolio. One of the major advances in the study of investments over the past couple of decades has been the explicit recognition that creating a portfolio of individual investments requires more than lumping together individual securities with desirable risk–return characteristics. Studies have shown that the relationship among the investments is important in building a portfolio that will best meet your investment objectives. Portfolio theory recognizes the important factors in creating a portfolio.

This chapter explains portfolio theory step by step. This involves introducing you to the basic portfolio risk formula that you must understand to combine different assets. Understanding this formula and its implications will increase your understanding of *why* you should diversify your portfolio, and also *how* you should diversify. Chapter 21 introduces capital market theory with an emphasis on the risk measure that is appropriate for individual assets.

Some Background Assumptions

Before presenting portfolio theory, we need to clarify some of its general assumptions. This includes the idea of an optimum portfolio, as well as the meanings of the terms *risk aversion* and *risk*. Therefore, these concepts are considered in this section before the presentation of portfolio theory begins.

One basic assumption of portfolio theory is that investors want to maximize the returns from their investments for given levels of risk. Such an assumption requires certain ground rules. First, consideration of a portfolio should extend to all of the investor's assets and liabilities. Rather than focusing only on your stocks, or even your marketable securities, you must include such items as your car, your house, and less marketable investments like coins, stamps, antiques, furniture, and so forth. You must consider the full spectrum of investments because the returns from all of them interact, and this interaction between returns is very important. Hence, a good portfolio is more than a collection of good individual investments.

Risk Aversion

A second assumption is that investors are basically risk averse. Given a choice between two assets with equal rates of return, they will select the asset with the lower level of risk. As evidence that most investors are risk averse, remember that they purchase various types of insurance. Buyers of insurance make current, certain outlays to guard against uncertain, possibly larger outlays in the future. Buying insurance implies that you are willing to pay the current known cost of the insurance policy to avoid the uncertainty of a potentially large future cost related to a car accident or a major illness.

As further evidence of risk aversion, consider the difference in promised yields (required rates of return) for different grades of bonds. As you know from our prior discussion of bonds, their promised yields increase as their ratings fall from AAA (the lowest-risk class) to AA, A, and so on. Yields must increase because investors require higher rates of return in order to accept higher risk.

This assumption does not imply that every investor is risk averse, or that investors are completely risk averse regarding all financial commitments. In fact, everybody does not buy insurance for everything. Some people have no insurance against anything, either by choice or because they cannot afford it.

In addition, some individuals who insure against some risks, such as auto accidents and illness, also gamble at race tracks or in Las Vegas despite known negative expected returns. These people are willing to pay for the excitement of risk. This combination of risk preference in Las Vegas and risk aversion indicates an attitude that is not completely risk averse or risk preferring, but that combines the two depending upon the amount of money involved. Friedman and Savage speculate that such an attitude characterizes people who like to gamble for small amounts (in lotteries or nickel slot machines), but buy insurance to protect themselves against large losses from catastrophic events like fire or accidents.[1]

While recognizing such attitudes, our basic assumption is that most investors who commit large sums of money to develop investment portfolios are risk averse. Therefore, we expect a positive relationship between the expected rate of return and risk.

Definition of Risk

While specific definitions of the terms *risk* and *uncertainty* differ, for our purposes, and in most financial literature, the two terms are interchangeable. In fact, we could define risk as the uncertainty of future outcomes. An alternative definition might call it the probability of an adverse outcome. In our discussion of portfolio theory, we will consider several measures of risk.

Markowitz Portfolio Theory

In the 1950s and early 1960s the investment community talked about risk, but lacked any specific measure. Building a portfolio model, however, required a quantifiable risk variable. Harry Markowitz developed the basic portfolio model by deriving the expected rate of return for a portfolio of assets and an expected risk measure.[2] Markowitz showed that the variance of the rate of return was a meaningful measure of portfolio risk under a reasonable set of assumptions, and he

---

[1]Milton Friedman and Leonard J. Savage, "The Utility Analysis of Choices Involving Risk," *Journal of Political Economy* 56, no. 3 (August 1948): 279–304.

[2]Harry Markowitz, "Portfolio Selection," *Journal of Finance* 7, no. 1 (March 1952): 77–91; and Harry Markowitz, *Portfolio Selection—Efficient Diversification of Investments* (New Haven, Conn.: Yale University Press, 1959).

derived the formulas for computing that variance for a portfolio. This formula for portfolio variance indicated both the importance of diversifying investments to reduce total portfolio risk, and also how to effectively diversify.

Assumptions Regarding Investor Behavior

The Markowitz model makes several assumptions regarding investor behavior:

1. Investors consider each investment alternative as being represented by a probability distribution of expected returns over some holding period.
2. Investors maximize 1-period expected utility, and their utility curves demonstrate diminishing marginal utility of wealth.
3. Investors estimate the risks of portfolios on the basis of the variability of expected returns.
4. Investors base decisions solely on expected return and risk, so their utility curves are functions of expected return and expected variance (or standard deviation) of returns only.
5. For a given risk level, investors prefer higher returns to lower returns. Similarly, for a given level of expected return, investors prefer less risk to more risk.

Under these assumptions, a single asset or portfolio of assets is considered to be *efficient* if no other asset or portfolio of assets offers higher expected return with the same (or lower) risk, or lower risk with the same (or higher) expected return.

Alternative Measures of Risk

One of the best-known measures of risk is the variance, or standard deviation, of expected returns.[3] This is a statistical measure of the dispersion of returns around the expected value with a larger variance or standard deviation indicating greater dispersion, all other factors being equal. More dispersed expected returns indicate greater uncertainty of those returns in any future period.

Another measure of risk is the range of returns. This assumes that a larger range of expected returns,

---

[3]We consider variance and standard deviation as one measure of risk because the standard deviation is the square root of the variance.

Table 20.1	Computation of the Expected Return for an Individual Risky Asset		

Probability	Potential Return (%)	Expected Return (%)
0.25	0.08	0.0200
0.25	0.10	0.0250
0.25	0.12	0.0300
0.25	0.14	0.0350
		E(R) = 0.1100

from the lowest to the highest, means greater uncertainty (risk) regarding future expected returns.

Some observers avoid measures that analyze all deviations from expectations. They believe that an investor should be concerned only with the risk of returns below expectations, or deviations below the mean. One measure, semivariance, considers these deviations. As an extension of semivariance, you might compute only returns that fall below zero, or negative returns. Both of these measures of risk implicitly assume that investors want to minimize the damage from below-average returns and would welcome positive returns, so the chance of returns above expectations is not considered when measuring risk.

From the numerous measures of risk, we will choose the variance or standard deviation of returns, because (1) this measure is somewhat intuitive, (2) it is a correct and widely recognized risk measure, and (3) it has been used in most of the theoretical asset pricing models.

Expected Rate of Return for the Portfolio

The expected rate of return for a portfolio of investments is simply the weighted average of the expected rates of return for the individual investments in the portfolio. The weights reflect the investments' values as proportions of the total portfolio value.

The expected rate of return for an individual investment is computed as shown in Table 20.1, which assumes equal probabilities for all the potential returns. The expected return for an individual investment (or *risky asset*) with the set of potential returns and probabilities in the example would be 11 percent.

Table 20.2   *Computation of the Expected Return for a Portfolio of Risky Assets*

Weight (W_i) (% of Portfolio)	Expected Security Return (R_i)	Expected Portfolio Return ($W_i \times R_i$)
0.20	0.10	0.0200
0.30	0.11	0.0330
0.30	0.12	0.0360
0.20	0.13	0.0260
		$E(R_{port}) = 0.1150$

Covariance   A measure of the degree to which two variables, such as rates of return for investment assets, move together over time.

The expected return for a hypothetical portfolio of four individual investments is computed in Table 20.2 to be 11.5 percent. The effect of additions to or deletions from the portfolio would be easy to determine, given the new weights based on revised values and the expected return for each investment. This formula for the expected return for the portfolio [$E(R_{port})$] can be generalized as follows:

$$E(R_{port}) = \sum_{i=1}^{n} W_i R_i$$

where:

W_i = the percent of the portfolio in asset i

R_i = the expected rate of return for asset i

Variance (Standard Deviation) of Returns for an Individual Investment

As noted, we will be using the variance, or standard deviation, of returns as the measure of risk. (Recall that standard deviation is the square root of variance.) Therefore, at this point we will demonstrate how to compute the standard deviation of returns for an individual investment. After discussing some other statistical concepts, we will consider the standard deviation for a portfolio of investments.

Variance, or standard deviation, measures the variation of possible rates of return (R_i) from the expected rate of return [$E(R_i)$] as follows:

$$\text{Variance } (\sigma^2) = \sum_{i=1}^{n} [R_i - E(R_i)]^2 P_i$$

where:

P_i = probability of the possible rate of return, R_i

$$\text{Standard deviation } (\sigma) = \sqrt{\sum_{i=1}^{n} [R_i - E(R_i)]^2 P_i}$$

Table 20.3 shows how to compute the variance and standard deviation of returns for the individual investment in Table 20.1.

Variance (Standard Deviation) of Returns for the Portfolio

You need to understand two basic statistical concepts, covariance and correlation, before we discuss the formula for the variance of the rate of return for a portfolio.

Covariance of Returns   In this subsection we discuss the covariance of returns measures, the formula for computing it, and a computational example. **Covariance** is a measure of the degree to which two variables move together over time. Portfolio analysis usually focuses on the covariance of rates of return rather than prices or some other variable.[4] A positive covariance means that the rates of return for two investments tend to move in the same direction at the same time. A negative covariance indicates that their

---

[4]Returns, of course, can be measured in a variety of ways to suit various types of assets. Recall that in Chapter 1 we defined returns (R_i) as:

$$R_i = \frac{EV - BV + CF}{BV}$$

where EV is ending value, BV is beginning value, and CF is the cash flow during the period.

Table 20.3   *Computation of the Variance for an Individual Risky Asset*

Potential Return (R_i)	Expected Return $E(R_i)$	$R_i - E(R_i)$	$[R_i - E(R_i)]^2$	P_i	$[R_i - E(R_i)^2 P_i]$
0.08	0.11	−0.03	0.0009	0.25	0.000225
0.10	0.11	−0.01	0.0001	0.25	0.000025
0.12	0.11	0.01	0.0001	0.25	0.000025
0.14	0.11	0.03	0.0009	0.25	0.000225
					0.000500

Variance $(\sigma^2) = 0.00050$
Standard Deviation $(\sigma) = 0.02236$

Table 20.4   *Computation of Monthly Rates of Return*

Date	Avon Closing Price	Dividend	Rate of Return (%)	IBM Closing Price	Dividend	Rate of Return (%)
12/88	19.500			121.875		
1/89	22.125		13.46	130.625		7.18
2/89	24.000		8.47	121.500		−6.99
3/89	22.875	0.25	−3.65	109.125	1.10	−9.28
4/89	28.625		25.14	114.000		4.47
5/89	35.375		23.58	109.625		−3.84
6/89	35.875	0.25	2.12	111.875	1.21	3.16
7/89	35.750		−0.35	115.000		2.79
8/89	36.500		2.10	117.125		1.85
9/89	31.375	0.25	−13.36	109.250	1.21	−5.69
10/89	27.500		−12.35	100.250		−8.24
11/89	36.125		31.36	97.625		−2.62
12/89	36.875	0.25	2.77	94.125	1.21	−2.35
			$E(R_{Avon}) = 6.61$			$E(R_{IBM}) = -1.63$

rates of return tend to move in different directions over a period of time. The magnitude of the covariance depends upon the variances of the individual returns and the relationship between them.

Table 20.4 lists the monthly closing prices and dividends for Avon and IBM stock. From these data, you can compute monthly rates of return for these two stocks during 1989. Figures 20.1 and 20.2 show time-series plots of these monthly rates of return. While the rates of return for the two stocks moved together during some months, in other months they moved in opposite directions. The covariance statistic provides an absolute measure of how the rates of return for the two stocks moved together over time.

Figure 20.1   *Time Series of Returns for Avon, 1989*

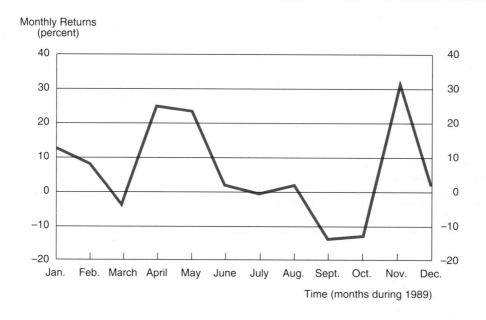

Figure 20.2   *Time Series of Returns for IBM, 1989*

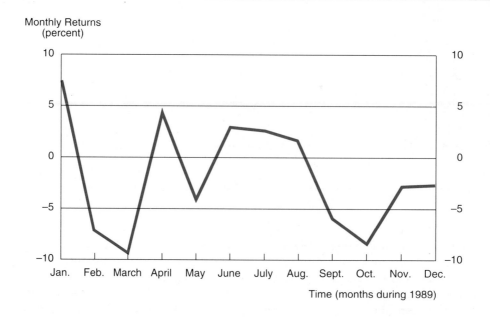

Table 20.5   *Computation of Covariance of Returns for Avon and IBM: 1989*

Date	Monthly Return (%) Avon (R)	IBM (R)	Avon R − E(R)	IBM R − E(R)	Avon IBM [R − E(R)] × [R − E(R)]
1/89	13.46	7.18	6.85	8.81	60.367
2/89	8.47	− 6.99	1.87	− 5.36	− 9.995
3/89	− 3.65	− 9.28	− 10.25	− 7.65	78.451
4/89	25.14	4.47	18.53	6.10	112.959
5/89	23.58	− 3.84	16.97	− 2.21	− 37.482
6/89	2.12	3.16	− 4.49	4.79	− 21.479
7/89	− 0.35	2.79	− 6.96	4.42	− 30.768
8/89	2.10	1.85	− 4.51	3.48	− 15.684
9/89	− 13.36	− 5.69	− 19.96	− 4.06	81.081
10/89	− 12.35	− 8.24	− 18.96	− 6.61	125.295
11/89	31.36	− 2.62	24.76	− 0.99	− 24.486
12/89	2.77	− 2.35	− 3.84	− 0.72	2.751
	$E(R_{Avon}) = 6.61$	$E(R_{IBM}) = -1.63$			Sum = 321.009

$$\text{Cov} = \tfrac{1}{12} \times 321.009 = 26.75$$

For two assets, i and j, the covariance of rates of return is defined as:

$$\text{Cov}_{ij} = E\{[R_i - E(R_i)][R_j - E(R_j)]\}$$

When we apply this formula to the monthly rates of return for Avon and IBM during 1989, we get:

$$\frac{1}{12}\sum_{i=1}^{12}[R_i - E(R_i)][R_j - E(R_j)]$$

If the rates of return for the stocks are either both above or both below their mean rates of return during a given period, the product of these deviations from the mean is positive. If this happens consistently, the covariance of returns between these two stocks will be a large positive value. If, however, the rate of return for one of the securities is above its mean return while the rate of return on the other security is below its mean return, the product of the two deviations will be negative. If this contrary movement happens consistently, the covariance measure between the two rate of return series will be a large negative value.

As an example, Table 20.5 shows monthly rates of return during 1989 for Avon and IBM, as computed in Table 20.4. One might expect the returns for the two stocks to have reasonably low covariance because the firms' products differ so much.

To find the expected returns [E(R)], we take the arithmetic mean of the monthly returns:

$$E(R_i) = 1/12 \sum_{i=1}^{12} R_{it}$$

and

$$E(R_j) = 1/12 \sum_{i=1}^{12} R_{jt}$$

All figures except those in the last column were rounded to the nearest hundredth of 1 percent. Table 20.4 gives average monthly returns of 6.61 percent on Avon and −1.63 percent on IBM. Using the results of the last column in Table 20.5, we can derive the covariance between these two stocks as follows:

$$\text{Cov}_{ij} = \frac{1}{12} \times 321.009$$
$$= 26.75$$

Interpretation of such a number is difficult; does 26.75 indicate a high or low covariance? We know the relationship between the two stocks is generally posi-

Figure 20.3 *Scatter Plot of Monthly Returns for IBM and Avon, 1989*

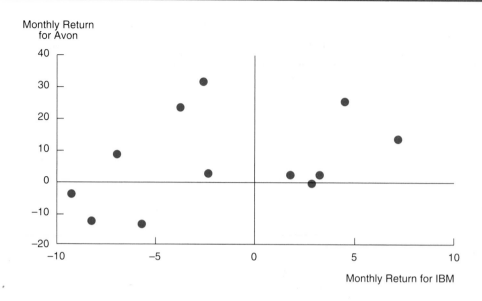

Correlation coefficient A standardized measure of the relationship between two series that ranges from −1.00 to +1.00.

---

tive, but it is not possible to be more specific. The scatter diagram in Figure 20.3 plots paired values of R_{it} and R_{jt} against each other to demonstrate the linear nature and strength of the relationship. It shows several instances during 1989 when IBM experienced negative returns while Avon had positive rates of return.

Correlation Coefficient Covariance is affected by the variability of the returns on the two individual stocks. The value of 26.75 in our example might indicate a weak positive relationship if the two individual series were very volatile, but would indicate a strong positive relationship if they were very stable. To evaluate the relative strength of the relationship, you want to standardize this covariance measure, taking into consideration the variability of the individual sets of two returns, as follows:

$$r_{ij} = \frac{\text{Cov}_{ij}}{\sigma_i \sigma_j}$$

where:

r_{ij} = the correlation coefficient of returns

σ_i = the standard deviation of R_{it}

σ_j = the standard deviation of R_{jt}

Standardizing the covariance by the individual standard deviations yields the **correlation coefficient** (r_{ij}) which can vary only in the range −1 to +1. A value of +1 would indicate a perfect positive linear relationship between R_i and R_j, meaning that the returns for the two stocks move together in a completely linear manner. A value of −1 would indicate a completely negative linear relationship between the two return series so that when the rate of return for one stock was above its mean, the return for the other stock would be below its mean by the comparable amount.

To calculate this standardized measure of the relationship, you need to compute the standard deviation for the two individual returns. We already have the values for $R_{it} − E(R_i)$ and $R_{jt} − E(R_j)$ in Table 20.5. We can square each of these values and sum the results as shown in Table 20.6 to calculate the variance of each return:

Table 20.6 **Computation of Standard Deviation of Returns for Avon and IBM**

Date	Avon		IBM	
	$R - E(R)$	$[R - E(R)]^2$	$R - E(R)$	$[R - E(R)]^2$
1/89	6.85	46.96	8.81	77.59
2/89	1.87	3.48	−5.36	28.69
3/89	−10.25	105.15	−7.65	58.53
4/89	18.53	343.29	6.10	37.17
5/89	16.97	288.06	−2.21	4.88
6/89	−4.49	20.15	4.79	22.90
7/89	−6.96	48.40	4.42	19.56
8/89	−4.51	20.35	3.48	12.09
9/89	−19.96	398.59	−4.06	16.49
10/89	−18.96	359.45	−6.61	43.67
11/89	24.76	612.82	−0.99	0.98
12/89	−3.84	14.75	−0.72	0.51
Sums		2,261.44		323.07

$$\sigma^2_{Avon} = \frac{2261.44}{12} = 188.45 \qquad \sigma^2_{IBM} = \frac{323.07}{12} = 26.92$$

$$\sigma_{Avon} = \sqrt{188.45} = 13.73 \qquad \sigma_{IBM} = \sqrt{26.92} = 5.19$$

$$\sigma_i^2 = \frac{1}{12}(2,261.44) = 188.45$$

and

$$\sigma_j^2 = \frac{1}{12}(323.07) = 26.92$$

The standard deviation for each series is the square root of the variance for each, as follows:

$$\sigma_i = \sqrt{188.45} = 13.73$$
$$\sigma_j = \sqrt{26.92} = 5.19$$

Based upon the covariance between the returns on Avon and IBM stock and their individual standard deviations, we can calculate the correlation coefficient between their returns:

$$r_{ij} = \frac{Cov_{ij}}{\sigma_i\sigma_j} = \frac{26.75}{(13.73)(5.19)} = 0.38$$

As noted, a correlation of +1.0 would indicate perfect positive correlation and a value of −1.0 would mean that the returns moved in completely opposite direc-

tions. A value of zero would mean that the returns had no linear relationship, that is, they were uncorrelated statistically. That does not mean that they are independent.

The value of $r_{ij} = 0.38$ is significant, but not very high. This is not unusual for stocks in diverse industries. Correlations between stocks within some industries approach 0.85.

Portfolio Standard Deviation Formula Now that we have discussed the concepts of covariance and correlation, we can consider the formula for computing the standard deviation of returns on a *portfolio* of assets, our measure of risk for portfolio management. As noted, Harry Markowitz derived the formula for computing the standard deviation of a portfolio of assets.[5]

Table 20.2 showed that the expected rate of return of the portfolio was the weighted average of the ex-

[5]Markowitz, "Portfolio Selection," pp. 80–85.

pected returns for the individual assets in the portfolio with weights that reflected the assets' values as percentages of value of the portfolio. Under such conditions, we can easily see the impact on the portfolio's expected return of adding or deleting an asset.

One might assume that it is possible to derive the standard deviation of the portfolio in the same manner, that is, by computing the weighted average of the standard deviations for the individual assets. This would be a mistake. Markowitz derived the general formula for the standard deviation of a portfolio as follows:[6]

$$\sigma_{port} = \sqrt{\sum_{i=1}^{N} W_i^2 \sigma_i^2 + \sum_{i=1}^{N}\sum_{j=1}^{N} W_i W_j Cov_{ij}}$$
$$\scriptstyle i \neq j$$

where:

σ_{port} = the standard deviation of the portfolio

W_i = the weights of the individual assets in the portfolio, where weights are determined by the proportion of value in the portfolio

σ_i^2 = the variance of asset i

Cov_{ij} = the covariance between the returns for assets i and j

Stated in words, this formula indicates that the standard deviation for a portfolio of assets is a function of the weighted average of the individual variances with the weights squared, *plus* the weighted covariances between all the assets in the portfolio. The standard deviation for a portfolio of investments encompasses not only the variances of the individual investments, but *also* the covariances between pairs of individual investments in the portfolio.

Further, it can be shown that, in a portfolio with a large number of securities, this formula reduces to the sum of the weighted covariances. This means that the important factor to consider when adding an investment to a portfolio with a number of other investments is not the investment's own variance, but its average covariance with all the other investments in the portfolio. In the following examples, we will consider the simple case of a two-asset portfolio. We do these relatively simple calculations with two assets to demonstrate the impact of different covariances on the total risk (standard deviation) of the portfolio.

[6]For the detailed derivation of this formula, see Markowitz, *Portfolio Selection—Efficient Diversification*, Chapter 4.

Demonstration of the Portfolio Standard Deviation Calculation

The assumptions that underlie the Markowitz model allow us to describe any asset or portfolio of assets by two characteristics: the expected rate of return and the expected standard deviation of returns. Therefore, the following demonstrations can be applied to two individual assets with the indicated return–standard deviation characteristics and correlation coefficients, or to two portfolios of assets with the same indicated characteristics and correlation coefficients.

Equal Risk and Return—Changing Correlations
Consider first a case in which both assets have the same expected return and expected standard deviation of return. As an example, let us assume:

$$E(R_1) = 0.20$$
$$E(\sigma_1) = 0.10$$
$$E(R_2) = 0.20$$
$$E(\sigma_2) = 0.10$$

To show the effects of different covariances, assume different levels of correlation between the two assets. Consider the following examples where the two assets have equal weights in the portfolio ($W_1 = 0.50$; $W_2 = 0.50$). The only value that changes in each example is the correlation coefficient between the returns for the two assets.

Recall that

$$Cov_{ij} = r_{ij}\sigma_i\sigma_j$$

Consider the following correlation coefficients and the covariances they yield. (The covariances will equal $r_{1,2}(0.10)(0.10)$, because both standard deviations are 0.10.)

a. $r_{1,2} = 1.00$: $Cov_{1,2} = (1.00)(0.10)(0.10) = 0.01$
b. $r_{1,2} = 0.50$: $Cov_{1,2} = 0.005$
c. $r_{1,2} = 0.00$: $Cov_{1,2} = 0.000$
d. $r_{1,2} = -0.50$: $Cov_{1,2} = -0.005$
e. $r_{1,2} = -1.00$: $Cov_{1,2} = -0.01$.

Now let us see what happens to the standard deviation of the portfolio under these five conditions. Recall that:

$$\sigma_{port} = \sqrt{\sum_{i=1}^{N} W_i^2 \sigma_i^2 + \sum_{i=1}^{N}\sum_{j=1}^{N} W_i W_j Cov_{ij}}$$
$$\scriptstyle i \neq j$$

When this general formula is applied to a two-asset portfolio, it is:

$$\sigma_{port} = \sqrt{W_1^2\sigma_1^2 + W_2^2\sigma_2^2 + 2W_1W_2r_{1,2}\sigma_1\sigma_2}$$

or

$$\sigma_{port} = \sqrt{W_1^2\sigma_1^2 + W_2^2\sigma_2^2 + 2W_1W_2Cov_{1,2}}$$

Thus, in Case a:

$$
\begin{aligned}
\sigma_{port\ (a)} &= \sqrt{(0.5)^2(0.10)^2 + (0.5)^2(0.10)^2 + 2(0.5)(0.5)(0.01)} \\
&= \sqrt{(0.25)(0.01) + (0.25)(0.01) + 2(0.25)(0.01)} \\
&= \sqrt{0.01} \\
&= 0.10
\end{aligned}
$$

In this special case where the returns for the two assets are perfectly positively correlated, the standard deviation for the portfolio is in fact the weighted average of the individual standard deviations. This shows that we get no real benefit from combining two assets that are perfectly correlated; they are like one asset because their returns move together.

Now consider Case b, where $r_{1,2}$ equals 0.50.

$$
\begin{aligned}
\sigma_{port\ (b)} &= \sqrt{(0.5)^2(0.10)^2 + (0.5)^2(0.10)^2 + 2(0.5)(0.5)(0.005)} \\
&= \sqrt{(0.0025) + (0.0025) + (0.50)(0.005)} \\
&= \sqrt{0.0075} \\
&= 0.0866
\end{aligned}
$$

Only one term changed from Case a. The last term, $Cov_{1,2}$, changed from 0.01 to 0.005. The ultimate result was that the standard deviation of the portfolio declined by about 13 percent, from 0.10 to 0.0866. Note that the expected return did not change; it remains the weighted average of the individual expected returns, or 0.20 in both cases.

You should be able to confirm through your own calculations that the standard deviations for Cases c and d are 0.0707 and 0.05, respectively. The final case, where the correlation between the two assets is -1.00 indicates the ultimate benefits of diversification.

$$
\begin{aligned}
\sigma_{port\ (e)} &= \sqrt{(0.5)^2(0.10)^2 + (0.5)^2(0.10)^2 + 2(0.5)(0.5)(-0.01)} \\
&= \sqrt{(0.0050) + (-0.0050)} \\
&= \sqrt{0} \\
&= 0
\end{aligned}
$$

Here, the covariance term exactly offsets the individual variance terms, leaving an overall standard deviation for the portfolio of zero. This would be a risk-free portfolio.

Figure 20.4 illustrates a graph of such a pattern. Perfect negative correlation gives a mean combined return for the two securities over time equal to the mean for each of them, so returns for the portfolio show no variability. Any return above or below the

Figure 20.4   *Time Patterns of Returns for Two Assets with Perfect Negative Correlation*

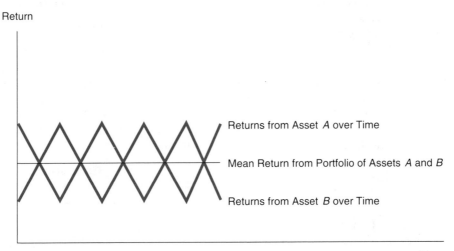

Figure 20.5 *Risk–Return Plot for Portfolios with Equal Returns and Standard Deviations but Different Correlations*

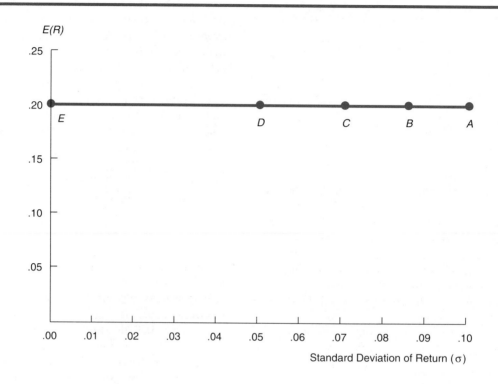

mean for each asset is completely offset by the return for the other asset, leaving no variability in total returns, that is no risk, for the portfolio. This combination of two assets that are completely negatively correlated provides the maximum benefits of diversification—it completely eliminates risk.

The graph in Figure 20.5 shows the differences in the risk–return postures for these five cases. As noted, the only impact of the change in correlation is the change in the standard deviation of this two-asset portfolio. Combining assets that are not perfectly correlated does not affect the expected return of the portfolio, but it does reduce the risk of the portfolio (as measured by its standard deviation). When we eventually reach the ultimate combination of perfect negative correlation, risk is eliminated.

Combining Stocks with Different Returns and Risk Levels The previous discussion indicated what happens when only the correlation coefficient (covariance) differs between the assets. We now move on to consider two assets (or portfolios) with different expected rates of return and individual standard deviations. We will show what happens when we vary the correlations between them. We will assume two assets with the following characteristics:

Stock	$E(R_i)$	W_i	σ_i^2	σ_i
1	0.10	0.50	0.0049	0.07
2	0.20	0.50	0.0100	0.10

The previous set of correlation coefficients give a different set of covariances because the standard deviations are different.

Case	Correlation Coefficient	Covariance $(r_{ij}\sigma_i\sigma_j)$
a	+1.00	+0.0070
b	+0.50	+0.0035
c	0.00	0.0000
d	−0.50	−0.0035
e	−1.00	−0.0070

Figure 20.6 *Risk–Return Plot for Portfolios with Different Returns, Standard Deviations, and Correlations*

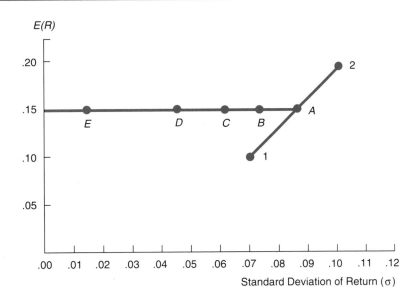

Because we are assuming the same weights in all cases (0.50–0.50), the expected return in every instance will be:

$$E(R_{port}) = 0.5(0.10) + 0.5(0.20)$$

$$= 0.15$$

The standard deviation for Case a will be

$$\sigma_{port\ (a)} = \sqrt{(0.5)^2(0.07)^2 + (0.5)^2(0.10)^2 + 2(0.5)(0.5)(0.0070)}$$

$$= \sqrt{0.007225}$$

$$= 0.085$$

Again, with perfect positive correlation, the standard deviation of the portfolio is the weighted average of the standard deviations of the individual assets:

$$(0.5)(0.07) + (0.5)(0.10) = 0.085$$

As you might envision, changing the weights with perfect positive correlation causes the standard deviation for the portfolio to change in a linear fashion. This is an important point to remember when we discuss the capital asset pricing model (CAPM) in a later chapter.

For Cases b, c, d, and e, the standard deviation for the portfolio would be as follows:[7]

$$\sigma_{port\ (b)} = \sqrt{(0.001225) + (0.0025) + (0.5)(0.0035)}$$

$$= \sqrt{0.005475}$$

$$= 0.07399$$

$$\sigma_{port\ (c)} = \sqrt{(0.001225) + (0.0025) + (0.5)(0.00)}$$

$$= 0.0610$$

$$\sigma_{port\ (d)} = \sqrt{(0.001225) + (0.0025) + (0.5)(-0.0035)}$$

$$= 0.0444$$

$$\sigma_{port\ (e)} = \sqrt{(0.003725) + 0.5(-0.00700)}$$

$$= 0.015$$

Note that perfect negative correlation no longer gives a standard deviation of the portfolio of zero. This is because the different cases have equal weights, but unequal individual standard deviations.

Figure 20.6 shows the results for the two assets and the portfolio of the two assets, assuming the correlation coefficients vary as set forth in Cases a through e. As before, the expected return does not

---

[7]In all of the following examples, we will skip some steps, because you are now aware that only the last term changes. We encourage you to work out the intervening steps to ensure that you understand the computation.

Efficient frontier The curve that defines the set of portfolios with the maximum rate of return for a given level of risk, or the minimum risk for a given rate of return.

change because the proportions remain constant at 0.50–0.50, so all the portfolios lie along the horizontal line at the return, R = 0.15.

Constant Correlation with Changing Weights If we changed the weights of the two assets while holding the correlation coefficient constant, the graph of the results would trace an ellipse starting at Stock 2, going through the 0.50–0.50 point, and ending at Stock 1. We can demonstrate this with Case c, in which the correlation coefficient of zero eases the computation.

We change the weights as follows:

Case	W_1	W_2	$E(R_i)$
f	0.20	0.80	0.18
g	0.40	0.60	0.16
h	0.50	0.50	0.15
i	0.60	0.40	0.14
j	0.80	0.20	0.12

In Cases f, g, i, and j, the standard deviations would be:

$$\sigma_{\text{port (f)}} = \sqrt{(0.20)^2(0.07)^2 + (0.80)^2(0.10)^2 + 2(0.20)(0.80)(0.00)}$$
$$= \sqrt{(0.04)(0.0049) + (0.64)(0.01) + (0)}$$
$$= \sqrt{0.006596}$$
$$= 0.0812$$

$$\sigma_{\text{port (g)}} = \sqrt{(0.40)^2(0.07)^2 + (0.60)^2(0.10)^2 + 2(0.40)(0.60)(0.00)}$$
$$= \sqrt{0.004384}$$
$$= 0.0662$$

$$\sigma_{\text{port (i)}} = \sqrt{(0.60)^2(0.07)^2 + (0.40)^2(0.10)^2 + 2(0.60)(0.40)(0.00)}$$
$$= \sqrt{0.003364}$$
$$= 0.0580$$

$$\sigma_{\text{port (j)}} = \sqrt{(0.80)^2(0.07)^2 + (0.20)^2(0.10)^2 + 2(0.80)(0.20)(0.00)}$$
$$= \sqrt{0.003536}$$
$$= 0.0595$$

We already know the standard deviation (σ) for Case h.[8] These values for alternative weights with

constant correlations would yield the following risk–return combinations:

Case	W_1	W_2	$E(R_i)$	$E(\sigma_{\text{port}})$
f	0.20	0.80	0.18	0.0812
g	0.40	0.60	0.16	0.0662
h	0.50	0.50	0.15	0.0610
i	0.60	0.40	0.14	0.0580
j	0.80	0.20	0.12	0.0595

A graph of these combinations appears in Figure 20.7. You could derive a more complete curve by simply varying the weights in smaller increments.

As noted, the curvature in the graph will depend upon the correlation between the two assets or portfolios. With $r_{ij} + 1.00$, the combinations would lie along a straight line between the two assets. With r_{ij} equal to -1.00, the graph would look like two straight lines touching at the vertical line at a point indicating some combination. Some specific set of weights would give a portfolio with zero risk.

The Efficient Frontier

If we derived curves for all possible weights for a number of two-asset combinations, we would have a graph like that in Figure 20.8. The envelope curve that contains the best of all these possible combinations is the **efficient frontier.** Specifically, the efficient frontier represents the set of portfolios with the maximum rate of return for every given level of risk, or the minimum risk for every level of return.

An example of such a frontier is shown in Figure 20.9. Every portfolio that lies on the efficient frontier has either a higher rate of return for equal risk or lower risk for an equal rate of return than portfolios that lie beneath the frontier. Thus, we would say that Portfolio A *dominates* Portfolio C because it has an equal rate of return, but substantially less risk. Similarly, Portfolio B dominates Portfolio C because it has equal risk, but a higher expected rate of return. Because of the benefits of diversification among imperfectly correlated assets, we would expect the efficient frontier to reflect risk–return combinations for portfolios of investments rather than individual securities.

---

[8]Again, we encourage you to fill in the steps we skipped in the computations.

Figure 20.7   *Portfolio Risk–Return Plot for Different Weights When $r_{ij} = 0.00$*

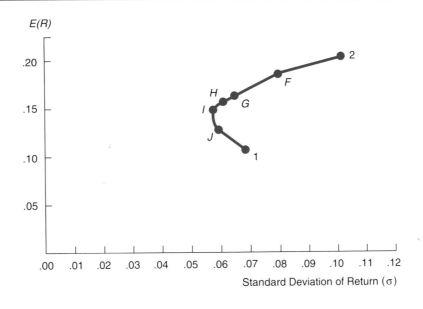

Figure 20.8   *Numerous Portfolio Combinations of Available Assets*

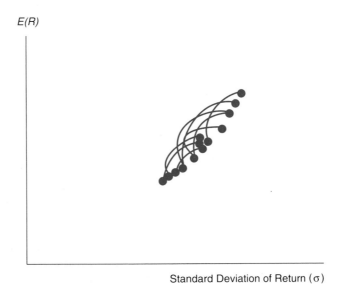

Figure 20.9 *Efficient Frontier for Alternative Portfolios*

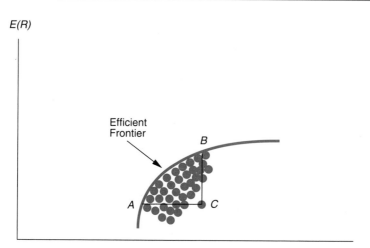

> **Optimal portfolio** The efficient portfolio with the highest utility for a given investor, found by the point of tangency between the efficient frontier and the investor's utility function.

Two possible exceptions arise at the end points, which represent the asset with the highest return and that with the lowest risk.

As an investor, you target a point along the efficient frontier based upon your utility function and your attitude toward risk. No portfolio on the efficient frontier can dominate any other portfolio on the efficient frontier. All of these portfolios have different return and risk measures, with expected rates of return that increase with higher risk.

The Efficient Frontier and Investor Utility

As Figure 20.9 shows, the shape of the typical efficient frontier for risky assets requires that you tolerate more and more risk to achieve higher returns. To evaluate this shape, we calculate the slope of the efficient frontier, as follows:

$$\frac{\Delta E(R_{port})}{\Delta E(\sigma_{port})}$$

The curve in Figure 20.9 shows that this slope decreases steadily as you move upward. This implies that adding equal increments of risk as you move up the efficient frontier gives you diminishing increments of expected return.

An individual investor's utility curves specify the trade-offs he or she is willing to make between expected return and risk. In conjunction with the efficient frontier, these utility curves determine which particular efficient portfolio best suits the individual investor. Two investors will choose the same portfolio from the efficient set only if their utility curves are identical.

Figure 20.10 shows two sets of utility curves along with an efficient frontier of investments. The curves labeled U_1 through U_3 would suit a very risk-averse investor (with $U_3 > U_2 > U_1$). These utility curves are quite steep, indicating that the investor will not tolerate much additional risk to obtain additional returns. The investor is equally disposed toward any $E(R)$, $E(\sigma)$ combination along a specific utility curve such as U_1.

The curves labeled U_1' through U_3' ($U_3' > U_2' > U_1'$) characterize a less risk-averse investor. Such an investor is willing to tolerate a bit more risk to get a higher expected return.

The **optimal portfolio** is the efficient portfolio that has the highest utility for a given investor. It lies at the point of tangency between the efficient frontier

Figure 20.10 *Optimal Risky Portfolio*

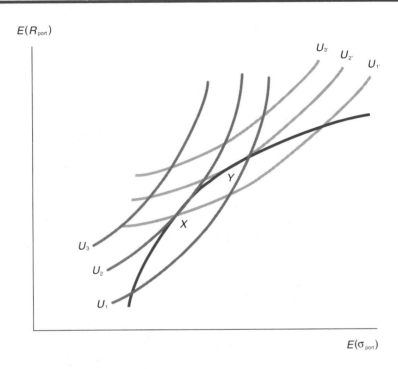

and the curve with the highest possible utility. A conservative investor's highest utility would lie at point X in Figure 20.10 where the curve U_2 just touches the efficient frontier. A less risk-averse investor's highest utility occurs at point Y, which represents a portfolio with higher expected returns and higher risk than the portfolio at X.

Summary

■ The basic Markowitz portfolio model derived the expected rate of return for a portfolio of assets and a measure of expected risk, which is the standard deviation of the expected rate of return. Markowitz showed that the expected rate of return of a portfolio is the weighted average of the expected returns for the individual investments in the portfolio. The standard deviation of a portfolio is a function not only of the standard deviations for the individual investments, but also of the covariance between the rates of return for all the pairs of assets in the portfolio. In a large portfolio, these covariances are important.

■ Different weights, or amounts of a portfolio held in various assets, yield a curve of potential combinations. Correlation coefficients critically affect selection of investments because it was demonstrated that you can maintain a rate of return while reducing the risk level of your portfolio by combining assets or portfolios with low positive or negative correlations.

■ Among numerous assets and a multitude of combination curves, the efficient frontier is the envelope curve that encompasses all of the best combinations. It defines the set of portfolios that has the highest expected return for each given level of risk, or the minimum risk for each given level of return. From this set of dominant portfolios, you select the one that lies at the point of tangency between the efficient frontier and your highest utility curve. Since risk–return utility functions differ, your point of tangency, and therefore your portfolio choice, will probably differ from those of other investors.

■ At this point, we understand that an optimum portfolio is a combination of investments, each with desirable risk–return characteristics that also fit together based upon their correlations. This deeper understanding of portfolio theory could lead you to reflect back upon our earlier discussion of global investing. Since many foreign stock and bond investments provide superior rates of return compared to U.S. securities *along with* very low correlations with portfolios of U.S. stocks and bonds, it means that including these foreign securities will help you to reduce the overall risk of your portfolio while possibly increasing your rate of return.

Questions

1. Why do most investors hold diversified portfolios?
2. What is covariance, and why is it important in portfolio theory?
3. Why do returns on most assets of the same type show positive covariances with each other? Would you expect positive covariances of returns between different types of assets, such as Treasury bills, General Electric common stock, and commercial real estate? Why or why not?
4. What is the relationship between covariance and the correlation coefficient? Why is the correlation coefficient considered more useful?
5. Explain the shape of the efficient frontier.
6. Draw a properly labeled graph of the Markowitz efficient frontier. Describe the efficient frontier in exact terms. Discuss the concept of dominant portfolios and show an example of one on your efficient frontier graph.
7. Assume you want to run a computer program to derive the efficient frontier for your feasible set of stocks. What information must you input to the program?
8. Why are investors' utility curves important in portfolio theory?
9. Explain how a given investor chooses an optimal portfolio. Will this choice always be a diversified portfolio, or could it be a single asset? Explain your answer.
10. Assume that you and a business associate develop an efficient frontier for a set of investments. Why might you select different portfolios on the frontier?
11. Draw a hypothetical graph of an efficient frontier of U.S. common stocks. On the same graph, draw an efficient frontier assuming the inclusion of U.S. bonds, as well. Finally, on the same graph draw an efficient frontier that includes U.S. common stocks, U.S. bonds, and stocks and bonds

from around the world. Discuss the changes in these frontiers.

Problems

1. Considering the world economic outlook for the coming year and estimates of sales and earnings for the pharmaceutical industry, you expect the rate of return for Abbott Labs common stock to fall between −20 percent and +40 percent with the following range of probabilities:

Probability	Rate of Return
0.10	−0.20
0.15	−0.05
0.20	0.10
0.25	0.15
0.20	0.20
0.10	0.40

Compute the expected rate of return $[E(R_i)]$ for Abbott Labs.

2. Given the following market values of stocks in your portfolio and their expected rates of return, what is the expected rate of return for your common stock portfolio?

Stock	Market Value	$E(R_i)$
Phillips Petroleum	$15,000	0.14
Caterpillar	17,000	−0.04
International Paper	32,000	0.18
Hewlett-Packard	23,000	0.16
Dow Chemical	7,000	0.05

3. The following table gives the monthly rates of return for Coca-Cola and Time-Warner during a 6-month period.

Month	Coca-Cola	Time-Warner
1	0.04	0.07
2	0.03	−0.02
3	−0.07	−0.10
4	0.12	0.15
5	−0.02	−0.06
6	0.05	0.02

Compute the following:

a. Expected monthly rate of return $[E(R_i)]$ for each stock

b. Standard deviation for each stock

c. Covariance between the rates of return

d. Correlation coefficient of rates of return

What level of correlation did you expect? How did your expectations compare to the computed correlation? Would these two stocks offer good chances for diversification? Why or why not?

4. You are considering two assets with the following characteristics:

$E(R_1) = 0.15$
$E(R_2) = 0.20$
$E(\sigma_1) = 0.10$
$E(\sigma_2) = 0.20$
$W_1 = 0.5$
$W_2 = 0.5$

Compute the mean and standard deviation of two portfolios if $r_{1,2} = 0.40$ and -0.60, respectively. Plot the two portfolios on a risk–return graph. Which would you select? Explain your choice.

5. Given the following characteristics for two assets:

$E(R_1) = 0.10$
$E(R_2) = 0.15$
$E(\sigma_1) = 0.03$
$E(\sigma_2) = 0.05$

Calculate the expected returns and expected standard deviations of a portfolio of these assets in which Asset 1 has a weight of 60 percent under the following conditions:

a. $r_{1,2} = 1.00$
b. $r_{1,2} = 0.75$
c. $r_{1,2} = 0.25$
d. $r_{1,2} = 0.00$
e. $r_{1,2} = -0.25$
f. $r_{1,2} = -0.75$
g. $r_{1,2} = -1.00$

6. Given the following characteristics for two assets:

$E(R_1) = 0.12$
$E(R_2) = 0.16$
$E(\sigma_1) = 0.04$
$E(\sigma_2) = 0.06$

Calculate the expected returns and expected standard deviations of a portfolio of these assets assuming a correlation coefficient of 0.70 under the following conditions:

a. $W_1 = 1.00$
b. $W_1 = 0.75$
c. $W_1 = 0.50$
d. $W_1 = 0.25$
e. $W_1 = 0.06$

7. The following table gives monthly percentage price changes for four market indicator series:

Month	DJIA	S&P 400	AMEX	Nikkei
1	0.03	0.02	0.04	0.02
2	0.07	0.06	0.10	−0.02
3	−0.02	−0.01	−0.04	0.03
4	0.01	0.03	0.03	0.02
5	0.05	0.07	0.11	0.01
6	−0.06	−0.04	−0.08	0.03

Compute the following:

a. Expected monthly rate of return for each series

b. Standard deviation for each series

c. Covariances between rates of return for the following series:
DJIA–S&P 400
S&P 400–AMEX
S&P 400–Nikkei
AMEX–Nikkei

d. Correlation coefficients for the same four combinations

Based upon these results, which combination of domestic series would provide the best diversification? Which domestic–foreign combination is best for diversification? What does this imply regarding international diversification?

References

Farrell, James L., Jr. *Guide to Portfolio Management.* New York: McGraw-Hill, 1983.

Hagin, Robert. *Modern Portfolio Theory.* Homewood, Ill.: Dow Jones-Irwin, 1979.

Harrington, Diana R. *Modern Portfolio Theory, the Capital Asset Pricing Model, and Arbitrage Pricing Theory: A User's Guide,* 2d ed. Englewood Cliffs, N.J.: Prentice-Hall, 1987.

Maginn, John L., and Donald L. Tuttle, eds. *Managing Investment Portfolios: A Dynamic Process,* 2d ed. Sponsored by The Institute of Chartered Financial Analysts. Boston: Warren, Gorham and Lamont, 1990.

Markowitz, Harry. "Portfolio Selection." *Journal of Finance* 7, no. 1 (March 1952).

Markowitz, Harry. *Portfolio Selection: Diversification of Investments.* New York: John Wiley & Sons, 1959.

21

Capital Market
Theory

Since capital market theory builds on portfolio theory, this chapter begins where the discussion of the Markowitz efficient frontier ended. We assume that you have examined the set of risky assets and derived the aggregate efficient frontier. Further we assume that you and all other investors want to maximize your utility in terms of risk and return, so you will choose portfolios of risky assets on the efficient frontier at points where your utility maps are tangent to the frontier as shown in Figure 20.10. When you make your investment decisions in this manner, you are referred to as *Markowitz efficient investors*.

Capital market theory extends portfolio theory to develop a model for *pricing all risky assets*. The final product, the capital asset pricing model (CAPM), will allow you to determine the required rate of return for any risky asset.

We begin with the background of capital market theory covering topics such as the underlying assumptions of the theory and the factors that led to its development from the Markowitz portfolio theory. Principal among these factors was the analysis of the effect of assuming the existence of a risk-free asset. This is the subject of the next section.

We will see that assuming a risk-free rate has significant implications for a portfolio's potential return and risk and also its risk–return combinations. This discussion implies a central portfolio of risky assets on the efficient frontier, which we call the *market portfolio*. We discuss this market portfolio in the third section along with its implications for different types of risk.

The fourth section considers which types of risk are relevant to an investor who believes in capital market theory. Having defined a measure of risk, we can consider how you determine your required rate of return on an investment. You can then compare this required rate of return to your estimate of the asset's expected rate of return during your investment horizon to determine whether it is undervalued or overvalued. The section ends with a demonstration of how you calculate the risk measure implied by capital market theory.

The final section discusses an alternative asset pricing model, the arbitrage pricing theory (APT). This model requires fewer assumptions than the CAPM, and contends that the required rate of return for a risky asset is a function of multiple factors. This is in contrast to the CAPM, which is a single-factor model. There is a brief demonstration of how you would determine the required rate of return using this model.

Background for Capital Market Theory

When dealing with any theory in science, economics, or finance, it is necessary to articulate a set of assumptions about how the world should act. From these assumptions, the theoretician can develop a theory that explains specific responses to changes in the environment. In this section, we will consider the main assumptions that underlie development of capital market theory. The second section considers the major assumptions that allowed theoreticians to extend the portfolio model's techniques for combining investments into an optimal portfolio to build a model that yields values for those investments (or other assets).

Assumptions of Capital Market Theory

Because capital market theory builds upon the Markowitz portfolio model, it requires the same assumptions, along with some additional ones:

1. All investors are Markowitz efficient investors who target points on the efficient frontier. The exact location on the efficient frontier, and therefore the specific portfolio selected, will depend upon the individual investor's risk–return utility function.

2. Investors can borrow or lend any amount of money at the risk-free rate of return (RFR). Clearly, it is always possible to lend money at the nominal risk-free rate by buying risk-free securities such as government T-bills. It is not always possible to borrow at this risk-free rate, but we will see that assuming a higher borrowing rate does not change the general results.
3. All investors have homogeneous expectations, that is, they all estimate identical probability distributions for future rates of return. This assumption can be relaxed, as well. As long as differences in expectations are not vast, their effects are minor.
4. All investors have the same 1-period time horizon, such as 1 month, 6 months, or 1 year. The model will be developed for a single hypothetical period, and its results could be affected by a different assumption. A difference would require the investors to derive risk measures that were consistent with their horizons.
5. All investments are infinitely divisible, which means that one can buy or sell fractional shares of any asset or portfolio. This assumption allows us to discuss investment alternatives as continuous curves, but changing it would have little impact on the theory.
6. Buying or selling assets entails no taxes or transaction costs. This is a reasonable assumption in many instances. Neither pension funds nor religious groups have to pay taxes, and the transaction costs for most financial institutions are less than 1 percent on most financial instruments. Again, relaxing this assumption modifies the results, but it does not change the basic thrust.
7. There is no inflation or any change in interest rates, or inflation is fully anticipated. This reasonable initial assumption can be modified.
8. Capital markets are in equilibrium. This means that we begin with all investments properly priced in line with their risk levels.

You may consider some of these assumptions unrealistic and wonder how useful a theory we can derive from them. In this regard, two points are important. First, as mentioned, relaxing many of these assumptions would have only minor impacts on the model without changing its main implications or conclusions. Second, a theory should never be judged on the basis of its assumptions, but rather on how well it explains and helps us predict behavior in the real world. If this theory and the model it implies help us explain the rates of return on a wide variety of risky assets, it is very useful, even if some of its assumptions are unrealistic. This kind of success implies that the questionable assumptions must not be important in the ultimate objective of the model, which is to explain the pricing and rates of return on assets.

Development of Capital Market Theory

The major factor that allowed portfolio theory to become capital market theory is the concept of a risk-free asset. Following the development of the Markowitz portfolio model, several authors considered the implications of assuming the existence of a **risk-free asset,** that is, an asset with zero variance. As we will show, such an asset would have zero correlation with all other risky assets and would yield the risk-free rate of return (RFR). It would lie on the vertical axis of a portfolio graph.

This assumption allows us to derive a generalized theory of capital asset pricing under conditions of uncertainty from the Markowitz portfolio theory. This achievement is generally attributed to William Sharpe, for which he received the Nobel prize, but Lintner and Mossin derived similar theories independently.[1] Consequently, you may see references to the Sharpe-Lintner-Mossin (SLM) capital asset pricing model.

Risk-Free Asset

As noted, the assumption of a risk-free asset in the economy is critical to asset pricing theory. This section explains the meaning of a risk-free asset and then shows the effects on the risk and return measures when this risk-free asset is combined with a portfolio on the Markowitz efficient frontier.

We have defined a **risky asset** as one for which future returns are uncertain and we have measured this uncertainty by the variance or standard deviation of returns. Since the expected rate of return on a risk-free asset is entirely certain, the standard deviation of its returns is zero ($\sigma_{RF} = 0$). The rate of return earned on such an asset should be the risk-free rate of return (RFR), which, as we discussed in Chapter 1, should equal the expected long-run real growth rate of the

[1]William F. Sharpe, "Capital Asset Prices: A Theory of Market Equilibrium under Conditions of Risk," *Journal of Finance* 19, no. 3 (September 1964): 425–442; John Lintner, "Security Prices, Risk and Maximal Gains from Diversification," *Journal of Finance* 20, no. 4 (December 1965): 587–615; and J. Mossin, "Equilibrium in a Capital Asset Market," *Econometrica* 34, no. 4 (October 1966): 768–783.

> **Risk-free asset** An asset with returns that exhibit zero variance.
> **Risky asset** An asset with uncertain future returns.

economy modified somewhat for short-run liquidity. The next subsections show what happens when we introduce this risk-free asset into the risky world of the Markowitz portfolio model.

Covariance with a Risk-Free Asset

Recall that the covariance between two sets of returns is:

$$\text{Cov}_{ij} = \sum_{i=1}^{n} [R_i - E(R_i)][R_j - E(R_j)]/n$$

Because the returns for the risk-free asset are certain, σ_{RF} equals 0, which means R_i equals $E(R_i)$ during all periods. Thus, R_i minus $E(R_i)$ will also equal zero and the product of this expression with any other expression will equal zero. Consequently, the covariance of the risk-free asset with any risky asset or portfolio of risky assets will always equal zero. Similarly, the correlation between any risky asset and the risk-free asset would be zero, since it is equal to:

$$r_{RFi} = \text{Cov}_{RFi}/\sigma_{RF}\,\sigma_i$$

Combining a Risk-Free Asset with a Risky Portfolio

What happens to the average rate of return and the standard deviation when we combine a risk-free asset with a portfolio of risky assets such as those that exist on the Markowitz efficient frontier?

Expected Return Like the expected return for a portfolio of two risky assets, the expected rate of return on a portfolio with a risk-free asset is the weighted average of the two returns:

$$E(R_{port}) = W_{RF}(RFR) + (1 - W_{RF})E(R_i)$$

where:

W_{RF} = the proportion of the portfolio invested in the risk-free asset

$E(R_i)$ = the expected rate of return on risky Portfolio i

Standard Deviation Recall from Chapter 20 that the expected variance for a two-asset portfolio is:

$$E(\sigma_{port}^2) = W_1^2\sigma_1^2 + W_2^2\sigma_2^2 + 2W_1W_2r_{1,2}\sigma_1\sigma_2$$

Substituting the risk-free asset for the first security and the risky asset portfolio for the second, this formula would become:

$$E(\sigma_{port}^2) = W_{RF}^2\sigma_{RF}^2 + (1 - W_{RF})^2\sigma_i^2$$
$$+ 2W_{RF}(1 - W_{RF})r_{RFi}\sigma_{RF}\sigma_i$$

We know that the variance of the risk-free asset is zero, that is, $\sigma_{RF}^2 = 0$. Since the correlation between the risk-free asset and any risky asset is also zero, the factor r_{RFi} in the equation above also equals zero. Therefore, any component of the variance formula that has either of these terms will equal zero. When you make these adjustments, the formula becomes:

$$E(\sigma_{port}^2) = (1 - W_{RF})^2\sigma_i^2$$

The standard deviation is:

$$E(\sigma_{port}) = \sqrt{(1 - W_{RF})^2\sigma_i^2}$$
$$= (1 - W_{RF})\sigma_i$$

Therefore the standard deviation of a portfolio that combines the risk-free asset with risky assets is *the linear proportion of the standard deviation of the risky asset portfolio.*

The Risk–Return Combination Since the expected return and the standard deviation for such a portfolio are linear combinations, a graph of possible portfolio returns and risks looks like a straight line between the two assets. Figure 21.1 shows a graph depicting portfolio possibilities when a risk-free asset is combined with alternative risky portfolios on the Markowitz efficient frontier.

You can attain any point along the straight line RFR–A by investing some portion of your portfolio in the risk-free asset W_{RF} and the remainder $(1 - W_{RF})$ in the risky asset portfolio at point A on the efficient frontier. This set of portfolio possibilities dominates all the risky asset portfolios on the efficient frontier below point A because some portfolio along RFR–A has equal variance with a higher rate of return. Likewise, you can attain any point along line RFR–B by investing in some combination of the risk-free asset and the risky asset portfolio at point B. Again, these

---

Figure 21.1   *Portfolio Possibilities Combining the Risk-Free Asset and Risky Portfolios on the Efficient Frontier*

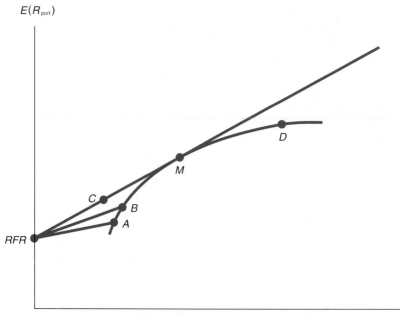

potential combinations dominate all portfolio possibilities on the original efficient frontier below point B (including line RFR–A).

You can draw further lines from the RFR to the efficient frontier at higher and higher points until you reach a line that is tangent to the frontier, which occurs in Figure 21.1 at point M. The set of portfolio possibilities along line RFR–M dominates all portfolios below point M. For example, you could attain a risk and return combination midway between the RFR and point M (point C) by investing one-half of your portfolio in the risk-free asset (that is, lending money at the RFR) and the other half in the risky portfolio at point M.

Risk–Return Possibilities with Leverage An investor may want to attain a higher expected return than is available at point M in exchange for accepting higher risk. One alternative would be to invest in one of the risky asset portfolios on the efficient frontier beyond point M such as the portfolio at point D. A second alternative is to add leverage to the portfolio by *borrowing* money at the risk-free rate and investing the proceeds in the risky asset portfolio at point M. What effect would this have on the return and risk for your portfolio?

If you borrow an amount equal to 50 percent of your original wealth, W_{RF} will not be a positive fraction, but rather a negative 50 percent ($W_{RF} = -0.50$). The effect on the expected return for your portfolio is:

$$E(R_{port}) = -W_{RF}(RFR) + (1 - W_{RF})E(R_m)$$
$$= -0.50(RFR) + [1 - (-0.50)]E(R_m)$$
$$= -0.50(RFR) + 1.50E(R_m)$$

The return will increase in a linear fashion along line RFR–M because the gross return increases by 50 percent, but you must pay interest at the RFR on the money borrowed. As an example, assume that E(RFR) equals 0.06 and $E(R_m)$ equals 0.12. The return on your leveraged portfolio would be:

$$E(R_{port}) = -0.50(0.06) + 1.5(0.12)$$
$$= -0.03 + 0.18$$
$$= 0.15$$

The effect on the standard deviation of the leveraged portfolio is similar.

$$E(\sigma_{port}) = (1 - W_{RF})\sigma_m$$
$$= [1 - (-0.50)]\sigma_m = 1.50\sigma_m$$

> **Capital market line (CML)** The line from the intercept point that represents the risk-free rate tangent to the original efficient frontier; it becomes the new efficient frontier.
> **Market portfolio** The portfolio that includes all risky assets with relative weights equal to their proportional market values.

Both return and risk increase in a linear fashion along the original line RFR–M, and this extension dominates everything below the line on the original efficient frontier. Thus, you have a new efficient frontier: the straight line from the RFR tangent to point M. This line, referred to as the **capital market line (CML)**, is shown in Figure 21.2.

Our discussion of portfolio theory stated that, when two assets are perfectly correlated, the set of portfolio possibilities falls along a straight line. Therefore, because the CML is a straight line, all the portfolios along it are perfectly positively correlated. This positive correlation appeals to our intuition, because all these portfolios combine the risky asset Portfolio M and the risk-free asset. You either invest part of your portfolio in the risk-free asset or you borrow at the risk-free rate and invest these funds in the risky asset portfolio. In either case, all the variability comes from the risky asset portfolio. The only difference between the portfolios on the CML is the magnitude of variability caused by the proportion of the risky asset portfolio in the total portfolio.

The Market Portfolio

Because it lies at the point of tangency, Portfolio M has the highest portfolio possibility line, and everybody will want to invest in it and borrow or lend to be somewhere on the CML. This portfolio must, therefore, include all risky assets. If a risky asset were not in this portfolio in which everyone wants to invest, it would have no demand and therefore no value.

Because the market is in equilibrium, all assets must also be included in this portfolio in proportion to their market values. If, for example, an asset accounts for a higher proportion of the M portfolio than its value justifies, excess demand for this asset will increase its price until its relative market value becomes consistent with its proportion in the portfolio.

This portfolio that includes all risky assets is referred to as the **market portfolio.** It includes not only common stocks, but *all* risky assets, such as non-U.S.

Figure 21.2   ***Derivation of Capital Market Line Assuming Lending or Borrowing at the Risk-Free Rate***

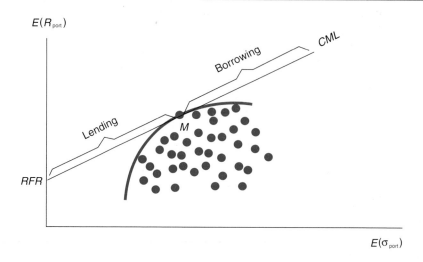

> **Completely diversified portfolio** A portfolio in which all unsystematic risk has been eliminated by diversification.
>
> **Unsystematic risk** Risk that is unique to an asset, derived from its particular characteristics.
>
> **Systematic risk** The variability of returns that is due to macroeconomic factors that affect all risky assets. Because it affects all risky assets, it cannot be eliminated by diversification.

stocks, U.S. and non-U.S. bonds, options, real estate, coins, stamps, art, antiques, and so on. Since the market portfolio contains all risky assets, it is a **completely diversified portfolio,** which means that all the risk unique to individual assets in the portfolio is diversified away. The unique risk of any asset is offset by the unique variability of the other assets in the portfolio.

This risk that is unique to an asset is referred to as **unsystematic risk.** This implies that only **systematic risk,** which is defined as the variability in all risky assets caused by macroeconomic variables, remains in the market portfolio. This systematic risk, measured by the standard deviation of returns on the market portfolio, can change over time with changes in the macroeconomic variables that affect the valuation of all risky assets.[2] Examples of such macroeconomic variables would be variability of growth in the money supply, interest rate volatility, and variability in factors

like industrial production, corporate earnings, and cash flow.

How to Measure Diversification

All portfolios on the CML are perfectly positively correlated, which means that all portfolios on the CML are perfectly correlated with the completely diversified market portfolio since it lies on the CML. This implies a measure of complete diversification.[3] Specifically, a completely diversified portfolio would have a correlation with the market portfolio of + 1.00. This is logical because complete diversification means elimination of unsystematic or unique risk. Once you have eliminated unsystematic risk, only systematic risk is left because it cannot be diversified away. Therefore, a completely diversified portfolio would correlate perfectly with the market portfolio, since it also has only systematic risk.

[2]For an analysis of changes in stock price volatility see Peter S. Spiro, "The Impact of Interest Rate Changes on Stock Price Volatility," *Journal of Portfolio Management* 16, no. 2 (Winter 1990): 63–68; Dennis W. Logue, "Are Stock Markets Becoming Riskier?" *Journal of Portfolio Management* 2, no. 3 (Spring 1976): 13–19; R. R. Officer, "The Variability of the Market Factor of the New York Stock Exchange," *Journal of Business* 46, no. 3 (July 1973): 434–453.

[3]James Lorie, "Diversification: Old and New," *Journal of Portfolio Management* 1, no. 2 (Winter 1975): 25–28.

Figure 21.3 **Number of Stocks in a Portfolio and the Standard Deviation of Portfolio Return**

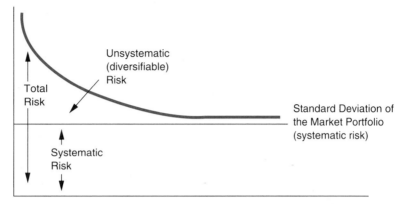

Diversification and the Elimination of Unsystematic Risk

As discussed in Chapter 20, the purpose of diversification is to reduce the standard deviation of the total portfolio. This assumes imperfect correlation among securities.[4] Ideally, as you add securities, the average covariance for the portfolio declines. So how many securities must you include in a completely diversified portfolio? To discover the answer, you must observe what happens as you increase the sample size of the portfolio by adding securities that have some positive correlation. The typical correlation between U.S. securities is about 0.5 to 0.6.

One set of studies examined the average standard deviation for numerous portfolios of randomly selected stocks of different sample sizes.[5] For example, they computed the standard deviation for portfolios of increasing numbers of stocks up to 20. The results indicated quite a large initial impact with the major benefits of diversification achieved rather quickly.

Specifically, about 90 percent of the maximum benefit from diversification was derived from portfolios of 12 to 18 stocks. Figure 21.3 shows a graph of the effect.

A more recent study by Statman compared the benefits of lower risk from diversification to the added transaction costs with more securities. It concluded that a well-diversified stock portfolio must include at least 30 stocks for a borrowing investor and 40 stocks for a lending investor.[6]

By adding stocks that are not perfectly correlated to a portfolio, you can reduce the overall standard deviation of the portfolio, but you *cannot eliminate variability.* The standard deviation of your portfolio will eventually reach the level of the market portfolio, where you will have diversified away all unsystematic risk, but you still have market or systematic risk. You cannot eliminate variability and uncertainty caused by macroeconomic factors that affect all risky assets.

The CML and the Separation Theorem

The CML leads all investors toward the same risky asset portfolio, the M portfolio. Individual investors should differ only in their positions on the CML, which is determined by their risk preferences. In turn,

---

[4]The discussion in Chapter 20 might lead one to conclude that securities with negative correlation would be ideal. While this is true in theory, it is very difficult to find such assets in the real world.

[5]John L. Evans and Stephen H. Archer, "Diversification and the Reduction of Dispersion: An Empirical Analysis," *Journal of Finance* 23, no. 5 (December 1968): 761–767; Thomas M. Tole, "You Can't Diversify without Diversifying," *Journal of Portfolio Management* 8, no. 2 (Winter 1982): 5–11.

[6]Meir Statman, "How Many Stocks Make a Diversified Portfolio?" *Journal of Financial and Quantitative Analysis* 22, no. 3 (September 1987): 353–363.

Figure 21.4 *Choice of Optimal Portfolio Combinations on the CML*

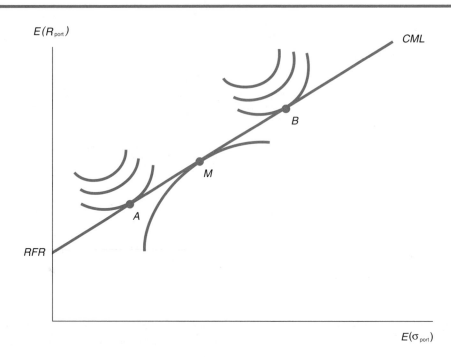

<table>
<tr><td>

Separation theorem The proposition that the investment decision, which involves investing in the market portfolio on the capital market line, is separate from the financing decision, which targets a specific point on the CML based upon the investor's risk preferences.

</td></tr>
</table>

how they get to a point on the CML is based upon their financing decisions.

If you are relatively risk averse, you will lend some part of your portfolio at the RFR by buying some risk-free securities and investing the remainder in the market portfolio. For example, you might invest in the portfolio combination at point A in Figure 21.4. In contrast, if you prefer more risk, you might borrow funds at the RFR and invest everything (all of your capital plus what you borrowed) in the market portfolio, to build the portfolio at point B. This financing decision gives you more risk, but greater returns than the market portfolio. As discussed earlier, because portfolios on the CML dominate other portfolio possibilities, the CML becomes the efficient frontier of portfolios along which investors choose positions.

Tobin called this division of the investment decision from the financing decision the **separation theorem**.[7] To reach the CML efficient frontier, you initially decide to invest in the market portfolio, M. This is your investment decision. Subsequently, based upon your risk preferences, you make a separate financing decision either to borrow or to lend to attain your preferred point on the CML.

A Risk Measure for the CML

In this section we will show that the relevant risk measure for risky assets is their covariance with the market (M) portfolio, which is referred to as their systematic risk. The importance of this covariance is apparent from two points of view.

First, in discussing the Markowitz portfolio, we noted that the relevant risk to consider for a security being added to a portfolio is its average covariance with all other assets in the portfolio. In this chapter

---

[7]James Tobin, "Liquidity Preference as Behavior towards Risk," *Review of Economic Studies* 25, no. 2 (February 1958): 65–85.

we have shown that the only relevant portfolio is the M portfolio. Together, these two findings mean that the only important consideration for any individual risky asset is its average covariance with all the risky assets in the M portfolio, or simply, *its covariance with the market portfolio*. This, then, is the relevant risk measure for an individual risky asset.

Second, because all individual risky assets are a part of the M portfolio, one can describe their rates of return in relation to the returns for the M portfolio using the following linear model:

$$R_{it} = a_i + b_i R_{mt} + \epsilon$$

where:

R_{it} = return for asset i during period t

a_i = constant term for asset i

b_i = slope coefficient for asset i

R_{mt} = return for the M portfolio during period t

ϵ = random error term

The variance of returns for a risky asset could be described as:

$$
\begin{aligned}
\text{Var}(R_{it}) &= \text{Var}(a_i + b_i R_{mt} + \epsilon) \\
&= \text{Var}(a_i) + \text{Var}(b_i R_{mt}) + \text{Var}(\epsilon) \\
&= 0 + \text{Var}(b_i R_{mt}) + \text{Var}(\epsilon)
\end{aligned}
$$

Note that $\text{Var}(b_i R_{mt})$ is the variance of the return for the asset related to the variance of the market return, or the systematic variance or risk. Also, $\text{Var}(\epsilon)$ is the residual variance of return for the individual asset that is not related to the market portfolio. This residual variance is the variability that we have referred to as unsystematic or unique risk or variance because it arises from the unique features of the asset. Therefore:

$$\text{Var}(R_{it}) = \text{Systematic variance} + \text{Unsystematic variance}$$

We know that a completely diversified portfolio such as the market portfolio eliminates all unsystematic variance. Therefore, the unsystematic variance is not relevant to investors because they can and do eliminate it when making an asset part of a market portfolio, and they should not expect to receive added returns for assuming this risk. Only the systematic variance is relevant since it *cannot* be diversified away because it is caused by macroeconomic influences that affect all risky assets.

> **Capital Asset Pricing Model (CAPM)** A theory concerned with deriving the expected or required rates of return on risky assets based upon the assets' systematic risk levels.

The Capital Asset Pricing Model: Expected Return and Risk

Up to this point, we have considered how investors make their portfolio decisions, including the significant effects of a risk-free asset. The existence of this asset resulted in the derivation of a capital market line (CML) that became the relevant efficient frontier. Because all investors want to be on the CML, an asset's covariance with the market portfolio of risky assets emerged as the relevant risk measure.

Now that we understand this relevant measure of risk, we can proceed to use it to determine an appropriate expected rate of return on a risky asset. This step takes us into the **Capital Asset Pricing Model (CAPM),** which is a technique for predicting expected or required rates of return on risky assets. This transition is important because it helps you to value an asset by providing a discount rate for use in dividend valuation models. Alternatively, if you have already estimated the rate of return that you think you will earn on an investment, you can compare it to the required rate of return implied by the CAPM to determine whether the asset is undervalued, overvalued, or properly valued.

In order to accomplish all this, we demonstrate the creation of a security market line that visually represents the relationship between risk and the expected or required rate of return on an asset. The equation of this SML together with estimates for the return on a risk-free asset and the market portfolio, can yield expected or required rates of return for any asset based upon its systematic risk. You compare this required rate of return to your estimate of the investment's estimated rate of return to determine whether it is under- or overvalued. After demonstrating this procedure, we finish the chapter with a demonstration of how to calculate systematic risk for a risky asset.

The Security Market Line

We know that the relevant risk measure for an individual risky asset is its covariance with the market portfolio (Cov_{im}). Therefore, we can draw the risk–return relationship as shown in Figure 21.5 with the systematic covariance variable as the risk measure.

Figure 21.5   **Graph of SML**

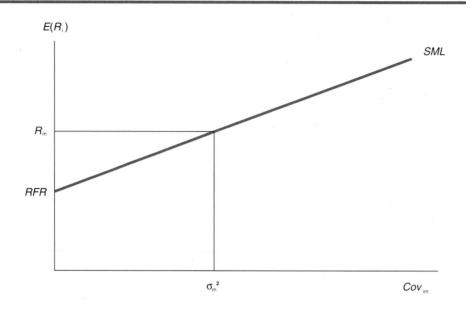

Beta A standardized measure of systematic risk found by an asset's covariance with the market portfolio.

Market risk premium The amount of return above the risk-free rate that investors expect from the market in general as compensation for systematic risk.

The return for the market portfolio (R_m) should be consistent with its own risk, which is the covariance of the market with itself. Since the covariance of any asset with itself is its variance ($Cov_{ii} = \sigma_i^2$), the covariance of the market with itself is the variance of the market rate of return ($Cov_{mm} = \sigma_m^2$). The equation for the risk–return line in Figure 21.5 is:

$$E(R_i) = RFR + \frac{R_m - RFR}{\sigma_m^2}(COV_{im})$$

$$= RFR + \frac{Cov_{im}}{\sigma_m^2}(R_m - RFR)$$

Defining Cov_{im}/σ_m^2 as beta (β_i), this equation can be stated:

$$E(R_i) = RFR + \beta_i(R_m - RFR)$$

Beta can be viewed as a *standardized* measure of systematic risk. Specifically, we already know that the covariance of any asset i with the market portfolio (Cov_{im}) is the relevant risk measure. With beta, it is standardized by relating it to the variance of the market portfolio. As a result, the market portfolio has a beta of 1. Therefore, if the β_i for an asset is above 1.0, the asset has higher systematic risk than the market, which means that it is more volatile than the overall market portfolio.

Given this standardized measure of systematic risk, the SML graph can be expressed as shown in Figure 21.6. This is the same graph as Figure 21.5 except that there is a different measure of risk. Specifically, it replaces the covariance of an asset's returns with the market portfolio as the risk measure with the standardized measure of systematic risk (beta), which is the covariance divided by the variance of the market portfolio.

Determining the Expected Rate of Return for a Risky Asset The equation above and the graph in Figure 21.6 tell us that the expected rate of return for a risky asset is determined by the RFR plus a risk premium for the individual asset, which is determined by its systematic risk (β_i) and the prevailing **market**

Figure 21.6 *Graph of SML with Normalized Systematic Risk*

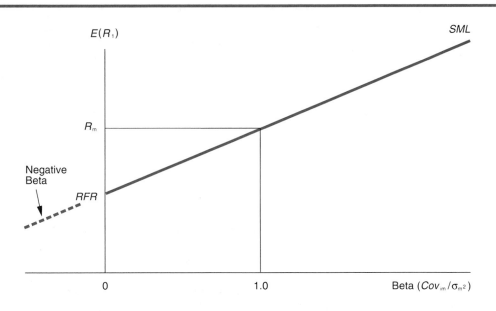

risk premium (R_m − RFR). To demonstrate how you would compute the expected or required rates of return, consider the following example stocks, assuming you have already computed betas:

Stock	Beta
A	0.70
B	1.00
C	1.15
D	1.40
E	−0.30

Assume that we expect the economy's RFR to be 8 percent (0.08) and the return on the market portfolio (R_m) to be 14 percent (0.14). This implies a market risk premium of 6 percent (0.06). With these inputs, the SML equation would yield expected (required) rates of return for these five stocks of:

$$E(R_i) = RFR + \beta_i (R_m - RFR)$$
$$E(R_a) = 0.08 + 0.70 (0.14 - 0.08)$$
$$= 0.122 = 12.2 \text{ percent}$$
$$E(R_b) = 0.08 + 1.00 (0.14 - 0.08)$$
$$= 0.14 = 14 \text{ percent}$$

$$E(R_c) = 0.08 + 1.15 (0.14 - 0.08)$$
$$= 0.149 = 14.9 \text{ percent}$$
$$E(R_d) = 0.08 + 1.40 (0.14 - 0.08)$$
$$= 0.164 = 16.4 \text{ percent}$$
$$E(R_e) = 0.08 + (-0.30) (0.14 - 0.08)$$
$$= 0.08 - 0.018$$
$$= 0.062 = 6.2 \text{ percent}$$

As stated, these are the expected (required) rates of return that these stocks should provide based upon their systematic risks and the prevailing SML.

Stock A has lower risk than the aggregate market, so an investor should not expect (require) its return to be as high as the return on the market portfolio of risky assets. You should expect (require) stock A to return 12.2 percent. Stock B has systematic risk equal to the market's (beta = 1.00), so its required rate of return should likewise be equal to the expected market return (14 percent). Stocks C and D have systematic risk greater than the market's, so they should provide returns consistent with this risk. Finally, stock E has a negative beta (which is quite rare in practice), so its required rate of return, if such a stock could be found, would be below the RFR.

In equilibrium, all assets and all portfolios of assets should plot on the SML. That is, all assets should

Table 21.1 *Price, Dividend, and Rate of Return Estimates*

Stock	Current Price (P_t)	Expected Price (P_{t+1})	Expected Dividend (D_{t+1})	Estimated Future Rate of Return
A	25	27	1.00	12.0%
B	40	42	1.25	8.1
C	33	40	1.00	24.2
D	64	65	2.40	5.3
E	50	55	—	10.0

Estimated rate of return The rate of return an investor anticipates earning from a specific investment over a particular future holding period.

be priced so that their **estimated rates of return**, which are the actual holding period rates of return that you anticipate, are consistent with their levels of systematic risk. Any security with an estimated rate of return plotted above the SML would be considered underpriced, because you expect to earn a rate of return on it that is above its required rate of return based upon its systematic risk. In contrast, assets with estimated rates of return plotted below the SML would be considered overpriced because this position relative to the SML implies that you expect to receive a rate of return on this asset that is below what you should require based upon the asset's systematic risk.

In an efficient market in equilibrium, you would not expect any assets to plot off the SML because, in equilibrium, all stocks are expected to provide holding period returns equal to their required rates of return. A market that is fairly efficient but not completely efficient, may misprice certain assets because not everyone will be aware of all the relevant information for the asset. As we will discuss in Chapter 23 when we deal with efficient markets, a superior investor is one who derives value estimates for assets that are consistently superior to the consensus market evaluations. As a result, such an investor will earn better rates of return than the average investor on a risk-adjusted basis.

Identifying Undervalued and Overvalued Assets
Now that we understand how to compute the rate of return one should expect or require for a specific risky

asset using the SML, we can compare this required rate of return to the asset's estimated rate of return over a specific investment horizon to determine whether it would be an appropriate investment. To make this comparison, you need an independent estimate of the rate of return outlook for the security based upon either fundamental or technical analysis, as discussed in earlier chapters. Let us continue the example for the five assets discussed in the previous section.

Analysts in a major trust department have been following these five stocks. Their extensive fundamental analysis has produced the price and dividend outlooks in Table 21.1. Given these expectations, you can compute the estimated rates of return the analysts would anticipate during this holding period. Table 21.2 summarizes the relationship between the required rate of return for each stock based on its systematic risk as computed earlier and its estimated rate of return based upon its current and future prices and dividend outlook.

Plotting these estimated rates of return and stock betas on the SML we specified earlier gives the graph shown in Figure 21.7. Stock A is almost exactly on the line, so it is properly valued because its estimated rate of return is almost equal to its required rate of return. Stocks B and D are overvalued, because their estimated rates of return during the coming period are not consistent with the risk involved as indicated by their positions below the SML. In contrast, stocks C and E are expected to provide rates of return greater than we would require based upon their systematic risk. Therefore, both stocks plot above the SML, indicating that they are undervalued.

Assuming that you trusted your analysts to forecast estimated returns, you would take no action re-

Table 21.2 *Comparison of Required Rate of Return and Estimated Rate of Return*

Stock	Beta	Required Return $E(R_i)$	Estimated Return	Estimated Return minus $E(R_i)$	Evaluation
A	0.70	12.2	12.0	−0.2	Properly valued
B	1.00	14.0	8.1	−5.9	Overvalued
C	1.15	14.9	24.2	9.3	Undervalued
D	1.40	16.4	5.3	−11.1	Overvalued
E	−0.30	6.2	10.0	3.8	Undervalued

Figure 21.7 *Plot of Estimated Returns on SML Graph*

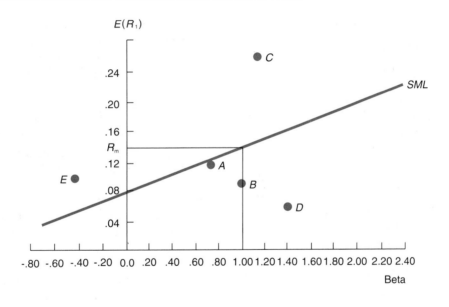

Characteristic line The line that best fits a scatter plot of rates of return for a risky asset and the market portfolio over a past time period.

garding stock A, but you would buy stocks C and E and sell stocks B and D. You might even sell stocks B and D short if you favored such aggressive tactics.

Calculating Systematic Risk: The Characteristic Line

The systematic risk input for an individual asset is derived from a regression model that yields the asset's

characteristic line with the market portfolio. The equation is:

$$R_{it} = \alpha_i + \beta_i R_{mt} + \epsilon$$

where:

R_{it} = the rate of return for asset i during period t

R_{mt} = the rate of return for the market portfolio during period t

α_i = the constant term, or intercept, of the regression, which equals $\overline{R}_i - \beta_i \overline{R}_m$

Figure 21.8   Scatter Plot of Rates of Return

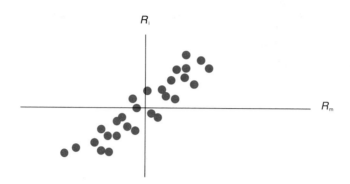

β_i = the slope coefficient for the regression,
        which is equal to Cov_{im}/σ^2_m

ϵ = the random error term

The characteristic line is the line that best fits a scatter plot of rates of return for the individual risky asset and the market portfolio of risky assets over some designated past period, as shown in Figure 21.8.

In practice the number of observations and the time interval vary. Value Line Investment Services derives characteristic lines for common stocks using weekly rates of return for the most recent 5 years (i.e., 260 weekly observations). Merrill Lynch, Pierce, Fenner & Smith uses monthly rates of return for the most recent 5 years (60 monthly observations). In the absence of any theoretically correct time interval of analysis, we must make a trade-off between enough observations to eliminate the impact of random rates of return and a length of time, such as 15 or 20 years, over which the subject company may have changed dramatically. Remember that what you really want is the *expected* systematic risk for the potential investment. In this analysis you are analyzing historical data to help you derive a reasonable estimate.

A couple of studies have considered the impact of the time interval used to compute betas (weekly versus monthly). Statman examined the relationship between Value Line (VL) and Merrill Lynch (ML) betas and found a relatively weak relationship.[8] Reilly and

Wright examined a larger sample and analyzed the differential effects of return computation, market index, and interval, likewise finding a weak relationship between VL and ML betas.[9] They showed that the major cause of the significant differences in beta was the monthly versus weekly intervals.

They also found that the interval effect depended somewhat on the sizes of the firms. The shorter weekly interval gave a larger beta for large firms, and a smaller beta for small firms. For example, from 1975 to 1979 monthly data gave an average beta for the smallest decile of firms of 1.682, but weekly data gave only 1.080. The authors concluded that the time interval over which you compute beta makes a difference, and the impact of the interval increases as the size of the firm declines.

Also, we must decide which indicator series to use as a proxy for the market portfolio. Obviously, no market series tracks all the risky assets in the economy. As a matter of practice, most investigators use the Standard & Poor's 500 Composite Index as a proxy for the market portfolio because the stocks in this index encompass a large proportion of the total market value of U.S. stocks. Also, it is a value-weighted series, which is consistent with the theoretical market series. Still, this series covers only U.S. stocks, most of them listed on the NYSE. The "ideal" market portfolio of risky assets should include U.S. stocks and bonds, non-U.S. stocks and bonds, real estate, coins, stamps, art,

[8]Meir Statman, "Betas Compared: Merrill Lynch vs. Value Line," *Journal of Portfolio Management* 7, no. 2 (Winter 1981): 41–44.

[9]Frank K. Reilly and David J. Wright, "A Comparison of Published Betas," *Journal of Portfolio Management* 14, no. 3 (Spring 1988): 64–69.

Table 21.3	Computation of Covariance between IBM and the S&P 500: 1989

Date	Month-End Price: S&P 500	S&P 500 Return	IBM Return[a]	S&P 500 R − E(R)	IBM R − E(R)	S&P 500 R − E(R) × IBM R − E(R)
12/88	276.51					
1/89	297.47	7.58	7.18	5.45	9.17	49.99
2/89	288.86	− 2.89	− 6.99	− 5.02	− 5.00	25.10
3/89	294.87	2.08	− 10.19	− 0.05	− 8.20	0.37
4/89	309.64	5.01	4.47	2.88	6.45	18.61
5/89	320.52	3.51	− 3.84	1.39	− 1.85	− 2.57
6/89	317.98	− 0.79	2.05	− 2.92	4.04	− 11.78
7/89	346.08	8.84	2.79	6.71	4.78	32.08
8/89	351.45	1.55	1.85	− 0.57	3.83	− 2.20
9/89	349.15	− 0.65	− 6.72	− 2.78	− 4.73	13.16
10/89	340.06	− 2.60	− 8.24	− 4.73	− 6.25	29.57
11/89	345.99	1.74	− 2.62	− 0.38	− 0.63	0.24
12/89	353.40	2.14	− 3.59	0.02	− 1.60	− 0.03
Average		2.13	− 1.99			Total = 152.54
Standard deviation		3.53	5.32			

$$\text{Cov (IBM, mkt.)} = 152.54/12 = 12.712$$

$$\text{Var (mkt.)} = (3.53)^2 = 12.44$$

$$\text{B (IBM)} = \frac{12.71}{12.44} = 1.02$$

$$\text{R (IBM, mkt.)} = \frac{12.71}{(3.53)(5.32)} = 0.68$$

$$\text{Alpha} = \text{R (avg., IBM)} - [\text{B(IBM)} \times \text{R (avg., mkt.)}]$$
$$= - 1.99 - (1.02 \times 2.13)$$
$$= - 1.99 - 2.17$$
$$= -4.16$$

[a]The IBM returns were calculated in Chapter 20.

antiques, and any other marketable risky asset from around the world.[10]

Example Computation of a Characteristic Line
The following example shows how to compute the characteristic line for IBM based upon its monthly rates of return during 1989.[11] Though the 12 observations we have are not sufficient, the exercise should provide a good example. Likewise, we use the S&P 500 Index as a proxy for the market portfolio, although we recognize that it is not ideal. We compute the monthly price changes using closing prices for the last day of each month.

[10]Substantial discussion has focused on the market index used and its impact on the empirical results and usefulness of the CAPM.

[11]This beta is computed using only monthly price changes for both IBM and the S&P 500 (i.e., dividends are not included). We do this for simplicity, but the technique is based upon a study indicating that betas derived with and without dividends are correlated 0.99: William Sharpe and Guy M. Cooper, "Risk-Return Classes of New York Stock Exchange Common Stocks," *Financial Analysts Journal* 28, no. 2 (March–April 1972): 35–43.

Figure 21.9   *Scatter Plot of IBM and S&P 500 with Characteristic Line for IBM*

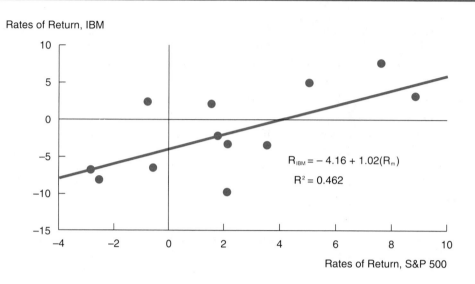

These data appear in Table 21.3, and Figure 21.9 shows a scatter plot of the percentage price changes for IBM and the S&P 500. During most months, IBM's returns were consistent with the aggregate market returns. In only four instances did one series experience a return above or below its mean while the other series did not do the same. This performance gave a positive covariance between IBM and the S&P 500 series. The covariance divided by the market variance indicates a beta for IBM of 1.02. This limited time-period analysis indicates that IBM is about as risky as the aggregate market.

When we draw this characteristic line on Figure 21.9, it matches the scatter plots reasonably closely, which is consistent with the correlation coefficient of 0.68.

Arbitrage Pricing Theory

Up to this point we have been discussing the CAPM in terms of the basic theory, including the assumptions that investors have quadratic utility functions, that the distribution of returns is normal, and that a market portfolio of all risky assets exists. While the empirical results generally provided support for the theory, a set of papers by Roll criticized the tests and the usefulness of the model because of its dependence on a true mar-

ket portfolio of risky assets that is not actually available.[12] When the CAPM is used to evaluate portfolio performance, it is necessary to select a proxy for the market portfolio as a benchmark for performance. It has been shown that the results can be changed because of the market proxy used.

Given these questions, the academic community has considered an alternative asset pricing theory that is reasonably intuitive and requires only limited assumptions. The arbitrage pricing theory (APT) was developed by Ross in the early 1970s and initially published in 1976.[13] The APT has three major assumptions:

[12]Richard Roll, "A Critique of the Asset Pricing Theory's Tests," *Journal of Financial Economics* 4, no. 4 (March 1977): 129–176; Richard Roll, "Ambiguity when Performance Is Measured by the Securities Market Line," *Journal of Finance* 33, no. 4 (September 1978): 1051–1069; Richard Roll, "Performance Evaluation and Benchmark Error I," *Journal of Portfolio Management* 6, no. 4 (Summer 1980): 5–12; Richard Roll, "Performance Evaluation and Benchmark Error II," *Journal of Portfolio Management* 7, no. 2 (Winter 1981): 17–22.

[13]Stephen Ross, "The Arbitrage Theory of Capital Asset Pricing," *Journal of Economic Theory* 13, no. 2 (December 1976): 341–360; Stephen Ross, "Return, Risk, and Arbitrage," in I. Friend and J. Bicksler, eds., *Risk and Return in Finance* (Cambridge: Ballinger, 1977): 189–218.

1. Capital markets are perfectly competitive.
2. Investors always prefer more wealth to less wealth with certainty.
3. The stochastic process generating asset returns can be represented as a K factor model (to be described).

There are several major assumptions that are *not* required. This theory does not require that investors have quadratic utility functions, that security returns be normally distributed, or that there be a market portfolio that contains all risky assets and is mean-variance efficient. Obviously, if such a theory were able to explain differential security prices, it would be considered superior to alternative asset pricing theories because it is simpler (that is, it requires fewer assumptions).

As noted, the theory assumes that the process generating rates of returns on assets can be represented as a K factor model of the form:

$$R_i = E_i + b_{i1}\delta_1 + b_{i2}\delta_2 + \cdots + b_{ik}\delta_k + \epsilon_i$$
$$\text{for i} = 1 \text{ to N}$$

where:

R_i = return on asset i during a specified time period

E_i = expected return for asset i

b_{ik} = reaction in asset i's returns to movements in a common factor δ_k

δ_k = a set of common factors with a zero mean that influences the returns on all assets

ϵ_i = a unique effect on asset i's return which, by assumption, is completely diversifiable in large portfolios and has a mean of zero

N = number of assets

Two terms require elaboration: δ_k and b. As indicated, the δ_k terms are the *multiple* factors that are expected to affect the returns of *all* assets. Examples might include inflation, growth in GNP, major political upheavals, or changes in interest rates. The point is, the APT contends that there are a *number* of such factors that influence returns. This is in contrast to the CAPM, where the only variable of importance is the covariance of the asset with the market portfolio. As a result, you will hear references to the CAPM as a single-factor model and the APT as a multi-factor model.

Given these common factors, the b_{ik} terms determine how individual assets react to one of these common factors. To extend the earlier example, while all assets may be affected by growth in GNP, the impact will differ between assets; stocks of cyclical firms will have larger b_{ik} values for this common factor than noncyclical firms, such as grocery chains. Likewise, you will hear discussions about interest-sensitive stocks: the implication is that all stocks are affected by changes in interest rates, but some stocks experience larger impacts.

The theory contends that there are a number of common factors and we can envision some likely examples of common factors, such as inflation, changes in interest rates, the growth rate of the economy, and other significant macroeconomic events. Still, in the application of the theory, the factors are not identified. As we will see when we discuss the empirical studies, the results indicate that there are three, four, or five factors that affect security returns, but there is no indication of what these factors represent.

As with the CAPM, it is assumed that the unique effects (ϵ_i) are independent and, therefore, that they will be diversified away in a large portfolio.

The APT assumes that, in equilibrium, the return on a zero investment, zero systematic risk portfolio is zero when the unique effects are diversified away. This assumption and some theory from linear algebra imply that the expected return on any asset i (E_i) can be expressed as:

$$E_i = \lambda_0 + \lambda_1\beta_{i1} + \lambda_2\beta_{i2} + \cdots + \lambda_k\beta_{ik}$$

where:

λ_0 = the expected return on an asset with zero systematic risk where $\lambda_0 = E_0$

λ_i = the risk premium related to each of the common factors—for example, the risk premium related to the interest rate risk factor ($\lambda_i = E_i - E_0$)

β_i = the pricing relationship between the risk premium and asset i—that is, how responsive asset i is to this common factor K

Consider the following example of two stocks and a two factor model:

K_1 = changes in the rate of inflation. The risk premium related to this factor is 1 percent for every 1 percent change in the rate ($\lambda_1 = 0.01$)

K_2 = percent growth in real GNP. The average risk premium related to this factor is 2 percent for every 1 percent change in the rate ($\lambda_2 = 0.02$)

λ_0 = the rate of return on an asset with zero systematic risk (zero beta: $\beta_{0j} = 0$) asset is 3 percent ($\lambda_0 = 0.03$)

The two assets (X,Y) have the following response coefficients to these factors:

β_{X1} = the response of asset X to changes in the rate of inflation is 0.50 ($\beta_{X1} = 0.50$)
(This asset is not very responsive to changes in the rate of inflation)

β_{Y1} = the response of asset Y to changes in the rate of inflation is 2.00 ($\beta_{Y1} = 2.00$)

β_{X2} = the response of asset X to changes in the growth rate of real GNP is 1.50 ($\beta_{X2} = 1.50$)

β_{Y2} = the response of asset Y to changes in the growth rate of real GNP is 1.75 ($\beta_{Y2} = 1.75$)

These response coefficients indicate that if these are the major factors influencing asset returns, overall asset Y has higher risk and, therefore, its expected return should be greater, as shown below:

$$E_i = \lambda_0 + \lambda_1\beta_{i1} + \lambda_2\beta_{i2}$$
$$= 0.03 + (0.01)\beta_{i1} + (0.02)\beta_{i2}$$

Therefore:

$$E_X = 0.03 + (0.01)(0.50) + (0.02)(1.50)$$
$$= 0.065 = 6.5 \text{ percent}$$
$$E_Y = 0.03 + (0.01)(2.00) + (0.02)(1.75)$$
$$= 0.085 = 8.5 \text{ percent}$$

If the prices of the assets do not reflect these expected returns, we would expect investors to enter into arbitrage arrangements whereby they would sell overpriced assets short. With the proceeds they would purchase the underpriced assets until the relevant prices were corrected. The point is, given these linear relationships, it should be possible to find an asset or a combination of assets that have higher expected returns with risk equal to the mispriced asset.

Empirical Tests of the APT

Studies by Roll and Ross and also by Chen have provided results that support the APT since the model was able to explain different rates of return, in some cases with results that were superior to those of the CAPM.[14] In contrast, results of Reinganum's study do not support the model because it did not explain small-firm results.[15] Finally, Dhrymes and Shanken both questioned the usefulness of the model when it was not possible to identify the factors; under these conditions, is the theory testable?[16]

At this time, the theory is relatively new and will be subject to continued testing. The important points to remember are that the model requires fewer assumptions and considers multiple factors to explain the risk of an asset, in contrast to the single-factor CAPM.[17]

Summary

■ The assumptions of capital market theory expand on those of the Markowitz portfolio model and include consideration of the risk-free rate of return. The correlation and covariance of any asset with a risk-free asset is zero, so that any combination of an asset or portfolio with the risk-free asset generates a linear return and risk function. Therefore, when you combine the risk-free asset with any risky asset on the Markowitz efficient frontier, you derive a set of straight-line portfolio possibilities.

■ The dominant line is the one that is tangent to the efficient frontier. This dominant line is referred

[14]Richard Roll and Stephen A. Ross, "An Empirical Investigation of the Arbitrage Pricing Theory," *Journal of Finance* 35, no. 5 (December 1980): 1073–1103; and Nai-fu Chen, "Some Empirical Tests of Theory of Arbitrage Pricing," *Journal of Finance* 38, no. 5 (December 1983): 1393–1414.

[15]Marc R. Reinganum, "The Arbitrage Pricing Theory: Some Empirical Results," *Journal of Finance* 36, no. 2 (May 1981): 313–321.

[16]Phoebus J. Dhrymes, "The Empirical Relevance of Arbitrage Pricing Models," *Journal of Portfolio Management* 10, no. 4 (Summer 1984): 35–44; Jay Shanken, "The Arbitrage Pricing Theory: Is It Testable?" *Journal of Finance* 37, no. 5 (December 1982): 1129–1140.

[17]For a discussion of how these models relate to each other, see William F. Sharpe, "Factor Models, CAPMs, and the APT," *Journal of Portfolio Management* 11, no. 1 (Fall 1984): 21–25.

to as the *capital market line (CML)*, and all investors should target points along this line depending upon their risk preferences.

■ Because all investors want to invest in the risky portfolio at the point of tangency, this portfolio, referred to as the market portfolio, must contain all risky assets in proportion to their relative market values. Moreover, the investment decision and the financing decision can be separated, because, while everyone will want to invest in the market portfolio, investors will make different financing decisions about whether to lend or borrow, based upon their individual risk preferences.

■ Given the CML and the dominance of the market portfolio, the relevant risk measure for an individual risky asset is its covariance with the market portfolio, that is, its *systematic risk*. When this covariance is standardized by the covariance for the market portfolio, we derive the well-known beta measure of systematic risk and a security market line (SML) that relates the expected or required rate of return for an asset to its beta. Since all individual securities and portfolios should plot on this SML, you can determine the expected (required) return on a security based upon its systematic risk (its beta).

■ Alternatively, assuming security markets are not always completely efficient, you can identify undervalued and overvalued securities by comparing your estimate of the rate of return to be earned on an investment to its required rate of return. The systematic risk variable (beta) for an individual risky asset is computed using a regression model that generates an equation referred to as the asset's *characteristic line*.

■ We concluded the chapter with a discussion of an alternative asset pricing model—the arbitrage pricing theory (APT) model. This included a discussion of the necessary assumptions and the basics of the model as well as an example of its use. We also considered some of the tests of the model that have generated mixed results. Because of the mixed results and the importance of the topic, it is likely that testing of this model will continue.

Questions

1. Define the term *risk-free asset*.
2. What is the covariance between a risk-free asset and a portfolio of risky assets? Explain your answer.
3. Explain why the set of points between the risk-free asset and a portfolio on the Markowitz efficient frontier is a straight line.
4. What happens to the Markowitz efficient frontier when you combine a risk-free asset with alternative risky asset portfolios on the Markowitz efficient frontier? Draw a graph to show this effect, and explain it.
5. Explain why the line from the RFR that is tangent to the efficient frontier defines the dominant set of portfolio possibilities. Demonstrate it graphically.
6. It has been shown that the capital market line (CML) is tangent to one portfolio, portfolio M, on the Markowitz efficient frontier. Discuss what risky assets are in portfolio M and why they are in it.
7. Discuss leverage and its effect on the CML.
8. Why is the CML considered the new efficient frontier?
9. Define complete diversification in terms of capital market theory.
10. Discuss and justify a measure of diversification for a portfolio.
11. What changes would you expect in the standard deviations of portfolios of between 4 and 10 stocks, between 10 and 20 stocks, and between 50 and 100 stocks?
12. Discuss why the investment and financing decisions are separate when you have a CML.
13. Given the CML, discuss and justify the relevant measure of risk for an individual security.
14. Capital market theory divides the total variance of returns for a security into systematic variance and unsystematic or unique variance. Describe what each of these terms means.
15. The capital asset pricing model (CAPM) assumes systematic and unsystematic risk for an individual security. Which is the relevant risk variable and why is it relevant? Why is the other risk variable not relevant?
16. Draw a properly labeled graph of the security market line (SML) and explain it. How does the SML differ from the CML?

Problems

1. Assume that you expect the economy's rate of inflation to be 3 percent, giving an RFR of 6 percent and a market return (R_m) of 12 percent.

a. Draw the SML under these assumptions.
b. Subsequently, you expect the rate of inflation to increase from 3 percent to 6 percent. What effect would this have on the RFR and the R_m? Draw another SML on the graph from part a.
c. Draw an SML on the same graph to reflect an RFR of 9 percent and an R_m of 17 percent. How does this SML differ from that derived in part b? Explain what has transpired.

2. You expect an RFR of 10 percent and a market return (R_m) of 14 percent. Compute the expected (required) returns for the following stocks, and plot them on an SML graph.

Stock	Beta	$E(R_i)$
U	0.85	
N	1.25	
D	−0.20	

3. You ask a stockbroker what the firm's research department expects for these three stocks. The broker responds with the following information:

Stock	Current Price	Expected Price	Expected Dividend
U	22	24	0.75
N	48	51	2.00
D	37	40	1.25

Compute your estimated returns and plot them on the graph from problem 2. Indicate what actions you would take with regard to these stocks. Discuss your decisions.

4. Select a stock from the NYSE and collect its month-end prices for the latest 13 months in order to compute 12 monthly percentage price changes ignoring dividends. Do the same for the S&P 500 series. Prepare a scatter plot of these series on a graph and draw a visually fitted characteristic line (the line from which the points deviate the least). Compute the slope of this line from the graph.

5. Given the returns derived in problem 4, compute the beta coefficient using the formula and techniques employed in Table 21.3. How many negative products did you have for the covariance?

How does this computed beta compare to the visual beta derived in problem 4?

6. Look up the stock you selected for problem 4 in *Value Line* and record the listed beta. How does *VL*'s beta compare to yours? Discuss reasons why the betas might differ.

7. Select a stock that is listed on the AMEX and plot its returns during the last 12 months relative to the S&P 500. Compute its beta coefficient. In general, did you expect this stock to have a higher or lower beta than the NYSE stock? Explain your answer.

8. Plot the returns for the AMEX stock in problem 7 relative to monthly rates of return for the AMEX Market Value Index and compute the beta coefficient. Does this beta differ from that derived in problem 7? If so, how can you explain this? Hint: Analyze the specific components of the beta coefficient formula. How did the components differ between problems 7 and 8?

9. Using the data from the prior questions, compute the beta coefficient for the AMEX Index relative to the S&P 500 Index. A priori, would you expect a beta less than or greater than 1.00? Discuss your expectations and the actual results.

10. Based upon 5 years of monthly data, you have derived the following information for the companies listed:

Company	a_i (Intercept)	σ_i	r_{im}
Apple Computer	0.22	12.10%	0.72
Chrysler	0.10	14.60	0.33
Anheuser Busch	0.17	7.60	0.55
Monsanto	0.05	10.20	0.60
S&P 500	0.00	5.50	1.00

a. Compute the beta coefficient for each stock.
b. Assuming a risk-free rate of 8 percent and an expected return for the market portfolio of 15 percent, compute the expected (required) return for all the stocks and plot them on the SML.
c. Plot the following estimated returns for the next year on the SML and indicate which stocks are undervalued or overvalued.

■ Apple Computer: 20 percent
■ Chrysler: 15 percent

- Anheuser Busch: 19 percent
- Monsanto: 10 percent

11. Calculate the expected return for each of the following stocks when the risk-free rate is 0.08 and you expect the market return to be 0.15.

Stock	Beta
A	1.72
B	1.14
C	0.76
D	0.44
E	0.03
F	−0.79

12. Compute the beta for Dome Computer Company based upon the following historic returns:

Year	Dome Computer	General Index
1	12	15
2	9	13
3	−11	14
4	8	−9
5	11	12
6	4	9

13. With the information in problem 12, compute the following:
   a. The correlation coefficient between Dome Computer and the General Index.

   b. The intercept of the characteristic line.
   c. The equation of the characteristic line.

References

Chen, F. N., Richard Roll and Steve Ross. "Economic Forces and the Stock Market." *Journal of Business* (July 1986).

Hagin, Robert. *Modern Portfolio Theory.* Homewood, Ill.: Dow Jones-Irwin, 1979.

Hawawini, Gabriel A. "Why Beta Shifts as the Return Interval Changes." *Financial Analysts Journal* 39, no. 3 (May–June 1983).

Lintner, John. "The Valuation of Risk Assets and the Selection of Risky Investments in Stock Portfolios and Capital Budgets." *Review of Economics and Statistics* 47, no. 2 (February 1965).

Mossin, Jan. "Equilibrium in a Capital Asset Market." *Econometrica* 34, no. 10 (October 1966).

Mullins, David. "Does the Capital Asset Pricing Model Work?" *Harvard Business Review*, January–February 1982.

Reilly, Frank K., and David J. Wright. "A Comparison of Published Betas." *Journal of Portfolio Management* 14, no. 3 (Spring 1988).

Rosenberg, Barr, and J. Guy. "Predictions of Beta from Investment Fundamentals." *Financial Analysts Journal* 32, no. 3 (May–June 1976).

Sharpe, William F. "Capital Asset Prices: A Theory of Market Equilibrium under Conditions of Risk." *Journal of Finance* 19, no. 3 (September 1964).

Statman, Meir. "How Many Stocks Make a Diversified Portfolio?" *Journal of Financial and Quantitative Analysis* 22, no. 3 (September 1987).

22

Efficient Capital Markets

Efficient capital market A market in which security prices rapidly reflect all information about securities.

An **efficient capital market** is one in which security prices adjust rapidly to the arrival of new information and, therefore, they reflect all information about the security. Some of the most interesting and important academic research over the past 10 years has analyzed whether our capital markets are efficient. This extensive research is important because its results have significant real-world implications for investors and portfolio managers. In addition, the efficiency of capital markets is one of the most controversial areas in investment research because opinions differ widely.

Therefore, you need to understand the meaning of the term *efficient capital market* and the efficient market hypothesis (EMH). You need to be familiar with the nature of the analysis performed to test the EMH and the results of studies that either support or contradict the hypothesis. Finally, you should be aware of the implications of these results for your analysis of alternative investments and the construction of a portfolio.

We consider the topic of efficient capital markets at this point for two reasons. First, the discussion in previous chapters has given you an understanding of how the capital markets function, so it now seems natural to consider the efficiency of the markets in terms of how prices react to new information. Second, the overall evidence on capital market efficiency is best described as mixed since some studies support the hypothesis and some do not. The implications of these diverse results are very important for you as an investor working to build a portfolio.

> **Informationally efficient market** A more technical term for an efficient capital market that emphasizes the role of information.

There are four major sections in this chapter. The first discusses why we would expect capital markets to be efficient and what factors contribute to an efficient market where the prices of securities reflect available information. The single efficient market hypothesis has been divided into three sub-hypotheses to facilitate testing. The second section describes these three sub-hypotheses along with their implications.

The next section, the largest, discusses how to test the three sub-hypotheses and reviews the results of numerous studies. This review of the research shows that a large body of evidence supports the EMH, but a growing number of other studies do not. The final section considers what these results mean for an investor who uses either technical analysis or fundamental analysis, and for a portfolio manager who has access to superior or inferior analysts. We conclude with a brief discussion of the evidence for markets in foreign countries.

We discuss numerous empirical studies of efficient markets in this chapter. Because space limitations preclude dealing with them in depth, we encourage you to consult the literature cited in the reference section at the end of this chapter.

Why Should Capital Markets Be Efficient?

As noted earlier, in an efficient capital market, security prices adjust rapidly to the infusion of new information and, therefore, current security prices fully reflect all available information. To be absolutely correct, this is referred to as an **informationally efficient market.** Although the idea of an efficient capital market is relatively straightforward, we often fail to consider why a capital market should be efficient.

What set of assumptions imply an efficient capital market?

As an initial, and very important, premise, an efficient market requires that *a large number of profit-maximizing participants analyze and value securities,* each independently of the others. A second assumption is that new information regarding securities comes to the market in a random fashion so that the timing of one announcement is generally independent of others.

The third assumption is especially crucial: *investors adjust security prices rapidly to reflect new information.* Although the price adjustment may be imperfect, it is unbiased. This means that sometimes the market will overadjust and other times it will underadjust, but you cannot predict which will occur at any given time. Security prices adjust rapidly because many profit-maximizing investors are competing against one another.

The combined effects of (1) information coming in a random, independent fashion and (2) numerous competing investors adjusting stock price expectations rapidly to reflect this new information keep prices changing independently and at random. You can see that the adjustment process requires a large number of investors following the movements of a security, analyzing the impact of new information on its value, and buying or selling it until its price adjusts to reflect the new information. This scenario implies that informational efficiency requires some minimum amount of trading and that more trading by a large number of competing investors should make price adjustment faster, making the market more efficient. We will return to this need for trading and attention when we discuss some anomalies of the EMH.

Finally, because security prices adjust to all new information, they should reflect all information that is publicly available at any point in time. This adjustment should keep the security prices that prevail at any time as unbiased reflections of all currently available information, including the risk involved in owning the security. Therefore, *the expected returns implicit in the current price of the security should reflect its risk.*

Alternative Efficient Market Hypotheses

Most of the early work related to efficient capital markets was based upon the random walk hypothesis, which contended that changes in stock prices occurred randomly. This early academic work featured extensive empirical analysis without much theory behind it. Fama made the first attempt to formalize the theory and organize the growing empirical evidence in a 1970 *Journal of Finance* article.[1] Fama presented the efficient market theory in terms of a fair game model, contending that investors can be confident that a current market price fully reflects all available information about a security and is consistent with its risk. In addition, Fama divided the overall efficient market hypothesis (EMH), and its empirical tests, into three sub-hypotheses by their information sets: (1) weak-form EMH, (2) semistrong-form EMH, and (3) strong-form EMH. The following discussion is organized to follow these categories. In the balance of this section we describe the three sub-hypotheses and their implications. In the following section, we describe how researchers have tested each of the hypotheses and the results of these tests.

Weak-Form Efficient Market Hypothesis

The **weak-form efficient market hypothesis** assumes that current stock prices fully reflect all *security market* information, including historical price sequences, price changes, trading volume data, and any other market-generated information such as odd-lot transactions, block-trades, and transactions by specialists or other unique groups. Because it assumes that current market prices already reflect all past price changes and any other security market information, this hypothesis implies that past price changes should have no relationship with future price changes, i.e., price changes should be independent. Therefore, you should gain little from any **trading rule** that decides whether to buy or sell a security based upon past price changes or any past market data.

Semistrong-Form Efficient Market Hypothesis

The **semistrong-form efficient market hypothesis** asserts that security prices adjust rapidly to the release of *all public information*, that is, current security prices fully reflect all public information. The semistrong-form hypothesis encompasses the weak-form hypoth-

> **Weak-form efficient market hypothesis** The belief that security prices fully reflect all security market information.
> **Trading rule** A formula for deciding on current transactions based on historical data.
> **Semistrong-form efficient market hypothesis** The belief that security prices fully reflect all publicly available information, including information from security transactions and company, economic, and political news.
> **Strong-form efficient market hypothesis** The belief that security prices fully reflect all information from both public and private sources.

esis because all the market information considered by the weak-form hypothesis, such as stock prices and trading volume, is public. Public information also includes all nonmarket information such as earnings and dividend announcements, stock splits, and economic and political news. This hypothesis implies that investors who base their decisions upon important new information *after it is public* should not derive above-average profits from their transactions considering the cost of trading, because the security price already reflects the new public information.

Strong-Form Efficient Market Hypothesis

The **strong-form efficient market hypothesis** contends that stock prices fully reflect *all information* from public sources and any others. This means that no group of investors has monopolistic access to information relevant to the formation of prices. Therefore, no group of investors should be able to consistently derive above-average profits. The strong-form EMH encompasses both the weak-form and semistrong-form EMHs. Further, the strong-form EMH extends the assumption of efficient markets in which prices adjust rapidly to the release of new public information to assume perfect markets in which all information is cost-free and available to everyone at the same time.

Tests and Results of Alternative Efficient Market Hypotheses

Now that you understand the three components of the EMH and what each of them implies regarding the effect on security prices of different sets of informa-

[1]Eugene F. Fama, "Efficient Capital Markets: A Review of Theory and Empirical Work," *Journal of Finance* 25, no. 2 (May 1970): 383–417.

> **Anomalies** Security price relationships that appear to contradict a well-regarded hypothesis, in this case, the efficient market hypothesis.
>
> **Autocorrelation test** A test of the efficient market hypothesis that compares security price changes over time to check for predictable correlation patterns.
>
> **Runs test** A test of the weak-form efficient market hypothesis that checks for trends that persist longer in terms of positive or negative price changes than one would expect for a random series.

tion, we can consider how a person doing research in this area tests to see whether data support the hypotheses. Therefore, in this section we discuss the specific tests used to gauge support for the hypotheses and we summarize the results of these tests.

Like most hypotheses in finance and economics, the evidence on the EMH is mixed. Some studies have supported the hypothesis and indicated that capital markets are efficient. Other studies have revealed some **anomalies** related to these hypotheses, raising questions about support for them.

Weak-Form Hypothesis: Tests and Results

Researchers have formulated two groups of tests of the weak-form EMH. The first category involves statistical tests of independence between stock-price changes. The second entails comparison of risk–return results for trading rules based on past market information to results from a simple buy-and-hold policy, which assumes that you buy stock at the beginning of a test period and hold it to the end.

Statistical Tests of Independence As discussed earlier, security-price changes over time should be independent of one another because the efficient market hypothesis contends that new information comes to the market in a random, independent fashion, and that security prices adjust rapidly to this new information. Two major statistical tests have been employed to verify this independence.

First, **autocorrelation tests** of independence measure the significance of positive or negative cor-

relation in price changes over time. Does the percentage price change on day t correlate with the percentage price change on days t − 1, t − 2, or t − 3?[2] Those who believe that capital markets are efficient would expect insignificant correlations for all such combinations.

Several researchers have examined the serial correlations among stock price changes for several different time intervals including 1 day, 4 days, 9 days, and 16 days.[3] The results consistently indicated that the correlation coefficients typically ranged from +0.10 to −0.10, but these were typically not statistically significant. These results have consistently indicated that stock price changes over time are generally statistically independent. This implies that past price changes cannot help you project future price changes.

The second statistical test of independence is the **runs test.**[4] Each increase in a series of price changes is designated with a plus sign (+) while a minus sign (−) is assigned to any decrease in price. The result is a set of pluses and minuses, as follows: + + + − + − − + + − − + +. A run occurs when two consecutive changes match; two or more consecutive positive or negative price changes constitutes one run. When the price changes in a different direction, such as when a negative price change is followed by a positive price change, the run ends and a new run may begin. To test for independence, you would compare the number of runs for a given series to the number in a table of expected values for the number of such runs that should occur in a random series.

Studies that have examined stock price runs have confirmed the independence of stock-price changes over time. The actual number of runs for stock-price series consistently fell into the range expected for a random series. Therefore, these statistical tests likewise indicated that stock-price changes over time are independent. These statistical tests of independence have been repeated for stocks traded on the OTC market, and the results likewise supported the EMH.[5]

---

[2]For a discussion of tests of independence, see S. Christian Albright, *Statistics for Business and Economics* (New York: Macmillan, 1987): 515–517.

[3]Eugene F. Fama, "The Behavior of Stock Market Prices," *Journal of Business* 38, no. 1 (January 1965): 34–105; Eugene Fama and James MacBeth, "Risk, Return and Equilibrium: Empirical Tests," *Journal of Political Economy* 81, no. 3 (May–June 1973): 607–636.

[4]For the details of a runs test see Albright, *Statistics for Business and Economics:* 695–699.

[5]Robert L. Hagerman and Richard D. Richmond, "Random Walks, Martingales and the OTC," *Journal of Finance* 28, no. 4 (September 1973): 897–909.

Although daily, weekly, and monthly aggregate stock price changes consistently supported the weak-form EMH, the evidence from individual transaction price changes did not. In several studies, researchers who examined price changes for individual transactions on the NYSE found significant serial correlations. None of these studies measured whether the dependence of transaction price movements could help an investor earn above-average risk-adjusted returns, though. The significant correlation among individual transactions seems to derive from the market-making activities of the specialist. Investors could probably not use this small imperfection in the market to derive excess profits, however, after considering the substantial transaction costs involved in such a trading rule.[6]

Tests of Trading Rules   The second group of tests of the weak-form EMH was developed in response to the assertion that the prior statistical tests of independence were too rigid to identify the intricate price patterns examined by technical analysts. As you know from the discussion in Chapter 15, technical analysts do not accept a set number of positive or negative price changes as a signal of a move to a new equilibrium in the market. They typically look for a general consistency in the price trend over time. Such a trend might include both positive and negative changes. For this reason, technical analysts felt that their trading rules were too sophisticated and complicated to be simulated by a rigid statistical test.

In response to this objection, investigators attempted to examine alternative technical trading rules through simulation. Advocates of an efficient market hypothesized that investors could not derive profits above a buy-and-hold policy, or abnormal profits, using any trading rule that depended solely on past market information about factors such as price, volume, odd-lot sales, or specialist activity. Trading rule studies compared the risk–return results derived from such a simulation, including transaction costs, to the results from a simple buy-and-hold policy.

Three major pitfalls can negate the results of such a study:

1.   The investigator should use only publicly available data in the decision rule. As an example, the earn-

> **Filter rule**   A trading rule that recommends security transactions when price changes exceed a previously determined percentage.

ings for a firm as of December 31 may not be publicly available until April 1 so you should not factor in an earnings report until then.
2.   When computing the returns from a trading rule, you should include all transaction costs involved in implementing the trading strategy because most trading rules generate many more transactions than a simple buy-and-hold policy.
3.   You must adjust the results for risk because a trading rule might simply select a portfolio of high-risk securities that should experience higher returns.

Researchers have encountered two operational problems in carrying out these tests of specific trading rules. First, some trading rules require too much subjective interpretation of data to simulate mechanically. Second, the almost infinite number of potential trading rules makes it impossible to test all of them. As a result, only the better-known technical trading rules have been examined.

Another factor that you should recognize is that some studies have been somewhat biased. Specifically, the operational problems noted above have restricted studies to the simple trading rules, which many technicians contend are rather naive.

In addition, these studies typically employ readily available data from the NYSE which is biased toward well-known, heavily traded stocks that certainly should trade in efficient markets. Since markets are likely to be more efficient with higher numbers of aggressive, profit-maximizing investors attempting to adjust stock prices to reflect new information, market efficiency depends on trading volume. Specifically, more trading in a security should promote market efficiency. Alternatively, for securities with relatively few stockholders and little trading activity, you could envision that the market could be inefficient because few investors would be analyzing the effect of new information and this limited interest would result in insufficient trading activity to move the price of the security quickly to a new equilibrium value that would reflect the new information. Therefore, using only active, heavily traded stocks in the tests could bias the results toward finding efficiency.

Results of Simulations of Specific Trading Rules   In the most popular trading technique, **filter rules,** an

[6]Victor Niederhoffer and M. F. Osborn, "Market-Making and Reversal on the Stock Exchange," *Journal of American Statistical Association* 61, no. 316 (December 1966): 897–916; Kenneth Carey, "A Model of Individual Transaction Stock Prices" (Ph.D. dissertation, University of Kansas, 1971).

investor trades a stock when the price change exceeds a filter value set for it. As an example, an investor using a 5 percent filter would see a positive breakout if the stock were to rise 5 percent from some base, suggesting that the stock price would continue to rise. He or she would acquire the stock to take advantage of the continued rise. In contrast, a 5 percent decline from some peak price would be considered a breakout on the downside and the technician would expect a further price decline and sell any holdings of the stock, even sell it short.

Studies of this trading rule have used a range of filters from 0.5 percent to 50 percent. The results indicated that small filters would yield above-average profits before taking account of trading commissions. However, small filters generate numerous trades and therefore substantial commissions. When these trading commissions were considered, all the trading profits turned to losses. Alternatively, larger filters did not yield returns above those of a simple buy-and-hold policy.[7]

Researchers have simulated other trading rules that used past market data other than stock prices.[8] Trading rules have been devised that use odd-lot figures, advance–decline ratios, and short sales. A few such rules earned slight profits, but the results of these simulations have suggested that they generally would not outperform a buy-and-hold policy on a risk-adjusted basis after taking account of commissions.[9] Therefore, most evidence from simulations of specific trading rules indicates that these trading rules cannot beat a buy-and-hold policy. These results support the weak-form EMH.

[7]Eugene Fama and Marshall Blume, "Filter Rules and Stock Market Trading Profits," *Journal of Business* 39, no. 1 (January 1966 Supplement): 226–241.

[8]Many of these trading rules are discussed in Chapter 15 on technical analysis.

[9]George Pinches, "The Random Walk Hypothesis and Technical Analysis," *Financial Analysts Journal* 26, no. 2 (March–April 1970): 104–110. Two studies provide support for some technical trading rules that use three-part filters or adjust relative strength for the January effect. See John S. Brush, "Eight Relative Strength Models Compared," *Journal of Portfolio Management* 13, no. 1 (Fall 1986): 21–28; and Stephen W. Pruitt and Richard E. White, "Who Says Technical Analysis Can't Beat the Market?" *Journal of Portfolio Management* 14, no. 3 (Spring 1988): 55–58.

Semistrong-Form Hypothesis: Tests and Results

Recall that the semistrong-form EMH asserts that security prices adjust rapidly to the release of all new public information; that is, security prices fully reflect all public information. Therefore, studies that have tested the semistrong-form EMH have examined one or both of the following factors:

1. Price movements around the time of an important public announcement measure the timing of the price adjustment: did security prices adjust before, during, or after the announcement was made? The EMH would imply that the price change would occur either before the public announcement due to a news leak, or during the period of announcement.
2. The potential for above-average risk-adjusted rates of return, assuming an investor acted after the information became public: would an investor who acquired the security after a public announcement have enjoyed above-average risk-adjusted returns compared to those experienced with a buy-and-hold policy after transaction costs? The EMH would imply that buying or selling after the information is public would not provide excess profits because the price would already reflect the new information.

Some have extended this analysis to consider the potential for abnormal profits from any trading that uses public information. While the weak-form EMH test used public *market* information, these tests of the semistrong-form EMH consider other public information like company earnings, economic information, company size, day of the week, or month of the year. Again, the semistrong-form EMH would contend that no trading rule that uses public information should beat the risk-adjusted returns from a buy-and-hold policy after transaction costs.

Adjustment for Market Effects For any such test, you need to adjust the security's price movements (or returns) for price movements (or rates of return) in the overall market during the period considered. The point is, a 5 percent price change in a stock during the period surrounding an announcement is not meaningful until you know what the aggregate stock market did during the same period and how this stock normally acts under such conditions. If the market had changed by 10 percent during this period, the 5 percent change for the stock might be lower than expected.

Authors of studies undertaken prior to 1970 generally recognized the need to make such adjustments for market movements. They typically assumed that individual stocks should experience returns equal to the aggregate stock market. This assumption reduced the adjustment process to subtracting the market return from the return for the individual security to derive its **abnormal rate of return,** as follows:

$$AR_{it} = R_{it} - R_{mt}$$

where:

AR_{it} = abnormal rate of return on security i during period t

R_{it} = rate of return on security i during period t

R_{mt} = rate of return on a market index during period t

A stock that experienced a 5 percent price increase while the market increased 10 percent would have an abnormal price change of minus 5 percent.

Some authors have adjusted the rates of return for securities by amounts other than the average market rate of return, recognizing that all stocks do not change by the same amount as the market; some stocks are more volatile than the market, and some are less volatile. These possibilities require that you determine an **expected rate of return** for the stock based upon the market rate of return and the stock's relationship with the market. As an example, suppose a stock is generally 20 percent more volatile than the market. When the market experiences a 10 percent rate of return, you would expect this stock to experience a 12 percent rate of return. You would determine the abnormal return by computing the difference between the stock's actual rate of return and its expected rate of return as follows:

$$AR_{it} = R_{it} - E(R_{it})$$

where:

$E(R_{it})$ = the expected rate of return for stock i during period t, based on the market rate of return and the stock's normal relationship with the market (its beta)

Abnormal rate of return The amount by which a security's return differs from the market's expected rate of return based upon the market's rate of return and the security's relationship with the market.

Expected rate of return The return analysts' calculations suggest a security should provide, based upon the market's rate of return during the period and the security's relationship to the market.

Event study Research that examines the reaction of a security's price to a specific company or world event or news announcements.

Continuing with the example, if the stock from which you expected a 12 percent return had only a 5 percent return, its abnormal rate of return during the period would be minus 7 percent. Over the normal long-run period, you would expect the abnormal returns for a stock to sum to zero. During one period the returns might exceed expectations, and in the next period they might fall short.

To summarize, there are two types of tests of the semistrong-form EMH. In the first, investigators examine abnormal price changes surrounding announcements of new information to see when the price adjustment took place. In the second set of tests, they examine abnormal rates of return for the period immediately after an announcement to determine whether an investor could derive above-average risk-adjusted rates of return on the basis of public information, or whether an investor could earn abnormal returns based upon a trading rule that uses any public information. Both sets of tests emphasize the analysis of abnormal rates of returns that are adjusted for overall market rates of return during the period.

Results of Semistrong-Form EMH Studies Numerous studies have examined price changes in reaction to specific events such as stock splits, exchange listings, and earnings announcements. Authors have also analyzed the potential for excess returns from investing on the basis of other public information, such as the size of the firm or its price–earnings ratio. Therefore, it is best to organize the discussion of results by event or item of public information.

First we will review the results of several **event studies** that have examined price movements and profit potential surrounding stock splits, initial public offerings, exchange listings, unexpected world or economic events, and announcements of significant accounting changes. We will see that the results for most of these studies have supported the semistrong-form EMH. In contrast, a number of more recent studies have examined events such as quarterly earnings reports or public information on size, price–earnings ratios, and neglected firms and found that this public information can be used to generate positive abnormal rates of return. These events or public information items are referred to as *anomalies*, meaning that the test results are inconsistent with the implications of the currently prevailing theory.

Studies Supporting the Semistrong-Form EMH

Stock-Split Studies Several studies have examined stock splits. Some investors believe that the prices of stocks that split increase because the shares' lower prices increase demand for them. In contrast, advocates of efficient markets would expect no change in value because such firms merely issue additional stock with correspondingly lower value leaving the value of the firm fundamentally unaffected.

Although the results of the numerous studies that have examined the profit potential of stock splits have not been unanimous, most have indicated that investors who acquire stock after it splits do not experience above-average rates of return. In fact, in many instances when a company split its stock and did not raise the dividend on the new shares, the stock fell short of expectations. Investors generally expect the company to raise the dividend rate at the time of a split since others have done it about 80 percent of the time.

In addition, several studies have examined the profit opportunities from acquiring a stock right after the announcement of an impending split. These studies have likewise generally agreed that investors have not experienced abnormal profits from such acquisitions after transaction costs.

In summary, it appears that, unless you know about a proposed stock split before it is announced, you should not expect to experience above-average risk-adjusted returns on these stocks. These results support the semistrong-form EMH.[10]

Initial Public Offerings During the past 3 decades a number of closely held companies have decided to go public by selling common stock. These new issues are referred to as *initial public offerings (IPOs)*. Since it is difficult to determine an appropriate price for such

stocks, it is risky to underwrite IPOs. Hence, most observers have expected investment bankers to underprice new issues, so investors who acquire IPOs at their offering prices should receive abnormal profits. If a new issue is underpriced, it allows us to test the EMH by analyzing how long it takes the market to adjust the IPO's price to the correct level.

The studies typically examined the returns received by original investors who acquired stock at its offering price, as well as the returns to investors who purchased the same stock after the initial offering and held it for various periods. These studies considered two questions: (1) Are IPOs generally underpriced? (2) How quickly does the market adjust its prices to correct the underpricing? The studies gave consistent answers to these questions.[11] All indicated that, on average, new issues purchased at their offering prices yield positive abnormal short-run returns.

Table 22.1 lists the number of annual offerings and their average initial returns during the period 1960 to 1987. Most authors attribute these excess returns to underpricing by underwriters. The results tend to support the semistrong-form EMH because the prices adjusted almost immediately. Therefore, investors would not receive abnormal returns from acquiring IPO shares shortly after the offering. The evidence for rapid adjustment is most evident in the Miller-Reilly study, which indicates that prices adjust within a day after the offering.[12]

Exchange Listings Another significant economic event is a firm's decision to list its stock on a national exchange, especially the NYSE. Such a listing is expected to increase the market liquidity of the stock and, possibly, to add to the prestige of the firm. Two questions are important. First, does listing on a major exchange cause a permanent change in the value of a firm? Second, can you derive abnormal returns from

[10]The classic study on this topic is Eugene Fama, Lawrence Fisher, Michael Jensen, and Richard Roll, "The Adjustment of Stock Prices to New Information," *International Economic Review* 10, no. 1 (February 1969): 1–20. A study that reviews the prior research and examines the question using daily data is Frank K. Reilly and Eugene F. Drzycimski, "Short-Run Profits from Stock Splits," *Financial Management* 10, no. 3 (Summer 1981): 64–74.

[11]For a review of past studies in this area, see Roger Ibbotson, Jody L. Sindelar, and Jay Ritter, "Initial Public Offerings," *Journal of Applied Corporate Finance* 1, no. 2 (Summer 1988): 37–45.

[12]Robert E. Miller and Frank K. Reilly, "An Examination of Mispricing, Returns, and Uncertainty for Initial Public Offerings," *Financial Management* 16, no. 3 (Summer 1987): 33–38.

Table 22.1	Number and Average Initial Return of Initial Public Offerings, 1960–1987	

	Number of Offerings[a]	Average Initial Return[b]
1960	269	17.83%
1961	435	34.11
1962	298	−1.61
1963	83	3.93
1964	97	5.32
1965	146	12.75
1966	85	7.06
1967	100	37.67
1968	368	55.86
1969	780	12.53
1970	358	−0.67
1971	391	21.16
1972	562	7.51
1973	105	−17.82
1974	9	−6.98
1975	14	−1.86
1976	34	2.90
1977	40	21.02
1978	42	25.66
1979	103	24.61
1980	259	49.36
1981	438	16.76
1982	198	20.31
1983	848	20.79
1984	516	11.52
1985	507	12.36
1986	953	9.99
1987	630	10.39
Total	8,668	16.37

[a]The number of offerings excludes Regulation A offerings (small issues, raising less than $1.5 million currently). Data are from Ibbotson and Jaffe (1975) for 1960–70, Ritter (1984) for 1971–82, *Going Public: The IPO Reporter* for 1983–85, and *Venture* magazine for 1986–87. The authors have excluded real estate investment trusts (REITs) and closed-end mutual funds.

[b]Initial returns are computed as the percentage return from the offering price to the end-of-the-calendar-month bid price, less the market return, for offerings in 1960–76. For 1977–87, initial returns are calculated as the percentage return from the offering price to the end-of-the-first-day bid price, without adjusting for market movements. Data are from Ibbotson and Jaffe (1975) for 1960, Ritter (1984) for 1971–82, and prepared by the authors for 1983–87. The latter numbers have been prepared with the assistance of Choo-Huang Teoh, using data supplied by Robert E. Miller.

Source: Roger G. Ibbotson, Jody L. Sindelar, and Jay R. Ritter, "Initial Public Offerings," *Journal of Applied Corporate Finance* 1, no. 2 (Summer 1988): 41.

investing in a stock when a new listing is announced or around the time of the actual listing?

Although the results differed slightly, the overall consensus was that listing on a national exchange did not cause a permanent change in the value of a firm.[13] The results about abnormal returns from investing in such stocks were mixed. All the studies agreed that the stocks' prices increased before any announcements of their listings and then consistently declined after their actual listings. The crucial question is, what happens between the announcement of the intent to apply for listing and the actual listing (a period of 4 to 6 weeks)? Although the evidence varies, the more recent studies point toward profit opportunities immediately after the announcement of application for listing and the possibility of excess returns from price declines after the actual listing.[14] Finally, studies that have examined the impact of listing on risk found no significant change in systematic risk or the firm's cost of equity.[15]

In summary, these studies on exchange listings indicate no long-run effects on value or risk. They do, however, give some evidence of short-run profit opportunities. This implies profit opportunities from public information, which does not support the semistrong-form EMH.

Unexpected World Events and Economic News
Almost all investors at one time or another receive major information from television broadcasts or newspapers and wonder whether they should call their brokers and try to make quick killings. Several studies indicate that you should not waste your time or your money on commissions attempting to beat the market on the basis of news flashes.

A study that examined the reaction of stock prices to unexpected world events such as President Eisen-

[13]In this regard, see James C. VanHorne, "New Listings and Their Price Behavior," *Journal of Finance* 25, no. 4 (September 1970): 783–794; Waldemar M. Goulet, "Price Changes, Managerial Actions and Insider Trading at the Time of Listing," *Financial Management* 3, no. 1 (Spring 1974): 30–36.

[14]See Gary Sanger and John McConnell, "Stock Exchange Listings, Firm Value and Security Market Efficiency: The Impact of NASDAQ," *Journal of Financial and Quantitative Analysis* 21, no. 1 (March 1986): 1–25; John J. McConnell and Gary Sanger, "A Trading Strategy for New Listings on the NYSE," *Financial Analysts Journal* 40, no. 1 (January/February 1989): 29–38.

[15]Frank J. Fabozzi, "Does Listing on the AMEX Increase the Value of Equity?" *Financial Management* 10, no. 1 (Spring 1981): 43–50; Kent Baker and James Spitzfaden, "The Impact of Exchange Listing on the Cost of Equity Capital," *The Financial Review* 17, no. 3 (September 1982): 128–141.

hower's heart attack, President Kennedy's assassination, or President Nixon's resignation indicated that prices adjusted to the news before the market first opened after the announcement. Many major economic announcements come when the market is closed and security exchanges will close temporarily for a critical event such as Kennedy's assassination.

A study that examined the response to announcements about the money supply, inflation, real economic activity, and the discount rate found either no impact, or an impact that did not persist beyond the announcement day. An analysis of hourly stock returns and trading volume at times of surprise announcements about money supply, prices, industrial production, and the unemployment rate found that news about money supply and prices had an impact that was reflected in about 1 hour.[16]

Announcements of Accounting Changes Numerous studies have analyzed the impact of announcements of accounting changes on stock prices. In efficient markets security prices should react quickly and predictably to announcements of accounting changes. An announcement of an accounting change that would affect the economic value of the firm should cause a rapid change in stock prices. An accounting change that would affect reported earnings, but that has no economic significance such as a change in the depreciation computation for bookkeeping purposes, should not affect stock prices. A study of annual earnings reports indicated that the stock market reacted as an efficient market advocate would expect to abnormally good or bad earnings reports, but the reaction occurred during the year, rather than when the final earnings numbers became available.

When a firm changes the accounting method by which it reports depreciation from the accelerated method to straight-line depreciation, its reported earnings increase, but this change has no economic consequence. An analysis of stock price movements surrounding these changes in depreciation method generally supported the EMH, finding no indication

[16]Frank K. Reilly and Eugene F. Drzycimski, "Tests of Stock Market Efficiency Following Major World Events," *Journal of Business Research* 1, no. 1 (Summer 1973): 57–72; Douglas Pierce and Vance Roley, "Stock Prices and Economic News," *Journal of Business* 59, no. 1 (Summer 1985): 49–67; Prom C. Jain, "Response of Hourly Stock Prices and Trading Volume to Economic News," *Journal of Business* 61, no. 2 (April 1988): 219–231.

Earnings surprise A company announcement of earnings that differ from analysts' prevailing expectations.

of positive price changes following such accounting changes. In fact, it found some negative effects.

The high rate of inflation during the late 1970s led many firms to change from the first in–first out (FIFO) inventory method to last in–first out (LIFO). Such a change reduces reported earnings, but benefits the firm because it reduces taxable earnings and, therefore, tax expenses. Advocates of efficient markets would expect positive price changes from the tax savings and study results confirmed this expectation. Although earnings were lower than they would have been with FIFO, stock prices generally increased for firms that changed their inventory methods.

Some Anomalies of the Semistrong-Form EMH While the results of numerous studies support the semistrong-form EMH, a growing number of studies have provided evidence that is inconsistent with this hypothesis. In this subsection we discuss a number of these studies. As before, we organize the discussion around specific events such as the release of quarterly earnings reports or items of public information like a firm's market value or price–earnings ratio. In some areas the evidence is clear and consistent, in others it is divided, while in others it has changed over time based upon new data or analytical techniques.

Quarterly Earnings Reports Studies that have focused on the usefulness of quarterly earnings reports have not supported the semistrong-form efficient market hypothesis. Our earlier discussion indicated that stock prices react before the release of annual earnings reports. Another set of studies examined the potential for abnormal profits from investing on the basis of quarterly earnings reports. The investigators typically examined a group of quarterly earnings reports after they were made public and assumed that investors acquired the stocks that had the lowest price–quarterly earnings ratios or those that had the largest **earnings surprises,** which is the difference between a firm's actual and expected quarterly earnings based upon analysts' forecasts.

The results have consistently shown that if you purchased stocks on the basis of strong quarterly earnings or earning surprises after the quarterly earnings reports became public and held them for 6 months, you would receive above-average risk-adjusted rates of return. These results indicate that the information in quarterly income statements has some value.[17] Apparently the market does not adjust stock prices to reflect the release of unexpected quarterly earnings reports as fast as it should according to the semistrong-form EMH.[18]

Differential Price–Earnings Ratios Another area where the evidence does not support the EMH are differential price–earnings ratios. Recall that the P/E ratio is typically computed as the current price of a stock divided by its earnings for the past 12 months. As an example, a stock selling for $60 a share that had earnings for the latest 12 months of $5 a share would have a price–earnings ratio (P/E ratio) of 12 times ($60/$5).

Our prior discussion of fundamental valuation indicated that a stock's P/E ratio should reflect its risk and growth potential. Therefore, in an efficient market you should not expect a difference in the risk-adjusted rate of return for stocks with high P/E ratios (perhaps 20 times earnings) compared to stocks with low P/E ratios (perhaps 5 times earnings). Most investors would probably expect that if there is any bias in P/E ratios, stocks with high P/Es would be more profitable because these stocks are expected to have higher growth rates.

In fact, several studies on this topic have indicated an *inverse* relationship between realized rates of re-

turn and P/E ratios. Specifically, these studies showed that investors could have derived above-average risk-adjusted rates of return by investing in stocks with relatively low P/E ratios, while portfolios of stocks with relatively high P/E ratios experienced rates of return that were below normal for the risk involved. Because these results indicate that investors could experience these abnormal risk-adjusted rates of return using available information on prices and earnings, this should be considered an anomaly that contradicts the semistrong-form EMH.[19]

The Firm Size Effect The impact of firm size on rates of return has received extensive attention during the past decade.[20] Size is measured in terms of the total market value of the firm, which equals the number of common shares outstanding times the current market price of a share. The studies followed a standard procedure, ranking all the stocks in a sample on the basis of market value and dividing the sample into 10 portfolios with equal numbers of stocks. Using beta as the measure of risk, the investigators derived risk-adjusted abnormal returns for the 10 portfolios over extended time periods (10 to 15 years). The results indicated a significant inverse relationship. Small firms consistently experienced above-average risk-adjusted rates of return and the largest firms experienced below-average risk-adjusted returns.

These studies on market efficiency test both the EMH and the CAPM by which we derive expected rates of return. These results may have occurred because markets are not efficient, or because the market model does not provide a correct estimate of a stock's required return. The model may underestimate expected return for small firms. Roll and Dimson contended that small firms' beta coefficients were

[17]Articles that review these studies include O. Maurice Joy and Charles P. Jones, "Earnings Reports and Market Efficiencies: An Analysis of Contrary Evidence," *Journal of Financial Research* 2, no. 1 (Spring 1979): 51–64; Ray Ball, "Anomalies in Relationships between Securities' Yields and Yield-Surrogates," *Journal of Financial Economics* 6, no. 2/3 (June–September 1978): 103–126; Ross L. Watts, "Systematic 'Abnormal' Returns after Quarterly Earnings Announcements," *Journal of Financial Economics* 6, no. 2/3 (June–September 1978): 127–150; Charles P. Jones, Richard J. Rendleman, Jr., and Henry A. Latane, "Earnings Announcements: Pre-and-Post Responses," *Journal of Portfolio Management* 11, no. 3 (Spring 1985): 28–33; Richard R. Mendenhall, "An Investigation of Anomalies Based on Unexpected Earnings" (Ph.D. dissertation, Indiana University, 1986); and Victor L. Bernard and Jacob K. Thomas, "Post-Earnings-Announcement Drift: Delayed Price Response or Risk Premium?" *Journal of Accounting Research* 27, supplement (1989).

[18]Studies indicating the importance of unexpected earnings have led *The Wall Street Journal* to publish a section on "earnings surprises" twice a week in connection with reports of regular quarterly earnings.

[19]The most widely quoted studies in this area are S. Basu, "Investment Performance of Common Stocks in Relation to Their Price–Earnings Ratios: A Test of the Efficient Market Hypothesis," *Journal of Finance* 32, no. 2 (June 1977): 663–682; and S. Basu, "The Information Content of Price–Earnings Ratios," *Financial Management* 4, no. 2 (Summer 1975): 53–64.

[20]The major initial studies were R. W. Banz, "The Relationship between Return and the Market Value of Common Stocks," *Journal of Financial Economics* 9, no. 1 (March 1981): 3–18; Marc Reinganum, "Misspecification of Capital Asset Pricing: Empirical Anomalies Based on Earnings Yield and Market Values," *Journal of Financial Economics* 9, no. 1 (March 1981): 19–46; Marc Reinganum, "Abnormal Returns in Small Firm Portfolios," *Financial Analysts Journal* 37, no. 2 (March–April 1981): 52–57.

underestimated because of infrequent trading.[21] Reinganum confirmed that the risk measures (betas) of small firms were underestimated, but he also showed that even with reestimated betas, small firms still experienced superior risk-adjusted returns.[22]

Another factor suggested to explain the abnormal returns was the higher costs of transactions for small versus large firms.[23] The study showed larger bid–ask spreads and higher commission percentages for small firms. With these higher transaction costs, if you adjust and rebalance your portfolio daily, the results reverse. If, however, you only adjust the portfolio once a year, the original differential in favor of small firms returns. Reinganum confirmed that annual rebalancing preserved the small-firm effect compared to a buy-and-hold policy, and found that transaction costs were not a factor when you assumed annual rebalancing.[24]

Researchers have also suggested that investors should consider firms that are not heavily followed by analysts (neglected firms). These neglected firms have been shown to provide excess returns even after taking account of the size effect.[25] After adjustment for firm size, industry effects, and infrequent trading, the risk-adjusted returns for the low P/E stocks were superior to those for the high P/E stocks.[26] A study that examined the relationship of returns, market size, and trading volume confirmed the negative relationship between size and rates of return, but indicated that trading activity had no impact on the rate of return.[27]

Finally, an examination of the performance of small firms over various time periods indicated that the small-firm effect is not stable.[28] During most periods, the negative relationship between size and rate of return derived by others held, but during some periods, such as 1967 to 1975, the authors found *positive* relationships with the stock of large firms experiencing higher risk-adjusted performance than that of small firms. Incidentally, analysis of recent returns indicates that this positive relationship held during the 4-year period from 1984 to 1987 and also during 1989.

The January Anomaly Some have suggested that our tax laws encourage investors to sell securities that have declined toward the end of the year to take tax losses and after the new year to reacquire these stocks or others that look attractive. This scenario would produce downward pressure on stock prices in late November and December and positive pressure in early January. Those who believe in efficient markets would not expect such a seasonal pattern to persist, because arbitrageurs' or speculators' attempts to profit from such a scenario by buying in December and selling in early January should correct the imbalance.

Some early work indicated that this trading rule could yield excess returns and more recent studies have confirmed these results.[29] Another study supported the January anomaly, and also showed a small-firm impact beyond the January effect.[30] Keim found a negative relationship between size and abnormal

[21]Richard Roll, "A Possible Explanation of the Small Firm Effect," *Journal of Finance* 36, no. 4 (September 1981): 879–888; and Elroy Dimson, "Risk Measurement When Shares Are Subject to Infrequent Trading," *Journal of Financial Economics* 7, no. 2 (June 1979): 197–226.

[22]Marc R. Reinganum, "A Direct Test of Roll's Conjecture on the Firm Size Effect," *Journal of Finance* 37, no. 1 (March 1982): 27–35.

[23]Hans Stoll and Robert E. Whaley, "Transactions Costs and the Small Firm Effect," *Journal of Financial Economics* 12, no. 1 (June 1983): 57–80.

[24]Marc R. Reinganum, "Portfolio Strategies Based on Market Capitalization," *Journal of Portfolio Management* 9, no. 2 (Winter 1983): 29–36.

[25]Avner Arbel and Paul Strebel, "Pay Attention to Neglected Firms," *Journal of Portfolio Management* 9, no. 2 (Winter 1983): 37–42.

[26]John W. Peavy III and David A. Goodman, "The Significance of P/Es for Portfolio Returns," *Journal of Portfolio Management* 9, no. 2 (Winter 1983): 43–47.

[27]Christopher James and Robert Edmister, "The Relation between Common Stock Returns, Trading Activity, and Market Values," *Journal of Finance* 38, no. 4 (September 1983): 1075–1086.

[28]Philip Brown, Allen W. Kleidon, and Terry A. Marsh, "New Evidence on the Nature of the Size-Related Anomalies in Stock Prices," *Journal of Financial Economics* 12, no. 1 (June 1983): 33–56.

[29]The early studies included Ben Branch, "A Tax Loss Trading Rule," *Journal of Business* 50, no. 2 (April 1977): 198–207; and Edward A. Dyl, "Capital Gains Taxation and Year-End Stock Market Behavior," *Journal of Finance* 32, no. 1 (March 1977): 165–175. Recent studies are, Marc R. Reinganum, "The Anomalous Stock Market Behavior of Small Firms in January: Empirical Tests for Tax-Loss Selling Effects," *Journal of Financial Economics* 12, no. 1 (January 1983): 89–104; and Ben Branch and Kyungchun Chang, "Tax-Loss Trading—Is the Game Over or Have the Rules Changed?" *Financial Review* 20, no. 1 (February 1985): 55–69.

[30]Richard Roll, "Vas Ist Das?" *Journal of Portfolio Management* 9, no. 2 (Winter 1983): 18–28.

returns, but the strongest relationship, accounting for nearly 50 percent of the overall size effect, always occurred in January.[31] In fact, more than 50 percent of the January effect was concentrated in the first week of trading, particularly on the first trading day of the year.

While the original rationale for the January effect cited tax selling, several studies in foreign countries confirm the January effect, despite differences in tax laws.[32] Finally, further support for a January effect has been derived from a study that indicated that the risk-return relationship for stocks occurred only in January, and that a dividend yield–stock return relationship was likewise concentrated in January.[33]

In summary, the January anomaly is intriguing because it is so pervasive. The original tax loss explanation of this anomaly has, however, received mixed support. The combined January small-firm effect is fascinating because it also indicates very rapid adjustment of returns. This seasonal January effect also influences the dividend yield effect and trading volume. Despite a plethora of studies, the January anomaly persists in posing as many questions as it answers.[34]

Other Calendar Effects While not as significant as the January anomaly, several other calendar effects disrupt efficiency including a monthly effect, a weekend/day-of-the-week effect, and an intraday effect. Ongoing research on the weekend–Monday effect has provided several changes. The early work examined daily returns, measuring the return from the close on Friday to the close on Monday. This research consistently found a significant negative return for Monday and positive average returns for the other four days.

This Monday effect was confirmed for listed and OTC stocks, for Treasury bills, different-sized firms, and for individual stocks.

A later study decomposed Monday returns into two components: a pure weekend return from the Friday close to the Monday open, and a pure Monday return from the Monday open to the Monday close. It found that all of the negative Monday effect was due to the pure weekend return, while the pure Monday effect was positive.[35]

A subsequent analysis examining hourly observations on Monday for the period 1963 to 1983 confirmed these results for the latter half of the period (1974 to 1983), but found the negative effective on Monday from 1963 to 1974.[36] Also it discovered that the pure Monday effect has turned positive because the negative Monday *morning* effect is swamped by a positive Monday *afternoon* effect.

Finally, an analysis of transaction data showed that the Monday effect differed by firm size. For large firms, the negative returns occurred on the weekend; for small firms, the negative impact occurred on Monday.[37] It was also discovered that prices declined only during the first 45 minutes of the day, while on other weekday mornings they increased. Otherwise, price patterns during the rest of Mondays were similar to those for other days, including a strong tendency for prices to rise on the last trade of the day. The evolution of the findings on the Monday effect is a prime example of how conclusions change over time as new research applies new statistical techniques to more detailed data.

The Value Line Enigma Value Line (VL), a large, well-known advisory service, publishes financial information on approximately 1,700 stocks. (See Chapter 5 for an example of a Value Line company report.) One of the items included in a VL report is a timing rank, which indicates Value Line's expectation regarding a common stock's performance over the coming 12

[31]Donald B. Keim, "Size-Related Anomalies and Stock Return Seasonality," *Journal of Financial Economics* 12, no. 1 (June 1983): 13–22.

[32]Philip Brown, Donald B. Keim, Allan W. Kleidon, and Terry A. Marsh, "Stock Return Seasonalities and the Tax-Loss Selling Hypothesis," *Journal of Financial Economics* 12, no. 1 (June 1983): 105–127; and Angel Berges, John J. McConnell, and Gary G. Schlarbaum, "The Turn-of-the-Year in Canada," *Journal of Finance* 39, no. 1 (March 1984): 185–192.

[33]Seha M. Tinic and Richard R. West, "Risk and Return! January vs. the Rest of the Year," *Journal of Financial Economics* 13, no. 4 (December 1984): 561–574; and Donald B. Keim, "Dividend Yields and the January Effect," *Journal of Portfolio Management* 12, no. 2 (Winter 1986): 54–60.

[34]An article that reviews these studies and others is Donald B. Keim, "The CAPM and Equity Return Regularities," *Financial Analysts Journal* 41, no. 3 (May/June 1986): 19–34.

[35]Richard J. Rogalski, "New Findings Regarding Day-of-the-Week Returns over Trading and Non-Trading Periods: A Note," *Journal of Finance* 39, no. 5 (December 1984): 1603–1614.

[36]Michael Smirlock and Laura Stacks, "Day-of-the-Week and Intraday Effects in Stock Returns," *Journal of Financial Economics* 17, no. 1 (September 1986): 197–210.

[37]Lawrence Harris, "A Transaction Data Study of Weekly and Intradaily Patterns in Stock Returns," *Journal of Financial Economics* 16, no. 1 (May 1986): 99–117.

months. A rank of 1 indicates the most favorable performance outlook and a rank of 5 the worst.

This ranking system, initiated in April 1965, is based upon a filter rule that considers several publicly available price and earnings factors. The top 100 firms are ranked 1 and the bottom 100 are ranked 5. The next 300 down from the top and up from the bottom are ranked 2 and 4, respectively, and the rest (approximately 900 firms) are ranked 3. The firm assigns rankings every week based upon the latest data. With the publication listing the new rankings ready on Wednesday, Value Line attempts a staggered mailing so that all subscribers receive it on Friday.

Several years after starting the ranking system, Value Line indicated that the performance of the stocks in the various classes differed substantially. Stocks rated 1 substantially outperformed the aggregate stock market, and stocks rated 5 seriously underperformed the market based upon performance figures that included neither dividend income nor commissions. This claim challenged the semistrong-form EMH because it implied that investors could create superior portfolios simply by using the VL rankings after they became public.

Studies of this phenomenon have considered many alternative trading rules including buying all stocks ranked 1 and selling stocks ranked 5 continuously or annually, buying and selling stocks the ranks of which changed from 2 to 1 or 4 to 5, concentrating on different-sized firms, or examining new additions to the stock universe. All of these investigators were very conscious of the effect of transaction costs, which depended on how often they revised the sample portfolios, and also the effect of having the transactions on Thursday, Friday, Monday, or Tuesday.

The results of these studies indicate that there is information in the VL rankings (especially ranks 1 and 5) and in changes in the rankings (especially going from 2 to 1). While these changes in rank have larger effects on smaller firms, the studies found no direct relationship between the VL rankings and the size anomaly. Further, most of the recent evidence indicates that the market is fairly efficient, since the abnormal adjustments appear to be complete by Tuesday, which is two trading days after the release. More recent studies have indicated even faster adjustment to this information. Also, although the price changes are statistically significant, mounting evidence suggests that realistic transaction costs prevent abnormal returns from these price changes.[38]

Dividend Yields Some relatively recent research has term stock returns as indicated by correlations that increase with the return horizon. It has been suggested that dividend yields and future returns maintain this relationship because dividend yields are a proxy for the risk premium on stocks.[39] The most recent study by Balvers, Cosimano, and McDonald provides a theoretical model to explain the phenomenon.[40] Their model and test results show that within an efficient market framework, stock prices do not have to follow a random walk and it is possible to predict long-run returns on stocks as long as you can predict aggregate output.

Summary Regarding Semistrong-Form EMH Results The evidence regarding the semistrong-form EMH is mixed. Numerous studies that have examined specific events such as stock splits, world events, and accounting changes have consistently supported the semistrong-form EMH. They have indicated swift reactions of security prices to new information and shown the ability of dividend yields to forecast long-suggested that investors generally could not derive abnormal returns by acting after announcements of events.

In contrast, some recent studies have suggested and tested a number of anomalies. The evidence from studies that analyzed unexpected quarterly earnings and those that examined the performance of stocks with low P/E ratios and stocks of small and neglected firms does not support the hypothesis. Further, a January anomaly and other calendar effects clearly affect

---

[38]For a fairly typical study of the enigma that discusses some of the prior research, see Scott E. Stickel, "The Effect of Value Line Investment Survey Changes on Common Stock Prices," *Journal of Financial Economics* 14, no. 1 (March 1985): 121–143. A recent review and reconciliation of the Value Line results with the EMH are contained in Gur Huberman and Shmuel Kandel, "Market Efficiency and Value Line's Record," *Journal of Business* 63, no. 2 (April 1990): 187–216.

[39]An analysis of this relationship and the explanation is contained in Eugene F. Fama and Kenneth R. French, "Dividend Yields and Expected Stock Returns," *Journal of Financial Economics* 22, no. 1 (October 1988): 3–25; Eugene F. Fama and Kenneth R. French, "Business Conditions and Expected Returns on Stocks and Bonds," *Journal of Financial Economics* 25, no. 1 (November 1989): 23–49; and Michael Rozeff, "Dividend Yields are Equity Risk Premiums," *Journal of Portfolio Management* 11, no. 1 (Fall 1984): 68–75.

[40]Ronald J. Balvers, Thomas F. Cosimano, and Bill McDonald, "Predicting Stock Returns in an Efficient Market," *Journal of Finance* 45, no. 4 (September 1990): 1109–1128.

numerous other areas such as size, the risk–return relationship, and the effect of the dividend yield. Finally, some studies have suggested that information in Value Line rankings can bring excess returns even after the rankings have been published. The results indicate that only certain rankings or rank changes have valuable information and the price adjustment to these rankings is getting faster. Further, the most recent evidence suggests that transaction costs probably prevent excess returns from this information and also indicates that the high returns may be justified by the systematic risk of these stocks. Some recent studies on the use of dividend yields indicate that long-term stock returns are predictable, but it is also shown that these results are consistent with an efficient market.

Strong-Form Hypothesis: Tests and Results

The strong-form EMH contends that stock prices fully reflect all information, public and private. This implies that no group of investors has information that will allow them to consistently experience above-average profits. This extremely rigid hypothesis requires not only that stock prices must adjust rapidly to new public information, but also that no group can have monopoly access to specific information.

Tests of the strong-form EMH have analyzed returns over time for different identifiable investment groups to determine whether any group consistently received above-average risk-adjusted returns. To consistently earn excess returns, a group must have monopolistic access to important information or an ability to act on public information before other investors. This would indicate that security prices were not adjusting rapidly to all new information.

Investigators interested in testing this form of the EMH have analyzed the performance of three major groups of investors. First, several researchers have analyzed the returns to corporate insiders from their stock trading. Another group of studies have analyzed the returns available to stock exchange specialists. The third group of tests have examined the overall performance of professional money managers, emphasizing the risk-adjusted returns experienced by mutual funds because of access to their results.

Corporate Insider Trading Insiders typically include major corporate officers, members of the board of directors, and significant stockholders of a given firm. Securities laws require that these individuals submit monthly reports to the SEC regarding their transactions in the stock of the firm. About 6 weeks after the reporting period, the SEC makes this insider trading information public. Thus it is possible to identify corporate insider transactions over a period of time and to determine whether these transactions (purchases or sales) were generally profitable. The question is, on balance, did insiders buy before abnormally good price movements and sell before poor market periods for their stocks?

The results of these studies generally indicated that corporate insiders consistently enjoyed significantly above-average profits, especially on purchase transactions.[41] This implies that many corporate insiders had otherwise unavailable information from which they derived above-average returns on investments in their companies' stocks. These results would be considered evidence against the strong-form EMH.

Other evidence suggests that public investors whose trades consistently followed insiders based upon SEC announcements of insider transactions would also have enjoyed excess returns after commissions. These results constitute evidence against the semistrong-form EMH, as well, because they imply that investors could derive above-average returns by trading on the basis of public information. This has led *The Wall Street Journal* to publish a monthly column entitled "Inside Track" that discusses the largest insider transactions.

Stock Exchange Specialists Several studies examining the function of stock exchange specialists have determined that specialists have monopolistic access to certain very important information about unfilled limit orders. One would expect specialists to derive above-average returns from this information. This expectation is generally supported by the data.

Specialists seem to generally make money because they typically sell shares at higher prices than they purchase shares. Also, they apparently make money when they are required to buy or sell after unexpected announcements and when they trade in large blocks of stock.

[41]For an article that discusses prior studies and analyzes subsets of insiders, see Kenneth P. Nunn, Jr., Gerald P. Madden, and Michael J. Gombolo, "Are Some Insiders More 'Inside' than Others?" *Journal of Portfolio Management* 9, no. 3 (Spring 1983): 18–22.

An SEC study in the early 1970s examined specialists' rates of return on their capital.[42] The results indicated that these rates of return were substantially above normal, which would not support the strong-form EMH. In fairness to current specialists, the prevailing environment differs substantially from that in the early 1970s. More recent results indicate that specialists are experiencing much lower rates of return following the introduction of competitive rates and other trading practices that have reduced specialists' fees.

Performance of Professional Money Managers
The prior discussion considered tests of the strong-form EMH that examined the risk–return experience of two unique groups of investors who consistently enjoyed above-average returns through monopolistic access to important information. A third group of investors, professional money managers, are more representative because they should not have consistent monopolistic access to important new information. They are, however, highly trained professionals who work full time at investment management. Therefore, if any "normal" investors should be able to derive above-average profits without inside information, this group should. Also, if any noninsider should be able to obtain inside information, it should be professional money managers because they and the security analysts who advise them constantly visit firms and interview corporate officers.

Although investigators would like to examine the performance of a wide range of money managers, most studies have focused on the performance of mutual funds because data on them are readily available. Only recently have data for bank trust departments, insurance companies, and investment advisers been made available.

Several studies of the performance of mutual funds over extended periods have indicated that few have been able to match the performance of a buy-and-hold policy, as measured by the performance of a market series such as the S&P 500 Index. Slightly more than half of a large sample of mutual funds had higher risk-adjusted rates of return before commission costs than the overall market. When commission costs for the funds' trades, the costs of buying fund shares,

and management fees were considered, approximately two-thirds of the mutual funds failed to match the performance of the overall market.

In addition, studies have found that funds do not perform consistently. A fund that did well one year was as likely to perform poorly as to do well the next year. A fund with better-than-average performance two years in a row was no more likely to do well for a third year than one would expect on the basis of random chance. These studies concluded that we cannot predict money managers' future performance based upon their past performance.[43]

Recently, some companies have been collecting performance figures for other institutional investors such as bank trust departments and insurance companies. An example of such results gathered by Frank Russell, Inc. appears in Table 22.2. As can be seen, the results have been quite consistent with the findings on mutual funds.

Studies of the performance of professional money managers have provided support for the strong-form EMH. The results have indicated that most mutual fund managers and other professional money managers using information available both publicly and otherwise could not consistently outperform a buy-and-hold policy.

Conclusions Regarding the Strong-Form EMH
Tests of the strong-form EMH have generated mixed results, but the bulk of relevant evidence has supported the hypothesis. The results for two unique groups of investors (corporate insiders and stock exchange specialists) have not supported the hypothesis because both groups apparently have monopolistic access to important information from which they derive above-average returns.

In contrast, the performance of professional money managers has supported the strong-form EMH. Numerous studies have indicated that these highly trained, full-time investors could not consistently outperform a simple buy-and-hold policy on a risk-adjusted basis. Because this last group most closely resembles common investors who lack consistent access to inside information, these results are considered most relevant to the hypothesis. Therefore, we find substantial support for the strong-form EMH as applied to most investors.

[42]U.S. Securities and Exchange Commission, *Institutional Investor Study Report*, 92d Congress, 1st Session, House Document No. 92–64 (Washington, D.C.: U.S. Government Printing Office, 1971).

[43]A number of studies on mutual fund performance are discussed in detail in Chapter 19.

| Table 22.2 | Annual Rates of Return during Alternative Periods ending December 31, 1989 |

	Years					
	1	2	4	6	8	10
U.S. Equity Broad Universes						
Equity accounts	26.99%	20.95%	15.80%	16.31%	17.65%	16.92%
Equity pooled accounts	27.32	20.53	15.41	15.50	17.02	16.51
Equity-oriented separate accounts	26.99	21.35	16.06	17.02	18.72	18.15
Special equity	27.62	23.27	13.81	12.75	15.89	16.96
Mutual Fund Universes						
Balanced and income funds	23.59	19.64	14.31	15.33	16.97	15.69
Growth funds	27.17	19.60	14.44	13.68	15.57	15.29
U.S. Equity Style Universes						
Earnings growth	35.63	22.22	17.22	16.55	18.43	18.17
Small-capitalization	24.08	21.98	13.09	14.08	18.05	17.77
Price-driven	23.23	22.77	16.05	16.42	19.41	18.85
Market-oriented	29.91	22.40	17.16	17.96	19.19	18.74
S&P 500 Index	31.43	23.74	17.46	17.96	18.75	17.41
Number of universes with returns above S&P 500	1	0	0	0	2	5

Source: Frank Russell Analytical Services, Tacoma, Wash.

Implications of Efficient Capital Markets

Overall, we can safely conclude that the capital markets are generally efficient for the great majority of investors. The substantial and consistent empirical results that support an efficient market suggest that anyone who assumes otherwise takes great risk. This evidence supporting the existence of efficient capital markets has important implications for several groups: technical analysts, investment analysts, and portfolio managers.

Efficient Markets and Technical Analysis

It is widely recognized that the assumptions of technical analysis directly oppose the notion of efficient markets. As a basic premise, technical analysis supposes that stock prices move in trends that persist.[44] Technicians believe that when new information comes to the market, it is not immediately available to everyone, but is typically disseminated from the informed professional to the aggressive investing public, and then to the great bulk of investors. Also, technicians contend that investors do not analyze information and act immediately. This process takes time. Therefore, they hypothesize that stock prices move to new equilibriums after the release of new information in a gradual manner, which causes trends in stock price movements that persist for certain periods.

Technical analysts feel that nimble traders can develop systems to detect the beginning of a movement to a new equilibrium (called a *breakout*). Hence, they hope to buy or sell a stock immediately after its breakout to take advantage of the subsequent price adjustment.

[44]Chapter 15 contains an extensive discussion of technical analysis.

The belief in this pattern of price adjustment directly contradicts the belief of advocates of the EMH that security prices adjust to new information very rapidly. These EMH advocates do not contend, however, that prices adjust perfectly, which means there is a chance of overadjustment or underadjustment. Still, because it is not certain whether the market will over- or underadjust at any given time, you cannot derive abnormal profits from adjustment errors.

If the capital market is efficient and prices fully reflect all relevant information, no technical trading system that depends only upon past trading data can have any value. By the time the information is public, the price adjustment has taken place. Therefore, no purchase or sale using a technical trading rule should generate abnormal returns after taking account of risk and commissions.

Efficient Markets and Fundamental Analysis

As you know from our prior discussion, fundamental analysts believe that, at any time, the aggregate stock market, various industries, or individual securities have basic, intrinsic values and that these values depend upon underlying economic factors. You determine the intrinsic value at a point in time by examining the variables that determine value such as current and future earnings, interest rates, and risk variables. If the prevailing market price differs from the intrinsic value by enough to cover transaction costs, you take appropriate action: you buy if market price is substantially below intrinsic value and sell if it is above. Investors who engage in fundamental analysis believe that occasionally, for short periods of time, market price and intrinsic value differ, but eventually investors recognize any discrepancy and correct it.

If you can do a superior job of *estimating* intrinsic value, you can consistently make superior market timing decisions or acquire undervalued securities and generate above-average returns. Fundamental analysis involves aggregate market analysis, industry analysis, company analysis, and portfolio management. The EMH has important implications for all of these components.

Aggregate Market Analysis with Efficient Capital Markets Chapter 12 makes a strong case that intrinsic value analysis should begin with aggregate market analysis. Still, the EMH implies that any analysis that examines only past economic events is unlikely to

help you outperform a buy-and-hold policy because the market adjusts very rapidly to known economic events. Evidence suggests that the market does experience long-run price movements, but to take advantage of these movements in an efficient market you must do a superior job of *estimating* the variables that cause them. Put another way, if you use only historical data to estimate future values and invest on the basis of these estimates, you will not experience superior risk-adjusted returns.

Industry and Company Analysis with Efficient Capital Markets The wide distribution of returns from different industries and companies clearly justifies industry and company analysis. Again, the EMH does not contradict the value of such analyses, but implies that you need to both understand the variables that affect returns and do a superior job of estimating movements in these variables. To demonstrate this, a model was developed that did an excellent job of explaining *past* stock price movements using historical data. When it was employed to project future stock price changes using past company data, however, the results were consistently inferior to those of a buy-and-hold policy.[45] This result implies that, even with a good valuation model, you cannot select stocks using only past data.

Another study showed that the crucial difference between the stocks with the best and worst price performance during a given year was the relationship between earnings expected by professional analysts and actual earnings; that is, if actual earnings substantially exceeded expected earnings, stock prices increased, and prices fell when earnings did not reach expected levels.[46] Thus, if you can do a superior job of projecting earnings and your expectations differ from the consensus, you will probably have a superior stock selection record.

How to Evaluate Analysts or Investors If you want to determine if an individual is a superior analyst or investor, you should examine the performance of numerous securities that this individual recommends

[45]Burton G. Malkiel and John G. Cragg, "Expectations and the Structure of Share Prices," *American Economic Review* 60, no. 4 (September 1970): 601–617.

[46]Gary A. Benesh and Pamela P. Peterson, "On the Relation Between Earnings Changes, Analysts' Forecasts and Stock Price Fluctuations," *Financial Analysts Journal* 41, no. 6 (November–December 1986).

over time in relation to the performance of a set of randomly selected stocks of the same risk class. The selections of a superior analyst or investor should consistently outperform a random selection. The consistency requirement is crucial because you would expect a portfolio developed by random selection to outperform the market about half the time.

Conclusions about Fundamental Analysis A text on investments can indicate the relevant variables that you should analyze and describe the important techniques, but actually estimating the relevant variables is as much an art as a science. If some mechanical formula could yield accurate estimates, you could program a computer to do it, and there would be no need for analysts. The superior analyst or successful investor must understand what variables are relevant to the valuation process and have the ability to do a superior job of *estimating* these variables.

Efficient Markets and Portfolio Management

As noted, a number of studies have indicated that few professional money managers can beat a buy-and-hold policy on a risk-adjusted basis. One explanation for this generally inferior performance is that there are no superior analysts. The cost of research forces the results of merely adequate analysis into the inferior category. Another explanation, which the author favors with no specific empirical support, is that money management firms employ both superior and inferior analysts and the gains from the recommendations by the few superior analysts are offset by costs and the poor results due to the inferior analysts' recommendations.

This raises the question, should a portfolio be managed actively or passively? A portfolio manager with superior analysts or an investor who feels that he or she has the time and expertise to be a superior investor can manage a portfolio actively, looking for undervalued securities and trading accordingly. In contrast, without superior analysts or the time and ability to be a superior investor, one should manage passively and assume that all securities are properly priced based upon their levels of risk.

Portfolio Management with Superior Analysts A portfolio manager with superior security analysts who have unique insights and analytical ability should follow their recommendations. The superior analysts

should make investment recommendations for a certain proportion of the portfolio, ensuring that the risk preferences of the client are maintained.

Also, the superior analysts should be encouraged to concentrate their efforts in the second tier of stocks. These stocks possess the liquidity required by institutional portfolio managers, but because they do not receive the attention given top-tier stocks, the markets for these neglected stocks may be less efficient than those for large, well-known stocks.[47]

Recall that capital markets should be efficient because many investors receive new information and analyze its effect on security values. If the numbers of analysts following stocks differ, one could conceive of differences in the efficiency of the markets. New information on top-tier stocks is well-publicized and rigorously analyzed, so the prices of these securities should adjust rapidly to reflect the new information. Since middle-tier firms receive less publicity and fewer analysts follow these firms, prices adjust less rapidly to new information. Therefore, the possibilities of finding temporarily undervalued securities among these neglected stocks are greater.

You should handle the part of the portfolio not assigned to the superior analysts, which might be the majority, like the passive portfolio created without superior analysts (discussed next). As a result, the overall performance of the portfolio should beat the market, assuming the pay for the superior analysts did not exceed the value of their recommendations.

Portfolio Management without Superior Analysts As you know, risk is an important determinant of the return an investor expects from an asset: higher risk increases expected return. Whether measured as total risk (the standard deviation of returns) or systematic risk (beta), the risk for a portfolio of stocks is relatively stable over time. Studies have confirmed that this stability is common, and that a good relationship holds between the returns for a portfolio of stocks in one period and the systematic risk of that portfolio in the previous period.[48] This means that you can build a portfolio of stocks with the desired risk characteristics by using historical risk information and receive a rate of return that is fairly consistent with the risk level.

[47]Recall the discussion in Chapter 4 on tiered markets.
[48]William F. Sharpe and Guy M. Cooper, "Risk–Return Classes of New York Stock Exchange Common Stocks, 1931–1967," *Financial Analysts Journal* 28, no. 2 (March–April 1972): 46–54, 81.

If you do not have access to superior analysts, first you should determine your risk preferences. You should then build a portfolio to match this risk level by investing a certain proportion of the portfolio in risky assets and the rest in a risk-free asset, as discussed in Chapters 20 and 21.

You must completely diversify the risky asset portfolio on a global basis so that it moves consistently with the world market. In this context, proper diversification means eliminating all unsystematic (unique) variability. In our prior discussion, we estimated the number of securities needed to gain most of the benefits (over 90 percent) of a completely diversified portfolio at about 15 to 20 securities. More than 100 stocks are required for complete diversification. To decide how many securities to actually include in your portfolio, you must balance the added benefits of worldwide diversification against the costs of researching the additional stocks.

Assuming that you cannot predict future market movements, you must maintain the specified risk level instead of attempting to adjust the risk of the portfolio to match market expectations. Still, changing market values will change the weights for different securities and the overall risk of the portfolio. Therefore, even to maintain a constant risk level, you will have to rebalance your holdings.

Finally, you should minimize transaction costs. Assuming that the portfolio is completely diversified and structured for the desired risk level, excessive transaction costs that do not generate added returns will detract from your expected rate of return. Three factors are involved in minimizing total transaction costs.

1. Minimize taxes. Methods of accomplishing this objective vary, but it should receive primary consideration.
2. Reduce trading turnover. You should trade only to liquidate part of the portfolio or to maintain a given risk level.
3. When you trade, minimize liquidity costs by trading relatively liquid stocks. To accomplish this, you should submit limit orders to buy or sell several stocks at prices that approximate specialists' quotes. That is, you would put in limit orders to buy stock at the bid price or sell at the ask price. The stock that is bought or sold first is the most liquid one; withdraw all other orders.

In summary, if you do not have access to superior analysts, you should do the following:

1. Determine and quantify your risk preferences.
2. Construct the appropriate portfolio by dividing the total portfolio between risk-free and risky assets.
3. Diversify completely on a global basis to eliminate all unsystematic risk.
4. Maintain the specified risk level by rebalancing when necessary.
5. Minimize total transaction costs.

The Rationale and Use of Index Funds As the prior discussion indicates, efficient capital markets and a lack of superior analysts imply that many portfolios should be managed so that their performance matches that of the aggregate market, minimizing the costs of research and trading. In response to this desire, several institutions have introduced market funds, also referred to as *index funds*, which are security portfolios designed to duplicate the composition, and therefore the performance, of a selected market index series.

Three major services started equity index funds in the early 1970s: American National Bank and Trust Company of Chicago, Batterymarch Financial Management Corporation of Boston, and Wells Fargo Investment Advisors, a division of Wells Fargo Bank in San Francisco. All these firms designed equity portfolios to match the performance of the S&P 500 Index. Analysis by the author has documented that the correlation of quarterly rates of return for the index funds and the S&P 500 from 1975 to 1989 exceeded 0.98. This shows that the funds generally fulfill their stated goal of matching market performance.

While these initial funds were only available to institutional investors, at least five index mutual funds are currently available to individuals. In addition, this concept has been extended to other areas of investment. Index bond funds attempt to emulate bond market indexes discussed in Chapter 5 such as the Shearson Lehman bond indexes. Also, there are indexes that focus on several segments of the market including international bond index funds, international stock index funds, funds that target specific countries, and even those that target small-capitalization stocks in the United States and Japan.[49] When portfolio managers decide that they want a

---

[49]For a discussion of some of these indexes, see James A. White, "The Index Boom: It's No Longer Just the S&P 500 Stock Index," *The Wall Street Journal*, May 29, 1991: C1, C3.

given asset class in their portfolios to aid diversification, they often look for index funds for that asset class. This may be easier and less costly in terms of research and commissions, and it may provide the same or better performance available from specific security selection.

Efficiency in European Equity Markets

With rare exceptions, the discussion in this chapter has been concerned with the efficiency of U.S. markets. The growing importance of world markets raises a natural question about the efficiency of securities markets outside the United States. Numerous studies have dealt with this set of questions, and a discussion of them would substantially lengthen the chapter. Fortunately, a monograph by Hawawini reviews numerous studies that examined the behavior of European stock prices and evaluated the efficiency of European equity markets.[50]

The monograph lists over 280 studies covering 14 western European countries from Austria to the United Kingdom classified by country and, within each country, into five categories:

1. Market model, beta estimation, and diversification
2. Capital asset pricing model and arbitrage pricing model
3. Weak-form tests of market efficiency
4. Semistrong-form tests of market efficiency
5. Strong-form tests of market efficiency

The author offers the following overall conclusion after acknowledging that European markets are smaller and less active than U.S. markets:

> Our review of the literature indicates that despite the peculiarities of European equity markets, the behavior of European stock prices is, with few exceptions, surprisingly similar to that of U.S. common stocks. That is true even for countries with extremely narrow equity markets such as Finland. The view that most European equity markets, particularly those of smaller countries, are informationally inefficient does not seem to be borne out by the data. We will see that most of the results of empirical tests performed on European common stock

prices are generally in line with those reported by researchers who used U.S. data.

This implies that when one considers securities outside the United States, it is appropriate to assume a level of efficiency similar to that for U.S. markets.

Summary

■ You need to consider the efficiency of capital markets because of its implications for your investment analysis and portfolio management. Capital markets should be efficient, because numerous rational, profit-maximizing investors react quickly to the release of new information. Assuming prices reflect new information, they are unbiased estimates of the securities' true, intrinsic values, and the relationship between the return on an investment and its risk should be consistent.

■ The voluminous research on the efficient market hypothesis has been divided into three segments that have been tested separately. The weak-form EMH states that stock prices fully reflect all market information, so any trading rule that uses past market data to predict future returns should have no value. The results of studies consistently supported this hypothesis.

■ The semistrong-form EMH asserts that security prices adjust rapidly to the release of all public information. The tests of this hypothesis examine either abnormal price movements surrounding announcements of important new information or whether investors could derive above-average returns from trading on the basis of public information. The test results have been mixed. On the one hand, the results for numerous studies related to economic events such as stock splits and accounting changes consistently support the semistrong-form EMH. In contrast, some recent studies that examined exchange listings, unexpected quarterly earnings, low P/E stocks, small firms, neglected stocks, stocks ranked by Value Line, and the January effect have not supported the hypothesis. Finally, it appears that dividend yields can predict long-run expected returns on stocks, but it is shown that these results are not inconsistent with an efficient market.

■ The strong-form EMH states that security prices reflect all information. This implies that nobody has monopolistic access to important information so no group should be able to derive above-average returns consistently. Studies that examined the results for cor-

[50]Gabriel Hawawini. *European Equity Markets: Price Behavior and Efficiency*, Monograph 1984–4/5, Monograph Series in Finance and Economics, Salomon Brothers Center for the Study of Financial Institutions, Graduate School of Business, New York University, 1984.

porate insiders and stock exchange specialists do not support the strong-form hypothesis. In contrast, analysis of the performance of professional money managers has supported the hypothesis finding that their investment performance was typically inferior to results achieved with buy-and-hold policies.

■ The EMH indicates that technical analysis should have no value. All forms of fundamental analysis are useful, but they are difficult to implement because they require the ability to estimate future values for relevant economic variables. Superior analysis is very difficult because it requires superior projections. Those who manage portfolios should consistently evaluate investment advice to determine whether it is superior.

■ Without access to superior analytical advice, you should run your portfolio like an index fund. In contrast, those with superior analytical ability should be allowed to make decisions, but they should concentrate their efforts on middle-tier firms, where there is a higher probability of discovering misvalued stocks.

■ This chapter reported some good news and some bad news. The good news is that the practices of investment analysis and portfolio management are not arts that we have lost to the great computer in the sky. Viable professions still await those willing to extend the effort and able to accept the pressures. The bad news is that many bright, hard-working people with extensive resources make the game tough. In fact, these competitors have created a fairly efficient capital market in which it is extremely difficult for most analysts and portfolio managers to achieve superior results.

Questions

1. Discuss the rationale for expecting an efficient capital market.
2. Several factors contribute to an efficient market. What factor would you look for to differentiate the market for two alternative stocks? Specifically, why should the efficiency of the markets for the stocks differ?
3. Define and discuss the weak-form EMH.
4. Describe the two sets of tests used to examine the weak-form EMH.
5. Define and discuss the semistrong-form EMH.
6. Describe the two general tests used to examine the semistrong-form EMH. Would you expect the two tests to yield consistent results? Why?
7. Define the term *abnormal rate of return*.
8. Describe how you would compute the abnormal rate of return for a stock for a period surrounding an economic event. Give a brief example for a stock with a beta of 0.70.
9. When testing the EMH by comparing alternative trading rules to a buy-and-hold policy, three common mistakes can bias the results against the EMH. Discuss each individually and explain why it would cause a bias.
10. Describe the results of a study that supported the semistrong-form EMH. Discuss specifically why the results supported the hypothesis.
11. Describe the results of a study that *did not* support the semistrong-form EMH. Discuss specifically why the results did not support the hypothesis.
12. Define and discuss the strong-form EMH. Why do some observers contend that the strong-form hypothesis really requires a perfect market rather than simply an efficient market? Be specific.
13. Discuss how you would test the strong-form EMH. Why are these tests relevant? Give a brief example.
14. Describe the results of a study that *did not* support the strong-form EMH. Discuss specifically why these results did not support the hypothesis.
15. Describe the results of a study that supported the strong-form EMH. Discuss specifically why these results supported the hypothesis.
16. What does the EMH imply for the use of technical analysis?
17. What does the EMH imply for fundamental analysis? Discuss specifically what it does and does not imply.
18. In a world where capital markets are efficient, what do you have to do to be a superior analyst? Be specific.
19. How would you test whether an investor or analyst were truly superior?
20. How should a portfolio manager without any superior analysts run a portfolio?
21. Describe an index fund. What are its goals?
22. Discuss the contention that index funds are the ultimate answer in a world with efficient capital markets.
23. At a social gathering you meet the portfolio manager for the trust department of a local bank. He confides to you that he has been following the recommendations of the department's six analysts for an extended period and has found that two are

superior, two are average, and two are clearly inferior. What would you recommend that he do to run his portfolio?

24. Discuss whether you were surprised by Hawawini's summary of findings related to the EMH for European equity markets.

25. Describe a test of the weak-form EMH for the Japanese stock market and indicate where you would get the required data.

Problems

1. Compute the abnormal rates of return for the following stocks during period t (ignore differential systematic risk):

Stock	R_{it}	R_{mt}
W	11.5%	12.0%
F	10.0	8.5
T	14.0	9.6
C	12.0	13.3
E	13.9	12.4

where:

R_{it} = return for stock i during period t

R_{mt} = return for the aggregate market during period t

2. Compute the abnormal rates of return for the five stocks in Problem 1 assuming the following systematic risk measures (betas):

Stock	β_i
W	0.90
F	1.20
T	1.65
C	0.60
E	−0.20

3. Compare the abnormal returns in Problems 1 and 2 and discuss the reason for the difference in each case.

4. You are given the following data regarding the performance of a group of stocks recommended by an analyst and another set of stocks with matching betas:

Stock	Beginning Price	Ending Price	Dividend
C	43	47	1.50
C-match	22	24	1.00
R	75	73	2.00
R-match	42	38	1.00
L	28	34	1.25
L-match	18	16	1.00
W	52	57	2.00
W-match	38	44	1.50
S	63	68	1.75
S-match	32	34	1.00

Based upon the composite results for these stocks, would you judge this individual to be a superior analyst? Discuss your reasoning.

5. Look up the daily trading volume for the following stocks during a recent 5-day period.

- International Business Machines (IBM)
- General Electric
- Xerox
- General Motors
- Apple Computers

Randomly select five NYSE stocks and examine their daily trading volumes for the same 5 days.

a. What are the average daily volumes for the two samples?

b. Would you expect this difference to have an impact on the efficiency of the markets for the two samples? Why or why not?

References

Ariel, Robert A. "A Monthly Effect in Stock Returns." *Journal of Financial Economics* 18, no. 1 (March 1987).

Ball, Ray. "Anomalies in Relationships between Securities' Yields and Yield-Surrogates." *Journal of Financial Economics* 6, no. 2/3 (June–September 1978).

Balvers, Ronald J., Thomas F. Cosimano, and Bill McDonald. "Predicting Stock Returns in an Efficient Market." *Journal of Finance* 45, no. 4 (September 1990).

Banz, R. W. "The Relationship between Return and Market Value of Common Stocks." *Journal of Financial Economics* 9, no. 1 (March 1981).

Barry, Christopher B., and Stephen J. Brown. "Differential Information and the Small Firm Effect." *Journal of Financial Economics* 13, no. 2 (June 1984).

Basu, Senjoy. "The Relationship between Earnings Yield, Market Value and Return for NYSE Common Stocks." *Journal of Financial Economics* 12, no. 1 (June 1983).

Beatty, Randolph, and Jay Ritter. "Investments Banking, Reputation, and the Underpricing of Initial Public Offerings." *Journal of Financial Economics* 15, no. 1 (March 1986).

Bernard, Victor L., and Jacob K. Thomas. "Post-Earnings–Announcement Drift: Delayed Price Response or Risk Premium." *Journal of Accounting Research* supplement 27 (1989).

Black, Fischer. "Yes, Virginia, There Is Hope: Tests of the Value Line Ranking System." *Financial Analysts Journal* 29, no. 5 (September/October 1973).

Copeland, Thomas E., and David Mayers. "The Value Line Enigma (1965–1978): A Case Study of Performance Evaluation Issues." *Journal of Financial Economics* 10, no. 3 (November 1982).

Fama, Eugene F. "Efficient Capital Markets: A Review of Theory and Empirical Work." *Journal of Finance* 25, no. 2 (May 1970).

Fama, Eugene F., L. Fisher, M. Jensen, and R. Roll. "The Adjustment of Stock Prices to New Information." *International Economic Review* 10, no. 1 (February 1969).

Fama, Eugene F., and Kenneth R. French. "Business Conditions and Expected Returns on Stocks and Bonds." *Journal of Financial Economics* 25, no. 1 (November 1989).

Finnerty, Joseph E. "Insiders and Market Efficiency." *Journal of Finance* 31, no. 4 (September 1976).

Foster, George, Chris Olsen, and Terry Shevlin. "Earnings Releases, Anomalies, and the Behavior of Security Returns." *Accounting Review* 59, no. 4 (October 1984).

French, Kenneth R. "Stock Returns and the Weekend Effect." *Journal of Financial Economics* 8, no. 1 (March 1980).

Gibbons, Michael R., and Patrick Hess. "Day of the Week Effects and Asset Returns." *Journal of Business* 54, no. 4 (October 1981).

Grinblatt, Mark S., Ronald W. Masulis, and Sheridan Titman. "The Valuation Effects of Stock Splits and Stock Dividends." *Journal of Financial Economics* 13, no. 4 (December 1984).

Hawawini, Gabriel. *European Equity Markets: Price Behavior and Efficiency.* Monograph 1984–4/5. Monograph Series in Finance and Economics, Salomon Brothers Center for the Study of Financial Institutions, Graduate School of Business, New York University, 1984.

Huberman, Gur, and Shmuel Kandel. "Market Efficiency and Value Line's Record." *Journal of Business* 63, no. 2 (April 1990).

Keim, Donald B. "Dividend Yields and Stock Returns: Implications of Abnormal January Returns." *Journal of Financial Economics* 14, no. 3 (September 1985).

Keim, Donald B. "Size-Related Anomalies and Stock Return Seasonality." *Journal of Financial Economics* 12, no. 1 (June 1983).

Lakonishok, Josef, and Maurice Lev. "Weekend Effects on Stock Returns: A Note." *Journal of Finance* 37, no. 2 (June 1987).

Lakonishok, Josef, and Seymour Smidt. "Volume and Turn-of-the-Year Behavior." *Journal of Financial Economics* 13, no. 3 (September 1984).

Latane, H. A., and Charles Jones. "Standardized Unexpected Earnings: 1971–1977." *Journal of Finance* 34, no. 3 (June 1979).

Lee, Wayne Y., and Michael E. Solt. "Insider Trading: A Poor Guide to Market Timing." *Journal of Portfolio Management* 12, no. 4 (Summer 1986).

Lorie, James H., Peter Dodd, and Mary Hamilton Kimpton. *The Stock Market: Theories and Evidence*, 2d ed. Homewood, Ill.: Richard D. Irwin, 1985.

Malkiel, Barton G. *A Random Walk Down Wall Street.* New York: W. W. Norton & Co., 1990.

Miller, Robert E., and Frank K. Reilly. "Examination of Mispricing, Returns, and Uncertainty for Initial Public Offerings." *Financial Management* 16, no. 2 (January 1987).

Peterson, David R. "Security Price Reactions to Initial Reviews of Common Stock by the Value Line Investment Survey." *Journal of Financial and Quantitative Analysis* 22, no. 4 (December 1987).

Reilly, Frank K., and Eugene F. Drzycimski. "Short-Run Profits from Stock Splits." *Financial Management* 10, no. 3 (Summer 1981).

Reinganum, Marc R. "Misspecification of Capital Asset Pricing: Empirical Anomalies Based on Earnings Yield and Market Values." *Journal of Financial Economics* 9, no. 1 (March 1981).

Reinganum, Marc R. "The Anomalous Stock Market Behavior of Small Firms in January: Empirical Tests for Tax-Loss Selling Effect." *Journal of Financial Economics* 12, no. 1 (January 1983).

Rendlemen, Richard J. Jr., Charles P. Jones, and Henry A. Latane. "Empirical Anomalies Based on Unexpected Earnings and the Importance of Risk Adjustments." *Journal of Financial Economics* 10, no. 3 (November 1982).

Roll, Richard. "A Possible Explanation of the Small Firm Effect." *Journal of Finance* 36, no. 4 (September 1981).

Seyhun, H. Nejat. "Insiders' Profits, Costs of Trading, and Market Efficiency." *Journal of Financial Economics* 16, no. 2 (June 1986).

Tinic, Seha M., and Richard R. West. "Risk and Return: January vs. the Rest of the Year." *Journal of Financial Economics* 13, no. 4 (December 1984).

Watts, Ross L. "Systematic 'Abnormal' Returns after Quarterly Earnings Announcements." *Journal of Financial Economics* 6, no. 2/3 (June–September 1978).

C H A P T E R

23

Evaluation of Portfolio Performance

Investors are always interested in evaluating the performance of their portfolios. It is both expensive and time-consuming to analyze and select securities for a portfolio, so an individual, company, or institution must determine whether this effort was worth the money and time invested in it. Investors who manage their own portfolios should evaluate their own performance just as those who pay professional money managers must. In the latter case, it is imperative to determine whether the investment performance justifies the cost of the service.

This chapter outlines the theory and practice of evaluating the performance of an investment portfolio. In the initial section we consider what we want from a portfolio manager. We need to pinpoint what to look for before we discuss the techniques used to evaluate the portfolio managers.

In the second section, we begin with a brief discussion of how one evaluated performance before Markowitz created portfolio theory and Sharpe developed the CAPM. The rest of this section discusses in detail three performance evaluation techniques for common stock portfolios called *composite performance measures* because they consider both return and risk.

The third section demonstrates these composite measures by applying them to gauge the performance of a sample of mutual funds. This demonstration includes an analysis of how the three measures relate to each other. You should recognize that while there is some redundancy among the measures, each provides some unique perspectives so they are best viewed as complementary. This section also includes a discussion of factors to consider when applying these measures, with consideration of the work of Roll that questions any evaluation technique that depends upon the CAPM and a market portfolio. This controversy is referred to as the *benchmark problem*. We also discuss why the benchmark problem becomes larger when you begin investing globally. We also discuss studies that have evaluated the reliability of the composite measures' predictions of future performance.

In the final section, we recognize that the factors that determine the performance of a bond portfolio differ from those that affect common stocks. Therefore, we consider several models that attempt specifically to evaluate the performance of fixed-income portfolios.

What Is Required of a Portfolio Manager?

We have two major requirements of a portfolio manager:

1. The ability to derive above-average returns for a given risk class.
2. The ability to completely diversify the portfolio to eliminate all unsystematic risk.

The first requirement, above-average returns, is obvious, but the need to simultaneously consider risk was not generally acknowledged prior to awareness of the work of Markowitz in portfolio theory in the 1960s. As we have noted on several occasions, superior risk-adjusted returns for a stock or bond portfolio can be derived through either superior timing or superior security selection.

An equity portfolio manager who can do a superior job of predicting the peaks and troughs of the equity market can adjust the portfolio's composition to anticipate the market, holding a completely diversified portfolio of high-beta stocks through rising markets and favoring low-beta stocks and money market instruments during declining markets. Bigger gains in rising markets and smaller losses in declining markets would give the portfolio manager above average risk-adjusted returns.

A fixed-income portfolio manager with superior timing ability can change the portfolio's duration in anticipation of interest rate changes, increasing dura-

tion in anticipation of falling interest rates and reducing duration when rates rise. If properly executed, this bond market timing strategy would likewise provide superior risk-adjusted returns.

As an alternative strategy, a portfolio manager could try to consistently select undervalued stocks or bonds for a given risk class. Even without superior market timing, such a portfolio would experience above-average risk-adjusted returns.

The second factor to consider in evaluating a portfolio manager is the ability to diversify completely. As noted in Chapter 21, the market rewards investors only for bearing systematic (market) risk. Unsystematic risk is not considered when determining required returns because it can be eliminated in a diversified market portfolio. Investors consequently want their portfolios completely diversified, which means that they want unsystematic risk eliminated. You can measure the level of diversification by computing the correlation between the returns of the portfolio and the market portfolio. A completely diversified portfolio correlates perfectly with the completely diversified market portfolio because both include only systematic risk.

You need to be constantly aware of these two distinct requirements of a portfolio manager: high risk-adjusted returns and complete diversification. Some portfolio evaluation techniques consider one requirement and not the other, and other techniques implicitly consider both factors, but do not differentiate between them.

Composite Equity Portfolio Performance Measures

At one time investors evaluated portfolio performance almost entirely on the basis of the rate of return. They were aware of the concept of risk, but they did not know how to quantify or measure it so they could not consider it explicitly. Developments in portfolio theory in the early 1960s showed how to quantify and measure risk in terms of the variability of returns. Still, because no single measure combined both return and risk, it was necessary to consider the two factors separately, as researchers had done in several early studies.[1] These investigators grouped portfolios

---

[1] Irwin Friend, Marshall Blume, and Jean Crockett, *Mutual Funds and Other Institutional Investors* (New York: McGraw-Hill, 1970).

into similar risk classes based upon a measure of risk such as the variance of return and then compared the rates of return for alternative portfolios within risk classes.

This section describes in detail the three major composite equity portfolio performance measures that combine risk and return levels into a single value. We describe each measure and what it is meant to do and then demonstrate how to compute it and interpret the results. Also, we directly compare two measures and discuss how they differ and why they would rank portfolios differently.

Treynor Portfolio Performance Measure

Treynor developed the first composite measure of portfolio performance that included risk.[2] He postulated two components of risk: risk produced by general market fluctuations and risk resulting from unique fluctuations in the securities in the portfolio. To identify risk due to market fluctuations, he introduced the characteristic line, which defines the relationship between the rate of return for a portfolio over time and the rate of return for an appropriate market portfolio, as we discussed in Chapter 21. He noted that the slope of the characteristic line measures the relative volatility of the portfolio's returns in relation to returns for the aggregate market, or the portfolio's beta coefficient. A higher slope (beta) characterizes a portfolio that is more sensitive to market returns and has greater market risk.

Deviations from the characteristic line indicate unique returns for the portfolio relative to the market. These differences arise from the returns on individual stocks in the portfolio. In a completely diversified portfolio, these unique returns for individual stocks should cancel out. As the correlation of the portfolio with the market increases, unique risk declines and diversification improves. Because Treynor was not interested in this aspect of portfolio performance, he gave no further consideration to the measure of diversification.

Treynor's Composite Performance Measure

Treynor was interested in a measure of performance that would apply to all investors regardless of their risk preferences. Building upon developments in capital market theory, he introduced a risk-free asset that could be combined with different portfolios to form a straight portfolio possibility line. He showed that rational, risk-averse investors would always prefer portfolio possibility lines with larger slopes because such high-slope lines would place investors on higher indifference curves. The slope of this portfolio possibility line (designated T) is equal to:[3]

$$T_i = \frac{R_i - RFR}{\beta_i}$$

where:

R_i = the average rate of return for portfolio i during a specified time period

RFR = the average rate of return on a risk-free investment during the same time period

β_i = the slope of the portfolio's characteristic line during that time period (this indicates the portfolio's relative volatility).

As noted, a larger T value indicates a larger slope and a better portfolio for all investors, regardless of their risk preferences. Since the numerator of this ratio ($R_i - RFR$) is the risk premium and the denominator is a measure of risk, the total expression indicates the portfolio's return per unit of risk. All risk-averse investors would prefer to maximize this value.

Note that the risk variable beta measures systematic risk and indicates nothing about the diversification of the portfolio. It *implicitly assumes* a completely diversified portfolio, which means that systematic risk is the relevant risk measure.

Comparing a portfolio's T value to a similar measure for the market portfolio indicates whether the portfolio would plot above the SML. You calculate the T value for the aggregate market as follows:

$$T_m = \frac{R_m - RFR}{\beta_m}$$

Note that in this expression β_m equals 1.0, the market's beta, which indicates the slope of the SML.

[2]Jack L. Treynor, "How to Rate Management of Investment Funds," *Harvard Business Review* 43, no. 1 (January–February 1965): 63–75.

[3]The terms used in the formula differ from those used by Treynor, but are consistent with our earlier discussion. Also, our discussion is concerned with general *portfolio* performance, rather than being limited to mutual funds.

Therefore, a portfolio with a higher T value than the market portfolio would plot above the SML. This would indicate superior risk-adjusted performance.

Demonstration of Comparative Treynor Measures To understand how to use and interpret this measure of performance, consider an example. Assume that during the most recent 10-year period, the average annual total rate of return (including dividends) on an aggregate market portfolio such as the S&P 500 was 14 percent ($R_m = 0.14$) and the average nominal rate of return on government T-bills was 8 percent ($RFR = 0.08$). Assume that, as administrator of a large pension fund that has been divided among three money managers during the past 10 years, you must decide whether to renew your investment management contracts with all three money managers. To do this, you must measure how they have performed.

A later section will show how the numbers have been derived. For now, assume you are given the following results:

Investment Manager	Average Annual Rate of Return	Beta
Z	0.12	0.90
B	0.16	1.05
Y	0.18	1.20

On the basis of this information, you can compute T values for the market portfolio and for each of the individual portfolio managers, as follows:

$$T_m = \frac{0.14 - 0.08}{1.00} = 0.060$$

$$T_z = \frac{0.12 - 0.08}{0.90} = 0.044$$

$$T_b = \frac{0.16 - 0.08}{1.05} = 0.076$$

$$T_y = \frac{0.18 - 0.08}{1.20} = 0.083$$

These results would indicate that investment manager Z not only ranked the lowest of three managers, but did not do as well as the aggregate market did. In contrast, both B and Y beat the market portfolio, and manager Y performed somewhat better than manager B. In terms of the SML, both of their portfolios plotted above the line, as shown in Figure 23.1.

Very poor performance or very good performance with very low risk can yield negative T values. An example of poor performance would be a portfolio with both an average rate of return below the risk-free rate and a positive beta. As an example, in the preceding case assume that a fourth portfolio manager, X, had a portfolio beta of 0.50, but an average rate of return of only 0.07. The T value would be:

$$T_x = \frac{0.07 - 0.08}{0.50} = -0.02$$

Obviously, this performance would plot below the SML in Figure 23.1.

A portfolio with a negative beta and an average rate of return above the risk-free rate of return would likewise have a negative T value. In this case, however, it would indicate exemplary performance. As an example, assume that a portfolio manager invested heavily in gold mining stocks during a period of great political and economic uncertainty. Because gold typically has a negative correlation with most stocks, this portfolio's beta could be negative. If you were examining this portfolio after gold prices had increased as a result of the uncertainty, you might find excellent returns. Assume that our gold bug portfolio had a beta of -0.20 and yet experienced an average rate of return of 10 percent. Its T value would be:

$$T = \frac{0.10 - 0.08}{-0.20} = -0.100$$

Although the T value is -0.100, you can see that plotting these results on the graph in Figure 23.1 would indicate a position substantially above the SML.

Since negative betas can yield T values that give confusing results, it is preferable either to plot the portfolio on an SML graph or to compute the expected return using the SML equation and compare it to the actual return. This comparison will tell you whether the actual return was above or below expectations. In the preceding example, the expected return would be:

$$
\begin{aligned}
E(R_i) &= RFR + \beta_i (R_m - RFR) \\
&= 0.08 + (-0.20)(0.06) \\
&= 0.08 - 0.012 \\
&= 0.068
\end{aligned}
$$

| Figure 23.1 | *Plot of Performance on SML (T Measure)* |

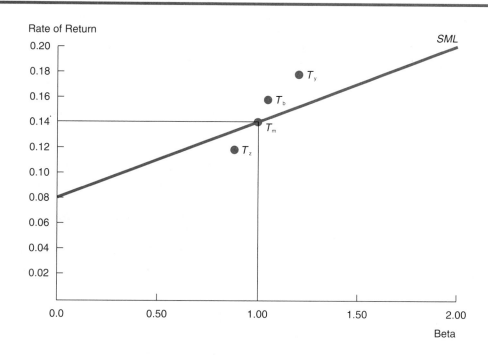

Comparing this expected (required) rate of return of 6.8 percent to the actual return of 10 percent shows that the portfolio manager has done a superior job.

Sharpe Portfolio Performance Measure

Sharpe likewise conceived of a composite measure to evaluate the performance of mutual funds.[4] The measure followed closely his earlier work on the capital asset pricing model (CAPM), dealing specifically with the capital market line (CML). The Sharpe portfolio performance measure (designated S) is stated as follows:

$$S_i = \frac{R_i - RFR}{SD_i}$$

where:

S_i = Sharpe portfolio performance measure for portfolio i

R_i = the average rate of return for portfolio i during a specified time period

RFR = the average rate of return on risk-free assets during the same period

SD_i = the standard deviation of the rate of return for portfolio i during the same period

This composite measure of portfolio performance is clearly similar to the Treynor measure, but it seeks to measure the *total* risk of the portfolio by including the standard deviation of returns rather than considering only the systematic risk by including beta. Because the numerator is the portfolio's risk premium, this measure indicates the risk premium earned per unit of total risk. In terms of capital market theory, this portfolio performance measure uses total risk to compare portfolios to the CML, whereas the Treynor measure examines portfolio performance in relation to the SML.

Demonstration of Comparative Sharpe Measures The following examples use the Sharpe mea-

[4]William F. Sharpe, "Mutual Fund Performance," *Journal of Business* 39, no. 1, Part 2 (January 1966): 119–138.

sure of performance. Again assume that $R_m = 0.14$ and $RFR = 0.08$. Suppose you are told that the standard deviation of the annual rate of return for the market portfolio over the past 10 years was 20 percent ($SD_m = 0.20$). Now you want to examine the performance of the following portfolios:

Portfolio	Average Annual Rate of Return	Standard Deviation of Return
B	0.13	0.18
O	0.17	0.22
P	0.16	0.23

The Sharpe measures for these portfolios would be as follows:

$$S_m = \frac{0.14 - 0.08}{0.20} = 0.300$$

$$S_b = \frac{0.13 - 0.08}{0.18} = 0.278$$

$$S_o = \frac{0.17 - 0.08}{0.22} = 0.409$$

$$S_p = \frac{0.16 - 0.08}{0.23} = 0.348$$

The B portfolio had the lowest risk premium per unit of total risk, failing even to perform as well as the aggregate market portfolio. In contrast, portfolios O and P performed better than the aggregate market: portfolio O did better than portfolio P.

Given the results for the market portfolio during this period, it is possible to draw the CML. If we then plot the results for portfolios B, O, and P on this graph, as shown in Figure 23.2, we see that portfolio B plots below the line, whereas the O and P portfolios are above the line, indicating superior risk-adjusted performance.

Treynor Measure versus Sharpe Measure The Sharpe portfolio performance measure uses the standard deviation of returns as the measure of risk, whereas the Treynor performance measure employs beta. The Sharpe measure, therefore, evaluates the portfolio manager on the basis of both rate of return performance and diversification.

For a completely diversified portfolio, one without any unsystematic risk, the two measures would give identical rankings because the total variance of the completely diversified portfolio is its systematic variance. A poorly diversified portfolio could have a high ranking on the basis of the Treynor performance measure, but a much lower ranking on the basis of the Sharpe performance measure. Any difference in rank would come directly from a difference in diversification.

These two measures provide complementary information, and both should be used. If you are dealing with a group of portfolios that are well-diversified, as are most mutual funds, then the two measures should provide very similar rankings.

Jensen Portfolio Performance Measure

The Jensen measure is similar to the measures already discussed since it is based upon the capital asset pricing model (CAPM).[5] All versions of the CAPM calculate the expected 1-period return on any security or portfolio by the following expression:

$$E(R_j) = RFR + \beta_j[E(R_m) - RFR]$$

where:

$E(R_j)$ = the expected return on security or portfolio j

RFR = the 1-period risk-free interest rate

β_j = the systematic risk for security or portfolio j

$E(R_m)$ = the expected return on the market portfolio of risky assets

The expected return and the risk-free return differ for different periods. Therefore, we are concerned with the time series of expected rates of return for security or portfolio j. Moreover, assuming that the asset pricing model is empirically valid, you can express the expectations formula in terms of realized rates of return as follows:

$$R_{jt} = RFR_t + \beta_j(R_{mt} - RFR_t) + U_{jt}$$

This equation indicates that the realized rate of return on a security or portfolio during a given time period should be a linear function of the risk-free rate of return, plus some risk premium that depends on the systematic risk of the security or portfolio plus a random error term.

---

[5]Michael C. Jensen, "The Performance of Mutual Funds in the Period 1945–1964," *Journal of Finance* 23, no. 2 (May 1968): 389–416.

Figure 23.2 *Plot of Performance on CML (S Measure)*

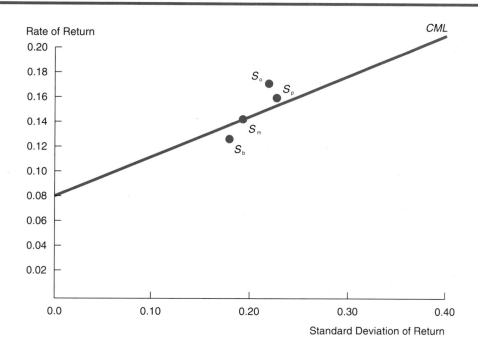

Subtracting the risk-free return from both sides, we have:

$$R_{jt} - RFR_t = \beta_j(R_{mt} - RFR_t) + U_{jt}$$

This indicates that the risk premium earned on security or portfolio j equals β_j times a market risk premium plus a random error term. In this form, one would not expect an intercept for the regression if all assets and portfolios were in equilibrium.

Alternatively, certain superior portfolio managers who could forecast market turns or consistently select undervalued securities would earn higher risk premiums than those implied by this model. Specifically, superior portfolio managers would have consistently positive random error terms because the actual returns for their portfolios would consistently exceed expected returns. To detect and measure this superior performance, you need to allow for an intercept (a nonzero constant) that measures any positive difference from the model. The positive difference would cause a positive intercept. With an intercept or nonzero constant, the earlier equation becomes:

$$R_{jt} - RFR_t = \alpha_j + \beta_j(R_{mt} - RFR_t) + U_{jt}$$

In this equation, the α_j value indicates whether the portfolio manager is superior or inferior in market timing and/or stock selection. A superior manager would have a significant positive α_j value because of the consistent positive residuals. In contrast, an inferior portfolio manager's returns would consistently fall short of expectations based upon the CAPM model giving consistently negative residuals. In such a case, the nonzero constant (α_j) would be a significant negative value.

The performance of a portfolio manager who had no forecasting ability but was not clearly inferior would equal that of a naive buy-and-hold policy. In the equation, since the rate of return on such a portfolio would typically match the returns that you expect on the basis of the CAPM, the residual returns would generally be randomly positive and negative. This would give a constant term that would differ insignificantly from zero, indicating that the portfolio manager basically matched the market on a risk-adjusted basis.

Therefore, the α_j represents how much of the rate of return on the portfolio is attributable to the manager's ability to derive above-average returns adjusted for risk. Superior risk-adjusted returns indicate that the manager is good at predicting market turns and/or selecting undervalued issues for the portfolio.

Applying the Jensen Measure The Jensen measure of performance requires that you use a different RFR for each time interval during the sample period. As an example, to examine the performance of a fund manager over a 10-year period using yearly intervals, you need to subtract the return on risk-free assets for each year from the annual returns for the fund and relate this to the annual return on the market portfolio less the same risk-free rate. This contrasts with the Treynor or Sharpe composite measures of performance, which examine the average returns for the total period for all variables.

Also, like the Treynor measure, the Jensen performance measure does not evaluate the ability of the portfolio manager to diversify, since it calculates risk premiums in terms of systematic risk. As noted earlier, to evaluate the performance of a group of well-diversified portfolios such as mutual funds, this is probably a fairly legitimate assumption. Jensen's analysis of mutual fund performance showed that complete diversification was a fairly reasonable assumption because the funds typically correlated with the market at rates above 0.90.

Application of Portfolio Performance Measures

To demonstrate how to apply these measures, we selected 20 open-end mutual funds for which data were available for the 15-year period from 1975 to 1989. The annual rates of return for the first fund (Affiliated Fund, Inc.) and the S&P 500 appear in Table 23.1. The total rate of return for each year is computed as follows:

$$R_{it} = \frac{EP_{it} + Div._{it} + Cap.\ Dist._{it} - BP_{it}}{BP_{it}}$$

Table 23.1 *Computation of Annual Rates of Return for Affiliated Fund, Inc. and Standard & Poor's 500: 1975–1989*

	Affiliated Fund, Inc.				S&P 500		
	Ending Price	Dividends	Capital Gains Distributions	Return (percentage)	Ending Price	Dividends	Return (percentage)
1974	5.54	—	—	—	68.56	—	—
1975	7.29	0.26	0.12	38.45	90.19	3.68	36.92
1976	9.15	0.34	0.22	33.20	107.46	4.05	23.64
1977	7.99	0.37	0.15	−6.99	95.10	4.67	−7.16
1978	7.52	0.39	0.31	2.88	96.11	5.07	6.39
1979	8.69	0.45	0.44	27.39	107.94	5.65	18.19
1980	9.47	0.51	0.71	23.01	135.76	6.16	31.48
1981	8.36	0.56	0.49	−0.63	122.55	6.63	−4.85
1982	9.26	0.56	0.33	21.41	140.64	6.87	20.37
1983	10.15	0.52	0.82	24.08	164.93	7.09	22.31
1984	9.68	0.53	0.48	5.32	164.48	7.53	4.29
1985	10.68	0.56	0.81	24.48	207.26	7.90	30.81
1986	11.32	0.55	1.14	21.82	248.61	8.28	23.95
1987	9.63	0.58	1.34	2.03	240.96	8.81	0.47
1988	9.92	0.48	0.35	11.63	276.51	9.73	18.79
1989	11.31	0.47	0.36	22.38	353.40	11.05	31.80
Average return				16.70			17.16

where:

R_{it} = the total return on fund i during year t

EP_{it} = the ending price for fund i during year t

Cap. Dist.$_{it}$ = the capital gain distributions made by fund i during year t

Div.$_{it}$ = the dividend payments made by fund i during year t

BP_{it} = the beginning price for fund i during year t

These return computations do not take into account any sales charges by the funds. Given the annual results for the fund and the aggregate market (as represented by the S&P 500), you can compute the composite measures presented in Table 23.2.

The arithmetic average annual rate of return for Affiliated was slightly lower than that for the market (16.70 percent versus 17.16 percent), but the fund's beta was likewise below 1.00 (0.89). Using the average rate on T-bills of 8.31 percent as the RFR, the Treynor measure for the Affiliated Fund beat the same measure for the market (9.427 percent versus 8.850 percent). Likewise, the standard deviation of returns

Table 23.2 *Computation of Portfolio Evaluation Measures: Affiliated Fund, Inc. and the S&P 500*

	R_{it}	R_{mt}	RFR_t	$R_{it} - RFR_t$	$R_{mt} - RFR_t$
1975	38.45	36.92	5.8	32.6	31.1
1976	33.20	23.64	5.1	28.1	18.5
1977	−6.99	−7.16	5.1	−12.1	−12.2
1978	2.88	6.39	7.2	−4.3	−0.8
1979	27.39	18.19	10.4	17.0	7.8
1980	23.01	31.48	11.2	11.8	20.3
1981	−0.63	−4.85	14.7	−15.3	−19.6
1982	21.41	20.37	10.5	10.9	9.9
1983	24.08	22.31	8.8	15.3	13.5
1984	5.32	4.29	9.8	−4.5	−5.5
1985	24.48	30.81	7.7	16.8	23.1
1986	21.82	23.95	6.2	15.6	17.8
1987	2.03	0.47	6.3	−4.3	−5.8
1988	11.63	18.79	8.2	3.4	10.6
1989	22.38	31.80	7.6	14.8	24.2
Mean	16.70	17.16	8.31		
Standard Deviation	12.98	13.18	2.56		
S_i	0.646				
S_m	0.671				
T_i	9.427				
T_m	8.850				
$R_{it} - RFR_t$	1.078				
$R_{mt} - RFR_t$	0.912				
β_i	0.890				
R^2_{im}	0.831				

Note: Annual rates of return from Table 23.1.

Source: Standard & Poor's Statistical Service; *Federal Reserve Bulletin.*

on Affiliated showed less total risk than the market (12.98 percent versus 13.18 percent). This difference in total risk was not enough to offset the difference in the rates of return, however, and the fund's Sharpe measure was slightly lower than the market's (0.646 versus 0.671).

Finally, a regression of the fund's annual risk premium $(R_{jt} - RFR_t)$ and the market's annual risk premium $(R_{mt} - RFR_t)$ indicated a positive intercept (constant) value of 1.078. This was not statistically significant. If this intercept value had been significant,

it would have indicated that Affiliated's risk-adjusted annual rate of return averaged about 1 percent above the market.

Total Sample Results Analysis of the results for all 20 funds, shown in Table 23.3, indicates that they are generally consistent with the findings of earlier studies. Our sample was rather casually selected because we intended it for demonstration purposes only. The mean annual rate of return for all the funds came quite close to the market return (17.55 percent versus 17.16

Table 23.3							
Performance Measures for 20 Selected Mutual Funds, 1975–1989							
	Annual Rate of Return	Standard Deviation	Beta	R^2	Treynor[a]	Sharpe[a]	Jensen[a]
Affiliated Fund, Inc.	16.83	12.98	0.89	0.831	9.574(14)	0.656(10)	1.078(10)
Dividend Shares, Inc.	13.92	11.79	0.87	0.705	6.447(16)	0.476(16)	−1.283(16)
Dreyfus Growth Opportunity Funds, Inc.	19.20	18.50	0.83	0.472	13.116(3)	0.589(13)	1.783(8)
Energy Fund, Inc.	17.44	16.20	0.83	0.547	10.996(8)	0.563(14)	0.741(11)
Fidelity Magellan Fund	31.92	18.57	1.08	0.532	21.866(1)	1.272(1)	14.989[b](1)
Guardian Mutual Fund	18.98	13.84	0.98	0.726	10.885(9)	0.771(7)	2.516(5)
IDS Mutual, Inc.	14.52	10.11	0.55	0.785	11.294(5)	0.615(12)	−0.269(14)
Istel Fund, Inc.	11.87	13.01	0.65	0.484	5.478(18)	0.274(19)	−2.694(18)
Massachusetts Investors Growth Stock Fund	14.88	14.21	1.08	0.710	6.086(17)	0.463(17)	−1.378(17)
Oppenheimer Fund, Inc.	12.81	17.25	1.04	0.686	4.330(20)	0.261(20)	−5.034[b](20)
Philadelphia Fund, Inc.	18.05	13.25	0.87	0.650	11.192(7)	0.735(8)	1.968(6)
T. Rowe Price Growth Stock Fund	12.90	13.33	0.94	0.882	4.880(19)	0.344(18)	−4.255[b](19)
Putnam Growth Fund Inc.	16.73	10.66	0.80	0.881	10.530(12)	0.790(6)	1.404(9)
Scudder Capital Growth	20.14	13.14	1.10	0.744	10.758(10)	0.900(3)	3.860(4)
Security Equity Fund, Inc.	18.40	15.82	1.03	0.757	9.800(13)	0.638(11)	0.600(13)
Sigma Investment Shares, Inc.	17.74	11.95	0.84	0.821	11.228(6)	0.790(5)	1.967(7)
Technology Fund, Inc.	17.12	16.24	1.12	0.692	7.862(15)	0.542(15)	−0.536(15)
Templeton Growth Fund, Inc.	20.85	12.68	0.77	0.422	16.285(2)	0.989(2)	6.051[b](2)
Value Line Special Situations Fund	21.60	19.02	1.16	0.420	11.458(4)	0.699(9)	4.818[b](3)
Wellington Fund, Inc.	15.19	9.57	0.65	0.877	10.585(11)	0.719(4)	0.656(12)
Mean	17.55	14.11	0.90	0.680	10.277	0.657	1.350
S&P 500	17.16	13.18	1.00	1.000	8.850	0.671	
90-Day T-Bill Rate	8.31	2.56					

[a]Numbers in parentheses indicate fund ranks.
[b]Intercept was statistically significant at the 0.05 level.

percent). Considering only the rate of return, 10 of the 20 funds outperformed the market.

The R^2 for a portfolio with the market can serve as a measure of diversification. The closer it comes to 1.00, the more completely diversified the portfolio is. The average R^2 for our sample was not very high at 0.68, and the range was quite large, from 0.42 to 0.88. This indicates that many of the funds were not well-diversified, especially the four with R^2 values less than 0.50. Of the 20, 15 had R^2 values less than 0.80.

The two risk measures (standard deviation and beta) likewise show a wide range, but are generally consistent with expectations. Specifically, 11 of the 20 funds had larger standard deviations than the market and the mean standard deviation was also larger (14.11 percent versus 13.18 percent). This larger standard deviation is consistent with the lack of complete diversification. Only seven of the funds had betas above 1.00; the average beta was 0.90.

Alternative measures rated the performance of individual funds very consistently. The Sharpe measures of 9 of the 20 funds were higher than the market's value. The Treynor measures of 12 of the 20 funds likewise indicated better performance than the market. The Jensen measures indicated that 13 of the 20 had positive intercepts, but only three of these intercepts were statistically significant. The mean value for the Sharpe measure was lower than the figure for the aggregate market, while the average fund did better than the market based upon the Treynor and Jensen measures. These results indicate that, on average, this sample of funds closely matched the market during this time period.

Relationship among Portfolio Performance Measures

We discussed the relationship between the Treynor and Sharpe measures of performance, noting that the main difference between them is that the Treynor measure examines the risk premium per unit of systematic risk (beta), whereas the Sharpe measure derives the risk premium per unit of total risk (standard deviation of return). Therefore, analysis of a well-diversified portfolio in which total risk approaches systematic risk should provide similar rankings by these measures. Later, we pointed out that the Jensen measure is also based on the CAPM and relates actual returns to expected returns based on the fund's systematic risk. Therefore, you should expect this measure to provide rankings similar to those from the

other two measures, especially for well-diversified portfolios.

Analysis of the rankings using the three measures generally confirms that they provide similar rankings. A rank correlation that relates ranks rather than exact values can provide a more exact measure. The rank correlations for the funds in Table 23.3 are:

- Sharpe–Treynor: 0.92
- Sharpe–Jensen: 0.90
- Treynor–Jensen: 0.90

Since the alternative measures give similar, but not identical, rankings, we recommend that you employ all three measures. Each provides somewhat different information about both return and diversification performance, risk, and the significance of the differential performance. The importance of evaluating portfolio performance leads us to suggest that you use as many techniques as possible.

Factors That Affect Use of Performance Measures

These performance measures are only as good as their data inputs. You need to be careful when computing rates of return and take proper account of all inflows and outflows. More importantly, you should use judgment and be patient in the evaluation process. It is not possible to evaluate a portfolio manager on the basis of performance over a quarter or even a year. Your evaluation should extend over several years and cover at least a full market cycle. This will allow you to determine whether the manager's performance differs during rising and declining markets.[6] Beyond these general considerations, there are several specific factors that you should consider when using these measures.

Measurement Problems As noted, all of the equity portfolio performance measures we have discussed are derived from the CAPM. They assume the existence of a market portfolio that defines the point of tangency on the Markowitz efficient frontier. Theoretically, the market portfolio should be an efficient

[6]In this regard, see Robert C. Kirby, "You Need More than Numbers to Measure Performance," paper presented at Institute of Chartered Financial Analysts seminar, Chicago, April 2, 1976. For a formal presentation related to the importance of the time element, see Mark Kritzman, "How to Detect Skill in Management Performance," *Journal of Portfolio Management* 12, no. 2 (Winter 1986): 16–20.

> **Benchmark error** An inaccuracy in evaluation of
> portfolio performance due to poor representation of
> market performance by the market indicator series
> chosen as a proxy for the market portfolio.

portfolio because it is on the efficient frontier. We also
noted that this market portfolio should contain all
risky assets in the economy so it will be completely
diversified.

The problem arises in finding a real-world proxy
for this theoretical market portfolio. As noted previously, analysts typically take the Standard & Poor's
500 Index as a proxy for the market portfolio because
it contains a fairly diversified portfolio of stocks, and
the sample is market value-weighted. Unfortunately, it
does not represent the true composition of the market
portfolio. Specifically, it includes *only* common stocks
and most of them are listed on the NYSE. It excludes
many other risky assets that theoretically should be
considered, such as numerous AMEX and OTC
stocks, foreign stocks, foreign and domestic bonds,
real estate, coins, stamps, and antiques.

This lack of completeness has always been recognized, but it was not highlighted until several articles
by Roll detailing the problem with the market proxy
and pointing out its implications for measuring portfolio performance.[7] Although a detailed discussion of
Roll's critique is not possible here, we can consider his
major problem with the measurement of the market
portfolio, which he refers to as a **benchmark error.**

When evaluating portfolio performance, various
techniques employ the market portfolio as the benchmark. We also use the market portfolio to derive our
risk measures (betas). Roll showed that if the proxy for
the market portfolio is not a truly efficient portfolio,
then the betas derived using it are incorrect. Similarly,
the security market line derived from this proxy may
not be the true SML; the true SML could have a
higher slope. Therefore, a portfolio that plotted above
the SML derived using a poor benchmark could actually plot below the true SML derived from the true
market portfolio. Also, the beta could differ from that
computed by using the true market portfolio. For ex-

ample, if the "true" beta were larger than the beta
computed using the proxy, the true position of the
portfolio would shift to the right.

Global Investing The concern with benchmark error only increases with global investing. The studies
on international diversification discussed in Chapter
2 state clearly that adding non-U.S. securities to the
portfolio universe almost certainly will move the efficient frontier to the left since including foreign securities reduces risk. You will recall that this movement
continues as you add countries that have less economic
interaction with the United States, such as some Asian
and third-world countries. Also, some of these additions increase the expected returns of the universe so
that the efficient frontier moves upward as well as
leftward. The point is, the efficient frontier will almost certainly change when you invest in foreign
securities.

The extent of the shift in the efficient frontier
depends upon the relationships among countries, and
these relationships will change dramatically in the
coming decade. Since our trade with European and
Asian countries will continue its rapid growth from
recent years, the interdependence of our economies
and the correlation of our financial markets should
increase. Also, individual European countries will certainly become more interdependent after 1992, when
numerous barriers to trade and travel in the European
Economic Community will be eliminated.[8]

Benchmark Problems This benchmark criticism
has several significant effects. First, the benchmark
problems noted by Roll, which increased with global
investing, do *not* negate the value of the CAPM as a
normative model of equilibrium pricing; the theory is
still viable. The problem is one of measurement when
using the theory to evaluate portfolio performance.

You need to find a better proxy for the market
portfolio or to adjust measured performance for
benchmark errors. In fact, in one of his later articles,
Roll made several suggestions to help overcome this

---

[7]Richard Roll, "Performance Evaluation and Benchmark Error I,"
Journal of Portfolio Management 6, no. 4 (Summer 1980): 5–12; and
Richard Roll, "Performance Evaluation and Benchmark Error II,"
Journal of Portfolio Management 7, no. 2 (Winter 1981): 17–22.

[8]A paper that initiates discussion of the procedure for evaluating non-U.S. equity portfolios is Gary P. Brinson and Nimrod
Fachler, "Measuring Non-U.S. Equity Portfolio Performance,"
Journal of Portfolio Management 11, no. 3 (Spring 1985): 73–76. It
discusses the problems with developing appropriate indices and
considers market (country) selection and stock selection within
countries.

problem.[9] From Chapter 4, we know that new, comprehensive stock market and bond market series are being developed that will be available as market portfolio proxies. These new series will reduce the problem, but they will not solve it because they include world stocks and bonds, but they do not include current data for other assets.

Alternatively, you might consider giving greater weight to the Sharpe portfolio performance measure because it does not depend so heavily on the market portfolio. Recall that this measure relates excess returns to standard deviations of returns, that is, to total risk. While the evaluation process generally uses a benchmark portfolio as an example of an unmanaged portfolio for comparison purposes, the risk measure does not directly depend upon a market portfolio. Also, note that ranks from the Sharpe measure typically correlate very highly with those from alternative performance measures.

Reliability of Performance Measures
Another concern is how reliably these measures rank managers and indicate their ability to significantly outperform the market. An examination of the performance measures under ideal conditions indicated that, when you eliminate the random noise, these measures of performance do an excellent job of ranking portfolios consistently with their true rankings.[10] At the same time, the random noise in stock and portfolio data complicates detecting performance that is statistically superior or inferior relative to the market portfolio. The fact is, a manager must be much better or worse than average before a difference shows up.

Evaluation of Bond Portfolio Performance

As discussed, the analysis of risk-adjusted performance for equity portfolios started in the late 1960s following the development of portfolio theory and the capital asset pricing model (CAPM). The common stock risk measures have been fairly simple indicators of either total risk (the standard deviation of returns) or systematic risk (betas). No such development has simplified analysis for the bond market, where more numerous and complex factors can influence portfolio returns. One reason for this lack of development of bond portfolio performance measures was that prior to the 1970s most bond portfolio managers followed buy-and-hold strategies, so their performance probably did not differ much. A reason for this buy-and-hold strategy is that interest rates were very stable, so one could gain little from the active management of bond portfolios.

The environment in the bond market changed dramatically in the 1970s, and especially in the 1980s, when interest rates increased dramatically and also became more volatile. This created an incentive to trade bonds and this trend toward more active management led to substantially more dispersed performance by bond portfolio managers. This dispersion in performance in turn created a demand for techniques that would help investors evaluate the performance of bond portfolio managers.

As with the equity market, the critical questions are: (1) How did performance compare among portfolio managers relative to the overall bond market? and (2) What factors explain or contribute to superior or inferior bond portfolio performance? In this section, we present several attempts to develop bond portfolio performance evaluation systems that consider multiple-risk factors.[11]

Bond Market Line
Wagner and Tito made an early attempt to apply asset pricing techniques to bond portfolios.[12] A prime factor needed to evaluate bond performance properly is a measure of risk like the beta coefficient for equities. This is difficult to achieve because a bond's maturity and coupon have significant effects on the volatility of its price.

[9]Richard Roll, "Performance Evaluation and Benchmark Error II": 17–22.

[10]Don W. French and Glenn V. Henderson, Jr., "How Well Does Performance Evaluation Perform?" *Journal of Portfolio Management* 11, no. 2 (Winter 1985): 15–18.

[11]An overview of this area and a discussion of the historical development appears in Arthur Williams III, "Performance Evaluation in Fixed Income Securities," in *The Handbook of Fixed Income Securities*, 2d ed., edited by Frank J. Fabozzi and Irving M. Pollack (Homewood, Ill.: Dow Jones-Irwin, 1987).

[12]Wayne H. Wagner and Dennis A. Tito, "Definitive New Measures of Bond Performance and Risk," *Pension World*, May 1977: 17–26; and Dennis A. Tito and Wayne H. Wagner, "Is Your Bond Manager Skillful?" *Pension World*, June 1977: 10–16.

| Figure 23.3 | *Bond Market Line Using Shearson Lehman Bond Index* |

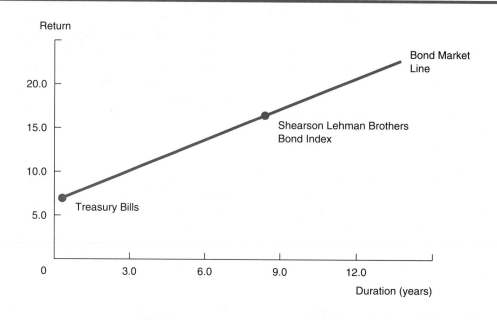

Source: Dennis A. Tito and Wayne H. Wagner, "Definitive New Measures of Bond Performance and Risk," *Pension World* (June 1977).

> **Policy effect** A difference in performance of a bond portfolio from that of a chosen index due to differences in duration, which result from a fund's investment policy.

You know from our discussion in Chapter 11 that an appropriate composite risk measure that indicates the relative price volatility for a bond compared to interest rate changes is the bond's duration. Using this as a measure of risk, the authors derived a bond market line much like the security market line used to evaluate equity performance. Duration simply replaces beta as the risk variable. The bond market line in Figure 23.3 is drawn from points defined by returns on Treasury bills and the Shearson Lehman Government–Corporate Bond Index rather than the S&P 500 Index.[13] The return for the Shearson Lehman index gives the market's average annual rate of return during

some common period, and the duration for the index is the value-weighted duration for the individual bonds in the index.

Deviations from the Bond Market Line We can divide differences in the return for a bond portfolio from the bond market line defined by the return on the Shearson Lehman index into four components: (1) a policy effect, (2) a rate anticipation effect, (3) an analysis effect, and (4) a trading effect. The latter three effects combined are referred to as the *management effect*.

The **policy effect** measures the difference in the expected return for a given bond portfolio due to the difference in its duration from that of the Shearson Lehman index. This assumes that the duration of an unmanaged portfolio would equal the duration of the Shearson Lehman index. A difference in the duration for a portfolio from the SL index duration indicates a management policy decision regarding relative risk. Expected return should differ consistently with that risk policy decision.

Besides the expected return and duration for a long-term portfolio, all other deviations from the in-

---

[13]As you know from the presentation in Chapter 4, it would be equally reasonable to use a comparable bond-market indicator series from Merrill Lynch or Salomon Brothers, or the Ryan Index.

dex portfolio are caused by *management effects*. This includes (1) an interest rate anticipation effect, (2) an analysis effect, and (3) a trading effect.

The **interest rate anticipation effect** attempts to measure the difference in return from changing the duration during a period as compared to the portfolio's long-term duration. A successful manager would increase the duration of the bond portfolio in anticipation of a period of declining interest rates in an effort to increase price volatility and, therefore, the price appreciation of a portfolio. The manager should reduce duration in times of rising rates.

The **analysis effect** is the difference in return attributable to acquiring bonds that are temporarily mispriced relative to their risk. To measure the analysis effect, you would compare the expected return for the portfolio at the beginning of the period in relation to the bond market line to the actual return on this portfolio. If the actual return is greater than the expected return, it implies that the portfolio manager acquired some underpriced issues that became properly priced and provided excess returns during the period.

Finally, the **trading effect** occurs due to short-run changes in the portfolio during the period. It is measured as the difference in return that remains after subtracting the analysis effect from the total excess return based upon duration.

This technique appears to be a very useful way to break down the return on a bond portfolio based upon duration as a comprehensive risk measure. The only concern is that duration does not consider differences in the risk of default. Specifically, the technique does not appear to differentiate between an Aaa bond with

Interest rate anticipation effect The difference in return from changing the duration of the portfolio during a period as compared with the portfolio's long-term duration.

Analysis effect A difference in performance of a bond portfolio from that of a chosen index due to acquisition of temporarily mispriced issues which then move to their correct prices.

Trading effect A difference in performance of a bond portfolio from that of a chosen index due to short-run changes in the portfolio.

Yield-to-maturity effect The return on a bond portfolio caused by the characteristics of the yield curve.

a duration of 8 years and a Baa bond with the same duration. This could clearly affect performance. You can avoid this problem by constructing different market lines for alternative ratings or by deriving a benchmark line that matches the quality makeup of the portfolio being evaluated.[14]

Decomposing Portfolio Returns

Dietz, Fogler, and Hardy derived a technique to decompose bond portfolio returns into maturity, sector, and quality effects.[15] The total return for a bond during a period of time is composed of a known income effect, which is due to normal yield-to-maturity factors, and an unknown price change effect, which is due to an interest rate effect, a sector/quality effect, and a residual effect. A graph of this breakdown might look like this:

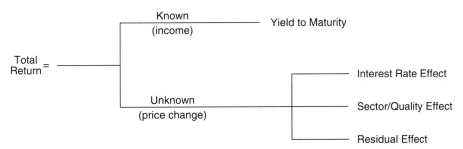

[14]This problem is briefly discussed in Frank K. Reilly and Rupinder Sidhu, "The Many Uses of Bond Duration," *Financial Analysts Journal* 36, no. 4 (July/August 1980): 58–72.

[15]Peter O. Dietz, H. Russell Fogler, and Donald J. Hardy, "The Challenge of Analyzing Bond Portfolio Returns," *Journal of Portfolio Management* 6, no. 3 (Spring 1980): 53–58.

The **yield-to-maturity effect** accounts for the return you would receive on a bond if the yield curve remained unchanged during the period. That is, it covers the interest income, any price change relative to par, and any price change due to the shape of the yield curve.

Sector/quality effect The return on a bond portfolio caused by the selection of the sector in which the bonds fall and their quality.

Residual effect The return on a bond portfolio not caused by the yield-to-maturity, interest rate, and sector/quality effects.

Maturity management component The part of the return on a bond portfolio caused by the manager's manipulation of maturity or duration in anticipation of interest rate changes.

Spread/quality management component The part of the return on a bond portfolio caused by the manager's selection of bonds from various sectors and quality groups.

Selectivity component The part of the return on a bond portfolio caused by the manager's selection of individual bond issues to implement maturity and quality decisions.

The interest rate effect is the same as before. The **sector/quality effect** measures the expected impact on the returns of the sector in which the bonds fall (corporates, utilities, financial issues, GNMA bonds, etc.) and also their quality (Aaa, Aa, A, Baa).

The **residual effect** is what remains after taking account of the yield-to-maturity, interest rate, and sector/quality effects. A consistently large positive residual effect would indicate superior selection capabilities. Specifically, this residual effect indicates that after taking account of all market effects caused by interest rate changes and the sector/quality characteristics of the portfolio, some additional positive returns may come from the selection of individual bonds.

For a given portfolio, you should probably prepare a time-series plot of these effects to determine the strengths and weaknesses of a manager. You should also compare these results, net of transaction costs, to the results for a static portfolio bought and held from the beginning of the period. In addition, you should compare these results to the overall performance of a broad bond-market indicator series, which should represent an unmanaged portfolio.

Analyzing Sources of Return

Fong, Pearson, and Vasicek proposed another performance evaluation technique that divides the total returns on a bond portfolio into several components.[16] The first breakdown divides the total return (R) between the effect of the external interest rate environment (I), which is beyond the control of the portfolio manager, and the impact of the management process (C):

$$R = I + C$$

In turn, C, the management contribution, is composed of three factors:

- M, the return from maturity management
- S, the return from spread/quality management
- B, the return from the selection of specific securities

The **maturity management component** (M) is a function of how well the portfolio manager changes maturity or duration in anticipation of interest rate changes. The **spread/quality management component** indicates the effect on the return of the manager's selection of bonds from various sectors and quality groups.

The **selectivity component** (B) is the remaining return. It is attributable to the performance of specific bonds beyond their maturity or sector/quality effects. It is based upon the performance of individual bonds selected within the other two constraints.

As before, you should compare these effects to some market index series that represents an unmanaged portfolio. You should also examine the components over time to determine any consistent strengths or weaknesses.

Consistency of Bond Portfolio Performance

You will recall from Chapter 19 that numerous investigators have documented inconsistent performance for managers of equity portfolios. A similar analysis for bonds ranked 32 bond managers employed by AT&T.[17] The analyst divided a 10-year period into two 5-year periods, determined each manager's percentile rank in each period, and correlated the rankings.

The results revealed no relationship between performance in the two periods. Another test revealed no relationship between past and future performance, even among the best and worst performers. Based

[16]Gifford Fong, Charles Pearson, and Oldrich Vasicek, "Bond Performance: Analyzing Sources of Return," *Journal of Portfolio Management* 9, no. 3 (Spring 1983): 46–50.

[17]Mark Kritzman, "Can Bond Managers Perform Consistently?" *Journal of Portfolio Management* 9, no. 4 (Summer 1983): 54–56.

upon these results, it was concluded that it would be necessary to examine something besides past performance to identify superior managers.

Summary

■ This chapter has discussed portfolio performance evaluation and reviewed several techniques by which to make such an evaluation. The first major goal of portfolio management is to derive rates of return that equal or exceed the returns on a naively selected portfolio with equal risk. The second goal is to attain complete diversification. Prior to the development of capital market theory, portfolio managers were judged only on the basis of rate of return with no consideration of risk. Risk was considered later, but not in a very rigorous manner.

■ Three major techniques have been derived to provide composite measures of equity portfolio performance. The first, developed by Treynor, measures the risk premium earned per unit of systematic risk. The Sharpe measure indicates the risk premium per unit of total risk. The third technique, Jensen's, likewise evaluates performance in terms of systematic risk and allows one to determine whether any positive or negative difference in risk-adjusted performance is statistically significant.

■ The application of the evaluation techniques to a selected sample of 20 mutual funds indicates the importance of considering both risk and return because of the wide range of total risk and systematic risk. We discussed how differences in diversification could influence the rankings generated by different performance measures. Still, the rank correlations among the alternative measures were very high.

■ Some general factors should be considered when analyzing performance, including nonquantitative factors and an adequate time period. You must also consider some benchmark problems. Notably, these measurement problems related to a proxy for the market portfolio do not negate the overall theoretical value of the CAPM or the portfolio evaluation measures. They simply mean that you need to watch for a measurement problem and adjust for it.

■ While the techniques for evaluating equity portfolio performance have been in existence for almost 30 years, comparable techniques for examining bond portfolio performance were developed only about 10 years ago. Evaluation models for bonds need to consider several important decision variables: the overall market factor, decisions related to duration, sector and quality, and individual bond selection.

■ Investors need to evaluate their own performance and the performance of hired portfolio managers. The various techniques discussed here provide theoretically justifiable measures that differ slightly. We contend that all the measures should be used in the evaluation process because they provide different information. Finally, a portfolio manager should be evaluated a number of times in different market environments before a final judgment is reached.

Questions

1. Assuming you are managing your own portfolio, do you think you should evaluate your own performance? Why or why not? Against what would you compare your performance?

2. What two major factors should you consider when evaluating a portfolio manager? What should the portfolio manager try to do?

3. How can a portfolio manager derive superior risk-adjusted returns?

4. What is the purpose of diversification according to the CAPM? How can you measure whether a portfolio is completely diversified? Explain why this measure of diversification makes sense.

5. Before the development of composite portfolio performance measures, how could you evaluate risk-adjusted portfolio performance?

6. Define the Treynor measure of portfolio performance. Discuss this measure in terms of what it measures.

7. Define the Sharpe measure of performance and discuss what it indicates.

8. Why is it suggested that you use both the Treynor and Sharpe measures of performance? What information do you gain by comparing the rankings from the two measures?

9. Define the Jensen measure of performance and indicate whether it should produce results similar to those produced by the Treynor or Sharpe methods. Why?

10. Assuming that a poor proxy is used for the market portfolio, discuss the potential problem with the measurement of portfolio beta. Show by an example the effect on a portfolio evaluation graph if the measured beta is significantly lower than the true beta.

11. Assuming that the market proxy is a poor one, show an example of the potential impact on the

security market line (SML). Demonstrate with an example how a portfolio that was superior relative to the proxy SML could be inferior when compared to the true SML.

12. Show with a graph the effect of global investing on the aggregate efficient frontier. What will this do to the world SML and individual betas?

13. It is more difficult to derive an appropriate model for evaluating the performance of a bond portfolio manager than for an equity portfolio manager because bond managers must make more decisions. Discuss some of the specific factors that need to be considered when evaluating a bond portfolio manager.

14. Briefly describe what you are trying to measure in tests for:
    a. The interest rate effect (i.e., market effect)
    b. The maturity effect (duration)
    c. The sector/quality effect
    d. The selection effect

15. Which of the effects in Question 14 are under the control of the bond portfolio manager?

16. *CFA Examination III* (June 1981) Richard Roll, in an article on using the capital asset pricing model (CAPM) to evaluate portfolio performance, indicated that it may not be possible to evaluate portfolio management ability if there is an error in the benchmark used.
    a. Describe the general portfolio performance evaluation procedure, with emphasis on the benchmark employed. [5 minutes]
    b. Explain what Roll meant by *benchmark error* and identify the specific problem with this benchmark. [5 minutes]
    c. Draw a graph that shows how a portfolio that has been judged as superior relative to a measured security market line (SML) can be inferior relative to the true SML. [10 minutes]
    d. Assume that you are informed that a given portfolio manager has been evaluated as superior when compared to the DJIA, the S&P 500, and the NYSE Composite Index. Explain whether this consensus would make you feel more comfortable regarding the portfolio manager's true ability. [5 minutes]
    e. While conceding the possible problem with benchmark errors as set forth by Roll, some contend that this does not mean the CAPM is incorrect, but only that there is a measurement problem when implementing the

theory. Others contend that because of benchmark errors, the whole technique should be scrapped. Take and defend one of these positions. [5 minutes]

17. *CFA Examination III* (June 1982) During a quarterly review session, a client of Fixed-Income Investors, a pension fund advisory firm, asks Fred Raymond, the portfolio manager for the company's account, if he could provide a more detailed analysis of portfolio performance than total return alone. Specifically, the client had recently seen an article by Dietz, Fogler, and Hardy on the analysis of bond portfolio returns. The authors attempted to decompose total return into four components: yield-to-maturity effect, interest rate effect, sector/quality effect, and residual effect.

While the customer does not expect you to provide such an analysis this year, you should explain each of these components so the customer will be better prepared to understand such an analysis when you do it for the company's portfolio next year. [20 minutes]

Problems

1. Assume that during the previous 10-year period, the risk-free rate was 6 percent (RFR = 0.06), and three portfolios had the following characteristics:

Portfolio	Return	Beta
A	0.11	1.10
B	0.09	0.90
C	0.14	1.20

   a. Compute the Treynor measure of portfolio performance for each portfolio and indicate which portfolio had the best performance.
   b. Assume the market return during this period was 12 percent (R_m = 0.12). How did these managers fare in relation to the market?

2. Assume the three portfolios in Problem 1 have standard deviations of 0.14, 0.10, and 0.20, respectively. Compute the Sharpe measure of performance. Is there any difference in the ranks determined by the Treynor measure versus those determined by the Sharpe measure? Discuss the probable cause of the difference.

3. Assume that the market return in Problem 2 was 12 percent and the standard deviation for the market was 12 percent. Using the Sharpe measure, how did the three portfolios perform in relation to the market portfolio?

4. The portfolios described below are being considered for investment. During the period under consideration, the risk-free rate was 7 percent (RFR = 0.07).

Portfolio	Return	Beta	σ
P	0.15	1.0	0.05
Q	0.20	1.5	0.10
R	0.10	0.6	0.03
S	0.17	1.1	0.06
Market	0.13	1.0	0.04

   a. Compute the Sharpe measure for each portfolio and the market portfolio.
   b. Compute the Treynor measure for each portfolio and the market portfolio.
   c. Rank the portfolios using each measure.

References

Brinson, Gary P., and Nimrod Fachler. "Measuring Non-U.S. Equity Portfolio Performance." *Journal of Portfolio Management* 11, no. 3 (Spring 1985).

Brinson, Gary P., Brian D. Singer, and Gilbert L. Beebower, "Determinants of Portfolio Performance II: An Update," *Financial Analysts Journal* 47, no. 3 (May/June 1991).

Dybvig, Philip H., and Stephen A. Ross. "The Analytics of Performance Measurement Using a Security Market Line." *Journal of Finance* 4, no. 2 (June 1985).

French, Dan W., and Glenn V. Henderson, Jr. "How Well Does Performance Evaluation Perform?" *Journal of Portfolio Management* 11, no. 2 (Winter 1985).

Jobson, J. D., and B. M. Korkie. "Performance Testing with the Sharpe and Treynor Measures." *Journal of Finance* 35, no. 4 (September 1981).

Maginn, John L., and Donald L. Tuttle. *Managing Investment Portfolios*, 2d ed. Boston: Warren, Gorham and Lamont, 1990.

Roll, Richard. "Performance Evaluation and Benchmark Error I." *Journal of Portfolio Management* 6, no. 4 (Summer 1980).

Roll, Richard. "Performance Evaluation and Benchmark Error II." *Journal of Portfolio Management* 7, no. 2 (Winter 1981).

Williams, Arthur, III. *Managing Your Investment Manager—The Complete Guide to Selection, Measurement, and Control.* Homewood, Ill.: Dow Jones-Irwin, 1986.

A   *How to Become a Chartered Financial Analyst*

As mentioned in the section on career opportunities, the professional designation of Chartered Financial Analyst (CFA) is becoming a significant requirement for a career in investment analysis and/or portfolio management. For that reason, this section presents the history and objectives of the Institute of Chartered Financial Analysts and general guidelines for acquiring the CFA designation. If you are interested in the program, you can write to the Institute for more information.

The Institute of Chartered Financial Analysts (ICFA) was formed in 1959 in Charlottesville, Virginia. The CFA candidate examinations were first offered in 1963. The ICFA, along with the Financial Analysts Federation, form the Association for Investment Management and Research (AIMR).

The Institute of Chartered Financial Analysts (ICFA) was organized to enhance the professionalism of those involved in various aspects of the investment decision-making process and to recognize those who achieve a high level of professionalism by awarding the designation of Chartered Financial Analyst (CFA).

The basic missions and purposes of the AIMR/ICFA are

- To develop and keep current a "body of knowledge" applicable to the investment decision-making process. The principal components of this knowledge are financial accounting, economics, both fixed-income and equity securities analysis, portfolio management, ethical and professional standards, and quantitative techniques.
- To administer a study and examination program for eligible candidates, the primary objectives of which are to assist the candidate in mastering and applying the body of knowledge and to test the candidate's competency in the knowledge gained.
- To award the professional CFA designation to those candidates who have passed three examination levels (encompassing a total of 18 hours of testing over a minimum of three years), who meet stipulated standards of professional conduct, and who otherwise are eligible for membership in the ICFA.
- To provide a useful and informative program of continuing education through seminars, publications, and other formats that enable members, candidates, and others in the investment constituency to be more aware of and to better utilize the changing and expanding body of knowledge.
- To sponsor and enforce a *Code of Ethics and Standards of Professional Conduct* that apply to enrolled candidates and to all members.

A college degree is necessary to enter the program. A candidate may sit for all three examinations without having had investment experience *per se* or having joined a constituent Society of the Financial Analysts Federation. However, after passing the three examination levels, the CFA Charter will not be awarded unless or until the candidate

- has at least three years of experience as a financial analyst, which is defined as a person who has spent and/or is spending a substantial portion of his/her professional time collecting, evaluating, and applying financial, economic, and related data to the investment decision-making process, and
- has applied for membership or is a member of a constituent Society of the Financial Analysts Federation, if such a Society exists within 50 miles of the candidate's principal place of business.

The curriculum of the CFA study program covers:

1. Ethical and Professional Standards
2. Financial Accounting
3. Economics
4. Fixed-Income Securities Analysis
5. Equity Securities Analysis
6. Portfolio Management
7. Quantitative Techniques

Members and candidates are typically employed in the investment field. From 1963 to 1991, over 13,000 charters have been awarded. More than 13,000 individuals currently are registered in the CFA Candidate Program. If you are interested in learning more about the CFA program, the Institute has a booklet that describes the program and includes an application form. The address is Institute of Chartered Financial Analysts, P.O. Box 3668, Charlottesville, Virginia 22903.

Source: Reprinted with permission from The Financial Analysts Federation and The Institute of Chartered Financial Analysts, Charlottesville, Virginia.

B

Code of Ethics and Standards of Professional Conduct

CODE OF ETHICS AND STANDARDS OF PROFESSIONAL CONDUCT
Effective January 1, 1990

CODE OF ETHICS

A financial analyst should conduct himself* with integrity and dignity and act in an ethical manner in his dealings with the public, clients, customers, employers, employees, and fellow analysts.

A financial analyst should conduct himself and should encourage others to practice financial analysis in a professional and ethical manner that will reflect credit on himself and his profession.

A financial analyst should act with competence and should strive to maintain and improve his competence and that of others in the profession.

A financial analyst should use proper care and exercise independent professional judgment.

THE STANDARDS OF PROFESSIONAL CONDUCT

I. **Obligation to Inform Employer of Code and Standards**
The financial analyst shall inform his employer, through his direct supervisor, that the analyst is obligated to comply with the Code of Ethics and Standards of Professional Conduct, and is subject to disciplinary sanctions for violations thereof. He shall deliver a copy of the Code and Standards to his employer if the employer does not have a copy.

II. **Compliance with Governing Laws and Regulations and the Code and Standards**
   A. **Required Knowledge and Compliance**
   The financial analyst shall maintain knowledge of and shall comply with all applicable laws, rules, and regulations of any government, governmental agency, and regulatory organization governing his professional, financial, or business activities, as well as with these Standards of Professional Conduct and the accompanying Code of Ethics.

   B. **Prohibition Against Assisting Legal and Ethical Violations**
   The financial analyst shall not knowingly participate in, or assist, any acts in violation of any applicable law, rule, or regulation of any government, governmental agency, or regulatory organization governing his professional, financial, or business activities, nor any act which would violate any provision of these Standards of Professional Conduct or the accompanying Code of Ethics.

   C. **Prohibition Against Use of Material Nonpublic Information**
   The financial analyst shall comply with all laws and regulations relating to the use and communication of material nonpublic information. The financial analyst's duty is generally defined as to not trade while in possession of, nor communicate, material nonpublic information in breach of a duty, or if the information is misappropriated.
   Duties under the Standard include the following: (1) If the analyst acquires such information as a result of a special or confidential relationship with the issuer or others, he shall not communicate the information (other than within the relationship), or take investment action on the basis of such information, if it violates that relationship. (2) If the analyst is not in a special or confidential relationship with the issuer or others, he shall not communicate or act on material nonpublic

information if he knows, or should have known, that such information (a) was disclosed to him, or would result in a breach of a duty, or (b) was misappropriated.
   If such a breach of duty exists, the analyst shall make reasonable efforts to achieve public dissemination of such information.

   D. **Responsibilities of Supervisors**
   A financial analyst with supervisory responsibility shall exercise reasonable supervision over those subordinate employees subject to his control, to prevent any violation by such persons of applicable statutes, regulations, or provisions of the Code of Ethics or Standards of Professional Conduct. In so doing the analyst is entitled to rely upon reasonable procedures established by his employer.

III. **Research Reports, Investment Recommendations and Actions**
   A. **Reasonable Basis and Representations**
   1. The financial analyst shall exercise diligence and thoroughness in making an investment recommendation to others or in taking an investment action for others.
   2. The financial analyst shall have a reasonable and adequate basis for such recommendations and actions, supported by appropriate research and investigation.
   3. The financial analyst shall make reasonable and diligent efforts to avoid any material misrepresentation in any research report or investment recommendation.
   4. The financial analyst shall maintain appropriate records to support the reasonableness of such recommendations and actions.

   B. **Research Reports**
   1. The financial analyst shall use reasonable judgment as to the inclusion of relevant factors in research reports.
   2. The financial analyst shall distinguish between facts and opinions in research reports.
   3. The financial analyst shall indicate the basic characteristics of the investment involved when preparing for general public distribution a research report that is not directly related to a specific portfolio or client.

   C. **Portfolio Investment Recommendations and Actions**
   The financial analyst shall, when making an investment recommendation or taking an investment action for a specific portfolio or client, consider its appropriateness and suitability for such portfolio or client. In considering such matters, the financial analyst shall take into account (1) the needs and circumstances of the

---
*Masculine personal pronouns, used throughout the Code and Standards to simplify sentence structure, shall apply to all persons, regardless of sex.

client, (2) the basic characteristics of the investment involved, and (3) the basic characteristics of the total portfolio. The financial analyst shall use reasonable judgment to determine the applicable relevant factors. The financial analyst shall distinguish between facts and opinions in the presentation of investment recommendations.

D. Prohibition Against Plagiarism

The financial analyst shall not, when presenting material to his employer, associates, customers, clients, or the general public, copy or use in substantially the same form material prepared by other persons without acknowledging its use and identifying the name of the author or publisher of such material. The analyst may, however, use without acknowledgement factual information published by recognized financial and statistical reporting services or similar sources.

E. Prohibition Against Misrepresentation of Services

The financial analyst shall not make any statements, orally or in writing, which misrepresent (1) the services that the analyst or his firm is capable of performing for the client, (2) the qualifications of such analyst or his firm, (3) the investment performance that the analyst or his firm has accomplished or can reasonably be expected to achieve for the client, or (4) the expected performance of any investment.

The financial analyst shall not make, orally or in writing, explicitly or implicitly, any assurances about or guarantees of any investment or its return except communication of accurate information as to the terms of the investment instrument and the issuer's obligations under the instrument.

F. Fair Dealing with Customers and Clients

The financial analyst shall act in a manner consistent with his obligation to deal fairly with all customers and clients when (1) disseminating investment recommendations, (2) disseminating material changes in prior investment advice, and (3) taking investment action.

IV. Priority of Transactions

The financial analyst shall conduct himself in such a manner that transactions for his customers, clients, and employer have priority over personal transactions, and so that his personal transactions do not operate adversely to their interests. If an analyst decides to make a recommendation about the purchase or sale of a security or other investment, he shall give his customers, clients, and employer adequate opportunity to act on this recommendation before acting on his own behalf.

V. Disclosure of Conflicts

The financial analyst, when making investment recommendations, or taking investment actions, shall disclose to his customers and clients any material conflict of interest relating to him and any material beneficial ownership of the securities or other investments involved that could reasonably be expected to impair his ability to render unbiased and objective advice.

The financial analyst shall disclose to his employer all matters that could reasonably be expected to interfere with his duty to the employer, or with his ability to render unbiased and objective advice.

The financial analyst shall also comply with all requirements as to disclosure of conflicts of interest imposed by law and by rules and regulations of organizations governing his activities and shall comply with any prohibitions on his activities if a conflict of interest exists.

VI. Compensation

A. Disclosure of Additional Compensation Arrangements

The financial analyst shall inform his customers, clients, and employer of compensation or other benefit arrangements in connection with his services to them which are in addition to compensation from them for such services.

B. Disclosure of Referral Fees

The financial analyst shall make appropriate disclosure to a prospective client or customer of any consideration paid or other benefit delivered to others for recommending his services to that prospective client or customer.

C. Duty to Employer

The financial analyst shall not undertake independent practice for compensation or other benefit in competition with his employer unless he has received written consent from both his employer and the person for whom he undertakes independent employment.

VII. Relationships with Others

A. Preservation of Confidentiality

A financial analyst shall preserve the confidentiality of information communicated by the client concerning matters within the scope of the confidential relationship, unless the financial analyst receives information concerning illegal activities on the part of the client.

B. Maintenance of Independence and Objectivity

The financial analyst, in relationships and contacts with an issuer of securities, whether individually or as a member of a group, shall use particular care and good judgment to achieve and maintain independence and objectivity.

C. Fiduciary Duties

The financial analyst, in relationships with clients, shall use particular care in determining applicable fiduciary duty and shall comply with such duty as to those persons and interests to whom it is owed.

VIII. Use of Professional Designation

The qualified financial analyst may use, as applicable, the professional designation "Member of the Association for Investment Management and Research", "Member of the Financial Analysts Federation", and "Member of the Institute of Chartered Financial Analysts", and is encouraged to do so, but only in a dignified and judicious manner. The use of the designations may be accompanied by an accurate explanation (1) of the requirements that have been met to obtain the designation, and (2) of the Association for Investment Management and Research, the Financial Analysts Federation, and the Institute of Chartered Financial Analysts, as applicable.

The Chartered Financial Analyst may use the professional designation "Chartered Financial Analyst", or the abbreviation "CFA", and is encouraged to do so, but only in a dignified and judicious manner. The use of the designation may be accompanied by an accurate explanation (1) of the requirements that have been met to obtain the designation, and (2) of the Association for Investment Management and Research, and the Institute of Chartered Financial Analysts.

IX. Professional Misconduct

The financial analyst shall not (1) commit a criminal act that upon conviction materially reflects adversely on his honesty, trustworthiness or fitness as a financial analyst in other respects, or (2) engage in conduct involving dishonesty, fraud, deceit or misrepresentation.

C Interest Tables

Table C.1 Present Value of $1: PVIF = $1/(1 + k)^t$

Period	1%	2%	3%	4%	5%	6%	7%	8%	9%	10%	12%	14%	15%	16%	18%	20%	24%	28%	32%	36%
1	.9901	.9804	.9709	.9615	.9524	.9434	.9346	.9259	.9174	.9091	.8929	.8772	.8696	.8621	.8475	.8333	.8065	.7813	.7576	.7353
2	.9803	.9612	.9426	.9246	.9070	.8900	.8734	.8573	.8417	.8264	.7972	.7695	.7561	.7432	.7182	.6944	.6504	.6104	.5739	.5407
3	.9706	.9423	.9151	.8890	.8638	.8396	.8163	.7938	.7722	.7513	.7118	.6750	.6575	.6407	.6086	.5787	.5245	.4768	.4348	.3975
4	.9610	.9238	.8885	.8548	.8227	.7921	.7629	.7350	.7084	.6830	.6355	.5921	.5718	.5523	.5158	.4823	.4230	.3725	.3294	.2923
5	.9515	.9057	.8626	.8219	.7835	.7473	.7130	.6806	.6499	.6209	.5674	.5194	.4972	.4761	.4371	.4019	.3411	.2910	.2495	.2149
6	.9420	.8880	.8375	.7903	.7462	.7050	.6663	.6302	.5963	.5645	.5066	.4556	.4323	.4104	.3704	.3349	.2751	.2274	.1890	.1580
7	.9327	.8706	.8131	.7599	.7107	.6651	.6227	.5835	.5470	.5132	.4523	.3996	.3759	.3538	.3139	.2791	.2218	.1776	.1432	.1162
8	.9235	.8535	.7894	.7307	.6768	.6274	.5820	.5403	.5019	.4665	.4039	.3506	.3269	.3050	.2660	.2326	.1789	.1388	.1085	.0854
9	.9143	.8368	.7664	.7026	.6446	.5919	.5439	.5002	.4604	.4241	.3606	.3075	.2843	.2630	.2255	.1938	.1443	.1084	.0822	.0628
10	.9053	.8203	.7441	.6756	.6139	.5584	.5083	.4632	.4224	.3855	.3220	.2697	.2472	.2267	.1911	.1615	.1164	.0847	.0623	.0462
11	.8963	.8043	.7224	.6496	.5847	.5268	.4751	.4289	.3875	.3505	.2875	.2366	.2149	.1954	.1619	.1346	.0938	.0662	.0472	.0340
12	.8874	.7885	.7014	.6246	.5568	.4970	.4440	.3971	.3555	.3186	.2567	.2076	.1869	.1685	.1372	.1122	.0757	.0517	.0357	.0250
13	.8787	.7730	.6810	.6006	.5303	.4688	.4150	.3677	.3262	.2897	.2292	.1821	.1625	.1452	.1163	.0935	.0610	.0404	.0271	.0184
14	.8700	.7579	.6611	.5775	.5051	.4423	.3878	.3405	.2992	.2633	.2046	.1597	.1413	.1252	.0985	.0779	.0492	.0316	.0205	.0135
15	.8613	.7430	.6419	.5553	.4810	.4173	.3624	.3152	.2745	.2394	.1827	.1401	.1229	.1079	.0835	.0649	.0397	.0247	.0155	.0099
16	.8528	.7284	.6232	.5339	.4581	.3936	.3387	.2919	.2519	.2176	.1631	.1229	.1069	.0930	.0708	.0541	.0320	.0193	.0118	.0073
17	.8444	.7142	.6050	.5134	.4363	.3714	.3166	.2703	.2311	.1978	.1456	.1078	.0929	.0802	.0600	.0451	.0258	.0150	.0089	.0054
18	.8360	.7002	.5874	.4936	.4155	.3503	.2959	.2502	.2120	.1799	.1300	.0946	.0808	.0691	.0508	.0376	.0208	.0118	.0068	.0039
19	.8277	.6864	.5703	.4746	.3957	.3305	.2765	.2317	.1945	.1635	.1161	.0829	.0703	.0596	.0431	.0313	.0168	.0092	.0051	.0029
20	.8195	.6730	.5537	.4564	.3769	.3118	.2584	.2145	.1784	.1486	.1037	.0728	.0611	.0514	.0365	.0261	.0135	.0072	.0039	.0021
25	.7798	.6095	.4776	.3751	.2953	.2330	.1842	.1460	.1160	.0923	.0588	.0378	.0304	.0245	.0160	.0105	.0046	.0021	.0010	.0005
30	.7419	.5521	.4120	.3083	.2314	.1741	.1314	.0994	.0754	.0573	.0334	.0196	.0151	.0116	.0070	.0042	.0016	.0006	.0002	.0001
40	.6717	.4529	.3066	.2083	.1420	.0972	.0668	.0460	.0318	.0221	.0107	.0053	.0037	.0026	.0013	.0007	.0002	.0001	•	•
50	.6080	.3715	.2281	.1407	.0872	.0543	.0339	.0213	.0134	.0085	.0035	.0014	.0009	.0006	.0003	.0001	•	•	•	•
60	.5504	.3048	.1697	.0951	.0535	.0303	.0173	.0099	.0057	.0033	.0011	.0004	.0002	.0001	•	•	•	•	•	•

*The factor is zero to four decimal places.

Table C.2   *Present Value of an Annuity of $1 Per Period for n Periods:*

$$PVIFA = \sum_{t=1}^{n} \frac{1}{(1+k)^t} = \frac{1 - \dfrac{1}{(1+k)^n}}{k}$$

Number of Payments	1%	2%	3%	4%	5%	6%	7%	8%	9%	10%	12%	14%	15%	16%	18%	20%	24%	28%	32%
1	0.9901	0.9804	0.9709	0.9615	0.9524	0.9434	0.9346	0.9259	0.9174	0.9091	0.8929	0.8772	0.8696	0.8621	0.8475	0.8333	0.8065	0.7813	0.7576
2	1.9704	1.9416	1.9135	1.8861	1.8594	1.8334	1.8080	1.7833	1.7591	1.7355	1.6901	1.6467	1.6257	1.6052	1.5656	1.5278	1.4568	1.3916	1.3315
3	2.9410	2.8839	2.8286	2.7751	2.7232	2.6730	2.6243	2.5771	2.5313	2.4869	2.4018	2.3216	2.2832	2.2459	2.1743	2.1065	1.9813	1.8684	1.7663
4	3.9020	3.8077	3.7171	3.6299	3.5460	3.4651	3.3872	3.3121	3.2397	3.1699	3.0373	2.9137	2.8550	2.7982	2.6901	2.5887	2.4043	2.2410	2.0957
5	4.8534	4.7135	4.5797	4.4518	4.3295	4.2124	4.1002	3.9927	3.8897	3.7908	3.6048	3.4331	3.3522	3.2743	3.1272	2.9906	2.7454	2.5320	2.3452
6	5.7955	5.6014	5.4172	5.2421	5.0757	4.9173	4.7665	4.6229	4.4859	4.3553	4.1114	3.8887	3.7845	3.6847	3.4976	3.3255	3.0205	2.7594	2.5342
7	6.7282	6.4720	6.2303	6.0021	5.7864	5.5824	5.3893	5.2064	5.0330	4.8684	4.5638	4.2883	4.1604	4.0386	3.8115	3.6046	3.2423	2.9370	2.6775
8	7.6517	7.3255	7.0197	6.7327	6.4632	6.2098	5.9713	5.7466	5.5348	5.3349	4.9676	4.6389	4.4873	4.3436	4.0776	3.8372	3.4212	3.0758	2.7860
9	8.5660	8.1622	7.7861	7.4353	7.1078	6.8017	6.5152	6.2469	5.9952	5.7590	5.3282	4.9464	4.7716	4.6065	4.3030	4.0310	3.5655	3.1842	2.8681
10	9.4713	8.9826	8.5302	8.1109	7.7217	7.3601	7.0236	6.7101	6.4177	6.1446	5.6502	5.2161	5.0188	4.8332	4.4941	4.1925	3.6819	3.2689	2.9304
11	10.3676	9.7868	9.2526	8.7605	8.3064	7.8869	7.4987	7.1390	6.8052	6.4951	5.9377	5.4527	5.2337	5.0286	4.6560	4.3271	3.7757	3.3351	2.9776
12	11.2551	10.5753	9.9540	9.3851	8.8633	8.3838	7.9427	7.5361	7.1607	6.8137	6.1944	5.6603	5.4206	5.1971	4.7932	4.4392	3.8514	3.3868	3.0133
13	12.1337	11.3484	10.6350	9.9856	9.3936	8.8527	8.3577	7.9038	7.4869	7.1034	6.4235	5.8424	5.5831	5.3423	4.9095	4.5327	3.9124	3.4272	3.0404
14	13.0037	12.1062	11.2961	10.5631	9.8986	9.2950	8.7455	8.2442	7.7862	7.3667	6.6282	6.0021	5.7245	5.4675	5.0081	4.6106	3.9616	3.4587	3.0609
15	13.8651	12.8493	11.9379	11.1184	10.3797	9.7122	9.1079	8.5595	8.0607	7.6061	6.8109	6.1422	5.8474	5.5755	5.0916	4.6755	4.0013	3.4834	3.0764
16	14.7179	13.5777	12.5611	11.6523	10.8378	10.1059	9.4466	8.8514	8.3126	7.8237	6.9740	6.2651	5.9542	5.6685	5.1624	4.7296	4.0333	3.5026	3.0882
17	15.5623	14.2919	13.1661	12.1657	11.2741	10.4773	9.7632	9.1216	8.5436	8.0216	7.1196	6.3729	6.0472	5.7487	5.2223	4.7746	4.0591	3.5177	3.0971
18	16.3983	14.9920	13.7535	12.6593	11.6896	10.8276	10.0591	9.3719	8.7556	8.2014	7.2497	6.4674	6.1280	5.8178	5.2732	4.8122	4.0799	3.5294	3.1039
19	17.2260	15.6785	14.3238	13.1339	12.0853	11.1581	10.3356	9.6036	8.9501	8.3649	7.3658	6.5504	6.1982	5.8775	5.3162	4.8435	4.0967	3.5386	3.1090
20	18.0456	16.3514	14.8775	13.5903	12.4622	11.4699	10.5940	9.8181	9.1285	8.5136	7.4694	6.6231	6.2593	5.9288	5.3527	4.8696	4.1103	3.5458	3.1129
25	22.0232	19.5235	17.4131	15.6221	14.0939	12.7834	11.6536	10.6748	9.8226	9.0770	7.8431	6.8729	6.4641	6.0971	5.4669	4.9476	4.1474	3.5640	3.1220
30	25.8077	22.3965	19.6004	17.2920	15.3725	13.7648	12.4090	11.2578	10.2737	9.4269	8.0552	7.0027	6.5660	6.1772	5.5168	4.9789	4.1601	3.5693	3.1242
40	32.8347	27.3555	23.1148	19.7928	17.1591	15.0463	13.3317	11.9246	10.7574	9.7791	8.2438	7.1050	6.6418	6.2335	5.5482	4.9966	4.1659	3.5712	3.1250
50	39.1961	31.4236	25.7298	21.4822	18.2559	15.7619	13.8007	12.2335	10.9617	9.9148	8.3045	7.1327	6.6605	6.2463	5.5541	4.9995	4.1666	3.5714	3.1250
60	44.9550	34.7609	27.6756	22.6235	18.9293	16.1614	14.0392	12.3766	11.0480	9.9672	8.3240	7.1401	6.6651	6.2402	5.5553	4.9999	4.1667	3.5714	3.1250

Table C.3 Future Value of $1 at the End of n Periods: $FVIF_{k,n} = (1 + k)^n$

Period	1%	2%	3%	4%	5%	6%	7%	8%	9%	10%	12%	14%	15%	16%	18%	20%	24%	28%	32%	36%
1	1.0100	1.0200	1.0300	1.0400	1.0500	1.0600	1.0700	1.0800	1.0900	1.1000	1.1200	1.1400	1.1500	1.1600	1.1800	1.2000	1.2400	1.2800	1.3200	1.3600
2	1.0201	1.0404	1.0609	1.0816	1.1025	1.1236	1.1449	1.1664	1.1881	1.2100	1.2544	1.2996	1.3225	1.3456	1.3924	1.4400	1.5376	1.6384	1.7424	1.8496
3	1.0303	1.0612	1.0927	1.1249	1.1576	1.1910	1.2250	1.2597	1.2950	1.3310	1.4049	1.4815	1.5209	1.5609	1.6430	1.7280	1.9066	2.0972	2.3000	2.5155
4	1.0406	1.0824	1.1255	1.1699	1.2155	1.2625	1.3108	1.3605	1.4116	1.4641	1.5735	1.6890	1.7490	1.8106	1.9388	2.0736	2.3642	2.6844	3.0360	3.4210
5	1.0510	1.1041	1.1593	1.2167	1.2763	1.3382	1.4026	1.4693	1.5386	1.6105	1.7623	1.9254	2.0114	2.1003	2.2878	2.4883	2.9316	3.4360	4.0075	4.6526
6	1.0615	1.1262	1.1941	1.2653	1.3401	1.4185	1.5007	1.5869	1.6771	1.7716	1.9738	2.1950	2.3131	2.4364	2.6996	2.9860	3.6352	4.3980	5.2899	6.3275
7	1.0721	1.1487	1.2299	1.3159	1.4071	1.5036	1.6058	1.7138	1.8280	1.9487	2.2107	2.5023	2.6600	2.8262	3.1855	3.5832	4.5077	5.6295	6.9826	8.6054
8	1.0829	1.1717	1.2668	1.3686	1.4775	1.5938	1.7182	1.8509	1.9926	2.1436	2.4760	2.8526	3.0590	3.2784	3.7589	4.2998	5.5895	7.2058	9.2170	11.703
9	1.0937	1.1951	1.3048	1.4233	1.5513	1.6895	1.8385	1.9990	2.1719	2.3579	2.7731	3.2519	3.5179	3.8030	4.4355	5.1598	6.9310	9.2234	12.166	15.916
10	1.1046	1.2190	1.3439	1.4802	1.6289	1.7908	1.9672	2.1589	2.3674	2.5937	3.1058	3.7072	4.0456	4.4114	5.2338	6.1917	8.5944	11.805	16.059	21.646
11	1.1157	1.2434	1.3842	1.5395	1.7103	1.8983	2.1049	2.3316	2.5804	2.8531	3.4785	4.2262	4.6524	5.1173	6.1759	7.4301	10.657	15.111	21.198	29.439
12	1.1268	1.2682	1.4258	1.6010	1.7959	2.0122	2.2522	2.5182	2.8127	3.1384	3.8960	4.8179	5.3502	5.9360	7.2876	8.9161	13.214	19.342	27.982	40.037
13	1.1381	1.2936	1.4685	1.6651	1.8856	2.1329	2.4098	2.7196	3.0658	3.4523	4.3635	5.4924	6.1528	6.8858	8.5994	10.699	16.386	24.758	36.937	54.451
14	1.1495	1.3195	1.5126	1.7317	1.9799	2.2609	2.5785	2.9372	3.3417	3.7975	4.8871	6.2613	7.0757	7.9875	10.147	12.839	20.319	31.691	48.756	74.053
15	1.1610	1.3459	1.5580	1.8009	2.0789	2.3966	2.7590	3.1722	3.6425	4.1772	5.4736	7.1379	8.1371	9.2655	11.973	15.407	25.195	40.564	64.358	100.71
16	1.1726	1.3728	1.6047	1.8730	2.1829	2.5404	2.9522	3.4259	3.9703	4.5950	6.1304	8.1372	9.3576	10.748	14.129	18.488	31.242	51.923	84.953	136.96
17	1.1843	1.4002	1.6528	1.9479	2.2920	2.6928	3.1588	3.7000	4.3276	5.0545	6.8660	9.2765	10.761	12.467	16.672	22.186	38.740	66.461	112.13	186.27
18	1.1961	1.4282	1.7024	2.0258	2.4066	2.8543	3.3799	3.9960	4.7171	5.5599	7.6900	10.575	12.375	14.462	19.673	26.623	48.038	85.070	148.02	253.33
19	1.2081	1.4568	1.7535	2.1068	2.5270	3.0256	3.6165	4.3157	5.1417	6.1159	8.6128	12.055	14.231	16.776	23.214	31.948	59.567	108.89	195.39	344.53
20	1.2202	1.4859	1.8061	2.1911	2.6533	3.2071	3.8697	4.6610	5.6044	6.7275	9.6463	13.743	16.366	19.460	27.393	38.337	73.864	139.37	257.91	468.57
21	1.2324	1.5157	1.8603	2.2788	2.7860	3.3996	4.1406	5.0338	6.1088	7.4002	10.803	15.667	18.821	22.574	32.323	46.005	91.591	178.40	340.44	637.26
22	1.2447	1.5460	1.9161	2.3699	2.9253	3.6035	4.4304	5.4365	6.6586	8.1403	12.100	17.861	21.644	26.186	38.142	55.206	113.57	228.35	449.39	866.67
23	1.2572	1.5769	1.9736	2.4647	3.0715	3.8197	4.7405	5.8715	7.2579	8.9543	13.552	20.361	24.891	30.376	45.007	66.247	140.83	292.30	593.19	1178.6
24	1.2697	1.6084	2.0328	2.5633	3.2251	4.0489	5.0724	6.3412	7.9111	9.8497	15.178	23.212	28.625	35.236	53.108	79.496	174.63	374.14	783.02	1602.9
25	1.2824	1.6406	2.0938	2.6658	3.3864	4.2919	5.4274	6.8485	8.6231	10.834	17.000	26.461	32.918	40.874	62.668	95.396	216.54	478.90	1033.5	2180.0
26	1.2953	1.6734	2.1566	2.7725	3.5557	4.5494	5.8074	7.3964	9.3992	11.918	19.040	30.166	37.856	47.414	73.948	114.47	268.51	612.99	1364.3	2964.9
27	1.3082	1.7069	2.2213	2.8834	3.7335	4.8223	6.2139	7.9881	10.245	13.110	21.324	34.389	43.535	55.000	87.259	137.37	332.95	784.63	1800.9	4032.2
28	1.3213	1.7410	2.2879	2.9987	3.9201	5.1117	6.6488	8.6271	11.167	14.421	23.883	39.204	50.065	63.800	102.96	164.84	412.86	1004.3	2377.2	5483.8
29	1.3345	1.7758	2.3566	3.1187	4.1161	5.4184	7.1143	9.3173	12.172	15.863	26.749	44.693	57.575	74.008	121.50	197.81	511.95	1285.5	3137.9	7458.0
30	1.3478	1.8114	2.4273	3.2434	4.3219	5.7435	7.6123	10.062	13.267	17.449	29.959	50.950	66.211	85.849	143.37	237.37	634.81	1645.5	4142.0	10143.
40	1.4889	2.2080	3.2620	4.8010	7.0400	10.285	14.974	21.724	31.409	45.259	93.050	188.88	267.86	378.72	750.37	1469.7	5455.9	19426.	66520.	•
50	1.6446	2.6916	4.3839	7.1067	11.467	18.420	29.457	46.901	74.357	117.39	289.00	700.23	1083.6	1670.7	3927.3	9100.4	46890.	•	•	•
60	1.8167	3.2810	5.8916	10.519	18.679	32.987	57.946	101.25	176.03	304.48	897.59	2595.9	4383.9	7370.1	20555.	56347.	•	•	•	•

*FVIFA > 99,999

644

Table C.4 — Sum of an Annuity of $1 Per Period for n Periods:

$$FVIFA_{k,n} = \sum_{t=1}^{n}(1+k)^{t-1} = \frac{(1+k)^{n}-1}{k}$$

Number of Periods	1%	2%	3%	4%	5%	6%	7%	8%	9%	10%	12%	14%	15%	16%	18%	20%	24%	28%	32%	36%
1	1.0000	1.0000	1.0000	1.0000	1.0000	1.0000	1.0000	1.0000	1.0000	1.0000	1.0000	1.0000	1.0000	1.0000	1.0000	1.0000	1.0000	1.0000	1.0000	1.0000
2	2.0100	2.0200	2.0300	2.0400	2.0500	2.0600	2.0700	2.0800	2.0900	2.1000	2.1200	2.1400	2.1500	2.1600	2.1800	2.2000	2.2400	2.2800	2.3200	2.3600
3	3.0301	3.0604	3.0909	3.1216	3.1525	3.1836	3.2149	3.2464	3.2781	3.3100	3.3744	3.4396	3.4725	3.5056	3.5724	3.6400	3.7776	3.9184	4.0624	4.2096
4	4.0604	4.1216	4.1836	4.2465	4.3101	4.3746	4.4399	4.5061	4.5731	4.6410	4.7793	4.9211	4.9934	5.0665	5.2154	5.3680	5.6842	6.0156	6.3624	6.7251
5	5.1010	5.2040	5.3091	5.4163	5.5256	5.6371	5.7507	5.8666	5.9847	6.1051	6.3528	6.6101	6.7424	6.8771	7.1542	7.4416	8.0484	8.6999	9.3983	10.146
6	6.1520	6.3081	6.4684	6.6330	6.8019	6.9753	7.1533	7.3359	7.5233	7.7156	8.1152	8.5355	8.7537	8.9775	9.4420	9.9299	10.980	12.135	13.405	14.798
7	7.2135	7.4343	7.6625	7.8983	8.1420	8.3938	8.6540	8.9228	9.2004	9.4872	10.089	10.730	11.066	11.413	12.141	12.915	14.615	16.533	18.695	21.126
8	8.2857	8.5830	8.8923	9.2142	9.5491	9.8975	10.259	10.636	11.028	11.435	12.299	13.232	13.726	14.240	15.327	16.499	19.122	22.163	25.678	29.731
9	9.3685	9.7546	10.159	10.582	11.026	11.491	11.978	12.487	13.021	13.579	14.775	16.085	16.785	17.518	19.085	20.798	24.712	29.369	34.895	41.435
10	10.462	10.949	11.463	12.006	12.577	13.180	13.816	14.486	15.192	15.937	17.548	19.337	20.303	21.321	23.521	25.958	31.643	38.592	47.061	57.351
11	11.566	12.168	12.807	13.486	14.206	14.971	15.783	16.645	17.560	18.531	20.654	23.044	24.349	25.732	28.755	32.150	40.237	50.398	63.121	78.998
12	12.682	13.412	14.192	15.025	15.917	16.869	17.888	18.977	20.140	21.384	24.133	27.270	29.001	30.850	34.931	39.580	50.894	65.510	84.320	108.43
13	13.809	14.680	15.617	16.626	17.713	18.882	20.140	21.495	22.953	24.522	28.029	32.088	34.351	36.786	42.218	48.496	64.109	84.852	112.30	148.47
14	14.947	15.973	17.086	18.291	19.598	21.015	22.550	24.214	26.019	27.975	32.392	37.581	40.504	43.672	50.818	59.195	80.496	109.61	149.23	202.92
15	16.096	17.293	18.598	20.023	21.578	23.276	25.129	27.152	29.360	31.772	37.279	43.842	47.580	51.659	60.965	72.035	100.81	141.30	197.99	276.97
16	17.257	18.639	20.156	21.824	23.657	25.672	27.888	30.324	33.003	35.949	42.753	50.980	55.717	60.925	72.939	87.442	126.01	181.86	262.35	377.69
17	18.430	20.012	21.761	23.697	25.840	28.212	30.840	33.750	36.973	40.544	48.883	59.117	65.075	71.673	87.068	105.93	157.25	233.79	347.30	514.66
18	19.614	21.412	23.414	25.645	28.132	30.905	33.999	37.450	41.301	45.599	55.749	68.394	75.836	84.140	103.74	128.11	195.99	300.25	459.44	700.93
19	20.810	22.840	25.116	27.671	30.539	33.760	37.379	41.446	46.018	51.159	63.439	78.969	88.211	98.603	123.41	154.74	244.03	385.32	607.47	954.27
20	22.019	24.297	26.870	29.778	33.066	36.785	40.995	45.762	51.160	57.275	72.052	91.024	102.44	115.37	146.62	186.68	303.60	494.21	802.86	1298.8
21	23.239	25.783	28.676	31.969	35.719	39.992	44.865	50.422	56.764	64.002	81.698	104.76	118.81	134.84	174.02	225.02	377.46	633.59	1060.7	1767.3
22	24.471	27.299	30.536	34.248	38.505	43.392	49.005	55.456	62.873	71.402	92.502	120.43	137.63	157.41	206.34	271.03	469.05	811.99	1401.2	2404.6
23	25.716	28.845	32.452	36.617	41.430	46.995	53.436	60.893	69.531	79.543	104.60	138.29	159.27	183.60	244.48	326.23	582.62	1040.3	1850.6	3271.3
24	26.973	30.421	34.426	39.082	44.502	50.815	58.176	66.764	76.789	88.497	118.15	158.65	184.16	213.97	289.49	392.48	723.46	1332.6	2443.8	4449.9
25	28.243	32.030	36.459	41.645	47.727	54.864	63.249	73.105	84.700	98.347	133.33	181.87	212.79	249.21	342.60	471.98	898.09	1706.8	3226.8	6052.9
26	29.525	33.670	38.553	44.311	51.113	59.156	68.676	79.954	93.323	109.18	150.33	208.33	245.71	290.08	405.27	567.37	1114.6	2185.7	4260.4	8233.0
27	30.820	35.344	40.709	47.084	54.669	63.705	74.483	87.350	102.72	121.09	169.37	238.49	283.56	337.50	479.22	681.85	1383.1	2798.7	5624.7	11197.9
28	32.129	37.051	42.930	49.967	58.402	68.528	80.697	95.338	112.96	134.20	190.69	272.88	327.10	392.50	566.48	819.22	1716.0	3583.3	7425.6	15230.2
29	33.450	38.792	45.218	52.966	62.322	73.639	87.346	103.96	124.13	148.63	214.58	312.09	377.16	456.30	669.44	984.06	2128.9	4587.6	9802.9	20714.1
30	34.784	40.568	47.575	56.084	66.438	79.058	94.460	113.28	136.30	164.49	241.33	356.78	434.74	530.31	790.94	1181.8	2640.9	5873.2	12940.	28172.2
40	48.886	60.402	75.401	95.025	120.79	154.76	199.63	259.05	337.88	442.59	767.09	1342.0	1779.0	2360.7	4163.2	7343.8	22728.	69377.	•	•
50	64.463	84.579	112.79	152.66	209.34	290.33	406.52	573.76	815.08	1163.9	2400.0	4994.5	7217.7	10435.	21813.	45497.	•	•	•	•
60	81.669	114.05	163.05	237.99	353.58	533.12	813.52	1253.2	1944.7	3034.8	7471.6	18535.	29219.	46057.	•	•	•	•	•	•

*FVIF > 99,999

D *Cumulative Probability Distributions*

Values of N(x) for Given Values of x for a Cumulative Normal Probability Distribution with Zero Mean and Unit Variance

x	N(x)	x	N(x)	x	N(x)	x	N(x)	x	N(x)	x	N(x)
		−1.00	.1587	1.00	.8413	−2.00	.0228	.00	.5000	2.00	.9773
−2.95	.0016	−.95	.1711	1.05	.8531	−1.95	.0256	.05	.5199	2.05	.9798
−2.90	.0019	−.90	.1841	1.10	.8643	−1.90	.0287	.10	.5398	2.10	.9821
−2.85	.0022	−.85	.1977	1.15	.8749	−1.85	.0322	.15	.5596	2.15	.9842
−2.80	.0026	−.80	.2119	1.20	.8849	−1.80	.0359	.20	.5793	2.20	.9861
−2.75	.0030	−.75	.2266	1.25	.8944	−1.75	.0401	.25	.5987	2.25	.9878
−2.70	.0035	−.70	.2420	1.30	.9032	−1.70	.0446	.30	.6179	2.30	.9893
−2.65	.0040	−.65	.2578	1.35	.9115	−1.65	.0495	.35	.6368	2.35	.9906
−2.60	.0047	−.60	.2743	1.40	.9192	−1.60	.0548	.40	.6554	2.40	.9918
−2.55	.0054	−.55	.2912	1.45	.9265	−1.55	.0606	.45	.6736	2.45	.9929
−2.50	.0062	−.50	.3085	1.50	.9332	−1.50	.0668	.50	.6915	2.50	.9938
−2.45	.0071	−.45	.3264	1.55	.9394	−1.45	.0735	.55	.7088	2.55	.9946
−2.40	.0082	−.40	.3446	1.60	.9452	−1.40	.0808	.60	.7257	2.60	.9953
−2.35	.0094	−.35	.3632	1.65	.9505	−1.35	.0885	.65	.7422	2.65	.9960
−2.30	.0107	−.30	.3821	1.70	.9554	−1.30	.0968	.70	.7580	2.70	.9965
−2.25	.0122	−.25	.4013	1.75	.9599	−1.25	.1057	.75	.7734	2.75	.9970
−2.20	.0139	−.20	.4207	1.80	.9641	−1.20	.1151	.80	.7881	2.80	.9974
−2.15	.0158	−.15	.4404	1.85	.9678	−1.15	.1251	.85	.8023	2.85	.9978
−2.10	.0179	−.10	.4602	1.90	.9713	−1.10	.1357	.90	.8159	2.90	.9981
−2.05	.0202	−.05	.4801	1.95	.9744	−1.05	.1469	.95	.8289	2.95	.9984

Glossary

Abnormal rate of return The amount by which a security's return differs from the security's expected rate of return based on the market's rate of return during the period and the security's relationship to the market.

American Depository Receipts (ADRs) Certificates of ownership of a foreign firm issued by a bank, which holds the firm's common stock in safekeeping.

Americus Trust A trust that holds common stock tendered by investors and in return issues units made up of primes and scores, which may be traded separately.

Analysis effect A difference in performance of a bond portfolio from that of a chosen index due to acquisition of temporarily mispriced issues which then move to their correct prices.

Anomalies Security price relationships that appear to contradict a well-regarded hypothesis, in this case, the efficient market hypothesis.

Arithmetic mean A measure of central tendency equal to the sum of annual returns divided by the number of years.

At-the-money option An option with an exercise price approximately equal to the stock's market price.

Autocorrelation test A test of the efficient market hypothesis that examines the relationship of security price changes over time to check for predictable correlation patterns.

Balance sheet A financial statement that shows what assets the firm controls at a point in time and how it has financed these assets.

Barbell A portfolio with capital divided between short and long maturities, avoiding intermediate-term bonds.

Basis The difference between an asset's prices in the cash market and the futures market.

Bearer bond An unregistered bond for which ownership is determined by possession. The holder receives interest payments by clipping coupons attached to the security and sending them to the issuer.

Benchmark error An inaccuracy in evaluation of portfolio performance due to poor representation of market performance by the security market index chosen as a proxy for the market portfolio.

Benchmark issue A Japanese government bond selected to dominate trading in that market.

Beta A standardized measure of systematic risk determined by an asset's covariance with the market portfolio.

Bond price volatility The percentage changes in bond prices over time.

Bond swap An active bond portfolio management strategy that exchanges one position for another to take advantage of some difference between them.

Breakeven time The time required for the added income from a convertible bond relative to the common stock to offset the conversion premium. Also referred to as the *payback period*.

Breakup value The estimated value of a firm's divisions if sold to other firms.

Bullet A portfolio with maturities concentrated in a single sector.

***Business Week* Leading Indicator Series** An indicator series composed of seven individual series that measure production, foreign exchange, prices, and monetary indicators. The goal is to develop a composite series that turns before the aggregate economy at peaks and troughs.

Business risk Uncertainty due to the nature of a firm's business.

Buy-and-hold strategy A passive portfolio management strategy in which bonds are bought and held to maturity.

Call options Options to buy a firm's common stock within a certain period at a specified price.

Call provision Part of a bond indenture that gives the issuer the right to redeem the bond at a stated time before maturity by paying its face value plus a premium.

Capital Asset Pricing Model (CAPM) A theory concerned with deriving the expected or required rates of return on risky assets based upon the assets' systematic risk levels.

Capital market instruments Fixed-income investments that trade in the secondary market.

Capital market line (CML) The line from the intercept point that represents the risk-free rate tangent to the original efficient frontier; it becomes the new efficient frontier.

Cash (spot) contract An agreement for the immediate delivery of some asset.

Certificates for automobile receivables (CARs) Asset-backed securities backed by pools of loans to individuals to finance car purchases.

Certificates of deposit (CDs) Instruments issued by banks and S&Ls that require minimum deposits for specified terms, and pay higher rates of interest than deposit accounts.

Characteristic line The line that best fits a scatter plot of rates of return for a risky asset and the market portfolio over a past time period.

Closed-end investment company An investment company that issues only a limited number of shares which it does not redeem (buy back). Shares are traded in securities markets at prices determined by supply and demand.

Closing purchase transaction Acquiring an option that exactly offsets another option to which you previously agreed. The purpose is to liquidate the position.

Coefficient of variation (CV) A measure of relative variability that indicates risk per unit of return.

Coincident indicators Indicator series that reach peaks or troughs at about the same time as the aggregate economy.

Collateral trust bond A bond secured by financial assets held by a trustee for the benefit of the bondholders.

Collateralized mortgage obligation (CMO) A debt security based on a pool of mortgage loans that provides a stable stream of payments for a relatively predictable term.

Common stock An equity investment that represents ownership of a firm, with full participation in its success or failure. The firm's directors must approve dividend payments.

Competitive environment The level of intensity of competition among firms in an industry, determined by an examination of five competitive sources.

Competitive strategy The search by a firm for a favorable competitive position within an industry, which is influenced by the industry's prospects.

Completely diversified portfolio A portfolio in which all unsystematic risk has been eliminated.

Composite leading indicator index A combination of leading indicators designed to indicate the overall current and likely future state of the economy.

Conversion parity price The market value of a convertible bond divided by the number of shares to which it can be converted (i.e., its conversion ratio).

Conversion premium The excess of the market value of a convertible bond compared to the market value of the common stock into which it can be converted (i.e., its conversion value). Typically expressed as a percentage of the conversion value.

Conversion ratio The number of shares into which a bond can be converted.

Conversion value The value of a convertible bond if converted into common stock at the stock's current market price. It is equal to the market price of the stock times the number of shares into which the bonds convert.

Convertible bond A bond, usually subordinated, that the holder can exchange for a stated number of shares of the issuer's common stock.

Convertible preferred stock A preferred stock issue that the holder can exchange for a stated number of shares of common stock.

Convexity A measure of the degree to which a bond's price-yield curve departs from a straight line, which affects estimates of price volatility.

Correlation coefficient A standardized measure of the relationship between two series that ranges from -1.00 to $+1.00$.

Country risk Uncertainty due to the possibility of major political or economic change in the country where an investment is located.

Coupon Indicates the interest payment on a debt security. It is the coupon rates times the par value that indicates the interest payments on a debt security.

Coupon reinvestment risk The component of interest rate risk due to the uncertainty of the rate at which coupon payments will be reinvested.

Covariance A measure of the degree to which two variables, such as rates of return for investment assets, move together over time.

Covered call option Selling an option contract against stock that you own.

Credit analysis An active bond portfolio management strategy designed to identify bonds that are expected to experience changes in rating. This strategy is critical when investing in high-yield bonds.

Crossover point The price at which it becomes profitable for an issuer to call a bond. Above this price, yield to call is the appropriate yield measure.

Currency exchange warrant (CEW) A warrant that entitles the holder to buy a specific number of U.S. dollars for a non-U.S. currency at a stated exchange rate.

Current yield A bond's yield as measured by its coupon income as a percentage of its current price.

Cyclical indicator model An attempt to predict future behavior of securities markets and the economy based on indicator series for the business cycle.

Debentures Bonds that promise payments of interest and principal, but pledge no specific assets. Holders have first claim on the issuer's income and unpledged assets.

Declining trend channel The range defined by security prices as they move progressively lower.

Dedicated portfolio management A bond portfolio management technique designed to service a particular stream of liabilities.

Default premium A risk premium defined as the return on long-term corporate bonds minus the return on long-term, riskless government bonds.

Deferred-delivery contract An agreement for delivery of an asset in the future. Forward and futures contracts are types of deferred-delivery contracts.

Diffusion index An indicator of the number of stocks rising during a specified period of time relative to the number declining and not changing price.

Discount A bond selling at a price below par value due to capital market conditions.

Dividend discount model (DDM) A technique for estimating the value of a stock issue as the present value of all future dividends.

Downtick An incremental movement downward in a transaction price compared to the previous transaction price.

Duration A composite measure of a bond's time characteristics influenced by its coupon and term to maturity.

Earnings multiplier model A technique for estimating the value of a stock issue as a multiple of its earnings per share.

Earnings surprise A company announcement of earnings that differ from analysts' prevailing previous expectations.

Efficient capital market A market in which security prices rapidly reflect all information about securities.

Efficient frontier The curve that defines the set of portfolios with the maximum rate of return for a given level of risk, or the minimum risk for a given rate of return.

Ending-wealth value The total amount of money derived from investment in a bond until maturity, including principal, coupon payments, and income from reinvestment of coupon payments.

Equipment trust certificate A debt security issued by a transportation firm to finance the purchase of equipment (railroad rolling stock, airplanes), which serves as collateral for the debt.

Estimated rate of return The rate of return an investor anticipates earning from a specific investment over a particular holding period.

Eurobonds Bonds denominated in a currency not native to the country in which they are issued.

Event study Research that examines the reaction of a security's price to a specific company or world event or news announcements.

Excess liquidity The amount of money in excess of that required to support economic growth, measured by subtracting the annual percentage change in nominal GNP from the annual percentage change in M2.

Exchange rate risk Uncertainty due to the denomination of an investment in a currency other than that native to the investor.

Exercise price The transaction price specified in an option contract. Also called the *strike price*.

Expected rate of return The return analysts' calculations suggest a security should provide based upon the market's rate of return during the period and the security's relationship to the market.

Expiration date The last date before a holder of an option contract loses the right to control the stock.

Filter rule A trading rule that recommends security transactions when price changes exceed a previously determined percentage.

Financial futures contract An agreement for future delivery of a specified amount of a particular financial instrument at a stated price.

Financial risk Uncertainty due to the method by which a firm finances an investment.

Fixed-income investments Loans with contractually mandated payment schedules from firms or governments to investors.

Flat trend channel The range defined by security prices as they maintain a relatively steady level.

Flower bond A Treasury issue that can be redeemed at face value in payment of federal estate taxes.

Foreign fund An investment company that holds non-U.S. securities.

Forward contract An agreement between two traders for delivery of an asset at a fixed time in the future for a specified price.

Fourth market Direct trading of securities between owners, usually institutions, without any broker's intermediation.

Fully taxable equivalent yield A yield on a tax-exempt bond that adjusts for its tax benefits to allow comparisons with taxable bonds.

Futures clearinghouse A subsidiary of a futures exchange that takes the other side of all trades to ensure a liquid, orderly market.

Futures contract An agreement between a trader and an exchange clearinghouse for the exchange of an asset at a fixed, standardized time in the future for a specified price.

General obligation bond (GO) A municipal issue serviced from and guaranteed by the issuer's full taxing authority.

Geometric mean A measure of dispersion equal to the nth root of annual returns for N years.

Global fund An investment company that holds both U.S. and non-U.S. securities.

Group rotation The tendency for demand to shift among industry groups or other market segments.

Growth company A company that consistently has the opportunities and ability to invest in projects that provide rates of return that exceed the firm's cost of capital. Because of these investment opportunities, it retains a high proportion of earnings and its earnings grow faster than those of average firms.

Growth stock A stock issue that generates a higher rate of return than other stocks in the market with similar risk characteristics.

Hedge Combining two or more securities into a single position such that price increases offset decreases to limit the effects of adverse price movements.

High yield bond A bond rated below investment grade. Also referred to as speculative-grade bonds or junk bonds. These are typically issued by relatively small firms or used to finance leveraged buyouts.

Holding period return (HPR) The total return from an investment, including all sources of income, for a given period of time. A value of 1.0 indicates no gain or loss.

Holding period yield (HPY) The total return from an investment for a given period of time stated as a percentage.

In-the-money option An option with a favorable exercise price in relation to the stock's market price.

Income bonds Debentures that stipulate interest payments only if the issuer earns the income to make the payments by specified dates.

Income statement A financial statement that shows the firm's earnings and costs over a period of time.

Indenture The legal agreement that lists the issuer's obligations to the bondholder, including payment schedule and special features.

Index arbitrage Simultaneous purchase (sale) and sale (purchase) of stock index futures and stocks in the index portfolio to profit from price differences between them.

Index fund An investment company that matches the portfolio composition, and therefore the performance, of a chosen market indicator series.

Indexing A passive portfolio management strategy that seeks to copy the composition, and therefore the performance, of a selected market index.

Indicator series A statistical measure of the performance of an entire market based on that of a sample of securities.

Industry analysis Study of the relationships between firms' return and risk levels within an industry and between the industry's levels and those of the aggregate market to identify superior investment opportunities.

Industry life cycle analysis Industry analysis that focuses on the industry's stage of development.

Informationally efficient market A more technical term for an efficient capital market that emphasizes the role of information.

Initial public offering (IPO) A new issue by a firm that has no existing public market.

Input-output analysis Industry analysis that evaluates an industry's prospects based on those of its suppliers and customers.

Interest rate anticipation An active bond portfolio management strategy designed to preserve capital or take advantage of capital gains opportunities by predicting interest rates and their effects on bond prices.

Interest rate anticipation effect The difference in return from changing the duration of the portfolio during a period as compared with the portfolio's long-term duration.

Interest rate risk The uncertainty of returns on an investment due to possible changes in interest rates over time. It has two components: price risk and reinvestment risk.

Interest-on-interest Bond income from reinvestment of coupon payments.

Internal liquidity (solvency) ratios Relationships between items of financial data that indicate the firm's ability to meet short-term financial obligations.

Internal rate of return The discount rate at which cash outflows of an investment equal cash inflows.

International domestic bonds Bonds issued by a foreign firm denominated in its native currency and sold within its own country.

International fund An investment company that holds only non-U.S. securities, sometimes focusing on a specific segment of the non-U.S. market.

International Leading Indicator Series Indicator series designed to predict economic activity outside the United States.

Investment The current commitment of dollars over time to derive future payments to compensate the investor for the time the funds are committed, the expected rate of inflation, and the uncertainty of future payments.

Investment companies Companies that sell shares in their diversified portfolios of investments to people who want to avoid the risk of direct investment in a few securities and who want professional management.

Investment decision process Estimation of value for comparison with market price to determine whether or not to invest.

Investment horizon The future time at which the investor requires the funds an investment is intended to provide.

Investment management company A company separate from the investment company that manages the portfolio and performs administrative functions.

Investment premium The difference between the market price of a convertible bond and its investment value as a straight bond as a percentage of investment value.

Investment value The price at which a convertible bond would probably sell as a straight debt instrument.

Ladder A portfolio with approximately equal amounts allotted among various maturity segments.

Lagging indicators Indicator series that reach peaks or troughs after the aggregate economy.

Leading Employment Index An indicator series designed to forecast changes in U.S. employment.

Leading indicator Indicator series that reach peaks or troughs in advance of the aggregate economy.

Leading Inflation Index An indicator series designed to forecast U.S. inflation rates.

Limit order An order to buy or sell a security when and if it trades at a specified price.

Liquidity risk Uncertainty due to the ability to quickly buy or sell an investment in secondary market for an investment.

Load fund A mutual fund that imposes sales charges on share purchases to compensate salespeople.

Long hedge The purchase of a financial futures contract to hedge against adverse price movements in a security a trader plans to purchase.

Long-Leading Index An indicator series designed to predict economic movements far in advance based on bond prices, a ratio of prices to labor costs, M2, and building permits.

Macroeconomic approach An attempt to project the outlook for securities markets based on their underlying relationship to the aggregate economy.

Maintenance margin A minimum amount for a margin account, typically about 75 percent of the initial margin.

Management fee The compensation an investment company pays to the investment management company for its services.

Margin The amount of cash a buyer pays for a security, borrowing the balance from the broker. This leverage increases the risk of the transaction.

Margin account An account that holds a trader's deposits toward the total cost of his or her position.

Margin call Notice that a trader's margin account balance has fallen below the maintenance margin, requiring additional deposits.

Marked to market The daily adjustment of the value of a trader's account to reflect that day's price changes.

Market index fund An investment company that attempts to match the composition, and performance, of a chosen market indicator series.

Market liquidity The ability to buy or sell an asset quickly with little price change from a prior transaction assuming no new information.

Market order An order to buy or sell a security immediately at the best price possible.

Market portfolio The portfolio that includes all risky assets the relative weights equal to their proportional market values.

Market risk premium The amount of return above the risk-free rate that investors expect from the market in general as compensation for systematic risk.

Maturity management component The part of the return on a bond portfolio caused by the manager's manipulation of maturity or duration in anticipation of interest rate changes.

Maturity premium A measure of the cost of longer-term investing defined as the return on long-term government bonds minus the return on T-bills.

Maturity strategy A portfolio immunization technique in which the investor acquires bonds with maturities that match the investment horizon.

Mean rate of return The average of an investment's returns over time.

Micro-analysis approach An attempt to estimate the value of the aggregate stock market based on an application of the dividend discount model.

Modified duration A measure of Macaulay duration adjusted to help you estimate a bond's price volatility.

Money market The market for short-term debt securities with maturities of less than 1 year.

Money market funds Investment companies that hold portfolios of high-quality, short-term securities like T-bills. High liquidity and superior returns make them a good alternative to bank savings accounts.

Money supply A measure of the amount of extremely liquid assets in the economy. Alternative specifications include currency plus demand deposits, sometimes adding time deposits and money market funds.

Mortgage bonds Bonds that pledge specific assets, the proceeds of which are used to pay off bondholders in case of bankruptcy.

Moving average The continually recalculated average of security prices for a period, often 200 days, to serve as an indication of the general trend of prices and also as a benchmark price.

National Association of Securities Dealers Automated Quotation (NASDAQ) system An electronic system for providing bid–ask quotes on OTC securities.

National Bureau of Economic Research (NBER) A nonprofit organization devoted to monitoring business cycles and other economic phenomena.

Net asset value (NAV) The market value of an investment company's assets after deducting liabilities divided by the number of shares outstanding.

New issue Securities issued for the first time by the firm or other entity that underlies them.

No-load fund A mutual fund that sells its shares at net asset value without adding sales charges.

Nominal yield A bond's yield as measured by its coupon rate.

Normal range The proportion of a portfolio an investor should hold in a particular set of assets under normal conditions.

Notes Intermediate-term debt securities with maturities longer than 1 year, but less than 10 years.

Open interest The number of contracts in a particular future outstanding at a point in time.

Open-end investment company A more formal name for a mutual fund, which derives from the fact that it continuously offers new shares to investors and redeems them on demand.

Operating efficiency ratios Relationships between sales and assets in various categories that indicate how effectively management uses the firm's capital.

Operating profitability ratios Relationships of profits to sales and to the capital employed to generate those profits.

Optimal portfolio The efficient portfolio with the highest utility for a given investor, found by the point of tangency between the efficient frontier and the investor's utility function.

Option Clearing Corporation (OCC) A central organization affiliated with the CBOE that guarantees the writer's performance. The OCC is the intermediary in each transaction between the buyer and the writer of an option contract.

Option contract An investment vehicle that gives the holder the right to either buy or sell 100 shares of a stock issue at a stated price within a set period of time.

Out-of-the-money option An option with an unfavorable exercise price in relation to the stock's market price.

Par value The principal of the debt underlying a bond that is payable at maturity. Rarely less than $1,000.

Peak The cumulation of a bull market when prices stop rising and begin declining.

Perpetuity An investment without any maturity date. It provides returns to its owners indefinitely.

Policy effect A difference in performance of a bond portfolio from that of a chosen index due to differences in duration, which result from a fund's investment policy.

Portfolio A group of investments with different patterns of returns over time.

Portfolio immunization A bond portfolio management technique of matching modified duration to the investment horizon to eliminate interest rate risk.

Preferred stock An equity investment that stipulates the dividend payment either as a coupon or a stated dollar amount. The firm's directors can withhold payments.

Premium A bond selling at a price above par value due to capital market conditions.

Premium The price a buyer pays for a stock option.

Price/book value ratio The relationship between a firm's stock price and the total book value of its assets, which can indicate its attractiveness as an investment.

Price/cash flow ratio The relationship between a firm's stock price and its cash flows. The analysis of this ratio supplements the analysis of price-earnings ratios because cash flows are less easily manipulated by accounting techniques than are earnings measures.

Price continuity A feature of a liquid market in which prices change little from one transaction to the next.

Price-earnings (P/E) ratio The number by which earnings per share is multiplied to estimate a stock's value. Also called the *earnings multiple*.

Price risk The component of interest rate risk due to the uncertainty of the market price of a bond caused by possible changes in market interest rates.

Price spread Simultaneously buying and selling options that are identical except for their exercise prices.

Price-weighted series An indicator series calculated as an arithmetic average of the current prices of the sampled securities.

Primary market The market in which newly issued securities are sold by their issuers.

Prime Part of a unit issued by an Americus Trust that entitles the holder to all dividend payments for the term of the trust, plus shares of the common stock at termination worth the number of shares originally tendered times the termination claim price.

Private placement A new issue sold directly to a small group of investors, usually institutions.

Program trading Index arbitrage using automatic transactions according to instructions from sophisticated computer programs.

Promised yield to call A bond's yield if held until the first available call date, with reinvestment of all coupon payments at the yield-to-call rate.

Promised yield to maturity The most widely used measure of a bond's yield that states the fully com-pounded rate of return on a bond bought at market price and held to maturity with reinvestment of all coupon payments at the promised YTM.

Prospectus A condensed version of a new issue's SEC registration statement designed to provide authoritative information about the issue for prospective investors.

Public bond A long-term, fixed obligation debt security in a convenient, affordable denomination for sale to individuals and financial institutions.

Put options Options to sell a firm's common stock within a certain period at a specified price.

Real estate investment trusts (REITs) Investment funds that hold portfolios of real estate investments.

Realized yield The expected compounded yield on a bond that is sold before it matures assuming the reinvestment of all cash flows at an explicit rate.

Registered bond A bond for which ownership is registered with the issuer. The holder receives interest payments directly from the issuer.

Relative-strength ratio The ratio of a stock price or an industry index value to a market indicator series, indicating performance relative to the overall market.

Required rate of return The minimum return that will induce the investor to invest. It is composed of a real risk-free rate, the expected rate of inflation, and a risk premium.

Residual effect The return on a bond portfolio not caused by the yield-to-maturity, interest rate, and sector/quality effects.

Resistance level A price at which a technician would expect a substantial increase in supply for a stock to reverse a rising trend.

Reversing trade A transaction that offsets a previous transaction leaving a trader with a zero balance between the two trades.

Rising trend channel The range defined by security prices as they move progressively higher.

Risk The uncertainty that an investment will earn its expected rate of return.

Risk averse The assumption about investors that they will choose the least risky alternative, all else being equal.

Risk-free asset An asset with returns that exhibit zero variance.

Risk-free rate (RFR) The basic interest rate with no accommodation for uncertainty. It is determined by the real growth rate of the economy and temporary ease of tightness in the capital market.

Risk premium The rate of return over the risk-free rate that investors demand as compensation for an investment's uncertainty.

Risky asset An asset with uncertain future returns.

Runs test A test of the weak-form efficient market hypothesis that checks for trends that persist longer in terms of positive or negative price changes than one would expect for random series.

Score Part of a unit issued by an Americus Trust that entitles the holder at termination to shares of stock worth the number of shares originally tendered times any surplus of the market price of the stock over the termination claim price.

Secondary market The market in which outstanding securities are bought and sold by owners other than the issuers. The purpose of this market is to provide liquidity for the owners.

Sector/quality effect The return on a bond portfolio caused by the selection of the sector in which the bonds fall and their quality.

Secured (senior) bond A bond backed by a legal claim on specified assets of the issuer.

Security market line (SML) A curve that represents the combination of risk and return characteristic of investments in a market.

Selectivity component The part of the return on a bond portfolio caused by the manager's selection of individual bond issues to implement maturity and quality decisions.

Semistrong-form efficient market hypothesis The belief that security prices fully reflect all publicly available information, including information from security transactions and company, economic, and political news.

Separation theorem The proposition that the investment decision, which involves selecting a portfolio that falls along the capital market line, is separate from the financing decision, which targets a specific point on the CML, based on the risk preferences of the investor.

Short hedge The sale of a financial futures contract to hedge a current position in the underlying security.

Short sale Sale of borrowed stock with the intention of repurchasing it later at a lower price and earning the difference.

Sinking fund A fund accumulated by a bond issuer to redeem a stated percentage of the issue prior to maturity.

Small stock premium A risk premium defined as the return on small capitalization stocks minus the return on total stocks.

Spread analysis An active bond portfolio management strategy designed to capitalize on corrections in temporarily abnormal yield spreads between alternative issues.

Spread/quality management component The part of the return on a bond portfolio caused by the manager's selection of bonds from various sectors and quality groups.

Standard deviation A measure of variability equal to the square root of the variance.

Statement of cash flows A financial statement that shows the effect on the firm's cash flows of sales, earnings, and changes in its balance sheet.

Stock index futures contract An agreement for delivery of cash based on movements in a stock market index.

Strong-form efficient market hypothesis The belief that security prices fully reflect all information from both public and private sources.

Subordinated bonds Debentures that, in case of default, entitle holders to claims on the issuer's assets only after the claims of holders of senior debentures and mortgage bonds are satisfied.

Suggested weighting The proportion of a portfolio an investor should hold in a particular class of investment assets under current economic and market conditions.

Support level A price at which a technician would expect a substantial increase in demand for a stock to reverse a declining trend that was due to profit taking.

Systematic risk The relationship between the rate of return for a security and that for a market portfolio of risky assets.

Technical analysis A security selection technique that contends that it is possible to estimate future security price movements based on past movements.

10-K Form An annual report required by the SEC of a firm's revenues, expenses, and other pertinent data.

Term structure of interest rates The relationship between term to maturity and yield for a sample of equal risk bonds at a given time.

Third market OTC trading in exchange-listed securities.

Time-series analysis Comparison of performance data over alternative time periods.

Time spread Simultaneously buying and selling options that are identical except for their expiration dates.

Trading effect A difference in performance of a bond portfolio from that of a chosen index due to short-run changes in the portfolio.

Trading rule A formula for deciding on current transactions based on historical data.

Transaction cost The cost of executing a trade. Low costs characterize good markets.

Treasury bill A negotiable U.S. government security with a maturity less than 1 year that pays no periodic interest, but yields the difference between its par value and its discounted purchase price.

Treasury bond A U.S. government security with a maturity longer than 10 years that pays interest periodically.

Treasury note A U.S. government security with a maturity between 1 year and 10 years that pays interest periodically.

Trough The culmination of a bear market at which prices cease declining and begin rising.

Uncovered (naked) call option Selling an option contract on a stock that you do not own; you would have to acquire it if the option owner called for the stock.

Underlying security The stock to which an option contract gives the holder rights.

Underweighted A condition in which a portfolio, for whatever reason, includes less of a class of securities than the relative market value alone would justify.

Unsecured (junior) bond A bond backed only by the issuer's promise of timely interest and principal payments.

Unsystematic risk Risk that is unique to an asset, derived from its particular characteristics. It is this risk that can be eliminated in a diversified portfolio.

Unweighted index An indicator series affected equally by the performance of each security in the sample regardless of price or market value.

Uptick An incremental movement upward in a transaction price over the previous transaction price.

Valuation analysis An active bond portfolio management strategy designed to capitalize on expected price increases in temporarily undervalued issues.

Valuation process Part of the investment decision process in which you estimate the value of a security.

Value-weighted series An indicator series calculated as the total market value of the securities in the sample.

Variable margin The amount a trader must deposit in cash to return his or her margin account to its initial level.

Variable-rate note A debt security for which the interest rate changes to follow some specified short-term rate (e.g., the T-bill rate).

Variance A measure of variability equal to the square of a return's deviation from the mean.

Volatility The variability of an asset's rates of return over time. The typical measure used for this is the standard deviation of returns.

Warrants Bond provisions that allow the holder to purchase the firm's common stock directly from the firm at a specified price during a stated period of time.

Weak-form efficient market hypothesis The belief that security prices fully reflect all information generated by security transactions.

Writing an option Selling an option contract, that is, giving another party control over stock you own, or will acquire if need be.

Yankee bonds Bonds sold in the United States and denominated in U.S. dollars, but issued by a foreign firm or government.

Yield The promised rate of return on an investment under certain assumptions.

Yield illusion The erroneous expectation that a bond will provide its stated yield to maturity without recognizing the implicit reinvestment assumption related to coupon payments.

Yield spread The difference between the promised yields of alternative bond issues or market segments at a given time.

Yield-to-maturity effect The return on a bond portfolio caused by the characteristics of the yield curve.

Zero coupon bond A bond that pays its par value at maturity, but no periodic interest payments. Its yield is the difference between its par value and its discounted purchase price.

Index